Happy 20th anniversary to NYC FIRST and StuyPulse FRC Team 694.
—Jeanne

For my daughter, Olivia, your determination and strength of heart are one of a kind. Your smile brightens even the darkest days. May your life be filled with happiness and love.
—Scott

Acknowledgments

Jeanne and Scott would like to thank numerous individuals for their contribution to this book. Thank you to Kathryn Duggan for guiding us through the process and making the book better in so many ways. Thank you to Janeice DelVecchio for being our technical editor as we wrote this book. Janeice pointed out many subtle errors in addition to the big ones. And thank you to Elena Felder for being our technical proofreader and finding the errors that we managed to sneak by Janeice. This book also wouldn't be possible without many people at Wiley, including Kenyon Brown, Pete Gaughan, Christine O'Connor, Barath Kumar Rajasekaran, Kim Wimpsett, Johnna VanHoose Dinse, and so many others.

Jeanne would personally like to thank Chris Kreussling for knowing more than a decade ago that she would someday write a book. He was a great mentor for many years and definitely shaped her career. Sibon Barman was helpful in getting feedback on the modules chapter, and Susanta Chattopadhyay provided real-life use cases for both service locator and serialization. Stuart Dabbs Halloway's 2001 book provided examples of `serialPeristentFields`. Scott was a great co-author, improving everything Jeanne wrote while writing his own chapters. A big thank you to everyone at `CodeRanch.com` who asked and responded to questions and comments about our books. Finally, Jeanne would like to thank all of the new programmers at `CodeRanch.com` and FIRST robotics teams FRC 694, FTC 310, and FTC 479 for the constant reminders of how new programmers think.

Scott could not have reached this point without his wife, Patti, and family, whose love and support makes this book possible. He would like to thank his twin daughters, Olivia and Sophia, and youngest daughter, Elysia, for their patience and understanding especially when it was "time for Daddy to work in his office!" Scott would like to extend his gratitude to his wonderfully patient co-author, Jeanne, on this, their fifth book. He doesn't know how she puts up with him, but he's glad she does and thrilled at the quality of books we produce. A big thanks to Matt Dalen, who has been a great friend, sounding board, and caring father to Olivia, Adeline, and newborn Henry. Finally, Scott would like to thank his mother and retired teacher, Barbara Selikoff, for teaching him the value of education, and his father, Mark Selikoff, for instilling in him the benefits of working hard.

We'd both like to thank Marcus Biel for providing a European's take on our localization content. Last but not least, both Jeanne and Scott would like to give a big thank you to the readers of all our books. Hearing from all of you who enjoyed the book and passed the exam is a great feeling. We'd also like to thank those who pointed out errors and made suggestions for improvements in the 1Z0-815 Java 11 book. As of May 2020, the top two were Nikolai Vinoku and Edmond Yong. Also, an honorable mention to Jakub Chrobak. Finally, thank you to Atanas Gegov for submitting a pull request to improve the 1Z0-815 modules examples readme.

About the Authors

Jeanne Boyarsky was selected as a Java Champion in 2019. She has worked as a Java developer for more than 18 years at a bank in New York City where she develops, mentors, and conducts training. Besides being a senior moderator at CodeRanch.com in her free time, she works on the forum code base. Jeanne also mentors the programming division of a FIRST robotics team where she works with students just getting started with Java. She also speaks at several conferences each year.

Jeanne got her Bachelor of Arts degree in 2002 and her Master in Computer Information Technology degree in 2005. She enjoyed getting her Master's degree in an online program while working full-time. This was before online education was cool! Jeanne is also a Distinguished Toastmaster and a Scrum Master. You can find out more about Jeanne at www.jeanneboyarsky.com or follow her on Twitter @JeanneBoyarsky.

Scott Selikoff is a professional software consultant, author, and owner of Selikoff Solutions, LLC, which provides software development solutions to businesses in the tri-state New York City area. Skilled in a plethora of software languages and platforms, Scott specializes in full-stack database-driven systems, cloud-based applications, microservice architectures, and service-oriented architectures.

A native of Toms River, New Jersey, Scott achieved his Bachelor of Arts degree from Cornell University in Mathematics and Computer Science in 2002, after three years of study. In 2003, he received his Master of Engineering degree in Computer Science, also from Cornell University.

As someone with a deep love of education, Scott has always enjoyed teaching others new concepts. He's given lectures at Cornell University and Rutgers University, as well as conferences including Oracle Code One and The Server Side Java Symposium. Scott lives in New Jersey with his loving wife, Patti; three amazing daughters, twins Olivia and Sophia and little Elysia; and two very playful dogs, Webby and Georgette. You can find out more about Scott at www.linkedin.com/in/selikoff or follow him on Twitter @ScottSelikoff.

Jeanne and Scott are both moderators on the CodeRanch.com forums and can be reached there for question and comments. They also co-author a technical blog called Down Home Country Coding at www.selikoff.net.

In addition to this book, Jeanne and Scott are also authors of the following best-selling Java 8 certification books: *OCA Oracle Certified Associate Java SE 8 Programmer I Study Guide* (Sybex, 2015) and *OCP Oracle Certified Professional Java SE 8 Programmer II Study Guide* (Sybex, 2016). These two books have been combined into the single release: *OCA/OCP Java SE 8 Programmer Certification Kit: Exam 1Z0-808 and Exam 1Z0-809* (Sybex 2016). They have also written a book of practice test questions for the Java 8 certification exams: *OCA/OCP Java SE 8 Programmer Practice Tests* (Sybex, 2017). Their most recent books are *OCP Oracle Certified Professional Java SE 11 Programmer I Study Guide: Exam 1Z0-815* (Sybex, 2019) and *OCP Oracle Certified Professional Java SE 11 Programmer II Study Guide: Exam 1Z0-816* (Sybex, 2020).

Contents at a Glance

Contents

Chapter   20   NIO.2   969

Introduction

This book is for those looking to obtain an Oracle Certified Professional Java SE 11 Developer or Java Foundations Certified Junior Associate title. This book is also for those looking to gain a deeper understanding and appreciation of Java. Not only do we want you to pass your exams, but we want to help you to improve yourself and become a better professional software developer.

The book provides detailed preparation for the following Oracle certifications exams:

1Z0-819 Exam: Java SE 11 Developer   The Developer Exam covers a wide variety of core topics in Java 11 including classes, interfaces, lambda expressions, operators, decision constructs, basic collections, and modules. These topics form the foundation of most Java applications. The Developer Exam also delves into select topics such as streams, modular applications, generics, advanced collections, I/O and NIO.2, concurrency, annotations, and security.

IZ0-817 Exam: Upgrade OCP Java 6, 7 & 8 to Java SE 11 Developer   The Upgrade Exam is meant for those who hold an existing OCP certification to be able to obtain the Java 11 OCP certification title with a single exam. It contains a selection of Java 11 topics from both the Programmer I and Programmer II exams.

1Z0-811 Exam: Java Foundations   The Foundations Exam a junior level certification exam that contains a variety of introductory and basic Java 8 topics. It is not meant for existing Java professionals, but rather those who use Java infrequently in their job or don't want to dive as deep into Java.

In the introduction, we start by covering important information about the various exams. Depending on your certification history, you may have a choice of which exam you can take. We then move on to information about how this book is structured. Finally, we conclude with two assessment tests so you can see how much studying lies ahead of you.

Understanding the Exam

At the end of the day, the exam is a list of questions. The more you know about the structure of the exam, the better you are likely to do. For example, knowing how many questions the exam contains allows you to manage your progress and time remaining better. In this section, we discuss the details of the exam, along with some history of previous certification exams.

Broader Objectives

In previous certification exams, the list of exam objectives tended to include specific topics, classes, and APIs that you needed to know for the exam. For example, take a look at an objective for the 1Z0-809 (OCP 8) exam:

- Use BufferedReader, BufferedWriter, File, FileReader, FileWriter, FileInputStream, FileOutputStream, ObjectOutputStream, ObjectInputStream, and PrintWriter in the java.io package.

    Now compare it with the equivalent objective for the 1Z0-816 (OCP 11) exam:

- Use I/O Streams to read and write files

Notice the difference? The older version is more detailed and describes specific classes you will need to understand. The newer version is a lot vaguer. It also gives the exam writers a lot more freedom to insert a new feature without having to update the list of objectives.

So how do you know what to study? By reading this study guide of course! We've spent years studying the certification exams, in all of their forms, and have carefully cultivated topics, material, and practice questions that we are confident can lead to successfully passing the exam.

Choosing Which Exam to Take

Java is now 25 years old, celebrating being "born" in 1995. As with anything 25 years old, there is a good amount of history and variation between different versions of Java. Over the years, the certification exams have changed to cover different topics. The names of the exams have even changed. This book covers the Java 11 exam.

Those with more recent certifications might remember that Oracle released two exams each for Java 7 and Java 8. The first exam tended to be easier, and completing it granted you the title of Oracle Certified Associate (OCA). The second exam was a lot more difficult, with much longer questions, and completing it granted you the title of Oracle Certified Professional (OCP).

Oracle did not release an exam for Java 9 or Java 10, probably because neither of these is a Long Term Support (LTS) release. With Java 11, Oracle decided to discontinue both the OCA certification and its associated exam. You still have to take two exams to earn an OCP title. Both are more difficult than the old OCA exams. The difference is that now you do not obtain a certification title from completing the first exam.

Figure I.1 shows these past and current Java certifications. This image is helpful if you run into material online that references older exams. It is also helpful if you have an older certification and are trying to determine where it fits in.

FIGURE I.1   Past and current Java certifications

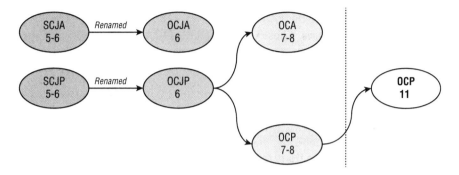

Figure I.2 shows the exams you need to take in order to earn the latest Java certification if you are new to certification.

FIGURE I.2   Latest Java certification exams

For those who already hold a Java certification, Figure I.3 shows common scenarios for which exam(s) you should target.

FIGURE I.3   Exam prerequisites

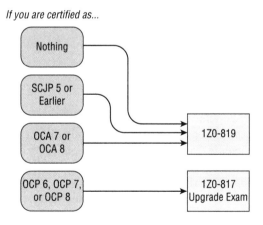

In a nutshell, you can take the 1Z0-819 exam if you hold the OCA 7 or 8 title. Oracle's goal here is to help people get to Java 11 OCP certification if they are halfway through the journey to OCP certification. Similarly, those with an OCP certification can take the 1Z0-817 upgrade exam to get to Java 11 OCP with one exam. Those with an older certification will have to start over and take the 1Z0-819 exam.

There are also two edge cases. Those who passed the OCA 6 exam must still take the 1Z0-819 exam. The OCA 6 exam covered far less material than the OCA 7 or 8.

Additionally, those who passed the OCP 7 or 8 exam but never received the OCP title because they didn't pass the OCA exam, need to take the 1Z0-819 exam.

If you're not sure which exam you should take, you can post questions on CodeRanch.com and the community will be happy to help. You might even get a response from Jeanne or Scott!

Taking the Upgrade Exam

The chapters of this book are structured for those taking 1Z0-819 exam. Those taking the 1Z0-817 Upgrade Exam can also rely on this book to prepare for the exam, and you don't need to read all 22 chapters!

While we think every chapter is worth reading, the following is a list of chapters that you should focus on if you are preparing for the 1Z0-817 exam and the order you should read them:

- Chapter 2, "Java Building Blocks"
- Chapter 11, "Modules"
- Chapter 12, "Java Fundamentals"
- Chapter 14, "Generics and Collections" (Lambda expressions and method references)
- Chapter 15, "Functional Programming"
- Chapter 16, "Exceptions, Assertions, and Localization"
- Chapter 17, "Modular Applications"
- Chapter 18, "Concurrency"
- Chapter 20, "NIO.2"

The 1Z0-817 exam is cumulative. For instance, the 1Z0-817 exam does not have any objectives on while and for loops, but they are certainly likely to appear in questions. In other words, if it's been awhile since you took the previous OCP exam, we recommend reading all of the chapters in Part I of this book.

We've included a mapping of all of the upgrade exam objectives and their associated chapters in the "Objective Maps" section of this introduction.

Changes to the Exam

Table I.1 shows the information about the exams at the time of publishing.

TABLE I.1 Exam information

Exam	Length	# Questions	Passing Score
1Z0-819 Java Developer	3 hours	50	68%
1Z0-817 Upgrade OCP Java 6, 7 & 8 to Java SE 11 Developer	3 hours	80	61%
1Z0-811 Java Foundations	2.5 hours	75	65%

Oracle has a tendency to fiddle with the length of the exam and the passing score once it comes out. Oracle also likes to "tweak" the exam topics over time. It wouldn't be a surprise for Oracle to make minor changes to the exam objectives, the number of questions, or the passing score after this book goes to print.

If there are any changes to the exam after this book is published, we will note them on the book page of our blog:

www.selikoff.net/ocp11-complete/

Exam Questions

Each exam consists entirely of multiple choice questions. There are between four and seven possible answers. If a question has more than one answer, the question specifically states exactly how many correct answers there are. This book does not do that. We say "Choose all that apply" to make the questions harder. This means the questions in this book are generally harder than those on the exam. The idea is to give you more practice so you can spot the correct answer more easily on the real exam.

If you read about older versions of the exams online, you might see references to drag-and-drop questions. These questions had you do a puzzle on how to complete a piece of code. Luckily these are no longer on any of the exams.

Many of the questions on each exam are code snippets rather than full classes. Saving space by not including imports and/or class definitions leaves room for lots of other code. For example, it is common to come across classes on the exam with portions omitted, like so:

```java
public class Zoo {
   String name;
   // Getters/Setters/Constructors omitted
}
```

In this case, you would assume methods like getName() and setName(), as well as related constructors exist. For instance, we would expect this code to compile:

```
var name = new Zoo("Java Zoo").getName();
```

Out-of-Scope Material

When you take an exam, you may see some questions that appear to be out of scope. *Don't panic!* Often, these questions do not require knowing anything about the topic to answer the question. For example, after reading this book you should be able to spot that the following does not compile, even if you've never heard of LocalDate and ChronoUnit:

```
final LocalDate holiday = LocalDate.now();
holiday = LocalDate.now().plus(5,ChronoUnit.HOURS);
```

The classes and enums used in this question are not in scope for the exam, but the reason it does not compile is in scope. In particular, you should know that you cannot reassign a variable marked final.

See, not so scary is it? Expect to see at least a few structures on the exam that you are not familiar with. If they aren't part of your exam preparation material, then you don't need to understand them to answer the question.

Question Topic Tips

The following list of topics is meant to give you an idea of the types of questions and oddities that you might come across on the exam. Being aware of these categories of such questions will help you get a higher score on an exam.

Questions with Extra Information Provided   Imagine the question includes a statement that XMLParseException is a checked exception. It's fine if you don't know what an XMLParseException is or what XML is for that matter. (If you are wondering, it is a format for data.) This question is a gift. You know the question is about checked and unchecked exceptions.

Questions with Embedded Questions   To answer some questions on the exam, you may have to actually answer two or three subquestions. For example, the question may contain two blank lines and the question may ask you to choose the two answers that fill in each blank. In some cases, the two answer choices are not related, which means you're really answering multiple questions, not just one! These questions are among the most difficult and time-consuming on the exam because they contain multiple, often independent, questions to answer. Unfortunately, the exam does not give partial credit, so take care when answering questions like these.

Questions with Unfamiliar APIs   If you see a class or method that wasn't covered in this book, assume it works as you would expect. Some of these APIs you might come across, such as LocalDate, were on the Java 8 exam and are not part of the Java 11 exams. Assume that the part of the code using that API is correct and look very hard for other errors.

Questions with Made-Up or Incorrect Concepts   In the context of a word problem, the exam may bring up a term or concept that does not make any sense such as saying an interface inherits from a class, which is not a correct statement. In other cases, they may use a keyword that does not exist in Java, like `struct`. For these, you just have to read them carefully and recognize when the exam is using invalid terminology.

Questions That Are Really Out of Scope   When introducing new questions, Oracle includes them as unscored questions at first. This allows them to see how real exam takers do without impacting your score. You will still receive the number of questions as the exam lists. However, a few of them may not count. These unscored questions may contain out-of-scope material or even errors. They will not be marked as unscored so you still have to do your best to answer them. Follow the previous advice to assume that anything you haven't seen before is correct. That will cover you if the question is being counted!

Reading This Book

It might help to have some idea about how this book has been written. This section contains details about some of the common structures and features you will find in this book, where to go for additional help, and how to obtain bonus material for this book.

Who Should Buy This Book

If you want to obtain the OCP 11 Java Developer certification, this book is definitely for you. If you want to acquire a solid foundation in Java and your goal is to prepare for the exam, then this book is also for you. You'll find clear explanations of the concepts you need to grasp and plenty of help to achieve the high level of professional competency you need in order to succeed in your chosen field.

This book is intended to be understandable to anyone who has a tiny bit of Java knowledge. If you've never read a Java book before, we recommend starting with a book that teaches programming from the beginning and then returning to this study guide.

This book is for anyone from high school students to those beginning their programming journey to experienced professionals who need a review for the certification.

How This Book Is Organized

This book is divided into two parts consisting of 11 chapters each, plus supplementary information: an online glossary, this introduction, and multiple bonus exams. You might have noticed that there are more than 11 objectives for each exam. We organized what you need to know to make it easy to learn and remember. Each chapter begins with a list of the objectives that are covered in that chapter.

Part I:

- **Chapter 1: Welcome to Java** describes the basics of Java such as how to run a program. It also includes the benefits of Java and key terminology.

- **Chapter 2: Java Building Blocks** focuses on variables such as primitives and object data types and scoping variables. It also discusses garbage collection.

- **Chapter 3: Operators** explains operations with variables. It also talks about casting and the precedence of operators.

- **Chapter 4: Making Decisions** covers on core logical constructs such as conditionals and loops.

- **Chapter 5: Core Java APIs** introduces you to `String`, `StringBuilder`, array, and various types.

- **Chapter 6: Lambdas and Functional Interfaces** shows how to use lambdas and four key functional interfaces. The focus is implementing and calling `Predicate`, `Consumer`, `Supplier`, and `Comparator`.

- **Chapter 7: Methods and Encapsulation** explains how to write methods. It also shows the four access modifiers.

- **Chapter 8: Class Design** covers constructors and superclasses. It also includes method overriding.

- **Chapter 9: Advanced Class Design** adds interfaces and abstract classes. It also introduces inner classes.

- **Chapter 10: Exceptions** shows the different types of exception classes and how to use them. It also includes different uses of `try` statements.

- **Chapter 11: Modules** details the benefits of the new module feature. It shows how to compile and run module programs from the command line.

Part II:

- **Chapter 12: Java Fundamentals** covers core Java topics including enums, the `final` modifier, inner classes, and interfaces. There are now many types of functional interface methods that you need to know for the exam. It also includes an introduction to creating functional interfaces and lambda expressions.

- **Chapter 13: Annotations** describes how to define and apply your own custom annotations, as well as how to use the common built-in ones.

- **Chapter 14: Generics and Collections** goes beyond the basics and demonstrates method references, generics with wildcards, and Collections. The Collections portion covers many common interfaces, classes, and methods that are useful for the exam and in every day software development.

- **Chapter 15: Functional Programming** explains lambdas and stream pipelines in detail. It also covers the built-in functional interfaces and the `Optional` class. If you want to become skilled at creating streams, read this chapter more than once!

- **Chapter 16: Exceptions, Assertions, and Localization** shows advanced exception handling topics including creating custom exceptions, try-with-resources statements, and suppressed exceptions. It also covers how to use assertions to validate your program. It concludes with localization and formatting, which allows your program to gracefully support multiple countries or languages.

- **Chapter 17: Modular Applications** shows advanced modularization concepts including services and how to migrate an application to a modular infrastructure.

- **Chapter 18: Concurrency** introduces the concept of thread management, and teaches you how to build multi-threaded programs using the concurrency API and parallel streams.

- **Chapter 19: I/O** introduces you to managing files and directories using the java.io API. It covers a number of I/O stream classes, teaches you how to serialize data, and shows how to interact with a user.

- **Chapter 20: NIO.2** shows you to manage files and directories using the newer NIO.2 API. It includes techniques for using streams to traverse and search the file system.

- **Chapter 21: JDBC** provides the basics of working with databases in Java including working with stored procedures.

- **Chapter 22: Security** describes how to securely build your program and protect against common malicious attacks.

At the end of each chapter, you'll find a few elements you can use to prepare for the exam:

Summary   This section reviews the most important topics that were covered in the chapter and serves as a good review.

Exam Essentials   This section summarizes highlights that were covered in the chapter. You should be able to convey the information described.

Review Questions   Each chapter concludes with at least 20 review questions. You should answer these questions and check your answers against the ones provided in the Appendix. If you can't answer at least 80 percent of these questions correctly, go back and review the chapter, or at least those sections that seem to be giving you difficulty.

The review questions, assessment tests, and other testing elements included in this book are *not* derived from the real exam questions, so don't memorize the answers to these questions and assume that doing so will enable you to pass the exam. You should focus on understanding the topic, as described in the text of the book. This will let you answer the questions provided with this book *and* pass the exam. Learning the underlying topic is also the approach that will serve you best in the workplace—the ultimate goal of a certification.

To get the most out of this book, you should read each chapter from start to finish before going to the chapter-end elements. They are most useful for checking and reinforcing your understanding. Even if you're already familiar with a topic, you should skim the chapter. There are a number of subtleties to Java that you could easily not encounter even when working with Java for years.

Conventions Used in This Book

This book uses certain typographic styles to help you quickly identify important information and to avoid confusion over the meaning of words such as on-screen prompts. In particular, look for the following styles:

- *Italicized text* indicates key terms that are described at length for the first time in a chapter. (Italics are also used for emphasis.)
- A `monospaced` font indicates code or command-line text.
- *`Italicized monospaced text`* indicates a variable.

In addition to these text conventions, which can apply to individual words or entire paragraphs, a few conventions highlight segments of text.

A tip is something to call particular attention to an aspect of working with a language feature or API.

A note indicates information that's useful or interesting. It is often something to pay special attention to for the exam.

Sidebars

A sidebar is like a note but longer. The information in a sidebar is useful, but it doesn't fit into the main flow of the text.

 Real World Scenario

A real-world scenario is a type of sidebar that describes a task or an example that's particularly grounded in the real world. This is something that is useful in the real world, but is not going to show up on the exam.

Getting Help

Both of the authors are moderators at CodeRanch.com. This site is a quite large and active programming forum that is friendly toward Java beginners. It has a forum just for this exam called Programmer Certification. It also has a forum called Beginning Java for non-exam-specific questions. As you read the book, feel free to ask your questions in either of those forums. It could be you are having trouble compiling a class or that you are just plain confused about something. You'll get an answer from a knowledgeable Java programmer. It might even be one of us.

Interactive Online Learning Environment and Test Bank

We've put together some really great online tools to help you pass the exams. The interactive online learning environment that accompanies this study guide provides a test bank and study tools to help you prepare for the exam. By using these tools you can dramatically increase your chances of passing the exam on your first try.

The online test bank includes the following:

Practice Exams   Many sample tests are provided throughout this book and online, including the assessment tests, which you'll find at the end of this introduction, and the chapter tests that include the review questions at the end of each chapter. In addition, there are four bonus practice exams. Use these questions to test your knowledge of the study guide material. The online test bank runs on multiple devices.

Flashcards   The online text bank includes two sets of flashcards specifically written to hit you hard, so don't get discouraged if you don't ace your way through them at first! They're there to ensure that you're really ready for the exam. And no worries— armed with the review questions, practice exams, and flashcards, you'll be more than prepared when exam day comes! Questions are provided in digital flashcard format (a question followed by a single correct answer). You can use the flashcards to reinforce your learning and provide last-minute test prep before the exam.

Resources   A glossary of key terms from this book and their definitions is available as a fully searchable PDF.

To register and gain access to this interactive online learning environment, please visit this URL:

www.wiley.com/go/Sybextestprep

Preparing for the Exam

This section includes suggestions and recommendations for how you should prepare for the certification exam. If you're an experienced test taker or you've taken a certification test before, most of this should be common knowledge. For those who are taking the exam for the first time, don't worry! We'll present a number of tips and strategies to help you prepare for the exam.

Creating a Study Plan

Rome wasn't built in a day, so you shouldn't attempt to study for the exam in only one day. Even if you have been certified with a previous version of Java, the new test includes features and components unique to Java 9, 10, and 11 that are covered in this text.

Once you have decided to take the test, you should construct a study plan that fits with your schedule. We recommend that you set aside some amount of time each day, even if it's just a few minutes during lunch, to read or practice for the exam. The idea is to keep your momentum going throughout the exam preparation process. The more consistent you are in how you study, the better prepared you will be for the exam. Try to avoid taking a few days or weeks off from studying or you're likely to spend a lot of time relearning existing material instead of moving on to new material.

Creating and Running the Code

Although some people can learn Java just by reading a textbook, that's not how we recommend that you study for a certification exam. We want you to be writing your own Java sample applications throughout this book so that you don't just learn the material, but that you understand the material as well. For example, it may not be obvious why the following line of code does not compile, but if you try to compile it yourself, the Java compiler will tell you the problem:

```
float value = 102.0; // DOES NOT COMPILE
```

 A lot of people post the question "Why does this code not compile?" on the CodeRanch.com forum. If you're stuck or just curious about a behavior in Java, we encourage you to post to the forum. There are a lot of nice people in the Java community standing by to help you.

Sample Test Class

Throughout this book, we present numerous code snippets and ask you whether they'll compile or not and what their output will be. You will place these snippets inside a simple

Java application that starts, executes the code, and terminates. You can accomplish this by compiling and running a public class containing a
public static void main(String[] args) method and adding the necessary import statements, such as the following:

```java
// Add any necessary import statements here
public class TestClass {
    public static void main(String[] args) {
        // Add test code here

        // Add any print statements here
        System.out.println("Hello World!");
    }
}
```

This application isn't particularly interesting—it just outputs Hello World! and exits. That said, you could insert many of the code snippets presented in this book in the main() method to determine whether the code compiles, as well as what the code outputs when it does compile.

 Real World Scenario

IDE Software

While studying for an exam, you should develop code using a text editor and command-line Java compiler. Some of you may have prior experience with integrated development environments (IDEs), such as Eclipse, IntelliJ, or Visual Studio Code. An IDE is a software application that facilitates software development for computer programmers. Although such tools are extremely valuable in developing software, they can interfere with your ability to spot problems readily on an exam.

Identifying Your Weakest Link

The review questions in each chapter are designed to help you hone in on those features of the Java language where you may be weak and that are required knowledge for the exam. For each chapter, you should note which questions you got wrong, understand why you got them wrong, and study those areas even more. After you've reread the chapter and written lots of code, you can do the review questions again. In fact, you can take the review questions over and over to reinforce your learning as long as you explain to yourself why it is correct.

> **"Overstudying" the Online Practice Exam**
>
> Although we recommend reading this book and writing your own sample applications multiple times, redoing the online practice exam over and over can have a negative impact in the long run. For example, some individuals study the practice exam so much that they end up memorizing the answers. In this scenario, they can easily become over-confident; that is, they can achieve perfect scores on the practice exams but may fail the actual exam.

Understanding the Question

The majority of questions on each exam will contain code snippets and ask you to answer questions about them. For those items containing code snippets, the number-one question we recommend that you answer before attempting to solve the question is this:

Does the code compile?

It sounds simple, but many people dive into answering the question without checking whether the code actually compiles. If you can determine whether a particular set of code compiles and what line or lines cause it to not compile, answering the question often becomes easy.

Applying the Process of Elimination

Although you might not immediately know the correct answer to a question, if you can reduce the question from five answers to three, your odds of guessing the correct answer will be markedly improved. Moreover, if you can reduce a question from four answers to two, you'll double your chances of guessing the correct answer!

The exam software allows you to eliminate answer choices by right-clicking an answer choice, which causes the text to be struck through, as shown in the following example:

~~A.   123~~

B.   Elephant

~~C.   Vulture~~

D.   The code does not compile due to line n1.

Even better, the exam software remembers which answer choices you have eliminated anytime you go back to the question. You can undo the crossed-out answer simply by right-clicking the choice again.

Sometimes you can eliminate answer choices quickly without reading the entire question. In some cases, you may even be able to solve the question based solely on the answer choices. If you come across such questions on the exam, consider it a gift.

Can you correctly answer the following question in which the application code has been left out?

5. Which line, when inserted independently at line m1, allows the code to compile?

- Code Omitted -

   A. `public abstract final int swim();`

   B. `public abstract void swim();`

   C. `public abstract swim();`

   D. `public abstract void swim() {}`

   E. `public void swim() {}`

Without reading the code or knowing what line m1 is, we can actually eliminate three of the five answer choices. Options A, C, and D contain invalid declarations, leaving us with options B and E as the only possible correct answers.

Skipping Difficult Questions

The exam software also includes an option to "mark" a question and review all marked questions at the end of the exam. If you are pressed for time, answer a question as best you can and then mark it to come back to later.

All questions are weighted equally, so spending 10 minutes answering five questions correctly is a lot better use of your time than spending 10 minutes on a single question. If you finish the exam early, you have the option of reviewing the marked questions, as well as all of the questions on the exam if you so choose.

Being Suspicious of Strong Words

Many questions on each exam include answer choices with descriptive sentences rather than lines of code. When you see such questions, be wary of any answer choice that includes strong words such as "must," "all," or "cannot." If you think about the complexities of programming languages, it is rare for a rule to have no exceptions or special cases. Therefore, if you are stuck between two answers and one of them uses "must" while the other uses "can" or "may," you are better off picking the one with the weaker word since it is a more ambiguous statement.

Using the Provided Writing Material

Depending on your particular testing center, you will be provided with a sheet of blank paper or a whiteboard to use to help you answer questions. In our experience, a whiteboard with a marker and an eraser are more commonly handed out. If you sit down and you are not provided with anything, make sure to ask for such materials.

After you have determined that the program does compile, it is time to understand what the program does! One of the most useful applications of writing material is tracking the state of primitive and reference variables. For example, let's say you encountered the following code snippet on a question about garbage collection:

```
Object o = new Turtle();
Mammal m = new Monkey();
Animal a = new Rabbit();
o = m;
```

In a situation like this, it can be helpful to draw a diagram of the current state of the variable references. As each reference variable changes which object it points to, you would erase or cross out the arrow between them and draw a new one to a different object.

Using the writing material to track state is also useful for complex questions that involve a loop, especially questions with embedded loops. For example, the value of a variable might change 5 or more times during a loop execution. You should make use of the provided writing material to improve your score.

N⦸TE   While you cannot bring any outside material into an exam, you can write down material at the start of the exam. For example, if you have trouble remembering which functional interfaces take which generic arguments, then it might be helpful to draw a table at the start of the exam on the provided writing material. You can then use this information to answer multiple questions.

Choosing the Best Answer

Sometimes you read a question and immediately spot a compiler error that tells you exactly what the question is asking. Other times, though, you may stare at a method declaration for a couple of minutes and have no idea what the question is asking. While you might not know for sure which answer is correct in these situations, there are some test-taking tips that can improve the probability that you will pick the correct answer.

Unlike some other standardized tests, there's no penalty for answering a question incorrectly versus leaving it blank. If you're nearly out of time or you just can't decide on an answer, select a random answer and move on. If you've been able to eliminate even one answer, then your guess will be better than blind luck.

Answer All Questions!

You should set a hard stop at five minutes of time remaining on the exam to ensure that you've answered each and every question. Remember, if you fail to answer a question, you'll definitely get it wrong and lose points, but if you guess, there's at least a chance that you'll be correct. There's no harm in guessing!

When in doubt, we generally recommend picking a random answer that includes "Does not compile" if available, although which choice you select is not nearly as important as making sure that you do not leave any questions unanswered on the exam!

Getting a Good Night's Rest

Although a lot of people are inclined to cram as much material as they can in the hours leading up to an exam, most studies have shown that this is a poor test-taking strategy. The best thing we can recommend that you do before taking an exam is to get a good night's rest!

Given the length of each exam and number of questions, the exam can be quite draining, especially if this is your first time taking a certification exam. You might come in expecting to be done 30 minutes early, only to discover that you are only a quarter of the way through the exam with half the time remaining. At some point, you may begin to panic, and it is in these moments that these test-taking skills are most important. Just remember to take a deep breath, stay calm, eliminate as many wrong answers as you can, and make sure to answer each and every question. It is for stressful moments like these that being well rested with a good night's sleep will be most beneficial!

Taking the Exam

So you've decided to take the exam? We hope so if you've bought this book! In this section, we discuss the process of scheduling and taking the exam, along with various options for each.

Scheduling the Exam

The exam is administered by Pearson VUE and can be taken at any Pearson VUE testing center. To find a testing center or register for the exam, go to:

    www.pearsonvue.com

Next, search for *Oracle* as the exam provider. If you haven't been to the test center before, we recommend visiting in advance. Some testing centers are nice and professionally run. Others stick you in a closet with lots of people talking around you. You don't want to be taking the test with people complaining about their broken laptops nearby!

At this time, you can reschedule the exam without penalty until up to 24 hours before. This means you can register for a convenient time slot well in advance, knowing that you can delay if you aren't ready by that time. Rescheduling is easy and can be done completely on the Pearson VUE website. This may change, so check the rules before paying.

The At-Home Online Option

Oracle now offers online-proctored exams that can be taken in the comfort of your own home. You choose a specific date and time, like a proctored exam, and take it at your computer.

While this option may be appealing for a lot of people, especially if you live far away from a testing center, there are a number of restrictions.

- Your session will be closely monitored by another individual from a remote location.

- You must set up a camera and microphone, and they must be on for the entire exam. At the start, you will also need to turn the camera around the room to show your workspace to prove you are not in reach of exam material.

- The exam software will also monitor your facial expressions and track eye movement. We've heard reports that it will warn you if you are looking away from the screen too much.

- You must be alone in a completely isolated space for the duration of the test. If someone comes in during your test, your test will be invalidated.

- You cannot have any papers, material, or items in your immediate vicinity.

- Unlike exam centers that provide writing material, writing down any notes or the use of scratch paper is prohibited. You do get to make notes on a digital whiteboard within the exam software.

- Stopping for any reason, including a restroom break, is prohibited.

With so many rules, you want to think carefully before taking the test at home. If you do plan to go this route, please visit Oracle's website for a complete set of rules and requirements.

The Day of the Exam

When you go to take the exam, remember to bring two forms of ID including one that is government issued. See Pearson's list of acceptable IDs here:

www.pearsonvue.com/policies/1S.pdf

Try not to bring too much extra with you as it will not be allowed into the exam room. While you will be allowed to check your belongings, it is better to leave extra items at home or in the car.

You will not be allowed to bring paper, your phone, and the like into the exam room with you. Some centers are stricter than others. At one center, tissues were even taken away from us! Most centers allow keeping your ID and money. They watch you taking the exam, though, so don't even think about writing notes on money.

As we mentioned earlier, the exam center will give you writing materials to use during the exam, either scratch paper or a whiteboard. If you aren't given these materials, remember to ask. These items will be collected at the end of the exam.

Finding Out Your Score

In the past, you would find out right after finishing the exam if you passed. Now you have to wait nervously until you can check your score online. Many test takers check their score from a mobile device as they are walking out of the test center.

If you go onto the Pearson VUE website, it will just have a status of "Taken" rather than your result. Oracle uses a separate system for scores. You'll need to go to Oracle's CertView website to find out whether you passed and your score.

```
certview.oracle.com
```

It usually updates shortly after you finish your exam but can take up to an hour in some cases. In addition to your score, you'll also see objectives for which you got a question wrong. Once you have passed the 1Z0-816 exam or the 1Z0-817 exam and fulfilled the required perquisites, the OCP 11 title will be granted within a few days.

 Oracle has partnered with Acclaim, which is an Open Badge platform. Upon obtaining a certification from Oracle, you also receive a "badge" that you can choose to share publicly with current or prospective employers.

Objective Map

This book has been written to cover every objective on the two exams.

Java SE 11 Developer (1Z0-819)

The following table provides a breakdown of this book's exam coverage for the Java SE 11 Developer (1Z0-819) exam, showing you the chapter where each objective or subobjective is covered:

Exam Objective	Chapter
Understanding Java Technology and environment	
Describe Java Technology and the Java development	1
Identify key features of the Java language	1

Exam Objective	Chapter
Creating a Simple Java Program	
Create an executable Java program with a main class	1
Compile and run a Java program from the command line	1
Create and import packages	1
Working with Java Primitive Data Types and String APIs	
Declare and initialize variables (including casting and promoting primitive data types)	2, 3
Identify the scope of variables	2
Use local variable type inference	2
Create and manipulate Strings	5
Manipulate data using the StringBuilder class and its methods	5
Using Operators and Decision Constructs	
Use Java operators including the use of parentheses to override operator precedence	3
Use Java control statements including if, if/else, switch	4
Create and use do/while, while, for and for each loops, including nested loops, use break and continue statements	4
Working with Java Arrays	
Declare, instantiate, initialize and use a one-dimensional array	5
Declare, instantiate, initialize and use a two-dimensional array	5
Describing and using Objects and Classes	
Declare and instantiate Java objects, and explain objects' lifecycles (including creation, dereferencing by reassignment, and garbage collection)	2
Define the structure of a Java class	1
Read or write to object fields	2
Creating and Using Methods	
Create methods and constructors with arguments and return values	7, 8
Create and invoke overloaded methods	7
Apply the static keyword to methods and fields	7

Upgrade OCP Java 6, 7 & 8 to Java SE 11 Developer (1Z0–817)

The following table provides a breakdown of this book's exam coverage for the Upgrade OCP Java 6, 7 & 8 to Java SE 11 Developer (1Z0–817) exam, showing you the chapter where each objective or subobjective is covered.

Exam Objective	Chapter
Language Enhancements	
Use try-with-resources construct	16
Develop code that handles multiple Exception types in a single catch block	16

Java Foundations (1Z0-811)

The following table provides a breakdown of this book's exam coverage for the Java Foundations (1Z0-811) exam, showing you the chapter where each objective or subobjective is covered.

A few topics are on the Java Foundations exam, but not the 1Z0-815. Those are covered here:

www.selikoff.net/java-foundations

Additionally, the objectives may be updated when Oracle updates the Java Foundations exam for Java 11. Check our website for those updates as well.

Exam Objective	Chapter
What is Java?	
Describe the features of Java	1
Describe the real-world applications of Java	1 + online
Java Basics	
Describe the Java Development Kit (JDK) and the Java Runtime Environment (JRE)	1
Describe the components of object-oriented programming	1
Describe the components of a basic Java program	1
Compile and execute a Java program	1
Basic Java Elements	
Identify the conventions to be followed in a Java program	1
Use Java reserved words	2

Exam Objective	Chapter
Using Looping Statements	
Describe looping statements	4
Use a for loop including an enhanced for loop	4
Use a while loop	4
Use a do- while loop	4
Compare and contrast the for, while, and do-while loops	4
Develop code that uses break and continue statements	4
Debugging and Exception Handling	
Identify syntax and logic errors	1, 2, 3, 4, 5
Use exception handling	10
Handle common exceptions thrown	10
Use try and catch blocks	10
Arrays and ArrayLists	
Use a one-dimensional array	5
Create and manipulate an ArrayList	5
Traverse the elements of an ArrayList by using iterators and loops including the enhanced for loop	5 + online
Compare an array and an ArrayList	5
Classes and Constructors	
Create a new class including a main method	1
Use the private modifier	7
Describe the relationship between an object and its members	8
Describe the difference between a class variable, an instance variable, and a local variable	2, 8
Develop code that creates an object's default constructor and modifies the object's fields	8
Use constructors with and without parameters	8
Develop code that overloads constructors	8
Java Methods	
Describe and create a method	7

Assessment Tests

Use the following assessment tests to gauge your current level of skill in Java for Exam 1Z0-819. These tests are designed to highlight some topics for your strengths and weaknesses so that you know which chapters you might want to read multiple times. Even if you do well on the assessment tests, you should still read the book from cover to cover, as the real exams are quite challenging.

If you are taking the 1Z0-817 exam, you can still take the 1Z0-819 assessments respectively. If you get a question wrong on the Part I assessment test, you should review the associated chapter to make sure you understand the material. Remember, the 1Z0-817 exam is cumulative. On the other hand, if you get a question wrong on the Part II assessment test, you should check the list of objectives and see if it is in scope for the upgrade exam. For example, the 1Z0-817 exam will not test you on annotations or security.

Part I:

1. What is the result of the following program?

```
1: public class MathFunctions {
2:     public static void addToInt(int x, int amountToAdd) {
3:         x = x + amountToAdd;
4:     }
5:     public static void main(String[] args) {
6:         var a = 15;
7:         var b = 10;
8:         MathFunctions.addToInt(a, b);
9:         System.out.println(a);    } }
```

   A. 10
   B. 15
   C. 25
   D. Compiler error on line 3
   E. Compiler error on line 8
   F. None of the above

2. What is the output of the following program? (Choose all that apply.)

```
1:  interface HasTail { int getTailLength(); }
2:  abstract class Puma implements HasTail {
3:      protected int getTailLength() { return 4; }
4:  }
```

```
5:  public class Cougar implements HasTail {
6:      public static void main(String[] args) {
7:          var puma = new Puma();
8:          System.out.println(puma.getTailLength());
9:      }
10:     public int getTailLength(int length) { return 2; }
11: }
```

A. 2

B. 4

C. The code will not compile because of line 3.

D. The code will not compile because of line 5.

E. The code will not compile because of line 7.

F. The code will not compile because of line 10.

G. The output cannot be determined from the code provided.

3. What is the output of the following code snippet?

```
int moon = 9, star = 2 + 2 * 3;
float sun = star>10 ? 1 : 3;
double jupiter = (sun + moon) - 1.0f;
int mars = --moon <= 8 ? 2 : 3;
System.out.println(sun+"-"+jupiter+"-"+mars);
```

A. 1–11–2

B. 3.0–11.0–2

C. 1.0–11.0–3

D. 3.0–13.0–3

E. 3.0f–12–2

F. The code does not compile because one of assignments requires an explicit numeric cast.

4. How many times is the word true printed?

```
var s1 = "Java";
var s2 = "Java";
var s3 = "Ja".concat("va");
var s4 = s3.intern();
var sb1 = new StringBuilder();
sb1.append("Ja").append("va");
```

```
System.out.println(s1 == s2);
System.out.println(s1.equals(s2));
System.out.println(s1 == s3);
System.out.println(s1 == s4);
System.out.println(sb1.toString() == s1);
System.out.println(sb1.toString().equals(s1));
```

A. Once

B. Twice

C. Three times

D. Four times

E. Five times

F. Six times

G. The code does not compile.

5. The following code appears in a file named `Flight.java`. What is the result of compiling this source file?

```
1: public class Flight {
2:     private FlightNumber number;
3:
4:     public Flight(FlightNumber number) {
5:         this.number = number;
6:     } }
7: public class FlightNumber {
8:     public int value;
9:     public String code; }
```

A. The code compiles successfully and two bytecode files are generated: `Flight.class` and `FlightNumber.class`.

B. The code compiles successfully and one bytecode file is generated: `Flight.class`.

C. A compiler error occurs on line 2.

D. A compiler error occurs on line 4.

E. A compiler error occurs on line 7.

6. Which of the following will run a modular program?

A. `java -cp modules mod/class`

B. `java -cp modules -m mod/class`

C. `java -cp modules -p mod/class`

D. `java -m modules mod/class`

E. `java -m modules -p mod/class`

F. `java -p modules mod/class`

G. `java -p modules -m mod/class`

7. What is the result of executing the following code snippet?

```
final int score1 = 8, score2 = 3;
char myScore = 7;
switch (myScore) {
   default:
   score1:
   2: 6: System.out.print("great-");
   4: System.out.print("good-"); break;
   score2:
   1: System.out.print("not good-");
}
```

A. great-good-

B. good-

C. not good-

D. great-good-not-good-

E. The code does not compile because default is not a keyword in Java.

F. The code does not compile for a different reason.

8. Which of the following lines can fill in the blank to print true? (Choose all that apply.)

```
10: public static void main(String[] args) {
11:     System.out.println(_____);
12: }
13: private static boolean test(Predicate<Integer> p) {
14:     return p.test(5);
15: }
```

A. test(i -> i == 5)

B. test(i -> {i == 5;})

C. test((i) -> i == 5)

D. test((int i) -> i == 5)

E. test((int i) -> {return i == 5;})

F. test((i) -> {return i == 5;})

9. Which of the following are valid instance members of a class? (Choose all that apply.)

A. var var = 3;

B. Var case = new Var();

C. void var() {}

D. int Var() { var _ = 7; return _;}

E. `String new = "var";`

F. `var var() { return null; }`

10. Which of the following types can be inserted into the blank that allows the program to compile successfully? (Choose all that apply.)

```
1:  import java.util.*;
2:  interface CanSwim {}
3:  class Amphibian implements CanSwim {}
4:  abstract class Tadpole extends Amphibian {}
5:  public class FindAllTadPole {
6:      public static void main(String[] args) {
7:          var tadpoles = new ArrayList<Tadpole>();
8:          for (Amphibian amphibian : tadpoles) {
9:              _____ tadpole = amphibian;
10: } } }
```

A. CanSwim

B. Boolean

C. Amphibian

D. Tadpole

E. Object

F. None of the above; the program contains a compilation error.

11. Which of the following expressions compile without error? (Choose all that apply.)

A. `int monday = 3 + 2.0;`

B. `double tuesday = 5_6L;`

C. `boolean wednesday = 1 > 2 ? !true;`

D. `short thursday = (short)Integer.MAX_VALUE;`

E. `long friday = 8.0L;`

F. `var saturday = 2_.0;`

G. None of the above

12. Suppose you have a module named `com.vet`. Where could you place the following `module-info.java` file to create a valid module?

```
public module com.vet {
    exports com.vet;
}
```

A. At the same level as the `com` folder

B. At the same level as the `vet` folder

C. Inside the `vet` folder

D. None of the above

13. What is the result of compiling and executing the following program?

```
1:  public class FeedingSchedule {
2:      public static void main(String[] args) {
3:          var x = 5;
4:          var j = 0;
5:          OUTER: for (var i = 0; i < 3;)
6:              INNER: do {
7:                  i++;
8:                  x++;
9:                  if (x > 10) break INNER;
10:                 x += 4;
11:                 j++;
12:             } while (j <= 2);
13:         System.out.println(x);
14: } }
```

A. 10

B. 11

C. 12

D. 17

E. The code will not compile because of line 5.

F. The code will not compile because of line 6.

14. Which statement about the following method is true?

```
5:  public static void main(String... unused) {
6:      System.out.print("a");
7:      try (StringBuilder reader = new StringBuilder()) {
8:          System.out.print("b");
9:          throw new IllegalArgumentException();
10:     } catch (Exception e || RuntimeException e) {
11:         System.out.print("c");
12:         throw new FileNotFoundException();
13:     } finally {
14:         System.out.print("d");
15: } }
```

A. It compiles and prints abc.

B. It compiles and prints abd.

C. It compiles and prints abcd.

D. One line contains a compiler error.

E. Two lines contain a compiler error.

F. Three lines contain a compiler error.

G. It compiles but prints an exception at runtime.

15. Which of the following are true statements? (Choose all that apply.)

A. The JDK contains a compiler.

B. The JVM contains a compiler.

C. The javac command creates a file containing bytecode.

D. The java command creates a file containing bytecode.

E. The JDK is contained in the JVM.

F. The JVM is contained in the JDK.

16. Which lines in Tadpole give a compiler error? (Choose all that apply.)

```
1:  package animal;
2:  public class Frog {
3:      protected void ribbit() { }
4:      void jump() { }
5:  }
```

```
1:   package other;
2:   import animal.*;
3:   public class Tadpole extends Frog {
4:       public static void main(String[] args) {
5:           Tadpole t = new Tadpole();
6:           t.ribbit();
7:           t.jump();
8:           Frog f = new Tadpole();
9:           f.ribbit();
10:          f.jump();
11:      } }
```

A. 5

B. 6

C. 7

D. 8

E. 9

F. 10

17. What is the output of the following program?

```
1:  class Deer {
2:      public Deer() {System.out.print("Deer");}
3:      public Deer(int age) {System.out.print("DeerAge");}
4:      protected boolean hasHorns() { return false; }
5:  }
6:  public class Reindeer extends Deer {
7:      public Reindeer(int age) {System.out.print("Reindeer");}
8:      public boolean hasHorns() { return true; }
9:      public static void main(String[] args) {
10:         Deer deer = new Reindeer(5);
11:         System.out.println("," + deer.hasHorns());
12: } }
```

A. ReindeerDeer,false

B. DeerAgeReindeer,true

C. DeerReindeer,true

D. DeerReindeer,false

E. ReindeerDeer,true

F. DeerAgeReindeer,false

G. The code will not compile because of line 4.

H. The code will not compile because of line 12.

18. What is printed by the following code? (Choose all that apply.)

```
int[] array = {6,9,8};
List<Integer> list = new ArrayList<>();
list.add(array[0]);
list.add(array[2]);
list.set(1, array[1]);
list.remove(0);
System.out.println(list);
System.out.println("C" + Arrays.compare(array,
    new int[] {6, 9, 8}));
System.out.println("M" + Arrays.mismatch(array,
    new int[] {6, 9, 8}));
```

A. [8]

B. [9]

C. [Ljava.lang.String;@160bc7c0

D. C-1

E. C0

F. M-1

G. M0

H. The code does not compile.

19. Which statements about the following program are true? (Choose all that apply.)

```
1:  public class Grasshopper {
2:      public Grasshopper(String n) {
3:          name = n;
4:      }
5:      public static void main(String[] args) {
6:          Grasshopper one = new Grasshopper("g1");
7:          Grasshopper two = new Grasshopper("g2");
8:          one = two;
9:          two = null;
10:         one = null;
11:     }
12:     private String name;
13: }
```

A. Immediately after line 8, no `Grasshopper` objects are eligible for garbage collection.

B. Immediately after line 9, no `Grasshopper` objects are eligible for garbage collection.

C. Immediately after line 8, only one `Grasshopper` object is eligible for garbage collection.

D. Immediately after line 9, only one `Grasshopper` object is eligible for garbage collection.

E. Immediately after line 10, only one `Grasshopper` object is eligible for garbage collection.

F. The code does not compile.

20. Which of the following statements about error handling in Java are correct? (Choose all that apply.)

A. Checked exceptions are intended to be thrown by the JVM (and not the programmer).

B. Checked exceptions are required to be handled or declared.

C. Errors are intended to be thrown by the JVM (and not the programmer).

D. Errors are required to be caught or declared.

E. Runtime exceptions are intended to be thrown by the JVM (and not the programmer).

F. Runtime exceptions are required to be handled or declared.

21. Which of the following are valid method modifiers that cannot be used together in a method declaration? (Choose all that apply.)

A. null and final

B. abstract and private

C. public and private

D. nonstatic and abstract

E. private and final

F. abstract and static

G. protected and abstract

22. Which of the following are true to sort the list? (Choose all that apply.)

```
13: int multiplier = 1;
14: multiplier *= -1;
15: List<Integer> list = List.of(99, 66, 77, 88);
16: list.sort(_____);
```

A. Line 14 must be removed for any of the following lambdas to compile.

B. Line 14 may remain for any of the following lambdas to compile.

C. (x, y) -> multiplier * y.compareTo(x)

D. x, y -> multiplier * y.compareTo(x)

E. (x, y) -> return multiplier * y.compareTo(x)

F. x, y -> return multiplier * y.compareTo(x)

Part II:

1. Which operations in the CRUD acronym are not allowed in an `executeUpdate()` call? (Choose all that apply.)

   A. Delete

   B. Deletion

   C. Disable

   D. Read

   E. Reading

   F. Select

   G. None of the above. All operations are allowed.

2. Assume the current directory is `/bats/day` and all of the files and directories referenced exist. What is the result of executing the following code?

   ```
   var path1 = Path.of("/bats/night","..")
       .resolve(Paths.get( "./sleep.txt")).normalize();
   var path2 = new File("../sleep.txt").toPath().toRealPath();
   System.out.print(Files.isSameFile(path1,path2));
   System.out.print(" " + path1.equals(path2));
   ```

   A. `true true`

   B. `true false`

   C. `false true`

   D. `false false`

   E. The code does not compile.

   F. The code compiles but throws an exception at runtime.

3. A(n) ——————————— module always contains a `module-info` file while a(n) ——————————— module always exports all its packages to other modules.

   A. automatic, named

   B. automatic, unnamed

   C. named, automatic

   D. named, unnamed

   E. unnamed, automatic

   F. unnamed, named

   G. None of the above

4. Which of the following lines of code do not compile? (Choose all that apply.)

   ```
   1:  import java.lang.annotation.*;
   2:  class IsAware {}
   ```

```
3:   enum Mode {AUTONOMOUS,DEPENDENT}
4:   @interface CleaningProgram {
5:      Mode mode();
6:   }
7:   @Documented public @interface Robot {
8:      CleaningProgram cp()
9:         default @CleaningProgram(Mode.AUTONOMOUS);
10:     final int MAX_CYCLES = 10;
11:     IsAware aware();
12:     String name() = 10;
13: }
```

A. Line 5

B. Line 7

C. Line 8

D. Line 9

E. Line 10

F. Line 11

G. Line 12

H. All of the lines compile.

5. What is the result of executing the following application?

```
final var cb = new CyclicBarrier(3,
    () -> System.out.println("Clean!"));   // u1
ExecutorService service = Executors.newSingleThreadExecutor();
try {
   IntStream.generate(() -> 1)
       .limit(12)
       .parallel()
       .forEach(i -> service.submit(
              () -> cb.await())));   // u2
} finally {
    if (service != null) service.shutdown();
}
```

A. It outputs Clean! at least once.

B. It outputs Clean! exactly four times.

C. The code will not compile because of line u1.

D. The code will not compile because of line u2.

E. It compiles but throws an exception at runtime.

F. It compiles but waits forever at runtime.

6. What modifiers must be used with the `serialPersistentFields` field in a class? (Choose all that apply.)

A. `final`

B. `private`

C. `protected`

D. `public`

E. `transient`

F. `static`

7. What is the output of the following code?

```java
import java.io.*;
public class RaceCar {
    static class Door implements AutoCloseable {
        public void close() { System.out.print("D"); }
    }
    static class Window implements Closeable {
        public void close() { System.out.print("W"); }
    }
    public static void main(String[] args) {
        Window w = new Window() {};
        Door d = new Door();
        try (w; d) {
            System.out.print("T");
        } catch (Exception e) {
            System.out.print("E");
        } finally {
            System.out.print("F");
        }
        d = null;
        w = null;
    }
}
```

A. TF

B. TEF

C. TDWF

D. TWDF

E. A compilation error occurs.

8. What are possible results of executing the following code snippet? (Choose all that apply.)

```
String line;
Console c = System.console();
if ((line = c.readLine()) != null)
    System.out.print("Your requested meal: "+line);
```

A. Nothing is printed.

B. A message followed by the text the user entered is printed.

C. An `ArrayIndexOutOfBoundsException` is thrown.

D. A `NullPointerException` is thrown.

E. An `IOException` is thrown.

F. None of the above, as the code does not compile

9. Suppose you have separate modules for a service provider interface, service provider, service locator, and consumer. If you add a new `abstract` method to the service provider interface and call it from the consumer module, how many of these modules do you need to re-compile?

A. Zero

B. One

C. Two

D. Three

E. Four

10. Which of the following statements can fill in the blank to make the code compile successfully? (Choose all that apply.)

```
Set<? extends RuntimeException> mySet = new _____();
```

A. `HashSet<? extends RuntimeException>`

B. `HashSet<Exception>`

C. `TreeSet<RuntimeException>`

D. `TreeSet<NullPointerException>`

E. None of the above

11. Suppose that we have the following property files and code. Which bundle is used on lines 8 and 9, respectively?

Dolphins.properties
```
name=The Dolphin
age=0
```

Dolphins_de.properties
```
name=Dolly
age=4
```

Dolphins_en.properties
name=Dolly

```
5: Locale fr = new Locale("fr");
6: Locale.setDefault(new Locale("en", "US"));
7: var b = ResourceBundle.getBundle("Dolphins", fr);
8: b.getString("name");
9: b.getString("age");
```

A. Dolphins.properties and Dolphins.properties are used.

B. Dolphins.properties and Dolphins_en.properties are used.

C. Dolphins_en.properties and Dolphins.properties are used.

D. Dolphins_en.properties and Dolphins_en.properties are used.

E. Dolphins_de.properties and Dolphins_en.properties are used.

F. The code does not compile.

12. Given the following program, what can be inserted into the blank line that would allow it to compile and print Poof! at runtime? (Choose all that apply.)

```
class Wizard {
    private enum Hat {
        BIG, SMALL
    }
    protected class MagicWand {
        void abracadabra() {
            System.out.print("Poof!");
        }
    }
}
public class CastSpells {
    public static void main(String[] args) {
        var w = new Wizard();
        _____.abracadabra();
    }
}
```

A. class DarkWizard extends Wizard {}.new MagicWand()

B. new Wizard().new MagicWand()

C. Wizard.new MagicWand()

D. w.new MagicWand(){
```
    void abracadabra(int spell) {
        System.out.print("Oops!"); } }
```

    E. `new MagicWand()`

    F. `w.new MagicWand()`

    G. None of the above, as the code does not compile.

13. Assume `birds.dat` exists, is accessible, and contains data for a `Bird` object. What is the result of executing the following code? (Choose all that apply.)

```
1:  import java.io.*;
2:  public class Bird {
3:      private String name;
4:      private transient Integer age;
5:
6:      // Getters/setters omitted
7:
8:      public static void main(String[] args) {
9:          try(var is = new ObjectInputStream(
10:                 new BufferedInputStream(
11:                 new FileInputStream("birds.dat")))) {
12:             Bird b = is.readObject();
13:             System.out.println(b.age);
14:      } } }
```

    A. It compiles and prints 0 at runtime.

    B. It compiles and prints `null` at runtime.

    C. It compiles and prints a number at runtime.

    D. The code will not compile because of lines 9–11.

    E. The code will not compile because of line 12.

    F. It compiles but throws an exception at runtime.

14. Which of the following are true? (Choose all that apply.)

```
private static void magic(Stream<Integer> s) {
    Optional o = s
        .filter(x -> x < 5)
        .limit(3)
        .max((x, y) -> x-y);
    System.out.println(o.get());
}
```

    A. `magic(Stream.empty());` runs infinitely.

    B. `magic(Stream.empty());` throws an exception.

    C. `magic(Stream.iterate(1, x -> x++));` runs infinitely.

    D. `magic(Stream.iterate(1, x -> x++));` throws an exception.

E. `magic(Stream.of(5, 10));` runs infinitely.

F. `magic(Stream.of(5, 10));` throws an exception.

G. The method does not compile.

15. Assume the file `/gorilla/signs.txt` exists within the file system. Which statements about the following code snippet are correct? (Choose all that apply.)

```
var x = Path.of("/gorilla/signs.txt");
Files.find(x.getParent(), 10.0, // k1
    (Path p) -> p.toString().endsWith(".txt")) // k2
    .collect(Collectors.toList())
    .forEach(System.out::println);

Files.readAllLines(x) // k3
    .flatMap(p -> Stream.of(p.split(" "))) // k4
    .map(s -> s.toLowerCase())
    .forEach(System.out::println);
```

A. Nothing is printed.

B. All of the `.txt` files and directories in the directory tree are printed.

C. All of the words in `signs.txt` are printed.

D. Line k1 contains a compiler error.

E. Line k2 contains a compiler error.

F. Line k3 contains a compiler error.

G. Line k4 contains a compiler error.

16. Which interface is used to run stored procedures?

A. `Callable`

B. `CallableStatement`

C. `PreparedStatement`

D. `ProceduralStatement`

E. `Statement`

F. `StoredStatement`

17. What is the result of the following class?

```
1: public class Box<T> {
2:     T value;
3:
4:     public Box(T value) {
5:         this.value = value;
6:     }
```

```
7:      public T getValue() {
8:          return value;
9:      }
10:     public static void main(String[] args) {
11:         var one = new Box<String>("a string");
12:         var two = new Box<Integer>(123);
13:         System.out.print(one.getValue());
14:         System.out.print(two.getValue());
15: } }
```

A. Compiler error on line 1

B. Compiler error on line 2

C. Compiler error on line 11

D. Compiler error on line 12

E. a string123

F. An exception is thrown.

18. Which changes, when made independently, guarantee the following code snippet prints 100 at runtime? (Choose all that apply.)

```
List<Integer> data = new ArrayList<>();
IntStream.range(0,100).parallel().forEach(s -> data.add(s));
System.out.println(data.size());
```

A. Change the data implementation class to a CopyOnWriteArrayList.

B. Remove parallel() in the stream operation.

C. Change forEach() to forEachOrdered() in the stream operation.

D. Change parallel() to serial() in the stream operation.

E. Wrap the data implementation class with a call to Collections.synchronizedList().

F. The code snippet will always print 100 as is.

19. Fill in the blanks: The _____ annotation can be used to indicate a method may be removed in a future version, while the _____ annotation can be used to ignore it.

A. @Ignore, @Suppress

B. @Retention, @SuppressWarnings

C. @Deprecated, @Suppress

D. @ForRemoval, @Ignore

E. @Deprecated, @SuppressWarnings

F. @Deprecated, @Ignore

20. What is the output of this code?

```
20: Predicate<String> empty = String::isEmpty;
21: Predicate<String> notEmpty = empty.negate();
22:
23: var result = Stream.generate(() -> "")
24:     .filter(notEmpty)
25:     .collect(Collectors.groupingBy(k -> k))
26:     .entrySet()
27:     .stream()
28:     .map(Entry::getValue)
29:     .flatMap(Collection::stream)
30:     .collect(Collectors.partitioningBy(notEmpty));
31: System.out.println(result);
```

A. It outputs: `{}`

B. It outputs: `{false=[], true=[]}`

C. The code does not compile.

D. The code does not terminate.

21. Which attack could exploit this code?

```
public boolean isValid(String hashedPassword)
        throws SQLException {

    var sql = "SELECT * FROM users WHERE password = '"
        + hashedPassword +"'";
    try (var stmt = conn.prepareStatement(sql);
        var rs = stmt.executeQuery(sql)) {
        return rs.next();
    }
}
```

A. Command injection

B. Confidential data exposure

C. Denial of service

D. SQL injection

E. SQL stealing

F. None of the above

22. Which lines of the following interface do not compile? (Choose all that apply.)

```
1: @FunctionalInterface
2: public interface PlayDnD {
3:     public static void roll() { roll(); }
4:     private int takeBreak() { roll(); return 1; }
5:     void startGame();
6:     default void win();
7:     static void end() { win(); }
8:     boolean equals(Object o);
9: }
```

- **A.** Line 1
- **B.** Line 3
- **C.** Line 4
- **D.** Line 5
- **E.** Line 6
- **F.** Line 7
- **G.** Line 8
- **H.** All of the lines compile.

Answers to Assessment Tests

Part I:

1. B. The code compiles successfully, so options D and E are incorrect. The value of a cannot be changed by the addToInt() method, no matter what the method does, because only a copy of the variable is passed into the parameter x. Therefore, a does not change, and the output on line 9 is 15. For more information, see Chapter 7.

2. C, D, E. The program contains three compiler errors. First, the method getTailLength() in the interface HasTail is implicitly to be public, since it is an abstract interface method. Therefore, line 3 does not compile since it is an invalid override, reducing the visibility of the method, making option C correct. Next, the class Cougar implements an overloaded version of getTailLength() with a different signature than the abstract interface method it inherits. For this reason, the declaration of Cougar is invalid, and option D is correct. Finally, option E is correct, since Puma is marked abstract and cannot be instantiated. For more information, see Chapter 9.

3. B. Initially, moon is assigned a value of 9, while star is assigned a value of 8. The multiplication operator (*) has a higher order of precedence than the addition operator (+), so it gets evaluated first. Since star is not greater than 10, sun is assigned a value of 3, which is promoted to 3.0f as part of the assignment. The value of jupiter is (3.0f + 9) - 1.0, which is 11.0f. This value is implicitly promoted to double when it is assigned. In the last assignment, moon is predecremented from 9 to 8, with the value of the expression returned as 8. Since 8 less than or equal to 8 is true, mars is set to a value of 2. The final output is 3.0–11.0–2, making option B the correct answer. Note that while Java outputs the decimal for both float and double values, it does not output the f for float values. For more information, see Chapter 3.

4. D. String literals are used from the string pool. This means that s1 and s2 refer to the same object and are equal. Therefore, the first two print statements print true. The concat() method forces a new String to be created making the third print statement print false. The intern() method reverts the String to the one from the string pool. Therefore, the fourth print statement prints true. The fifth print statement prints false because toString() uses a method to compute the value, and it is not from the string pool. The final print statement again prints true because equals() looks at the values of String objects. For more information, see Chapter 5.

5. E. The code does not compile because Java allows at most one public class in the same file. Either the FlightNumber class must not be declared public or it should be moved to its own source file named FlightNumber.java. The compiler error occurs on line 7, so the answer is option E. For more information, see Chapter 1.

6. G. This exam requires knowing how to run at the command line. The new -p option specifies the module path. The new -m option precedes the program to be run in the format moduleName/fullyQualifiedClassName. Option G is the only one that matches these

requirements. For more information, see Chapter 11.

7. F. The code does not compile because `switch` statements require case statements before the colon (:). For example, `case score1:` would compile. For this reason, option F is the correct answer. If the six missing `case` statements were added throughout this snippet, then the `default` branch would be executed as 7 is not matched in any of the `case` statements, resulting in an output of `great-good-` and making option A correct. For more information, see Chapter 4.

8. A, C, F. The `Predicate` interface takes a single parameter and returns a `boolean`. Lambda expressions with one parameter are allowed to omit the parentheses around the parameter list, making options A and C equivalent and both correct. The `return` statement is optional when a single statement is in the body, making option F correct. Option B is incorrect because a `return` statement must be used if braces are included around the body. Options D and E are incorrect because the type is `Integer` in the predicate and `int` in the lambda. Auto-boxing works for collections not inferring predicates. If these two were changed to `Integer`, they would be correct. For more information, see Chapter 6.

9. C. Option A is incorrect because `var` is only allowed as a type for local variables, not instance members. Options B and E are incorrect because `new` and `case` are reserved words and cannot be used as identifiers. Option C is correct, as `var` can be used as a method name. Option D is incorrect because a single underscore (_) cannot be used as an identifier starting with Java 9. Finally, option F is incorrect because `var` cannot be specified as the return type of a method. For more information, see Chapter 2.

10. A, C, E. The for-each loop implicitly casts each `Tadpole` object to an `Amphibian` reference, which is permitted because `Tadpole` is a subclass of `Amphibian`. From there, any supertype of `Amphibian` is permitted without an explicit cast. This includes `CanSwim`, which `Amphibian` implements, and `Object`, which all classes extend from, making options A and E correct. Option C is also correct since the reference is being cast to the same type. Option B is incorrect, since `Boolean` is not a supertype of `Amphibian`. Option D is also incorrect. Even though the underlying object is a `Tadpole` instance, it requires an explicit cast on line 9 since the reference type is `Amphibian`. Option F is incorrect because there are options that allow the code to compile. For more information, see Chapter 8.

11. B, D. Option A does not compile, as the expression `3 + 2.0` is evaluated as a `double`, and a `double` requires an explicit cast to be assigned to an `int`. Option B compiles without issue, as a `long` value can be implicitly cast to a `double`. Option C does not compile because the ternary operator (? :) is missing a colon (:), followed by a second expression. Option D is correct. Even though the `int` value is larger than a `short`, it is implicitly cast to a `short`, which means the value will wrap around to fit in a `short`. Option E is incorrect, as you cannot use a decimal (.) with the `long` (L) postfix. Finally, option F is incorrect, as an underscore cannot be used next to a decimal point. For more information, see Chapter 3.

12. D. If this were a valid `module-info.java` file, it would need to be placed at the root directory of the module, which is option A. However, a module is not allowed to use the `public` access modifier. Option D is correct because the provided file does not compile regardless of placement in the project. For more information, see Chapter 11.

13. C. The code compiles and runs without issue; therefore, options E and F are incorrect. This type of problem is best examined one loop iteration at a time:

- On the first iteration of the outer loop i is 0, so the loop continues.

- On the first iteration of the inner loop, i is updated to 1 and x to 6. The if statement branch is not executed, and x is increased to 10 and j to 1.

- On the second iteration of the inner loop (since j = 1 and 1 <= 2), i is updated to 2 and x to 11. At this point, the if branch will evaluate to true for the remainder of the program run, which causes the flow to break out of the inner loop each time it is reached.

- On the second iteration of the outer loop (since i = 2), i is updated to 3 and x to 12. As before, the inner loop is broken since x is still greater than 10.

- On the third iteration of the outer loop, the outer loop is broken, as i is already not less than 3. The most recent value of x, 12, is output, so the answer is option C.

For more information, see Chapter 4.

14. F. Line 5 does not compile as the FileNotFoundException thrown on line 12 is not handled or declared by the method. Line 7 does not compile because StringBuilder does not implement AutoCloseable and is therefore not compatible with a try-with-resource statement. Finally, line 10 does not compile as RuntimeException is a subclass of Exception in the multicatch block, making it redundant. Since this method contains three compiler errors, option F is the correct answer. For more information, see Chapter 10.

15. A, C, F. The Java Development Kit (JDK) is used when creating Java programs. It contains a compiler since it is a development tool making option A correct and option B incorrect. The JDK contains a Java Virtual Machine (JVM) making option F correct and option E incorrect. The compiler creates bytecode making option C correct and option D incorrect. For more information, see Chapter 1.

16. C, E, F. The jump() method has default (package-private) access, which means it can be accessed only from the same package. Tadpole is not in the same package as Frog, causing lines 7 and 10 to give a compiler error, making options C and F correct. The ribbit() method has protected access, which means it can only be accessed from a subclass reference or in the same package. Line 6 is fine because Tadpole is a subclass. Line 9 does not compile because the variable reference is to a Frog, making option E correct. This is the trickiest question you can get on this topic on the exam. For more information, see Chapter 7.

17. C. The code compiles and runs without issue, so options G and H are incorrect. First, the Reindeer object is instantiated using the constructor that takes an int value. Since there is no explicit call to the parent constructor, the compiler inserts super()as the first line of the constructor on line 7. The parent constructor is called, and Deer is printed on line 2. The flow returns to the constructor on line 7, which prints Reindeer. Next, the method hasHorns() is called. The reference type is Deer, and the underlying object type is Reindeer. Since Reindeer correctly overrides the hasHorns() method, the version in Reindeer is called, printing true. For these reasons, option C is the correct answer. For more information, see Chapter 8.

18. B, E, F. The array is allowed to use an anonymous initializer because it is in the same line as the declaration. The `ArrayList` uses the diamond operator. This specifies the type matches the one on the left without having to retype it. After adding the two elements, `list` contains [6, 8]. We then replace the element at index 1 with 9, resulting in [6, 9]. Finally, we remove the element at index 0, leaving [9]and making option B correct. Option C is incorrect because arrays output something that looks like a reference rather than a nicely printed list of values.

Option E is correct because the `compare()` method returns 0 when the arrays are the same length and have the same elements. Option F is correct because the `mismatch()` method returns a −1 when the arrays are equivalent. For more information, see Chapter 5.

19. C, D. Immediately after line 8, only `Grasshopper g1`, created on line 6, is eligible for garbage collection since both one and two point to `Grasshopper g2`, making option C correct and option A incorrect. Immediately after line 9, we still only have `Grasshopper g1` eligible for garbage collection, since one points to it. For this reason, option B is incorrect and option D is correct. Reference two now points to `null`. Immediately after line 10, both `Grasshopper` objects are eligible for garbage collection since both one and two point to `null`, making option E incorrect. The code does compile, so option F is incorrect. Although it is traditional to declare instance variables early in the class, you don't have to. For more information, see Chapter 2.

20. B, C. Only checked exceptions are required to be handled or declared, making option B correct and option F incorrect. An `Error` is intended to be thrown by the JVM and never caught by the programmer, making option C correct and options A, D, and E incorrect. While a programmer could throw or catch an `Error`, this would be a horrible practice. For more information, see Chapter 10.

21. B, C, F. First, `null` and `nonstatic` are not valid method modifiers, making options A and D incorrect. Options B and F are correct, as abstract methods cannot be marked `private` or `static`, since they then would not be able to be overridden. Option C is also correct, as you cannot declare two access modifiers on the same method. Finally, options E and G are two sets of valid modifiers that can be used together in a method declaration. Using `private` with `final` is allowed, albeit redundant. For more information, see Chapter 9.

22. A. This is a great example to practice the process of elimination. The first thing to notice is that `multiplier` is not effectively final since it is reassigned. None of the lambdas will compile, making option A correct. The next step is to look at the lambda syntax. Options D and F are invalid because lambdas with more than one parameter must have parentheses. Options E and F are invalid because a `return` statement may not be used in a lambda without a block present. While option C at least compiles, the code fails at runtime because `List.of()` creates an immutable list. This is tricky as none of the lambdas will work successfully. Therefore, option A is the only correct answer. For more information, see Chapter 6.

Part II:

1. D. CRUD stands for Create Read Update Delete, making options B, C, E, and F incorrect. The `executeUpdate()` method is not allowed to make read operations. Option F is tricky, but incorrect, because it is a SQL keyword and not part of the CRUD acronym. Option D is the correct answer since it is a read operation. For more information, see Chapter 21.

2. A. The code compiles and runs without issue, so options E and F are incorrect. First, `path1` simplifies to /bats/sleep.txt after the path symbols have been removed and the `normalize()` method applied. The `path2` variable using the current directory of /bats/day is assigned a path value of /bats/sleep.txt. The `toRealPath()` method will also remove path symbols. Since the file `Path` objects represent the same path within the file system, they will return `true` for both `equals()` and `isSameFile()`, making option A correct. For more information, see Chapter 20.

3. C. Only named modules are required to have a `module-info` file, ruling out options A, B, E, and F. Unnamed modules are not readable by any other types of modules, ruling out option D. Automatic modules always export all packages to other modules, making the answer option C. For more information, see Chapter 17.

4. D, F, G. Line 9 does not compile because the use of `@CleaningProgram` is missing the element name `mode`. The element name can be dropped only if the element is named `value()` in the annotation type declaration. Line 11 does not compile because an annotation element must be a primitive, `String`, `Class`, enum, another annotation, or an array of these types. Line 12 does not compile because an element uses the keyword `default` to assign a default value, not the equal (=) sign. For more information, see Chapter 13.

5. F. The code compiles without issue, so options C and D are incorrect. The key to understanding this code is to notice that our thread executor contains only one thread, but our `CyclicBarrier` limit is 3. Even though 12 tasks are all successfully submitted to the service, the first task will block forever on the call to `await()`. Since the barrier is never reached, nothing is printed, and the program hangs, making option F correct. For more information, see Chapter 18.

6. A, B, F. The `serialPersistentFields` field is used to specify which fields should be used in serialization. It must be declared `private static final`, or it will be ignored. Therefore options A, B, and F are correct. For more information, see Chapter 22.

7. E. A resource must be marked `final` or be effectively `final` to be used in a try-with-resources statement. Since the variables d and w are reassigned after the try-with-resources statement, they are not effectively final. Therefore, the code does not compile, making option E correct. If those two lines were removed, then the program would compile and print TDWF at runtime. Remember that resources in a try-with-resources statement are closed in the reverse order in which they are declared. For more information, see Chapter 16.

8. B, D. If the console is not available, `System.console()` returns `null`, making option D correct. On the other hand, if the console is available, it will read the user input and print the result, making option B correct. For more information, see Chapter 19.

9. D. Since you are changing the service provider interface, you have to re-compile it. Similarly, you need to re-compile the service provider because it now needs to implement the new method. The consumer module needs to be re-compiled as well since the code has changed to call the new method. Therefore, three modules need to be re-compiled, and option D is correct. The service locator does not need to be re-compiled since it simply

looks up the interface. For more information, see Chapter 17.

10. C, D. The `mySet` declaration defines an upper bound of type `RuntimeException`. This means that classes may specify `RuntimeException` or any subclass of `RuntimeException` as the type parameter. Option B is incorrect because `Exception` is a superclass, not a subclass, of `RuntimeException`. Option A is incorrect because the wildcard cannot occur on the right side of the assignment. Options C and D compile and are the answers. For more information, see Chapter 14.

11. C. Java will use `Dolphins_en.properties` as the matching resource bundle on line 7. Since there is no match for French, the default locale is used. Line 8 finds a matching key in this file. Line 9 does not find a match in that file; therefore, it has to look higher up in the hierarchy. For more information, see Chapter 16.

12. B, D, F. The `MagicWand` class is an inner class that requires an instance of the outer class `Wizard` to instantiate. Option A is incorrect, as `DarkWizard` declares a local class but does not create an instance of the local class. Options B and F both correctly create an inner class instance from an outer class instance, printing `Poof!` at runtime. Options C and E are incorrect, as they each require an instance of the outer class. Remember, `MagicWand` is not a `static` nested class. Finally, option D is correct, as it creates an anonymous class of `Magic-Wand`. The method declared in the anonymous class is never called, though, since it is an overload of the original method with a different signature, not an override. In this manner, `Poof!` is still printed at runtime. For more information, see Chapter 12.

13. D, E. Line 10 includes an unhandled checked `IOException`, while line 11 includes an unhandled checked `FileNotFoundException`, making option D correct. Line 12 does not compile because `is.readObject()` must be cast to a `Bird` object to be assigned to b. It also does not compile because it includes two unhandled checked exceptions, `IOException` and `ClassNotFoundException`, making option E correct. If a cast operation were added on line 13 and the `main()` method were updated on line 8 to declare the various checked exceptions, then the code would compile but throw an exception at runtime since `Bird` does not implement `Serializable`. Finally, if the class did implement `Serializable`, then the program would print `null` at runtime, as that is the default value for the `transient` field `age`. For more information, see Chapter 19.

14. B, F. Calling `get()` on an empty `Optional` causes an exception to be thrown, making option B correct. Option F is also correct because `filter()` makes the Optional empty before it calls `get()`. Option C is incorrect because the infinite stream is made finite by the intermediate `limit()` operation. Options A and E are incorrect because the source streams are not infinite. Therefore, the call to `max()` sees only three elements and terminates. For more information, see Chapter 15.

15. D, E, G. The code contains multiple compiler errors. First, the second parameter of `Files.find()` takes an `int` depth limit, not `double`, so line k1 does not compile. Next, the lambda expression on line k2 does not compile. The parameter must be of type `BiPredicate<Path,BasicFileAttributes>`. Finally, `readAllLines()` on line k3 returns a `List<String>`, not a `Stream<String>`, resulting in line k4 not compiling. For this code to compile, the `Files.lines()` method should be used. If the code was corrected, then the first stream operation would print all of the files and directories that end with `.txt` in the directory tree up to a

depth limit of 10. The second stream operation would print each word in the sign.txt as lowercase on a separate line. For more information, see Chapter 20.

16. B. Option A is incorrect because Callable is used for concurrency rather than JDBC code. Option B is the correct answer as CallableStatement is used to run a stored procedure. Option C is incorrect because PreparedStatement is used for SQL specified in your application. Option E is incorrect because Statement is the generic interface and does not have functionality specific to stored procedures. Options D and F are incorrect because they are not interfaces in the JDK. For more information, see Chapter 21.

17. E. This class is a proper use of generics. Box uses a generic type named T. On line 11, the generic type is String. On line 12, the generic type is Integer. Both lines 11 and 12 use var for local variables to represent the types so you have to keep track of them yourself. For more information, see Chapter 14.

18. A, B, C, E. The code may print 100 without any changes, but since the data class is not thread-safe, the code may print other values. For this reason, option F is incorrect. Options A and E both change the data class to a thread-safe class and guarantee 100 will be printed at runtime. Options B and C are also correct, as they both cause the stream to apply the add() operation in a serial manner. Option D is incorrect, as serial() is not a stream method. For more information, see Chapter 18.

19. E. The @Deprecated annotation can be used to indicate that a method or class may be removed in a future version. The @SuppressWarnings with the "deprecation" value can be used to ignore deprecated warnings. For these reasons, option E is correct. The @Retention annotation is used to specify when/if the annotation information should be discarded. The other options are not built-in Java annotations. For more information, see Chapter 13.

20. D. First, this mess of code does compile. However, the source is an infinite stream. The filter operation will check each element in turn to see whether any are not empty. While nothing passes the filter, the code does not terminate. Therefore, option D is correct. For more information, see Chapter 15.

21. D. Option E is incorrect because SQL stealing is not the name of an attack. Option C is incorrect because the PreparedStatement and ResultSet are closed in a try-with-resources block. While we do not see the Connection closed, we also don't see it opened. The exam allows us to assume code that we can't see is correct.

Option D is the answer because bind variables are not used. The potentially unsafe provided method parameter hashedPassword is passed directly to the SQL statement. Remember that using a PreparedStatement is a necessary, but not sufficient, step to prevent SQL injection. For more information, see Chapter 22.

22. E, F. Line 1 compiles, as this is a functional interface and contains exactly one abstract method startGame(). Note that equals(Object) on line 8 does not contribute to the abstract method count, as it is always provided by java.lang.Object. Line 3 compiles, although if executed it would generate an infinite recursive call at runtime. Line 4 compiles since private interface methods can call static interface methods. Line 6 does not compile because the default interface methods must include a body. Line 7 also does not compile, as static interface methods are not permitted to call default, abstract, or non-static private interface methods. For these reasons, options E and F are correct. For more information, see Chapter 12.

Exam 1Z0-815, OCP Java SE 11 Programmer I

Chapter 1

Welcome to Java

Welcome to the beginning of your journey to achieve a Java 11 certification. We assume this isn't the first Java programming book you've read. Although we do talk about the basics, we do so only because we want to make sure you have all the terminology and detail you'll need for the 1Z0-815 exam. If you've never written a Java program before, we recommend you pick up an introductory book on any version of Java. Examples include *Head First Java, 2nd Edition* (O'Reilly Media, 2009); *Java for Dummies* (For Dummies, 2017), *Murach's Java Programming* (Murach, 2017), or *Thinking in Java, 4th Edition* (Prentice Hall, 2006). It's okay if the book covers an older version of Java—even Java 1.3 is fine. Then come back to this certification study guide.

This chapter covers the fundamentals of Java. You'll better understand the Java environments and benefits of Java. You'll also see how to define and run a Java class and learn about packages.

Learning About the Java Environment

The Java environment consists of understanding a number of technologies. In the following sections, we will go over the key terms and acronyms you need to know for the exam and then discuss what software you need to study for the exam.

Major Components of Java

The *Java Development Kit* (JDK) contains the minimum software you need to do Java development. Key pieces include the compiler (javac), which converts .java files to .class files, and the launcher java, which creates the virtual machine and executes the program. We will use both later in this chapter when running programs at the command line. The JDK also contains other tools including the archiver (jar) command, which can package files together, and the API documentation (javadoc) command for generating documentation.

The javac program generates instructions in a special format that the java command can run called *bytecode*. Then java launches the *Java Virtual Machine* (JVM) before running the code. The JVM knows how to run bytecode on the actual machine it is on. You can think of the JVM as a special magic box on your machine that knows how to run your .class file.

Where Did the JRE Go?

In previous versions of Java, you could download a Java Runtime Environment (JRE) instead of the full JDK. The JRE was a subset of the JDK that was used for running a program but could not compile one. It was literally a subset. In fact, if you looked inside the directory structure of a JDK in older versions of Java, you would see a folder named jre.

In Java 11, the JRE is no longer available as a stand-alone download or a subdirectory of the JDK. People can use the full JDK when running a Java program. Alternatively, developers can supply an executable that contains the required pieces that would have been in the JRE. The jlink command creates this executable.

While the JRE is not in scope for the exam, knowing what changed may help you eliminate wrong answers.

When writing a program, there are common pieces of functionality and algorithms that developers need. Luckily, we do not have to write each of these ourselves. Java comes with a large suite of *application programming interfaces* (APIs) that you can use. For example, there is a StringBuilder class to create a large String and a method in Collections to sort a list. When writing a program, it is helpful to look what pieces of your assignment can be accomplished by existing APIs.

You might have noticed that we said the JDK contains the minimum software you need. Many developers use an *integrated development environment* (IDE) to make writing and running code easier. While we do not recommend using one while studying for the exam, it is still good to know that they exist. Common Java IDEs include Eclipse, IntelliJ IDEA, and NetBeans.

Downloading a JDK

Every six months, the version number of Java gets incremented. Java 11 came out in September 2018. This means that Java 11 will not be the latest version when you download the JDK to study for the exam. However, you should still use Java 11 to study with since this is a Java 11 exam. The rules and behavior can change with later versions of Java. You wouldn't want to get a question wrong because you studied with a different version of Java!

Every three years, Oracle has a *long-term support* (LTS) release. Unlike non-LTS versions that are supported for only six months, LTS releases have patches and upgrades available for at least three years. Even after the next LTS, Java 17, comes out, be sure to use Java 11 to study for the Java 11 certification exam.

Oracle changed the licensing model for its JDK. While this isn't on the exam, you can read more about the licensing changes and other JDKs from the links on our book's website:

http://www.selikoff.net/ocp11-complete/

We recommend using the Oracle distribution of Java 11 to study for this exam. Note that Oracle's JDK is free for personal use as well as other scenarios. Alternatively, you can use OpenJDK, which is based on the same source code.

The Oracle distribution requires you to register for an Oracle account if you don't already have one. This is the same Oracle account you will use to get your exam scores, so you will have to do this at some point anyway.

Identifying Benefits of Java

Java has some key benefits that you'll need to know for the exam.

Object Oriented   Java is an object-oriented language, which means all code is defined in classes, and most of those classes can be instantiated into objects. We'll discuss this more throughout the book. Many languages before Java were procedural, which meant there were routines or methods but no classes. Another common approach is functional programming. Java allows for functional programming within a class, but object-oriented is still the main organization of code.

Encapsulation   Java supports access modifiers to protect data from unintended access and modification. Most people consider encapsulation to be an aspect of object-oriented languages. Since the exam objectives call attention to it specifically, so do we. In fact, Chapter 7, "Methods and Encapsulation," covers it extensively.

Platform Independent   Java is an interpreted language that gets compiled to bytecode. A key benefit is that Java code gets compiled once rather than needing to be recompiled for different operating systems. This is known as "write once, run everywhere." The portability allows you to easily share pre-compiled pieces of software. When studying for the 1Z0-816 exam, you'll learn that it is possible to write code that throws an exception in some environments, but not others. For example, you might refer to a file in a specific directory. If you get asked about running Java on different operating systems on the 1Z0-815 exam, the answer is that the same class files run everywhere.

Robust   One of the major advantages of Java over C++ is that it prevents memory leaks. Java manages memory on its own and does garbage collection automatically. Bad memory management in C++ is a big source of errors in programs.

Simple   Java was intended to be simpler to understand than C++. In addition to eliminating pointers, it got rid of operator overloading. In C++, you could write a + b and have it mean almost anything.

Secure   Java code runs inside the JVM. This creates a sandbox that makes it hard for Java code to do evil things to the computer it is running on. On the 1Z0-816 exam, there is even an exam objective for security.

Multithreaded　Java is designed to allow multiple pieces of code to run at the same time. There are also many APIs to facilitate this task. You'll learn about some of them when studying for the 1Z0-816 exam.

Backward Compatibility　The Java language architects pay careful attention to making sure old programs will work with later versions of Java. While this doesn't always occur, changes that will break backward compatibility occur slowly and with notice. *Deprecation* is a technique to accomplish this where code is flagged to indicate it shouldn't be used. This lets developers know a different approach is preferred so they can start changing the code.

Understanding the Java Class Structure

In Java programs, classes are the basic building blocks. When defining a *class*, you describe all the parts and characteristics of one of those building blocks. To use most classes, you have to create objects. An *object* is a runtime instance of a class in memory. An object is often referred to as an *instance* since it represents a single representation of the class. All the various objects of all the different classes represent the state of your program. A *reference* is a variable that points to an object.

In the following sections, we'll look at fields, methods, and comments. We'll also explore the relationship between classes and files.

Fields and Methods

Java classes have two primary elements: *methods*, often called functions or procedures in other languages, and *fields*, more generally known as variables. Together these are called the *members* of the class. Variables hold the state of the program, and methods operate on that state. If the change is important to remember, a variable stores that change. That's all classes really do. It's the programmer who creates and arranges these elements in such a way that the resulting code is useful and, ideally, easy for other programmers to understand.

Other building blocks include interfaces, which you'll learn about in Chapter 9, "Advanced Class Design," and enums, which you'll learn about in detail when you study for the 1Z0-816 exam.

The simplest Java class you can write looks like this:

```
1: public class Animal {
2: }
```

Java calls a word with special meaning a *keyword*. Other classes can use this class since there is a public keyword on line 1. The class keyword indicates you're defining a class. Animal gives the name of the class. Granted, this isn't an interesting class, so let's add your first field.

```
1: public class Animal {
2:     String name;
3: }
```

NOTE   The line numbers aren't part of the program; they're just there to make the code easier to talk about.

On line 2, we define a variable named name. We also define the type of that variable to be a String. A String is a value that we can put text into, such as "this is a string". String is also a class supplied with Java. Next you can add methods.

```
1: public class Animal {
2:     String name;
3:     public String getName() {
4:         return name;
5:     }
6:     public void setName(String newName) {
7:         name = newName;
8:     }
9: }
```

On lines 3–5, you've defined your first method. A method is an operation that can be called. Again, public is used to signify that this method may be called from other classes. Next comes the return type—in this case, the method returns a String. On lines 6–8 is another method. This one has a special return type called *void*. The void keyword means that no value at all is returned. This method requires information be supplied to it from the calling method; this information is called a *parameter*. The setName() method has one parameter named newName, and it is of type String. This means the caller should pass in one String parameter and expect nothing to be returned.

Two pieces of the method are special. The method name and parameter types are called the *method signature*. In this example, can you identify the method name and parameters?

```
public int numberVisitors(int month)
```

The method name is numberVisitors. There's one parameter named month, which is of type int, which is a numeric type.

The *method declaration* consists of additional information such as the return type. In this example, the return type is int.

Comments

Another common part of the code is called a *comment*. Because comments aren't executable code, you can place them in many places. Comments can make your code easier to read. You won't see many comments on the exam since the exam creators are trying to make the code harder to read. You will see them in this book as we explain the code. And we hope you use them in your own code. There are three types of comments in Java. The first is called a single-line comment:

```
// comment until end of line
```

A single-line comment begins with two slashes. The compiler ignores anything you type after that on the same line. Next comes the multiple-line comment:

```
/* Multiple
 * line comment
 */
```

A multiple-line comment (also known as a multiline comment) includes anything starting from the symbol /* until the symbol */. People often type an asterisk (*) at the beginning of each line of a multiline comment to make it easier to read, but you don't have to. Finally, we have a Javadoc comment:

```
/**
 * Javadoc multiple-line comment
 * @author Jeanne and Scott
 */
```

This comment is similar to a multiline comment except it starts with /**. This special syntax tells the Javadoc tool to pay attention to the comment. Javadoc comments have a specific structure that the Javadoc tool knows how to read. You probably won't see a Javadoc comment on the exam. Just remember it exists so you can read up on it online when you start writing programs for others to use.

As a bit of practice, can you identify which type of comment each of the following six words is in? Is it a single-line or a multiline comment?

```
/*
 * // anteater
 */
// bear
// // cat
// /* dog */
/* elephant */
/*
 * /* ferret */
 */
```

Did you look closely? Some of these are tricky. Even though comments technically aren't on the exam, it is good to practice to look at code carefully.

OK, on to the answers. The comment containing anteater is in a multiline comment. Everything between /* and */ is part of a multiline comment—even if it includes a single-line comment within it! The comment containing bear is your basic single-line comment. The comments containing cat and dog are also single-line comments. Everything from // to the end of the line is part of the comment, even if it is another type of comment. The comment containing elephant is your basic multiline comment.

The line with ferret is interesting in that it doesn't compile. Everything from the first /* to the first */ is part of the comment, which means the compiler sees something like this:

```
/* */ */
```

We have a problem. There is an extra `*/`. That's not valid syntax—a fact the compiler is happy to inform you about.

Classes vs. Files

Most of the time, each Java class is defined in its own `.java` file. It is usually `public`, which means any code can call it. Interestingly, Java does not require that the class be `public`. For example, this class is just fine:

```
1: class Animal {
2:     String name;
3: }
```

You can even put two classes in the same file. When you do so, at most one of the classes in the file is allowed to be public. That means a file containing the following is also fine:

```
1: public class Animal {
2:     private String name;
3: }
4: class Animal2 {
5: }
```

If you do have a public class, it needs to match the filename. The declaration `public class Animal2` would not compile in a file named `Animal.java`. In Chapter 7, we will discuss what access options are available other than `public`.

Writing a *main()* Method

A Java program begins execution with its `main()` method. A `main()` method is the gateway between the startup of a Java process, which is managed by the Java Virtual Machine (JVM), and the beginning of the programmer's code. The JVM calls on the underlying system to allocate memory and CPU time, access files, and so on. In this section, you will learn how to create a `main()` method, pass a parameter, and run a program both with and without the `javac` step.

Checking Your Version of Java

Before we go any further, please take this opportunity to ensure you have the right version of Java on your path.

```
javac -version
java -version
```

Both of these commands should include a version number that begins with the number 11.

Creating a *main()* Method

The main() method lets the JVM call our code. The simplest possible class with a main() method looks like this:

```
1: public class Zoo {
2:    public static void main(String[] args) {
3:
4:    }
5: }
```

This code doesn't do anything useful (or harmful). It has no instructions other than to declare the entry point. It does illustrate, in a sense, that what you can put in a main() method is arbitrary. Any legal Java code will do. In fact, the only reason we even need a class structure to start a Java program is because the language requires it. To compile and execute this code, type it into a file called Zoo.java and execute the following:

```
javac Zoo.java
java Zoo
```

If you don't get any error messages, you were successful. If you do get error messages, check that you've installed the Java 11 JDK, that you have added it to the PATH, and that you didn't make any typos in the example. If you have any of these problems and don't know what to do, post a question with the error message you received in the Beginning Java forum at CodeRanch (www.coderanch.com/forums/f-33/java).

To compile Java code, the file must have the extension .java. The name of the file must match the name of the class. The result is a file of bytecode by the same name, but with a .class filename extension. Remember that bytecode consists of instructions that the JVM knows how to execute. Notice that we must omit the .class extension to run Zoo.java.

The rules for what a Java code file contains, and in what order, are more detailed than what we have explained so far (there is more on this topic later in the chapter). To keep things simple for now, we'll follow this subset of the rules:

- Each file can contain only one public class.

- The filename must match the class name, including case, and have a .java extension.

Suppose we replace line 3 in Zoo.java with the following:

```
3: System.out.println("Welcome!");
```

When we compile and run the code again, we'll get the line of output that matches what's between the quotes. In other words, the program will output Welcome!.

Let's first review the words in the main() method's signature, one at a time. The keyword public is what's called an *access modifier*. It declares this method's level of exposure to potential callers in the program. Naturally, public means anyplace in the program. You'll learn more about access modifiers in Chapter 7.

The keyword *static* binds a method to its class so it can be called by just the class name, as in, for example, Zoo.main(). Java doesn't need to create an object to call the main()

method—which is good since you haven't learned about creating objects yet! In fact, the JVM does this, more or less, when loading the class name given to it. If a main() method isn't present in the class we name with the .java executable, the process will throw an error and terminate. Even if a main() method is present, Java will throw an exception if it isn't static. A nonstatic main() method might as well be invisible from the point of view of the JVM. You'll see static again in Chapter 7.

The keyword void represents the *return type*. A method that returns no data returns control to the caller silently. In general, it's good practice to use void for methods that change an object's state. In that sense, the main() method changes the program state from started to finished. We will explore return types in Chapter 7 as well. (Are you excited for Chapter 7 yet?)

Finally, we arrive at the main() method's parameter list, represented as an array of java.lang.String objects. In practice, you can write any of the following:

```
String[] args
String args[]
String... args;
```

The compiler accepts any of these. The variable name args hints that this list contains values that were read in (arguments) when the JVM started. The characters [] are brackets and represent an array. An array is a fixed-size list of items that are all of the same type. The characters ... are called varargs (variable argument lists). You will learn about String in Chapter 2, "Java Building Blocks." Arrays and varargs will follow in Chapter 5, "Core Java APIs."

While the previous example used the common args parameter name, you can use any valid variable name you like. The following three are also allowed:

```
String[] options
String options []
String... options;
```

Passing Parameters to a Java Program

Let's see how to send data to our program's main() method. First we modify the Zoo program to print out the first two arguments passed in:

```java
public class Zoo {
    public static void main(String[] args) {
        System.out.println(args[0]);
        System.out.println(args[1]);
    }
}
```

The code args[0] accesses the first element of the array. That's right: array indexes begin with 0 in Java. To run it, type this:

```
javac Zoo.java
java Zoo Bronx Zoo
```

The output is what you might expect:

```
Bronx
Zoo
```

The program correctly identifies the first two "words" as the arguments. Spaces are used to separate the arguments. If you want spaces inside an argument, you need to use quotes as in this example:

```
javac Zoo.java
java Zoo "San Diego" Zoo
```

Now we have a space in the output:

```
San Diego
Zoo
```

To see if you follow that, what do you think this outputs?

```
javac Zoo.java
java Zoo San Diego Zoo
```

The answer is two lines. The first one is San, and the second is Diego. Since the program doesn't read from args[2], the third element (Zoo) is ignored.

All command-line arguments are treated as String objects, even if they represent another data type like a number:

```
javac Zoo.java
java Zoo Zoo 2
```

No matter. You still get the values output as String values. In Chapter 2, you'll learn how to convert String values to numbers.

```
Zoo
2
```

Finally, what happens if you don't pass in enough arguments?

```
javac Zoo.java
java Zoo Zoo
```

Reading args[0] goes fine, and Zoo is printed out. Then Java panics. There's no second argument! What to do? Java prints out an exception telling you it has no idea what to do with this argument at position 1. (You'll learn about exceptions in Chapter 10, "Exceptions.")

```
Zoo
Exception in thread "main" java.lang.ArrayIndexOutOfBoundsException:
Index 1 out of bounds for length 1
    at Zoo.main(Zoo.java:4)
```

To review, the JDK contains a compiler. Java class files run on the JVM and therefore run on any machine with Java rather than just the machine or operating system they happened to have been compiled on.

Running a Program in One Line

Starting in Java 11, you can run a program without compiling it first—well, without typing the javac command that is. Let's create a new class:

```
public class SingleFileZoo {
   public static void main(String[] args) {
      System.out.println("Single file: " + args[0]);
   }
}
```

We can run our SingleFileZoo example without actually having to compile it.

```
java SingleFileZoo.java Cleveland
```

Notice how this command passes the name of the Java file. When we compiled earlier, we wrote java Zoo. When running it as a one-liner, we write java SingleFileZoo.java. This is a key difference. After you first compiled with javac, you then passed the java command the name of the class. When running it directly, you pass the java command the name of the file. This feature is called launching *single-file source-code* programs. The name cleverly tells you that it can be used only if your program is one file. This means if your program has two .java files, you still need to use javac.

Now, suppose you have a class with invalid syntax in it. What do you think happens when we run java Learning.java?

```
public class Learning {
   public static void main(String[] args) {
      UhOh;   // DOES NOT COMPILE
      System.out.println("This works!");
   }
}
```

Java is still a compiled language, which means the code is being compiled in memory and the java command can give you a compiler error.

```
Learning.java:3: error: not a statement
   UhOh; // DOES NOT COMPILE
   ^
1 error
error: compilation failed
```

Notice how we said "in memory." Even if the code compiles properly, no `.class` file is created. This faster way of launching single-file source-code programs will save you time as you study for the exam. You'll be writing a lot of tiny programs. Having to write one line to run them instead of two will be a relief! However, compiling your code in advance using javac will result in the program running faster, and you will definitely want to do that for real programs.

Table 1.1 highlights the differences between this new feature and the traditional way of compiling. You'll learn about imports in the next section, but for now, just know they are a way of using code written by others.

TABLE 1.1   Running programs

Full command	Single-file source-code command
`javac HelloWorld.java` `java HelloWorld`	`java HelloWorld.java`
Produces a class file	Fully in memory
For any program	For programs with one file
Can import code in any available Java library	Can only import code that came with the JDK

Understanding Package Declarations and Imports

Java comes with thousands of built-in classes, and there are countless more from developers like you. With all those classes, Java needs a way to organize them. It handles this in a way similar to a file cabinet. You put all your pieces of paper in folders. Java puts classes in *packages*. These are logical groupings for classes.

We wouldn't put you in front of a file cabinet and tell you to find a specific paper. Instead, we'd tell you which folder to look in. Java works the same way. It needs you to tell it which packages to look in to find code.

Suppose you try to compile this code:

```
public class ImportExample {
   public static void main(String[] args) {
      Random r = new Random();   // DOES NOT COMPILE
      System.out.println(r.nextInt(10));
   }
}
```

The Java compiler helpfully gives you an error that looks like this:

```
Random cannot be resolved to a type
```

This error could mean you made a typo in the name of the class. You double-check and discover that you didn't. The other cause of this error is omitting a needed *import* statement. Import statements tell Java which packages to look in for classes. Since you didn't tell Java where to look for Random, it has no clue.

Trying this again with the import allows you to compile.

```java
import java.util.Random;  // import tells us where to find Random
public class ImportExample {
    public static void main(String[] args) {
        Random r = new Random();
        System.out.println(r.nextInt(10));  // print a number 0-9
    }
}
```

Now the code runs; it prints out a random number between 0 and 9. Just like arrays, Java likes to begin counting with 0.

As you can see in the previous example, Java classes are grouped into packages. The import statement tells the compiler which package to look in to find a class. This is similar to how mailing a letter works. Imagine you are mailing a letter to 123 Main St., Apartment 9. The mail carrier first brings the letter to 123 Main St. Then she looks for the mailbox for apartment number 9. The address is like the package name in Java. The apartment number is like the class name in Java. Just as the mail carrier only looks at apartment numbers in the building, Java only looks for class names in the package.

Package names are hierarchical like the mail as well. The postal service starts with the top level, looking at your country first. You start reading a package name at the beginning too. If it begins with java or javax, this means it came with the JDK. If it starts with something else, it likely shows where it came from using the website name in reverse. For example, com.amazon.javabook tells us the code came from Amazon.com. After the website name, you can add whatever you want. For example, com.amazon.java.my.name also came from Amazon.com. Java calls more detailed packages *child packages*. The package com.amazon.javabook is a child package of com.amazon. You can tell because it's longer and thus more specific.

You'll see package names on the exam that don't follow this convention. Don't be surprised to see package names like a.b.c. The rule for package names is that they are mostly letters or numbers separated by periods (.). Technically, you're allowed a couple of other characters between the periods (.). The rules are the same as for variable names, which you'll see in Chapter 2. The exam may try to trick you with invalid variable names. Luckily, it doesn't try to trick you by giving invalid package names.

In the following sections, we'll look at imports with wildcards, naming conflicts with imports, how to create a package of your own, and how the exam formats code.

Wildcards

Classes in the same package are often imported together. You can use a shortcut to `import` all the classes in a package.

```
import java.util.*;     // imports java.util.Random among other things
public class ImportExample {
   public static void main(String[] args) {
      Random r = new Random();
      System.out.println(r.nextInt(10));
   }
}
```

In this example, we imported `java.util.Random` and a pile of other classes. The `*` is a wildcard that matches all classes in the package. Every class in the `java.util` package is available to this program when Java compiles it. It doesn't `import` child packages, fields, or methods; it imports only classes. (There is a special type of `import` called the *static import* that imports other types, which you'll learn more about in Chapter 7.)

You might think that including so many classes slows down your program execution, but it doesn't. The compiler figures out what's actually needed. Which approach you choose is personal preference—or team preference if you are working with others on a team. Listing the classes used makes the code easier to read, especially for new programmers. Using the wildcard can shorten the `import` list. You'll see both approaches on the exam.

Redundant Imports

Wait a minute! We've been referring to `System` without an `import`, and Java found it just fine. There's one special package in the Java world called `java.lang`. This package is special in that it is automatically imported. You can type this package in an `import` statement, but you don't have to. In the following code, how many of the imports do you think are redundant?

```
1:  import java.lang.System;
2:  import java.lang.*;
3:  import java.util.Random;
4:  import java.util.*;
5:  public class ImportExample {
6:     public static void main(String[] args) {
7:        Random r = new Random();
8:        System.out.println(r.nextInt(10));
9:     }
10: }
```

The answer is that three of the imports are redundant. Lines 1 and 2 are redundant because everything in java.lang is automatically considered to be imported. Line 4 is also redundant in this example because Random is already imported from java.util.Random. If line 3 wasn't present, java.util.* wouldn't be redundant, though, since it would cover importing Random.

Another case of redundancy involves importing a class that is in the same package as the class importing it. Java automatically looks in the current package for other classes.

Let's take a look at one more example to make sure you understand the edge cases for imports. For this example, Files and Paths are both in the package java.nio.file. You don't need to memorize this package for the 1Z0-815 exam (but you should know it for the 1Z0-816 exam). When testing your understanding of packages and imports, the 1Z0-815 exam may use packages you may never have seen before. The question will let you know which package the class is in if you need to know that in order to answer the question.

What imports do you think would work to get this code to compile?

```java
public class InputImports {
    public void read(Files files) {
        Paths.get("name");
    }
}
```

There are two possible answers. The shorter one is to use a wildcard to import both at the same time.

```java
import java.nio.file.*;
```

The other answer is to import both classes explicitly.

```java
import java.nio.file.Files;
import java.nio.file.Paths;
```

Now let's consider some imports that don't work.

```java
import java.nio.*;          // NO GOOD - a wildcard only matches
                            // class names, not "file.Files"

import java.nio.*.*;        // NO GOOD - you can only have one wildcard
                            // and it must be at the end

import java.nio.file.Paths.*; // NO GOOD - you cannot import methods
                              // only class names
```

Naming Conflicts

One of the reasons for using packages is so that class names don't have to be unique across all of Java. This means you'll sometimes want to import a class that can be found in multiple places. A common example of this is the `Date` class. Java provides implementations of `java.util.Date` and `java.sql.Date`. This is another example where you don't need to know the package names for the 1Z0-815 exam—they will be provided to you. What `import` could we use if we want the `java.util.Date` version?

```java
public class Conflicts {
    Date date;
    // some more code
}
```

The answer should be easy by now. You can write either `import java.util.*;` or `import java.util.Date;`. The tricky cases come about when other imports are present.

```java
import java.util.*;
import java.sql.*; // causes Date declaration to not compile
```

When the class is found in multiple packages, Java gives you a compiler error.

```
error: reference to Date is ambiguous
    Date date;
    ^
    both class java.sql.Date in java.sql and class java.util.Date in java.util match
```

In our example, the solution is easy—remove the `import java.sql.Date` that we don't need. But what do we do if we need a whole pile of other classes in the `java.sql` package?

```java
import java.util.Date;
import java.sql.*;
```

Ah, now it works. If you explicitly `import` a class name, it takes precedence over any wildcards present. Java thinks, "The programmer really wants me to assume use of the `java.util.Date` class."

One more example. What does Java do with "ties" for precedence?

```java
import java.util.Date;
import java.sql.Date;
```

Java is smart enough to detect that this code is no good. As a programmer, you've claimed to explicitly want the default to be both the `java.util.Date` and `java.sql.Date` implementations. Because there can't be two defaults, the compiler tells you the following:

```
error: reference to Date is ambiguous
    Date date;
    ^
    both class java.util.Date in java.util and class java.sql.Date in java.sql match
```

If You Really Need to Use Two Classes with the Same Name

Sometimes you really do want to use Date from two different packages. When this happens, you can pick one to use in the import and use the other's fully qualified class name [the package name, a period (.), and the class name] to specify that it's special. Here's an example:

```java
import java.util.Date;

public class Conflicts {
   Date date;
   java.sql.Date sqlDate;

}
```

Or you could have neither with an import and always use the fully qualified class name.

```java
public class Conflicts {
   java.util.Date date;
   java.sql.Date sqlDate;

}
```

Creating a New Package

Up to now, all the code we've written in this chapter has been in the *default package*. This is a special unnamed package that you should use only for throwaway code. You can tell the code is in the default package, because there's no package name. On the exam, you'll see the default package used a lot to save space in code listings. In real life, always name your packages to avoid naming conflicts and to allow others to reuse your code.

Now it's time to create a new package. The directory structure on your computer is related to the package name. In this section, just read along. We will cover how to compile and run the code in the next section.

Suppose we have these two classes in the C:\temp directory:

```java
package packagea;
public class ClassA {
}

package packageb;
import packagea.ClassA;
public class ClassB {
   public static void main(String[] args) {
```

```
        ClassA a;
        System.out.println("Got it");
    }
}
```

When you run a Java program, Java knows where to look for those package names. In this case, running from `C:\temp` works because both packagea and packageb are underneath it.

What do you think happens if you run `java packageb/ClassB.java`? This does not work. Remember that you can use the `java` command to run a file directly only when that program is contained within a single file. Here, `ClassB.java` relies on `ClassA`.

Compiling and Running Code with Packages

You'll learn Java much more easily by using the command line to compile and test your examples. Once you know the Java syntax well, you can switch to an IDE. But for the exam, your goal is to know details about the language and not have the IDE hide them for you.

Follow this example to make sure you know how to use the command line. If you have any problems following this procedure, post a question in the Beginning Java forum at CodeRanch (www.coderanch.com/forums/f-33/java). Describe what you tried and what the error said.

The first step is to create the two files from the previous section. Table 1.2 shows the expected fully qualified filenames and the command to get into the directory for the next steps.

TABLE 1.2   Setup procedure by operating system

Step	Windows	Mac/Linux
1. Create first class.	`C:\temp\packagea\ClassA.java`	`/tmp/packagea/ClassA.java`
2. Create second class.	`C:\temp\packageb\ClassB.java`	`/tmp/packageb/ClassB.java`
3. Go to directory.	`cd C:\temp`	`cd /tmp`

Now it is time to compile the code. Luckily, this is the same regardless of the operating system. To compile, type the following command:

```
javac packagea/ClassA.java packageb/ClassB.java
```

If this command doesn't work, you'll get an error message. Check your files carefully for typos against the provided files. If the command does work, two new files will be created: `packagea/ClassA.class` and `packageb/ClassB.class`.

Compiling with Wildcards

You can use an asterisk to specify that you'd like to include all Java files in a directory. This is convenient when you have a lot of files in a package. We can rewrite the previous javac command like this:

```
javac packagea/*.java packageb/*.java
```

However, you cannot use a wildcard to include subdirectories. If you were to write javac *.java, the code in the packages would not be picked up.

Now that your code has compiled, you can run it by typing the following command:

```
java packageb.ClassB
```

If it works, you'll see Got it printed. You might have noticed that we typed ClassB rather than ClassB.class. As discussed earlier, you don't pass the extension when running a program.

Figure 1.1 shows where the .class files were created in the directory structure.

FIGURE 1.1   Compiling with packages

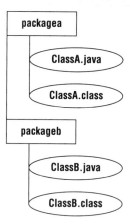

Using an Alternate Directory

By default, the javac command places the compiled classes in the same directory as the source code. It also provides an option to place the class files into a different directory. The -d option specifies this target directory.

   Java options are case sensitive. This means you cannot pass -D instead of -d.

If you are following along, delete the ClassA.class and ClassB.class files that were created in the previous section.

Where do you think this command will create the file ClassA.class?

```
javac -d classes packagea/ClassA.java packageb/ClassB.java
```

The correct answer is classes/packagea/ClassA.class. The package structure is preserved under the requested target directory. Figure 1.2 shows this new structure.

FIGURE 1.2   Compiling with packages and directories

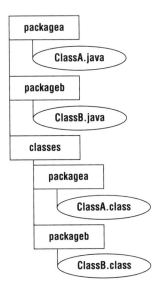

To run the program, you specify the classpath so Java knows where to find the classes. There are three options you can use. All three of these do the same thing:

```
java -cp classes packageb.ClassB
java -classpath classes packageb.ClassB
java --class-path classes packageb.ClassB
```

Notice that the last one requires two dashes (--), while the first two require one dash (-). If you have the wrong number of dashes, the program will not run.

Three Classpath Options

You might wonder why there are three options for the classpath. The -cp option is the short form. Developers frequently choose the short form because we are lazy typists. The -classpath and --class-path versions can be clearer to read but require more typing. The exam can use any of these, so be sure to learn all three.

Table 1.3 and Table 1.4 review the options you need to know for the exam. In Chapter 11, "Modules," you will learn additional options specific to modules.

TABLE 1.3 Options you need to know for the exam: javac

Option	Description
-cp <classpath> -classpath <classpath> --class-path <classpath>	Location of classes needed to compile the program
-d <dir>	Directory to place generated class files

TABLE 1.4 Options you need to know for the exam: java

Option	Description
-cp <classpath> -classpath <classpath> --class-path <classpath>	Location of classes needed to run the program

Compiling with JAR Files

Just like the classes directory in the previous example, you can also specify the location of the other files explicitly using a classpath. This technique is useful when the class files are located elsewhere or in special JAR files. A *Java archive* (JAR) file is like a zip file of mainly Java class files.

On Windows, you type the following:

```
java -cp ".;C:\temp\someOtherLocation;c:\temp\myJar.jar" myPackage.MyClass
```

And on macOS/Linux, you type this:

```
java -cp ".:/tmp/someOtherLocation:/tmp/myJar.jar" myPackage.MyClass
```

The period (.) indicates you want to include the current directory in the classpath. The rest of the command says to look for loose class files (or packages) in someOtherLocation and within myJar.jar. Windows uses semicolons (;) to separate parts of the classpath; other operating systems use colons.

Just like when you're compiling, you can use a wildcard (*) to match all the JARs in a directory. Here's an example:

```
java -cp "C:\temp\directoryWithJars\*" myPackage.MyClass
```

This command will add all the JARs to the classpath that are in directoryWithJars. It won't include any JARs in the classpath that are in a subdirectory of directoryWithJars.

Creating a JAR File

Some JARs are created by others, such as those downloaded from the Internet or created by a teammate. Alternatively, you can create a JAR file yourself. To do so, you use the jar command. The simplest commands create a jar containing the files in the current directory. You can use the short or long form for each option.

```
jar -cvf myNewFile.jar .
jar --create --verbose --file myNewFile.jar .
```

Alternatively, you can specify a directory instead of using the current directory.

```
jar -cvf myNewFile.jar -C dir .
```

There is no long form of the -C option. Table 1.5 lists the options you need to use the jar command to create a jar file. In Chapter 11, you will learn another option specific to modules.

TABLE 1.5   Options you need to know for the exam: jar

Option	Description
-c --create	Creates a new JAR file
-v --verbose	Prints details when working with JAR files
-f \<fileName\> --file \<fileName\>	JAR filename
-C \<directory\>	Directory containing files to be used to create the JAR

Running a Program in One Line with Packages

You can use single-file source-code programs from within a package as long as they rely only on classes supplied by the JDK. This code meets the criteria.

```java
package singleFile;

import java.util.*;

public class Learning {
   private ArrayList list;
   public static void main(String[] args) {
      System.out.println("This works!");
   }
}
```

You can run either of these commands:

```
java Learning.java          // from within the singleFile directory
java singleFile/Learning.java // from the directory above singleFile
```

Ordering Elements in a Class

Now that you've seen the most common parts of a class, let's take a look at the correct order to type them into a file. Comments can go anywhere in the code. Beyond that, you need to memorize the rules in Table 1.6.

TABLE 1.6 Order for declaring a class

Element	Example	Required?	Where does it go?
Package declaration	package abc;	No	First line in the file
Import statements	import java.util.*;	No	Immediately after the package (if present)
Class declaration	public class C	Yes	Immediately after the import (if any)
Field declarations	int value;	No	Any top-level element in a class
Method declarations	void method()	No	Any top-level element in a class

Let's look at a few examples to help you remember this. The first example contains one of each element:

```
package structure;      // package must be first non-comment
import java.util.*;     // import must come after package
public class Meerkat {  // then comes the class
   double weight;       // fields and methods can go in either order
   public double getWeight() {
      return weight; }
   double height;    // another field - they don't need to be together
}
```

So far, so good. This is a common pattern that you should be familiar with. How about this one?

```
/* header */
package structure;
// class Meerkat
public class Meerkat { }
```

Still good. We can put comments anywhere, and imports are optional. In the next example, we have a problem:

```
import java.util.*;
package structure;        // DOES NOT COMPILE
String name;              // DOES NOT COMPILE
public class Meerkat { } // DOES NOT COMPILE
```

There are two problems here. One is that the `package` and `import` statements are reversed. Though both are optional, package must come before import if present. The other issue is that a field attempts a declaration outside a class. This is not allowed. Fields and methods must be within a class.

Got all that? Think of the acronym PIC (picture): package, import, and class. Fields and methods are easier to remember because they merely have to be inside a class.

You need to know one more thing about class structure for the 1Z0-815 exam: multiple classes can be defined in the same file, but only one of them is allowed to be public. The public class matches the name of the file. For example, these two classes must be in a file named `Meerkat.java`:

```
1: public class Meerkat { }
2: class Paw { }
```

A file is also allowed to have neither class be public. As long as there isn't more than one public class in a file, it is okay.

Now you know how to create and arrange a `class`. Later chapters will show you how to create classes with more powerful operations.

Code Formatting on the Exam

Not all questions will include package declarations and imports. Don't worry about missing package statements or imports unless you are asked about them. The following are common cases where you don't need to check the imports:

- Code that begins with a class name
- Code that begins with a method declaration
- Code that begins with a code snippet that would normally be inside a class or method
- Code that has line numbers that don't begin with 1

This point is so important that we are going to reinforce it with an example. Does this code compile?

```
public class MissingImports {
   Date date;
   public void today() {}
}
```

Yes! The question was not about imports, so you have to assume that import java.util is present.

On the other hand, a question that asks you about packages, imports, or the correct order of elements in a class is giving you clues that the question is virtually guaranteed to be testing you on these topics! Also note that imports will be not removed to save space if the package statement is present. This is because imports go after the package statement.

You'll see code that doesn't have a main() method. When this happens, assume any necessary plumbing code like the main() method and class definition were written correctly. You're just being asked if the part of the code you're shown compiles when dropped into valid surrounding code.

Another thing the exam does to save space is to merge code on the same line. You should expect to see code like the following and to be asked whether it compiles. (You'll learn about ArrayList in Chapter 5—assume that part is good for now.)

```
6: public void getLetter(ArrayList list) {
7:    if (list.isEmpty()) { System.out.println("e");
8:    } else { System.out.println("n");
9: }  }
```

The answer here is that it does compile because the line break between the if statement and println() is not necessary. Additionally, you still get to assume the necessary class definition and imports are present. Now, what about this one? Does it compile?

```
1: public class LineNumbers {
2:    public void getLetter(ArrayList list) {
3:       if (list.isEmpty()) { System.out.println("e");
4:       } else { System.out.println("n");
5: }  } }
```

For this one, you would answer "Does not compile." Since the code begins with line 1, you don't get to assume that valid imports were provided earlier. The exam will let you know what package classes are in unless they're covered in the objectives. You'll be expected to know that ArrayList is in java.util—at least you will once you get to Chapter 5 of this book!

> Remember that extra whitespace doesn't matter in Java syntax. The exam may use varying amounts of whitespace to trick you.

Summary

The Java Development Kit (JDK) is used to do software development. It contains the compiler (javac), which turns source code into bytecode. It also contains the Java Virtual Machine (JVM) launcher (java), which launches the JVM and then calls the code. Application programming interfaces (APIs) are available to call reusable pieces of code.

Java code is object-oriented, meaning all code is defined in classes. Access modifiers allow classes to encapsulate data. Java is platform independent, compiling to bytecode. It is robust and simple by not providing pointers or operator overloading. Java is secure because it runs inside a virtual machine. Finally, the language facilitates multithreaded programming and strives for backward compatibility.

Java classes consist of members called fields and methods. An object is an instance of a Java class. There are three styles of comments: a single-line comment (//), a multiline comment (/* */), and a Javadoc comment (/** */).

Java begins program execution with a main() method. The most common signature for this method run from the command line is public static void main(String[] args). Arguments are passed in after the class name, as in java NameOfClass firstArgument. Arguments are indexed starting with 0.

Java code is organized into folders called packages. To reference classes in other packages, you use an import statement. A wildcard ending an import statement means you want to import all classes in that package. It does not include packages that are inside that one. The package java.lang is special in that it does not need to be imported.

For some class elements, order matters within the file. The package statement comes first if present. Then come the import statements if present. Then comes the class declaration. Fields and methods are allowed to be in any order within the class.

Exam Essentials

Identify benefits of Java.   Benefits of Java include object-oriented design, encapsulation, platform independence, robustness, simplicity, security, multithreading, and backward compatibility.

Define common acronyms.   The JDK stands for Java Development Kit and contains the compiler and JVM launcher. The JVM stands for Java Virtual Machine, and it runs byte-code. API is an application programming interface, which is code that you can call.

Be able to write code using a *main()* method.   A main() method is usually written as public static void main(String[] args). Arguments are referenced starting with args[0]. Accessing an argument that wasn't passed in will cause the code to throw an exception.

Understand the effect of using packages and imports.   Packages contain Java classes. Classes can be imported by class name or wildcard. Wildcards do not look at subdirectories. In the event of a conflict, class name imports take precedence.

Be able to recognize misplaced statements in a class.   Package and import statements are optional. If present, both go before the class declaration in that order. Fields and methods are also optional and are allowed in any order within the class declaration.

Review Questions

The answers to the chapter review questions can be found in the Appendix.

1. Which of the following are true statements? (Choose all that apply.)

    A. Java allows operator overloading.

    B. Java code compiled on Windows can run on Linux.

    C. Java has pointers to specific locations in memory.

    D. Java is a procedural language.

    E. Java is an object-oriented language.

    F. Java is a functional programming language.

2. Which of the following are true? (Choose all that apply.)

    A. javac compiles a `.class` file into a `.java` file.

    B. javac compiles a `.java` file into a `.bytecode` file.

    C. javac compiles a `.java` file into a `.class` file.

    D. java accepts the name of the class as a parameter.

    E. java accepts the filename of the `.bytecode` file as a parameter.

    F. java accepts the filename of the `.class` file as a parameter.

3. Which of the following are true if this command completes successfully assuming the CLASSPATH is not set? (Choose all that apply.)

    `java MyProgram.java`

    A. A `.class` file is created.

    B. MyProgram can reference classes in the package `com.sybex.book`.

    C. MyProgram can reference classes in the package `java.lang`.

    D. MyProgram can reference classes in the package `java.util`.

    E. None of the above. The program needs to be run as `java MyProgram`.

4. Given the following classes, which of the following can independently replace INSERT IMPORTS HERE to make the code compile? (Choose all that apply.)

    ```
    package aquarium;
    public class Tank { }

    package aquarium.jellies;
    public class Jelly { }

    package visitor;
    INSERT IMPORTS HERE
    public class AquariumVisitor {
        public void admire(Jelly jelly) { } }
    ```

    A. `import aquarium.*;`

    B. `import aquarium.*.Jelly;`

    C. `import aquarium.jellies.Jelly;`

    D. `import aquarium.jellies.*;`

    E. `import aquarium.jellies.Jelly.*;`

    F. None of these can make the code compile.

5. Which are included in the JDK? (Choose all that apply.)

    A. javac

    B. Eclipse

    C. JVM

    D. javadoc

    E. jar

    F. None of the above

6. Given the following classes, what is the maximum number of imports that can be removed and have the code still compile?

```
package aquarium;
public class Water { }

package aquarium;
import java.lang.*;
import java.lang.System;
import aquarium.Water;
import aquarium.*;
public class Tank {
    public void print(Water water) {
        System.out.println(water); } }
```

    A. 0

    B. 1

    C. 2

    D. 3

    E. 4

    F. Does not compile

7. Given the following classes, which of the following snippets can independently be inserted in place of INSERT IMPORTS HERE and have the code compile? (Choose all that apply.)

```
package aquarium;
public class Water {
    boolean salty = false;
```

```
   }
   package aquarium.jellies;
   public class Water {
      boolean salty = true;
   }

   package employee;
   INSERT IMPORTS HERE
   public class WaterFiller {
      Water water;
   }
```

A. import aquarium.*;

B. import aquarium.Water;
       import aquarium.jellies.*;

C. import aquarium.*;
       import aquarium.jellies.Water;

D. import aquarium.*;
       import aquarium.jellies.*;

E. import aquarium.Water;
       import aquarium.jellies.Water;

F. None of these imports can make the code compile.

8. Given the following command, which of the following classes would be included for compilation? (Choose all that apply.)

```
javac *.java
```

A. Hyena.java

B. Warthog.java

C. land/Hyena.java

D. land/Warthog.java

E. Hyena.groovy

F. Warthog.groovy

9. Given the following class, which of the following calls print out Blue Jay? (Choose all that apply.)

```
public class BirdDisplay {
   public static void main(String[] name) {
      System.out.println(name[1]);
} }
```

   A. `java BirdDisplay Sparrow Blue Jay`

   B. `java BirdDisplay Sparrow "Blue Jay"`

   C. `java BirdDisplay Blue Jay Sparrow`

   D. `java BirdDisplay "Blue Jay" Sparrow`

   E. `java BirdDisplay.class Sparrow "Blue Jay"`

   F. `java BirdDisplay.class "Blue Jay" Sparrow`

10. Which of the following are legal entry point methods that can be run from the command line? (Choose all that apply.)

   A. `private static void main(String[] args)`

   B. `public static final main(String[] args)`

   C. `public void main(String[] args)`

   D. `public static void test(String[] args)`

   E. `public static void main(String[] args)`

   F. `public static main(String[] args)`

11. Which of the following are true statements about Java? (Choose all that apply.)

   A. Bug-free code is guaranteed.

   B. Deprecated features are never removed.

   C. Multithreaded code is allowed.

   D. Security is a design goal.

   E. Sideways compatibility is a design goal.

12. Which options are valid on the `javac` command without considering module options? (Choose all that apply.)

   A. `-c`

   B. `-C`

   C. `-cp`

   D. `-CP`

   E. `-d`

   F. `-f`

   G. `-p`

13. Which options are valid on the `java` command without considering module options? (Choose all that apply.)

   A. `-c`

   B. `-C`

   C. `-cp`

   D. `-d`

   E. `-f`

   F. `-p`

14. Which options are valid on the `jar` command without considering module options? (Choose all that apply.)

A. -c

B. -C

C. -cp

D. -d

E. -f

F. -p

15. What does the following code output when run as `java Duck Duck Goose`?

```
public class Duck {
   public void main(String[] args) {
      for (int i = 1; i <= args.length; i++)
         System.out.println(args[i]);
} }
```

A. Duck Goose

B. Duck ArrayIndexOutOfBoundsException

C. Goose

D. Goose ArrayIndexOutOfBoundsException

E. None of the above

16. Suppose we have the following class in the file `/my/directory/named/A/Bird.java`. Which of the answer options replaces `INSERT CODE HERE` when added independently if we compile from `/my/directory`? (Choose all that apply.)

```
INSERT CODE HERE
public class Bird { }
```

A. package my.directory.named.a;

B. package my.directory.named.A;

C. package named.a;

D. package named.A;

E. package a;

F. package A;

17. Which of the following are true? (Choose all that apply.)

```
public class Bunny {
   public static void main(String[] x) {
      Bunny bun = new Bunny();
} }
```

A. Bunny is a class.

B. bun is a class.

C. main is a class.

D. Bunny is a reference to an object.

E. bun is a reference to an object.

F. main is a reference to an object.

G. The main() method doesn't run because the parameter name is incorrect.

18. Which answer options represent the order in which the following statements can be assembled into a program that will compile successfully? (Choose all that apply.)

```
X: class Rabbit {}
Y: import java.util.*;
Z: package animals;
```

A. X, Y, Z

B. Y, Z, X

C. Z, Y, X

D. Y, X

E. Z, X

F. X, Z

19. Which are not available for download from Oracle for Java 11? (Choose all that apply.)

A. JDK

B. JRE

C. Eclipse

D. All of these are available from Oracle.

20. Which are valid ways to specify the classpath when compiling? (Choose all that apply.)

A. -cp

B. -classpath

C. --classpath

D. -class-path

E. --class-path

Chapter

2

Java Building Blocks

OCP EXAM OBJECTIVES COVERED IN THIS CHAPTER:

✓ **Working With Java Primitive Data Types and String APIs**

- Declare and initialize variables (including casting and promoting primitive data types)
- Identify the scope of variables
- Use local variable type inference

✓ **Describing and Using Objects and Classes**

- Declare and instantiate Java objects, and explain objects' lifecycles (including creation, dereferencing by reassignment, and garbage collection)
- Read or write to object fields

As the old saying goes, you have to learn how to walk before you can run. Likewise, you have to learn the basics of Java before you can build complex programs. In this chapter, we'll be presenting the basic structure of Java classes, variables, and data types, along with the aspects of each that you need to know for the exam. For example, you might use Java every day but be unaware you cannot create a variable called 3dMap or this. The exam expects you to know and understand the rules behind these principles. While most of this chapter should be review, there may be aspects of the Java language that are new to you since they don't come up in practical use often.

Creating Objects

Our programs wouldn't be able to do anything useful if we didn't have the ability to create new objects. Remember from Chapter 1, "Welcome to Java," that an object is an instance of a class. In the following sections, we'll look at constructors, object fields, instance initializers, and the order in which values are initialized.

Calling Constructors

To create an instance of a class, all you have to do is write new before the class name and add parentheses after it. Here's an example:

```
Park p = new Park();
```

First you declare the type that you'll be creating (Park) and give the variable a name (p). This gives Java a place to store a reference to the object. Then you write new Park() to actually create the object.

Park() looks like a method since it is followed by parentheses. It's called a *constructor*, which is a special type of method that creates a new object. Now it's time to define a constructor of your own:

```java
public class Chick {
    public Chick() {
        System.out.println("in constructor");
    }
}
```

There are two key points to note about the constructor: the name of the constructor matches the name of the class, and there's no return type. You'll likely see a method like this on the exam:

```
public class Chick {
   public void Chick() { }  // NOT A CONSTRUCTOR
}
```

When you see a method name beginning with a capital letter and having a return type, pay special attention to it. It is *not* a constructor since there's a return type. It's a regular method that does compile but will not be called when you write new Chick().

The purpose of a constructor is to initialize fields, although you can put any code in there. Another way to initialize fields is to do so directly on the line on which they're declared. This example shows both approaches:

```
public class Chicken {
   int numEggs = 12;   // initialize on line
   String name;
   public Chicken() {
      name = "Duke";   // initialize in constructor
   }
}
```

For most classes, you don't have to code a constructor—the compiler will supply a "do nothing" default constructor for you. There are some scenarios that do require you declare a constructor. You'll learn all about them in Chapter 8, "Class Design."

> Some classes provide built-in methods that allow you to create new instances without using a constructor or the new keyword. For example, in Chapter 5, "Core Java APIs," you'll create instances of Integer using the valueOf() method. Methods like this will often use new with a constructor in their method definition. For the exam, remember that anytime a constructor is used, the new keyword is required.

Reading and Writing Member Fields

It's possible to read and write instance variables directly from the caller. In this example, a mother swan lays eggs:

```
public class Swan {
   int numberEggs;                          // instance variable
   public static void main(String[] args) {
      Swan mother = new Swan();
      mother.numberEggs = 1;                // set variable
```

```
      System.out.println(mother.numberEggs);  // read variable
   }
}
```

The "caller" in this case is the main() method, which could be in the same class or in another class. Reading a variable is known as *getting* it. The class gets numberEggs directly to print it out. Writing to a variable is known as *setting* it. This class sets numberEggs to 1.

In Chapter 7, "Methods and Encapsulation," you'll learn how to use encapsulation to protect the Swan class from having someone set a negative number of eggs.

You can even read values of already initialized fields on a line initializing a new field:

```
1: public class Name {
2:    String first = "Theodore";
3:    String last = "Moose";
4:    String full = first + last;
5: }
```

Lines 2 and 3 both write to fields. Line 4 both reads and writes data. It reads the fields first and last. It then writes the field full.

Executing Instance Initializer Blocks

When you learned about methods, you saw braces ({}). The code between the braces (sometimes called "inside the braces") is called a *code block*. Anywhere you see braces is a code block.

Sometimes code blocks are inside a method. These are run when the method is called. Other times, code blocks appear outside a method. These are called *instance initializers*. In Chapter 7, you'll learn how to use a static initializer.

How many blocks do you see in the following example? How many instance initializers do you see?

```
1: public class Bird {
2:    public static void main(String[] args) {
3:        { System.out.println("Feathers"); }
4:    }
5:    { System.out.println("Snowy"); }
6: }
```

There are four code blocks in this example: a class definition, a method declaration, an inner block, and an instance initializer. Counting code blocks is easy: you just count the number of pairs of braces. If there aren't the same number of open ({) and close (}) braces or they aren't defined in the proper order, the code doesn't compile. For example, you cannot use a closed brace (}) if there's no corresponding open brace ({) that it matches written earlier in the code. In programming, this is referred to as the *balanced parentheses problem*, and it often comes up in job interview questions.

When you're counting instance initializers, keep in mind that they cannot exist inside of a method. Line 5 is an instance initializer, with its braces outside a method. On the other hand, line 3 is not an instance initializer, as it is only called when the `main()` method is executed. There is one additional set of braces on lines 1 and 6 that constitute the class declaration.

Following Order of Initialization

When writing code that initializes fields in multiple places, you have to keep track of the order of initialization. This is simply the order in which different methods, constructors, or blocks are called when an instance of the class is created. We'll add some more rules to the order of initialization in Chapter 8. In the meantime, you need to remember:

- Fields and instance initializer blocks are run in the order in which they appear in the file.
- The constructor runs after all fields and instance initializer blocks have run.

Let's look at an example:

```
1:  public class Chick {
2:      private String name = "Fluffy";
3:      { System.out.println("setting field"); }
4:      public Chick() {
5:          name = "Tiny";
6:          System.out.println("setting constructor");
7:      }
8:      public static void main(String[] args) {
9:          Chick chick = new Chick();
10:         System.out.println(chick.name); } }
```

Running this example prints this:

```
setting field
setting constructor
Tiny
```

Let's look at what's happening here. We start with the `main()` method because that's where Java starts execution. On line 9, we call the constructor of `Chick`. Java creates a new object. First it initializes `name` to `"Fluffy"` on line 2. Next it executes the `println()` statement in the instance initializer on line 3. Once all the fields and instance initializers have run, Java returns to the constructor. Line 5 changes the value of `name` to `"Tiny"`, and line 6 prints another statement. At this point, the constructor is done, and then the execution goes back to the `println()` statement on line 10.

Order matters for the fields and blocks of code. You can't refer to a variable before it has been defined:

```
{ System.out.println(name); }   // DOES NOT COMPILE
private String name = "Fluffy";
```

You should expect to see a question about initialization on the exam. Let's try one more. What do you think this code prints out?

```
public class Egg {
   public Egg() {
      number = 5;
   }
   public static void main(String[] args) {
      Egg egg = new Egg();
      System.out.println(egg.number);
   }
   private int number = 3;
   { number = 4; } }
```

If you answered 5, you got it right. Fields and blocks are run first in order, setting number to 3 and then 4. Then the constructor runs, setting number to 5. You will see a lot more of rules and examples covering order of initialization in Chapter 8.

Understanding Data Types

Java applications contain two types of data: primitive types and reference types. In this section, we'll discuss the differences between a primitive type and a reference type.

Using Primitive Types

Java has eight built-in data types, referred to as the Java *primitive types*. These eight data types represent the building blocks for Java objects, because all Java objects are just a complex collection of these primitive data types. That said, a primitive is not an object in Java nor does it represent an object. A primitive is just a single value in memory, such as a number or character.

The Primitive Types

The exam assumes you are well versed in the eight primitive data types, their relative sizes, and what can be stored in them. Table 2.1 shows the Java primitive types together with their size in bits and the range of values that each holds.

TABLE 2.1   Primitive types

Keyword	Type	Example
boolean	true or false	true
byte	8-bit integral value	123
short	16-bit integral value	123
int	32-bit integral value	123
long	64-bit integral value	123L
float	32-bit floating-point value	123.45f
double	64-bit floating-point value	123.456
char	16-bit Unicode value	'a'

Is String a Primitive?

No, it is not. That said, String is often mistaken for a ninth primitive because Java includes built-in support for String literals and operators. You'll learn more about String in Chapter 5, but for now just remember they are objects, not primitives.

There's a lot of information in Table 2.1. Let's look at some key points:

- The float and double types are used for floating-point (decimal) values.
- A float requires the letter f following the number so Java knows it is a float.
- The byte, short, int, and long types are used for numbers without decimal points. In mathematics, these are all referred to as integral values, but in Java, int and Integer refer to specific types.
- Each numeric type uses twice as many bits as the smaller similar type. For example, short uses twice as many bits as byte does.
- All of the numeric types are signed in Java. This means that they reserve one of their bits to cover a negative range. For example, byte ranges from –128 to 127. You might be surprised that the range is not –128 to 128. Don't forget, 0 needs to be accounted for too in the range.

You won't be asked about the exact sizes of most of these types, although you should know that a byte can hold a value from –128 to 127.

Real World Scenario

Signed and Unsigned: *short* and *char*

For the exam, you should be aware that short and char are closely related, as both are stored as integral types with the same 16-bit length. The primary difference is that short is *signed*, which means it splits its range across the positive and negative integers. Alternatively, char is *unsigned*, which means range is strictly positive including 0. Therefore, char can hold a higher positive numeric value than short, but cannot hold any negative numbers.

The compiler allows them to be used interchangeably in some cases, as shown here:

```
short bird = 'd';
char mammal = (short)83;
```

Printing each variable displays the value associated with their type.

```
System.out.println(bird);   // Prints 100
System.out.println(mammal); // Prints S
```

This usage is not without restriction, though. If you try to set a value outside the range of short or char, the compiler will report an error.

```
short reptile = 65535;  // DOES NOT COMPILE
char fish = (short)-1;  // DOES NOT COMPILE
```

Both of these examples would compile if their data types were swapped because the values would then be within range for their type. You'll learn more about casting in Chapter 3, "Operators."

So you aren't stuck memorizing data type ranges, let's look at how Java derives it from the number of bits. A byte is 8 bits. A bit has two possible values. (These are basic computer science definitions that you should memorize.) 2^8 is $2 \times 2 = 4 \times 2 = 8 \times 2 = 16 \times 2 = 32 \times 2 = 64 \times 2 = 128 \times 2 = 256$. Since 0 needs to be included in the range, Java takes it away from the positive side. Or if you don't like math, you can just memorize it.

Floating-Point Numbers and Scientific Notation

While integer values like short and int are relatively easy to calculate the range for, floating-point values like double and float are decidedly not. In most computer systems, floating-point numbers are stored in scientific notation. This means the numbers are stored as two numbers, a and b, of the form $a \times 10^b$.

This notation allows much larger values to be stored, at the cost of accuracy. For example, you can store a value of 3×10^{200} in a double, which would require a lot more than 8 bytes if every digit were stored without scientific notation (84 bytes in case you were wondering). To accomplish this, you only store the first dozen or so digits of the number. The name *scientific notation* comes from science, where often only the first few significant digits are required for a calculation.

Don't worry, for the exam you are not required to know scientific notation or how floating-point values are stored.

The number of bits is used by Java when it figures out how much memory to reserve for your variable. For example, Java allocates 32 bits if you write this:

```
int num;
```

Writing Literals

There are a few more things you should know about numeric primitives. When a number is present in the code, it is called a *literal*. By default, Java assumes you are defining an int value with a numeric literal. In the following example, the number listed is bigger than what fits in an int. Remember, you aren't expected to memorize the maximum value for an int. The exam will include it in the question if it comes up.

```
long max = 3123456789;  // DOES NOT COMPILE
```

Java complains the number is out of range. And it is—for an int. However, we don't have an int. The solution is to add the character L to the number:

```
long max = 3123456789L;  // now Java knows it is a long
```

Alternatively, you could add a lowercase l to the number. But please use the uppercase L. The lowercase l looks like the number 1.

Another way to specify numbers is to change the "base." When you learned how to count, you studied the digits 0–9. This numbering system is called *base 10* since there are 10 numbers. It is also known as the *decimal number system*. Java allows you to specify digits in several other formats:

- Octal (digits 0–7), which uses the number 0 as a prefix—for example, 017

- Hexadecimal (digits 0–9 and letters A–F/a–f), which uses 0x or 0X as a prefix—for example, 0xFF, 0xff, 0XFf. Hexadecimal is case insensitive so all of these examples mean the same value.

- Binary (digits 0–1), which uses the number 0 followed by b or B as a prefix—for example, 0b10, 0B10

You won't need to convert between number systems on the exam. You'll have to recognize valid literal values that can be assigned to numbers.

Literals and the Underscore Character

The last thing you need to know about numeric literals is that you can have underscores in numbers to make them easier to read:

```
int million1 = 1000000;
int million2 = 1_000_000;
```

We'd rather be reading the latter one because the zeros don't run together. You can add underscores anywhere except at the beginning of a literal, the end of a literal, right before a decimal point, or right after a decimal point. You can even place multiple underscore characters next to each other, although we don't recommend it.

Let's look at a few examples:

```
double notAtStart = _1000.00;         // DOES NOT COMPILE
double notAtEnd = 1000.00_;           // DOES NOT COMPILE
double notByDecimal = 1000_.00;       // DOES NOT COMPILE
double annoyingButLegal = 1_00_0.0_0; // Ugly, but compiles
double reallyUgly = 1_____2;      // Also compiles
```

Using Reference Types

A *reference type* refers to an object (an instance of a class). Unlike primitive types that hold their values in the memory where the variable is allocated, references do not hold the value of the object they refer to. Instead, a reference "points" to an object by storing the memory address where the object is located, a concept referred to as a *pointer*. Unlike other languages, Java does not allow you to learn what the physical memory address is. You can only use the reference to refer to the object.

Let's take a look at some examples that declare and initialize reference types. Suppose we declare a reference of type java.util.Date and a reference of type String:

```
java.util.Date today;
String greeting;
```

The today variable is a reference of type Date and can only point to a Date object. The greeting variable is a reference that can only point to a String object. A value is assigned to a reference in one of two ways:

- A reference can be assigned to another object of the same or compatible type.
- A reference can be assigned to a new object using the new keyword.

For example, the following statements assign these references to new objects:

```
today = new java.util.Date();
greeting = new String("How are you?");
```

The today reference now points to a new Date object in memory, and today can be used to access the various fields and methods of this Date object. Similarly, the greeting reference points to a new `String` object, `"How are you?"`. The `String` and `Date` objects do not have names and can be accessed only via their corresponding reference. Figure 2.1 shows how the reference types appear in memory.

FIGURE 2.1   An object in memory can be accessed only via a reference.

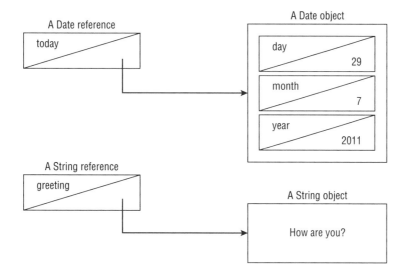

Distinguishing between Primitives and Reference Types

There are a few important differences you should know between primitives and reference types. First, reference types can be assigned `null`, which means they do not currently refer to an object. Primitive types will give you a compiler error if you attempt to assign them `null`. In this example, `value` cannot point to `null` because it is of type `int`:

```
int value = null;   // DOES NOT COMPILE
String s = null;
```

But what if you don't know the value of an `int` and want to assign it to `null`? In that case, you should use a numeric wrapper class, such as `Integer`, instead of `int`. Wrapper classes will be covered in Chapter 5.

Next, reference types can be used to call methods, assuming the reference is not `null`. Primitives do not have methods declared on them. In this example, we can call a method on `reference` since it is of a reference type. You can tell `length` is a method because it has `()` after it. See if you can understand why the following snippet does not compile:

```
4: String reference = "hello";
5: int len = reference.length();
6: int bad = len.length(); // DOES NOT COMPILE
```

Line 6 is gibberish. No methods exist on `len` because it is an `int` primitive. Primitives do not have methods. Remember, a `String` is not a primitive, so you can call methods like `length()` on a `String` reference, as we did on line 5.

Finally, notice that all the primitive types have lowercase type names. All classes that come with Java begin with uppercase. Although not required, it is a standard practice, and you should follow this convention for classes you create as well.

Declaring Variables

You've seen some variables already. A *variable* is a name for a piece of memory that stores data. When you declare a variable, you need to state the variable type along with giving it a name. For example, the following code declares two variables. One is named `zooName` and is of type `String`. The other is named `numberAnimals` and is of type `int`.

```
String zooName;
int numberAnimals;
```

Now that we've declared a variable, we can give it a value. This is called *initializing* a variable. To initialize a variable, you just type the variable name followed by an equal sign, followed by the desired value:

```
zooName = "The Best Zoo";
numberAnimals = 100;
```

Since you often want to initialize a variable right away, you can do so in the same statement as the declaration. For example, here we merge the previous declarations and initializations into more concise code:

```
String zooName = "The Best Zoo";
int numberAnimals = 100;
```

In the following sections, we'll look at how to properly define variables in one or multiple lines.

Identifying Identifiers

It probably comes as no surprise to you that Java has precise rules about identifier names. An *identifier* is the name of a variable, method, class, interface, or package. Luckily, the rules for identifiers for variables apply to all of the other types that you are free to name.

There are only four rules to remember for legal identifiers:

- Identifiers must begin with a letter, a $ symbol, or a _ symbol.
- Identifiers can include numbers but not start with them.

- Since Java 9, a single underscore _ is not allowed as an identifier.

- You cannot use the same name as a Java reserved word. A *reserved word* is special word that Java has held aside so that you are not allowed to use it. Remember that Java is case sensitive, so you can use versions of the keywords that only differ in case. Please don't, though.

Don't worry—you won't need to memorize the full list of reserved words. The exam will only ask you about ones that are commonly used, such as class and for. Table 2.2 lists all of the reserved words in Java.

TABLE 2.2 Reserved words

abstract	assert	boolean	break	byte
case	catch	char	class	const*
continue	default	do	double	else
enum	extends	false**	final	finally
float	for	goto*	if	implements
import	instanceof	int	interface	long
native	new	null**	package	private
protected	public	return	short	static
strictfp	super	switch	synchronized	this
throw	throws	transient	true**	try
void	volatile	while	_ (*underscore*)	

* The reserved words const and goto aren't actually used in Java. They are reserved so that people coming from other programming languages don't use them by accident—and in theory, in case Java wants to use them one day.
** true/false/null are not actually reserved words, but literal values. Since they cannot be used as identifier names, we include them in this table.

Prepare to be tested on these rules. The following examples are legal:

```
long okidentifier;
float $OK2Identifier;
boolean _alsoOK1d3ntifi3r;
char __SStillOkbutKnotsonice$;
```

These examples are not legal:

```
int 3DPointClass;     // identifiers cannot begin with a number
byte hollywood@vine;  // @ is not a letter, digit, $ or _
String *$coffee;      // * is not a letter, digit, $ or _
double public;        // public is a reserved word
short _;              // a single underscore is not allowed
```

Style: camelCase

Although you can do crazy things with identifier names, please don't. Java has conventions so that code is readable and consistent. This consistency includes *camel case*, often written as camelCase for emphasis. In camelCase, the first letter of each word is capitalized.

The camelCase format makes identifiers easier to read. Which would you rather read: `Thisismyclass` name or `ThisIsMyClass` name? The exam will mostly use common conventions for identifiers, but not always. When you see a nonstandard identifier, be sure to check if it is legal. If it's not, you get to mark the answer "does not compile" and skip analyzing everything else in the question.

 Real World Scenario

Identifiers in the Real World

Most Java developers follow these conventions for identifier names:

- Method and variable names are written in camelCase with the first letter being lowercase.

- Class and interface names are written in camelCase with the first letter being uppercase. Also, don't start any class name with $, as the compiler uses this symbol for some files.

Also, know that valid letters in Java are not just characters in the English alphabet. Java supports the Unicode character set, so there are thousands of characters that can start a legal Java identifier. Some are non-Arabic numerals that may appear after the first character in a legal identifier. Luckily, you don't have to worry about memorizing those for the exam. If you are in a country that doesn't use the English alphabet, this is useful to know for a job.

Style: snake_case

Another style you might see both on the exam and in the real world or in other languages is called *snake case*, often written as snake_case for emphasis. It simply uses an underscore (_) to separate words, often entirely in lowercase. The previous example would be written as `this_is_my_class` name in snake_case.

While both camelCase and snake_case are perfectly valid syntax in Java, the development community functions better when everyone adopts the same style convention. With that in mind, Oracle (and Sun before it) recommends everyone use camelCase for class and variable names. There are some exceptions, though. Constant static final values are often written in snake_case, such as THIS_IS_A_CONSTANT. In addition, enum values tend to be written with snake_case, as in Color.RED, Color.DARK_GRAY, and so on.

Declaring Multiple Variables

You can also declare and initialize multiple variables in the same statement. How many variables do you think are declared and initialized in the following example?

```
void sandFence() {
    String s1, s2;
    String s3 = "yes", s4 = "no";
}
```

Four String variables were declared: s1, s2, s3, and s4. You can declare many variables in the same declaration as long as they are all of the same type. You can also initialize any or all of those values inline. In the previous example, we have two initialized variables: s3 and s4. The other two variables remain declared but not yet initialized.

This is where it gets tricky. Pay attention to tricky things! The exam will attempt to trick you. Again, how many variables do you think are declared and initialized in the following code?

```
void paintFence() {
    int i1, i2, i3 = 0;
}
```

As you should expect, three variables were declared: i1, i2, and i3. However, only one of those values was initialized: i3. The other two remain declared but not yet initialized. That's the trick. Each snippet separated by a comma is a little declaration of its own. The initialization of i3 only applies to i3. It doesn't have anything to do with i1 or i2 despite being in the same statement. As you will see in the next section, you can't actually use i1 or i2 until they have been initialized.

Another way the exam could try to trick you is to show you code like this line:

```
int num, String value; // DOES NOT COMPILE
```

This code doesn't compile because it tries to declare multiple variables of *different* types in the same statement. The shortcut to declare multiple variables in the same statement is legal only when they share a type.

Legal, *valid*, and *compiles* are all synonyms in the Java exam world. We try to use all the terminology you could encounter on the exam.

To make sure you understand this, see if you can figure out which of the following are legal declarations:

```
4: boolean b1, b2;
5: String s1 = "1", s2;
6: double d1, double d2;
7: int i1; int i2;
8: int i3; i4;
```

The first statement on line 4 is legal. It declares two variables without initializing them. The second statement on line 5 is also legal. It declares two variables and initializes only one of them.

The third statement on line 6 is *not* legal. Java does not allow you to declare two different types in the same statement. Wait a minute! Variables d1 and d2 are the same type. They are both of type double. Although that's true, it still isn't allowed. If you want to declare multiple variables in the same statement, they must share the same type declaration and not repeat it. double d1, d2; would have been legal.

The fourth statement on line 7 is legal. Although int does appear twice, each one is in a separate statement. A semicolon (;) separates statements in Java. It just so happens there are two completely different statements on the same line. The fifth statement on line 8 is *not* legal. Again, we have two completely different statements on the same line. The second one on line 8 is not a valid declaration because it omits the type. When you see an oddly placed semicolon on the exam, pretend the code is on separate lines and think about whether the code compiles that way. In this case, the last two lines of code could be rewritten as follows:

```
int i1;
int i2;
int i3;
i4;
```

Looking at the last line on its own, you can easily see that the declaration is invalid. And yes, the exam really does cram multiple statements onto the same line—partly to try to trick you and partly to fit more code on the screen. In the real world, please limit yourself to one declaration per statement and line. Your teammates will thank you for the readable code.

Initializing Variables

Before you can use a variable, it needs a value. Some types of variables get this value set automatically, and others require the programmer to specify it. In the following sections, we'll look at the differences between the defaults for local, instance, and class variables.

Creating Local Variables

A *local variable* is a variable defined within a constructor, method, or initializer block. For simplicity, we will focus primarily on local variables within methods in this section, although the rules for the others are the same.

Local variables do not have a default value and must be initialized before use. Furthermore, the compiler will report an error if you try to read an uninitialized value. For example, the following code generates a compiler error:

```
4: public int notValid() {
5:    int y = 10;
6:    int x;
7:    int reply = x + y; // DOES NOT COMPILE
8:    return reply;
9: }
```

The y variable is initialized to 10. However, because x is not initialized before it is used in the expression on line 7, the compiler generates the following error:

```
Test.java:7: variable x might not have been initialized
   int reply = x + y; // DOES NOT COMPILE
            ^
```

Until x is assigned a value, it cannot appear within an expression, and the compiler will gladly remind you of this rule. The compiler knows your code has control of what happens inside the method and can be expected to initialize values.

The compiler is smart enough to recognize variables that have been initialized after their declaration but before they are used. Here's an example:

```
public int valid() {
   int y = 10;
   int x; // x is declared here
   x = 3; // and initialized here
   int reply = x + y;
   return reply;
}
```

The compiler is also smart enough to recognize initializations that are more complex. In this example, there are two branches of code:

```
public void findAnswer(boolean check) {
   int answer;
   int otherAnswer;
   int onlyOneBranch;
   if (check) {
      onlyOneBranch = 1;
```

```
      answer = 1;
   } else {
      answer = 2;
   }
   System.out.println(answer);
   System.out.println(onlyOneBranch); // DOES NOT COMPILE
}
```

The answer variable is initialized in both branches of the if statement, so the compiler is perfectly happy. It knows that regardless of whether check is true or false, the value answer will be set to something before it is used. The otherAnswer variable is not initialized but never used, and the compiler is equally as happy. Remember, the compiler is only concerned if you try to use uninitialized local variables; it doesn't mind the ones you never use.

The onlyOneBranch variable is initialized only if check happens to be true. The compiler knows there is the possibility for check to be false, resulting in uninitialized code, and gives a compiler error. You'll learn more about the if statement in Chapter 4, "Making Decisions."

On the exam, be wary of any local variable that is declared but not initialized in a single line. This is a common place on the exam that could result in a "Does not compile" answer. As you saw in the previous examples, you are not required to initialize the variable on the same line it is defined, but be sure to check to make sure it's initialized before it's used on the exam.

Passing Constructor and Method Parameters

Variables passed to a constructor or method are called *constructor parameters* or *method parameters*, respectively. These parameters are local variables that have been pre-initialized. In other words, they are like local variables that have been initialized before the method is called, by the caller. The rules for initializing constructor and method parameters are the same, so we'll focus primarily on method parameters.

In the previous example, check is a method parameter.

```
public void findAnswer(boolean check) {}
```

Take a look at the following method checkAnswer() in the same class:

```
public void checkAnswer() {
   boolean value;
   findAnswer(value);  // DOES NOT COMPILE
}
```

The call to findAnswer() does not compile because it tries to use a variable that is not initialized. While the caller of a method checkAnswer() needs to be concerned about the variable being initialized, once inside the method findAnswer(), we can assume the local variable has been initialized to some value.

Defining Instance and Class Variables

Variables that are not local variables are defined either as instance variables or as class variables. An *instance variable*, often called a field, is a value defined within a specific instance of an object. Let's say we have a Person class with an instance variable name of type String. Each instance of the class would have its own value for name, such as Elysia or Sarah. Two instances could have the same value for name, but changing the value for one does not modify the other.

On the other hand, a *class variable* is one that is defined on the class level and shared among all instances of the class. It can even be publicly accessible to classes outside the class without requiring an instance to use. In our previous Person example, a shared class variable could be used to represent the list of people at the zoo today. You can tell a variable is a class variable because it has the keyword static before it. You'll learn about this in Chapter 7. For now, just know that a variable is a class variable if it has the static keyword in its declaration.

Instance and class variables do not require you to initialize them. As soon as you declare these variables, they are given a default value. You'll need to memorize everything in Table 2.3 except the default value of char. To make this easier, remember that the compiler doesn't know what value to use and so wants the simplest value it can give the type: null for an object and 0/false for a primitive.

TABLE 2.3 Default initialization values by type

Variable type	Default initialization value
boolean	false
byte, short, int, long	0
float, double	0.0
char	'\u0000' (NUL)
All object references (everything else)	null

Introducing *var*

Starting in Java 10, you have the option of using the keyword var instead of the type for local variables under certain conditions. To use this feature, you just type var instead of the primitive or reference type. Here's an example:

```
public void whatTypeAmI() {
   var name = "Hello";
   var size = 7;
}
```

The formal name of this feature is *local variable type inference*. Let's take that apart. First comes *local variable*. This means just what it sounds like. You can only use this feature for local variables. The exam may try to trick you with code like this:

```
public class VarKeyword {
   var tricky = "Hello"; // DOES NOT COMPILE
}
```

Wait a minute! We just learned the difference between instance and local variables. The variable `tricky` is an instance variable. Local variable type inference works with local variables and not instance variables.

In Chapter 4, you'll learn that var can be used in for loops, and as you'll see in Chapter 6, "Lambdas and Functional Interfaces," with some lambdas as well. In Chapter 10, "Exceptions," you'll also learn that var can be used with try-with-resources. All of these cases are still internal to a method and therefore consistent with what you learn in this chapter.

Type Inference of *var*

Now that you understand the local variable part, it is time to go on to what *type inference* means. The good news is that this also means what it sounds like. When you type var, you are instructing the compiler to determine the type for you. The compiler looks at the code on the line of the declaration and uses it to infer the type. Take a look at this example:

```
7:  public void reassignment() {
8:     var number = 7;
9:     number = 4;
10:    number = "five";  // DOES NOT COMPILE
11: }
```

On line 8, the compiler determines that we want an int variable. On line 9, we have no trouble assigning a different int to it. On line 10, Java has a problem. We've asked it to assign a String to an int variable. This is not allowed. It is equivalent to typing this:

```
int number = "five";
```

If you know a language like JavaScript, you might be expecting var to mean a variable that can take on any type at runtime. In Java, var is still a specific type defined at compile time. It does not change type at runtime.

So, the type of var can't change at runtime, but what about the value? Take a look at the following code snippet:

```
var apples = (short)10;
apples = (byte)5;
apples = 1_000_000;  // DOES NOT COMPILE
```

The first line creates a var named apples with a type of short. It then assigns a byte of 5 to it, but did that change the data type of apples to byte? Nope! As you will learn in Chapter 3, the byte can be automatically promoted to a short, because a byte is small enough that it can fit inside of short. Therefore, the value stored on the second line is a short. In fact, let's rewrite the example showing what the compiler is really doing when it sees the var:

```
short apples = (short)10;
apples = (byte)5;
apples = 1_000_000;  // DOES NOT COMPILE
```

The last line does not compile, as one million is well beyond the limits of short. The compiler treats the value as an int and reports an error indicating it cannot be assigned to apples.

If you didn't follow that last example, don't worry, we'll be covering numeric promotion and casting in the next chapter. For now, you just need to know that the value for a var can change after it is declared but the type never does.

For simplicity when discussing var in the following sections, we are going to assume a variable declaration statement is completed in a single line. For example, you could insert a line break between the variable name and its initialization value, as in the following example:

```
7:  public void breakingDeclaration() {
8:      var silly
9:          = 1;
10: }
```

This example is valid and does compile, but we consider the declaration and initialization of silly to be happening on the same line.

Examples with *var*

Let's go through some more scenarios so the exam doesn't trick you on this topic! Do you think the following compiles?

```
3:  public void doesThisCompile(boolean check) {
4:      var question;
5:      question = 1;
6:      var answer;
7:      if (check) {
8:          answer = 2;
9:      } else {
10:         answer = 3;
11:     }
12:     System.out.println(answer);
13: }
```

The code does not compile. Remember that for local variable type inference, the compiler looks only at the line with the declaration. Since question and answer are not assigned values on the lines where they are defined, the compiler does not know what to make of them. For this reason, both lines 4 and 6 do not compile.

You might find that strange since both branches of the if/else do assign a value. Alas, it is not on the same line as the declaration, so it does not count for var. Contrast this behavior with what we saw a short while ago when we discussed branching and initializing a local variable in our findAnswer() method.

Now we know the initial value used to determine the type needs to be part of the same statement. Can you figure out why these two statements don't compile?

```
4: public void twoTypes() {
5:    int a, var b = 3;  // DOES NOT COMPILE
6:    var n = null;      // DOES NOT COMPILE
7: }
```

Line 5 wouldn't work even if you replaced var with a real type. All the types declared on a single line must be the same type and share the same declaration. We couldn't write int a, int v = 3; either. Likewise, this is not allowed:

```
5:    var a = 2, b = 3;  // DOES NOT COMPILE
```

In other words, Java does not allow var in multiple variable declarations.

Line 6 is a single line. The compiler is being asked to infer the type of null. This could be any reference type. The only choice the compiler could make is Object. However, that is almost certainly not what the author of the code intended. The designers of Java decided it would be better not to allow var for null than to have to guess at intent.

---

var and *null*

While a var cannot be initialized with a null value without a type, it can be assigned a null value after it is declared, provided that the underlying data type of the var is an object. Take a look at the following code snippet:

```
13: var n = "myData";
14: n = null;
15: var m = 4;
16: m = null;  // DOES NOT COMPILE
```

Line 14 compiles without issue because n is of type String, which is an object. On the other hand, line 16 does not compile since the type of m is a primitive int, which cannot be assigned a null value.

It might surprise you to learn that a var can be initialized to a null value if the type is specified. You'll learn about casting in Chapter 3, but the following does compile:

```
17: var o = (String)null;
```

Since the type is provided, the compiler can apply type inference and set the type of the var to be String.

Let's try another example. Do you see why this does not compile?

```java
public int addition(var a, var b) {  // DOES NOT COMPILE
    return a + b;
}
```

In this example, a and b are method parameters. These are not local variables. Be on the lookout for var used with constructors, method parameters, or instance variables. Using var in one of these places is a good exam trick to see if you are paying attention. Remember that var is only used for local variable type inference!

Time for two more examples. Do you think this is legal?

```java
package var;

public class Var {
    public void var() {
        var var = "var";
    }
    public void Var() {
        Var var = new Var();
    }
}
```

Believe it or not, this code does compile. Java is case sensitive, so Var doesn't introduce any conflicts as a class name. Naming a local variable var is legal. Please don't write code that looks like this at your job! But understanding why it works will help get you ready for any tricky exam questions Oracle could throw at you!

There's one last rule you should be aware of. While var is not a reserved word and allowed to be used as an identifier, it is considered a reserved type name. A *reserved type name* means it cannot be used to define a type, such as a class, interface, or enum. For example, the following code snippet does not compile because of the class name:

```java
public class var {  // DOES NOT COMPILE
    public var() {
    }
}
```

We're sure if the writers of Java had a time machine, they would likely go back and make var a reserved word in Java 1.0. They could have made var a reserved word starting in Java 10 or 11, but this would have broken older code where var was used as a variable name. For a large enough project, making var a reserved word could involve checking and recompiling millions of lines of code! On the other hand, since having a class or interface start with a lowercase letter is considered a bad practice prior to Java 11, they felt pretty safe marking it as a reserved type name.

It is often inappropriate to use var as the type for every local variable in your code. That just makes the code difficult to understand. If you are ever unsure of whether it is appropriate to use var, there are numerous style guides out there that can help. We recommend the one titled "Style Guidelines for Local Variable Type Inference in Java," which is available at the following location. This resource includes great style suggestions.

```
https://openjdk.java.net/projects/amber/LVTIstyle.html
```

Review of *var* Rules

We complete this section by summarizing all of the various rules for using var in your code. Here's a quick review of the var rules:

1. A var is used as a local variable in a constructor, method, or initializer block.

2. A var cannot be used in constructor parameters, method parameters, instance variables, or class variables.

3. A var is always initialized on the same line (or statement) where it is declared.

4. The value of a var can change, but the type cannot.

5. A var cannot be initialized with a null value without a type.

6. A var is not permitted in a multiple-variable declaration.

7. A var is a reserved type name but not a reserved word, meaning it can be used as an identifier except as a class, interface, or enum name.

That's a lot of rules, but we hope most are pretty straightforward. Since var is new to Java since the last exam, expect to see it used frequently on the exam. You'll also be seeing numerous ways var can be used throughout this book.

 Real World Scenario

var in the Real World

The var keyword is great for exam authors because it makes it easier to write tricky code. When you work on a real project, you want the code to be easy to read.

Once you start having code that looks like the following, it is time to consider using var:

```
PileOfPapersToFileInFilingCabinet pileOfPapersToFile =
    new PileOfPapersToFileInFilingCabinet();
```

You can see how shortening this would be an improvement without losing any information:

```
var pileOfPapersToFile = new PileOfPapersToFileInFilingCabinet();
```

Managing Variable Scope

You've learned that local variables are declared within a method. How many local variables do you see in this example?

```
public void eat(int piecesOfCheese) {
   int bitesOfCheese = 1;
}
```

There are two local variables in this method. The `bitesOfCheese` variable is declared inside the method. The `piecesOfCheese` variable is a method parameter and, as discussed earlier, it also acts like a local variable in terms of garbage collection and scope. Both of these variables are said to have a *scope* local to the method. This means they cannot be used outside of where they are defined.

Limiting Scope

Local variables can never have a scope larger than the method they are defined in. However, they can have a smaller scope. Consider this example:

```
3: public void eatIfHungry(boolean hungry) {
4:    if (hungry) {
5:       int bitesOfCheese = 1;
6:    }  // bitesOfCheese goes out of scope here
7:    System.out.println(bitesOfCheese);  // DOES NOT COMPILE
8: }
```

The variable `hungry` has a scope of the entire method, while variable `bitesOfCheese` has a smaller scope. It is only available for use in the `if` statement because it is declared inside of it. When you see a set of braces ({}) in the code, it means you have entered a new block of code. Each block of code has its own scope. When there are multiple blocks, you match them from the inside out. In our case, the `if` statement block begins at line 4 and ends at line 6. The method's block begins at line 3 and ends at line 8.

Since `bitesOfCheese` is declared in an `if` statement block, the scope is limited to that block. When the compiler gets to line 7, it complains that it doesn't know anything about this `bitesOfCheese` thing and gives an error:

```
error: cannot find symbol
   System.out.println(bitesOfCheese);  // DOES NOT COMPILE
                      ^
   symbol:   variable bitesOfCheese
```

Nesting Scope

Remember that blocks can contain other blocks. These smaller contained blocks can reference variables defined in the larger scoped blocks, but not vice versa. Here's an example:

```
16: public void eatIfHungry(boolean hungry) {
17:    if (hungry) {
18:       int bitesOfCheese = 1;
19:       {
20:          var teenyBit = true;
21:          System.out.println(bitesOfCheese);
22:       }
23:    }
24:    System.out.println(teenyBit);   // DOES NOT COMPILE
25: }
```

The variable defined on line 18 is in scope until the block ends on line 23. Using it in the smaller block from lines 19 to 22 is fine. The variable defined on line 20 goes out of scope on line 22. Using it on line 24 is not allowed.

Tracing Scope

The exam will attempt to trick you with various questions on scope. You'll probably see a question that appears to be about something complex and fails to compile because one of the variables is out of scope.

Let's try one. Don't worry if you aren't familiar with if statements or while loops yet. It doesn't matter what the code does since we are talking about scope. See if you can figure out on which line each of the five local variables goes into and out of scope:

```
11: public void eatMore(boolean hungry, int amountOfFood) {
12:    int roomInBelly = 5;
13:    if (hungry) {
14:       var timeToEat = true;
15:       while (amountOfFood > 0) {
16:          int amountEaten = 2;
17:          roomInBelly = roomInBelly - amountEaten;
18:          amountOfFood = amountOfFood - amountEaten;
19:       }
20:    }
21:    System.out.println(amountOfFood);
22: }
```

The first step in figuring out the scope is to identify the blocks of code. In this case, there are three blocks. You can tell this because there are three sets of braces. Starting from the innermost set, we can see where the while loop's block starts and ends. Repeat this as we go out for the `if` statement block and method block. Table 2.4 shows the line numbers that each block starts and ends on.

TABLE 2.4   Tracking scope by block

Line	First line in block	Last line in block
`while`	15	19
`if`	13	20
Method	11	22

Now that we know where the blocks are, we can look at the scope of each variable. `hungry` and `amountOfFood` are method parameters, so they are available for the entire method. This means their scope is lines 11 to 22. The variable `roomInBelly` goes into scope on line 12 because that is where it is declared. It stays in scope for the rest of the method and so goes out of scope on line 22. The variable `timeToEat` goes into scope on line 14 where it is declared. It goes out of scope on line 20 where the `if` block ends. Finally, the variable `amountEaten` goes into scope on line 16 where it is declared. It goes out of scope on line 19 where the `while` block ends.

You'll want to practice this skill a lot! Identifying blocks and variable scope needs to be second nature for the exam. The good news is that there are lots of code examples to practice on. You can look at any code example on any topic in this book and match up braces.

Applying Scope to Classes

All of that was for local variables. Luckily the rule for instance variables is easier: they are available as soon as they are defined and last for the entire lifetime of the object itself. The rule for class, aka `static`, variables is even easier: they go into scope when declared like the other variable types. However, they stay in scope for the entire life of the program.

Let's do one more example to make sure you have a handle on this. Again, try to figure out the type of the four variables and when they go into and out of scope.

```
1:  public class Mouse {
2:     final static int MAX_LENGTH = 5;
3:     int length;
4:     public void grow(int inches) {
5:        if (length < MAX_LENGTH) {
6:           int newSize = length + inches;
7:           length = newSize;
8:        }
9:     }
10: }
```

In this class, we have one class variable, MAX_LENGTH; one instance variable, length; and two local variables, inches and newSize. The MAX_LENGTH variable is a class variable because it has the static keyword in its declaration. In this case, MAX_LENGTH goes into scope on line 2 where it is declared. It stays in scope until the program ends.

Next, length goes into scope on line 3 where it is declared. It stays in scope as long as this Mouse object exists. inches goes into scope where it is declared on line 4. It goes out of scope at the end of the method on line 9. newSize goes into scope where it is declared on line 6. Since it is defined inside the if statement block, it goes out of scope when that block ends on line 8.

Reviewing Scope

Got all that? Let's review the rules on scope:

- *Local variables*: In scope from declaration to end of block
- *Instance variables*: In scope from declaration until object eligible for garbage collection
- *Class variables*: In scope from declaration until program ends

Not sure what garbage collection is? Relax, that's our next and final section for this chapter.

Destroying Objects

Now that we've played with our objects, it is time to put them away. Luckily, the JVM automatically takes care of that for you. Java provides a garbage collector to automatically look for objects that aren't needed anymore.

Remember from Chapter 1, your code isn't the only process running in your Java program. Java code exists inside of a Java Virtual Machine (JVM), which includes numerous processes independent from your application code. One of the most important of those is a built-in garbage collector.

All Java objects are stored in your program memory's *heap*. The heap, which is also referred to as the *free store*, represents a large pool of unused memory allocated to your Java application. The heap may be quite large, depending on your environment, but there is always a limit to its size. After all, there's no such thing as a computer with infinite memory. If your program keeps instantiating objects and leaving them on the heap, eventually it will run out of memory and crash.

In the following sections, we'll look at garbage collection.

 Real World Scenario

Garbage Collection in Other Languages

One of the distinguishing characteristics of Java since its very first version is that it automatically performs garbage collection for you. In fact, other than removing references to an object, there's very little you can do to control garbage collection directly in Java.

While garbage collection is pretty standard in most programming languages now, some languages, such as C, do not have automatic garbage collection. When a developer finishes using an object in memory, they have to manually deallocate it so the memory can be reclaimed and reused.

Failure to properly handle garbage collection can lead to catastrophic performance and security problems, the most common of which is for an application to run out of memory. Another similar problem, though, is if secure data like a credit card number stays in memory long after it is used and is able to be read by other programs. Luckily, Java handles a lot of these complex issues for you.

Understanding Garbage Collection

Garbage collection refers to the process of automatically freeing memory on the heap by deleting objects that are no longer reachable in your program. There are many different algorithms for garbage collection, but you don't need to know any of them for the exam. If you are curious, though, one algorithm is to keep a counter on the number of places an object is accessible at any given time and mark it eligible for garbage collection if the counter ever reaches zero.

Eligible for Garbage Collection

As a developer, the most interesting part of garbage collection is determining when the memory belonging to an object can be reclaimed. In Java and other languages, *eligible for garbage collection* refers to an object's state of no longer being accessible in a program and therefore able to be garbage collected.

Does this mean an object that's eligible for garbage collection will be immediately garbage collected? Definitely not. When the object actually is discarded is not under your control, but for the exam, you will need to know at any given moment which objects are eligible for garbage collection.

Think of garbage-collection eligibility like shipping a package. You can take an item, seal it in a labeled box, and put it in your mailbox. This is analogous to making an item eligible for garbage collection. When the mail carrier comes by to pick it up, though, is not in your control. For example, it may be a postal holiday or there could be a severe weather event. You can even call the post office and ask them to come pick it up right away, but there's no way to guarantee when and if this will actually happen. Hopefully, they come by before your mailbox fills with packages!

As a programmer, the most important thing you can do to limit out-of-memory problems is to make sure objects are eligible for garbage collection once they are no longer needed. It is the JVM's responsibility to actually perform the garbage collection.

Calling *System.gc()*

Java includes a built-in method to help support garbage collection that can be called at any time.

```
public static void main(String[] args) {
   System.gc();
}
```

What is the System.gc() command *guaranteed* to do? Nothing, actually. It merely *suggests* that the JVM kick off garbage collection. The JVM may perform garbage collection at that moment, or it might be busy and choose not to. The JVM is free to ignore the request.

When is System.gc() *guaranteed* to be called by the JVM? Never, actually. While the JVM will likely run it over time as available memory decreases, it is not guaranteed to ever actually run. In fact, shortly before a program runs out of memory and throws an OutOfMemoryError, the JVM will *try* to perform garbage collection, but it's not guaranteed to succeed.

For the exam, you need to know that System.gc() is not guaranteed to run or do anything, and you should be able to recognize when objects become eligible for garbage collection.

Tracing Eligibility

How does the JVM know when an object is eligible for garbage collection? The JVM waits patiently and monitors each object until it determines that the code no longer needs that memory. An object will remain on the heap until it is no longer reachable. An object is no longer reachable when one of two situations occurs:

- The object no longer has any references pointing to it.
- All references to the object have gone out of scope.

Objects vs. References

Do not confuse a reference with the object that it refers to; they are two different entities. The reference is a variable that has a name and can be used to access the contents of an object. A reference can be assigned to another reference, passed to a method, or returned from a method. All references are the same size, no matter what their type is.

An object sits on the heap and does not have a name. Therefore, you have no way to access an object except through a reference. Objects come in all different shapes and sizes and consume varying amounts of memory. An object cannot be assigned to another object, and an object cannot be passed to a method or returned from a method. It is the object that gets garbage collected, not its reference.

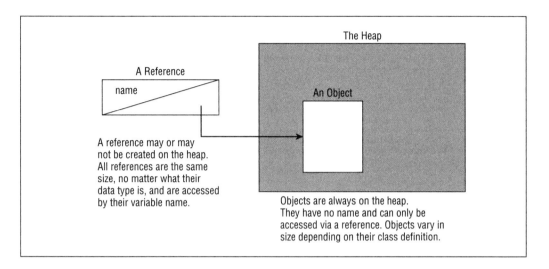

Realizing the difference between a reference and an object goes a long way toward understanding garbage collection, the new operator, and many other facets of the Java language. Look at this code and see whether you can figure out when each object first becomes eligible for garbage collection:

```
1: public class Scope {
2:     public static void main(String[] args) {
3:         String one, two;
4:         one = new String("a");
5:         two = new String("b");
6:         one = two;
7:         String three = one;
8:         one = null;
9:     } }
```

When you get asked a question about garbage collection on the exam, we recommend you draw what's going on. There's a lot to keep track of in your head, and it's easy to make a silly mistake trying to keep it all in your memory. Let's try it together now. Really. Get a pencil and paper. We'll wait.

Got that paper? Okay, let's get started. On line 3, write **one** and **two** (just the words— no need for boxes or arrows yet since no objects have gone on the heap yet). On line 4, we have our first object. Draw a box with the string **"a"** in it and draw an arrow from the word one to that box. Line 5 is similar. Draw another box with the string **"b"** in it this time and an arrow from the word two. At this point, your work should look like Figure 2.2.

FIGURE 2.2   Your drawing after line 5

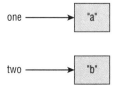

On line 6, the variable one changes to point to "b". Either erase or cross out the arrow from one and draw a new arrow from one to "b". On line 7, we have a new variable, so write the word **three** and draw an arrow from three to "b". Notice that three points to what one is pointing to right now and not what it was pointing to at the beginning. This is why you are drawing pictures. It's easy to forget something like that. At this point, your work should look like Figure 2.3.

FIGURE 2.3   Your drawing after line 7

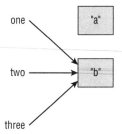

Finally, cross out the line between one and "b" since line 8 sets this variable to null. Now, we were trying to find out when the objects were first eligible for garbage collection. On line 6, we got rid of the only arrow pointing to "a", making that object eligible for garbage collection. "b" has arrows pointing to it until it goes out of scope. This means "b" doesn't go out of scope until the end of the method on line 9.

---

finalize()

Java allows objects to implement a method called finalize(). This feature can be confusing and hard to use properly. In a nutshell, the garbage collector would call the finalize() method once. If the garbage collector didn't run, there was no call to finalize(). If the garbage collector failed to collect the object and tried again later, there was no second call to finalize().

This topic is no longer on the exam. In fact, it is deprecated in Object as of Java 9, with the official documentation stating, "The finalization mechanism is inherently problematic." We mention the finalize() method in case Oracle happens to borrow from an old exam question. Just remember that finalize() can run zero or one times. It cannot run twice.

Summary

In this chapter, we described the building blocks of Java—most important, what a Java object is, how it is referenced and used, and how it is destroyed. This chapter lays the foundation for many topics that we will revisit throughout this book.

For example, we will go into a lot more detail on primitive types and how to use them in Chapter 3. Creating methods will be covered in Chapter 7. And in Chapter 8, we will discuss numerous rules for creating and managing objects. In other words, learn the basics, but don't worry if you didn't follow everything in this chapter. We will go a lot deeper into many of these topics in the rest of the book.

To begin with, constructors create Java objects. A constructor is a method matching the class name and omitting the return type. When an object is instantiated, fields and blocks of code are initialized first. Then the constructor is run.

Next, primitive types are the basic building blocks of Java types. They are assembled into reference types. Reference types can have methods and be assigned to null. Numeric literals are allowed to contain underscores (_) as long as they do not start or end the literal and are not next to a decimal point (.).

Declaring a variable involves stating the data type and giving the variable a name. Variables that represent fields in a class are automatically initialized to their corresponding 0, null, or false values during object instantiation. Local variables must be specifically initialized before they can be used. Identifiers may contain letters, numbers, $, or _. Identifiers may not begin with numbers. Local variables may use the var keyword instead of the actual type. When using var, the type is set once at compile time and does not change.

Moving on, scope refers to that portion of code where a variable can be accessed. There are three kinds of variables in Java, depending on their scope: instance variables, class variables, and local variables. Instance variables are the non-static fields of your class. Class variables are the static fields within a class. Local variables are declared within a constructor, method, or initializer block.

Finally, garbage collection is responsible for removing objects from memory when they can never be used again. An object becomes eligible for garbage collection when there are no more references to it or its references have all gone out of scope.

Exam Essentials

Be able to recognize a constructor.   A constructor has the same name as the class. It looks like a method without a return type.

Be able to identify legal and illegal declarations and initialization.   Multiple variables can be declared and initialized in the same statement when they share a type. Local variables require an explicit initialization; others use the default value for that type. Identifiers may contain letters, numbers, $, or _, although they may not begin with numbers. Also, you cannot define an identifier that is just a single underscore character _. Numeric literals may contain underscores between two digits, such as 1_000, but not in other places, such as _100_.0_. Numeric literals can begin with 1-9, 0, 0x, 0X, 0b, and 0B, with the latter four indicating a change of numeric base.

Be able to use var correctly. A var is used for a local variable inside a constructor, a method, or an initializer block. It cannot be used for constructor parameters, method parameters, instance variables, or class variables. A var is initialized on the same line where it is declared, and while it can change value, it cannot change type. A var cannot be initialized with a null value without a type, nor can it be used in multiple variable declarations. Finally, var is not a reserved word in Java and can be used as a variable name.

Be able to determine where variables go into and out of scope. All variables go into scope when they are declared. Local variables go out of scope when the block they are declared in ends. Instance variables go out of scope when the object is eligible for garbage collection. Class variables remain in scope as long as the program is running.

Know how to identify when an object is eligible for garbage collection. Draw a diagram to keep track of references and objects as you trace the code. When no arrows point to a box (object), it is eligible for garbage collection.

Review Questions

The answers to the chapter review questions can be found in the Appendix.

1. Which of the following are valid Java identifiers? (Choose all that apply.)

   A. `_`

   B. `_helloWorld$`

   C. `true`

   D. `java.lang`

   E. `Public`

   F. `1980_s`

   G. `_Q2_`

2. What lines are printed by the following program? (Choose all that apply.)

   ```
   1:  public class WaterBottle {
   2:      private String brand;
   3:      private boolean empty;
   4:      public static float code;
   5:      public static void main(String[] args) {
   6:          WaterBottle wb = new WaterBottle();
   7:          System.out.println("Empty = " + wb.empty);
   8:          System.out.println("Brand = " + wb.brand);
   9:          System.out.println("Code = " + code);
   10:     } }
   ```

   A. Line 8 generates a compiler error.

   B. Line 9 generates a compiler error.

   C. `Empty =`

   D. `Empty = false`

   E. `Brand =`

   F. `Brand = null`

   G. `Code = 0.0`

   H. `Code = 0f`

3. Which of the following code snippets about var compile without issue when used in a method? (Choose all that apply.)

   A. `var spring = null;`

   B. `var fall = "leaves";`

   C. `var evening = 2; evening = null;`

   D. `var night = new Object();`

   E. `var day = 1/0;`

F. `var winter = 12, cold;`

G. `var fall = 2, autumn = 2;`

H. `var morning = ""; morning = null;`

4. Which of the following statements about the code snippet are true? (Choose all that apply.)

```
4: short numPets = 5L;
5: int numGrains = 2.0;
6: String name = "Scruffy";
7: int d = numPets.length();
8: int e = numGrains.length;
9: int f = name.length();
```

A. Line 4 generates a compiler error.

B. Line 5 generates a compiler error.

C. Line 6 generates a compiler error.

D. Line 7 generates a compiler error.

E. Line 8 generates a compiler error.

F. Line 9 generates a compiler error.

5. Which statements about the following class are true? (Choose all that apply.)

```
1:  public class River {
2:      int Depth = 1;
3:      float temp = 50.0;
4:      public void flow() {
5:          for (int i = 0; i < 1; i++) {
6:              int depth = 2;
7:              depth++;
8:              temp--;
9:          }
10:         System.out.println(depth);
11:         System.out.println(temp); }
12:     public static void main(String... s) {
13:         new River().flow();
14: } }
```

A. Line 3 generates a compiler error.

B. Line 6 generates a compiler error.

C. Line 7 generates a compiler error.

D. Line 10 generates a compiler error.

E. The program prints 3 on line 10.

    F. The program prints 4 on line 10.

    G. The program prints 50.0 on line 11.

    H. The program prints 49.0 on line 11.

6. Which of the following are correct? (Choose all that apply.)

    A. An instance variable of type float defaults to 0.

    B. An instance variable of type char defaults to null.

    C. An instance variable of type double defaults to 0.0.

    D. An instance variable of type int defaults to null.

    E. An instance variable of type String defaults to null.

    F. An instance variable of type String defaults to the empty string "".

    G. None of the above

7. Which of the following are correct? (Choose all that apply.)

    A. A local variable of type boolean defaults to null.

    B. A local variable of type float defaults to 0.0f.

    C. A local variable of type double defaults to 0.

    D. A local variable of type Object defaults to null.

    E. A local variable of type boolean defaults to false.

    F. A local variable of type float defaults to 0.0.

    G. None of the above

8. Which of the following are true? (Choose all that apply.)

    A. A class variable of type boolean defaults to 0.

    B. A class variable of type boolean defaults to false.

    C. A class variable of type boolean defaults to null.

    D. A class variable of type long defaults to null.

    E. A class variable of type long defaults to 0L.

    F. A class variable of type long defaults to 0.

    G. None of the above

9. Which of the following statements about garbage collection are correct? (Choose all that apply.)

    A. Calling System.gc() is guaranteed to free up memory by destroying objects eligible for garbage collection.

    B. Garbage collection runs on a set schedule.

    C. Garbage collection allows the JVM to reclaim memory for other objects.

    D. Garbage collection runs when your program has used up half the available memory.

E. An object may be eligible for garbage collection but never removed from the heap.

F. An object is eligible for garbage collection once no references to it are accessible in the program.

G. Marking a variable final means its associated object will never be garbage collected.

10. Which statements about the following class are correct? (Choose all that apply.)

```
1:  public class PoliceBox {
2:      String color;
3:      long age;
4:      public void PoliceBox() {
5:          color = "blue";
6:          age = 1200;
7:      }
8:      public static void main(String []time) {
9:          var p = new PoliceBox();
10:         var q = new PoliceBox();
11:         p.color = "green";
12:         p.age = 1400;
13:         p = q;
14:         System.out.println("Q1="+q.color);
15:         System.out.println("Q2="+q.age);
16:         System.out.println("P1="+p.color);
17:         System.out.println("P2="+p.age);
18: } }
```

A. It prints Q1=blue.

B. It prints Q2=1200.

C. It prints P1=null.

D. It prints P2=1400.

E. Line 4 does not compile.

F. Line 12 does not compile.

G. Line 13 does not compile.

H. None of the above

11. Which of the following legally fill in the blank so you can run the main() method from the command line? (Choose all that apply.)

```
public static void main(_____) {}
```

A. String... var

B. String My.Names[]

    C. `String[] 123`

    D. `String[] _names`

    E. `String... $n`

    F. `var names`

    G. `String myArgs`

12. Which of the following expressions, when inserted independently into the blank line, allow the code to compile? (Choose all that apply.)

```
public void printMagicData() {
    double magic = _____;
    System.out.println(magic);
}
```

    A. `3_1`

    B. `1_329_.0`

    C. `3_13.0_`

    D. `5_291._2`

    E. `2_234.0_0`

    F. `9___6`

    G. `_1_3_5_0`

    H. None of the above

13. Suppose we have a class named `Rabbit`. Which of the following statements are true? (Choose all that apply.)

```
1:  public class Rabbit {
2:      public static void main(String[] args) {
3:          Rabbit one = new Rabbit();
4:          Rabbit two = new Rabbit();
5:          Rabbit three = one;
6:          one = null;
7:          Rabbit four = one;
8:          three = null;
9:          two = null;
10:         two = new Rabbit();
11:         System.gc();
12: } }
```

    A. The `Rabbit` object created on line 3 is first eligible for garbage collection immediately following line 6.

    B. The `Rabbit` object created on line 3 is first eligible for garbage collection immediately following line 8.

C. The Rabbit object created on line 3 is first eligible for garbage collection immediately following line 12.

D. The Rabbit object created on line 4 is first eligible for garbage collection immediately following line 9.

E. The Rabbit object created on line 4 is first eligible for garbage collection immediately following line 11.

F. The Rabbit object created on line 4 is first eligible for garbage collection immediately following line 12.

G. The Rabbit object created on line 10 is first eligible for garbage collection immediately following line 11.

H. The Rabbit object created on line 10 is first eligible for garbage collection immediately following line 12.

14. Which of the following statements about var are true? (Choose all that apply.)

A. A var can be used as a constructor parameter.

B. The type of var is known at compile time.

C. A var cannot be used as an instance variable.

D. A var can be used in a multiple variable assignment statement.

E. The value of var cannot change at runtime.

F. The type of var cannot change at runtime.

G. The word var is a reserved word in Java.

15. Given the following class, which of the following lines of code can independently replace INSERT CODE HERE to make the code compile? (Choose all that apply.)

```java
public class Price {
   public void admission() {
      INSERT CODE HERE
      System.out.print(amount);
   } }
```

A. `int Amount = 0b11;`

B. `int amount = 9L;`

C. `int amount = 0xE;`

D. `int amount = 1_2.0;`

E. `double amount = 1_0_.0;`

F. `int amount = 0b101;`

G. `double amount = 9_2.1_2;`

H. `double amount = 1_2_.0_0;`

16. Which statements about the following class are correct? (Choose all that apply.)

```
1: public class ClownFish {
2:    int gills = 0, double weight=2;
3:    { int fins = gills; }
4:    void print(int length = 3) {
5:       System.out.println(gills);
6:       System.out.println(weight);
7:       System.out.println(fins);
8:       System.out.println(length);
9: } }
```

- **A.** Line 2 contains a compiler error.
- **B.** Line 3 contains a compiler error.
- **C.** Line 4 contains a compiler error.
- **D.** Line 7 contains a compiler error.
- **E.** The code prints 0.
- **F.** The code prints 2.0.
- **G.** The code prints 2.
- **H.** The code prints 3.

17. Which statements about classes and its members are correct? (Choose all that apply.)

- **A.** A variable declared in a loop cannot be referenced outside the loop.
- **B.** A variable cannot be declared in an instance initializer block.
- **C.** A constructor argument is in scope for the life of the instance of the class for which it is defined.
- **D.** An instance method can only access instance variables declared before the instance method declaration.
- **E.** A variable can be declared in an instance initializer block but cannot be referenced outside the block.
- **F.** A constructor can access all instance variables.
- **G.** An instance method can access all instance variables.

18. Which statements about the following code snippet are correct? (Choose all that apply.)

```
3:   var squirrel = new Object();
4:   int capybara = 2, mouse, beaver = -1;
5:   char chipmunk = -1;
6:   squirrel = "";
7:   beaver = capybara;
```

```
8:  System.out.println(capybara);
9:  System.out.println(mouse);
10: System.out.println(beaver);
11: System.out.println(chipmunk);
```

A. The code prints 2.

B. The code prints -1.

C. The code prints the empty String.

D. The code prints: null.

E. Line 4 contains a compiler error.

F. Line 5 contains a compiler error.

G. Line 9 contains a compiler error.

H. Line 10 contains a compiler error.

19. Assuming the following class compiles, how many variables defined in the class or method are in scope on the line marked // SCOPE on line 14?

```
1:  public class Camel {
2:      { int hairs = 3_000_0; }
3:      long water, air=2;
4:      boolean twoHumps = true;
5:      public void spit(float distance) {
6:          var path = "";
7:          { double teeth = 32 + distance++; }
8:          while(water > 0) {
9:              int age = twoHumps ? 1 : 2;
10:             short i=-1;
11:             for(i=0; i<10; i++) {
12:                 var Private = 2;
13:             }
14:             // SCOPE
15:         }
16:     }
17: }
```

A. 2

B. 3

C. 4

D. 5

E. 6

F. 7

G. None of the above

20. What is the output of executing the following class?

```
1:   public class Salmon {
2:       int count;
3:       { System.out.print(count+"-"); }
4:       { count++; }
5:       public Salmon() {
6:           count = 4;
7:           System.out.print(2+"-");
8:       }
9:       public static void main(String[] args) {
10:          System.out.print(7+"-");
11:          var s = new Salmon();
12:          System.out.print(s.count+"-"); } }
```

A. 7-0-2-1-

B. 7-0-1-

C. 0-7-2-1-

D. 7-0-2-4-

E. 0-7-1-

F. The class does not compile because of line 3.

G. The class does not compile because of line 4.

H. None of the above.

21. Which statements about the following program are correct? (Choose all that apply.)

```
1:   public class Bear {
2:       private Bear pandaBear;
3:       protected void finalize() {}
4:       private void roar(Bear b) {
5:           System.out.println("Roar!");
6:           pandaBear = b;
7:       }
8:       public static void main(String[] args) {
9:           Bear brownBear = new Bear();
10:          Bear polarBear = new Bear();
11:          brownBear.roar(polarBear);
12:          polarBear = null;
13:          brownBear = null;
14:          System.gc(); } }
```

A. The object created on line 9 is eligible for garbage collection after line 13.

B. The object created on line 9 is eligible for garbage collection after line 14.

    C. The object created on line 10 is eligible for garbage collection after line 12.

    D. The object created on line 10 is eligible for garbage collection after line 13.

    E. Garbage collection is guaranteed to run.

    F. Garbage collection might or might not run.

    G. Garbage collection is guaranteed not to run.

    H. The code does not compile.

22. Which of the following are valid instance variable declarations? (Choose all that apply.)

    A. `var _ = 6000_.0;`

    B. `var null = 6_000;`

    C. `var $_ = 6_000;`

    D. `var $2 = 6_000f;`

    E. `var var = 3_0_00.0;`

    F. `var #CONS = 2_000.0;`

    G. `var %C = 6_000_L;`

    H. None of the above

Chapter

3

Operators

OCP EXAM OBJECTIVES COVERED IN THIS CHAPTER:

✓ **Using Operators and Decision Constructs**

- Use Java operators including the use of parentheses to override operator precedence

✓ **Working With Java Primitive Data Types and String APIs**

- Declare and initialize variables (including casting and promoting primitive data types)

In the previous chapter, we talked a lot about defining variables, but what can you do with a variable once it is created? This chapter introduces operators and shows how you can use them to combine existing values and create new values. We'll show you how to apply operators to various primitive data types, including introducing you to operators that can be applied to objects.

Understanding Java Operators

Before we get into the fun stuff, let's cover a bit of terminology. A Java *operator* is a special symbol that can be applied to a set of variables, values, or literals—referred to as operands—and that returns a result. The term *operand*, which we'll use throughout this chapter, refers to the value or variable the operator is being applied to. The output of the operation is simply referred to as the result. For example, in a + b, the operator is the addition operator (+), and values a and b are the operands. If we then store the result in a variable c, such as c = a + b, then the variable c and the result of a + b become the new operands for our assignment operator (=).

We're sure you have been using the addition (+) and subtraction (-) operators since you were a little kid. Java supports many other operators that you need to know for the exam. While many should be review for you, some (such as the compound assignment operators) may be new to you.

Types of Operators

In general, three flavors of operators are available in Java: unary, binary, and ternary. These types of operators can be applied to one, two, or three operands, respectively. For the exam, you'll need to know a specific subset of Java operators, how to apply them, and the order in which they should be applied.

Java operators are not necessarily evaluated from left-to-right order. For example, the second expression of the following Java code is actually evaluated from right to left given the specific operators involved:

```java
int cookies = 4;
double reward = 3 + 2 * --cookies;
System.out.print("Zoo animal receives: "+reward+" reward points");
```

In this example, you would first decrement `cookies` to 3, then multiply the resulting value by 2, and finally add 3. The value would then be automatically promoted from 9 to 9.0 and assigned to `reward`. The final values of `reward` and `cookies` would be 9.0 and 3, respectively, with the following printed:

```
Zoo animal receives: 9.0 reward points
```

If you didn't follow that evaluation, don't worry. By the end of this chapter, solving problems like this should be second nature.

Operator Precedence

When reading a book or a newspaper, some written languages are evaluated from left to right, while some are evaluated from right to left. In mathematics, certain operators can override other operators and be evaluated first. Determining which operators are evaluated in what order is referred to as *operator precedence*. In this manner, Java more closely follows the rules for mathematics. Consider the following expression:

```
var perimeter = 2 * height + 2 * length;
```

The multiplication operator (*) has a higher precedence than the addition operator (+), so the *height* and *length* are both multiplied by 2 before being added together. The assignment operator (=) has the lowest order of precedence, so the assignment to the *perimeter* variable is performed last.

Unless overridden with parentheses, Java operators follow *order of operation*, listed in Table 3.1, by decreasing order of operator precedence. If two operators have the same level of precedence, then Java guarantees left-to-right evaluation. For the exam, you only need to know the operators shown in bold in Table 3.1.

TABLE 3.1   Order of operator precedence

Operator	Symbols and examples
Post-unary operators	*expression*++, *expression*--
Pre-unary operators	++*expression*, --*expression*
Other unary operators	-, !, ~, +, **(type)**
Multiplication/division/modulus	***, /, %**
Addition/subtraction	**+, -**
Shift operators	<<, >>, >>>
Relational operators	**<, >, <=, >=, instanceof**

TABLE 3.1   Order of operator precedence *(continued)*

Operator	Symbols and examples
Equal to/not equal to	**==, !=**
Logical operators	**&, ^, |**
Short-circuit logical operators	**&&, ||**
Ternary operators	*boolean expression* **?** *expression1* **:** *expression2*
Assignment operators	**=, +=, -=, *=, /=,** %=, &=, ^=, |=, <<=, >>=, >>>=

We recommend that you keep Table 3.1 handy throughout this chapter. For the exam, you need to memorize the order of precedence in this table. Note that you won't be tested on some operators, like the shift operators, although we recommend that you be aware of their existence.

Applying Unary Operators

By definition, a *unary* operator is one that requires exactly one operand, or variable, to function. As shown in Table 3.2, they often perform simple tasks, such as increasing a numeric variable by one or negating a boolean value.

TABLE 3.2   Unary operators

Operator	Description
!	Inverts a boolean's logical value
+	Indicates a number is positive, although numbers are assumed to be positive in Java unless accompanied by a negative unary operator
-	Indicates a literal number is negative or negates an expression
++	Increments a value by 1
--	Decrements a value by 1
(*type*)	Casts a value to a specific type.

Even though Table 3.2 includes the casting operator, we'll postpone discussing casting until the "Assigning Values" section later in this chapter, since that is where it is commonly used.

Logical Complement and Negation Operators

Since we're going to be working with a lot of numeric operators in this chapter, let's get the boolean one out of the way first. The *logical complement operator* (!) flips the value of a boolean expression. For example, if the value is true, it will be converted to false, and vice versa. To illustrate this, compare the outputs of the following statements:

```
boolean isAnimalAsleep = false;
System.out.println(isAnimalAsleep);   // false
isAnimalAsleep = !isAnimalAsleep;
System.out.println(isAnimalAsleep);   // true
```

Likewise, the *negation operator*, -, reverses the sign of a numeric expression, as shown in these statements:

```
double zooTemperature = 1.21;
System.out.println(zooTemperature);   // 1.21
zooTemperature = -zooTemperature;
System.out.println(zooTemperature);   // -1.21
zooTemperature = -(-zooTemperature);
System.out.println(zooTemperature);   // -1.21
```

Notice that in the last example we used parentheses, (), for the negation operator, -, to apply the negation twice. If we had instead written --, then it would have been interpreted as the decrement operator and printed -2.21. You will see more of that decrement operator shortly.

Based on the description, it might be obvious that some operators require the variable or expression they're acting upon to be of a specific type. For example, you cannot apply a negation operator (-) to a boolean expression, nor can you apply a logical complement operator (!) to a numeric expression. Be wary of questions on the exam that try to do this, as they'll cause the code to fail to compile. For example, none of the following lines of code will compile:

```
int pelican = !5;         // DOES NOT COMPILE
boolean penguin = -true;  // DOES NOT COMPILE
boolean peacock = !0;     // DOES NOT COMPILE
```

The first statement will not compile because in Java you cannot perform a logical inversion of a numeric value. The second statement does not compile because you cannot numerically negate a boolean value; you need to use the logical inverse operator. Finally, the last statement does not compile because you cannot take the logical complement of a numeric value, nor can you assign an integer to a boolean variable.

NOTE

Keep an eye out for questions on the exam that use the logical complement operator or numeric values with boolean expressions or variables. Unlike some other programming languages, in Java, 1 and true are not related in any way, just as 0 and false are not related.

Increment and Decrement Operators

Increment and decrement operators, ++ and --, respectively, can be applied to numeric variables and have a high order of precedence, as compared to binary operators. In other words, they often get applied first in an expression.

Increment and decrement operators require special care because the order in which they are attached to their associated variable can make a difference in how an expression is processed. If the operator is placed before the operand, referred to as the *pre-increment operator* and the *pre-decrement operator*, then the operator is applied first and the value returned is the *new value* of the expression. Alternatively, if the operator is placed after the operand, referred to as the *post-increment operator* and the *post-decrement operator*, then the *original value* of the expression is returned, with operator applied after the value is returned.

The following code snippet illustrates this distinction:

```
int parkAttendance = 0;
System.out.println(parkAttendance);      // 0
System.out.println(++parkAttendance);    // 1
System.out.println(parkAttendance);      // 1
System.out.println(parkAttendance--);    // 1
System.out.println(parkAttendance);      // 0
```

The first pre-increment operator updates the value for parkAttendance and outputs the new value of 1. The next post-decrement operator also updates the value of parkAttendance but outputs the value before the decrement occurs.

NOTE

For the exam, it is critical that you know the difference between expressions like parkAttendance++ and ++parkAttendance. The increment and decrement operators will be in multiple questions, and confusion about which value is returned could cause you to lose a lot of points on the exam.

One common practice in a certification exam, albeit less common in the real world, is to apply multiple increment or decrement operators to a single variable on the same line:

```
int lion = 3;
int tiger = ++lion * 5 / lion--;
System.out.println("lion is " + lion);
System.out.println("tiger is " + tiger);
```

This one is more complicated than the previous example because lion is modified two times on the same line. Each time it is modified, the value of lion changes, with different values being assigned to the variable. As you'll recall from our discussion on operator precedence, order of operation plays an important part in evaluating this example.

So how do you read this code? First, lion is decremented. We can simplify this:

```
int tiger = ++lion * 5 / 3;   // lion assigned value of 2
```

Next, lion is incremented with the new value of 3 used in the expression, leading to this:

```
int tiger = 3 * 5 / 3;   // lion assigned value of 3
```

Finally, we evaluate multiplication and division from left to right. The product of the first two numbers is 15. The divisor 3 divides 15 evenly, resulting in an assignment of 5 to tiger. The result is then printed:

```
lion is 3
tiger is 5
```

Working with Binary Arithmetic Operators

Next, we move on to operators that take two arguments, called *binary operators*. Binary operators are by far the most common operators in the Java language. They can be used to perform mathematical operations on variables, create logical expressions, and perform basic variable assignments. Binary operators are often combined in complex expressions with other binary operators; therefore, operator precedence is very important in evaluating expressions containing binary operators.

In this section, we'll start with binary arithmetic operators, shown in Table 3.3. In the following sections, we'll expand to other binary operators that you need to know for the exam.

TABLE 3.3   Binary arithmetic operators

Operator	Description
+	Adds two numeric values
−	Subtracts two numeric values
*	Multiplies two numeric values
/	Divides one numeric value by another
%	Modulus operator returns the remainder after division of one numeric value by another

Arithmetic Operators

Arithmetic operators are often encountered in early mathematics and include addition (+), subtraction (-), multiplication (*), division (/), and modulus (%). If you don't know what modulus is, don't worry—we'll cover that shortly. Arithmetic operators also include the unary operators, ++ and --, which we covered already. As you may have noticed in Table 3.1, the *multiplicative* operators (*, /, %) have a higher order of precedence than the *additive* operators (+, -). Take a look at the following expression:

```
int price = 2 * 5 + 3 * 4 - 8;
```

First, you evaluate the 2 * 5 and 3 * 4, which reduces the expression to this:

```
int price = 10 + 12 - 8;
```

Then, you evaluate the remaining terms in left-to-right order, resulting in a value of price of 14. Make sure you understand why the result is 14 because you'll likely see this kind of operator precedence question on the exam.

> All of the arithmetic operators may be applied to any Java primitives, with the exception of boolean. Furthermore, only the addition operators + and += may be applied to String values, which results in String concatenation. You will learn more about these operators and how they apply to String values in Chapter 5, "Core Java APIs."

Adding Parentheses

You might have noticed we said "Unless overridden with parentheses" prior to presenting Table 3.1 on operator precedence. That's because you can change the order of operation explicitly by wrapping parentheses around the sections you want evaluated first.

Changing the Order of Operation

Let's return to the previous price example. The following code snippet contains the same values and operators, in the same order, but with two sets of parentheses added:

```
int price = 2 * ((5 + 3) * 4 - 8);
```

This time you would evaluate the addition operator 5 + 3, which reduces the expression to the following:

```
int price = 2 * (8 * 4 - 8);
```

You can further reduce this expression by multiplying the first two values within the parentheses:

```
int price = 2 * (32 - 8);
```

Next, you subtract the values within the parentheses before applying terms outside the parentheses:

```
int price = 2 * 24;
```

Finally, you would multiply the result by 2, resulting in a value of 48 for price.

Parentheses can appear in nearly any question on the exam involving numeric values, so make sure you understand how they are changing the order of operation when you see them.

Verifying Parentheses Syntax

When working with parentheses, you need to make sure they are always valid and balanced. Consider the following examples:

```
long pigeon = 1 + ((3 * 5) / 3;        // DOES NOT COMPILE
int blueJay = (9 + 2) + 3) / (2 * 4;   // DOES NOT COMPILE
short robin = 3 + [(4 * 2) + 4];       // DOES NOT COMPILE
```

The first example does not compile because the parentheses are not balanced. There is a left-parenthesis with no matching right-parenthesis. The second example has an equal number of left and right parentheses, but they are not balanced properly. When reading from left to right, a new right-parenthesis must match a previous left-parenthesis. Likewise, all left-parentheses must be closed by right-parentheses before the end of the expression. The last example does not compile because Java, unlike some other programming languages, does not allow brackets, [], to be used in place of parentheses. If you replace the brackets with parentheses, the last example will compile just fine.

Division and Modulus Operators

Although we are sure you have seen most of the arithmetic operators before, the modulus operator, %, may be new to you. The modulus operator, often called the *remainder operator*, is simply the remainder when two numbers are divided. For example, 9 divided by 3 divides evenly and has no remainder; therefore, the result of 9 % 3 is 0. On the other hand, 11 divided by 3 does not divide evenly; therefore, the result of 11 % 3, is 2.

The following examples illustrate this distinction:

```
System.out.println(9 / 3);    // 3
System.out.println(9 % 3);    // 0

System.out.println(10 / 3);   // 3
System.out.println(10 % 3);   // 1

System.out.println(11 / 3);   // 3
System.out.println(11 % 3);   // 2

System.out.println(12 / 3);   // 4
System.out.println(12 % 3);   // 0
```

As you can see, the division results increase only when the value on the left side goes from 11 to 12, whereas the modulus remainder value increases by 1 each time the left side is increased until it wraps around to zero. For a given divisor y, which is 3 in these examples, the modulus operation results in a value between 0 and (y - 1) for positive dividends. This means that the result of this modulus operation is always 0, 1, or 2.

Be sure to understand the difference between arithmetic division and modulus. For integer values, division results in the floor value of the nearest integer that fulfills the operation, whereas modulus is the remainder value. If you hear the phrase *floor value*, it just means the value without anything after the decimal point. For example, the floor value is 4 for each of the values 4.0, 4.5, and 4.9999999. Unlike rounding, which we'll cover in Chapter 5, you just take the value before the decimal point, regardless of what is after the decimal point.

The modulus operation is not limited to positive integer values in Java; it may also be applied to negative integers and floating-point numbers. For example, if the divisor is 5, then the modulus value of a negative number is between -4 and 0. For the exam, though, you are not required to be able to take the modulus of a negative integer or a floating-point number.

Numeric Promotion

Now that you understand the basics of arithmetic operators, it is vital to talk about primitive *numeric promotion*, as Java may do things that seem unusual to you at first. As we showed in Chapter 2, "Java Building Blocks," each primitive numeric type has a bit-length. You don't need to know the exact size of these types for the exam, but you should know which are bigger than others. For example, you should know that a long takes up more space than an int, which in turn takes up more space than a short, and so on.

You need to memorize certain rules Java will follow when applying operators to data types:

Numeric Promotion Rules

1. If two values have different data types, Java will automatically promote one of the values to the larger of the two data types.

2. If one of the values is integral and the other is floating-point, Java will automatically promote the integral value to the floating-point value's data type.

3. Smaller data types, namely, byte, short, and char, are first promoted to int any time they're used with a Java binary arithmetic operator, even if neither of the operands is int.

4. After all promotion has occurred and the operands have the same data type, the resulting value will have the same data type as its promoted operands.

The last two rules are the ones most people have trouble with and the ones likely to trip you up on the exam. For the third rule, note that unary operators are excluded from this rule. For example, applying ++ to a short value results in a short value.

Let's tackle some examples for illustrative purposes:

▪ What is the data type of x * y?

```
int x = 1;
long y = 33;
var z = x * y;
```

If we follow the first rule, since one of the values is `long` and the other is `int` and since `long` is larger than `int`, then the `int` value is promoted to a `long`, and the resulting value is `long`.

- What is the data type of `x + y`?

  ```
  double x = 39.21;
  float y = 2.1;
  var z = x + y;
  ```

  This is actually a trick question, as this code will not compile! As you may remember from Chapter 2, floating-point literals are assumed to be `double`, unless postfixed with an `f`, as in `2.1f`. If the value of y was set properly to `2.1f`, then the promotion would be similar to the previous example, with both operands being promoted to a `double`, and the result would be a `double` value.

- What is the data type of `x * y`?

  ```
  short x = 10;
  short y = 3;
  var z = x * y;
  ```

  On the last line, we must apply the third rule, namely, that x and y will both be promoted to `int` before the binary multiplication operation, resulting in an output of type `int`. If you were to try to assign the value to a `short` variable without casting, the code would not compile. Pay close attention to the fact that the resulting output is not a `short`, as we'll come back to this example in the upcoming "Assigning Values" section.

- What is the data type of `w * x / y`?

  ```
  short w = 14;
  float x = 13;
  double y = 30;
  var z = w * x / y;
  ```

  In this case, we must apply all of the rules. First, w will automatically be promoted to `int` solely because it is a `short` and it is being used in an arithmetic binary operation. The promoted w value will then be automatically promoted to a `float` so that it can be multiplied with x. The result of `w * x` will then be automatically promoted to a `double` so that it can be divided by y, resulting in a `double` value.

When working arithmetic operators in Java, you should always be aware of the data type of variables, intermediate values, and resulting values. You should apply operator precedence and parentheses and work outward, promoting data types along the way. In the next section, we'll discuss the intricacies of assigning these values to variables of a particular type.

Assigning Values

Compilation errors from assignment operators are often overlooked on the exam, in part because of how subtle these errors can be. To master the assignment operators, you should be fluent in understanding how the compiler handles numeric promotion and when casting is required. Being able to spot these issues is critical to passing the exam, as assignment operators appear in nearly every question with a code snippet.

Assignment Operator

An *assignment operator* is a binary operator that modifies, or *assigns*, the variable on the left side of the operator, with the result of the value on the right side of the equation. The simplest assignment operator is the = assignment, which you have seen already:

```
int herd = 1;
```

This statement assigns the herd variable the value of 1.

Java will automatically promote from smaller to larger data types, as you saw in the previous section on arithmetic operators, but it will throw a compiler exception if it detects that you are trying to convert from larger to smaller data types without casting. Table 3.4 lists the first assignment operator that you need to know for the exam. We will present additional assignment operators later in this section.

TABLE 3.4 Simple assignment operator

Operator	Description
=	Assigns the value on the right to the variable on the left

Casting Values

Seems easy so far, right? Well, we can't really talk about the assignment operator in detail until we've covered casting. *Casting* is a unary operation where one data type is explicitly interpreted as another data type. Casting is optional and unnecessary when converting to a larger or widening data type, but it is required when converting to a smaller or narrowing data type. Without casting, the compiler will generate an error when trying to put a larger data type inside a smaller one.

Casting is performed by placing the data type, enclosed in parentheses, to the left of the value you want to cast. Here are some examples of casting:

```
int fur = (int)5;
int hair = (short) 2;
String type = (String)  "Bird";
```

```
short tail = (short)(4 + 10);
long feathers = 10(long);  // DOES NOT COMPILE
```

Spaces between the cast and the value are optional. As shown in the second-to-last example, it is common for the right side to also be in parentheses. Since casting is a unary operation, it would only be applied to the 4 if we didn't enclose 4 + 10 in parentheses. The last example does not compile because the type is on the wrong side of the value.

On the one hand, it is convenient that the compiler automatically casts smaller data types to larger ones. On the other hand, it makes for great exam questions when they do the opposite to see whether you are paying attention. See if you can figure out why none of the following lines of code compile:

```
float egg = 2.0 / 9;       // DOES NOT COMPILE
int tadpole = (int)5 * 2L;  // DOES NOT COMPILE
short frog = 3 - 2.0;      // DOES NOT COMPILE
```

All of these examples involve putting a larger value into a smaller data type. Don't worry if you don't follow this yet; we will be covering many examples like these in this part of the chapter.

In this chapter, casting is primarily concerned with converting numeric data types into other data types. As you will see in later chapters, casting can also be applied to objects and references. In those cases, though, no conversion is performed, as casting is allowed only if the underlying object is already a member of the class or interface.

And during the exam, remember to keep track of parentheses and return types any time casting is involved!

Reviewing Primitive Assignments

Let's return to some examples similar to what you saw in Chapter 2 to show how casting can resolve these issues:

```
int fish = 1.0;         // DOES NOT COMPILE
short bird = 1921222;   // DOES NOT COMPILE
int mammal = 9f;        // DOES NOT COMPILE
long reptile = 192301398193810323;  // DOES NOT COMPILE
```

The first statement does not compile because you are trying to assign a double 1.0 to an integer value. Even though the value is a mathematic integer, by adding .0, you're instructing the compiler to treat it as a double. The second statement does not compile because the literal value 1921222 is outside the range of short and the compiler detects this. The third statement does not compile because of the f added to the end of the number that instructs the compiler to treat the number as a floating-point value, but the assignment is to an int. Finally, the last statement does not compile because Java interprets the literal as an int and notices that the value is larger than int allows. The literal would need a postfix L or l to be considered a long.

Applying Casting

We can fix the previous set of examples by casting the results to a smaller data type. Remember, casting primitives is required any time you are going from a larger numerical data type to a smaller numerical data type, or converting from a floating-point number to an integral value.

```
int trainer = (int)1.0;
short ticketTaker = (short)1921222;  // Stored as 20678
int usher = (int)9f;
long manager = 192301398193810323L;
```

Overflow and Underflow

The expressions in the previous example now compile, although there's a cost. The second value, 1,921,222, is too large to be stored as a short, so numeric overflow occurs and it becomes 20,678. *Overflow* is when a number is so large that it will no longer fit within the data type, so the system "wraps around" to the lowest negative value and counts up from there, similar to how modulus arithmetic works. There's also an analogous *underflow*, when the number is too low to fit in the data type, such as storing −200 in a byte field.

This is beyond the scope of the exam, but something to be careful of in your own code. For example, the following statement outputs a negative number:

```
System.out.print(2147483647+1);  // −2147483648
```

Since 2147483647 is the maximum int value, adding any strictly positive value to it will cause it to wrap to the smallest negative number.

Let's return to a similar example from the "Numeric Promotion" section earlier in the chapter.

```
short mouse = 10;
short hamster = 3;
short capybara = mouse * hamster;  // DOES NOT COMPILE
```

Based on everything you have learned up until now about numeric promotion and casting, do you understand why the last line of this statement will not compile? As you may remember, short values are automatically promoted to int when applying any arithmetic operator, with the resulting value being of type int. Trying to assign a short variable with an int value results in a compiler error, as Java thinks you are trying to implicitly convert from a larger data type to a smaller one.

We can fix this expression by casting, as there are times that you may want to override the compiler's default behavior. In this example, we know the result of 10 ∗ 3 is 30, which can easily fit into a short variable, so we can apply casting to convert the result back to a short.

```
short mouse = 10;
short hamster = 3;
short capybara = (short)(mouse * hamster);
```

By casting a larger value into a smaller data type, you are instructing the compiler to ignore its default behavior. In other words, you are telling the compiler that you have taken additional steps to prevent overflow or underflow. It is also possible that in your particular application and scenario, overflow or underflow would result in acceptable values.

Last but not least, casting can appear anywhere in an expression, not just on the assignment. For example, let's take a look at a modified form of the previous example:

```
short mouse = 10;
short hamster = 3;
short capybara = (short)mouse * hamster;      // DOES NOT COMPILE
short gerbil = 1 + (short)(mouse * hamster);  // DOES NOT COMPILE
```

So, what's going on in the last two lines? Well, remember when we said casting was a unary operation? That means the cast in the first line is applied to mouse, and mouse alone. After the cast is complete, both operands are promoted to int since they are used with the binary multiplication operator (∗), making the result an int and causing a compiler error.

In the second example, casting is performed successfully, but the resulting value is automatically promoted to int because it is used with the binary arithmetic operator (+).

Compound Assignment Operators

Besides the simple assignment operator (=) Java supports numerous *compound assignment operators*. For the exam, you should be familiar with the compound operators in Table 3.5.

TABLE 3.5   Compound assignment operators

Operator	Description
+=	Adds the value on the right to the variable on the left and assigns the sum to the variable
−=	Subtracts the value on the right from the variable on the left and assigns the difference to the variable
∗=	Multiplies the value on the right with the variable on the left and assigns the product to the variable
/=	Divides the variable on the left by the value on the right and assigns the quotient to the variable

Complex operators are really just glorified forms of the simple assignment operator, with a built-in arithmetic or logical operation that applies the left and right sides of the statement and stores the resulting value in the variable on the left side of the statement. For example, the following two statements after the declaration of `camel` and `giraffe` are equivalent when run independently:

```
int camel = 2, giraffe = 3;
camel = camel * giraffe;    // Simple assignment operator
camel *= giraffe;           // Compound assignment operator
```

The left side of the compound operator can be applied only to a variable that is already defined and cannot be used to declare a new variable. In this example, if `camel` were not already defined, then the expression `camel *= giraffe` would not compile.

Compound operators are useful for more than just shorthand—they can also save us from having to explicitly cast a value. For example, consider the following example. Can you figure out why the last line does not compile?

```
long goat = 10;
int sheep = 5;
sheep = sheep * goat;    // DOES NOT COMPILE
```

From the previous section, you should be able to spot the problem in the last line. We are trying to assign a `long` value to an `int` variable. This last line could be fixed with an explicit cast to `(int)`, but there's a better way using the compound assignment operator:

```
long goat = 10;
int sheep = 5;
sheep *= goat;
```

The compound operator will first cast `sheep` to a `long`, apply the multiplication of two `long` values, and then cast the result to an `int`. Unlike the previous example, in which the compiler reported an error, in this example we see that the compiler will automatically cast the resulting value to the data type of the value on the left side of the compound operator.

Assignment Operator Return Value

One final thing to know about assignment operators is that the result of an assignment is an expression in and of itself, equal to the value of the assignment. For example, the following snippet of code is perfectly valid, if not a little odd-looking:

```
long wolf = 5;
long coyote = (wolf=3);
System.out.println(wolf);   // 3
System.out.println(coyote); // 3
```

The key here is that (wolf=3) does two things. First, it sets the value of the variable wolf to be 3. Second, it returns a value of the assignment, which is also 3.

The exam creators are fond of inserting the assignment operator (=) in the middle of an expression and using the value of the assignment as part of a more complex expression. For example, don't be surprised if you see an if statement on the exam similar to the following:

```
boolean healthy = false;
if(healthy = true)
    System.out.print("Good!");
```

While this may look like a test if healthy is true, it's actually assigning healthy a value of true. The result of the assignment is the value of the assignment, which is true, resulting in this snippet printing Good!. We'll cover this in more detail in the upcoming "Equality Operators" section.

Comparing Values

The last set of binary operators revolves around comparing values. They can be used to check if two values are the same, check if one numeric value is less than or greater than another, and perform boolean arithmetic. Chances are you have used many of the operators in this section in your development experience.

Equality Operators

Determining equality in Java can be a nontrivial endeavor as there's a semantic difference between "two objects are the same" and "two objects are equivalent." It is further complicated by the fact that for numeric and boolean primitives, there is no such distinction.

Table 3.6 lists the equality operators. The equals operator (==) and not equals operator (!=) compare two operands and return a boolean value determining whether the expressions or values are equal or not equal, respectively.

TABLE 3.6   Equality operators

Operator	Apply to primitives	Apply to objects
==	Returns true if the two values represent the same value	Returns true if the two values reference the same object
!=	Returns true if the two values represent different values	Returns true if the two values do not reference the same object

The equality operators are used in one of three scenarios:

- Comparing two numeric or character primitive types. If the numeric values are of different data types, the values are automatically promoted. For example, 5 == 5.00 returns `true` since the left side is promoted to a double.
- Comparing two `boolean` values
- Comparing two objects, including `null` and `String` values

The comparisons for equality are limited to these three cases, so you cannot mix and match types. For example, each of the following would result in a compiler error:

```
boolean monkey = true == 3;        // DOES NOT COMPILE
boolean ape = false != "Grape";    // DOES NOT COMPILE
boolean gorilla = 10.2 == "Koko";  // DOES NOT COMPILE
```

Pay close attention to the data types when you see an equality operator on the exam. As we mentioned in the previous section, the exam creators also have a habit of mixing assignment operators and equality operators.

```
boolean bear = false;
boolean polar = (bear = true);
System.out.println(polar);  // true
```

At first glance, you might think the output should be `false`, and if the expression were (bear == true), then you would be correct. In this example, though, the expression is assigning the value of `true` to bear, and as you saw in the section on assignment operators, the assignment itself has the value of the assignment. Therefore, polar is also assigned a value of `true`, and the output is true.

For object comparison, the equality operator is applied to the references to the objects, not the objects they point to. Two references are equal if and only if they point to the same object or both point to `null`. Let's take a look at some examples:

```
File monday = new File("schedule.txt");
File tuesday = new File("schedule.txt");
File wednesday = tuesday;
System.out.println(monday == tuesday);      // false
System.out.println(tuesday == wednesday);  // true
```

Even though all of the variables point to the same file information, only two references, tuesday and wednesday, are equal in terms of == since they point to the same object.

NOTE   Wait, what's the `File` class? In this example, as well as during the exam, you may be presented with class names that are unfamiliar, such as `File`. Many times you can answer questions about these classes without knowing the specific details of these classes. In the previous example, you should be able to answer questions that indicate monday and tuesday are two separate and distinct objects because the new keyword is used, even if you are not familiar with the data types of these objects.

In some languages, comparing null with any other value is always false, although this is not the case in Java.

```
System.out.print(null == null);   // true
```

In Chapter 5, we'll continue the discussion of object equality by introducing what it means for two different objects to be equivalent. We'll also cover String equality and show how this can be a nontrivial topic.

Relational Operators

We now move on to *relational operators*, which compare two expressions and return a boolean value. Table 3.7 describes the relational operators you need to know for the exam.

TABLE 3.7 Relational operators

Operator	Description
<	Returns true if the value on the left is strictly less than the value on the right
<=	Returns true if the value on the left is less than or equal to the value on the right
>	Returns true if the value on the left is strictly greater than the value on the right
>=	Returns true if the value on the left is greater than or equal to the value on the right
a instanceof b	Returns true if the reference that a points to is an instance of a class, subclass, or class that implements a particular interface, as named in b

Numeric Comparison Operators

The first four relational operators in Table 3.7 apply only to numeric values. If the two numeric operands are not of the same data type, the smaller one is promoted as previously discussed.

Let's look at examples of these operators in action:

```
int gibbonNumFeet = 2, wolfNumFeet = 4, ostrichNumFeet = 2;
System.out.println(gibbonNumFeet < wolfNumFeet);       // true
System.out.println(gibbonNumFeet <= wolfNumFeet);      // true
System.out.println(gibbonNumFeet >= ostrichNumFeet);   // true
System.out.println(gibbonNumFeet > ostrichNumFeet);    // false
```

Notice that the last example outputs false, because although gibbonNumFeet and ostrichNumFeet have the same value, gibbonNumFeet is not strictly greater than ostrichNumFeet.

instanceof Operator

The final relational operator you need to know for the exam is the instanceof operator, shown in Table 3.7. It is useful for determining whether an arbitrary object is a member of a particular class or interface at runtime.

Why wouldn't you know what class or interface an object is? As we will get into in Chapter 8, "Class Design," Java supports polymorphism. For now, that just means some objects can be passed around using a variety of references. For example, all classes inherit from java.lang.Object. This means that any instance can be assigned to an Object reference. For example, how many objects are created and used in the following code snippet?

```
Integer zooTime = Integer.valueOf(9);
Number num = zooTime;
Object obj = zooTime;
```

In this example, there is only one object created in memory but three different references to it because Integer inherits both Number and Object. This means that you can call instanceof on any of these references with three different data types and it would return true for each of them.

Where polymorphism often comes into play is when you create a method that takes a data type with many possible subclasses. For example, imagine we have a function that opens the zoo and prints the time. As input, it takes a Number as an input parameter.

```
public void openZoo(Number time) {}
```

Now, we want the function to add O'clock to the end of output if the value is a whole number type, such as an Integer; otherwise, it just prints the value.

```
public static void openZoo(Number time) {
   if(time instanceof Integer)
      System.out.print((Integer)time + " O'clock");
   else
      System.out.print(time);
}
```

We now have a method that can intelligently handle both Integer and other values. A good exercise left for the reader is to add checks for other numeric data types.

Notice that we cast the Integer value in this example. It is common to use casting and instanceof together when working with objects that can be various different types, since it can give you access to fields available only in the more specific classes. It is considered a good coding practice to use the instanceof operator prior to casting from one object to a narrower type.

Invalid *instanceof*

One area the exam might try to trip you up on is using `instanceof` with incompatible types. For example, `Number` cannot possibly hold a `String` value, so the following would cause a compilation error:

```
public static void openZoo(Number time) {
    if(time instanceof String) // DOES NOT COMPILE
    ...
```

It gets even more complicated as the previous rule applies to classes, but not interfaces. Don't worry if this is all new to you; we will go into more detail when we discuss polymorphism in Chapter 9, "Advanced Class Design."

null and the *instanceof* operator

What happens if you call `instanceof` on a null variable? For the exam, you should know that calling `instanceof` on the null literal or a null reference always returns `false`.

```
System.out.print(null instanceof Object);

Object noObjectHere = null;
System.out.print(noObjectHere instanceof String);
```

The preceding examples both print `false`. It almost doesn't matter what the right side of the expression is. We say "almost" because there are exceptions. The last example does not compile, since null is used on the right side of the `instanceof` operator:

```
System.out.print(null instanceof null);  // DOES NOT COMPILE
```

Logical Operators

If you have studied computer science, you may have already come across logical operators before. If not, no need to panic—we'll be covering them in detail in this section.

The logical operators, (&), (|), and (^), may be applied to both numeric and `boolean` data types; they are listed in Table 3.8. When they're applied to `boolean` data types, they're referred to as *logical operators*. Alternatively, when they're applied to numeric data types, they're referred to as *bitwise operators*, as they perform bitwise comparisons of the bits that compose the number. For the exam, though, you don't need to know anything about numeric bitwise comparisons, so we'll leave that educational aspect to other books.

TABLE 3.8   Logical operators

Operator	Description
&	Logical AND is true only if both values are true.
|	Inclusive OR is true if at least one of the values is true.
^	Exclusive XOR is true only if one value is true and the other is false.

You should familiarize yourself with the truth tables in Figure 3.1, where x and y are assumed to be boolean data types.

FIGURE 3.1   The logical truth tables for &, |, and ^

x & y (AND)	y = true	y = false
x = true	true	false
x = false	false	false

x | y (INCLUSIVE OR)	y = true	y = false
x = true	true	true
x = false	true	false

x ^ y (EXCLUSIVE OR)	y = true	y = false
x = true	false	true
x = false	true	false

Here are some tips to help you remember this table:

- AND is only true if both operands are true.
- Inclusive OR is only false if both operands are false.
- Exclusive OR is only true if the operands are different.

Let's take a look at some examples:

```
boolean eyesClosed = true;
boolean breathingSlowly = true;

boolean resting = eyesClosed | breathingSlowly;
boolean asleep = eyesClosed & breathingSlowly;
boolean awake = eyesClosed ^ breathingSlowly;
System.out.println(resting);   // true
System.out.println(asleep);    // true
System.out.println(awake);     // false
```

You should try these out yourself, changing the values of eyesClosed and breathingSlowly and studying the results.

Short-Circuit Operators

Next, we present the conditional operators, && and ||, which are often referred to as *short-circuit operators* and are shown in Table 3.9.

TABLE 3.9   Short-circuit operators

Operator	Description
&&	Short-circuit AND is true only if both values are true. If the left side is false, then the right side will not be evaluated.
||	Short-circuit OR is true if at least one of the values is true. If the left side is true, then the right side will not be evaluated.

The *short-circuit operators* are nearly identical to the logical operators, & and |, except that the right side of the expression may never be evaluated if the final result can be determined by the left side of the expression. For example, consider the following statement:

```
int hour = 10;
boolean zooOpen = true || (hour < 4);
System.out.println(zooOpen);   // true
```

Referring to the truth tables, the value zooOpen can be false only if both sides of the expression are false. Since we know the left side is true, there's no need to evaluate the right side, since no value of hour will ever make this code print false. In other words, hour could have been -10 or 892; the output would have been the same. Try it yourself with different values for hour!

Avoiding a NullPointerException

A more common example of where short-circuit operators are used is checking for null objects before performing an operation. In the following example, if duck is null, then the program will throw a NullPointerException at runtime:

```
if(duck!=null & duck.getAge()<5) { // Could throw a NullPointerException
   // Do something
}
```

The issue is that the logical AND (&) operator evaluates both sides of the expression. We could add a second if statement, but this could get unwieldy if we have a lot of variables to check. An easy-to-read solution is to use the short-circuit AND operator (&&):

```
if(duck!=null && duck.getAge()<5) {
   // Do something
}
```

In this example, if duck was null, then the short-circuit prevents a NullPointerException from ever being thrown, since the evaluation of duck.getAge() < 5 is never reached.

Checking for Unperformed Side Effects

Be wary of short-circuit behavior on the exam, as questions are known to alter a variable on the right side of the expression that may never be reached. This is referred to as an *unperformed side effect*. For example, what is the output of the following code?

```
int rabbit = 6;
boolean bunny = (rabbit >= 6) || (++rabbit <= 7);
System.out.println(rabbit);
```

Because rabbit >= 6 is true, the increment operator on the right side of the expression is never evaluated, so the output is 6.

Making Decisions with the Ternary Operator

The final operator you should be familiar with for the exam is the conditional operator, ? :, otherwise known as the *ternary operator*. It is notable in that it is the only operator that takes three operands. The ternary operator has the following form:

```
booleanExpression ? expression₁ : expression₂
```

The first operand must be a `boolean` expression, and the second and third operands can be any expression that returns a value. The ternary operation is really a condensed form of a combined `if` and `else` statement that returns a value. We will be covering `if`/`else` statements in a lot more detail in Chapter 4, "Making Decisions," so for now we will just use simple examples.

For example, consider the following code snippet that calculates the food amount for an owl:

```
int owl = 5;
int food;
if(owl < 2) {
    food = 3;
} else {
    food = 4;
}
System.out.println(food);  // 4
```

Compare the previous code snippet with the following ternary operator code snippet:

```
int owl = 5;
int food = owl < 2 ? 3 : 4;
System.out.println(food);  // 4
```

These two code snippets are equivalent to each other. Note that it is often helpful for readability to add parentheses around the expressions in ternary operations, although it is certainly not required.

```
int food = (owl < 2) ? 3 : 4;
```

For the exam, you should know that there is no requirement that second and third expressions in ternary operations have the same data types, although it does come into play when combined with the assignment operator. Compare the two statements following the variable declaration:

```
int stripes = 7;

System.out.print((stripes > 5) ? 21 : "Zebra");

int animal = (stripes < 9) ? 3 : "Horse";  // DOES NOT COMPILE
```

Both expressions evaluate similar boolean values and return an int and a String, although only the first one will compile. System.out.print() does not care that the expressions are completely different types, because it can convert both to Object values and call toString() on them. On the other hand, the compiler does know that "Horse" is of the wrong data type and cannot be assigned to an int; therefore, it will not allow the code to be compiled.

Ternary Expression and Unperformed Side Effects

Like we saw with the short-circuit operator, a ternary expression can contain an unperformed side effect, as only one of the expressions on the right side will be evaluated at runtime. Let's illustrate this principle with the following example:

```
int sheep = 1;
int zzz = 1;
int sleep = zzz<10 ? sheep++ : zzz++;
System.out.print(sheep+","+zzz);  // 2,1
```

Notice that since the left-hand boolean expression was true, only sheep was incremented. Contrast the preceding example with the following modification:

```
int sheep = 1;
int zzz = 1;
int sleep = sheep>=10 ? sheep++ : zzz++;
System.out.print(sheep+","+zzz);  // 1,2
```

Now that the left-hand boolean expression evaluates to false, only zzz was incremented. In this manner, we see how the expressions in a ternary operator may not be applied if the particular expression is not used.

For the exam, be wary of any question that includes a ternary expression in which a variable is modified in one of the right-hand side expressions.

Summary

This chapter covered a wide variety of Java operator topics for unary, binary, and ternary operators. Hopefully, most of these operators were review for you. If not, you'll need to study them in detail. It is important that you understand how to use all of the required Java operators covered in this chapter and know how operator precedence and parentheses influence the way a particular expression is interpreted.

There will likely be numerous questions on the exam that appear to test one thing, such as StringBuilder or exception handling, when in fact the answer is related to the misuse of a particular operator that causes the application to fail to compile. When you see an operator involving numbers on the exam, always check that the appropriate data types are used and that they match each other where applicable.

Operators are used throughout the exam, in nearly every code sample, so the better you understand this chapter, the more prepared you will be for the exam.

Exam Essentials

Be able to write code that uses Java operators.   This chapter covered a wide variety of operator symbols. Go back and review them several times so that you are familiar with them throughout the rest of the book.

Be able to recognize which operators are associated with which data types.   Some operators may be applied only to numeric primitives, some only to boolean values, and some only to objects. It is important that you notice when an operator and operand(s) are mismatched, as this issue is likely to come up in a couple of exam questions.

Understand when casting is required or numeric promotion occurs.   Whenever you mix operands of two different data types, the compiler needs to decide how to handle the resulting data type. When you're converting from a smaller to a larger data type, numeric promotion is automatically applied. When you're converting from a larger to a smaller data type, casting is required.

Understand Java operator precedence.   Most Java operators you'll work with are binary, but the number of expressions is often greater than two. Therefore, you must understand the order in which Java will evaluate each operator symbol.

Be able to write code that uses parentheses to override operator precedence.   You can use parentheses in your code to manually change the order of precedence.

Review Questions

The answers to the chapter review questions can be found in the Appendix.

1. Which of the following Java operators can be used with `boolean` variables? (Choose all that apply.)

    A. `==`

    B. `+`

    C. `--`

    D. `!`

    E. `%`

    F. `<=`

    G. Cast with `(boolean)`

2. What data type (or types) will allow the following code snippet to compile? (Choose all that apply.)

    ```
    byte apples = 5;
    short oranges = 10;
    _____ bananas = apples + oranges;
    ```

    A. `int`

    B. `long`

    C. `boolean`

    D. `double`

    E. `short`

    F. `byte`

3. What change, when applied independently, would allow the following code snippet to compile? (Choose all that apply.)

    ```
    3: long ear = 10;
    4: int hearing = 2 * ear;
    ```

    A. No change; it compiles as is.

    B. Cast `ear` on line 4 to `int`.

    C. Change the data type of `ear` on line 3 to `short`.

    D. Cast `2 * ear` on line 4 to `int`.

    E. Change the data type of `hearing` on line 4 to `short`.

    F. Change the data type of `hearing` on line 4 to `long`.

4. What is the output of the following code snippet?

    ```
    3: boolean canine = true, wolf = true;
    4: int teeth = 20;
    ```

```
5: canine = (teeth != 10) ^ (wolf=false);
6: System.out.println(canine+", "+teeth+", "+wolf);
```

A. true, 20, true

B. true, 20, false

C. false, 10, true

D. false, 20, false

E. The code will not compile because of line 5.

F. None of the above

5. Which of the following operators are ranked in increasing or the same order of precedence? Assume the + operator is binary addition, not the unary form. (Choose all that apply.)

A. +, *, %, --

B. ++, (int), *

C. =, ==, !

D. (short), =, !, *

E. *, /, %, +, ==

F. !, ||, &

G. ^, +, =, +=

6. What is the output of the following program?

```
1: public class CandyCounter {
2:     static long addCandy(double fruit, float vegetables) {
3:         return (int)fruit+vegetables;
4:     }
5:
6:     public static void main(String[] args) {
7:         System.out.print(addCandy(1.4, 2.4f) + "-");
8:         System.out.print(addCandy(1.9, (float)4) + "-");
9:         System.out.print(addCandy((long)(int)(short)2, (float)4)); } }
```

A. 4-6-6.0

B. 3-5-6

C. 3-6-6

D. 4-5-6

E. The code does not compile because of line 9.

F. None of the above

7. What is the output of the following code snippet?

```
int ph = 7, vis = 2;
boolean clear = vis > 1 & (vis < 9 || ph < 2);
boolean safe = (vis > 2) && (ph++ > 1);
boolean tasty = 7 <= --ph;
System.out.println(clear+"-"+safe+"-"+tasty);
```

- **A.** true-true-true
- **B.** true-true-false
- **C.** true-false-true
- **D.** true-false-false
- **E.** false-true-true
- **F.** false-true-false
- **G.** false-false-true
- **H.** false-false-false

8. What is the output of the following code snippet?

```
4: int pig = (short)4;
5: pig = pig++;
6: long goat = (int)2;
7: goat -= 1.0;
8: System.out.print(pig + " - " + goat);
```

- **A.** 4 - 1
- **B.** 4 - 2
- **C.** 5 - 1
- **D.** 5 - 2
- **E.** The code does not compile due to line 7.
- **F.** None of the above

9. What are the unique outputs of the following code snippet? (Choose all that apply.)

```
int a = 2, b = 4, c = 2;
System.out.println(a > 2 ? --c : b++);
System.out.println(b = (a!=c ? a : b++));
System.out.println(a > b ? b < c ? b : 2 : 1);
```

- **A.** 1
- **B.** 2
- **C.** 3

D. 4

E. 5

F. 6

G. The code does not compile.

10. What are the unique outputs of the following code snippet? (Choose all that apply.)

```
short height = 1, weight = 3;
short zebra = (byte) weight * (byte) height;
double ox = 1 + height * 2 + weight;
long giraffe = 1 + 9 % height + 1;
System.out.println(zebra);
System.out.println(ox);
System.out.println(giraffe);
```

A. 1

B. 2

C. 3

D. 4

E. 5

F. 6

G. The code does not compile.

11. What is the output of the following code?

```
1: public class ArithmeticSample {
2:     public static void main(String[] args) {
3:         int sample1 = (2 * 4) % 3;
4:         int sample2 = 3 * 2 % 3;
5:         int sample3 = 5 * (1 % 2);
6:         System.out.println(sample1+"-"+sample2+"-"+sample3);
7: }}
```

A. 0-0-5

B. 1-2-10

C. 2-1-5

D. 2-0-5

E. 3-1-10

F. 3-2-6

G. The code does not compile.

12. The _____ operator increases a value and returns the original value, while the _____ operator decreases a value and returns the new value.

   A. post-increment, post-increment

   B. pre-decrement, post-decrement

   C. post-increment, post-decrement

   D. post-increment, pre-decrement

   E. pre-increment, pre-decrement

   F. pre-increment, post-decrement

13. What is the output of the following code snippet?

```
boolean sunny = true, raining = false, sunday = true;
boolean goingToTheStore = sunny & raining ^ sunday;
boolean goingToTheZoo = sunday && !raining;
boolean stayingHome = !(goingToTheStore && goingToTheZoo);
System.out.println(goingToTheStore + "-" + goingToTheZoo
    + "-" +stayingHome);
```

   A. true-false-false

   B. false-true-false

   C. true-true-true

   D. false-true-true

   E. false-false-false

   F. true-true-false

   G. None of the above

14. Which of the following statements are correct? (Choose all that apply.)

   A. The return value of an assignment operation expression can be void.

   B. The inequality operator (!=) can be used to compare objects.

   C. The equality operator (==) can be used to compare a boolean value with a numeric value.

   D. During runtime, the && and | operators may cause only the left side of the expression to be evaluated.

   E. The return value of an assignment operation expression is the value of the newly assigned variable.

   F. In Java, 0 and false may be used interchangeably.

   G. The logical complement operator (!) cannot be used to flip numeric values.

15. Which operators take three operands or values? (Choose all that apply.)

    A.   =

    B.   &&

    C.   *=

    D.   ? :

    E.   &

    F.   ++

    G.   /

16. How many lines of the following code contain compiler errors?

```
int note = 1 * 2 + (long)3;
short melody = (byte)(double)(note *= 2);
double song = melody;
float symphony = (float)((song == 1_000f) ? song * 2L : song);
```

    A.   0

    B.   1

    C.   2

    D.   3

    E.   4

17. Given the following code snippet, what is the value of the variables after it is executed? (Choose all that apply.)

```
int ticketsTaken = 1;
int ticketsSold = 3;
ticketsSold += 1 + ticketsTaken++;
ticketsTaken *= 2;
ticketsSold += (long)1;
```

    A.   ticketsSold is 8

    B.   ticketsTaken is 2

    C.   ticketsSold is 6

    D.   ticketsTaken is 6

    E.   ticketsSold is 7

    F.   ticketsTaken is 4

    G.   The code does not compile.

18. Which of the following can be used to change the order of operation in an expression? (Choose all that apply.)

    A. [ ]

    B. < >

    C. ( )

    D. \ /

    E. { }

    F. " "

19. What is the result of executing the following code snippet? (Choose all that apply.)

```
3: int start = 7;
4: int end = 4;
5: end += ++start;
6: start = (byte)(Byte.MAX_VALUE + 1);
```

    A. start is 0

    B. start is –128

    C. start is 127

    D. end is 8

    E. end is 11

    F. end is 12

    G. The code does not compile.

    H. The code compiles but throws an exception at runtime.

20. Which of the following statements about unary operators are true? (Choose all that apply.)

    A. Unary operators are always executed before any surrounding binary or ternary operators.

    B. The - operator can be used to flip a boolean value.

    C. The pre-increment operator (++) returns the value of the variable before the increment is applied.

    D. The post-decrement operator (--) returns the value of the variable before the decrement is applied.

    E. The ! operator cannot be used on numeric values.

    F. None of the above

Chapter

4

Making Decisions

OCP EXAM OBJECTIVES COVERED IN THIS CHAPTER:

✓ **Using Operators and Decision Constructs**

  ▪ Use Java control statements including if, if/else, switch

  ▪ Create and use do/while, while, for and for each loops, including nested loops, use break and continue statements

Like many programming languages, Java is composed primarily of variables, operators, and statements put together in some logical order. Previously, we covered how to create and manipulate variables. Writing software is about more than managing variables, though; it is about creating applications that can make intelligent decisions. In this chapter, we present the various decision-making statements available to you within the language. This knowledge will allow you to build complex functions and class structures that you'll see throughout this book.

Creating Decision-Making Statements

Java operators allow you to create a lot of complex expressions, but they're limited in the manner in which they can control program flow. Imagine you want a method to be executed only under certain conditions that cannot be evaluated until runtime. For example, on rainy days, a zoo should remind patrons to bring an umbrella, or on a snowy day, the zoo might need to close. The software doesn't change, but the behavior of the software should, depending on the inputs supplied in the moment. In this section, we will discuss decision-making statements including if, else, and switch statements.

Statements and Blocks

As you may recall from Chapter 2, "Java Building Blocks," a Java *statement* is a complete unit of execution in Java, terminated with a semicolon (;). For the remainder of the chapter, we'll be introducing you to various Java control flow statements. *Control flow statements* break up the flow of execution by using decision-making, looping, and branching, allowing the application to selectively execute particular segments of code.

These statements can be applied to single expressions as well as a block of Java code. As described in Chapter 2, a *block* of code in Java is a group of zero or more statements between balanced braces ({}) and can be used anywhere a single statement is allowed. For example, the following two snippets are equivalent, with the first being a single expression and the second being a block of statements:

```
// Single statement
patrons++;

// Statement inside a block
{
    patrons++;
}
```

A statement or block often functions as the target of a decision-making statement. For example, we can prepend the decision-making if statement to these two examples:

```
// Single statement
if(ticketsTaken > 1)
    patrons++;

// Statement inside a block
if(ticketsTaken > 1)
{
    patrons++;
}
```

Again, both of these code snippets are equivalent. Just remember that the target of a decision-making statement can be a single statement or block of statements. For the rest of the chapter, we will use both forms to better prepare you for what you will see on the exam.

> While both of the previous examples are equivalent, stylistically the second form is often preferred, even if the block has only one statement. The second form has the advantage that you can quickly insert new lines of code into the block, without modifying the surrounding structure. While either of these forms is correct, it might explain why you often see developers who always use blocks with all decision-making statements.

The *if* Statement

Oftentimes, we want to execute a block of code only under certain circumstances. The *if* statement, as shown in Figure 4.1, accomplishes this by allowing our application to execute a particular block of code if and only if a boolean expression evaluates to true at runtime.

FIGURE 4.1   The structure of an if statement

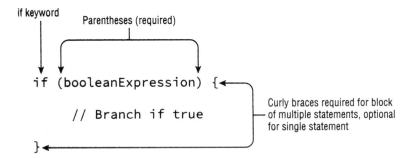

For example, imagine we had a function that used the hour of day, an integer value from 0 to 23, to display a message to the user:

```
if(hourOfDay < 11)
    System.out.println("Good Morning");
```

If the hour of the day is less than 11, then the message will be displayed. Now let's say we also wanted to increment some value, morningGreetingCount, every time the greeting is printed. We could write the if statement twice, but luckily Java offers us a more natural approach using a block:

```
if(hourOfDay < 11) {
    System.out.println("Good Morning");
    morningGreetingCount++;
}
```

The block allows multiple statements to be executed based on the if evaluation. Notice that the first statement didn't contain a block around the print section, but it easily could have. As discussed in the previous section, it is often considered good coding practice to put blocks around the execution component of if statements, as well as many other control flow statements, although it is certainly not required.

Watch Indentation and Braces

One area where the exam writers will try to trip you up is on if statements without braces ({}). For example, take a look at this slightly modified form of our example:

```
if(hourOfDay < 11)
    System.out.println("Good Morning");
    morningGreetingCount++;
```

Based on the indentation, you might be inclined to think the variable morningGreetingCount is only going to be incremented if the hourOfDay is less than 11, but that's not what this code does. It will execute the print statement only if the condition is met, but it will always execute the increment operation.

Remember that in Java, unlike some other programming languages, tabs are just whitespace and are not evaluated as part of the execution. When you see a control flow statement in a question, be sure to trace the open and close braces of the block, ignoring any indentation you may come across.

The *else* Statement

Let's expand our example a little. What if we want to display a different message if it is 11 a.m. or later? Could we do it using only the tools we have? Of course we can!

```
if(hourOfDay < 11) {
    System.out.println("Good Morning");
```

```
}
if(hourOfDay >= 11) {
    System.out.println("Good Afternoon");
}
```

This seems a bit redundant, though, since we're performing an evaluation on hourOfDay twice. It's also wasteful because in some circumstances the cost of the boolean expression we're evaluating could be computationally expensive. Luckily, Java offers us a more useful approach in the form of an else statement, as shown in Figure 4.2.

FIGURE 4.2   The structure of an else statement

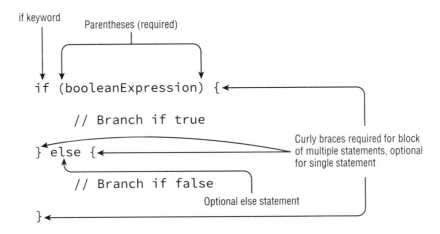

Let's return to this example:

```
if(hourOfDay < 11) {
    System.out.println("Good Morning");
} else {
    System.out.println("Good Afternoon");
}
```

Now our code is truly branching between one of the two possible options, with the boolean evaluation happening only once. The else operator takes a statement or block of statements, in the same manner as the if statement does. Similarly, we can append additional if statements to an else block to arrive at a more refined example:

```
if(hourOfDay < 11) {
    System.out.println("Good Morning");
} else if(hourOfDay < 15) {
    System.out.println("Good Afternoon");
} else {
    System.out.println("Good Evening");
}
```

In this example, the Java process will continue execution until it encounters an if statement that evaluates to true. If neither of the first two expressions is true, it will execute the final code of the else block. One thing to keep in mind in creating complex if and else statements is that order is important. For example, see what happens if we reorder the previous snippet of code as follows:

```java
if(hourOfDay < 15) {
    System.out.println("Good Afternoon");
} else if(hourOfDay < 11) {
    System.out.println("Good Morning");  // COMPILES BUT IS UNREACHABLE
} else {
    System.out.println("Good Evening");
}
```

For hours of the day less than 11, this code behaves very differently than the previous set of code. Do you see why the second block can never be executed regardless of the value of hourOfDay?

If a value is less than 11, then it must be also less than 15 by definition. Therefore, if the second branch in the example can be reached, the first branch can also be reached. Since execution of each branch is mutually exclusive in this example (that is, only one branch can be executed), then if the first branch is executed, the second cannot be executed. Therefore, there is no way the second branch will ever be executed, and the code is deemed unreachable.

Verifying That the *if* Statement Evaluates to a Boolean Expression

Another common place the exam may try to lead you astray is by providing code where the boolean expression inside the if statement is not actually a boolean expression. For example, take a look at the following lines of code:

```java
int hourOfDay = 1;
if(hourOfDay) {  // DOES NOT COMPILE
    ...
}
```

This statement may be valid in some other programming and scripting languages, but not in Java, where 0 and 1 are not considered boolean values.

Also, like you saw in Chapter 3, "Operators," be wary of assignment operators being used as if they were equals (==) operators in if statements:

```java
int hourOfDay = 1;
if(hourOfDay = 5) {  // DOES NOT COMPILE
    ...
}
```

The *switch* Statement

What if we have a lot of possible branches for a single value? For example, we might want to print a different message based on the day of the week. We could certainly accomplish this with a combination of seven if or else statements, but that tends to create code that is long, difficult to read, and often not fun to maintain. For example, the following code prints a different value based on the day of the week using various different styles for each decision statement:

```
int dayOfWeek = 5;

if(dayOfWeek == 0) System.out.print("Sunday");
else if(dayOfWeek == 1)
{
   System.out.print("Monday");
}
else if(dayOfWeek == 2) {
   System.out.print("Tuesday");
} else if(dayOfWeek == 3)
   System.out.print("Wednesday");
...
```

Luckily, Java, along with many other languages, provides a cleaner approach. A *switch* statement, as shown in Figure 4.3, is a complex decision-making structure in which a single value is evaluated and flow is redirected to the first matching branch, known as a *case* statement. If no such case statement is found that matches the value, an optional *default* statement will be called. If no such default option is available, the entire switch statement will be skipped.

FIGURE 4.3 The structure of a switch statement

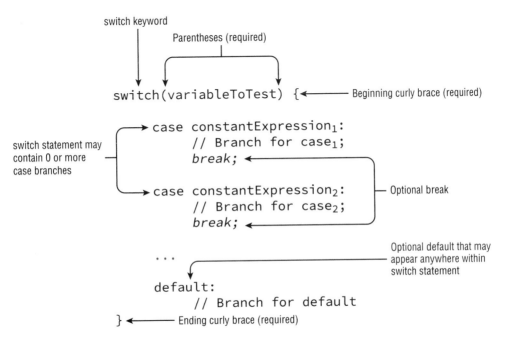

Proper Switch Syntax

Because switch statements can be longer than most decision-making statements, the exam may present invalid switch syntax to see whether you are paying attention. See if you can figure out why each of the following switch statements does not compile:

```
int month = 5;

switch month {  // DOES NOT COMPILE
   case 1: System.out.print("January");
}

switch (month)  // DOES NOT COMPILE
   case 1: System.out.print("January");

switch (month) {
   case 1: 2: System.out.print("January"); // DOES NOT COMPILE
}

switch (month) {
   case 1 || 2: System.out.print("January"); // DOES NOT COMPILE
}
```

The first switch statement does not compile because it is missing parentheses around the switch variable. The second statement does not compile because it is missing braces around the switch body. The third statement does not compile because the case keyword is missing before the 2: label. Each case statement requires the keyword case, followed by a value and a colon (:).

Finally, the last switch statement does not compile because 1 || 2 uses the short-circuit boolean operator, which cannot be applied to numeric values. A single bitwise operator (|) would have allowed the code to compile, although the interpretation of this might not be what you expect. It would then only match a value of month that is the bitwise result of 1 | 2, which is 3, and would *not* match month having a value 1 or 2. You don't need to know bitwise arithmetic for the exam, but you do need to know proper syntax for case statements.

Notice that these last two statements both try to combine case statements in ways that are not valid. One last note you should be aware of for the exam: a switch statement is not required to contain any case statements. For example, this statement is perfectly valid:

```
switch (month) {}
```

For the exam, make sure you memorize the syntax used in Figure 4.3. As you will see in the next section, while some aspects of switch statements have changed over the years, many things have not changed.

Switch Data Types

As shown in Figure 4.3, a switch statement has a target variable that is not evaluated until runtime. Prior to Java 5.0, this variable could only be int values or those values that could be promoted to int, specifically byte, short, char, or int, which we refer to as *primitive numeric types*.

The switch statement also supports any of the wrapper class versions of these primitive numeric types, such as Byte, Short, Character, or Integer. Don't worry if you haven't seen numeric wrapper classes—we'll be covering them in Chapter 5, "Core Java APIs." For now, you just need to know that they are objects that can store primitive values.

 Notice that boolean, long, float, and double are excluded from switch statements, as are their associated Boolean, Long, Float, and Double classes. The reasons are varied, such as boolean having too small a range of values and floating-point numbers having quite a wide range of values. For the exam, though, you just need to know that they are not permitted in switch statements.

When enumeration, denoted enum, was added in Java 5.0, support was added to switch statements to support enum values. An enumeration is a fixed set of constant values, which can also include methods and class variables, similar to a class definition. For the exam, you do not need to know how to create enums, but you should be aware they can be used as the target of switch statements.

In Java 7, switch statements were further updated to allow matching on String values. In Java 10, if the type a var resolves to is one of the types supported by a switch statement, then var can be used in a switch statement too.

Switch History and Changes

As you can see, switch statements have been modified in numerous versions of Java. You don't have to worry about remembering the history—just know what types are now allowed. The history lesson is for experienced Java developers who have been using an older version of Java and may not be aware of the numerous changes to switch statements over the years.

But wait, there's more. Java 12 launched with a Preview release of a powerful new feature called Switch Expressions, a construct that combines switch statements with lambda expressions and allows switch statements to return a value. You won't need to know Switch Expressions for the exam, but it's just a sign that the writers of Java are far from done making enhancements to switch statements.

The following is a list of all data types supported by switch statements:

- int and Integer
- byte and Byte
- short and Short
- char and Character
- String
- enum values
- var (if the type resolves to one of the preceding types)

For the exam, we recommend you memorize this list. Remember, boolean, long, float, double, and each of their associated wrapper classes are not supported by switch statements.

Switch Control Flow

Let's look at a simple switch example using the day of the week, with 0 for Sunday, 1 for Monday, and so on:

```java
int dayOfWeek = 5;
switch(dayOfWeek) {
    default:
        System.out.println("Weekday");
    break;
        case 0:
    System.out.println("Sunday");
        break;
    case 6:
        System.out.println("Saturday");
    break;
}
```

With a value of dayOfWeek of 5, this code will output the following:

```
Weekday
```

The first thing you may notice is that there is a break statement at the end of each case and default section. We'll discuss break statements in more detail when we discuss branching, but for now all you need to know is that they terminate the switch statement and return flow control to the enclosing statement. As you'll soon see, if you leave out the break statement, flow will continue to the next proceeding case or default block automatically.

Another thing you might notice is that the default block is not at the end of the switch statement. There is no requirement that the case or default statement be in a particular order, unless you are going to have pathways that reach multiple sections of the switch block in a single execution.

To illustrate both of the preceding points, consider the following variation:

```java
var dayOfWeek = 5;
switch(dayOfWeek) {
    case 0:
        System.out.println("Sunday");
    default:
        System.out.println("Weekday");
    case 6:
        System.out.println("Saturday");
    break;
}
```

This code looks a lot like the previous example. Notice that we used a var for the switch variable, which is allowed because it resolves to an int by the compiler. Next, two of the break statements have been removed, and the order has been changed. This means that for the given value of dayOfWeek, 5, the code will jump to the default block and then execute all of the proceeding case statements in order until it finds a break statement or finishes the switch statement:

```
Weekday
Saturday
```

The order of the case and default statements is now important since placing the default statement at the end of the switch statement would cause only one word to be output.

What if the value of dayOfWeek was 6 in this example? Would the default block still be executed? The output of this example with dayOfWeek set to 6 would be as follows:

```
Saturday
```

Even though the default block was before the case block, only the case block was executed. If you recall the definition of the default block, it is branched to only if there is no matching case value for the switch statement, regardless of its position within the switch statement.

Finally, if the value of dayOfWeek was 0, all three statements would be output:

```
Sunday
Weekday
Saturday
```

Notice that in this last example, the default statement is executed since there was no break statement at the end of the preceding case block. While the code will not branch to the default statement if there is a matching case value within the switch statement, it will execute the default statement if it encounters it after a case statement for which there is no terminating break statement.

The exam creators are fond of switch *examples that are missing* break *statements!* When evaluating switch statements on the exam, always consider that multiple branches may be visited in a single execution.

Acceptable Case Values

We conclude our discussion of switch statements by talking about acceptable values for case statements, given a particular switch variable. Not just any variable or value can be used in a case statement!

First off, the values in each case statement must be compile-time constant values of the same data type as the switch value. This means you can use only literals, enum constants, or final constant variables of the same data type. By final constant, we mean that the variable must be marked with the final modifier and initialized with a literal value in the same expression in which it is declared. For example, you can't have a case statement value that requires executing a method at runtime, even if that method always returns the same value. For these reasons, only the first and last case statements in the following example compiles:

```
final int getCookies() { return 4; }
void feedAnimals() {
   final int bananas = 1;
   int apples = 2;
   int numberOfAnimals = 3;
   final int cookies = getCookies();
   switch (numberOfAnimals) {
      case bananas:
      case apples:  // DOES NOT COMPILES
      case getCookies():  // DOES NOT COMPILE
      case cookies :  // DOES NOT COMPILE
      case 3 * 5 :
   }
}
```

The bananas variable is marked final, and its value is known at compile-time, so it is valid. The apples variable is not marked final, even though its value is known, so it is not permitted. The next two case statements, with values getCookies() and cookies, do not compile because methods are not evaluated until runtime, so they cannot be used as the value of a case statement, even if one of the values is stored in a final variable. The last case statement, with value 3 * 5, does compile, as expressions are allowed as case values, provided the value can be resolved at compile-time. They also must be able to fit in the switch data type without an explicit cast. We'll go into that in more detail shortly.

Next, the data type for case statements must all match the data type of the switch variable. For example, you can't have a case statement of type String, if the switch statement variable is of type int, since the types are incomparable.

A More Complex Example

We now present a large switch statement, not unlike what you could see on the exam, with numerous broken case statements. See if you can figure out why certain case statements compile and others do not.

```
private int getSortOrder(String firstName, final String lastName) {
   String middleName = "Patricia";
   final String suffix = "JR";
   int id = 0;
   switch(firstName) {
      case "Test":
         return 52;
      case middleName:  // DOES NOT COMPILE
         id = 5;
         break;
      case suffix:
```

```
          id = 0;
          break;
      case lastName:     // DOES NOT COMPILE
          id = 8;
          break;
      case 5:            // DOES NOT COMPILE
          id = 7;
          break;
      case 'J':          // DOES NOT COMPILE
          id = 10;
          break;
      case java.time.DayOfWeek.SUNDAY:  // DOES NOT COMPILE
          id=15;
          break;
   }
   return id;
}
```

The first case statement, "Test", compiles without issue since it is a String literal and is a good example of how a return statement, like a break statement, can be used to exit the switch statement early. The second case statement does not compile because middleName is not a constant value, despite having a known value at this particular line of execution. If a final modifier was added to the declaration of middleName, this case statement would have compiled. The third case statement compiles without issue because suffix is a final constant variable.

In the fourth case statement, despite lastName being final, it is not constant as it is passed to the function; therefore, this line does not compile as well. Finally, the last three case statements do not compile because none of them has a matching type of String, the last one being an enum value.

Numeric Promotion and Casting

Last but not least, switch statements support numeric promotion that does not require an explicit cast. For example, see if you can understand why only two of these case statements compile:

```
short size = 4;
final int small = 15;
final int big = 1_000_000;
switch(size) {
   case small:
   case 1+2 :
   case big:  // DOES NOT COMPILE
}
```

As you may recall from our discussion of numeric promotion and casting in Chapter 3, the compiler can easily cast small from int to short at compile-time because the value 15 is small enough to fit inside a short. This would not be permitted if small was not a compile-time constant. Likewise, it can convert the expression 1+2 from int to short at compile-time. On the other hand, 1_000_000 is too large to fit inside of short without an explicit cast, so the last case statement does not compile.

Writing *while* Loops

A common practice when writing software is the need to do the same task some number of times. You could use the decision structures we have presented so far to accomplish this, but that's going to be a pretty long chain of if or else statements, especially if you have to execute the same thing 100 times or more.

Enter loops! A *loop* is a repetitive control structure that can execute a statement of code multiple times in succession. By making use of variables being able to be assigned new values, each repetition of the statement may be different. In the following example, the loop increments a counter variable that causes the value of price to increase by 10 on each execution of the loop. The loop continues for a total of 10 times.

```
int counter = 0;
while (counter < 10) {
    double price = counter * 10;
    System.out.println(price);
    counter++;
}
```

If you don't follow this code, don't panic—we'll be covering it shortly. In this section, we're going to discuss the while loop and its two forms. In the next section, we'll move onto for loops, which have their roots in while loops.

The *while* Statement

The simplest repetitive control structure in Java is the while statement, described in Figure 4.4. Like all repetition control structures, it has a termination condition, implemented as a boolean expression, that will continue as long as the expression evaluates to true.

FIGURE 4.4   The structure of a while statement

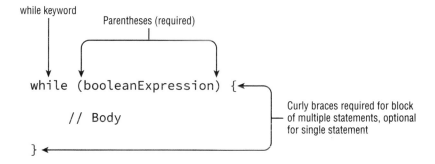

As shown in Figure 4.4, a `while` loop is similar to an `if` statement in that it is composed of a `boolean` expression and a statement, or a block of statements. During execution, the `boolean` expression is evaluated before each iteration of the loop and exits if the evaluation returns `false`.

Let's return to our mouse example from Chapter 2 and show how a loop can be used to model a mouse eating a meal.

```
int roomInBelly = 5;
public void eatCheese(int bitesOfCheese) {
    while (bitesOfCheese > 0 && roomInBelly > 0) {
        bitesOfCheese--;
        roomInBelly--;
    }
    System.out.println(bitesOfCheese+" pieces of cheese left");
}
```

This method takes an amount of food, in this case cheese, and continues until the mouse has no room in its belly or there is no food left to eat. With each iteration of the loop, the mouse "eats" one bite of food and loses one spot in its belly. By using a compound `boolean` statement, you ensure that the `while` loop can end for either of the conditions.

One thing to remember is that a `while` loop may terminate after its first evaluation of the `boolean` expression. For example, how many times is `Not full!` printed in the following example?

```
int full = 5;
while(full < 5) {
    System.out.println("Not full!");
    full++;
}
```

The answer? Zero! On the first iteration of the loop, the condition is reached, and the loop exits. This is why `while` loops are often used in places where you expect zero or more executions of the loop. Simply put, the body of the loop may not execute at all or may execute many times.

The *do/while* Statement

The second form a `while` loop can take is called a *do/while* loop, which like a `while` loop is a repetition control structure with a termination condition and statement, or a block of statements, as shown in Figure 4.5. Unlike a `while` loop, though, a `do/while` loop guarantees that the statement or block will be executed at least once. Whereas a `while` loop is executed zero or more times, a `do/while` loop is executed one or more times.

FIGURE 4.5 The structure of a do/while statement

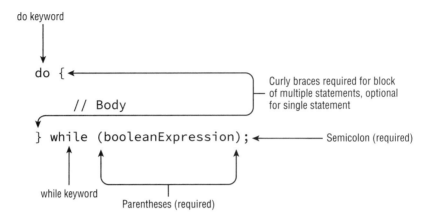

The primary difference between the syntactic structure of a do/while loop and a while loop is that a do/while loop purposely orders the body before the conditional expression so that the body will be executed at least once. For example, what is the output of the following statements?

```
int lizard = 0;
do {
    lizard++;
} while(false);
System.out.println(lizard);  // 1
```

Java will execute the statement block first and then check the loop condition. Even though the loop exits right away, the statement block is still executed once, and the program prints 1.

Comparing *while* and *do/while* Loops

In practice, it might be difficult to determine when you should use a while loop and when you should use a do/while loop. The short answer is that it does not actually matter. Any while loop can be converted to a do/while loop, and vice versa. For example, compare this while loop:

```
while(llama > 10) {
    System.out.println("Llama!");
    llama--;
}
```

and this do/while loop:

```
if(llama > 10) {
    do {
```

```
      System.out.println("Llama!");
      llama--;
   } while(llama > 10);
}
```

Although one of the loops is certainly easier to read, they are functionally equivalent. Think about it. If `llama` is less than or equal to `10` at the start, then both code snippets will exit without printing anything. If `llama` is greater than `10`, say `15`, then both loops will print `Llama!` exactly five times.

We recommend you use a `while` loop when the code will execute zero or more times and a do/while loop when the code will execute one or more times. To put it another way, you should use a do/while loop when you want your loop to execute at least once.

That said, determining whether you should use a `while` loop or a do/while loop in practice is sometimes about personal preference and about code readability.

For example, although the first statement in our previous example is shorter, the do/while statement has the advantage that you could leverage the existing `if` statement and perform some other operation in a new `else` branch, as shown in the following example:

```
if(llama > 10) {
   do {
      System.out.println("Llama!");
      llama--;
   } while(llama > 10);
} else {
   llama++;
}
```

For fun, try taking a do/while loop you've written in the past and convert it to a `while` loop, or vice versa.

Infinite Loops

The single most important thing you should be aware of when you are using any repetition control structure is to make sure they always terminate! Failure to terminate a loop can lead to numerous problems in practice including overflow exceptions, memory leaks, slow performance, and even bad data. Let's take a look at an example:

```
int pen = 2;
int pigs = 5;
while(pen < 10)
   pigs++;
```

You may notice one glaring problem with this statement: it will never end. The variable pen is never modified, so the expression (pen < 10) will always evaluate to true. The result is that the loop will never end, creating what is commonly referred to as an infinite loop. An *infinite loop* is a loop whose termination condition is never reached during runtime.

Anytime you write a loop, you should examine it to determine whether the termination condition is always eventually met under some condition. For example, a loop in which no variables are changing between two executions suggests that the termination condition may not be met. The loop variables should always be moving in a particular direction.

In other words, make sure the loop condition, or the variables the condition is dependent on, are changing between executions. Then, ensure that the termination condition will be eventually reached in all circumstances. As you'll see in the last section of this chapter, a loop may also exit under other conditions, such as a break statement.

 Real World Scenario

A Practical Use of an Infinite Loop

In practice, infinite loops can be used to monitor processes that exist for the life of the program—for example, a process that wakes up every 30 seconds to look for work to be done and then goes back to sleep afterward.

When creating an infinite loop like this, you need to make sure there are only a fixed number of them created by the application, or you could run out of memory. You also have to make sure that there is a way to stop them, often as part of the application shutting down. Finally, there are modern alternatives to creating infinite loops, such as using a scheduled thread executor, that are well beyond the scope of the exam.

If you're not familiar with how to create and execute multiple processes at once, don't worry, you don't need to be for this exam. When you continue on to exam 1Z0-816, you will study these topics as part of concurrency.

Constructing *for* Loops

Even though while and do/while statements are quite powerful, some tasks are so common in writing software that special types of loops were created—for example, iterating over a statement exactly 10 times or iterating over a list of names. You could easily accomplish these tasks with various while loops that you've seen so far, but they usually require writing multiple lines of code and managing variables manually. Wouldn't it be great if there was a looping structure that could do the same thing in a single line of code?

With that, we present the most convenient repetition control structure, for loops. There are two types of for loops, although both use the same for keyword. The first is referred to as the *basic* for loop, and the second is often called the *enhanced* for loop. For clarity, we'll refer to them as the for loop and the for-each loop, respectively, throughout the book.

The *for* Loop

A basic *for loop* has the same conditional boolean expression and statement, or block of statements, as the while loops, as well as two new sections: an *initialization block* and an *update* statement. Figure 4.6 shows how these components are laid out.

FIGURE 4.6   The structure of a basic for loop

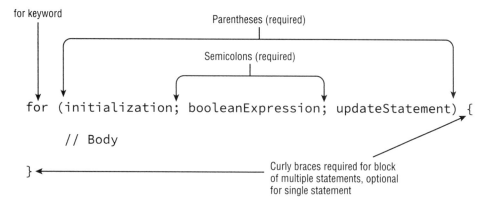

1. Initialization statement executes
2. If booleanExpression is true continue, else exit loop
3. Body executes
4. Execute updateStatement
5. Return to Step 2

Although Figure 4.6 might seem a little confusing and almost arbitrary at first, the organization of the components and flow allow us to create extremely powerful statements in a single line that otherwise would take multiple lines with a while loop. Note that each section is separated by a semicolon. Also, the initialization and update sections may contain multiple statements, separated by commas.

Variables declared in the initialization block of a for loop have limited scope and are accessible only within the for loop. Be wary of any exam questions in which a variable is declared within the initialization block of a for loop and then read outside the loop. For example, this code does not compile because the loop variable i is referenced outside the loop:

```
for(int i=0; i < 10; i++)
    System.out.print("Value is: "+i);
System.out.println(i);  // DOES NOT COMPILE
```

Alternatively, variables declared before the for loop and assigned a value in the initialization block may be used outside the for loop because their scope precedes the creation of the for loop.

Let's take a look at an example that prints the first five numbers, starting with zero:

```java
for(int i = 0; i < 5; i++) {
    System.out.print(i + " ");
}
```

The local variable i is initialized first to 0. The variable i is only in scope for the duration of the loop and is not available outside the loop once the loop has completed. Like a while loop, the boolean condition is evaluated on every iteration of the loop *before* the loop executes. Since it returns true, the loop executes and outputs the 0 followed by a space. Next, the loop executes the update section, which in this case increases the value of i to 1. The loop then evaluates the boolean expression a second time, and the process repeats multiple times, printing the following:

```
0 1 2 3 4
```

On the fifth iteration of the loop, the value of i reaches 4 and is incremented by 1 to reach 5. On the sixth iteration of the loop, the boolean expression is evaluated, and since (5 < 5) returns false, the loop terminates without executing the statement loop body.

 Real World Scenario

Why *i* in *for* Loops?

You may notice it is common practice to name a for loop variable i. Long before Java existed, programmers started using i as short for increment variable, and the practice exists today, even though many of those programming languages no longer do!

For double or triple loops, where i is already used, the next letters in the alphabet, j and k, are often used, respectively. One advantage of using a single-letter variable name in a for loop is that it doesn't take up a lot of space, allowing the for loop declaration to fit on a single line.

For the exam, and for your own coding experience, you should know that using a single-letter variable name is not required. That said, you are likely to encounter i in for loops throughout your professional software development experience.

Printing Elements in Reverse

Let's say you wanted to print the same first five numbers from zero as we did in the previous section, but this time in reverse order. The goal then is to print 4 3 2 1 0.

How would you do that? Starting with Java 10, you may now see var used in a for loop, so let's use that for this example. An initial implementation might look like the following:

```java
for (var counter = 5; counter > 0; counter--) {
    System.out.print(counter + " ");
}
```

First, how is var interpreted? Since it is assigned a value of 5, the compiler treats it as having a type of int. Next, what does the example output? While this snippet does output five distinct values and it resembles our first for loop example, it does not output the same five values. Instead, this is the output:

```
5 4 3 2 1
```

Wait, that's not what we wanted! We wanted 4 3 2 1 0. It starts with 5, because that is the first value assigned to it. Let's fix that by starting with 4 instead:

```
for (var counter = 4; counter > 0; counter--) {
    System.out.print(counter + " ");
}
```

What does this print now? This prints the following:

```
4 3 2 1
```

So close! The problem is it ends with 1, not 0, because we told it to exit as soon as the value was not strictly greater than 0. If we want to print the same 0 through 4 as our first example, we need to update the termination condition, like this:

```
for (var counter = 4; counter >= 0; counter--) {
    System.out.print(counter + " ");
}
```

Finally! We have code that now prints 4 3 2 1 0 and matches the reverse of our for loop example in the previous section. We could have instead used counter > -1 as the loop termination condition in this example, although counter >= 0 tends to be more readable.

 For the exam, you are going to have to know how to read forward and backward for loops. When you see a for loop on the exam, pay close attention to the loop variable and operations if the decrement operator, --, is used. While incrementing from 0 in a for loop is often straightforward, decrementing tends to be less intuitive. In fact, if you do see a for loop with a decrement operator on the exam, you should assume they are trying to test your knowledge of loop operations.

Working with *for* Loops

Although most for loops you are likely to encounter in your professional development experience will be well defined and similar to the previous examples, there are a number of variations and edge cases you could see on the exam. You should familiarize yourself with the following five examples; variations of these are likely to be seen on the exam.

Let's tackle some examples for illustrative purposes:

1. Creating an Infinite Loop

```
for( ; ; )
    System.out.println("Hello World");
```

Although this for loop may look like it does not compile, it will in fact compile and run without issue. It is actually an infinite loop that will print the same statement repeatedly. This example reinforces the fact that the components of the for loop are each optional. Note that the semicolons separating the three sections are required, as for( ) without any semicolons will not compile.

2. Adding Multiple Terms to the for Statement

```
int x = 0;
for(long y = 0, z = 4; x < 5 && y < 10; x++, y++) {
    System.out.print(y + " "); }
System.out.print(x + " ");
```

This code demonstrates three variations of the for loop you may not have seen. First, you can declare a variable, such as x in this example, before the loop begins and use it after it completes. Second, your initialization block, boolean expression, and update statements can include extra variables that may or may not reference each other. For example, z is defined in the initialization block and is never used. Finally, the update statement can modify multiple variables. This code will print the following when executed:

```
0 1 2 3 4 5
```

3. Redeclaring a Variable in the Initialization Block

```
int x = 0;
for(int x = 4; x < 5; x++) {    // DOES NOT COMPILE
    System.out.print(x + " ");
}
```

This example looks similar to the previous one, but it does not compile because of the initialization block. The difference is that x is repeated in the initialization block after already being declared before the loop, resulting in the compiler stopping because of a duplicate variable declaration. We can fix this loop by removing the declaration of x from the for loop as follows:

```
int x = 0;
for(x = 0; x < 5; x++) {
    System.out.print(x + " ");
}
```

Note that this variation will now compile because the initialization block simply assigns a value to x and does not declare it.

4. Using Incompatible Data Types in the Initialization Block

```java
int x = 0;
for(long y = 0, int z = 4; x < 5; x++) {   // DOES NOT COMPILE
    System.out.print(y + " ");
}
```

Like the third example, this code will not compile, although this time for a different reason. The variables in the initialization block must all be of the same type. In the multiple terms example, y and z were both long, so the code compiled without issue, but in this example they have differing types, so the code will not compile.

5. Using Loop Variables Outside the Loop

```java
for(long y = 0, x = 4; x < 5 && y < 10; x++, y++) {
    System.out.print(y + " ");
}
System.out.print(x);   // DOES NOT COMPILE
```

We covered this already at the start of this section, but this is so important for passing the exam that we discuss it again here. If you notice, x is defined in the initialization block of the loop and then used after the loop terminates. Since x was only scoped for the loop, using it outside the loop will cause a compiler error.

Modifying Loop Variables

What happens if you modify a variable in a for loop, or any other loop for that matter? Does Java even let you modify these variables? Take a look at the following three examples, and see whether you can determine what will happen if they are each run independently:

```java
for(int i=0; i<10; i++)
    i = 0;

for(int j=1; j<10; j++)
    j--;

for(int k=0; k<10; )
    k++;
```

All three of these examples compile, as Java does let you modify loop variables, whether they be in for, while, or do/while loops. The first two examples create infinite loops, as loop conditions i<10 and j<10 are never reached, independently. In the first example, i is reset during every loop to 0, then incremented to 1, then reset to 0, and so on. In the second example, j is decremented to 0, then incremented to 1, then decremented to 0, and so on. The last example executes the loop exactly 10 times, so it is valid, albeit a little unusual.

Java does allow modification of loop variables, but you should be wary if you see questions on the exam that do this. While it is normally straightforward to look at a for loop and get an idea of how many times the loop will execute, once we start modifying loop variables, the behavior can be extremely erratic. This is especially true when nested loops are involved, which we cover later in this chapter.

There are also some special considerations when modifying a Collection object within a loop. For example, if you delete an element from a List while iterating over it, you could run into a ConcurrentModificationException. This topic is out of scope for the exam, though. You'll revisit this when studying for the 1Z0-816 exam.

> As a general rule, it is considered a poor coding practice to modify loop variables due to the unpredictability of the result. It also tends to make code difficult for other people to read. If you need to exit a loop early or change the flow, you can use break, continue, or return, which we'll discuss later in this chapter.

The for-each Loop

Let's say you want to iterate over a set of values, such as a list of names, and print each of them. Using a for loop, this can be accomplished with a counter variable:

```java
public void printNames(String[] names) {
    for(int counter=0; counter<names.length; counter++)
        System.out.println(names[counter]);
}
```

This works, although it's a bit verbose. We're creating a counter variable, but we really don't care about its value—just that it loops through the array in order.

After almost 20 years of programming for loops like this, the writers of Java took a page from some other programming languages and added the enhanced for loop, or for-each loop as we like to call it. The *for-each* loop is a specialized structure designed to iterate over arrays and various Collection Framework classes, as presented in Figure 4.7.

FIGURE 4.7   The structure of an enhanced for-each loop

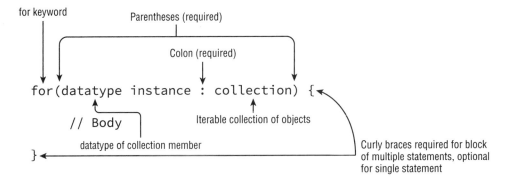

The for-each loop declaration is composed of an initialization section and an object to be iterated over. The right side of the for-each loop must be one of the following:

- A built-in Java array
- An object whose type implements `java.lang.Iterable`

We'll cover what implements means in Chapter 9, "Advanced Class Design," but for now you just need to know the right side must be an array or collection of items, such as a `List` or a `Set`. For the exam, you should know that this does not include all of the Collections Framework classes or interfaces, but only those that implement or extend that `Collection` interface. For example, `Map` is not supported in a for-each loop, although `Map` does include methods that return `Collection` instances.

In Chapter 5, we'll go into detail about how to create `List` objects and how they differ from traditional Java arrays. Likewise, `String` and `StringBuilder`, which you will also see in the next chapter, do not implement `Iterable` and cannot be used as the right side of a for-each statement.

The left side of the for-each loop must include a declaration for an instance of a variable whose type is compatible with the type of the array or collection on the right side of the statement. A var may also be used for the variable type declaration, with the specific type determined by the right side of the for-each statement. On each iteration of the loop, the named variable on the left side of the statement is assigned a new value from the array or collection on the right side of the statement.

Let's return to our previous example and see how we can apply a for-each loop to it.

```
public void printNames(String[] names) {
   for(String name : names)
      System.out.println(name);
}
```

A lot shorter, isn't it? We no longer have a counter loop variable that we need to create, increment, and monitor. Like using a `for` loop in place of a `while` loop, for-each loops are meant to make code easier to read/write, freeing you to focus on the parts of your code that really matter.

Tackling the for-each Statement

Let's work with some examples:

- What will this code output?

```
final String[] names = new String[3];
names[0] = "Lisa";
names[1] = "Kevin";
names[2] = "Roger";

for(String name : names) {
   System.out.print(name + ", ");
}
```

This is a simple one, with no tricks. The code will compile and print the following:

```
Lisa, Kevin, Roger,
```

- What will this code output?

```
List<String> values = new ArrayList<String>();
values.add("Lisa");
values.add("Kevin");
values.add("Roger");

for(var value : values) {
    System.out.print(value + ", ");
}
```

This code will compile and print the same values:

```
Lisa, Kevin, Roger,
```

Like the regular `for` loop, the for-each loop also accepts var for the loop variable, with the type implied by the data type being iterated over.

When you see a for-each loop on the exam, make sure the right side is an array or Iterable object and the left side has a matching type.

- Why does this fail to compile?

```
String names = "Lisa";
for(String name : names) {   // DOES NOT COMPILE
    System.out.print(name + " ");
}
```

In this example, the String names is not an array, nor does it define a list of items, so the compiler will throw an exception since it does not know how to iterate over the String. As a developer, you could iterate over each character of a String, but this would require using the charAt() method, which is not compatible with a for-each loop. The charAt() method, along with other String methods, will be covered in Chapter 5.

- Why does this fail to compile?

```
String[] names = new String[3];
for(int name : names) {   // DOES NOT COMPILE
    System.out.print(name + " ");
}
```

This code will fail to compile because the left side of the for-each statement does not define an instance of String. Notice that in this last example, the array is initialized with three null pointer values. In and of itself, that will not cause the code to not compile, as a corrected loop would just output null three times.

Switching Between *for* and for-each Loops

You may have noticed that in the previous for-each examples, there was an extra comma printed at the end of the list:

```
Lisa, Kevin, Roger,
```

While the for-each statement is convenient for working with lists in many cases, it does hide access to the loop iterator variable. If we wanted to print only the comma between names, we could convert the example into a standard for loop, as in the following example:

```
List<String> names = new ArrayList<String>();
names.add("Lisa");
names.add("Kevin");
names.add("Roger");

for(int i=0; i<names.size(); i++) {
   String name = names.get(i);
   if(i > 0) {
      System.out.print(", ");
   }
   System.out.print(name);
}
```

This sample code would output the following:

```
Lisa, Kevin, Roger
```

This is not as short as our for-each example, but it does create the output we wanted, without the extra comma.

It is also common to use a standard for loop over a for-each loop if comparing multiple elements in a loop within a single iteration, as in the following example:

```
int[] values = new int[3];
values[0] = 1;
values[1] = Integer.valueOf(3);
values[2] = 6;

for(int i=1; i<values.length; i++) {
   System.out.print((values[i]-values[i-1]) + ", ");
}
```

This sample code would output the following:

```
2, 3,
```

Notice that we skip the first index of the array, since value[-1] is not defined and would throw an IndexOutOfBoundsException error if called with i=0. When comparing n elements of a list with each other, our loop should be executed n-1 times.

Despite these examples, enhanced for-each loops are extremely convenient in a variety of circumstances. As a developer, though, you can always revert to a standard for loop if you need fine-grained control.

 Real World Scenario

Comparing *for* and for-each Loops

Since for and for-each both use the same keyword, you might be wondering how they are related. While this discussion is out of scope for the exam, let's take a moment to explore how for-each loops are converted to for loops by the compiler.

When for-each was introduced in Java 5, it was added as a compile-time enhancement. This means that Java actually converts the for-each loop into a standard for loop during compilation. For example, assuming names is an array of String as we saw in the first example, the following two loops are equivalent:

```
for(String name : names) {
    System.out.print(name + ", ");
}
for(int i=0; i < names.length; i++) {
    String name = names[i];
    System.out.print(name + ", ");
}
```

For objects that inherit Iterable, there is a different, but similar, conversion. For example, assuming values is an instance of List<Integer>, the following two loops are equivalent:

```
for(int value : values) {
    System.out.print(value + ", ");
}
for(Iterator<Integer> i = values.iterator(); i.hasNext(); ) {
    int value = i.next();
    System.out.print(value + ", ");
}
```

Notice that in the second version, there is no update statement in the for loop as next() both retrieves the next available value and moves the iterator forward.

Controlling Flow with Branching

The final type of control flow structures we will cover in this chapter are branching statements. Up to now, we have been dealing with single loops that ended only when their boolean expression evaluated to false. We'll now show you other ways loops could end, or branch, and you'll see that the path taken during runtime may not be as straightforward as in the previous examples.

Nested Loops

Before we move into branching statements, we need to introduce the concept of nested loops. A *nested loop* is a loop that contains another loop including while, do/while, for, and for-each loops. For example, consider the following code that iterates over a two-dimensional array, which is an array that contains other arrays as its members. We'll cover multidimensional arrays in detail in Chapter 5, but for now assume the following is how you would declare a two-dimensional array:

```
int[][] myComplexArray = {{5,2,1,3},{3,9,8,9},{5,7,12,7}};

for(int[] mySimpleArray : myComplexArray) {
   for(int i=0; i<mySimpleArray.length; i++) {
      System.out.print(mySimpleArray[i]+"\t");
   }
   System.out.println();
}
```

Notice that we intentionally mix a for and for-each loop in this example. The outer loop will execute a total of three times. Each time the outer loop executes, the inner loop is executed four times. When we execute this code, we see the following output:

```
5       2       1       3
3       9       8       9
5       7       12      7
```

Nested loops can include while and do/while, as shown in this example. See whether you can determine what this code will output:

```
int hungryHippopotamus = 8;
while(hungryHippopotamus>0) {
   do {
      hungryHippopotamus -= 2;
   } while (hungryHippopotamus>5);
   hungryHippopotamus--;
   System.out.print(hungryHippopotamus+", ");
}
```

The first time this loop executes, the inner loop repeats until the value of hungryHippopotamus is 4. The value will then be decremented to 3, and that will be the output at the end of the first iteration of the outer loop.

On the second iteration of the outer loop, the inner do/while will be executed once, even though hungryHippopotamus is already not greater than 5. As you may recall, do/while statements always execute the body at least once. This will reduce the value to 1, which will be further lowered by the decrement operator in the outer loop to 0. Once the value reaches 0, the outer loop will terminate. The result is that the code will output the following:

3, 0,

The examples in the rest of this section will include many nested loops. You will also encounter nested loops on the exam, so the more practice you have with them, the more prepared you will be.

 Some of the most time-consuming questions you may see on the exam could involve nested loops with lots of branching. We recommend you try to answer the question right away, but if you start to think it is going to take too long, you should mark it and come back to it later. Remember, all questions on the exam are weighted evenly!

Adding Optional Labels

One thing we intentionally skipped when we presented if statements, switch statements, and loops is that they can all have optional labels. A *label* is an optional pointer to the head of a statement that allows the application flow to jump to it or break from it. It is a single identifier that is proceeded by a colon (:). For example, we can add optional labels to one of the previous examples:

```
int[][] myComplexArray = {{5,2,1,3},{3,9,8,9},{5,7,12,7}};

OUTER_LOOP: for(int[] mySimpleArray : myComplexArray) {
   INNER_LOOP: for(int i=0; i<mySimpleArray.length; i++) {
      System.out.print(mySimpleArray[i]+"\t");
   }
   System.out.println();
}
```

Labels follow the same rules for formatting as identifiers. For readability, they are commonly expressed using uppercase letters, with underscores between words, to distinguish them from regular variables. When dealing with only one loop, labels do not add any value, but as we'll see in the next section, they are extremely useful in nested structures.

While this topic is not on the exam, it is possible to add optional labels to control and block statements. For example, the following is permitted by the compiler, albeit extremely uncommon:

```
int frog = 15;
BAD_IDEA: if(frog>10)
EVEN_WORSE_IDEA: {
    frog++;
}
```

The *break* Statement

As you saw when working with switch statements, a *break* statement transfers the flow of control out to the enclosing statement. The same holds true for a break statement that appears inside of a while, do/while, or for loop, as it will end the loop early, as shown in Figure 4.8.

FIGURE 4.8 The structure of a break statement

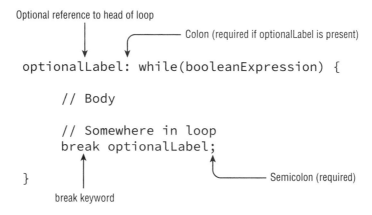

Notice in Figure 4.8 that the break statement can take an optional label parameter. Without a label parameter, the break statement will terminate the nearest inner loop it is currently in the process of executing. The optional label parameter allows us to break out of a higher-level outer loop. In the following example, we search for the first (x,y) array index position of a number within an unsorted two-dimensional array:

```
public class FindInMatrix {
    public static void main(String[] args) {
        int[][] list = {{1,13},{5,2},{2,2}};
        int searchValue = 2;
        int positionX = -1;
```

```
    int positionY = -1;

    PARENT_LOOP: for(int i=0; i<list.length; i++) {
        for(int j=0; j<list[i].length; j++) {
            if(list[i][j]==searchValue) {
                positionX = i;
                positionY = j;
                break PARENT_LOOP;
            }
        }
    }
    if(positionX==-1 || positionY==-1) {
        System.out.println("Value "+searchValue+" not found");
    } else {
        System.out.println("Value "+searchValue+" found at: " +
            "("+positionX+","+positionY+")");
    }
}
}
```

When executed, this code will output the following:

```
Value 2 found at: (1,1)
```

In particular, take a look at the statement break PARENT_LOOP. This statement will break out of the entire loop structure as soon as the first matching value is found. Now, imagine what would happen if we replaced the body of the inner loop with the following:

```
            if(list[i][j]==searchValue) {
                positionX = i;
                positionY = j;
                break;
            }
```

How would this change our flow, and would the output change? Instead of exiting when the first matching value is found, the program will now only exit the inner loop when the condition is met. In other words, the structure will now find the first matching value of the last inner loop to contain the value, resulting in the following output:

```
Value 2 found at: (2,0)
```

Finally, what if we removed the break altogether?

```
            if(list[i][j]==searchValue) {
                positionX = i;
                positionY = j;
            }
```

In this case, the code will search for the last value in the entire structure that has the matching value. The output will look like this:

```
Value 2 found at: (2,1)
```

You can see from this example that using a label on a break statement in a nested loop, or not using the break statement at all, can cause the loop structure to behave quite differently.

The *continue* Statement

Let's now extend our discussion of advanced loop control with the *continue* statement, a statement that causes flow to finish the execution of the current loop, as shown in Figure 4.9.

FIGURE 4.9   The structure of a continue statement

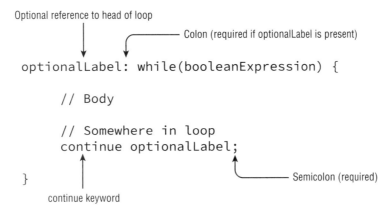

You may notice the syntax of the continue statement mirrors that of the break statement. In fact, the statements are identical in how they are used, but with different results. While the break statement transfers control to the enclosing statement, the continue statement transfers control to the boolean expression that determines if the loop should continue. In other words, it ends the current iteration of the loop. Also, like the break statement, the continue statement is applied to the nearest inner loop under execution using optional label statements to override this behavior.

Let's take a look at an example. Imagine we have a zookeeper who is supposed to clean the first leopard in each of four stables but skip stable b entirely.

```
1: public class CleaningSchedule {
2:     public static void main(String[] args) {
3:         CLEANING: for(char stables = 'a'; stables<='d'; stables++) {
4:             for(int leopard = 1; leopard<4; leopard++) {
5:                 if(stables=='b' || leopard==2) {
```

```
6:                         continue CLEANING;
7:                    }
8:                    System.out.println("Cleaning: "+stables+","+leopard);
9: } } } }
```

With the structure as defined, the loop will return control to the parent loop any time the first value is b or the second value is 2. On the first, third, and fourth executions of the outer loop, the inner loop prints a statement exactly once and then exits on the next inner loop when leopard is 2. On the second execution of the outer loop, the inner loop immediately exits without printing anything since b is encountered right away. The following is printed:

```
Cleaning: a,1
Cleaning: c,1
Cleaning: d,1
```

Now, imagine we removed the CLEANING label in the continue statement so that control is returned to the inner loop instead of the outer. Line 6 becomes the following:

```
6:                    continue;
```

This corresponds to the zookeeper skipping all leopards except those labeled 2 or in stable b. The output would then be the following:

```
Cleaning: a,1
Cleaning: a,3
Cleaning: c,1
Cleaning: c,3
Cleaning: d,1
Cleaning: d,3
```

Finally, if we remove the continue statement and associated if statement altogether by removing lines 5–7, we arrive at a structure that outputs all the values, such as this:

```
Cleaning: a,1
Cleaning: a,2
Cleaning: a,3
Cleaning: b,1
Cleaning: b,2
Cleaning: b,3
Cleaning: c,1
Cleaning: c,2
Cleaning: c,3
Cleaning: d,1
Cleaning: d,2
Cleaning: d,3
```

The *return* Statement

Given that this book shouldn't be your first foray into programming, we hope you've come across methods that contain return statements. Regardless, we'll be covering how to design and create methods that use them in detail in Chapter 7, "Methods and Encapsulation."

For now, though, you should be familiar with the idea that creating methods and using return statements can be used as an alternative to using labels and break statements. For example, take a look at this rewrite of our earlier FindInMatrix class:

```java
public class FindInMatrixUsingReturn {
   private static int[] searchForValue(int[][] list, int v) {
      for (int i = 0; i < list.length; i++) {
         for (int j = 0; j < list[i].length; j++) {
            if (list[i][j] == v) {
               return new int[] {i,j};
            }
         }
      }
      return null;
   }

   public static void main(String[] args) {
      int[][] list = { { 1, 13 }, { 5, 2 }, { 2, 2 } };
      int searchValue = 2;
      int[] results = searchForValue(list,searchValue);

      if (results == null) {
         System.out.println("Value " + searchValue + " not found");
      } else {
         System.out.println("Value " + searchValue + " found at: " +
            "(" + results[0] + "," + results[1] + ")");
      }
   }
}
```

This class is functionally the same as the first FindInMatrix class we saw earlier using break. If you need finer-grained control of the loop with multiple break and continue statements, the first class is probably better. That said, we find code without labels and break statements a lot easier to read and debug. Also, making the search logic an independent function makes the code more reusable and the calling main() method a lot easier to read.

For the exam, you will need to know both forms. Just remember that return statements can be used to exit loops quickly and can lead to more readable code in practice, especially when used with nested loops.

Unreachable Code

One facet of break, continue, and return that you should be aware of is that any code placed immediately after them in the same block is considered unreachable and will not compile. For example, the following code snippet does not compile:

```
int checkDate = 0;
while(checkDate<10) {
   checkDate++;
   if(checkDate>100) {
      break;
      checkDate++;  // DOES NOT COMPILE
   }
}
```

Even though it is not logically possible for the if statement to evaluate to true in this code sample, the compiler notices that you have statements immediately following the break and will fail to compile with "unreachable code" as the reason. The same is true for continue and return statements too, as shown in the following two examples:

```
int minute = 1;
WATCH: while(minute>2) {
   if(minute++>2) {
      continue WATCH;
      System.out.print(minute);  // DOES NOT COMPILE
   }
}

int hour = 2;
switch(hour) {
   case 1: return; hour++;  // DOES NOT COMPILE
   case 2:
}
```

One thing to remember is that it does not matter if loop or decision structure actually visits the line of code. For example, the loop could execute zero or infinite times at runtime. Regardless of execution, the compiler will report an error if it finds any code it deems unreachable, in this case any statements immediately following a break, continue, or return statement.

Reviewing Branching

We conclude this section with Table 4.1, which will help remind you when labels, break, and continue statements are permitted in Java. Although for illustrative purposes our examples have included using these statements in nested loops, they can be used inside single loops as well.

TABLE 4.1   Advanced flow control usage

	Allows optional labels	Allows *break* statement	Allows *continue* statement
while	Yes	Yes	Yes
do while	Yes	Yes	Yes
for	Yes	Yes	Yes
switch	Yes	Yes	No

Last but not least, all testing centers should offer some form of scrap paper or dry-erase board to use during the exam. We strongly recommend you make use of these testing aids should you encounter complex questions involving nested loops and branching statements.

Summary

This chapter presented how to make intelligent decisions in Java. We covered basic decision-making constructs such as if, else, and switch statements and showed how to use them to change the path of process at runtime. Remember that the switch statement allows a lot of data types it did not in the past, such as String, enum, and in certain cases var.

We then moved our discussion to repetition control structures, starting with while and do/while loops. We showed how to use them to create processes that looped multiple times and also showed how it is important to make sure they eventually terminate. Remember that most of these structures require the evaluation of a particular boolean expression to complete.

Next, we covered the extremely convenient repetition control structures, for and for-each loops. While their syntax is more complex than the traditional while or do/while loops, they are extremely useful in everyday coding and allow you to create complex expressions in a single line of code. With a for-each loop you don't need to explicitly write a boolean expression, since the compiler builds one for you. For clarity, we referred to an enhanced for loop as a for-each loop, but syntactically both are written using the for keyword.

We concluded this chapter by discussing advanced control options and how flow can be enhanced through nested loops, coupled with break, continue, and return statements. Be wary of questions on the exam that use nested loops, especially ones with labels, and verify they are being used correctly.

This chapter is especially important because at least one component of this chapter will likely appear in every exam question with sample code. Many of the questions on the exam focus on proper syntactic use of the structures, as they will be a large source of questions that end in "Does not compile." You should be able to answer all of the review questions correctly or fully understand those that you answered incorrectly before moving on to later chapters.

Exam Essentials

Understand if and else decision control statements. The if and else statements come up frequently throughout the exam in questions unrelated to decision control, so make sure you fully understand these basic building blocks of Java.

Understand switch statements and their proper usage. You should be able to spot a poorly formed switch statement on the exam. The switch value and data type should be compatible with the case statements, and the values for the case statements must evaluate to compile-time constants. Finally, at runtime a switch statement branches to the first matching case, or default if there is no match, or exits entirely if there is no match and no default branch. The process then continues into any proceeding case or default statements until a break or return statement is reached.

Understand while loops. Know the syntactical structure of all while and do/while loops. In particular, know when to use one versus the other.

Be able to use for loops. You should be familiar with for and for-each loops and know how to write and evaluate them. Each loop has its own special properties and structures. You should know how to use for-each loops to iterate over lists and arrays.

Understand how break, continue, and return can change flow control. Know how to change the flow control within a statement by applying a break, continue, or return statement. Also know which control statements can accept break statements and which can accept continue statements. Finally, you should understand how these statements work inside embedded loops or switch statements.

Review Questions

The answers to the chapter review questions can be found in the Appendix.

1. Which of the following data types can be used in a `switch` statement? (Choose all that apply.)

    A. enum

    B. int

    C. Byte

    D. long

    E. String

    F. char

    G. var

    H. double

2. What is the output of the following code snippet? (Choose all that apply.)

    ```
    3: int temperature = 4;
    4: long humidity = -temperature + temperature * 3;
    5: if (temperature>=4)
    6: if (humidity < 6) System.out.println("Too Low");
    7: else System.out.println("Just Right");
    8: else System.out.println("Too High");
    ```

    A. Too Low

    B. Just Right

    C. Too High

    D. A `NullPointerException` is thrown at runtime.

    E. The code will not compile because of line 7.

    F. The code will not compile because of line 8.

3. What is the output of the following code snippet?

    ```
    List<Integer> myFavoriteNumbers = new ArrayList<>();
    myFavoriteNumbers.add(10);
    myFavoriteNumbers.add(14);
    for (var a : myFavoriteNumbers) {
       System.out.print(a + ", ");
       break;
    }

    for (int b : myFavoriteNumbers) {
    ```

```
        continue;
        System.out.print(b + ", ");
    }

    for (Object c : myFavoriteNumbers)
        System.out.print(c + ", ");
```

A. It compiles and runs without issue but does not produce any output.

B. `10, 14,`

C. `10, 10, 14,`

D. `10, 10, 14, 10, 14,`

E. Exactly one line of code does not compile.

F. Exactly two lines of code do not compile.

G. Three or more lines of code do not compile.

H. The code contains an infinite loop and does not terminate.

4. Which statements about decision structures are true? (Choose all that apply.)

A. A for-each loop can be executed on any Collections Framework object.

B. The body of a while loop is guaranteed to be executed at least once.

C. The conditional expression of a for loop is evaluated before the first execution of the loop body.

D. A switch statement with no matching case statement requires a default statement.

E. The body of a do/while loop is guaranteed to be executed at least once.

F. An if statement can have multiple corresponding else statements.

5. Assuming weather is a well-formed nonempty array, which code snippet, when inserted independently into the blank in the following code, prints all of the elements of weather? (Choose all that apply.)

```
private void print(int[] weather) {
    for(_____) {
        System.out.println(weather[i]);
    }
}
```

A. `int i=weather.length; i>0; i--`

B. `int i=0; i<=weather.length-1; ++i`

C. `var w : weather`

D. `int i=weather.length-1; i>=0; i--`

E. `int i=0, int j=3; i<weather.length; ++i`

F. `int i=0; ++i<10 && i<weather.length;`

G. None of the above

6. Which statements, when inserted independently into the following blank, will cause the code to print 2 at runtime? (Choose all that apply.)

```
int count = 0;
BUNNY: for(int row = 1; row <=3; row++)
    RABBIT: for(int col = 0; col <3 ; col++) {
        if((col + row) % 2 == 0)
            _____;
        count++;
    }
System.out.println(count);
```

A. break BUNNY

B. break RABBIT

C. continue BUNNY

D. continue RABBIT

E. break

F. continue

G. None of the above, as the code contains a compiler error

7. Given the following method, how many lines contain compilation errors? (Choose all that apply.)

```
private DayOfWeek getWeekDay(int day, final int thursday) {
    int otherDay = day;
    int Sunday = 0;
    switch(otherDay) {
        default:
        case 1: continue;
        case thursday: return DayOfWeek.THURSDAY;
        case 2: break;
        case Sunday: return DayOfWeek.SUNDAY;
        case DayOfWeek.MONDAY: return DayOfWeek.MONDAY;
    }
    return DayOfWeek.FRIDAY;
}
```

A. None, the code compiles without issue.

B. 1

C. 2

D. 3

E. 4

F.   5

G.   6

H.   The code compiles but may produce an error at runtime.

8.   What is the result of the following code snippet?

```
3: int sing = 8, squawk = 2, notes = 0;
4: while(sing > squawk) {
5:     sing--;
6:     squawk += 2;
7:     notes += sing + squawk;
8: }
9: System.out.println(notes);
```

A.   11

B.   13

C.   23

D.   33

E.   50

F.   The code will not compile because of line 7.

9.   What is the output of the following code snippet?

```
2: boolean keepGoing = true;
3: int result = 15, meters = 10;
4: do {
5:     meters--;
6:     if(meters==8) keepGoing = false;
7:     result -= 2;
8: } while keepGoing;
9: System.out.println(result);
```

A.   7

B.   9

C.   10

D.   11

E.   15

F.   The code will not compile because of line 6.

G.   The code does not compile for a different reason.

10. Which statements about the following code snippet are correct? (Choose all that apply.)

```
for(var penguin : new int[2])
   System.out.println(penguin);

var ostrich = new Character[3];
for(var emu : ostrich)
   System.out.println(emu);

List parrots = new ArrayList();
for(var macaw  : parrots)
   System.out.println(macaw);
```

- **A.** The data type of penguin is Integer.
- **B.** The data type of penguin is int.
- **C.** The data type of emu is undefined.
- **D.** The data type of emu is Character.
- **E.** The data type of macaw is undefined.
- **F.** The data type of macaw is Object.
- **G.** None of the above, as the code does not compile

11. What is the result of the following code snippet?

```
final char a = 'A', e = 'E';
char grade = 'B';
switch (grade) {
   default:
   case a:
   case 'B': 'C': System.out.print("great ");
   case 'D': System.out.print("good "); break;
   case e:
   case 'F': System.out.print("not good ");
}
```

- **A.** great
- **B.** great good
- **C.** good
- **D.** not good
- **E.** The code does not compile because the data type of one or more case statements does not match the data type of the switch variable.
- **F.** None of the above

12. Given the following array, which code snippets print the elements in reverse order from how they are declared? (Choose all that apply.)

```
char[] wolf = {'W', 'e', 'b', 'b', 'y'};
```

A.
```
int q = wolf.length;
for( ; ; ) {
   System.out.print(wolf[--q]);
   if(q==0) break;
}
```

B.
```
for(int m=wolf.length-1; m>=0; --m)
   System.out.print(wolf[m]);
```

C.
```
for(int z=0; z<wolf.length; z++)
   System.out.print(wolf[wolf.length-z]);
```

D.
```
int x = wolf.length-1;
for(int j=0; x>=0 && j==0; x--)
   System.out.print(wolf[x]);
```

E.
```
final int r = wolf.length;
for(int w = r-1; r>-1; w = r-1)
   System.out.print(wolf[w]);
```

F.
```
for(int i=wolf.length; i>0; --i)
   System.out.print(wolf[i]);
```

G. None of the above

13. What distinct numbers are printed when the following method is executed? (Choose all that apply.)

```
private void countAttendees() {
   int participants = 4, animals = 2, performers = -1;

   while((participants = participants+1) < 10) {}
   do {} while (animals++ <= 1);
   for( ; performers<2; performers+=2) {}

   System.out.println(participants);
   System.out.println(animals);
   System.out.println(performers);
}
```

A. 6

B. 3

C. 4

D. 5

E. 10

F. 9

G. The code does not compile.

H. None of the above

14. What is the output of the following code snippet?

```
2: double iguana = 0;
3: do {
4:     int snake = 1;
5:     System.out.print(snake++ + " ");
6:     iguana--;
7: } while (snake <= 5);
8: System.out.println(iguana);
```

A. 1 2 3 4 -4.0

B. 1 2 3 4 -5.0

C. 1 2 3 4 5 -4.0

D. 0 1 2 3 4 5 -5.0

E. The code does not compile.

F. The code compiles but produces an infinite loop at runtime.

G. None of the above

15. Which statements, when inserted into the following blanks, allow the code to compile and run without entering an infinite loop? (Choose all that apply.)

```
4:  int height = 1;
5:  L1: while(height++ <10) {
6:      long humidity = 12;
7:      L2: do {
8:          if(humidity-- % 12 == 0) _____;
9:          int temperature = 30;
10:         L3: for( ; ; ) {
11:             temperature++;
12:             if(temperature>50) _____;
13:         }
14:     } while (humidity > 4);
15: }
```

A. break `L2` on line 8; continue `L2` on line 12

B. continue on line 8; continue on line 12

C. break `L3` on line 8; break `L1` on line 12

D. continue `L2` on line 8; continue `L3` on line 12

E. continue `L2` on line 8; continue `L2` on line 12

F. None of the above, as the code contains a compiler error.

16. What is the output of the following code snippet? (Choose all that apply.)

```
2: var tailFeathers = 3;
3: final var one = 1;
4: switch (tailFeathers) {
5:    case one: System.out.print(3 + " ");
6:    default: case 3: System.out.print(5 + " ");
7: }
8: while (tailFeathers > 1) {
9:    System.out.print(--tailFeathers + " "); }
```

A. 3

B. 5 1

C. 5 2

D. 3 5 1

E. 5 2 1

F. The code will not compile because of lines 3–5.

G. The code will not compile because of line 6.

17. What is the output of the following code snippet?

```
15: int penguin = 50, turtle = 75;
16: boolean older = penguin >= turtle;
17: if (older = true) System.out.println("Success");
18: else System.out.println("Failure");
19: else if(penguin != 50) System.out.println("Other");
```

A. Success

B. Failure

C. Other

D. The code will not compile because of line 17.

E. The code compiles but throws an exception at runtime.

F. None of the above

18. Which of the following are possible data types for `olivia` that would allow the code to compile? (Choose all that apply.)

```
for(var sophia : olivia) {
   System.out.println(sophia);
}
```

A. Set

B. Map

C. String

D. int[]

E. Collection

F. StringBuilder

G. None of the above

19. What is the output of the following code snippet?

```
6:  String instrument = "violin";
7:  final String CELLO = "cello";
8:  String viola = "viola";
9:  int p = -1;
10: switch(instrument) {
11:    case "bass" : break;
12:    case CELLO : p++;
13:    default: p++;
14:    case "VIOLIN": p++;
15:    case "viola" : ++p; break;
16: }
17: System.out.print(p);
```

A. -1

B. 0

C. 1

D. 2

E. 3

F. The code does not compile.

20. What is the output of the following code snippet? (Choose all that apply.)

```
9:  int w = 0, r = 1;
10: String name = "";
11: while(w < 2) {
12:    name += "A";
```

```
13:    do {
14:        name += "B";
15:        if(name.length()>0) name += "C";
16:        else break;
17:    } while (r <=1);
18:    r++; w++; }
19: System.out.println(name);
```

A. ABC

B. ABCABC

C. ABCABCABC

D. Line 15 contains a compilation error.

E. Line 18 contains a compilation error.

F. The code compiles but never terminates at runtime.

G. The code compiles but throws a `NullPointerException` at runtime.

Chapter

5

Core Java APIs

OCP EXAM OBJECTIVES COVERED IN THIS CHAPTER:

✓ **Working with Java Primitive Data Types and String APIs**

- Create and manipulate Strings
- Manipulate data using the StringBuilder class and its methods

✓ **Working with Java Arrays**

- Declare, instantiate, initialize and use a one-dimensional array
- Declare, instantiate, initialize and use a two-dimensional array

✓ **Programming Abstractly Through Interfaces**

- Declare and use List and ArrayList instances

In the context of an Application Programming Interface (API), an interface refers to a group of classes or Java interface definitions giving you access to a service or functionality.

In this chapter, you will learn about many core data structures in Java, along with the most common APIs to access them. For example, String and StringBuilder, along with their associated APIs, are used to create and manipulate text data. An array, List, Set, or Map are used to manage often large groups of data. You'll also learn how to determine whether two objects are equivalent.

This chapter is long, so we recommend reading it in multiple sittings. On the bright side, it contains most of the APIs you need to know for the exam.

Creating and Manipulating Strings

The String class is such a fundamental class that you'd be hard-pressed to write code without it. After all, you can't even write a main() method without using the String class. A *string* is basically a sequence of characters; here's an example:

```
String name = "Fluffy";
```

As you learned in Chapter 2, "Java Building Blocks," this is an example of a reference type. You also learned that reference types are created using the new keyword. Wait a minute. Something is missing from the previous example: It doesn't have new in it! In Java, these two snippets both create a String:

```
String name = "Fluffy";
String name = new String("Fluffy");
```

Both give you a reference variable named name pointing to the String object "Fluffy". They are subtly different, as you'll see in the section "The *String* Pool" later in this chapter. For now, just remember that the String class is special and doesn't need to be instantiated with new.

Since a String is a sequence of characters, you probably won't be surprised to hear that it implements the interface CharSequence. This interface is a general way of representing several classes, including String and StringBuilder. You'll learn more about interfaces later in the book.

In this section, we'll look at concatenation, immutability, common methods, and method chaining.

Concatenation

In Chapter 3, "Operators," you learned how to add numbers. 1 + 2 is clearly 3. But what is "1" + "2"? It's actually "12" because Java combines the two String objects. Placing one String before the other String and combining them is called string *concatenation*. The exam creators like string concatenation because the + operator can be used in two ways within the same line of code. There aren't a lot of rules to know for this, but you have to know them well:

1. If both operands are numeric, + means numeric addition.

2. If either operand is a String, + means concatenation.

3. The expression is evaluated left to right.

Now let's look at some examples:

```
System.out.println(1 + 2);          // 3
System.out.println("a" + "b");      // ab
System.out.println("a" + "b" + 3);  // ab3
System.out.println(1 + 2 + "c");    // 3c
System.out.println("c" + 1 + 2);    // c12
```

The first example uses the first rule. Both operands are numbers, so we use normal addition. The second example is simple string concatenation, described in the second rule. The quotes for the String are only used in code—they don't get output.

The third example combines both the second and third rules. Since we start on the left, Java figures out what "a" + "b" evaluates to. You already know that one: It's "ab". Then Java looks at the remaining expression of "ab" + 3. The second rule tells us to concatenate since one of the operands is a String.

In the fourth example, we start with the third rule, which tells us to consider 1 + 2. Both operands are numeric, so the first rule tells us the answer is 3. Then we have 3 + "c", which uses the second rule to give us "3c". Notice all three rules get used in one line?

Finally, the fifth example shows the importance of the third rule. First we have "c" + 1, which uses the second rule to give us "c1". Then we have "c1" + 2, which uses the second rule again to give us "c12".

The exam takes this a step further and will try to trick you with something like this:

```
int three = 3;
String four = "4";
System.out.println(1 + 2 + three + four);
```

When you see this, just take it slow and remember the three rules—and be sure to check the variable types. In this example, we start with the third rule, which tells us to consider 1 + 2. The first rule gives us 3. Next we have 3 + three. Since three is of type int, we still use the first rule, giving us 6. Next we have 6 + four. Since four is of type String, we switch to the second rule and get a final answer of "64". When you see questions like this, just take your time and check the types. Being methodical pays off.

There is only one more thing to know about concatenation, but it is an easy one. In this example, you just have to remember what += does. s += "2" means the same thing as s = s + "2".

```
4: String s = "1";              // s currently holds "1"
5: s += "2";                    // s currently holds "12"
6: s += 3;                      // s currently holds "123"
7: System.out.println(s);       // 123
```

On line 5, we are "adding" two strings, which means we concatenate them. Line 6 tries to trick you by adding a number, but it's just like we wrote s = s + 3. We know that a string "plus" anything else means to use concatenation.

To review the rules one more time: Use numeric addition if two numbers are involved, use concatenation otherwise, and evaluate from left to right. Have you memorized these three rules yet? Be sure to do so before the exam!

Immutability

Once a String object is created, it is not allowed to change. It cannot be made larger or smaller, and you cannot change one of the characters inside it.

You can think of a String as a storage box you have perfectly full and whose sides can't bulge. There's no way to add objects, nor can you replace objects without disturbing the entire arrangement. The trade-off for the optimal packing is zero flexibility.

Mutable is another word for changeable. *Immutable* is the opposite—an object that can't be changed once it's created. On the exam, you need to know that String is immutable.

More on Immutability

You won't be asked to identify whether custom classes are immutable on the OCP part 1 exam, but it's helpful to see an example. Consider the following code:

```
class Mutable {
   private String s;
   public void setS(String newS){ s = newS; }  // Setter makes it mutable
   public String getS() { return s; }
}
final class Immutable {
   private String s = "name";
   public String getS() { return s; }
}
```

Immutable has only a getter. There's no way to change the value of s once it's set. Mutable has a setter. This allows the reference s to change to point to a different String

---

later. Note that even though the String class is immutable, it can still be used in a mutable class. You can even make the instance variable final so the compiler reminds you if you accidentally change s.

Also, immutable classes in Java are final, which prevents subclasses creation. You wouldn't want a subclass adding mutable behavior.

You learned that + is used to do String concatenation in Java. There's another way, which isn't used much on real projects but is great for tricking people on the exam. What does this print out?

```java
String s1 = "1";
String s2 = s1.concat("2");
s2.concat("3");
System.out.println(s2);
```

Did you say "12"? Good. The trick is to see if you forget that the String class is immutable by throwing a method call at you.

Important *String* Methods

The String class has dozens of methods. Luckily, you need to know only a handful for the exam. The exam creators pick most of the methods developers use in the real world.

For all these methods, you need to remember that a string is a sequence of characters and Java counts from 0 when indexed. Figure 5.1 shows how each character in the string "animals" is indexed.

FIGURE 5.1   Indexing for a string

a	n	i	m	a	l	s
0	1	2	3	4	5	6

Let's look at a number of methods from the String class. Many of them are straightforward, so we won't discuss them at length. You need to know how to use these methods. We left out public from the signatures in the following sections so you can focus on the important parts.

length()

The method length() returns the number of characters in the String. The method signature is as follows:

```java
int length()
```

The following code shows how to use length():

```
String string = "animals";
System.out.println(string.length());  // 7
```

Wait. It outputs 7? Didn't we just tell you that Java counts from 0? The difference is that zero counting happens only when you're using indexes or positions within a list. When determining the total size or length, Java uses normal counting again.

charAt()

The method charAt() lets you query the string to find out what character is at a specific index. The method signature is as follows:

```
char charAt(int index)
```

The following code shows how to use charAt():

```
String string = "animals";
System.out.println(string.charAt(0));  // a
System.out.println(string.charAt(6));  // s
System.out.println(string.charAt(7));  // throws exception
```

Since indexes start counting with 0, charAt(0) returns the "first" character in the sequence. Similarly, charAt(6) returns the "seventh" character in the sequence. charAt(7) is a problem. It asks for the "eighth" character in the sequence, but there are only seven characters present. When something goes wrong that Java doesn't know how to deal with, it throws an exception, as shown here. You'll learn more about exceptions in Chapter 10, "Exceptions."

```
java.lang.StringIndexOutOfBoundsException: String index out of range: 7
```

indexOf()

The method indexOf() looks at the characters in the string and finds the first index that matches the desired value. indexOf can work with an individual character or a whole String as input. It can also start from a requested position. Remember that a char can be passed to an int parameter type. On the exam, you'll only see a char passed to the parameters named ch. The method signatures are as follows:

```
int indexOf(int ch)
int indexOf(int ch, int fromIndex)
int indexOf(String str)
int indexOf(String str, int fromIndex)
```

The following code shows how to use indexOf():

```
String string = "animals";
System.out.println(string.indexOf('a'));        // 0
System.out.println(string.indexOf("al"));       // 4
```

```
System.out.println(string.indexOf('a', 4));      // 4
System.out.println(string.indexOf("al", 5));     // -1
```

Since indexes begin with 0, the first 'a' matches at that position. The second statement looks for a more specific string, so it matches later. The third statement says Java shouldn't even look at the characters until it gets to index 4. The final statement doesn't find anything because it starts looking after the match occurred. Unlike charAt(), the indexOf() method doesn't throw an exception if it can't find a match. indexOf() returns –1 when no match is found. Because indexes start with 0, the caller knows that –1 couldn't be a valid index. This makes it a common value for a method to signify to the caller that no match is found.

substring()

The method substring() also looks for characters in a string. It returns parts of the string. The first parameter is the index to start with for the returned string. As usual, this is a zero-based index. There is an optional second parameter, which is the end index you want to stop at.

Notice we said "stop at" rather than "include." This means the endIndex parameter is allowed to be 1 past the end of the sequence if you want to stop at the end of the sequence. That would be redundant, though, since you could omit the second parameter entirely in that case. In your own code, you want to avoid this redundancy. Don't be surprised if the exam uses it, though. The method signatures are as follows:

```
String substring(int beginIndex)
String substring(int beginIndex, int endIndex)
```

It helps to think of indexes a bit differently for the substring methods. Pretend the indexes are right before the character they would point to. Figure 5.2 helps visualize this. Notice how the arrow with the 0 points to the character that would have index 0. The arrow with the 1 points between characters with indexes 0 and 1. There are seven characters in the String. Since Java uses zero-based indexes, this means the last character has an index of 6. The arrow with the 7 points immediately after this last character. This will help you remember that endIndex doesn't give an out-of-bounds exception when it is one past the end of the String.

FIGURE 5.2   Indexes for a substring

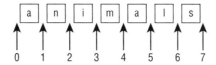

The following code shows how to use substring():

```
String string = "animals";
System.out.println(string.substring(3));                  // mals
System.out.println(string.substring(string.indexOf('m'))); // mals
```

```
System.out.println(string.substring(3, 4));                    // m
System.out.println(string.substring(3, 7));                    // mals
```

The substring() method is the trickiest String method on the exam. The first example says to take the characters starting with index 3 through the end, which gives us "mals". The second example does the same thing, but it calls indexOf() to get the index rather than hard-coding it. This is a common practice when coding because you may not know the index in advance.

The third example says to take the characters starting with index 3 until, but not including, the character at index 4—which is a complicated way of saying we want a String with one character: the one at index 3. This results in "m". The final example says to take the characters starting with index 3 until we get to index 7. Since index 7 is the same as the end of the string, it is equivalent to the first example.

We hope that wasn't too confusing. The next examples are less obvious:

```
System.out.println(string.substring(3, 3)); // empty string
System.out.println(string.substring(3, 2));  // throws exception
System.out.println(string.substring(3, 8)); // throws exception
```

The first example in this set prints an empty string. The request is for the characters starting with index 3 until you get to index 3. Since we start and end with the same index, there are *no* characters in between. The second example in this set throws an exception because the indexes can't be backward. Java knows perfectly well that it will never get to index 2 if it starts with index 3. The third example says to continue until the eighth character. There is no eighth position, so Java throws an exception. Granted, there is no seventh character either, but at least there is the "end of string" invisible position.

Let's review this one more time since substring() is so tricky. The method returns the string starting from the requested index. If an end index is requested, it stops right before that index. Otherwise, it goes to the end of the string.

toLowerCase() and *toUpperCase()*

Whew. After that mental exercise, it is nice to have methods that do exactly what they sound like! These methods make it easy to convert your data. The method signatures are as follows:

```
String toLowerCase()
String toUpperCase()
```

The following code shows how to use these methods:

```
String string = "animals";
System.out.println(string.toUpperCase());  // ANIMALS
System.out.println("Abc123".toLowerCase());  // abc123
```

These methods do what they say. toUpperCase() converts any lowercase characters to uppercase in the returned string. toLowerCase() converts any uppercase characters to lowercase in the returned string. These methods leave alone any characters other than letters. Also, remember that strings are immutable, so the original string stays the same.

equals() and equalsIgnoreCase()

The equals() method checks whether two String objects contain exactly the same characters in the same order. The equalsIgnoreCase() method checks whether two String objects contain the same characters with the exception that it will convert the characters' case if needed. The method signatures are as follows:

```
boolean equals(Object obj)
boolean equalsIgnoreCase(String str)
```

You might have noticed that equals() takes an Object rather than a String. This is because the method is the same for all objects. If you pass in something that isn't a String, it will just return false. By contrast, the equalsIgnoreCase method only applies to String objects so it can take the more specific type as the parameter.

The following code shows how to use these methods:

```
System.out.println("abc".equals("ABC"));  // false
System.out.println("ABC".equals("ABC"));  // true
System.out.println("abc".equalsIgnoreCase("ABC"));  // true
```

This example should be fairly intuitive. In the first example, the values aren't exactly the same. In the second, they are exactly the same. In the third, they differ only by case, but it is okay because we called the method that ignores differences in case.

startsWith() and endsWith()

The startsWith() and endsWith() methods look at whether the provided value matches part of the String. The method signatures are as follows:

```
boolean startsWith(String prefix)
boolean endsWith(String suffix)
```

The following code shows how to use these methods:

```
System.out.println("abc".startsWith("a")); // true
System.out.println("abc".startsWith("A")); // false
System.out.println("abc".endsWith("c")); // true
System.out.println("abc".endsWith("a")); // false
```

Again, nothing surprising here. Java is doing a case-sensitive check on the values provided.

replace()

The replace() method does a simple search and replace on the string. There's a version that takes char parameters as well as a version that takes CharSequence parameters. The method signatures are as follows:

```
String replace(char oldChar, char newChar)
String replace(CharSequence target, CharSequence replacement)
```

The following code shows how to use these methods:

```
System.out.println("abcabc".replace('a', 'A')); // AbcAbc
System.out.println("abcabc".replace("a", "A")); // AbcAbc
```

The first example uses the first method signature, passing in char parameters. The second example uses the second method signature, passing in String parameters.

contains()

The contains() method looks for matches in the String. It isn't as particular as startsWith() and endsWith()—the match can be anywhere in the String. The method signature is as follows:

```
boolean contains(CharSequence charSeq)
```

The following code shows how to use these methods:

```
System.out.println("abc".contains("b")); // true
System.out.println("abc".contains("B")); // false
```

Again, we have a case-sensitive search in the String. The contains() method is a convenience method so you don't have to write str.indexOf(otherString) != -1.

trim(), strip(), stripLeading(), and stripTrailing()

You've made it through almost all the String methods you need to know. Next up is removing blank space from the beginning and/or end of a String. The strip() and trim() methods remove whitespace from the beginning and end of a String. In terms of the exam, whitespace consists of spaces along with the \t (tab) and \n (newline) characters. Other characters, such as \r (carriage return), are also included in what gets trimmed. The strip() method is new in Java 11. It does everything that trim() does, but it supports Unicode.

 You don't need to know about Unicode for the exam. But if you want to test the difference, one of Unicode whitespace characters is as follows:

```
char ch = '\u2000';
```

Additionally, the stripLeading() and stripTrailing() methods were added in Java 11. The stripLeading() method removes whitespace from the beginning of the String and leaves it at the end. The stripTrailing() method does the opposite. It removes whitespace from the end of the String and leaves it at the beginning.

The method signatures are as follows:

```
String strip()
String stripLeading()
String stripTrailing()
String trim()
```

The following code shows how to use these methods:

```
System.out.println("abc".strip());                      // abc
System.out.println("\t   a b c\n".strip());             // a b c

String text = " abc\t ";
System.out.println(text.trim().length());          // 3
System.out.println(text.strip().length());         // 3
System.out.println(text.stripLeading().length());  // 5
System.out.println(text.stripTrailing().length()); // 4
```

First, remember that \t is a single character. The backslash escapes the t to represent a tab. The first example prints the original string because there are no whitespace characters at the beginning or end. The second example gets rid of the leading tab, subsequent spaces, and the trailing newline. It leaves the spaces that are in the middle of the string.

The remaining examples just print the number of characters remaining. You can see that both trim() and strip() leave the same three characters "abc" because they remove both the leading and trailing whitespace. The stripLeading() method only removes the one whitespace character at the beginning of the String. It leaves the tab and space at the end. The stripTrailing() method removes these two characters at the end but leaves the character at the beginning of the String.

intern()

The intern() method returns the value from the string pool if it is there. Otherwise, it adds the value to the string pool. We will explain about the string pool and give examples for intern() later in the chapter. The method signature is as follows:

```
String intern()
```

Method Chaining

It is common to call multiple methods as shown here:

```
String start = "AniMaL   ";
String trimmed = start.trim();                 // "AniMaL"
String lowercase = trimmed.toLowerCase();      // "animal"
String result = lowercase.replace('a', 'A');   // "AnimAl"
System.out.println(result);
```

This is just a series of String methods. Each time one is called, the returned value is put in a new variable. There are four String values along the way, and AnimAl is output.

However, on the exam there is a tendency to cram as much code as possible into a small space. You'll see code using a technique called method chaining. Here's an example:

```
String result = "AniMaL   ".trim().toLowerCase().replace('a', 'A');
System.out.println(result);
```

This code is equivalent to the previous example. It also creates four `String` objects and outputs `AnimAl`. To read code that uses method chaining, start at the left and evaluate the first method. Then call the next method on the returned value of the first method. Keep going until you get to the semicolon.

Remember that `String` is immutable. What do you think the result of this code is?

```
5: String a = "abc";
6: String b = a.toUpperCase();
7: b = b.replace("B", "2").replace('C', '3');
8: System.out.println("a=" + a);
9: System.out.println("b=" + b);
```

On line 5, we set a to point to "abc" and never pointed a to anything else. Since we are dealing with an immutable object, none of the code on lines 6 and 7 changes a, and the value remains "abc".

b is a little trickier. Line 6 has b pointing to "ABC", which is straightforward. On line 7, we have method chaining. First, "ABC".replace("B", "2") is called. This returns "A2C". Next, "A2C".replace('C', '3') is called. This returns "A23". Finally, b changes to point to this returned `String`. When line 9 executes, b is "A23".

Using the *StringBuilder* Class

A small program can create a lot of `String` objects very quickly. For example, how many do you think this piece of code creates?

```
10: String alpha = "";
11: for(char current = 'a'; current <= 'z'; current++)
12:     alpha += current;
13: System.out.println(alpha);
```

The empty `String` on line 10 is instantiated, and then line 12 appends an "a". However, because the `String` object is immutable, a new `String` object is assigned to alpha, and the "" object becomes eligible for garbage collection. The next time through the loop, alpha is assigned a new `String` object, "ab", and the "a" object becomes eligible for garbage collection. The next iteration assigns alpha to "abc", and the "ab" object becomes eligible for garbage collection, and so on.

This sequence of events continues, and after 26 iterations through the loop, a total of 27 objects are instantiated, most of which are immediately eligible for garbage collection.

This is very inefficient. Luckily, Java has a solution. The `StringBuilder` class creates a `String` without storing all those interim `String` values. Unlike the `String` class, `StringBuilder` is not immutable.

```
15: StringBuilder alpha = new StringBuilder();
16: for(char current = 'a'; current <= 'z'; current++)
```

```
17:     alpha.append(current);
18: System.out.println(alpha);
```

On line 15, a new StringBuilder object is instantiated. The call to append() on line 17 adds a character to the StringBuilder object each time through the for loop appending the value of current to the end of alpha. This code reuses the same StringBuilder without creating an interim String each time.

In old code, you might see references to StringBuffer. It works the same way except it supports threads, which you'll learn about when preparing for the 1Z0-816 exam. StringBuffer is no longer on either exam. It performs slower than StringBuilder, so just use StringBuilder.

In this section, we'll look at creating a StringBuilder and using its common methods.

Mutability and Chaining

We're sure you noticed this from the previous example, but StringBuilder is not immutable. In fact, we gave it 27 different values in the example (blank plus adding each letter in the alphabet). The exam will likely try to trick you with respect to String and StringBuilder being mutable.

Chaining makes this even more interesting. When we chained String method calls, the result was a new String with the answer. Chaining StringBuilder methods doesn't work this way. Instead, the StringBuilder changes its own state and returns a reference to itself. Let's look at an example to make this clearer:

```
4: StringBuilder sb = new StringBuilder("start");
5: sb.append("+middle");                    // sb = "start+middle"
6: StringBuilder same = sb.append("+end");  // "start+middle+end"
```

Line 5 adds text to the end of sb. It also returns a reference to sb, which is ignored. Line 6 also adds text to the end of sb and returns a reference to sb. This time the reference is stored in same—which means sb and same point to the same object and would print out the same value.

The exam won't always make the code easy to read by having only one method per line. What do you think this example prints?

```
4: StringBuilder a = new StringBuilder("abc");
5: StringBuilder b = a.append("de");
6: b = b.append("f").append("g");
7: System.out.println("a=" + a);
8: System.out.println("b=" + b);
```

Did you say both print "abcdefg"? Good. There's only one StringBuilder object here. We know that because new StringBuilder() was called only once. On line 5, there are two variables referring to that object, which has a value of "abcde". On line 6, those two variables are still referring to that same object, which now has a value of "abcdefg".

Incidentally, the assignment back to b does absolutely nothing. b is already pointing to that StringBuilder.

Creating a *StringBuilder*

There are three ways to construct a StringBuilder:

```
StringBuilder sb1 = new StringBuilder();
StringBuilder sb2 = new StringBuilder("animal");
StringBuilder sb3 = new StringBuilder(10);
```

The first says to create a StringBuilder containing an empty sequence of characters and assign sb1 to point to it. The second says to create a StringBuilder containing a specific value and assign sb2 to point to it. For the first two, it tells Java to manage the implementation details. The final example tells Java that we have some idea of how big the eventual value will be and would like the StringBuilder to reserve a certain capacity, or number of slots, for characters.

Important *StringBuilder* Methods

As with String, we aren't going to cover every single method in the StringBuilder class. These are the ones you might see on the exam.

charAt(), indexOf(), length(), and substring()

These four methods work exactly the same as in the String class. Be sure you can identify the output of this example:

```
StringBuilder sb = new StringBuilder("animals");
String sub = sb.substring(sb.indexOf("a"), sb.indexOf("al"));
int len = sb.length();
char ch = sb.charAt(6);
System.out.println(sub + " " + len + " " + ch);
```

The correct answer is anim 7 s. The indexOf() method calls return 0 and 4, respectively. substring() returns the String starting with index 0 and ending right before index 4.

length() returns 7 because it is the number of characters in the StringBuilder rather than an index. Finally, charAt() returns the character at index 6. Here we do start with 0 because we are referring to indexes. If any of this doesn't sound familiar, go back and read the section on String again.

Notice that substring() returns a String rather than a StringBuilder. That is why sb is not changed. substring() is really just a method that inquires about what the state of the StringBuilder happens to be.

append()

The append() method is by far the most frequently used method in StringBuilder. In fact, it is so frequently used that we just started using it without comment. Luckily, this method does just what it sounds like: It adds the parameter to the `StringBuilder` and returns a reference to the current `StringBuilder`. One of the method signatures is as follows:

```
StringBuilder append(String str)
```

Notice that we said *one* of the method signatures. There are more than 10 method signatures that look similar but that take different data types as parameters. All those methods are provided so you can write code like this:

```
StringBuilder sb = new StringBuilder().append(1).append('c');
sb.append("-").append(true);
System.out.println(sb);        // 1c-true
```

Nice method chaining, isn't it? `append()` is called directly after the constructor. By having all these method signatures, you can just call `append()` without having to convert your parameter to a `String` first.

insert()

The `insert()` method adds characters to the `StringBuilder` at the requested index and returns a reference to the current `StringBuilder`. Just like `append()`, there are lots of method signatures for different types. Here's one:

```
StringBuilder insert(int offset, String str)
```

Pay attention to the offset in these examples. It is the index where we want to insert the requested parameter.

```
3: StringBuilder sb = new StringBuilder("animals");
4: sb.insert(7, "-");                  // sb = animals-
5: sb.insert(0, "-");                  // sb = -animals-
6: sb.insert(4, "-");                  // sb = -ani-mals-
7: System.out.println(sb);
```

Line 4 says to insert a dash at index 7, which happens to be the end of the sequence of characters. Line 5 says to insert a dash at index 0, which happens to be the very beginning. Finally, line 6 says to insert a dash right before index 4. The exam creators will try to trip you up on this. As we add and remove characters, their indexes change. When you see a question dealing with such operations, draw what is going on so you won't be confused.

delete() and deleteCharAt()

The `delete()` method is the opposite of the `insert()` method. It removes characters from the sequence and returns a reference to the current `StringBuilder`. The `deleteCharAt()` method is convenient when you want to delete only one character. The method signatures are as follows:

```
StringBuilder delete(int startIndex, int endIndex)
StringBuilder deleteCharAt(int index)
```

The following code shows how to use these methods:

```
StringBuilder sb = new StringBuilder("abcdef");
sb.delete(1, 3);                    // sb = adef
sb.deleteCharAt(5);                 // throws an exception
```

First, we delete the characters starting with index 1 and ending right before index 3. This gives us adef. Next, we ask Java to delete the character at position 5. However, the remaining value is only four characters long, so it throws a StringIndexOutOfBoundsException.

The delete() method is more flexible than some others when it comes to array indexes. If you specify a second parameter that is past the end of the StringBuilder, Java will just assume you meant the end. That means this code is legal:

```
StringBuilder sb = new StringBuilder("abcdef");
sb.delete(1, 100);                  // sb = a
```

replace()

The replace() method works differently for StringBuilder than it did for String. The method signature is as follows:

```
StringBuilder replace(int startIndex, int endIndex, String newString)
```

The following code shows how to use this method:

```
StringBuilder builder = new StringBuilder("pigeon dirty");
builder.replace(3, 6, "sty");
System.out.println(builder);  // pigsty dirty
```

First, Java deletes the characters starting with index 3 and ending right before index 6. This gives us pig dirty. Then Java inserts to the value "sty" in that position.

In this example, the number of characters removed and inserted is the same. However, there is no reason that it has to be. What do you think this does?

```
StringBuilder builder = new StringBuilder("pigeon dirty");
builder.replace(3, 100, "");
System.out.println(builder);
```

It actually prints "pig". Remember the method is first doing a logical delete. The replace() method allows specifying a second parameter that is past the end of the StringBuilder. That means only the first three characters remain.

reverse()

After all that, it's time for a nice, easy method. The reverse() method does just what it sounds like: it reverses the characters in the sequences and returns a reference to the current StringBuilder. The method signature is as follows:

```
StringBuilder reverse()
```

The following code shows how to use this method:

```
StringBuilder sb = new StringBuilder("ABC");
sb.reverse();
System.out.println(sb);
```

As expected, this prints CBA. This method isn't that interesting. Maybe the exam creators like to include it to encourage you to write down the value rather than relying on memory for indexes.

toString()

The last method converts a StringBuilder into a String. The method signature is as follows:

```
String toString()
```

The following code shows how to use this method:

```
StringBuilder sb = new StringBuilder("ABC");
String s = sb.toString();
```

Often StringBuilder is used internally for performance purposes, but the end result needs to be a String. For example, maybe it needs to be passed to another method that is expecting a String.

Understanding Equality

In Chapter 3, you learned how to use == to compare numbers and that object references refer to the same object. In this section, we will look at what it means for two objects to be equivalent or the same. We will also look at the impact of the String pool on equality.

Comparing *equals()* and ==

Consider the following code that uses == with objects:

```
StringBuilder one = new StringBuilder();
StringBuilder two = new StringBuilder();
StringBuilder three = one.append("a");
System.out.println(one == two); // false
System.out.println(one == three); // true
```

Since this example isn't dealing with primitives, we know to look for whether the references are referring to the same object. one and two are both completely separate StringBuilder objects, giving us two objects. Therefore, the first print statement gives us false. three is more interesting. Remember how StringBuilder methods like to return the current reference for chaining? This means one and three both point to the same object, and the second print statement gives us true.

You saw earlier that you can say you want logical equality rather than object equality for String objects:

```
String x = "Hello World";
String z = " Hello World".trim();
System.out.println(x.equals(z)); // true
```

This works because the authors of the String class implemented a standard method called equals to check the values inside the String rather than the string reference itself. If a class doesn't have an equals method, Java determines whether the references point to the same object—which is exactly what == does.

In case you are wondering, the authors of StringBuilder did not implement equals(). If you call equals() on two StringBuilder instances, it will check reference equality. You can call toString() on StringBuilder to get a String to check for equality instead.

The exam will test you on your understanding of equality with objects they define too. For example, the following Tiger class works just like StringBuilder but is easier to understand:

```
1:  public class Tiger {
2:      String name;
3:      public static void main(String[] args) {
4:          Tiger t1 = new Tiger();
5:          Tiger t2 = new Tiger();
6:          Tiger t3 = t1;
7:          System.out.println(t1 == t3);      // true
8:          System.out.println(t1 == t2);      // false
9:          System.out.println(t1.equals(t2)); // false
10: } }
```

The first two statements check object reference equality. Line 7 prints true because we are comparing references to the same object. Line 8 prints false because the two object references are different. Line 9 prints false since Tiger does not implement equals(). Don't worry—you aren't expected to know how to implement equals() for this exam.

Finally, the exam might try to trick you with a question like this. Can you guess why the code doesn't compile?

```
String string = "a";
StringBuilder builder = new StringBuilder("a");
System.out.println(string == builder); //DOES NOT COMPILE
```

Remember that == is checking for object reference equality. The compiler is smart enough to know that two references can't possibly point to the same object when they are completely different types.

The *String* Pool

Since strings are everywhere in Java, they use up a lot of memory. In some production applications, they can use a large amount of memory in the entire program. Java realizes that many strings repeat in the program and solves this issue by reusing common ones. The *string pool*, also known as the intern pool, is a location in the Java virtual machine (JVM) that collects all these strings.

The string pool contains literal values and constants that appear in your program. For example, "name" is a literal and therefore goes into the string pool. myObject.toString() is a string but not a literal, so it does not go into the string pool.

Let's now visit the more complex and confusing scenario, String equality, made so in part because of the way the JVM reuses String literals.

```java
String x = "Hello World";
String y = "Hello World";
System.out.println(x == y);     // true
```

Remember that Strings are immutable and literals are pooled. The JVM created only one literal in memory. x and y both point to the same location in memory; therefore, the statement outputs true. It gets even trickier. Consider this code:

```java
String x = "Hello World";
String z = " Hello World".trim();
System.out.println(x == z); // false
```

In this example, we don't have two of the same String literal. Although x and z happen to evaluate to the same string, one is computed at runtime. Since it isn't the same at compile-time, a new String object is created. Let's try another one. What do you think is output here?

```java
String singleString = "hello world";
String concat = "hello ";
concat += "world";
System.out.println(singleString == concat);
```

This prints false. Concatenation is just like calling a method and results in a new String. You can even force the issue by creating a new String:

```java
String x = "Hello World";
String y = new String("Hello World");
System.out.println(x == y); // false
```

The former says to use the string pool normally. The second says "No, JVM, I really don't want you to use the string pool. Please create a new object for me even though it is less efficient."

You can also do the opposite and tell Java to use the string pool. The `intern()` method will use an object in the string pool if one is present. If the literal is not yet in the string pool, Java will add it at this time.

```
String name = "Hello World";
String name2 = new String("Hello World").intern();
System.out.println(name == name2);     // true
```

First we tell Java to use the string pool normally for name. Then for name2, we tell Java to create a new object using the constructor but to intern it and use the string pool anyway. Since both variables point to the same reference in the string pool, we can use the `==` operator.

Let's try another one. What do you think this prints out? Be careful. It is tricky.

```
15: String first = "rat" + 1;
16: String second = "r" + "a" + "t" + "1";
17: String third = "r" + "a" + "t" + new String("1");
18: System.out.println(first == second);
19: System.out.println(first == second.intern());
20: System.out.println(first == third);
21: System.out.println(first == third.intern());
```

On line 15, we have a compile-time constant that automatically gets placed in the string pool as "rat1". On line 16, we have a more complicated expression that is also a compile-time constant. Therefore, `first` and `second` share the same string pool reference. This makes line 18 and 19 print true.

On line 17, we have a `String` constructor. This means we no longer have a compile-time constant, and `third` does not point to a reference in the string pool. Therefore, line 20 prints `false`. On line 21, the `intern()` call looks in the string pool. Java notices that `first` points to the same `String` and prints true.

When you write programs, you wouldn't want to create a `String` of a `String` or use the `intern()` method. For the exam, you need to know that both are allowed and how they behave.

Remember to never use `intern()` or `==` to compare `String` objects in your code. The only time you should have to deal with these is on the exam.

Understanding Java Arrays

Up to now, we've been referring to the `String` and `StringBuilder` classes as a "sequence of characters." This is true. They are implemented using an *array* of characters. An array is an area of memory on the heap with space for a designated number of elements. A `String` is implemented as an array with some methods that you might want to use when dealing with characters specifically. A `StringBuilder` is implemented as an array where the array object is replaced with a new bigger array object when it runs out of space to store all the characters. A big difference is that an array can be of any other Java type. If we didn't want to use a `String` for some reason, we could use an array of `char` primitives directly:

```
char[] letters;
```

This wouldn't be very convenient because we'd lose all the special properties `String` gives us, such as writing `"Java"`. Keep in mind that `letters` is a reference variable and not a primitive. `char` is a primitive. But `char` is what goes into the array and not the type of the array itself. The array itself is of type `char[]`. You can mentally read the brackets (`[]`) as "array."

In other words, an array is an ordered list. It can contain duplicates. In this section, we'll look at creating an array of primitives and objects, sorting, searching, varargs, and multidimensional arrays.

Creating an Array of Primitives

The most common way to create an array looks like this:

```
int[] numbers1 = new int[3];
```

The basic parts are shown in Figure 5.3. It specifies the type of the array (`int`) and the size (3). The brackets tell you this is an array.

FIGURE 5.3   The basic structure of an array

When you use this form to instantiate an array, all elements are set to the default value for that type. As you learned in Chapter 2, the default value of an `int` is 0. Since numbers1 is a reference variable, it points to the array object, as shown in Figure 5.4. As you can see, the default value for all the elements is 0. Also, the indexes start with 0 and count up, just as they did for a `String`.

FIGURE 5.4   An empty array

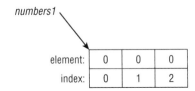

Another way to create an array is to specify all the elements it should start out with:

```
int[] numbers2 = new int[] {42, 55, 99};
```

In this example, we also create an `int` array of size 3. This time, we specify the initial values of those three elements instead of using the defaults. Figure 5.5 shows what this array looks like.

FIGURE 5.5   An initialized array

Java recognizes that this expression is redundant. Since you are specifying the type of the array on the left side of the equal sign, Java already knows the type. And since you are specifying the initial values, it already knows the size. As a shortcut, Java lets you write this:

```
int[] numbers2 = {42, 55, 99};
```

This approach is called an *anonymous array*. It is anonymous because you don't specify the type and size.

Finally, you can type the [] before or after the name, and adding a space is optional. This means that all five of these statements do the exact same thing:

```
int[] numAnimals;
int [] numAnimals2;
int []numAnimals3;
int numAnimals4[];
int numAnimals5 [];
```

Most people use the first one. You could see any of these on the exam, though, so get used to seeing the brackets in odd places.

Multiple "Arrays" in Declarations

What types of reference variables do you think the following code creates?

```
int[] ids, types;
```

The correct answer is two variables of type `int[]`. This seems logical enough. After all, `int a, b;` created two `int` variables. What about this example?

```
int ids[], types;
```

All we did was move the brackets, but it changed the behavior. This time we get one variable of type int[] and one variable of type int. Java sees this line of code and thinks something like this: "They want two variables of type int. The first one is called ids[]. This one is an int[] called ids. The second one is just called types. No brackets, so it is a regular integer."

Needless to say, you shouldn't write code that looks like this. But you do need to understand it for the exam.

Creating an Array with Reference Variables

You can choose any Java type to be the type of the array. This includes classes you create yourself. Let's take a look at a built-in type with String:

```
public class ArrayType {
    public static void main(String args[]) {
        String [] bugs = { "cricket", "beetle", "ladybug" };
        String [] alias = bugs;
        System.out.println(bugs.equals(alias));     // true
        System.out.println(
            bugs.toString()); //[Ljava.lang.String;@160bc7c0
} }
```

We can call equals() because an array is an object. It returns true because of reference equality. The equals() method on arrays does not look at the elements of the array. Remember, this would work even on an int[] too. int is a primitive; int[] is an object.

The second print statement is even more interesting. What on earth is [Ljava.lang .String;@160bc7c0? You don't have to know this for the exam, but [L means it is an array, java.lang.String is the reference type, and 160bc7c0 is the hash code. You'll get different numbers and letters each time you run it since this is a reference.

 Since Java 5, Java has provided a method that prints an array nicely: Arrays.toString(bugs) would print [cricket, beetle, ladybug].

Make sure you understand Figure 5.6. The array does not allocate space for the String objects. Instead, it allocates space for a reference to where the objects are really stored.

FIGURE 5.6 An array pointing to strings

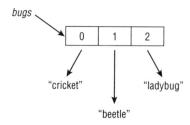

As a quick review, what do you think this array points to?

```
class Names {
    String names[];
}
```

You got us. It was a review of Chapter 2 and not our discussion on arrays. The answer is null. The code never instantiated the array, so it is just a reference variable to null. Let's try that again—what do you think this array points to?

```
class Names {
    String names[] = new String[2];
}
```

It is an array because it has brackets. It is an array of type String since that is the type mentioned in the declaration. It has two elements because the length is 2. Each of those two slots currently is null but has the potential to point to a String object.

Remember casting from the previous chapter when you wanted to force a bigger type into a smaller type? You can do that with arrays too:

```
3: String[] strings = { "stringValue" };
4: Object[] objects = strings;
5: String[] againStrings = (String[]) objects;
6: againStrings[0] = new StringBuilder();   // DOES NOT COMPILE
7: objects[0] = new StringBuilder();        // careful!
```

Line 3 creates an array of type String. Line 4 doesn't require a cast because Object is a broader type than String. On line 5, a cast is needed because we are moving to a more specific type. Line 6 doesn't compile because a String[] only allows String objects and StringBuilder is not a String.

Line 7 is where this gets interesting. From the point of view of the compiler, this is just fine. A StringBuilder object can clearly go in an Object[]. The problem is that we don't actually have an Object[]. We have a String[] referred to from an Object[] variable. At runtime, the code throws an ArrayStoreException. You don't need to memorize the name of this exception, but you do need to know that the code will throw an exception.

Using an Array

Now that you know how to create an array, let's try accessing one:

```
4: String[] mammals = {"monkey", "chimp", "donkey"};
5: System.out.println(mammals.length);          // 3
6: System.out.println(mammals[0]);              // monkey
7: System.out.println(mammals[1]);              // chimp
8: System.out.println(mammals[2]);              // donkey
```

Line 4 declares and initializes the array. Line 5 tells us how many elements the array can hold. The rest of the code prints the array. Notice elements are indexed starting with 0. This should be familiar from String and StringBuilder, which also start counting with 0. Those classes also counted length as the number of elements. Note that there are no parentheses after length since it is not a method.

To make sure you understand how length works, what do you think this prints?

```
String[] birds = new String[6];
System.out.println(birds.length);
```

The answer is 6. Even though all six elements of the array are null, there are still six of them. length does not consider what is in the array; it only considers how many slots have been allocated.

It is very common to use a loop when reading from or writing to an array. This loop sets each element of numbers to five higher than the current index:

```
5: int[] numbers = new int[10];
6: for (int i = 0; i < numbers.length; i++)
7:     numbers[i] = i + 5;
```

Line 5 simply instantiates an array with 10 slots. Line 6 is a for loop that uses an extremely common pattern. It starts at index 0, which is where an array begins as well. It keeps going, one at a time, until it hits the end of the array. Line 7 sets the current element of numbers.

The exam will test whether you are being observant by trying to access elements that are not in the array. Can you tell why each of these throws an ArrayIndexOutOfBoundsException for our array of size 10?

```
numbers[10] = 3;
numbers[numbers.length] = 5;
for (int i = 0; i <= numbers.length; i++) numbers[i] = i + 5;
```

The first one is trying to see whether you know that indexes start with 0. Since we have 10 elements in our array, this means only numbers[0] through numbers[9] are valid. The second example assumes you are clever enough to know 10 is invalid and disguises it by using the length field. However, the length is always one more than the maximum valid index. Finally, the for loop incorrectly uses <= instead of <, which is also a way of referring to that 10th element.

Sorting

Java makes it easy to sort an array by providing a sort method—or rather, a bunch of sort methods. Just like StringBuilder allowed you to pass almost anything to append(), you can pass almost any array to Arrays.sort().

Arrays is the first class provided by Java we have used that requires an import. To use it, you must have either of the following two statements in your class:

```
import java.util.*;       // import whole package including Arrays
import java.util.Arrays;  // import just Arrays
```

There is one exception, although it doesn't come up often on the exam. You can write java.util.Arrays every time it is used in the class instead of specifying it as an import.

Remember that if you are shown a code snippet with a line number that doesn't begin with 1, you can assume the necessary imports are there. Similarly, you can assume the imports are present if you are shown a snippet of a method.

This simple example sorts three numbers:

```
int[] numbers = { 6, 9, 1 };
Arrays.sort(numbers);
for (int i = 0; i < numbers.length; i++)
    System.out.print(numbers[i] +  " ");
```

The result is 1 6 9, as you should expect it to be. Notice that we looped through the output to print the values in the array. Just printing the array variable directly would give the annoying hash of [I@2bd9c3e7. Alternatively, we could have printed Arrays .toString(numbers) instead of using the loop. That would have output [1, 6, 9].

Try this again with String types:

```
String[] strings = { "10", "9", "100" };
Arrays.sort(strings);
for (String string : strings)
    System.out.print(string + " ");
```

This time the result might not be what you expect. This code outputs 10 100 9. The problem is that String sorts in alphabetic order, and 1 sorts before 9. (Numbers sort before letters, and uppercase sorts before lowercase, in case you were wondering.) For the 1Z0-816 exam, you'll learn how to create custom sort orders using something called a *comparator*.

Did you notice we snuck in the enhanced for loop in this example? Since we aren't using the index, we don't need the traditional for loop. That won't stop the exam creators from using it, though, so we'll be sure to use both to keep you sharp!

Searching

Java also provides a convenient way to search—but only if the array is already sorted. Table 5.1 covers the rules for binary search.

TABLE 5.1   Binary search rules

Scenario	Result
Target element found in sorted array	Index of match
Target element not found in sorted array	Negative value showing one smaller than the negative of the index, where a match needs to be inserted to preserve sorted order
Unsorted array	A surprise—this result isn't predictable

Let's try these rules with an example:

```
3: int[] numbers = {2,4,6,8};
4: System.out.println(Arrays.binarySearch(numbers, 2)); // 0
5: System.out.println(Arrays.binarySearch(numbers, 4)); // 1
6: System.out.println(Arrays.binarySearch(numbers, 1)); // -1
7: System.out.println(Arrays.binarySearch(numbers, 3)); // -2
8: System.out.println(Arrays.binarySearch(numbers, 9)); // -5
```

Take note of the fact that line 3 is a sorted array. If it wasn't, we couldn't apply either of the other rules. Line 4 searches for the index of 2. The answer is index 0. Line 5 searches for the index of 4, which is 1.

Line 6 searches for the index of 1. Although 1 isn't in the list, the search can determine that it should be inserted at element 0 to preserve the sorted order. Since 0 already means something for array indexes, Java needs to subtract 1 to give us the answer of −1. Line 7 is similar. Although 3 isn't in the list, it would need to be inserted at element 1 to preserve the sorted order. We negate and subtract 1 for consistency, getting −1 −1, also known as −2. Finally, line 8 wants to tell us that 9 should be inserted at index 4. We again negate and subtract 1, getting −4 −1, also known as −5.

What do you think happens in this example?

```
5: int[] numbers = new int[] {3,2,1};
6: System.out.println(Arrays.binarySearch(numbers, 2));
7: System.out.println(Arrays.binarySearch(numbers, 3));
```

Note that on line 5, the array isn't sorted. This means the output will not be predictable. When testing this example, line 6 correctly gave 1 as the output. However, line 7 gave the wrong answer. The exam creators will not expect you to know what incorrect values come out. As soon as you see the array isn't sorted, look for an answer choice about unpredictable output.

On the exam, you need to know what a binary search returns in various scenarios. Oddly, you don't need to know why "binary" is in the name. In case you are curious, a binary search splits the array into two equal pieces (remember 2 is binary) and determines which half the target is in. It repeats this process until only one element is left.

Comparing

Java also provides methods to compare two arrays to determine which is "smaller." First we will cover the `compare()` method and then go on to `mismatch()`.

compare()

There are a bunch of rules you need to know before calling `compare()`. Luckily, these are the same rules you'll need to know for the 1Z0-816 exam when writing a `Comparator`.

First you need to learn what the return value means. You do not need to know the exact return values, but you do need to know the following:

- A negative number means the first array is smaller than the second.
- A zero means the arrays are equal.
- A positive number means the first array is larger than the second.

    Here's an example:

```
System.out.println(Arrays.compare(new int[] {1}, new int[] {2}));
```

This code prints a negative number. It should be pretty intuitive that 1 is smaller than 2, making the first array smaller.

Now that you know how to compare a single value, let's look at how to compare arrays of different lengths:

- If both arrays are the same length and have the same values in each spot in the same order, return zero.
- If all the elements are the same but the second array has extra elements at the end, return a negative number.
- If all the elements are the same but the first array has extra elements at the end, return a positive number.
- If the first element that differs is smaller in the first array, return a negative number.
- If the first element that differs is larger in the first array, return a positive number.

    Finally, what does smaller mean? Here are some more rules that apply here and to `compareTo()`, which you'll see in Chapter 6, "Lambdas and Functional Interfaces":

- null is smaller than any other value.
- For numbers, normal numeric order applies.
- For strings, one is smaller if it is a prefix of another.
- For strings/characters, numbers are smaller than letters.
- For strings/characters, uppercase is smaller than lowercase.

Table 5.2 shows examples of these rules in action.

TABLE 5.2 Arrays.compare() examples

First array	Second array	Result	Reason
new int[] {1, 2}	new int[] {1}	Positive number	The first element is the same, but the first array is longer.
new int[] {1, 2}	new int[] {1, 2}	Zero	Exact match
new String[] {"a"}	new String[] {"aa"}	Negative number	The first element is a substring of the second.
new String[] {"a"}	new String[] {"A"}	Positive number	Uppercase is smaller than lowercase.
new String[] {"a"}	new String[] {null}	Positive number	null is smaller than a letter.

Finally, this code does not compile because the types are different. When comparing two arrays, they must be the same array type.

```
System.out.println(Arrays.compare(
    new int[] {1}, new String[] {"a"})); // DOES NOT COMPILE
```

mismatch()

Now that you are familiar with compare(), it is time to learn about mismatch(). If the arrays are equal, mismatch() returns -1. Otherwise, it returns the first index where they differ. Can you figure out what these print?

```
System.out.println(Arrays.mismatch(new int[] {1}, new int[] {1}));
System.out.println(Arrays.mismatch(new String[] {"a"},
    new String[] {"A"}));
System.out.println(Arrays.mismatch(new int[] {1, 2}, new int[] {1}));
```

In the first example, the arrays are the same, so the result is -1. In the second example, the entries at element 0 are not equal, so the result is 0. In the third example, the entries at element 0 are equal, so we keep looking. The element at index 1 is not equal. Or more specifically, one array has an element at index 1, and the other does not. Therefore, the result is 1.

To make sure you understand the compare() and mismatch() methods, study Table 5.3. If you don't understand why all of the values are there, please go back and study this section again.

TABLE 5.3   Equality vs. comparison vs. mismatch

Method	When arrays are the same	When arrays are different
equals()	true	false
compare()	0	Positive or negative number
mismatch()	−1	Zero or positive index

Varargs

When you're creating an array yourself, it looks like what we've seen thus far. When one is passed to your method, there is another way it can look. Here are three examples with a main() method:

```
public static void main(String[] args)
public static void main(String args[])
public static void main(String... args) // varargs
```

The third example uses a syntax called *varargs* (variable arguments), which you saw in Chapter 1, "Welcome to Java." You'll learn how to call a method using varargs in Chapter 7, "Methods and Encapsulation." For now, all you need to know is that you can use a variable defined using varargs as if it were a normal array. For example, args.length and args[0] are legal.

Multidimensional Arrays

Arrays are objects, and of course array components can be objects. It doesn't take much time, rubbing those two facts together, to wonder whether arrays can hold other arrays, and of course they can.

Creating a Multidimensional Array

Multiple array separators are all it takes to declare arrays with multiple dimensions. You can locate them with the type or variable name in the declaration, just as before:

```
int[][] vars1;          // 2D array
int vars2 [][];         // 2D array
int[] vars3[];          // 2D array
int[] vars4 [], space [][];  // a 2D AND a 3D array
```

The first two examples are nothing surprising and declare a two-dimensional (2D) array. The third example also declares a 2D array. There's no good reason to use this style other than to confuse readers with your code. The final example declares two arrays on the same line. Adding up the brackets, we see that the vars4 is a 2D array and space is a 3D array. Again, there's no reason to use this style other than to confuse readers of your code. The exam creators like to try to confuse you, though. Luckily, you are on to them and won't let this happen to you!

You can specify the size of your multidimensional array in the declaration if you like:

```
String [][] rectangle = new String[3][2];
```

The result of this statement is an array rectangle with three elements, each of which refers to an array of two elements. You can think of the addressable range as [0][0] through [2][1], but don't think of it as a structure of addresses like [0,0] or [2,1].

Now suppose we set one of these values:

```
rectangle[0][1] = "set";
```

You can visualize the result as shown in Figure 5.7. This array is sparsely populated because it has a lot of null values. You can see that rectangle still points to an array of three elements and that we have three arrays of two elements. You can also follow the trail from reference to the one value pointing to a String. First you start at index 0 in the top array. Then you go to index 1 in the next array.

FIGURE 5.7 A sparsely populated multidimensional array

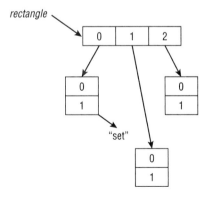

While that array happens to be rectangular in shape, an array doesn't need to be. Consider this one:

```
int[][] differentSizes = {{1, 4}, {3}, {9,8,7}};
```

We still start with an array of three elements. However, this time the elements in the next level are all different sizes. One is of length 2, the next length 1, and the last length 3 (see Figure 5.8). This time the array is of primitives, so they are shown as if they are in the array themselves.

FIGURE 5.8   An asymmetric multidimensional array

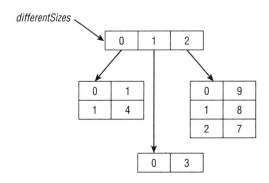

Another way to create an asymmetric array is to initialize just an array's first dimension and define the size of each array component in a separate statement:

```
int [][] args = new int[4][];
args[0] = new int[5];
args[1] = new int[3];
```

This technique reveals what you really get with Java: arrays of arrays that, properly managed, offer a multidimensional effect.

Using a Multidimensional Array

The most common operation on a multidimensional array is to loop through it. This example prints out a 2D array:

```
int[][] twoD = new int[3][2];
for (int i = 0; i < twoD.length; i++) {
   for (int j = 0; j < twoD[i].length; j++)
      System.out.print(twoD[i][j] + " "); // print element
   System.out.println();                  // time for a new row
}
```

We have two loops here. The first uses index i and goes through the first subarray for twoD. The second uses a different loop variable j. It is important that these be different variable names so the loops don't get mixed up. The inner loop looks at how many elements are in the second-level array. The inner loop prints the element and leaves a space for readability. When the inner loop completes, the outer loop goes to a new line and repeats the process for the next element.

This entire exercise would be easier to read with the enhanced for loop.

```
for (int[] inner : twoD) {
   for (int num : inner)
      System.out.print(num + " ");
   System.out.println();
}
```

We'll grant you that it isn't fewer lines, but each line is less complex, and there aren't any loop variables or terminating conditions to mix up.

Understanding an *ArrayList*

An array has one glaring shortcoming: You have to know how many elements will be in the array when you create it, and then you are stuck with that choice. Just like a StringBuilder, an ArrayList can change capacity at runtime as needed. Like an array, an ArrayList is an ordered sequence that allows duplicates.

As when we used Arrays.sort, ArrayList requires an import. To use it, you must have either of the following two statements in your class:

```
import java.util.*;         // import whole package
import java.util.ArrayList; // import just ArrayList
```

In this section, we'll look at creating an ArrayList, common methods, autoboxing, conversion, and sorting.

Experienced programmers, take note: This section is simplified and doesn't cover a number of topics that are out of scope for this exam.

Creating an *ArrayList*

As with StringBuilder, there are three ways to create an ArrayList:

```
ArrayList list1 = new ArrayList();
ArrayList list2 = new ArrayList(10);
ArrayList list3 = new ArrayList(list2);
```

The first says to create an ArrayList containing space for the default number of elements but not to fill any slots yet. The second says to create an ArrayList containing a specific number of slots, but again not to assign any. The final example tells Java that we want to make a copy of another ArrayList. We copy both the size and contents of that ArrayList. Granted, list2 is empty in this example, so it isn't particularly interesting.

Although these are the only three constructors you need to know, you do need to learn some variants of it. The previous examples were the old pre–Java 5 way of creating an ArrayList. They still work, and you still need to know they work. You also need to know the new and improved way. Java 5 introduced *generics*, which allow you to specify the type of class that the ArrayList will contain.

```
ArrayList<String> list4 = new ArrayList<String>();
ArrayList<String> list5 = new ArrayList<>();
```

Java 5 allows you to tell the compiler what the type would be by specifying it between < and >. Starting in Java 7, you can even omit that type from the right side. The < and > are still required, though. This is called the *diamond operator* because <> looks like a diamond.

Using var with ArrayList

Now that var can be used to obscure data types, there is a whole new group of questions that can be asked with generics. Consider this code mixing the two:

```
var strings = new ArrayList<String>();
strings.add("a");
for (String s: strings) {  }
```

The type of var is ArrayList<String>. This means you can add a String or loop through the String objects. What if we use the diamond operator with var?

```
var list = new ArrayList<>();
```

Believe it or not, this does compile. The type of the var is ArrayList<Object>. Since there isn't a type specified for the generic, Java has to assume the ultimate superclass. This is a bit silly and unexpected, so please don't write this. But if you see it on the exam, you'll know what to expect. Now can you figure out why this doesn't compile?

```
var list = new ArrayList<>();
list.add("a");
for (String s: list) { } // DOES NOT COMPILE
```

The type of var is ArrayList<Object>. Since there isn't a type in the diamond operator, Java has to assume the most generic option it can. Therefore, it picks Object, the ultimate superclass. Adding a String to the list is fine. You can add any subclass of Object. However, in the loop, we need to use the Object type rather than String.

Just when you thought you knew everything about creating an ArrayList, there is one more thing you need to know. ArrayList implements an interface called List. In other words, an ArrayList is a List. You will learn about interfaces later in the book. In the meantime, just know that you can store an ArrayList in a List reference variable but not vice versa. The reason is that List is an interface and interfaces can't be instantiated.

```
List<String> list6 = new ArrayList<>();
ArrayList<String> list7 = new List<>(); // DOES NOT COMPILE
```

Using an *ArrayList*

ArrayList has many methods, but you only need to know a handful of them—even fewer than you did for String and StringBuilder.

Before reading any further, you are going to see something new in the method signatures: a "class" named E. Don't worry—it isn't really a class. E is used by convention in generics to mean "any class that this array can hold." If you didn't specify a type when creating the ArrayList, E means Object. Otherwise, it means the class you put between < and >.

You should also know that ArrayList implements toString(), so you can easily see the contents just by printing it. Arrays do not produce such pretty output by default.

add()

The add() methods insert a new value in the ArrayList. The method signatures are as follows:

```
boolean add(E element)
void add(int index, E element)
```

Don't worry about the boolean return value. It always returns true. As we'll see later in the chapter, it is there because other classes in the Collections family need a return value in the signature when adding an element.

Since add() is the most critical ArrayList method you need to know for the exam, we are going to show a few examples for it. Let's start with the most straightforward case:

```
ArrayList list = new ArrayList();
list.add("hawk");           // [hawk]
list.add(Boolean.TRUE);     // [hawk, true]
System.out.println(list);   // [hawk, true]
```

add() does exactly what we expect: It stores the String in the no longer empty ArrayList. It then does the same thing for the Boolean. This is okay because we didn't specify a type for ArrayList; therefore, the type is Object, which includes everything except primitives. It may not have been what we intended, but the compiler doesn't know that. Now, let's use generics to tell the compiler we only want to allow String objects in our ArrayList:

```
ArrayList<String> safer = new ArrayList<>();
safer.add("sparrow");
safer.add(Boolean.TRUE);    // DOES NOT COMPILE
```

This time the compiler knows that only String objects are allowed in and prevents the attempt to add a Boolean. Now let's try adding multiple values to different positions.

```
4: List<String> birds = new ArrayList<>();
5: birds.add("hawk");          // [hawk]
6: birds.add(1, "robin");      // [hawk, robin]
7: birds.add(0, "blue jay");   // [blue jay, hawk, robin]
8: birds.add(1, "cardinal");   // [blue jay, cardinal, hawk, robin]
9: System.out.println(birds);  // [blue jay, cardinal, hawk, robin]
```

When a question has code that adds objects at indexed positions, draw it so that you won't lose track of which value is at which index. In this example, line 5 adds "hawk" to the end of birds. Then line 6 adds "robin" to index 1 of birds, which happens to be the end. Line 7 adds "blue jay" to index 0, which happens to be the beginning of birds. Finally, line 8 adds "cardinal" to index 1, which is now near the middle of birds.

remove()

The remove() methods remove the first matching value in the ArrayList or remove the element at a specified index. The method signatures are as follows:

```
boolean remove(Object object)
E remove(int index)
```

This time the boolean return value tells us whether a match was removed. The E return type is the element that actually got removed. The following shows how to use these methods:

```
3: List<String> birds = new ArrayList<>();
4: birds.add("hawk");     // [hawk]
5: birds.add("hawk");     // [hawk, hawk]
6: System.out.println(birds.remove("cardinal")); // prints false
7: System.out.println(birds.remove("hawk"));     // prints true
8: System.out.println(birds.remove(0));          // prints hawk
9: System.out.println(birds);                    // []
```

Line 6 tries to remove an element that is not in birds. It returns false because no such element is found. Line 7 tries to remove an element that is in birds and so returns true. Notice that it removes only one match. Line 8 removes the element at index 0, which is the last remaining element in the ArrayList.

Since calling remove() with an int uses the index, an index that doesn't exist will throw an exception. For example, birds.remove(100) throws an IndexOutOfBoundsException.

There is also a removeIf() method. We'll cover it in the next chapter because it uses lambda expressions (a topic in that chapter).

set()

The set() method changes one of the elements of the ArrayList without changing the size. The method signature is as follows:

```
E set(int index, E newElement)
```

The E return type is the element that got replaced. The following shows how to use this method:

```
15: List<String> birds = new ArrayList<>();
16: birds.add("hawk");                  // [hawk]
17: System.out.println(birds.size());   // 1
18: birds.set(0, "robin");              // [robin]
19: System.out.println(birds.size());   // 1
20: birds.set(1, "robin");              // IndexOutOfBoundsException
```

Line 16 adds one element to the array, making the size 1. Line 18 replaces that one element, and the size stays at 1. Line 20 tries to replace an element that isn't in the ArrayList. Since the size is 1, the only valid index is 0. Java throws an exception because this isn't allowed.

isEmpty() and size()

The isEmpty() and size() methods look at how many of the slots are in use. The method signatures are as follows:

```
boolean isEmpty()
int size()
```

The following shows how to use these methods:

```
List<String> birds = new ArrayList<>();
System.out.println(birds.isEmpty());    // true
System.out.println(birds.size());       // 0
birds.add("hawk");                      // [hawk]
birds.add("hawk");                      // [hawk, hawk]
System.out.println(birds.isEmpty());    // false
System.out.println(birds.size());       // 2
```

At the beginning, birds has a size of 0 and is empty. It has a capacity that is greater than 0. However, as with StringBuilder, we don't use the capacity in determining size or length. After adding elements, the size becomes positive, and it is no longer empty. Notice how isEmpty() is a convenience method for size() == 0.

clear()

The clear() method provides an easy way to discard all elements of the ArrayList. The method signature is as follows:

```
void clear()
```

The following shows how to use this method:

```
List<String> birds = new ArrayList<>();
birds.add("hawk");                      // [hawk]
birds.add("hawk");                      // [hawk, hawk]
```

```
System.out.println(birds.isEmpty());   // false
System.out.println(birds.size());      // 2
birds.clear();                         // []
System.out.println(birds.isEmpty());   // true
System.out.println(birds.size());      // 0
```

After we call clear(), birds is back to being an empty ArrayList of size 0.

contains()

The contains() method checks whether a certain value is in the ArrayList. The method signature is as follows:

```
boolean contains(Object object)
```

The following shows how to use this method:

```
List<String> birds = new ArrayList<>();
birds.add("hawk");                                 // [hawk]
System.out.println(birds.contains("hawk"));   // true
System.out.println(birds.contains("robin"));  // false
```

This method calls equals() on each element of the ArrayList to see whether there are any matches. Since String implements equals(), this works out well.

equals()

Finally, ArrayList has a custom implementation of equals(),so you can compare two lists to see whether they contain the same elements in the same order.

```
boolean equals(Object object)
```

The following shows an example:

```
31: List<String> one = new ArrayList<>();
32: List<String> two = new ArrayList<>();
33: System.out.println(one.equals(two));   // true
34: one.add("a");                          // [a]
35: System.out.println(one.equals(two));   // false
36: two.add("a");                          // [a]
37: System.out.println(one.equals(two));   // true
38: one.add("b");                          // [a,b]
39: two.add(0, "b");                       // [b,a]
40: System.out.println(one.equals(two));   // false
```

On line 33, the two ArrayList objects are equal. An empty list is certainly the same elements in the same order. On line 35, the ArrayList objects are not equal because the size is different. On line 37, they are equal again because the same one element is in each. On line

40, they are not equal. The size is the same and the values are the same, but they are not in the same order.

Wrapper Classes

Up to now, we've only put `String` objects in the `ArrayList`. What happens if we want to put primitives in? Each primitive type has a wrapper class, which is an object type that corresponds to the primitive. Table 5.4 lists all the wrapper classes along with how to create them.

TABLE 5.4   Wrapper classes

Primitive type	Wrapper class	Example of creating
boolean	Boolean	Boolean.valueOf(true)
byte	Byte	Byte.valueOf((byte) 1)
short	Short	Short.valueOf((short) 1)
int	Integer	Integer.valueOf(1)
long	Long	Long.valueOf(1)
float	Float	Float.valueOf((float) 1.0)
double	Double	Double.valueOf(1.0)
char	Character	Character.valueOf('c')

Each wrapper class also has a constructor. It works the same way as `valueOf()` but isn't recommended for new code. The `valueOf()` allows object caching. Remember how a `String` could be shared when the value is the same? The wrapper classes are immutable and take advantage of some caching as well.

The wrapper classes also have a method that converts back to a primitive. You don't need to know much about the `valueOf()` or `intValue()` type methods for the exam because autoboxing has removed the need for them (see the next section). You just need to be able to read the code and not look for tricks in it.

There are also methods for converting a `String` to a primitive or wrapper class. You do need to know these methods. The parse methods, such as `parseInt()`, return a primitive, and the `valueOf()` method returns a wrapper class. This is easy to remember because the name of the returned primitive is in the method name. Here's an example:

```
int primitive = Integer.parseInt("123");
Integer wrapper = Integer.valueOf("123");
```

The first line converts a String to an int primitive. The second converts a String to an Integer wrapper class. If the String passed in is not valid for the given type, Java throws an exception. In these examples, letters and dots are not valid for an integer value:

```
int bad1 = Integer.parseInt("a");        // throws NumberFormatException
Integer bad2 = Integer.valueOf("123.45"); // throws NumberFormatException
```

Before you worry, the exam won't make you recognize that the method parseInt() is used rather than parseInteger(). You simply need to be able to recognize the methods when put in front of you. Also, the Character class doesn't participate in the parse/valueOf methods. Since a String consists of characters, you can just call charAt() normally.

Table 5.5 lists the methods you need to recognize for creating a primitive or wrapper class object from a String. In real coding, you won't be so concerned about which is returned from each method due to autoboxing.

TABLE 5.5   Converting from a String

Wrapper class	Converting String to a primitive	Converting String to a wrapper class
Boolean	Boolean.parseBoolean("true")	Boolean.valueOf("TRUE")
Byte	Byte.parseByte("1")	Byte.valueOf("2")
Short	Short.parseShort("1")	Short.valueOf("2")
Integer	Integer.parseInt("1")	Integer.valueOf("2")
Long	Long.parseLong("1")	Long.valueOf("2")
Float	Float.parseFloat("1")	Float.valueOf("2.2")
Double	Double.parseDouble("1")	Double.valueOf("2.2")
Character	None	None

Wrapper Classes and Null

When we presented numeric primitives in Chapter 2, we mentioned they could not be used to store null values. One advantage of a wrapper class over a primitive is that because it's an object, it can be used to store a null value. While null values aren't particularly useful for numeric calculations, they are quite useful in data-based services. For example, if you are storing a user's location data using (latitude,longitude), it would be a bad idea to store a missing point as (0,0) since that refers to an actual location off the coast of Africa where the user could theoretically be.

Autoboxing and Unboxing

Why won't you need to be concerned with whether a primitive or wrapper class is returned, you ask? Since Java 5, you can just type the primitive value, and Java will convert it to the relevant wrapper class for you. This is called *autoboxing*. The reverse conversion of wrapper class to primitive value is called *unboxing*. Let's look at an example:

```
3: List<Integer> weights = new ArrayList<>();
4: Integer w = 50;
5: weights.add(w);                   // [50]
6: weights.add(Integer.valueOf(60));    // [50, 60]
7: weights.remove(new Integer(50)); // [60]
8: double first = weights.get(0);   // 60.0
```

Line 4 autoboxes the `int` primitive into an `Integer` object, and line 5 adds that to the `List`. Line 6 shows that you can still write code the long way and pass in a wrapper object. Line 8 retrieves the first `Integer` in the list, unboxes it as a primitive and implicitly casts it to double.

What do you think happens if you try to unbox a `null`?

```
3: List<Integer> heights = new ArrayList<>();
4: heights.add(null);
5: int h = heights.get(0);          // NullPointerException
```

On line 4, we add a `null` to the list. This is legal because a `null` reference can be assigned to any reference variable. On line 5, we try to unbox that `null` to an `int` primitive. This is a problem. Java tries to get the `int` value of `null`. Since calling any method on `null` gives a `NullPointerException`, that is just what we get. Be careful when you see `null` in relation to autoboxing.

Also be careful when autoboxing into `Integer`. What do you think this code outputs?

```
List<Integer> numbers = new ArrayList<>();
numbers.add(1);
numbers.add(2);
numbers.remove(1);
System.out.println(numbers);
```

It actually outputs [1]. After adding the two values, the `List` contains [1, 2]. We then request the element with index 1 be removed. That's right: index 1. Because there's already a `remove()` method that takes an `int` parameter, Java calls that method rather than autoboxing. If you want to remove the 1, you can write `numbers.remove(new Integer(1))` to force wrapper class use.

Converting Between *array* and *List*

You should know how to convert between an array and a `List`. Let's start with turning an `ArrayList` into an array:

```
13: List<String> list = new ArrayList<>();
14: list.add("hawk");
15: list.add("robin");
16: Object[] objectArray = list.toArray();
17: String[] stringArray = list.toArray(new String[0]);
18: list.clear();
19: System.out.println(objectArray.length);     // 2
20: System.out.println(stringArray.length);     // 2
```

Line 16 shows that an ArrayList knows how to convert itself to an array. The only problem is that it defaults to an array of class Object. This isn't usually what you want. Line 17 specifies the type of the array and does what we actually want. The advantage of specifying a size of 0 for the parameter is that Java will create a new array of the proper size for the return value. If you like, you can suggest a larger array to be used instead. If the ArrayList fits in that array, it will be returned. Otherwise, a new one will be created.

Also, notice that line 18 clears the original List. This does not affect either array. The array is a newly created object with no relationship to the original List. It is simply a copy.

Converting from an array to a List is more interesting. We will show you two methods to do this conversion. Note that you aren't guaranteed to get a java.util.ArrayList from either. This means each has special behavior to learn about.

One option is to create a List that is linked to the original array. When a change is made to one, it is available in the other. It is a fixed-size list and is also known as a backed List because the array changes with it. Pay careful attention to the values here:

```
20: String[] array = { "hawk", "robin" };     // [hawk, robin]
21: List<String> list = Arrays.asList(array); // returns fixed size list
22: System.out.println(list.size());          // 2
23: list.set(1, "test");                       // [hawk, test]
24: array[0] = "new";                          // [new, test]
25: System.out.print(Arrays.toString(array));// [new, test]
26: list.remove(1);      // throws UnsupportedOperationException
```

Line 21 converts the array to a List. Note that it isn't the java.util.ArrayList we've grown used to. It is a fixed-size, backed version of a List. Line 23 is okay because set() merely replaces an existing value. It updates both array and list because they point to the same data store. Line 24 also changes both array and list. Line 25 shows the array has changed to [new, test]. Line 26 throws an exception because we are not allowed to change the size of the list.

Another option is to create an immutable List. That means you cannot change the values or the size of the List. You can change the original array, but changes will not be reflected in the immutable List. Again, pay careful attention to the values:

```
32: String[] array = { "hawk", "robin" };         // [hawk, robin]
33: List<String> list = List.of(array);       // returns immutable list
34: System.out.println(list.size());              // 2
```

```
35: array[0] = "new";
36: System.out.println(Arrays.toString(array)); // [new, robin]
37: System.out.println(list);                    // [hawk, robin]
38: list.set(1, "test");       // throws UnsupportedOperationException
```

Line 33 creates the immutable List. It contains the two values that array happened to contain at the time the List was created. On line 35, there is a change to the array. Line 36 shows that array has changed. Line 37 shows that list still has the original values. This is because it is an immutable copy of the original array. Line 38 shows that changing a list value in an immutable list is not allowed.

Using Varargs to Create a List

Using varargs allows you to create a List in a cool way:

```
List<String> list1 = Arrays.asList("one", "two");
List<String> list2 = List.of("one", "two");
```

Both of these methods take varargs, which let you pass in an array or just type out the String values. This is handy when testing because you can easily create and populate a List on one line. Both methods create fixed-size arrays. If you will need to later add or remove elements, you'll still need to create an ArrayList using the constructor. There's a lot going on here, so let's study Table 5.6.

TABLE 5.6   Array and list conversions

	toArray()	Arrays.asList()	List.of()
Type converting from	List	Array (or varargs)	Array (or varargs)
Type created	Array	List	List
Allowed to remove values from created object	No	No	No
Allowed to change values in the created object	Yes	Yes	No
Changing values in the created object affects the original or vice versa.	No	Yes	N/A

Notice that none of the options allows you to change the number of elements. If you want to do that, you'll need to actually write logic to create the new object. Here's an example:

```
List<String> fixedSizeList  = Arrays.asList("a", "b", "c");
List<String> expandableList = new ArrayList<>(fixedSizeList);
```

Sorting

Sorting an `ArrayList` is similar to sorting an array. You just use a different helper class:

```
List<Integer> numbers = new ArrayList<>();
numbers.add(99);
numbers.add(5);
numbers.add(81);
Collections.sort(numbers);
System.out.println(numbers); // [5, 81, 99]
```

As you can see, the numbers got sorted, just like you'd expect. Isn't it nice to have something that works just like you think it will?

Creating Sets and Maps

Although advanced collections topics are not covered until the 1Z0-816 exam, you should still know the basics of `Set` and `Map` now.

Introducing Sets

A `Set` is a collection of objects that cannot contain duplicates. If you try to add a duplicate to a set, the API will not fulfill the request. You can imagine a set as shown in Figure 5.9.

FIGURE 5.9   Example of a Set

All the methods you learned for `ArrayList` apply to a `Set` with the exception of those taking an index as a parameter. Why is this? Well, a `Set` isn't ordered, so it wouldn't make sense to talk about the first element. This means you cannot call `set(index, value)` or `remove(index)`. You can call other methods like `add(value)` or `remove(value)`.

Do you remember that `boolean` return value on `add()` that always returned `true` for an `ArrayList`? `Set` is a reason it needs to exist. When trying to add a duplicate value, the method returns `false` and does not add the value.

There are two common classes that implement Set that you might see on the exam. HashSet is the most common. TreeSet is used when sorting is important.

To make sure you understand a Set, follow along with this code:

```
3: Set<Integer> set = new HashSet<>();
4: System.out.println(set.add(66)); // true
5: System.out.println(set.add(66)); // false
6: System.out.println(set.size()); // 1
7: set.remove(66);
8: System.out.println(set.isEmpty()); // true
```

Line 3 creates a new set that declares only unique elements are allowed. Both lines 4 and 5 attempt to add the same value. Only the first one is allowed, making line 4 print true and line 5 false. Line 6 confirms there is only one value in the set. Removing an element on line 7 works normally, and the set is empty on line 8.

Introducing Maps

A Map uses a key to identify values. For example, when you use the contact list on your phone, you look up "George" rather than looking through each phone number in turn. Figure 5.10 shows how to visualize a Map.

FIGURE 5.10   Example of a Map

George	555-555-5555
Mary	777-777-7777

The most common implementation of Map is HashMap. Some of the methods are the same as those in ArrayList like clear(), isEmpty(), and size().

There are also methods specific to dealing with key and value pairs. Table 5.7 shows these minimal methods you need to know.

TABLE 5.7   Common Map methods

Method	Description
V get(Object key)	Returns the value mapped by key or null if none is mapped
V getOrDefault(Object key, V other)	Returns the value mapped by key or other if none is mapped
V put(K key, V value)	Adds or replaces key/value pair. Returns previous value or null

TABLE 5.7   Common Map methods *(continued)*

Method	Description
`V remove(Object key)`	Removes and returns value mapped to key. Returns `null` if none
`boolean containsKey(Object key)`	Returns whether key is in map
`boolean containsValue(Object value)`	Returns whether value is in map
`Set<K> keySet()`	Returns set of all keys
`Collection<V> values()`	Returns `Collection` of all values

Now let's look at an example to confirm this is clear:

```
8:  Map<String, String> map = new HashMap<>();
9:  map.put("koala", "bamboo");
10: String food = map.get("koala"); // bamboo
11: String other = map.getOrDefault("ant", "leaf"); // leaf
12: for (String key: map.keySet())
13:     System.out.println(key + " " + map.get(key)); // koala bamboo
```

In this example, we create a new map and store one key/value pair inside. Line 10 gets this value by key. Line 11 looks for a key that isn't there, so it returns the second parameter leaf as the default value. Lines 12 and 13 list all the key and value pairs.

Calculating with Math APIs

It should come as no surprise that computers are good at computing numbers. Java comes with a powerful Math class with many methods to make your life easier. We will just cover a few common ones here that are most likely to appear on the exam. When doing your own projects, look at the Math Javadoc to see what other methods can help you.

Pay special attention to return types in math questions. They are an excellent opportunity for trickery!

min() and max()

The min() and max() methods compare two values and return one of them.

The method signatures for min() are as follows:

```
double min(double a, double b)
float min(float a, float b)
```

```
int min(int a, int b)
long min(long a, long b)
```

There are four overloaded methods, so you always have an API available with the same type. Each method returns whichever of a or b is smaller. The max() method works the same way except it returns the larger value.

The following shows how to use these methods:

```
int first = Math.max(3, 7);   // 7
int second = Math.min(7, -9);  // -9
```

The first line returns 7 because it is larger. The second line returns -9 because it is smaller. Remember from school that negative values are smaller than positive ones.

round()

The round() method gets rid of the decimal portion of the value, choosing the next higher number if appropriate. If the fractional part is .5 or higher, we round up.

The method signatures for round() are as follows:

```
long round(double num)
int round(float num)
```

There are two overloaded methods to ensure there is enough room to store a rounded double if needed. The following shows how to use this method:

```
long low = Math.round(123.45); // 123
long high = Math.round(123.50); // 124
int fromFloat = Math.round(123.45f); // 123
```

The first line returns 123 because .45 is smaller than a half. The second line returns 124 because the fractional part is just barely a half. The final line shows that an explicit float triggers the method signature that returns an int.

pow()

The pow() method handles exponents. As you may recall from your elementary school math class, 3^2 means three squared. This is 3 * 3 or 9. Fractional exponents are allowed as well. Sixteen to the .5 power means the square root of 16, which is 4. (Don't worry, you won't have to do square roots on the exam.)

The method signature is as follows:

```
double pow(double number, double exponent)
```

The following shows how to use this method:

```
double squared = Math.pow(5, 2); // 25.0
```

Notice that the result is 25.0 rather than 25 since it is a double. (Again, don't worry, the exam won't ask you to do any complicated math.)

random()

The random() method returns a value greater than or equal to 0 and less than 1. The method signature is as follows:

```
double random()
```

The following shows how to use this method:

```
double num = Math.random();
```

Since it is a random number, we can't know the result in advance. However, we can rule out certain numbers. For example, it can't be negative because that's less than 0. It can't be 1.0 because that's not less than 1.

Summary

In this chapter, you learned that Strings are immutable sequences of characters. The new operator is optional. The concatenation operator (+) creates a new String with the content of the first String followed by the content of the second String. If either operand involved in the + expression is a String, concatenation is used; otherwise, addition is used. String literals are stored in the string pool. The String class has many methods.

StringBuilders are mutable sequences of characters. Most of the methods return a reference to the current object to allow method chaining. The StringBuilder class has many methods.

Calling == on String objects will check whether they point to the same object in the pool. Calling == on StringBuilder references will check whether they are pointing to the same StringBuilder object. Calling equals() on String objects will check whether the sequence of characters is the same. Calling equals() on StringBuilder objects will check whether they are pointing to the same object rather than looking at the values inside.

An array is a fixed-size area of memory on the heap that has space for primitives or pointers to objects. You specify the size when creating it—for example, int[] a = new int[6];. Indexes begin with 0, and elements are referred to using a[0]. The Arrays.sort() method sorts an array. Arrays.binarySearch() searches a sorted array and returns the index of a match. If no match is found, it negates the position where the element would need to be inserted and subtracts 1. Arrays.compare() and Arrays .mismatch() check whether two arrays are the equivalent. Methods that are passed varargs (...) can be used as if a normal array was passed in. In a multidimensional array, the second-level arrays and beyond can be different sizes.

An ArrayList can change size over its life. It can be stored in an ArrayList or List reference. Generics can specify the type that goes in the ArrayList. Although an ArrayList is not allowed to contain primitives, Java will autobox parameters passed in to the proper wrapper type. Collections.sort() sorts an ArrayList.

A `Set` is a collection with unique values. A `Map` consists of key/value pairs. The `Math` class provides many static methods to facilitate programming.

Exam Essentials

Be able to determine the output of code using `String`. Know the rules for concatenating `String`s and how to use common `String` methods. Know that `String`s are immutable. Pay special attention to the fact that indexes are zero-based and that `substring()` gets the string up until right before the index of the second parameter.

Be able to determine the output of code using `StringBuilder`. Know that `StringBuilder` is mutable and how to use common `StringBuilder` methods. Know that `substring()` does not change the value of a `StringBuilder`, whereas `append()`, `delete()`, and `insert()` do change it. Also note that most `StringBuilder` methods return a reference to the current instance of `StringBuilder`.

Understand the difference between `==` and `equals()`. `==` checks object equality. `equals()` depends on the implementation of the object it is being called on. For `String`s, `equals()` checks the characters inside of it.

Be able to determine the output of code using arrays. Know how to declare and instantiate one-dimensional and multidimensional arrays. Be able to access each element and know when an index is out of bounds. Recognize correct and incorrect output when searching and sorting.

Be able to determine the output of code using `ArrayList`. Know that `ArrayList` can increase in size. Be able to identify the different ways of declaring and instantiating an `ArrayList`. Identify correct output from `ArrayList` methods, including the impact of autoboxing.

Review Questions

The answers to the chapter review questions can be found in the Appendix.

1. What is output by the following code? (Choose all that apply.)

```
1: public class Fish {
2:     public static void main(String[] args) {
3:         int numFish = 4;
4:         String fishType = "tuna";
5:         String anotherFish = numFish + 1;
6:         System.out.println(anotherFish + " " + fishType);
7:         System.out.println(numFish + " " + 1);
8: } }
```

A. 4 1
B. 5
C. 5 tuna
D. 5tuna
E. 51tuna
F. The code does not compile.

2. Which of the following are output by this code? (Choose all that apply.)

```
3: var s = "Hello";
4: var t = new String(s);
5: if ("Hello".equals(s)) System.out.println("one");
6: if (t == s) System.out.println("two");
7: if (t.intern() == s) System.out.println("three");
8: if ("Hello" == s) System.out.println("four");
9: if ("Hello".intern() == t) System.out.println("five");
```

A. one
B. two
C. three
D. four
E. five
F. The code does not compile.
G. None of the above

3. Which statements about the following code snippet are correct? (Choose all that apply.)

```
List<String> gorillas = new ArrayList<>();
for(var koko : gorillas)
```

```
System.out.println(koko);

var monkeys = new ArrayList<>();
for(var albert : monkeys)
    System.out.println(albert);

List chimpanzees = new ArrayList<Integer>();
for(var ham : chimpanzees)
    System.out.println(ham);
```

A. The data type of koko is String.

B. The data type of koko is Object.

C. The data type of albert is Object.

D. The data type of albert is undefined.

E. The data type of ham is Integer.

F. The data type of ham is Object.

G. None of the above, as the code does not compile

4. What is the result of the following code?

```
7: StringBuilder sb = new StringBuilder();
8: sb.append("aaa").insert(1, "bb").insert(4, "ccc");
9: System.out.println(sb);
```

A. abbaaccc

B. abbaccca

C. bbaaaccc

D. bbaaccca

E. An empty line

F. The code does not compile.

5. What is the result of the following code?

```
12: int count = 0;
13: String s1 = "java";
14: String s2 = "java";
15: StringBuilder s3 = new StringBuilder("java");
16: if (s1 == s2) count++;
17: if (s1.equals(s2)) count++;
18: if (s1 == s3) count++;
19: if (s1.equals(s3)) count++;
20: System.out.println(count);
```

A. 0

B. 1

C. 2

D. 3

E. 4

F. An exception is thrown.

G. The code does not compile.

6. What is the result of the following code?

```
public class Lion {
    public void roar(String roar1, StringBuilder roar2) {
        roar1.concat("!!!");
        roar2.append("!!!");
    }
    public static void main(String[] args) {
        String roar1 = "roar";
        StringBuilder roar2 = new StringBuilder("roar");
        new Lion().roar(roar1, roar2);
        System.out.println(roar1 + " " + roar2);
} }
```

A. roar roar

B. roar roar!!!

C. roar!!! roar

D. roar!!! roar!!!

E. An exception is thrown.

F. The code does not compile.

7. Which of the following return the number 5 when run independently? (Choose all that apply.)

```
var string = "12345";
var builder = new StringBuilder("12345");
```

A. builder.charAt(4)

B. builder.replace(2, 4, "6").charAt(3)

C. builder.replace(2, 5, "6").charAt(2)

D. string.charAt(5)

E. string.length

F. string.replace("123", "1").charAt(2)

G. None of the above

8. What is output by the following code? (Choose all that apply.)

```
String numbers = "012345678";
System.out.println(numbers.substring(1, 3));
System.out.println(numbers.substring(7, 7));
```

```
System.out.println(numbers.substring(7));
```

A. 12

B. 123

C. 7

D. 78

E. A blank line

F. The code does not compile.

G. An exception is thrown.

9. What is the result of the following code? (Choose all that apply.)

```
14: String s1 = "purr";
15: String s2 = "";
16:
17: s1.toUpperCase();
18: s1.trim();
19: s1.substring(1, 3);
20: s1 += "two";
21:
22: s2 += 2;
23: s2 += 'c';
24: s2 += false;
25:
26: if ( s2 == "2cfalse") System.out.println("==");
27: if ( s2.equals("2cfalse")) System.out.println("equals");
28: System.out.println(s1.length());
```

A. 2

B. 4

C. 7

D. 10

E. ==

F. equals

G. An exception is thrown.

H. The code does not compile.

10. Which of these statements are true? (Choose all that apply.)

```
var letters = new StringBuilder("abcdefg");
```

A. `letters.substring(1, 2)` returns a single character String.

B. `letters.substring(2, 2)` returns a single character String.

C. `letters.substring(6, 5)` returns a single character String.

   D. `letters.substring(6, 6)` returns a single character `String`.

   E. `letters.substring(1, 2)` throws an exception.

   F. `letters.substring(2, 2)` throws an exception.

   G. `letters.substring(6, 5)` throws an exception.

   H. `letters.substring(6, 6)` throws an exception.

11. What is the result of the following code?

```
StringBuilder numbers = new StringBuilder("0123456789");
numbers.delete(2,  8);
numbers.append("-").insert(2, "+");
System.out.println(numbers);
```

   A. `01+89-`

   B. `012+9-`

   C. `012+-9`

   D. `0123456789`

   E. An exception is thrown.

   F. The code does not compile.

12. What is the result of the following code?

```
StringBuilder b = "rumble";
b.append(4).deleteCharAt(3).delete(3, b.length() - 1);
System.out.println(b);
```

   A. `rum`

   B. `rum4`

   C. `rumb4`

   D. `rumble4`

   E. An exception is thrown.

   F. The code does not compile.

13. Which of the following can replace line 4 to print `"avaJ"`? (Choose all that apply.)

```
3: var puzzle = new StringBuilder("Java");
4: // INSERT CODE HERE
5: System.out.println(puzzle);
```

   A. `puzzle.reverse();`

   B. `puzzle.append("vaJ$").substring(0, 4);`

   C. `puzzle.append("vaJ$").delete(0, 3).deleteCharAt(puzzle.length() - 1);`

   D. `puzzle.append("vaJ$").delete(0, 3).deleteCharAt(puzzle.length());`

   E. None of the above

14. Which of these array declarations is not legal? (Choose all that apply.)

A. `int[][] scores = new int[5][];`

B. `Object[][][] cubbies = new Object[3][0][5];`

C. `String beans[] = new beans[6];`

D. `java.util.Date[] dates[] = new java.util.Date[2][];`

E. `int[][] types = new int[];`

F. `int[][] java = new int[][];`

15. Which of the following can fill in the blanks so the code compiles? (Choose two.)

```
6: char[]c = new char[2];
7: ArrayList l = new ArrayList();
8: int length = _____ + _____;
```

A. `c.length`

B. `c.length()`

C. `c.size`

D. `c.size()`

E. `l.length`

F. `l.length()`

G. `l.size`

H. `l.size()`

16. Which of the following are true? (Choose all that apply.)

A. An array has a fixed size.

B. An `ArrayList` has a fixed size.

C. An array is immutable.

D. An `ArrayList` is immutable.

E. Calling `equals()` on two equivalent arrays returns `true`.

F. Calling `equals()` on two equivalent `ArrayList` objects returns `true`.

G. If you call `remove(0)` using an empty `ArrayList` object, it will compile successfully.

H. If you call `remove(0)` using an empty `ArrayList` object, it will run successfully.

17. What is the result of the following statements?

```
6:  var list = new ArrayList<String>();
7:  list.add("one");
8:  list.add("two");
9:  list.add(7);
10: for(var s : list)  System.out.print(s);
```

A. `onetwo`

B. `onetwo7`

   C. onetwo followed by an exception

   D. Compiler error on line 6

   E. Compiler error on line 7

   F. Compiler error on line 9

   G. Compiler error on line 10

18. Which of the following pairs fill in the blanks to output 6?

```
3: var values = new _____<Integer>();
4: values.add(4);
5: values.add(4);
6: values._____;
7: values.remove(0);
8: for (var v : values) System.out.print(v);
```

   A. ArrayList and put(1, 6)

   B. ArrayList and replace(1, 6)

   C. ArrayList and set(1, 6)

   D. HashSet and put(1, 6)

   E. HashSet and replace(1, 6)

   F. HashSet and set(1, 6)

   G. The code does not compile with any of these options.

19. What is output by the following? (Choose all that apply.)

```
8:  List<Integer> list = Arrays.asList(10, 4, -1, 5);
9:  int[] array = { 6, -4, 12, 0, -10 };
10: Collections.sort(list);
11:
12: Integer converted[] = list.toArray(new Integer[4]);
13: System.out.println(converted[0]);
14: System.out.println(Arrays.binarySearch(array, 12));
```

   A. -1

   B. 2

   C. 4

   D. 6

   E. 10

   F. One of the outputs is undefined.

   G. An exception is thrown.

   H. The code does not compile.

20. Which of the lines contain a compiler error? (Choose all that apply.)

```
23: double one = Math.pow(1, 2);
24: int two = Math.round(1.0);
25: float three = Math.random();
26: var doubles = new double[] { one, two, three};
27:
28: String [] names = {"Tom", "Dick", "Harry"};
29: List<String> list = names.asList();
30: var other = Arrays.asList(names);
31: other.set(0, "Sue");
```

A. Line 23

B. Line 24

C. Line 25

D. Line 26

E. Line 29

F. Line 30

G. Line 31

21. What is the result of the following?

```
List<String> hex = Arrays.asList("30", "8", "3A", "FF");
Collections.sort(hex);
int x = Collections.binarySearch(hex, "8");
int y = Collections.binarySearch(hex, "3A");
int z = Collections.binarySearch(hex, "4F");
System.out.println(x + " " + y + " " + z);
```

A. 0 1 −2

B. 0 1 −3

C. 2 1 −2

D. 2 1 −3

E. None of the above

F. The code doesn't compile.

22. Which of the following are true statements about the following code? (Choose all that apply.)

```
4: List<Integer> ages = new ArrayList<>();
5: ages.add(Integer.parseInt("5"));
6: ages.add(Integer.valueOf("6"));
7: ages.add(7);
8: ages.add(null);
9: for (int age : ages) System.out.print(age);
```

A. The code compiles.

B. The code throws a runtime exception.

C. Exactly one of the add statements uses autoboxing.

D. Exactly two of the add statements use autoboxing.

E. Exactly three of the add statements use autoboxing.

23. What is the result of the following?

```java
List<String> one = new ArrayList<String>();
one.add("abc");
List<String> two = new ArrayList<>();
two.add("abc");
if (one == two)
    System.out.println("A");
else if (one.equals(two))
    System.out.println("B");
else
    System.out.println("C");
```

A. A

B. B

C. C

D. An exception is thrown.

E. The code does not compile.

24. Which statements are true about the following code? (Choose all that apply.)

```java
public void run(Integer[] ints, Double[] doubles) {
    List<Integer> intList = Arrays.asList(ints);
    List<Double> doubleList = List.of(doubles);
    // more code
}
```

A. Adding an element to doubleList is allowed.

B. Adding an element to intList is allowed.

C. Changing the first element in doubleList changes the first element in doubles.

D. Changing the first element in intList changes the first element in ints.

E. doubleList is immutable.

F. intList is immutable.

25. Which of the following statements are true of the following code? (Choose all that apply.)

```
String[] s1 = { "Camel", "Peacock", "Llama"};
String[] s2 = { "Camel", "Llama", "Peacock"};
String[] s3 = { "Camel"};
String[] s4 = { "Camel", null};
```

A. Arrays.compare(s1, s2) returns a positive integer.

B. Arrays.mismatch(s1, s2) returns a positive integer.

C. Arrays.compare(s3, s4) returns a positive integer.

D. Arrays.mismatch(s3, s4) returns a positive integer.

E. Arrays.compare(s4, s4) returns a positive integer.

F. Arrays.mismatch(s4, s4) returns a positive integer.

Chapter

6

Lambdas and Functional Interfaces

OCP EXAM OBJECTIVES COVERED IN THIS CHAPTER:

✓ **Programming Abstractly Through Interfaces**

- Declare and use List and ArrayList instances

- Understanding Lambda Expressions

When we covered the Java APIs in the previous chapter, we didn't cover the ones that use lambda syntax. This chapter remedies that! You'll learn what a lambda is used for, about common functional interfaces, how to write a lambda with variables, and the APIs on the exam that rely on lambdas.

Writing Simple Lambdas

Java is an object-oriented language at heart. You've seen plenty of objects by now. In Java 8, the language added the ability to write code using another style.

Functional programming is a way of writing code more declaratively. You specify what you want to do rather than dealing with the state of objects. You focus more on expressions than loops.

Functional programming uses lambda expressions to write code. A *lambda expression* is a block of code that gets passed around. You can think of a lambda expression as an unnamed method. It has parameters and a body just like full-fledged methods do, but it doesn't have a name like a real method. Lambda expressions are often referred to as *lambdas* for short. You might also know them as closures if Java isn't your first language. If you had a bad experience with closures in the past, don't worry. They are far simpler in Java.

In other words, a lambda expression is like a method that you can pass as if it were a variable. For example, there are different ways to calculate age. One human year is equivalent to seven dog years. You want to write a method that takes an age() method as input. To do this in an object-oriented program, you'd need to define a Human subclass and a Dog subclass. With lambdas, you can just pass in the relevant expression to calculate age.

Lambdas allow you to write powerful code in Java. Only the simplest lambda expressions are on this exam. The goal is to get you comfortable with the syntax and the concepts. You'll see lambdas again on the 1Z0-816 exam.

In this section, we'll cover an example of why lambdas are helpful and the syntax of lambdas.

Lambda Example

Our goal is to print out all the animals in a list according to some criteria. We'll show you how to do this without lambdas to illustrate how lambdas are useful. We start out with the Animal class:

```
public class Animal {
   private String species;
   private boolean canHop;
   private boolean canSwim;
   public Animal(String speciesName, boolean hopper, boolean swimmer){
      species = speciesName;
      canHop = hopper;
      canSwim = swimmer;
   }
   public boolean canHop() { return canHop; }
   public boolean canSwim() { return canSwim; }
   public String toString() { return species; }
}
```

The Animal class has three instance variables, which are set in the constructor. It has two methods that get the state of whether the animal can hop or swim. It also has a toString() method so we can easily identify the Animal in programs.

We plan to write a lot of different checks, so we want an interface. You'll learn more about interfaces in Chapter 9, "Advanced Class Design." For now, it is enough to remember that an interface specifies the methods that our class needs to implement:

```
public interface CheckTrait {
   boolean test(Animal a);
}
```

The first thing we want to check is whether the Animal can hop. We provide a class that can check this:

```
public class CheckIfHopper implements CheckTrait {
   public boolean test(Animal a) {
      return a.canHop();
   }
}
```

This class may seem simple—and it is. This is actually part of the problem that lambdas solve. Just bear with us for a bit. Now we have everything that we need to write our code to find the Animals that hop:

```
1:  import java.util.*;
2:  public class TraditionalSearch {
3:     public static void main(String[] args) {
4:
```

```
 5:        // list of animals
 6:        List<Animal> animals = new ArrayList<Animal>();
 7:        animals.add(new Animal("fish", false, true));
 8:        animals.add(new Animal("kangaroo", true, false));
 9:        animals.add(new Animal("rabbit", true, false));
10:        animals.add(new Animal("turtle", false, true));
11:
12:        // pass class that does check
13:        print(animals, new CheckIfHopper());
14:    }
15:    private static void print(List<Animal> animals,
16:        CheckTrait checker) {
17:        for (Animal animal : animals) {
18:
19:            // the general check
20:            if (checker.test(animal))
21:                System.out.print(animal + " ");
22:        }
23:        System.out.println();
24:    }
25: }
```

The print() method on line 13 method is very general—it can check for any trait. This is good design. It shouldn't need to know what specifically we are searching for in order to print a list of animals.

Now what happens if we want to print the Animals that swim? Sigh. We need to write another class, CheckIfSwims. Granted, it is only a few lines. Then we need to add a new line under line 13 that instantiates that class. That's two things just to do another check.

Why can't we just specify the logic we care about right here? Turns out that we can with lambda expressions. We could repeat that whole class here and make you find the one line that changed. Instead, we'll just show you. We could replace line 13 with the following, which uses a lambda:

```
13:    print(animals, a -> a.canHop());
```

Don't worry that the syntax looks a little funky. You'll get used to it, and we'll describe it in the next section. We'll also explain the bits that look like magic. For now, just focus on how easy it is to read. We are telling Java that we only care about Animals that can hop.

It doesn't take much imagination to figure out how we would add logic to get the Animals that can swim. We only have to add one line of code—no need for an extra class to do something simple. Here's that other line:

```
print(animals, a -> a.canSwim());
```

How about Animals that cannot swim?

```
print(animals, a -> ! a.canSwim());
```

The point here is that it is really easy to write code that uses lambdas once you get the basics in place. This code uses a concept called deferred execution. *Deferred execution* means that code is specified now but will run later. In this case, later is when the print() method calls it.

Lambda Syntax

One of the simplest lambda expressions you can write is the one you just saw:

```
a -> a.canHop()
```

Lambdas work with interfaces that have only one abstract method. In this case, Java looks at the CheckTrait interface that has one method. The lambda indicates that Java should call a method with an Animal parameter that returns a boolean value that's the result of a.canHop(). We know all this because we wrote the code. But how does Java know?

Java relies on context when figuring out what lambda expressions mean. We are passing this lambda as the second parameter of the print() method. That method expects a CheckTrait as the second parameter. Since we are passing a lambda instead, Java tries to map our lambda to that interface:

```
boolean test(Animal a);
```

Since that interface's method takes an Animal, that means the lambda parameter has to be an Animal. And since that interface's method returns a boolean, we know the lambda returns a boolean.

The syntax of lambdas is tricky because many parts are optional. These two lines do the exact same thing:

```
a -> a.canHop()
```

```
(Animal a) -> { return a.canHop(); }
```

Let's look at what is going on here. The first example, shown in Figure 6.1, has three parts:

- A single parameter specified with the name a
- The arrow operator to separate the parameter and body
- A body that calls a single method and returns the result of that method

FIGURE 6.1   Lambda syntax omitting optional parts

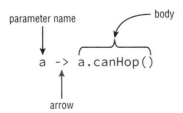

The second example shows the most verbose form of a lambda that returns a `boolean` (see Figure 6.2):

- A single parameter specified with the name a and stating the type is `Animal`
- The arrow operator to separate the parameter and body
- A body that has one or more lines of code, including a semicolon and a `return` statement

FIGURE 6.2   Lambda syntax, including optional parts

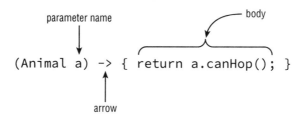

The parentheses can be omitted only if there is a single parameter and its type is not explicitly stated. Java does this because developers commonly use lambda expressions this way and they can do as little typing as possible.

It shouldn't be news to you that we can omit braces when we have only a single statement. We did this with `if` statements and loops already. What is different here is that the rules change when you omit the braces. Java doesn't require you to type `return` or use a semicolon when no braces are used. This special shortcut doesn't work when we have two or more statements. At least this is consistent with using {} to create blocks of code elsewhere.

    Here's a fun fact: s -> {} is a valid lambda. If there is no code on the right side of the expression, you don't need the semicolon or `return` statement.

Table 6.1 shows examples of valid lambdas that return a `boolean`.

TABLE 6.1   Valid lambdas

Lambda	# parameters
() -> true	0
a -> a.startsWith("test")	1
(String a) -> a.startsWith("test")	1
(a, b) -> a.startsWith("test")	2
(String a, String b) -> a.startsWith("test")	2

Notice that all of these examples have parentheses around the parameter list except the one that takes only one parameter and doesn't specify the type. The first row takes zero parameters and always returns the boolean value true. The second row takes one parameter and calls a method on it, returning the result. The third row does the same except that it explicitly defines the type of the variable. The final two rows take two parameters and ignore one of them—there isn't a rule that says you must use all defined parameters.

Now let's make sure you can identify invalid syntax for each row in Table 6.2 where each is supposed to return a boolean. Make sure you understand what's wrong with each of these.

TABLE 6.2   Invalid lambdas that return boolean

Invalid lambda	Reason
`a, b -> a.startsWith("test")`	Missing parentheses
`a -> { a.startsWith("test"); }`	Missing return
`a -> { return a.startsWith("test") }`	Missing semicolon

Remember that the parentheses are optional *only* when there is one parameter and it doesn't have a type declared.

Introducing Functional Interfaces

In our earlier example, we created an interface with one method:

```
boolean test(Animal a);
```

Lambdas work with interfaces that have only one abstract method. These are called *functional interfaces*. (It's actually more complicated than this, but for this exam the simplified definition is fine. On the 1Z0-816 exam, you'll get to deal with the full definition of a functional interface.)

We mentioned that a functional interface has only one abstract method. Your friend Sam can help you remember this because it is officially known as a *Single Abstract Method (SAM)* rule.

Java provides an annotation @FunctionalInterface on some, but not all, functional interfaces. This annotation means the authors of the interface promise it will be safe to use in a lambda in the future. However, just because you don't see the annotation doesn't mean it's not a functional interface. Remember that having exactly one abstract method is what makes it a functional interface, not the annotation.

There are four functional interfaces you are likely to see on the exam. The next sections take a look at Predicate, Consumer, Supplier, and Comparator.

Predicate

You can imagine that we'd have to create lots of interfaces like this to use lambdas. We want to test Animals and Strings and Plants and anything else that we come across.

Luckily, Java recognizes that this is a common problem and provides such an interface for us. It's in the package java.util.function and the gist of it is as follows:

```
public interface Predicate<T> {
   boolean test(T t);
}
```

That looks a lot like our test(Animal) method. The only difference is that it uses the type T instead of Animal. That's the syntax for generics. It's like when we created an ArrayList and got to specify any type that goes in it.

This means we don't need our own interface anymore and can put everything related to our search in one class:

```
1:   import java.util.*;
2:   import java.util.function.*;
3:   public class PredicateSearch {
4:      public static void main(String[] args) {
5:         List<Animal> animals = new ArrayList<Animal>();
6:         animals.add(new Animal("fish", false, true));
7:
8:         print(animals, a -> a.canHop());
9:      }
10:     private static void print(List<Animal> animals,
11:        Predicate<Animal>  checker) {
12:        for (Animal animal : animals) {
13:           if (checker.test(animal))
14:              System.out.print(animal + " ");
15:        }
16:        System.out.println();
17:     }
18: }
```

This time, line 11 is the only one that changed. We expect to have a Predicate passed in that uses type Animal. Pretty cool. We can just use it without having to write extra code.

Consumer

The Consumer functional interface has one method you need to know:

```
void accept(T t)
```

Why might you want to receive a value and not return it? A common reason is when printing a message:

```
Consumer<String> consumer = x -> System.out.println(x);
```

We've declared functionality to print out the value we were given. It's okay that we don't have a value yet. When the consumer is called, the value will be provided and printed then. Let's take a look at code that uses a Consumer:

```
public static void main(String[] args) {
   Consumer<String> consumer = x -> System.out.println(x);
   print(consumer, "Hello World");
}
private static void print(Consumer<String> consumer, String value) {
   consumer.accept(value);
}
```

This code prints Hello World. It's a more complicated version than the one you learned as your first program. The print() method accepts a Consumer that knows how to print a value. When the accept() method is called, the lambda actually runs, printing the value.

Supplier

The Supplier functional interface has only one method:

```
T get()
```

A good use case for a Supplier is when generating values. Here are two examples:

```
Supplier<Integer> number = () ->  42;
Supplier<Integer> random = () ->  new Random().nextInt();
```

The first example returns 42 each time the lambda is called. The second generates a random number each time it is called. It could be the same number but is likely to be a different one. After all, it's random. Let's take a look at code that uses a Supplier:

```
public static void main(String[] args) {
   Supplier<Integer> number = () ->  42;
   System.out.println(returnNumber(number));
}

private static int returnNumber(Supplier<Integer> supplier) {
   return supplier.get();
}
```

When the returnNumber() method is called, it invokes the lambda to get the desired value. In this case, the method returns 42.

Comparator

In Chapter 5, "Core Java APIs," we compared numbers. We didn't supply a Comparator because we were using the default sort order. We did learn the rules. A negative number means the first value is smaller, zero means they are equal, and a positive number means the first value is bigger. The method signature is as follows:

```
int compare(T o1, T o2)
```

This interface is a functional interface since it has only one unimplemented method. It has many static and default methods to facilitate writing complex comparators.

> The Comparator interface existed prior to lambdas being added to Java. As a result, it is in a different package. You can find Comparator in java.util.

You only have to know compare() for the exam. Can you figure out whether this sorts in ascending or descending order?

```
Comparator<Integer> ints = (i1, i2) -> i1 - i2;
```

The ints comparator uses natural sort order. If the first number is bigger, it will return a positive number. Try it. Suppose we are comparing 5 and 3. The comparator subtracts 5-3 and gets 2. This is a positive number that means the first number is bigger and we are sorting in ascending order.

Let's try another one. Do you think these two statements would sort in ascending or descending order?

```
Comparator<String> strings = (s1, s2) -> s2.compareTo(s1);
Comparator<String> moreStrings = (s1, s2) -> - s1.compareTo(s2);
```

Both of these comparators actually do the same thing: sort in descending order. In the first example, the call to compareTo() is "backwards," making it descending. In the second example, the call uses the default order; however, it applies a negative sign to the result, which reverses it.

Be sure you understand Table 6.3 to identify what type of lambda you are looking at.

TABLE 6.3 Basic functional interfaces

Functional interface	# parameters	Return type
Comparator	Two	int
Consumer	One	void
Predicate	One	boolean
Supplier	None	One (type varies)

Working with Variables in Lambdas

Variables can appear in three places with respect to lambdas: the parameter list, local variables declared inside the lambda body, and variables referenced from the lambda body. All three of these are opportunities for the exam to trick you. We will explore each one so you'll be alert when tricks show up!

Parameter List

Earlier in this chapter, you learned that specifying the type of parameters is optional. Additionally, var can be used in place of the specific type. That means that all three of these statements are interchangeable:

```
Predicate<String> p = x -> true;
Predicate<String> p = (var x) -> true;
Predicate<String> p = (String x) -> true;
```

The exam might ask you to identify the type of the lambda parameter. In our example, the answer is String. How did we figure that out? A lambda infers the types from the surrounding context. That means you get to do the same.

In this case, the lambda is being assigned to a Predicate that takes a String. Another place to look for the type is in a method signature. Let's try another example. Can you figure out the type of x?

```
public void whatAmI() {
   consume((var x) -> System.out.print(x), 123);
}
public void consume(Consumer<Integer> c, int num) {
   c.accept(num);
}
```

If you guessed Integer, you were right. The whatAmI() method creates a lambda to be passed to the consume() method. Since the consume() method expects an Integer as the generic, we know that is what the inferred type of x will be.

But wait; there's more. In some cases, you can determine the type without even seeing the method signature. What do you think the type of x is here?

```
   public void counts(List<Integer> list) {
      list.sort((var x, var y) -> x.compareTo(y));
   }
```

The answer is again Integer. Since we are sorting a list, we can use the type of the list to determine the type of the lambda parameter.

Local Variables inside the Lambda Body

While it is most common for a lambda body to be a single expression, it is legal to define a block. That block can have anything that is valid in a normal Java block, including local variable declarations.

The following code does just that. It creates a local variable named c that is scoped to the lambda block.

```
(a, b) -> { int c = 0; return 5;}
```

When writing your own code, a lambda block with a local variable is a good hint that you should extract that code into a method.

Now let's try another one. Do you see what's wrong here?

```
(a, b) -> { int a = 0; return 5;}      // DOES NOT COMPILE
```

We tried to redeclare a, which is not allowed. Java doesn't let you create a local variable with the same name as one already declared in that scope. Now let's try a hard one. How many syntax errors do you see in this method?

```
11: public void variables(int a) {
12:    int b = 1;
13:    Predicate<Integer> p1 = a -> {
14:       int b = 0;
15:       int c = 0;
16:       return b == c;}
17: }
```

There are three syntax errors. The first is on line 13. The variable a was already used in this scope as a method parameter, so it cannot be reused. The next syntax error comes on line 14 where the code attempts to redeclare local variable b. The third syntax error is quite subtle and on line 16. See it? Look really closely.

The variable p1 is missing a semicolon at the end. There is a semicolon before the }, but that is inside the block. While you don't normally have to look for missing semicolons, lambdas are tricky in this space, so beware!

Variables Referenced from the Lambda Body

Lambda bodies are allowed to reference some variables from the surrounding code. The following code is legal:

```
public class Crow {
   private String color;
   public void caw(String name) {
      String volume = "loudly";
      Consumer<String> consumer = s ->
          System.out.println(name + " says "
              + volume + " that she is " + color);
   }
}
```

This shows that lambda can access an instance variable, method parameter, or local variable under certain conditions. Instance variables (and class variables) are always allowed.

Method parameters and local variables are allowed to be referenced if they are *effectively final*. This means that the value of a variable doesn't change after it is set, regardless of whether it is explicitly marked as final. If you aren't sure whether a variable is effectively final, add the final keyword. If the code would still compile, the variable is effectively final. You can think of it as if we had written this:

```
public class Crow {
    private String color;
    public void caw(final String name) {
        final String volume = "loudly";
        Consumer<String> consumer = s ->
            System.out.println(name + " says "
                + volume + " that she is " + color);
    }
}
```

It gets even more interesting when you look at where the compiler errors occur when the variables are not effectively final.

```
2:  public class Crow {
3:      private String color;
4:      public void caw(String name) {
5:          String volume = "loudly";
6:          name = "Caty";
7:          color = "black";
8:
9:          Consumer<String> consumer = s ->
10:             System.out.println(name + " says "
11:                 + volume + " that she is " + color);
12:         volume = "softly";
13:     }
14: }
```

In this example, name is not effectively final because it is set on line 6. However, the compiler error occurs on line 10. It's not a problem to assign a value to a nonfinal variable. However, once the lambda tries to use it, we do have a problem. The variable is no longer effectively final, so the lambda is not allowed to use the variable.

The variable volume is not effectively final either since it is updated on line 12. In this case, the compiler error is on line 11. That's before the assignment! Again, the act of assigning a value is only a problem from the point of view of the lambda. Therefore, the lambda has to be the one to generate the compiler error.

To review, make sure you've memorized Table 6.4.

TABLE 6.4 Rules for accessing a variable from a lambda body inside a method

Variable type	Rule
Instance variable	Allowed
Static variable	Allowed
Local variable	Allowed if effectively final
Method parameter	Allowed if effectively final
Lambda parameter	Allowed

Calling APIs with Lambdas

Now that you are familiar with lambdas and functional interfaces, we can look at the most common methods that use them on the exam. The 1Z0-816 will cover streams and many more APIs that use lambdas.

removeIf()

List and Set declare a removeIf() method that takes a Predicate. Imagine we have a list of names for pet bunnies. We decide we want to remove all of the bunny names that don't begin with the letter h because our little cousin really wants us to choose an h name. We could solve this problem by writing a loop. Or we could solve it in one line:

```
3: List<String> bunnies = new ArrayList<>();
4: bunnies.add("long ear");
5: bunnies.add("floppy");
6: bunnies.add("hoppy");
7: System.out.println(bunnies);      // [long ear, floppy, hoppy]
8: bunnies.removeIf(s -> s.charAt(0) != 'h');
9: System.out.println(bunnies);      // [hoppy]
```

Line 8 takes care of everything for us. It defines a predicate that takes a String and returns a boolean. The removeIf() method does the rest.

The removeIf() method works the same way on a Set. It removes any values in the set that match the Predicate. There isn't a removeIf() method on a Map. Remember that maps have both keys and values. It wouldn't be clear what one was removing!

sort()

While you can call `Collections.sort(list)`, you can now sort directly on the list object.

```
3: List<String> bunnies = new ArrayList<>();
4: bunnies.add("long ear");
5: bunnies.add("floppy");
6: bunnies.add("hoppy");
7: System.out.println(bunnies);     // [long ear, floppy, hoppy]
8: bunnies.sort((b1, b2) -> b1.compareTo(b2));
9: System.out.println(bunnies);     // [floppy, hoppy, long ear]
```

On line 8, we sort the list alphabetically. The `sort()` method takes `Comparator` that provides the sort order. Remember that `Comparator` takes two parameters and returns an `int`. If you need a review of what the return value of a `compare()` operation means, check the `Comparator` section in this chapter or the Comparing section in Chapter 5. This is really important to memorize!

There is not a sort method on `Set` or `Map`. Neither of those types has indexing, so it wouldn't make sense to sort them.

forEach()

Our final method is `forEach()`. It takes a `Consumer` and calls that lambda for each element encountered.

```
3: List<String> bunnies = new ArrayList<>();
4: bunnies.add("long ear");
5: bunnies.add("floppy");
6: bunnies.add("hoppy");
7:
8: bunnies.forEach(b -> System.out.println(b));
9: System.out.println(bunnies);
```

This code prints the following:

```
long ear
floppy
hoppy
[long ear, floppy, hoppy]
```

The method on line 8 prints one entry per line. The method on line 9 prints the entire list on one line.

We can use `forEach()` with a `Set` or `Map`. For a `Set`, it works the same way as a `List`.

```
Set<String> bunnies = Set.of("long ear", "floppy", "hoppy");
bunnies.forEach(b -> System.out.println(b));
```

For a Map, you have to choose whether you want to go through the keys or values:

```
Map<String, Integer> bunnies =  new HashMap<>();
bunnies.put("long ear", 3);
bunnies.put("floppy", 8);
bunnies.put("hoppy", 1);
bunnies.keySet().forEach(b -> System.out.println(b));
bunnies.values().forEach(b -> System.out.println(b));
```

It turns out the keySet() and values() methods each return a Set. Since we know how to use forEach() with a Set, this is easy!

 Real World Scenario

Using *forEach()* with a Map Directly

You don't need to know this for the exam, but Java has a functional interface called BiConsumer. It works just like Consumer except it can take two parameters. This functional interface allows you to use forEach() with key/value pairs from Map.

```
Map<String, Integer> bunnies = new HashMap<>();
bunnies.put("long ear", 3);
bunnies.put("floppy", 8);
bunnies.put("hoppy", 1);
bunnies.forEach((k, v) -> System.out.println(k + " " + v));
```

Summary

Lambda expressions, or lambdas, allow passing around blocks of code. The full syntax looks like this:

```
(String a, String b) -> { return a.equals(b); }
```

The parameter types can be omitted. When only one parameter is specified without a type the parentheses can also be omitted. The braces and return statement can be omitted for a single statement, making the short form as follows:

```
a -> a.equals(b)
```

Lambdas are passed to a method expecting an instance of a functional interface.

A functional interface is one with a single abstract method. Predicate is a common interface that returns a boolean and takes any type. Consumer takes any type and doesn't return a value. Supplier returns a value and does not take any parameters. Comparator takes two parameters and returns an int.

A lambda can define parameters or variables in the body as long as their names are different from existing local variables. The body of a lambda is allowed to use any instance or class variables. Additionally, it can use any local variables or method parameters that are effectively final.

We covered three common APIs that use lambdas. The removeIf() method on a List and a Set takes a Predicate. The sort() method on a List interface takes a Comparator. The forEach() methods on a List and a Set interface both take a Consumer.

Exam Essentials

Write simple lambda expressions. Look for the presence or absence of optional elements in lambda code. Parameter types are optional. Braces and the return keyword are optional when the body is a single statement. Parentheses are optional when only one parameter is specified and the type is implicit.

Identify common functional interfaces. From a code snippet, identify whether the lambda is a Comparator, Consumer, Predicate, or Supplier. You can use the number of parameters and return type to tell them apart.

Determine whether a variable can be used in a lambda body. Local variables and method parameters must be effectively final to be referenced. This means the code must compile if you were to add the final keyword to these variables. Instance and class variables are always allowed.

Use common APIs with lambdas. Be able to read and write code using forEach(), removeIf(), and sort().

Review Questions

The answers to the chapter review questions can be found in the Appendix.

1. What is the result of the following class?

```
1:   import java.util.function.*;
2:
3:   public class Panda {
4:       int age;
5:       public static void main(String[] args) {
6:           Panda p1 = new Panda();
7:           p1.age = 1;
8:           check(p1, p -> p.age < 5);
9:       }
10:      private static void check(Panda panda,
11:          Predicate<Panda> pred) {
12:          String result =
13:              pred.test(panda) ? "match" : "not match";
14:          System.out.print(result);
15: } }
```

   A. match
   B. not match
   C. Compiler error on line 8.
   D. Compiler error on lines 10 and 11.
   E. Compiler error on lines 12 and 13.
   F. A runtime exception is thrown.

2. What is the result of the following code?

```
1:   interface Climb {
2:       boolean isTooHigh(int height, int limit);
3:   }
4:
5:   public class Climber {
6:       public static void main(String[] args) {
7:           check((h, m) -> h.append(m).isEmpty(), 5);
8:       }
9:       private static void check(Climb climb, int height) {
10:          if (climb.isTooHigh(height, 10))
11:              System.out.println("too high");
12:          else
```

```
13:          System.out.println("ok");
14:     }
15: }
```

A. `ok`

B. `too high`

C. Compiler error on line 7.

D. Compiler error on line 10.

E. Compiler error on a different line.

F. A runtime exception is thrown.

3. Which of the following lambda expressions can fill in the blank? (Choose all that apply.)

```
List<String> list = new ArrayList<>();
list.removeIf(_____);
```

A. `s -> s.isEmpty()`

B. `s -> {s.isEmpty()}`

C. `s -> {s.isEmpty();}`

D. `s -> {return s.isEmpty();}`

E. `String s -> s.isEmpty()`

F. `(String s) -> s.isEmpty()`

4. Which lambda can replace the `MySecret` class to return the same value? (Choose all that apply.)

```
interface Secret {
   String magic(double d);
}

class MySecret implements Secret {
   public String magic(double d) {
      return "Poof";
   }
}
```

A. `(e) -> "Poof"`

B. `(e) -> {"Poof"}`

C. `(e) -> { String e = ""; "Poof" }`

D. `(e) -> { String e = ""; return "Poof"; }`

E. `(e) -> { String e = ""; return "Poof" }`

F. `(e) -> { String f = ""; return "Poof"; }`

5. Which of the following lambda expressions can be passed to a function of Predicate<String> type? (Choose all that apply.)

   A. `() -> s.isEmpty()`

   B. `s -> s.isEmpty()`

   C. `String s -> s.isEmpty()`

   D. `(String s) -> s.isEmpty()`

   E. `(s1) -> s.isEmpty()`

   F. `(s1, s2) -> s1.isEmpty()`

6. Which of these statements is true about the following code?

```java
public void method() {
    x((var x) -> {}, (var x, var y) -> 0);
}
public void x(Consumer<String> x, Comparator<Boolean> y) {
}
```

   A. The code does not compile because of one of the variables named x.

   B. The code does not compile because of one of the variables named y.

   C. The code does not compile for another reason.

   D. The code compiles, and the var in each lambda refers to the same type.

   E. The code compiles, and the var in each lambda refers to a different type.

7. Which of the following will compile when filling in the blank? (Choose all that apply.)

```java
List list = List.of(1, 2, 3);
Set set = Set.of(1, 2, 3);
Map map = Map.of(1, 2, 3, 4);

_____.forEach(x -> System.out.println(x));
```

   A. `list`

   B. `set`

   C. `map`

   D. `map.keys()`

   E. `map.keySet()`

   F. `map.values()`

   G. `map.valueSet()`

8. Which statements are true?

   A. The Consumer interface is best for printing out an existing value.

   B. The Supplier interface is best for printing out an existing value.

   C. The Comparator interface returns an int.

   D. The Predicate interface returns an int.

E. The `Comparator` interface has a method named `test()`.

F. The `Predicate` interface has a method named `test()`.

9. Which of the following can be inserted without causing a compilation error? (Choose all that apply.)

```
public void remove(List<Character> chars) {
    char end = 'z';
    chars.removeIf(c -> {
        char start = 'a'; return start <= c && c <= end; });
    // INSERT LINE HERE
}
```

A. `char start = 'a';`

B. `char c = 'x';`

C. `chars = null;`

D. `end = '1';`

E. None of the above

10. How many lines does this code output?

```
Set<String> set = Set.of("mickey", "minnie");
List<String> list = new ArrayList<>(set);

set.forEach(s -> System.out.println(s));
list.forEach(s -> System.out.println(s));
```

A. 0

B. 2

C. 4

D. The code does not compile.

E. A runtime exception is thrown.

11. What is the output of the following code?

```
List<String> cats = new ArrayList<>();
cats.add("leo");
cats.add("Olivia");

cats.sort((c1, c2) -> -c1.compareTo(c2)); // line X
System.out.println(cats);
```

A. `[leo, Olivia]`

B. `[Olivia, leo]`

C. The code does not compile because of line X.

D. The code does not compile for another reason.

E. A runtime exception is thrown.

12. Which pieces of code can fill in the blanks? (Choose all that apply.)

```
_____ first = () -> Set.of(1.23);
_____ second = x -> true;
```

A. Consumer<Set<Double>>

B. Consumer<Set<Float>>

C. Predicate<Set<Double>>

D. Predicate<Set<Float>>

E. Supplier<Set<Double>>

F. Supplier<Set<Float>>

13. Which is true of the following code?

```
int length = 3;

for (int i = 0; i<3; i++) {
   if (i%2 == 0) {
      Supplier<Integer> supplier = () -> length; // A
      System.out.println(supplier.get());        // B
   } else {
      int j = i;
      Supplier<Integer> supplier = () -> j;       // C
      System.out.println(supplier.get());         // D
   }
}
```

A. The first compiler error is on line A.

B. The first compiler error is on line B.

C. The first compiler error is on line C.

D. The first compiler error is on line D.

E. The code compiles successfully.

14. Which of the following can be inserted without causing a compilation error? (Choose all that apply.)

```
public void remove(List<Character> chars) {
   char end = 'z';
   // INSERT LINE HERE
   chars.removeIf(c -> {
      char start = 'a'; return start <= c && c <= end; });
}
```

A. char start = 'a';

B. char c = 'x';

C. `chars = null;`

D. `end = '1';`

E. None of the above

15. What is the output of the following code?

```
Set<String> cats = new HashSet<>();
cats.add("leo");
cats.add("Olivia");

cats.sort((c1, c2) -> -c1.compareTo(c2)); // line X
System.out.println(cats);
```

A. `[leo, Olivia]`

B. `[Olivia, leo]`

C. The code does not compile because of line X.

D. The code does not compile for another reason.

E. A runtime exception is thrown.

16. Which variables are effectively final? (Choose all that apply.)

```
public void isIt(String param1, String param2) {
    String local1 = param1 + param2;
    String local2 = param1 + param2;

    param1 = null;
    local2 = null;
}
```

A. `local1`

B. `local2`

C. `param1`

D. `param2`

E. None of the above

17. What is the result of the following class?

```
1:  import java.util.function.*;
2:
3:  public class Panda {
4:      int age;
5:      public static void main(String[] args) {
6:          Panda p1 = new Panda();
7:          p1.age = 1;
8:          check(p1, p -> {p.age < 5});
9:      }
```

```
10:     private static void check(Panda panda,
11:         Predicate<Panda> pred) {
12:         String result = pred.test(panda)
13:             ? "match" : "not match";
14:         System.out.print(result);
15: } }
```

A. match

B. not match

C. Compiler error on line 8.

D. Compiler error on line 10.

E. Compile error on line 12.

F. A runtime exception is thrown.

18. How many lines does this code output?

```
Set<String> s = Set.of("mickey", "minnie");
List<String> x = new ArrayList<>(s);

s.forEach(s -> System.out.println(s));
x.forEach(x -> System.out.println(x));
```

A. 0

B. 2

C. 4

D. The code does not compile.

E. A runtime exception is thrown.

19. Which lambda can replace the MySecret class? (Choose all that apply.)

```
interface Secret {
    String concat(String a, String b);
}

class MySecret implements Secret {
    public String concat(String a, String b) {
        return a + b;
    }
}
```

A. (a, b) -> a + b

B. (String a, b) -> a + b

C. (String a, String b) -> a + b

  D. `(a, b) , a + b`

  E. `(String a, b) , a + b`

  F. `(String a, String b) , a + b`

20. Which of the following lambda expressions can be passed to a function of `Predicate<String>` type? (Choose all that apply.)

  A. `s -> s.isEmpty()`

  B. `s --> s.isEmpty()`

  C. `(String s) -> s.isEmpty()`

  D. `(String s) --> s.isEmpty()`

  E. `(StringBuilder s) -> s.isEmpty()`

  F. `(StringBuilder s) --> s.isEmpty()`

Chapter

7

Methods and Encapsulation

OCP EXAM OBJECTIVES COVERED IN THIS CHAPTER:

✓ **Creating and Using Methods**

- Create methods and constructors with arguments and return values

- Create and invoke overloaded methods

- Apply the static keyword to methods and fields

✓ **Applying Encapsulation**

- Apply access modifiers

- Apply encapsulation principles to a class

In previous chapters, you learned how to use methods without examining them in detail. In this chapter, you'll explore methods in depth, including overloading. This chapter discusses instance variables, access modifiers, and encapsulation.

Designing Methods

Every interesting Java program we've seen has had a main() method. You can write other methods, too. For example, you can write a basic method to take a nap, as shown in Figure 7.1.

FIGURE 7.1 Method declaration

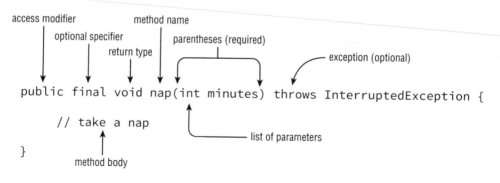

This is called a *method declaration*, which specifies all the information needed to call the method. There are a lot of parts, and we'll cover each one in more detail. Two of the parts—the method name and parameter list—are called the *method signature*.

Table 7.1 is a brief reference to the elements of a method declaration. Don't worry if it seems like a lot of information—by the time you finish this chapter, it will all fit together.

TABLE 7.1 Parts of a method declaration

Element	Value in nap() example	Required?
Access modifier	public	No
Optional specifier	final	No

Element	Value in nap() example	Required?
Return type	`void`	Yes
Method name	`nap`	Yes
Parameter list	`(int minutes)`	Yes, but can be empty parentheses
Optional exception list	`throws InterruptedException`	No

Method body*	`{`
	`  // take a nap`
	`}`
		Yes, but can be empty braces

* Body omitted for abstract methods, which we will cover in the later in the book.

To call this method, just type its name, followed by a single `int` value in parentheses:

`nap(10);`

Let's start by taking a look at each of these parts of a basic method.

Access Modifiers

Java offers four choices of access modifier:

private   The `private` modifier means the method can be called only from within the same class.

Default (Package-Private) Access   With default access, the method can be called only from classes in the same package. This one is tricky because there is no keyword for default access. You simply omit the access modifier.

protected   The `protected` modifier means the method can be called only from classes in the same package or subclasses. You'll learn about subclasses in Chapter 8, "Class Design."

public   The `public` modifier means the method can be called from any class.

There's a `default` keyword in Java. You saw it in the `switch` statement in Chapter 4, "Making Decisions," and you'll see it again in the Chapter 9, "Advanced Class Design," when I discuss interfaces. It's not used for access control.

We'll explore the impact of the various access modifiers later in this chapter. For now, just master identifying valid syntax of methods. The exam creators like to trick you by putting method elements in the wrong order or using incorrect values.

We'll see practice examples as we go through each of the method elements in this section. Make sure you understand why each of these is a valid or invalid method declaration. Pay attention to the access modifiers as you figure out what is wrong with the ones that don't compile when inserted into a class:

```
public void walk1() {}
default void walk2() {} // DOES NOT COMPILE
void public walk3() {}  // DOES NOT COMPILE
void walk4() {}
```

The walk1() method is a valid declaration with public access. The walk4() method is a valid declaration with default access. The walk2() method doesn't compile because default is not a valid access modifier. The walk3() method doesn't compile because the access modifier is specified after the return type.

Optional Specifiers

There are a number of optional specifiers, but most of them aren't on the exam. Optional specifiers come from the following list. Unlike with access modifiers, you can have multiple specifiers in the same method (although not all combinations are legal). When this happens, you can specify them in any order. And since these specifiers are optional, you are allowed to not have any of them at all. This means you can have zero or more specifiers in a method declaration.

static   The static modifier is used for class methods and will be covered later in this chapter.

abstract   The abstract modifier is used when a method body is not provided. It will be covered in Chapter 9.

final   The final modifier is used when a method is not allowed to be overridden by a subclass. It will also be covered in Chapter 8.

synchronized   The synchronized modifier is used with multithreaded code. It is on the 1Z0-816 exam, but not the 1Z0-815 exam.

native   The native modifier is used when interacting with code written in another language such as C++. It is not on either OCP 11 exam.

strictfp   The strictfp modifier is used for making floating-point calculations portable. It is not on either OCP 11 exam.

Again, just focus on syntax for now. Do you see why these compile or don't compile?

```
public void walk1() {}
public final void walk2() {}
public static final void walk3() {}
public final static void walk4() {}
public modifier void walk5() {}       // DOES NOT COMPILE
public void final walk6() {}          // DOES NOT COMPILE
final public void walk7() {}
```

The walk1() method is a valid declaration with no optional specifier. This is okay—it is optional after all. The walk2() method is a valid declaration, with final as the optional specifier. The walk3() and walk4() methods are valid declarations with both final and static as optional specifiers. The order of these two keywords doesn't matter. The walk5() method doesn't compile because modifier is not a valid optional specifier. The walk6() method doesn't compile because the optional specifier is after the return type.

The walk7() method does compile. Java allows the optional specifiers to appear before the access modifier. This is a weird case and not one you need to know for the exam. We are mentioning it so you don't get confused when practicing.

Return Type

The next item in a method declaration is the return type. The return type might be an actual Java type such as String or int. If there is no return type, the void keyword is used. This special return type comes from the English language: *void* means without contents. In Java, there is no type there.

 Remember that a method must have a return type. If no value is returned, the return type is void. You cannot omit the return type.

When checking return types, you also have to look inside the method body. Methods with a return type other than void are required to have a return statement inside the method body. This return statement must include the primitive or object to be returned. Methods that have a return type of void are permitted to have a return statement with no value returned or omit the return statement entirely.

Ready for some examples? Can you explain why these methods compile or don't?

```
public void walk1() {}
public void walk2() { return; }
public String walk3() { return ""; }
public String walk4() {}                   // DOES NOT COMPILE
public walk5() {}                          // DOES NOT COMPILE
public String int walk6() { }              // DOES NOT COMPILE
String walk7(int a) { if (a == 4) return ""; } // DOES NOT COMPILE
```

Since the return type of the walk1() method is void, the return statement is optional. The walk2() method shows the optional return statement that correctly doesn't return anything. The walk3() method is a valid declaration with a String return type and a return statement that returns a String. The walk4() method doesn't compile because the return statement is missing. The walk5() method doesn't compile because the return type is missing. The walk6() method doesn't compile because it attempts to use two return types. You get only one return type.

The walk7() method is a little tricky. There is a return statement, but it doesn't always get run. If a is 6, the return statement doesn't get executed. Since the String always needs to be returned, the compiler complains.

When returning a value, it needs to be assignable to the return type. Imagine there is a local variable of that type to which it is assigned before being returned. Can you think of how to add a line of code with a local variable in these two methods?

```java
int integer() {
   return 9;
}
int longMethod() {
   return 9L; // DOES NOT COMPILE
}
```

It is a fairly mechanical exercise. You just add a line with a local variable. The type of the local variable matches the return type of the method. Then you return that local variable instead of the value directly:

```java
int integerExpanded() {
   int temp = 9;
   return temp;
}
int longExpanded() {
   int temp = 9L; // DOES NOT COMPILE
   return temp;
}
```

This shows more clearly why you can't return a long primitive in a method that returns an int. You can't stuff that long into an int variable, so you can't return it directly either.

Method Name

Method names follow the same rules as we practiced with variable names in Chapter 2, "Java Building Blocks." To review, an identifier may only contain letters, numbers, $, or _. Also, the first character is not allowed to be a number, and reserved words are not allowed. Finally, the single underscore character is not allowed. By convention, methods begin with a lowercase letter but are not required to. Since this is a review of Chapter 2, we can jump right into practicing with some examples:

```java
public void walk1() {}
public void 2walk() {}     // DOES NOT COMPILE
public walk3 void() {}     // DOES NOT COMPILE
public void Walk_$() {}
public _() {}              // DOES NOT COMPILE
public void() {}           // DOES NOT COMPILE
```

The walk1() method is a valid declaration with a traditional name. The 2walk() method doesn't compile because identifiers are not allowed to begin with numbers. The walk3() method doesn't compile because the method name is before the return type. The Walk_$() method is a valid declaration. While it certainly isn't good practice to start a method name with a capital letter and end with punctuation, it is legal. The _ method is not allowed since it consists of a single underscore. The final line of code doesn't compile because the method name is missing.

Parameter List

Although the parameter list is required, it doesn't have to contain any parameters. This means you can just have an empty pair of parentheses after the method name, as follows:

```
void nap(){}
```

If you do have multiple parameters, you separate them with a comma. There are a couple more rules for the parameter list that you'll see when we cover varargs shortly. For now, let's practice looking at method declaration with "regular" parameters:

```
public void walk1() {}
public void walk2 {}                    // DOES NOT COMPILE
public void walk3(int a) {}
public void walk4(int a; int b) {}  // DOES NOT COMPILE
public void walk5(int a, int b) {}
```

The walk1() method is a valid declaration without any parameters. The walk2() method doesn't compile because it is missing the parentheses around the parameter list. The walk3() method is a valid declaration with one parameter. The walk4() method doesn't compile because the parameters are separated by a semicolon rather than a comma. Semicolons are for separating statements, not for parameter lists. The walk5() method is a valid declaration with two parameters.

Optional Exception List

In Java, code can indicate that something went wrong by throwing an exception. We'll cover this in Chapter 10, "Exceptions." For now, you just need to know that it is optional and where in the method declaration it goes if present. For example, InterruptedException is a type of Exception. You can list as many types of exceptions as you want in this clause separated by commas. Here's an example:

```
public void zeroExceptions() {}
public void oneException() throws IllegalArgumentException {}
public void twoExceptions() throws
   IllegalArgumentException, InterruptedException {}
```

You might be wondering what methods do with these exceptions. The calling method can throw the same exceptions or handle them. You'll learn more about this in Chapter 10.

Method Body

The final part of a method declaration is the method body (except for abstract methods and interfaces, but you don't need to know about either of those yet). A method body is simply a code block. It has braces that contain zero or more Java statements. We've spent several chapters looking at Java statements by now, so you should find it easy to figure out why these compile or don't:

```
public void walk1() {}
public void walk2()      // DOES NOT COMPILE
public void walk3(int a) { int name = 5; }
```

The walk1() method is a valid declaration with an empty method body. The walk2() method doesn't compile because it is missing the braces around the empty method body. The walk3() method is a valid declaration with one statement in the method body.

You've made it through the basics of identifying correct and incorrect method declarations. Now you can delve into more detail.

Working with Varargs

As you saw in Chapter 5, "Core Java APIs," a method may use a varargs parameter (variable argument) as if it is an array. It is a little different than an array, though. A varargs parameter must be the last element in a method's parameter list. This means you are allowed to have only one varargs parameter per method.

Can you identify why each of these does or doesn't compile? (Yes, there is a lot of practice in this chapter. You have to be really good at identifying valid and invalid methods for the exam.)

```
public void walk1(int... nums) {}
public void walk2(int start, int... nums) {}
public void walk3(int... nums, int start) {}    // DOES NOT COMPILE
public void walk4(int... start, int... nums) {} // DOES NOT COMPILE
```

The walk1() method is a valid declaration with one varargs parameter. The walk2() method is a valid declaration with one int parameter and one varargs parameter. The walk3() and walk4() methods do not compile because they have a varargs parameter in a position that is not the last one.

When calling a method with a varargs parameter, you have a choice. You can pass in an array, or you can list the elements of the array and let Java create it for you. You can even omit the varargs values in the method call and Java will create an array of length zero for you.

Finally! You get to do something other than identify whether method declarations are valid. Instead, you get to look at method calls. Can you figure out why each method call outputs what it does?

```
15: public static void walk(int start, int... nums) {
16:     System.out.println(nums.length);
17: }
18: public static void main(String[] args) {
19:     walk(1);                        // 0
20:     walk(1, 2);                     // 1
21:     walk(1, 2, 3);                  // 2
22:     walk(1, new int[] {4, 5});      // 2
23: }
```

Line 19 passes 1 as start but nothing else. This means Java creates an array of length 0 for nums. Line 20 passes 1 as start and one more value. Java converts this one value to an array of length 1. Line 21 passes 1 as start and two more values. Java converts these two values to an array of length 2. Line 22 passes 1 as start and an array of length 2 directly as nums.

You've seen that Java will create an empty array if no parameters are passed for a vararg. However, it is still possible to pass null explicitly:

```
walk(1, null);      // throws a NullPointerException in walk()
```

Since null isn't an int, Java treats it as an array reference that happens to be null. It just passes on the null array object to walk. Then the walk() method throws an exception because it tries to determine the length of null.

Accessing a varargs parameter is just like accessing an array. It uses array indexing. Here's an example:

```
16: public static void run(int... nums) {
17:     System.out.println(nums[1]);
18: }
19: public static void main(String[] args) {
20:     run(11, 22);    // 22
21: }
```

Line 20 calls a varargs method with two parameters. When the method gets called, it sees an array of size 2. Since indexes are 0 based, 22 is printed.

Applying Access Modifiers

You already saw that there are four access modifiers: `public`, `private`, `protected`, and default access. We are going to discuss them in order from most restrictive to least restrictive:

- **private:** Only accessible within the same class
- **Default (package-private) access:** `private` plus other classes in the same package
- **protected:** Default access plus child classes
- **public:** `protected` plus classes in the other packages

We will explore the impact of these four levels of access on members of a class. As you learned in Chapter 1, "Welcome to Java," a member is an instance variable or instance method.

Private Access

Private access is easy. Only code in the same class can call private methods or access private fields.

First, take a look at Figure 7.2. It shows the classes you'll use to explore private and default access. The big boxes are the names of the packages. The smaller boxes inside them are the classes in each package. You can refer back to this figure if you want to quickly see how the classes relate.

FIGURE 7.2   Classes used to show private and default access

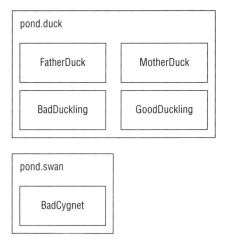

This is perfectly legal code because everything is one class:

```
1: package pond.duck;
2: public class FatherDuck {
3:    private String noise = "quack";
4:    private void quack() {
5:        System.out.println(noise);     // private access is ok
6:    }
7:    private void makeNoise() {
8:        quack();                       // private access is ok
9:    } }
```

So far, so good. FatherDuck makes a call to private method quack() on line 8 and uses private instance variable noise on line 5.

Now we add another class:

```
1: package pond.duck;
2: public class BadDuckling {
3:    public void makeNoise() {
4:        FatherDuck duck = new FatherDuck();
5:        duck.quack();                      // DOES NOT COMPILE
6:        System.out.println(duck.noise);    // DOES NOT COMPILE
7:    } }
```

BadDuckling is trying to access an instance variable and a method it has no business touching. On line 5, it tries to access a private method in another class. On line 6, it tries to access a private instance variable in another class. Both generate compiler errors. Bad duckling!

Our bad duckling is only a few days old and doesn't know better yet. Luckily, you know that accessing private members of other classes is not allowed and you need to use a different type of access.

Default (Package-Private) Access

Luckily, MotherDuck is more accommodating about what her ducklings can do. She allows classes in the same package to access her members. When there is no access modifier, Java uses the default, which is package-private access. This means that the member is "private" to classes in the same package. In other words, only classes in the package may access it.

```
package pond.duck;
public class MotherDuck {
   String noise = "quack";
   void quack() {
      System.out.println(noise);     // default access is ok
```

```
    }
    private void makeNoise() {
        quack();                        // default access is ok
    }
}
```

MotherDuck can refer to noise and call quack(). After all, members in the same class are certainly in the same package. The big difference is MotherDuck lets other classes in the same package access members (due to being package-private), whereas FatherDuck doesn't (due to being private). GoodDuckling has a much better experience than BadDuckling:

```
package pond.duck;
public class GoodDuckling {
    public void makeNoise() {
        MotherDuck duck = new MotherDuck();
        duck.quack();                               // default access
        System.out.println(duck.noise);             // default access
    }
}
```

GoodDuckling succeeds in learning to quack() and make noise by copying its mother. Notice that all the classes covered so far are in the same package pond.duck. This allows default (package-private) access to work.

In this same pond, a swan just gave birth to a baby swan. A baby swan is called a *cygnet*. The cygnet sees the ducklings learning to quack and decides to learn from MotherDuck as well.

```
package pond.swan;
import pond.duck.MotherDuck;            // import another package
public class BadCygnet {
    public void makeNoise() {
        MotherDuck duck = new MotherDuck();
        duck.quack();                       // DOES NOT COMPILE
        System.out.println(duck.noise);     // DOES NOT COMPILE
    }
}
```

Oh no! MotherDuck only allows lessons to other ducks by restricting access to the pond.duck package. Poor little BadCygnet is in the pond.swan package, and the code doesn't compile.

Remember that when there is no access modifier on a member, only classes in the same package can access the member.

Protected Access

Protected access allows everything that default (package-private) access allows and more. The protected access modifier adds the ability to access members of a parent class. We'll cover creating subclasses in depth in Chapter 8. For now, we'll cover the simplest possible use of a child class.

Figure 7.3 shows the many classes we will create in this section. There are a number of classes and packages, so don't worry about keeping them all in your head. Just check back with this figure as you go.

FIGURE 7.3   Classes used to show protected access

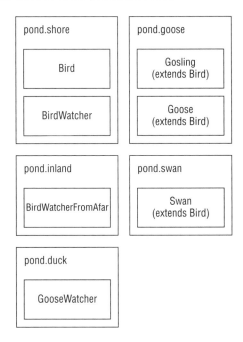

First, create a `Bird` class and give protected access to its members:

```
package pond.shore;
public class Bird {
    protected String text = "floating";          // protected access
    protected void floatInWater() {              // protected access
        System.out.println(text);
    }
}
```

Next, we create a subclass:

```
package pond.goose;
import pond.shore.Bird;          // in a different package
public class Gosling extends Bird {   // extends means create subclass
   public void swim() {
      floatInWater();            // calling protected member
      System.out.println(text);  // accessing protected member
   }
}
```

This is a simple subclass. It *extends* the Bird class. Extending means creating a subclass that has access to any protected or public members of the parent class. Running this code prints floating twice: once from calling floatInWater(), and once from the print statement in swim(). Since Gosling is a subclass of Bird, it can access these members even though it is in a different package.

Remember that protected also gives us access to everything that default access does. This means that a class in the same package as Bird can access its protected members.

```
package pond.shore;               // same package as Bird
public class BirdWatcher {
   public void watchBird() {
      Bird bird = new Bird();
      bird.floatInWater();        // calling protected member
      System.out.println(bird.text);   // accessing protected member
   }
}
```

Since Bird and BirdWatcher are in the same package, BirdWatcher can access members of the bird variable. The definition of protected allows access to subclasses and classes in the same package. This example uses the same package part of that definition.

Now let's try the same thing from a different package:

```
package pond.inland;
import pond.shore.Bird;           // different package than Bird
public class BirdWatcherFromAfar {
   public void watchBird() {
      Bird bird = new Bird();
      bird.floatInWater();        // DOES NOT COMPILE
      System.out.println(bird.text);   // DOES NOT COMPILE
   }
}
```

BirdWatcherFromAfar is not in the same package as Bird, and it doesn't inherit from Bird. This means that it is not allowed to access protected members of Bird.

Got that? Subclasses and classes in the same package are the only ones allowed to access protected members.

There is one gotcha for protected access. Consider this class:

```
1:   package pond.swan;
2:   import pond.shore.Bird;      // in different package than Bird
3:   public class Swan extends Bird {      // but subclass of Bird
4:       public void swim() {
5:           floatInWater();                // subclass access to superclass
6:           System.out.println(text);      // subclass access to superclass
7:       }
8:       public void helpOtherSwanSwim() {
9:           Swan other = new Swan();
10:          other.floatInWater();          // subclass access to superclass
11:          System.out.println(other.text); // subclass access
12:                                          // to superclass
13:      }
14:      public void helpOtherBirdSwim() {
15:          Bird other = new Bird();
16:          other.floatInWater();              // DOES NOT COMPILE
17:          System.out.println(other.text);    // DOES NOT COMPILE
18:      }
19: }
```

Take a deep breath. This is interesting. Swan is not in the same package as Bird but does extend it—which implies it has access to the protected members of Bird since it is a subclass. And it does. Lines 5 and 6 refer to protected members via inheriting them.

Lines 10 and 11 also successfully use protected members of Bird. This is allowed because these lines refer to a Swan object. Swan inherits from Bird, so this is okay. It is sort of a two-phase check. The Swan class is allowed to use protected members of Bird, and we are referring to a Swan object. Granted, it is a Swan object created on line 9 rather than an inherited one, but it is still a Swan object.

Lines 16 and 17 do *not* compile. Wait a minute. They are almost exactly the same as lines 10 and 11! There's one key difference. This time a Bird reference is used rather than inheritance. It is created on line 15. Bird is in a different package, and this code isn't inheriting from Bird, so it doesn't get to use protected members. Say what now? We just got through saying repeatedly that Swan inherits from Bird. And it does. However, the variable reference isn't a Swan. The code just happens to be in the Swan class.

It's okay to be confused. This is arguably one of the most confusing points on the exam. Looking at it a different way, the protected rules apply under two scenarios:

- A member is used without referring to a variable. This is the case on lines 5 and 6. In this case, we are taking advantage of inheritance and protected access is allowed.

- A member is used through a variable. This is the case on lines 10, 11, 16, and 17. In this case, the rules for the reference type of the variable are what matter. If it is a subclass, protected access is allowed. This works for references to the same class or a subclass.

We're going to try this again to make sure you understand what is going on. Can you figure out why these examples don't compile?

```
package pond.goose;
import pond.shore.Bird;
public class Goose extends Bird {
   public void helpGooseSwim() {
      Goose other = new Goose();
      other.floatInWater();
      System.out.println(other.text);
   }
   public void helpOtherGooseSwim() {
      Bird other = new Goose();
      other.floatInWater();            // DOES NOT COMPILE
      System.out.println(other.text); // DOES NOT COMPILE
   }
}
```

The first method is fine. In fact, it is equivalent to the Swan example. Goose extends Bird. Since we are in the Goose subclass and referring to a Goose reference, it can access protected members. The second method is a problem. Although the object happens to be a Goose, it is stored in a Bird reference. We are not allowed to refer to members of the Bird class since we are not in the same package and the reference type of other is not a subclass of Goose.

What about this one?

```
package pond.duck;
import pond.goose.Goose;
public class GooseWatcher {
   public void watch() {
      Goose goose = new Goose();
      goose.floatInWater();      // DOES NOT COMPILE
   }
}
```

This code doesn't compile because we are not in the goose object. The floatInWater() method is declared in Bird. GooseWatcher is not in the same package as Bird, nor does it extend Bird. Goose extends Bird. That only lets Goose refer to floatInWater() and not callers of Goose.

If this is still puzzling, try it. Type in the code and try to make it compile. Then reread this section. Don't worry—it wasn't obvious to us the first time either!

Public Access

Protected access was a tough concept. Luckily, the last type of access modifier is easy: public means anyone can access the member from anywhere.

 The Java module system redefines "anywhere," and it becomes possible to restrict access to public code. When given a code sample, you can assume it isn't in a module unless explicitly stated otherwise.

Let's create a class that has public members:

```
package pond.duck;
public class DuckTeacher {
    public String name = "helpful";    // public access
    public void swim() {                // public access
        System.out.println("swim");
    }
}
```

DuckTeacher allows access to any class that wants it. Now we can try it:

```
package pond.goose;
import pond.duck.DuckTeacher;
public class LostDuckling {
    public void swim() {
        DuckTeacher teacher = new DuckTeacher();
        teacher.swim();                                  // allowed
        System.out.println("Thanks" + teacher.name);     // allowed
    }
}
```

LostDuckling is able to refer to swim() and name on DuckTeacher because they are public. The story has a happy ending. LostDuckling has learned to swim and can find its parents—all because DuckTeacher made members public.

To review access modifiers, make sure you know why everything in Table 7.2 is true. Remember that a member is a method or field.

TABLE 7.2 Access modifiers

A method in _____ can access a _____ member	private	Default (package-private)	protected	public
the same class	Yes	Yes	Yes	Yes
another class in the same package	No	Yes	Yes	Yes
in a subclass in a different package	No	No	Yes	Yes
an unrelated class in a different package	No	No	No	Yes

Applying the *static* Keyword

When the static keyword is applied to a variable, method, or class, it applies to the class rather than a specific instance of the class. In this section, you will see that the static keyword can also be applied to import statements.

Designing *static* Methods and Fields

Except for the main() method, we've been looking at instance methods. static methods don't require an instance of the class. They are shared among all users of the class. You can think of a static variable as being a member of the single class object that exists independently of any instances of that class.

You have seen one static method since Chapter 1. The main() method is a static method. That means you can call it using the class name:

```
public class Koala {
    public static int count = 0;              // static variable
    public static void main(String[] args) {  // static method
        System.out.println(count);
    }
}
```

Here the JVM basically calls Koala.main() to get the program started. You can do this too. We can have a KoalaTester that does nothing but call the main() method:

```
public class KoalaTester {
    public static void main(String[] args) {
        Koala.main(new String[0]);            // call static method
    }
}
```

Quite a complicated way to print 0, isn't it? When we run KoalaTester, it makes a call to the main() method of Koala, which prints the value of count. The purpose of all these examples is to show that main() can be called just like any other static method.

In addition to main() methods, static methods have two main purposes:

- For utility or helper methods that don't require any object state. Since there is no need to access instance variables, having static methods eliminates the need for the caller to instantiate an object just to call the method.

- For state that is shared by all instances of a class, like a counter. All instances must share the same state. Methods that merely use that state should be static as well.

In the following sections, we will look at some examples covering other static concepts.

Accessing a *static* Variable or Method

Usually, accessing a static member like count is easy. You just put the class name before the method or variable and you are done. Here's an example:

```
System.out.println(Koala.count);
Koala.main(new String[0]);
```

Both of these are nice and easy. There is one rule that is trickier. You can use an instance of the object to call a static method. The compiler checks for the type of the reference and uses that instead of the object—which is sneaky of Java. This code is perfectly legal:

```
5: Koala k = new Koala();
6: System.out.println(k.count);        // k is a Koala
7: k = null;
8: System.out.println(k.count);        // k is still a Koala
```

Believe it or not, this code outputs 0 twice. Line 6 sees that k is a Koala and count is a static variable, so it reads that static variable. Line 8 does the same thing. Java doesn't care that k happens to be null. Since we are looking for a static, it doesn't matter.

Remember to look at the reference type for a variable when you see a static method or variable. The exam creators will try to trick you into thinking a NullPointerException is thrown because the variable happens to be null. Don't be fooled!

One more time because this is really important: what does the following output?

```
Koala.count = 4;
Koala koala1 = new Koala();
Koala koala2 = new Koala();
koala1.count = 6;
koala2.count = 5;
System.out.println(Koala.count);
```

We hope you answered 5. There is only one count variable since it is static. It is set to 4, then 6, and finally winds up as 5. All the Koala variables are just distractions.

Static vs. Instance

There's another way the exam creators will try to trick you regarding static and instance members. A static member cannot call an instance member without referencing an instance of the class. This shouldn't be a surprise since static doesn't require any instances of the class to even exist.

The following is a common mistake for rookie programmers to make:

```java
public class Static {
   private String name = "Static class";
   public static void first() {  }
   public static void second() {  }
   public void third() {  System.out.println(name); }
   public static void main(String args[]) {
      first();
      second();
      third();            // DOES NOT COMPILE
   }
}
```

The compiler will give you an error about making a static reference to a nonstatic method. If we fix this by adding static to third(), we create a new problem. Can you figure out what it is?

All this does is move the problem. Now, third() is referring to nonstatic name. Adding static to name as well would solve the problem. Another solution would have been to call third as an instance method—for example, new Static().third();.

The exam creators like this topic. A static method or instance method can call a static method because static methods don't require an object to use. Only an instance method can call another instance method on the same class without using a reference variable, because instance methods do require an object. Similar logic applies for the instance and static variables.

Suppose we have a Giraffe class:

```java
public class Giraffe {
   public void eat(Giraffe g) {}
   public void drink() {};
   public static void allGiraffeGoHome(Giraffe g) {}
   public static void allGiraffeComeOut() {}
}
```

Make sure you understand Table 7.3 before continuing.

TABLE 7.3   Static vs. instance calls

Type	Calling	Legal?
allGiraffeGoHome()	allGiraffeComeOut()	Yes
allGiraffeGoHome()	drink()	No
allGiraffeGoHome()	g.eat()	Yes
eat()	allGiraffeComeOut()	Yes
eat()	drink()	Yes
eat()	g.eat()	Yes

Let's try one more example so you have more practice at recognizing this scenario. Do you understand why the following lines fail to compile?

```
1:  public class Gorilla {
2:     public static int count;
3:     public static void addGorilla() { count++; }
4:     public void babyGorilla() { count++; }
5:     public void announceBabies() {
6:        addGorilla();
7:        babyGorilla();
8:     }
9:     public static void announceBabiesToEveryone() {
10:       addGorilla();
11:       babyGorilla();      // DOES NOT COMPILE
12:    }
13:    public int total;
14:    public static double average
15:       = total / count;  // DOES NOT COMPILE
16: }
```

Lines 3 and 4 are fine because both static and instance methods can refer to a static variable. Lines 5–8 are fine because an instance method can call a static method. Line 11 doesn't compile because a static method cannot call an instance method. Similarly, line 15 doesn't compile because a static variable is trying to use an instance variable.

A common use for static variables is counting the number of instances:

```java
public class Counter {
    private static int count;
    public Counter() { count++; }
    public static void main(String[] args) {
        Counter c1 = new Counter();
        Counter c2 = new Counter();
        Counter c3 = new Counter();
        System.out.println(count);          // 3
    }
}
```

Each time the constructor gets called, it increments count by 1. This example relies on the fact that static (and instance) variables are automatically initialized to the default value for that type, which is 0 for int. See Chapter 2 to review the default values.

Also notice that we didn't write Counter.count. We could have. It isn't necessary because we are already in that class so the compiler can infer it.

Does Each Instance Have Its Own Copy of the Code?

Each object has a copy of the instance variables. There is only one copy of the code for the instance methods. Each instance of the class can call it as many times as it would like. However, each call of an instance method (or any method) gets space on the stack for method parameters and local variables.

The same thing happens for static methods. There is one copy of the code. Parameters and local variables go on the stack.

Just remember that only data gets its "own copy." There is no need to duplicate copies of the code itself.

---

static Variables

Some static variables are meant to change as the program runs. Counters are a common example of this. We want the count to increase over time. Just as with instance variables, you can initialize a static variable on the line it is declared:

```java
public class Initializers {
    private static int counter = 0;          // initialization
}
```

Other static variables are meant to never change during the program. This type of variable is known as a *constant*. It uses the final modifier to ensure the variable never changes. Constants use the modifier static final and a different naming convention than other variables. They use all uppercase letters with underscores between "words." Here's an example:

```java
public class Initializers {
   private static final int NUM_BUCKETS = 45;
   public static void main(String[] args) {
      NUM_BUCKETS = 5;  // DOES NOT COMPILE
   }
}
```

The compiler will make sure that you do not accidentally try to update a final variable. This can get interesting. Do you think the following compiles?

```java
private static final ArrayList<String> values = new ArrayList<>();
public static void main(String[] args) {
   values.add("changed");
}
```

It actually does compile since values is a reference variable. We are allowed to call methods on reference variables. All the compiler can do is check that we don't try to reassign the final values to point to a different object.

Static Initialization

In Chapter 2, we covered instance initializers that looked like unnamed methods—just code inside braces. Static initializers look similar. They add the static keyword to specify they should be run when the class is first loaded. Here's an example:

```java
private static final int NUM_SECONDS_PER_MINUTE;
private static final int NUM_MINUTES_PER_HOUR;
private static final int NUM_SECONDS_PER_HOUR;
static {
   NUM_SECONDS_PER_MINUTE = 60;
   NUM_MINUTES_PER_HOUR = 60;
}
static {
   NUM_SECONDS_PER_HOUR
      = NUM_SECONDS_PER_MINUTE * NUM_MINUTES_PER_HOUR;
}
```

All static initializers run when the class is first used in the order they are defined. The statements in them run and assign any static variables as needed. There is something interesting about this example. We just got through saying that `final` variables aren't allowed to be reassigned. The key here is that the `static` initializer is the first assignment. And since it occurs up front, it is okay.

Let's try another example to make sure you understand the distinction:

```
14: private static int one;
15: private static final int two;
16: private static final int three = 3;
17: private static final int four;     // DOES NOT COMPILE
18: static {
19:     one = 1;
20:     two = 2;
21:     three = 3;                      // DOES NOT COMPILE
22:     two = 4;                        // DOES NOT COMPILE
23: }
```

Line 14 declares a `static` variable that is not `final`. It can be assigned as many times as we like. Line 15 declares a `final` variable without initializing it. This means we can initialize it exactly once in a `static` block. Line 22 doesn't compile because this is the second attempt. Line 16 declares a `final` variable and initializes it at the same time. We are not allowed to assign it again, so line 21 doesn't compile. Line 17 declares a `final` variable that never gets initialized. The compiler gives a compiler error because it knows that the `static` blocks are the only place the variable could possibly get initialized. Since the programmer forgot, this is clearly an error.

Try to Avoid Static and Instance Initializers

Using `static` and instance initializers can make your code much harder to read. Everything that could be done in an instance initializer could be done in a constructor instead. Many people find the constructor approach is easier to read.

There is a common case to use a `static` initializer: when you need to initialize a `static` field and the code to do so requires more than one line. This often occurs when you want to initialize a collection like an `ArrayList`. When you do need to use a `static` initializer, put all the `static` initialization in the same block. That way, the order is obvious.

Static Imports

In Chapter 1, you saw that we could import a specific class or all the classes in a package:

```
import java.util.ArrayList;
import java.util.*;
```

We could use this technique to import two classes:

```
import java.util.List;
import java.util.Arrays;
public class Imports {
   public static void main(String[] args) {
      List<String> list = Arrays.asList("one", "two");
   }
}
```

Imports are convenient because you don't need to specify where each class comes from each time you use it. There is another type of import called a *static import*. Regular imports are for importing classes. Static imports are for importing static members of classes. Just like regular imports, you can use a wildcard or import a specific member. The idea is that you shouldn't have to specify where each static method or variable comes from each time you use it. An example of when static imports shine is when you are referring to a lot of constants in another class.

 In a large program, static imports can be overused. When importing from too many places, it can be hard to remember where each static member comes from.

The previous method has one static method call: `Arrays.asList`. Rewriting the code to use a static import yields the following:

```
import java.util.List;
import static java.util.Arrays.asList;          // static import
public class StaticImports {
   public static void main(String[] args) {
      List<String> list = asList("one", "two"); // no Arrays.
   }
}
```

In this example, we are specifically importing the `asList` method. This means that any time we refer to `asList` in the class, it will call `Arrays.asList()`.

An interesting case is what would happen if we created an `asList` method in our `StaticImports` class. Java would give it preference over the imported one, and the method we coded would be used.

The exam will try to trick you with misusing static imports. This example shows almost everything you can do wrong. Can you figure out what is wrong with each one?

```
1: import static java.util.Arrays;       // DOES NOT COMPILE
2: import static java.util.Arrays.asList;
3: static import java.util.Arrays.*;      // DOES NOT COMPILE
```

```
4: public class BadStaticImports {
5:    public static void main(String[] args) {
6:       Arrays.asList("one");              // DOES NOT COMPILE
7:    } }
```

Line 1 tries to use a static import to import a class. Remember that static imports are only for importing static members. Regular imports are for importing a class. Line 3 tries to see whether you are paying attention to the order of keywords. The syntax is import static and not vice versa. Line 6 is sneaky. The asList method is imported on line 2. However, the Arrays class is not imported anywhere. This makes it okay to write asList("one") but not Arrays.asList("one").

There's only one more scenario with static imports. In Chapter 1, you learned that importing two classes with the same name gives a compiler error. This is true of static imports as well. The compiler will complain if you try to explicitly do a static import of two methods with the same name or two static variables with the same name. Here's an example:

```
import static statics.A.TYPE;
import static statics.B.TYPE;        // DOES NOT COMPILE
```

Luckily, when this happens, we can just refer to the static members via their class name in the code instead of trying to use a static import.

Passing Data among Methods

Java is a "pass-by-value" language. This means that a copy of the variable is made and the method receives that copy. Assignments made in the method do not affect the caller. Let's look at an example:

```
2: public static void main(String[] args) {
3:    int num = 4;
4:    newNumber(num);
5:    System.out.println(num);     // 4
6: }
7: public static void newNumber(int num) {
8:    num = 8;
9: }
```

On line 3, num is assigned the value of 4. On line 4, we call a method. On line 8, the num parameter in the method gets set to 8. Although this parameter has the same name as the variable on line 3, this is a coincidence. The name could be anything. The exam will often use the same name to try to confuse you. The variable on line 3 never changes because no assignments are made to it.

Now that you've seen primitives, let's try an example with a reference type. What do you think is output by the following code?

```
public static void main(String[] args) {
   String name = "Webby";
   speak(name);
   System.out.println(name);
}
public static void speak(String name) {
   name = "Sparky";
}
```

The correct answer is Webby. Just as in the primitive example, the variable assignment is only to the method parameter and doesn't affect the caller.

Notice how we keep talking about variable assignments. This is because we can call methods on the parameters. As an example, here is code that calls a method on the StringBuilder passed into the method:

```
public static void main(String[] args) {
   StringBuilder name = new StringBuilder();
   speak(name);
   System.out.println(name); // Webby
}
public static void speak(StringBuilder s) {
   s.append("Webby");
}
```

In this case, the output is Webby because the method merely calls a method on the parameter. It doesn't reassign name to a different object. In Figure 7.4, you can see how pass-by-value is still used. The variable s is a copy of the variable name. Both point to the same StringBuilder, which means that changes made to the StringBuilder are available to both references.

FIGURE 7.4   Copying a reference with pass-by-value

Real World Scenario

Pass-by-Value vs. Pass-by-Reference

Different languages handle parameters in different ways. Pass-by-value is used by many languages, including Java. In this example, the swap method does not change the original values. It only changes a and b within the method.

```java
public static void main(String[] args) {
    int original1 = 1;
    int original2 = 2;
    swap(original1, original2);
    System.out.println(original1);    // 1
    System.out.println(original2);    // 2
}
public static void swap(int a, int b) {
    int temp = a;
    a = b;
    b = temp;
}
```

The other approach is pass-by-reference. It is used by default in a few languages, such as Perl. We aren't going to show you Perl code here because you are studying for the Java exam and we don't want to confuse you. The following example is in a made-up language that shows pass-by-reference:

```
original1 = 1;
original2 = 2;
swapByReference(original1, original2);
print(original1);    // 2 (not in Java)
print(original2);    // 1 (not in Java)

swapByReference(a, b) {
    temp = a;
    a = b;
    b = temp;
}
```

See the difference? In our made-up language, the caller is affected by variable assignments made in the method.

To review, Java uses pass-by-value to get data into a method. Assigning a new primitive or reference to a parameter doesn't change the caller. Calling methods on a reference to an object can affect the caller.

Getting data back from a method is easier. A copy is made of the primitive or reference and returned from the method. Most of the time, this returned value is used. For example, it might be stored in a variable. If the returned value is not used, the result is ignored. Watch for this on the exam. Ignored returned values are tricky.

Let's try an example. Pay attention to the return types.

```
1:  public class ReturningValues {
2:     public static void main(String[] args) {
3:        int number = 1;                        // number=1
4:        String letters = "abc";                // letters=abc
5:        number(number);                        // number=1
6:        letters = letters(letters);            // letters=abcd
7:        System.out.println(number + letters);  // 1abcd
8:     }
9:     public static int number(int number) {
10:       number++;
11:       return number;
12:    }
13:    public static String letters(String letters) {
14:       letters += "d";
15:       return letters;
16:    }
17: }
```

This is a tricky one because there is a lot to keep track of. When you see such questions on the exam, write down the values of each variable. Lines 3 and 4 are straightforward assignments. Line 5 calls a method. Line 10 increments the method parameter to 2 but leaves the number variable in the main() method as 1. While line 11 returns the value, the caller ignores it. The method call on line 6 doesn't ignore the result, so letters becomes "abcd". Remember that this is happening because of the returned value and not the method parameter.

Overloading Methods

Now that you are familiar with the rules for declaring methods, it is time to look at creating methods with the same name in the same class. *Method overloading* occurs when methods have the same name but different method signatures, which means they differ by method parameters. (Overloading differs from overriding, which you'll learn about in Chapter 8.)

We've been showing how to call overloaded methods for a while. `System.out.println` and `StringBuilder`'s append methods provide many overloaded versions, so you can pass just about anything to them without having to think about it. In both of these examples, the only change was the type of the parameter. Overloading also allows different numbers of parameters.

Everything other than the method name can vary for overloading methods. This means there can be different access modifiers, specifiers (like `static`), return types, and exception lists.

These are all valid overloaded methods:

```
public void fly(int numMiles) {}
public void fly(short numFeet) {}
public boolean fly() { return false; }
void fly(int numMiles, short numFeet) {}
public void fly(short numFeet, int numMiles) throws Exception {}
```

As you can see, we can overload by changing anything in the parameter list. We can have a different type, more types, or the same types in a different order. Also notice that the return type, access modifier, and exception list are irrelevant to overloading.

Now let's look at an example that is not valid overloading:

```
public void fly(int numMiles) {}
public int fly(int numMiles) {}     // DOES NOT COMPILE
```

This method doesn't compile because it differs from the original only by return type. The parameter lists are the same, so they are duplicate methods as far as Java is concerned.

What about these two? Why does the second not compile?

```
public void fly(int numMiles) {}
public static void fly(int numMiles) {}     // DOES NOT COMPILE
```

Again, the parameter list is the same. You cannot have methods where the only difference is that one is an instance method and one is a `static` method.

Calling overloaded methods is easy. You just write code and Java calls the right one. For example, look at these two methods:

```
public void fly(int numMiles) {
   System.out.println("int");
}
public void fly(short numFeet) {
   System.out.println("short");
}
```

The call `fly((short) 1)` prints `short`. It looks for matching types and calls the appropriate method. Of course, it can be more complicated than this.

Now that you know the basics of overloading, let's look at some more complex scenarios that you may encounter on the exam.

Varargs

Which method do you think is called if we pass an `int[]`?

```
public void fly(int[] lengths) {}
public void fly(int... lengths) {}      // DOES NOT COMPILE
```

Trick question! Remember that Java treats varargs as if they were an array. This means that the method signature is the same for both methods. Since we are not allowed to overload methods with the same parameter list, this code doesn't compile. Even though the code doesn't look the same, it compiles to the same parameter list.

Now that we've just gotten through explaining that they are the same, it is time to mention how they are not the same. It shouldn't be a surprise that you can call either method by passing an array:

```
fly(new int[] { 1, 2, 3 });
```

However, you can only call the varargs version with stand-alone parameters:

```
fly(1, 2, 3);
```

Obviously, this means they don't compile *exactly* the same. The parameter list is the same, though, and that is what you need to know with respect to overloading for the exam.

Autoboxing

In Chapter 5, you saw how Java will convert a primitive `int` to an object `Integer` to add it to an `ArrayList` through the wonders of autoboxing. This works for code you write too.

```
public void fly(Integer numMiles) {}
```

This means calling `fly(3)` will call the previous method as expected. However, what happens if you have both a primitive and an integer version?

```
public void fly(int numMiles) {}
public void fly(Integer numMiles) {}
```

Java will match the `int numMiles` version. Java tries to use the most specific parameter list it can find. When the primitive `int` version isn't present, it will autobox. However, when the primitive `int` version is provided, there is no reason for Java to do the extra work of autoboxing.

Reference Types

Given the rule about Java picking the most specific version of a method that it can, what do you think this code outputs?

```
public class ReferenceTypes {
   public void fly(String s) {
```

```
        System.out.print("string");
    }


    public void fly(Object o) {
        System.out.print("object");
    }
    public static void main(String[] args) {
        ReferenceTypes r = new ReferenceTypes();
        r.fly("test");
        System.out.print("-");
        r.fly(56);
    }
}
```

The answer is string-object. The first call is a String and finds a direct match. There's no reason to use the Object version when there is a nice String parameter list just waiting to be called. The second call looks for an int parameter list. When it doesn't find one, it autoboxes to Integer. Since it still doesn't find a match, it goes to the Object one.

Let's try another one. What does this print?

```
public static void print(Iterable i) {
    System.out.print("I");
}
public static void print(CharSequence c) {
    System.out.print("C");
}
public static void print(Object o) {
    System.out.print("O");
}
public static void main(String[] args){
    print("abc");
    print(new ArrayList<>());
    print(LocalDate.of(2019, Month.JULY, 4));
}
```

The answer is CIO. The code is due for a promotion! The first call to print() passes a String. As you learned in Chapter 5, String and StringBuilder implement the CharSequence interface.

The second call to print() passes an ArrayList. Remember that you get to assume unknown APIs do what they sound like. In this case, Iterable is an interface for classes you can iterate over.

The final call to print() passes a LocalDate. This is another class you might not know, but that's okay. It clearly isn't a sequence of characters or something to loop through. That means the Object method signature is used.

Primitives

Primitives work in a way that's similar to reference variables. Java tries to find the most specific matching overloaded method. What do you think happens here?

```java
public class Plane {
   public void fly(int i) {
      System.out.print("int");
   }
   public void fly(long l) {
      System.out.print("long");
   }
   public static void main(String[] args) {
      Plane p = new Plane();
      p.fly(123);
      System.out.print("-");
      p.fly(123L);
   }
}
```

The answer is int-long. The first call passes an int and sees an exact match. The second call passes a long and also sees an exact match. If we comment out the overloaded method with the int parameter list, the output becomes long-long. Java has no problem calling a larger primitive. However, it will not do so unless a better match is not found.

Note that Java can only accept wider types. An int can be passed to a method taking a long parameter. Java will not automatically convert to a narrower type. If you want to pass a long to a method taking an int parameter, you have to add a cast to explicitly say narrowing is okay.

Generics

You might be surprised to learn that these are not valid overloads:

```java
public void walk(List<String> strings) {}
public void walk(List<Integer> integers) {}    // DOES NOT COMPILE
```

Java has a concept called *type erasure* where generics are used only at compile time. That means the compiled code looks like this:

```java
public void walk(List strings) {}
public void walk(List integers) {}    // DOES NOT COMPILE
```

We clearly can't have two methods with the same method signature, so this doesn't compile. Remember that method overloads must differ in at least one of the method parameters.

Arrays

Unlike the previous example, this code is just fine:

```
public static void walk(int[] ints) {}
public static void walk(Integer[] integers) {}
```

Arrays have been around since the beginning of Java. They specify their actual types and don't participate in type erasure.

Putting It All Together

So far, all the rules for when an overloaded method is called should be logical. Java calls the most specific method it can. When some of the types interact, the Java rules focus on backward compatibility. A long time ago, autoboxing and varargs didn't exist. Since old code still needs to work, this means autoboxing and varargs come last when Java looks at overloaded methods. Ready for the official order? Table 7.4 lays it out for you.

TABLE 7.4   The order that Java uses to choose the right overloaded method

Rule	Example of what will be chosen for `glide(1,2)`
Exact match by type	`String glide(int i, int j)`
Larger primitive type	`String glide(long i, long j)`
Autoboxed type	`String glide(Integer i, Integer j)`
Varargs	`String glide(int... nums)`

Let's give this a practice run using the rules in Table 7.4. What do you think this outputs?

```
public class Glider2 {
   public static String glide(String s) {
      return "1";
   }
   public static String glide(String... s) {
      return "2";
   }
   public static String glide(Object o) {
      return "3";
   }
   public static String glide(String s, String t) {
```

```
        return "4";
    }
    public static void main(String[] args) {
        System.out.print(glide("a"));
        System.out.print(glide("a", "b"));
        System.out.print(glide("a", "b", "c"));
    }
}
```

It prints out 142. The first call matches the signature taking a single `String` because that is the most specific match. The second call matches the signature, taking two `String` parameters since that is an exact match. It isn't until the third call that the varargs version is used since there are no better matches.

As accommodating as Java is with trying to find a match, it will do only one conversion:

```
public class TooManyConversions {
    public static void play(Long l) {}
    public static void play(Long... l) {}
    public static void main(String[] args) {
        play(4);        // DOES NOT COMPILE
        play(4L);       // calls the Long version
    }
}
```

Here we have a problem. Java is happy to convert the `int` 4 to a `long` 4 or an `Integer` 4. It cannot handle converting to a `long` and then to a `Long`. If we had `public static void play(Object o) {}`, it would match because only one conversion would be necessary: from `int` to `Integer`. Remember, if a variable is not a primitive, it is an `Object`, as you'll see in Chapter 8.

Encapsulating Data

In Chapter 2, you saw an example of a class with a field that wasn't private:

```
public class Swan {
    int numberEggs;     // instance variable
}
```

Why do we care? Since there is default (package-private) access, that means any class in the package can set `numberEggs`. We no longer have control of what gets set in your own class. A caller could even write this:

```
mother.numberEggs = -1;
```

This is clearly no good. We do not want the mother Swan to have a negative number of eggs!

Encapsulation to the rescue. *Encapsulation* means only methods in the class with the variables can refer to the instance variables. Callers are required to use these methods. Let's take a look at the newly encapsulated Swan class:

```
1: public class Swan {
2:     private int numberEggs;                    // private
3:     public int getNumberEggs() {               // getter
4:         return numberEggs;
5:     }
6:     public void setNumberEggs(int newNumber) { // setter
7:         if (newNumber >= 0)                     // guard condition
8:             numberEggs = newNumber;
9:     } }
```

Note that numberEggs is now private on line 2. This means only code within the class can read or write the value of numberEggs. Since we wrote the class, we know better than to set a negative number of eggs. We added a method on lines 3–5 to read the value, which is called an *accessor method* or a getter. We also added a method on lines 6–9 to update the value, which is called a *mutator method* or a setter. The setter has an if statement in this example to prevent setting the instance variable to an invalid value. This guard condition protects the instance variable.

For encapsulation, remember that data (an instance variable) is private and getters/setters are public. Java defines a naming convention for getters and setters listed in Table 7.5.

TABLE 7.5 Naming conventions for getters and setters

Rule	Example
Getter methods most frequently begin with is if the property is a boolean.	```public boolean isHappy() { return happy; }```
Getter methods begin with get if the property is not a boolean.	```public int getNumberEggs() { return numberEggs; }```
Setter methods begin with set.	```public void setHappy(boolean _happy) { happy = _happy; }```

In the last example in Table 7.5, you probably noticed that you can name the method parameter to anything you want. Only the method name and property name have naming conventions here.

It's time for some practice. See whether you can figure out which lines follow these naming conventions:

```
12: private boolean playing;
13: private String name;
14: public boolean isPlaying() { return playing; }
15: public String name() { return name; }
16: public void updateName(String n) { name = n; }
17: public void setName(String n) { name = n; }
```

Lines 12 and 13 are good. They are private instance variables. Line 14 is correct. Since playing is a boolean, line 14 is a correct getter. Line 15 doesn't follow the naming conventions because it should be called getName(). Line 16 does not follow the naming convention for a setter, but line 17 does.

For data to be encapsulated, you don't have to provide getters and setters. As long as the instance variables are private, you are good. For example, this is a well-encapsulated class:

```
public class Swan {
    private int numEggs;
    public void layEgg() {
        numEggs++;
    }
    public void printEggCount() {
        System.out.println(numEggs);
    }
}
```

To review, you can tell it is a well-encapsulated class because the numEggs instance variable is private. Only methods can retrieve and update the value.

Summary

As you learned in this chapter, Java methods start with an access modifier of public, private, protected, or blank (default access). This is followed by an optional specifier such as static, final, or abstract. Next comes the return type, which is void or a Java type. The method name follows, using standard Java identifier rules. Zero or more parameters go in parentheses as the parameter list. Next come any optional exception types. Finally, zero or more statements go in braces to make up the method body.

Using the private keyword means the code is only available from within the same class. Default (package-private) access means the code is available only from within the same package. Using the protected keyword means the code is available from the same package or subclasses. Using the public keyword means the code is available from anywhere. Both static methods and static variables are shared by all instances of the class. When referenced from outside the class, they are called using the classname—for example, StaticClass.method(). Instance members are allowed to call static members, but static members are not allowed to call instance members. Static imports are used to import static members.

Java uses pass-by-value, which means that calls to methods create a copy of the parameters. Assigning new values to those parameters in the method doesn't affect the caller's variables. Calling methods on objects that are method parameters changes the state of those objects and is reflected in the caller.

Overloaded methods are methods with the same name but a different parameter list. Java calls the most specific method it can find. Exact matches are preferred, followed by wider primitives. After that comes autoboxing and finally varargs.

Encapsulation refers to preventing callers from changing the instance variables directly. This is done by making instance variables private and getters/setters public.

Exam Essentials

Be able to identify correct and incorrect method declarations.   A sample method declaration is public static void method(String... args) throws Exception {}.

Identify when a method or field is accessible.   Recognize when a method or field is accessed when the access modifier (private, protected, public, or default access) does not allow it.

Recognize valid and invalid uses of static imports.   Static imports import static members. They are written as import static, not *static import*. Make sure they are importing static methods or variables rather than class names.

State the output of code involving methods.   Identify when to call static rather than instance methods based on whether the class name or object comes before the method. Recognize that instance methods can call static methods and that static methods need an instance of the object in order to call an instance method.

Recognize the correct overloaded method.   Exact matches are used first, followed by wider primitives, followed by autoboxing, followed by varargs. Assigning new values to method parameters does not change the caller, but calling methods on them does.

Identify properly encapsulated classes.   Instance variables in encapsulated classes are private. All code that retrieves the value or updates it uses methods. These methods are allowed to be public.

Review Questions

The answers to the chapter review questions can be found in the Appendix.

1. Which of the following can fill in the blank in this code to make it compile? (Choose all that apply.)

```
public class Ant {
    _____ void method() {}
}
```

   A. default
   B. final
   C. private
   D. Public
   E. String
   F. zzz:

2. Which of the following methods compile? (Choose all that apply.)

   A. final static void method4() {}
   B. public final int void method() {}
   C. private void int method() {}
   D. static final void method3() {}
   E. void final method() {}
   F. void public method() {}

3. Which of the following methods compile? (Choose all that apply.)

   A. public void methodA() { return;}
   B. public int methodB() { return null;}
   C. public void methodC() {}
   D. public int methodD() { return 9;}
   E. public int methodE() { return 9.0;}
   F. public int methodF() { return;}

4. Which of the following methods compile? (Choose all that apply.)

   A. public void moreA(int... nums) {}
   B. public void moreB(String values, int... nums) {}
   C. public void moreC(int... nums, String values) {}
   D. public void moreD(String... values, int... nums) {}
   E. public void moreE(String[] values, ...int nums) {}
   F. public void moreG(String[] values, int[] nums) {}

5. Given the following method, which of the method calls return 2? (Choose all that apply.)

```
public int howMany(boolean b, boolean... b2) {
 return b2.length;
}
```

- **A.** howMany();
- **B.** howMany(true);
- **C.** howMany(true, true);
- **D.** howMany(true, true, true);
- **E.** howMany(true, {true, true});
- **F.** howMany(true, new boolean[2]);

6. Which of the following statements is true?

- **A.** Package-private access is more lenient than protected access.
- **B.** A public class that has private fields and package-private methods is not visible to classes outside the package.
- **C.** You can use access modifiers so only some of the classes in a package see a particular package-private class.
- **D.** You can use access modifiers to allow access to all methods and not any instance variables.
- **E.** You can use access modifiers to restrict access to all classes that begin with the word Test.

7. Given the following my.school.Classroom and my.city.School class definitions, which line numbers in main() generate a compiler error? (Choose all that apply.)

```
1: package my.school;
2: public class Classroom {
3:     private int roomNumber;
4:     protected static String teacherName;
5:     static int globalKey = 54321;
6:     public static int floor = 3;
7:     Classroom(int r, String t) {
8:         roomNumber = r;
9:         teacherName = t; } }
```

```
1: package my.city;
2: import my.school.*;
3: public class School {
4:     public static void main(String[] args) {
5:         System.out.println(Classroom.globalKey);
6:         Classroom room = new Classroom(101, "Mrs. Anderson");
7:         System.out.println(room.roomNumber);
```

```
8:          System.out.println(Classroom.floor);
9:          System.out.println(Classroom.teacherName); } }
```

A. None, the code compiles fine.

B. Line 5

C. Line 6

D. Line 7

E. Line 8

F. Line 9

8. Which of the following are true about encapsulation? (Choose all that apply.)

   A. It allows getters.

   B. It allows setters.

   C. It requires specific naming conventions.

   D. It uses package-private instance variables.

   E. It uses private instance variables.

9. Which pairs of methods are valid overloaded pairs? (Choose all that apply.)

   A.
   ```
   public void hiss(Iterable i) {}
   ```
   and
   ```
   public int hiss(Iterable i) { return 0; }
   ```
   B.
   ```
   public void baa(CharSequence c) {}
   ```
   and
   ```
   public void baa(String s) {}
   ```
   C.
   ```
   public var meow(List<String> l) {}
   ```
   and
   ```
   public var meow(String s) {}
   ```
   D.
   ```
   public void moo(Object o) {}
   ```
   and
   ```
   public void moo(String s) {}
   ```
   E.
   ```
   public void roar(List<Boolean> b) {}
   ```
   and
   ```
   public void roar(List<Character> c) {}
   ```
   F.
   ```
   public void woof(boolean[] b1) {}
   ```
   and
   ```
   public void woof(Boolean[] b) {}
   ```

10. What is the output of the following code?

```
1: package rope;
2: public class Rope {
3:    public static int LENGTH = 5;
4:    static {
5:        LENGTH = 10;
6:    }
7:    public static void swing() {
8:        System.out.print("swing ");
9:    } }
```

```
1: import rope.*;
2: import static rope.Rope.*;
3: public class Chimp {
4:    public static void main(String[] args) {
5:        Rope.swing();
6:        new Rope().swing();
7:        System.out.println(LENGTH);
8:    } }
```

A. swing swing 5

B. swing swing 10

C. Compiler error on line 2 of Chimp

D. Compiler error on line 5 of Chimp

E. Compiler error on line 6 of Chimp

F. Compiler error on line 7 of Chimp

11. Which statements are true of the following code? (Choose all that apply.)

```
1:  public class Rope {
2:     public static void swing() {
3:        System.out.print("swing");
4:     }
5:     public void climb() {
6:        System.out.println("climb");
7:     }
8:     public static void play() {
9:        swing();
10:       climb();
11:    }
12:    public static void main(String[] args) {
13:       Rope rope = new Rope();
```

```
14:        rope.play();
15:        Rope rope2 = null;
16:        System.out.print("-");
17:        rope2.play();
18:    } }
```

A. The code compiles as is.

B. There is exactly one compiler error in the code.

C. There are exactly two compiler errors in the code.

D. If the line(s) with compiler errors are removed, the output is `swing-climb`.

E. If the line(s) with compiler errors are removed, the output is `swing-swing`.

F. If the line(s) with compile errors are removed, the code throws a `NullPointerException`.

12. What is the output of the following code?

```
import rope.*;
import static rope.Rope.*;
public class RopeSwing {
    private static Rope rope1 = new Rope();
    private static Rope rope2 = new Rope();
    {
        System.out.println(rope1.length);
    }
    public static void main(String[] args) {
        rope1.length = 2;
        rope2.length = 8;
        System.out.println(rope1.length);
    }
}

package rope;
public class Rope {
    public static int length = 0;
}
```

A. 02

B. 08

C. 2

D. 8

E. The code does not compile.

F. An exception is thrown.

13. How many lines in the following code have compiler errors?

```
1:  public class RopeSwing {
2:      private static final String leftRope;
3:      private static final String rightRope;
4:      private static final String bench;
5:      private static final String name = "name";
6:      static {
7:          leftRope = "left";
8:          rightRope = "right";
9:      }
10:     static {
11:         name = "name";
12:         rightRope = "right";
13:     }
14:     public static void main(String[] args) {
15:         bench = "bench";
16:     }
17: }
```

- **A.** 0
- **B.** 1
- **C.** 2
- **D.** 3
- **E.** 4
- **F.** 5

14. Which of the following can replace line 2 to make this code compile? (Choose all that apply.)

```
1: import java.util.*;
2: // INSERT CODE HERE
3: public class Imports {
4:     public void method(ArrayList<String> list) {
5:         sort(list);
6:     }
7: }
```

- **A.** import static java.util.Collections;
- **B.** import static java.util.Collections.*;
- **C.** import static java.util.Collections.sort(ArrayList<String>);
- **D.** static import java.util.Collections;
- **E.** static import java.util.Collections.*;
- **F.** static import java.util.Collections.sort(ArrayList<String>);

15. What is the result of the following statements?

```
1:  public class Test {
2:     public void print(byte x) {
3:        System.out.print("byte-");
4:     }
5:     public void print(int x) {
6:        System.out.print("int-");
7:     }
8:     public void print(float x) {
9:        System.out.print("float-");
10:    }
11:    public void print(Object x) {
12:       System.out.print("Object-");
13:    }
14:    public static void main(String[] args) {
15:       Test t = new Test();
16:       short s = 123;
17:       t.print(s);
18:       t.print(true);
19:       t.print(6.789);
20:    }
21: }
```

A. byte-float-Object-

B. int-float-Object-

C. byte-Object-float-

D. int-Object-float-

E. int-Object-Object-

F. byte-Object-Object-

16. What is the result of the following program?

```
1:  public class Squares {
2:     public static long square(int x) {
3:        var y = x * (long) x;
4:        x = -1;
5:        return y;
6:     }
7:     public static void main(String[] args) {
8:        var value = 9;
9:        var result = square(value);
10:       System.out.println(value);
11:    } }
```

A. -1

B. 9

C. 81

D. Compiler error on line 9

E. Compiler error on a different line

17. Which of the following are output by the following code? (Choose all that apply.)

```java
public class StringBuilders {
    public static StringBuilder work(StringBuilder a,
        StringBuilder b) {
        a = new StringBuilder("a");
        b.append("b");
        return a;
    }
    public static void main(String[] args) {
        var s1 = new StringBuilder("s1");
        var s2 = new StringBuilder("s2");
        var s3 = work(s1, s2);
        System.out.println("s1 = " + s1);
        System.out.println("s2 = " + s2);
        System.out.println("s3 = " + s3);
    }
}
```

A. s1 = a

B. s1 = s1

C. s2 = s2

D. s2 = s2b

E. s3 = a

F. The code does not compile.

18. Which of the following will compile when independently inserted in the following code? (Choose all that apply.)

```java
1:  public class Order3 {
2:      final String value1 = "red";
3:      static String value2 = "blue";
4:      String value3 = "yellow";
5:      {
6:          // CODE SNIPPET 1
7:      }
```

```
 8:      static {
 9:          // CODE SNIPPET 2
10:      } }
```

A. Insert at line 6: `value1 = "green";`

B. Insert at line 6: `value2 = "purple";`

C. Insert at line 6: `value3 = "orange";`

D. Insert at line 9: `value1 = "magenta";`

E. Insert at line 9: `value2 = "cyan";`

F. Insert at line 9: `value3 = "turquoise";`

19. Which of the following are true about the following code? (Choose all that apply.)

```
public class Run {
   static void execute() {
      System.out.print("1-");
   }
   static void execute(int num) {
      System.out.print("2-");
   }
   static void execute(Integer num) {
      System.out.print("3-");
   }
   static void execute(Object num) {
      System.out.print("4-");
   }
   static void execute(int... nums) {
      System.out.print("5-");
   }
   public static void main(String[] args) {
      Run.execute(100);
      Run.execute(100L);
   }
}
```

A. The code prints out 2-4-.

B. The code prints out 3-4-.

C. The code prints out 4-2-.

D. The code prints out 4-4-.

E. The code prints 3-4- if you remove the method `static void execute(int num)`.

F. The code prints 4-4- if you remove the method `static void execute(int num)`.

20. Which pairs of methods are valid overloaded pairs? (Choose all that apply.)

A.
```
public void hiss(Set<String> s) {}
```
and
```
public void hiss(List<String> l) {}
```

B.
```
public void baa(var c) {}
```
and
```
public void baa(String s) {}
```

C.
```
public void meow(char ch) {}
```
and
```
public void meow(String s) {}
```

D.
```
public void moo(char ch) {}
```
and
```
public void moo(char ch) {}
```

E.
```
public void roar(long... longs){}
```
and
```
public void roar(long long) {}
```

F.
```
public void woof(char... chars) {}
```
and
```
public void woof(Character c) {}
```

21. Which can fill in the blank to create a properly encapsulated class? (Choose all that apply.)

```
public class Rabbits {
    _____ int numRabbits = 0;
    _____ void multiply() {
       numRabbits *= 6;
    }
    _____ int getNumberOfRabbits() {
       return numRabbits;
    }
}
```

A. private, public, and public

B. private, protected, and private

C. private, private, and protected

D. public, public, and public

E. None of the above since multiply() does not begin with set

F. None of the above for a reason other than the multiply() method

Chapter

8

Class Design

OCP EXAM OBJECTIVES COVERED IN THIS CHAPTER:

✓ **Creating and Using Methods**

- Create methods and constructors with arguments and return values

✓ **Reusing Implementations Through Inheritance**

- Create and use subclasses and superclasses

- Enable polymorphism by overriding methods

- Utilize polymorphism to cast and call methods, differentiating object type versus reference type

- Distinguish overloading, overriding, and hiding

In Chapter 2, "Java Building Blocks," we introduced the basic definition for a class in Java. In Chapter 7, "Methods and Encapsulation," we delved into methods and modifiers and showed how you can use them to build more structured classes. In this chapter, we'll take things one step further and show how class structure and inheritance is one of the most powerful features in the Java language.

At its core, proper Java class design is about code reusability, increased functionality, and standardization. For example, by creating a new class that extends an existing class, you may gain access to a slew of inherited primitives, objects, and methods, which increases code reuse. Through polymorphism, you may also gain access to a dynamic hierarchy that supports replacing method implementations in subclasses at runtime.

This chapter is the culmination of some of the most important topics in Java including class design, constructor overloading and inheritance, order of initialization, overriding/hiding methods, and polymorphism. Read this chapter carefully and make sure you understand all of the topics well. This chapter forms the basis of Chapter 9, "Advanced Class Design," in which we will expand our discussion of types to include abstract classes and interfaces.

Understanding Inheritance

When creating a new class in Java, you can define the class as inheriting from an existing class. *Inheritance* is the process by which a subclass automatically includes any public or protected members of the class, including primitives, objects, or methods, defined in the parent class.

For illustrative purposes, we refer to any class that inherits from another class as a *subclass* or *child class*, as it is considered a descendant of that class. Alternatively, we refer to the class that the child inherits from as the *superclass* or *parent class*, as it is considered an ancestor of the class. And inheritance is transitive. If child class X inherits from parent class Y, which in turn inherits from a parent class Z, then class X would be considered a subclass, or descendant, of class Z. By comparison, X is a direct descendant only of class Y, and Y is a direct descendant only of class Z.

In the last chapter, you learned that there are four access levels: public, protected, package-private, and private. When one class inherits from a parent class, all public and protected members are automatically available as part of the child class. Package-private members are available if the child class is in the same package as the parent class. Last but not least, `private` members are restricted to the class they are defined in and are never available via inheritance. This doesn't mean the parent class doesn't have `private` members that can hold data or modify an object; it just means the child class has no direct reference to them.

Let's take a look at a simple example with the `BigCat` and `Jaguar` classes. In this example, `Jaguar` is a subclass or child of `BigCat`, making `BigCat` a superclass or parent of `Jaguar`.

```
public class BigCat {
   public double size;
}

public class Jaguar extends BigCat {
   public Jaguar() {
      size = 10.2;
   }
   public void printDetails() {
      System.out.println(size);
   }
}
```

In the `Jaguar` class, `size` is accessible because it is marked `public`. Via inheritance, the `Jaguar` subclass can read or write `size` as if it were its own member.

Single vs. Multiple Inheritance

Java supports *single inheritance*, by which a class may inherit from only one direct parent class. Java also supports multiple levels of inheritance, by which one class may extend another class, which in turn extends another class. You can have any number of levels of inheritance, allowing each descendant to gain access to its ancestor's members.

To truly understand single inheritance, it may helpful to contrast it with *multiple inheritance*, by which a class may have multiple direct parents. By design, Java doesn't support multiple inheritance in the language because multiple inheritance can lead to complex, often difficult-to-maintain data models. Java does allow one exception to the single inheritance rule that you'll see in Chapter 9—a class may implement multiple interfaces.

Figure 8.1 illustrates the various types of inheritance models. The items on the left are considered single inheritance because each child has exactly one parent. You may notice that single inheritance doesn't preclude parents from having multiple children. The right side shows items that have multiple inheritance. As you can see, a `Dog` object has multiple parent designations. Part of what makes multiple inheritance complicated is determining which parent to inherit values from in case of a conflict. For example, if you have an object or method defined in all of the parents, which one does the child inherit? There is no natural ordering for parents in this example, which is why Java avoids these issues by disallowing multiple inheritance altogether.

FIGURE 8.1 Types of inheritance

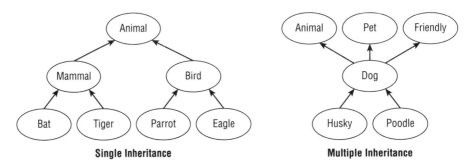

It is possible in Java to prevent a class from being extended by marking the class with the final modifier. If you try to define a class that inherits from a final class, then the class will fail to compile. Unless otherwise specified, throughout this chapter you can assume the classes we work with are not marked final.

Inheriting *Object*

Throughout our discussion of Java in this book, we have thrown around the word *object* numerous times—and with good reason. In Java, all classes inherit from a single class: java.lang.Object, or Object for short. Furthermore, Object is the only class that doesn't have a parent class.

You might be wondering, "None of the classes I've written so far extend Object, so how do all classes inherit from it?" The answer is that the compiler has been automatically inserting code into any class you write that doesn't extend a specific class. For example, consider the following two equivalent class definitions:

```
public class Zoo { }
```

```
public class Zoo extends java.lang.Object { }
```

The key is that when Java sees you define a class that doesn't extend another class, it automatically adds the syntax extends java.lang.Object to the class definition. The result is that every class gains access to any accessible methods in the Object class. For example, the toString() and equals() methods are available in Object; therefore, they are accessible in all classes. Without being overridden in a subclass, though, they may not be particularly useful. We will cover overriding methods later in this chapter.

On the other hand, when you define a new class that extends an existing class, Java does not automatically extend the Object class. Since all classes inherit from Object, extending an existing class means the child already inherits from Object by definition. If you look at the inheritance structure of any class, it will always end with Object on the top of the tree, as shown in Figure 8.2.

FIGURE 8.2 Java object inheritance

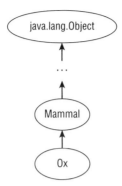

All objects inherit java.lang.Object

Primitive types such as `int` and `boolean` do not inherit from `Object`, since they are not classes. As you learned in Chapter 5, "Core Java APIs," through autoboxing they can be assigned or passed as an instance of an associated wrapper class, which does inherit `Object`.

Creating Classes

Now that we've established how inheritance works in Java, we can use it to define and create complex class relationships. In this section, we will review the basics for creating and working with classes.

Extending a Class

The full syntax of defining and extending a class using the `extends` keyword is shown in Figure 8.3.

FIGURE 8.3 Defining and extending a class

`public` or default (package-private) access modifier

`abstract` or `final` keyword (optional)

Class name (required)

extends parent class (optional)

`class` keyword (required)

```
public abstract class ElephantSeal extends Seal {

    // Methods and Variables defined here

}
```

Remember that final means a class cannot be extended. We'll discuss what it means for a class to be abstract in Chapter 9.

Let's create two files, Animal.java and Lion.java, in which the Lion class extends the Animal class. Assuming they are in the same package, an import statement is not required in Lion.java to access the Animal class.

Here are the contents of Animal.java:

```java
public class Animal {
   private int age;
   protected String name;
   public int getAge() {
      return age;
   }
   public void setAge(int newAge) {
      age = newAge;
   }
}
```

And here are the contents of Lion.java:

```java
public class Lion extends Animal {
   public void setProperties(int age, String n) {
      setAge(age);
      name = n;
   }
   public void roar() {
      System.out.print(name + ", age " + getAge() + ", says: Roar!");
   }
   public static void main(String[] args) {
      var lion = new Lion();
      lion.setProperties(3, "kion");
      lion.roar();
   }
}
```

The extends keyword is used to express that the Lion class inherits the Animal class. When executed, the Lion program prints the following:

```
kion, age 3, says: Roar!
```

Let's take a look at the members of the Lion class. The instance variable age is marked as private and is not directly accessible from the subclass Lion. Therefore, the following would not compile:

```
public class Lion extends Animal {
   ...
   public void roar() {
      System.out.print("Lions age: "+age);  // DOES NOT COMPILE
   }
   ...
}
```

The age variable can be accessed indirectly through the getAge() and setAge() methods, which are marked as public in the Animal class. The name variable can be accessed directly in the Lion class since it is marked protected in the Animal class.

Applying Class Access Modifiers

You already know that you can apply access modifiers to both methods and variables. It probably comes as little surprise that you can also apply access modifiers to class definitions, since we have been adding the public access modifier to most classes up to now.

In Java, a *top-level class* is a class that is not defined inside another class. Most of the classes in this book are top-level classes. They can only have public or package-private access. Applying public access to a class indicates that it can be referenced and used in any class. Applying default (package-private) access, which you'll remember is the lack of any access modifier, indicates the class can be accessed only by a class within the same package.

 An *inner class* is a class defined inside of another class and is the opposite of a top-level class. In addition to public and package-private access, inner classes can also have protected and private access. We will discuss inner classes in Chapter 9.

As you might recall, a Java file can have many top-level classes but at most one public top-level class. In fact, it may have no public class at all. There's also no requirement that the single public class be the first class in the file. One benefit of using the package-private access is that you can define many classes within the same Java file. For example, the following definition could appear in a single Java file named Groundhog.java, since it contains only one public class:

```
class Rodent {}
```

```
public class Groundhog extends Rodent {}
```

If we were to update the Rodent class with the public access modifier, the Groundhog.java file would not compile unless the Rodent class was moved to its own Rodent.java file.

 For simplicity, any time you see multiple public classes or interfaces defined in the same code sample in this book, assume each class is defined in its own Java file.

Accessing the *this* Reference

What happens when a method parameter has the same name as an existing instance variable? Let's take a look at an example. What do you think the following program prints?

```java
public class Flamingo {
   private String color;
   public void setColor(String color) {
      color = color;
   }
   public static void main(String... unused) {
      Flamingo f = new Flamingo();
      f.setColor("PINK");
      System.out.println(f.color);
   }
}
```

If you said null, then you'd be correct. Java uses the most granular scope, so when it sees color = color, it thinks you are assigning the method parameter value to itself. The assignment completes successfully within the method, but the value of the instance variable color is never modified and is null when printed in the main() method.

The fix when you have a local variable with the same name as an instance variable is to use the this reference or keyword. The this reference refers to the current instance of the class and can be used to access any member of the class, including inherited members. It can be used in any instance method, constructor, and instance initializer block. It cannot be used when there is no implicit instance of the class, such as in a static method or static initializer block. We apply this to our previous method implementation as follows:

```java
   public void setColor(String color) {
      this.color = color;
   }
```

The corrected code will now print PINK as expected. In many cases, the this reference is optional. If Java encounters a variable or method it cannot find, it will check the class hierarchy to see if it is available.

Now let's look at some examples that aren't common but that you might see on the exam.

```java
1:  public class Duck {
2:      private String color;
3:      private int height;
4:      private int length;
5:
6:      public void setData(int length, int theHeight) {
7:          length = this.length;  // Backwards - no good!
```

```
8:           height = theHeight;    // Fine because a different name
9:           this.color = "white";  // Fine, but this. not necessary
10:    }
11:
12:    public static void main(String[] args) {
13:        Duck b = new Duck();
14:        b.setData(1,2);
15:        System.out.print(b.length + " " + b.height + " " + b.color);
16:    } }
```

This code compiles and prints the following:

```
0 2 white
```

This might not be what you expected, though. Line 7 is incorrect, and you should watch for it on the exam. The instance variable length starts out with a 0 value. That 0 is assigned to the method parameter length. The instance variable stays at 0. Line 8 is more straightforward. The parameter theHeight and instance variable height have different names. Since there is no naming collision, this is not required. Finally, line 9 shows that a variable assignment is allowed to use this even when there is no duplication of variable names.

Calling the *super* Reference

In Java, a variable or method can be defined in both a parent class and a child class. When this happens, how do we reference the version in the parent class instead of the current class?

To achieve this, you can use the super reference or keyword. The super reference is similar to the this reference, except that it excludes any members found in the current class. In other words, the member must be accessible via inheritance. The following class shows how to apply super to use two variables with the same name in a method:

```
class Mammal {
   String type = "mammal";
}

public class Bat extends Mammal {
   String type = "bat";
   public String getType() {
      return super.type + ":" + this.type;
   }
   public static void main(String... zoo) {
      System.out.print(new Bat().getType());
   }
}
```

The program prints mammal:bat. What do you think would happen if the super reference was dropped? The program would then print bat:bat. Java uses the narrowest scope it can—in this case, the type variable defined in the Bat class. Note that the this reference in the previous example was optional, with the program printing the same output as it would if this was dropped.

Let's see if you've gotten the hang of this and super. What does the following program output?

```
1:   class Insect {
2:       protected int numberOfLegs = 4;
3:       String label = "buggy";
4:   }
5:
6:   public class Beetle extends Insect {
7:       protected int numberOfLegs = 6;
8:       short age = 3;
9:       public void printData() {
10:          System.out.print(this.label);
11:          System.out.print(super.label);
12:          System.out.print(this.age);
13:          System.out.print(super.age);
14:          System.out.print(numberOfLegs);
15:      }
16:      public static void main(String []n) {
17:          new Beetle().printData();
18:      }
19: }
```

That was a trick question—this program code would not compile! Let's review each line of the printData() method. Since label is defined in the parent class, it is accessible via both this and super references. For this reason, lines 10 and 11 compile and would both print buggy if the class compiled. On the other hand, the variable age is defined only in the current class, making it accessible via this but not super. For this reason, line 12 compiles, but line 13 does not. Remember, while this includes current and inherited members, super only includes inherited members. In this example, line 12 would print 3 if the code compiled.

Last but least, what would line 14 print if line 13 was commented out? Even though both numberOfLegs variables are accessible in Beetle, Java checks outward starting with the narrowest scope. For this reason, the value of numberOfLegs in the Beetle class is used and 6 would be printed. In this example, this.numberOfLegs and super.numberOfLegs refer to different variables with distinct values.

Since this includes inherited members, you often only use super when you have a naming conflict via inheritance. For example, you have a method or variable defined in the current class that matches a method or variable in a parent class. This commonly comes up in method overriding and variable hiding, which will be discussed later in this chapter.

Declaring Constructors

As you learned in Chapter 2, a constructor is a special method that matches the name of the class and has no return type. It is called when a new instance of the class is created. For the exam, you'll need to know a lot of rules about constructors. In this section, we'll show how to create a constructor. Then, we'll look at default constructors, overloading constructors, calling parent constructors, final fields, and the order of initialization in a class.

Creating a Constructor

Let's start with a simple constructor:

```
public class Bunny {
   public Bunny() {
      System.out.println("constructor");
   }
}
```

The name of the constructor, Bunny, matches the name of the class, Bunny, and there is no return type, not even void. That makes this a constructor. Can you tell why these two are not valid constructors for the Bunny class?

```
public class Bunny {
   public bunny() { }      // DOES NOT COMPILE
   public void Bunny() { }
}
```

The first one doesn't match the class name because Java is case sensitive. Since it doesn't match, Java knows it can't be a constructor and is supposed to be a regular method. However, it is missing the return type and doesn't compile. The second method is a perfectly good method but is not a constructor because it has a return type.

Like method parameters, constructor parameters can be any valid class, array, or primitive type, including generics, but may not include var. The following does not compile:

```
class Bonobo {
   public Bonobo(var food) { // DOES NOT COMPILE
   }
}
```

A class can have multiple constructors, so long as each constructor has a unique signature. In this case, that means the constructor parameters must be distinct. Like methods with the same name but different signatures, declaring multiple constructors with different signatures is referred to as *constructor overloading*. The following Turtle class has four distinct overloaded constructors:

```
public class Turtle {
   private String name;
   public Turtle() {
      name = "John Doe";
   }
   public Turtle(int age) {}
   public Turtle(long age) {}
   public Turtle(String newName, String... favoriteFoods) {
      name = newName;
   }
}
```

Constructors are used when creating a new object. This process is called *instantiation* because it creates a new instance of the class. A constructor is called when we write new followed by the name of the class we want to instantiate. Here's an example:

```
new Turtle()
```

When Java sees the new keyword, it allocates memory for the new object. It then looks for a constructor with a matching signature and calls it.

Default Constructor

Every class in Java has a constructor whether you code one or not. If you don't include any constructors in the class, Java will create one for you without any parameters. This Java-created constructor is called the *default constructor* and is added anytime a class is declared without any constructors. We often refer to it as the default no-argument constructor for clarity. Here's an example:

```
public class Rabbit {
   public static void main(String[] args) {
      Rabbit rabbit = new Rabbit();     // Calls default constructor
   }
}
```

In the Rabbit class, Java sees no constructor was coded and creates one. This default constructor is equivalent to typing this:

```
public Rabbit() {}
```

The default constructor has an empty parameter list and an empty body. It is fine for you to type this in yourself. However, since it doesn't do anything, Java is happy to generate it for you and save you some typing.

We keep saying *generated*. This happens during the compile step. If you look at the file with the .java extension, the constructor will still be missing. It is only in the compiled file with the .class extension that it makes an appearance.

Remember that a default constructor is only supplied if there are no constructors present. Which of these classes do you think has a default constructor?

```
public class Rabbit1 {}

public class Rabbit2 {
   public Rabbit2() {}
}
public class Rabbit3 {
   public Rabbit3(boolean b) {}
}
public class Rabbit4 {
   private Rabbit4() {}
}
```

Only Rabbit1 gets a default no-argument constructor. It doesn't have a constructor coded, so Java generates a default no-argument constructor. Rabbit2 and Rabbit3 both have public constructors already. Rabbit4 has a private constructor. Since these three classes have a constructor defined, the default no-argument constructor is not inserted for you.

Let's take a quick look at how to call these constructors:

```
1: public class RabbitsMultiply {
2:    public static void main(String[] args) {
3:       Rabbit1 r1 = new Rabbit1();
4:       Rabbit2 r2 = new Rabbit2();
5:       Rabbit3 r3 = new Rabbit3(true);
6:       Rabbit4 r4 = new Rabbit4();  // DOES NOT COMPILE
7:    } }
```

Line 3 calls the generated default no-argument constructor. Lines 4 and 5 call the user-provided constructors. Line 6 does not compile. Rabbit4 made the constructor private so that other classes could not call it.

Having only private constructors in a class tells the compiler not to provide a default no-argument constructor. It also prevents other classes from instantiating the class. This is useful when a class has only static methods or the developer wants to have full control of all calls to create new instances of the class. Remember, static methods in the class, including a main() method, may access private members, including private constructors.

Calling Overloaded Constructors with *this()*

Remember, a single class can have multiple constructors. This is referred to as constructor overloading because all constructors have the same inherent name but a different signature. Let's take a look at this in more detail using a Hamster class.

```
public class Hamster {
   private String color;
   private int weight;
   public Hamster(int weight) {                    // First constructor
      this.weight = weight;
      color = "brown";
   }
   public Hamster(int weight, String color) {   // Second constructor
      this.weight = weight;
      this.color = color;
   }
}
```

One of the constructors takes a single int parameter. The other takes an int and a String. These parameter lists are different, so the constructors are successfully overloaded. There is a problem here, though.

There is a bit of duplication, as this.weight is assigned twice in the same way in both constructors. In programming, even a bit of duplication tends to turn into a lot of duplication as we keep adding "just one more thing." For example, imagine we had 20 variables being set like this.weight, rather than just one. What we really want is for the first constructor to call the second constructor with two parameters. So, how can you have a constructor call another constructor? You might be tempted to write this:

```
public Hamster(int weight) {
   Hamster(weight, "brown");       // DOES NOT COMPILE
}
```

This will not work. Constructors can be called only by writing new before the name of the constructor. They are not like normal methods that you can just call. What happens if we stick new before the constructor name?

```
public Hamster(int weight) {
   new Hamster(weight, "brown");  // Compiles, but incorrect
}
```

This attempt does compile. It doesn't do what we want, though. When this constructor is called, it creates a new object with the default weight and color. It then constructs a different object with the desired weight and color and ignores the new object. In this manner, we end up with two objects, with one being discarded after it is created. That's not what we want. We want `weight` and `color` set on the object we are trying to instantiate in the first place.

Java provides a solution: `this()`—yes, the same keyword we used to refer to instance members. When `this()` is used with parentheses, Java calls another constructor on the same instance of the class.

```java
public Hamster(int weight) {
    this(weight, "brown");
}
```

Success! Now Java calls the constructor that takes two parameters, with `weight` and color set as expected.

Calling `this()` has one special rule you need to know. If you choose to call it, the `this()` call must be the first statement in the constructor. The side effect of this is that there can be only one call to `this()` in any constructor.

```java
3:    public Hamster(int weight) {
4:        System.out.println("in constructor");
5:        // Set weight and default color
6:        this(weight, "brown");      // DOES NOT COMPILE
7:    }
```

Even though a print statement on line 4 doesn't change any variables, it is still a Java statement and is not allowed to be inserted before the call to `this()`. The comment on line 5 is just fine. Comments aren't considered statements and are allowed anywhere.

There's one last rule for overloaded constructors you should be aware of. Consider the following definition of the Gopher class:

```java
public class Gopher {
    public Gopher(int dugHoles) {
        this(5);  // DOES NOT COMPILE
    }
}
```

The compiler is capable of detecting that this constructor is calling itself infinitely. Since this code can never terminate, the compiler stops and reports this as an error. Likewise, this also does not compile:

```java
public class Gopher {
    public Gopher() {
        this(5);  // DOES NOT COMPILE
    }
    public Gopher(int dugHoles) {
        this();   // DOES NOT COMPILE
    }
}
```

In this example, the constructors call each other, and the process continues infinitely. Since the compiler can detect this, it reports this as an error.

---

this vs. *this()*

Despite using the same keyword, this and this() are very different. The first, this, refers to an instance of the class, while the second, this(), refers to a constructor call within the class. The exam may try to trick you by using both together, so make sure you know which one to use and why.

Calling Parent Constructors with *super()*

In Java, the first statement of every constructor is either a call to another constructor within the class, using this(), or a call to a constructor in the direct parent class, using super(). If a parent constructor takes arguments, then the super() call also takes arguments. For simplicity in this section, we refer to the super() command as any parent constructor, even those that take arguments. Let's take a look at the Animal class and its subclass Zebra and see how their constructors can be properly written to call one another:

```
public class Animal {
    private int age;
    public Animal(int age) {
        super();      // Refers to constructor in java.lang.Object
        this.age = age;
    }
}

public class Zebra extends Animal {
    public Zebra(int age) {
        super(age);  // Refers to constructor in Animal
    }
    public Zebra() {
        this(4);      // Refers to constructor in Zebra with int argument
    }
}
```

In the first class, Animal, the first statement of the constructor is a call to the parent constructor defined in java.lang.Object, which takes no arguments. In the second class, Zebra, the first statement of the first constructor is a call to Animal's constructor, which takes a single argument. The class Zebra also includes a second no-argument constructor that doesn't call super() but instead calls the other constructor within the Zebra class using this(4).

Like calling this(), calling super() can only be used as the first statement of the constructor. For example, the following two class definitions will not compile:

```java
public class Zoo {
    public Zoo() {
        System.out.println("Zoo created");
        super();      // DOES NOT COMPILE
    }
}

public class Zoo {
    public Zoo() {
        super();
        System.out.println("Zoo created");
        super();      // DOES NOT COMPILE
    }
}
```

The first class will not compile because the call to the parent constructor must be the first statement of the constructor. In the second code snippet, super() is the first statement of the constructor, but it is also used as the third statement. Since super() can only be called once as the first statement of the constructor, the code will not compile.

If the parent class has more than one constructor, the child class may use any valid parent constructor in its definition, as shown in the following example:

```java
public class Animal {
    private int age;
    private String name;
    public Animal(int age, String name) {
        super();
        this.age = age;
        this.name = name;
    }
    public Animal(int age) {
        super();
        this.age = age;
        this.name = null;
    }
}

public class Gorilla extends Animal {
    public Gorilla(int age) {
        super(age,"Gorilla");
```

```
    }
    public Gorilla() {
        super(5);
    }
}
```

In this example, the first child constructor takes one argument, age, and calls the parent constructor, which takes two arguments, age and name. The second child constructor takes no arguments, and it calls the parent constructor, which takes one argument, age. In this example, notice that the child constructors are not required to call matching parent constructors. Any valid parent constructor is acceptable as long as the appropriate input parameters to the parent constructor are provided.

---

super vs. _super()_

Like this and this(), super and super() are unrelated in Java. The first, super, is used to reference members of the parent class, while the second, super(), calls a parent constructor. Anytime you see the super keyword on the exam, make sure it is being used properly.

Understanding Compiler Enhancements

Wait a second, we said the first line of every constructor is a call to either this() or super(), but we've been creating classes and constructors throughout this book, and we've rarely done either. How did these classes compile? The answer is that the Java compiler automatically inserts a call to the no-argument constructor super() if you do not explicitly call this() or super() as the first line of a constructor. For example, the following three class and constructor definitions are equivalent, because the compiler will automatically convert them all to the last example:

```
public class Donkey {}
```

```
public class Donkey {
    public Donkey() {}
}
```

```
public class Donkey {
    public Donkey() {
        super();
    }
}
```

Make sure you understand the differences between these three Donkey class definitions and why Java will automatically convert them all to the last definition. Keep the process that the Java compiler performs in mind while reading the next section.

Are Classes with Only *private* Constructors Considered *final*?

Remember, a final class cannot be extended. What happens if you have a class that is not marked final but only contains private constructors—can you extend the class? The answer is "yes," but only an inner class defined in the class itself can extend it. An inner class is the only one that would have access to a private constructor and be able to call super(). Other top-level classes cannot extend such a class. Don't worry—knowing this fact is not required for the exam. We include it here for those who were curious about declaring only private constructors.

Missing a Default No-Argument Constructor

What happens if the parent class doesn't have a no-argument constructor? Recall that the default no-argument constructor is not required and is inserted by the compiler only if there is no constructor defined in the class. For example, do you see why the following Elephant class declaration does not compile?

```
public class Mammal {
   public Mammal(int age) {}
}
```

```
public class Elephant extends Mammal {  // DOES NOT COMPILE
}
```

Since Elephant does not define any constructors, the Java compiler will attempt to insert a default no-argument constructor. As a second compile-time enhancement, it will also auto-insert a call to super() as the first line of the default no-argument constructor. Our previous Elephant declaration is then converted by the compiler to the following declaration:

```
public class Elephant extends Mammal {
   public Elephant() {
      super();  // DOES NOT COMPILE
   }
}
```

Since the Mammal class has at least one constructor declared, the compiler does not insert a default no-argument constructor. Therefore, the super() call in the Elephant class declaration does not compile. In this case, the Java compiler will not help, and you must create at least one constructor in your child class that explicitly calls a parent constructor via the super() command. We can fix this by adding a call to a parent constructor that takes a fixed argument.

```java
public class Elephant extends Mammal {
    public Elephant() {
        super(10);
    }
}
```

This code will compile because we have added a constructor with an explicit call to a parent constructor. Notice that the class Elephant now has a no-argument constructor even though its parent class Mammal doesn't. Subclasses may define explicit no-argument constructors even if their parent classes do not, provided the constructor of the child maps to a parent constructor via an explicit call of the super() command. This means that subclasses of the Elephant can rely on compiler enhancements. For example, the following class compiles because Elephant now has a no-argument constructor, albeit one defined explicitly:

```java
public class AfricanElephant extends Elephant {}
```

You should be wary of any exam question in which a class defines a constructor that takes arguments and doesn't define a no-argument constructor. Be sure to check that the code compiles before answering a question about it, especially if any classes inherit it. For the exam, you should be able to spot right away why classes such as our first Elephant implementation did not compile.

---

super() Always Refers to the Most Direct Parent

A class may have multiple ancestors via inheritance. In our previous example, AfricanElephant is a subclass of Elephant, which in turn is a subclass of Mammal. For constructors, though, super() always refers to the most direct parent. In this example, calling super() inside the AfricanElephant class always refers to the Elephant class, and never the Mammal class.

Constructors and *final* Fields

As you might recall from Chapter 7, final static variables must be assigned a value exactly once. You saw this happen in the line of the declaration and in a static initializer. Instance variables marked final follow similar rules. They can be assigned values in the line in which they are declared or in an instance initializer.

```java
public class MouseHouse {
    private final int volume;
```

```
   private final String name = "The Mouse House";
   {
      volume = 10;
   }
}
```

Like other final variables, once the value is assigned, it cannot be changed. There is one more place they can be assigned a value—the constructor. The constructor is part of the initialization process, so it is allowed to assign final instance variables in it. For the exam, you need to know one important rule. By the time the constructor completes, all final instance variables must be assigned a value. Let's try this out in an example:

```
public class MouseHouse {
   private final int volume;
   private final String type;
   public MouseHouse() {
      this.volume = 10;
      type = "happy";
   }
}
```

In our MouseHouse implementation, the values for volume and type are assigned in the constructor. Remember that the this keyword is optional since the instance variables are part of the class declaration, and there are no constructor parameters with the same name.

Unlike local final variables, which are not required to have a value unless they are actually used, final instance variables *must* be assigned a value. Default values are not used for these variables. If they are not assigned a value in the line where they are declared or in an instance initializer, then they must be assigned a value in the constructor declaration. Failure to do so will result in a compiler error on the line that declares the constructor.

```
public class MouseHouse {
   private final int volume;
   private final String type;
   {
      this.volume = 10;
   }
   public MouseHouse(String type) {
      this.type = type;
   }
   public MouseHouse() {  // DOES NOT COMPILE
      this.volume = 2;     // DOES NOT COMPILE
   }
}
```

In this example, the first constructor that takes a String argument compiles. Although a final instance variable can be assigned a value only once, each constructor is considered independently in terms of assignment. The second constructor does not compile for two reasons. First, the constructor fails to set a value for the type variable. The compiler detects that a value is never set for type and reports an error on the line where the constructor is declared. Second, the constructor sets a value for the volume variable, even though it was already assigned a value by the instance initializer. The compiler reports this error on the line where volume is set.

On the exam, be wary of any instance variables marked final. Make sure they are assigned a value in the line where they are declared, in an instance initializer, or in a constructor. They should be assigned a value only once, and failure to assign a value is considered a compiler error in the constructor.

What about final instance variables when a constructor calls another constructor in the same class? In that case, you have to follow the constructor logic pathway carefully, making sure every final instance variable is assigned a value exactly once. We can replace our previous bad constructor with the following one that does compile:

```
public MouseHouse() {
    this(null);
}
```

This constructor does not perform any assignments to any final instance variables, but it calls the MouseHouse(String) constructor, which we observed compiles without issue. We use null here to demonstrate that the variable does not need to be an object value. We can assign a null value to final instance variables, so long as they are explicitly set.

Order of Initialization

In Chapter 2, we presented the order of initialization. With inheritance, though, the order of initialization for an instance gets a bit more complicated. We'll start with how to initialize the class and then expand to initializing the instance.

Class Initialization

First, you need to initialize the class, which involves invoking all static members in the class hierarchy, starting with the highest superclass and working downward. This is often referred to as loading the class. The JVM controls when the class is initialized, although you can assume the class is loaded before it is used. The class may be initialized when the program first starts, when a static member of the class is referenced, or shortly before an instance of the class is created.

The most important rule with class initialization is that it happens at most once for each class. The class may also never be loaded if it is not used in the program. We summarize the order of initialization for a class as follows:

Initialize Class X

1. If there is a superclass Y of X, then initialize class Y first.

2. Process all `static` variable declarations in the order they appear in the class.

3. Process all `static` initializers in the order they appear in the class.

Taking a look at an example, what does the following program print?

```java
public class Animal {
    static { System.out.print("A"); }
}
```

```java
public class Hippo extends Animal {
    static { System.out.print("B"); }
    public static void main(String[] grass) {
        System.out.print("C");
        new Hippo();
        new Hippo();
        new Hippo();
    }
}
```

It prints ABC exactly once. Since the `main()` method is inside the `Hippo` class, the class will be initialized first, starting with the superclass and printing AB. Afterward, the `main()` method is executed, printing C. Even though the `main()` method creates three instances, the class is loaded only once.

Why the Hippo Program Printed *C* After *AB*

In the previous example, the `Hippo` class was initialized before the `main()` method was executed. This happened because our `main()` method was inside the class being executed, so it had to be loaded on startup. What if you instead called `Hippo` inside another program?

```java
public class HippoFriend {
    public static void main(String[] grass) {
        System.out.print("C");
        new Hippo();
    }
}
```

Assuming the class isn't referenced anywhere else, this program will likely print CAB, with the Hippo class not being loaded until it is needed inside the main() method. We say *likely*, because the rules for when classes are loaded are determined by the JVM at runtime. For the exam, you just need to know that a class must be initialized before it is referenced or used. Also, the class containing the program entry point, aka the main() method, is loaded before the main() method is executed.

Instance Initialization

An instance is initialized anytime the new keyword is used. In our previous example, there were three new Hippo() calls, resulting in three Hippo instances being initialized. Instance initialization is a bit more complicated than class initialization, because a class or superclass may have many constructors declared but only a handful used as part of instance initialization.

First, start at the lowest-level constructor where the new keyword is used. Remember, the first line of every constructor is a call to this() or super(), and if omitted, the compiler will automatically insert a call to the parent no-argument constructor super(). Then, progress upward and note the order of constructors. Finally, initialize each class starting with the superclass, processing each instance initializer and constructor in the reverse order in which it was called. We summarize the order of initialization for an instance as follows:

Initialize Instance of X

1. If there is a superclass Y of X, then initialize the instance of Y first.
2. Process all instance variable declarations in the order they appear in the class.
3. Process all instance initializers in the order they appear in the class.
4. Initialize the constructor including any overloaded constructors referenced with this().

Let's try a simple example with no inheritance. See if you can figure out what the following application outputs:

```
1:  public class ZooTickets {
2:      private String name = "BestZoo";
3:      { System.out.print(name+"-"); }
4:      private static int COUNT = 0;
5:      static { System.out.print(COUNT+"-"); }
6:      static { COUNT += 10; System.out.print(COUNT+"-"); }
7:
8:      public ZooTickets() {
9:          System.out.print("z-");
10:     }
11:
12:     public static void main(String... patrons) {
```

```
13:        new ZooTickets();
14:    }
15: }
```

The output is as follows:

```
0-10-BestZoo-z-
```

First, we have to initialize the class. Since there is no superclass declared, which means the superclass is `Object`, we can start with the `static` components of `ZooTickets`. In this case, lines 4, 5, and 6 are executed, printing `0-` and `10-`. Next, we initialize the instance. Again, since there is no superclass declared, we start with the instance components. Lines 2 and 3 are executed, which prints `BestZoo-`. Finally, we run the constructor on lines 8–10, which outputs `z-`.

Next, let's try a simple example with inheritance.

```
class Primate {
    public Primate() {
        System.out.print("Primate-");
    }
}

class Ape extends Primate {
    public Ape(int fur) {
        System.out.print("Ape1-");
    }
    public Ape() {
        System.out.print("Ape2-");
    }
}

public class Chimpanzee extends Ape {
    public Chimpanzee() {
        super(2);
        System.out.print("Chimpanzee-");
    }
    public static void main(String[] args) {
        new Chimpanzee();
    }
}
```

The compiler inserts the `super()` command as the first statement of both the `Primate` and `Ape` constructors. The code will execute with the parent constructors called first and yields the following output:

```
Primate-Ape1-Chimpanzee-
```

Notice that only one of the two Ape() constructors is called. You need to start with the call to new Chimpanzee() to determine which constructors will be executed. Remember, constructors are executed from the bottom up, but since the first line of every constructor is a call to another constructor, the flow actually ends up with the parent constructor executed before the child constructor.

The next example is a little harder. What do you think happens here?

```java
1:  public class Cuttlefish {
2:      private String name = "swimmy";
3:      { System.out.println(name); }
4:      private static int COUNT = 0;
5:      static { System.out.println(COUNT); }
6:      { COUNT++; System.out.println(COUNT); }
7:
8:      public Cuttlefish() {
9:          System.out.println("Constructor");
10:     }
11:
12:     public static void main(String[] args) {
13:         System.out.println("Ready");
14:         new Cuttlefish();
15:     }
16: }
```

The output looks like this:

```
0
Ready
swimmy
1
Constructor
```

There is no superclass declared, so we can skip any steps that relate to inheritance. We first process the static variables and static initializers—lines 4 and 5, with line 5 printing 0. Now that the static initializers are out of the way, the main() method can run, which prints Ready. Lines 2, 3, and 6 are processed, with line 3 printing swimmy and line 6 printing 1. Finally, the constructor is run on lines 8–10, which print Constructor.

Ready for a more difficult example? What does the following output?

```java
1:  class GiraffeFamily {
2:      static { System.out.print("A"); }
3:      { System.out.print("B"); }
4:
5:      public GiraffeFamily(String name) {
```

```
6:          this(1);
7:          System.out.print("C");
8:      }
9:
10:     public GiraffeFamily() {
11:         System.out.print("D");
12:     }
13:
14:     public GiraffeFamily(int stripes) {
15:         System.out.print("E");
16:     }
17: }
18: public class Okapi extends GiraffeFamily {
19:     static { System.out.print("F"); }
20:
21:     public Okapi(int stripes) {
22:         super("sugar");
23:         System.out.print("G");
24:     }
25:     { System.out.print("H"); }
26:
27:     public static void main(String[] grass) {
28:         new Okapi(1);
29:         System.out.println();
30:         new Okapi(2);
31:     }
32: }
```

The program prints the following:

```
AFBECHG
BECHG
```

Let's walk through it. Start with initializing the Okapi class. Since it has a superclass GiraffeFamily, initialize it first, printing A on line 2. Next, initialize the Okapi class, printing F on line 19.

After the classes are initialized, execute the main() method on line 27. The first line of the main() method creates a new Okapi object, triggering the instance initialization process. Per the first rule, the superclass instance of GiraffeFamily is initialized first. Per our third rule, the instance initializer in the superclass GiraffeFamily is called, and B is printed on line 3. Per the fourth rule, we initialize the constructors. In this case, this involves calling the constructor on line 5, which in turn calls the overloaded constructor on line 14. The result is that EC is printed, as the constructor bodies are unwound in the reverse order that they were called.

The process then continues with the initialization of the Okapi instance itself. Per the third and fourth rules, H is printed on line 25, and G is printed on line 23, respectively. The process is a lot simpler when you don't have to call any overloaded constructors. Line 29 then inserts a line break in the output. Finally, line 30 initializes a new Okapi object. The order and initialization are the same as line 28, sans the class initialization, so BECHG is printed again. Notice that D is never printed, as only two of the three constructors in the superclass GiraffeFamily are called.

This example is tricky for a few reasons. There are multiple overloaded constructors, lots of initializers, and a complex constructor pathway to keep track of. Luckily, questions like this are rare on the exam. If you see one, just write down what is going on as you read the code.

Reviewing Constructor Rules

Let's review some of the most important constructor rules that we covered in this part of the chapter.

1.   The first statement of every constructor is a call to an overloaded constructor via this(), or a direct parent constructor via super().

2.   If the first statement of a constructor is not a call to this() or super(), then the compiler will insert a no-argument super() as the first statement of the constructor.

3.   Calling this() and super() after the first statement of a constructor results in a compiler error.

4.   If the parent class doesn't have a no-argument constructor, then every constructor in the child class must start with an explicit this() or super() constructor call.

5.   If the parent class doesn't have a no-argument constructor and the child doesn't define any constructors, then the child class will not compile.

6.   If a class only defines private constructors, then it cannot be extended by a top-level class.

7.   All final instance variables must be assigned a value exactly once by the end of the constructor. Any final instance variables not assigned a value will be reported as a compiler error on the line the constructor is declared.

Make sure you understand these rules. The exam will often provide code that breaks one or many of these rules and therefore doesn't compile.

When taking the exam, pay close attention to any question involving two or more classes related by inheritance. Before even attempting to answer the question, you should check that the constructors are properly defined using the previous set of rules. You should also verify the classes include valid access modifiers for members. Once those are verified, you can continue answering the question.

Inheriting Members

Now that we've created a class, what can we do with it? One of Java's biggest strengths is leveraging its inheritance model to simplify code. For example, let's say you have five animal classes that each extend from the `Animal` class. Furthermore, each class defines an `eat()` method with identical implementations. In this scenario, it's a lot better to define `eat()` once in the `Animal` class with the proper access modifiers than to have to maintain the same method in five separate classes. As you'll also see in this section, Java allows any of the five subclasses to replace, or override, the parent method implementation at runtime.

Calling Inherited Members

Java classes may use any `public` or `protected` member of the parent class, including methods, primitives, or object references. If the parent class and child class are part of the same package, then the child class may also use any package-private members defined in the parent class. Finally, a child class may never access a `private` member of the parent class, at least not through any direct reference. As you saw earlier in this chapter, a `private` member age was accessed indirectly via a `public` or `protected` method.

To reference a member in a parent class, you can just call it directly, as in the following example with the output function `displaySharkDetails()`:

```java
class Fish {
   protected int size;
   private int age;

   public Fish(int age) {
      this.age = age;
   }

   public int getAge() {
      return age;
   }
}

public class Shark extends Fish {
   private int numberOfFins = 8;

   public Shark(int age) {
      super(age);
      this.size = 4;
   }

   public void displaySharkDetails() {
```

```
        System.out.print("Shark with age: "+getAge());
        System.out.print(" and "+size+" meters long");
        System.out.print(" with "+numberOfFins+" fins");
    }
}
```

In the child class, we use the public method getAge() and protected member size to access values in the parent class. Remember, you can use this to access visible members of the current or a parent class, and you can use super to access visible members of a parent class.

```
    public void displaySharkDetails() {
        System.out.print("Shark with age: "+super.getAge());
        System.out.print(" and "+super.size+" meters long");
        System.out.print(" with "+this.numberOfFins+" fins");
    }
```

In this example, getAge() and size can be accessed with this or super since they are defined in the parent class, while numberOfFins can only be accessed with this and not super since it is not an inherited property.

Inheriting Methods

Inheriting a class not only grants access to inherited methods in the parent class but also sets the stage for collisions between methods defined in both the parent class and the subclass. In this section, we'll review the rules for method inheritance and how Java handles such scenarios.

Overriding a Method

What if there is a method defined in both the parent and child classes with the same signature? For example, you may want to define a new version of the method and have it behave differently for that subclass. The solution is to override the method in the child class. In Java, *overriding* a method occurs when a subclass declares a new implementation for an inherited method with the same signature and compatible return type. Remember that a method signature includes the name of the method and method parameters.

When you override a method, you may reference the parent version of the method using the super keyword. In this manner, the keywords this and super allow you to select between the current and parent versions of a method, respectively. We illustrate this with the following example:

```
public class Canine {
    public double getAverageWeight() {
        return 50;
    }
}
```

```
public class Wolf extends Canine {
   public double getAverageWeight() {
      return super.getAverageWeight()+20;
   }
   public static void main(String[] args) {
      System.out.println(new Canine().getAverageWeight());
      System.out.println(new Wolf().getAverageWeight());
   }
}
```

In this example, in which the child class Wolf overrides the parent class Canine, the method getAverageWeight() runs, and the program displays the following:

```
50.0
70.0
```

Method Overriding and Recursive Calls

You might be wondering whether the use of super in the previous example was required. For example, what would the following code output if we removed the super keyword?

```
public double getAverageWeight() {
   return getAverageWeight()+20;   // StackOverflowError
}
```

In this example, the compiler would not call the parent Canine method; it would call the current Wolf method since it would think you were executing a recursive method call. A *recursive method* is one that calls itself as part of execution. It is common in programming but must have a termination condition that triggers the end to recursion at some point or depth. In this example, there is no termination condition; therefore, the application will attempt to call itself infinitely and produce a StackOverflowError at runtime.

To override a method, you must follow a number of rules. The compiler performs the following checks when you override a method:

1. The method in the child class must have the same signature as the method in the parent class.

2. The method in the child class must be at least as accessible as the method in the parent class.

3. The method in the child class may not declare a checked exception that is new or broader than the class of any exception declared in the parent class method.

4. If the method returns a value, it must be the same or a subtype of the method in the parent class, known as *covariant return types*.

Defining Subtype and Supertype

When discussing inheritance and polymorphism, we often use the word *subtype* rather than *subclass*, since Java includes interfaces. A *subtype* is the relationship between two types where one type inherits the other. If we define X to be a subtype of Y, then one of the following is true:

- X and Y are classes, and X is a subclass of Y.

- X and Y are interfaces, and X is a subinterface of Y.

- X is a class and Y is an interface, and X implements Y (either directly or through an inherited class).

Likewise, a *supertype* is the reciprocal relationship between two types where one type is the ancestor of the other. Remember, a subclass is a subtype, but not all subtypes are subclasses.

The first rule of overriding a method is somewhat self-explanatory. If two methods have the same name but different signatures, the methods are overloaded, not overridden. Overloaded methods are considered independent and do not share the same polymorphic properties as overridden methods.

Overloading vs. Overriding

Overloading and overriding a method are similar in that they both involve redefining a method using the same name. They differ in that an overloaded method will use a different list of method parameters. This distinction allows overloaded methods a great deal more freedom in syntax than an overridden method would have. For example, compare the overloaded fly() with the overridden eat() in the Eagle class.

```java
public class Bird {
    public void fly() {
        System.out.println("Bird is flying");
    }
    public void eat(int food) {
        System.out.println("Bird is eating "+food+" units of food");
    }
}

public class Eagle extends Bird {
    public int fly(int height) {
        System.out.println("Bird is flying at "+height+" meters");
```

```
      return height;
   }
   public int eat(int food) {  // DOES NOT COMPILE
      System.out.println("Bird is eating "+food+" units of food");
      return food;
   }
}
```

The fly() method is overloaded in the subclass Eagle, since the signature changes from a no-argument method to a method with one int argument. Because the method is being overloaded and not overridden, the return type can be changed from void to int.

The eat() method is overridden in the subclass Eagle, since the signature is the same as it is in the parent class Bird—they both take a single argument int. Because the method is being overridden, the return type of the method in the Eagle class must be compatible with the return type for the method in the Bird class. In this example, the return type int is not a subtype of void; therefore, the compiler will throw an exception on this method definition.

Any time you see a method on the exam with the same name as a method in the parent class, determine whether the method is being overloaded or overridden first; doing so will help you with questions about whether the code will compile.

What's the purpose of the second rule about access modifiers? Let's try an illustrative example:

```
public class Camel {
   public int getNumberOfHumps() {
      return 1;
   }
}

public class BactrianCamel extends Camel {
   private int getNumberOfHumps() {  // DOES NOT COMPILE
      return 2;
   }
}

public class Rider {
   public static void main(String[] args) {
      Camel c = new BactrianCamel();
      System.out.print(c.getNumberOfHumps());
   }
}
```

In this example, `BactrianCamel` attempts to override the `getNumberOfHumps()` method defined in the parent class but fails because the access modifier `private` is more restrictive than the one defined in the parent version of the method. Let's say `BactrianCamel` was allowed to compile, though. Would the call to `getNumberOfHumps()` in `Rider.main()` succeed or fail? As you will see when we get into polymorphism later in this chapter, the answer is quite ambiguous. The reference type for the object is `Camel`, where the method is declared `public`, but the object is actually an instance of type `BactrianCamel`, which is declared `private`. Java avoids these types of ambiguity problems by limiting overriding a method to access modifiers that are as accessible or more accessible than the version in the inherited method.

The third rule says that overriding a method cannot declare new checked exceptions or checked exceptions broader than the inherited method. This is done for similar polymorphic reasons as limiting access modifiers. In other words, you could end up with an object that is more restrictive than the reference type it is assigned to, resulting in a checked exception that is not handled or declared. We will discuss what it means for an exception to be checked in Chapter 10, "Exceptions." For now, you should just recognize that if a broader checked exception is declared in the overriding method, the code will not compile. Let's try an example:

```
public class Reptile {
    protected void sleepInShell() throws IOException {}

    protected void hideInShell() throws NumberFormatException {}

    protected void exitShell() throws FileNotFoundException {}
}

public class GalapagosTortoise extends Reptile {
    public void sleepInShell() throws FileNotFoundException {}

    public void hideInShell() throws IllegalArgumentException {}

    public void exitShell() throws IOException {} // DOES NOT COMPILE
}
```

In this example, we have three overridden methods. These overridden methods use the more accessible `public` modifier, which is allowed per our second rule over overridden methods. The overridden `sleepInShell()` method declares `FileNotFoundException`, which is a subclass of the exception declared in the inherited method, `IOException`. Per our third rule of overridden methods, this is a successful override since the exception is narrower in the overridden method.

The overridden `hideInShell()` method declares an `IllegalArgumentException`, which is a superclass of the exception declared in the inherited method, `NumberFormatException`. While this seems like an invalid override since the overridden method uses a broader exception, both of these exceptions are unchecked, so the third rule does not apply.

The third overridden exitShell() method declares IOException, which is a superclass of the exception declared in the inherited method, FileNotFoundException. Since these are checked exceptions and IOException is broader, the overridden exitShell() method does not compile in the GalapagosTortoise class. We'll revisit these exception classes, including memorizing which ones are subclasses of each other, in Chapter 10.

The fourth and final rule around overriding a method is probably the most complicated, as it requires knowing the relationships between the return types. The overriding method must use a return type that is covariant with the return type of the inherited method.

Let's try an example for illustrative purposes:

```
public class Rhino {
    protected CharSequence getName() {
        return "rhino";
    }
    protected String getColor() {
        return "grey, black, or white";
    }
}

class JavanRhino extends Rhino {
    public String getName() {
        return "javan rhino";
    }
    public CharSequence getColor() {  // DOES NOT COMPILE
        return "grey";
    }
}
```

The subclass JavanRhino attempts to override two methods from Rhino: getName() and getColor(). Both overridden methods have the same name and signature as the inherited methods. The overridden methods also have a broader access modifier, public, than the inherited methods. Per the second rule, a broader access modifier is acceptable.

From Chapter 5, you should already know that String implements the CharSequence interface, making String a subtype of CharSequence. Therefore, the return type of getName() in JavanRhino is covariant with the return type of getName() in Rhino.

On the other hand, the overridden getColor() method does not compile because CharSequence is not a subtype of String. To put it another way, all String values are CharSequence values, but not all CharSequence values are String values. For example, a StringBuilder is a CharSequence but not a String. For the exam, you need to know if the return type of the overriding method is the same or a subtype of the return type of the inherited method.

A simple test for covariance is the following: Given an inherited return type A and an overriding return type B, can you assign an instance of B to a reference variable for A without a cast? If so, then they are covariant. This rule applies to primitive types and object types alike. If one of the return types is void, then they both must be void, as nothing is covariant with void except itself.

The last three rules of overriding a method may seem arbitrary or confusing at first, but as you'll see later in this chapter when we discuss polymorphism, they are needed for consistency. Without these rules in place, it is possible to create contradictions within the Java language.

Overriding a Generic Method

Overriding methods is complicated enough, but add generics to it and things only get more challenging. In this section, we'll provide a discussion of the aspects of overriding generic methods that you'll need to know for the exam.

Review of Overloading a Generic Method

In Chapter 7, you learned that you cannot overload methods by changing the generic type due to type erasure. To review, only one of the two methods is allowed in a class because type erasure will reduce both sets of arguments to (List input).

```
public class LongTailAnimal {
   protected void chew(List<Object> input) {}
   protected void chew(List<Double> input) {}  // DOES NOT COMPILE
}
```

For the same reason, you also can't overload a generic method in a parent class.

```
public class LongTailAnimal {
   protected void chew(List<Object> input) {}
}

public class Anteater extends LongTailAnimal {
   protected void chew(List<Double> input) {}  // DOES NOT COMPILE
}
```

Both of these examples fail to compile because of type erasure. In the compiled form, the generic type is dropped, and it appears as an invalid overloaded method.

Generic Method Parameters

On the other hand, you can override a method with generic parameters, but you must match the signature including the generic type exactly. For example, this version of the

Anteater class does compile because it uses the same generic type in the overridden method as the one defined in the parent class:

```
public class LongTailAnimal {
    protected void chew(List<String> input) {}
}

public class Anteater extends LongTailAnimal {
    protected void chew(List<String> input) {}
}
```

The generic type parameters have to match, but what about the generic class or interface? Take a look at the following example. From what you know so far, do you think these classes will compile?

```
public class LongTailAnimal {
    protected void chew(List<Object> input) {}
}

public class Anteater extends LongTailAnimal {
    protected void chew(ArrayList<Double> input) {}
}
```

Yes, these classes do compile. However, they are considered overloaded methods, not overridden methods, because the signature is not the same. Type erasure does not change the fact that one of the method arguments is a List and the other is an ArrayList.

Generics and Wildcards

Java includes support for generic wildcards using the question mark (?) character. It even supports bounded wildcards.

```
void sing1(List<?> v) {}                    // unbounded wildcard
void sing2(List<? super String> v) {}       // lower bounded wildcard
void sing3(List<? extends String> v) {}     // upper bounded wildcard
```

Using generics with wildcards, overloaded methods, and overridden methods can get quite complicated. Luckily, wildcards are out of scope for the 1Z0-815 exam. They are required knowledge, though, when you take the 1Z0-816 exam.

Generic Return Types

When you're working with overridden methods that return generics, the return values must be covariant. In terms of generics, this means that the return type of the class or interface declared in the overriding method must be a subtype of the class defined in the parent class. The generic parameter type must match its parent's type exactly.

Given the following declaration for the Mammal class, which of the two subclasses, Monkey and Goat, compile?

```
public class Mammal {
   public List<CharSequence> play() { ... }
   public CharSequence sleep() { ... }
}

public class Monkey extends Mammal {
   public ArrayList<CharSequence> play() { ... }
}

public class Goat extends Mammal {
   public List<String> play() { ... }  // DOES NOT COMPILE
   public String sleep() { ... }
}
```

The Monkey class compiles because ArrayList is a subtype of List. The play() method in the Goat class does not compile, though. For the return types to be covariant, the generic type parameter must match. Even though String is a subtype of CharSequence, it does not exactly match the generic type defined in the Mammal class. Therefore, this is considered an invalid override.

Notice that the sleep() method in the Goat class does compile since String is a subtype of CharSequence. This example shows that covariance applies to the return type, just not the generic parameter type.

For the exam, it might be helpful for you to apply type erasure to questions involving generics to ensure that they compile properly. Once you've determined which methods are overridden and which are being overloaded, work backward, making sure the generic types match for overridden methods. And remember, generic methods cannot be overloaded by changing the generic parameter type only.

Redeclaring *private* Methods

What happens if you try to override a private method? In Java, you can't override private methods since they are not inherited. Just because a child class doesn't have access to the parent method doesn't mean the child class can't define its own version of the method. It just means, strictly speaking, that the new method is not an overridden version of the parent class's method.

Java permits you to redeclare a new method in the child class with the same or modified signature as the method in the parent class. This method in the child class is a separate and independent method, unrelated to the parent version's method, so none of the rules for overriding methods is invoked. Let's return to the `Camel` example we used in the previous section and show two related classes that define the same method:

```
public class Camel {
    private String getNumberOfHumps() {
        return "Undefined";
    }
}

public class DromedaryCamel extends Camel {
    private int getNumberOfHumps() {
        return 1;
    }
}
```

This code compiles without issue. Notice that the return type differs in the child method from `String` to `int`. In this example, the method `getNumberOfHumps()` in the parent class is redeclared, so the method in the child class is a new method and not an override of the method in the parent class. As you saw in the previous section, if the method in the parent class were `public` or `protected`, the method in the child class would not compile because it would violate two rules of overriding methods. The parent method in this example is `private`, so there are no such issues.

Hiding Static Methods

A *hidden method* occurs when a child class defines a `static` method with the same name and signature as an inherited `static` method defined in a parent class. Method hiding is similar but not exactly the same as method overriding. The previous four rules for overriding a method must be followed when a method is hidden. In addition, a new rule is added for hiding a method:

5. The method defined in the child class must be marked as `static` if it is marked as `static` in a parent class.

Put simply, it is method hiding if the two methods are marked `static`, and method overriding if they are not marked `static`. If one is marked `static` and the other is not, the class will not compile.

Let's review some examples of the new rule:

```
public class Bear {
    public static void eat() {
        System.out.println("Bear is eating");
    }
}

public class Panda extends Bear {
```

```
   public static void eat() {
      System.out.println("Panda is chewing");
   }
   public static void main(String[] args) {
      eat();
   }
}
```

In this example, the code compiles and runs. The eat() method in the Panda class hides the eat() method in the Bear class, printing "Panda is chewing" at runtime. Because they are both marked as static, this is not considered an overridden method. That said, there is still some inheritance going on. If you remove the eat() method in the Panda class, then the program prints "Bear is eating" at runtime.

Let's contrast this with an example that violates the fifth rule:

```
public class Bear {
   public static void sneeze() {
      System.out.println("Bear is sneezing");
   }
   public void hibernate() {
      System.out.println("Bear is hibernating");
   }
   public static void laugh() {
      System.out.println("Bear is laughing");
   }
}

public class Panda extends Bear {
   public void sneeze() {              // DOES NOT COMPILE
      System.out.println("Panda sneezes quietly");
   }
   public static void hibernate() { // DOES NOT COMPILE
      System.out.println("Panda is going to sleep");
   }
   protected static void laugh() {  // DOES NOT COMPILE
      System.out.println("Panda is laughing");
   }
}
```

In this example, sneeze() is marked static in the parent class but not in the child class. The compiler detects that you're trying to override using an instance method. However, sneeze() is a static method that should be hidden, causing the compiler to generate an error. In the second method, hibernate() is an instance member in the parent class but a static method in the child class. In this scenario, the compiler thinks that you're trying to hide a static method. Because hibernate() is an instance method that should be overridden, the compiler generates an error. Finally, the laugh() method does not compile. Even though both versions of method are marked static, the version in Panda has a more restrictive access modifier than the one it inherits, and it breaks the second rule for overriding methods. Remember, the four rules for overriding methods must be followed when hiding static methods.

Creating *final* Methods

We conclude our discussion of method inheritance with a somewhat self-explanatory rule—final methods cannot be replaced.

By marking a method final, you forbid a child class from replacing this method. This rule is in place both when you override a method and when you hide a method. In other words, you cannot hide a static method in a child class if it is marked final in the parent class.

Let's take a look at an example:

```
public class Bird {
    public final boolean hasFeathers() {
        return true;
    }
    public final static void flyAway() {}
}

public class Penguin extends Bird {
    public final boolean hasFeathers() {  // DOES NOT COMPILE
        return false;
    }
    public final static void flyAway() {}  // DOES NOT COMPILE
}
```

In this example, the instance method hasFeathers() is marked as final in the parent class Bird, so the child class Penguin cannot override the parent method, resulting in a compiler error. The static method flyAway() is also marked final, so it cannot be hidden in the subclass. In this example, whether or not the child method used the final keyword is irrelevant—the code will not compile either way.

This rule applies only to inherited methods. For example, if the two methods were marked private in the parent Bird class, then the Penguin class, as defined, would compile. In that case, the private methods would be redeclared, not overridden or hidden.

Real World Scenario

Why Mark a Method as *final*?

Although marking methods as final prevents them from being overridden, it does have advantages in practice. For example, you'd mark a method as final when you're defining a parent class and want to guarantee certain behavior of a method in the parent class, regardless of which child is invoking the method.

In the previous example with Bird, the author of the parent class may want to ensure the method hasFeathers() always returns true, regardless of the child class instance on which it is invoked. The author is confident that there is no example of a Bird in which feathers are not present.

The reason methods are not commonly marked as final in practice, though, is that it may be difficult for the author of a parent class method to consider all of the possible ways her child class may be used. For example, although all adult birds have feathers, a baby chick doesn't; therefore, if you have an instance of a Bird that is a chick, it would not have feathers. For this reason, the final modifier is often used when the author of the parent class wants to guarantee certain behavior at the cost of limiting polymorphism.

Hiding Variables

As you saw with method overriding, there are a lot of rules when two methods have the same signature and are defined in both the parent and child classes. Luckily, the rules for variables with the same name in the parent and child classes are a lot simpler. In fact, Java doesn't allow variables to be overridden. Variables can be hidden, though.

A *hidden variable* occurs when a child class defines a variable with the same name as an inherited variable defined in the parent class. This creates two distinct copies of the variable within an instance of the child class: one instance defined in the parent class and one defined in the child class.

As when hiding a static method, you can't override a variable; you can only hide it. Let's take a look at a hidden variable. What do you think the following application prints?

```
class Carnivore {
    protected boolean hasFur = false;
}

public class Meerkat extends Carnivore {
    protected boolean hasFur = true;

    public static void main(String[] args) {
        Meerkat m = new Meerkat();
        Carnivore c = m;
        System.out.println(m.hasFur);
```

```
        System.out.println(c.hasFur);
    }
}
```

It prints true followed by false. Confused? Both of these classes define a hasFur vari-able, but with different values. Even though there is only one object created by the main() method, both variables exist independently of each other. The output changes depending on the reference variable used.

If you didn't understand the last example, don't worry. The next section on polymorphism will expand on how overriding and hiding differ. For now, you just need to know that overrid-ing a method replaces the parent method on all reference variables (other than super), whereas hiding a method or variable replaces the member only if a child reference type is used.

Understanding Polymorphism

Java supports *polymorphism*, the property of an object to take on many different forms. To put this more precisely, a Java object may be accessed using a reference with the same type as the object, a reference that is a superclass of the object, or a reference that defines an interface the object implements, either directly or through a superclass. Furthermore, a cast is not required if the object is being reassigned to a super type or interface of the object.

Interface Primer

We'll be discussing interfaces in detail in the next chapter. For this chapter, you need to know the following:

- An interface can define abstract methods.

- A class can implement any number of interfaces.

- A class implements an interface by overriding the inherited abstract methods.

- An object that implements an interface can be assigned to a reference for that interface.

As you'll see in the next chapter, the same rules for overriding methods and polymor-phism apply.

Let's illustrate this polymorphism property with the following example:

```
public class Primate {
    public boolean hasHair() {
        return true;
```

```
      }
}

public interface HasTail {
   public abstract boolean isTailStriped();
}

public class Lemur extends Primate implements HasTail {
   public boolean isTailStriped() {
      return false;
   }
   public int age = 10;
   public static void main(String[] args) {
      Lemur lemur = new Lemur();
      System.out.println(lemur.age);

      HasTail hasTail = lemur;
      System.out.println(hasTail.isTailStriped());

      Primate primate = lemur;
      System.out.println(primate.hasHair());
   }
}
```

This code compiles and prints the following output:

```
10
false
true
```

The most important thing to note about this example is that only one object, Lemur, is created and referenced. Polymorphism enables an instance of Lemur to be reassigned or passed to a method using one of its supertypes, such as Primate or HasTail.

Once the object has been assigned to a new reference type, only the methods and variables available to that reference type are callable on the object without an explicit cast. For example, the following snippets of code will not compile:

```
      HasTail hasTail = lemur;
      System.out.println(hasTail.age);               // DOES NOT COMPILE

      Primate primate = lemur;
      System.out.println(primate.isTailStriped()); // DOES NOT COMPILE
```

In this example, the reference hasTail has direct access only to methods defined with the HasTail interface; therefore, it doesn't know the variable age is part of the object. Likewise, the reference primate has access only to methods defined in the Primate class, and it doesn't have direct access to the isTailStriped() method.

Object vs. Reference

In Java, all objects are accessed by reference, so as a developer you never have direct access to the object itself. Conceptually, though, you should consider the object as the entity that exists in memory, allocated by the Java runtime environment. Regardless of the type of the reference you have for the object in memory, the object itself doesn't change. For example, since all objects inherit java.lang.Object, they can all be reassigned to java.lang.Object, as shown in the following example:

```
Lemur lemur = new Lemur();

Object lemurAsObject = lemur;
```

Even though the Lemur object has been assigned to a reference with a different type, the object itself has not changed and still exists as a Lemur object in memory. What has changed, then, is our ability to access methods within the Lemur class with the lemurAsObject reference. Without an explicit cast back to Lemur, as you'll see in the next section, we no longer have access to the Lemur properties of the object.

We can summarize this principle with the following two rules:

1. The type of the object determines which properties exist within the object in memory.

2. The type of the reference to the object determines which methods and variables are accessible to the Java program.

It therefore follows that successfully changing a reference of an object to a new reference type may give you access to new properties of the object, but remember, those properties existed before the reference change occurred.

Let's illustrate this property using the previous example in Figure 8.4.

FIGURE 8.4   Object vs. reference

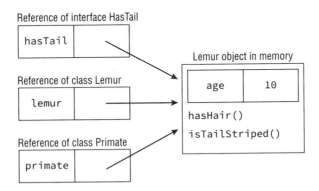

As you can see in the figure, the same object exists in memory regardless of which reference is pointing to it. Depending on the type of the reference, we may only have access to certain methods. For example, the hasTail reference has access to the method isTailStriped() but doesn't have access to the variable age defined in the Lemur class.

As you'll learn in the next section, it is possible to reclaim access to the variable age by explicitly casting the hasTail reference to a reference of type Lemur.

Casting Objects

In the previous example, we created a single instance of a Lemur object and accessed it via superclass and interface references. Once we changed the reference type, though, we lost access to more specific members defined in the subclass that still exist within the object. We can reclaim those references by casting the object back to the specific subclass it came from:

```
Primate primate = new Lemur();   // Implicit Cast

Lemur lemur2 = primate;          // DOES NOT COMPILE
System.out.println(lemur2.age);

Lemur lemur3 = (Lemur)primate;   // Explicit Cast
System.out.println(lemur3.age);
```

In this example, we first create a Lemur object and implicitly cast it to a Primate reference. Since Lemur is a subclass of Primate, this can be done without a cast operator. Next, we try to convert the primate reference back to a lemur reference, lemur2, without an explicit cast. The result is that the code will not compile. In the second example, though, we explicitly cast the object to a subclass of the object Primate, and we gain access to all the methods and fields available to the Lemur class.

Casting objects is similar to casting primitives, as you saw in Chapter 3, "Operators." When casting objects, you do not need a cast operator if the current reference is a subtype of the target type. This is referred to as an implicit cast or type conversion. Alternatively, if the current reference is not a subtype of the target type, then you need to perform an explicit cast with a compatible type. If the underlying object is not compatible with the type, then a ClassCastException will be thrown at runtime.

We summarize these concepts into a set of rules for you to memorize for the exam:

1. Casting a reference from a subtype to a supertype doesn't require an explicit cast.
2. Casting a reference from a supertype to a subtype requires an explicit cast.
3. The compiler disallows casts to an unrelated class.
4. At runtime, an invalid cast of a reference to an unrelated type results in a ClassCastException being thrown.

The third rule is important; the exam may try to trick you with a cast that the compiler doesn't allow. In our previous example, we were able to cast a Primate reference to a Lemur reference, because Lemur is a subclass of Primate and therefore related. Consider this example instead:

```
public class Bird {}

public class Fish {
    public static void main(String[] args) {
```

```
        Fish fish = new Fish();
        Bird bird = (Bird)fish;  // DOES NOT COMPILE
    }
}
```

In this example, the classes Fish and Bird are not related through any class hierarchy that the compiler is aware of; therefore, the code will not compile. While they both extend Object implicitly, they are considered unrelated types since one cannot be a subtype of the other.

> While the compiler can enforce rules about casting to unrelated types for classes, it cannot do the same for interfaces, since a subclass may implement the interface. We'll revisit this topic in the next chapter. For now, you just need to know the third rule on casting applies to class types only, not interfaces.

Casting is not without its limitations. Even though two classes share a related hierarchy, that doesn't mean an instance of one can automatically be cast to another. Here's an example:

```
public class Rodent {}

public class Capybara extends Rodent {
    public static void main(String[] args) {
        Rodent rodent = new Rodent();
        Capybara capybara = (Capybara)rodent;  // ClassCastException
    }
}
```

This code creates an instance of Rodent and then tries to cast it to a subclass of Rodent, Capybara. Although this code will compile, it will throw a ClassCastException at runtime since the object being referenced is not an instance of the Capybara class. The thing to keep in mind in this example is the Rodent object created does not inherit the Capybara class in any way.

When reviewing a question on the exam that involves casting and polymorphism, be sure to remember what the instance of the object actually is. Then, focus on whether the compiler will allow the object to be referenced with or without explicit casts.

The *instanceof* Operator

In Chapter 3, we presented the instanceof operator, which can be used to check whether an object belongs to a particular class or interface and to prevent ClassCastExceptions at runtime. Unlike the previous example, the following code snippet doesn't throw an exception at runtime and performs the cast only if the instanceof operator returns true:

```
if(rodent instanceof Capybara) {
    Capybara capybara = (Capybara)rodent;
}
```

Just as the compiler does not allow casting an object to unrelated types, it also does not allow instanceof to be used with unrelated types. We can demonstrate this with our unrelated Bird and Fish classes:

```
public static void main(String[] args) {
    Fish fish = new Fish();
    if (fish instanceof Bird) {  // DOES NOT COMPILE
        Bird bird = (Bird) fish;  // DOES NOT COMPILE
    }
}
```

In this snippet, neither the instanceof operator nor the explicit cast operation compile.

Polymorphism and Method Overriding

In Java, polymorphism states that when you override a method, you replace all calls to it, even those defined in the parent class. As an example, what do you think the following code snippet outputs?

```
class Penguin {
    public int getHeight() { return 3; }
    public void printInfo() {
        System.out.print(this.getHeight());
    }
}

public class EmperorPenguin extends Penguin {
    public int getHeight() { return 8; }
    public static void main(String []fish) {
        new EmperorPenguin().printInfo();
    }
}
```

If you said 8, then you are well on your way to understanding polymorphism. In this example, the object being operated on in memory is an EmperorPenguin. The getHeight() method is overridden in the subclass, meaning all calls to it are replaced at runtime. Despite printInfo() being defined in the Penguin class, calling getHeight() on the object calls the method associated with the precise object in memory, not the current reference type where it is called. Even using the `this` reference, which is optional in this example, does not call the parent version because the method has been replaced.

The facet of polymorphism that replaces methods via overriding is one of the most important properties in all of Java. It allows you to create complex inheritance models, with subclasses that have their own custom implementation of overridden methods. It also means the parent class does not need to be updated to use the custom or overridden method. If the method is properly overridden, then the overridden version will be used in all places that it is called.

Remember, you can choose to limit polymorphic behavior by marking methods `final`, which prevents them from being overridden by a subclass.

Calling the Parent Version of an Overridden Method

As you saw earlier in the chapter, there is one exception to overriding a method where the parent method can still be called, and that is when the `super` reference is used. How can you modify our `EmperorPenguin` example to print 3, as defined in the `Penguin getHeight()` method? You could try calling `super.getHeight()` in the `printInfo()` method of the `Penguin` class.

```
class Penguin {
   ...
   public void printInfo() {
      System.out.print(super.getHeight());   // DOES NOT COMPILE
   }
}
```

Unfortunately, this does not compile, as `super` refers to the superclass of `Penguin`, in this case `Object`. The solution is to override `printInfo()` in the `EmperorPenguin` class and use `super` there.

```
public class EmperorPenguin extends Penguin {
   ...
   public void printInfo() {
      System.out.print(super.getHeight());
   }
   ...
}
```

This new version of `EmperorPenguin` uses the `getHeight()` method declared in the parent class and prints 3.

Overriding vs. Hiding Members

While method overriding replaces the method everywhere it is called, static method and variable hiding does not. Strictly speaking, hiding members is not a form of polymorphism since the methods and variables maintain their individual properties. Unlike method overriding, hiding members is very sensitive to the reference type and location where the member is being used.

Let's take a look at an example:

```java
class Penguin {
    public static int getHeight() { return 3; }
    public void printInfo() {
        System.out.println(this.getHeight());
    }
}
public class CrestedPenguin extends Penguin {
    public static int getHeight() { return 8; }
    public static void main(String... fish) {
        new CrestedPenguin().printInfo();
    }
}
```

The CrestedPenguin example is nearly identical to our previous EmporerPenguin example, although as you probably already guessed, it prints 3 instead of 8. The getHeight() method is static and is therefore hidden, not overridden. The result is that calling getHeight() in CrestedPenguin returns a different value than calling it in the Penguin, even if the underlying object is the same. Contrast this with overriding a method, where it returns the same value for an object regardless of which class it is called in.

What about the fact that we used this to access a static method in this.getHeight()? As discussed in Chapter 7, while you are permitted to use an instance reference to access a static variable or method, it is often discouraged. In fact, the compiler will warn you when you access static members in a non-static way. In this case, the this reference had no impact on the program output.

Besides the location, the reference type can also determine the value you get when you are working with hidden members. Ready? Let's try a more complex example:

```java
class Marsupial {
    protected int age = 2;
    public static boolean isBiped() {
        return false;
    }
}

public class Kangaroo extends Marsupial {
```

```
    protected int age = 6;
    public static boolean isBiped() {
        return true;
    }

    public static void main(String[] args) {
        Kangaroo joey = new Kangaroo();
        Marsupial moey = joey;
        System.out.println(joey.isBiped());
        System.out.println(moey.isBiped());
        System.out.println(joey.age);
        System.out.println(moey.age);
    }
}
```

The program prints the following:

```
true
false
6
2
```

Remember, in this example, only *one object*, of type Kangaroo, is created and stored in memory. Since static methods can only be hidden, not overridden, Java uses the reference type to determine which version of isBiped() should be called, resulting in joey.isBiped() printing true and moey.isBiped() printing false.

Likewise, the age variable is hidden, not overridden, so the reference type is used to determine which value to output. This results in joey.age returning 6 and moey.age returning 2.

 Real World Scenario

Don't Hide Members in Practice

Although Java allows you to hide variables and static methods, it is considered an extremely poor coding practice. As you saw in the previous example, the value of the variable or method can change depending on what reference is used, making your code very confusing, difficult to follow, and challenging for others to maintain. This is further compounded when you start modifying the value of the variable in both the parent and child methods, since it may not be clear which variable you're updating.

When you're defining a new variable or static method in a child class, it is considered good coding practice to select a name that is not already used by an inherited member. Redeclaring private methods and variables is considered less problematic, though, because the child class does not have access to the variable in the parent class to begin with.

For the exam, make sure you understand these examples as they show how hidden and overridden methods are fundamentally different. In practice, overriding methods is the cornerstone of polymorphism and is an extremely powerful feature.

Summary

This chapter took the basic class structures we've presented throughout the book and expanded them by introducing the notion of inheritance. Java classes follow a multilevel single-inheritance pattern in which every class has exactly one direct parent class, with all classes eventually inheriting from java.lang.Object.

Inheriting a class gives you access to all of the public and protected members of the class. It also gives you access to package-private members of the class if the classes are in the same package. All instance methods, constructors, and instance initializers have access to two special reference variables: this and super. Both this and super provide access to all inherited members, with only this providing access to all members in the current class declaration.

Constructors are special methods that use the class name and do not have a return type. They are used to instantiate new objects. Declaring constructors requires following a number of important rules. If no constructor is provided, the compiler will automatically insert a default no-argument constructor in the class. The first line of every constructor is a call to an overloaded constructor, this(), or a parent constructor, super(); otherwise, the compiler will insert a call to super() as the first line of the constructor. In some cases, such as if the parent class does not define a no-argument constructor, this can lead to compilation errors. Pay close attention on the exam to any class that defines a constructor with arguments and doesn't define a no-argument constructor.

Classes are initialized in a predetermined order: superclass initialization; static variables and static initializers in the order that they appear; instance variables and instance initializers in the order they appear; and finally, the constructor. All final instance variables must be assigned a value exactly once. If by the time a constructor finishes, a final instance variable is not assigned a value, then the constructor will not compile.

We reviewed overloaded, overridden, hidden, and redeclared methods and showed how they differ, especially in terms of polymorphism. A method is overloaded if it has the same name but a different signature as another accessible method. A method is overridden if it has the same signature as an inherited method, with access modifiers, exceptions, and a return type that are compatible. A static method is hidden if it has the same signature as an inherited static method. Finally, a method is redeclared if it has the same name and possibly the same signature as an uninherited method.

We also introduced the notion of hiding variables, although we strongly discourage this in practice as it often leads to confusing, difficult-to-maintain code.

Finally, this chapter introduced the concept of polymorphism, central to the Java language, and showed how objects can be accessed in a variety of forms. Make sure you understand when casts are needed for accessing objects, and be able to spot the difference between compile-time and runtime cast problems.

Exam Essentials

Be able to write code that extends other classes. A Java class that extends another class inherits all of its `public` and `protected` methods and variables. If the class is in the same package, it also inherits all package-private members of the class. Classes that are marked `final` cannot be extended. Finally, all classes in Java extend `java.lang.Object` either directly or from a superclass.

Be able to distinguish and make use of *this*, *this()*, *super*, and *super()*. To access a current or inherited member of a class, the `this` reference can be used. To access an inherited member, the `super` reference can be used. The `super` reference is often used to reduce ambiguity, such as when a class reuses the name of an inherited method or variable. The calls to `this()` and `super()` are used to access constructors in the same class and parent class, respectively.

Evaluate code involving constructors. The first line of every constructor is a call to another constructor within the class using `this()` or a call to a constructor of the parent class using the `super()` call. The compiler will insert a call to `super()` if no constructor call is declared. If the parent class doesn't contain a no-argument constructor, an explicit call to the parent constructor must be provided. Be able to recognize when the default constructor is provided. Remember that the order of initialization is to initialize all classes in the class hierarchy, starting with the superclass. Then, the instances are initialized, again starting with the superclass. All `final` variables must be assigned a value exactly once by the time the constructor is finished.

Understand the rules for method overriding. Java allows methods to be overridden, or replaced, by a subclass if certain rules are followed: a method must have the same signature, be at least as accessible as the parent method, must not declare any new or broader exceptions, and must use covariant return types. The generic parameter types must exactly match in any of the generic method arguments or a generic return type. Methods marked `final` may not be overridden or hidden.

Understand the rules for hiding methods and variables. When a `static` method is overridden in a subclass, it is referred to as method hiding. Likewise, variable hiding is when an inherited variable name is reused in a subclass. In both situations, the original method or variable still exists and is accessible depending on where it is accessed and the reference type used. For method hiding, the use of `static` in the method declaration must be the same between the parent and child class. Finally, variable and method hiding should generally be avoided since it leads to confusing and difficult-to-follow code.

Recognize the difference between method overriding and method overloading. Both method overloading and overriding involve creating a new method with the same name as an existing method. When the method signature is the same, it is referred to as method overriding and must follow a specific set of override rules to compile. When the method signature is different, with the method taking different inputs, it is referred to as method overloading, and none of the override rules are required. Method overriding is important to polymorphism because it replaces all calls to the method, even those made in a superclass.

Understand polymorphism.   An object may take on a variety of forms, referred to as polymorphism. The object is viewed as existing in memory in one concrete form but is accessible in many forms through reference variables. Changing the reference type of an object may grant access to new members, but the members always exist in memory.

Recognize valid reference casting.   An instance can be automatically cast to a superclass or interface reference without an explicit cast. Alternatively, an explicit cast is required if the reference is being narrowed to a subclass of the object. The Java compiler doesn't permit casting to unrelated class types. Be able to discern between compiler-time casting errors and those that will not occur until runtime and that throw a `ClassCastException`.

Review Questions

The answers to the chapter review questions can be found in the Appendix.

1. Which code can be inserted to have the code print 2?

```java
public class BirdSeed {
    private int numberBags;
    boolean call;

    public BirdSeed() {
        // LINE 1
        call = false;
        // LINE 2
    }

    public BirdSeed(int numberBags) {
        this.numberBags = numberBags;
    }

    public static void main(String[] args) {
        BirdSeed seed = new BirdSeed();
        System.out.print(seed.numberBags);
    } }
```

   A. Replace line 1 with `BirdSeed(2);`

   B. Replace line 2 with `BirdSeed(2);`

   C. Replace line 1 with `new BirdSeed(2);`

   D. Replace line 2 with `new BirdSeed(2);`

   E. Replace line 1 with `this(2);`

   F. Replace line 2 with `this(2);`

   G. The code prints 2 without any changes.

2. Which of the following statements about methods are true? (Choose all that apply.)

   A. Overloaded methods must have the same signature.

   B. Overridden methods must have the same signature.

   C. Hidden methods must have the same signature.

   D. Overloaded methods must have the same return type.

   E. Overridden methods must have the same return type.

   F. Hidden methods must have the same return type.

3. What is the output of the following program?

```
1:  class Mammal {
2:      private void sneeze() {}
3:      public Mammal(int age) {
4:          System.out.print("Mammal");
5:      } }
6:  public class Platypus extends Mammal {
7:      int sneeze() { return 1; }
8:      public Platypus() {
9:          System.out.print("Platypus");
10:     }
11:     public static void main(String[] args) {
12:         new Mammal(5);
13:     } }
```

A. Platypus

B. Mammal

C. PlatypusMammal

D. MammalPlatypus

E. The code will compile if line 7 is changed.

F. The code will compile if line 9 is changed.

4. Which of the following complete the constructor so that this code prints out 50? (Choose all that apply.)

```
class Speedster {
    int numSpots;
}
public class Cheetah extends Speedster {
    int numSpots;

    public Cheetah(int numSpots) {
        // INSERT CODE HERE
    }

    public static void main(String[] args) {
        Speedster s = new Cheetah(50);
        System.out.print(s.numSpots);
    }
}
```

A. numSpots = numSpots;

B. numSpots = this.numSpots;

  C. `this.numSpots = numSpots;`

  D. `numSpots = super.numSpots;`

  E. `super.numSpots = numSpots;`

  F. The code does not compile, regardless of the code inserted into the constructor.

  G. None of the above

5. What is the output of the following code?

```
1:  class Arthropod {
2:      protected void printName(long input) {
3:          System.out.print("Arthropod");
4:      }
5:      void printName(int input) {
6:          System.out.print("Spooky");
7:      } }
8:  public class Spider extends Arthropod {
9:      protected void printName(int input) {
10:         System.out.print("Spider");
11:     }
12:     public static void main(String[] args) {
13:         Arthropod a = new Spider();
14:         a.printName((short)4);
15:         a.printName(4);
16:         a.printName(5L);
17:     } }
```

  A. SpiderSpiderArthropod

  B. SpiderSpiderSpider

  C. SpiderSpookyArthropod

  D. SpookySpiderArthropod

  E. The code will not compile because of line 5.

  F. The code will not compile because of line 9.

  G. None of the above

6. Which of the following statements about overridden methods are true? (Choose all that apply.)

  A. An overridden method must contain method parameters that are the same or covariant with the method parameters in the inherited method.

  B. An overridden method may declare a new exception, provided it is not checked.

  C. An overridden method must be more accessible than the method in the parent class.

  D. An overridden method may declare a broader checked exception than the method in the parent class.

E. If an inherited method returns void, then the overridden version of the method must return void.

F. None of the above

7. Which of the following pairs, when inserted into the blanks, allow the code to compile? (Choose all that apply.)

```
1:  public class Howler {
2:      public Howler(long shadow) {
3:          _____;
4:      }
5:      private Howler(int moon) {
6:          super();
7:      }
8:  }
9:  class Wolf extends Howler {
10:     protected Wolf(String stars) {
11:         super(2L);
12:     }
13:     public Wolf() {
14:         _____;
15:     }
16: }
```

A. this(3) at line 3, this("") at line 14

B. this() at line 3, super(1) at line 14

C. this((short)1) at line 3, this(null) at line 14

D. super() at line 3, super() at line 14

E. this(2L) at line 3, super((short)2) at line 14

F. this(5) at line 3, super(null) at line 14

G. Remove lines 3 and 14.

8. What is the result of the following?

```
1:  public class PolarBear {
2:      StringBuilder value = new StringBuilder("t");
3:      { value.append("a"); }
4:      { value.append("c"); }
5:      private PolarBear() {
6:          value.append("b");
7:      }
8:      public PolarBear(String s) {
```

```
 9:         this();
10:         value.append(s);
11:     }
12:     public PolarBear(CharSequence p) {
13:         value.append(p);
14:     }
15:     public static void main(String[] args) {
16:         Object bear = new PolarBear();
17:         bear = new PolarBear("f");
18:         System.out.println(((PolarBear)bear).value);
19:     } }
```

A. tacb

B. tacf

C. tacbf

D. tcafb

E. taftacb

F. The code does not compile.

G. An exception is thrown.

9. Which of the following method signatures are valid overrides of the hairy() method in the Alpaca class? (Choose all that apply.)

```
import java.util.*;

public class Alpaca {
    protected List<String> hairy(int p) { return null; }
}
```

A. `List<String> hairy(int p) { return null; }`

B. `public List<String> hairy(int p) { return null; }`

C. `public List<CharSequence> hairy(int p) { return null; }`

D. `private List<String> hairy(int p) { return null; }`

E. `public Object hairy(int p) { return null; }`

F. `public ArrayList<String> hairy(int p) { return null; }`

G. None of the above

10. How many lines of the following program contain a compilation error?

```
1: public class Rodent {
2:     public Rodent(var x) {}
3:     protected static Integer chew() throws Exception {
4:         System.out.println("Rodent is chewing");
```

```
5:          return 1;
6:      }
7:  }
8:  class Beaver extends Rodent {
9:      public Number chew() throws RuntimeException {
10:         System.out.println("Beaver is chewing on wood");
11:         return 2;
12:     } }
```

A. None

B. 1

C. 2

D. 3

E. 4

F. 5

11. Which of the following statements about polymorphism are true? (Choose all that apply.)

   A. An object may be cast to a subtype without an explicit cast.

   B. If the type of a method argument is an interface, then a reference variable that implements the interface may be passed to the method.

   C. A method that takes a parameter with type `java.lang.Object` can be passed any variable.

   D. All cast exceptions can be detected at compile-time.

   E. By defining a `final` instance method in the superclass, you guarantee that the specific method will be called in the parent class at runtime.

   F. Polymorphism applies only to classes, not interfaces.

12. Which of the following statements can be inserted in the blank so that the code will compile successfully? (Choose all that apply.)

```
public class Snake {}
public class Cobra extends Snake {}
public class GardenSnake extends Cobra {}
public class SnakeHandler {
   private Snake snake;
   public void setSnake(Snake snake) { this.snake = snake; }
   public static void main(String[] args) {
      new SnakeHandler().setSnake(_____);
   }
}
```

   A. `new Cobra()`

   B. `new Snake()`

    C. `new Object()`

    D. `new String("Snake")`

    E. `new GardenSnake()`

    F. `null`

    G. None of the above. The class does not compile, regardless of the value inserted in the blank.

13. Which of these classes compile and will include a default constructor created by the compiler? (Choose all that apply.)

    A. `public class Bird {}`

    B.
```
public class Bird {
    public bird() {}
}
```

    C.
```
public class Bird {
    public bird(String name) {}
}
```

    D.
```
public class Bird {
    public Bird() {}
}
```

    E.
```
public class Bird {
    Bird(String name) {}
}
```

    F.
```
public class Bird {
    private Bird(int age) {}
}
```

    G.
```
public class Bird {
    public Bird bird() {return null;}
}
```

14. Which of the following statements about inheritance are correct? (Choose all that apply.)

    A. A class can directly extend any number of classes.

    B. A class can implement any number of interfaces.

    C. All variables inherit `java.lang.Object`.

    D. If class A is extended by B, then B is a superclass of A.

    E. If class C implements interface D, then C is subtype of D.

    F. Multiple inheritance is the property of a class to have multiple direct superclasses.

15. What is the result of the following?

```
1:  class Arachnid {
2:      static StringBuilder sb = new StringBuilder();
3:      { sb.append("c"); }
```

```
4:      static
5:      { sb.append("u"); }
6:      { sb.append("r"); }
7:  }
8:  public class Scorpion extends Arachnid {
9:      static
10:     { sb.append("q"); }
11:     { sb.append("m"); }
12:     public static void main(String[] args) {
13:         System.out.print(Scorpion.sb + " ");
14:         System.out.print(Scorpion.sb + " ");
15:         new Arachnid();
16:         new Scorpion();
17:         System.out.print(Scorpion.sb);
18:     } }
```

A. qu qu qumrcrc

B. u u ucrcrm

C. uq uq uqmcrcr

D. uq uq uqcrcrm

E. qu qu qumcrcr

F. qu qu qucrcrm

G. The code does not compile.

16. Which of the following methods are valid overrides of the friendly() method in the Llama class? (Choose all that apply.)

```
import java.util.*;

public class Llama {
    void friendly(List<String> laugh, Iterable<Short> s) {}
}
```

A. void friendly(List<CharSequence> laugh, Iterable<Short> s) {}

B. void friendly(List<String> laugh, Iterable<Short> s) {}

C. void friendly(ArrayList<String> laugh, Iterable<Short> s) {}

D. void friendly(List<String> laugh, Iterable<Integer> s) {}

E. void friendly(ArrayList<CharSequence> laugh, Object s) {}

F. void friendly(ArrayList<String> laugh, Iterable... s) {}

G. None of the above

17. Which of the following statements about inheritance and variables are true? (Choose all that apply.)

   A. Instance variables can be overridden in a subclass.

   B. If an instance variable is declared with the same name as an inherited variable, then the type of the variable must be covariant.

   C. If an instance variable is declared with the same name as an inherited variable, then the access modifier must be at least as accessible as the variable in the parent class.

   D. If a variable is declared with the same name as an inherited `static` variable, then it must also be marked `static`.

   E. The variable in the child class may not throw a checked exception that is new or broader than the class of any exception thrown in the parent class variable.

   F. None of the above

18. Which of the following are true? (Choose all that apply.)

   A. `this()` can be called from anywhere in a constructor.

   B. `this()` can be called from anywhere in an instance method.

   C. `this.variableName` can be called from any instance method in the class.

   D. `this.variableName` can be called from any `static` method in the class.

   E. You can call the default constructor written by the compiler using `this()`.

   F. You can access a `private` constructor with the `main()` method in the same class.

19. Which statements about the following classes are correct? (Choose all that apply.)

```
1:  public class Mammal {
2:      private void eat() {}
3:      protected static void drink() {}
4:      public Integer dance(String p) { return null; }
5:  }
6:  class Primate extends Mammal {
7:      public void eat(String p) {}
8:  }
9:  class Monkey extends Primate {
10:     public static void drink() throws RuntimeException {}
11:     public Number dance(CharSequence p) { return null; }
12:     public int eat(String p) {}
13: }
```

   A. The `eat()` method in `Mammal` is correctly overridden on line 7.

   B. The `eat()` method in `Mammal` is correctly overloaded on line 7.

C. The drink() method in Mammal is correctly hidden on line 10.

D. The drink() method in Mammal is correctly overridden on line 10.

E. The dance() method in Mammal is correctly overridden on line 11.

F. The dance() method in Mammal is correctly overloaded on line 11.

G. The eat() method in Primate is correctly hidden on line 12.

H. The eat() method in Primate is correctly overloaded on line 12.

20. What is the output of the following code?

```
1:  class Reptile {
2:      {System.out.print("A");}
3:      public Reptile(int hatch) {}
4:      void layEggs() {
5:          System.out.print("Reptile");
6:      } }
7:  public class Lizard extends Reptile {
8:      static {System.out.print("B");}
9:      public Lizard(int hatch) {}
10:     public final void layEggs() {
11:         System.out.print("Lizard");
12:     }
13:     public static void main(String[] args) {
14:         Reptile reptile = new Lizard(1);
15:         reptile.layEggs();
16:     } }
```

A. AALizard

B. BALizard

C. BLizardA

D. ALizard

E. The code will not compile because of line 10.

F. None of the above

21. Which statement about the following program is correct?

```
1:  class Bird {
2:      int feathers = 0;
3:      Bird(int x) { this.feathers = x; }
4:      Bird fly() {
5:          return new Bird(1);
```

```
6:     } }
7:  class Parrot extends Bird {
8:     protected Parrot(int y) { super(y); }
9:     protected Parrot fly() {
10:        return new Parrot(2);
11:     } }
12: public class Macaw extends Parrot {
13:     public Macaw(int z) { super(z); }
14:     public Macaw fly() {
15:        return new Macaw(3);
16:     }
17:     public static void main(String... sing) {
18:        Bird p = new Macaw(4);
19:        System.out.print(((Parrot)p.fly()).feathers);
20:     } }
```

A. One line contains a compiler error.

B. Two lines contain compiler errors.

C. Three lines contain compiler errors.

D. The code compiles but throws a `ClassCastException` at runtime.

E. The program compiles and prints 3.

F. The program compiles and prints 0.

22. What does the following program print?

```
1:  class Person {
2:     static String name;
3:     void setName(String q) { name = q; } }
4:  public class Child extends Person {
5:     static String name;
6:     void setName(String w) { name = w; }
7:     public static void main(String[] p) {
8:        final Child m = new Child();
9:        final Person t = m;
10:       m.name = "Elysia";
11:       t.name = "Sophia";
12:       m.setName("Webby");
13:       t.setName("Olivia");
14:       System.out.println(m.name + " " + t.name);
15:    } }
```

A. Elysia Sophia

B. Webby Olivia

C. Olivia Olivia

D. Olivia Sophia

E. The code does not compile.

F. None of the above

23. What is the output of the following program?

```
1:  class Canine {
2:      public Canine(boolean t) { logger.append("a"); }
3:      public Canine() { logger.append("q"); }
4:
5:      private StringBuilder logger = new StringBuilder();
6:      protected void print(String v) { logger.append(v); }
7:      protected String view() { return logger.toString(); }
8:  }
9:
10: class Fox extends Canine {
11:     public Fox(long x) { print("p"); }
12:     public Fox(String name) {
13:         this(2);
14:         print("z");
15:     }
16: }
17:
18: public class Fennec extends Fox {
19:     public Fennec(int e) {
20:         super("tails");
21:         print("j");
22:     }
23:     public Fennec(short f) {
24:         super("eevee");
25:         print("m");
26:     }
27:
28:     public static void main(String... unused) {
29:         System.out.println(new Fennec(1).view());
30:     } }
```

A. qpz

B. qpzj

C. jzpa

D. apj

E. apjm

F. The code does not compile.

G. None of the above

24. Which statements about polymorphism and method inheritance are correct? (Choose all that apply.)

A. It cannot be determined until runtime which overridden method will be executed in a parent class.

B. It cannot be determined until runtime which hidden method will be executed in a parent class.

C. Marking a method static prevents it from being overridden or hidden.

D. Marking a method final prevents it from being overridden or hidden.

E. The reference type of the variable determines which overridden method will be called at runtime.

F. The reference type of the variable determines which hidden method will be called at runtime.

25. What is printed by the following program?

```
1:  class Antelope {
2:      public Antelope(int p) {
3:          System.out.print("4");
4:      }
5:      { System.out.print("2"); }
6:      static { System.out.print("1"); }
7:  }
8:  public class Gazelle extends Antelope {
9:      public Gazelle(int p) {
10:         super(6);
11:         System.out.print("3");
12:     }
13:     public static void main(String hopping[]) {
14:         new Gazelle(0);
15:     }
16:     static { System.out.print("8"); }
17:     { System.out.print("9"); }
18: }
```

A. 182640

B. 182943

C. 182493

D. 421389

E. The code does not compile.

F. The output cannot be determined until runtime.

26. How many lines of the following program contain a compilation error?

```
1:  class Primate {
2:      protected int age = 2;
3:      { age = 1; }
4:      public Primate() {
5:          this().age = 3;
6:      }
7:  }
8:  public class Orangutan {
9:      protected int age = 4;
10:     { age = 5; }
11:     public Orangutan() {
12:         this().age = 6;
13:     }
14:     public static void main(String[] bananas) {
15:         final Primate x = (Primate)new Orangutan();
16:         System.out.println(x.age);
17:     }
18: }
```

A. None, and the program prints 1 at runtime.

B. None, and the program prints 3 at runtime.

C. None, but it causes a ClassCastException at runtime.

D. 1

E. 2

F. 3

G. 4

Chapter

9

Advanced Class Design

OCP EXAM OBJECTIVES COVERED IN THIS CHAPTER:

✓ **Reusing Implementations Through Inheritance**

  ▪ Create and extend abstract classes

✓ **Programming Abstractly Through Interfaces**

  ▪ Create and implement interfaces

  ▪ Distinguish class inheritance from interface inheritance including abstract classes

In Chapter 8, "Class Design," we showed you how to create classes utilizing inheritance and polymorphism. In this chapter, we will continue our discussion of class design starting with abstract classes. By creating abstract class definitions, you're defining a platform that other developers can extend and build on top of. We'll then move on to interfaces and show how to use them to design a standard set of methods across classes with varying implementations. Finally, we'll conclude this chapter with a brief presentation of inner classes.

Creating Abstract Classes

We start our discussion of advanced class design with abstract classes. As you will see, abstract classes have important uses in defining a framework that other developers can use.

Introducing Abstract Classes

In Chapter 8, you learned that a subclass can override an inherited method defined in a parent class. Overriding a method potentially changes the behavior of a method in the parent class. For example, take a look at the following Bird class and its Stork subclass:

```
class Bird {
    public String getName() { return null; }
    public void printName() {
        System.out.print(getName());
    }
}


public class Stork extends Bird {
    public String getName() { return "Stork!"; }
    public static void main(String[] args) {
        new Stork().printName();
    }
}
```

This program prints Stork! at runtime. Notice that the getName() method is overridden in the subclass. Even though the implementation of printName() is defined in the Bird class, the fact that getName() is overridden in the subclass means it is replaced everywhere, even in the parent class.

Let's take this one step further. Suppose you want to define a Bird class that other developers can extend and use, but you want the developers to specify the particular type of Bird. Also, rather than having the Bird version of getName() return null (or throw an exception), you want to ensure every class that extends Bird is required to provide its own overridden version of the getName() method.

Enter abstract classes. An *abstract class* is a class that cannot be instantiated and may contain abstract methods. An *abstract method* is a method that does not define an implementation when it is declared. Both abstract classes and abstract methods are denoted with the abstract modifier. Compare our previous implementation with this new one using an abstract Bird class:

```java
abstract class Bird {
    public abstract String getName();
    public void printName() {
        System.out.print(getName());
    }
}

public class Stork extends Bird {
    public String getName() { return "Stork!"; }
    public static void main(String[] args) {
        new Stork().printName();
    }
}
```

What's different? First, the Bird class is marked abstract. Next, the getName() method in Bird is also marked abstract. Finally, the implementation of getName(), including the braces ({}), have been replaced with a single semicolon (;).

What about the Stork class? It's exactly the same as before. While it may look the same, though, the rules around how the class must be implemented have changed. In particular, the Stork class *must* now override the abstract getName() method. For example, the following implementation does not compile because Stork does not override the required abstract getName() method:

```java
public class Stork extends Bird {}  // DOES NOT COMPILE
```

While these differences may seem small, imagine the Bird and Stork class are each written by different people. By one person marking getName() as abstract in the Bird class, they are sending a message to the other developer writing the Stork class: "Hey, to use this class, you need to write a getName() method!"

An abstract class is most commonly used when you want another class to inherit properties of a particular class, but you want the subclass to fill in some of the implementation details. In our example, the author of the Bird class wrote the printName() method but did not know what it was going to do at runtime, since the getName() implementation had yet to be provided.

> **Override vs. Implement**
>
> Oftentimes, when an abstract method is overridden in a subclass, it is referred to as implementing the method. It is described this way because the subclass is providing an implementation for a method that does not yet have one. While we tend to use the terms *implement* and *override* interchangeably for abstract methods, the term *override* is more accurate.
>
> When overriding an abstract method, all of the rules you learned about overriding methods in Chapter 8 are applicable. For example, you can override an abstract method with a covariant return type. Likewise, you can declare new unchecked exceptions but not checked exceptions in the overridden method. Furthermore, you can override an abstract method in one class and then override it again in a subclass of that class.
>
> The method override rules apply whether the abstract method is declared in an abstract class or, as we shall see later in this chapter, an interface. We will continue to use override and implement interchangeably in this chapter, as this is common in software development. Just remember that providing an implementation for an abstract method is considered a method override and all of the associated rules for overriding methods apply.

Earlier, we said that an abstract class is one that cannot be instantiated. This means that if you attempt to instantiate it, the compiler will report an exception, as in this example:

```
abstract class Alligator {
   public static void main(String... food) {
      var a = new Alligator();  // DOES NOT COMPILE
   }
}
```

An abstract class can be initialized, but only as part of the instantiation of a nonabstract subclass.

Defining Abstract Methods

As you saw in the previous example, an abstract class may include nonabstract methods, in this case with the printName() method. In fact, an abstract class can include all of the same members as a nonabstract class, including variables, static and instance methods, and inner classes. As you will see in the next section, abstract classes can also include constructors.

One of the most important features of an abstract class is that it is not actually required to include any abstract methods. For example, the following code compiles even though it doesn't define any abstract methods:

```
public abstract class Llama {
   public void chew() {}
}
```

Although an abstract class doesn't have to declare any abstract methods, an abstract method can only be defined in an abstract class (or an interface, as you will see shortly). For example, the following code won't compile because the class is not marked abstract:

```
public class Egret {  // DOES NOT COMPILE
   public abstract void peck();
}
```

The exam creators like to include invalid class declarations like the Egret class, which mixes nonabstract classes with abstract methods. If you see a class that contains an abstract method, make sure the class is marked abstract.

Like the final modifier, the abstract modifier can be placed before or after the access modifier in class and method declarations, as shown in this Tiger class:

```
abstract public class Tiger {
   abstract public int claw();
}
```

There are some restrictions on the placement of the abstract modifier. The abstract modifier cannot be placed after the class keyword in a class declaration, nor after the return type in a method declaration. The following Jackal and howl() declarations do not compile for these reasons:

```
public class abstract Jackal {  // DOES NOT COMPILE
   public int abstract howl();  // DOES NOT COMPILE
}
```

It is not possible to define an abstract method that has a body, or default implementation. You can still define a method with a body—you just can't mark it as abstract. As long as you do not mark the method as final, the subclass has the option to override an inherited method.

Constructors in Abstract Classes

Even though abstract classes cannot be instantiated, they are still initialized through constructors by their subclasses. For example, does the following program compile?

```
abstract class Bear {
   abstract CharSequence chew();
   public Bear() {
      System.out.println(chew());  // Does this compile?
   }
}

public class Panda extends Bear {
   String chew() { return "yummy!"; }
```

```
    public static void main(String[] args) {
        new Panda();
    }
}
```

Using the constructor rules you learned in Chapter 8, the compiler inserts a default no-argument constructor into the Panda class, which first calls super() in the Bear class. The Bear constructor is only called when the abstract class is being initialized through a subclass; therefore, there is an implementation of chew() at the time the constructor is called. This code compiles and prints yummy! at runtime.

For the exam, remember that abstract classes are initialized with constructors in the same way as nonabstract classes. For example, if an abstract class does not provide a constructor, the compiler will automatically insert a default no-argument constructor.

The primary difference between a constructor in an abstract class and a nonabstract class is that a constructor in abstract class can be called only when it is being initialized by a nonabstract subclass. This makes sense, as abstract classes cannot be instantiated.

Invalid Abstract Method Declarations

The exam writers are also fond of questions with methods marked as abstract for which an implementation is also defined. For example, can you see why each of the following methods does not compile?

```
public abstract class Turtle {
    public abstract long eat()      // DOES NOT COMPILE
    public abstract void swim() {}; // DOES NOT COMPILE
    public abstract int getAge() {  // DOES NOT COMPILE
        return 10;
    }
    public void sleep;              // DOES NOT COMPILE
    public void goInShell();        // DOES NOT COMPILE
}
```

The first method, eat(), does not compile because it is marked abstract but does not end with as semicolon (;). The next two methods, swim() and getAge(), do not compile because they are marked abstract, but they provide an implementation block enclosed in braces ({}). For the exam, remember that an abstract method declaration must end in a semicolon without any braces. The next method, sleep, does not compile because it is missing parentheses, (), for method arguments. The last method, goInShell(), does not compile because it is not marked abstract and therefore must provide a body enclosed in braces.

Make sure you understand why each of the previous methods does not compile and that you can spot errors like these on the exam. If you come across a question on the exam in which a class or method is marked abstract, make sure the class is properly implemented before attempting to solve the problem.

Invalid Modifiers

In Chapter 7, "Methods and Encapsulation," you learned about various modifiers for methods and classes. In this section, we review the abstract modifier and which modifiers it is not compatible with.

abstract and *final* Modifiers

What would happen if you marked a class or method both abstract and final? If you mark something abstract, you are intending for someone else to extend or implement it. But, if you mark something final, you are preventing anyone from extending or implementing it. These concepts are in direct conflict with each other.

Due to this incompatibility, Java does not permit a class or method to be marked both abstract and final. For example, the following code snippet will not compile:

```
public abstract final class Tortoise {  // DOES NOT COMPILE
   public abstract final void walk();   // DOES NOT COMPILE
}
```

In this example, neither the class or method declarations will compile because they are marked both abstract and final. The exam doesn't tend to use final modifiers on classes or methods often, so if you see them, make sure they aren't used with the abstract modifier.

abstract and *private* Modifiers

A method cannot be marked as both abstract and private. This rule makes sense if you think about it. How would you define a subclass that implements a required method if the method is not inherited by the subclass? The answer is you can't, which is why the compiler will complain if you try to do the following:

```
public abstract class Whale {
   private abstract void sing();  // DOES NOT COMPILE
}

public class HumpbackWhale extends Whale {
   private void sing() {
      System.out.println("Humpback whale is singing");
   }
}
```

In this example, the abstract method sing() defined in the parent class Whale is not visible to the subclass HumpbackWhale. Even though HumpbackWhale does provide an implementation, it is not considered an override of the abstract method since the abstract method is not inherited. The compiler recognizes this in the parent class and reports an error as soon as private and abstract are applied to the same method.

While it is not possible to declare a method abstract and private, it is possible (albeit redundant) to declare a method final and private.

If we changed the access modifier from `private` to `protected` in the parent class `Whale`, would the code compile? Let's take a look:

```java
public abstract class Whale {
   protected abstract void sing();
}

public class HumpbackWhale extends Whale {
   private void sing() {  // DOES NOT COMPILE
      System.out.println("Humpback whale is singing");
   }
}
```

In this modified example, the code will still not compile, but for a completely different reason. If you remember the rules for overriding a method, the subclass cannot reduce the visibility of the parent method, `sing()`. Because the method is declared `protected` in the parent class, it must be marked as `protected` or `public` in the child class. Even with abstract methods, the rules for overriding methods must be followed.

abstract and *static* Modifiers

As you saw in Chapter 8, a `static` method cannot be overridden. It is defined as belonging to the class, not an instance of the class. If a `static` method cannot be overridden, then it follows that it also cannot be marked `abstract` since it can never be implemented. For example, the following class does not compile:

```java
abstract class Hippopotamus {
   abstract static void swim();  // DOES NOT COMPILE
}
```

For the exam, make sure you know which modifiers can and cannot be used with one another, especially for abstract classes and interfaces.

Creating a Concrete Class

An abstract class becomes usable when it is extended by a concrete subclass. A *concrete class* is a nonabstract class. The first concrete subclass that extends an abstract class is required to implement all inherited abstract methods. This includes implementing any inherited abstract methods from inherited interfaces, as we will see later in this chapter.

When you see a concrete class extending an abstract class on the exam, check to make sure that it implements all of the required abstract methods. Can you see why the following `Walrus` class does not compile?

```java
public abstract class Animal {
   public abstract String getName();
}

public class Walrus extends Animal { // DOES NOT COMPILE
}
```

In this example, we see that `Animal` is marked as `abstract` and `Walrus` is not, making `Walrus` a concrete subclass of `Animal`. Since `Walrus` is the first concrete subclass, it must implement all inherited abstract methods—`getName()` in this example. Because it doesn't, the compiler reports an error with the declaration of `Walrus`.

We highlight the *first* concrete subclass for a reason. An abstract class can extend a non-abstract class, and vice versa. Any time a concrete class is extending an abstract class, it must implement all of the methods that are inherited as abstract. Let's illustrate this with a set of inherited classes:

```java
abstract class Mammal {
    abstract void showHorn();
    abstract void eatLeaf();
}

abstract class Rhino extends Mammal {
    void showHorn() {}
}

public class BlackRhino extends Rhino {
    void eatLeaf() {}
}
```

In this example, the `BlackRhino` class is the first concrete subclass, while the `Mammal` and `Rhino` classes are abstract. The `BlackRhino` class inherits the `eatLeaf()` method as abstract and is therefore required to provide an implementation, which it does.

What about the `showHorn()` method? Since the parent class, `Rhino`, provides an implementation of `showHorn()`, the method is inherited in the `BlackRhino` as a nonabstract method. For this reason, the `BlackRhino` class is permitted but not required to override the `showHorn()` method. The three classes in this example are correctly defined and compile.

What if we changed the `Rhino` declaration to remove the abstract modifier?

```java
class Rhino extends Mammal {  // DOES NOT COMPILE
    void showHorn() {}
}
```

By changing `Rhino` to a concrete class, it becomes the first nonabstract class to extend the abstract `Mammal` class. Therefore, it must provide an implementation of both the `showHorn()` and `eatLeaf()` methods. Since it only provides one of these methods, the modified `Rhino` declaration does not compile.

Let's try one more example. The following concrete class `Lion` inherits two abstract methods, `getName()` and `roar()`:

```java
public abstract class Animal {
    abstract String getName();
```

```
}

public abstract class BigCat extends Animal {
   protected abstract void roar();
}

public class Lion extends BigCat {
   public String getName() {
      return "Lion";
   }
   public void roar() {
      System.out.println("The Lion lets out a loud ROAR!");
   }
}
```

In this sample code, BigCat extends Animal but is marked as abstract; therefore, it is not required to provide an implementation for the getName() method. The class Lion is not marked as abstract, and as the first concrete subclass, it must implement all of the inherited abstract methods not defined in a parent class. All three of these classes compile successfully.

Reviewing Abstract Class Rules

For the exam, you should know the following rules about abstract classes and abstract methods. While it may seem like a lot to remember, most of these rules are pretty straightforward. For example, marking a class or method abstract and final makes it unusable. Be sure you can spot contradictions such as these if you come across them on the exam.

Abstract Class Definition Rules

1. Abstract classes cannot be instantiated.

2. All top-level types, including abstract classes, cannot be marked protected or private.

3. Abstract classes cannot be marked final.

4. Abstract classes may include zero or more abstract and nonabstract methods.

5. An abstract class that extends another abstract class inherits all of its abstract methods.

6. The first concrete class that extends an abstract class must provide an implementation for all of the inherited abstract methods.

7. Abstract class constructors follow the same rules for initialization as regular constructors, except they can be called only as part of the initialization of a subclass.

These rules for abstract methods apply regardless of whether the abstract method is defined in an abstract class or interface.

Abstract Method Definition Rules

1. Abstract methods can be defined only in abstract classes or interfaces.

2. Abstract methods cannot be declared `private` or `final`.

3. Abstract methods must not provide a method body/implementation in the abstract class in which they are declared.

4. Implementing an abstract method in a subclass follows the same rules for overriding a method, including covariant return types, exception declarations, etc.

Implementing Interfaces

Although Java doesn't allow multiple inheritance of state, it does allow a class to implement any number of interfaces. An *interface* is an abstract data type are that declares a list of abstract methods that any class implementing the interface must provide. An interface can also include constant variables. Both abstract methods and constant variables included with an interface are implicitly assumed to be `public`.

Interfaces and Nonabstract Methods

For the 1Z0-815 exam, you only need to know about two members for interfaces: abstract methods and constant variables. With Java 8, interfaces were updated to include `static` and `default` methods. A `default` method is one in which the interface method has a body and is not marked `abstract`. It was added for backward compatibility, allowing an older class to use a new version of an interface that contains a new method, without having to modify the existing class.

In Java 9, interfaces were updated to support `private` and `private static` methods. Both of these types were added for code reusability within an interface declaration and cannot be called outside the interface definition.

When you study for the 1Z0-816 exam, you will need to know about other kinds of interface members. For the 1Z0-815 exam, you only need to know about abstract methods and constant variables.

Defining an Interface

In Java, an interface is defined with the `interface` keyword, analogous to the `class` keyword used when defining a class. Refer to Figure 9.1 for a proper interface declaration.

FIGURE 9.1 Defining an interface

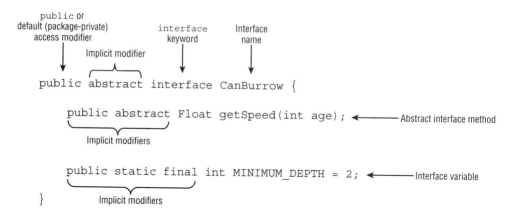

In Figure 9.1, our interface declaration includes a constant variable and an abstract method. Interface variables are referred to as constants because they are assumed to be public, static, and final. They are initialized with a constant value when they are declared. Since they are public and static, they can be used outside the interface declaration without requiring an instance of the interface. Figure 9.1 also includes an abstract method that, like an interface variable, is assumed to be public.

 For brevity, we sometimes say "an instance of an interface" to mean an instance of a class that implements the interface.

What does it mean for a variable or method to be assumed to be something? One aspect of an interface declaration that differs from an abstract class is that it contains implicit modifiers. An *implicit modifier* is a modifier that the compiler automatically adds to a class, interface, method, or variable declaration. For example, an interface is always considered to be abstract, even if it is not marked so. We'll cover rules and examples for implicit modifiers in more detail later in the chapter.

Let's start with an example. Imagine we have an interface WalksOnTwoLegs, defined as follows:

```
public abstract interface WalksOnTwoLegs {}
```

It compiles because interfaces are not required to define any methods. The abstract modifier in this example is optional for interfaces, with the compiler inserting it if it is not provided. Now, consider the following two examples, which do not compile:

```
public class Biped {
    public static void main(String[] args) {
        var e = new WalksOnTwoLegs();        // DOES NOT COMPILE
    }
```

```
}

public final interface WalksOnEightLegs {}  // DOES NOT COMPILE
```

The first example doesn't compile, as WalksOnTwoLegs is an interface and cannot be instantiated. The second example, WalksOnEightLegs, doesn't compile because interfaces cannot be marked as final for the same reason that abstract classes cannot be marked as final. In other words, marking an interface final implies no class could ever implement it.

How do you use an interface? Let's say we have an interface Climb, defined as follows:

```
interface Climb {
    Number getSpeed(int age);
}
```

Next, we have a concrete class FieldMouse that invokes the Climb interface by using the implements keyword in its class declaration, as shown in Figure 9.2.

FIGURE 9.2   Implementing an interface

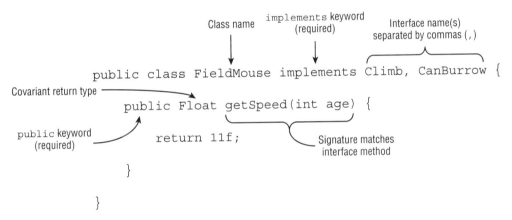

The FieldMouse class declares that it implements the Climb interface and includes an overridden version of getSpeed() inherited from the Climb interface. The method signature of getSpeed() matches exactly, and the return type is covariant. The access modifier of the interface method is assumed to be public in Climb, although the concrete class FieldMouse must explicitly declare it.

As shown in Figure 9.2, a class can implement multiple interfaces, each separated by a comma (,). If any of the interfaces define abstract methods, then the concrete class is required to override them. In this case, FieldMouse also implements the CanBurrow interface that we saw in Figure 9.1. In this manner, the class overrides two abstract methods at the same time with one method declaration. You'll learn more about duplicate and compatible interface methods shortly.

Like a class, an interface can extend another interface using the extends keyword.

```java
interface Nocturnal {}

public interface HasBigEyes extends Nocturnal {}
```

Unlike a class, which can extend only one class, an interface can extend multiple interfaces.

```java
interface Nocturnal {
    public int hunt();
}

interface CanFly {
    public void flap();
}

interface HasBigEyes extends Nocturnal, CanFly {}

public class Owl implements Nocturnal, CanFly {
    public int hunt() { return 5; }
    public void flap() { System.out.println("Flap!"); }
}
```

In this example, the Owl class implements the HasBigEyes interface and must implement the hunt() and flap() methods. Extending two interfaces is permitted because interfaces are not initialized as part of a class hierarchy. Unlike abstract classes, they do not contain constructors and are not part of instance initialization. Interfaces simply define a set of rules that a class implementing them must follow. They also include various static members, including constants that do not require an instance of the class to use.

Many of the rules for class declarations also apply to interfaces including the following:

- A Java file may have at most one public top-level class or interface, and it must match the name of the file.
- A top-level class or interface can only be declared with public or package-private access.

It may help to think of an interface as a specialized abstract class, as many of the rules carry over. Just remember that an interface does not follow the same rules for single inheritance and instance initialization with constructors, as a class does.

What About Enums?

In this section, we described how a Java class can have at most one public top-level element, a class or interface. This public top-level element could also be an enumeration, or *enum* for short. An enum is a specialized type that defines a set of fixed values. It is declared with the enum keyword. The following demonstrates a simple example of an enum for Color:

```
public enum Color {
    RED, YELOW, BLUE, GREEN, ORANGE, PURPLE
}
```

Like classes and interfaces, enums can have more complex formations including meth-ods, `private` constructors, and instance variables.

Luckily for you, enums are out of scope for the 1Z0-815 exam. Like some of the more advanced interface members we described earlier, you will need to study enums when preparing for the 1Z0-816 exam.

Inserting Implicit Modifiers

As mentioned earlier, an implicit modifier is one that the compiler will automatically insert. It's reminiscent of the compiler inserting a default no-argument constructor if you do not define a constructor, which you learned about in Chapter 8. You can choose to insert these implicit modifiers yourself or let the compiler insert them for you.

The following list includes the implicit modifiers for interfaces that you need to know for the exam:

- Interfaces are assumed to be `abstract`.
- Interface variables are assumed to be `public`, `static`, and `final`.
- Interface methods without a body are assumed to be `abstract` and `public`.

For example, the following two interface definitions are equivalent, as the compiler will convert them both to the second declaration:

```
public interface Soar {
    int MAX_HEIGHT = 10;
    final static boolean UNDERWATER = true;
    void fly(int speed);
    abstract void takeoff();
    public abstract double dive();
}
public abstract interface Soar {
    public static final int MAX_HEIGHT = 10;
    public final static boolean UNDERWATER = true;
    public abstract void fly(int speed);
    public abstract void takeoff();
    public abstract double dive();
}
```

In this example, we've marked in bold the implicit modifiers that the compiler automatically inserts. First, the abstract keyword is added to the interface declaration. Next, the public, static, and final keywords are added to the interface variables if they do not exist. Finally, each abstract method is prepended with the abstract and public keywords if they do not contain them already.

Conflicting Modifiers

What happens if a developer marks a method or variable with a modifier that conflicts with an implicit modifier? For example, if an abstract method is assumed to be public, then can it be explicitly marked protected or private?

```
public interface Dance {
    private int count = 4;   // DOES NOT COMPILE
    protected void step();   // DOES NOT COMPILE
}
```

Neither of these interface member declarations compiles, as the compiler will apply the public modifier to both, resulting in a conflict.

While issues with private and protected access modifiers in interfaces are easy to spot, what about the package-private access? For example, what is the access level of the following two elements volume and start()?

```
public interface Sing {
    float volume = 10;
    abstract void start();
}
```

If you said public, then you are correct! When working with class members, omitting the access modifier indicates default (package-private) access. When working with interface members, though, the lack of access modifier always indicates public access.

Let's try another one. Which line or lines of this top-level interface declaration do not compile?

```
1: private final interface Crawl {
2:     String distance;
3:     private int MAXIMUM_DEPTH = 100;
4:     protected abstract boolean UNDERWATER = false;
5:     private void dig(int depth);
6:     protected abstract double depth();
7:     public final void surface(); }
```

Every single line of this example, including the interface declaration, does not compile! Line 1 does not compile for two reasons. First, it is marked as final, which cannot be applied to an interface since it conflicts with the implicit abstract keyword. Next, it is marked as private, which conflicts with the public or package-private access for top-level interfaces.

Line 2 does not compile because the `distance` variable is not initialized. Remember that interface variables are assumed to be `static final` constants and initialized when they are declared. Lines 3 and 4 do not compile because interface variables are also assumed to be `public`, and the access modifiers on these lines conflict with this. Line 4 also does not compile because variables cannot be marked `abstract`.

Next, lines 5 and 6 do not compile because all interface abstract methods are assumed to be `public` and marking them as `private` or `protected` is not permitted. Finally, the last line doesn't compile because the method is marked as `final`, and since interface methods without a body are assumed to be `abstract`, the compiler throws an exception for using both `abstract` and `final` keywords on a method.

Study these examples with conflicting modifiers carefully and make sure you know why they fail to compile. On the exam, you are likely to get at least one question in which an interface includes a member that contains an invalid modifier.

Differences between Interfaces and Abstract Classes

Even though abstract classes and interfaces are both considered abstract types, only interfaces make use of implicit modifiers. This means that an abstract class and interface with similar declarations may have very different properties. For example, how do the `play()` methods differ in the following two definitions?

```
abstract class Husky {
    abstract void play();
}

interface Poodle {
    void play();
}
```

Both of these method definitions are considered abstract. That said, the Husky class will not compile if the `play()` method is not marked `abstract`, whereas the method in the Poodle interface will compile with or without the `abstract` modifier.

What about the access level of the `play()` method? Even though neither has an access modifier, they do not have the same access level. The `play()` method in Husky class is considered default (package-private), whereas the method in the Poodle interface is assumed to be `public`. This is especially important when you create classes that inherit these definitions. For example, can you spot anything wrong with the following class definitions that use our abstract types?

```
class Webby extends Husky {
    void play() {}
}
class Georgette implements Poodle {
    void play() {}
}
```

The Webby class compiles, but the Georgette class does not. Even though the two method implementations are identical, the method in the Georgette class breaks the rules of method overriding. From the Poodle interface, the inherited abstract method is assumed to be public. The definition of play() in the Georgette class therefore reduces the visibility of a method from public to package-private, resulting in a compiler error. The following is the correct implementation of the Georgette class:

```
class Georgette implements Poodle {
   public void play() {}
}
```

Inheriting an Interface

An interface can be inherited in one of three ways.

- An interface can extend another interface.

- A class can implement an interface.

- A class can extend another class whose ancestor implements an interface.

When an interface is inherited, all of the abstract methods are inherited. Like we saw with abstract classes, if the type inheriting the interface is also abstract, such as an interface or abstract class, it is not required to implement the interface methods. On the other hand, the first concrete subclass that inherits the interface must implement all of the inherited abstract methods.

We illustrate this principle in Figure 9.3. How many abstract methods does the concrete Swan class inherit?

FIGURE 9.3   Interface Inheritance

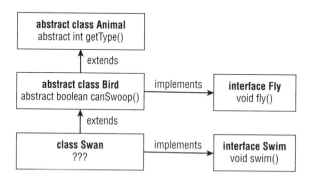

The Swan class inherits four methods: the public fly() and swim() methods, along with the package-private getType() and canSwoop() methods.

Let's take a look at another example involving an abstract class that implements an interface:

```
public interface HasTail {
   public int getTailLength();
}
public interface HasWhiskers {
   public int getNumberOfWhiskers();
}
public abstract class HarborSeal implements HasTail, HasWhiskers {
}
public class CommonSeal extends HarborSeal {  // DOES NOT COMPILE
}
```

The HarborSeal class is not required to implement any of the abstract methods it inherits from the HasTail and HasWhiskers because it is marked abstract. The concrete class CommonSeal, which extends HarborSeal, is required to implement all inherited abstract methods. In this example, CommonSeal doesn't provide an implementation for the inherited abstract interface methods, so CommonSeal doesn't compile.

Mixing Class and Interface Keywords

The exam creators are fond of questions that mix class and interface terminology. Although a class can implement an interface, a class cannot extend an interface. Likewise, while an interface can extend another interface, an interface cannot implement another interface. The following examples illustrate these principles:

```
public interface CanRun {}
public class Cheetah extends CanRun {}   // DOES NOT COMPILE

public class Hyena {}
public interface HasFur extends Hyena {} // DOES NOT COMPILE
```

The first example shows a class trying to extend an interface that doesn't compile. The second example shows an interface trying to extend a class, which also doesn't compile. Be wary of examples on the exam that mix class and interface definitions. The following is the only valid syntax for relating classes and interfaces in their declarations:

```
class1 extends class2

interface1 extends interface2, interface3, ...

class1 implements interface2, interface3, ...
```

Duplicate Interface Method Declarations

Since Java allows for multiple inheritance via interfaces, you might be wondering what will happen if you define a class that inherits from two interfaces that contain the same abstract method.

```java
public interface Herbivore {
   public void eatPlants();
}

public interface Omnivore {
   public void eatPlants();
   public void eatMeat();
}
```

In this scenario, the signatures for the two interface methods eatPlants() are duplicates. As they have identical method declarations, they are also considered *compatible*. By compatibility, we mean that the compiler can resolve the differences between the two declarations without finding any conflicts. You can define a class that fulfills both interfaces simultaneously.

```java
public class Bear implements Herbivore, Omnivore {
   public void eatMeat() {
      System.out.println("Eating meat");
   }
   public void eatPlants() {
      System.out.println("Eating plants");
   }
}
```

As we said earlier, interfaces simply define a set of rules that a class implementing them must follow. If two abstract interface methods have identical behaviors—or in this case the same method declaration—you just need to be able to create a single method that overrides both inherited abstract methods at the same time.

What if the duplicate methods have different signatures? If the method name is the same but the input parameters are different, there is no conflict because this is considered a method overload. We demonstrate this principle in the following example:

```java
public interface Herbivore {
   public int eatPlants(int quantity);
}

public interface Omnivore {
   public void eatPlants();
}

public class Bear implements Herbivore, Omnivore {
```

```
   public int eatPlants(int quantity) {
      System.out.println("Eating plants: "+quantity);
      return quantity;
   }
   public void eatPlants() {
      System.out.println("Eating plants");
   }
}
```

In this example, we see that the class that implements both interfaces must provide implementations of both versions of eatPlants(), since they are considered separate methods.

What if the duplicate methods have the same signature but different return types? In that case, you need to review the rules for overriding methods. Let's try an example:

```
interface Dances {
   String swingArms();
}
interface EatsFish {
   CharSequence swingArms();
}
public class Penguin implements Dances, EatsFish {
   public String swingArms() {
      return "swing!";
   }
}
```

In this example, the Penguin class compiles. The Dances version of the swingArms() method is trivially overridden in the Penguin class, as the declaration in Dances and Penguin have the same method declarations. The EatsFish version of swingArms() is also overridden as String and CharSequence are covariant return types.

Let's take a look at a sample where the return types are not covariant:

```
interface Dances {
   int countMoves();
}
interface EatsFish {
   boolean countMoves();
}
public class Penguin implements Dances, EatsFish { // DOES NOT COMPILE
   ...
}
```

Since it is not possible to define a version of countMoves() that returns both int and boolean, there is no implementation of the Penguin that will allow this declaration to compile. It is the equivalent of trying to define two methods in the same class with the same signature and different return types.

The compiler would also throw an exception if you define an abstract class or interface that inherits from two conflicting abstract types, as shown here:

```java
interface LongEars {
    int softSkin();
}
interface LongNose {
    void softSkin();
}

interface Donkey extends LongEars, LongNose {}  // DOES NOT COMPILE

abstract class Aardvark implements LongEars, LongNose {}
                                                // DOES NOT COMPILE
```

All of the types in this example are abstract, with none being concrete. Despite the fact they are all abstract, the compiler detects that Donkey and Aardvark contain incompatible methods and prevents them from compiling.

Polymorphism and Interfaces

In Chapter 8, we introduced polymorphism and showed how an object in Java can take on many forms through references. While many of the same rules apply, the fact that a class can inherit multiple interfaces limits some of the checks the compiler can perform.

Abstract Reference Types

When working with abstract types, you may prefer to work with the abstract reference types, rather than the concrete class. This is especially common when defining method parameters. Consider the following implementation:

```java
import java.util.*;
public class Zoo {
    public void sortAndPrintZooAnimals(List<String> animals) {
        Collections.sort(animals);
        for(String a : animals) {
            System.out.println(a);
        }
    }
}
```

This class defines a method that sorts and prints animals in alphabetical order. At no point is this class interested in what the actual underlying object for animals is. It might be an ArrayList, which you have seen before, but it may also be a LinkedList or a Vector (neither of which you need to know for the exam).

Casting Interfaces

Let's say you have an abstract reference type variable, which has been instantiated by a concrete subclass. If you need access to a method that is only declared in the concrete subclass, then you will need to cast the interface reference to that type, assuming the cast is supported at runtime. That brings us back to a rule we discussed in Chapter 8, namely, that the compiler does not allow casts to unrelated types. For example, the following is not permitted as the compiler detects that the String and Long class cannot be related:

```
String lion = "Bert";
Long tiger = (Long)lion;
```

With interfaces, there are limitations to what the compiler can validate. For example, does the following program compile?

```
1: interface Canine {}
2: class Dog implements Canine {}
3: class Wolf implements Canine {}
4:
5: public class BadCasts {
6:    public static void main(String[] args) {
7:        Canine canine = new Wolf();
8:        Canine badDog = (Dog)canine;
9:    } }
```

In this program, a Wolf object is created and then assigned to a Canine reference type on line 7. Because of polymorphism, Java cannot be sure which specific class type the canine instance on line 8 is. Therefore, it allows the invalid cast to the Dog reference type, even though Dog and Wolf are not related. The code compiles but throws a ClassCastException at runtime.

This limitation aside, the compiler can enforce one rule around interface casting. The compiler does not allow a cast from an interface reference to an object reference if the object type does not implement the interface. For example, the following change to line 8 causes the program to fail to compile:

```
8:        Object badDog = (String)canine;   // DOES NOT COMPILE
```

Since String does not implement Canine, the compiler recognizes that this cast is not possible.

Interfaces and the *instanceof* Operator

In Chapter 3, "Operators," we showed that the compiler will report an error if you attempt to use the instanceof operator with two unrelated classes, as follows:

```
Number tickets = 4;
if(tickets instanceof String) {}  // DOES NOT COMPILE
```

With interfaces, the compiler has limited ability to enforce this rule because even though a reference type may not implement an interface, one of its subclasses could. For example, the following does compile:

```
Number tickets = 5;
if(tickets instanceof List) {}
```

Even though Number does not inherit List, it's possible the tickets variable may be a reference to a subclass of Number that does inherit List. As an example, the tickets variable could be assigned to an instance of the following MyNumber class (assuming all inherited methods were implemented):

```
public class MyNumber extends Number implements List
```

That said, the compiler can check for unrelated interfaces if the reference is a class that is marked final.

```
Integer tickets = 6;
if(tickets instanceof List) {}  // DOES NOT COMPILE
```

The compiler rejects this code because the Integer class is marked final and does not inherit List. Therefore, it is not possible to create a subclass of Integer that inherits the List interface.

Reviewing Interface Rules

We summarize the interface rules in this part of the chapter in the following list. If you compare the list to our list of rules for an abstract class definition, the first four rules are similar.

Interface Definition Rules

1. Interfaces cannot be instantiated.
2. All top-level types, including interfaces, cannot be marked protected or private.
3. Interfaces are assumed to be abstract and cannot be marked final.
4. Interfaces may include zero or more abstract methods.
5. An interface can extend any number of interfaces.
6. An interface reference may be cast to any reference that inherits the interface, although this may produce an exception at runtime if the classes aren't related.

7. The compiler will only report an unrelated type error for an `instanceof` operation with an interface on the right side if the reference on the left side is a `final` class that does not inherit the interface.

8. An interface method with a body must be marked `default`, `private`, `static`, or `private static` (covered when studying for the 1Z0-816 exam).

The following are the five rules for abstract methods defined in interfaces.

Abstract Interface Method Rules

1. Abstract methods can be defined only in abstract classes or interfaces.

2. Abstract methods cannot be declared `private` or `final`.

3. Abstract methods must not provide a method body/implementation in the abstract class in which is it declared.

4. Implementing an abstract method in a subclass follows the same rules for overriding a method, including covariant return types, exception declarations, etc.

5. Interface methods without a body are assumed to be `abstract` and `public`.

Notice anything? The first four rules for abstract methods, whether they be defined in abstract classes or interfaces, are exactly the same! The only new rule you need to learn for interfaces is the last one.

Finally, there are two rules to remember for interface variables.

Interface Variables Rules

1. Interface variables are assumed to be `public`, `static`, and `final`.

2. Because interface variables are marked `final`, they must be initialized with a value when they are declared.

It may be helpful to think of an interface as a specialized kind of abstract class, since it shares many of the same properties and rules as an abstract class. The primary differences between the two are that interfaces include implicit modifiers, do not contain constructors, do not participate in the instance initialization process, and support multiple inheritance.

 Real World Scenario

Using an Interface vs. Implementing an Interface

An interface provides a way for one individual to develop code that uses another individual's code, without having access to the other individual's underlying implementation. Interfaces can facilitate rapid application development by enabling development teams to create applications in parallel, rather than being directly dependent on each other.

For example, two teams can work together to develop a one-page standard interface at the start of a project. One team then develops code that *uses* the interface, while the other team develops code that *implements* the interface. The development teams can then combine their implementations toward the end of the project, and as long as both teams developed with the same interface, they will be compatible. Of course, testing will still be required to make sure that the class implementing the interface behaves as expected.

Introducing Inner Classes

We conclude this chapter with a brief discussion of inner classes. For the 1Z0-815 exam, you only need to know the basics of inner classes. In particular, you should know the difference between a top-level class and an inner class, permitted access modifiers for an inner class, and how to define a member inner class.

For simplicity, we will often refer to inner or nested interfaces as *inner classes*, as the rules described in this chapter for inner classes apply to both class and interface types.

Defining a Member Inner Class

A *member inner class* is a class defined at the member level of a class (the same level as the methods, instance variables, and constructors). It is the opposite of a top-level class, in that it cannot be declared unless it is inside another class.

Developers often define a member inner class inside another class if the relationship between the two classes is very close. For example, a Zoo sells tickets for its patrons; therefore, it may want to manage the lifecycle of the Ticket object.

For the 1Z0-816 exam, there are four types of nested classes you will need to know about: member inner classes, local classes, anonymous classes, and static nested classes. You'll also need to know more detail about member inner classes. For this chapter, we limit our discussion to just the basics of member inner classes, as this is all you need to know on the 1Z0-815 exam.

The following is an example of an outer class Zoo with an inner class Ticket:

```
public class Zoo {
    public class Ticket {}
}
```

We can expand this to include an interface.

```
public class Zoo {
   private interface Paper {}
   public class Ticket implements Paper {}
}
```

While top-level classes and interfaces can only be set with `public` or package-private access, member inner classes do not have the same restriction. A member inner class can be declared with all of the same access modifiers as a class member, such as `public`, `protected`, default (package-private), or `private`.

A member inner class can contain many of the same methods and variables as a top-level class. Some members are disallowed in member inner classes, such as `static` members, although you don't need to know that for the 1Z0-815 exam. Let's update our example with some instance members.

```
public class Zoo {
   private interface Paper {
      public String getId();
   }
   public class Ticket implements Paper {
      private String serialNumber;
      public String getId() { return serialNumber;}
   }
}
```

Our Zoo and Ticket examples are starting to become more interesting. In the next section, we will show you how to use them.

Using a Member Inner Class

One of the ways a member inner class can be used is by calling it in the outer class. Continuing with our previous example, let's define a method in Zoo that makes use of the member inner class with a new `sellTicket()` method.

```
public class Zoo {
   private interface Paper {
      public String getId();
   }
   public class Ticket implements Paper {
      private String serialNumber;
      public String getId() { return serialNumber; }
   }
   public Ticket sellTicket(String serialNumber) {
```

```
      var t = new Ticket();
      t.serialNumber = serialNumber;
      return t;
   }
}
```

The advantage of using a member inner class in this example is that the Zoo class completely manages the lifecycle of the Ticket class.

Let's add an entry point to this example.

```
public class Zoo {
   ...
   public static void main(String... unused) {
      var z = new Zoo();
      var t = z.sellTicket("12345");
      System.out.println(t.getId()+" Ticket sold!");
   }
}
```

This compiles and prints 12345 Ticket sold! at runtime.

For the 1Z0-815 exam, this is the extent of what you need to know about inner classes. As discussed, when you study for the 1Z0-816 exam, there is a lot more you will need to know.

Summary

In this chapter, we presented advanced topics in class design, starting with abstract classes. An abstract class is just like a regular class except that it cannot be instantiated and may contain abstract methods. An abstract class can extend a nonabstract class, and vice versa. Abstract classes can be used to define a framework that other developers write subclasses against.

An abstract method is one that does not include a body when it is declared. An abstract method may be placed inside an abstract class or interface. Next, an abstract method can be overridden with another abstract declaration or a concrete implementation, provided the rules for overriding methods are followed. The first concrete class must implement all of the inherited abstract methods, whether they are inherited from an abstract class or interface.

An interface is a special type of abstract structure that primarily contains abstract methods and constant variables. Interfaces include implicit modifiers, which are modifiers that the compiler will automatically apply to the interface declaration. For the 1Z0-815 exam, you should know which modifiers are assumed in interfaces and be able to spot potential conflicts. When you prepare for the 1Z0-816 exam, you will study the four additional nonabstract methods that interfaces now support. Finally, while the compiler can often prevent casting to unrelated types, it has limited ability to prevent invalid casts when working with interfaces.

We concluded this chapter with a brief presentation of member inner classes. For the exam, you should be able to recognize member inner classes and know which access modifiers are allowed. Member inner classes, along with the other types of nested classes, will be covered in much more detail when you study for the 1Z0-816 exam.

Exam Essentials

Be able to write code that creates and extends abstract classes.   In Java, classes and methods can be declared as abstract. An abstract class cannot be instantiated. An instance of an abstract class can be obtained only through a concrete subclass. Abstract classes can include any number, including zero, of abstract and nonabstract methods. Abstract methods follow all the method override rules and may be defined only within abstract classes. The first concrete subclass of an abstract class must implement all the inherited methods. Abstract classes and methods may not be marked as final.

Be able to write code that creates, extends, and implements interfaces.   Interfaces are specialized abstract types that focus on abstract methods and constant variables. An interface may extend any number of interfaces and, in doing so, inherits their abstract methods. An interface cannot extend a class, nor can a class extend an interface. A class may implement any number of interfaces.

Know the implicit modifiers that the compiler will automatically apply to an interface. All interfaces are assumed to be abstract. An interface method without a body is assumed to be public and abstract. An interface variable is assumed to be public, static, and final and initialized with a value when it is declared. Using a modifier that conflicts with one of these implicit modifiers will result in a compiler error.

Distinguish between top-level and inner classes/interfaces and know which access modifiers are allowed.   A top-level class or interface is one that is not defined within another class declaration, while an inner class or interface is one defined within another class. Inner classes can be marked public, protected, package-private, or private.

Review Questions

The answers to the chapter review questions can be found in the Appendix.

1. What modifiers are implicitly applied to all interface methods that do not declare a body? (Choose all that apply.)

   A. protected

   B. public

   C. static

   D. void

   E. abstract

   F. default

2. Which of the following statements can be inserted in the blank line so that the code will compile successfully? (Choose all that apply.)

```
interface CanHop {}
public class Frog implements CanHop {
    public static void main(String[] args) {
        _____ frog = new TurtleFrog();
    }
}
class BrazilianHornedFrog extends Frog {}
class TurtleFrog extends Frog {}
```

   A. Frog

   B. TurtleFrog

   C. BrazilianHornedFrog

   D. CanHop

   E. Object

   F. Long

   G. None of the above; the code contains a compilation error.

3. Which of the following is true about a concrete class? (Choose all that apply.)

   A. A concrete class can be declared as abstract.

   B. A concrete class must implement all inherited abstract methods.

   C. A concrete class can be marked as final.

   D. If a concrete class inherits an interface from one of its superclasses, then it must declare an implementation for all methods defined in that interface.

   E. A concrete method that implements an abstract method must match the method declaration of the abstract method exactly.

4. Which statements about the following program are correct? (Choose all that apply.)

```
1:  interface HasExoskeleton {
2:      double size = 2.0f;
3:      abstract int getNumberOfSections();
4:  }
5:  abstract class Insect implements HasExoskeleton {
6:      abstract int getNumberOfLegs();
7:  }
8:  public class Beetle extends Insect {
9:      int getNumberOfLegs() { return 6; }
10:     int getNumberOfSections(int count) { return 1; }
11: }
```

A. It compiles without issue.

B. The code will produce a `ClassCastException` if called at runtime.

C. The code will not compile because of line 2.

D. The code will not compile because of line 5.

E. The code will not compile because of line 8.

F. The code will not compile because of line 10.

5. What modifiers are implicitly applied to all interface variables? (Choose all that apply.)

A. `private`

B. `nonstatic`

C. `final`

D. `const`

E. `abstract`

F. `public`

G. default (package-private)

6. Which statements about the following program are correct? (Choose all that apply.)

```
1: public abstract interface Herbivore {
2:     int amount = 10;
3:     public void eatGrass();
4:     public abstract int chew() { return 13; }
5: }
6:
7: abstract class IsAPlant extends Herbivore {
8:     Object eatGrass(int season) { return null; }
9: }
```

A. It compiles and runs without issue.

B. The code will not compile because of line 1.

C. The code will not compile because of line 2.

D. The code will not compile because of line 4.

E. The code will not compile because of line 7.

F. The code will not compile because line 8 contains an invalid method override.

7. Which statements about the following program are correct? (Choose all that apply.)

```
1: abstract class Nocturnal {
2:     boolean isBlind();
3: }
4: public class Owl extends Nocturnal {
5:     public boolean isBlind() { return false; }
6:     public static void main(String[] args) {
7:         var nocturnal = (Nocturnal)new Owl();
8:         System.out.println(nocturnal.isBlind());
9: } }
```

A. It compiles and prints true.

B. It compiles and prints false.

C. The code will not compile because of line 2.

D. The code will not compile because of line 5.

E. The code will not compile because of line 7.

F. The code will not compile because of line 8.

G. None of the above

8. Which statements are true about the following code? (Choose all that apply.)

```
interface Dog extends CanBark, HasVocalCords {
    abstract int chew();
}

public interface CanBark extends HasVocalCords {
    public void bark();
}

interface HasVocalCords {
    public abstract void makeSound();
}
```

A. The CanBark declaration doesn't compile.

B. A class that implements HasVocalCords must override the makeSound() method.

C. A class that implements `CanBark` inherits both the `makeSound()` and `bark()` methods.

D. A class that implements `Dog` must be marked `final`.

E. The `Dog` declaration does not compile because an interface cannot extend two interfaces.

9. Which access modifiers can be applied to member inner classes? (Choose all that apply.)

   A. `static`

   B. `public`

   C. default (package-private)

   D. `final`

   E. `protected`

   F. `private`

10. Which statements are true about the following code? (Choose all that apply.)

```
5:  public interface CanFly {
6:     int fly()
7:     String fly(int distance);
8:  }
9:  interface HasWings {
10:    abstract String fly();
11:    public abstract Object getWingSpan();
12: }
13: abstract class Falcon implements CanFly, HasWings {}
```

   A. It compiles without issue.

   B. The code will not compile because of line 5.

   C. The code will not compile because of line 6.

   D. The code will not compile because of line 7.

   E. The code will not compile because of line 9.

   F. The code will not compile because of line 10.

   G. The code will not compile because of line 13.

11. Which modifier pairs can be used together in a method declaration? (Choose all that apply.)

    A. `static` and `final`

    B. `private` and `static`

    C. `static` and `abstract`

    D. `private` and `abstract`

    E. `abstract` and `final`

    F. `private` and `final`

12. Which of the following statements about the `FruitStand` program are correct? (Choose all that apply.)

```
1:  interface Apple {}
2:  interface Orange {}
3:  class Gala implements Apple {}
4:  class Tangerine implements Orange {}
5:  final class Citrus extends Tangerine {}
6:  public class FruitStand {
7:     public static void main(String... farm) {
8:        Gala g = new Gala();
9:        Tangerine t = new Tangerine();
10:        Citrus c = new Citrus();
11:        System.out.print(t instanceof Gala);
12:        System.out.print(c instanceof Tangerine);
13:        System.out.print(g instanceof Apple);
14:        System.out.print(t instanceof Apple);
15:        System.out.print(c instanceof Apple);
16: } }
```

A. Line 11 contains a compiler error.

B. Line 12 contains a compiler error.

C. Line 13 contains a compiler error.

D. Line 14 contains a compiler error.

E. Line 15 contains a compiler error.

F. None of the above

13. What is the output of the following code?

```
1:  interface Jump {
2:     static public int MAX = 3;
3:  }
4:  public abstract class Whale implements Jump {
5:     public abstract void dive();
6:     public static void main(String[] args) {
7:        Whale whale = new Orca();
8:        whale.dive(3);
9:     }
10: }
11: class Orca extends Whale {
12:    public void dive() {
13:       System.out.println("Orca diving");
14:    }
```

```
15:    public void dive(int... depth) {
16:        System.out.println("Orca diving deeper "+MAX);
17: } }
```

A. Orca diving

B. Orca diving deeper 3

C. The code will not compile because of line 2.

D. The code will not compile because of line 4.

E. The code will not compile because of line 11.

F. The code will not compile because of line 16.

G. None of the above

14. Which statements are true for both abstract classes and interfaces? (Choose all that apply.)

A. Both can be extended using the extends keyword.

B. All methods within them are assumed to be abstract.

C. Both can contain public static final variables.

D. The compiler will insert the implicit abstract modifier automatically on methods declared without a body, if they are not marked as such.

E. Both interfaces and abstract classes can be declared with the abstract modifier.

F. Both inherit java.lang.Object.

15. What is the result of the following code?

```
1:    abstract class Bird {
2:        private final void fly() { System.out.println("Bird"); }
3:        protected Bird() { System.out.print("Wow-"); }
4:    }
5:    public class Pelican extends Bird {
6:        public Pelican() { System.out.print("Oh-"); }
7:        protected void fly() { System.out.println("Pelican"); }
8:        public static void main(String[] args) {
9:            var chirp = new Pelican();
10:           chirp.fly();
11: } }
```

A. Oh-Bird

B. Oh-Pelican

C. Wow-Oh-Bird

D. Wow-Oh-Pelican

E. The code contains a compilation error.

F. None of the above

16. Which of the following statements about this program is correct?

```
1: interface Aquatic {
2:    int getNumOfGills(int p);
3: }
4: public class ClownFish implements Aquatic {
5:    String getNumOfGills() { return "14"; }
6:    int getNumOfGills(int input) { return 15; }
7:    public static void main(String[] args) {
8:        System.out.println(new ClownFish().getNumOfGills(-1));
9: } }
```

A. It compiles and prints 14.

B. It compiles and prints 15.

C. The code will not compile because of line 4.

D. The code will not compile because of line 5.

E. The code will not compile because of line 6.

F. None of the above

17. Which statements about top-level types and member inner classes are correct? (Choose all that apply.)

A. A member inner class can be marked `final`.

B. A top-level type can be marked `protected`.

C. A member inner class cannot be marked `public` since that would make it a top-level class.

D. A top-level type must be stored in a `.java` file with a name that matches the class name.

E. If a member inner class is marked `private`, then it can be referenced only in the outer class for which it is defined.

18. What types can be inserted in the blanks on the lines marked X and Z that allow the code to compile? (Choose all that apply.)

```
interface Walk { public List move(); }
interface Run extends Walk { public ArrayList move(); }
public class Leopard {
    public _____ move() { // X
        return null;
    }
}
public class Panther implements Run {
    public _____ move() { // Z
        return null;
    }
}
```

A. Integer on the line marked X

B. ArrayList on the line marked X

C. List on the line marked Z

D. ArrayList on the line marked Z

E. None of the above, since the Run interface does not compile.

F. The code does not compile for a different reason.

19. Which statements about interfaces are correct? (Choose all that apply.)

A. A class cannot extend multiple interfaces.

B. Java enables true multiple inheritance via interfaces.

C. Interfaces cannot be declared abstract.

D. If an interface does not contain a constructor, the compiler will insert one automatically.

E. An interface can extend multiple interfaces.

F. An interface cannot be instantiated.

20. Which of the following classes and interfaces are correct and compile? (Choose all that apply.)

```
abstract class Camel {
    void travel();
}
interface EatsGrass {
    protected int chew();
}
abstract class Elephant {
    abstract private class SleepsAlot {
        abstract int sleep();
    }
}
class Eagle {
    abstract soar();
}
```

A. SleepsAlot

B. Eagle

C. Camel

D. Elephant

E. EatsGrass

F. None of the classes or interfaces compile.

Chapter

10

Exceptions

OCP EXAM OBJECTIVES COVERED IN THIS CHAPTER:

✓ **Handling Exceptions**

- ▪ Describe the advantages of Exception handling and differentiate among checked, unchecked exceptions, and Errors

- ▪ Create try-catch blocks and determine how exceptions alter program flow

- ▪ Create and invoke a method that throws an exception

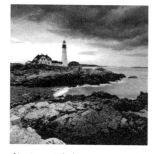

Many things can go wrong in a program. Java uses exceptions to deal with some of these scenarios. This chapter focuses on how exceptions are created, how to handle them, and how to distinguish between various types of exceptions and errors.

Understanding Exceptions

A program can fail for just about any reason. Here are just a few possibilities:

- The code tries to connect to a website, but the Internet connection is down.
- You made a coding mistake and tried to access an invalid index in an array.
- One method calls another with a value that the method doesn't support.

As you can see, some of these are coding mistakes. Others are completely beyond your control. Your program can't help it if the Internet connection goes down. What it *can* do is deal with the situation.

First, we'll look at the role of exceptions. Then we'll cover the various types of exceptions, followed by an explanation of how to throw an exception in Java.

The Role of Exceptions

An *exception* is Java's way of saying, "I give up. I don't know what to do right now. You deal with it." When you write a method, you can either deal with the exception or make it the calling code's problem.

As an example, think of Java as a child who visits the zoo. The *happy path* is when nothing goes wrong. The child continues to look at the animals until the program nicely ends. Nothing went wrong, and there were no exceptions to deal with.

This child's younger sister doesn't experience the happy path. In all the excitement she trips and falls. Luckily, it isn't a bad fall. The little girl gets up and proceeds to look at more animals. She has handled the issue all by herself. Unfortunately, she falls again later in the day and starts crying. This time, she has declared she needs help by crying. The story ends well. Her daddy rubs her knee and gives her a hug. Then they go back to seeing more animals and enjoy the rest of the day.

These are the two approaches Java uses when dealing with exceptions. A method can handle the exception case itself or make it the caller's responsibility. You saw both in the trip to the zoo.

You saw an exception in Chapter 1, "Welcome to Java," with a simple Zoo example. You wrote a class that printed out the name of the zoo:

```
1: public class Zoo {
2:    public static void main(String[] args) {
3:       System.out.println(args[0]);
4:       System.out.println(args[1]);
5: } }
```

Then you tried to call it without enough arguments:

```
$ javac Zoo.java
$ java Zoo Zoo
```

On line 4, Java realized there's only one element in the array and index 1 is not allowed. Java threw up its hands in defeat and threw an exception. It didn't try to handle the exception. It just said, "I can't deal with it," and the exception was displayed:

```
Zoo
Exception in thread "main" java.lang.ArrayIndexOutOfBoundsException:
Index 1 out of bounds for length 1
   at Zoo.main(Zoo.java:4)
```

Exceptions can and do occur all the time, even in solid program code. In our example, toddlers falling are a fact of life. When you write more advanced programs, you'll need to deal with failures in accessing files, networks, and outside services. On the exam, exceptions deal largely with mistakes in programs. For example, a program might try to access an invalid position in an array. The key point to remember is that exceptions alter the program flow.

 Real World Scenario

Return Codes vs. Exceptions

Exceptions are used when "something goes wrong." However, the word *wrong* is subjective. The following code returns –1 instead of throwing an exception if no match is found:

```
public int indexOf(String[] names, String name) {
   for (int i = 0; i < names.length; i++) {
      if (names[i].equals(name)) { return i; }
   }
   return -1;
}
```

This approach is common when writing a method that does a search. For example, imagine being asked to find the name Joe in the array. It is perfectly reasonable that Joe might not appear in the array. When this happens, a special value is returned. An exception should be reserved for exceptional conditions like names being null.

In general, try to avoid return codes. Return codes are commonly used in searches, so programmers are expecting them. In other methods, you will take your callers by surprise by returning a special value. An exception forces the program to deal with the problem or end with the exception if left unhandled, whereas a return code could be accidentally ignored and cause problems later in the program. Even worse, a return value could be confused with real data. In the context of a school, does –1 mean an error or the number of students removed from a class? An exception is like shouting, "Deal with me!" and avoids possible ambiguity.

Understanding Exception Types

As we've explained, an exception is an event that alters program flow. Java has a Throwable superclass for all objects that represent these events. Not all of them have the word *exception* in their class name, which can be confusing. Figure 10.1 shows the key subclasses of Throwable.

FIGURE 10.1 Categories of exception

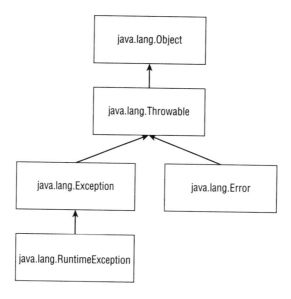

Error means something went so horribly wrong that your program should not attempt to recover from it. For example, the disk drive "disappeared" or the program ran out of memory. These are abnormal conditions that you aren't likely to encounter and cannot recover from.

For the exam, the only thing you need to know about Throwable is that it's the parent class of all exceptions, including the Error class. While you can handle Throwable and Error exceptions, it is not recommended you do so in your application code. In this chapter, when we refer to exceptions, we generally mean any class that inherits Throwable, although we are almost always working with the Exception class or subclasses of it.

Checked Exceptions

A *checked exception* is an exception that must be declared or handled by the application code where it is thrown. In Java, checked exceptions all inherit Exception but not RuntimeException. Checked exceptions tend to be more anticipated—for example, trying to read a file that doesn't exist.

Checked exceptions also include any class that inherits Throwable, but not Error or RuntimeException. For example, a class that directly extends Throwable would be a checked exception. For the exam, though, you just need to know about checked exceptions that extend Exception.

Checked exceptions? What are we checking? Java has a rule called the handle or declare rule. The *handle or declare rule* means that all checked exceptions that could be thrown within a method are either wrapped in compatible try and catch blocks or declared in the method signature.

Because checked exceptions tend to be anticipated, Java enforces the rule that the programmer must do something to show the exception was thought about. Maybe it was handled in the method. Or maybe the method declares that it can't handle the exception and someone else should.

While only checked exceptions must be handled or declared in Java, unchecked exceptions (which we will present in the next section) may also be handled or declared. The distinction is that checked exceptions must be handled or declared, while unchecked exceptions can be optionally handled or declared.

Let's take a look at an example. The following fall() method declares that it might throw an IOException, which is a checked exception:

```
void fall(int distance) throws IOException {
    if(distance > 10) {
        throw new IOException();
    }
}
```

Notice that you're using two different keywords here. The throw keyword tells Java that you want to throw an Exception, while the throws keyword simply declares that the method might throw an Exception. It also might not. You will see the throws keyword again later in the chapter.

Now that you know how to declare an exception, how do you instead handle it? The following alternate version of the fall() method handles the exception:

```
void fall(int distance) {
   try {
      if(distance > 10) {
         throw new IOException();
      }
   } catch (Exception e) {
      e.printStackTrace();
   }
}
```

Notice that the catch statement uses Exception, not IOException. Since IOException is a subclass of Exception, the catch block is allowed to catch it. We'll cover try and catch blocks in more detail later in this chapter.

Unchecked Exceptions

An *unchecked exception* is any exception that does not need to be declared or handled by the application code where it is thrown. Unchecked exceptions are often referred to as runtime exceptions, although in Java, unchecked exceptions include any class that inherits RuntimeException or Error.

A *runtime exception* is defined as the RuntimeException class and its subclasses. Runtime exceptions tend to be unexpected but not necessarily fatal. For example, accessing an invalid array index is unexpected. Even though they do inherit the Exception class, they are not checked exceptions.

Runtime vs. at the Time the Program Is Run

A runtime (unchecked) exception is a specific type of exception. All exceptions occur at the time that the program is run. (The alternative is compile time, which would be a compiler error.) People don't refer to them as "run time" exceptions because that would be too easy to confuse with runtime! When you see *runtime*, it means unchecked.

An unchecked exception can often occur on nearly any line of code, as it is not required to be handled or declared. For example, a NullPointerException can be thrown in the body of the following method if the input reference is null:

```
void fall(String input) {
   System.out.println(input.toLowerCase());
}
```

We work with objects in Java so frequently, a `NullPointerException` can happen almost anywhere. If you had to declare unchecked exceptions everywhere, every single method would have that clutter! The code will compile if you declare an unchecked exception. However, it is redundant.

Checked vs. Unchecked (Runtime) Exceptions

In the past, developers used checked exceptions more often than they do now. According to Oracle, they are intended for issues a programmer "might reasonably be expected to recover from." Then developers started writing code where a chain of methods kept declaring the same exception and nobody actually handled it. Some libraries started using unchecked exceptions for issues a programmer might reasonably be expected to recover from. Many programmers can hold a debate with you on which approach is better. For the exam, you need to know the rules for how checked versus unchecked exceptions function. You don't have to decide philosophically whether an exception should be checked or unchecked.

Throwing an Exception

Any Java code can throw an exception; this includes code you write. The exam is limited to exceptions that someone else has created. Most likely, they will be exceptions that are provided with Java. You might encounter an exception that was made up for the exam. This is fine. The question will make it obvious that these are exceptions by having the class name end with `Exception`. For example, `MyMadeUpException` is clearly an exception.

On the exam, you will see two types of code that result in an exception. The first is code that's wrong. Here's an example:

```java
String[] animals = new String[0];
System.out.println(animals[0]);
```

This code throws an `ArrayIndexOutOfBoundsException` since the array has no elements. That means questions about exceptions can be hidden in questions that appear to be about something else.

 On the exam, many questions have a choice about not compiling and about throwing an exception. Pay special attention to code that calls a method on a `null` reference or that references an invalid array or `List` index. If you spot this, you know the correct answer is that the code throws an exception at runtime.

The second way for code to result in an exception is to explicitly request Java to throw one. Java lets you write statements like these:

```
throw new Exception();
throw new Exception("Ow! I fell.");
throw new RuntimeException();
throw new RuntimeException("Ow! I fell.");
```

The throw keyword tells Java you want some other part of the code to deal with the exception. This is the same as the young girl crying for her daddy. Someone else needs to figure out what to do about the exception.

---

throw vs. throws

Anytime you see throw or throws on the exam, make sure the correct one is being used. The throw keyword is used as a statement inside a code block to throw a new exception or rethrow an existing exception, while the throws keyword is used only at the end of a method declaration to indicate what exceptions it supports. On the exam, you might start reading a long class definition only to realize the entire thing does not compile due to the wrong keyword being used.

When creating an exception, you can usually pass a String parameter with a message, or you can pass no parameters and use the defaults. We say *usually* because this is a convention. Someone could create an exception class that does not have a constructor that takes a message. The first two examples create a new object of type Exception and throw it. The last two show that the code looks the same regardless of which type of exception you throw.

Additionally, you should know that an Exception is an Object. This means you can store in a variable, and this is legal:

```
Exception e = new RuntimeException();
throw e;
```

The code instantiates an exception on one line and then throws on the next. The exception can come from anywhere, even passed into a method. As long as it is a valid exception, it can be thrown.

The exam might also try to trick you. Do you see why this code doesn't compile?

```
throw RuntimeException();    // DOES NOT COMPILE
```

If your answer is that there is a missing keyword, you're absolutely right. The exception is never instantiated with the new keyword.

Let's take a look at another place the exam might try to trick you. Can you see why the following does not compile?

```
3: try {
4:     throw new RuntimeException();
5:     throw new ArrayIndexOutOfBoundsException();  // DOES NOT COMPILE
6: } catch (Exception e) {
7: }
```

Since line 4 throws an exception, line 5 can never be reached during runtime. The compiler recognizes this and reports an unreachable code error.

The types of exceptions are important. Be sure to closely study everything in Table 10.1. Remember that a `Throwable` is either an `Exception` or an `Error`. You should not catch `Throwable` directly in your code.

TABLE 10.1   Types of exceptions and errors

Type	How to recognize	Okay for program to catch?	Is program required to handle or declare?
Runtime exception	Subclass of `RuntimeException`	Yes	No
Checked exception	Subclass of `Exception` but not subclass of `RuntimeException`	Yes	Yes
Error	Subclass of `Error`	No	No

Recognizing Exception Classes

You need to recognize three groups of exception classes for the exam: `RuntimeException`, checked `Exception`, and `Error`. We'll look at common examples of each type. For the exam, you'll need to recognize which type of an exception it is and whether it's thrown by the Java virtual machine (JVM) or a programmer. So that you can recognize them, we'll show you some code examples for those exceptions. For some exceptions, you also need to know which are inherited from one another.

RuntimeException Classes

`RuntimeException` and its subclasses are unchecked exceptions that don't have to be handled or declared. They can be thrown by the programmer or by the JVM. Common `RuntimeException` classes include the following:

`ArithmeticException`   Thrown when code attempts to divide by zero

`ArrayIndexOutOfBoundsException`   Thrown when code uses an illegal index to access an array

`ClassCastException`   Thrown when an attempt is made to cast an object to a class of which it is not an instance

`NullPointerException`   Thrown when there is a null reference where an object is required

`IllegalArgumentException`   Thrown by the programmer to indicate that a method has been passed an illegal or inappropriate argument

NumberFormatException Subclass of IllegalArgumentException thrown when an attempt is made to convert a string to a numeric type but the string doesn't have an appropriate format

ArithmeticException

Trying to divide an int by zero gives an undefined result. When this occurs, the JVM will throw an ArithmeticException:

```
int answer = 11 / 0;
```

Running this code results in the following output:

```
Exception in thread "main" java.lang.ArithmeticException: / by zero
```

Java doesn't spell out the word *divide*. That's okay, though, because we know that / is the division operator and that Java is trying to tell you division by zero occurred.

The thread "main" is telling you the code was called directly or indirectly from a program with a main method. On the exam, this is all the output you will see. Next comes the name of the exception, followed by extra information (if any) that goes with the exception.

ArrayIndexOutOfBoundsException

You know by now that array indexes start with 0 and go up to 1 less than the length of the array—which means this code will throw an ArrayIndexOutOfBoundsException:

```
int[] countsOfMoose = new int[3];
System.out.println(countsOfMoose[-1]);
```

This is a problem because there's no such thing as a negative array index. Running this code yields the following output:

```
Exception in thread "main" java.lang.ArrayIndexOutOfBoundsException:
Index -1 out of bounds for length 3
```

At least Java tells us what index was invalid. Can you see what's wrong with this one?

```
int total = 0;
int[] countsOfMoose = new int[3];
for (int i = 0; i <= countsOfMoose.length; i++)
   total += countsOfMoose[i];
```

The problem is that the for loop should have < instead of <=. On the final iteration of the loop, Java tries to call countsOfMoose[3], which is invalid. The array includes only three elements, making 2 the largest possible index. The output looks like this:

```
Exception in thread "main" java.lang.ArrayIndexOutOfBoundsException:
Index 3 out of bounds for length 3
```

ClassCastException

Java tries to protect you from impossible casts. This code doesn't compile because Integer is not a subclass of String:

```
String type = "moose";
Integer number = (Integer) type;  // DOES NOT COMPILE
```

More complicated code thwarts Java's attempts to protect you. When the cast fails at runtime, Java will throw a ClassCastException:

```
String type = "moose";
Object obj = type;
Integer number = (Integer) obj;
```

The compiler sees a cast from Object to Integer. This could be okay. The compiler doesn't realize there's a String in that Object. When the code runs, it yields the following output:

```
Exception in thread "main" java.lang.ClassCastException:
java.base/java.lang.String
cannot be cast to java.lang.base/java.lang.Integer
```

Java tells you both types that were involved in the problem, making it apparent what's wrong.

NullPointerException

Instance variables and methods must be called on a non-null reference. If the reference is null, the JVM will throw a NullPointerException. It's usually subtle, such as in the following example, which checks whether you remember instance variable references default to null:

```
String name;
public void printLength() {
   System.out.println(name.length());
}
```

Running this code results in this output:

```
Exception in thread "main" java.lang.NullPointerException
```

IllegalArgumentException

IllegalArgumentException is a way for your program to protect itself. You first saw the following setter method in the Swan class in Chapter 7, "Methods and Encapsulation."

```
6: public void setNumberEggs(int numberEggs) { // setter
7:    if (numberEggs >= 0) // guard condition
8:       this.numberEggs = numberEggs;
9: }
```

This code works, but you don't really want to ignore the caller's request when they tell you a Swan has -2 eggs. You want to tell the caller that something is wrong—preferably in an obvious way that the caller can't ignore so that the programmer will fix the problem. Exceptions are an efficient way to do this. Seeing the code end with an exception is a great reminder that something is wrong:

```
public void setNumberEggs(int numberEggs) {
    if (numberEggs < 0)
        throw new IllegalArgumentException(
            "# eggs must not be negative");
    this.numberEggs = numberEggs;
}
```

The program throws an exception when it's not happy with the parameter values. The output looks like this:

```
Exception in thread "main"
java.lang.IllegalArgumentException: # eggs must not be negative
```

Clearly this is a problem that must be fixed if the programmer wants the program to do anything useful.

NumberFormatException

Java provides methods to convert strings to numbers. When these are passed an invalid value, they throw a NumberFormatException. The idea is similar to IllegalArgumentException. Since this is a common problem, Java gives it a separate class. In fact, NumberFormatException is a subclass of IllegalArgumentException. Here's an example of trying to convert something non-numeric into an int:

```
Integer.parseInt("abc");
```

The output looks like this:

```
Exception in thread "main"
java.lang.NumberFormatException: For input string: "abc"
```

For the exam, you need to know that NumberFormatException is a subclass of IllegalArgumentException. We'll cover more about why that is important later in the chapter.

Checked *Exception* Classes

Checked exceptions have Exception in their hierarchy but not RuntimeException. They must be handled or declared. Common checked exceptions include the following:

IOException   Thrown programmatically when there's a problem reading or writing a file

FileNotFoundException   Subclass of IOException thrown programmatically when code tries to reference a file that does not exist

For the exam, you need to know that these are both checked exceptions. You also need to know that `FileNotFoundException` is a subclass of `IOException`. You'll see shortly why that matters.

Error Classes

Errors are unchecked exceptions that extend the `Error` class. They are thrown by the JVM and should not be handled or declared. Errors are rare, but you might see these:

ExceptionInInitializerError   Thrown when a static initializer throws an exception and doesn't handle it

StackOverflowError   Thrown when a method calls itself too many times (This is called *infinite recursion* because the method typically calls itself without end.)

NoClassDefFoundError   Thrown when a class that the code uses is available at compile time but not runtime

ExceptionInInitializerError

Java runs `static` initializers the first time a class is used. If one of the `static` initializers throws an exception, Java can't start using the class. It declares defeat by throwing an `ExceptionInInitializerError`. This code throws an `ArrayIndexOutOfBounds` in a `static` initializer:

```
static {
    int[] countsOfMoose = new int[3];
    int num = countsOfMoose[-1];
}
public static void main(String... args) { }
```

This code yields information about the error and the underlying exception:

```
Exception in thread "main" java.lang.ExceptionInInitializerError
Caused by: java.lang.ArrayIndexOutOfBoundsException: -1 out of bounds for length 3
```

When executed, you get an `ExceptionInInitializerError` because the error happened in a `static` initializer. That information alone wouldn't be particularly useful in fixing the problem. Therefore, Java also tells you the original cause of the problem: the `ArrayIndexOutOfBoundsException` that you need to fix.

The `ExceptionInInitializerError` is an error because Java failed to load the whole class. This failure prevents Java from continuing.

StackOverflowError

When Java calls methods, it puts parameters and local variables on the stack. After doing this a very large number of times, the stack runs out of room and overflows. This is called a StackOverflowError. Most of the time, this error occurs when a method calls itself.

```
public static void doNotCodeThis(int num) {
    doNotCodeThis(1);
}
```

The output contains this line:

```
Exception in thread "main" java.lang.StackOverflowError
```

Since the method calls itself, it will never end. Eventually, Java runs out of room on the stack and throws the error. This is called infinite recursion. It is better than an infinite loop because at least Java will catch it and throw the error. With an infinite loop, Java just uses all your CPU until you can kill the program.

NoClassDefFoundError

A NoClassDefFoundError occurs when Java can't find the class at runtime. Generally, this means a library available when the code was compiled is not available when the code is executed.

Handling Exceptions

What do you do when you encounter an exception? How do you handle or recover from the exception? In this section, we will show the various statements in Java that support handling exceptions and ensuring certain code, like closing a resource, is always executed.

Using *try* and *catch* Statements

Now that you know what exceptions are, let's explore how to handle them. Java uses a try statement to separate the logic that might throw an exception from the logic to handle that exception. Figure 10.2 shows the syntax of a *try statement*.

FIGURE 10.2   The syntax of a try statement

The code in the try block is run normally. If any of the statements throws an exception that can be caught by the exception type listed in the catch block, the try block stops running and execution goes to the catch statement. If none of the statements in the try block throws an exception that can be caught, the *catch clause* is not run.

You probably noticed the words *block* and *clause* used interchangeably. The exam does this as well, so get used to it. Both are correct. *Block* is correct because there are braces present. *Clause* is correct because they are part of a try statement.

There aren't a ton of syntax rules here. The curly braces are required for the try and catch blocks.

In our example, the little girl gets up by herself the first time she falls. Here's what this looks like:

```
3:  void explore() {
4:      try {
5:          fall();
6:          System.out.println("never get here");
7:      } catch (RuntimeException e) {
8:          getUp();
9:      }
10:     seeAnimals();
11: }
12: void fall() {  throw new RuntimeException(); }
```

First, line 5 calls the fall() method. Line 12 throws an exception. This means Java jumps straight to the catch block, skipping line 6. The girl gets up on line 8. Now the try statement is over, and execution proceeds normally with line 10.

Now let's look at some invalid try statements that the exam might try to trick you with. Do you see what's wrong with this one?

```
try  // DOES NOT COMPILE
    fall();
catch (Exception e)
    System.out.println("get up");
```

The problem is that the braces {} are missing. It needs to look like this:

```
try {
    fall();
} catch (Exception e) {
    System.out.println("get up");
}
```

The try statements are like methods in that the curly braces are required even if there is only one statement inside the code blocks, while if statements and loops are special and allow you to omit the curly braces.

What about this one?

```
try { // DOES NOT COMPILE
    fall();
}
```

This code doesn't compile because the try block doesn't have anything after it. Remember, the point of a try statement is for something to happen if an exception is thrown. Without another clause, the try statement is lonely. As you will see shortly, there is a special type of try statement that includes an implicit finally block, although the syntax for this is quite different from this example.

Chaining *catch* Blocks

So far, you have been catching only one type of exception. Now let's see what happens when different types of exceptions can be thrown from the same try/catch block.

For the exam, you won't be asked to create your own exception, but you may be given exception classes and need to understand how they function. Here's how to tackle them. First, you must be able to recognize if the exception is a checked or an unchecked exception. Second, you need to determine whether any of the exceptions are subclasses of the others.

```
class AnimalsOutForAWalk extends RuntimeException { }
class ExhibitClosed extends RuntimeException { }
class ExhibitClosedForLunch extends ExhibitClosed { }
```

In this example, there are three custom exceptions. All are unchecked exceptions because they directly or indirectly extend RuntimeException. Now we chain both types of exceptions with two catch blocks and handle them by printing out the appropriate message:

```
public void visitPorcupine() {
    try {
        seeAnimal();
    } catch (AnimalsOutForAWalk e) { // first catch block
        System.out.print("try back later");
    } catch (ExhibitClosed e) { // second catch block
        System.out.print("not today");
    }
}
```

There are three possibilities for when this code is run. If seeAnimal() doesn't throw an exception, nothing is printed out. If the animal is out for a walk, only the first catch block runs. If the exhibit is closed, only the second catch block runs. It is not possible for both catch blocks to be executed when chained together like this.

A rule exists for the order of the catch blocks. Java looks at them in the order they appear. If it is impossible for one of the catch blocks to be executed, a compiler error about unreachable code occurs. For example, this happens when a superclass catch block appears before a subclass catch block. Remember, we warned you to pay attention to any subclass exceptions.

In the porcupine example, the order of the catch blocks could be reversed because the exceptions don't inherit from each other. And yes, we have seen a porcupine be taken for a walk on a leash.

The following example shows exception types that do inherit from each other:

```java
public void visitMonkeys() {
    try {
        seeAnimal();
    } catch (ExhibitClosedForLunch e) {  // subclass exception
        System.out.print("try back later");
    } catch (ExhibitClosed e) {  // superclass exception
        System.out.print("not today");
    }
}
```

If the more specific ExhibitClosedForLunch exception is thrown, the first catch block runs. If not, Java checks whether the superclass ExhibitClosed exception is thrown and catches it. This time, the order of the catch blocks does matter. The reverse does not work.

```java
public void visitMonkeys() {
    try {
        seeAnimal();
    } catch (ExhibitClosed e) {
        System.out.print("not today");
    } catch (ExhibitClosedForLunch e) {  // DOES NOT COMPILE
        System.out.print("try back later");
    }
}
```

This time, if the more specific ExhibitClosedForLunch exception is thrown, the catch block for ExhibitClosed runs—which means there is no way for the second catch block to ever run. Java correctly tells you there is an unreachable catch block.

Let's try this one more time. Do you see why this code doesn't compile?

```java
public void visitSnakes() {
    try {
    } catch (IllegalArgumentException e) {
    } catch (NumberFormatException e) {  // DOES NOT COMPILE
    }
}
```

Remember we said earlier you needed to know that NumberFormatException is a subclass of IllegalArgumentException? This example is the reason why. Since NumberFormatException is a subclass, it will always be caught by the first catch block, making the second catch block unreachable code that does not compile. Likewise, for the exam you need to know that FileNotFoundException is subclass of IOException and cannot be used in a similar manner.

To review multiple catch blocks, remember that at most one catch block will run, and it will be the first catch block that can handle it. Also, remember that an exception defined by the catch statement is only in scope for that catch block. For example, the following causes a compiler error since it tries to use the exception class outside the block for which it was defined:

```java
public void visitManatees() {
   try {
   } catch (NumberFormatException e1) {
      System.out.println(e1);
   } catch (IllegalArgumentException e2) {
      System.out.println(e1);  // DOES NOT COMPILE
   }
}
```

Applying a Multi-catch Block

Oftentimes, we want the result of an exception being thrown to be the same, regardless of which particular exception is thrown. For example, take a look at this method:

```java
public static void main(String args[]) {
   try {
      System.out.println(Integer.parseInt(args[1]));
   } catch (ArrayIndexOutOfBoundsException e) {
      System.out.println("Missing or invalid input");
   } catch (NumberFormatException e) {
      System.out.println("Missing or invalid input");
   }
}
```

Notice that we have the same println() statement for two different catch blocks. How can you reduce the duplicate code? One way is to have the related exception classes all inherit the same interface or extend the same class. For example, you can have a single catch block that just catches Exception. This will catch everything and anything. Another way is to move the println() statements into a separate method and have every related catch block call that method.

While these solutions are valid, Java provides another structure to handle this more gracefully called a *multi-catch* block. A multi-catch block allows multiple exception types to be caught by the same catch block. Let's rewrite the previous example using a multi-catch block:

```
public static void main(String[] args) {
    try {
        System.out.println(Integer.parseInt(args[1]));
    } catch (ArrayIndexOutOfBoundsException | NumberFormatException e) {
        System.out.println("Missing or invalid input");
    }
}
```

This is much better. There's no duplicate code, the common logic is all in one place, and the logic is exactly where you would expect to find it. If you wanted, you could still have a second catch block for Exception in case you want to handle other types of exceptions differently.

Figure 10.3 shows the syntax of multi-catch. It's like a regular catch clause, except two or more exception types are specified separated by a pipe. The pipe (|) is also used as the "or" operator, making it easy to remember that you can use either/or of the exception types. Notice how there is only one variable name in the catch clause. Java is saying that the variable named e can be of type Exception1 or Exception2.

FIGURE 10.3   The syntax of a multi-catch block

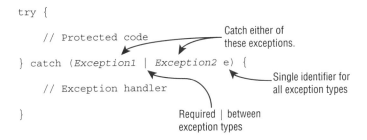

The exam might try to trick you with invalid syntax. Remember that the exceptions can be listed in any order within the catch clause. However, the variable name must appear only once and at the end. Do you see why these are valid or invalid?

```
catch(Exception1 e | Exception2 e | Exception3 e) // DOES NOT COMPILE

catch(Exception1 e1 | Exception2 e2 | Exception3 e3) // DOES NOT COMPILE

catch(Exception1 | Exception2 | Exception3 e)
```

The first line is incorrect because the variable name appears three times. Just because it happens to be the same variable name doesn't make it okay. The second line is incorrect because the variable name again appears three times. Using different variable names doesn't make it any better. The third line does compile. It shows the correct syntax for specifying three exceptions.

Java intends multi-catch to be used for exceptions that aren't related, and it prevents you from specifying redundant types in a multi-catch. Do you see what is wrong here?

```
try {
   throw new IOException();
} catch (FileNotFoundException | IOException p) {} // DOES NOT COMPILE
```

Specifying it in the multi-catch is redundant, and the compiler gives a message such as this:

```
The exception FileNotFoundException is already caught by the alternative IOException
```

Since `FileNotFoundException` is a subclass of `IOException`, this code will not compile. A multi-catch block follows similar rules as chaining `catch` blocks together that you saw in the previous section. For example, both trigger compiler errors when they encounter unreachable code or duplicate exceptions being caught. The one difference between multi-catch blocks and chaining `catch` blocks is that order does not matter for a multi-catch block within a single `catch` expression.

Getting back to the example, the correct code is just to drop the extraneous subclass reference, as shown here:

```
try {
   throw new IOException();
} catch (IOException e) { }
```

To review multi-catch, see how many errors you can find in this `try` statement:

```
11: public void doesNotCompile() { // METHOD DOES NOT COMPILE
12:    try {
13:       mightThrow();
14:    } catch (FileNotFoundException | IllegalStateException e) {
15:    } catch (InputMismatchException e | MissingResourceException e) {
16:    } catch (FileNotFoundException | IllegalArgumentException e) {
17:    } catch (Exception e) {
18:    } catch (IOException e) {
19:    }
20: }
21: private void mightThrow() throws DateTimeParseException, IOException { }
```

This code is just swimming with errors. In fact, some errors hide others, so you might not see them all in the compiler. Once you start fixing some errors, you'll see the others. Here's what's wrong:

- Line 15 has an extra variable name. Remember that there can be only one exception variable per catch block.

- Line 16 cannot catch `FileNotFoundException` because that exception was already caught on line 14. You can't list the same exception type more than once in the same try statement, just like with "regular" catch blocks.

- Lines 17 and 18 are reversed. The more general superclasses must be caught after their subclasses. While this doesn't have anything to do with multi-catch, you'll see "regular" catch block problems mixed in with multi-catch.

Don't worry—you won't see this many problems in the same example on the exam!

Adding a *finally* Block

The try statement also lets you run code at the end with a *finally clause* regardless of whether an exception is thrown. Figure 10.4 shows the syntax of a try statement with this extra functionality.

FIGURE 10.4 The syntax of a try statement with finally

There are two paths through code with both a catch and a finally. If an exception is thrown, the finally block is run after the catch block. If no exception is thrown, the finally block is run after the try block completes.

Let's go back to our young girl example, this time with finally:

```
12: void explore() {
13:     try {
14:         seeAnimals();
15:         fall();
16:     } catch (Exception e) {
17:         getHugFromDaddy();
18:     } finally {
19:         seeMoreAnimals();
20:     }
21:     goHome();
22: }
```

The girl falls on line 15. If she gets up by herself, the code goes on to the `finally` block and runs line 19. Then the `try` statement is over, and the code proceeds on line 21. If the girl doesn't get up by herself, she throws an exception. The catch block runs, and she gets a hug on line 17. With that hug she is ready to see more animals on line 19. Then the `try` statement is over, and the code proceeds on line 21. Either way, the ending is the same. The `finally` block is executed, and execution continues after the try statement.

The exam will try to trick you with missing clauses or clauses in the wrong order. Do you see why the following do or do not compile?

```
25: try { // DOES NOT COMPILE
26:    fall();
27: } finally {
28:    System.out.println("all better");
29: } catch (Exception e) {
30:    System.out.println("get up");
31: }
32:
33: try { // DOES NOT COMPILE
34:    fall();
35: }
36:
37: try {
38:    fall();
39: } finally {
40:    System.out.println("all better");
41: }
```

The first example (lines 25–31) does not compile because the `catch` and `finally` blocks are in the wrong order. The second example (lines 33–35) does not compile because there must be a `catch` or `finally` block. The third example (lines 37–41) is just fine. The `catch` block is not required if `finally` is present.

One problem with `finally` is that any realistic uses for it are out of the scope of the exam. A `finally` block is typically used to close resources such as files or databases—neither of which is a topic on this exam. This means most of the examples you encounter on the exam with `finally` are going to look contrived. For example, you'll get asked questions such as what this code outputs:

```
public static void main(String[] unused) {
   StringBuilder sb = new StringBuilder();
   try {
      sb.append("t");
   } catch (Exception e) {
      sb.append("c");
   } finally {
      sb.append("f");
```

```
    }
    sb.append("a");
    System.out.print(sb.toString());
}
```

The answer is tfa. The try block is executed. Since no exception is thrown, Java goes straight to the finally block. Then the code after the try statement is run. We know that this is a silly example, but you can expect to see examples like this on the exam.

There is one additional rule you should know for finally blocks. If a try statement with a finally block is entered, then the finally block will always be executed, regardless of whether the code completes successfully. Take a look at the following goHome() method. Assuming an exception may or may not be thrown on line 14, what are the possible values that this method could print? Also, what would the return value be in each case?

```
12: int goHome() {
13:     try {
14:         // Optionally throw an exception here
15:         System.out.print("1");
16:         return -1;
17:     } catch (Exception e) {
18:         System.out.print("2");
19:         return -2;
20:     } finally {
21:         System.out.print("3");
22:         return -3;
23:     }
24: }
```

If an exception is not thrown on line 14, then the line 15 will be executed, printing 1. Before the method returns, though, the finally block is executed, printing 3. If an exception is thrown, then lines 15–16 will be skipped, and lines 17–19 will be executed, printing 2, followed by 3 from the finally block. While the first value printed may differ, the method always prints 3 last since it's in the finally block.

What is the return value of the goHome() method? In this case, it's always -3. Because the finally block is executed shortly before the method completes, it interrupts the return statement from inside both the try and catch blocks.

For the exam, you need to remember that a finally block will always be executed. That said, it may not complete successfully. Take a look at the following code snippet. What would happen if info was null on line 32?

```
31: } finally {
32:     info.printDetails();
33:     System.out.print("Exiting");
34:     return "zoo";
35: }
```

If info is null, then the finally block would be executed, but it would stop on line 32 and throw a NullPointerException. Lines 33–34 would not be executed. In this example, you see that while a finally block will always be executed, it may not finish.

System.exit()

There is one exception to "the finally block always be executed" rule: Java defines a method that you call as System.exit(). It takes an integer parameter that represents the error code that gets returned.

```
try {
   System.exit(0);
} finally {
   System.out.print("Never going to get here");  // Not printed
}
```

System.exit() tells Java, "Stop. End the program right now. Do not pass go. Do not collect $200." When System.exit() is called in the try or catch block, the finally block does not run.

Finally Closing Resources

Oftentimes, your application works with files, databases, and various connection objects. Commonly, these external data sources are referred to as *resources*. In many cases, you *open* a connection to the resource, whether it's over the network or within a file system. You then *read/write* the data you want. Finally, you *close* the resource to indicate you are done with it.

What happens if you don't close a resource when you are done with it? In short, a lot of bad things could happen. If you are connecting to a database, you could use up all available connections, meaning no one can talk to the database until you release your connections. Although you commonly hear about memory leaks as causing programs to fail, a *resource leak* is just as bad and occurs when a program fails to release its connections to a resource, resulting in the resource becoming inaccessible.

Writing code that simplifies closing resources is what this section is about. Let's take a look at a method that opens a file, reads the data, and closes it:

```
4:  public void readFile(String file) {
5:     FileInputStream is = null;
6:     try {
7:        is = new FileInputStream("myfile.txt");
8:        // Read file data
9:     } catch (IOException e) {
10:        e.printStackTrace();
```

```
11:    } finally {
12:       if(is != null) {
13:          try {
14:             is.close();
15:          } catch (IOException e2) {
16:             e2.printStackTrace();
17:          }
18:       }
19:    }
20: }
```

Wow, that's a long method! Why do we have two `try` and `catch` blocks? Well, the code on lines 7 and 14 both include checked `IOException` calls, so they both need to be caught in the method or rethrown by the method. Half the lines of code in this method are just closing a resource. And the more resources you have, the longer code like this becomes. For example, you may have multiple resources and they need to be closed in a particular order. You also don't want an exception from closing one resource to prevent the closing of another resource.

To solve this, Java includes the *try-with-resources* statement to automatically close all resources opened in a `try` clause. This feature is also known as *automatic resource management*, because Java automatically takes care of the closing.

 For the 1Z0-815 exam, you are not required to know any File IO, network, or database classes, although you are required to know try-with-resources. If you see a question on the exam or in this chapter that uses these types of resources, assume that part of the code compiles without issue. In other words, these questions are actually a gift, since you know the problem must be about basic Java syntax or exception handling. That said, for the 1Z0-816 exam, you will need to know numerous resources classes.

Let's take a look at our same example using a try-with-resources statement:

```
4:  public void readFile(String file) {
5:     try (FileInputStream is = new FileInputStream("myfile.txt")) {
6:        // Read file data
7:     } catch (IOException e) {
8:        e.printStackTrace();
9:     }
10: }
```

Functionally, they are both quite similar, but our new version has half as many lines. More importantly, though, by using a try-with-resources statement, we guarantee that as soon as a connection passes out of scope, Java will attempt to close it within the same method.

In the following sections, we will look at the try-with-resources syntax and how to indicate a resource can be automatically closed.

Implicit *finally* Blocks

Behind the scenes, the compiler replaces a try-with-resources block with a try and finally block. We refer to this "hidden" finally block as an implicit finally block since it is created and used by the compiler automatically. You can still create a programmer-defined finally block when using a try-with-resources statement; just be aware that the implicit one will be called first.

Basics of Try-with-Resources

Figure 10.5 shows what a try-with-resources statement looks like. Notice that one or more resources can be opened in the try clause. When there are multiple resources opened, they are closed in the *reverse* order from which they were created. Also, notice that parentheses are used to list those resources, and semicolons are used to separate the declarations. This works just like declaring multiple indexes in a for loop.

FIGURE 10.5   The syntax of a basic try-with-resources

What happened to the catch block in Figure 10.5? Well, it turns out a catch block is optional with a try-with-resources statement. For example, we can rewrite the previous readFile() example so that the method rethrows the exception to make it even shorter:

```
4: public void readFile(String file) throws IOException {
5:     try (FileInputStream is = new FileInputStream("myfile.txt")) {
6:         // Read file data
7:     }
8: }
```

Earlier in the chapter, you learned that a try statement must have one or more catch blocks or a finally block. This is still true. The finally clause exists implicitly. You just don't have to type it.

Remember that only a try-with-resources statement is permitted to omit both the catch and finally blocks. A traditional try statement must have either or both. You can easily distinguish between the two by the presence of parentheses, (), after the try keyword.

Figure 10.6 shows that a try-with-resources statement is still allowed to have catch and/or finally blocks. In fact, if the code within the try block throws a checked exception not declared by the method in which it is defined or handled by another try/catch block, then it will need to be handled by the catch block. Also, the catch and finally blocks are run in addition to the implicit one that closes the resources. For the exam, you need to know that the implicit finally block runs *before* any programmer-coded ones.

FIGURE 10.6   The syntax of try-with-resources including catch/finally

```
Any resources that should
automatically be closed

try (FileInputStream in = new FileInputStream("data.txt");
        FileOutputStream out = new FileOutputStream("output.txt");) {

    // Protected code

} catch (IOException  e) {

    // Exception handler           Optional catch and
                                    finally clauses
} finally {

    // finally block

}
```

Resources are closed at this point.

To make sure that you've wrapped your head around the differences, you should be able to fill in Table 10.2 and Table 10.3 with whichever combinations of catch and finally blocks are legal configurations.

TABLE 10.2   Legal vs. illegal configurations with a traditional try statement

	0 finally blocks	**1 finally block**	**2 or more finally blocks**
0 catch blocks	Not legal	Legal	Not legal
1 or more catch blocks	Legal	Legal	Not legal

TABLE 10.3   Legal vs. illegal configurations with a try-with-resources statement

	0 finally blocks	1 finally block	2 or more finally blocks
0 catch blocks	Legal	Legal	Not legal
1 or more catch blocks	Legal	Legal	Not legal

You can see that for both of these try statements, two or more programmer-defined finally blocks are not allowed. Remember that the implicit finally block defined by the compiler is not counted here.

AutoCloseable

You can't just put any random class in a try-with-resources statement. Java requires classes used in a try-with-resources implement the AutoCloseable interface, which includes a void close() method. You'll learn more about resources that implement this method when you study for the 1Z0-816 exam.

Declaring Resources

While try-with-resources does support declaring multiple variables, each variable must be declared in a separate statement. For example, the following do not compile:

```
try (MyFileClass is = new MyFileClass(1),  // DOES NOT COMPILE
     os = new MyFileClass(2)) {
}


try (MyFileClass ab = new MyFileClass(1),  // DOES NOT COMPILE
     MyFileClass cd = new MyFileClass(2)) {
}
```

A try-with-resources statement does not support multiple variable declarations. The first example does not compile because it is missing the data type and it uses a comma (,) instead of a semicolon (;). The second example does not compile because it also uses a comma (,) instead of a semicolon (;). Each resource must include the data type and be separated by a semicolon (;).

You can declare a resource using var as the data type in a try-with-resources statement, since resources are local variables.

```
try (var f = new BufferedInputStream(new FileInputStream("it.txt"))) {
    // Process file
}
```

Declaring resources is a common situation where using var is quite helpful, as it shortens the already long line of code.

Scope of Try-with-Resources

The resources created in the try clause are in scope only within the try block. This is another way to remember that the implicit finally runs before any catch/finally blocks that you code yourself. The implicit close has run already, and the resource is no longer available. Do you see why lines 6 and 8 don't compile in this example?

```
3: try (Scanner s = new Scanner(System.in)) {
4:    s.nextLine();
5: } catch(Exception e) {
6:    s.nextInt(); // DOES NOT COMPILE
7: } finally {
8:    s.nextInt(); // DOES NOT COMPILE
9: }
```

The problem is that Scanner has gone out of scope at the end of the try clause. Lines 6 and 8 do not have access to it. This is actually a nice feature. You can't accidentally use an object that has been closed. In a traditional try statement, the variable has to be declared before the try statement so that both the try and finally blocks can access it, which has the unpleasant side effect of making the variable in scope for the rest of the method, just inviting you to call it by accident.

Following Order of Operation

You've learned two new rules for the order in which code runs in a try-with-resources statement:

- Resources are closed after the try clause ends and before any catch/finally clauses.
- Resources are closed in the reverse order from which they were created.

Let's review these principles with a more complex example. First, we define a custom class that you can use with a try-with-resources statement, as it implements AutoCloseable.

```
public class MyFileClass implements AutoCloseable {
   private final int num;
   public MyFileClass(int num) { this.num = num; }
   public void close() {
      System.out.println("Closing: " + num);
   }
}
```

This is a pretty simple class that prints the number, set by the constructor, when a resource is closed. Based on these rules, can you figure out what this method prints?

```java
public static void main(String... xyz) {
    try (MyFileClass a1 = new MyFileClass(1);
         MyFileClass a2 = new MyFileClass(2)) {
        throw new RuntimeException();
    } catch (Exception e) {
        System.out.println("ex");
    } finally {
        System.out.println("finally");
    }
}
```

Since the resources are closed in the reverse order from which they were opened, we have `Closing: 2` and then `Closing: 1`. After that, the catch block and finally block are run—just as they are in a regular try statement. The output is as follows:

```
Closing: 2
Closing: 1
ex
finally
```

For the exam, make sure you understand why the method prints the statements in this order. Remember, the resources are closed in the reverse order from which they are declared, and the implicit finally is executed before the programmer-defined finally.

 Real World Scenario

Try-with-Resources Guarantees

Does a try-with-resources statement guarantee a resource will be closed? Although this is beyond the scope of the exam, the short answer is "no." The try-with-resources statement guarantees only the close() method will be called. If the close() method encounters an exception of its own or the method is implemented poorly, a resource leak can still occur. For the exam, you just need to know try-with-resources is guaranteed to call the close() method on the resource.

Throwing Additional Exceptions

A catch or finally block can have any valid Java code in it—including another try statement. What happens when an exception is thrown inside of a catch or finally block?

To answer this, let's take a look at a concrete example:

```
16: public static void main(String[] a) {
17:     FileReader reader = null;
18:     try {
19:         reader = read();
20:     } catch (IOException e) {
21:         try {
22:             if (reader != null)  reader.close();
23:         } catch (IOException inner) {
24:         }
25:     }
26: }
27: private static FileReader read() throws IOException {
28:     // CODE GOES HERE
29: }
```

The easiest case is if line 28 doesn't throw an exception. Then the entire catch block on lines 20–25 is skipped. Next, consider if line 28 throws a NullPointerException. That isn't an IOException, so the catch block on lines 20–25 will still be skipped, resulting in the main() method terminating early.

If line 28 does throw an IOException, the catch block on lines 20–25 gets run. Line 22 tries to close the reader. If that goes well, the code completes, and the main() method ends normally. If the close() method does throw an exception, Java looks for more catch blocks. This exception is caught on line 23. Regardless, the exception on line 28 is handled. A different exception might be thrown, but the one from line 28 is done.

Most of the examples you see with exception handling on the exam are abstract. They use letters or numbers to make sure you understand the flow. This one shows that only the last exception to be thrown matters:

```
26: try {
27:     throw new RuntimeException();
28: } catch (RuntimeException e) {
29:     throw new RuntimeException();
30: } finally {
31:     throw new Exception();
32: }
```

Line 27 throws an exception, which is caught on line 28. The catch block then throws an exception on line 29. If there were no finally block, the exception from line 29 would be thrown. However, the finally block runs after the catch block. Since the finally block throws an exception of its own on line 31, this one gets thrown. The exception from the catch block gets forgotten about. This is why you often see another try/catch inside a finally block—to make sure it doesn't mask the exception from the catch block.

Next we are going to show you one of the hardest examples you can be asked related to exceptions. What do you think this method returns? Go slowly. It's tricky.

```
30: public String exceptions() {
31:     StringBuilder result = new StringBuilder();
32:     String v = null;
33:     try {
34:         try {
35:             result.append("before_");
36:             v.length();
37:             result.append("after_");
38:         } catch (NullPointerException e) {
39:             result.append("catch_");
40:             throw new RuntimeException();
41:         } finally {
42:             result.append("finally_");
43:             throw new Exception();
44:         }
45:     } catch (Exception e) {
46:         result.append("done");
47:     }
48:     return result.toString();
49: }
```

The correct answer is before_catch_finally_done. First on line 35, "before_" is added. Line 36 throws a NullPointerException. Line 37 is skipped as Java goes straight to the catch block. Line 38 does catch the exception, and "catch_" is added on line 39. Then line 40 throws a RuntimeException. The finally block runs after the catch regardless of whether an exception is thrown; it adds "finally_" to result. At this point, we have completed the inner try statement that ran on lines 34–44. The outer catch block then sees an exception was thrown and catches it on line 45; it adds "done" to result.

Did you get that right? If so, you are well on your way to acing this part of the exam. If not, we recommend reading this section again before moving on.

Calling Methods That Throw Exceptions

When you're calling a method that throws an exception, the rules are the same as within a method. Do you see why the following doesn't compile?

```
class NoMoreCarrotsException extends Exception {}
public class Bunny {
    public static void main(String[] args) {
        eatCarrot(); // DOES NOT COMPILE
```

```
    }
    private static void eatCarrot() throws NoMoreCarrotsException {
    }
}
```

The problem is that NoMoreCarrotsException is a checked exception. Checked exceptions must be handled or declared. The code would compile if you changed the main() method to either of these:

```
    public static void main(String[] args)
            throws NoMoreCarrotsException { // declare exception
        eatCarrot();
    }

    public static void main(String[] args) {
        try {
            eatCarrot();
        } catch (NoMoreCarrotsException e ) { // handle exception
            System.out.print("sad rabbit");
        }
    }
```

You might have noticed that eatCarrot() didn't actually throw an exception; it just declared that it could. This is enough for the compiler to require the caller to handle or declare the exception.

The compiler is still on the lookout for unreachable code. Declaring an unused exception isn't considered unreachable code. It gives the method the option to change the implementation to throw that exception in the future. Do you see the issue here?

```
public void bad() {
    try {
        eatCarrot();
    } catch (NoMoreCarrotsException e ) { // DOES NOT COMPILE
        System.out.print("sad rabbit");
    }
}

public void good() throws NoMoreCarrotsException {
    eatCarrot();
}

private void eatCarrot() { }
```

Java knows that eatCarrot() can't throw a checked exception—which means there's no way for the catch block in bad() to be reached. In comparison, good() is free to declare other exceptions.

 NOTE When you see a checked exception declared inside a catch block on the exam, check and make sure the code in the associated try block is capable of throwing the exception or a subclass of the exception. If not, the code is unreachable and does not compile. Remember that this rule does not extend to unchecked exceptions or exceptions declared in a method signature.

Declaring and Overriding Methods with Exceptions

Now that you have a deeper understanding of exceptions, let's look at overriding methods with exceptions in the method declaration. When a class overrides a method from a superclass or implements a method from an interface, it's not allowed to add new checked exceptions to the method signature. For example, this code isn't allowed:

```
class CanNotHopException extends Exception { }
class Hopper {
    public void hop() { }
}
class Bunny extends Hopper {
    public void hop() throws CanNotHopException { } // DOES NOT COMPILE
}
```

Java knows hop() isn't allowed to throw any checked exceptions because the hop() method in the superclass Hopper doesn't declare any. Imagine what would happen if the subclasses versions of the method could add checked exceptions—you could write code that calls Hopper's hop() method and not handle any exceptions. Then if Bunny were used in its place, the code wouldn't know to handle or declare CanNotHopException.

An overridden method in a subclass is allowed to declare fewer exceptions than the superclass or interface. This is legal because callers are already handling them.

```
class Hopper {
    public void hop() throws CanNotHopException { }
}
class Bunny extends Hopper {
    public void hop()  { }
}
```

An overridden method not declaring one of the exceptions thrown by the parent method is similar to the method declaring it throws an exception that it never actually throws. This is perfectly legal.

Similarly, a class is allowed to declare a subclass of an exception type. The idea is the same. The superclass or interface has already taken care of a broader type. Here's an example:

```java
class Hopper {
    public void hop() throws Exception { }
}
class Bunny extends Hopper {
    public void hop() throws CanNotHopException { }
}
```

Bunny could declare that it throws Exception directly, or it could declare that it throws a more specific type of Exception. It could even declare that it throws nothing at all.

This rule applies only to checked exceptions. The following code is legal because it has an unchecked exception in the subclass's version:

```java
class Hopper {
    public void hop() { }
}
class Bunny extends Hopper {
    public void hop() throws IllegalStateException { }
}
```

The reason that it's okay to declare new unchecked exceptions in a subclass method is that the declaration is redundant. Methods are free to throw any unchecked exceptions they want without mentioning them in the method declaration.

Printing an Exception

There are three ways to print an exception. You can let Java print it out, print just the message, or print where the stack trace comes from. This example shows all three approaches:

```java
5:  public static void main(String[] args) {
6:      try {
7:          hop();
8:      } catch (Exception e) {
9:          System.out.println(e);
10:         System.out.println(e.getMessage());
11:         e.printStackTrace();
12:     }
13: }
14: private static void hop() {
15:     throw new RuntimeException("cannot hop");
16: }
```

This code results in the following output:

```
java.lang.RuntimeException: cannot hop
cannot hop
java.lang.RuntimeException: cannot hop
   at Handling.hop(Handling.java:15)
   at Handling.main(Handling.java:7)
```

The first line shows what Java prints out by default: the exception type and message. The second line shows just the message. The rest shows a stack trace.

The stack trace is usually the most helpful one because it is a picture in time the moment the exception is thrown. It shows the hierarchy of method calls that were made to reach the line that threw the exception. On the exam, you will mostly see the first approach. This is because the exam often shows code snippets.

The stack trace shows all the methods on the stack. Figure 10.7 shows what the stack looks like for this code. Every time you call a method, Java adds it to the stack until it completes. When an exception is thrown, it goes through the stack until it finds a method that can handle it or it runs out of stack.

FIGURE 10.7 A method stack

 Real World Scenario

Why Swallowing Exceptions Is Bad

Because checked exceptions require you to handle or declare them, there is a temptation to catch them so they "go away." But doing so can cause problems. In the following code, there's a problem reading the file:

```
public static void main(String... p) {
   String textInFile = null;
   try {
      textInFile = readInFile();
```

```
    } catch (IOException e) {
        // ignore exception
    }
    // imagine many lines of code here
    System.out.println(textInFile.replace(" ", ""));
}
private static String readInFile() throws IOException {
    throw new IOException();
}
```

The code results in a `NullPointerException`. Java doesn't tell you anything about the original `IOException` because it was handled. Granted, it was handled poorly, but it was handled.

When writing this book, we tend to swallow exceptions because many of our examples are artificial in nature. However, when you're writing your own code, you should print out a stack trace or at least a message when catching an exception. Also, consider whether continuing is the best course of action. In our example, the program can't do anything after it fails to read in the file. It might as well have just thrown the `IOException`.

Summary

An exception indicates something unexpected happened. A method can handle an exception by catching it or declaring it for the caller to deal with. Many exceptions are thrown by Java libraries. You can throw your own exceptions with code such as `throw new Exception()`.

All exceptions inherit `Throwable`. Subclasses of `Error` are exceptions that a programmer should not attempt to handle. Classes that inherit `RuntimeException` and `Error` are runtime (unchecked) exceptions. Classes that inherit `Exception`, but not `RuntimeException`, are checked exceptions. Java requires checked exceptions to be handled with a `catch` block or declared with the `throws` keyword.

A `try` statement must include at least one `catch` block or a `finally` block. A multi-catch block is one that catches multiple unrelated exceptions in a single `catch` block. If a `try` statement has multiple `catch` blocks chained together, at most one `catch` block can run. Java looks for an exception that can be caught by each `catch` block in the order they appear, and the first match is run. Then execution continues after the `try` statement. If both `catch` and `finally` throw an exception, the one from `finally` gets thrown.

A try-with-resources block is used to ensure a resource like a database or a file is closed properly after it is created. A try-with-resources statement does not require a `catch` or `finally` block but may optionally include them. The implicit `finally` block is executed before any programmer-defined `catch` or `finally` blocks.

RuntimeException classes you should know for the exam include the following:

- ArithmeticException
- ArrayIndexOutOfBoundsException
- ClassCastException
- IllegalArgumentException
- NullPointerException
- NumberFormatException

IllegalArgumentException is typically thrown by the programmer, whereas the others are typically thrown by the standard Java library.

Checked Exception classes you should know for the exam include the following:

- IOException
- FileNotFoundException

Error classes you should know for the exam include the following:

- ExceptionInInitializerError
- StackOverflowError
- NoClassDefFoundError

For the exam, remember that NumberFormatException is a subclass of IllegalArgumentException, and FileNotFoundException is a subclass of IOException.

When a method overrides a method in a superclass or interface, it is not allowed to add checked exceptions. It is allowed to declare fewer exceptions or declare a subclass of a declared exception. Methods declare exceptions with the keyword throws.

Exam Essentials

Understand the various types of exceptions.   All exceptions are subclasses of java.lang.Throwable. Subclasses of java.lang.Error should never be caught. Only subclasses of java.lang.Exception should be handled in application code.

Differentiate between checked and unchecked exceptions.   Unchecked exceptions do not need to be caught or handled and are subclasses of java.lang.RuntimeException and java.lang.Error. All other subclasses of java.lang.Exception are checked exceptions and must be handled or declared.

Understand the flow of a try statement.   A try statement must have a catch or a finally block. Multiple catch blocks can be chained together, provided no superclass exception type appears in an earlier catch block than its subclass. A multi-catch expression may be used to handle multiple exceptions in the same catch block, provided one exception is not a subclass of another. The finally block runs last regardless of whether an exception is thrown.

Be able to follow the order of a try-with-resources statement.   A try-with-resources statement is a special type of `try` block in which one or more resources are declared and automatically closed in the reverse order of which they are declared. It can be used with or without a `catch` or `finally` block, with the implicit `finally` block always executed first.

Identify whether an exception is thrown by the programmer or the JVM. `IllegalArgumentException` and `NumberFormatException` are commonly thrown by the programmer. Most of the other unchecked exceptions are typically thrown by the JVM or built-in Java libraries.

Write methods that declare exceptions.   The `throws` keyword is used in a method declaration to indicate an exception might be thrown. When overriding a method, the method is allowed to throw fewer or narrower checked exceptions than the original version.

Recognize when to use throw versus throws.   The `throw` keyword is used when you actually want to throw an exception—for example, `throw new RuntimeException()`. The `throws` keyword is used in a method declaration.

Review Questions

The answers to the chapter review questions can be found in the Appendix.

1. Which of the following statements are true? (Choose all that apply.)

   A. Exceptions of type `RuntimeException` are unchecked.

   B. Exceptions of type `RuntimeException` are checked.

   C. You can declare unchecked exceptions.

   D. You can declare checked exceptions.

   E. You can handle only `Exception` subclasses.

   F. All exceptions are subclasses of `Throwable`.

2. Which of the following pairs fill in the blanks to make this code compile? (Choose all that apply.)

   ```
   6: public void ohNo(ArithmeticException ae) _____ Exception {
   7:    if(ae==null) _____ Exception();
   8:    else _____ ae;
   9: }
   ```

   A. On line 6, fill in `throw`

   B. On line 6, fill in `throws`

   C. On line 7, fill in `throw`

   D. On line 7, fill in `throw new`

   E. On line 8, fill in `throw`

   F. On line 8, fill in `throw new`

   G. None of the above

3. What is printed by the following? (Choose all that apply.)

   ```
   1: public class Mouse {
   2:    public String name;
   3:    public void findCheese() {
   4:       System.out.print("1");
   5:       try {
   6:          System.out.print("2");
   7:          name.toString();
   8:          System.out.print("3");
   9:       } catch (NullPointerException e | ClassCastException e) {
   10:          System.out.print("4");
   11:          throw e;
   12:       }
   13:       System.out.print("5");
   14:    }
   ```

```
15:    public static void main(String... tom) {
16:        Mouse jerry = new Mouse();
17:        jerry.findCheese();
18:    } }
```

A. 1

B. 2

C. 3

D. 4

E. 5

F. The stack trace for a NullPointerException

G. None of the above

4. Which of the following statements about finally blocks are true? (Choose all that apply.)

   A. A finally block is never required with a regular try statement.

   B. A finally block is required when there are no catch blocks in a regular try statement.

   C. A finally block is required when the program code doesn't terminate on its own.

   D. A finally block is never required with a try-with-resources statement.

   E. A finally block is required when there are no catch blocks in a try-with-resources statement.

   F. A finally block is required in order to make sure all resources are closed in a try-with-resources statement.

   G. A finally block is executed before the resources declared in a try-with-resources statement are closed.

5. Which exception will the following method throw?

```
3: public static void main(String[] other) {
4:    Object obj = Integer.valueOf(3);
5:    String str = (String) obj;
6:    obj = null;
7:    System.out.println(obj.equals(null));
8: }
```

   A. ArrayIndexOutOfBoundsException

   B. IllegalArgumentException

   C. ClassCastException

   D. NumberFormatException

   E. NullPointerException

   F. None of the above

6. What does the following method print?

```
11: public void tryAgain(String s) {
12:    try(FileReader r = null, p = new FileReader("")) {
13:       System.out.print("X");
14:       throw new IllegalArgumentException();
15:    } catch (Exception s) {
16:       System.out.print("A");
17:       throw new FileNotFoundException();
18:    } finally {
19:       System.out.print("O");
20:    }
21: }
```

A. XAO

B. XOA

C. One line of this method contains a compiler error.

D. Two lines of this method contain compiler errors.

E. Three lines of this method contain compiler errors.

F. The code compiles, but a NullPointerException is thrown at runtime.

G. None of the above

7. What will happen if you add the following statement to a working main() method?

```
System.out.print(4 / 0);
```

A. It will not compile.

B. It will not run.

C. It will run and throw an ArithmeticException.

D. It will run and throw an IllegalArgumentException.

E. None of the above

8. What is printed by the following program?

```
1:  public class DoSomething {
2:     public void go() {
3:        System.out.print("A");
4:        try {
5:           stop();
6:        } catch (ArithmeticException e) {
7:           System.out.print("B");
8:        } finally {
9:           System.out.print("C");
10:       }
11:       System.out.print("D");
12:    }
13:    public void stop() {
```

```
14:        System.out.print("E");
15:        Object x = null;
16:        x.toString();
17:        System.out.print("F");
18:    }
19:    public static void main(String n[]) {
20:        new DoSomething().go();
21:    }
22: }
```

A. AE

B. AEBCD

C. AEC

D. AECD

E. AE followed by a stack trace

F. AEBCD followed by a stack trace

G. AEC followed by a stack trace

H. A stack trace with no other output

9. What is the output of the following snippet, assuming a and b are both 0?

```
3:  try {
4:      System.out.print(a / b);
5:  } catch (RuntimeException e) {
6:      System.out.print(-1);
7:  } catch (ArithmeticException e) {
8:      System.out.print(0);
9:  } finally {
10:     System.out.print("done");
11: }
```

A. -1

B. 0

C. done-1

D. done0

E. The code does not compile.

F. An uncaught exception is thrown.

G. None of the above

10. What is the output of the following program?

```
1:  public class Laptop {
2:      public void start() {
3:          try {
4:              System.out.print("Starting up_");
```

```
5:              throw new Exception();
6:          } catch (Exception e) {
7:              System.out.print("Problem_");
8:              System.exit(0);
9:          } finally {
10:             System.out.print("Shutting down");
11:         }
12:     }
13:     public static void main(String[] w) {
14:         new Laptop().start();
15:     } }
```

A. Starting up_

B. Starting up_Problem_

C. Starting up_Problem_Shutting down

D. Starting up_Shutting down

E. The code does not compile.

F. An uncaught exception is thrown.

11. What is the output of the following program?

```
1:  public class Dog {
2:      public String name;
3:      public void runAway() {
4:          System.out.print("1");
5:          try {
6:              System.out.print("2");
7:              int x = Integer.parseInt(name);
8:              System.out.print("3");
9:          } catch (NumberFormatException e) {
10:             System.out.print("4");
11:         }
12:     }
13:     public static void main(String... args) {
14:         Dog webby = new Dog();
15:         webby.name = "Webby";
16:         webby.runAway();
17:         System.out.print("5");
18:     } }
```

A. 1234

B. 1235

C. 124

D. 1245

E. The code does not compile.

F. An uncaught exception is thrown.

G. None of the above

12. What is the output of the following program?

```
1:  public class Cat {
2:      public String name;
3:      public void knockStuffOver() {
4:          System.out.print("1");
5:          try {
6:              System.out.print("2");
7:              int x = Integer.parseInt(name);
8:              System.out.print("3");
9:          } catch (NullPointerException e) {
10:              System.out.print("4");
11:          }
12:          System.out.print("5");
13:      }
14:      public static void main(String args[]) {
15:          Cat loki = new Cat();
16:          loki.name = "Loki";
17:          loki.knockStuffOver();
18:          System.out.print("6");
19:      } }
```

A. The output is 12, followed by a stack trace for a `NumberFormatException`.

B. The output is 124, followed by a stack trace for a `NumberFormatException`.

C. The output is 12456.

D. The output is 1256, followed by a stack trace for a `NumberFormatException`.

E. The code does not compile.

F. An uncaught exception is thrown.

G. None of the above

13. Which of the following statements are true? (Choose all that apply.)

A. You can declare a method with `Exception` as the return type.

B. You can declare a method with `RuntimeException` as the return type.

C. You can declare any subclass of `Error` in the throws part of a method declaration.

D. You can declare any subclass of `Exception` in the throws part of a method declaration.

E. You can declare any subclass of `Object` in the throws part of a method declaration.

F. You can declare any subclass of `RuntimeException` in the throws part of a method declaration.

14. Which of the following can be inserted on line 8 to make this code compile? (Choose all that apply.)

```
7: public void whatHappensNext() throws IOException {
8:     // INSERT CODE HERE
9: }
```

A. `System.out.println("it's ok");`

B. `throw new Exception();`

C. `throw new IllegalArgumentException();`

D. `throw new java.io.IOException();`

E. `throw new RuntimeException();`

F. None of the above

15. What is printed by the following program? (Choose all that apply.)

```
1:  public class Help {
2:      public void callSuperhero() {
3:          try (String raspberry = new String("Olivia")) {
4:              System.out.print("Q");
5:          } catch (Error e) {
6:              System.out.print("X");
7:          } finally {
8:              System.out.print("M");
9:          }
10:     }
11:     public static void main(String[] args) {
12:         new Help().callSuperhero();
13:         System.out.print("S");
14:     } }
```

A. SQM

B. QXMS

C. QSM

D. QMS

E. A stack trace

F. The code does not compile because `NumberFormatException` is not declared or caught.

G. None of the above

16. Which of the following do not need to be handled or declared? (Choose all that apply.)

A. `ArrayIndexOutOfBoundsException`

B. `IllegalArgumentException`

C. `IOException`

D. `Error`

E. `NumberFormatException`

F. Any exception that extends `RuntimeException`

G. Any exception that extends `Exception`

17. Which lines can fill in the blank to make the following code compile? (Choose all that apply.)

```
void rollOut() throws ClassCastException {}

  public void transform(String c) {
    try {
      rollOut();
    } catch (IllegalArgumentException | _____) {
    }
  }
}
```

A. `IOException a`

B. `Error b`

C. `NullPointerException c`

D. `RuntimeException d`

E. `NumberFormatException e`

F. `ClassCastException f`

G. None of the above. The code contains a compiler error regardless of what is inserted into the blank.

18. Which scenario is the best use of an exception?

A. An element is not found when searching a list.

B. An unexpected parameter is passed into a method.

C. The computer caught fire.

D. You want to loop through a list.

E. You don't know how to code a method.

19. Which of the following can be inserted into `Lion` to make this code compile? (Choose all that apply.)

```
class HasSoreThroatException extends Exception {}
class TiredException extends RuntimeException {}
interface Roar {
    void roar() throws HasSoreThroatException;
}
class Lion implements Roar {
    // INSERT CODE HERE
}
```

    A. `public void roar() {}`

    B. `public int roar() throws RuntimeException {}`

    C. `public void roar() throws Exception {}`

    D. `public void roar() throws HasSoreThroatException {}`

    E. `public void roar() throws IllegalArgumentException {}`

    F. `public void roar() throws TiredException {}`

20. Which of the following are true? (Choose all that apply.)

    A. Checked exceptions are allowed, but not required, to be handled or declared.

    B. Checked exceptions are required to be handled or declared.

    C. Errors are allowed, but not required, to be handled or declared.

    D. Errors are required to be handled or declared.

    E. Unchecked exceptions are allowed, but not required, to be handled or declared.

    F. Unchecked exceptions are required to be handled or declared.

21. Which of the following pairs fill in the blanks to make this code compile? (Choose all that apply.)

```
6: public void ohNo(IOException ie) _____ Exception {
7:       _____ FileNotFoundException();
8:       _____ ie;
9: }
```

    A. On line 6, fill in `throw`

    B. On line 6, fill in `throws`

    C. On line 7, fill in `throw`

    D. On line 7, fill in `throw new`

    E. On line 8, fill in `throw`

    F. On line 8, fill in `throw new`

    G. None of the above

22. Which of the following can be inserted in the blank to make the code compile? (Choose all that apply.)

```
public void dontFail() {
    try {
        System.out.println("work real hard");
    } catch (_____ e) {
    } catch (RuntimeException e) {}
}
```

    A. `var`

    B. `Exception`

    C. `IOException`

D. `IllegalArgumentException`

E. `RuntimeException`

F. `StackOverflowError`

G. None of the above

23. What does the output of the following method contain? (Choose all that apply.)

```
12: public static void main(String[] args) {
13:     System.out.print("a");
14:     try {
15:         System.out.print("b");
16:         throw new IllegalArgumentException();
17:     } catch (IllegalArgumentException e) {
18:         System.out.print("c");
19:         throw new RuntimeException("1");
20:     } catch (RuntimeException e) {
21:         System.out.print("d");
22:         throw new RuntimeException("2");
23:     } finally {
24:         System.out.print("e");
25:         throw new RuntimeException("3");
26:     }
27: }
```

A. abce

B. abde

C. An exception with the message set to "1"

D. An exception with the message set to "2"

E. An exception with the message set to "3"

F. Nothing; the code does not compile.

24. What does the following class output?

```
1:  public class MoreHelp {
2:      class Sidekick implements AutoCloseable {
3:          protected String n;
4:          public Sidekick(String n) { this.n = n; }
5:          public void close() { System.out.print("L"); }
6:      }
7:      public void requiresAssistance() {
8:          try (Sidekick is = new Sidekick("Adeline")) {
9:              System.out.print("O");
10:         } finally {
```

```
11:            System.out.print("K");
12:        }
13:    }
14:    public static void main(String... league) {
15:        new MoreHelp().requiresAssistance();
16:        System.out.print("I");
17:    } }
```

A. LOKI

B. OKLI

C. OLKI

D. OKIL

E. The output cannot be determined until runtime.

F. Nothing; the code does not compile.

G. None of the above

25. What does the following code snippet return, assuming a and b are both 1?

```
13: try {
14:     return a / b;
15: } catch (ClassCastException e) {
16:     return 10;
17: } catch (RuntimeException e) {
18:     return 20;
19: } finally {
20:     return 30;
21: }
```

A. 1

B. 10

C. 20

D. 30

E. The code does not compile.

F. An uncaught exception is thrown.

G. None of the above

Chapter 11

Modules

OCP EXAM OBJECTIVES COVERED IN THIS CHAPTER:

✓ **Understanding Modules**

- Describe the Modular JDK
- Declare modules and enable access between modules
- Describe how a modular project is compiled and run

Since Java 9, packages can be grouped into modules. In this chapter, we will explain the purpose of modules and how to build your own. We will also show how to run them and how to discover existing modules. This book only covers the basics of modules that you need to know for the 1Z0-815 exam.

We've made the code in this chapter available online. Since it can be tedious to create the directory structure, this will save you some time. Additionally, the commands need to be exactly right, so we've included those online so you can copy and paste them and compare them with what you typed. Both are available in the resources section of the online test bank and in our GitHub repo linked to from:

```
http://www.selikoff.net/ocp11-complete/
```

Introducing Modules

When writing code for the exam, you generally see small classes. After all, exam questions have to fit on a single screen! When you work on real programs, they are much bigger. A real project will consist of hundreds or thousands of classes grouped into packages. These packages are grouped into *Java archive (JAR)* files. A JAR is a zip file with some extra information, and the extension is .jar.

In addition to code written by your team, most applications also use code written by others. *Open source* is software with the code supplied and is often free to use. Java has a vibrant open-source software (OSS) community, and those libraries are also supplied as JAR files. For example, there are libraries to read files, connect to a database, and much more.

Some open source projects even depend on functionality in other open source projects. For example, Spring is a commonly used framework, and JUnit is a commonly used testing library. To use either, you need to make sure you had compatible versions of all the relevant JARs available at runtime. This complex chain of dependencies and minimum versions is often referred to by the community as *JAR hell*. Hell is an excellent way of describing the wrong version of a class being loaded or even a ClassNotFoundException at runtime.

The *Java Platform Module System* (JPMS) was introduced in Java 9 to group code at a higher level and tries to solve the problems that Java has been plagued with since the beginning. The main purpose of a module is to provide groups of related packages to offer a particular set of functionality to developers. It's like a JAR file except a developer chooses which packages are accessible outside the module. Let's look at what modules are and what problems they are designed to solve.

The Java Platform Module System includes the following:

- A format for module JAR files
- Partitioning of the JDK into modules
- Additional command-line options for Java tools

Exploring a Module

In Chapter 1, "Welcome to Java," we had a small Zoo application. It had only one class and just printed out one thing. Now imagine we had a whole staff of programmers and were automating the operations of the zoo. There are many things that need to be coded including the interactions with the animals, visitors, the public website, and outreach.

A *module* is a group of one or more packages plus a special file called `module-info .java`. Figure 11.1 lists just a few of the modules a zoo might need. We decided to focus on the animal interactions in our example. The full zoo could easily have a dozen modules. In Figure 11.1, notice that there are arrows between many of the modules. These represent *dependencies* where one module relies on code in another. The staff needs to feed the animals to keep their jobs. The line from `zoo.staff` to `zoo.animal.feeding` shows the former depends on the latter.

FIGURE 11.1   Design of a modular system

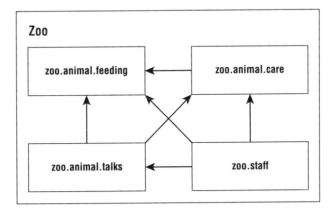

Now let's drill down into one of these modules. Figure 11.2 shows what is inside the `zoo.animal.talks` module. There are three packages with two classes each. (It's a small zoo.) There is also a strange file called `module-info.java`. This file is required to be inside all modules. We will explain this in more detail later in the chapter.

FIGURE 11.2   Looking inside a module

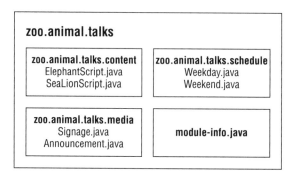

Benefits of Modules

Modules look like another layer of things you need to know in order to program. While using modules is optional, it is important to understand the problems they are designed to solve. Besides, knowing why modules are useful is required for the exam!

Better Access Control

In Chapter 7, "Methods and Encapsulation," you saw the traditional four levels of access control available in Java 8: private, package-private, protected, and public access. These levels of access control allowed you to restrict access to a certain class or package. You could even allow access to subclasses without exposing them to the world.

However, what if we wrote some complex logic that we wanted to restrict to just some packages? For example, we would like the packages in the zoo.animal.talks module to just be available to the packages in the zoo.staff module without making them available to any other code. Our traditional access modifiers cannot handle this scenario.

Developers would resort to hacks like naming a package zoo.animal.internal. That didn't work, though, because other developers could still call the "internal" code. There was a class named sun.misc.Unsafe, and it got used in places. And that class had Unsafe in the name. Clearly, relying on naming conventions was insufficient at preventing developers from calling it in the past.

Modules solve this problem by acting as a fifth level of access control. They can expose packages within the modular JAR to specific other packages. This stronger form of encapsulation really does create internal packages. You'll see how to code it when we talk about the module-info.java file later in this chapter.

Clearer Dependency Management

It is common for libraries to depend on other libraries. For example, the JUnit 4 testing library depends on the Hamcrest library for matching logic. Developers would have to find this out by reading the documentation or files in the project itself.

If you forgot to include Hamcrest in your classpath, your code would run fine until you used a Hamcrest class. Then it would blow up at runtime with a message about not finding a required class. (We did mention JAR hell, right?)

In a fully modular environment, each of the open source projects would specify their dependencies in the module-info.java file. When launching the program, Java would complain that Hamcrest isn't in the module path and you'd know right away.

Custom Java Builds

The Java Development Kit (JDK) is larger than 150 MB. Even the Java Runtime Environment (JRE) was pretty big when it was available as a separate download. In the past, Java attempted to solve this with a *compact profile*. The three compact profiles provided a subset of the built-in Java classes so there would be a smaller package for mobile and embedded devices.

However, the compact profiles lacked flexibility. Many packages were included that developers were unlikely to use, such as Java Native Interface (JNI), which is for working with OS-specific programs. At the same time, using other packages like Image I/O required the full JRE.

The Java Platform Module System allows developers to specify what modules they actually need. This makes it possible to create a smaller runtime image that is customized to what the application needs and nothing more. Users can run that image without having Java installed at all.

A tool called jlink is used to create this runtime image. Luckily, you only need to know that custom smaller runtimes are possible. How to create them is out of scope for the exam.

In addition to the smaller scale package, this approach improves security. If you don't use AWT and a security vulnerability is reported for AWT, applications that packaged a runtime image without AWT aren't affected.

Improved Performance

Since Java now knows which modules are required, it only needs to look at those at class loading time. This improves startup time for big programs and requires less memory to run.

While these benefits may not seem significant for the small programs we've been writing, they are far more important for big applications. A web application can easily take a minute to start. Additionally, for some financial applications, every millisecond of performance is important.

Unique Package Enforcement

Another manifestation of JAR hell is when the same package is in two JARs. There are a number of causes of this problem including renaming JARs, clever developers using a package name that is already taken, and having two versions of the same JAR on the classpath.

The Java Platform Module System prevents this scenario. A package is only allowed to be supplied by one module. No more unpleasant surprises about a package at runtime.

Creating and Running a Modular Program

In this section, we will create, build, and run the zoo.animal.feeding module. We chose this one to start with because all the other modules depend on it. Figure 11.3 shows the design of this module. In addition to the module-info.java file, it has one package with one class inside.

FIGURE 11.3   Contents of zoo.animal.feeding

In the next sections, we will create, compile, run, and package the zoo.animal.feeding module.

Creating the Files

First we have a really simple class that prints one line in a main() method. We know, that's not much of an implementation. All those programmers we hired can fill it in with business logic. In this book, we will focus on what you need to know for the exam. So, let's create a simple class.

```
package zoo.animal.feeding;

public class Task {
   public static void main(String... args) {
      System.out.println("All fed!");
   }
}
```

Next comes the module-info.java file. This is the simplest possible one.

```
module zoo.animal.feeding {
}
```

There are a few key differences between a module-info file and a regular Java class:

- The module-info file must be in the root directory of your module. Regular Java classes should be in packages.

- The module-info file must use the keyword module instead of class, interface, or enum.

- The module name follows the naming rules for package names. It often includes periods (.) in its name. Regular class and package names are not allowed to have dashes (-). Module names follow the same rule.

That's a lot of rules for the simplest possible file. There will be many more rules when we flesh out this file later in the chapter.

Can a *module-info.java* File Be Empty?

Yes. As a bit of trivia, it was legal to compile any empty file with a .java extension even before modules. The compiler sees there isn't a class in there and exits without creating a .class file.

The next step is to make sure the files are in the right directory structure. Figure 11.4 shows the expected directory structure.

FIGURE 11.4   Module zoo.animal.feeding directory structure

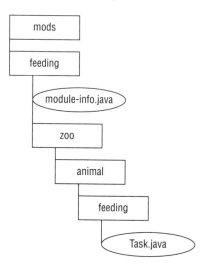

In particular, feeding is the module directory, and the module-info file is directly under it. Just as with a regular JAR file, we also have the zoo.animal.feeding package with one sub-folder per portion of the name. The Task class is in the appropriate subfolder for its package.

Also, note that we created a directory called mods at the same level as the module. We will use it for storing the module artifacts a little later in the chapter. This directory can be named anything, but mods is a common name. If you are following along with the online code example, note that the mods directory is not included, because it is empty.

Compiling Our First Module

Before we can run modular code, we need to compile it. Other than the module-path option, this code should look familiar from Chapter 1:

```
javac --module-path mods
   -d feeding
   feeding/zoo/animal/feeding/*.java
   feeding/module-info.java
```

When you're entering commands at the command line, they should be typed all on one line. We use line breaks in the book to make the commands easier to read and study. If you wanted to use multiple lines at the command prompt, the approach varies by operating system. Linux uses a backslash (\) as the line break.

As a review, the -d option specifies the directory to place the class files in. The end of the command is a list of the .java files to compile. You can list the files individually or use a wildcard for all .java files in a subdirectory.

The new part is the module-path. This option indicates the location of any custom module files. In this example, module-path could have been omitted since there are no dependencies. You can think of module-path as replacing the classpath option when you are working on a modular program.

What Happened to the Classpath?

In the past, you would reference JAR files using the classpath option. It had three possible forms: -cp, --class-path, and -classpath. You can still use these options in Java 11. In fact, it is common to do so when writing nonmodular programs.

Just like classpath, you can use an abbreviation in the command. The syntax --module-path and -p are equivalent. That means we could have written many other commands in place of the previous command. The following four commands show the -p option:

```
javac -p mods
   -d feeding
   feeding/zoo/animal/feeding/*.java
   feeding/*.java

javac -p mods
   -d feeding
   feeding/zoo/animal/feeding/*.java
   feeding/module-info.java

javac -p mods
   -d feeding
   feeding/zoo/animal/feeding/Task.java
   feeding/module-info.java

javac -p mods
   -d feeding
   feeding/zoo/animal/feeding/Task.java
   feeding/*.java
```

While you can use whichever you like best, be sure that you can recognize all valid forms for the exam. Table 11.1 lists the options you need to know well when compiling modules. There are many more options you can pass to the javac command, but these are the ones you can expect to be tested on.

TABLE 11.1   Options you need to know for using modules with `javac`

Use for	Abbreviation	Long form
Directory for class files	`-d <dir>`	n/a
Module path	`-p <path>`	`--module-path <path>`

> ### 🌐 Real World Scenario
>
> #### Building Modules
>
> Even before modules, it was rare to run `javac` and `java` commands manually on a real project. They get long and complicated very quickly. Most developers use a build tool such as Maven or Gradle. These build tools suggest directories to place the class files like `target/classes`.
>
> With modules, there is even more typing to run these commands by hand. After all, with modules, you are using more directories by definition. This means that it is likely the only time you need to know the syntax of these commands is when you take the exam. The concepts themselves are useful regardless.
>
> Do be sure to memorize the module command syntax. You will be tested on it on the exam. We will be sure to give you lots of practice questions on the syntax to reinforce it.

Running Our First Module

Before we package our module, we should make sure it works by running it. To do that, we need to learn the full syntax. Suppose there is a module named book.module. Inside that module is a package named com.sybex, which has a class named OCP with a main() method. Figure 11.5 shows the syntax for running a module. Pay special attention to the book.module/com.sybex.OCP part. It is important to remember that you specify the module name followed by a slash (/) followed by the fully qualified class name.

FIGURE 11.5 Running a module using java

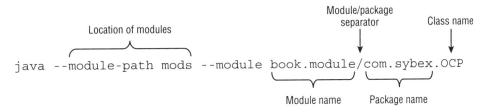

Now that we've seen the syntax, we can write the command to run the Task class in the zoo.animal.feeding package. In the following example, the package name and module name are the same. It is common for the module name to match either the full package name or the beginning of it.

```
java --module-path feeding
    --module zoo.animal.feeding/zoo.animal.feeding.Task
```

Since you already saw that --module-path uses the short form of -p, we bet you won't , be surprised to learn there is a short form of --module as well. The short option is -m. That means the following command is equivalent:

```
java -p feeding
    -m zoo.animal.feeding/zoo.animal.feeding.Task
```

In these examples, we used feeding as the module path because that's where we compiled the code. This will change once we package the module and run that.

Table 11.2 lists the options you need to know for the java command.

TABLE 11.2 Options you need to know for using modules with java

Use for	Abbreviation	Long form
Module name	-m <name>	--module <name>
Module path	-p <path>	--module-path <path>

Packaging Our First Module

A module isn't much use if we can run it only in the folder it was created in. Our next step is to package it. Be sure to create a mods directory before running this command:

```
jar -cvf mods/zoo.animal.feeding.jar -C feeding/ .
```

There's nothing module-specific here. In fact, you might remember seeing this command in Chapter 1. We are packaging everything under the feeding directory and storing it in a JAR file named zoo.animal.feeding.jar under the mods folder. This represents how the module JAR will look to other code that wants to use it.

It is possible to version your module using the --module-version option. This isn't on the exam but is good to do when you are ready to share your module with others.

Now let's run the program again, but this time using the mods directory instead of the loose classes:

```
java -p mods
   -m zoo.animal.feeding/zoo.animal.feeding.Task
```

You might notice that this command looks identical to the one in the previous section except for the directory. In the previous example, it was feeding. In this one, it is the module path of mods. Since the module path is used, a module JAR is being run.

Figure 11.6 shows what the directory structure looks like now that we've compiled and packaged the code.

FIGURE 11.6   Module zoo.animal.feeding directory structure with class and jar files

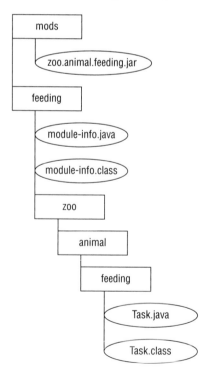

Updating Our Example for Multiple Modules

Now that our zoo.animal.feeding module is solid, we can start thinking about our other modules. As you can see in Figure 11.7, all three of the other modules in our system depend on the zoo.animal.feeding module.

FIGURE 11.7   Modules depending on zoo.animal.feeding

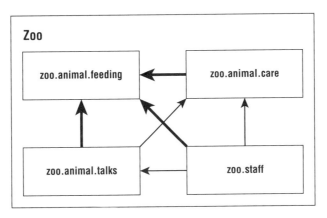

Updating the Feeding Module

Since we will be having our other modules call code in the zoo.animal.feeding package, we need to declare this intent in the module-info file.

The exports keyword is used to indicate that a module intends for those packages to be used by Java code outside the module. As you might expect, without an exports keyword, the module is only available to be run from the command line on its own. In the following example, we export one package:

```
module zoo.animal.feeding {
   exports zoo.animal.feeding;
}
```

Recompiling and repackaging the module will update the module-info inside our zoo.animal.feeding.jar file. These are the same javac and jar commands you ran previously.

```
javac -p mods
   -d feeding
   feeding/zoo/animal/feeding/*.java
   feeding/module-info.java
```

```
jar -cvf mods/zoo.animal.feeding.jar -C feeding/ .
```

Creating a Care Module

Next, let's create the zoo.animal.care module. This time, we are going to have two packages. The zoo.animal.care.medical package will have the classes and methods that are intended for use by other modules. The zoo.animal.care.details package is only going to be used by this module. It will not be exported from the module. Think of it as healthcare privacy for the animals.

Figure 11.8 shows the contents of this module. Remember that all modules must have a module-info file.

FIGURE 11.8   Contents of zoo.animal.care

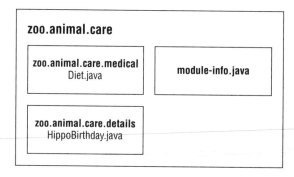

The module contains two basic packages and classes in addition to the module-info.java file:

```
// HippoBirthday.java
package zoo.animal.care.details;
import zoo.animal.feeding.*;
public class HippoBirthday {
    private Task task;
}


// Diet.java
package zoo.animal.care.medical;
public class Diet { }
```

This time the module-info.java file specifies three things.

```
1: module zoo.animal.care {
2:     exports zoo.animal.care.medical;
3:     requires zoo.animal.feeding;
4: }
```

Line 1 specifies the name of the module. Line 2 lists the package we are exporting so it can be used by other modules. So far, this is similar to the zoo.animal.feeding module.

On line 3, we see a new keyword. The requires statement specifies that a module is needed. The zoo.animal.care module depends on the zoo.animal.feeding module.

Next we need to figure out the directory structure. We will create two packages. The first is zoo.animal.care.details and contains one class named HippoBirthday. The second is zoo.animal.care.medical and contains one class named Diet. Try to draw the directory structure on paper or create it on your computer. If you are trying to run these examples without using the online code, just create classes without variables or methods for everything except the module-info.java files.

Figure 11.9 shows the directory structure of this module. Note that module-info.java is in the root of the module. The two packages are underneath it.

FIGURE 11.9 Module zoo.animal.care directory structure

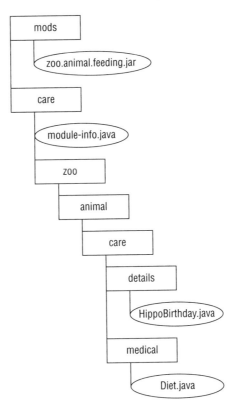

You might have noticed that the packages begin with the same prefix as the module name. This is intentional. You can think of it as if the module name "claims" the matching package and all subpackages.

To review, we now compile and package the module:

```
javac -p mods
   -d care
   care/zoo/animal/care/details/*.java
   care/zoo/animal/care/medical/*.java
   care/module-info.java
```

We compile both packages and the module-info file. In the real world, you'll use a build tool rather than doing this by hand. For the exam, you just list all the packages and/or files you want to compile.

Order Matters!

Note that order matters when compiling a module. Suppose we list the module-info file first when trying to compile:

```
javac -p mods
   -d care
   care/module-info.java
   care/zoo/animal/care/details/*.java
   care/zoo/animal/care/medical/*.java
```

The compiler complains that it doesn't know anything about the package zoo.animal.care.medical.

```
care/module-info.java:3: error: package is empty or does not exist:
zoo.animal.care.medical
exports zoo.animal.care.medical;
```

A package must have at least one class in it in order to be exported. Since we haven't yet compiled zoo.animal.care.medical.Diet, the compiler acts as if it doesn't exist. If you get this error message, you can reorder the javac statement. Alternatively, you can compile the packages in a separate javac command, before compiling the module-info file.

Now that we have compiled code, it's time to create the module JAR:

```
jar -cvf mods/zoo.animal.care.jar -C care/ .
```

Creating the Talks Module

So far, we've used only one exports and requires statement in a module. Now you'll learn how to handle exporting multiple packages or requiring multiple modules. In Figure 11.10, observe that the zoo.animal.talks module depends on two modules: zoo.animal.feeding and zoo.animal.care. This means that there must be two requires statements in the module-info.java file.

FIGURE 11.10   Dependencies for zoo.animal.talks

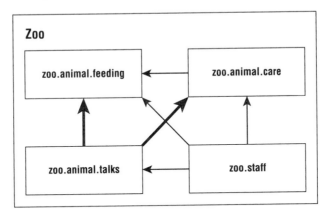

Figure 11.11 shows the contents of this module. We are going to export all three packages in this module.

FIGURE 11.11   Contents of zoo.animal.talks

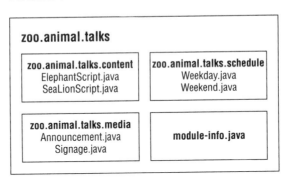

First let's look at the module-info.java file for zoo.animal.talks:

```
1: module zoo.animal.talks {
2:     exports zoo.animal.talks.content;
3:     exports zoo.animal.talks.media;
4:     exports zoo.animal.talks.schedule;
5:
6:     requires zoo.animal.feeding;
7:     requires zoo.animal.care;
8: }
```

Line 1 shows the module name. Lines 2–4 allow other modules to reference all three packages. Lines 6–7 specify the two modules that this module depends on.

Then we have the six classes, as shown here:

```
// ElephantScript.java
package zoo.animal.talks.content;
public class ElephantScript { }


// SeaLionScript.java
package zoo.animal.talks.content;
public class SeaLionScript { }


// Announcement.java
package zoo.animal.talks.media;
public class Announcement {
   public static void main(String[] args) {
      System.out.println("We will be having talks");
   }
}


// Signage.java
package zoo.animal.talks.media;
public class Signage { }


// Weekday.java
package zoo.animal.talks.schedule;
public class Weekday { }


// Weekend.java
package zoo.animal.talks.schedule;
public class Weekend {}
```

If you are still following along on your computer, create empty classes in the packages. The following are the commands to compile and build the module:

```
javac -p mods
   -d talks
   talks/zoo/animal/talks/content/*.java
   talks/zoo/animal/talks/media/*.java
   talks/zoo/animal/talks/schedule/*.java
   talks/module-info.java

jar -cvf mods/zoo.animal.talks.jar -C talks/ .
```

Creating the Staff Module

Our final module is zoo.staff. Figure 11.12 shows there is only one package inside. We will not be exposing this package outside the module.

FIGURE 11.12   Contents of zoo.staff

Based on this information, do you know what should go in the module-info?

```
module zoo.staff {
    requires zoo.animal.feeding;
    requires zoo.animal.care;
    requires zoo.animal.talks;
}
```

There are three arrows in Figure 11.13 pointing from zoo.staff to other modules. These represent the three modules that are required. Since no packages are to be exposed from zoo.staff, there are no exports statements.

FIGURE 11.13   Dependencies for zoo.staff

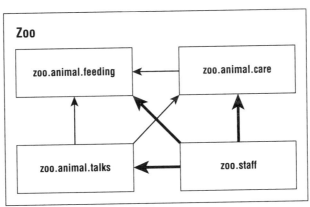

In this module, we have a single class in file Jobs.java:

```
package zoo.staff;
public class Jobs { }
```

For those of you following along on your computer, create an empty class in the package. The following are the commands to compile and build the module:

```
javac -p mods
   -d staff
   staff/zoo/staff/*.java
   staff/module-info.java

jar -cvf mods/zoo.staff.jar -C staff/ .
```

Diving into the *module-info* File

Now that we've successfully created modules, we can learn more about the module-info file. In these sections, we will look at exports, requires, provides, uses, and opens. Now would be a good time to mention that these keywords can appear in any order in the module-info file.

Real World Scenario

Are *exports* and *requires* Keywords?

In Chapter 2, "Java Building Blocks," we provided a list of keywords. However, exports wasn't on that list. Nor was module or requires or any of the other special words in a module-info file.

Java is a bit sneaky here. These "keywords" are only keywords inside a module-info .java file. In other files, like classes and interfaces, you are free to name your variable exports. These special keywords are called directives.

Backward compatibility is really important to the Java language designers so they don't want to risk preventing existing code from compiling just to introduce new global keywords. However, the module file type is new. Since there are no legacy module files, it is safe to introduce new keywords in that context.

exports

We've already seen how exports *packageName* exports a package to other modules. It's also possible to export a package to a specific module. Suppose the zoo decides that only staff members should have access to the talks. We could update the module declaration as follows:

```
module zoo.animal.talks {
    exports zoo.animal.talks.content to zoo.staff;
    exports zoo.animal.talks.media;
    exports zoo.animal.talks.schedule;

    requires zoo.animal.feeding;
    requires zoo.animal.care;
}
```

From the `zoo.staff` module, nothing has changed. However, no other modules would be allowed to access that package.

You might have noticed that none of our other modules requires `zoo.animal.talks` in the first place. However, we don't know what other modules will exist in the future. It is important to consider future use when designing modules. Since we want only the one module to have access, we only allow access for that module.

Exported Types

We've been talking about exporting a package. But what does that mean exactly? All `public` classes, interfaces, and enums are exported. Further, any `public` and `protected` fields and methods in those files are visible.

Fields and methods that are `private` are not visible because they are not accessible outside the class. Similarly, package-private fields and methods are not visible because they are not accessible outside the package.

The exports keyword essentially gives us more levels of access control. Table 11.3 lists the full access control options.

TABLE 11.3 Access control with modules

Level	Within module code	Outside module
private	Available only within class	No access
default (package-private)	Available only within package	No access
protected	Available only within package or to subclasses	Accessible to subclasses only if package is exported
public	Available to all classes	Accessible only if package is exported

requires transitive

As you saw earlier in this chapter, requires *moduleName* specifies that the current module depends on *moduleName*. There's also a requires transitive *moduleName*, which means that any module that requires this module will also depend on *moduleName*.

Well, that was a mouthful. Let's look at an example. Figure 11.14 shows the modules with dashed lines for the redundant relationships and solid lines for relationships specified in the module-info. This shows how the module relationships would look if we were to only use transitive dependencies.

FIGURE 11.14   Transitive dependency version of our modules

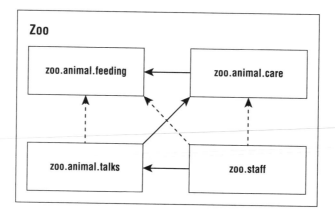

For example, zoo.animal.talks depends on zoo.animal.care, which depends on zoo.animal.feeding. That means the arrow between zoo.animal.talks and zoo.animal.feeding no longer appears in Figure 11.14.

Now let's look at the four module-info files. The first module remains unchanged. We are exporting one package to any packages that use the module.

```
module zoo.animal.feeding {
    exports zoo.animal.feeding;
}
```

The zoo.animal.care module is the first opportunity to improve things. Rather than forcing all remaining modules to explicitly specify zoo.animal.feeding, the code uses requires transitive.

```
module zoo.animal.care {
    exports zoo.animal.care.medical;
    requires transitive zoo.animal.feeding;
}
```

In the zoo.animal.talks module, we make a similar change and don't force other modules to specify zoo.animal.care. We also no longer need to specify zoo.animal.feeding, so that line is commented out.

```
module zoo.animal.talks {
    exports zoo.animal.talks.content to zoo.staff;
    exports zoo.animal.talks.media;
    exports zoo.animal.talks.schedule;

    // no longer needed requires zoo.animal.feeding;
    // no longer needed requires zoo.animal.care;
    requires transitive zoo.animal.care;
}
```

Finally, in the zoo.staff module, we can get rid of two requires statements.

```
module zoo.staff {
    // no longer needed requires zoo.animal.feeding;
    // no longer needed requires zoo.animal.care;
    requires zoo.animal.talks;
}
```

The more modules you have, the more benefits of requires transitive compound. It is also more convenient for the caller. If you were trying to work with this zoo, you could just require zoo.staff and have the remaining dependencies automatically inferred.

Effects of *requires transitive*

Given our newly updated module-info files and using Figure 11.14, what is the effect of applying the transitive modifier to the requires statement in our zoo.animal.care module? Applying the transitive modifiers has the following effect:

- Module zoo.animal.talks can optionally declare it requires the zoo.animal.feeding module, but it is not required.
- Module zoo.animal.care cannot be compiled or executed without access to the zoo.animal.feeding module.
- Module zoo.animal.talks cannot be compiled or executed without access to the zoo.animal.feeding module.

These rules hold even if the zoo.animal.care and zoo.animal.talks modules do not explicitly reference any packages in the zoo.animal.feeding module. On the other hand, without the transitive modifier in our module-info file of zoo.animal.care, the other modules would have to explicitly use requires in order to reference any packages in the zoo.animal.feeding module.

Duplicate *requires* Statements

One place the exam might try to trick you is mixing requires and requires transitive together. Can you think of a reason this code doesn't compile?

```
module bad.module {
    requires zoo.animal.talks;
    requires transitive zoo.animal.talks;
}
```

Java doesn't allow you to repeat the same module in a requires clause. It is redundant and most like an error in coding. Keep in mind that requires transitive is like requires plus some extra behavior.

provides, uses, and *opens*

For the remaining three keywords (provides, uses, and opens), you only need to be aware they exist rather than understanding them in detail for the 1Z0-815 exam.

The provides keyword specifies that a class provides an implementation of a service. The topic of services is covered on the 1Z0-816 exam, so for now, you can just think of a service as a fancy interface. To use it, you supply the API and class name that implements the API:

```
provides zoo.staff.ZooApi with zoo.staff.ZooImpl
```

The uses keyword specifies that a module is relying on a service. To code it, you supply the API you want to call:

```
uses zoo.staff.ZooApi
```

Java allows callers to inspect and call code at runtime with a technique called *reflection*. This is a powerful approach that allows calling code that might not be available at compile time. It can even be used to subvert access control! Don't worry—you don't need to know how to write code using reflection for the exam.

Since reflection can be dangerous, the module system requires developers to explicitly allow reflection in the module-info if they want calling modules to be allowed to use it. Here are two examples:

```
opens zoo.animal.talks.schedule;
opens zoo.animal.talks.media to zoo.staff;
```

The first example allows any module using this one to use reflection. The second example only gives that privilege to the zoo.staff package.

Discovering Modules

So far, we've been working with modules that we wrote. Since Java 9, the classes built into the JDK were modularized as well. In this section, we will show you how to use commands to learn about modules.

You do not need to know the output of the commands in this section. You do, however, need to know the syntax of the commands and what they do. We include the output where it facilitates remembering what is going on. But you don't need to memorize that (which frees up more space in your head to memorize command-line options).

The *java* Command

The java command has three module-related options. One describes a module, another lists the available modules, and the third shows the module resolution logic.

 It is also possible to add modules, exports, and more at the command line. But please don't. It's confusing and hard to maintain. Note these flags are available on java, but not all commands.

Describing a Module

Suppose you are given the zoo.animal.feeding module JAR file and want to know about its module structure. You could "unjar" it and open the module-info file. This would show you that the module exports one package and doesn't require any modules.

```
module zoo.animal.feeding {
    exports zoo.animal.feeding;
}
```

However, there is an easier way. The java command now has an option to describe a module. The following two commands are equivalent:

```
java -p mods
   -d zoo.animal.feeding
```

```
java -p mods
   --describe-module zoo.animal.feeding
```

Each prints information about the module. For example, it might print this:

```
zoo.animal.feeding file:///absolutePath/mods/zoo.animal.feeding.jar
exports zoo.animal.feeding
requires java.base mandated
```

The first line is the module we asked about: zoo.animal.feeding. The second line starts information about the module. In our case, it is the same package exports statement we had in the module-info file.

On the third line, we see requires java.base mandated. Now wait a minute. The module-info file very clearly does not specify any modules that zoo.animal.feeding has as dependencies.

The java.base module is special. It is automatically added as a dependency to all modules. This module has frequently used packages like java.util. That's what the mandated is about. You get java.base whether you asked for it or not.

In classes, the java.lang package is automatically imported whether you type it or not. The java.base module works the same way. It is automatically available to all other modules.

More About Describing Modules

You only need to know how to run --describe-module for the exam. However, you might encounter some surprises when experimenting with this feature, so we describe them in a bit more detail here.

As a reminder, the following are the contents of module-info in zoo.animal.care:

```
module zoo.animal.care {
    exports zoo.animal.care.medical to zoo.staff;
    requires transitive zoo.animal.feeding;
}
```

Now we have the command to describe the module and the output.

```
java -p mods -d zoo.animal.care


zoo.animal.care file:///absolutePath/mods/zoo.animal.care.jar
requires zoo.animal.feeding transitive
requires java.base mandated
qualified exports zoo.animal.care.medical to zoo.staff
contains zoo.animal.care.details
```

The first line of the output is the absolute path of the module file. The two requires lines should look familiar as well. The first is in the module-info, and the other is added to all modules. Next comes something new. The qualified exports is the full name of exporting to a specific module.

Finally, the contains means that there is a package in the module that is not exported at all. This is true. Our module has two packages, and one is available only to code inside the module.

Listing Available Modules

In addition to describing modules, you can use the java command to list the modules that are available. The simplest form lists the modules that are part of the JDK:

```
java --list-modules
```

When we ran it, the output went on for 70 lines and looked like this:

```
java.base@11.0.2
java.compiler@11.0.2
java.datatransfer@11.0.2
```

This is a listing of all the modules that come with Java and their version numbers. You can tell that we were using Java 11.0.2 when testing this example.

More interestingly, you can use this command with custom code. Let's try again with the directory containing our zoo modules.

```
java -p mods --list-modules
```

How many lines do you expect to be in the output this time? There are 74 lines now: the 70 built-in modules plus the four in our zoo system. The custom lines look like this:

```
zoo.animal.care file:///absolutePath/mods/zoo.animal.care.jar
zoo.animal.feeding file:///absolutePath/mods/zoo.animal.feeding.jar
zoo.animal.talks file:///absolutePath/mods/zoo.animal.talks.jar
zoo.staff file:///absolutePath/mods/zoo.staff.jar
```

Since these are custom modules, we get a location on the file system. If the project had a module version number, it would have both the version number and the file system path.

 Note that --list-modules exits as soon as it prints the observable modules. It does not run the program.

Showing Module Resolution

In case listing the modules didn't give you enough output, you can also use the --show-module-resolution option. You can think of it as a way of debugging modules. It spits out a lot of output when the program starts up. Then it runs the program.

```
java --show-module-resolution
   -p feeding
   -m zoo.animal.feeding/zoo.animal.feeding.Task
```

Luckily you don't need to understand this output. That said, having seen it will make it easier to remember. Here's a snippet of the output:

```
root zoo.animal.feeding file:///absolutePath/feeding/
java.base binds java.desktop jrt:/java.desktop
java.base binds jdk.jartool jrt:/jdk.jartool
...
jdk.security.auth requires java.naming jrt:/java.naming
jdk.security.auth requires java.security.jgss jrt:/java.security.jgss
...
All fed!
```

It starts out by listing the root module. That's the one we are running: zoo.animal .feeding. Then it lists many lines of packages included by the mandatory java.base module. After a while, it lists modules that have dependencies. Finally, it outputs the result of the program All fed!. The total output of this command is 66 lines.

The *jar* Command

Like the java command, the jar command can describe a module. Both of these commands are equivalent:

```
jar -f mods/zoo.animal.feeding.jar -d
jar --file mods/zoo.animal.feeding.jar --describe-module
```

The output is slightly different from when we used the java command to describe the module. With jar, it outputs the following:

```
zoo.animal.feeding jar:file:///absolutePath/mods/zoo.animal.feeding.jar
/!module-info.class
exports zoo.animal.feeding
requires java.base mandated
```

The JAR version includes the module-info in the filename, which is not a particularly significant difference in the scheme of things. You don't need to know this difference. You do need to know that both commands can describe a module.

The *jdeps* Command

The jdeps command gives you information about dependencies within a module. Unlike describing a module, it looks at the code in addition to the module-info file. This tells you what dependencies are actually used rather than simply declared.

Let's start with a simple example and ask for a summary of the dependencies in zoo.animal.feeding. Both of these commands give the same output:

```
jdeps -s mods/zoo.animal.feeding.jar

jdeps -summary mods/zoo.animal.feeding.jar
```

Notice that there is one dash (-) before -summary rather than two. Regardless, the output tells you that there is only one package and it depends on the built-in java.base module.

```
zoo.animal.feeding -> java.base
```

Alternatively, you can call jdeps without the summary option and get the long form:

```
jdeps mods/zoo.animal.feeding.jar
[file:///absolutePath/mods/zoo.animal.feeding.jar]
   requires mandated java.base (@11.0.2)
zoo.animal.feeding -> java.base
   zoo.animal.feeding       -> java.io
      java.base
   zoo.animal.feeding       -> java.lang
      java.base
```

The first part of the output shows the module filename and path. The second part lists the required java.base dependency and version number. This has the high-level summary that matches the previous example.

Finally, the last four lines of the output list the specific packages within the java.base modules that are used by zoo.animal.feeding.

Now, let's look at a more complicated example. This time, we pick a module that depends on zoo.animal.feeding. We need to specify the module path so jdeps knows where to find information about the dependent module. We didn't need to do that before because all dependent modules were built into the JDK.

Following convention, these two commands are equivalent:

```
jdeps -s
   --module-path mods
   mods/zoo.animal.care.jar
```

```
jdeps -summary
   --module-path mods
   mods/zoo.animal.care.jar
```

There is not a short form of --module-path in the jdeps command. The output is only two lines:

```
zoo.animal.care -> java.base
zoo.animal.care -> zoo.animal.feeding
```

We can see that the zoo.animal.care module depends on our custom zoo.animal.feeding module along with the built-in java.base.

In case you were worried the output was too short, we can run it in full mode:

```
jdeps --module-path mods
   mods/zoo.animal.care.jar
```

This time we get lots of output:

```
zoo.animal.care
   [file:///absolutePath/mods/zoo.animal.care.jar]
      requires mandated java.base (@11.0.2)
      requires transitive zoo.animal.feeding
   zoo.animal.care -> java.base
   zoo.animal.care -> zoo.animal.feeding
      zoo.animal.care.details     -> java.lang
         java.base
      zoo.animal.care.details     -> zoo.animal.feeding
         zoo.animal.feeding
      zoo.animal.care.medical     -> java.lang
         java.base
```

As before, there are three sections. The first section is the filename and required dependencies. The second section is the summary showing the two module dependencies with an arrow. The last six lines show the package-level dependencies.

The *jmod* Command

The final command you need to know for the exam is jmod. You might think a JMOD file is a Java module file. Not quite. Oracle recommends using JAR files for most modules. JMOD files are recommended only when you have native libraries or something that can't go inside a JAR file. This is unlikely to affect you in the real world.

The most important thing to remember is that jmod is only for working with the JMOD files. Conveniently, you don't have to memorize the syntax for jmod. Table 11.4 lists the common modes.

TABLE 11.4 Modes using jmod

Operation	Description
create	Creates a JMOD file.
extract	Extracts all files from the JMOD. Works like unzipping.
describe	Prints the module details such as requires.
list	Lists all files in the JMOD file.
hash	Shows a long string that goes with the file

Reviewing Command-Line Options

Congratulations on reaching the last section of the book. This section is a number of tables that cover what you need to know about running command-line options for the 1Z0-815 exam.

Table 11.5 shows the command lines you should expect to encounter on the exam.

TABLE 11.5 Comparing command-line operations

Description	Syntax
Compile nonmodular code	`javac -cp` *classpath* `-d` *directory* *classesToCompile* `javac --class-path` *classpath* `-d` *directory* *classesToCompile* `javac -classpath` *classpath* `-d` *directory* *classesToCompile*
Run nonmodular code	`java -cp` *classpath* *package.className* `java -classpath` *classpath* *package.className* `java --class-path` *classpath* *package.className*
Compile a module	`javac -p` *moduleFolderName* `-d` *directory* *classesToCompileIncludingModuleInfo* `javac --module-path` *moduleFolderName* `-d` *directory* *classesToCompileIncludingModuleInfo*
Run a module	`java -p` *moduleFolderName* `-m` *moduleName/package.className* `java --module-path` *moduleFolderName* `--module` *moduleName/package.className*

Describe a module	`java -p` *moduleFolderName* `-d` *moduleName*
	`java --module-path` *moduleFolderName* `--describe-module` *moduleName*
	`jar --file` *jarName* `--describe-module`
	`jar -f` *jarName* `-d`

List available modules	`java --module-path` *moduleFolderName* `--list-modules`
	`java -p` *moduleFolderName* `--list-modules`
	`java --list-modules`

View dependencies	`jdeps -summary --module-path` *moduleFolderName* *jarName* `jdeps -s --module-path` *moduleFolderName* *jarName*
Show module resolution	`java --show-module-resolution -p` *moduleFolderName* `-m` *moduleName* `java --show-module-resolution --module-path` *moduleFolderName* `--module` *moduleName*

Since there are so many commands you need to know, we've made a number of tables to review the available options that you need to know for the exam. There are many more options in the documentation. For example, there is a --module option on javac that limits compilation to that module. Luckily, you don't need to know those.

Table 11.6 shows the options for javac, Table 11.7 shows the options for java, Table 11.8 shows the options for jar, and Table 11.9 shows the options for jdeps.

TABLE 11.6   Options you need to know for the exam: javac

Option	Description
-cp <classpath> -classpath <classpath> --class-path <classpath>	Location of JARs in a nonmodular program
-d <dir>	Directory to place generated class files
-p <path> --module-path <path>	Location of JARs in a modular program

TABLE 11.7   Options you need to know for the exam: java

Option	Description
-p <path> --module-path <path>	Location of JARs in a modular program
-m <name> --module <name>	Module name to run
-d --describe-module	Describes the details of a module
--list-modules	Lists observable modules without running a program
--show-module-resolution	Shows modules when running program

TABLE 11.8 Options you need to know for the exam: `jar`

Option	Description
`-c` `--create`	Create a new JAR file
`-v` `--verbose`	Prints details when working with JAR files
`-f` `--file`	JAR filename
`-C`	Directory containing files to be used to create the JAR
`-d` `--describe-module`	Describes the details of a module

TABLE 11.9 Options you need to know for the exam: `jdeps`

Option	Description
`--module-path <path>`	Location of JARs in a modular program
`-s` `-summary`	Summarizes output

Summary

The Java Platform Module System organizes code at a higher level than packages. Each module contains one or more packages and a `module-info` file. Advantages of the JPMS include better access control, clearer dependency management, custom runtime images, improved performance, and unique package enforcement.

The process of compiling and running modules uses the `--module-path`, also known as `-p`. Running a module uses the `--module` option, also known as `-m`. The class to run is specified in the format `moduleName/className`.

The module-info file supports a number of keywords. The exports keyword specifies that a package should be accessible outside the module. It can optionally restrict that export to a specific package. The requires keyword is used when a module depends on code in another module. Additionally, requires transitive can be used when all modules that require one module should always require another. The provides and uses keywords are used when sharing and consuming an API. Finally, the opens keyword is used for allowing access via reflection.

Both the java and jar commands can be used to describe the contents of a module. The java command can additionally list available modules and show module resolution. The jdeps command prints information about packages used in addition to module-level information. Finally, the jmod command is used when dealing with files that don't meet the requirements for a JAR.

Exam Essentials

Identify benefits of the Java Platform Module System.   Be able to identify benefits of the JPMS from a list such as access control, dependency management, custom runtime images, performance, and unique package enforcement. Also be able to differentiate benefits of the JPMS from benefits of Java as a whole. For example, garbage collection is not a benefit of the JPMS.

Use command-line syntax with modules.   Use the command-line options for javac, java, and jar. In particular, understand the module (-m) and module path (-p) options.

Create basic module-info files.   Place the module-info.java file in the root directory of the module. Know how to code using exports to expose a package and how to export to a specific module. Also, know how to code using requires and requires transitive to declare a dependency on a package or to share that dependency with any modules using the current module.

Identify advanced module-info keywords.   The provides keyword is used when exposing an API. The uses keyword is for consuming an API. The opens keyword is for allowing the use of reflection.

Display information about modules.   The java command can describe a module, list available modules, or show the module resolution. The jar command can describe a module similar to how the java command does. The jdeps command prints details about a module and packages. The jmod command provides various modes for working with JMOD files rather than JAR files.

Review Questions

The answers to the chapter review questions can be found in the Appendix.

1. Which of the following is an advantage of the Java Platform Module System?

    A. A central repository of all modules

    B. Encapsulating packages

    C. Encapsulating objects

    D. No defined types

    E. Platform independence

2. Which statement is true of the following module?

    ```
    zoo.staff
    |---zoo
        |-- staff
          |-- Vet.java
    ```

    A. The directory structure shown is a valid module.

    B. The directory structure would be a valid module if `module.java` were added directly underneath `zoo.staff`.

    C. The directory structure would be a valid module if `module.java` were added directly underneath `zoo`.

    D. The directory structure would be a valid module if `module-info.java` were added directly underneath `zoo.staff`.

    E. The directory structure would be a valid module if `module-info.java` were added directly underneath `zoo`.

    F. None of these changes would make this directory structure a valid module.

3. Suppose module puppy depends on module dog and module dog depends on module animal. Fill in the blank so that code in module dog can access the `animal.behavior` package in module `animal`.

    ```
    module animal {
        _____ animal.behavior;
    }
    ```

    A. `export`

    B. `exports`

    C. `require`

    D. `requires`

    E. `require transitive`

    F. `requires transitive`

    G. None of the above

4. Fill in the blanks so this command to run the program is correct:

   ```
   java
   _____ zoo.animal.talks/zoo/animal/talks/Peacocks
   _____ modules
   ```

   A. -d and -m

   B. -d and -p

   C. -m and -d

   D. -m and -p

   E. -p and -d

   F. -p and -m

   G. None of the above

5. Which of the following statements are true in a `module-info.java` file? (Choose all that apply.)

   A. The opens keyword allows the use of reflection.

   B. The opens keyword declares an API is called.

   C. The use keyword allows the use of reflection.

   D. The use keyword declares an API is called.

   E. The uses keyword allows the use of reflection.

   F. The uses keyword declares an API is called.

   G. The file can be empty (zero bytes).

6. What is true of a module containing a file named `module-info.java` with the following contents? (Choose all that apply.)

   ```
   module com.food.supplier {}
   ```

   A. All packages inside the module are automatically exported.

   B. No packages inside the module are automatically exported.

   C. A main method inside the module can be run.

   D. A main method inside the module cannot be run since the class is not exposed.

   E. The `module-info.java` file contains a compiler error.

   F. The `module-info.java` filename is incorrect.

7. Suppose module puppy depends on module dog and module dog depends on module animal. Which two lines allow module puppy to access the `animal.behavior` package in module animal? (Choose two.)

   ```
   module animal {
       exports animal.behavior to dog;
   }
   module dog {
       _____ animal;   // line S
   }
   ```

```
module puppy {
    _____ dog;      // line T
}
```

A. require on line S

B. require on line T

C. requires on line S

D. requires on line T

E. require transitive on line S

F. require transitive on line T

G. requires transitive on line S

H. requires transitive on line T

8. Which commands take a --module-path parameter? (Choose all that apply.)

A. javac

B. java

C. jar

D. jdeps

E. jmod

F. None of the above

9. Which of the following are legal commands to run a modular program? (Choose all that apply.)

A. java -p x -m x/x

B. java -p x-x -m x/x

C. java -p x -m x-x/x

D. java -p x -m x/x-x

E. java -p x -m x.x

F. java -p x.x -m x.x

G. None of the above

10. Which would best fill in the blank to complete the following code?

```
module _____ {
    exports com.unicorn.horn;
    exports com.unicorn.magic;
}
```

A. com

B. com.unicorn

C. com.unicorn.horn

D. com.unicorn.magic

E. The code does not compile.

F. The code compiles, but none of these would be a good choice.

11. Which are valid modes for the jmod command? (Choose all that apply.)

    A. add

    B. create

    C. delete

    D. describe

    E. extract

    F. list

    G. show

12. Suppose you have the commands javac, java, and jar. How many of them support a --show-module-resolution option?

    A. 0

    B. 1

    C. 2

    D. 3

13. Which are true statements about the following module? (Choose all that apply.)

    ```
    class dragon {
        exports com.dragon.fire;
        exports com.dragon.scales to castle;
    }
    ```

    A. All modules can reference the com.dragon.fire package.

    B. All modules can reference the com.dragon.scales package.

    C. Only the castle module can reference the com.dragon.fire package.

    D. Only the castle module can reference the com.dragon.scales package.

    E. None of the above

14. Which would you expect to see when describing any module?

    A. requires java.base mandated

    B. requires java.core mandated

    C. requires java.lang mandated

    D. requires mandated java.base

    E. requires mandated java.core

    F. requires mandated java.lang

    G. None of the above

15. Which of the following statements are correct? (Choose all that apply.)

   A. The `jar` command allows adding exports as command-line options.

   B. The `java` command allows adding exports as command-line options.

   C. The `jdeps` command allows adding exports as command-line options.

   D. Adding an export at the command line is discouraged.

   E. Adding an export at the command line is recommended.

16. Which are valid calls to list a summary of the dependencies? (Choose all that apply.)

   A. `jdeps flea.jar`

   B. `jdeps -s flea.jar`

   C. `jdeps -summary flea.jar`

   D. `jdeps --summary flea.jar`

   E. None of the above

17. Which is the first line to contain a compiler error?

```
1: module snake {
2:     exports com.snake.tail;
3:     exports com.snake.fangs to bird;
4:     requires skin;
5:     requires transitive skin;
6: }
```

   A. Line 1.

   B. Line 2.

   C. Line 3.

   D. Line 4.

   E. Line 5.

   F. The code does not contain any compiler errors.

18. Which of the following would be a legal module name? (Choose all that apply.)

   A. `com.book`

   B. `com-book`

   C. `com.book$`

   D. `com-book$`

   E. `4com.book`

   F. `4com-book`

19. What can be created using the Java Platform Module System that could not be created without it? (Choose all that apply.)

 A. JAR file

 B. JMOD file

 C. Smaller runtime images for distribution

 D. Operating system specific bytecode

 E. TAR file

 F. None of the above

20. Which of the following options does not have a one-character shortcut in any of the commands studied in this chapter? (Choose all that apply.)

 A. `describe-module`

 B. `list-modules`

 C. `module`

 D. `module-path`

 E. `show-module-resolution`

 F. `summary`

21. Which of the following are legal commands to run a modular program where n is the package name and c is the class name? (Choose all that apply.)

 A. `java -module-path x -m n.c`

 B. `java --module-path x -p n.c`

 C. `java --module-path x -m n/c`

 D. `java --module-path x -p n/c`

 E. `java --module-path x -m n c`

 F. `java --module-path x -p n c`

 G. None of the above

Exam 1Z0-816, OCP Java SE 11 Programmer II

Exam 1Z0-817, Upgrade OCP Java SE 11

Chapter 12

Java Fundamentals

OCP EXAM OBJECTIVES COVERED IN THIS CHAPTER:

✓ **Java Fundamentals**

- Create and use final classes
- Create and use inner, nested and anonymous classes
- Create and use enumerations

✓ **Java Interfaces**

- Create and use interfaces with default methods
- Create and use interfaces with private methods

✓ **Functional Interface and Lambda Expressions**

- Define and write functional interfaces
- Create and use lambda expressions including statement lambdas, local-variable for lambda parameters

Welcome to the first chapter on your road to taking the 1Z0-816 Programmer II exam! If you've recently taken the 1Z0-815 Programmer I exam, then you should be well versed in class structure, inheritance, scope, abstract types, etc. If not, you might want to review earlier chapters. The exam expects you to have a solid foundation on these topics.

In this chapter, we are going to expand your understanding of Java fundamentals including enums and nested classes, various interface members, functional interfaces, and lambda expressions. Pay attention in this chapter, as many of these topics will be used throughout the rest of this book. Even if you use them all the time, there are subtle rules you might not be aware of.

Finally, we want to wish you a hearty congratulations on beginning your journey to prepare for the 1Z0-816 Programmer II exam!

Applying the *final* Modifier

From previous chapters, you should remember the final modifier can be applied to variables, methods, and classes. Marking a variable final means the value cannot be changed after it is assigned. Marking a method or class final means it cannot be overridden or extended, respectively. In this section, we will review the rules for using the final modifier.

If you studied final classes for the 1Z0-815 exam recently, then you can probably skip this section and go straight to enums.

Declaring *final* Local Variables

Let's start by taking a look at some local variables marked with the final modifier:

```java
private void printZooInfo(boolean isWeekend) {
    final int giraffe = 5;
    final long lemur;
    if(isWeekend) lemur = 5;
    else lemur = 10;
    System.out.println(giraffe+" "+lemur);
}
```

As shown with the lemur variable, we don't need to assign a value when a final variable is declared. The rule is only that it must be assigned a value before it can be used. Contrast this with the following example:

```
private void printZooInfo(boolean isWeekend) {
    final int giraffe = 5;
    final long lemur;
    if(isWeekend) lemur = 5;
    giraffe = 3;                                // DOES NOT COMPILE
    System.out.println(giraffe+" "+lemur);  // DOES NOT COMPILE
}
```

This snippet contains two compilation errors. The giraffe variable is already assigned a value, so attempting to assign it a new value is not permitted. The second compilation error is from attempting to use the lemur variable, which would not be assigned a value if isWeekend is false. The compiler does not allow the use of local variables that may not have been assigned a value, whether they are marked final or not.

Just because a variable reference is marked final does not mean the object associated with it cannot be modified. Consider the following code snippet:

```
final StringBuilder cobra = new StringBuilder();
cobra.append("Hssssss");
cobra.append("Hssssss!!!");
```

In the cobra example, the object reference is constant, but that doesn't mean the data in the class is constant.

> Throughout this book, you'll see a lot of examples involving zoos and animals. We chose this topic because it is a fruitful topic for data modeling. There are a wide variety of species, with very interesting attributes, relationships, and hierarchies. In addition, there are a lot of complex tasks involved in managing a zoo. Ideally, you enjoy the topic and learn about animals along the way!

Adding *final* to Instance and *static* Variables

Instance and static class variables can also be marked final. If an instance variable is marked final, then it must be assigned a value when it is declared or when the object is instantiated. Like a local `final` variable, it cannot be assigned a value more than once, though. The following `PolarBear` class demonstrates these properties:

```
public class PolarBear {
    final int age = 10;
    final int fishEaten;
    final String name;

    { fishEaten = 10; }

    public PolarBear() {
        name = "Robert";
    }
    public PolarBear(int height) {
        this();
    }
}
```

The age variable is given a value when it is declared, while the `fishEaten` variable is assigned a value in an instance initializer. The name variable is given a value in the no-argument constructor. Notice that the second constructor does not assign a value to name, but since it calls the no-argument constructor first, name is guaranteed to be assigned a value in the first line of this constructor.

The rules for `static final` variables are similar to instance `final` variables, except they do not use `static` constructors (there is no such thing!) and use `static` initializers instead of instance initializers.

```
public class Panda {
    final static String name = "Ronda";
    static final int bamboo;
    static final double height; // DOES NOT COMPILE
    static { bamboo = 5;}
}
```

The name variable is assigned a value when it is declared, while the bamboo variable is assigned a value in a `static` initializer. The height variable is not assigned a value any-where in the class definition, so that line does not compile.

Writing *final* Methods

Methods marked `final` cannot be overridden by a subclass. This essentially prevents any polymorphic behavior on the method call and ensures that a specific version of the method is always called.

Remember that methods can be assigned an abstract or final modifier. An abstract method is one that does not define a method body and can appear only inside an abstract class or interface. A final method is one that cannot be overridden by a subclass. Let's take a look at an example:

```
public abstract class Animal {
   abstract void chew();
}

public class Hippo extends Animal {
   final void chew() {}
}

public class PygmyHippo extends Hippo {
   void chew() {}  // DOES NOT COMPILE
}
```

The chew() method is declared abstract in the Animal class. It is then implemented in the concrete Hippo class, where it is marked final, thereby preventing a subclass of Hippo from overriding it. For this reason, the chew() method in PygmyHippo does not compile since it is inherited as final.

What happens if a method is marked both abstract and final? Well, that's like saying, "I want to declare a method that someone else will provide an implementation for, while also telling that person that they are not allowed to provide an implementation." For this reason, the compiler does not allow it.

```
abstract class ZooKeeper {
   public abstract final void openZoo();  // DOES NOT COMPILE
}
```

Marking Classes *final*

Lastly, the final modifier can be applied to class declarations as well. A final class is one that cannot be extended. For example, the following does not compile:

```
public final class Reptile {}

public class Snake extends Reptile {}  // DOES NOT COMPILE
```

Like we saw with final methods, classes cannot be marked both abstract and final. For example, the following two declarations do not compile:

```
public abstract final class Eagle {}  // DOES NOT COMPILE

public final interface Hawk {}        // DOES NOT COMPILE
```

It is not possible to write a class that provides a concrete implementation of the abstract Eagle class, as it is marked final and cannot be extended. The Hawk interface also does not compile, although the reason is subtler. The compiler automatically applies the implicit `abstract` modifier to each interface declaration. Just like abstract classes, interfaces cannot be marked `final`.

> As you may remember from Chapter 9, "Advanced Class Design," a modifier that is inserted automatically by the compiler is referred to as an *implicit modifier*. Think of an implicit modifier as being present, even if it is not written out. For example, a method that is implicitly `public` cannot be marked `private`. Implicit modifiers are common in interface members, as we will see later in this chapter.

Working with Enums

In programming, it is common to have a type that can only have a finite set of values, such as days of the week, seasons of the year, primary colors, etc. An *enumeration* is like a fixed set of constants. In Java, an *enum*, short for "enumerated type," can be a top-level type like a class or interface, as well as a nested type like an inner class.

Using an enum is much better than using a bunch of constants because it provides type-safe checking. With numeric or `String` constants, you can pass an invalid value and not find out until runtime. With enums, it is impossible to create an invalid enum value without introducing a compiler error.

Enumerations show up whenever you have a set of items whose types are known at compile time. Common examples include the compass directions, the months of the year, the planets in the solar system, or the cards in a deck (well, maybe not the planets in a solar system, given that Pluto had its planetary status revoked).

Creating Simple Enums

To create an enum, use the enum keyword instead of the `class` or `interface` keyword. Then list all of the valid types for that enum.

```
public enum Season {
    WINTER, SPRING, SUMMER, FALL
}
```

Keep the Season enum handy, as we will be using it throughout this section.

NOTE Enum values are considered constants and are commonly written using snake case, often stylized as snake_case. This style uses an underscore (_) to separate words with constant values commonly written in all uppercase. For example, an enum declaring a list of ice cream flavors might include values like VANILLA, ROCKY_ROAD, MINT_CHOCOLATE_CHIP, and so on.

Behind the scenes, an enum is a type of class that mainly contains `static` members. It also includes some helper methods like `name()`. Using an enum is easy.

```
Season s = Season.SUMMER;
System.out.println(Season.SUMMER);       // SUMMER
System.out.println(s == Season.SUMMER); // true
```

As you can see, enums print the name of the enum when `toString()` is called. They can be compared using `==` because they are like `static final` constants. In other words, you can use `equals()` or `==` to compare enums, since each enum value is initialized only once in the Java Virtual Machine (JVM).

An enum provides a `values()` method to get an array of all of the values. You can use this like any normal array, including in an enhanced `for` loop, often called a *for-each loop*.

```
for(Season season: Season.values()) {
    System.out.println(season.name() + " " + season.ordinal());
}
```

The output shows that each enum value has a corresponding `int` value, and the values are listed in the order in which they are declared.

```
WINTER 0
SPRING 1
SUMMER 2
FALL 3
```

The `int` value will remain the same during your program, but the program is easier to read if you stick to the human-readable enum value.

You can't compare an `int` and enum value directly anyway since an enum is a type, like a Java class, and *not* a primitive `int`.

```
if ( Season.SUMMER == 2) {} // DOES NOT COMPILE
```

Another useful feature is retrieving an enum value from a `String` using the `valueOf()` method. This is helpful when working with older code. The `String` passed in must match the enum value exactly, though.

```
Season s = Season.valueOf("SUMMER"); // SUMMER

Season t = Season.valueOf("summer"); // Throws an exception at runtime
```

The first statement works and assigns the proper enum value to s. Note that this line is not creating an enum value, at least not directly. Each enum value is created once when the enum is first loaded. Once the enum has been loaded, it retrieves the single enum value with the matching name.

The second statement encounters a problem. There is no enum value with the lowercase name summer. Java throws up its hands in defeat and throws an IllegalArgumentException.

```
Exception in thread "main" java.lang.IllegalArgumentException:
    No enum constant enums.Season.summer
```

One thing that you can't do is extend an enum.

```
public enum ExtendedSeason extends Season { } // DOES NOT COMPILE
```

The values in an enum are all that are allowed. You cannot add more by extending the enum.

Using Enums in *Switch* Statements

Enums can be used in switch statements. Pay attention to the case values in this code:

```
Season summer = Season.SUMMER;
switch (summer) {
    case WINTER:
        System.out.println("Get out the sled!");
        break;
    case SUMMER:
        System.out.println("Time for the pool!");
        break;
    default:
        System.out.println("Is it summer yet?");
}
```

The code prints "Time for the pool!" since it matches SUMMER. In each case statement, we just typed the value of the enum rather than writing Season.WINTER. After all, the compiler already knows that the only possible matches can be enum values. Java treats the enum type as implicit. In fact, if you were to type case Season.WINTER, it would not compile. Don't believe us? Take a look at the following example:

```
switch (summer) {
    case Season.FALL:   // DOES NOT COMPILE
        System.out.println("Rake some leaves!");
        break;
    case 0:             // DOES NOT COMPILE
        System.out.println("Get out the sled!");
        break;
}
```

The first case statement does not compile because Season is used in the case value. If we changed Season.FALL to just FALL, then the line would compile. What about the second case statement? Just as earlier we said that you can't compare enums with int values, you cannot use them in a switch statement with int values either. On the exam, pay special attention when working with enums that they are used only as enums.

Adding Constructors, Fields, and Methods

Enums can have more in them than just a list of values. Let's say our zoo wants to keep track of traffic patterns for which seasons get the most visitors.

```
1: public enum Season {
2:    WINTER("Low"), SPRING("Medium"), SUMMER("High"), FALL("Medium");
3:    private final String expectedVisitors;
4:    private Season(String expectedVisitors) {
5:        this.expectedVisitors = expectedVisitors;
6:    }
7:    public void printExpectedVisitors() {
8:        System.out.println(expectedVisitors);
9:    } }
```

There are a few things to notice here. On line 2, the list of enum values ends with a semicolon (;). While this is optional when our enum is composed solely of a list of values, it is required if there is anything in the enum besides the values.

Lines 3–9 are regular Java code. We have an instance variable, a constructor, and a method. We mark the instance variable final on line 3 so that our enum values are considered immutable. Although this is certainly not required, it is considered a good coding practice to do so. Since enum values are shared by all processes in the JVM, it would be problematic if one of them could change the value inside an enum.

 Real World Scenario

Creating Immutable Objects

The *immutable objects pattern* is an object-oriented design pattern in which an object cannot be modified after it is created. Instead of modifying an immutable object, you create a new object that contains any properties from the original object you want copied over.

Many Java libraries contain immutable objects, including String and classes in the java.time package, just to name a few. Immutable objects are invaluable in concurrent applications since the state of the object cannot change or be corrupted by a rogue thread. You'll learn more about threads in Chapter 18, "Concurrency."

All enum constructors are implicitly `private`, with the modifier being optional. This is reasonable since you can't extend an enum and the constructors can be called only within the enum itself. An enum constructor will not compile if it contains a `public` or `protected` modifier.

How do we call an enum method? It's easy.

```
Season.SUMMER.printExpectedVisitors();
```

Notice how we don't appear to call the constructor. We just say that we want the enum value. The first time that we ask for any of the enum values, Java constructs all of the enum values. After that, Java just returns the already constructed enum values. Given that explanation, you can see why this calls the constructor only once:

```
public enum OnlyOne {
   ONCE(true);
   private OnlyOne(boolean b) {
      System.out.print("constructing,");
   }
}
```

```
public class PrintTheOne {
   public static void main(String[] args) {
      System.out.print("begin,");
      OnlyOne firstCall = OnlyOne.ONCE;  // prints constructing,
      OnlyOne secondCall = OnlyOne.ONCE; // doesn't print anything
      System.out.print("end");
   }
}
```

This class prints the following:

```
begin,constructing,end
```

If the `OnlyOne` enum was used earlier, and therefore initialized sooner, then the line that declares the `firstCall` variable would not print anything.

This technique of a constructor and state allows you to combine logic with the benefit of a list of values. Sometimes, you want to do more. For example, our zoo has different seasonal hours. It is cold and gets dark early in the winter. We could keep track of the hours through instance variables, or we can let each enum value manage hours itself.

```
public enum Season {
   WINTER {
      public String getHours() { return "10am-3pm"; }
   },
   SPRING {
      public String getHours() { return "9am-5pm"; }
   },
```

```
    SUMMER {
        public String getHours() { return "9am-7pm"; }
    },
    FALL {
        public String getHours() { return "9am-5pm"; }
    };
    public abstract String getHours();
}
```

What's going on here? It looks like we created an abstract class and a bunch of tiny subclasses. In a way we did. The enum itself has an abstract method. This means that each and every enum value is required to implement this method. If we forget to implement the method for one of the values, then we get a compiler error.

```
The enum constant WINTER must implement the abstract method getHours()
```

If we don't want each and every enum value to have a method, we can create a default implementation and override it only for the special cases.

```
public enum Season {
    WINTER {
        public String getHours() { return "10am-3pm"; }
    },
    SUMMER {
        public String getHours() { return "9am-7pm"; }
    },
    SPRING, FALL;
    public String getHours() { return "9am-5pm"; }
}
```

This one looks better. We only code the special cases and let the others use the enum-provided implementation. Of course, overriding getHours() is possible only if it is not marked final.

Just because an enum can have lots of methods doesn't mean that it should. Try to keep your enums simple. If your enum is more than a page or two, it is way too long. Most enums are just a handful of lines. The main reason they get long is that when you start with a one- or two-line method and then declare it for each of your dozen enum types, it grows long. When they get too long or too complex, it makes the enum hard to read.

You might have noticed that in each of these enum examples, the list of values came first. This was not an accident. Whether the enum is simple or contains a ton of methods, constructors, and variables, the compiler requires that the list of values always be declared first.

Creating Nested Classes

A *nested class* is a class that is defined within another class. A nested class can come in one of four flavors.

- *Inner class*: A non-static type defined at the member level of a class
- *Static nested class:* A static type defined at the member level of a class
- *Local class*: A class defined within a method body
- *Anonymous class*: A special case of a local class that does not have a name

There are many benefits of using nested classes. They can encapsulate helper classes by restricting them to the containing class. They can make it easy to create a class that will be used in only one place. They can make the code cleaner and easier to read. This section covers all four types of nested classes.

By convention and throughout this chapter, we often use the term *inner* or *nested class* to apply to other Java types, including interfaces and enums. Although you are unlikely to encounter this on the exam, interfaces and enums can be declared as both inner classes and static nested classes, but not as local or anonymous classes.

When used improperly, though, nested classes can sometimes make the code harder to read. They also tend to tightly couple the enclosing and inner class, whereas there may be cases where you want to use the inner class by itself. In this case, you should move the inner class out into a separate top-level class.

Unfortunately, the exam tests these edge cases where programmers wouldn't typically use a nested class. For example, the exam might have an inner class within another inner class. This tends to create code that is difficult to read, so please never do this in practice!

Declaring an Inner Class

An *inner class*, also called a *member inner class*, is a non-static type defined at the member level of a class (the same level as the methods, instance variables, and constructors). Inner classes have the following properties:

- Can be declared public, protected, package-private (default), or private
- Can extend any class and implement interfaces
- Can be marked abstract or final
- Cannot declare static fields or methods, except for static final fields
- Can access members of the outer class including private members

The last property is actually pretty cool. It means that the inner class can access variables in the outer class without doing anything special. Ready for a complicated way to print Hi three times?

```
1:  public class Outer {
2:      private String greeting = "Hi";
3:
4:      protected class Inner {
5:          public int repeat = 3;
6:          public void go() {
7:              for (int i = 0; i < repeat; i++)
8:                  System.out.println(greeting);
9:          }
10:     }
11:
12:     public void callInner() {
13:         Inner inner = new Inner();
14:         inner.go();
15:     }
16:     public static void main(String[] args) {
17:         Outer outer = new Outer();
18:         outer.callInner();
19: } }
```

An inner class declaration looks just like a stand-alone class declaration except that it happens to be located inside another class. Line 8 shows that the inner class just refers to greeting as if it were available. This works because it is in fact available. Even though the variable is private, it is within that same class.

Since an inner class is not static, it has to be used with an instance of the outer class. Line 13 shows that an instance of the outer class can instantiate Inner normally. This works because callInner() is an instance method on Outer. Both Inner and callInner() are members of Outer. Since they are peers, they just write the name.

There is another way to instantiate Inner that looks odd at first. OK, well maybe not just at first. This syntax isn't used often enough to get used to it:

```
20:     public static void main(String[] args) {
21:         Outer outer = new Outer();
22:         Inner inner = outer.new Inner(); // create the inner class
23:         inner.go();
24:     }
```

Let's take a closer look at line 22. We need an instance of Outer to create Inner. We can't just call new Inner() because Java won't know with which instance of Outer it is associated. Java solves this by calling new as if it were a method on the outer variable.

.class Files for Inner Classes

Compiling the Outer.java class with which we have been working creates two class files. Outer.class you should be expecting. For the inner class, the compiler creates Outer$Inner.class. You don't need to know this syntax for the exam. We mention it so that you aren't surprised to see files with $ appearing in your directories. You do need to understand that multiple class files are created.

Inner classes can have the same variable names as outer classes, making scope a little tricky. There is a special way of calling this to say which variable you want to access. This is something you might see on the exam but ideally not in the real world.

In fact, you aren't limited to just one inner class. Please never do this in code you write. Here is how to nest multiple classes and access a variable with the same name in each:

```
1:  public class A {
2:      private int x = 10;
3:      class B {
4:          private int x = 20;
5:          class C {
6:              private int x = 30;
7:              public void allTheX() {
8:                  System.out.println(x);          // 30
9:                  System.out.println(this.x);     // 30
10:                 System.out.println(B.this.x); // 20
11:                 System.out.println(A.this.x); // 10
12:     } } }
13:     public static void main(String[] args) {
14:         A a = new A();
15:         A.B b = a.new B();
16:         A.B.C c = b.new C();
17:         c.allTheX();
18: }}
```

Yes, this code makes us cringe too. It has two nested classes. Line 14 instantiates the outermost one. Line 15 uses the awkward syntax to instantiate a B. Notice the type is A.B. We could have written B as the type because that is available at the member level of B. Java knows where to look for it. On line 16, we instantiate a C. This time, the A.B.C type is necessary to specify. C is too deep for Java to know where to look. Then line 17 calls a method on c.

Lines 8 and 9 are the type of code that we are used to seeing. They refer to the instance variable on the current class—the one declared on line 6 to be precise. Line 10 uses this in a special way. We still want an instance variable. But this time we want the one on the B class, which is the variable on line 4. Line 11 does the same thing for class A, getting the variable from line 2.

Inner Classes Require an Instance

Take a look at the following and see whether you can figure out why two of the three constructor calls do not compile:

```
public class Fox {
    private class Den {}
    public void goHome() {
        new Den();
    }
    public static void visitFriend() {
        new Den();  // DOES NOT COMPILE
    }
}

public class Squirrel {
    public void visitFox() {
        new Den();  // DOES NOT COMPILE
    }
}
```

The first constructor call compiles because goHome() is an instance method, and therefore the call is associated with the this instance. The second call does not compile because it is called inside a static method. You can still call the constructor, but you have to explicitly give it a reference to a Fox instance.

The last constructor call does not compile for two reasons. Even though it is an instance method, it is not an instance method inside the Fox class. Adding a Fox reference would not fix the problem entirely, though. Den is private and not accessible in the Squirrel class.

Creating a *static* Nested Class

A *static nested class* is a static type defined at the member level. Unlike an inner class, a static nested class can be instantiated without an instance of the enclosing class. The trade-off, though, is it can't access instance variables or methods in the outer class directly. It can be done but requires an explicit reference to an outer class variable.

In other words, it is like a top-level class except for the following:

- The nesting creates a namespace because the enclosing class name must be used to refer to it.
- It can be made `private` or use one of the other access modifiers to encapsulate it.
- The enclosing class can refer to the fields and methods of the `static` nested class.

Let's take a look at an example:

```
1: public class Enclosing {
2:     static class Nested {
3:         private int price = 6;
4:     }
5:     public static void main(String[] args) {
6:         Nested nested = new Nested();
7:         System.out.println(nested.price);
8: } }
```

Line 6 instantiates the nested class. Since the class is `static`, you do not need an instance of `Enclosing` to use it. You are allowed to access `private` instance variables, which is shown on line 7.

Importing a *static* Nested Class

Importing a `static` nested class is interesting. You can import it using a regular import.

```
// Toucan.java
package bird;
public class Toucan {
    public static class Beak {}
}
```

```
// BirdWatcher.java
package watcher;
import bird.Toucan.Beak; // regular import ok
public class BirdWatcher {
    Beak beak;
}
```

Since it is static, you can also use a static import.

```
import static bird.Toucan.Beak;
```

Either one will compile. Surprising, isn't it? Remember, Java treats the enclosing class as if it were a namespace.

Writing a Local Class

A *local class* is a nested class defined within a method. Like local variables, a local class declaration does not exist until the method is invoked, and it goes out of scope when the method returns. This means you can create instances only from within the method. Those instances can still be returned from the method. This is just how local variables work.

 Local classes are not limited to being declared only inside methods. They can be declared inside constructors and initializers too. For simplicity, we limit our discussion to methods in this chapter.

Local classes have the following properties:

- They do not have an access modifier.
- They cannot be declared `static` and cannot declare `static` fields or methods, except for `static final` fields.
- They have access to all fields and methods of the enclosing class (when defined in an instance method).
- They can access local variables if the variables are `final` or effectively final.

 As you saw in Chapter 6, "Lambdas and Functional Interfaces," *effectively final* refers to a local variable whose value does not change after it is set. A simple test for effectively final is to add the `final` modifier to the local variable declaration. If it still compiles, then the local variable is effectively final.

Ready for an example? Here's a complicated way to multiply two numbers:

```
1:  public class PrintNumbers {
2:      private int length = 5;
3:      public void calculate() {
4:          final int width = 20;
5:          class MyLocalClass {
6:              public void multiply() {
7:                  System.out.print(length * width);
8:              }
9:          }
10:         MyLocalClass local = new MyLocalClass();
11:         local.multiply();
12:     }
13:     public static void main(String[] args) {
14:         PrintNumbers outer = new PrintNumbers();
15:         outer.calculate();
16:     }
17: }
```

Lines 5 through 9 are the local class. That class's scope ends on line 12 where the method ends. Line 7 refers to an instance variable and a final local variable, so both variable references are allowed from within the local class.

Earlier, we made the statement that local variable references are allowed if they are final or effectively final. Let's talk about that now. The compiler is generating a .class file from your local class. A separate class has no way to refer to local variables. If the local variable is final, Java can handle it by passing it to the constructor of the local class or by storing it in the .class file. If it weren't effectively final, these tricks wouldn't work because the value could change after the copy was made.

As an illustrative example, consider the following:

```java
public void processData() {
    final int length = 5;
    int width = 10;
    int height = 2;
    class VolumeCalculator {
        public int multiply() {
            return length * width * height; // DOES NOT COMPILE
        }
    }
    width = 2;
}
```

The length and height variables are final and effectively final, respectively, so neither causes a compilation issue. On the other hand, the width variable is reassigned during the method so it cannot be effectively final. For this reason, the local class declaration does not compile.

Defining an Anonymous Class

An *anonymous class* is a specialized form of a local class that does not have a name. It is declared and instantiated all in one statement using the new keyword, a type name with parentheses, and a set of braces {}. Anonymous classes are required to extend an existing class or implement an existing interface. They are useful when you have a short implementation that will not be used anywhere else. Here's an example:

```java
1:  public class ZooGiftShop {
2:      abstract class SaleTodayOnly {
3:          abstract int dollarsOff();
4:      }
5:      public int admission(int basePrice) {
6:          SaleTodayOnly sale = new SaleTodayOnly() {
7:              int dollarsOff() { return 3; }
8:          };  // Don't forget the semicolon!
9:          return basePrice - sale.dollarsOff();
10: } }
```

Lines 2 through 4 define an abstract class. Lines 6 through 8 define the anonymous class. Notice how this anonymous class does not have a name. The code says to instantiate a new SaleTodayOnly object. But wait, SaleTodayOnly is abstract. This is OK because we provide the class body right there—anonymously. In this example, writing an anonymous class is equivalent to writing a local class with an unspecified name that extends SaleTodayOnly and then immediately using it.

Pay special attention to the semicolon on line 8. We are declaring a local variable on these lines. Local variable declarations are required to end with semicolons, just like other Java statements—even if they are long and happen to contain an anonymous class.

Now we convert this same example to implement an interface instead of extending an abstract class.

```
1:  public class ZooGiftShop {
2:      interface SaleTodayOnly {
3:          int dollarsOff();
4:      }
5:      public int admission(int basePrice) {
6:          SaleTodayOnly sale = new SaleTodayOnly() {
7:              public int dollarsOff() { return 3; }
8:          };
9:          return basePrice - sale.dollarsOff();
10: } }
```

The most interesting thing here is how little has changed. Lines 2 through 4 declare an interface instead of an abstract class. Line 7 is public instead of using default access since interfaces require public methods. And that is it. The anonymous class is the same whether you implement an interface or extend a class! Java figures out which one you want automatically. Just remember that in this second example, an instance of a class is created on line 6, not an interface.

But what if we want to implement both an interface and extend a class? You can't with an anonymous class, unless the class to extend is java.lang.Object. The Object class doesn't count in the rule. Remember that an anonymous class is just an unnamed local class. You can write a local class and give it a name if you have this problem. Then you can extend a class and implement as many interfaces as you like. If your code is this complex, a local class probably isn't the most readable option anyway.

There is one more thing that you can do with anonymous classes. You can define them right where they are needed, even if that is an argument to another method.

```
1:  public class ZooGiftShop {
2:      interface SaleTodayOnly {
3:          int dollarsOff();
4:      }
5:      public int pay() {
```

```
6:            return admission(5, new SaleTodayOnly() {
7:               public int dollarsOff() { return 3; }
8:            });
9:        }
10:    public int admission(int basePrice, SaleTodayOnly sale) {
11:            return basePrice - sale.dollarsOff();
12: }}
```

Lines 6 through 8 are the anonymous class. We don't even store it in a local variable. Instead, we pass it directly to the method that needs it. Reading this style of code does take some getting used to. But it is a concise way to create a class that you will use only once.

You can even define anonymous classes outside a method body. The following may look like we are instantiating an interface as an instance variable, but the {} after the interface name indicates that this is an anonymous inner class implementing the interface.

```
public class Gorilla {
    interface Climb {}
    Climb climbing = new Climb() {};
}
```

 Real World Scenario

Anonymous Classes and Lambda Expressions

Prior to Java 8, anonymous classes were frequently used for asynchronous tasks and event handlers. For example, the following shows an anonymous class used as an event handler in a JavaFX application:

```
Button redButton = new Button();
redButton.setOnAction(new EventHandler<ActionEvent>() {
    public void handle(ActionEvent e) {
        System.out.println("Red button pressed!");
    }
});
```

Since Java 8, though, lambda expressions are a much more concise way of expressing the same thing.

```
Button redButton = new Button();
redButton.setOnAction(e -> System.out.println("Red button pressed!"));
```

The only restriction is that the variable type must be a functional interface. If you haven't worked with functional interfaces and lambda expressions before, don't worry. We'll be reviewing them in this chapter.

Reviewing Nested Classes

For the exam, make sure that you know the information in Table 12.1 and Table 12.2 about which syntax rules are permitted in Java.

TABLE 12.1 Modifiers in nested classes

Permitted Modifiers	Inner class	static nested class	Local class	Anonymous class
Access modifiers	All	All	None	None
abstract	Yes	Yes	Yes	No
Final	Yes	Yes	Yes	No

TABLE 12.2 Members in nested classes

Permitted Members	Inner class	static nested class	Local class	Anonymous class
Instance methods	Yes	Yes	Yes	Yes
Instance variables	Yes	Yes	Yes	Yes
static methods	No	Yes	No	No
static variables	Yes (if final)	Yes	Yes (if final)	Yes (if final)

You should also know the information in Table 12.3 about types of access. For example, the exam might try to trick you by having a static class access an outer class instance variable without a reference to the outer class.

TABLE 12.3 Nested class access rules

	Inner class	static nested class	Local class	Anonymous class
Can extend any class or implement any number of interfaces	Yes	Yes	Yes	No—must have exactly one superclass or one interface
Can access instance members of enclosing class without a reference	Yes	No	Yes (if declared in an instance method)	Yes (if declared in an instance method)
Can access local variables of enclosing method	N/A	N/A	Yes (if final or effectively final)	Yes (if final or effectively final)

Understanding Interface Members

When Java was first released, there were only two types of members an interface declaration could include: abstract methods and constant (`static final`) variables. Since Java 8 and 9 were released, four new method types have been added that we will cover in this section. Keep Table 12.4 handy as we discuss the various interface types in this section.

TABLE 12.4 Interface member types

	Since Java version	Membership type	Required modifiers	Implicit modifiers	Has value or body?
Constant variable	1.0	Class	—	public static final	Yes
Abstract method	1.0	Instance	—	public abstract	No
Default method	8	Instance	default	public	Yes
Static method	8	Class	static	public	Yes

	Since Java version	Membership type	Required modifiers	Implicit modifiers	Has value or body?
Private method	9	Instance	`private`	—	Yes
Private static method	9	Class	`private` `static`	—	Yes

We assume from your previous studies that you know how to define a constant variable and abstract method, so we'll move on to the newer interface member types.

Relying on a *default* Interface Method

A *default method* is a method defined in an interface with the `default` keyword and includes a method body. Contrast `default` methods with abstract methods in an interface, which do not define a method body.

A `default` method may be overridden by a class implementing the interface. The name *default* comes from the concept that it is viewed as an abstract interface method with a default implementation. The class has the option of overriding the `default` method, but if it does not, then the default implementation will be used.

Purpose of *default* Methods

One motivation for adding `default` methods to the Java language was for backward compatibility. A `default` method allows you to add a new method to an existing interface, without the need to modify older code that implements the interface.

Another motivation for adding `default` methods to Java is for convenience. For instance, the Comparator interface includes a `default reversed()` method that returns a new Comparator in the order reversed. While these can be written in every class implementing the interface, having it defined in the interface as a `default` method is quite useful.

The following is an example of a `default` method defined in an interface:

```
public interface IsWarmBlooded {
   boolean hasScales();
```

```
default double getTemperature() {
    return 10.0;
}
}
```

This example defines two interface methods: one is the abstract hasScales()method, and the other is the default getTemperature()method. Any class that implements IsWarmBlooded may rely on the default implementation of getTemperature() or override the method with its own version. Both of these methods include the implicit public modifier, so overriding them with a different access modifier is not allowed.

 Note that the default interface method modifier is not the same as the default label used in switch statements. Likewise, although package-private access is commonly referred to as default access, that feature is implemented by omitting an access modifier. Sorry if this is confusing! We agree Java has overused the word *default* over the years.

For the exam, you should be familiar with various rules for declaring default methods.

Default Interface Method Definition Rules

1. A default method may be declared only within an interface.
2. A default method must be marked with the default keyword and include a method body.
3. A default method is assumed to be public.
4. A default method cannot be marked abstract, final, or static.
5. A default method may be overridden by a class that implements the interface.
6. If a class inherits two or more default methods with the same method signature, then the class must override the method.

The first rule should give you some comfort in that you'll only see default methods in interfaces. If you see them in a class or enum on the exam, something is wrong. The second rule just denotes syntax, as default methods must use the default keyword. For example, the following code snippets will not compile:

```
public interface Carnivore {
    public default void eatMeat();         // DOES NOT COMPILE
    public int getRequiredFoodAmount() {  // DOES NOT COMPILE
        return 13;
    }
}
```

The first method, eatMeat(), doesn't compile because it is marked as default but doesn't provide a method body. The second method, getRequiredFoodAmount(), also doesn't compile because it provides a method body but is not marked with the default keyword.

What about our third, fourth, and fifth rules? Like abstract interface methods, default methods are implicitly public. Unlike abstract methods, though, default interface methods cannot be marked abstract and must provide a body. They also cannot be marked as final, because they can always be overridden in classes implementing the interface. Finally, they cannot be marked static since they are associated with the instance of the class implementing the interface.

Inheriting Duplicate *default* Methods

We have one last rule for default methods that warrants some discussion. You may have realized that by allowing default methods in interfaces, coupled with the fact that a class may implement multiple interfaces, Java has essentially opened the door to multiple inheritance problems. For example, what value would the following code output?

```
public interface Walk {
    public default int getSpeed() { return 5; }
}

public interface Run {
    public default int getSpeed() { return 10; }
}

public class Cat implements Walk, Run {  // DOES NOT COMPILE
    public static void main(String[] args) {
        System.out.println(new Cat().getSpeed());
    }
}
```

In this example, Cat inherits the two default methods for getSpeed(), so which does it use? Since Walk and Run are considered siblings in terms of how they are used in the Cat class, it is not clear whether the code should output 5 or 10. In this case, Java throws up its hands and says "Too hard, I give up!" and fails to compile.

If a class implements two interfaces that have default methods with the same method signature, the compiler will report an error. This rule holds true even for abstract classes because the duplicate method could be called within a concrete method within the abstract class. All is not lost, though. If the class implementing the interfaces *overrides* the duplicate default method, then the code will compile without issue.

By overriding the conflicting method, the ambiguity about which version of the method to call has been removed. For example, the following modified implementation of Cat will compile and output 1:

```
public class Cat implements Walk, Run {
    public int getSpeed() { return 1; }
```

```
   public static void main(String[] args) {
      System.out.println(new Cat().getSpeed());
   }
}
```

 In this section, all of our conflicting methods had identical declarations. These rules also apply to methods with the same signature but different return types or declared exceptions. If a default method is overridden in the concrete class, then it must use a declaration that is compatible, following the rules for overriding methods introduced in Chapter 8, "Class Design".

Calling a Hidden *default* Method

Let's conclude our discussion of default methods by revisiting the Cat example, with two inherited default getSpeed() methods. Given our corrected implementation of Cat that overrides the getSpeed() method and returns 1, how would you call the version of the default method in the Walk interface? Take a few minutes to think about the following incomplete code:

```
public class Cat implements Walk, Run {
   public int getSpeed() { return 1; }

   public int getWalkSpeed() {
      return _____; // TODO: Call Walk's version of getSpeed()
   }

   public static void main(String[] args) {
      System.out.println(new Cat().getWalkSpeed());
   }
}
```

This is an area where a default method exhibits properties of both a static and instance method. Ready for the answer? Well, first off, you definitely can't call Walk.getSpeed(). A default method is treated as part of the instance since they can be overridden, so they cannot be called like a static method.

What about calling super.getSpeed()? That gets us a little closer, but which of the two inherited default methods is called? It's ambiguous and therefore not allowed. In fact, the compiler won't allow this even if there is only one inherited default method, as an interface is not part of the class hierarchy.

The solution is a combination of both of these answers. Take a look at the getWalkSpeed() method in this implementation of the Cat class:

```
public class Cat implements Walk, Run {
   public int getSpeed() {
      return 1;
   }

   public int getWalkSpeed() {
      return Walk.super.getSpeed();
   }

   public static void main(String[] args) {
      System.out.println(new Cat().getWalkSpeed());
   }
}
```

In this example, we first use the interface name, followed by the super keyword, followed by the default method we want to call. We also put the call to the inherited default method inside the instance method getWalkSpeed(), as super is not accessible in the main() method.

Congratulations—if you understood this section, then you are prepared for the most complicated thing the exam can throw at you on default methods!

Using *static* Interface Methods

If you've been using an older version of Java, you might not be aware that Java now supports static interface methods. These methods are defined explicitly with the static keyword and for the most part behave just like static methods defined in classes.

Static Interface Method Definition Rules

1. A static method must be marked with the static keyword and include a method body.

2. A static method without an access modifier is assumed to be public.

3. A static method cannot be marked abstract or final.

4. A static method is not inherited and cannot be accessed in a class implementing the interface without a reference to the interface name.

These rules should follow from what you know so far of classes, interfaces, and static methods. For example, you can't declare static methods without a body in classes either. Like default and abstract interface methods, static interface methods are implicitly public if they are declared without an access modifier. As we'll see shortly, you can use the private access modifier with static methods.

Let's take a look at a `static` interface method.

```
public interface Hop {
   static int getJumpHeight() {
      return 8;
   }
}
```

The method `getJumpHeight()` works just like a `static` method as defined in a class. In other words, it can be accessed without an instance of a class using the `Hop.getJumpHeight()` syntax. Since the method was defined without an access modifier, the compiler will automatically insert the `public` access modifier.

The fourth rule about inheritance might be a little confusing, so let's look at an example. The following is an example of a class Bunny that implements Hop and does not compile:

```
public class Bunny implements Hop {
   public void printDetails() {
      System.out.println(getJumpHeight());  // DOES NOT COMPILE
   }
}
```

Without an explicit reference to the name of the interface, the code will not compile, even though Bunny implements Hop. In this manner, the `static` interface methods are not inherited by a class implementing the interface, as they would if the method were defined in a parent class. Because `static` methods do not require an instance of the class, the problem can be easily fixed by using the interface name and calling the `public` static method.

```
public class Bunny implements Hop {
   public void printDetails() {
      System.out.println(Hop.getJumpHeight());
   }
}
```

Java "solved" the multiple inheritance problem of `static` interface methods by not allowing them to be inherited. This applies to both subinterfaces and classes that implement the interface. For example, a class that implements two interfaces containing `static` methods with the same signature will still compile. Contrast this with the behavior you saw for `default` interface methods in the previous section.

Introducing *private* Interface Methods

New to Java 9, interfaces may now include `private` interface methods. Putting on our thinking cap for a minute, what do you think `private` interface methods are useful for? Since they are `private`, they cannot be used outside the interface definition. They also cannot be used in static interface methods without a static method modifier, as we'll see in the next section. With all these restrictions, why were they added to the Java language?

Give up? The answer is that private interface methods can be used to reduce code duplication. For example, let's say we had a Schedule interface with a bunch of default methods. In each default method, we want to check some value and log some information based on the hour value. We could copy and paste the same code into each method, or we could use a private interface method. Take a look at the following example:

```java
public interface Schedule {
    default void wakeUp()       { checkTime(7);  }
    default void haveBreakfast() { checkTime(9);  }
    default void haveLunch()    { checkTime(12); }
    default void workOut()      { checkTime(18); }
    private void checkTime(int hour) {
        if (hour > 17) {
            System.out.println("You're late!");
        } else {
            System.out.println("You have "+(17-hour)+" hours left "
                    + "to make the appointment");
        }
    }
}
```

While you can write this code without using a private interface method by copying the contents of the checkTime() method into every default method, it's a lot shorter and easier to read if we don't. Since the authors of Java were nice enough to add this feature for our convenience, we might as well make use of it!

The rules for private interface methods are pretty straightforward.

Private Interface Method Definition Rules

1. A private interface method must be marked with the private modifier and include a method body.

2. A private interface method may be called only by default and private (non-static) methods within the interface definition.

Private interface methods behave a lot like instance methods within a class. Like private methods in a class, they cannot be declared abstract since they are not inherited.

Introducing *private static* Interface Methods

Alongside private interface methods, Java 9 added private static interface methods. As you might have already guessed, the purpose of private static interface methods is to reduce code duplication in static methods within the interface declaration. Furthermore, because instance methods can access static methods within a class, they can also be accessed by default and private methods.

The following is an example of a Swim interface that uses a `private static` method to reduce code duplication within other methods declared in the interface:

```java
public interface Swim {
    private static void breathe(String type) {
        System.out.println("Inhale");
        System.out.println("Performing stroke: " + type);
        System.out.println("Exhale");
    }
    static void butterfly()        { breathe("butterfly");   }
    public static void freestyle() { breathe("freestyle");   }
    default void backstroke()      { breathe("backstroke"); }
    private void breaststroke()    { breathe("breaststroke"); }
}
```

The `breathe()` method is able to be called in the `static butterfly()` and `freestyle()` methods, as well as the `default backstroke()` and `private breaststroke()` methods. Also, notice that `butterfly()` is assumed to be `public static` without any access modifier. The rules for `private static` interface methods are nearly the same as the rules for `private` interface methods.

Private Static Interface Method Definition Rules

1. A `private static` method must be marked with the `private` and `static` modifiers and include a method body.

2. A `private static` interface method may be called only by other methods within the interface definition.

Both `private` and `private static` methods can be called from `default` and `private` methods. This is equivalent to how an instance method is able to call both `static` and instance methods. On the other hand, a `private` method cannot be called from a `private static` method. This would be like trying to access an instance method from a `static` method in a class.

Why Mark Interface Methods *private*?

Instead of `private` and `private static` methods, we could have created `default` and `public static` methods, respectively. The code would have compiled just the same, so why mark them `private` at all?

The answer is to improve encapsulation, as we might not want these methods exposed outside the interface declaration. Encapsulation and security work best when the outside caller knows as little as possible about the internal implementation of a class or an interface. Using `private` interface methods doesn't just provide a way to reduce code duplication, but also a way to hide some of the underlying implementation details from users of the interface.

Reviewing Interface Members

We conclude our discussion of interface members with Table 12.5.

TABLE 12.5   Interface member access

	Accessible from `default` and `private` methods within the interface definition?	Accessible from `static` methods within the interface definition?	Accessible from instance methods implementing or extending the interface?	Accessible outside the interface without an instance of interface?
Constant variable	Yes	Yes	Yes	Yes
abstract method	Yes	No	Yes	No
default method	Yes	No	Yes	No
private method	Yes	No	No	No
static method	Yes	Yes	Yes	Yes
private static method	Yes	Yes	No	No

The first two data columns of Table 12.5 refer to access within the same interface definition. For example, a `private` method can access other `private` and `private static` methods defined within the same interface declaration.

When working with interfaces, we consider abstract, `default`, and `private` interface methods as instance methods. With that thought in mind, the last two columns of Table 12.5 should follow from what you know about class access modifiers and `private` members. Recall that instance methods can access `static` members within the class, but `static` members cannot access instance methods without a reference to the instance. Also, `private` members are never inherited, so they are never accessible directly by a class implementing an interface.

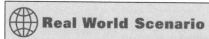

Real World Scenario

Abstract Classes vs. Interfaces

By introducing six different interface member types, Java has certainly blurred the lines between an abstract class and an interface. A key distinction, though, is that interfaces do not implement constructors and are not part of the class hierarchy. While a class can implement multiple interfaces, it can only directly extend a single class.

In fact, a common interview question is to ask an interviewee to describe the difference between an abstract class and an interface. These days, the question is more useful in determining which version of Java the candidate has most recently worked with. If you do happen to get this question on an interview, an appropriate tongue-in-cheek response would be, "How much time have you got?"

Introducing Functional Programming

Functional interfaces are used as the basis for lambda expressions in functional programming. A *functional interface* is an interface that contains a single abstract method. Your friend Sam can help you remember this because it is officially known as a *single abstract method (SAM)* rule.

A *lambda expression* is a block of code that gets passed around, sort of like an anonymous class that defines one method. As you'll see in this section, it can be written in a variety of short or long forms.

Since lambdas were part of the 1Z0-815 exam, some of this you should already know. Considering how important functional interfaces and lambda expressions are to passing the exam, you should read this section carefully, even if some of it is review.

Defining a Functional Interface

Let's take a look at an example of a functional interface and a class that implements it:

```java
@FunctionalInterface
public interface Sprint {
    public void sprint(int speed);
}
```

```
public class Tiger implements Sprint {
    public void sprint(int speed) {
        System.out.println("Animal is sprinting fast! " + speed);
    }
}
```

In this example, the Sprint interface is a functional interface, because it contains exactly one abstract method, and the Tiger class is a valid class that implements the interface.

 We'll cover the meaning of the @FunctionalInterface annotation in Chapter 13, "Annotations." For now, you just need to know that adding the annotation to a functional interface is optional.

Consider the following four interfaces. Given our previous Sprint functional interface, which of the following are functional interfaces?

```
public interface Dash extends Sprint {}
```

```
public interface Skip extends Sprint {
    void skip();
}
```

```
public interface Sleep {
    private void snore() {}
    default int getZzz() { return 1; }
}
```

```
public interface Climb {
    void reach();
    default void fall() {}
    static int getBackUp() { return 100; }
    private static boolean checkHeight() { return true; }
}
```

All four of these are valid interfaces, but not all of them are functional interfaces. The Dash interface is a functional interface because it extends the Sprint interface and inherits the single abstract method sprint(). The Skip interface is not a valid functional interface because it has two abstract methods: the inherited sprint() method and the declared skip() method.

The Sleep interface is also not a valid functional interface. Neither snore() nor getZzz() meet the criteria of a single abstract method. Even though default methods function like abstract methods, in that they can be overridden in a class implementing the interface, they are insufficient for satisfying the single abstract method requirement.

Finally, the Climb interface is a functional interface. Despite defining a slew of methods, it contains only one abstract method: reach().

Declaring a Functional Interface with *Object* Methods

As you may remember from your previous studies, all classes inherit certain methods from Object. For the exam, you should be familiar with the following Object method declarations:

- String toString()
- boolean equals(Object)
- int hashCode()

We bring this up now because there is one exception to the single abstract method rule that you should be familiar with. If a functional interface includes an abstract method with the same signature as a public method found in Object, then those methods do not count toward the single abstract method test. The motivation behind this rule is that any class that implements the interface will inherit from Object, as all classes do, and therefore always implement these methods.

 Since Java assumes all classes extend from Object, you also cannot declare an interface method that is incompatible with Object. For example, declaring an abstract method int toString() in an interface would not compile since Object's version of the method returns a String.

Let's take a look at an example. Is the Soar class a functional interface?

```
public interface Soar {
   abstract String toString();
}
```

It is not. Since toString() is a public method implemented in Object, it does not count toward the single abstract method test.

On the other hand, the following implementation of Dive is a functional interface:

```
public interface Dive {
   String toString();
   public boolean equals(Object o);
   public abstract int hashCode();
   public void dive();
}
```

The dive() method is the single abstract method, while the others are not counted since they are public methods defined in the Object class.

Be wary of examples that resemble methods in the Object class but are not actually defined in the Object class. Do you see why the following is not a valid functional interface?

```
public interface Hibernate {
    String toString();
    public boolean equals(Hibernate o);
    public abstract int hashCode();
    public void rest();
}
```

Despite looking a lot like our Dive interface, the Hibernate interface uses equals(Hibernate) instead of equals(Object). Because this does not match the method signature of the equals(Object) method defined in the Object class, this interface is counted as containing two abstract methods: equals(Hibernate) and rest().

 Real World Scenario

Overriding *toString()*, *equals(Object)*, and *hashCode()*

While knowing how to properly override toString(), equals(Object), and hashCode() was part of Java certification exams prior to Java 11, this requirement was removed on all of the Java 11 exams. As a professional Java developer, it is important for you to know at least the basic rules for overriding each of these methods.

- toString(): The toString() method is called when you try to print an object or concatenate the object with a String. It is commonly overridden with a version that prints a unique description of the instance using its instance fields.

- equals(Object): The equals(Object) method is used to compare objects, with the default implementation just using the == operator. You should override the equals(Object) method anytime you want to conveniently compare elements for equality, especially if this requires checking numerous fields.

- hashCode(): Any time you override equals(Object), you must override hash Code() to be consistent. This means that for any two objects, if a.equals(b) is true, then a.hashCode()==b.hashCode() must also be true. If they are not consistent, then this could lead to invalid data and side effects in hash-based collections such as HashMap and HashSet.

All of these methods provide a default implementation in Object, but if you want to make intelligent use out of them, then you should override them.

Implementing Functional Interfaces with Lambdas

In addition to functional interfaces you write yourself, Java provides a number of pre-defined ones. You'll learn about many of these in Chapter 15, "Functional Programming." For now, let's work with the Predicate interface. Excluding any static or default methods defined in the interface, we have the following:

```java
public interface Predicate<T> {
   boolean test(T t);
}
```

We'll review generics in Chapter 14, "Generics and Collections," but for now you just need to know that <T> allows the interface to take an object of a specified type. Now that we have a functional interface, we'll show you how to implement it using a lambda expression. The relationship between functional interfaces and lambda expressions is as follows: *any functional interface can be implemented as a lambda expression.*

Even older Java interfaces that pass the single abstract method test are functional interfaces, which can be implemented with lambda expressions.

Let's try an illustrative example. Our goal is to print out all the animals in a list according to some criteria. We start out with the Animal class.

```java
public class Animal {
   private String species;
   private boolean canHop;
   private boolean canSwim;
   public Animal(String speciesName, boolean hopper, boolean swimmer) {
      species = speciesName;
      canHop = hopper;
      canSwim = swimmer;
   }
   public boolean canHop()  { return canHop; }
   public boolean canSwim() { return canSwim; }
   public String toString() { return species; }
}
```

The Animal class has three instance variables, which are set in the constructor. It has two methods that get the state of whether the animal can hop or swim. It also has a toString() method so we can easily identify the Animal in programs.

Now we have everything that we need to write our code to find each Animal that hops.

```java
1:   import java.util.*;
2:   import java.util.function.Predicate;
```

```
3:  public class TraditionalSearch {
4:      public static void main(String[] args) {
5:
6:          // list of animals
7:          var animals = new ArrayList<Animal>();
8:          animals.add(new Animal("fish",     false, true));
9:          animals.add(new Animal("kangaroo", true,  true));
10:         animals.add(new Animal("rabbit",   true,  false));
11:         animals.add(new Animal("turtle",   false, true));
12:
13:         // Pass lambda that does check
14:         print(animals, a -> a.canHop());
15:     }
16:     private static void print(List<Animal> animals,
17:         Predicate<Animal> checker) {
18:         for (Animal animal : animals) {
19:             if (checker.test(animal))
20:                 System.out.print(animal + " ");
21:         }
22:     }
23: }
```

This program compiles and prints kangaroo rabbit at runtime. The print() method on line 14 method is very general—it can check for any trait. This is good design. It shouldn't need to know what specifically we are searching for in order to print a list of animals.

Now what happens if we want to print the Animals that swim? We only have to add one line of code—no need for an extra class to do something simple. Here's that other line:

```
14:         print(animals, a -> a.canSwim());
```

This prints fish kangaroo turtle at runtime. How about Animals that cannot swim?

```
14:         print(animals, a -> !a.canSwim());
```

This prints rabbit by itself. The point here is that it is really easy to write code that uses lambdas once you get the basics in place.

Lambda expressions rely on the notion of deferred execution. *Deferred execution* means that code is specified now but runs later. In this case, *later* is when the `print()` method calls it. Even though the execution is deferred, the compiler will still validate that the code syntax is correct.

Writing Lambda Expressions

The syntax of lambda expressions is tricky because many parts are optional. Despite this, the overall structure is the same. The left side of the lambda expression lists the variables. It must be compatible with the type and number of input parameters of the functional interface's single abstract method.

The right side of the lambda expression represents the body of the expression. It must be compatible with the return type of the functional interface's abstract method. For example, if the abstract method returns `int`, then the lambda expression must return an `int`, a value that can be implicitly cast to an `int`, or throw an exception.

Let's take a look at a functional interface in both its short and long forms. Figure 12.1 shows the short form of this functional interface and has three parts:

- A single parameter specified with the name a

- The arrow operator to separate the parameter and body

- A body that calls a single method and returns the result of that method

FIGURE 12.1   Lambda syntax omitting optional parts

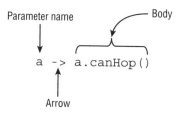

Now let's look at a more verbose version of this lambda expression, shown in Figure 12.2. It also contains three parts.

- A single parameter specified with the name a and stating the type is Animal

- The arrow operator to separate the parameter and body

- A body that has one or more lines of code, including a semicolon and a return statement

FIGURE 12.2   Lambda syntax, including optional parts

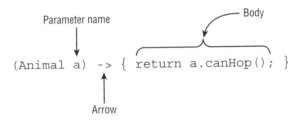

The parentheses can be omitted only if there is a single parameter and its type is not explicitly stated. Java does this because developers commonly use lambda expressions this way so they can do as little typing as possible.

It shouldn't be news to you that we can omit braces when we have only a single statement. We did this with `if` statements and loops already. What is different here is that the rules change when you omit the braces. Java doesn't require you to type `return` or use a semicolon when no braces are used. This special shortcut doesn't work when we have two or more statements. At least this is consistent with using {} to create blocks of code elsewhere.

As a fun fact, `s -> {}` is a valid lambda. If the return type of the functional interface method is `void`, then you don't need the semicolon or `return` statement.

Let's take a look at some examples. The following are all valid lambda expressions, assuming that there are functional interfaces that can consume them:

```
() -> new Duck()
d -> {return d.quack();}
(Duck d) -> d.quack()
(Animal a, Duck d) -> d.quack()
```

The first lambda expression could be used by a functional interface containing a method that takes no arguments and returns a `Duck` object. The second and third lambda expressions both can be used by a functional interface that takes a `Duck` as input and returns whatever the return type of `quack()` is. The last lambda expression can be used by a functional interface that takes as input `Animal` and `Duck` objects and returns whatever the return type of `quack()` is.

Now let's make sure you can identify invalid syntax. Let's assume we needed a lambda that returns a `boolean` value. Do you see what's wrong with each of these?

```
3: a, b -> a.startsWith("test")      // DOES NOT COMPILE
4: Duck d -> d.canQuack();           // DOES NOT COMPILE
```

```
5: a -> { a.startsWith("test"); }       // DOES NOT COMPILE
6: a -> { return a.startsWith("test") } // DOES NOT COMPILE
7: (Swan s, t) -> s.compareTo(t) != 0   // DOES NOT COMPILE
```

Lines 3 and 4 require parentheses around each parameter list. Remember that the parentheses are optional *only* when there is one parameter and it doesn't have a type declared. Line 5 is missing the return keyword, which is required since we said the lambda must return a boolean. Line 6 is missing the semicolon inside of the braces, {}. Finally, line 7 is missing the parameter type for t. If the parameter type is specified for one of the parameters, then it must be specified for all of them.

Working with Lambda Variables

Variables can appear in three places with respect to lambdas: the parameter list, local variables declared inside the lambda body, and variables referenced from the lambda body. All three of these are opportunities for the exam to trick you.

Parameter List

Earlier you learned that specifying the type of parameters is optional. Now var can be used in a lambda parameter list. That means that all three of these statements are interchangeable:

```
Predicate<String> p = x -> true;
Predicate<String> p = (var x) -> true;
Predicate<String> p = (String x) -> true;
```

The exam might ask you to identify the type of the lambda parameter. In the previous example, the answer is String. OK, but how did we figure that out? A lambda infers the types from the surrounding context. That means you get to do the same!

In this case, the lambda is being assigned to a Predicate that takes a String. Another place to look for the type is in a method signature. Let's try another example. Can you figure out the type of x?

```
public void whatAmI() {
    test((var x) -> x>2, 123);
}


public void test(Predicate<Integer> c, int num) {
    c.test(num);
}
```

If you guessed Integer, you were right. The whatAmI() method creates a lambda to be passed to the test() method. Since the test() method expects an Integer as the generic, we know that is what the inferred type of x will be.

But wait, there's more! In some cases, you can determine the type without even seeing the method signature. What do you think the type of x is here?

```
public void counts(List<Integer> list) {
    list.sort((var x, var y) -> x.compareTo(y));
}
```

The answer is again Integer. Since we are sorting a list, we can use the type of the list to determine the type of the lambda parameter.

Restrictions on Using *var* in the Parameter List

While you can use var inside a lambda parameter list, there is a rule you need to be aware of. If var is used for one of the types in the parameter list, then it must be used for all parameters in the list. Given this rule, which of the following lambda expressions do not compile if they were assigned to a variable?

```
3: (var num) -> 1
4: var w -> 99
5: (var a, var b) -> "Hello"
6: (var a, Integer b) -> true
7: (String x, var y, Integer z) -> true
8: (var b, var k, var m) -> 3.14159
9: (var x, y) -> "goodbye"
```

Line 3 compiles and is similar to our previous examples. Line 4 does not compile because parentheses, (), are required when using the parameter name. Lines 5 and 8 compile because all of the parameters in the list use var. Lines 6 and 7 do not compile, though, because the parameter types include a mix of var and type names. Finally, line 9 does not compile because the parameter type is missing for the second parameter, y. Even when using var for all the parameter types, each parameter type must be written out.

Local Variables Inside the Lambda Body

While it is most common for a lambda body to be a single expression, it is legal to define a block. That block can have anything that is valid in a normal Java block, including local variable declarations.

The following code does just that. It creates a local variable named c that is scoped to the lambda block.

```
(a, b) -> { int c = 0; return 5;}
```

When writing your own code, a lambda block with a local variable is a good hint that you should extract that code into a method.

Now let's try another one. Do you see what's wrong here?

```
(a, b) -> { int a = 0; return 5;}     // DOES NOT COMPILE
```

We tried to redeclare a, which is not allowed. Java doesn't let you create a local variable with the same name as one already declared in that scope. Now let's try a hard one. How many syntax errors do you see in this method?

```
11: public void variables(int a) {
12:     int b = 1;
13:     Predicate<Integer> p1 = a -> {
14:         int b = 0;
15:         int c = 0;
16:         return b == c;}
17: }
```

There are actually three syntax errors. The first is on line 13. The variable a was already used in this scope as a method parameter, so it cannot be reused. The next syntax error comes on line 14 where the code attempts to redeclare local variable b. The third syntax error is quite subtle and on line 16. See it? Look really closely.

The variable p1 is missing a semicolon at the end. There is a semicolon before the }, but that is inside the block. While you don't normally have to look for missing semicolons, lambdas are tricky in this space, so beware!

Variables Referenced from the Lambda Body

Lambda bodies are allowed to use static variables, instance variables, and local variables if they are final or effectively final. Sound familiar? Lambdas follow the same rules for access as local and anonymous classes! This is not a coincidence, as behind the scenes, anonymous classes are used for lambda expressions. Let's take a look at an example:

```
4:  public class Crow {
5:      private String color;
6:      public void caw(String name) {
7:          String volume = "loudly";
8:          Predicate<String> p = s -> (name+volume+color).length()==10;
9:      }
10: }
```

On the other hand, if the local variable is not final or effectively final, then the code does not compile.

```
4:  public class Crow {
5:      private String color;
6:      public void caw(String name) {
7:          String volume = "loudly";
8:          color = "allowed";
```

```
9:          name = "not allowed";
10:         volume = "not allowed";
11:         Predicate<String> p =
12:             s -> (name+volume+color).length()==9; // DOES NOT COMPILE
13:     }
14: }
```

In this example, the values of name and volume are assigned new values on lines 9 and 10. For this reason, the lambda expression declared on lines 11 and 12 does not compile since it references local variables that are not final or effectively final. If lines 9 and 10 were removed, then the class would compile.

Summary

This chapter focused on core fundamentals of the Java language that you will use throughout this book. We started with the final modifier and showed how it could be applied to local, instance, and static variables, as well as methods and classes.

We next moved on to enumerated types, which define a list of fixed values. Like boolean values, enums are not integers and cannot be compared this way. Enums can be used in switch statements. Besides the list of values, enums can include instance variables, constructors, and methods. Methods can even be abstract, in which case all enum values must provide an implementation. Alternatively, if an enum method is not marked final, then it can be overridden by one of its value declarations.

There are four types of nested classes. An inner class requires an instance of the outer class to use, while a static nested class does not. A local class is one defined within a method. Local classes can access final and effectively final local variables. Anonymous classes are a special type of local class that does not have a name. Anonymous classes are required to extend exactly one class by name or implement exactly one interface. Inner, local, and anonymous classes can access private members of the class in which they are defined, provided the latter two are used inside an instance method.

As of Java 9, interfaces now support six different members. Constant variables (static final) and abstract methods should have been familiar to you. Newer member types include default, static, private, and private static methods. While interfaces now contain a lot of member types, they are still distinct from abstract classes and do not participate in the class instantiation.

Last but certainly not least, this chapter included an introduction to functional interfaces and lambda expressions. A functional interface is an interface that contains exactly one abstract method. Any functional interface can be implemented with a lambda expression. A lambda expression can be written in a number of different forms, since many of the parts are optional. Make sure you understand the basics of writing lambda expressions as you will be using them throughout the book.

Exam Essentials

Be able to correctly apply the *final* modifier. Applying the `final` modifier to a variable means its value cannot change after it has been assigned, although its contents can be modified. An instance `final` variable must be assigned a value when it is declared, in an instance initializer, or in a constructor at most once. A `static final` variable must be assigned a value when it is declared or in a `static` initializer. A `final` method is one that cannot be overridden by a subclass, while a `final` class is one that cannot be extended.

Be able to create and use enum types. An enum is a data structure that defines a list of values. If the enum does not contain any other elements, then the semicolon (;) after the values is optional. An enum can have instance variables, constructors, and methods. Enum constructors are implicitly `private`. Enums can include methods, both as members or within individual enum values. If the enum declares an `abstract` method, each enum value must implement it.

Identify and distinguish between types of nested classes. There are four types of nested types: inner classes, `static` classes, local classes, and anonymous classes. The first two are defined as part of a class declaration. Local classes are used inside method bodies and scoped to the end of the current block of code. Anonymous classes are created and used once, often on the fly. More recently, they are commonly implemented as lambda expressions.

Be able to declare and use nested classes. Instantiating an inner class requires an instance of the outer class, such as calling new `Outer.new Inner()`. On the other hand, `static` nested classes can be created without a reference to the outer class, although they cannot access instance members of the outer class without a reference. Local and anonymous classes cannot be declared with an access modifier. Anonymous classes are limited to extending a single class or implementing one interface.

Be able to create *default, static, private*, and *private static* interface methods. A `default` interface method is a `public` interface that contains a body, which can be overridden by a class implementing the interface. If a class inherits two `default` methods with the same signature, then the class must override the `default` method with its own implementation. An interface can include `public static` and `private static` methods, the latter of which can be accessed only by methods declared within the interface. An interface can also include `private` methods, which can be called only by `default` and other `private` methods in the interface declaration.

Determine whether an interface is a functional interface. Use the single abstract method (SAM) rule to determine whether an interface is a functional interface. Other interface method types (`default`, `private`, `static`, and `private static`) do not count toward the single abstract method count, nor do any `public` methods with signatures found in `Object`.

Write simple lambda expressions.   Look for the presence or absence of optional elements in lambda code. Parameter types are optional. Braces and the `return` keyword are optional when the body is a single statement. Parentheses are optional when only one parameter is specified and the type is implicit. If one of the parameters is a var, then they all must use var.

Determine whether a variable can be used in a lambda body.   Local variables and method parameters must be `final` or effectively final to be referenced in a lambda expression. Class variables are always allowed. Instance variables are allowed if the lambda is used inside an instance method.

Review Questions

The answers to the chapter review questions can be found in the Appendix.

1. Which statements about the `final` modifier are correct? (Choose all that apply.)
   A. Instance and static variables can be marked `final`.
   B. A variable is effectively final if it is marked `final`.
   C. The `final` modifier can be applied to classes and interfaces.
   D. A `final` class cannot be extended.
   E. An object that is marked `final` cannot be modified.
   F. Local variables cannot be declared with type var and the `final` modifier.

2. What is the result of the following program?

   ```java
   public class FlavorsEnum {
       enum Flavors {
           VANILLA, CHOCOLATE, STRAWBERRY
           static final Flavors DEFAULT = STRAWBERRY;
       }
       public static void main(String[] args) {
           for(final var e : Flavors.values())
               System.out.print(e.ordinal()+" ");
       }
   }
   ```

   A. 0 1 2
   B. 1 2 3
   C. Exactly one line of code does not compile.
   D. More than one line of code does not compile.
   E. The code compiles but produces an exception at runtime.
   F. None of the above

3. What is the result of the following code? (Choose all that apply.)

   ```java
   1: public class Movie {
   2:     private int butter = 5;
   3:     private Movie() {}
   4:     protected class Popcorn {
   5:         private Popcorn() {}
   6:         public static int butter = 10;
   7:         public void startMovie() {
   8:             System.out.println(butter);
   ```

```
 9:          }
10:      }
11:      public static void main(String[] args) {
12:          var movie = new Movie();
13:          Movie.Popcorn in = new Movie().new Popcorn();
14:          in.startMovie();
15:      } }
```

A. The output is 5.

B. The output is 10.

C. Line 6 generates a compiler error.

D. Line 12 generates a compiler error.

E. Line 13 generates a compiler error.

F. The code compiles but produces an exception at runtime.

4. Which statements about `default` and `private` interface methods are correct? (Choose all that apply.)

A. A `default` interface method can be declared `private`.

B. A `default` interface method can be declared `public`.

C. A `default` interface method can be declared `static`.

D. A `private` interface method can be declared `abstract`.

E. A `private` interface method can be declared `protected`.

F. A `private` interface method can be declared `static`.

5. Which of the following are valid lambda expressions? (Choose all that apply.)

A. `(Wolf w, var c) -> 39`

B. `(final Camel c) -> {}`

C. `(a,b,c) -> {int b = 3; return 2;}`

D. `(x,y) -> new RuntimeException()`

E. `(var y) -> return 0;`

F. `() -> {float r}`

G. `(Cat a, b) -> {}`

6. What are some advantages of using `private` interface methods? (Choose all that apply.)

A. Improve polymorphism

B. Improve performance at runtime

C. Reduce code duplication

D. Backward compatibility

E. Encapsulate interface implementation

F. Portability

7. What is the result of the following program?

```java
public class IceCream {
    enum Flavors {
        CHOCOLATE, STRAWBERRY, VANILLA
    }

    public static void main(String[] args) {
        Flavors STRAWBERRY = null;
        switch (STRAWBERRY) {
            case Flavors.VANILLA: System.out.print("v");
            case Flavors.CHOCOLATE: System.out.print("c");
            case Flavors.STRAWBERRY: System.out.print("s");
            break;
            default: System.out.println("missing flavor"); }
    }
}
```

   A. v
   B. vc
   C. s
   D. `missing flavor`
   E. Exactly one line of code does not compile.
   F. More than one line of code does not compile.
   G. The code compiles but produces an exception at runtime.

8. Which statements about functional interfaces are true? (Choose all that apply.)
   A. A functional interface can contain `default` and `private` methods.
   B. A functional interface can be defined by a class or interface.
   C. Abstract methods with signatures that are contained in `public` methods of `java .lang.Object` do not count toward the abstract method count for a functional interface.
   D. A functional interface cannot contain `static` or `private static` methods.
   E. A functional interface contains at least one abstract method.
   F. A functional interface must be marked with the `@FunctionalInterface` annotation.

9. Which lines, when entered independently into the blank, allow the code to print `Not scared` at runtime? (Choose all that apply.)

```java
public class Ghost {
    public static void boo() {
        System.out.println("Not scared");
    }
```

```
     protected final class Spirit {
        public void boo() {
           System.out.println("Booo!!!");
        }
     }
     public static void main(String... haunt) {
        var g = new Ghost().new Spirit() {};
        _____;
     }
  }
}
```

A. g.boo()

B. g.super.boo()

C. new Ghost().boo()

D. g.Ghost.boo()

E. new Spirit().boo()

F. Ghost.boo()

G. None of the above

10. The following code appears in a file named Ostrich.java. What is the result of compiling the source file?

```
1: public class Ostrich {
2:     private int count;
3:     private interface Wild {}
4:     static class OstrichWrangler implements Wild {
5:         public int stampede() {
6:             return count;
7:         } } }
```

A. The code compiles successfully, and one bytecode file is generated: Ostrich.class.

B. The code compiles successfully, and two bytecode files are generated: Ostrich.class and OstrichWrangler.class.

C. The code compiles successfully, and two bytecode files are generated: Ostrich.class and Ostrich$OstrichWrangler.class.

D. A compiler error occurs on line 4.

E. A compiler error occurs on line 6.

11. What is the result of the following code?

```
1:  public interface CanWalk {
2:      default void walk() { System.out.print("Walking"); }
3:      private void testWalk() {}
4:  }
5:  public interface CanRun {
6:      abstract public void run();
7:      private void testWalk() {}
8:      default void walk() { System.out.print("Running"); }
9:  }
10: public interface CanSprint extends CanWalk, CanRun {
11:     void sprint();
12:     default void walk(int speed) {
13:         System.out.print("Sprinting");
14:     }
15:     private void testWalk() {}
16: }
```

A. The code compiles without issue.

B. The code will not compile because of line 6.

C. The code will not compile because of line 8.

D. The code will not compile because of line 10.

E. The code will not compile because of line 12.

F. None of the above

12. What is the result of executing the following program?

```
interface Sing {
   boolean isTooLoud(int volume, int limit);
}
public class OperaSinger {
   public static void main(String[] args) {
      check((h, l) -> h.toString(), 5);   // m1
   }
   private static void check(Sing sing, int volume) {
      if (sing.isTooLoud(volume, 10))     // m2
         System.out.println("not so great");
      else System.out.println("great");
   }
}
```

A. great

B. not so great

    C. Compiler error on line m1

    D. Compiler error on line m2

    E. Compiler error on a different line

    F. A runtime exception is thrown.

13. Which lines of the following interface declaration do not compile? (Choose all that apply.)

```
1: public interface Herbivore {
2:    int amount = 10;
3:    static boolean gather = true;
4:    static void eatGrass() {}
5:    int findMore() { return 2; }
6:    default float rest() { return 2; }
7:    protected int chew() { return 13; }
8:    private static void eatLeaves() {}
9: }
```

    A. All of the lines compile without issue.

    B. Line 2

    C. Line 3

    D. Line 4

    E. Line 5

    F. Line 6

    G. Line 7

    H. Line 8

14. What is printed by the following program?

```
public class Deer {
    enum Food {APPLES, BERRIES, GRASS}
    protected class Diet {
        private Food getFavorite() {
            return Food.BERRIES;
        }
    }
    public static void main(String[] seasons) {
        switch(new Diet().getFavorite()) {
            case APPLES: System.out.print("a");
            case BERRIES: System.out.print("b");
            default: System.out.print("c");
        }
    }
}
```

A. b

B. bc

C. abc

D. The code declaration of the `Diet` class does not compile.

E. The `main()` method does not compile.

F. The code compiles but produces an exception at runtime.

G. None of the above

15. Which of the following are printed by the `Bear` program? (Choose all that apply.)

```java
public class Bear {
    enum FOOD {
        BERRIES, INSECTS {
            public boolean isHealthy() { return true; }},
        FISH, ROOTS, COOKIES, HONEY;
        public abstract boolean isHealthy();
    }
    public static void main(String[] args) {
        System.out.print(FOOD.INSECTS);
        System.out.print(FOOD.INSECTS.ordinal());
        System.out.print(FOOD.INSECTS.isHealthy());
        System.out.print(FOOD.COOKIES.isHealthy());
    }
}
```

A. insects

B. INSECTS

C. 0

D. 1

E. false

F. true

G. The code does not compile.

16. Which of the following are valid functional interfaces? (Choose all that apply.)

```java
public interface Transport {
    public int go();
    public boolean equals(Object o);
}
```

```
public abstract class Car {
   public abstract Object swim(double speed, int duration);
}

public interface Locomotive extends Train {
   public int getSpeed();
}

public interface Train extends Transport {}

abstract interface Spaceship extends Transport {
   default int blastOff();
}

public interface Boat {
   int hashCode();
   int hashCode(String input);
}
```

- **A.** Boat
- **B.** Car
- **C.** Locomotive
- **D.** Tranport
- **E.** Train
- **F.** Spaceship
- **G.** None of these is a valid functional interface.

17. Which lambda expression when entered into the blank line in the following code causes the program to print hahaha? (Choose all that apply.)

```
import java.util.function.Predicate;
public class Hyena {
   private int age = 1;
   public static void main(String[] args) {
      var p = new Hyena();
      double height = 10;
      int age = 1;
      testLaugh(p, _____ );
      age = 2;
   }
```

```
        static void testLaugh(Hyena panda, Predicate<Hyena> joke) {
            var r = joke.test(panda) ? "hahaha" : "silence";
            System.out.print(r);
        }
    }
```

A. `var -> p.age <= 10`

B. `shenzi -> age==1`

C. `p -> true`

D. `age==1`

E. `shenzi -> age==2`

F. `h -> h.age < 5`

G. None of the above, as the code does not compile.

18. Which of the following can be inserted in the `rest()` method? (Choose all that apply.)

```
    public class Lion {
        class Cub {}
        static class Den {}
        static void rest() {

            _____;

        } }
```

A. `Cub a = Lion.new Cub()`

B. `Lion.Cub b = new Lion().Cub()`

C. `Lion.Cub c = new Lion().new Cub()`

D. `var d = new Den()`

E. `var e = Lion.new Cub()`

F. `Lion.Den f = Lion.new Den()`

G. `Lion.Den g = new Lion.Den()`

H. `var h = new Cub()`

19. Given the following program, what can be inserted into the blank line that would allow it to print Swim! at runtime?

```
    interface Swim {
        default void perform() { System.out.print("Swim!"); }
    }
    interface Dance {
        default void perform() { System.out.print("Dance!"); }
    }
    public class Penguin implements Swim, Dance {
```

```
public void perform() { System.out.print("Smile!"); }
private void doShow() {

    _____

}
public static void main(String[] eggs) {
    new Penguin().doShow();
}
}
```

A. `super.perform();`

B. `Swim.perform();`

C. `super.Swim.perform();`

D. `Swim.super.perform();`

E. The code does not compile regardless of what is inserted into the blank.

F. The code compiles, but due to polymorphism, it is not possible to produce the requested output without creating a new object.

20. Which statements about effectively final variables are true? (Choose all that apply.)

A. The value of an effectively final variable is not modified after it is set.

B. A lambda expression can reference effectively final variables.

C. A lambda expression can reference `final` variables.

D. If the `final` modifier is added, the code still compiles.

E. Instance variables can be effectively final.

F. Static variables can be effectively final.

21. Which lines of the following interface do not compile? (Choose all that apply.)

```
1: public interface BigCat {
2:     abstract String getName();
3:     static int hunt() { getName(); return 5; }
4:     default void climb() { rest(); }
5:     private void roar() { getName();  climb(); hunt(); }
6:     private static boolean sneak() { roar(); return true; }
7:     private int rest() { return 2; };
8: }
```

A. Line 2

B. Line 3

C. Line 4

D. Line 5

E. Line 6

F. Line 7

G. None of the above

22. What are some advantages of using `default` interface methods? (Choose all that apply.)

   A. Automatic resource management

   B. Improve performance at runtime

   C. Better exception handling

   D. Backward compatibility

   E. Highly concurrent execution

   F. Convenience in classes implementing the interface

23. Which statements about the following enum are true? (Choose all that apply.)

```
1:  public enum AnimalClasses {
2:     MAMMAL(true), INVERTIBRATE(Boolean.FALSE), BIRD(false),
3:     REPTILE(false), AMPHIBIAN(false), FISH(false) {
4:        public int swim() { return 4; }
5:     }
6:     final boolean hasHair;
7:     public AnimalClasses(boolean hasHair) {
8:        this.hasHair = hasHair;
9:     }
10:    public boolean hasHair() { return hasHair; }
11:    public int swim() { return 0; }
12: }
```

   A. Compiler error on line 2

   B. Compiler error on line 3

   C. Compiler error on line 7

   D. Compiler error on line 8

   E. Compiler error on line 10

   F. Compiler error on another line

   G. The code compiles successfully.

24. Which lambdas can replace the new `Sloth()` call in the `main()` method and produce the same output at runtime? (Choose all that apply.)

```
import java.util.List;
interface Yawn {
   String yawn(double d, List<Integer> time);
}
```

```
class Sloth implements Yawn {
    public String yawn(double zzz, List<Integer> time) {
        return "Sleep: " + zzz;
    }
}
public class Vet {
    public static String takeNap(Yawn y) {
        return y.yawn(10, null);
    }
    public static void main(String... unused) {
        System.out.print(takeNap(new Sloth()));
    }
}
```

A. (z,f) -> { String x = ""; return "Sleep: " + x }

B. (t,s) -> { String t = ""; return "Sleep: " + t; }

C. (w,q) -> {"Sleep: " + w}

D. (e,u) -> { String g = ""; "Sleep: " + e }

E. (a,b) -> "Sleep: " + (double)(b==null ? a : a)

F. (r,k) -> { String g = ""; return "Sleep:"; }

G. None of the above, as the program does not compile.

25. What does the following program print?

```
1:  public class Zebra {
2:      private int x = 24;
3:      public int hunt() {
4:          String message = "x is ";
5:          abstract class Stripes {
6:              private int x = 0;
7:              public void print() {
8:                  System.out.print(message + Zebra.this.x);
9:              }
10:         }
11:         var s = new Stripes() {};
12:         s.print();
13:         return x;
14:     }
```

```
15:    public static void main(String[] args) {
16:        new Zebra().hunt();
17:    } }
```

A. x is 0

B. x is 24

C. Line 6 generates a compiler error.

D. Line 8 generates a compiler error.

E. Line 11 generates a compiler error.

F. None of the above

Chapter

13

Annotations

OCP EXAM OBJECTIVES COVERED IN THIS CHAPTER:

✓ **Annotations**

- Describe the purpose of annotations and typical usage patterns

- Apply annotations to classes and methods

- Describe commonly used annotations in the JDK

- Declare custom annotations

There are some topics you need to know to pass the exam, some that are important in your daily development experience, and some that are important for both. Annotations definitely fall into this last category. Annotations were added to the Java language to make a developer's life a lot easier.

Prior to annotations, adding extra information about a class or method was often cumbersome and required a lot of extra classes and configuration files. Annotations solved this by having the data and the information about the data defined in the same location.

In this chapter, we define what an annotation is, how to create a custom annotation, and how to properly apply annotations. We will also teach you about built-in annotations that you will need to learn for the exam. We hope this chapter increases your understanding and usage of annotations in your professional development experience.

Introducing Annotations

Annotations are all about metadata. That might not sound very exciting at first, but they add a lot of value to the Java language. Or perhaps, better said, they allow you to add a lot of value to your code.

Understanding Metadata

What exactly is metadata? *Metadata* is data that provides information about other data. Imagine our zoo is having a sale on tickets. The *attribute data* includes the price, the expiration date, and the number of tickets purchased. In other words, the attribute data is the transactional information that makes up the ticket sale and its contents.

On the other hand, the *metadata* includes the rules, properties, or relationships surrounding the ticket sales. Patrons must buy at least one ticket, as a sale of zero or negative tickets is silly. Maybe the zoo is having a problem with scalpers, so they add a rule that each person can buy a maximum of five tickets a day. These metadata rules describe information about the ticket sale but are not part of the ticket sale.

As you'll learn in this chapter, annotations provide an easy and convenient way to insert metadata like this into your applications.

While annotations allow you to insert rules around data, it does not mean the values for these rules need to be defined in the code, aka "hard-coded." In many frameworks, you can define the rules and relationships in the code but read the values from elsewhere. In the previous example, you could define an annotation specifying a maximum number of tickets but load the value of 5 from a config file or database. For this chapter, though, you can assume the values are defined in the code.

Purpose of Annotations

The purpose of an *annotation* is to assign metadata attributes to classes, methods, variables, and other Java types. Let's start with a simple annotation for our zoo: @ZooAnimal. Don't worry about how this annotation is defined or the syntax of how to call it just yet; we'll delve into that shortly. For now, you just need to know that annotations start with the at (@) symbol and can contain attribute/value pairs called *elements*.

```
public class Mammal {}
public class Bird {}

@ZooAnimal public class Lion extends Mammal {}

@ZooAnimal public class Peacock extends Bird {}
```

In this case, the annotation is applied to the Lion and Peacock classes. We could have also had them extend a class called ZooAnimal, but then we have to change the class hierarchy. By using an annotation, we leave the class structure intact.

That brings us to our first rule about annotations: *annotations function a lot like interfaces*. In this example, annotations allow us to *mark* a class as a ZooAnimal without changing its inheritance structure.

So if annotations function like interfaces, why don't we just use interfaces? While interfaces can be applied only to classes, annotations can be applied to any declaration including classes, methods, expressions, and even other annotations. Also, unlike interfaces, annotations allow us to pass a set of values where they are applied.

Consider the following Veterinarian class:

```
public class Veterinarian {
    @ZooAnimal(habitat="Infirmary") private Lion sickLion;

    @ZooAnimal(habitat="Safari") private Lion healthyLion;

    @ZooAnimal(habitat="Special Enclosure") private Lion blindLion;
}
```

This class defines three variables, each with an associated habitat value. The habitat value is part of the type declaration of each variable, not an individual object. For example, the healthyLion may change the object it points to, but the value of the annotation does not. Without annotations, we'd have to define a new Lion type for each habitat value, which could become cumbersome given a large enough application.

That brings us to our second rule about annotations: *annotations establish relationships that make it easier to manage data about our application.*

Sure, we could write applications without annotations, but that often requires creating a lot of extra classes, interfaces, or data files (XML, JSON, etc.) to manage these complex relationships. Worse yet, because these extra classes or files may be defined outside the class where they are being used, we have to do a lot of work to keep the data and the relationships in sync.

 Real World Scenario

External Metadata Files

Prior to annotations, many early Java enterprise frameworks relied on external XML files to store metadata about an application. Imagine managing an application with dozens of services, hundreds of objects, and thousands of attributes. The data would be stored in numerous Java files alongside a large, ever-growing XML file. And a change to one often required a change to the other.

As you can probably imagine, this becomes untenable very quickly! Many of these frameworks were abandoned or rewritten to use annotations. These days, XML files are still used with Java projects but often serve to provide minimal configuration information, rather than low-level metadata.

Consider the following methods that use a hypothetical @ZooSchedule annotation to indicate when a task should be performed.

```java
// Lion.java
public class Lion {
    @ZooSchedule(hours={"9am","5pm","10pm"}) void feedLions() {
        System.out.print("Time to feed the lions!");
    }
}
```

```java
// Peacock.java
public class Peacock {
    @ZooSchedule(hours={"4am","5pm"}) void cleanPeacocksPen() {
        System.out.print("Time to sweep up!");
    }
}
```

These methods are defined in completely different classes, but the interpretation of the annotation is the same. With this approach, the task and its schedule are defined right next to each other. This brings us to our third rule about annotations: *an annotation ascribes custom information on the declaration where it is defined.* This turns out to be a powerful tool, as the same annotation can often be applied to completely unrelated classes or variables.

There's one final rule about annotations you should be familiar with: *annotations are optional metadata and by themselves do not do anything.* This means you can take a project filled with thousands of annotations and remove all of them, and it will still compile and run, albeit with potentially different behavior at runtime.

This last rule might seem a little counterintuitive at first, but it refers to the fact that annotations aren't utilized where they are defined. It's up to the rest of the application, or more likely the underlying framework, to enforce or use annotations to accomplish tasks. For instance, marking a method with @SafeVarargs informs other developers and development tools that no unsafe operations are present in the method body. It does not actually prevent unsafe operations from occurring!

 While an annotation can be removed from a class and it will still compile, the opposite is not true; adding an annotation can trigger a compiler error. As we will see in this chapter, the compiler validates that annotations are properly used and include all required fields.

For the exam, you need to know how to define your own custom annotations, how to apply annotations properly, and how to use common annotations. Writing code that processes or enforces annotations is not required for the exam.

 Real World Scenario

The Spring Framework

While there are many platforms that rely on annotations, one of the most recognized and one of the first to popularize using annotations is the Spring Framework, or Spring for short. Spring uses annotations for many purposes, including dependency injection, which is a common technique of decoupling a service and the clients that use it.

In Chapter 17, "Modular Applications," you'll learn all about Java's built-in service implementation, which uses module-info files rather than annotations to manage services. While modules and Spring are both providing dependencies dynamically, they are implemented in a very different manner.

Spring, along with the well-known convention over configuration Spring Boot framework, isn't on the exam, but we recommend professional Java developers be familiar with both of them.

Creating Custom Annotations

Creating your own annotation is surprisingly easy. You just give it a name, define a list of optional and required elements, and specify its usage. In this section, we'll start with the simplest possible annotation and work our way up from there.

Creating an Annotation

Let's say our zoo wants to specify the exercise metadata for various zoo inhabitants using annotations. We use the @interface annotation (all lowercase) to declare an annotation. Like classes and interfaces, they are commonly defined in their own file as a top-level type, although they can be defined inside a class declaration like an inner class.

```
public @interface Exercise {}
```

Yes, we use an annotation to create an annotation! The Exercise annotation is referred to as a *marker annotation*, since it does not contain any elements. In Chapter 19, "I/O," you'll actually learn about something called a marker interface, which shares a lot of similarities with annotations.

How do we use our new annotation? It's easy. We use the at (@) symbol, followed by the type name. In this case, the annotation is @Exercise. Then, we apply the annotation to other Java code, such as a class.

Let's apply @Exercise to some classes.

```
@Exercise() public class Cheetah {}
```

```
@Exercise public class Sloth {}
```

```
@Exercise
public class ZooEmployee {}
```

Oh no, we've mixed animals and zoo employees! That's perfectly fine. There's no rule that our @Exercise annotation has to be applied to animals. Like interfaces, annotations can be applied to unrelated classes.

You might have noticed that Cheetah and Sloth differ on their usage of the annotation. One uses parentheses, (), while the other does not. When using a marker annotation, parentheses are optional. Once we start adding elements, though, they are required if the annotation includes any values.

We also see ZooEmployee is not declared on the same line as its annotation. If an annotation is declared on a line by itself, then it applies to the next nonannotation type found on the proceeding lines. In fact, this applies when there are multiple annotations present.

```
@Scaley        @Flexible
   @Food("insect") @Food("rodent")      @FriendlyPet
@Limbless public class Snake {}
```

Some annotations are on the same line, some are on their own line, and some are on the line with the declaration of Snake. Regardless, all of the annotations apply to Snake. As with other declarations in Java, spaces and tabs between elements are ignored.

 Whether you put annotations on the same line as the type they apply to or on separate lines is a matter of style. Either is acceptable.

In this example, some annotations are all lowercase, while others are mixed case. Annotation names are case sensitive. Like class and interface names, it is common practice to have them start with an uppercase letter, although it is not required.

Finally, some annotations, like @Food, can be applied more than once. We'll cover repeatable annotations later in this chapter.

Specifying a Required Element

An *annotation element* is an attribute that stores values about the particular usage of an annotation. To make our previous example more useful, let's change @Exercise from a marker annotation to one that includes an element.

```
public @interface Exercise {
    int hoursPerDay();
}
```

The syntax for the hoursPerDay() element may seem a little strange at first. It looks a lot like an abstract method, although we're calling it an element (or attribute). Remember, annotations have their roots in interfaces. Behind the scenes, the JVM is creating elements as interface methods and annotations as implementations of these interfaces. Luckily, you don't need to worry about those details; the compiler does that for you.

Let's see how this new element changes our usage:

```
@Exercise(hoursPerDay=3) public class Cheetah {}

@Exercise hoursPerDay=0 public class Sloth {}      // DOES NOT COMPILE

@Exercise public class ZooEmployee {}              // DOES NOT COMPILE
```

The Cheetah class compiles and correctly uses the annotation, providing a value for the element. The Sloth class does not compile because it is missing parentheses around the annotation parameters. Remember, parentheses are optional only if no values are included.

What about ZooEmployee? This class does not compile because the hoursPerDay field is required. Remember earlier when we said annotations are optional metadata? While the annotation itself is optional, the compiler still cares that they are used correctly.

Wait a second, when did we mark hoursPerDay() as required? We didn't. But we also didn't specify a default value either. *When declaring an annotation, any element without a default value is considered required.* We'll show you how to declare an optional element next.

Providing an Optional Element

For an element to be optional, rather than required, it must include a default value. Let's update our annotation to include an optional value.

```
public @interface Exercise {
    int hoursPerDay();
    int startHour() default 6;
}
```

In Chapter 12, "Java Fundamentals," we mentioned that the default keyword can be used in switch statements and interface methods. Yep, they did it again. There is yet another use of the default keyword that is unrelated to any of the usages you were previously familiar with. And don't forget package-private access is commonly referred to as default access without any modifiers. Good grief!

Next, let's apply the updated annotation to our classes.

```
@Exercise(startHour=5, hoursPerDay=3) public class Cheetah {}

@Exercise(hoursPerDay=0) public class Sloth {}

@Exercise(hoursPerDay=7, startHour="8")   // DOES NOT COMPILE
public class ZooEmployee {}
```

There are a few things to unpack here. First, when we have more than one element value within an annotation, we separate them by a comma (,). Next, each element is written using the syntax *elementName=elementValue*. It's like a shorthand for a Map. Also, the order of each element does not matter. Cheetah could have listed hoursPerDay first.

We also see that Sloth does not specify a value for startHour, meaning it will be instantiated with the default value of 6.

In this version, the ZooEmployee class does not compile because it defines a value that is incompatible with the int type of startHour. The compiler is doing its duty validating the type!

Defining a Default Element Value

The default value of an annotation cannot be just any value. Similar to case statement values, *the default value of an annotation must be a non-null constant expression.*

```
public @interface BadAnnotation {
    String name() default new String("");  // DOES NOT COMPILE
    String address() default "";
    String title() default null;           // DOES NOT COMPILE
}
```

In this example, name() does not compile because it is not a constant expression, while title() does not compile because it is null. Only address() compiles. Notice that while null is not permitted as a default value, the empty String "" is.

Selecting an Element Type

Similar to a default element value, an annotation element cannot be declared with just any type. It must be a primitive type, a String, a Class, an enum, another annotation, or an array of any of these types.

Given this information and our previous Exercise annotation, which of the following elements compile?

```
public class Bear {}

public enum Size {SMALL, MEDIUM, LARGE}

public @interface Panda {
    Integer height();
    String[][] generalInfo();
    Size size() default Size.SMALL;
    Bear friendlyBear();
    Exercise exercise() default @Exercise(hoursPerDay=2);
}
```

The height() element does not compile. While primitive types like int and long are supported, wrapper classes like Integer and Long are not. The generalInfo() element also does not compile. The type String[] is supported, as it is an array of String values, but String[][] is not.

The size() and exercise() elements both compile, with one being an enum and the other being an annotation. To set a default value for exercise(), we use the @Exercise annotation. Remember, this is the only way to create an annotation value. Unlike instantiating a class, the new keyword is never used to create an annotation.

Finally, the friendlyBear() element does not compile. The type of friendlyBear() is Bear (not Class). Even if Bear were changed to an interface, the friendlyBear() element would still not compile since it is not one of the supported types.

Applying Element Modifiers

Like abstract interface methods, annotation elements are implicitly abstract and public, whether you declare them that way or not.

```
public @interface Material {}

public @interface Fluffy {
    int cuteness();
    public abstract int softness() default 11;
    protected Material material();   // DOES NOT COMPILE
    private String friendly();       // DOES NOT COMPILE
    final boolean isBunny();         // DOES NOT COMPILE
}
```

The elements cuteness() and softness() are both considered abstract and
public, even though only one of them is marked as such. The elements material()
and friendly() do not compile because the access modifier conflicts with the elements
being implicitly public. The element isBunny() does not compile because, like abstract
methods, it cannot be marked final.

Adding a Constant Variable

Annotations can include constant variables that can be accessed by other classes without
actually creating the annotation.

```
public @interface ElectricitySource {
    public int voltage();
    int MIN_VOLTAGE = 2;
    public static final int MAX_VOLTAGE = 18;
}
```

Yep, just like interface variables, annotation variables are implicitly public, static,
and final. These constant variables are not considered elements, though. For example,
marker annotations can contain constants.

Reviewing Annotation Rules

We conclude creating custom annotations with Figure 13.1, which summarizes many of the
syntax rules that you have learned thus far.

Figure 13.2 shows how to apply this annotation to a Java class. For contrast, it also
includes a simple marker annotation @Alert. Remember, a marker annotation is one that
does not contain any elements.

If you understand all of the parts of these two figures, then you are well on your way
to understanding annotations. If not, then we suggest rereading this section. The rest of
the chapter will build on this foundation; you will see more advanced usage, apply annotations to other annotations, and learn the built-in annotations that you will need to know
for the exam.

FIGURE 13.1   Annotation declaration

FIGURE 13.2   Using an annotation

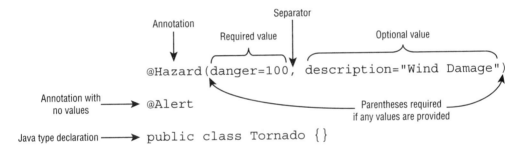

Applying Annotations

Now that we have described how to create and use simple annotations, it's time to discuss other ways to apply annotations.

Using Annotations in Declarations

Up until now, we've only been applying annotations to classes and methods, but they can be applied to any Java declaration including the following:

- Classes, interfaces, enums, and modules
- Variables (static, instance, local)
- Methods and constructors
- Method, constructor, and lambda parameters
- Cast expressions
- Other annotations

The following compiles, assuming the annotations referenced in it exist:

```
1:  @FunctionalInterface interface Speedster {
2:      void go(String name);
3:  }
4:  @LongEars
5:  @Soft @Cuddly public class Rabbit {
6:      @Deprecated public Rabbit(@NotNull Integer size) {}
7:
8:      @Speed(velocity="fast") public void eat(@Edible String input) {
9:          @Food(vegetarian=true) String m = (@Tasty String) "carrots";
10:
11:         Speedster s1 = new @Racer Speedster() {
12:             public void go(@FirstName @NotEmpty String name) {
13:                 System.out.print("Start! "+name);
14:             }
15:         };
16:
17:         Speedster s2 = (@Valid String n) -> System.out.print(n);
18:     }
19: }
```

It's a little contrived, we know. Lines 1, 4, and 5 apply annotations to the interface and class declarations. Some of the annotations, like @Cuddly, do not require any values, while others, like @Speed, do provide values. You would need to look at the annotation declaration to know if these values are optional or required.

Lines 6 and 8 contain annotations applied to constructor and method declarations. These lines also contain annotations applied to their parameters.

Line 9 contains the annotation @Food applied to a local variable, along with the annotation @Tasty applied to a cast expression.

> **NOTE**   When applying an annotation to an expression, a cast operation including the Java type is required. On line 9, the expression was cast to String, and the annotation @Tasty was applied to the type.

Line 11 applies an annotation to the type in the anonymous class declaration, and line 17 shows an annotation in a lambda expression parameter. Both of these examples may look a little odd at first, but they are allowed. In fact, you're more likely to see examples like this on the exam than you are in real life.

In this example, we applied annotations to various declarations, but this isn't always permitted. An annotation can specify which declaration type they can be applied to using the @Target annotation. We'll cover this, along with other annotation-specific annotations, in the next part of the chapter.

Mixing Required and Optional Elements

One of the most important rules when applying annotations is the following: *to use an annotation, all required values must be provided*. While an annotation may have many elements, values are required only for ones without default values.

Let's try this. Given the following annotation:

```
public @interface Swimmer {
    int armLength = 10;
    String stroke();
    String name();
    String favoriteStroke() default "Backstroke";
}
```

which of the following compile?

```
@Swimmer class Amphibian {}

@Swimmer(favoriteStroke="Breaststroke", name="Sally") class Tadpole {}

@Swimmer(stroke="FrogKick", name="Kermit") class Frog {}

@Swimmer(stroke="Butterfly", name="Kip", armLength=1) class Reptile {}

@Swimmer(stroke="", name="", favoriteStroke="") class Snake {}
```

Amphibian does not compile, because it is missing the required elements stroke() and name(). Likewise, Tadpole does not compile, because it is missing the required element stroke().

Frog provides all of the required elements and none of the optional ones, so it compiles. Reptile does not compile since armLength is a constant, not an element, and cannot be included in an annotation. Finally, Snake does compile, providing all required and optional values.

Creating a *value()* Element

In your development experience, you may have seen an annotation with a value, written without the *elementName*. For example, the following is valid syntax under the right condition:

```
@Injured("Broken Tail") public class Monkey {}
```

This is considered a shorthand or abbreviated annotation notation. What qualifies as *the right condition*? An annotation must adhere to the following rules to be used without a name:

- The annotation declaration must contain an element named value(), which may be optional or required.

- The annotation declaration must not contain any other elements that are required.
- The annotation usage must not provide values for any other elements.

Let's create an annotation that meets these requirements.

```
public @interface Injured {
    String veterinarian() default "unassigned";
    String value() default "foot";
    int age() default 1;
}
```

This annotation is composed of multiple optional elements. In this example, we gave value() a default value, but we could have also made it required. Using this declaration, the following annotations are valid:

```
public abstract class Elephant {
    @Injured("Legs") public void fallDown() {}
    @Injured(value="Legs") public abstract int trip();
    @Injured String injuries[];
}
```

The usage in the first two annotations are equivalent, as the compiler will convert the shorthand form to the long form with the value() element name. The last annotation with no values is permitted because @Injured does not have any required elements.

Typically, the value() of an annotation should be related to the name of the annotation. In our previous example, @Injured was the annotation name, and the value() referred to the item that was impacted. This is especially important since all shorthand elements use the same element name, value().

For the exam, make sure that if the shorthand notation is used, then there is an element named value(). Also, check that there are no other required elements. For example, the following annotation declarations cannot be used with a shorthand annotation:

```
public @interface Sleep {
    int value();
    String hours();
}

public @interface Wake {
    String hours();
}
```

The first declaration contains two required elements, while the second annotation does not include an element named value().

Likewise, the following annotation is not valid as it provides more than one value:

```
@Injured("Fur",age=2) public class Bear {}  // DOES NOT COMPILE
```

Passing an Array of Values

Annotations support a shorthand notation for providing an array that contains a single element. Let's say we have an annotation Music defined as follows:

```
public @interface Music {
    String[] genres();
}
```

If we want to provide only one value to the array, we have a choice of two ways to write the annotation. Either of the following is correct:

```
public class Giraffe {
    @Music(genres={"Rock and roll"}) String mostDisliked;
    @Music(genres="Classical") String favorite;
}
```

The first annotation is considered the regular form, as it is clear the usage is for an array. The second annotation is the shorthand notation, where the array braces ({}) are dropped for convenience. Keep in mind that this is still providing a value for an array element; the compiler is just inserting the missing array braces for you.

This notation can be used only if the array is composed of a single element. For example, only one of the following annotations compiles:

```
public class Reindeer {
    @Music(genres="Blues","Jazz") String favorite;    // DOES NOT COMPILE
    @Music(genres=) String mostDisliked;               // DOES NOT COMPILE
    @Music(genres=null) String other;                  // DOES NOT COMPILE
    @Music(genres={}) String alternate;
}
```

The first provides more than one value, while the next two do not provide any values. The last one does compile, as an array with no elements is still a valid array.

While this shorthand notation can be used for arrays, it does not work for List or Collection. As mentioned earlier, they are not in the list of supported element types for annotations.

Combining Shorthand Notations

It might not surprise you that we can combine both of our recent rules for shorthand notations. Consider this annotation:

(Continued)

```
public @interface Rhythm {
   String[] value();
}
```

Each of the following four annotations is valid:

```
public class Capybara {
   @Rhythm(value={"Swing"}) String favorite;
   @Rhythm(value="R&B") String secondFavorite;
   @Rhythm({"Classical"}) String mostDisliked;
   @Rhythm("Country") String lastDisliked;
}
```

The first annotation provides all of the details, while the last one applies both short-hand rules.

Declaring Annotation-Specific Annotations

Congratulations—if you've gotten this far, then you've learned all of the general rules for annotations we have to teach you! From this point on, you'll need to learn about specific annotations and their associated rules for the exam. Many of these rules are straightforward, although some will require memorization.

In this section, we'll cover built-in annotations applied to other annotations. Yes, metadata about metadata! Since these annotations are built into Java, they primarily impact the compiler. In the final section, we'll cover built-in annotations applied to various Java data types.

Limiting Usage with @*Target*

Earlier, we showed you examples of annotations applied to various Java types, such as classes, methods, and expressions. When defining your own annotation, you might want to limit it to a particular type or set of types. After all, it may not make sense for a particular annotation to be applied to a method parameter or local variable.

Many annotation declarations include @Target annotation, which limits the types the annotation can be applied to. More specifically, the @Target annotation takes an array of ElementType enum values as its value() element.

Learning the *ElementType* Values

Table 13.1 shows all of the values available for the @Target annotation.

TABLE 13.1   Values for the `@Target` annotation

ElementType value	Applies to
TYPE	Classes, interfaces, enums, annotations
FIELD	Instance and `static` variables, enum values
METHOD	Method declarations
PARAMETER	Constructor, method, and lambda parameters
CONSTRUCTOR	Constructor declarations
LOCAL_VARIABLE	Local variables
ANNOTATION_TYPE	Annotations
PACKAGE*	Packages declared in `package-info.java`
TYPE_PARAMETER*	Parameterized types, generic declarations
TYPE_USE	Able to be applied anywhere there is a Java type declared or used
MODULE*	Modules

*Applying these with annotations is out of scope for the exam.

You might notice that some of the `ElementType` applications overlap. For example, to create an annotation usable on other annotations, you could declare an `@Target` with `ANNOTATION_TYPE` or `TYPE`. Either will work for annotations, although the second option opens the annotation usage to other types like classes and interfaces.

While you are not likely to be tested on all of these types, you may see a few on the exam. Make sure you can recognize proper usage of them. Most are pretty self-explanatory.

 You can't add a package annotation to just any package declaration, only those defined in a special file, which must be named package-info.java. This file stores documentation metadata about a package. Don't worry, though, this isn't on the exam.

Consider the following annotation:

```
import java.lang.annotation.ElementType;
import java.lang.annotation.Target;

@Target({ElementType.METHOD,ElementType.CONSTRUCTOR})
public @interface ZooAttraction {}
```

NOTE   Even though the java.lang package is imported automatically by the compiler, the java.lang.annotation package is not. Therefore, import statements are required for many of the examples in the remainder of this chapter.

Based on this annotation, which of the following lines of code will compile?

```
1: @ZooAttraction class RollerCoaster {}
2: class Events {
3:     @ZooAttraction String rideTrain() {
4:         return (@ZooAttraction String) "Fun!";
5:     }
6:     @ZooAttraction Events(@ZooAttraction String description) {
7:         super();
8:     }
9:     @ZooAttraction int numPassengers; }
```

This example contains six uses of @ZooAttraction with only two of them being valid. Line 1 does not compile, because the annotation is applied to a class type. Line 3 compiles, because it is permitted on a method declaration. Line 4 does not compile, because it is not permitted on a cast operation.

Line 6 is tricky. The first annotation is permitted, because it is applied to the constructor declaration. The second annotation is not, as the annotation is not marked for use in a constructor parameter. Finally, line 9 is not permitted, because it cannot be applied to fields or variables.

Understanding the *TYPE_USE* Value

While most of the values in Table 13.1 are straightforward, TYPE_USE is without a doubt the most complex. The TYPE_USE parameter *can be used anywhere there is a Java type*. By including it in @Target, it actually includes nearly all the values in Table 13.1 including classes, interfaces, constructors, parameters, and more. There are a few exceptions; for example, it can be used only on a method that returns a value. Methods that return void would still need the METHOD value defined in the annotation.

It also allows annotations in places where types are *used*, such as cast operations, object creation with new, inside type declarations, etc. These might seem a little strange at first, but the following are valid TYPE_USE applications:

```
// Technical.java
import java.lang.annotation.ElementType;
import java.lang.annotation.Target;

@Target(ElementType.TYPE_USE)
@interface Technical {}
```

```
// NetworkRepair.java
import java.util.function.Predicate;
public class NetworkRepair {
    class OutSrc extends @Technical NetworkRepair {}
    public void repair() {
        var repairSubclass = new @Technical NetworkRepair() {};

        var o = new @Technical NetworkRepair().new @Technical OutSrc();

        int remaining = (@Technical int)10.0;
    }
}
```

For the exam, you don't need to know all of the places TYPE_USE can be used, nor what applying it to these locations actually does, but you do need to recognize that they can be applied in this manner if TYPE_USE is one of the @Target options.

Storing Annotations with @*Retention*

As you saw in Chapter 7, "Methods and Encapsulation," the compiler discards certain types of information when converting your source code into a .class file. With generics, this is known as *type erasure*.

In a similar vein, annotations *may* be discarded by the compiler or at runtime. We say "may," because we can actually specify how they are handled using the @Retention annotation. This annotation takes a value() of the enum RetentionPolicy. Table 13.2 shows the possible values, in increasing order of retention.

TABLE 13.2   Values for the @Retention annotation

RetentionPolicy value	Description
SOURCE	Used only in the source file, discarded by the compiler
CLASS	Stored in the .class file but not available at runtime (default compiler behavior)
RUNTIME	Stored in the .class file and available at runtime

Using it is pretty easy.

```
import java.lang.annotation.Retention;
import java.lang.annotation.RetentionPolicy;
```

```
@Retention(RetentionPolicy.CLASS) @interface Flier {}
@Retention(RetentionPolicy.RUNTIME) @interface Swimmer {}
```

In this example, both annotations will retain the annotation information in their .class files, although only Swimmer will be available (via reflection) at runtime.

Generating Javadoc with @*Documented*

When trying to determine what methods or classes are available in Java or a third-party library, you've undoubtedly relied on web pages built with Javadoc. Javadoc is a built-in standard within Java that generates documentation for a class or API.

In fact, you can generate Javadoc files for any class you write! Better yet, you can add additional metadata, including comments and annotations, that have no impact on your code but provide more detailed and user-friendly Javadoc files.

For the exam, you should be familiar with the marker annotation @Documented. If present, then the generated Javadoc will include annotation information defined on Java types. Because it is a marker annotation, it doesn't take any values; therefore, using it is pretty easy.

```
// Hunter.java
import java.lang.annotation.Documented;
@Documented public @interface Hunter {}


// Lion.java
@Hunter public class Lion {}
```

In this example, the @Hunter annotation would be published with the Lion Javadoc information because it's marked with the @Documented annotation.

Java vs. Javadoc Annotations

Javadoc has its own annotations that are used solely in generating data within a Javadoc file.

```
public class ZooLightShow {

   /**
    * Performs a light show at the zoo.
    *
    * @param     distance    length the light needs to travel.
    * @return    the result of the light show operation.
    * @author    Grace Hopper
    * @since     1.5
```

```
     * @deprecated Use EnhancedZooLightShow.lights() instead.
     */
    @Deprecated(since="1.5") public static String perform(int distance) {
        return "Beginning light show!";
    }
}
```

Be careful not to confuse Javadoc annotations with the Java annotations. Take a look at the
@deprecated and @Deprecated annotations in this example. The first, @deprecated,
is a Javadoc annotation used inside a comment, while @Deprecated is a Java annotation
applied to a class. Traditionally, Javadoc annotations are all lowercase, while Java annotations start with an uppercase letter.

Inheriting Annotations with *@Inherited*

Another marker annotation you should know for the exam is @Inherited. When this
annotation is applied to a class, subclasses will inherit the annotation information found
in the parent class.

// Vertebrate.java
```
import java.lang.annotation.Inherited;
@Inherited public @interface Vertebrate {}
```

// Mammal.java
```
@Vertebrate public class Mammal {}
```

// Dolphin.java
```
public class Dolphin extends Mammal {}
```

In this example, the @Vertebrate annotation will be applied to both Mammal and
Dolphin objects. Without the @Inherited annotation, @Vertebrate would apply only
to Mammal instances.

Supporting Duplicates with *@Repeatable*

The last annotation-specific annotation you need to know for the exam is arguably the most
complicated to use, as it actually requires creating two annotations. The @Repeatable
annotation is used when you want to specify an annotation more than once on a type.

Why would you want to specify twice? Well, if it's a marker annotation with no elements,
you probably wouldn't. Generally, you use repeatable annotations when you want to apply
the same annotation with different values.

Let's assume we have a repeatable annotation @Risk, which assigns a set of risk values
to a zoo animal. We'll show how it is used and then work backward to create it.

```
public class Zoo {
   public static class Monkey {}

   @Risk(danger="Silly")
   @Risk(danger="Aggressive",level=5)
   @Risk(danger="Violent",level=10)
   private Monkey monkey;
}
```

Next, let's define a simple annotation that implements these elements:

```
public @interface Risk {
   String danger();
   int level() default 1;
}
```

Now, as written, the Zoo class does not compile. Why? Well, the Risk annotation is missing the @Repeatable annotation! That brings us to our first rule: *without the @Repeatable annotation, an annotation can be applied only once.* So, let's add the @Repeatable annotation.

```
import java.lang.annotation.Repeatable;

@Repeatable   // DOES NOT COMPILE
public @interface Risk {
   String danger();
   int level() default 1;
}
```

This code also does not compile, but this time because the @Repeatable annotation is not declared correctly. It requires a reference to a second annotation. That brings us to our next rule: *to declare a @Repeatable annotation, you must define a containing annotation type value.*

A *containing annotation type* is a separate annotation that defines a value() array element. The type of this array is the particular annotation you want to repeat. By convention, the name of the annotation is often the plural form of the repeatable annotation.

Putting all of this together, the following Risks declaration is a containing annotation type for our Risk annotation:

```
public @interface Risks {
   Risk[] value();
}
```

Finally, we go back to our original Risk annotation and specify the containing annotation class:

```
import java.lang.annotation.Repeatable;

@Repeatable(Risks.class)
public @interface Risk {
    String danger();
    int level() default 1;
}
```

With these two annotations, our original Zoo class will now compile. Notice that we never actually use @Risks in our Zoo class. Given the declaration of the Risk and Risks annotations, the compiler takes care of applying the annotations for us.

The following summarizes the rules for declaring a repeatable annotation, along with its associated containing type annotation:

- The repeatable annotation must be declared with @Repeatable and contain a value that refers to the containing type annotation.

- The containing type annotation must include an element named value(), which is a primitive array of the repeatable annotation type.

Once you understand the basic structure of declaring a repeatable annotation, it's all pretty convenient.

Repeatable Annotations vs. an Array of Annotations

Repeatable annotations were added in Java 8. Prior to this, you would have had to use the @Risks containing annotation type directly:

```
@Risks({
    @Risk(danger="Silly"),
    @Risk(danger="Aggressive",level=5),
    @Risk(danger="Violent",level=10)
})
private Monkey monkey;
```

With this implementation, @Repeatable is not required in the Risk annotation declaration. The @Repeatable annotation is the preferred approach now, as it is easier than working with multiple nested statements.

Reviewing Annotation-Specific Annotations

We conclude this part of the chapter with Table 13.3, which shows the annotations that can be applied to other annotations that might appear on the exam.

TABLE 13.3 Annotation-specific annotations

Annotation	Marker annotation	Type of value()	Default compiler behavior (if annotation not present)
@Target	No	Array of ElementType	Annotation able to be applied to all locations except TYPE_USE and TYPE_PARAMETER
@Retention	No	RetentionPolicy	RetentionPolicy.CLASS
@Documented	Yes	—	Annotations are not included in the generated Javadoc.
@Inherited	Yes	—	Annotations in supertypes are not inherited.
@Repeatable	No	Annotation	Annotation cannot be repeated.

Prior to this section, we created numerous annotations, and we never used any of the annotations in Table 13.3. So, what did the compiler do? Like implicit modifiers and default no-arg constructors, the compiler auto-inserted information based on the lack of data.

The default behavior for most of the annotations in Table 13.3 is often intuitive. For example, without the @Documented or @Inherited annotation, these features are not supported. Likewise, the compiler will report an error if you try to use an annotation more than once without the @Repeatable annotation.

The @Target annotation is a bit of a special case. When @Target is not present, an annotation can be used in any place except TYPE_USE or TYPE_PARAMETER scenarios (cast operations, object creation, generic declarations, etc.).

Why Doesn't @*Target*'s Default Behavior Apply to All Types?

We learn from Table 13.3 that to use an annotation in a type use or type parameter location, such as a lambda expression or generic declaration, you must explicitly set the @Target to include these values. If an annotation is declared without the @Target annotation that includes these values, then these locations are prohibited.

One possible explanation for this behavior is backward compatibility. When these values were added to Java 8, it was decided that they would have to be explicitly declared to be used in these locations.

That said, when the authors of Java added the MODULE value in Java 9, they did not make this same decision. If @Target is absent, the annotation is permitted in a module declaration by default.

Using Common Annotations

For the exam, you'll need to know about a set of built-in annotations, which apply to various types and methods. Unlike custom annotations that you might author, many of these annotations have special rules. In fact, if they are used incorrectly, the compiler will report an error.

Some of these annotations (like @Override) are quite useful, and we recommend using them in practice. Others (like @SafeVarargs), you are likely to see only on a certification exam. For each annotation, you'll need to understand its purposes, identify when to use it (or not to use it), and know what elements it takes (if any).

Marking Methods with *@Override*

The @Override is a marker annotation that is used to indicate a method is overriding an inherited method, whether it be inherited from an interface or parent class. From Chapter 8, "Class Design," you should know that the overriding method must have the same signature, the same or broader access modifier, and a covariant return type, and not declare any new or broader checked exceptions.

Let's take a look at an example:

```
public interface Intelligence {
    int cunning();
}
public class Canine implements Intelligence {
    @Override public int cunning() { return 500; }
    void howl() { System.out.print("Woof!"); }
}
public class Wolf extends Canine {
    @Override
    public int cunning() { return Integer.MAX_VALUE; }
    @Override void howl() { System.out.print("Howl!"); }
}
```

In this example, the @Override annotation is applied to three methods that it inherits from the parent class or interface.

During the exam, you should be able to identify anywhere this annotation is used incorrectly. For example, using the same Canine class, this Dog class does not compile:

```
public class Dog extends Canine {
    @Override
    public boolean playFetch() { return true; }  // DOES NOT COMPILE
    @Override void howl(int timeOfDay) {}          // DOES NOT COMPILE
}
```

The playFetch() method does not compile, because there is no inherited method with that name. In the Dog class, howl() is an overloaded method, not an overridden one. While there is a howl() method defined in the parent class, it does not have the same signature. It is a method overload, not a method override.

Removing both uses of the @Override annotation in the Dog class would allow the class to compile. Using these annotations is not required, but using them incorrectly is prohibited.

> The annotations in this section are entirely optional but help improve the quality of the code. By adding these annotations, though, you help take the guesswork away from someone reading your code. It also enlists the compiler to help you spot errors. For example, applying @Override on a method that is not overriding another triggers a compilation error and could help you spot problems if a class or interface is later changed.

Declaring Interfaces with *@FunctionalInterface*

In Chapter 12, we showed you how to create and identify functional interfaces, which are interfaces with exactly one abstract method. The @FunctionalInterface marker annotation can be applied to any valid functional interface. For example, our previous Intelligence example was actually a functional interface.

```
@FunctionalInterface public interface Intelligence {
    int cunning();
}
```

The compiler will report an error, though, if applied to anything other than a valid functional interface. From what you learned in Chapter 12, which of the following declarations compile?

```
@FunctionalInterface abstract class Reptile {
    abstract String getName();
}
```

```
@FunctionalInterface interface Slimy {}
```

```
@FunctionalInterface interface Scaley {
    boolean isSnake();
}
```

```
@FunctionalInterface interface Rough extends Scaley {
    void checkType();
}
```

```
@FunctionalInterface interface Smooth extends Scaley {
    boolean equals(Object unused);
}
```

The `Reptile` declaration does not compile, because the `@FunctionalInterface` annotation can be applied only to interfaces. The `Slimy` interface does not compile, because it does not contain any abstract methods. The `Scaley` interface compiles, as it contains exactly one abstract method.

The Rough interface does not compile, because it contains two abstract methods, one of which it inherits from `Scaley`. Finally, the `Smooth` interface contains two abstract methods, although since one matches the signature of a method in `java.lang.Object`, it does compile.

Like we saw with the `@Override` annotation, removing the `@FunctionalInterface` annotation in the invalid declarations would allow the code to compile. Review functional interfaces in Chapter 12 if you had any trouble with these examples.

 If you are declaring a complex interface, perhaps one that contains `static`, `private`, and `default` methods, there's a simple test you can perform to determine whether it is a valid functional interface. Just add the `@FunctionalInterface` annotation to it! If it compiles, it is a functional interface and can be used with lambda expressions.

Retiring Code with *@Deprecated*

In professional software development, you rarely write a library once and never go back to it. More likely, libraries are developed and maintained over a period of years. Libraries change for external reasons, like new business requirements or new versions of Java, or internal reasons, like a bug is found and corrected.

Sometimes a method changes so much that we need to create a new version of it entirely with a completely different signature. We don't want to necessarily remove the old version of the method, though, as this could cause a lot of compilation headaches for our users if the method suddenly disappears. What we want is a way to notify our users that a new version of the method is available and give them time to migrate their code to the new version before we finally remove the old version.

With those ideas in mind, Java includes the `@Deprecated` annotation. The `@Deprecated` annotation is similar to a marker annotation, in that it can be used without any values, but it includes some optional elements. The `@Deprecated` annotation can be applied to nearly any Java declaration, such as classes, methods, or variables.

Let's say we have an older class `ZooPlanner`, and we've written a replacement `ParkPlanner`. We want to notify all users of the older class to switch to the new version.

```
/**
 * Design and plan a zoo.
 * @deprecated Use ParkPlanner instead.
 */
@Deprecated
public class ZooPlanner { ... }
```

That's it! The users of the ZooPlanner class will now receive a compiler warning if they are using ZooPlanner. In the next section, we'll show how they can use another annotation to ignore these warnings.

Always Document the Reason for Deprecation

Earlier, we discussed @Deprecated and @deprecated, the former being a Java annotation and the latter being a Javadoc annotation. Whenever you deprecate a method, you should add a Javadoc annotation to instruct users on how they should update their code.

For the exam, you should know that it is good practice to document why a type is being deprecated and be able to suggest possible alternatives.

While this may or may not appear on the exam, the @Deprecated annotation does support two optional values: String since() and boolean forRemoval(). They provide additional information about when the deprecation occurred in the past and whether or not the type is expected to be removed entirely in the future.

```
/**
 * Method to formulate a zoo layout.
 * @deprecated Use ParkPlanner.planPark(String... data) instead.
 */
@Deprecated(since="1.8", forRemoval=true)
public void plan() {}
```

Note that the @Deprecated annotation does not allow you to provide any suggested alternatives. For that, you should use the Javadoc annotation.

 NOTE When reviewing the Java JDK, you may encounter classes or methods that are marked deprecated, with the purpose that developers migrate to a new implementation. For example, the constructors of the wrapper classes (like Integer or Double) were recently marked @Deprecated, with the Javadoc note that you should use the factory method valueOf() instead. In this case, the advantage is that an immutable value from a pool can be reused, rather than creating a new object. This saves memory and improves performance.

Ignoring Warnings with *@SuppressWarnings*

One size does not fit all. While the compiler can be helpful in warning you of potential coding problems, sometimes you need to perform a particular operation, and you don't care whether or not it is a potential programming problem.

Enter @SuppressWarnings. Applying this annotation to a class, method, or type basically tells the compiler, "I know what I am doing; do not warn me about this." Unlike the previous annotations, it requires a String[] value() parameter. Table 13.4 lists some of the values available for this annotation.

TABLE 13.4 Common *@SuppressWarnings* values

Value	Description
"deprecation"	Ignore warnings related to types or methods marked with the @Deprecated annotation.
"unchecked"	Ignore warnings related to the use of raw types, such as List instead of List<String>.

The annotation actually supports a lot of other values, but for the exam, you only need to know the ones listed in this table. Let's try an example:

```
import java.util.*;

class SongBird {
    @Deprecated static void sing(int volume) {}
    static Object chirp(List<String> data) { return data.size(); }
}

public class Nightingale {
    public void wakeUp() {
        SongBird.sing(10);
    }
    public void goToBed() {
        SongBird.chirp(new ArrayList());
    }
    public static void main(String[] args) {
        var birdy = new Nightingale();
        birdy.wakeUp();
        birdy.goToBed();
    }
}
```

This code compiles and runs but produces two compiler warnings.

```
Nightingale.java uses or overrides a deprecated API.
Nightingale.java uses unchecked or unsafe operations.
```

The first warning is because we are using a method SongBird.sing() that is deprecated. The second warning is triggered by the call to new ArrayList(), which does not define a generic type. An improved implementation would be to use new ArrayList<String>().

Let's say we are absolutely sure that we don't want to change our Nightingale implementation, and we don't want the compiler to bother us anymore about these warnings. Adding the @SuppressWarnings annotation, with the correct values, accomplishes this.

```
@SuppressWarnings("deprecation") public void wakeUp() {
    SongBird.sing(10);
}


@SuppressWarnings("unchecked") public void goToBed() {
    SongBird.chirp(new ArrayList());
}
```

Now our code compiles, and no warnings are generated.

> You should use the @SuppressWarnings annotation sparingly. Oftentimes, the compiler is correct in alerting you to potential coding problems. In some cases, a developer may use this annotation as a way to ignore a problem, rather than refactoring code to solve it.

Protecting Arguments with @*SafeVarargs*

The @SafeVargs marker annotation indicates that a method does not perform any potential unsafe operations on its varargs parameter. It can be applied only to constructors or methods that cannot be overridden (aka methods marked private, static, or final).

Let's review varargs for a minute. A varargs parameter is used to indicate the method may be passed zero or more values of the same type, by providing an ellipsis (...). In addition, a method can have at most one varargs parameter, and it must be listed last.

Returning to @SafeVargs, the annotation is used to indicate to other developers that your method does not perform any unsafe operations. It basically tells other developers, "Don't worry about the varargs parameter; I promise this method won't do anything bad with it!" It also suppresses unchecked compiler warnings for the varargs parameter.

In the following example, thisIsUnsafe() performs an unsafe operation using its varargs parameter:

```
1:   import java.util.*;
2:
3:   public class NeverDoThis {
4:       final int thisIsUnsafe(List<Integer>... carrot) {
5:           Object[] stick = carrot;
```

```
6:          stick[0] = Arrays.asList("nope!");
7:          return carrot[0].get(0);  // ClassCastException at runtime
8:      }
9:      public static void main(String[] a) {
10:         var carrot = new ArrayList<Integer>();
11:         new NeverDoThis().thisIsUnsafe(carrot);
12:     }
13: }
```

This code compiles, although it generates two compiler warnings. Both are related to type safety.

```
[Line 4]  Type safety: Potential heap pollution via varargs
   parameter carrot
[Line 11] Type safety: A generic array of List<Integer> is created
   for a varargs parameter
```

We can remove both compiler warnings by adding the @SafeVarargs annotation to line 4.

```
3:      @SafeVarargs final int thisIsUnsafe(List<Integer>... carrot) {
```

Did we actually fix the unsafe operation? No! It still throws a ClassCastException at runtime on line 7. However, we made it so the compiler won't warn us about it anymore.

For the exam you don't need to know how to create or resolve unsafe operations, as that can be complex. You just need to be able to identify unsafe operations and know they often involve generics.

You should also know the annotation can be applied only to methods that contain a varargs parameter and are not able to be overridden. For example, the following do not compile:

```
@SafeVarargs
public static void eat(int meal) {}        // DOES NOT COMPILE

@SafeVarargs
protected void drink(String... cup) {}      // DOES NOT COMPILE

@SafeVarargs void chew(boolean... food) {}  // DOES NOT COMPILE
```

The eat() method is missing a varargs parameter, while the drink() and chew() methods are not marked static, final, or private.

Reviewing Common Annotations

Table 13.5 lists the common annotations that you will need to know for the exam along with how they are structured.

TABLE 13.5 Understanding common annotations

Annotation	Marker annotation	Type of value()	Optional members
@Override	Yes	—	—
@FunctionalInterface	Yes	—	—
@Deprecated	No	—	String since() boolean forRemoval()
@SuppressWarnings	No	String[]	—
@SafeVarargs	Yes	—	—

Some of these annotations have special rules that will trigger a compiler error if used incorrectly, as shown in Table 13.6.

TABLE 13.6 Applying common annotations

Annotation	Applies to	Compiler error when
@Override	Methods	Method signature does not match the signature of an inherited method
@FunctionalInterface	Interfaces	Interface does not contain a single abstract method
@Deprecated	Most Java declarations	—
@SuppressWarnings	Most Java declarations	—
@SafeVarargs	Methods, constructors	Method or constructor does not contain a varargs parameter or is applied to a method not marked private, static, or final

While none of these annotations is required, they do improve the quality of your code. They also help prevent you from making a mistake.

Let's say you override a method but accidentally alter the signature so that the compiler considers it an overload. If you use the @Override annotation, then the compiler will immediately report the error, rather than finding it later during testing.

Real World Scenario

JavaBean Validation

This chapter covered only the annotations you need to know for the exam, but there are many incredibly useful annotations available.

If you've ever used JavaBeans to transmit data, then you've probably written code to validate it. While this can be cumbersome for large data structures, annotations allow you to mark `private` fields directly. The following are some useful `javax.validation` annotations:

- `@NotNull`: Object cannot be `null`

- `@NotEmpty`: Object cannot be `null` or have size of `0`

- `@Size(min=5,max=10)`: Sets minimum and/or maximum sizes

- `@Max(600)` and `@Min(-5)`: Sets the maximum or minimum numeric values

- `@Email`: Validates that the email is in a valid format

These annotations can be applied to a variety of data types. For example, when `@Size` is applied to a `String`, it checks the number of characters in the `String`. When applied to an array or `Collection`, it checks the number of elements present.

Of course, using the annotations is only half the story. The service receiving or processing the data needs to perform the validation step. In some frameworks like Spring Boot, this can be performed automatically by adding the `@Valid` annotation to a service parameter.

Summary

In this chapter, we taught you everything you need to know about annotations for the exam. Ideally, we also taught you how to create and use custom annotations in your daily programming life. As we mentioned early on, annotations are one of the most convenient tools available in the Java language.

For the exam, you need to know the structure of an annotation declaration, including how to declare required elements, optional elements, and constant variables. You also need to know how to apply an annotation properly and ensure required elements have values. You should also be familiar with the two shorthand notations we discussed in this chapter. The first allows you to drop the *elementName* under certain conditions. The second allows you to specify a single value for an array element without the array braces ({}).

You need to know about the various built-in annotations available in the Java language. We sorted these into two groups: annotations that apply to other annotations and common annotations. The annotation-specific annotations provide rules for how annotations are handled by the compiler, such as specifying an inheritance or retention policy. They can also be used to disallow certain usage, such as using a method-targeted annotation applied to a class declaration.

The second set of annotations are common ones that you should know for the exam. Many, like @Override and @FunctionalInterface, are quite useful and provide other developers with additional information about your application.

Exam Essentials

Be able to declare annotations with required elements, optional elements, and variables. An annotation is declared with the @interface type. It may include elements and public static final constant variables. If it does not include any elements, then it is a marker annotation. Optional elements are specified with a default keyword and value, while required elements are those specified without one.

Be able to identify where annotations can be applied. An annotation is applied using the at (@) symbol, followed by the annotation name. Annotations must include a value for each required element and can be applied to types, methods, constructors, and variables. They can also be used in cast operations, lambda expressions, or inside type declarations.

Understand how to apply an annotation without an element name. If an annotation contains an element named value() and does not contain any other elements that are required, then it can be used without the elementName. For it to be used properly, no other values may be passed.

Understand how to apply an annotation with a single-element array. If one of the annotation elements is a primitive array and the array is passed a single value, then the annotation value may be written without the array braces ({}).

Apply built-in annotations to other annotations. Java includes a number of annotations that apply to annotation declarations. The @Target annotation allows you to specify where an annotation can and cannot be used. The @Retention annotation allows you to specify at what level the annotation metadata is kept or discarded. @Documented is a marker annotation that allows you to specify whether annotation information is included in the generated documentation. @Inherited is another marker annotation that determines whether annotations are inherited from super types. The @Repeatable annotation allows you to list an annotation more than once on a single declaration. It requires a second containing type annotation to be declared.

Apply common annotations to various Java types.   Java includes many built-in annotations that apply to classes, methods, variables, and expressions. The @Override annotation is used to indicate that a method is overriding an inherited method. The @FunctionalInterface annotation confirms that an interface contains exactly one abstract method. Marking a type @Deprecated means that the compiler will generate a depreciation warning when it is referenced. Adding @SuppressWarnings with a set of values to a declaration causes the compiler to ignore the set of specified warnings. Adding @SafeVarargs on a constructor or private, static, or final method instructs other developers that no unsafe operations will be performed on its varargs parameter. While all of these annotations are optional, they are quite useful and improve the quality of code when used.

Review Questions

The answers to the chapter review questions can be found in the Appendix.

1. What modifier is used to mark that an annotation element is required?

   A. optional

   B. default

   C. required

   D. *

   E. None of the above

2. Which of the following lines of code do not compile? (Choose all that apply.)

   ```
   1: import java.lang.annotation.Documented;
   2: enum Color {GREY, BROWN}
   3: @Documented public @interface Dirt {
   4:    boolean wet();
   5:    String type() = "unknown";
   6:    public Color color();
   7:    private static final int slippery = 5;
   8: }
   ```

   A. Line 2

   B. Line 3

   C. Line 4

   D. Line 5

   E. Line 6

   F. Line 7

   G. All of the lines compile.

3. Which built-in annotations can be applied to an annotation declaration? (Choose all that apply.)

   A. @Override

   B. @Deprecated

   C. @Document

   D. @Target

   E. @Repeatable

   F. @Functional

4. Given an automobile sales system, which of the following information is best stored using an annotation?

   A. The price of the vehicle

   B. A list of people who purchased the vehicle

   C. The sales tax of the vehicle

   D. The number of passengers a vehicle is rated for

   E. The quantity of models in stock

5. Which of the following lines of code do not compile? (Choose all that apply.)

```
1: import java.lang.annotation.*;
2: class Food {}
3: @Inherited public @interface Unexpected {
4:    public String rsvp() default null;
5:    Food food();
6:    public String[] dessert();
7:    final int numberOfGuests = 5;
8:    long startTime() default 0L;
9: }
```

   A. Line 3

   B. Line 4

   C. Line 5

   D. Line 6

   E. Line 7

   F. Line 8

   G. All of the lines compile.

6. Which annotations, when applied independently, allow the following program to compile? (Choose all that apply.)

```
import java.lang.annotation.*;
@Documented @Deprecated
public @interface Driver {
   int[] directions();
   String name() default "";
}
_____ class Taxi {}
```

A. @Driver

B. @Driver(1)

C. @Driver(3,4)

D. @Driver({5,6})

E. @Driver(directions=7)

F. @Driver(directions=8,9)

G. @Driver(directions={0,1})

H. None of the above

7. Annotations can be applied to which of the following? (Choose all that apply.)

A. Class declarations

B. Constructor parameters

C. Local variable declarations

D. Cast operations

E. Lambda expression parameters

F. Interface declarations

G. None of the above

8. Fill in the blanks with the correct answers that allow the entire program to compile. (Choose all that apply.)

```
@interface FerociousPack {
    _____;          // m1
}


@Repeatable(_____)  // m2
public @interface Ferocious {}


@Ferocious @Ferocious class Lion {}
```

A. Ferocious value() on line m1.

B. Ferocious[] value() on line m1.

C. Object[] value() on line m1.

D. @FerociousPack on line m2.

E. FerociousPack on line m2.

F. FerociousPack.class on line m2.

G. None of the above. The code will not compile due to its use of the Lion class.

9. What properties must be true to use an annotation with an element value, but no element name? (Choose all that apply.)

   A. The element must be named `values()`.

   B. The element must be required.

   C. The annotation declaration must not contain any other elements.

   D. The annotation must not contain any other values.

   E. The element value must not be array.

   F. None of the above

10. Which statement about the following code is correct?

```
import java.lang.annotation.*;
@Target(ElementType.TYPE) public @interface Furry {
    public String[] value();
    boolean cute() default true;
}
class Bunny {
    @Furry("Soft") public static int hop() {
        return 1;
    }
}
```

   A. The code compiles without any changes.

   B. The code compiles only if the type of `value()` is changed to a `String` in the annotation declaration.

   C. The code compiles only if `cute()` is removed from the annotation declaration.

   D. The code compiles only if @Furry includes a value for `cute()`.

   E. The code compiles only if @Furry includes the element name for `value`.

   F. The code compiles only if the value in @Furry is changed to an array.

   G. None of the above

11. What properties of applying @SafeVarargs are correct? (Choose all that apply.)

   A. By applying the annotation, the compiler verifies that all operations on parameters are safe.

   B. The annotation can be applied to `abstract` methods.

   C. The annotation can be applied to method and constructor declarations.

   D. When the annotation is applied to a method, the method must contain a varargs parameter.

   E. The annotation can be applied to method and constructor parameters.

   F. The annotation can be applied to `static` methods.

12. Which of the following lines of code do not compile? (Choose all that apply.)

```
1: import java.lang.annotation.*;
2: enum UnitOfTemp { C, F }
3: @interface Snow { boolean value(); }
4: @Target(ElementType.METHOD) public @interface Cold {
5:     private Cold() {}
6:     int temperature;
7:     UnitOfTemp unit default UnitOfTemp.C;
8:     Snow snow() default @Snow(true);
9: }
```

- **A.** Line 4
- **B.** Line 5
- **C.** Line 6
- **D.** Line 7
- **E.** Line 8
- **F.** All of the lines compile.

13. Which statements about an optional annotation are correct? (Choose all that apply.)

- **A.** The annotation declaration always includes a default value.
- **B.** The annotation declaration may include a default value.
- **C.** The annotation always includes a value.
- **D.** The annotation may include a value.
- **E.** The annotation must not include a value.
- **F.** None of the above

14. Fill in the blanks: The _____ annotation determines whether annotations are discarded at runtime, while the ───────── annotation determines whether they are discarded in generated Javadoc.

- **A.** @Target, @Deprecated
- **B.** @Discard, @SuppressWarnings
- **C.** @Retention, @Generated
- **D.** @Retention, @Documented
- **E.** @Inherited, @Retention
- **F.** @Target, @Repeatable
- **G.** None of the above

15. What statement about marker annotations is correct?

    A. A marker annotation does not contain any elements or constant variables.

    B. A marker annotation does not contain any elements but may contain constant variables.

    C. A marker annotation does not contain any required elements but may include optional elements.

    D. A marker annotation does not contain any optional elements but may include required elements.

    E. A marker annotation can be extended.

16. Which options, when inserted into the blank in the code, allow the code to compile without any warnings? (Choose all that apply.)

```
import java.util.*;
import java.lang.annotation.*;
public class Donkey {

    _____

    public String kick(List... t) {
        t[0] = new ArrayList();
        t[0].add(1);
        return (String)t[0].get(0);
    }
}
```

    A. @SafeVarargs

    B. @SafeVarargs("unchecked")

    C. @Inherited

    D. @SuppressWarnings

    E. @SuppressWarnings("ignore")

    F. @SuppressWarnings("unchecked")

    G. None of the above

17. What motivations would a developer have for applying the @FunctionalInterface annotation to an interface? (Choose all that apply.)

    A. To allow the interface to be used in a lambda expression

    B. To provide documentation to other developers

    C. To allow the interface to be used as a method reference

    D. There is no reason to use this annotation.

    E. To trigger a compiler error if the annotation is used incorrectly

18. Which of the following lines of code do not compile? (Choose all that apply.)

```
1: @interface Strong {
2:    int force(); }
3: @interface Wind {
4:    public static final int temperature = 20;
5:    Boolean storm() default true;
6:    public void kiteFlying();
7:    protected String gusts();
8:    Strong power() default @Strong(10);
9: }
```

A. Line 2

B. Line 4

C. Line 5

D. Line 6

E. Line 7

F. Line 8

G. All of the lines compile.

19. Which annotations can be added to an existing method declaration but could cause a compiler error depending on the method signature? (Choose all that apply.)

A. @Override

B. @Deprecated

C. @FunctionalInterface

D. @Repeatable

E. @Retention

F. @SafeVarargs

20. Given the Floats annotation declaration, which lines in the Birch class contain compiler errors? (Choose all that apply.)

// Floats.java
```
import java.lang.annotation.*;
@Target(ElementType.TYPE_USE)
public @interface Floats {
    int buoyancy() default 2;
}
```

// Birch.java
```
1: import java.util.function.Predicate;
2: interface Wood {}
```

```
3: @Floats class Duck {}
4: @Floats
5: public class Birch implements @Floats Wood {
6:    @Floats(10) boolean mill() {
7:       Predicate<Integer> t = (@Floats Integer a) -> a > 10;
8:       return (@Floats) t.test(12);
9:    } }
```

- **A.** Line 3
- **B.** Line 4
- **C.** Line 5
- **D.** Line 6
- **E.** Line 7
- **F.** Line 8
- **G.** None of the above. All of the lines compile without issue.

21. Fill in the blanks: The _____ annotation determines what annotations from a super-class or interface are applied, while the _____ annotation determines what declarations an annotation can be applied to.

- **A.** @Target, @Retention
- **B.** @Inherited, @ElementType
- **C.** @Documented, @Deprecated
- **D.** @Target, @Generated
- **E.** @Repeatable, @Element
- **F.** @Inherited, @Retention
- **G.** None of the above

22. Which annotation can cancel out a warning on a method using the @Deprecated API at compile time?

- **A.** @FunctionalInterface
- **B.** @Ignore
- **C.** @IgnoreDeprecated
- **D.** @Retention
- **E.** @SafeVarargs
- **F.** @SuppressWarnings
- **G.** None of the above

23. The main() method in the following program reads the annotation value() of Plumber at runtime on each member of Team. It compiles and runs without any errors. Based on this, how many times is Mario printed at runtime?

```java
import java.lang.annotation.*;
import java.lang.reflect.Field;
@interface Plumber {
    String value() default "Mario";
}

public class Team {
    @Plumber("") private String foreman = "Mario";
    @Plumber private String worker = "Kelly";
    @Plumber("Kelly") private String trainee;

    public static void main(String[] args) {
        var t = new Team();
        var fields = t.getClass().getDeclaredFields();
        for (Field field : fields)
            if(field.isAnnotationPresent(Plumber.class))
                System.out.print(field.getAnnotation(Plumber.class)
                    .value());
    }
}
```

A. Zero

B. One

C. Two

D. Three

E. The answer cannot be determined until runtime.

24. Which annotations, when applied independently, allow the following program to compile? (Choose all that apply.)

```
public @interface Dance {
    long rhythm() default 66;
    int[] value();
    String track() default "";
    final boolean fast = true;
}
class Sing {
                    _____ String album;

}
```

A. @Dance(77)

B. @Dance(33, 10)

C. @Dance(value=5, rhythm=2, fast=false)

D. @Dance(5, rhythm=9)

E. @Dance(value=5, rhythm=2, track="Samba")

F. @Dance()

G. None of the above

25. When using the @Deprecated annotation, what other annotation should be used and why?

A. @repeatable, along with a containing type annotation

B. @retention, along with a location where the value should be discarded

C. @deprecated, along with a reason why and a suggested alternative

D. @SuppressWarnings, along with a cause

E. @Override, along with an inherited reference

Chapter 14

Generics and Collections

THE OCP EXAM TOPICS COVERED IN THIS CHAPTER INCLUDE THE FOLLOWING:

✓ **Generics and Collections**

- Use wrapper classes, autoboxing and autounboxing

- Create and use generic classes, methods with diamond notation and wildcards

- Describe the Collections Framework and use key collection interfaces

- Use Comparator and Comparable interfaces

- Create and use convenience methods for collections

✓ **Java Stream API**

- Use lambda expressions and method references

You learned the basics of the Java Collections Framework in Chapter 5, "Core Java APIs," along with generics and the basics of sorting. We will review these topics while diving into them more deeply.

First, we will cover how to use method references. After a review of autoboxing and unboxing, we will explore more classes and APIs in the Java Collections Framework. The thread-safe collection types will be discussed in Chapter 18, "Concurrency."

Next, we will cover details about Comparator and Comparable. Finally, we will discuss how to create your own classes and methods that use generics so that the same class can be used with many types.

As you may remember from Chapter 6, "Lambdas and Functional Interfaces," we presented functional interfaces like Predicate, Consumer, Function, and Supplier. We will review all of these functional interfaces in Chapter 15, "Functional Programming," but since some will be used in this chapter, we provide Table 14.1 as a handy reference. The letters (R, T, and U) are generics that you can pass any type to when using these functional interfaces.

TABLE 14.1   Functional interfaces used in this chapter

Functional interfaces	Return type	Method name	# parameters
Supplier<T>	T	get()	0
Consumer<T>	void	accept(T)	1 (T)
BiConsumer<T, U>	void	accept(T,U)	2 (T, U)
Predicate<T>	boolean	test(T)	1 (T)
BiPredicate<T, U>	boolean	test(T, U)	2 (T, U)
Function<T, R>	R	apply(T)	1 (T)
BiFunction<T, U, R>	R	apply(T,U)	2 (T, U)
UnaryOperator<T>	T	apply(T)	1 (T)

For this chapter, you can just use these functional interfaces as is. In the next chapter, though, we'll be presenting and testing your knowledge of them.

Using Method References

In Chapter 12, we went over lambdas and showed how they make code shorter. *Method references* are another way to make the code easier to read, such as simply mentioning the name of the method. Like lambdas, it takes time to get used to the new syntax.

In this section, we will show the syntax along with the four types of method references. We will also mix in lambdas with method references. If you'd like to review using lambdas, see Chapter 12. This will prepare you well for the next chapter, which uses both heavily.

Suppose we are coding a duckling who is trying to learn how to quack. First, we have a functional interface. As you'll recall from Chapter 12, this is an interface with exactly one abstract method.

```java
@FunctionalInterface
public interface LearnToSpeak {
    void speak(String sound);
}
```

Next, we discover that our duckling is lucky. There is a helper class that the duckling can work with. We've omitted the details of teaching the duckling how to quack and left the part that calls the functional interface.

```java
public class DuckHelper {
    public static void teacher(String name, LearnToSpeak trainer) {

        // exercise patience

        trainer.speak(name);
    }
}
```

Finally, it is time to put it all together and meet our little `Duckling`. This code implements the functional interface using a lambda:

```java
public class Duckling {
    public static void makeSound(String sound) {
        LearnToSpeak learner = s -> System.out.println(s);
        DuckHelper.teacher(sound, learner);
    }
}
```

Not bad. There's a bit of redundancy, though. The lambda declares one parameter named s. However, it does nothing other than pass that parameter to another method. A method reference lets us remove that redundancy and instead write this:

```
LearnToSpeak learner = System.out::println;
```

The :: operator tells Java to call the `println()` method later. It will take a little while to get used to the syntax. Once you do, you may find your code is shorter and less distracting without writing as many lambdas.

Remember that :: is like a lambda, and it is used for deferred execution with a functional interface.

A method reference and a lambda behave the same way at runtime. You can pretend the compiler turns your method references into lambdas for you.

There are four formats for method references:

- Static methods

- Instance methods on a particular instance

- Instance methods on a parameter to be determined at runtime

- Constructors

Let's take a brief look at each of these in turn. In each example, we will show the method reference and its lambda equivalent. We are going to use some built-in functional interfaces in these examples. We will remind you what they do right before each example. In Chapter 15, we will cover many such interfaces.

Calling Static Methods

The Collections class has a `static` method that can be used for sorting. Per Table 14.1, the Consumer functional interface takes one parameter and does not return anything. Here we will assign a method reference and a lambda to this functional interface:

```
14: Consumer<List<Integer>> methodRef = Collections::sort;
15: Consumer<List<Integer>> lambda = x -> Collections.sort(x);
```

On line 14, we reference a method with one parameter, and Java knows that it's like a lambda with one parameter. Additionally, Java knows to pass that parameter to the method.

Wait a minute. You might be aware that the `sort()` method is overloaded. How does Java know that we want to call the version with only one parameter? With both lambdas and method references, Java is inferring information from the context. In this case, we said that we were declaring a Consumer, which takes only one parameter. Java looks for a method that matches that description. If it can't find it or it finds multiple ones that could match multiple methods, then the compiler will report an error. The latter is sometimes called an *ambiguous* type error.

Calling Instance Methods on a Particular Object

The String class has a startsWith() method that takes one parameter and returns a boolean. Conveniently, a Predicate is a functional interface that takes one parameter and returns a boolean. Let's look at how to use method references with this code:

```
18: var str = "abc";
19: Predicate<String> methodRef = str::startsWith;
20: Predicate<String> lambda = s -> str.startsWith(s);
```

Line 19 shows that we want to call str.startsWith() and pass a single parameter to be supplied at runtime. This would be a nice way of filtering the data in a list. In fact, we will do that later in the chapter.

A method reference doesn't have to take any parameters. In this example, we use a Supplier, which takes zero parameters and returns a value:

```
var random = new Random();
Supplier<Integer> methodRef = random::nextInt;
Supplier<Integer> lambda = () -> random.nextInt();
```

Since the methods on Random are instance methods, we call the method reference on an instance of the Random class.

Calling Instance Methods on a Parameter

This time, we are going to call an instance method that doesn't take any parameters. The trick is that we will do so without knowing the instance in advance.

```
23: Predicate<String> methodRef = String::isEmpty;
24: Predicate<String> lambda = s -> s.isEmpty();
```

Line 23 says the method that we want to call is declared in String. It looks like a static method, but it isn't. Instead, Java knows that isEmpty() is an instance method that does not take any parameters. Java uses the parameter supplied at runtime as the instance on which the method is called.

Compare lines 23 and 24 with lines 19 and 20 of our instance example. They look similar, although one references a local variable named str, while the other only references the functional interface parameters.

You can even combine the two types of instance method references. We are going to use a functional interface called a BiPredicate, which takes two parameters and returns a boolean.

```
26: BiPredicate<String, String> methodRef = String::startsWith;
27: BiPredicate<String, String> lambda = (s, p) -> s.startsWith(p);
```

Since the functional interface takes two parameters, Java has to figure out what they represent. The first one will always be the instance of the object for instance methods. Any others are to be method parameters.

Remember that line 26 may look like a `static` method, but it is really a method reference declaring that the instance of the object will be specified later. Line 27 shows some of the power of a method reference. We were able to replace two lambda parameters this time.

Calling Constructors

A *constructor reference* is a special type of method reference that uses new instead of a method, and it instantiates an object. It is common for a constructor reference to use a `Supplier` as shown here:

```
30: Supplier<List<String>> methodRef = ArrayList::new;
31: Supplier<List<String>> lambda = () -> new ArrayList();
```

It expands like the method references you have seen so far. In the previous example, the lambda doesn't have any parameters.

Method references can be tricky. In our next example, we will use the `Function` functional interface, which takes one parameter and returns a result. Notice that line 32 in the following example has the same method reference as line 30 in the previous example:

```
32: Function<Integer, List<String>> methodRef = ArrayList::new;
33: Function<Integer, List<String>> lambda = x -> new ArrayList(x);
```

This means you can't always determine which method can be called by looking at the method reference. Instead, you have to look at the context to see what parameters are used and if there is a return type. In this example, Java sees that we are passing an `Integer` parameter and calls the constructor of `ArrayList` that takes a parameter.

Reviewing Method References

Reading method references is helpful in understanding the code. Table 14.2 shows the four types of method references. If this table doesn't make sense, please reread the previous section. It can take a few tries before method references start to make sense.

TABLE 14.2 Method references

Type	Before colon	After colon	Example
Static methods	Class name	Method name	`Collections::sort`
Instance methods on a particular object	Instance variable name	Method name	`str::startsWith`
Instance methods on a parameter	Class name	Method name	`String::isEmpty`
Constructor	Class name	new	`ArrayList::new`

Number of Parameters in a Method Reference

We mentioned that a method reference can look the same even when it will behave differently based on the surrounding context. For example, given the following method:

```java
public class Penguin {
    public static Integer countBabies(Penguin... cuties) {
        return cuties.length;
    }
}
```

we show three ways that Penguin::countBabies can be interpreted. This method allows you to pass zero or more values and creates an array with those values.

```java
10: Supplier<Integer> methodRef1 = Penguin::countBabies;
11: Supplier<Integer> lambda1 = () -> Penguin.countBabies();
12:
13: Function<Penguin, Integer> methodRef2 = Penguin::countBabies;
14: Function<Penguin, Integer> lambda2 = (x) -> Penguin.countBabies(x);
15:
16: BiFunction<Penguin, Penguin, Integer> methodRef3 = Penguin::countBabies;
17: BiFunction<Penguin, Penguin, Integer> lambda3 =
18:     (x, y) -> Penguin.countBabies(x, y);
```

Lines 10 and 11 do not take any parameters because the functional interface is a Supplier. Lines 13 and 14 take one parameter. Lines 16 and 17 take two parameters. All six lines return an Integer from the method reference or lambda.

There's nothing special about zero, one, and two parameters. If we had a functional interface with 100 parameters of type Penguin and the final one of Integer, we could still implement it with Penguin::countBabies.

Using Wrapper Classes

As you read in Chapter 5, each Java primitive has a corresponding wrapper class, shown in Table 14.3. With *autoboxing*, the compiler automatically converts a primitive to the corresponding wrapper. Unsurprisingly, *unboxing* is the process in which the compiler automatically converts a wrapper class back to a primitive.

TABLE 14.3 Wrapper classes

Primitive type	Wrapper class	Example of initializing
boolean	Boolean	Boolean.valueOf(true)
byte	Byte	Byte.valueOf((byte) 1)
short	Short	Short.valueOf((short) 1)
int	Integer	Integer.valueOf(1)
long	Long	Long.valueOf(1)
float	Float	Float.valueOf((float) 1.0)
double	Double	Double.valueOf(1.0)
char	Character	Character.valueOf('c')

Can you spot the autoboxing and unboxing in this example?

```
12: Integer pounds = 120;
13: Character letter = "robot".charAt(0);
14: char r = letter;
```

Line 12 is an example of autoboxing as the int primitive is autoboxed into an Integer object. Line 13 demonstrates that autoboxing can involve methods. The charAt() method returns a primitive char. It is then autoboxed into the wrapper object Character. Finally, line 14 shows an example of unboxing. The Character object is unboxed into a primitive char.

There are two tricks in the space of autoboxing and unboxing. The first has to do with null values. This innocuous-looking code throws an exception:

```
15: var heights = new ArrayList<Integer>();
16: heights.add(null);
17: int h = heights.get(0); // NullPointerException
```

On line 16, we add a null to the list. This is legal because a null reference can be assigned to any reference variable. On line 17, we try to unbox that null to an int primitive. This is a problem. Java tries to get the int value of null. Since calling any method on null gives a NullPointerException, that is just what we get. Be careful when you see null in relation to autoboxing.

Wrapper Classes and *null*

Speaking of null, one advantage of a wrapper class over a primitive is that it can hold a null value. While null values aren't particularly useful for numeric calculations, they are quite useful in data-based services. For example, if you are storing a user's location data using (latitude, longitude), it would be a bad idea to store a missing point as (0,0) since that refers to an actual location off the cost of Africa where the user could theoretically be.

Also, be careful when autoboxing into Integer. What do you think this code outputs?

```
23: List<Integer> numbers = new ArrayList<Integer>();
24: numbers.add(1);
25: numbers.add(Integer.valueOf(3));
26: numbers.add(Integer.valueOf(5));
27: numbers.remove(1);
28: numbers.remove(Integer.valueOf(5));
29: System.out.println(numbers);
```

It actually outputs [1]. Let's walk through why that is. On lines 24 through 26, we add three Integer objects to numbers. The one on line 24 relies on autoboxing to do so, but it gets added just fine. At this point, numbers contains [1, 3, 5].

Line 27 contains the second trick. The remove() method is overloaded. One signature takes an int as the index of the element to remove. The other takes an Object that should be removed. On line 27, Java sees a matching signature for int, so it doesn't need to autobox the call to the method. Now numbers contains [1, 5]. Line 28 calls the other remove() method, and it removes the matching object, which leaves us with just [1].

Using the Diamond Operator

In the past, we would write code using generics like the following:

```
List<Integer> list = new ArrayList<Integer>();
Map<String,Integer> map = new HashMap<String,Integer>();
```

You might even have generics that contain other generics, such as this:

```
Map<Long,List<Integer>> mapLists = new HashMap<Long,List<Integer>>();
```

That's a lot of duplicate code to write! We'll cover expressions later in this chapter where the generic types might not be the same, but often the generic types for both sides of the expression are identical.

Luckily, the diamond operator, <>, was added to the language. The diamond operator is a shorthand notation that allows you to omit the generic type from the right side of a statement when the type can be inferred. It is called the *diamond operator* because <> looks like a diamond. Compare the previous declarations with these new, much shorter versions:

```
List<Integer> list = new ArrayList<>();
Map<String,Integer> map = new HashMap<>();
Map<Long,List<Integer>> mapOfLists = new HashMap<>();
```

The first is the variable declaration and fully specifies the generic type. The second is an expression that infers the type from the assignment operator, using the diamond operator. To the compiler, both these declarations and our previous ones are equivalent. To us, though, the latter is a lot shorter and easier to read.

The diamond operator cannot be used as the type in a variable declaration. It can be used only on the right side of an assignment operation. For example, none of the following compiles:

```
List<> list = new ArrayList<Integer>();      // DOES NOT COMPILE
Map<> map = new HashMap<String, Integer>();  // DOES NOT COMPILE
class InvalidUse {
    void use(List<> data) {}                 // DOES NOT COMPILE
}
```

Since var is new to Java, let's look at the impact of using var with the diamond operator. Do you think these two statements compile and are equivalent?

```
var list = new ArrayList<Integer>();
var list = new ArrayList<>();
```

While they both compile, they are not equivalent. The first one creates an ArrayList<Integer> just like the prior set of examples. The second one creates an ArrayList<Object>. Since there is no generic type specified, it cannot be inferred. Java happily assumes you wanted Object in this scenario.

Using Lists, Sets, Maps, and Queues

A *collection* is a group of objects contained in a single object. The *Java Collections Framework* is a set of classes in java.util for storing collections. There are four main interfaces in the Java Collections Framework.

- **List:** A *list* is an ordered collection of elements that allows duplicate entries. Elements in a list can be accessed by an int index.

- **Set:** A *set* is a collection that does not allow duplicate entries.

- **Queue:** A *queue* is a collection that orders its elements in a specific order for processing. A typical queue processes its elements in a first-in, first-out order, but other orderings are possible.
- **Map:** A *map* is a collection that maps keys to values, with no duplicate keys allowed. The elements in a map are key/value pairs.

Figure 14.1 shows the Collection interface, its subinterfaces, and some classes that implement the interfaces that you should know for the exam. The interfaces are shown in rectangles, with the classes in rounded boxes.

FIGURE 14.1   The Collection interface is the root of all collections except maps.

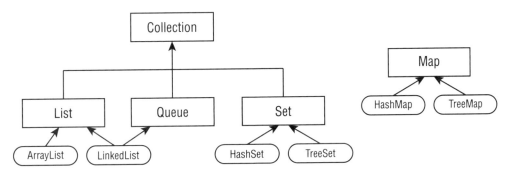

Notice that Map doesn't implement the Collection interface. It is considered part of the Java Collections Framework, even though it isn't technically a Collection. It is a collection (note the lowercase), though, in that it contains a group of objects. The reason why maps are treated differently is that they need different methods due to being key/value pairs.

We will first discuss the methods Collection provides to all implementing classes. Then we will cover the different types of collections, including when to use each one and the concrete subclasses. Then we will compare the different types.

Common Collections Methods

The Collection interface contains useful methods for working with lists, sets, and queues. In the following sections, we will discuss the most common ones. We will cover streams in the next chapter. Many of these methods are *convenience methods* that could be implemented in other ways but make your code easier to write and read. This is why they are convenient.

In this section, we use ArrayList and HashSet as our implementation classes, but they can apply to any class that inherits the Collection interface. We'll cover the specific properties of each Collection class in the next section.

add()

The add() method inserts a new element into the Collection and returns whether it was successful. The method signature is as follows:

```
boolean add(E element)
```

Remember that the Collections Framework uses generics. You will see E appear frequently. It means the generic type that was used to create the collection. For some Collection types, add() always returns true. For other types, there is logic as to whether the add() call was successful. The following shows how to use this method:

```
3: Collection<String> list = new ArrayList<>();
4: System.out.println(list.add("Sparrow")); // true
5: System.out.println(list.add("Sparrow")); // true
6:
7: Collection<String> set = new HashSet<>();
8: System.out.println(set.add("Sparrow")); // true
9: System.out.println(set.add("Sparrow")); // false
```

A List allows duplicates, making the return value true each time. A Set does not allow duplicates. On line 9, we tried to add a duplicate so that Java returns false from the add() method.

remove()

The remove() method removes a single matching value in the Collection and returns whether it was successful. The method signature is as follows:

```
boolean remove(Object object)
```

This time, the boolean return value tells us whether a match was removed. The following shows how to use this method:

```
3: Collection<String> birds = new ArrayList<>();
4: birds.add("hawk");                              // [hawk]
5: birds.add("hawk");                              // [hawk, hawk]
6: System.out.println(birds.remove("cardinal")); // false
7: System.out.println(birds.remove("hawk"));      // true
8: System.out.println(birds);                      // [hawk]
```

Line 6 tries to remove an element that is not in birds. It returns false because no such element is found. Line 7 tries to remove an element that is in birds, so it returns true. Notice that it removes only one match.

Since calling remove() on a List with an int uses the index, an index that doesn't exist will throw an exception. For example, birds.remove(100); throws an IndexOutOfBoundsException. Remember that there are overloaded remove() methods. One takes the element to remove. The other takes the index of the element to remove. The latter is being called here.

Deleting while Looping

Java does not allow removing elements from a list while using the enhanced for loop.

```
Collection<String> birds = new ArrayList<>();
birds.add("hawk");
birds.add("hawk");
birds.add("hawk");

for (String bird : birds) // ConcurrentModificationException
   birds.remove(bird);
```

Wait a minute. Concurrent modification? We don't get to concurrency until Chapter 18. That's right. It is possible to get a ConcurrentModificationException without threads. This is Java's way of complaining that you are trying to modify the list while looping through it. In Chapter 18, we'll return to this example and show how to fix it with the CopyOnWriteArrayList class.

---

isEmpty() and size()

The isEmpty() and size() methods look at how many elements are in the Collection. The method signatures are as follows:

```
boolean isEmpty()
int size()
```

The following shows how to use these methods:

```
Collection<String> birds = new ArrayList<>();
System.out.println(birds.isEmpty()); // true
System.out.println(birds.size());    // 0
birds.add("hawk");                   // [hawk]
birds.add("hawk");                   // [hawk, hawk]
System.out.println(birds.isEmpty()); // false
System.out.println(birds.size());    // 2
```

At the beginning, birds has a size of 0 and is empty. It has a capacity that is greater than 0. After we add elements, the size becomes positive, and it is no longer empty.

clear()

The clear() method provides an easy way to discard all elements of the Collection. The method signature is as follows:

```
void clear()
```

The following shows how to use this method:

```
Collection<String> birds = new ArrayList<>();
birds.add("hawk");                      // [hawk]
birds.add("hawk");                      // [hawk, hawk]
System.out.println(birds.isEmpty());   // false
System.out.println(birds.size());       // 2
birds.clear();                          // []
System.out.println(birds.isEmpty());   // true
System.out.println(birds.size());       // 0
```

After calling clear(), birds is back to being an empty ArrayList of size 0.

contains()

The contains() method checks whether a certain value is in the Collection. The method signature is as follows:

```
boolean contains(Object object)
```

The following shows how to use this method:

```
Collection<String> birds = new ArrayList<>();
birds.add("hawk"); // [hawk]
System.out.println(birds.contains("hawk"));   // true
System.out.println(birds.contains("robin")); // false
```

The contains() method calls equals() on elements of the ArrayList to see whether there are any matches.

removeIf()

The removeIf() method removes all elements that match a condition. We can specify what should be deleted using a block of code or even a method reference.

The method signature looks like the following. (We will explain what the ? super means in the "Working with Generics" section later in this chapter.)

```
boolean removeIf(Predicate<? super E> filter)
```

It uses a Predicate, which takes one parameter and returns a boolean. Let's take a look at an example:

```
4: Collection<String> list = new ArrayList<>();
5: list.add("Magician");
6: list.add("Assistant");
7: System.out.println(list);      // [Magician, Assistant]
8: list.removeIf(s -> s.startsWith("A"));
9: System.out.println(list);      // [Magician]
```

Line 8 shows how to remove all of the String values that begin with the letter A. This allows us to make the Assistant disappear.

How would you replace line 8 with a method reference? Trick question—you can't. The removeIf() method takes a Predicate. We can pass only one value with this method reference. Since startsWith takes a literal, it needs to be specified "the long way."

Let's try one more example that does use a method reference.

```
11: Collection<String> set = new HashSet<>();
12: set.add("Wand");
13: set.add("");
14: set.removeIf(String::isEmpty); // s -> s.isEmpty()
15: System.out.println(set);        // [Wand]
```

On line 14, we remove any empty String objects from the set. The comment on that line shows the lambda equivalent of the method reference. Line 15 shows that the removeIf() method successfully removed one element from the list.

forEach()

Looping through a Collection is common. On the 1Z0-815 exam, you wrote lots of loops. There's also a forEach() method that you can call on a Collection. It uses a Consumer that takes a single parameter and doesn't return anything. The method signature is as follows:

```
void forEach(Consumer<? super T> action)
```

Cats like to explore, so let's print out two of them using both method references and streams.

```
Collection<String> cats = Arrays.asList("Annie", "Ripley");
cats.forEach(System.out::println);
cats.forEach(c -> System.out.println(c));
```

The cats have discovered how to print their names. Now they have more time to play (as do we)!

Using the *List* Interface

Now that you're familiar with some common Collection interface methods, let's move on to specific classes. You use a list when you want an ordered collection that can contain duplicate entries. Items can be retrieved and inserted at specific positions in the list based on an int index much like an array. Unlike an array, though, many List implementations can change in size after they are declared.

Lists are commonly used because there are many situations in programming where you need to keep track of a list of objects.

For example, you might make a list of what you want to see at the zoo: First, see the lions because they go to sleep early. Second, see the pandas because there is a long line later in the day. And so forth.

Figure 14.2 shows how you can envision a List. Each element of the List has an index, and the indexes begin with zero.

FIGURE 14.2 Example of a List

List

Ordered Index	Data
0	lions
1	pandas
2	zebras
...	...

Sometimes, you don't actually care about the order of elements in a list. List is like the "go to" data type. When we make a shopping list before going to the store, the order of the list happens to be the order in which we thought of the items. We probably aren't attached to that particular order, but it isn't hurting anything.

While the classes implementing the List interface have many methods, you need to know only the most common ones. Conveniently, these methods are the same for all of the implementations that might show up on the exam.

The main thing that all List implementations have in common is that they are ordered and allow duplicates. Beyond that, they each offer different functionality. We will look at the implementations that you need to know and the available methods.

> Pay special attention to which names are classes and which are interfaces. The exam may ask you which is the best class or which is the best interface for a scenario.

Comparing *List* Implementations

An ArrayList is like a resizable array. When elements are added, the ArrayList automatically grows. When you aren't sure which collection to use, use an ArrayList.

The main benefit of an ArrayList is that you can look up any element in constant time. Adding or removing an element is slower than accessing an element. This makes an ArrayList a good choice when you are reading more often than (or the same amount as) writing to the ArrayList.

A LinkedList is special because it implements both List and Queue. It has all the methods of a List. It also has additional methods to facilitate adding or removing from the beginning and/or end of the list.

The main benefits of a LinkedList are that you can access, add, and remove from the beginning and end of the list in constant time. The trade-off is that dealing with an arbitrary index takes linear time. This makes a LinkedList a good choice when you'll be using it as Queue. As you saw in Figure 14.1, a LinkedList implements both the List and Queue interface.

Creating a *List* with a Factory

When you create a List of type ArrayList or LinkedList, you know the type. There are a few special methods where you get a List back but don't know the type. These methods let you create a List including data in one line using a factory method. This is convenient, especially when testing. Some of these methods return an immutable object. As we saw in Chapter 12, an immutable object cannot be changed or modified. Table 14.4 summarizes these three lists.

TABLE 14.4 Factory methods to create a List

Method	Description	Can add elements?	Can replace element?	Can delete elements?
Arrays .asList(varargs)	Returns fixed size list backed by an array	No	Yes	No
List.of(varargs)	Returns immutable list	No	No	No
List .copyOf(collection)	Returns immutable list with copy of original collection's values	No	No	No

Let's take a look at an example of these three methods.

```
16: String[] array = new String[] {"a", "b", "c"};
17: List<String> asList = Arrays.asList(array); // [a, b, c]
18: List<String> of = List.of(array);          // [a, b, c]
19: List<String> copy = List.copyOf(asList);    // [a, b, c]
20:
21: array[0] = "z";
22:
23: System.out.println(asList); // [z, b, c]
24: System.out.println(of);     // [a, b, c]
25: System.out.println(copy);   // [a, b, c]
26:
27: asList.set(0, "x");
28: System.out.println(Arrays.toString(array)); // [x, b, c]
29:
30: copy.add("y");  // throws UnsupportedOperationException
```

Line 17 creates a List that is backed by an array. Line 21 changes the array, and line 23 reflects that change. Lines 27 and 28 show the other direction where changing the List updates the underlying array. Lines 18 and 19 create an immutable List. Line 30 shows it is immutable by throwing an exception when trying to add a value. All three lists would throw an exception when adding or removing a value. The of and copy lists would also throw one on trying to update a reference.

Working with *List* Methods

The methods in the List interface are for working with indexes. In addition to the inherited Collection methods, the method signatures that you need to know are in Table 14.5.

TABLE 14.5 List methods

Method	Description
boolean add(E element)	Adds element to end (available on all Collection APIs)
void add(int index, E element)	Adds element at index and moves the rest toward the end
E get(int index)	Returns element at index
E remove(int index)	Removes element at index and moves the rest toward the front
void replaceAll (UnaryOperator<E> op)	Replaces each element in the list with the result of the operator
E set(int index, E e)	Replaces element at index and returns original. Throws IndexOutOfBoundsException if the index is larger than the maximum one set

The following statements demonstrate most of these methods for working with a List:

```
3:  List<String> list = new ArrayList<>();
4:  list.add("SD");                      // [SD]
5:  list.add(0, "NY");                   // [NY,SD]
6:  list.set(1, "FL");                   // [NY,FL]
7:  System.out.println(list.get(0));     // NY
8:  list.remove("NY");                   // [FL]
9:  list.remove(0);                      // []
10: list.set(0, "?");                    // IndexOutOfBoundsException
```

On line 3, list starts out empty. Line 4 adds an element to the end of the list. Line 5 adds an element at index 0 that bumps the original index 0 to index 1. Notice how the ArrayList is now automatically one larger. Line 6 replaces the element at index 1 with a new value.

Line 7 uses the get() method to print the element at a specific index. Line 8 removes the element matching NY. Finally, line 9 removes the element at index 0, and list is empty again.

Line 10 throws an IndexOutOfBoundsException because there are no elements in the List. Since there are no elements to replace, even index 0 isn't allowed. If line 10 were moved up between lines 4 and 5, the call would have succeeded.

The output would be the same if you tried these examples with LinkedList. Although the code would be less efficient, it wouldn't be noticeable until you have very large lists.

Now, let's look at using the replaceAll() method. It takes a UnaryOperator that takes one parameter and returns a value of the same type.

```
List<Integer> numbers = Arrays.asList(1, 2, 3);
numbers.replaceAll(x -> x*2);
System.out.println(numbers);    // [2, 4, 6]
```

This lambda doubles the value of each element in the list. The replaceAll() method calls the lambda on each element of the list and replaces the value at that index.

Iterating through a List

There are many ways to iterate through a list. For example, in Chapter 4, "Making Decisions," you saw how to loop through a list using an enhanced for loop.

```
for (String string: list) {
    System.out.println(string);
}
```

You may see another approach used.

```
Iterator<String> iter = list.iterator();
while(iter.hasNext()) {
    String string = iter.next();
    System.out.println(string);
}
```

Pay attention to the difference between these techniques. The hasNext() method checks whether there is a next value. In other words, it tells you whether next() will execute without throwing an exception. The next() method actually moves the Iterator to the next element.

Using the *Set* Interface

You use a set when you don't want to allow duplicate entries. For example, you might want to keep track of the unique animals that you want to see at the zoo. You aren't concerned with the order in which you see these animals, but there isn't time to see them more than once. You just want to make sure you see the ones that are important to you and remove them from the set of outstanding animals to see after you see them.

Figure 14.3 shows how you can envision a Set. The main thing that all Set implementations have in common is that they do not allow duplicates. We will look at each implementation that you need to know for the exam and how to write code using Set.

FIGURE 14.3   Example of a Set

Comparing *Set* Implementations

A HashSet stores its elements in a *hash table*, which means the keys are a hash and the values are an Object. This means that it uses the hashCode() method of the objects to retrieve them more efficiently.

The main benefit is that adding elements and checking whether an element is in the set both have constant time. The trade-off is that you lose the order in which you inserted the elements. Most of the time, you aren't concerned with this in a set anyway, making HashSet the most common set.

A TreeSet stores its elements in a sorted tree structure. The main benefit is that the set is always in sorted order. The trade-off is that adding and checking whether an element exists take longer than with a HashSet, especially as the tree grows larger.

Figure 14.4 shows how you can envision HashSet and TreeSet being stored. HashSet is more complicated in reality, but this is fine for the purpose of the exam.

Working with *Set* Methods

Like List, you can create an immutable Set in one line or make a copy of an existing one.

```
Set<Character> letters = Set.of('z', 'o', 'o');
Set<Character> copy = Set.copyOf(letters);
```

FIGURE 14.4   Examples of a HashSet and TreeSet

hashCode() Value	Data
−995544615	pandas
...	
−705903059	zebras
...	
102978519	lions

Those are the only extra methods you need to know for the Set interface for the exam! You do have to know how sets behave with respect to the traditional Collection methods. You also have to know the differences between the types of sets. Let's start with HashSet:

```
3: Set<Integer> set = new HashSet<>();
4: boolean b1 = set.add(66);    // true
5: boolean b2 = set.add(10);    // true
6: boolean b3 = set.add(66);    // false
7: boolean b4 = set.add(8);     // true
8: set.forEach(System.out::println);
```

This code prints three lines:

```
66
8
10
```

The add() methods should be straightforward. They return true unless the Integer is already in the set. Line 6 returns false, because we already have 66 in the set and a set must preserve uniqueness. Line 8 prints the elements of the set in an arbitrary order. In this case, it happens not to be sorted order, or the order in which we added the elements.

Remember that the equals() method is used to determine equality. The hashCode() method is used to know which bucket to look in so that Java doesn't have to look through the whole set to find out whether an object is there. The best case is that hash codes are unique, and Java has to call equals() on only one object. The worst case is that all implementations return the same hashCode(), and Java has to call equals() on every element of the set anyway.

Now let's look at the same example with TreeSet.

```
3: Set<Integer> set = new TreeSet<>();
4: boolean b1 = set.add(66); // true
5: boolean b2 = set.add(10); // true
```

```
6: boolean b3 = set.add(66); // false
7: boolean b4 = set.add(8);  // true
8: set.forEach(System.out::println);
```

This time, the code prints the following:

```
8
10
66
```

The elements are printed out in their natural sorted order. Numbers implement the Comparable interface in Java, which is used for sorting. Later in the chapter, you will learn how to create your own Comparable objects.

Using the *Queue* Interface

You use a queue when elements are added and removed in a specific order. Queues are typically used for sorting elements prior to processing them. For example, when you want to buy a ticket and someone is waiting in line, you get in line behind that person. And if you are British, you get in the queue behind that person, making this really easy to remember!

Unless stated otherwise, a queue is assumed to be *FIFO* (first-in, first-out). Some queue implementations change this to use a different order. You can envision a FIFO queue as shown in Figure 14.5. The other format is *LIFO* (last-in, first-out), which is commonly referred to as a *stack*. In Java, though, both can be implemented with the Queue interface.

FIGURE 14.5 Example of a Queue

Since this is a FIFO queue, Rover is first, which means he was the first one to arrive. Bella is last, which means she was last to arrive and has the longest wait remaining. All queues have specific requirements for adding and removing the next element. Beyond that, they each offer different functionality. We will look at the implementations that you need to know and the available methods.

Comparing *Queue* Implementations

You saw LinkedList earlier in the List section. In addition to being a list, it is a double-ended queue. A double-ended queue is different from a regular queue in that you can insert and remove elements from both the front and back of the queue. Think, "Mr. Woodie Flowers, come right to the front. You are the only one who gets this special treatment. Everyone else will have to start at the back of the line."

The main benefit of a LinkedList is that it implements both the List and Queue interfaces. The trade-off is that it isn't as efficient as a "pure" queue. You can use the ArrayDeque class (short for double-ended queue) if you need a more efficient queue. However, ArrayDeque is not in scope for the exam.

Working with *Queue* Methods

The Queue interface contains many methods. Luckily, there are only six methods that you need to focus on. These methods are shown in Table 14.6.

TABLE 14.6   Queue methods

Method	Description	Throws exception on failure
boolean add(E e)	Adds an element to the back of the queue and returns true or throws an exception	Yes
E element()	Returns next element or throws an exception if empty queue	Yes
boolean offer(E e)	Adds an element to the back of the queue and returns whether successful	No
E remove()	Removes and returns next element or throws an exception if empty queue	Yes
E poll()	Removes and returns next element or returns null if empty queue	No
E peek()	Returns next element or returns null if empty queue	No

As you can see, there are basically two sets of methods. One set throws an exception when something goes wrong. The other uses a different return value when something goes wrong. The offer()/poll()/peek() methods are more common. This is the standard language people use when working with queues.

Let's look at an example that uses some of these methods.

```
12: Queue<Integer> queue = new LinkedList<>();
13: System.out.println(queue.offer(10)); // true
14: System.out.println(queue.offer(4));  // true
15: System.out.println(queue.peek());    // 10
```

```
16: System.out.println(queue.poll());    // 10
17: System.out.println(queue.poll());    // 4
18: System.out.println(queue.peek());    // null
```

Figure 14.6 shows what the queue looks like at each step of the code. Lines 13 and 14 successfully add an element to the end of the queue. Some queues are limited in size, which would cause offering an element to the queue to fail. You won't encounter a scenario like that on the exam. Line 15 looks at the first element in the queue, but it does not remove it. Lines 16 and 17 actually remove the elements from the queue, which results in an empty queue. Line 18 tries to look at the first element of a queue, which results in null.

FIGURE 14.6   Working with a queue

Using the *Map* Interface

You use a map when you want to identify values by a key. For example, when you use the contact list in your phone, you look up "George" rather than looking through each phone number in turn.

You can envision a Map as shown in Figure 14.7. You don't need to know the names of the specific interfaces that the different maps implement, but you do need to know that TreeMap is sorted.

The main thing that all Map classes have in common is that they all have keys and values. Beyond that, they each offer different functionality. We will look at the implementations that you need to know and the available methods.

FIGURE 14.7   Example of a Map

Map

Key	Value
George	555-555-5555
May	777-777-7777

Map.of() and *Map.copyOf()*

Just like List and Set, there is a helper method to create a Map. You pass any number of pairs of keys and values.

```
Map.of("key1", "value1", "key2", "value2");
```

Unlike List and Set, this is less than ideal. Suppose you miscount and leave out a value.

```
Map.of("key1", "value1", "key2"); // INCORRECT
```

This code compiles but throws an error at runtime. Passing keys and values is also harder to read because you have to keep track of which parameter is which. Luckily, there is a better way. Map also provides a method that lets you supply key/value pairs.

```
Map.ofEntries(
    Map.entry("key1", "value1"),
    Map.entry("key1", "value1"));
```

Now we can't forget to pass a value. If we leave out a parameter, the entry() method won't compile. Conveniently, Map.copyOf(map) works just like the List and Set interface copyOf() methods.

Comparing *Map* Implementations

A HashMap stores the keys in a hash table. This means that it uses the hashCode() method of the keys to retrieve their values more efficiently.

The main benefit is that adding elements and retrieving the element by key both have constant time. The trade-off is that you lose the order in which you inserted the elements. Most of the time, you aren't concerned with this in a map anyway. If you were, you could use LinkedHashMap, but that's not in scope for the exam.

A TreeMap stores the keys in a sorted tree structure. The main benefit is that the keys are always in sorted order. Like a TreeSet, the trade-off is that adding and checking whether a key is present takes longer as the tree grows larger.

Working with *Map* Methods

Given that Map doesn't extend Collection, there are more methods specified on the Map interface. Since there are both keys and values, we need generic type parameters for both. The class uses K for key and V for value. The methods you need to know for the exam are in Table 14.7. Some of the method signatures are simplified to make them easier to understand.

TABLE 14.7 Map methods

Method	Description
void clear()	Removes all keys and values from the map.
boolean containsKey (Object key)	Returns whether key is in map.
boolean containsValue (Object value)	Returns whether value is in map.
Set<Map.Entry<K,V>> entrySet()	Returns a Set of key/value pairs.
void forEach(BiConsumer(K key, V value))	Loop through each key/value pair.
V get(Object key)	Returns the value mapped by key or null if none is mapped.
V getOrDefault(Object key, V defaultValue)	Returns the value mapped by the key or the default value if none is mapped.
boolean isEmpty()	Returns whether the map is empty.
Set<K> keySet()	Returns set of all keys.
V merge(K key, V value, Function(<V, V, V> func))	Sets value if key not set. Runs the function if the key is set to determine the new value. Removes if null.
V put(K key, V value)	Adds or replaces key/value pair. Returns previous value or null.
V putIfAbsent(K key, V value)	Adds value if key not present and returns null. Otherwise, returns existing value.
V remove(Object key)	Removes and returns value mapped to key. Returns null if none.

Method	Description
V replace(K key, V value)	Replaces the value for a given key if the key is set. Returns the original value or null if none.
void replaceAll (BiFunction<K, V, V> func)	Replaces each value with the results of the function.
int size()	Returns the number of entries (key/value pairs) in the map.
Collection<V> values()	Returns Collection of all values.

Basic Methods

Let's start out by comparing the same code with two Map types. First up is HashMap.

```
Map<String, String> map = new HashMap<>();
map.put("koala", "bamboo");
map.put("lion", "meat");
map.put("giraffe", "leaf");
String food = map.get("koala"); // bamboo
for (String key: map.keySet())
    System.out.print(key + ","); // koala,giraffe,lion,
```

Here we set the put() method to add key/value pairs to the map and get() to get a value given a key. We also use the keySet() method to get all the keys.

Java uses the hashCode() of the key to determine the order. The order here happens to not be sorted order, or the order in which we typed the values. Now let's look at TreeMap.

```
Map<String, String> map = new TreeMap<>();
map.put("koala", "bamboo");
map.put("lion", "meat");
map.put("giraffe", "leaf");
String food = map.get("koala"); // bamboo
for (String key: map.keySet())
    System.out.print(key + ","); // giraffe,koala,lion,
```

TreeMap sorts the keys as we would expect. If we were to have called values() instead of keySet(), the order of the values would correspond to the order of the keys.

With our same map, we can try some boolean checks.

```
System.out.println(map.contains("lion")); // DOES NOT COMPILE
System.out.println(map.containsKey("lion")); // true
System.out.println(map.containsValue("lion")); // false
System.out.println(map.size()); // 3
map.clear();
System.out.println(map.size()); // 0
System.out.println(map.isEmpty()); // true
```

The first line is a little tricky. The contains() method is on the Collection interface but not the Map interface. The next two lines show that keys and values are checked separately. We can see that there are three key/value pairs in our map. Then we clear out the contents of the map and see there are zero elements and it is empty.

In the following sections, we show Map methods you might not be as familiar with.

forEach() and entrySet()

You saw the forEach() method earlier in the chapter. Note that it works a little differently on a Map. This time, the lambda used by the forEach() method has two parameters; the key and the value. Let's look at an example, shown here:

```
Map<Integer, Character> map = new HashMap<>();
map.put(1, 'a');
map.put(2, 'b');
map.put(3, 'c');
map.forEach((k, v) -> System.out.println(v));
```

The lambda has both the key and value as the parameters. It happens to print out the value but could do anything with the key and/or value. Interestingly, if you don't care about the key, this particular code could have been written with the values() method and a method reference instead.

```
map.values().forEach(System.out::println);
```

Another way of going through all the data in a map is to get the key/value pairs in a Set. Java has a static interface inside Map called Entry. It provides methods to get the key and value of each pair.

```
map.entrySet().forEach(e ->
    System.out.println(e.getKey() + e.getValue()));
```

getOrDefault()

The get() method returns null if the requested key is not in map. Sometimes you prefer to have a different value returned. Luckily, the getOrDefault() method makes this easy. Let's compare the two methods.

```
3: Map<Character, String> map = new HashMap<>();
4: map.put('x', "spot");
```

```
5: System.out.println("X marks the " + map.get('x'));
6: System.out.println("X marks the " + map.getOrDefault('x', ""));
7: System.out.println("Y marks the " + map.get('y'));
8: System.out.println("Y marks the " + map.getOrDefault('y', ""));
```

This code prints the following:

```
X marks the spot
X marks the spot
Y marks the null
Y marks the
```

As you can see, lines 5 and 6 have the same output because get() and getOrDefault() behave the same way when the key is present. They return the value mapped by that key. Lines 7 and 8 give different output, showing that get() returns null when the key is not present. By contrast, getOrDefault() returns the empty string we passed as a parameter.

replace() and replaceAll()

These methods are similar to the Collection version except a key is involved.

```
21: Map<Integer, Integer> map = new HashMap<>();
22: map.put(1, 2);
23: map.put(2, 4);
24: Integer original = map.replace(2, 10); // 4
25: System.out.println(map);     // {1=2, 2=10}
26: map.replaceAll((k, v) -> k + v);
27: System.out.println(map);     // {1=3, 2=12}
```

Line 24 replaces the value for key 2 and returns the original value. Line 26 calls a function and sets the value of each element of the map to the result of that function. In our case, we added the key and value together.

putIfAbsent()

The putIfAbsent() method sets a value in the map but skips it if the value is already set to a non-null value.

```
Map<String, String> favorites = new HashMap<>();
favorites.put("Jenny", "Bus Tour");
favorites.put("Tom", null);
favorites.putIfAbsent("Jenny", "Tram");
favorites.putIfAbsent("Sam", "Tram");
favorites.putIfAbsent("Tom", "Tram");
System.out.println(favorites); // {Tom=Tram, Jenny=Bus Tour, Sam=Tram}
```

As you can see, Jenny's value is not updated because one was already present. Sam wasn't there at all, so he was added. Tom was present as a key but had a null value. Therefore, he was added as well.

merge()

The merge() method adds logic of what to choose. Suppose we want to choose the ride with the longest name. We can write code to express this by passing a mapping function to the merge() method.

```
11: BiFunction<String, String, String> mapper = (v1, v2)
12:    -> v1.length() > v2.length() ? v1: v2;
13:
14: Map<String, String> favorites = new HashMap<>();
15: favorites.put("Jenny", "Bus Tour");
16: favorites.put("Tom", "Tram");
17:
18: String jenny = favorites.merge("Jenny", "Skyride", mapper);
19: String tom = favorites.merge("Tom", "Skyride", mapper);
20:
21: System.out.println(favorites); // {Tom=Skyride, Jenny=Bus Tour}
22: System.out.println(jenny);     // Bus Tour
23: System.out.println(tom);       // Skyride
```

The code on lines 11 and 12 take two parameters and returns a value. Our implementation returns the one with the longest name. Line 18 calls this mapping function, and it sees that Bus Tour is longer than Skyride, so it leaves the value as Bus Tour. Line 19 calls this mapping function again. This time, Tram is not longer than Skyride, so the map is updated. Line 21 prints out the new map contents. Lines 22 and 23 show that the result gets returned from merge().

The merge() method also has logic for what happens if null values or missing keys are involved. In this case, it doesn't call the BiFunction at all, and it simply uses the new value.

```
BiFunction<String, String, String> mapper =
   (v1, v2) -> v1.length() > v2.length() ? v1 : v2;
Map<String, String> favorites = new HashMap<>();
favorites.put("Sam", null);
favorites.merge("Tom", "Skyride", mapper);
favorites.merge("Sam", "Skyride", mapper);
System.out.println(favorites);   // {Tom=Skyride, Sam=Skyride}
```

Notice that the mapping function isn't called. If it were, we'd have a NullPointerException. The mapping function is used only when there are two actual values to decide between.

The final thing to know about merge() is what happens when the mapping function is called and returns null. The key is removed from the map when this happens:

```
BiFunction<String, String, String> mapper = (v1, v2) -> null;
Map<String, String> favorites = new HashMap<>();
favorites.put("Jenny", "Bus Tour");
favorites.put("Tom", "Bus Tour");
```

```
favorites.merge("Jenny", "Skyride", mapper);
favorites.merge("Sam", "Skyride", mapper);
System.out.println(favorites);    // {Tom=Bus Tour, Sam=Skyride}
```

Tom was left alone since there was no merge() call for that key. Sam was added since that key was not in the original list. Jenny was removed because the mapping function returned null.

Table 14.8 shows all of these scenarios as a reference.

TABLE 14.8   Behavior of the merge() method

If the requested key _____	And mapping function returns _____	Then:
Has a null value in map	N/A (mapping function not called)	Update key's value in map with value parameter.
Has a non-null value in map	null	Remove key from map.
Has a non-null value in map	A non-null value	Set key to mapping function result.
Is not in map	N/A (mapping function not called)	Add key with value parameter to map directly without calling mapping function.

Comparing Collection Types

We conclude this section with a review of all the collection classes. Make sure that you can fill in Table 14.9 to compare the four collections types from memory.

TABLE 14.9   Java Collections Framework types

Type	Can contain duplicate elements?	Elements always ordered?	Has keys and values?	Must add/remove in specific order?
List	Yes	Yes (by index)	No	No
Map	Yes (for values)	No	Yes	No
Queue	Yes	Yes (retrieved in defined order)	No	Yes
Set	No	No	No	No

Additionally, make sure you can fill in Table 14.10 to describe the types on the exam.

TABLE 14.10   Collection attributes

Type	Java Collections Framework interface	Sorted?	Calls hashCode?	Calls compareTo?
ArrayList	List	No	No	No
HashMap	Map	No	Yes	No
HashSet	Set	No	Yes	No
LinkedList	List, Queue	No	No	No
TreeMap	Map	Yes	No	Yes
TreeSet	Set	Yes	No	Yes

Next, the exam expects you to know which data structures allow null values. The data structures that involve sorting do not allow null values.

Finally, the exam expects you to be able to choose the right collection type given a description of a problem. We recommend first identifying which type of collection the question is asking about. Figure out whether you are looking for a list, map, queue, or set. This lets you eliminate a number of answers. Then you can figure out which of the remaining choices is the best answer.

 Real World Scenario

Older Collections

There are a few collections that are no longer on the exam that you might come across in older code. All three were early Java data structures you could use with threads. In Chapter 18, you'll learn about modern alternatives if you need a concurrent collection.

- **Vector**: Implements List. If you don't need concurrency, use ArrayList instead.

- **Hashtable**: Implements Map. If you don't need concurrency, use HashMap instead.

- **Stack**: Implements Queue. If you don't need concurrency, use a LinkedList instead.

Sorting Data

We discussed "order" for the TreeSet and TreeMap classes. For numbers, order is obvious—it is numerical order. For String objects, order is defined according to the Unicode character mapping. As far as the exam is concerned, that means numbers sort before letters, and uppercase letters sort before lowercase letters.

 Remember that numbers sort before letters, and uppercase letters sort before lowercase letters.

We will be using Collections.sort() in many of these examples. It returns void because the method parameter is what gets sorted.

You can also sort objects that you create yourself. Java provides an interface called Comparable. If your class implements Comparable, it can be used in these data structures that require comparison. There is also a class called Comparator, which is used to specify that you want to use a different order than the object itself provides.

Comparable and Comparator are similar enough to be tricky. The exam likes to see if it can trick you into mixing up the two. Don't be confused! In this section, we will discuss Comparable first. Then, as we go through Comparator, we will point out all of the differences.

Creating a *Comparable* Class

The Comparable interface has only one method. In fact, this is the entire interface:

```
public interface Comparable<T> {
    int compareTo(T o);
}
```

The generic T lets you implement this method and specify the type of your object. This lets you avoid a cast when implementing compareTo(). Any object can be Comparable. For example, we have a bunch of ducks and want to sort them by name. First, we update the class declaration to inherit Comparable<Duck>, and then we implement the compareTo() method.

```
import java.util.*;
public class Duck implements Comparable<Duck> {
    private String name;
    public Duck(String name) {
        this.name = name;
    }
```

```
public String toString() { // use readable output
   return name;
}
public int compareTo(Duck d) {
   return name.compareTo(d.name); // sorts ascendingly by name
}
public static void main(String[] args) {
   var ducks = new ArrayList<Duck>();
   ducks.add(new Duck("Quack"));
   ducks.add(new Duck("Puddles"));
   Collections.sort(ducks);    // sort by name
   System.out.println(ducks); // [Puddles, Quack]
}}
```

Without implementing that interface, all we have is a method named compareTo(), but it wouldn't be a Comparable object. We could also implement Comparable<Object> or some other class for T, but this wouldn't be as useful for sorting a group of Duck objects with each other.

The Duck class overrides the toString() method from Object, which we described in Chapter 12. This override provides useful output when printing out ducks. Without this override, the output would be something like [Duck@70dea4e, Duck@5c647e05]—hardly useful in seeing which duck's name comes first.

Finally, the Duck class implements compareTo(). Since Duck is comparing objects of type String and the String class already has a compareTo() method, it can just delegate.

We still need to know what the compareTo() method returns so that we can write our own. There are three rules to know.

- The number 0 is returned when the current object is equivalent to the argument to compareTo().

- A negative number (less than 0) is returned when the current object is smaller than the argument to compareTo().

- A positive number (greater than 0) is returned when the current object is larger than the argument to compareTo().

Let's look at an implementation of compareTo() that compares numbers instead of String objects.

```
1: public class Animal implements Comparable<Animal> {
2:    private int id;
3:    public int compareTo(Animal a) {
4:       return id - a.id; // sorts ascending by id
```

```
5:      }
6:      public static void main(String[] args) {
7:          var a1 = new Animal();
8:          var a2 = new Animal();
9:          a1.id = 5;
10:         a2.id = 7;
11:         System.out.println(a1.compareTo(a2)); // -2
12:         System.out.println(a1.compareTo(a1)); // 0
13:         System.out.println(a2.compareTo(a1)); // 2
14:     } }
```

Lines 7 and 8 create two Animal objects. Lines 9 and 10 set their id values. This is not a good way to set instance variables. It would be better to use a constructor or setter method. Since the exam shows nontraditional code to make sure that you understand the rules, we throw in some non-traditional code as well.

Lines 3-5 show one way to compare two int values. We could have used Integer.compare(id, a.id) instead. Be sure to be able to recognize both approaches.

Remember that id - a.id sorts in ascending order, and a.id - id sorts in descending order.

Lines 11 through 13 confirm that we've implemented compareTo() correctly. Line 11 compares a smaller id to a larger one, and therefore it prints a negative number. Line 12 compares animals with the same id, and therefore it prints 0. Line 13 compares a larger id to a smaller one, and therefore it returns a positive number.

Casting the *compareTo()* Argument

When dealing with legacy code or code that does not use generics, the compareTo() method requires a cast since it is passed an Object.

```
public class LegacyDuck implements Comparable {
    private String name;
    public int compareTo(Object obj) {
        LegacyDuck d = (LegacyDuck) obj; // cast because no generics
        return name.compareTo(d.name);
    }
}
```

Since we don't specify a generic type for Comparable, Java assumes that we want an Object, which means that we have to cast to LegacyDuck before accessing instance variables on it.

Checking for *null*

When working with Comparable and Comparator in this chapter, we tend to assume the data has values, but this is not always the case. When writing your own compare methods, you should check the data before comparing it if is not validated ahead of time.

```java
public class MissingDuck implements Comparable<MissingDuck> {
    private String name;
    public int compareTo(MissingDuck quack) {
        if (quack == null)
            throw new IllegalArgumentException("Poorly formed duck!");
        if (this.name == null && quack.name == null)
            return 0;
        else if (this.name == null) return -1;
        else if (quack.name == null) return 1;
        else return name.compareTo(quack.name);
    }
}
```

This method throws an exception if it is passed a null MissingDuck object. What about the ordering? If the name of a duck is null, then it's sorted first.

Keeping *compareTo()* and *equals()* Consistent

If you write a class that implements Comparable, you introduce new business logic for determining equality. The compareTo() method returns 0 if two objects are equal, while your equals() method returns true if two objects are equal. A *natural ordering* that uses compareTo() is said to be *consistent with equals* if, and only if, x.equals(y) is true whenever x.compareTo(y) equals 0.

Similarly, x.equals(y) must be false whenever x.compareTo(y) is not 0. You are strongly encouraged to make your Comparable classes consistent with equals because not all collection classes behave predictably if the compareTo() and equals() methods are not consistent.

For example, the following Product class defines a compareTo() method that is not consistent with equals:

```java
public class Product implements Comparable<Product> {
    private int id;
    private String name;

    public int hashCode() { return id; }
    public boolean equals(Object obj) {
        if(!(obj instanceof Product)) return false;
        var other = (Product) obj;
        return this.id == other.id;
    }
```

```
    public int compareTo(Product obj) {
        return this.name.compareTo(obj.name);
} }
```

You might be sorting Product objects by name, but names are not unique. Therefore, the return value of compareTo() might not be 0 when comparing two equal Product objects, so this compareTo() method is not consistent with equals. One way to fix that is to use a Comparator to define the sort elsewhere.

Now that you know how to implement Comparable objects, you get to look at Comparators and focus on the differences.

Comparing Data with a *Comparator*

Sometimes you want to sort an object that did not implement Comparable, or you want to sort objects in different ways at different times. Suppose that we add weight to our Duck class. We now have the following:

```
1:   import java.util.ArrayList;
2:   import java.util.Collections;
3:   import java.util.Comparator;
4:
5:   public class Duck implements Comparable<Duck> {
6:       private String name;
7:       private int weight;
8:
9:       // Assume getters/setters/constructors provided
10:
11:      public String toString() { return name; }
12:
13:      public int compareTo(Duck d) {
14:          return name.compareTo(d.name);
15:      }
16:
17:      public static void main(String[] args) {
18:          Comparator<Duck> byWeight = new Comparator<Duck>() {
19:              public int compare(Duck d1, Duck d2) {
20:                  return d1.getWeight()-d2.getWeight();
21:              }
22:          };
23:          var ducks = new ArrayList<Duck>();
24:          ducks.add(new Duck("Quack", 7));
25:          ducks.add(new Duck("Puddles", 10));
```

```
26:        Collections.sort(ducks);
27:        System.out.println(ducks); // [Puddles, Quack]
28:        Collections.sort(ducks, byWeight);
29:        System.out.println(ducks); // [Quack, Puddles]
30:    }
31: }
```

First, notice that this program imports java.util.Comparator on line 3. We don't always show imports since you can assume they are present if not shown. Here, we do show the import to call attention to the fact that Comparable and Comparator are in different packages, namely, java.lang versus java.util, respectively. That means Comparable can be used without an import statement, while Comparator cannot.

The Duck class itself can define only one compareTo() method. In this case, name was chosen. If we want to sort by something else, we have to define that sort order outside the compareTo() method using a separate class or lambda expression.

Lines 18-22 of the main() method show how to define a Comparator using an inner class. On lines 26-29, we sort without the comparator and then with the comparator to see the difference in output.

Comparator is a functional interface since there is only one abstract method to implement. This means that we can rewrite the comparator on lines 18-22 using a lambda expression, as shown here:

```
Comparator<Duck> byWeight = (d1, d2) -> d1.getWeight()-d2.getWeight();
```

Alternatively, we can use a method reference and a helper method to specify we want to sort by weight.

```
Comparator<Duck> byWeight = Comparator.comparing(Duck::getWeight);
```

In this example, Comparator.comparing() is a static interface method that creates a Comparator given a lambda expression or method reference. Convenient, isn't it?

Is *Comparable* a Functional Interface?

We said that Comparator is a functional interface because it has a single abstract method. Comparable is also a functional interface since it also has a single abstract method. However, using a lambda for Comparable would be silly. The point of Comparable is to implement it inside the object being compared.

Comparing *Comparable* and *Comparator*

There are a good number of differences between Comparable and Comparator. We've listed them for you in Table 14.11.

TABLE 14.11   Comparison of Comparable and Comparator

Difference	Comparable	Comparator
Package name	java.lang	java.util
Interface must be implemented by class comparing?	Yes	No
Method name in interface	compareTo()	compare()
Number of parameters	1	2
Common to declare using a lambda	No	Yes

Memorize this table—really. The exam will try to trick you by mixing up the two and seeing if you can catch it. Do you see why this one doesn't compile?

```
var byWeight = new Comparator<Duck>() { // DOES NOT COMPILE
    public int compareTo(Duck d1, Duck d2) {
        return d1.getWeight()-d2.getWeight();
    }
};
```

The method name is wrong. A Comparator must implement a method named compare(). Pay special attention to method names and the number of parameters when you see Comparator and Comparable in questions.

Comparing Multiple Fields

When writing a Comparator that compares multiple instance variables, the code gets a little messy. Suppose that we have a Squirrel class, as shown here:

```
public class Squirrel {
    private int weight;
    private String species;
    // Assume getters/setters/constructors provided
}
```

We want to write a Comparator to sort by species name. If two squirrels are from the same species, we want to sort the one that weighs the least first. We could do this with code that looks like this:

```
public class MultiFieldComparator implements Comparator<Squirrel> {
    public int compare(Squirrel s1, Squirrel s2) {
        int result = s1.getSpecies().compareTo(s2.getSpecies());
```

```
      if (result != 0) return result;
      return s1.getWeight()-s2.getWeight();
  }}
```

This works assuming no species names are null. It checks one field. If they don't match, we are finished sorting. If they do match, it looks at the next field. This isn't that easy to read, though. It is also easy to get wrong. Changing != to == breaks the sort completely.

Alternatively, we can use method references and build the comparator. This code represents logic for the same comparison.

```
Comparator<Squirrel> c = Comparator.comparing(Squirrel::getSpecies)
    .thenComparingInt(Squirrel::getWeight);
```

This time, we chain the methods. First, we create a comparator on species ascending. Then, if there is a tie, we sort by weight. We can also sort in descending order. Some methods on Comparator, like thenComparingInt(), are default methods. As discussed in Chapter 12, default methods were introduced in Java 8 as a way of expanding APIs.

Suppose we want to sort in descending order by species.

```
var c = Comparator.comparing(Squirrel::getSpecies).reversed();
```

Table 14.12 shows the helper methods you should know for building Comparator. We've omitted the parameter types to keep you focused on the methods. They use many of the functional interfaces you'll be learning about in the next chapter.

TABLE 14.12 Helper static methods for building a Comparator

Method	Description
comparing(function)	Compare by the results of a function that returns any Object (or object autoboxed into an Object).
comparingDouble(function)	Compare by the results of a function that returns a double.
comparingInt(function)	Compare by the results of a function that returns an int.
comparingLong(function)	Compare by the results of a function that returns a long.
naturalOrder()	Sort using the order specified by the Comparable implementation on the object itself.
reverseOrder()	Sort using the reverse of the order specified by the Comparable implementation on the object itself.

Table 14.13 shows the methods that you can chain to a Comparator to further specify its behavior.

TABLE 14.13   Helper default methods for building a Comparator

Method	Description
reversed()	Reverse the order of the chained Comparator.
thenComparing(function)	If the previous Comparator returns 0, use this comparator that returns an Object or can be autoboxed into one.
thenComparingDouble(function)	If the previous Comparator returns 0, use this comparator that returns a double. Otherwise, return the value from the previous Comparator.
thenComparingInt(function)	If the previous Comparator returns 0, use this comparator that returns an int. Otherwise, return the value from the previous Comparator.
thenComparingLong(function)	If the previous Comparator returns 0, use this comparator that returns a long. Otherwise, return the value from the previous Comparator.

You've probably noticed by now that we often ignore null values in checking equality and comparing objects. This works fine for the exam. In the real world, though, things aren't so neat. You will have to decide how to handle null values or prevent them from being in your object.

Sorting and Searching

Now that you've learned all about Comparable and Comparator, we can finally do something useful with it, like sorting. The Collections.sort() method uses the compareTo() method to sort. It expects the objects to be sorted to be Comparable.

```
2: public class SortRabbits {
3:    static class Rabbit{ int id; }
4:    public static void main(String[] args) {
5:       List<Rabbit> rabbits = new ArrayList<>();
6:       rabbits.add(new Rabbit());
7:       Collections.sort(rabbits); // DOES NOT COMPILE
8:    } }
```

Java knows that the Rabbit class is not Comparable. It knows sorting will fail, so it doesn't even let the code compile. You can fix this by passing a Comparator to sort(). Remember that a Comparator is useful when you want to specify sort order without using a compareTo() method.

```
2: public class SortRabbits {
3:     static class Rabbit{ int id; }
4:     public static void main(String[] args) {
5:         List<Rabbit> rabbits = new ArrayList<>();
6:         rabbits.add(new Rabbit());
7:         Comparator<Rabbit> c = (r1, r2) -> r1.id - r2.id;
8:         Collections.sort(rabbits, c);
9:     } }
```

The sort() and binarySearch() methods allow you to pass in a Comparator object when you don't want to use the natural order.

Reviewing *binarySearch()*

The binarySearch() method requires a sorted List.

```
11: List<Integer> list = Arrays.asList(6,9,1,8);
12: Collections.sort(list); // [1, 6, 8, 9]
13: System.out.println(Collections.binarySearch(list, 6)); // 1
14: System.out.println(Collections.binarySearch(list, 3)); // -2
```

Line 12 sorts the List so we can call binary search properly. Line 13 prints the index at which a match is found. Line 14 prints one less than the negated index of where the requested value would need to be inserted. The number 3 would need to be inserted at index 1 (after the number 1 but before the number 6). Negating that gives us –1, and subtracting 1 gives us –2.

There is a trick in working with binarySearch(). What do you think the following outputs?

```
3: var names = Arrays.asList("Fluffy", "Hoppy");
4: Comparator<String> c = Comparator.reverseOrder();
5: var index = Collections.binarySearch(names, "Hoppy", c);
6: System.out.println(index);
```

The correct answer is –1. Before you panic, you don't need to know that the answer is –1. You do need to know that the answer is not defined. Line 3 creates a list, [Fluffy, Hoppy]. This list happens to be sorted in ascending order. Line 4 creates a Comparator that reverses the natural order. Line 5 requests a binary search in descending order. Since the list is in ascending order, we don't meet the precondition for doing a search.

Earlier in the chapter, we talked about collections that require classes to implement Comparable. Unlike sorting, they don't check that you have actually implemented Comparable at compile time.

Going back to our Rabbit that does not implement Comparable, we try to add it to a TreeSet.

```
2:  public class UseTreeSet {
3:      static class Rabbit{ int id; }
4:      public static void main(String[] args) {
5:          Set<Duck> ducks = new TreeSet<>();
6:          ducks.add(new Duck("Puddles"));
7:
8:          Set<Rabbit> rabbits = new TreeSet<>();
9:          rabbits.add(new Rabbit());  // ClassCastException
10: } }
```

Line 6 is fine. Duck does implement Comparable. TreeSet is able to sort it into the proper position in the set. Line 9 is a problem. When TreeSet tries to sort it, Java discovers the fact that Rabbit does not implement Comparable. Java throws an exception that looks like this:

```
Exception in thread "main" java.lang.ClassCastException:
   class Duck cannot be cast to class java.lang.Comparable
```

It may seem weird for this exception to be thrown when the first object is added to the set. After all, there is nothing to compare yet. Java works this way for consistency.

Just like searching and sorting, you can tell collections that require sorting that you want to use a specific Comparator, for example:

```
8: Set<Rabbit> rabbits = new TreeSet<>((r1, r2) -> r1.id-r2.id);
9: rabbits.add(new Rabbit());
```

Now Java knows that you want to sort by id and all is well. Comparators are helpful objects. They let you separate sort order from the object to be sorted. Notice that line 9 in both of the previous examples is the same. It's the declaration of the TreeSet that has changed.

Working with Generics

We conclude this chapter with one of the most useful, and at times most confusing, feature in the Java language: generics. Why do we need generics? Well, remember when we said that we had to hope the caller didn't put something in the list that we didn't expect? The following does just that:

```
14: static void printNames(List list) {
15:    for (int i = 0; i < list.size(); i++) {
16:       String name = (String) list.get(i); // ClassCastException
17:       System.out.println(name);
18:    }
19: }
20: public static void main(String[] args) {
21:    List names = new ArrayList();
22:    names.add(new StringBuilder("Webby"));
23:    printNames(names);
24: }
```

This code throws a ClassCastException. Line 22 adds a StringBuilder to list. This is legal because a nongeneric list can contain anything. However, line 16 is written to expect a specific class to be in there. It casts to a String, reflecting this assumption. Since the assumption is incorrect, the code throws a ClassCastException that java.lang .StringBuilder cannot be cast to java.lang.String.

Generics fix this by allowing you to write and use parameterized types. You specify that you want an ArrayList of String objects. Now the compiler has enough information to prevent you from causing this problem in the first place.

```
List<String> names = new ArrayList<String>();
names.add(new StringBuilder("Webby")); // DOES NOT COMPILE
```

Getting a compiler error is good. You'll know right away that something is wrong rather than hoping to discover it later.

Generic Classes

You can introduce generics into your own classes. The syntax for introducing a generic is to declare a *formal type parameter* in angle brackets. For example, the following class named Crate has a generic type variable declared after the name of the class.

```
public class Crate<T> {
   private T contents;
   public T emptyCrate() {
      return contents;
   }
   public void packCrate(T contents) {
      this.contents = contents;
   }
}
```

The generic type T is available anywhere within the Crate class. When you instantiate the class, you tell the compiler what T should be for that particular instance.

Naming Conventions for Generics

A type parameter can be named anything you want. The convention is to use single uppercase letters to make it obvious that they aren't real class names. The following are common letters to use:

- E for an element
- K for a map key
- V for a map value
- N for a number
- T for a generic data type
- S, U, V, and so forth for multiple generic types

For example, suppose an Elephant class exists, and we are moving our elephant to a new and larger enclosure in our zoo. (The San Diego Zoo did this in 2009. It was interesting seeing the large metal crate.)

```
Elephant elephant = new Elephant();
Crate<Elephant> crateForElephant = new Crate<>();
crateForElephant.packCrate(elephant);
Elephant inNewHome = crateForElephant.emptyCrate();
```

To be fair, we didn't pack the crate so much as the elephant walked into it. However, you can see that the Crate class is able to deal with an Elephant without knowing anything about it.

This probably doesn't seem particularly impressive yet. We could have just typed in Elephant instead of T when coding Crate. What if we wanted to create a Crate for another animal?

```
Crate<Zebra> crateForZebra = new Crate<>();
```

Now we couldn't have simply hard-coded Elephant in the Crate class since a Zebra is not an Elephant. However, we could have created an Animal superclass or interface and used that in Crate.

Generic classes become useful when the classes used as the type parameter can have absolutely nothing to do with each other. For example, we need to ship our 120-pound robot to another city.

```
Robot joeBot = new Robot();
Crate<Robot> robotCrate = new Crate<>();
robotCrate.packCrate(joeBot);
```

```
// ship to St. Louis
Robot atDestination = robotCrate.emptyCrate();
```

Now it is starting to get interesting. The Crate class works with any type of class. Before generics, we would have needed Crate to use the Object class for its instance variable, which would have put the burden on the caller of needing to cast the object it receives on emptying the crate.

In addition to Crate not needing to know about the objects that go into it, those objects don't need to know about Crate either. We aren't requiring the objects to implement an interface named Crateable or the like. A class can be put in the Crate without any changes at all.

Don't worry if you can't think of a use for generic classes of your own. Unless you are writing a library for others to reuse, generics hardly show up in the class definitions you write. They do show up frequently in the code you call, such as the Java Collections Framework.

Generic classes aren't limited to having a single type parameter. This class shows two generic parameters.

```
public class SizeLimitedCrate<T, U> {
    private T contents;
    private U sizeLimit;
    public SizeLimitedCrate(T contents, U sizeLimit) {
        this.contents = contents;
        this.sizeLimit = sizeLimit;
    } }
```

T represents the type that we are putting in the crate. U represents the unit that we are using to measure the maximum size for the crate. To use this generic class, we can write the following:

```
Elephant elephant = new Elephant();
Integer numPounds = 15_000;
SizeLimitedCrate<Elephant, Integer> c1
    = new SizeLimiteCrate<>(elephant, numPounds);
```

Here we specify that the type is Elephant, and the unit is Integer. We also throw in a reminder that numeric literals can contain underscores.

What Is Type Erasure?

Specifying a generic type allows the compiler to enforce proper use of the generic type. For example, specifying the generic type of Crate as Robot is like replacing the T in the Crate class with Robot. However, this is just for compile time.

Behind the scenes, the compiler replaces all references to T in Crate with Object. In other words, after the code compiles, your generics are actually just Object types. The Crate class looks like the following at runtime:

```
public class Crate {
    private Object contents;
    public Object emptyCrate() {
        return contents;
    }
    public void packCrate(Object contents) {
        this.contents = contents;
    }
}
```

This means there is only one class file. There aren't different copies for different parameterized types. (Some other languages work that way.)

This process of removing the generics syntax from your code is referred to as *type erasure*. Type erasure allows your code to be compatible with older versions of Java that do not contain generics.

The compiler adds the relevant casts for your code to work with this type of erased class. For example, you type the following:

```
Robot r = crate.emptyCrate();
```

The compiler turns it into the following:

```
Robot r = (Robot) crate.emptyCrate();
```

Generic Interfaces

Just like a class, an interface can declare a formal type parameter. For example, the following Shippable interface uses a generic type as the argument to its ship() method:

```
public interface Shippable<T> {
    void ship(T t);
}
```

There are three ways a class can approach implementing this interface. The first is to specify the generic type in the class. The following concrete class says that it deals only with robots. This lets it declare the ship() method with a Robot parameter.

```
class ShippableRobotCrate implements Shippable<Robot> {
    public void ship(Robot t) { }
}
```

The next way is to create a generic class. The following concrete class allows the caller to specify the type of the generic:

```
class ShippableAbstractCrate<U> implements Shippable<U> {
   public void ship(U t) { }
}
```

In this example, the type parameter could have been named anything, including T. We used U in the example so that it isn't confusing as to what T refers to. The exam won't mind trying to confuse you by using the same type parameter name.

Raw Types

The final way is to not use generics at all. This is the old way of writing code. It generates a compiler warning about Shippable being a *raw type*, but it does compile. Here the ship() method has an Object parameter since the generic type is not defined:

```
class ShippableCrate implements Shippable {
   public void ship(Object t) { }
}
```

 Real World Scenario

What You Can't Do with Generic Types

There are some limitations on what you can do with a generic type. These aren't on the exam, but it will be helpful to refer to this scenario when you are writing practice programs and run into one of these situations.

Most of the limitations are due to type erasure. Oracle refers to types whose information is fully available at runtime as *reifiable*. Reifiable types can do anything that Java allows. Nonreifiable types have some limitations.

Here are the things that you can't do with generics (and by "can't," we mean without resorting to contortions like passing in a class object):

- **Calling a constructor:** Writing new T() is not allowed because at runtime it would be new Object().

- **Creating an array of that generic type:** This one is the most annoying, but it makes sense because you'd be creating an array of Object values.

- **Calling instanceof:** This is not allowed because at runtime List<Integer> and List<String> look the same to Java thanks to type erasure.

- **Using a primitive type as a generic type parameter:** This isn't a big deal because you can use the wrapper class instead. If you want a type of `int`, just use `Integer`.

- **Creating a static variable as a generic type parameter:** This is not allowed because the type is linked to the instance of the class.

Generic Methods

Up until this point, you've seen formal type parameters declared on the class or interface level. It is also possible to declare them on the method level. This is often useful for `static` methods since they aren't part of an instance that can declare the type. However, it is also allowed on non-`static` methods.

In this example, both methods use a generic parameter:

```
public class Handler {
   public static <T> void prepare(T t) {
      System.out.println("Preparing " + t);
   }
   public static <T> Crate<T> ship(T t) {
      System.out.println("Shipping " + t);
      return new Crate<T>();
   }
}
```

The method parameter is the generic type T. Before the return type, we declare the formal type parameter of <T>. In the `ship()` method, we show how you can use the generic parameter in the return type, Crate<T>, for the method.

Unless a method is obtaining the generic formal type parameter from the class/interface, it is specified immediately before the return type of the method. This can lead to some interesting-looking code!

```
2: public class More {
3:    public static <T> void sink(T t) { }
4:    public static <T> T identity(T t) { return t; }
5:    public static T noGood(T t) { return t; } // DOES NOT COMPILE
6: }
```

Line 3 shows the formal parameter type immediately before the return type of void. Line 4 shows the return type being the formal parameter type. It looks weird, but it is correct. Line 5 omits the formal parameter type, and therefore it does not compile.

Real World Scenario

Optional Syntax for Invoking a Generic Method

You can call a generic method normally, and the compiler will try to figure out which one you want. Alternatively, you can specify the type explicitly to make it obvious what the type is.

```
Box.<String>ship("package");
Box.<String[]>ship(args);
```

As to whether this makes things clearer, it is up to you. You should at least be aware that this syntax exists.

When you have a method declare a generic parameter type, it is independent of the class generics. Take a look at this class that declares a generic T at both levels:

```
1: public class Crate<T> {
2:     public <T> T tricky(T t) {
3:         return t;
4:     }
5: }
```

See if you can figure out the type of T on lines 1 and 2 when we call the code as follows:

```
10: public static String createName() {
11:     Crate<Robot> crate = new Crate<>();
12:     return crate.tricky("bot");
13: }
```

Clearly, "T is for tricky." Let's see what is happening. On line 1, T is Robot because that is what gets referenced when constructing a Crate. On line 2, T is String because that is what is passed to the method. When you see code like this, take a deep breath and write down what is happening so you don't get confused.

Bounding Generic Types

By now, you might have noticed that generics don't seem particularly useful since they are treated as an Object and therefore don't have many methods available. Bounded wildcards solve this by restricting what types can be used in a wildcard. A *bounded parameter type* is a generic type that specifies a bound for the generic. Be warned that this is the hardest section in the chapter, so don't feel bad if you have to read it more than once.

A *wildcard generic type* is an unknown generic type represented with a question mark (?). You can use generic wildcards in three ways, as shown in Table 14.14. This section looks at each of these three wildcard types.

TABLE 14.14 Types of bounds

Type of bound	Syntax	Example
Unbounded wildcard	?	List<?> a = new ArrayList<String>();
Wildcard with an upper bound	? extends type	List<? extends Exception> a = new ArrayList<RuntimeException>();
Wildcard with a lower bound	? super type	List<? super Exception> a = new ArrayList<Object>();

Unbounded Wildcards

An unbounded wildcard represents any data type. You use ? when you want to specify that any type is okay with you. Let's suppose that we want to write a method that looks through a list of any type.

```
public static void printList(List<Object> list) {
for (Object x: list)
   System.out.println(x);
}
public static void main(String[] args) {
    List<String> keywords = new ArrayList<>();
    keywords.add("java");
    printList(keywords); // DOES NOT COMPILE
}
```

Wait. What's wrong? A String is a subclass of an Object. This is true. However, List<String> cannot be assigned to List<Object>. We know, it doesn't sound logical. Java is trying to protect us from ourselves with this one. Imagine if we could write code like this:

```
4: List<Integer> numbers = new ArrayList<>();
5: numbers.add(new Integer(42));
6: List<Object> objects = numbers; // DOES NOT COMPILE
7: objects.add("forty two");
8: System.out.println(numbers.get(1));
```

On line 4, the compiler promises us that only Integer objects will appear in numbers. If line 6 were to have compiled, line 7 would break that promise by putting a String in there since numbers and objects are references to the same object. Good thing that the compiler prevents this.

Going back to printing a list, we cannot assign a List<String> to a List<Object>. That's fine; we don't really need a List<Object>. What we really need is a List of "whatever." That's what List<?> is. The following code does what we expect:

```
public static void printList(List<?> list) {
for (Object x: list)
   System.out.println(x);
}
public static void main(String[] args) {
   List<String> keywords = new ArrayList<>();
   keywords.add("java");
   printList(keywords);
}
```

The printList() method takes any type of list as a parameter. The keywords variable is of type List<String>. We have a match! List<String> is a list of anything. "Anything" just happens to be a String here.

Finally, let's look at the impact of var. Do you think these two statements are equivalent?

```
List<?> x1 = new ArrayList<>();
var x2 = new ArrayList<>();
```

They are not. There are two key differences. First, x1 is of type List, while x2 is of type ArrayList. Additionally, we can only assign x2 to a List<Object>. These two variables do have one thing in common. Both return type Object when calling the get() method.

Upper-Bounded Wildcards

Let's try to write a method that adds up the total of a list of numbers. We've established that a generic type can't just use a subclass.

```
ArrayList<Number> list = new ArrayList<Integer>(); // DOES NOT COMPILE
```

Instead, we need to use a wildcard.

```
List<? extends Number> list = new ArrayList<Integer>();
```

The upper-bounded wildcard says that any class that extends Number or Number itself can be used as the formal parameter type:

```
public static long total(List<? extends Number> list) {
   long count = 0;
   for (Number number: list)
      count += number.longValue();
   return count;
}
```

Remember how we kept saying that type erasure makes Java think that a generic type is an Object? That is still happening here. Java converts the previous code to something equivalent to the following:

```
public static long total(List list) {
   long count = 0;
   for (Object obj: list) {
      Number number = (Number) obj;
      count += number.longValue();
   }
   return count;
}
```

Something interesting happens when we work with upper bounds or unbounded wild-cards. The list becomes logically immutable and therefore cannot be modified. Technically, you can remove elements from the list, but the exam won't ask about this.

```
2: static class Sparrow extends Bird { }
3: static class Bird { }
4:
5: public static void main(String[] args) {
6:    List<? extends Bird> birds = new ArrayList<Bird>();
7:    birds.add(new Sparrow()); // DOES NOT COMPILE
8:    birds.add(new Bird());    // DOES NOT COMPILE
9: }
```

The problem stems from the fact that Java doesn't know what type List<? extends Bird> really is. It could be List<Bird> or List<Sparrow> or some other generic type that hasn't even been written yet. Line 7 doesn't compile because we can't add a Sparrow to List<? extends Bird>, and line 8 doesn't compile because we can't add a Bird to List<Sparrow>. From Java's point of view, both scenarios are equally possible, so neither is allowed.

Now let's try an example with an interface. We have an interface and two classes that implement it.

```
interface Flyer { void fly(); }
class HangGlider implements Flyer { public void fly() {} }
class Goose implements Flyer { public void fly() {} }
```

We also have two methods that use it. One just lists the interface, and the other uses an upper bound.

```
private void anyFlyer(List<Flyer> flyer) {}
private void groupOfFlyers(List<? extends Flyer> flyer) {}
```

Note that we used the keyword extends rather than implements. Upper bounds are like anonymous classes in that they use extends regardless of whether we are working with a class or an interface.

You already learned that a variable of type List<Flyer> can be passed to either method. A variable of type List<Goose> can be passed only to the one with the upper bound. This shows one of the benefits of generics. Random flyers don't fly together. We want our groupOfFlyers() method to be called only with the same type. Geese fly together but don't fly with hang gliders.

Lower-Bounded Wildcards

Let's try to write a method that adds a string "quack" to two lists.

```
List<String> strings = new ArrayList<String>();
strings.add("tweet");

List<Object> objects = new ArrayList<Object>(strings);
addSound(strings);
addSound(objects);
```

The problem is that we want to pass a List<String> and a List<Object> to the same method. First, make sure that you understand why the first three examples in Table 14.15 do *not* solve this problem.

TABLE 14.15   Why we need a lower bound

public static void addSound(_____list) {list.add("quack");}	Method compiles	Can pass a List<String>	Can pass a List<Object>
List<?>	No (unbounded generics are immutable)	Yes	Yes
List<? extends Object>	No (upper-bounded generics are immutable)	Yes	Yes
List<Object>	Yes	No (with generics, must pass exact match)	Yes
List<? super String>	Yes	Yes	Yes

To solve this problem, we need to use a lower bound.

```
public static void addSound(List<? super String> list) {
    list.add("quack");
}
```

With a lower bound, we are telling Java that the list will be a list of String objects or a list of some objects that are a superclass of String. Either way, it is safe to add a String to that list.

Just like generic classes, you probably won't use this in your code unless you are writing code for others to reuse. Even then it would be rare. But it's on the exam, so now is the time to learn it!

Understand Generic Supertypes

When you have subclasses and superclasses, lower bounds can get tricky.

```
3: List<? super IOException> exceptions = new ArrayList<Exception>();
4: exceptions.add(new Exception()); // DOES NOT COMPILE
5: exceptions.add(new IOException());
6: exceptions.add(new FileNotFoundException());
```

Line 3 references a List that could be List<IOException> or List<Exception> or List<Object>. Line 4 does not compile because we could have a List<IOException> and an Exception object wouldn't fit in there.

Line 5 is fine. IOException can be added to any of those types. Line 6 is also fine. FileNotFoundException can also be added to any of those three types. This is tricky because FileNotFoundException is a subclass of IOException, and the keyword says super. What happens is that Java says, "Well, FileNotFoundException also happens to be an IOException, so everything is fine."

Putting It All Together

At this point, you know everything that you need to know to ace the exam questions on generics. It is possible to put these concepts together to write some *really* confusing code, which the exam likes to do.

This section is going to be difficult to read. It contains the hardest questions that you could possibly be asked about generics. The exam questions will probably be easier to read than these. We want you to encounter the really tough ones here so that you are ready for the exam. In other words, don't panic. Take it slow, and reread the code a few times. You'll get it.

Combining Generic Declarations

Let's try an example. First, we declare three classes that the example will use.

```
class A {}
class B extends A {}
class C extends B {}
```

Ready? Can you figure out why these do or don't compile? Also, try to figure out what they do.

```
6: List<?> list1 = new ArrayList<A>();
7: List<? extends A> list2 = new ArrayList<A>();
8: List<? super A> list3 = new ArrayList<A>();
```

Line 6 creates an `ArrayList` that can hold instances of class A. It is stored in a variable with an unbounded wildcard. Any generic type can be referenced from an unbounded wildcard, making this okay.

Line 7 tries to store a list in a variable declaration with an upper-bounded wildcard. This is okay. You can have `ArrayList<A>`, `ArrayList<B>`, or `ArrayList<C>` stored in that reference. Line 8 is also okay. This time, you have a lower-bounded wildcard. The lowest type you can reference is A. Since that is what you have, it compiles.

Did you get those right? Let's try a few more.

```
9:  List<? extends B> list4 = new ArrayList<A>(); // DOES NOT COMPILE
10: List<? super B> list5 = new ArrayList<A>();
11: List<?> list6 = new ArrayList<? extends A>(); // DOES NOT COMPILE
```

Line 9 has an upper-bounded wildcard that allows `ArrayList<B>` or `ArrayList<C>` to be referenced. Since you have `ArrayList<A>` that is trying to be referenced, the code does not compile. Line 10 has a lower-bounded wildcard, which allows a reference to `ArrayList<A>`, `ArrayList<B>`, or `ArrayList<Object>`.

Finally, line 11 allows a reference to any generic type since it is an unbounded wildcard. The problem is that you need to know what that type will be when instantiating the `ArrayList`. It wouldn't be useful anyway, because you can't add any elements to that `ArrayList`.

Passing Generic Arguments

Now on to the methods. Same question: try to figure out why they don't compile or what they do. We will present the methods one at a time because there is more to think about.

```
<T> T first(List<? extends T> list) {
   return list.get(0);
}
```

The first method, `first()`, is a perfectly normal use of generics. It uses a method-specific type parameter, T. It takes a parameter of `List<T>`, or some subclass of T, and it returns a single object of that T type. For example, you could call it with a `List<String>`

parameter and have it return a String. Or you could call it with a List<Number> parameter and have it return a Number. Or ... well, you get the idea.

Given that, you should be able to see what is wrong with this one:

```
<T> <? extends T> second(List<? extends T> list) { // DOES NOT COMPILE
  return list.get(0);
}
```

The next method, second(), does not compile because the return type isn't actually a type. You are writing the method. You know what type it is supposed to return. You don't get to specify this as a wildcard.

Now be careful—this one is extra tricky:

```
<B extends A> B third(List<B> list) {
  return new B(); // DOES NOT COMPILE
}
```

This method, third(), does not compile. <B extends A> says that you want to use B as a type parameter just for this method and that it needs to extend the A class. Coincidentally, B is also the name of a class. It isn't a coincidence. It's an evil trick. Within the scope of the method, B can represent class A, B, or C, because all extend the A class. Since B no longer refers to the B class in the method, you can't instantiate it.

After that, it would be nice to get something straightforward.

```
void fourth(List<? super B> list) {}
```

We finally get a method, fourth(), which is a normal use of generics. You can pass the types List<B>, List<A>, or List<Object>.

Finally, can you figure out why this example does not compile?

```
<X> void fifth(List<X super B> list) { // DOES NOT COMPILE
}
```

This last method, fifth(), does not compile because it tries to mix a method-specific type parameter with a wildcard. A wildcard must have a ? in it.

Phew. You made it through generics. That's the hardest topic in this chapter (and why we covered it last!). Remember that it's okay if you need to go over this material a few times to get your head around it.

Summary

A method reference is a compact syntax for writing lambdas that refer to methods. There are four types: static methods, instance methods on a particular object, instance methods on a parameter, and constructor references.

Each primitive class has a corresponding wrapper class. For example, `long`'s wrapper class is `Long`. Java can automatically convert between primitive and wrapper classes when needed. This is called autoboxing and unboxing. Java will use autoboxing only if it doesn't find a matching method signature with the primitive. For example, `remove(int n)` will be called rather than `remove(Object o)` when called with an `int`.

The diamond operator (`<>`) is used to tell Java that the generic type matches the declaration without specifying it again. The diamond operator can be used for local variables or instance variables as well as one-line declarations.

The Java Collections Framework includes four main types of data structures: lists, sets, queues, and maps. The `Collection` interface is the parent interface of `List`, `Set`, and `Queue`. The `Map` interface does not extend `Collection`. You need to recognize the following:

- **List**: An ordered collection of elements that allows duplicate entries
  - **ArrayList**: Standard resizable list
  - **LinkedList**: Can easily add/remove from beginning or end

- **Set**: Does not allow duplicates
  - **HashSet**: Uses hashCode() to find unordered elements
  - **TreeSet**: Sorted. Does not allow null values

- **Queue**: Orders elements for processing
  - **LinkedList**: Can easily add/remove from beginning or end

- **Map**: Maps unique keys to values
  - **HashMap**: Uses hashCode() to find keys
  - **TreeMap**: Sorted map. Does not allow null keys

The `Comparable` interface declares the `compareTo()` method. This method returns a negative number if the object is smaller than its argument, 0 if the two objects are equal, and a positive number otherwise. The `compareTo()` method is declared on the object that is being compared, and it takes one parameter. The `Comparator` interface defines the `compare()` method. A negative number is returned if the first argument is smaller, zero if they are equal, and a positive number otherwise. The `compare()` method can be declared in any code, and it takes two parameters. `Comparator` is often implemented using a lambda.

The `Arrays` and `Collections` classes have methods for `sort()` and `binarySearch()`. Both take an optional `Comparator` parameter. It is necessary to use the same sort order for both sorting and searching, so the result is not undefined.

Generics are type parameters for code. To create a class with a generic parameter, add `<T>` after the class name. You can use any name you want for the type parameter. Single uppercase letters are common choices.

Generics allow you to specify wildcards. `<?>` is an unbounded wildcard that means any type. `<? extends Object>` is an upper bound that means any type that is `Object` or extends it. `<? extends MyInterface>` means any type that implements `MyInterface`.

`<? super Number>` is a lower bound that means any type that is Number or a superclass. A compiler error results from code that attempts to add an item in a list with an unbounded or upper-bounded wildcard.

Exam Essentials

Translate method references to the "long form" lambda. Be able to convert method references into regular lambda expressions and vice versa. For example, `System.out::print` and `x -> System.out.print(x)` are equivalent. Remember that the order of method parameters is inferred for both based on usage.

Use autoboxing and unboxing. Autoboxing converts a primitive into an `Object`. For example, `int` is autoboxed into `Integer`. Unboxing converts an `Object` into a primitive. For example, `Character` is autoboxed into `char`.

Pick the correct type of collection from a description. A `List` allows duplicates and orders the elements. A `Set` does not allow duplicates. A `Queue` orders its elements to facilitate retrievals. A `Map` maps keys to values. Be familiar with the differences of implementations of these interfaces.

Work with convenience methods. The Collections Framework contains many methods such as `contains()`, `forEach()`, and `removeIf()` that you need to know for the exam. There are too many to list in this paragraph for review, so please do review the tables in this chapter.

Differentiate between Comparable and Comparator. Classes that implement `Comparable` are said to have a natural ordering and implement the `compareTo()` method. A class is allowed to have only one natural ordering. A `Comparator` takes two objects in the `compare()` method. Different Comparators can have different sort orders. A `Comparator` is often implemented using a lambda such as `(a, b) -> a.num - b.num`.

Write code using the diamond operator. The diamond operator (`<>`) is used to write more concise code. The type of the generic parameter is inferred from the surrounding code. For example, in `List<String> c = new ArrayList<>()`, the type of the diamond operator is inferred to be `String`.

Identify valid and invalid uses of generics and wildcards. `<T>` represents a type parameter. Any name can be used, but a single uppercase letter is the convention. `<?>` is an unbounded wildcard. `<? extends X>` is an upper-bounded wildcard and applies to both classes and interfaces. `<? super X>` is a lower-bounded wildcard.

Review Questions

The answers to the chapter review questions can be found in the Appendix.

1. Suppose that you have a collection of products for sale in a database and you need to display those products. The products are not unique. Which of the following collections classes in the `java.util` package best suits your needs for this scenario?

   A. `Arrays`

   B. `ArrayList`

   C. `HashMap`

   D. `HashSet`

   E. `LinkedList`

2. Suppose that you need to work with a collection of elements that need to be sorted in their natural order, and each element has a unique text `id` that you want to use to store and retrieve the record. Which of the following collections classes in the `java.util` package best suits your needs for this scenario?

   A. `ArrayList`

   B. `HashMap`

   C. `HashSet`

   D. `TreeMap`

   E. `TreeSet`

   F. None of the above

3. Which of the following are true? (Choose all that apply.)

   ```
   12: List<?> q = List.of("mouse", "parrot");
   13: var v = List.of("mouse", "parrot");
   14:
   15: q.removeIf(String::isEmpty);
   16: q.removeIf(s -> s.length() == 4);
   17: v.removeIf(String::isEmpty);
   18: v.removeIf(s -> s.length() == 4);
   ```

   A. This code compiles and runs without error.

   B. Exactly one of these lines contains a compiler error.

   C. Exactly two of these lines contain a compiler error.

   D. Exactly three of these lines contain a compiler error.

   E. Exactly four of these lines contain a compiler error.

   F. If any lines with compiler errors are removed, this code runs without throwing an exception.

   G. If all lines with compiler errors are removed, this code throws an exception.

4. What is the result of the following statements?

```
3:  var greetings = new LinkedList<String>();
4:  greetings.offer("hello");
5:  greetings.offer("hi");
6:  greetings.offer("ola");
7:  greetings.pop();
8:  greetings.peek();
9:  while (greetings.peek() != null)
10:     System.out.print(greetings.pop());
```

   A. hello

   B. hellohi

   C. hellohiola

   D. hiola

   E. ola

   F. The code does not compile.

   G. An exception is thrown.

5. Which of these statements compile? (Choose all that apply.)

   A. `HashSet<Number> hs = new HashSet<Integer>();`

   B. `HashSet<? super ClassCastException> set = new`
   `HashSet<Exception>();`

   C. `List<> list = new ArrayList<String>();`

   D. `List<Object> values = new HashSet<Object>();`

   E. `List<Object> objects = new ArrayList<? extends Object>();`

   F. `Map<String, ? extends Number> hm = new`
   `HashMap<String, Integer>();`

6. What is the result of the following code?

```
1:  public class Hello<T> {
2:      T t;
3:      public Hello(T t) { this.t = t; }
4:      public String toString() { return t.toString(); }
5:      private <T> void println(T message) {
6:          System.out.print(t + "-" + message);
7:      }
8:      public static void main(String[] args) {
9:          new Hello<String>("hi").println(1);
10:         new Hello("hola").println(true);
11:  } }
```

   A. hi followed by a runtime exception

   B. hi-1hola-true

   C. The first compiler error is on line 1.

   D. The first compiler error is on line 4.

   E. The first compiler error is on line 5.

   F. The first compiler error is on line 9.

   G. The first compiler error is on line 10.

7. Which of the following statements are true? (Choose all that apply.)

```
3:  var numbers = new HashSet<Number>();
4:  numbers.add(Integer.valueOf(86));
5:  numbers.add(75);
6:  numbers.add(Integer.valueOf(86));
7:  numbers.add(null);
8:  numbers.add(309L);
9:  Iterator iter = numbers.iterator();
10: while (iter.hasNext())
11:     System.out.print(iter.next());
```

   A. The code compiles successfully.

   B. The output is 8675null309.

   C. The output is 867586null309.

   D. The output is indeterminate.

   E. There is a compiler error on line 3.

   F. There is a compiler error on line 9.

   G. An exception is thrown.

8. Which of the following can fill in the blank to print [7, 5, 3]? (Choose all that apply.)

```
3:  public class Platypus {
4:      String name;
5:      int beakLength;
6:
7:      // Assume getters/setters/constructors provided
8:
9:      public String toString() {return "" + beakLength;}
10:
11:     public static void main(String[] args) {
12:         Platypus p1 = new Platypus("Paula", 3);
13:         Platypus p2 = new Platypus("Peter", 5);
14:         Platypus p3 = new Platypus("Peter", 7);
```

```
15:
16:        List<Platypus> list = Arrays.asList(p1, p2, p3);
17:
18:        Collections.sort(list, Comparator.comparing_____);
19:
20:        System.out.println(list);
21:    }
22: }
```

A.

```
(Platypus::getBeakLength)
```

B.

```
(Platypus::getBeakLength).reversed()
```

C.

```
(Platypus::getName)
    .thenComparing(Platypus::getBeakLength)
```

D.

```
(Platypus::getName)
    .thenComparing(
        Comparator.comparing(Platypus::getBeakLength)
    .reversed())
```

E.

```
(Platypus::getName)
    .thenComparingNumber(Platypus::getBeakLength)
    .reversed()
```

F.

```
(Platypus::getName)
    .thenComparingInt(Platypus::getBeakLength)
    .reversed()
```

G. None of the above

9. Which of the answer choices are valid given the following code? (Choose all that apply.)

```
Map<String, Double> map = new HashMap<>();
```

A. `map.add("pi", 3.14159);`

B. `map.add("e", 2L);`

C. `map.add("log(1)", new Double(0.0));`

D. `map.add('x', new Double(123.4));`

E. None of the above

10. What is the result of the following program?

```
3:  public class MyComparator implements Comparator<String> {
4:      public int compare(String a, String b) {
5:          return b.toLowerCase().compareTo(a.toLowerCase());
6:      }
7:      public static void main(String[] args) {
8:          String[] values = { "123", "Abb", "aab" };
9:          Arrays.sort(values, new MyComparator());
10:         for (var s: values)
11:             System.out.print(s + " ");
12:     }
13: }
```

A. Abb aab 123

B. aab Abb 123

C. 123 Abb aab

D. 123 aab Abb

E. The code does not compile.

F. A runtime exception is thrown.

11. What is the result of the following code?

```
3: var map = new HashMap<Integer, Integer>(10);
4: for (int i = 1; i <= 10; i++) {
5:     map.put(i, i * i);
6: }
7: System.out.println(map.get(4));
```

A. 16

B. 25

C. Compiler error on line 3.

D. Compiler error on line 5.

E. Compiler error on line 7.

F. A runtime exception is thrown.

12. Which of these statements can fill in the blank so that the Helper class compiles success-fully? (Choose all that apply.)

```
2:  public class Helper {
3:      public static <U extends Exception>
4:          void printException(U u) {
5:
```

```
6:          System.out.println(u.getMessage());
7:      }
8:      public static void main(String[] args) {
9:          Helper._____ ;
10:     } }
```

A. `printException(new FileNotFoundException("A"))`

B. `printException(new Exception("B"))`

C. `<Throwable>printException(new Exception("C"))`

D. `<NullPointerException>printException`
   `(new NullPointerException ("D"))`

E. `printException(new Throwable("E"))`

13. Which of these statements can fill in the blank so that the `Wildcard` class compiles successfully? (Choose all that apply.)

```
3:  public class Wildcard {
4:      public void showSize(List<?> list) {
5:          System.out.println(list.size());
6:      }
7:      public static void main(String[] args) {
8:          Wildcard card = new Wildcard();
9:          _____;
10:         card.showSize(list);
11:     } }
```

A. `List<?> list = new HashSet <String>()`

B. `ArrayList<? super Date> list = new ArrayList<Date>()`

C. `List<?> list = new ArrayList<?>()`

D. `List<Exception> list = new LinkedList<java.io.IOException>()`

E. `ArrayList <? extends Number> list = new ArrayList <Integer>()`

F. None of the above

14. What is the result of the following program?

```
3:  public class Sorted
4:      implements Comparable<Sorted>, Comparator<Sorted> {
5:
6:      private int num;
7:      private String text;
8:
9:      // Assume getters/setters/constructors provided
10:
```

```
11:    public String toString() { return "" + num; }
12:    public int compareTo(Sorted s) {
13:        return text.compareTo(s.text);
14:    }
15:    public int compare(Sorted s1, Sorted s2) {
16:        return s1.num - s2.num;
17:    }
18:    public static void main(String[] args) {
19:        var s1 = new Sorted(88, "a");
20:        var s2 = new Sorted(55, "b");
21:        var t1 = new TreeSet<Sorted>();
22:        t1.add(s1); t1.add(s2);
23:        var t2 = new TreeSet<Sorted>(s1);
24:        t2.add(s1); t2.add(s2);
25:        System.out.println(t1 + " " + t2);
26:    } }
```

A. [55, 88] [55, 88]
B. [55, 88] [88, 55]
C. [88, 55] [55, 88]
D. [88, 55] [88, 55]
E. The code does not compile.
F. A runtime exception is thrown.

15. What is the result of the following code? (Choose all that apply.)

```
Comparator<Integer> c1 = (o1, o2) -> o2 - o1;
Comparator<Integer> c2 = Comparator.naturalOrder();
Comparator<Integer> c3 = Comparator.reverseOrder();

var list = Arrays.asList(5, 4, 7, 2);
Collections.sort(list, _____);
System.out.println(Collections.binarySearch(list, 2));
```

A. One or more of the comparators can fill in the blank so that the code prints 0.
B. One or more of the comparators can fill in the blank so that the code prints 1.
C. One or more of the comparators can fill in the blank so that the code prints 2.
D. The result is undefined regardless of which comparator is used.
E. A runtime exception is thrown regardless of which comparator is used.
F. The code does not compile.

16. Which of the following statements are true? (Choose all that apply.)

A. Comparable is in the java.util package.

B. Comparator is in the java.util package.

C. compare() is in the Comparable interface.

D. compare() is in the Comparator interface.

E. compare() takes one method parameter.

F. compare() takes two method parameters.

17. Which options can fill in the blanks to make this code compile? (Choose all that apply.)

```
1: public class Generic_____ {
2:     public static void main(String[] args) {
3:         Generic<String> g = new Generic_____();
4:         Generic<Object> g2 = new Generic();
5:     }
6: }
```

A. On line 1, fill in with <>.

B. On line 1, fill in with <T>.

C. On line 1, fill in with <?>.

D. On line 3, fill in with <>.

E. On line 3, fill in with <T>.

F. On line 3, fill in with <?>.

18. Which of the following lines can be inserted to make the code compile? (Choose all that apply.)

```
class W {}
class X extends W {}
class Y extends X {}
class Z<Y> {
// INSERT CODE HERE
}
```

A. W w1 = new W();

B. W w2 = new X();

C. W w3 = new Y();

D. Y y1 = new W();

E. Y y2 = new X();

F. Y y1 = new Y();

19. Which options are true of the following code? (Choose all that apply.)

```
3: _____<Integer> q = new LinkedList<>();
4: q.add(10);
5: q.add(12);
6: q.remove(1);
7: System.out.print(q);
```

A. If we fill in the blank with List, the output is [10].

B. If we fill in the blank with List, the output is [10, 12].

C. If we fill in the blank with Queue, the output is [10].

D. If we fill in the blank with Queue, the output is [10, 12].

E. The code does not compile in either scenario.

F. A runtime exception is thrown.

20. What is the result of the following code?

```
4: Map m = new HashMap();
5: m.put(123, "456");
6: m.put("abc", "def");
7: System.out.println(m.contains("123"));
```

A. false

B. true

C. Compiler error on line 4

D. Compiler error on line 5

E. Compiler error on line 7

F. A runtime exception is thrown.

21. What is the result of the following code? (Choose all that apply.)

```
48: var map = Map.of(1,2, 3, 6);
49: var list = List.copyOf(map.entrySet());
50:
51: List<Integer> one = List.of(8, 16, 2);
52: var copy = List.copyOf(one);
53: var copyOfCopy = List.copyOf(copy);
54: var thirdCopy = new ArrayList<>(copyOfCopy);
55:
56: list.replaceAll(x -> x * 2);
57: one.replaceAll(x -> x * 2);
58: thirdCopy.replaceAll(x -> x * 2);
59:
60: System.out.println(thirdCopy);
```

A. One line fails to compile.

B. Two lines fail to compile.

C. Three lines fail to compile.

D. The code compiles but throws an exception at runtime.

E. If any lines with compiler errors are removed, the code throws an exception at runtime.

F. If any lines with compiler errors are removed, the code prints [16, 32, 4].

G. The code compiles and prints [16, 32, 4] without any changes.

22. What code change is needed to make the method compile assuming there is no class named T?

```
public static T identity(T t) {
   return t;
}
```

A. Add <T> after the `public` keyword.

B. Add <T> after the `static` keyword.

C. Add <T> after T.

D. Add <?> after the `public` keyword.

E. Add <?> after the `static` keyword.

F. No change required. The code already compiles.

23. Which of the answer choices make sense to implement with a lambda? (Choose all that apply.)

A. `Comparable` interface

B. `Comparator` interface

C. `remove` method on a `Collection`

D. `removeAll` method on a `Collection`

E. `removeIf` method on a `Collection`

24. Which of the following compiles and prints out the entire set? (Choose all that apply.)

```
Set<?> set = Set.of("lion", "tiger", "bear");
var s = Set.copyOf(set);
s.forEach(_____);
```

A. `() -> System.out.println(s)`

B. `s -> System.out.println(s)`

C. `(s) -> System.out.println(s)`

D. `System.out.println(s)`

E. `System::out::println`

F. `System.out::println`

G. None of the above

25. What is the result of the following?

```
var map = new HashMap<Integer, Integer>();
map.put(1, 10);
map.put(2, 20);
map.put(3, null);
map.merge(1, 3, (a,b) -> a + b);
map.merge(3, 3, (a,b) -> a + b);
System.out.println(map);
```

A. {1=10, 2=20}

B. {1=10, 2=20, 3=null}

C. {1=10, 2=20, 3=3}

D. {1=13, 2=20}

E. {1=13, 2=20, 3=null}

F. {1=13, 2=20, 3=3}

G. The code does not compile.

H. An exception is thrown.

Chapter

15

Functional Programming

THE OCP EXAM TOPICS COVERED IN THIS CHAPTER INCLUDE THE FOLLOWING:

✓ **Java Stream API**

- Describe the Stream interface and pipelines
- Use lambda expressions and method references

✓ **Built-in Functional Interfaces**

- Use interfaces from the java.util.function package
- Use core functional interfaces including Predicate, Consumer, Function and Supplier
- Use primitive and binary variations of base interfaces of java.util.function package

✓ **Lambda Operations on Streams**

- Extract stream data using map, peek and flatMap methods
- Search stream data using search findFirst, findAny, anyMatch, allMatch and noneMatch methods
- Use the Optional class
- Perform calculations using count, max, min, average and sum stream operations
- Sort a collection using lambda expressions
- Use Collectors with streams, including the groupingBy and partitioningBy operations

By now, you should be comfortable with the lambda and method reference syntax. Both are used when implementing functional interfaces. If you need more practice, you may want to go back and review Chapter 12, "Java Fundamentals," and Chapter 14, "Generics and Collections." You even used methods like forEach() and merge() in Chapter 14. In this chapter, we'll add actual functional programming to that, focusing on the Streams API.

Note that the Streams API in this chapter is used for functional programming. By contrast, there are also java.io streams, which we will talk about in Chapter 19, "I/O." Despite both using the word *stream*, they are nothing alike.

In this chapter, we will introduce many more functional interfaces and Optional classes. Then we will introduce the Stream pipeline and tie it all together. You might have noticed that this chapter covers a long list of objectives. Don't worry if you find the list daunting. By the time you finish the chapter, you'll see that many of the objectives cover similar topics. You might even want to read this chapter twice before doing the review questions so that you really get the hang of it. Functional programming tends to have a steep learning curve but can be really exciting once you get the hang of it.

Working with Built-in Functional Interfaces

In Table 14.1, we introduced some basic functional interfaces that we used with the Collections Framework. Now, we will learn them in more detail and more thoroughly. As discussed in Chapter 12, a functional interface has exactly one abstract method. We will focus on that method here.

All of the functional interfaces in Table 15.1 are provided in the java.util.function package. The convention here is to use the generic type T for the type parameter. If a second type parameter is needed, the next letter, U, is used. If a distinct return type is needed, R for *return* is used for the generic type.

TABLE 15.1   Common functional interfaces

Functional interface	Return type	Method name	# of parameters
Supplier<T>	T	get()	0
Consumer<T>	void	accept(T)	1 (T)
BiConsumer<T, U>	void	accept(T,U)	2 (T, U)
Predicate<T>	boolean	test(T)	1 (T)
BiPredicate<T, U>	boolean	test(T,U)	2 (T, U)
Function<T, R>	R	apply(T)	1 (T)
BiFunction<T, U, R>	R	apply(T,U)	2 (T, U)
UnaryOperator<T>	T	apply(T)	1 (T)
BinaryOperator<T>	T	apply(T,T)	2 (T, T)

There is one functional interface here that was not in Table 14.1 (BinaryOperator.) We introduced only what you needed in Chapter 14 at that point. Even Table 15.1 is a subset of what you need to know. Many functional interfaces are defined in the java.util .function package. There are even functional interfaces for handling primitives, which you'll see later in the chapter.

While you need to know a lot of functional interfaces for the exam, luckily many share names with the ones in Table 15.1. With that in mind, you need to memorize Table 15.1. We will give you lots of practice in this section to help make this memorable. Before you ask, most of the time we don't actually assign the implementation of the interface to a variable. The interface name is implied, and it gets passed directly to the method that needs it. We are introducing the names so that you can better understand and remember what is going on. Once we get to the streams part of the chapter, we will assume that you have this down and stop creating the intermediate variable.

As you saw in Chapter 12, you can name a functional interface anything you want. The only requirements are that it must be a valid interface name and contain a single abstract method. Table 15.1 is significant because these interfaces are often used in streams and other classes that come with Java, which is why you need to memorize them for the exam.

As you'll learn in Chapter 18, "Concurrency," there are two more functional interfaces called Runnable and Callable, which you need to know for the exam. They are used for concurrency the majority of the time. However, they may show up on the exam when you are asked to recognize which functional interface to use. All you need to know is that Runnable and Callable don't take any parameters, with Runnable returning void and Callable returning a generic type.

Let's look at how to implement each of these interfaces. Since both lambdas and method references show up all over the exam, we show an implementation using both where possible. After introducing the interfaces, we will also cover some convenience methods available on these interfaces.

Implementing *Supplier*

A Supplier is used when you want to generate or supply values without taking any input. The Supplier interface is defined as follows:

```
@FunctionalInterface
public interface Supplier<T> {
    T get();
}
```

You can create a LocalDate object using the factory method now(). This example shows how to use a Supplier to call this factory:

```
Supplier<LocalDate> s1 = LocalDate::now;
Supplier<LocalDate> s2 = () -> LocalDate.now();

LocalDate d1 = s1.get();
LocalDate d2 = s2.get();

System.out.println(d1);
System.out.println(d2);
```

This example prints a date such as 2020–02–20 twice. It's also a good opportunity to review static method references. The LocalDate::now method reference is used to create a Supplier to assign to an intermediate variable s1. A Supplier is often used when constructing new objects. For example, we can print two empty StringBuilder objects.

```
Supplier<StringBuilder> s1 = StringBuilder::new;
Supplier<StringBuilder> s2 = () -> new StringBuilder();

System.out.println(s1.get());
System.out.println(s2.get());
```

This time, we used a constructor reference to create the object. We've been using generics to declare what type of Supplier we are using. This can get a little long to read. Can you figure out what the following does? Just take it one step at a time.

```
Supplier<ArrayList<String>> s3 = ArrayList<String>::new;
ArrayList<String> a1 = s3.get();
System.out.println(a1);
```

We have a Supplier of a certain type. That type happens to be ArrayList<String>. Then calling get() creates a new instance of ArrayList<String>, which is the generic type of the Supplier—in other words, a generic that contains another generic. It's not hard to understand, so just look at the code carefully when this type of thing comes up.

Notice how we called get() on the functional interface. What would happen if we tried to print out s3 itself?

```
System.out.println(s3);
```

The code prints something like this:

```
functionalinterface.BuiltIns$$Lambda$1/0x0000000800066840@4909b8da
```

That's the result of calling toString() on a lambda. Yuck. This actually does mean something. Our test class is named BuiltIns, and it is in a package that we created named functionalinterface. Then comes $$, which means that the class doesn't exist in a class file on the file system. It exists only in memory. You don't need to worry about the rest.

Implementing *Consumer* and *BiConsumer*

You use a Consumer when you want to do something with a parameter but not return anything. BiConsumer does the same thing except that it takes two parameters. The interfaces are defined as follows:

```
@FunctionalInterface
public interface Consumer<T> {
    void accept(T t);
    // omitted default method
}

@FunctionalInterface
public interface BiConsumer<T, U> {
    void accept(T t, U u);
    // omitted default method
}
```

 You'll notice this pattern. *Bi* means two. It comes from Latin, but you can remember it from English words like *binary* (0 or 1) or *bicycle* (two wheels). Always add another parameter when you see *Bi* show up.

You used a Consumer in Chapter 14 with forEach(). Here's that example actually being assigned to the Consumer interface:

```
Consumer<String> c1 = System.out::println;
Consumer<String> c2 = x -> System.out.println(x);

c1.accept("Annie");
c2.accept("Annie");
```

This example prints Annie twice. BiConsumer is called with two parameters. They don't have to be the same type. For example, we can put a key and a value in a map using this interface:

```
var map = new HashMap<String, Integer>();
BiConsumer<String, Integer> b1 = map::put;
BiConsumer<String, Integer> b2 = (k, v) -> map.put(k, v);

b1.accept("chicken", 7);
b2.accept("chick", 1);

System.out.println(map);
```

The output is {chicken=7, chick=1}, which shows that both BiConsumer implementations did get called. When declaring b1, we used an instance method reference on an object since we want to call a method on the local variable map. The code to instantiate b1 is a good bit shorter than the code for b2. This is probably why the exam is so fond of method references.

As another example, we use the same type for both generic parameters.

```
var map = new HashMap<String, String>();
BiConsumer<String, String> b1 = map::put;
BiConsumer<String, String> b2 = (k, v) -> map.put(k, v);

b1.accept("chicken", "Cluck");
b2.accept("chick", "Tweep");

System.out.println(map);
```

The output is {chicken=Cluck, chick=Tweep}, which shows that a BiConsumer can use the same type for both the T and U generic parameters.

Implementing *Predicate* and *BiPredicate*

You saw Predicate with removeIf() in Chapter 14. Predicate is often used when filtering or matching. Both are common operations. A BiPredicate is just like a

Predicate except that it takes two parameters instead of one. The interfaces are defined as follows:

```
@FunctionalInterface
public interface Predicate<T> {
   boolean test(T t);
   // omitted default and static methods
}
```

```
@FunctionalInterface
public interface BiPredicate<T, U> {
   boolean test(T t, U u);
   // omitted default methods
}
```

It should be old news by now that you can use a Predicate to test a condition.

```
Predicate<String> p1 = String::isEmpty;
Predicate<String> p2 = x -> x.isEmpty();

System.out.println(p1.test(""));   // true
System.out.println(p2.test(""));   // true
```

This prints true twice. More interesting is a BiPredicate. This example also prints true twice:

```
BiPredicate<String, String> b1 = String::startsWith;
BiPredicate<String, String> b2 =
   (string, prefix) -> string.startsWith(prefix);

System.out.println(b1.test("chicken", "chick"));   // true
System.out.println(b2.test("chicken", "chick"));   // true
```

The method reference includes both the instance variable and parameter for startsWith(). This is a good example of how method references save a good bit of typing. The downside is that they are less explicit, and you really have to understand what is going on!

Implementing *Function* and *BiFunction*

In Chapter 14, we used Function with the merge() method. A Function is responsible for turning one parameter into a value of a potentially different type and returning it. Similarly, a BiFunction is responsible for turning two parameters into a value and returning it. The interfaces are defined as follows:

```
@FunctionalInterface
public interface Function<T, R> {
```

```
   R apply(T t);
   // omitted default and static methods
}
```

```
@FunctionalInterface
public interface BiFunction<T, U, R> {
   R apply(T t, U u);
   // omitted default method
}
```

For example, this function converts a String to the length of the String:

```
Function<String, Integer> f1 = String::length;
Function<String, Integer> f2 = x -> x.length();
```

```
System.out.println(f1.apply("cluck")); // 5
System.out.println(f2.apply("cluck")); // 5
```

This function turns a String into an Integer. Well, technically it turns the String into an int, which is autoboxed into an Integer. The types don't have to be different. The following combines two String objects and produces another String:

```
BiFunction<String, String, String> b1 = String::concat;
BiFunction<String, String, String> b2 =
   (string, toAdd) -> string.concat(toAdd);
```

```
System.out.println(b1.apply("baby ", "chick")); // baby chick
System.out.println(b2.apply("baby ", "chick")); // baby chick
```

The first two types in the BiFunction are the input types. The third is the result type. For the method reference, the first parameter is the instance that concat() is called on, and the second is passed to concat().

Creating Your Own Functional Interfaces

Java provides a built-in interface for functions with one or two parameters. What if you need more? No problem. Suppose that you want to create a functional interface for the wheel speed of each wheel on a tricycle. You could create a functional interface such as this:

```
@FunctionalInterface
interface TriFunction<T,U,V,R> {
   R apply(T t, U u, V v);
}
```

There are four type parameters. The first three supply the types of the three wheel speeds. The fourth is the return type. Now suppose that you want to create a function to determine how fast your quad-copter is going given the power of the four motors. You could create a functional interface such as the following:

```
@FunctionalInterface
interface QuadFunction<T,U,V,W,R> {
    R apply(T t, U u, V v, W w);
}
```

There are five type parameters here. The first four supply the types of the four motors. Ideally these would be the same type, but you never know. The fifth is the return type in this example.

Java's built-in interfaces are meant to facilitate the most common functional interfaces that you'll need. It is by no means an exhaustive list. Remember that you can add any functional interfaces you'd like, and Java matches them when you use lambdas or method references.

Implementing *UnaryOperator* and *BinaryOperator*

UnaryOperator and BinaryOperator are a special case of a Function. They require all type parameters to be the same type. A UnaryOperator transforms its value into one of the same type. For example, incrementing by one is a unary operation. In fact, UnaryOperator extends Function. A BinaryOperator merges two values into one of the same type. Adding two numbers is a binary operation. Similarly, BinaryOperator extends BiFunction. The interfaces are defined as follows:

```
@FunctionalInterface
public interface UnaryOperator<T> extends Function<T, T> { }

@FunctionalInterface
public interface BinaryOperator<T> extends BiFunction<T, T, T> {
    // omitted static methods
}
```

This means that method signatures look like this:

```
T apply(T t);          // UnaryOperator

T apply(T t1, T t2);  // BinaryOperator
```

In the Javadoc, you'll notice that these methods are actually inherited from the Function/BiFunction superclass. The generic declarations on the subclass are what force the type to be the same. For the unary example, notice how the return type is the same type as the parameter.

```
UnaryOperator<String> u1 = String::toUpperCase;
UnaryOperator<String> u2 = x -> x.toUpperCase();


System.out.println(u1.apply("chirp"));  // CHIRP
System.out.println(u2.apply("chirp"));  // CHIRP
```

This prints CHIRP twice. We don't need to specify the return type in the generics because UnaryOperator requires it to be the same as the parameter. And now here's the binary example:

```
BinaryOperator<String> b1 = String::concat;
BinaryOperator<String> b2 = (string, toAdd) -> string.concat(toAdd);


System.out.println(b1.apply("baby ", "chick")); // baby chick
System.out.println(b2.apply("baby ", "chick")); // baby chick
```

Notice that this does the same thing as the BiFunction example. The code is more succinct, which shows the importance of using the correct functional interface. It's nice to have one generic type specified instead of three.

Checking Functional Interfaces

It's really important to know the number of parameters, types, return value, and method name for each of the functional interfaces. Now would be a good time to memorize Table 15.1 if you haven't done so already. Let's do some examples to practice.

What functional interface would you use in these three situations?

- Returns a String without taking any parameters
- Returns a Boolean and takes a String
- Returns an Integer and takes two Integers

Ready? Think about what your answer is before continuing. Really. You have to know this cold. OK. The first one is a Supplier<String> because it generates an object and takes zero parameters. The second one is a Function<String,Boolean> because it takes one parameter and returns another type. It's a little tricky. You might think it is a Predicate<String>. Note that a Predicate returns a boolean primitive and not a Boolean object. Finally, the third one is either a BinaryOperator<Integer> or a BiFunction<Integer,Integer,Integer>. Since BinaryOperator is a special case of BiFunction, either is a correct answer. BinaryOperator<Integer> is the better answer of the two since it is more specific.

Let's try this exercise again but with code. It's harder with code. With code, the first thing you do is look at how many parameters the lambda takes and whether there is a return value. What functional interface would you use to fill in the blank for these?

```
6: _____<List> ex1 = x -> "".equals(x.get(0));
7: _____<Long> ex2 = (Long l) -> System.out.println(l);
8: _____<String, String> ex3 = (s1, s2) -> false;
```

Again, think about the answers before continuing. Ready? Line 6 passes one List parameter to the lambda and returns a boolean. This tells us that it is a Predicate or Function. Since the generic declaration has only one parameter, it is a Predicate.

Line 7 passes one Long parameter to the lambda and doesn't return anything. This tells us that it is a Consumer. Line 8 takes two parameters and returns a boolean. When you see a boolean returned, think Predicate unless the generics specify a Boolean return type. In this case, there are two parameters, so it is a BiPredicate.

Are you finding these easy? If not, review Table 15.1 again. We aren't kidding. You need to know the table really well. Now that you are fresh from studying the table, we are going to play "identify the error." These are meant to be tricky:

```
6: Function<List<String>> ex1 = x -> x.get(0); // DOES NOT COMPILE
7: UnaryOperator<Long> ex2 = (Long l) -> 3.14; // DOES NOT COMIPLE
8: Predicate ex4 = String::isEmpty;            // DOES NOT COMPILE
```

Line 6 claims to be a Function. A Function needs to specify two generics—the input parameter type and the return value type. The return value type is missing from line 6, causing the code not to compile. Line 7 is a UnaryOperator, which returns the same type as it is passed in. The example returns a double rather than a Long, causing the code not to compile.

Line 8 is missing the generic for Predicate. This makes the parameter that was passed an Object rather than a String. The lambda expects a String because it calls a method that exists on String rather than Object. Therefore, it doesn't compile.

Convenience Methods on Functional Interfaces

By definition, all functional interfaces have a single abstract method. This doesn't mean they can have only one method, though. Several of the common functional interfaces provide a number of helpful default methods.

Table 15.2 shows the convenience methods on the built-in functional interfaces that you need to know for the exam. All of these facilitate modifying or combining functional interfaces of the same type. Note that Table 15.2 shows only the main interfaces. The BiConsumer, BiFunction, and BiPredicate interfaces have similar methods available.

Let's start with these two Predicate variables.

```
Predicate<String> egg = s -> s.contains("egg");
Predicate<String> brown = s -> s.contains("brown");
```

TABLE 15.2   Convenience methods

Interface instance	Method return type	Method name	Method parameters
Consumer	Consumer	andThen()	Consumer
Function	Function	andThen()	Function
Function	Function	compose()	Function
Predicate	Predicate	and()	Predicate
Predicate	Predicate	negate()	—
Predicate	Predicate	or()	Predicate

Now we want a `Predicate` for brown eggs and another for all other colors of eggs. We could write this by hand, as shown here:

```
Predicate<String> brownEggs =
  s -> s.contains("egg") && s.contains("brown");
Predicate<String> otherEggs =
  s -> s.contains("egg") && ! s.contains("brown");
```

This works, but it's not great. It's a bit long to read, and it contains duplication. What if we decide the letter *e* should be capitalized in *egg*? We'd have to change it in three variables: egg, brownEggs, and otherEggs. A better way to deal with this situation is to use two of the default methods on Predicate.

```
Predicate<String> brownEggs = egg.and(brown);
Predicate<String> otherEggs = egg.and(brown.negate());
```

Neat! Now we are reusing the logic in the original `Predicate` variables to build two new ones. It's shorter and clearer what the relationship is between variables. We can also change the spelling of *egg* in one place, and the other two objects will have new logic because they reference it.

Moving on to `Consumer`, let's take a look at the andThen() method, which runs two functional interfaces in sequence.

```
Consumer<String> c1 = x -> System.out.print("1: " + x);
Consumer<String> c2 = x -> System.out.print(",2: " + x);

Consumer<String> combined = c1.andThen(c2);
combined.accept("Annie");              // 1: Annie,2: Annie
```

Notice how the same parameter gets passed to both c1 and c2. This shows that the Consumer instances are run in sequence and are independent of each other. By contrast, the compose() method on Function chains functional interfaces. However, it passes along the output of one to the input of another.

```
Function<Integer, Integer> before = x -> x + 1;
Function<Integer, Integer> after = x -> x * 2;

Function<Integer, Integer> combined = after.compose(before);
System.out.println(combined.apply(3));   // 8
```

This time the before runs first, turning the 3 into a 4. Then the after runs, doubling the 4 to 8. All of the methods in this section are helpful in simplifying your code as you work with functional interfaces.

Returning an *Optional*

Suppose that you are taking an introductory Java class and receive scores of 90 and 100 on the first two exams. Now, we ask you what your average is. An average is calculated by adding the scores and dividing by the number of scores, so you have (90+100)/2. This gives 190/2, so you answer with 95. Great!

Now suppose that you are taking your second class on Java, and it is the first day of class. We ask you what your average is in this class that just started. You haven't taken any exams yet, so you don't have anything to average. It wouldn't be accurate to say that your average is zero. That sounds bad, and it isn't true. There simply isn't any data, so you don't have an average yet.

How do we express this "we don't know" or "not applicable" answer in Java? We use the Optional type. An Optional is created using a factory. You can either request an empty Optional or pass a value for the Optional to wrap. Think of an Optional as a box that might have something in it or might instead be empty. Figure 15.1 shows both options.

FIGURE 15.1 Optional

Optional.empty()

Optional.of(95)

Creating an *Optional*

Here's how to code our average method:

```
10: public static Optional<Double> average(int... scores) {
11:     if (scores.length == 0) return Optional.empty();
12:     int sum = 0;
13:     for (int score: scores) sum += score;
14:     return Optional.of((double) sum / scores.length);
15: }
```

Line 11 returns an empty Optional when we can't calculate an average. Lines 12 and 13 add up the scores. There is a functional programming way of doing this math, but we will get to that later in the chapter. In fact, the entire method could be written in one line, but that wouldn't teach you how Optional works! Line 14 creates an Optional to wrap the average.

Calling the method shows what is in our two boxes.

```
System.out.println(average(90, 100)); // Optional[95.0]
System.out.println(average());        // Optional.empty
```

You can see that one Optional contains a value and the other is empty. Normally, we want to check whether a value is there and/or get it out of the box. Here's one way to do that:

```
20: Optional<Double> opt = average(90, 100);
21: if (opt.isPresent())
22:     System.out.println(opt.get()); // 95.0
```

Line 21 checks whether the Optional actually contains a value. Line 22 prints it out. What if we didn't do the check and the Optional was empty?

```
26: Optional<Double> opt = average();
27: System.out.println(opt.get()); // NoSuchElementException
```

We'd get an exception since there is no value inside the Optional.

```
java.util.NoSuchElementException: No value present
```

When creating an Optional, it is common to want to use empty() when the value is null. You can do this with an if statement or ternary operator. We use the ternary operator (? :) to simplify the code, which you saw Chapter 3, "Operators".

```
Optional o = (value == null) ? Optional.empty() : Optional.of(value);
```

If value is null, o is assigned the empty Optional. Otherwise, we wrap the value. Since this is such a common pattern, Java provides a factory method to do the same thing.

```
Optional o = Optional.ofNullable(value);
```

That covers the static methods you need to know about Optional. Table 15.3 summarizes most of the instance methods on Optional that you need to know for the exam. There are a few others that involve chaining. We will cover those later in the chapter.

TABLE 15.3 Optional instance methods

Method	When Optional is empty	When Optional contains a value
get()	Throws an exception	Returns value
ifPresent(Consumer c)	Does nothing	Calls Consumer with value
isPresent()	Returns false	Returns true
orElse(T other)	Returns other parameter	Returns value
orElseGet(Supplier s)	Returns result of calling Supplier	Returns value
orElseThrow()	Throws NoSuchElementException	Returns value
orElseThrow (Supplier s)	Throws exception created by calling Supplier	Returns value

You've already seen get() and isPresent(). The other methods allow you to write code that uses an Optional in one line without having to use the ternary operator. This makes the code easier to read. Instead of using an if statement, which we used when checking the average earlier, we can specify a Consumer to be run when there is a value inside the Optional. When there isn't, the method simply skips running the Consumer.

```
Optional<Double> opt = average(90, 100);
opt.ifPresent(System.out::println);
```

Using ifPresent() better expresses our intent. We want something done if a value is present. You can think of it as an if statement with no else.

Dealing with an Empty *Optional*

The remaining methods allow you to specify what to do if a value isn't present. There are a few choices. The first two allow you to specify a return value either directly or using a Supplier.

```
30: Optional<Double> opt = average();
31: System.out.println(opt.orElse(Double.NaN));
32: System.out.println(opt.orElseGet(() -> Math.random()));
```

This prints something like the following:

```
NaN
0.49775932295380165
```

Line 31 shows that you can return a specific value or variable. In our case, we print the "not a number" value. Line 32 shows using a Supplier to generate a value at runtime to return instead. I'm glad our professors didn't give us a random average, though!

Alternatively, we can have the code throw an exception if the Optional is empty.

```
30: Optional<Double> opt = average();
31: System.out.println(opt.orElseThrow());
```

This prints something like the following:

```
Exception in thread "main" java.util.NoSuchElementException:
  No value present
  at java.base/java.util.Optional.orElseThrow(Optional.java:382)
```

Without specifying a Supplier for the exception, Java will throw a NoSuchElementException. This method was added in Java 10. Remember that the stack trace looks weird because the lambdas are generated rather than named classes. Alternatively, we can have the code throw a custom exception if the Optional is empty.

```
30: Optional<Double> opt = average();
31: System.out.println(opt.orElseThrow(
32:     () -> new IllegalStateException()));
```

This prints something like the following:

```
Exception in thread "main" java.lang.IllegalStateException
   at optionals.Methods.lambda$orElse$1(Methods.java:30)
   at java.base/java.util.Optional.orElseThrow(Optional.java:408)
```

Line 32 shows using a Supplier to create an exception that should be thrown. Notice that we do not write throw new IllegalStateException(). The orElseThrow() method takes care of actually throwing the exception when we run it.

The two methods that take a Supplier have different names. Do you see why this code does not compile?

```
System.out.println(opt.orElseGet(
   () -> new IllegalStateException())); // DOES NOT COMPILE
```

The opt variable is an Optional<Double>. This means the Supplier must return a Double. Since this supplier returns an exception, the type does not match.

The last example with Optional is really easy. What do you think this does?

```
Optional<Double> opt = average(90, 100);
System.out.println(opt.orElse(Double.NaN));
System.out.println(opt.orElseGet(() -> Math.random()));
System.out.println(opt.orElseThrow());
```

It prints out 95.0 three times. Since the value does exist, there is no need to use the "or else" logic.

Is *Optional* the Same as *null*?

Before Java 8, programmers would return null instead of Optional. There were a few shortcomings with this approach. One was that there wasn't a clear way to express that null might be a special value. By contrast, returning an Optional is a clear statement in the API that there might not be a value in there.

Another advantage of Optional is that you can use a functional programming style with ifPresent() and the other methods rather than needing an if statement. Finally, you'll see toward the end of the chapter that you can chain Optional calls.

Using Streams

A *stream* in Java is a sequence of data. A *stream pipeline* consists of the operations that run on a stream to produce a result. First we will look at the flow of pipelines conceptually. After that, we will actually get into code.

Understanding the Pipeline Flow

Think of a stream pipeline as an assembly line in a factory. Suppose that we were running an assembly line to make signs for the animal exhibits at the zoo. We have a number of jobs. It is one person's job to take signs out of a box. It is a second person's job to paint the sign. It is a third person's job to stencil the name of the animal on the sign. It's the last person's job to put the completed sign in a box to be carried to the proper exhibit.

Notice that the second person can't do anything until one sign has been taken out of the box by the first person. Similarly, the third person can't do anything until one sign has been painted, and the last person can't do anything until it is stenciled.

The assembly line for making signs is finite. Once we process the contents of our box of signs, we are finished. *Finite* streams have a limit. Other assembly lines essentially run forever, like one for food production. Of course, they do stop at some point when the factory closes down, but pretend that doesn't happen. Or think of a sunrise/sunset cycle as *infinite*, since it doesn't end for an inordinately large period of time.

Another important feature of an assembly line is that each person touches each element to do their operation and then that piece of data is gone. It doesn't come back. The next person deals with it at that point. This is different than the lists and queues that you saw in the previous chapter. With a list, you can access any element at any time. With a queue, you are limited in which elements you can access, but all of the elements are there. With streams, the data isn't generated up front—it is created when needed. This is an example of *lazy evaluation*, which delays execution until necessary.

Many things can happen in the assembly line stations along the way. In functional programming, these are called *stream operations*. Just like with the assembly line, operations occur in a pipeline. Someone has to start and end the work, and there can be any number of stations in between. After all, a job with one person isn't an assembly line! There are three parts to a stream pipeline, as shown in Figure 15.2.

- **Source:** Where the stream comes from
- **Intermediate operations:** Transforms the stream into another one. There can be as few or as many intermediate operations as you'd like. Since streams use lazy evaluation, the intermediate operations do not run until the terminal operation runs.
- **Terminal operation:** Actually produces a result. Since streams can be used only once, the stream is no longer valid after a terminal operation completes.

FIGURE 15.2   Stream pipeline

Notice that the operations are unknown to us. When viewing the assembly line from the outside, you care only about what comes in and goes out. What happens in between is an implementation detail.

You will need to know the differences between intermediate and terminal operations well. Make sure you can fill in Table 15.4.

TABLE 15.4   Intermediate vs. terminal operations

Scenario	Intermediate operation	Terminal operation
Required part of a useful pipeline?	No	Yes
Can exist multiple times in a pipeline?	Yes	No
Return type is a stream type?	Yes	No
Executed upon method call?	No	Yes
Stream valid after call?	Yes	No

A factory typically has a foreman who oversees the work. Java serves as the foreman when working with stream pipelines. This is a really important role, especially when dealing with lazy evaluation and infinite streams. Think of declaring the stream as giving instructions to the foreman. As the foreman finds out what needs to be done, he sets up the stations and tells the workers what their duties will be. However, the workers do not start until the foreman tells them to begin. The foreman waits until he sees the terminal operation to actually kick off the work. He also watches the work and stops the line as soon as work is complete.

Let's look at a few examples of this. We aren't using code in these examples because it is really important to understand the stream pipeline concept before starting to write the code. Figure 15.3 shows a stream pipeline with one intermediate operation.

FIGURE 15.3   Steps in running a stream pipeline

Let's take a look at what happens from the point of the view of the foreman. First, he sees that the source is taking signs out of the box. The foreman sets up a worker at the table to unpack the box and says to await a signal to start. Then the foreman sees the intermediate operation to paint the sign. He sets up a worker with paint and says to await a signal to start. Finally, the foreman sees the terminal operation to put the signs into a pile. He sets up a worker to do this and yells out that all three workers should start.

Suppose that there are two signs in the box. Step 1 is the first worker taking one sign out of the box and handing it to the second worker. Step 2 is the second worker painting it and handing it to the third worker. Step 3 is the third worker putting it in the pile. Steps 4–6 are this same process for the other sign. Then the foreman sees that there are no more signs left and shuts down the entire enterprise.

The foreman is smart. He can make decisions about how to best do the work based on what is needed. As an example, let's explore the stream pipeline in Figure 15.4.

The foreman still sees a source of taking signs out of the box and assigns a worker to do that on command. He still sees an intermediate operation to paint and sets up another worker with instructions to wait and then paint. Then he sees an intermediate step that we need only two signs. He sets up a worker to count the signs that go by and notify him when the worker has seen two. Finally, he sets up a worker for the terminal operation to put the signs in a pile.

FIGURE 15.4 A stream pipeline with a limit

This time, suppose that there are 10 signs in the box. We start out like last time. The first sign makes its way down the pipeline. The second sign also makes its way down the pipeline. When the worker in charge of counting sees the second sign, she tells the foreman. The foreman lets the terminal operation worker finish her task and then yells out "stop the line." It doesn't matter that there are eight more signs in the box. We don't need them, so it would be unnecessary work to paint them. And we all want to avoid unnecessary work!

Similarly, the foreman would have stopped the line after the first sign if the terminal operation was to find the first sign that gets created.

In the following sections, we will cover the three parts of the pipeline. We will also discuss special types of streams for primitives and how to print a stream.

Creating Stream Sources

In Java, the streams we have been talking about are represented by the Stream<T> interface, defined in the java.util.stream package.

Creating Finite Streams

For simplicity, we'll start with finite streams. There are a few ways to create them.

```
11: Stream<String> empty = Stream.empty();          // count = 0
12: Stream<Integer> singleElement = Stream.of(1);   // count = 1
13: Stream<Integer> fromArray = Stream.of(1, 2, 3); // count = 3
```

Line 11 shows how to create an empty stream. Line 12 shows how to create a stream with a single element. Line 13 shows how to create a stream from a varargs. You've undoubtedly noticed that there isn't an array on line 13. The method signature uses varargs, which let you specify an array or individual elements.

Java also provides a convenient way of converting a Collection to a stream.

```
14: var list = List.of("a", "b", "c");
15: Stream<String> fromList = list.stream();
```

Line 15 shows that it is a simple method call to create a stream from a list. This is helpful since such conversions are common.

Creating a Parallel Stream

It is just as easy to create a parallel stream from a list.

```
24: var list = List.of("a", "b", "c");
25: Stream<String> fromListParallel = list.parallelStream();
```

This is a great feature because you can write code that uses concurrency before even learning what a thread is. Using parallel streams is like setting up multiple tables of workers who are able to do the same task. Painting would be a lot faster if we could have five painters painting signs instead of just one. Just keep in mind some tasks cannot be done in parallel, such as putting the signs away in the order that they were created in the stream. Also be aware that there is a cost in coordinating the work, so for smaller streams, it might be faster to do it sequentially. You'll learn much more about running tasks concurrently in Chapter 18.

Creating Infinite Streams

So far, this isn't particularly impressive. We could do all this with lists. We can't create an infinite list, though, which makes streams more powerful.

```
17: Stream<Double> randoms = Stream.generate(Math::random);
18: Stream<Integer> oddNumbers = Stream.iterate(1, n -> n + 2);
```

Line 17 generates a stream of random numbers. How many random numbers? However many you need. If you call randoms.forEach(System.out::println), the program will print random numbers until you kill it. Later in the chapter, you'll learn about operations like limit() to turn the infinite stream into a finite stream.

Line 18 gives you more control. The iterate() method takes a seed or starting value as the first parameter. This is the first element that will be part of the stream. The other parameter is a lambda expression that gets passed the previous value and generates the next value. As with the random numbers example, it will keep on producing odd numbers as long as you need them.

If you try to call System.out.print(stream), you'll get something like the following:

```
java.util.stream.ReferencePipeline$3@4517d9a3
```

This is different from a Collection where you see the contents. You don't need to know this for the exam. We mention it so that you aren't caught by surprise when writing code for practice.

What if you wanted just odd numbers less than 100? Java 9 introduced an overloaded version of iterate() that helps with just that.

```
19: Stream<Integer> oddNumberUnder100 = Stream.iterate(
20:    1,                  // seed
21:    n -> n < 100,       // Predicate to specify when done
22:    n -> n + 2);        // UnaryOperator to get next value
```

This method takes three parameters. Notice how they are separated by commas (,) just like all other methods. The exam may try to trick you by using semicolons since it is similar to a for loop. Similar to a for loop, you have to take care that you aren't accidentally creating an infinite stream.

Reviewing Stream Creation Methods

To review, make sure you know all the methods in Table 15.5. These are the ways of creating a source for streams, given a Collection instance coll.

TABLE 15.5   Creating a source

Method	Finite or infinite?	Notes
Stream.empty()	Finite	Creates Stream with zero elements
Stream.of(varargs)	Finite	Creates Stream with elements listed
coll.stream()	Finite	Creates Stream from a Collection
coll.parallelStream()	Finite	Creates Stream from a Collection where the stream can run in parallel
Stream.generate(supplier)	Infinite	Creates Stream by calling the Supplier for each element upon request
Stream.iterate(seed, unaryOperator)	Infinite	Creates Stream by using the seed for the first element and then calling the UnaryOperator for each subsequent element upon request
Stream.iterate(seed, predicate, unaryOperator)	Finite or infinite	Creates Stream by using the seed for the first element and then calling the UnaryOperator for each subsequent element upon request. Stops if the Predicate returns false

Using Common Terminal Operations

You can perform a terminal operation without any intermediate operations but not the other way around. This is why we will talk about terminal operations first. *Reductions* are a special type of terminal operation where all of the contents of the stream are combined into a single primitive or Object. For example, you might have an int or a Collection.

Table 15.6 summarizes this section. Feel free to use it as a guide to remember the most important points as we go through each one individually. We explain them from simplest to most complex rather than alphabetically.

TABLE 15.6 Terminal stream operations

Method	What happens for infinite streams	Return value	Reduction
count()	Does not terminate	long	Yes
min() max()	Does not terminate	Optional\<T>	Yes
findAny() findFirst()	Terminates	Optional\<T>	No
allMatch() anyMatch() noneMatch()	Sometimes terminates	boolean	No
forEach()	Does not terminate	void	No
reduce()	Does not terminate	Varies	Yes
collect()	Does not terminate	Varies	Yes

count()

The count() method determines the number of elements in a finite stream. For an infinite stream, it never terminates. Why? Count from 1 to infinity and let us know when you are finished. Or rather, don't do that because we'd rather you study for the exam than spend the rest of your life counting. The count() method is a reduction because it looks at each element in the stream and returns a single value. The method signature is as follows:

```
long count()
```

This example shows calling count() on a finite stream:

```
Stream<String> s = Stream.of("monkey", "gorilla", "bonobo");
System.out.println(s.count());    // 3
```

min() and max()

The min() and max() methods allow you to pass a custom comparator and find the smallest or largest value in a finite stream according to that sort order. Like the count() method, min() and max() hang on an infinite stream because they cannot be sure that a smaller or larger value isn't coming later in the stream. Both methods are reductions because they return a single value after looking at the entire stream. The method signatures are as follows:

```
Optional<T> min(Comparator<? super T> comparator)
Optional<T> max(Comparator<? super T> comparator)
```

This example finds the animal with the fewest letters in its name:

```
Stream<String> s = Stream.of("monkey", "ape", "bonobo");
Optional<String> min = s.min((s1, s2) -> s1.length()-s2.length());
min.ifPresent(System.out::println); // ape
```

Notice that the code returns an Optional rather than the value. This allows the method to specify that no minimum or maximum was found. We use the Optional method ifPresent() and a method reference to print out the minimum only if one is found. As an example of where there isn't a minimum, let's look at an empty stream.

```
Optional<?> minEmpty = Stream.empty().min((s1, s2) -> 0);
System.out.println(minEmpty.isPresent()); // false
```

Since the stream is empty, the comparator is never called, and no value is present in the Optional.

> **NOTE**   What if you need both the min() and max() values of the same stream? For now, you can't have both, at least not using these methods. Remember, a stream can have only one terminal operation. Once a terminal operation has been run, the stream cannot be used again. As we'll see later in this chapter, there are built-in summary methods for some numeric streams that will calculate a set of values for you.

findAny() and findFirst()

The findAny() and findFirst() methods return an element of the stream unless the stream is empty. If the stream is empty, they return an empty Optional. This is the first method you've seen that can terminate with an infinite stream. Since Java generates only the amount of stream you need, the infinite stream needs to generate only one element.

As its name implies, the findAny() method can return any element of the stream. When called on the streams you've seen up until now, it commonly returns the first element, although this behavior is not guaranteed. As you'll see in Chapter 18, the findAny() method is more likely to return a random element when working with parallel streams.

These methods are terminal operations but not reductions. The reason is that they sometimes return without processing all of the elements. This means that they return a value based on the stream but do not reduce the entire stream into one value.

The method signatures are as follows:

```
Optional<T> findAny()
Optional<T> findFirst()
```

This example finds an animal:

```
Stream<String> s = Stream.of("monkey", "gorilla", "bonobo");
Stream<String> infinite = Stream.generate(() -> "chimp");
```

```
s.findAny().ifPresent(System.out::println);        // monkey (usually)
infinite.findAny().ifPresent(System.out::println); // chimp
```

Finding any one match is more useful than it sounds. Sometimes we just want to sample the results and get a representative element, but we don't need to waste the processing generating them all. After all, if we plan to work with only one element, why bother looking at more?

allMatch(), anyMatch(), and noneMatch()

The allMatch(), anyMatch(), and noneMatch() methods search a stream and return information about how the stream pertains to the predicate. These may or may not terminate for infinite streams. It depends on the data. Like the find methods, they are not reductions because they do not necessarily look at all of the elements.

The method signatures are as follows:

```
boolean anyMatch(Predicate <? super T> predicate)
boolean allMatch(Predicate <? super T> predicate)
boolean noneMatch(Predicate <? super T> predicate)
```

This example checks whether animal names begin with letters:

```
var list = List.of("monkey", "2", "chimp");
Stream<String> infinite = Stream.generate(() -> "chimp");
Predicate<String> pred = x -> Character.isLetter(x.charAt(0));
```

```
System.out.println(list.stream().anyMatch(pred));  // true
System.out.println(list.stream().allMatch(pred));  // false
System.out.println(list.stream().noneMatch(pred)); // false
System.out.println(infinite.anyMatch(pred));       // true
```

This shows that we can reuse the same predicate, but we need a different stream each time. The `anyMatch()` method returns `true` because two of the three elements match. The `allMatch()` method returns `false` because one doesn't match. The `noneMatch()` method also returns `false` because one matches. On the infinite stream, one match is found, so the call terminates. If we called `allMatch()`, it would run until we killed the program.

> Remember that `allMatch()`, `anyMatch()`, and `noneMatch()` return a boolean. By contrast, the find methods return an `Optional` because they return an element of the stream.

forEach()

Like in the Java Collections Framework, it is common to iterate over the elements of a stream. As expected, calling `forEach()` on an infinite stream does not terminate. Since there is no return value, it is not a reduction.

Before you use it, consider if another approach would be better. Developers who learned to write loops first tend to use them for everything. For example, a loop with an `if` statement could be written with a filter. You will learn about filters in the intermediate operations section.

The method signature is as follows:

```
void forEach(Consumer<? super T> action)
```

Notice that this is the only terminal operation with a return type of `void`. If you want something to happen, you have to make it happen in the `Consumer`. Here's one way to print the elements in the stream (there are other ways, which we cover later in the chapter):

```
Stream<String> s = Stream.of("Monkey", "Gorilla", "Bonobo");
s.forEach(System.out::print); // MonkeyGorillaBonobo
```

> Remember that you can call `forEach()` directly on a `Collection` or on a `Stream`. Don't get confused on the exam when you see both approaches.

Notice that you can't use a traditional `for` loop on a stream.

```
Stream<Integer> s = Stream.of(1);
for (Integer i  : s) {} // DOES NOT COMPILE
```

While `forEach()` sounds like a loop, it is really a terminal operator for streams. Streams cannot be used as the source in a `for-each` loop to run because they don't implement the `Iterable` interface.

reduce()

The reduce() method combines a stream into a single object. It is a reduction, which means it processes all elements. The three method signatures are these:

```
T reduce(T identity, BinaryOperator<T> accumulator)

Optional<T> reduce(BinaryOperator<T> accumulator)

<U> U reduce(U identity,
    BiFunction<U,? super T,U> accumulator,
    BinaryOperator<U> combiner)
```

Let's take them one at a time. The most common way of doing a reduction is to start with an initial value and keep merging it with the next value. Think about how you would concatenate an array of String objects into a single String without functional programming. It might look something like this:

```
var array = new String[] { "w", "o", "l", "f" };
var result = "";
for (var s: array) result = result + s;
System.out.println(result); // wolf
```

The *identity* is the initial value of the reduction, in this case an empty String. The *accumulator* combines the current result with the current value in the stream. With lambdas, we can do the same thing with a stream and reduction:

```
Stream<String> stream = Stream.of("w", "o", "l", "f");
String word = stream.reduce("", (s, c) -> s + c);
System.out.println(word); // wolf
```

Notice how we still have the empty String as the identity. We also still concatenate the String objects to get the next value. We can even rewrite this with a method reference.

```
Stream<String> stream = Stream.of("w", "o", "l", "f");
String word = stream.reduce("", String::concat);
System.out.println(word); // wolf
```

Let's try another one. Can you write a reduction to multiply all of the Integer objects in a stream? Try it. Our solution is shown here:

```
Stream<Integer> stream = Stream.of(3, 5, 6);
System.out.println(stream.reduce(1, (a, b) -> a*b));  // 90
```

We set the identity to 1 and the accumulator to multiplication. In many cases, the identity isn't really necessary, so Java lets us omit it. When you don't specify an identity, an Optional is returned because there might not be any data. There are three choices for what is in the Optional.

- If the stream is empty, an empty `Optional` is returned.
- If the stream has one element, it is returned.
- If the stream has multiple elements, the accumulator is applied to combine them.

The following illustrates each of these scenarios:

```
BinaryOperator<Integer> op = (a, b) -> a * b;
Stream<Integer> empty = Stream.empty();
Stream<Integer> oneElement = Stream.of(3);
Stream<Integer> threeElements = Stream.of(3, 5, 6);
```

```
empty.reduce(op).ifPresent(System.out::println);          // no output
oneElement.reduce(op).ifPresent(System.out::println);     // 3
threeElements.reduce(op).ifPresent(System.out::println); // 90
```

Why are there two similar methods? Why not just always require the identity? Java could have done that. However, sometimes it is nice to differentiate the case where the stream is empty rather than the case where there is a value that happens to match the identity being returned from calculation. The signature returning an `Optional` lets us differentiate these cases. For example, we might return `Optional.empty()` when the stream is empty and `Optional.of(3)` when there is a value.

The third method signature is used when we are dealing with different types. It allows Java to create intermediate reductions and then combine them at the end. Let's take a look at an example that counts the number of characters in each `String`:

```
Stream<String> stream = Stream.of("w", "o", "l", "f!");
int length = stream.reduce(0, (i, s) -> i+s.length(), (a, b) -> a+b);
System.out.println(length); // 5
```

The first parameter (0) is the value for the initializer. If we had an empty stream, this would be the answer. The second parameter is the *accumulator*. Unlike the accumulators you saw previously, this one handles mixed data types. In this example, the first argument, i, is an `Integer`, while the second argument, s, is a `String`. It adds the length of the current `String` to our running total. The third parameter is called the *combiner*, which combines any intermediate totals. In this case, a and b are both `Integer` values.

The three-argument reduce() operation is useful when working with parallel streams because it allows the stream to be decomposed and reassembled by separate threads. For example, if we needed to count the length of four 100-character strings, the first two values and the last two values could be computed independently. The intermediate result (200 + 200) would then be combined into the final value.

collect()

The collect() method is a special type of reduction called a *mutable reduction*. It is more efficient than a regular reduction because we use the same mutable object while accumulating. Common mutable objects include `StringBuilder` and `ArrayList`. This is a really useful method, because it lets us get data out of streams and into another form. The method signatures are as follows:

```
<R> R collect(Supplier<R> supplier,
   BiConsumer<R, ? super T> accumulator,
   BiConsumer<R, R> combiner)

<R,A> R collect(Collector<? super T, A,R> collector)
```

Let's start with the first signature, which is used when we want to code specifically how collecting should work. Our wolf example from reduce can be converted to use collect().

```
Stream<String> stream = Stream.of("w", "o", "l", "f");

StringBuilder word = stream.collect(
   StringBuilder::new,
   StringBuilder::append,
   StringBuilder::append)

System.out.println(word); // wolf
```

The first parameter is the *supplier*, which creates the object that will store the results as we collect data. Remember that a Supplier doesn't take any parameters and returns a value. In this case, it constructs a new StringBuilder.

The second parameter is the *accumulator*, which is a BiConsumer that takes two parameters and doesn't return anything. It is responsible for adding one more element to the data collection. In this example, it appends the next String to the StringBuilder.

The final parameter is the *combiner*, which is another BiConsumer. It is responsible for taking two data collections and merging them. This is useful when we are processing in parallel. Two smaller collections are formed and then merged into one. This would work with StringBuilder only if we didn't care about the order of the letters. In this case, the accumulator and combiner have similar logic.

Now let's look at an example where the logic is different in the accumulator and combiner.

```
Stream<String> stream = Stream.of("w", "o", "l", "f");

TreeSet<String> set = stream.collect(
   TreeSet::new,
   TreeSet::add,
   TreeSet::addAll);

System.out.println(set); // [f, l, o, w]
```

The collector has three parts as before. The supplier creates an empty `TreeSet`. The accumulator adds a single `String` from the `Stream` to the `TreeSet`. The combiner adds all of the elements of one `TreeSet` to another in case the operations were done in parallel and need to be merged.

We started with the long signature because that's how you implement your own collector. It is important to know how to do this for the exam and to understand how collectors work. In practice, there are many common collectors that come up over and over. Rather than making developers keep reimplementing the same ones, Java provides a class with common collectors cleverly named `Collectors`. This approach also makes the code easier to read because it is more expressive. For example, we could rewrite the previous example as follows:

```
Stream<String> stream = Stream.of("w", "o", "l", "f");
TreeSet<String> set =
  stream.collect(Collectors.toCollection(TreeSet::new));
System.out.println(set); // [f, l, o, w]
```

If we didn't need the set to be sorted, we could make the code even shorter:

```
Stream<String> stream = Stream.of("w", "o", "l", "f");
Set<String> set = stream.collect(Collectors.toSet());
System.out.println(set); // [f, w, l, o]
```

You might get different output for this last one since `toSet()` makes no guarantees as to which implementation of `Set` you'll get. It is likely to be a `HashSet`, but you shouldn't expect or rely on that.

The exam expects you to know about common predefined collectors in addition to being able to write your own by passing a supplier, accumulator, and combiner.

Later in this chapter, we will show many `Collectors` that are used for grouping data. It's a big topic, so it's best to master how streams work before adding too many `Collectors` into the mix.

Using Common Intermediate Operations

Unlike a terminal operation, an intermediate operation produces a stream as its result. An intermediate operation can also deal with an infinite stream simply by returning another infinite stream. Since elements are produced only as needed, this works fine. The assembly line worker doesn't need to worry about how many more elements are coming through and instead can focus on the current element.

filter()

The filter() method returns a Stream with elements that match a given expression. Here is the method signature:

```
Stream<T> filter(Predicate<? super T> predicate)
```

This operation is easy to remember and powerful because we can pass any Predicate to it. For example, this filters all elements that begin with the letter *m*:

```
Stream<String> s = Stream.of("monkey", "gorilla", "bonobo");
s.filter(x -> x.startsWith("m"))
    .forEach(System.out::print); // monkey
```

distinct()

The distinct() method returns a stream with duplicate values removed. The duplicates do not need to be adjacent to be removed. As you might imagine, Java calls equals() to determine whether the objects are the same. The method signature is as follows:

```
Stream<T> distinct()
```

Here's an example:

```
Stream<String> s = Stream.of("duck", "duck", "duck", "goose");
s.distinct()
    .forEach(System.out::print); // duckgoose
```

limit() and skip()

The limit() and skip() methods can make a Stream smaller, or they could make a finite stream out of an infinite stream. The method signatures are shown here:

```
Stream<T> limit(long maxSize)
Stream<T> skip(long n)
```

The following code creates an infinite stream of numbers counting from 1. The skip() operation returns an infinite stream starting with the numbers counting from 6, since it skips the first five elements. The limit() call takes the first two of those. Now we have a finite stream with two elements, which we can then print with the forEach() method.

```
Stream<Integer> s = Stream.iterate(1, n -> n + 1);
s.skip(5)
    .limit(2)
    .forEach(System.out::print); // 67
```

map()

The map() method creates a one-to-one mapping from the elements in the stream to the elements of the next step in the stream. The method signature is as follows:

```
<R> Stream<R> map(Function<? super T, ? extends R> mapper)
```

This one looks more complicated than the others you have seen. It uses the lambda expression to figure out the type passed to that function and the one returned. The return type is the stream that gets returned.

The map() method on streams is for transforming data. Don't confuse it with the Map interface, which maps keys to values.

As an example, this code converts a list of String objects to a list of Integer objects representing their lengths.

```
Stream<String> s = Stream.of("monkey", "gorilla", "bonobo");
s.map(String::length)
    .forEach(System.out::print); // 676
```

Remember that String::length is shorthand for the lambda x -> x.length(), which clearly shows it is a function that turns a String into an Integer.

flatMap()

The flatMap() method takes each element in the stream and makes any elements it contains top-level elements in a single stream. This is helpful when you want to remove empty elements from a stream or you want to combine a stream of lists. We are showing you the method signature for consistency with the other methods, just so you don't think we are hiding anything. You aren't expected to be able to read this:

```
<R> Stream<R> flatMap(
    Function<? super T, ? extends Stream<? extends R>> mapper)
```

This gibberish basically says that it returns a Stream of the type that the function contains at a lower level. Don't worry about the signature. It's a headache.

What you should understand is the example. This gets all of the animals into the same level along with getting rid of the empty list.

```
List<String> zero = List.of();
var one = List.of("Bonobo");
var two = List.of("Mama Gorilla", "Baby Gorilla");
Stream<List<String>> animals = Stream.of(zero, one, two);

animals.flatMap(m -> m.stream())
    .forEach(System.out::println);
```

Here's the output:

```
Bonobo
Mama Gorilla
Baby Gorilla
```

As you can see, it removed the empty list completely and changed all elements of each list to be at the top level of the stream.

sorted()

The sorted() method returns a stream with the elements sorted. Just like sorting arrays, Java uses natural ordering unless we specify a comparator. The method signatures are these:

```
Stream<T> sorted()
Stream<T> sorted(Comparator<? super T> comparator)
```

Calling the first signature uses the default sort order.

```
Stream<String> s = Stream.of("brown-", "bear-");
s.sorted()
   .forEach(System.out::print); // bear-brown-
```

We can optionally use a Comparator implementation via a method or a lambda. In this example, we are using a method:

```
Stream<String> s = Stream.of("brown bear-", "grizzly-");
s.sorted(Comparator.reverseOrder())
   .forEach(System.out::print); // grizzly-brown bear-
```

Here we passed a Comparator to specify that we want to sort in the reverse of natural sort order. Ready for a tricky one? Do you see why this doesn't compile?

```
s.sorted(Comparator::reverseOrder); // DOES NOT COMPILE
```

Take a look at the method signatures again. Comparator is a functional interface. This means that we can use method references or lambdas to implement it. The Comparator interface implements one method that takes two String parameters and returns an int. However, Comparator::reverseOrder doesn't do that. It is a reference to a function that takes zero parameters and returns a Comparator. This is not compatible with the interface. This means that we have to use a method and not a method reference. We bring this up to remind you that you really do need to know method references well.

peek()

The peek() method is our final intermediate operation. It is useful for debugging because it allows us to perform a stream operation without actually changing the stream. The method signature is as follows:

```
Stream<T> peek(Consumer<? super T> action)
```

You might notice the intermediate peek() operation takes the same argument as the terminal forEach() operation Think of peek() as an intermediate version of forEach() that returns the original stream back to you.

The most common use for peek() is to output the contents of the stream as it goes by. Suppose that we made a typo and counted bears beginning with the letter *g* instead of *b*. We are puzzled why the count is 1 instead of 2. We can add a peek() method to find out why.

```
var stream = Stream.of("black bear", "brown bear", "grizzly");
long count = stream.filter(s -> s.startsWith("g"))
    .peek(System.out::println).count();          // grizzly
System.out.println(count);                       // 1
```

In Chapter 14, you saw that peek() looks only at the first element when working with a Queue. In a stream, peek() looks at each element that goes through that part of the stream pipeline. It's like having a worker take notes on how a particular step of the process is doing.

Danger: Changing State with *peek()*

Remember that peek() is intended to perform an operation without changing the result. Here's a straightforward stream pipeline that doesn't use peek():

```
var numbers = new ArrayList<>();
var letters = new ArrayList<>();
numbers.add(1);
letters.add('a');

Stream<List<?>> stream = Stream.of(numbers, letters);
stream.map(List::size).forEach(System.out::print); // 11
```

Now we add a peek() call and note that Java doesn't prevent us from writing bad peek code.

```
Stream<List<?>> bad = Stream.of(numbers, letters);
bad.peek(x -> x.remove(0))
    .map(List::size)
    .forEach(System.out::print); // 00
```

This example is bad because peek() is modifying the data structure that is used in the stream, which causes the result of the stream pipeline to be different than if the peek wasn't present.

Putting Together the Pipeline

Streams allow you to use chaining and express what you want to accomplish rather than how to do so. Let's say that we wanted to get the first two names of our friends alphabetically that are four characters long. Without streams, we'd have to write something like the following:

```
var list = List.of("Toby", "Anna", "Leroy", "Alex");
List<String> filtered = new ArrayList<>();
for (String name: list)
   if (name.length() == 4) filtered.add(name);

Collections.sort(filtered);
var iter = filtered.iterator();
if (iter.hasNext()) System.out.println(iter.next());
if (iter.hasNext()) System.out.println(iter.next());
```

This works. It takes some reading and thinking to figure out what is going on. The problem we are trying to solve gets lost in the implementation. It is also very focused on the how rather than on the what. With streams, the equivalent code is as follows:

```
var list = List.of("Toby", "Anna", "Leroy", "Alex");
list.stream().filter(n -> n.length() == 4).sorted()
   .limit(2).forEach(System.out::println);
```

Before you say that it is harder to read, we can format it.

```
var list = List.of("Toby", "Anna", "Leroy", "Alex");
list.stream()
   .filter(n -> n.length() == 4)
   .sorted()
   .limit(2)
   .forEach(System.out::println);
```

The difference is that we express what is going on. We care about String objects of length 4. Then we want them sorted. Then we want the first two. Then we want to print them out. It maps better to the problem that we are trying to solve, and it is simpler.

Once you start using streams in your code, you may find yourself using them in many places. Having shorter, briefer, and clearer code is definitely a good thing!

In this example, you see all three parts of the pipeline. Figure 15.5 shows how each intermediate operation in the pipeline feeds into the next.

FIGURE 15.5 Stream pipeline with multiple intermediate operations

Remember that the assembly line foreman is figuring out how to best implement the stream pipeline. He sets up all of the tables with instructions to wait before starting. He tells the limit() worker to inform him when two elements go by. He tells the sorted() worker that she should just collect all of the elements as they come in and sort them all at once. After sorting, she should start passing them to the limit() worker one at a time. The data flow looks like this:

1. The stream() method sends Toby to filter(). The filter() method sees that the length is good and sends Toby to sorted(). The sorted() method can't sort yet because it needs all of the data, so it holds Toby.

2. The stream() method sends Anna to filter(). The filter() method sees that the length is good and sends Anna to sorted(). The sorted() method can't sort yet because it needs all of the data, so it holds Anna.

3. The stream() method sends Leroy to filter(). The filter() method sees that the length is not a match, and it takes Leroy out of the assembly line processing.

4. The stream() method sends Alex to filter(). The filter() method sees that the length is good and sends Alex to sorted(). The sorted() method can't sort yet because it needs all of the data, so it holds Alex. It turns out sorted() does have all of the required data, but it doesn't know it yet.

5. The foreman lets sorted() know that it is time to sort and the sort occurs.

6. The sorted() method sends Alex to limit(). The limit() method remembers that it has seen one element and sends Alex to forEach(), printing Alex.

7. The sorted() method sends Anna to limit(). The limit() method remembers that it has seen two elements and sends Anna to forEach(), printing Anna.

8. The limit() method has now seen all of the elements that are needed and tells the foreman. The foreman stops the line, and no more processing occurs in the pipeline.

Make sense? Let's try a few more examples to make sure that you understand this well. What do you think the following does?

```
Stream.generate(() -> "Elsa")
    .filter(n -> n.length() == 4)
    .sorted()
    .limit(2)
    .forEach(System.out::println);
```

It actually hangs until you kill the program or it throws an exception after running out of memory. The foreman has instructed sorted() to wait until everything to sort is present. That never happens because there is an infinite stream. What about this example?

```
Stream.generate(() -> "Elsa")
    .filter(n -> n.length() == 4)
    .limit(2)
    .sorted()
    .forEach(System.out::println);
```

This one prints Elsa twice. The filter lets elements through, and limit() stops the earlier operations after two elements. Now sorted() can sort because we have a finite list. Finally, what do you think this does?

```
Stream.generate(() -> "Olaf Lazisson")
    .filter(n -> n.length() == 4)
    .limit(2)
    .sorted()
    .forEach(System.out::println);
```

This one hangs as well until we kill the program. The filter doesn't allow anything through, so limit() never sees two elements. This means we have to keep waiting and hope that they show up.

You can even chain two pipelines together. See if you can identify the two sources and two terminal operations in this code.

```
30: long count =  Stream.of("goldfish", "finch")
31:     .filter(s -> s.length() > 5)
32:     .collect(Collectors.toList())
33:     .stream()
34:     .count();
35: System.out.println(count);    // 1
```

Lines 30–32 are one pipeline, and lines 33 and 34 are another. For the first pipeline, line 30 is the source, and line 32 is the terminal operation. For the second pipeline, line 33 is the source, and line 34 is the terminal operation. Now that's a complicated way of outputting the number 1!

On the exam, you might see long or complex pipelines as answer choices. If this happens, focus on the differences between the answers. Those will be your clues to the correct answer. This approach will also save you time from not having to study the whole pipeline on each option.

When you see chained pipelines, note where the source and terminal operations are. This will help you keep track of what is going on. You can even rewrite the code in your head to have a variable in between so it isn't as long and complicated. Our prior example can be written as follows:

```
List<String> helper =  Stream.of("goldfish", "finch")
   .filter(s -> s.length() > 5)
   .collect(Collectors.toList());
long count = helper.stream()
   .count();
System.out.println(count);
```

Which style you use is up to you. However, you need to be able to read both styles before you take the exam.

 Real World Scenario

Peeking behind the Scenes

The peek() method is useful for seeing how a stream pipeline works behind the scenes. Remember that the methods run against each element one at a time until processing is done. Suppose that we have this code:

```
var infinite = Stream.iterate(1, x -> x + 1);
infinite.limit(5)
   .filter(x -> x % 2 == 1)
   .forEach(System.out::print); // 135
```

The source is an infinite stream of numbers. Only the first five elements are allowed through before the foreman instructs work to stop. The filter() operation is limited to seeing whether these five numbers from 1 to 5 are odd. Only three are, and those are the ones that get printed, giving 135.

Now what do you think this prints?

```
var infinite = Stream.iterate(1, x -> x + 1);
infinite.limit(5)
   .peek(System.out::print)
   .filter(x -> x % 2 == 1)
   .forEach(System.out::print);
```

The correct answer is 11233455. As the first element passes through, 1 shows up in the peek() and print(). The second element makes it past limit() and peek(), but it gets caught in filter(). The third and fifth elements behave like the first element. The fourth behaves like the second.

Reversing the order of the intermediate operations changes the result.

```
var infinite = Stream.iterate(1, x -> x + 1);
infinite.filter(x -> x % 2 == 1)
    .limit(5)
    .forEach(System.out::print); // 13579
```

The source is still an infinite stream of numbers. The first element still flows through the entire pipeline, and `limit()` remembers that it allows one element through. The second element doesn't make it past `filter()`. The third element flows through the entire pipeline, and `limit()` allows its second element. This proceeds until the ninth element flows through and `limit()` has allowed its fifth element through.

Finally, what do you think this prints?

```
var infinite = Stream.iterate(1, x -> x + 1);
infinite.filter(x -> x % 2 == 1)
    .peek(System.out::print)
    .limit(5)
    .forEach(System.out::print);
```

The answer is 1133557799. Since `filter()` is before `peek()`, we see only the odd numbers.

Working with Primitive Streams

Up until now, all of the streams we've created used the `Stream` class with a generic type, like `Stream<String>`, `Stream<Integer>`, etc. For numeric values, we have been using the wrapper classes you learned about in Chapter 14. We did this with the `Collections` API so it would feel natural.

Java actually includes other stream classes besides `Stream` that you can use to work with select primitives: `int`, `double`, and `long`. Let's take a look at why this is needed. Suppose that we want to calculate the sum of numbers in a finite stream.

```
Stream<Integer> stream = Stream.of(1, 2, 3);
System.out.println(stream.reduce(0, (s, n) -> s + n)); // 6
```

Not bad. It wasn't hard to write a reduction. We started the accumulator with zero. We then added each number to that running total as it came up in the stream. There is another way of doing that, shown here:

```
Stream<Integer> stream = Stream.of(1, 2, 3);
System.out.println(stream.mapToInt(x -> x).sum()); // 6
```

This time, we converted our Stream<Integer> to an IntStream and asked the IntStream to calculate the sum for us. An IntStream has many of the same intermediate and terminal methods as a Stream but includes specialized methods for working with numeric data. The primitive streams know how to perform certain common operations automatically.

So far, this seems like a nice convenience but not terribly important. Now think about how you would compute an average. You need to divide the sum by the number of elements. The problem is that streams allow only one pass. Java recognizes that calculating an average is a common thing to do, and it provides a method to calculate the average on the stream classes for primitives.

```
IntStream intStream = IntStream.of(1, 2, 3);
OptionalDouble avg = intStream.average();
System.out.println(avg.getAsDouble());  // 2.0
```

Not only is it possible to calculate the average, but it is also easy to do so. Clearly primitive streams are important. We will look at creating and using such streams, including optionals and functional interfaces.

Creating Primitive Streams

Here are three types of primitive streams.

- **IntStream:** Used for the primitive types int, short, byte, and char
- **LongStream:** Used for the primitive type long
- **DoubleStream:** Used for the primitive types double and float

Why doesn't each primitive type have its own primitive stream? These three are the most common, so the API designers went with them.

When you see the word *stream* on the exam, pay attention to the case. With a capital *S* or in code, Stream is the name of a class that contains an Object type. With a lowercase *s*, a stream is a concept that might be a Stream, DoubleStream, IntStream, or LongStream.

Table 15.7 shows some of the methods that are unique to primitive streams. Notice that we don't include methods in the table like empty() that you already know from the Stream interface.

TABLE 15.7   Common primitive stream methods

Method	Primitive stream	Description
OptionalDouble average()	IntStream LongStream DoubleStream	The arithmetic mean of the elements

TABLE 15.7 Common primitive stream methods *(continued)*

Method	Primitive stream	Description
Stream<T> boxed()	IntStream LongStream DoubleStream	A Stream<T> where T is the wrapper class associated with the primitive value
OptionalInt max() OptionalLong max() OptionalDouble max()	IntStream LongStream DoubleStream	The maximum element of the stream
OptionalInt min() OptionalLong min() OptionalDouble min()	IntStream LongStream DoubleStream	The minimum element of the stream
IntStream range(int a, int b) LongStream range(long a, long b)	IntStream LongStream	Returns a primitive stream from a (inclusive) to b (exclusive)
IntStream rangeClosed(int a, int b) LongStream rangeClosed(long a, long b)	IntStream LongStream	Returns a primitive stream from a (inclusive) to b (inclusive)
int sum() long sum() double sum()	IntStream LongStream DoubleStream	Returns the sum of the elements in the stream
IntSummaryStatistics summaryStatistics() LongSummaryStatistics summaryStatistics() DoubleSummaryStatistics summaryStatistics()	IntStream LongStream DoubleStream	Returns an object containing numerous stream statistics such as the average, min, max, etc.

Some of the methods for creating a primitive stream are equivalent to how we created the source for a regular Stream. You can create an empty stream with this:

```
DoubleStream empty = DoubleStream.empty();
```

Another way is to use the of() factory method from a single value or by using the varargs overload.

```
DoubleStream oneValue = DoubleStream.of(3.14);
oneValue.forEach(System.out::println);

DoubleStream varargs = DoubleStream.of(1.0, 1.1, 1.2);
varargs.forEach(System.out::println);
```

This code outputs the following:

```
3.14
1.0
1.1
1.2
```

You can also use the two methods for creating infinite streams, just like we did with Stream.

```
var random = DoubleStream.generate(Math::random);
var fractions = DoubleStream.iterate(.5, d -> d / 2);
random.limit(3).forEach(System.out::println);
fractions.limit(3).forEach(System.out::println);
```

Since the streams are infinite, we added a limit intermediate operation so that the output doesn't print values forever. The first stream calls a static method on Math to get a random double. Since the numbers are random, your output will obviously be different. The second stream keeps creating smaller numbers, dividing the previous value by two each time. The output from when we ran this code was as follows:

```
0.07890654781186413
0.28564363465842346
0.6311403511266134
0.5
0.25
0.125
```

You don't need to know this for the exam, but the Random class provides a method to get primitives streams of random numbers directly. Fun fact! For example, ints() generates an infinite IntStream of primitives.

It works the same way for each type of primitive stream. When dealing with `int` or `long` primitives, it is common to count. Suppose that we wanted a stream with the numbers from 1 through 5. We could write this using what we've explained so far:

```
IntStream count = IntStream.iterate(1, n -> n+1).limit(5);
count.forEach(System.out::println);
```

This code does print out the numbers 1–5, one per line. However, it is a lot of code to do something so simple. Java provides a method that can generate a range of numbers.

```
IntStream range = IntStream.range(1, 6);
range.forEach(System.out::println);
```

This is better. If we wanted numbers 1–5, why did we pass 1–6? The first parameter to the range() method is *inclusive*, which means it includes the number. The second parameter to the range() method is *exclusive*, which means it stops right before that number. However, it still could be clearer. We want the numbers 1–5 inclusive. Luckily, there's another method, rangeClosed(), which is inclusive on both parameters.

```
IntStream rangeClosed = IntStream.rangeClosed(1, 5);
rangeClosed.forEach(System.out::println);
```

Even better. This time we expressed that we want a closed range, or an inclusive range. This method better matches how we express a range of numbers in plain English.

Mapping Streams

Another way to create a primitive stream is by mapping from another stream type. Table 15.8 shows that there is a method for mapping between any stream types.

TABLE 15.8 Mapping methods between types of streams

Source stream class	To create `Stream`	To create `DoubleStream`	To create `IntStream`	To create `LongStream`
`Stream<T>`	`map()`	`mapToDouble()`	`mapToInt()`	`mapToLong()`
`DoubleStream`	`mapToObj()`	`map()`	`mapToInt()`	`mapToLong()`
`IntStream`	`mapToObj()`	`mapToDouble()`	`map()`	`mapToLong()`
`LongStream`	`mapToObj()`	`mapToDouble()`	`mapToInt()`	`map()`

Obviously, they have to be compatible types for this to work. Java requires a mapping function to be provided as a parameter, for example:

```
Stream<String> objStream = Stream.of("penguin", "fish");
IntStream intStream = objStream.mapToInt(s -> s.length());
```

This function takes an `Object`, which is a `String` in this case. The function returns an `int`. The function mappings are intuitive here. They take the source type and return the target type. In this example, the actual function type is `ToIntFunction`. Table 15.9 shows the mapping function names. As you can see, they do what you might expect.

TABLE 15.9 Function parameters when mapping between types of streams

Source stream class	To create Stream	To create DoubleStream	To create IntStream	To create LongStream
Stream<T>	Function<T,R>	ToDouble Function<T>	ToInt Function<T>	ToLong Function<T>
DoubleStream	Double Function<R>	DoubleUnary Operator	DoubleToInt Function	DoubleToLong Function
IntStream	IntFunction<R>	IntToDouble Function	IntUnary Operator	IntToLong Function
LongStream	Long Function<R>	LongToDouble Function	LongToInt Function	LongUnary Operator

You do have to memorize Table 15.8 and Table 15.9. It's not as hard as it might seem. There are patterns in the names if you remember a few rules. For Table 15.8, mapping to the same type you started with is just called `map()`. When returning an object stream, the method is `mapToObj()`. Beyond that, it's the name of the primitive type in the map method name.

For Table 15.9, you can start by thinking about the source and target types. When the target type is an object, you drop the `To` from the name. When the mapping is to the same type you started with, you use a unary operator instead of a function for the primitive streams.

Using *flatMap()*

The `flatMap()` method exists on primitive streams as well. It works the same way as on a regular `Stream` except the method name is different. Here's an example:

```
var integerList = new ArrayList<Integer>();
IntStream ints = integerList.stream()
   .flatMapToInt(x -> IntStream.of(x));
DoubleStream doubles = integerList.stream()
   .flatMapToDouble(x -> DoubleStream.of(x));
LongStream longs = integerList.stream()
   .flatMapToLong(x -> LongStream.of(x));
```

Additionally, you can create a Stream from a primitive stream. These methods show two ways of accomplishing this:

```
private static Stream<Integer> mapping(IntStream stream) {
    return stream.mapToObj(x -> x);
}
```

```
private static Stream<Integer> boxing(IntStream stream) {
    return stream.boxed();
}
```

The first one uses the mapToObj() method we saw earlier. The second one is more succinct. It does not require a mapping function because all it does is autobox each primitive to the corresponding wrapper object. The boxed() method exists on all three types of primitive streams.

Using *Optional* with Primitive Streams

Earlier in the chapter, we wrote a method to calculate the average of an int[] and promised a better way later. Now that you know about primitive streams, you can calculate the average in one line.

```
var stream = IntStream.rangeClosed(1,10);
OptionalDouble optional = stream.average();
```

The return type is not the Optional you have become accustomed to using. It is a new type called OptionalDouble. Why do we have a separate type, you might wonder? Why not just use Optional<Double>? The difference is that OptionalDouble is for a primitive and Optional<Double> is for the Double wrapper class. Working with the primitive optional class looks similar to working with the Optional class itself.

```
optional.ifPresent(System.out::println);               // 5.5
System.out.println(optional.getAsDouble());            // 5.5
System.out.println(optional.orElseGet(() -> Double.NaN)); // 5.5
```

The only noticeable difference is that we called getAsDouble() rather than get(). This makes it clear that we are working with a primitive. Also, orElseGet() takes a DoubleSupplier instead of a Supplier.

As with the primitive streams, there are three type-specific classes for primitives. Table 15.10 shows the minor differences among the three. You probably won't be surprised that you have to memorize it as well. This is really easy to remember since the primitive name is the only change. As you should remember from the terminal operations section, a number of stream methods return an optional such as min() or findAny(). These each return the corresponding optional type. The primitive stream implementations also add two new methods that you need to know. The sum() method does not return an optional. If you try to add up an empty stream, you simply get zero. The average() method always returns an OptionalDouble since an average can potentially have fractional data for any type.

TABLE 15.10 Optional types for primitives

	OptionalDouble	OptionalInt	OptionalLong
Getting as a primitive	getAsDouble()	getAsInt()	getAsLong()
orElseGet() parameter type	DoubleSupplier	IntSupplier	LongSupplier
Return type of max() and min()	OptionalDouble	OptionalInt	OptionalLong
Return type of sum()	double	int	long
Return type of average()	OptionalDouble	OptionalDouble	OptionalDouble

Let's try an example to make sure that you understand this.

```
5: LongStream longs = LongStream.of(5, 10);
6: long sum = longs.sum();
7: System.out.println(sum);      // 15
8: DoubleStream doubles = DoubleStream.generate(() -> Math.PI);
9: OptionalDouble min = doubles.min(); // runs infinitely
```

Line 5 creates a stream of long primitives with two elements. Line 6 shows that we don't use an optional to calculate a sum. Line 8 creates an infinite stream of double primitives. Line 9 is there to remind you that a question about code that runs infinitely can appear with primitive streams as well.

Summarizing Statistics

You've learned enough to be able to get the maximum value from a stream of int primitives. If the stream is empty, we want to throw an exception.

```
private static int max(IntStream ints) {
    OptionalInt optional = ints.max();
    return optional.orElseThrow(RuntimeException::new);
}
```

This should be old hat by now. We got an OptionalInt because we have an IntStream. If the optional contains a value, we return it. Otherwise, we throw a new RuntimeException.

Now we want to change the method to take an IntStream and return a range. The range is the minimum value subtracted from the maximum value. Uh-oh. Both min() and max() are terminal operations, which means that they use up the stream when they are run. We can't run two terminal operations against the same stream. Luckily, this is a common problem and the primitive streams solve it for us with summary statistics. *Statistic* is just a big word for a number that was calculated from data.

```
private static int range(IntStream ints) {
    IntSummaryStatistics stats = ints.summaryStatistics();
    if (stats.getCount() == 0) throw new RuntimeException();
    return stats.getMax()-stats.getMin();
}
```

Here we asked Java to perform many calculations about the stream. Summary statistics include the following:

- **Smallest number (minimum):** getMin()
- **Largest number (maximum):** getMax()
- **Average:** getAverage()
- **Sum:** getSum()
- **Number of values:** getCount()

If the stream were empty, we'd have a count and sum of zero. The other methods would return an empty optional.

Learning the Functional Interfaces for Primitives

Remember when we told you to memorize Table 15.1, with the common functional interfaces, at the beginning of the chapter? Did you? If you didn't, go do it now. We are about to make it more involved. Just as there are special streams and optional classes for primitives, there are also special functional interfaces.

Luckily, most of them are for the double, int, and long types that you saw for streams and optionals. There is one exception, which is BooleanSupplier. We will cover that before introducing the ones for double, int, and long.

Functional Interfaces for *boolean*

BooleanSupplier is a separate type. It has one method to implement:
```
boolean getAsBoolean()
```

It works just as you've come to expect from functional interfaces. Here's an example:

```
12: BooleanSupplier b1 = () -> true;
13: BooleanSupplier b2 = () -> Math.random() > .5;
14: System.out.println(b1.getAsBoolean());  // true
15: System.out.println(b2.getAsBoolean());  // false
```

Lines 12 and 13 each create a BooleanSupplier, which is the only functional interface for boolean. Line 14 prints true, since it is the result of b1. Line 15 prints out true or false, depending on the random value generated.

Functional Interfaces for *double*, *int*, and *long*

Most of the functional interfaces are for double, int, and long to match the streams and optionals that we've been using for primitives. Table 15.11 shows the equivalent of Table 15.1 for these primitives. You probably won't be surprised that you have to memorize it. Luckily, you've memorized Table 15.1 by now and can apply what you've learned to Table 15.11.

TABLE 15.11 Common functional interfaces for primitives

Functional interfaces	# parameters	Return type	Single abstract method
DoubleSupplier IntSupplier LongSupplier	0	double int long	getAsDouble getAsInt getAsLong
DoubleConsumer IntConsumer LongConsumer	1 (double) 1 (int) 1 (long)	void	accept
DoublePredicate IntPredicate LongPredicate	1 (double) 1 (int) 1 (long)	boolean	test
DoubleFunction<R> IntFunction<R> LongFunction<R>	1 (double) 1 (int) 1 (long)	R	apply
DoubleUnaryOperator IntUnaryOperator LongUnaryOperator	1 (double) 1 (int) 1 (long)	double int long	applyAsDouble applyAsInt applyAsLong
DoubleBinaryOperator IntBinaryOperator LongBinaryOperator	2 (double, double) 2 (int, int) 2 (long, long)	double int long	applyAsDouble applyAsInt applyAsLong

There are a few things to notice that are different between Table 15.1 and Table 15.11.

- Generics are gone from some of the interfaces, and instead the type name tells us what primitive type is involved. In other cases, such as IntFunction, only the return type generic is needed because we're converting a primitive int into an object.
- The single abstract method is often renamed when a primitive type is returned.

In addition to Table 15.1 equivalents, some interfaces are specific to primitives. Table 15.12 lists these.

TABLE 15.12   Primitive-specific functional interfaces

Functional interfaces	# parameters	Return type	Single abstract method
ToDoubleFunction<T>	1 (T)	double	applyAsDouble
ToIntFunction<T>		int	applyAsInt
ToLongFunction<T>		long	applyAsLong
ToDoubleBiFunction<T, U>	2 (T, U)	double	applyAsDouble
ToIntBiFunction<T, U>		int	applyAsInt
ToLongBiFunction<T, U>		long	applyAsLong
DoubleToIntFunction	1 (double)	int	applyAsInt
DoubleToLongFunction	1 (double)	long	applyAsLong
IntToDoubleFunction	1 (int)	double	applyAsDouble
IntToLongFunction	1 (int)	long	applyAsLong
LongToDoubleFunction	1 (long)	double	applyAsDouble
LongToIntFunction	1 (long)	int	applyAsInt
ObjDoubleConsumer<T>	2 (T, double)	void	accept
ObjIntConsumer<T>	2 (T, int)		
ObjLongConsumer<T>	2 (T, long)		

We've been using functional interfaces all chapter long, so you should have a good grasp of how to read the table by now. Let's do one example just to be sure. Which functional interface would you use to fill in the blank to make the following code compile?

```
var d = 1.0;
_____ f1 = x -> 1;
f1.applyAsInt(d);
```

When you see a question like this, look for clues. You can see that the functional interface in question takes a `double` parameter and returns an `int`. You can also see that it has a single abstract method named `applyAsInt`. The `DoubleToIntFunction` and `ToIntFunction` meet all three of those criteria.

Working with Advanced Stream Pipeline Concepts

You've almost reached the end of learning about streams. We have only a few more topics left. You'll see the relationship between streams and the underlying data, chaining Optional and grouping collectors.

Linking Streams to the Underlying Data

What do you think this outputs?

```
25: var cats = new ArrayList<String>();
26: cats.add("Annie");
27: cats.add("Ripley");
28: var stream = cats.stream();
29: cats.add("KC");
30: System.out.println(stream.count());
```

The correct answer is 3. Lines 25–27 create a List with two elements. Line 28 requests that a stream be created from that List. Remember that streams are lazily evaluated. This means that the stream isn't actually created on line 28. An object is created that knows where to look for the data when it is needed. On line 29, the List gets a new element. On line 30, the stream pipeline actually runs. The stream pipeline runs first, looking at the source and seeing three elements.

Chaining Optionals

By now, you are familiar with the benefits of chaining operations in a stream pipeline. A few of the intermediate operations for streams are available for Optional.

Suppose that you are given an Optional<Integer> and asked to print the value, but only if it is a three-digit number. Without functional programming, you could write the following:

```
private static void threeDigit(Optional<Integer> optional) {
   if (optional.isPresent()) {  // outer if
      var num = optional.get();
      var string = "" + num;
      if (string.length() == 3) // inner if
         System.out.println(string);
   }
}
```

It works, but it contains nested `if` statements. That's extra complexity. Let's try this again with functional programming.

```
private static void threeDigit(Optional<Integer> optional) {
    optional.map(n -> "" + n)              // part 1
        .filter(s -> s.length() == 3)      // part 2
        .ifPresent(System.out::println);   // part 3
}
```

This is much shorter and more expressive. With lambdas, the exam is fond of carving up a single statement and identifying the pieces with a comment. We've done that here to show what happens with both the functional programming and nonfunctional programming approaches.

Suppose that we are given an empty `Optional`. The first approach returns `false` for the outer `if` statement. The second approach sees an empty `Optional` and has both `map()` and `filter()` pass it through. Then `ifPresent()` sees an empty `Optional` and doesn't call the `Consumer` parameter.

The next case is where we are given an `Optional.of(4)`. The first approach returns `false` for the inner `if` statement. The second approach maps the number 4 to `"4"`. The `filter()` then returns an empty `Optional` since the filter doesn't match, and `ifPresent()` doesn't call the `Consumer` parameter.

The final case is where we are given an `Optional.of(123)`. The first approach returns `true` for both `if` statements. The second approach maps the number 123 to `"123"`. The `filter()` then returns the same `Optional`, and `ifPresent()` now does call the `Consumer` parameter.

Now suppose that we wanted to get an `Optional<Integer>` representing the length of the `String` contained in another `Optional`. Easy enough.

```
Optional<Integer> result = optional.map(String::length);
```

What if we had a helper method that did the logic of calculating something for us that returns `Optional<Integer>`? Using map doesn't work.

```
Optional<Integer> result = optional
    .map(ChainingOptionals::calculator); // DOES NOT COMPILE
```

The problem is that calculator returns `Optional<Integer>`. The map() method adds another `Optional`, giving us `Optional<Optional<Integer>>`. Well, that's no good. The solution is to call `flatMap()` instead.

```
Optional<Integer> result = optional
    .flatMap(ChainingOptionals::calculator);
```

This one works because `flatMap` removes the unnecessary layer. In other words, it flattens the result. Chaining calls to `flatMap()` is useful when you want to transform one `Optional` type to another.

Real World Scenario

Checked Exceptions and Functional Interfaces

You might have noticed by now that most functional interfaces do not declare checked exceptions. This is normally OK. However, it is a problem when working with methods that declare checked exceptions. Suppose that we have a class with a method that throws a checked exception.

```
import java.io.*;
import java.util.*;
public class ExceptionCaseStudy {
    private static List<String> create() throws IOException {
        throw new IOException();
    }
}
```

Now we use it in a stream.

```
public void good() throws IOException {
    ExceptionCaseStudy.create().stream().count();
}
```

Nothing new here. The create() method throws a checked exception. The calling method handles or declares it. Now what about this one?

```
public void bad() throws IOException {
    Supplier<List<String>> s = ExceptionCaseStudy::create; // DOES NOT COMPILE
}
```

The actual compiler error is as follows:

```
unhandled exception type IOException
```

Say what now? The problem is that the lambda to which this method reference expands does not declare an exception. The Supplier interface does not allow checked exceptions. There are two approaches to get around this problem. One is to catch the exception and turn it into an unchecked exception.

```
public void ugly() {
    Supplier<List<String>> s = () -> {
        try {
            return ExceptionCaseStudy.create();
        } catch (IOException e) {
```

```
        throw new RuntimeException(e);
      }
    };
  }
```

This works. But the code is ugly. One of the benefits of functional programming is that the code is supposed to be easy to read and concise. Another alternative is to create a wrapper method with the try/catch.

```
  private static List<String> createSafe() {
    try {
      return ExceptionCaseStudy.create();
    } catch (IOException e) {
      throw new RuntimeException(e);
    } }
```

Now we can use the safe wrapper in our Supplier without issue.

```
  public void wrapped() {
    Supplier<List<String>> s2 = ExceptionCaseStudy::createSafe;
  }
```

Collecting Results

You're almost finished learning about streams. The last topic builds on what you've learned so far to group the results. Early in the chapter, you saw the collect() terminal operation. There are many predefined collectors, including those shown in Table 15.13. These collectors are available via static methods on the Collectors interface. We will look at the different types of collectors in the following sections.

TABLE 15.13   Examples of grouping/partitioning collectors

Collector	Description	Return value when passed to collect
averagingDouble(ToDoubleFunction f) averagingInt(ToIntFunction f) averagingLong(ToLongFunction f)	Calculates the average for our three core primitive types	Double
counting()	Counts the number of elements	Long

TABLE 15.13 Examples of grouping/partitioning collectors *(continued)*

Collector	Description	Return value when passed to collect
groupingBy(Function f) groupingBy(Function f, Collector dc) groupingBy(Function f, Supplier s, Collector dc)	Creates a map grouping by the specified function with the optional map type supplier and optional downstream collector	Map<K, List<T>>
joining(CharSequence cs)	Creates a single String using cs as a delimiter between elements if one is specified	String
maxBy(Comparator c) minBy(Comparator c)	Finds the largest/smallest elements	Optional<T>
mapping(Function f, Collector dc)	Adds another level of collectors	Collector
partitioningBy(Predicate p) partitioningBy(Predicate p, Collector dc)	Creates a map grouping by the specified predicate with the optional further downstream collector	Map<Boolean, List<T>>
summarizingDouble(ToDoubleFunction f) summarizingInt(ToIntFunction f) summarizingLong(ToLongFunction f)	Calculates average, min, max, and so on	DoubleSummary Statistics IntSummary Statistics LongSummary Statistics
summingDouble(ToDoubleFunction f) summingInt(ToIntFunction f) summingLong(ToLongFunction f)	Calculates the sum for our three core primitive types	Double Integer Long
toList() toSet()	Creates an arbitrary type of list or set	List Set
toCollection(Supplier s)	Creates a Collection of the specified type	Collection

Collector	Description	Return value when passed to collect
toMap(Function k, Function v) toMap(Function k, Function v, BinaryOperator m) toMap(Function k, Function v, BinaryOperator m, Supplier s)	Creates a map using functions to map the keys, values, an optional merge function, and an optional map type supplier	Map

Collecting Using Basic Collectors

Luckily, many of these collectors work in the same way. Let's look at an example.

```
var ohMy = Stream.of("lions", "tigers", "bears");
String result = ohMy.collect(Collectors.joining(", "));
System.out.println(result); // lions, tigers, bears
```

Notice how the predefined collectors are in the Collectors class rather than the Collector interface. This is a common theme, which you saw with Collection versus Collections. In fact, you'll see this pattern again in Chapter 20, "NIO.2," when working with Paths and Path, and other related types.

We pass the predefined joining() collector to the collect() method. All elements of the stream are then merged into a String with the specified delimiter between each element. It is important to pass the Collector to the collect method. It exists to help collect elements. A Collector doesn't do anything on its own.

Let's try another one. What is the average length of the three animal names?

```
var ohMy = Stream.of("lions", "tigers", "bears");
Double result = ohMy.collect(Collectors.averagingInt(String::length));
System.out.println(result); // 5.333333333333333
```

The pattern is the same. We pass a collector to collect(), and it performs the average for us. This time, we needed to pass a function to tell the collector what to average. We used a method reference, which returns an int upon execution. With primitive streams, the result of an average was always a double, regardless of what type is being averaged. For collectors, it is a Double since those need an Object.

Often, you'll find yourself interacting with code that was written without streams. This means that it will expect a Collection type rather than a Stream type. No problem. You can still express yourself using a Stream and then convert to a Collection at the end, for example:

```
var ohMy = Stream.of("lions", "tigers", "bears");
TreeSet<String> result = ohMy
```

```
   .filter(s -> s.startsWith("t"))
   .collect(Collectors.toCollection(TreeSet::new));
System.out.println(result); // [tigers]
```

This time we have all three parts of the stream pipeline. `Stream.of()` is the source for the stream. The intermediate operation is `filter()`. Finally, the terminal operation is `collect()`, which creates a `TreeSet`. If we didn't care which implementation of `Set` we got, we could have written `Collectors.toSet()` instead.

At this point, you should be able to use all of the `Collectors` in Table 15.13 except `groupingBy()`, `mapping()`, `partitioningBy()`, and `toMap()`.

Collecting into Maps

Code using `Collectors` involving maps can get quite long. We will build it up slowly. Make sure that you understand each example before going on to the next one. Let's start with a straightforward example to create a map from a stream.

```
var ohMy = Stream.of("lions", "tigers", "bears");
Map<String, Integer> map = ohMy.collect(
   Collectors.toMap(s -> s, String::length));
System.out.println(map); // {lions=5, bears=5, tigers=6}
```

When creating a map, you need to specify two functions. The first function tells the collector how to create the key. In our example, we use the provided `String` as the key. The second function tells the collector how to create the value. In our example, we use the length of the `String` as the value.

Returning the same value passed into a lambda is a common operation, so Java provides a method for it. You can rewrite `s -> s` as `Function.identity()`. It is not shorter and may or may not be clearer, so use your judgment on whether to use it.

Now we want to do the reverse and map the length of the animal name to the name itself. Our first incorrect attempt is shown here:

```
var ohMy = Stream.of("lions", "tigers", "bears");
Map<Integer, String> map = ohMy.collect(Collectors.toMap(
   String::length,
   k -> k)); // BAD
```

Running this gives an exception similar to the following:

```
Exception in thread "main"
   java.lang.IllegalStateException: Duplicate key 5
```

What's wrong? Two of the animal names are the same length. We didn't tell Java what to do. Should the collector choose the first one it encounters? The last one it encounters? Concatenate the two? Since the collector has no idea what to do, it "solves" the problem by throwing an exception and making it our problem. How thoughtful. Let's suppose that our requirement is to create a comma-separated String with the animal names. We could write this:

```
var ohMy = Stream.of("lions", "tigers", "bears");
Map<Integer, String> map = ohMy.collect(Collectors.toMap(
    String::length,
    k -> k,
    (s1, s2) -> s1 + "," + s2));
System.out.println(map);              // {5=lions,bears, 6=tigers}
System.out.println(map.getClass()); // class java.util.HashMap
```

It so happens that the Map returned is a HashMap. This behavior is not guaranteed. Suppose that we want to mandate that the code return a TreeMap instead. No problem. We would just add a constructor reference as a parameter.

```
var ohMy = Stream.of("lions", "tigers", "bears");
TreeMap<Integer, String> map = ohMy.collect(Collectors.toMap(
    String::length,
    k -> k,
    (s1, s2) -> s1 + "," + s2,
    TreeMap::new));
System.out.println(map); //            // {5=lions,bears, 6=tigers}
System.out.println(map.getClass()); // class java.util.TreeMap
```

This time we got the type that we specified. With us so far? This code is long but not particularly complicated. We did promise you that the code would be long!

Collecting Using Grouping, Partitioning, and Mapping

Great job getting this far. The exam creators like asking about groupingBy() and partitioningBy(), so make sure you understand these sections very well. Now suppose that we want to get groups of names by their length. We can do that by saying that we want to group by length.

```
var ohMy = Stream.of("lions", "tigers", "bears");
Map<Integer, List<String>> map = ohMy.collect(
    Collectors.groupingBy(String::length));
System.out.println(map);     // {5=[lions, bears], 6=[tigers]}
```

The groupingBy() collector tells collect() that it should group all of the elements of the stream into a Map. The function determines the keys in the Map. Each value in the Map is a List of all entries that match that key.

Note that the function you call in groupingBy() cannot return null. It does not allow null keys.

Suppose that we don't want a List as the value in the map and prefer a Set instead. No problem. There's another method signature that lets us pass a *downstream collector*. This is a second collector that does something special with the values.

```
var ohMy = Stream.of("lions", "tigers", "bears");
Map<Integer, Set<String>> map = ohMy.collect(
   Collectors.groupingBy(
      String::length,
      Collectors.toSet()));
System.out.println(map);    // {5=[lions, bears], 6=[tigers]}
```

We can even change the type of Map returned through yet another parameter.

```
var ohMy = Stream.of("lions", "tigers", "bears");
TreeMap<Integer, Set<String>> map = ohMy.collect(
   Collectors.groupingBy(
      String::length,
      TreeMap::new,
      Collectors.toSet()));
System.out.println(map); // {5=[lions, bears], 6=[tigers]}
```

This is very flexible. What if we want to change the type of Map returned but leave the type of values alone as a List? There isn't a method for this specifically because it is easy enough to write with the existing ones.

```
var ohMy = Stream.of("lions", "tigers", "bears");
TreeMap<Integer, List<String>> map = ohMy.collect(
   Collectors.groupingBy(
      String::length,
      TreeMap::new,
      Collectors.toList()));
System.out.println(map);
```

Partitioning is a special case of grouping. With partitioning, there are only two possible groups—true and false. *Partitioning* is like splitting a list into two parts.

Suppose that we are making a sign to put outside each animal's exhibit. We have two sizes of signs. One can accommodate names with five or fewer characters. The other is needed for longer names. We can partition the list according to which sign we need.

```
var ohMy = Stream.of("lions", "tigers", "bears");
Map<Boolean, List<String>> map = ohMy.collect(
   Collectors.partitioningBy(s -> s.length() <= 5));
System.out.println(map);    // {false=[tigers], true=[lions, bears]}
```

Here we passed a `Predicate` with the logic for which group each animal name belongs in. Now suppose that we've figured out how to use a different font, and seven characters can now fit on the smaller sign. No worries. We just change the `Predicate`.

```
var ohMy = Stream.of("lions", "tigers", "bears");
Map<Boolean, List<String>> map = ohMy.collect(
    Collectors.partitioningBy(s -> s.length() <= 7));
System.out.println(map);     // {false=[], true=[lions, tigers, bears]}
```

Notice that there are still two keys in the map—one for each boolean value. It so happens that one of the values is an empty list, but it is still there. As with `groupingBy()`, we can change the type of `List` to something else.

```
var ohMy = Stream.of("lions", "tigers", "bears");
Map<Boolean, Set<String>> map = ohMy.collect(
    Collectors.partitioningBy(
        s -> s.length() <= 7,
        Collectors.toSet()));
System.out.println(map);     // {false=[], true=[lions, tigers, bears]}
```

Unlike `groupingBy()`, we cannot change the type of `Map` that gets returned. However, there are only two keys in the map, so does it really matter which `Map` type we use?

Instead of using the downstream collector to specify the type, we can use any of the collectors that we've already shown. For example, we can group by the length of the animal name to see how many of each length we have.

```
var ohMy = Stream.of("lions", "tigers", "bears");
Map<Integer, Long> map = ohMy.collect(
    Collectors.groupingBy(
        String::length,
        Collectors.counting()));
System.out.println(map);     // {5=2, 6=1}
```

Debugging Complicated Generics

When working with `collect()`, there are often many levels of generics, making compiler errors unreadable. Here are three useful techniques for dealing with this situation:

- Start over with a simple statement and keep adding to it. By making one tiny change at a time, you will know which code introduced the error.

- Extract parts of the statement into separate statements. For example, try writing `Collectors.groupingBy(String::length, Collectors.counting());`. If it compiles, you know that the problem lies elsewhere. If it doesn't compile, you have a much shorter statement to troubleshoot.

- Use generic wildcards for the return type of the final statement; for example, `Map<?, ?>`. If that change alone allows the code to compile, you'll know that the problem lies with the return type not being what you expect.

Finally, there is a mapping() collector that lets us go down a level and add another collector. Suppose that we wanted to get the first letter of the first animal alphabetically of each length. Why? Perhaps for random sampling. The examples on this part of the exam are fairly contrived as well. We'd write the following:

```
var ohMy = Stream.of("lions", "tigers", "bears");
Map<Integer, Optional<Character>> map = ohMy.collect(
    Collectors.groupingBy(
        String::length,
        Collectors.mapping(
            s -> s.charAt(0),
            Collectors.minBy((a, b) -> a -b))));
System.out.println(map);    // {5=Optional[b], 6=Optional[t]}
```

We aren't going to tell you that this code is easy to read. We will tell you that it is the most complicated thing you need to understand for the exam. Comparing it to the previous example, you can see that we replaced counting() with mapping(). It so happens that mapping() takes two parameters: the function for the value and how to group it further.

You might see collectors used with a static import to make the code shorter. The exam might even use var for the return value and less indentation than we used. This means that you might see something like this:

```
var ohMy = Stream.of("lions", "tigers", "bears");
var map = ohMy.collect(groupingBy(String::length,
    mapping(s -> s.charAt(0), minBy((a, b) -> a -b))));
System.out.println(map);    // {5=Optional[b], 6=Optional[t]}
```

The code does the same thing as in the previous example. This means that it is important to recognize the collector names because you might not have the Collectors class name to call your attention to it.

There is one more collector called reducing(). You don't need to know it for the exam. It is a general reduction in case all of the previous collectors don't meet your needs.

Summary

A functional interface has a single abstract method. You must know the functional interfaces.

- Supplier<T> with method: T get()
- Consumer<T> with method: void accept(T t)
- BiConsumer<T, U> with method: void accept(T t, U u)

- Predicate<T> with method: boolean test(T t)
- BiPredicate<T, U> with method: boolean test(T t, U u)
- Function<T, R> with method: R apply(T t)
- BiFunction<T, U, R> with method: R apply(T t, U u)
- UnaryOperator<T> with method: T apply(T t)
- BinaryOperator<T> with method: T apply(T t1, T t2)

An Optional<T> can be empty or store a value. You can check whether it contains a value with isPresent() and get() the value inside. You can return a different value with orElse(T t) or throw an exception with orElseThrow(). There are even three methods that take functional interfaces as parameters: ifPresent(Consumer c), orElseGet(Supplier s), and orElseThrow(Supplier s). There are three optional types for primitives: OptionalDouble, OptionalInt, and OptionalLong. These have the methods getAsDouble(), getAsInt(), and getAsLong(), respectively.

A stream pipeline has three parts. The source is required, and it creates the data in the stream. There can be zero or more intermediate operations, which aren't executed until the terminal operation runs. The first stream class we covered was Stream<T>, which takes a generic argument T. The Stream<T> class includes many useful intermediate operations including filter(), map(), flatMap(), and sorted(). Examples of terminal operations include allMatch(), count(), and forEach().

Besides the Stream<T> class, there are three primitive streams: DoubleStream, IntStream, and LongStream. In addition to the usual Stream<T> methods, IntStream and LongStream have range() and rangeClosed(). The call range(1, 10) on IntStream and LongStream creates a stream of the primitives from 1 to 9. By contrast, rangeClosed(1, 10) creates a stream of the primitives from 1 to 10. The primitive streams have math operations including average(), max(), and sum(). They also have summaryStatistics() to get many statistics in one call. There are also functional interfaces specific to streams. Except for BooleanSupplier, they are all for double, int, and long primitives as well.

You can use a Collector to transform a stream into a traditional collection. You can even group fields to create a complex map in one line. Partitioning works the same way as grouping, except that the keys are always true and false. A partitioned map always has two keys even if the value is empty for the key.

You should review the tables in the chapter. While there's a lot of tables, many share common patterns, making it easier to remember them. You absolutely must memorize Table 15.1. You should memorize Table 15.8 and Table 15.9 but be able to spot incompatibilities, such as type differences, if you can't memorize these two. Finally, remember that streams are lazily evaluated. They take lambdas or method references as parameters, which execute later when the method is run.

Exam Essentials

Identify the correct functional interface given the number of parameters, return type, and method name—and vice versa.   The most common functional interfaces are Supplier, Consumer, Function, and Predicate. There are also binary versions and primitive versions of many of these methods.

Write code that uses *Optional*.   Creating an Optional uses Optional.empty() or Optional.of(). Retrieval frequently uses isPresent() and get(). Alternatively, there are the functional ifPresent() and orElseGet() methods.

Recognize which operations cause a stream pipeline to execute.   Intermediate operations do not run until the terminal operation is encountered. If no terminal operation is in the pipeline, a Stream is returned but not executed. Examples of terminal operations include collect(), forEach(), min(), and reduce().

Determine which terminal operations are reductions.   Reductions use all elements of the stream in determining the result. The reductions that you need to know are collect(), count(), max(), min(), and reduce(). A mutable reduction collects into the same object as it goes. The collect() method is a mutable reduction.

Write code for common intermediate operations.   The filter() method returns a Stream<T> filtering on a Predicate<T>. The map() method returns a Stream transforming each element of type T to another type R through a Function <T,R>. The flatMap() method flattens nested streams into a single level and removes empty streams.

Compare primitive streams to *Stream<T>*.   Primitive streams are useful for performing common operations on numeric types including statistics like average(), sum(), etc. There are three primitive stream classes: DoubleStream, IntStream, and LongStream. There are also three primitive Optional classes: OptionalDouble, OptionalInt, and OptionalLong. Aside from BooleanSupplier, they all involve the double, int, or long primitives.

Convert primitive stream types to other primitive stream types. Normally when mapping, you just call the *map()* method.   When changing the class used for the stream, a different method is needed. To convert to Stream, you use mapToObj(). To convert to DoubleStream, you use mapToDouble(). To convert to IntStream, you use mapToInt(). To convert to LongStream, you use mapToLong().

Use *peek()* to inspect the stream.   The peek() method is an intermediate operation often used for debugging purposes. It executes a lambda or method reference on the input and passes that same input through the pipeline to the next operator. It is useful for printing out what passes through a certain point in a stream.

Search a stream. The findFirst() and findAny() methods return a single element from a stream in an Optional. The anyMatch(), allMatch(), and noneMatch() methods return a boolean. Be careful, because these three can hang if called on an infinite stream with some data. All of these methods are terminal operations.

Sort a stream. The sorted() method is an intermediate operation that sorts a stream. There are two versions: the signature with zero parameters that sorts using the natural sort order, and the signature with one parameter that sorts using that Comparator as the sort order.

Compare *groupingBy()* and *partitioningBy()*. The groupingBy() method is a terminal operation that creates a Map. The keys and return types are determined by the parameters you pass. The values in the Map are a Collection for all the entries that map to that key. The partitioningBy() method also returns a Map. This time, the keys are true and false. The values are again a Collection of matches. If there are no matches for that boolean, the Collection is empty.

Review Questions

The answers to the chapter review questions can be found in the Appendix.

1. What could be the output of the following?

```
var stream = Stream.iterate("", (s) -> s + "1");
System.out.println(stream.limit(2).map(x -> x + "2"));
```

A. 12112

B. 212

C. 212112

D. java.util.stream.ReferencePipeline$3@4517d9a3

E. The code does not compile.

F. An exception is thrown.

G. The code hangs.

2. What could be the output of the following?

```
Predicate<String> predicate = s -> s.startsWith("g");
var stream1 = Stream.generate(() -> "growl!");
var stream2 = Stream.generate(() -> "growl!");
var b1 = stream1.anyMatch(predicate);
var b2 = stream2.allMatch(predicate);
System.out.println(b1 + " " + b2);
```

A. true false

B. true true

C. java.util.stream.ReferencePipeline$3@4517d9a3

D. The code does not compile.

E. An exception is thrown.

F. The code hangs.

3. What could be the output of the following?

```
Predicate<String> predicate = s -> s.length() > 3;
var stream = Stream.iterate("-",
    s -> ! s.isEmpty(), (s) -> s + s);
var b1 = stream.noneMatch(predicate);
var b2 = stream.anyMatch(predicate);
System.out.println(b1 + " " + b2);
```

A. `false false`

B. `false true`

C. `java.util.stream.ReferencePipeline$3@4517d9a3`

D. The code does not compile.

E. An exception is thrown.

F. The code hangs.

4. Which are true statements about terminal operations in a stream that runs successfully? (Choose all that apply.)

A. At most, one terminal operation can exist in a stream pipeline.

B. Terminal operations are a required part of the stream pipeline in order to get a result.

C. Terminal operations have `Stream` as the return type.

D. The `peek()` method is an example of a terminal operation.

E. The referenced `Stream` may be used after calling a terminal operation.

5. Which of the following sets `result` to `8.0`? (Choose all that apply.)

A.
```
double result = LongStream.of(6L, 8L, 10L)
    .mapToInt(x -> (int) x)
    .collect(Collectors.groupingBy(x -> x))
    .keySet()
    .stream()
    .collect(Collectors.averagingInt(x -> x));
```

B.
```
double result = LongStream.of(6L, 8L, 10L)
    .mapToInt(x -> x)
    .boxed()
    .collect(Collectors.groupingBy(x -> x))
    .keySet()
    .stream()
    .collect(Collectors.averagingInt(x -> x));
```

C.
```
double result = LongStream.of(6L, 8L, 10L)
    .mapToInt(x -> (int) x)
    .boxed()
    .collect(Collectors.groupingBy(x -> x))
    .keySet()
    .stream()
    .collect(Collectors.averagingInt(x -> x));
```

D.

```
double result = LongStream.of(6L, 8L, 10L)
    .mapToInt(x -> (int) x)
    .collect(Collectors.groupingBy(x -> x, Collectors.toSet()))
    .keySet()
    .stream()
    .collect(Collectors.averagingInt(x -> x));
```

E.

```
double result = LongStream.of(6L, 8L, 10L)
    .mapToInt(x -> x)
    .boxed()
    .collect(Collectors.groupingBy(x -> x, Collectors.toSet()))
    .keySet()
    .stream()
    .collect(Collectors.averagingInt(x -> x));
```

F.

```
double result = LongStream.of(6L, 8L, 10L)
    .mapToInt(x -> (int) x)
    .boxed()
    .collect(Collectors.groupingBy(x -> x, Collectors.toSet()))
    .keySet()
    .stream()
    .collect(Collectors.averagingInt(x -> x));
```

6. Which of the following can fill in the blank so that the code prints out `false`? (Choose all that apply.)

```
var s = Stream.generate(() -> "meow");
var match = s._____(String::isEmpty);
System.out.println(match);
```

- **A.** allMatch
- **B.** anyMatch
- **C.** findAny
- **D.** findFirst
- **E.** noneMatch
- **F.** None of the above

7. We have a method that returns a sorted list without changing the original. Which of the following can replace the method implementation to do the same with streams?

```java
private static List<String> sort(List<String> list) {
   var copy = new ArrayList<String>(list);
   Collections.sort(copy, (a, b) -> b.compareTo(a));
   return copy;
}
```

A.
```java
return list.stream()
   .compare((a, b) -> b.compareTo(a))
   .collect(Collectors.toList());
```

B.
```java
return list.stream()
   .compare((a, b) -> b.compareTo(a))
   .sort();
```

C.
```java
return list.stream()
   .compareTo((a, b) -> b.compareTo(a))
   .collect(Collectors.toList());
```

D.
```java
return list.stream()
   .compareTo((a, b) -> b.compareTo(a))
   .sort();
```

E.
```java
return list.stream()
   .sorted((a, b) -> b.compareTo(a))
   .collect();
```

F.
```java
return list.stream()
   .sorted((a, b) -> b.compareTo(a))
   .collect(Collectors.toList());
```

8. Which of the following are true given this declaration? (Choose all that apply.)
```java
var is = IntStream.empty();
```
   A. `is.average()` returns the type `int`.
   B. `is.average()` returns the type `OptionalInt`.
   C. `is.findAny()` returns the type `int`.

D.   is.findAny() returns the type OptionalInt.

E.   is.sum() returns the type int.

F.   is.sum() returns the type OptionalInt.

9. Which of the following can we add after line 6 for the code to run without error and not produce any output? (Choose all that apply.)

```
4: var stream = LongStream.of(1, 2, 3);
5: var opt = stream.map(n -> n * 10)
6:    .filter(n -> n < 5).findFirst();
```

A.

```
if (opt.isPresent())
   System.out.println(opt.get());
```

B.

```
if (opt.isPresent())
   System.out.println(opt.getAsLong());
```

C.

```
opt.ifPresent(System.out.println);
```

D.

```
opt.ifPresent(System.out::println);
```

E.   None of these; the code does not compile.

F.   None of these; line 5 throws an exception at runtime.

10. Given the four statements (L, M, N, O), select and order the ones that would complete the expression and cause the code to output 10 lines. (Choose all that apply.)

```
Stream.generate(() -> "1")
   L: .filter(x -> x.length() > 1)
   M: .forEach(System.out::println)
   N: .limit(10)
   O: .peek(System.out::println)
;
```

A. L, N

B. L, N, O

C. L, N, M

D. L, N, M, O

E. L, O, M

F. N, M

G. N, O

11. What changes need to be made together for this code to print the string 12345? (Choose all that apply.)

```
Stream.iterate(1, x -> x++)
   .limit(5).map(x -> x)
   .collect(Collectors.joining());
```

A. Change `Collectors.joining()` to `Collectors.joining(",")`.

B. Change `map(x -> x)` to `map(x -> "" + x)`.

C. Change `x -> x++` to `x -> ++x`.

D. Add `forEach(System.out::print)` after the call to `collect()`.

E. Wrap the entire line in a `System.out.print` statement.

F. None of the above. The code already prints 12345.

12. Which functional interfaces complete the following code? For line 7, assume m and n are instances of functional interfaces that exist and have the same type as y. (Choose three.)

```
6: _____ x = String::new;
7: _____ y = m.andThen(n);
8: _____ z = a -> a + a;
```

A. `BinaryConsumer<String, String>`

B. `BiConsumer<String, String>`

C. `BinaryFunction<String, String>`

D. `BiFunction<String, String>`

E. `Predicate<String>`

F. `Supplier<String>`

G. `UnaryOperator<String>`

H. `UnaryOperator<String, String>`

13. Which of the following is true?

```
List<Integer> x1 = List.of(1, 2, 3);
List<Integer> x2 = List.of(4, 5, 6);
List<Integer> x3 = List.of();
Stream.of(x1, x2, x3).map(x -> x + 1)
   .flatMap(x -> x.stream())
   .forEach(System.out::print);
```

A. The code compiles and prints 123456.

B. The code compiles and prints 234567.

C. The code compiles but does not print anything.

D. The code compiles but prints stream references.

    E. The code runs infinitely.

    F. The code does not compile.

    G. The code throws an exception.

14. Which of the following is true? (Choose all that apply.)

```
4: Stream<Integer> s = Stream.of(1);
5: IntStream is = s.boxed();
6: DoubleStream ds = s.mapToDouble(x -> x);
7: Stream<Integer> s2 = ds.mapToInt(x -> x);
8: s2.forEach(System.out::print);
```

    A. Line 4 causes a compiler error.

    B. Line 5 causes a compiler error.

    C. Line 6 causes a compiler error.

    D. Line 7 causes a compiler error.

    E. Line 8 causes a compiler error.

    F. The code compiles but throws an exception at runtime.

    G. The code compiles and prints 1.

15. Given the generic type `String`, the `partitioningBy()` collector creates a `Map<Boolean, List<String>>` when passed to `collect()` by default. When a downstream collector is passed to `partitioningBy()`, which return types can be created? (Choose all that apply.)

    A. `Map<boolean, List<String>>`

    B. `Map<Boolean, List<String>>`

    C. `Map<Boolean, Map<String>>`

    D. `Map<Boolean, Set<String>>`

    E. `Map<Long, TreeSet<String>>`

    F. None of the above

16. Which of the following statements are true about this code? (Choose all that apply.)

```
20: Predicate<String> empty = String::isEmpty;
21: Predicate<String> notEmpty = empty.negate();
22:
23: var result = Stream.generate(() -> "")
24:     .limit(10)
25:     .filter(notEmpty)
26:     .collect(Collectors.groupingBy(k -> k))
27:     .entrySet()
28:     .stream()
29:     .map(Entry::getValue)
```

```
30:      .flatMap(Collection::stream)
31:      .collect(Collectors.partitioningBy(notEmpty));
32: System.out.println(result);
```

A. It outputs: {}

B. It outputs: {false=[], true=[]}

C. If we changed line 31 from `partitioningBy(notEmpty)` to `groupingBy(n -> n)`, it would output: {}

D. If we changed line 31 from `partitioningBy(notEmpty)` to `groupingBy(n -> n)`, it would output: {false=[], true=[]}

E. The code does not compile.

F. The code compiles but does not terminate at runtime.

17. Which of the following is equivalent to this code? (Choose all that apply.)

```
UnaryOperator<Integer> u = x -> x * x;
```

A. `BiFunction<Integer> f = x -> x*x;`

B. `BiFunction<Integer, Integer> f = x -> x*x;`

C. `BinaryOperator<Integer, Integer> f = x -> x*x;`

D. `Function<Integer> f = x -> x*x;`

E. `Function<Integer, Integer> f = x -> x*x;`

F. None of the above

18. What is the result of the following?

```
var s = DoubleStream.of(1.2, 2.4);
s.peek(System.out::println).filter(x -> x > 2).count();
```

A. 1

B. 2

C. 2.4

D. 1.2 and 2.4

E. There is no output.

F. The code does not compile.

G. An exception is thrown.

19. What does the following code output?

```
Function<Integer, Integer> s = a -> a + 4;
Function<Integer, Integer> t = a -> a * 3;
Function<Integer, Integer> c = s.compose(t);
System.out.println(c.apply(1));
```

A. 7

B. 15

    C. The code does not compile because of the data types in the lambda expressions.

    D. The code does not compile because of the `compose()` call.

    E. The code does not compile for another reason.

20. Which of the following functional interfaces contain an abstract method that returns a primitive value? (Choose all that apply.)

    A. `BooleanSupplier`

    B. `CharSupplier`

    C. `DoubleSupplier`

    D. `FloatSupplier`

    E. `IntSupplier`

    F. `StringSupplier`

21. What is the simplest way of rewriting this code?

```
List<Integer> x = IntStream.range(1, 6)
    .mapToObj(i -> i)
    .collect(Collectors.toList());
x.forEach(System.out::println);
```

    A.

```
IntStream.range(1, 6);
```

    B.

```
IntStream.range(1, 6)
    .forEach(System.out::println);
```

    C.

```
IntStream.range(1, 6)
    .mapToObj(i -> i)
    .forEach(System.out::println);
```

    D. None of the above is equivalent.

    E. The provided code does not compile.

22. Which of the following throw an exception when an `Optional` is empty? (Choose all that apply.)

    A. `opt.orElse("");`

    B. `opt.orElseGet(() -> "");`

    C. `opt.orElseThrow();`

    D. `opt.orElseThrow(() -> throw new Exception());`

    E. `opt.orElseThrow(RuntimeException::new);`

    F. `opt.get();`

    G. `opt.get("");`

Chapter

16

Exceptions, Assertions, and Localization

OCP EXAM OBJECTIVES COVERED IN THIS CHAPTER:

✓ **Exception Handling and Assertions**

- Use the try-with-resources construct

- Create and use custom exception classes

- Test invariants by using assertions

✓ **Localization**

- Use the Locale class

- Use resource bundles

- Format messages, dates, and numbers with Java

This chapter is about creating applications that adapt to change. What happens if a user enters invalid data on a web page, or our connection to a database goes down in the middle of a sale? How do we ensure rules about our data are enforced? Finally, how do we build applications that can support multiple languages or geographic regions?

In this chapter, we will discuss these problems and solutions to them using exceptions, assertions, and localization. One way to make sure your applications respond to change is to build in support early on. For example, supporting localization doesn't mean you actually need to support multiple languages right away. It just means your application can be more easily adapted in the future. By the end of this chapter, we hope we've provided structure for designing applications that better adapt to change.

Reviewing Exceptions

An *exception* is Java's way of saying, "I give up. I don't know what to do right now. You deal with it." When you write a method, you can either deal with the exception or make it the calling code's problem. In this section, we cover the fundamentals of exceptions.

If you've recently studied for the 1Z0-815 exam, then you can probably skip this section and go straight to "Creating Custom Exceptions." This section is meant only for review.

Handling Exceptions

A *try statement* is used to handle exceptions. It consists of a try clause, zero or more *catch clauses* to handle the exceptions that are thrown, and an optional *finally clause*, which runs regardless of whether an exception is thrown. Figure 16.1 shows the syntax of a try statement.

A traditional try statement must have at least one of the following: a catch block or a finally block. It can have more than one catch block, including multi-catch blocks, but at most one finally block.

Swallowing an exception is when you handle it with an empty catch block. When presenting a topic, we often do this to keep things simple. Please, *never do this in practice!* Oftentimes, it is added by developers who do not want to handle or declare an exception properly and can lead to bugs in production code.

FIGURE 16.1   The syntax of a try statement

```
try {

    // Protected code

} catch (IOException e) {
                    Exception identifier

    // Handler for IOException

} catch (ArithmeticException | IllegalArgumentException e) {
                                                    Exception identifier
                        Catch either of
    // Multi-catch handler    these exceptions.

} finally {

    // Always runs after try/catch blocks are finished

}
```

You can also create a *try-with-resources* statement to handle exceptions. A try-with-resources statement looks a lot like a try statement, except that it includes a list of resources inside a set of parentheses, (). These resources are automatically closed in the reverse order that they are declared at the conclusion of the try clause. The syntax of the try-with-resources statement is presented in Figure 16.2.

Like a regular try statement, a try-with-resources statement can include optional catch and finally blocks. Unlike a try statement, though, neither is required. We'll cover try-with-resources statements in more detail in this chapter.

FIGURE 16.2   The syntax of a try-with-resources statement

Did you notice we used var for the resource type? While var is not required, it is convenient when working with streams, database objects, and especially generics, whose declarations can be lengthy.

> While presenting try-with-resources statements, we include a number of examples that use I/O stream classes that we'll be covering later in this book. For this chapter, you can assume these resources are declared correctly. For example, you can assume the previous code snippet correctly creates FileInputStream and FileOutputStream objects. If you see a try-with-resources statement with an I/O stream on the exam, though, it could be testing either topic.

Distinguishing between *throw* and *throws*

By now, you should know the difference between throw and throws. The throw keyword means an exception is actually being thrown, while the throws keyword indicates that the method merely has the potential to throw that exception. The following example uses both:

```
10: public String getDataFromDatabase() throws SQLException {
11:     throw new UnsupportedOperationException();
12: }
```

Line 10 declares that the method might or might not throw a SQLException. Since this is a checked exception, the caller needs to handle or declare it. Line 11 actually does throw an UnsupportedOperationException. Since this is a runtime exception, it does not need to be declared on line 10.

Examining Exception Categories

In Java, all exceptions inherit from Throwable, although in practice, the only ones you should be handling or declaring extend from the Exception class. Figure 16.3 reviews the hierarchy of the top-level exception classes.

To begin with, a *checked exception* must be handled or declared by the application code where it is thrown. The *handle or declare rule* dictates that a checked exception must be either caught in a catch block or thrown to the caller by including it in the method declaration.

The ZooMaintenance class shows an example of a method that handles an exception, and one that declares an exception.

```
public class ZooMaintenance {
    public void open() {
        try {
            throw new Exception();
        } catch (Exception e) {
```

```
            // Handles exception
        }
    }

    public void close() throws Exception {  // Declares exceptions
        throw new Exception();
    }
}
```

FIGURE 16.3   Categories of exceptions

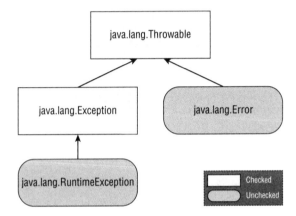

In Java, all exceptions that inherit Exception but not RuntimeException are considered checked exceptions.

On the other hand, an *unchecked exception* does not need to be handled or declared. Unchecked exceptions are often referred to as runtime exceptions, although in Java unchecked exceptions include any class that inherits RuntimeException or Error. An Error is fatal, and it is considered a poor practice to catch it.

For the exam, you need to memorize some common exception classes. You also need to know whether they are checked or unchecked exceptions. Table 16.1 lists the unchecked exceptions that inherit RuntimeException that you should be familiar with for the exam.

TABLE 16.1   Unchecked exceptions

ArithmeticException	ArrayIndexOutOfBoundsException
ArrayStoreException	ClassCastException
IllegalArgumentException	IllegalStateException
MissingResourceException	NullPointerException
NumberFormatException	UnsupportedOperationException

Table 16.2 presents the checked exceptions you should also be familiar with.

TABLE 16.2 Checked exceptions

FileNotFoundException	IOException
NotSerializableException	ParseException
SQLException	

Inheriting Exception Classes

When evaluating catch blocks, the inheritance of the exception types can be important. For the exam, you should know that NumberFormatException inherits from IllegalArgumentException. You should also know that FileNotFoundException and NotSerializableException both inherit from IOException.

This comes up often in multi-catch expressions. For example, why does the following not compile?

```
try {
   throw new IOException();
} catch (IOException | FileNotFoundException e) {} // DOES NOT COMPILE
```

Since FileNotFoundException is a subclass of IOException, listing both in a multi-catch expression is redundant, resulting in a compilation error.

Ordering of exceptions in consecutive catch blocks matters too. Do you understand why the following does not compile?

```
try {
   throw new IOException();
} catch (IOException e) {
} catch (FileNotFoundException e) {} // DOES NOT COMPILE
```

For the exam, remember that trying to catch a more specific exception (after already catching a broader exception) results in unreachable code and a compiler error.

If you're a bit rusty on exceptions, then you may want to review Chapter 10, "Exceptions". The rest of this book assumes you know the basics of exception handling.

Creating Custom Exceptions

Java provides many exception classes out of the box. Sometimes, you want to write a method with a more specialized type of exception. You can create your own exception class to do this.

Declaring Exception Classes

When creating your own exception, you need to decide whether it should be a checked or unchecked exception. While you can extend any exception class, it is most common to extend Exception (for checked) or RuntimeException (for unchecked).

Creating your own exception class is really easy. Can you figure out whether the exceptions are checked or unchecked in this example?

```
1: class CannotSwimException extends Exception {}
2: class DangerInTheWater extends RuntimeException {}
3: class SharkInTheWaterException extends DangerInTheWater {}
4: class Dolphin {
5:     public void swim() throws CannotSwimException {
6:         // logic here
7:     }
8: }
```

On line 1, we have a checked exception because it extends directly from Exception. Not being able to swim is pretty bad when we are trying to swim, so we want to force callers to deal with this situation. Line 2 declares an unchecked exception because it extends directly from RuntimeException. On line 3, we have another unchecked exception because it extends indirectly from RuntimeException. It is pretty unlikely that there will be a shark in the water. We might even be swimming in a pool where the odds of a shark are 0 percent! We don't want to force the caller to deal with everything that might remotely happen, so we leave this as an unchecked exception.

The method on lines 5–7 declares that it might throw the checked CannotSwimException. The method implementation could be written to actually throw it or not. The method implementation could also be written to throw a SharkInTheWaterException, an ArrayIndexOutOfBoundsException, or any other runtime exception.

Adding Custom Constructors

These one-liner exception declarations are pretty useful, especially on the exam where they need to communicate quickly whether an exception is checked or unchecked. Let's see how to pass more information in your exception.

The following example shows the three most common constructors defined by the Exception class:

```
public class CannotSwimException extends Exception {
    public CannotSwimException() {
        super();  // Optional, compiler will insert automatically
    }
    public CannotSwimException(Exception e) {
        super(e);
    }
    public CannotSwimException(String message) {
        super(message);
    }
}
```

The first constructor is the default constructor with no parameters. The second constructor shows how to wrap another exception inside yours. The third constructor shows how to pass a custom error message.

> **NOTE**   Remember from Chapter 8, "Class Design," that the default no-argument constructor is provided automatically if you don't write any constructors of your own.

In these examples, our constructors and parent constructors took the same parameters, but this is certainly not required. For example, the following constructor takes an Exception and calls the parent constructor that takes a String:

```
public CannotSwimException(Exception e) {
    super("Cannot swim because: " + e.toString());
}
```

Using a different constructor allows you to provide more information about what went wrong. For example, let's say we have a main() method with the following line:

```
15: public static void main(String[] unused) throws Exception {
16:     throw new CannotSwimException();
17: }
```

The output for this method is as follows:

```
Exception in thread "main" CannotSwimException
    at CannotSwimException.main(CannotSwimException.java:16)
```

The JVM gives us just the exception and its location. Useful, but we could get more. Now, let's change the main() method to include some text, as shown here:

```
15: public static void main(String[] unused) throws Exception {
16:    throw new CannotSwimException("broken fin");
17: }
```

The output of this new main() method is as follows:

```
Exception in thread "main" CannotSwimException: broken fin
   at CannotSwimException.main(CannotSwimException.java:16)
```

This time we see the message text in the result. You might want to provide more information about the exception depending on the problem.

We can even pass another exception, if there is an underlying cause for the exception. Take a look at this version of our main() method:

```
15: public static void main(String[] unused) throws Exception {
16:    throw new CannotSwimException(
17:       new FileNotFoundException("Cannot find shark file"));
18: }
```

This would yield the longest output so far:

```
Exception in thread "main" CannotSwimException:
   java.io.FileNotFoundException: Cannot find shark file
   at CannotSwimException.main(CannotSwimException.java:16)
Caused by: java.io.FileNotFoundException: Cannot find shark file
   ... 1 more
```

Printing Stack Traces

The error messages that we've been showing are called *stack traces*. A stack trace shows the exception along with the method calls it took to get there. The JVM automatically prints a stack trace when an exception is thrown that is not handled by the program.

You can also print the stack trace on your own. The advantage is that you can read or log information from the stack trace and then continue to handle or even rethrow it.

```
try {
   throw new CannotSwimException();
} catch (CannotSwimException e) {
   e.printStackTrace();
}
```

Automating Resource Management

As previously described, a try-with-resources statement ensures that any resources declared in the try clause are automatically closed at the conclusion of the try block. This feature is also known as *automatic resource management*, because Java automatically takes care of closing the resources for you.

For the exam, a *resource* is typically a file or a database that requires some kind of stream or connection to read or write data. In Chapter 19, "I/O," Chapter 20, "NIO.2," and Chapter 21, "JDBC," you'll create numerous resources that will need to be closed when you are finished with them. In Chapter 22, "Security," we'll discuss how failure to close resources can lead to resource leaks that could make your program more vulnerable to attack.

Resource Management vs. Garbage Collection

Java has great built-in support for garbage collection. When you are finished with an object, it will automatically (over time) reclaim the memory associated with it.

The same is not true for resource management without a try-with-resources statement. If an object connected to a resource is not closed, then the connection could remain open. In fact, it may interfere with Java's ability to garbage collect the object.

To eliminate this problem, it is recommended that you close resources in the same block of code that opens them. By using a try-with-resources statement to open all your resources, this happens automatically.

Constructing Try-With-Resources Statements

What types of resources can be used with a try-with-resources statement? The first rule you should know is: *try-with-resources statements require resources that implement the AutoCloseable interface.* For example, the following does not compile as String does not implement the AutoCloseable interface:

```
try (String reptile = "lizard") {
}
```

Inheriting AutoCloseable requires implementing a compatible close() method.

```
interface AutoCloseable {
    public void close() throws Exception;
}
```

From your studies of method overriding, this means that the implemented version of close() can choose to throw Exception or a subclass, or not throw any exceptions at all.

 In Chapter 19 and Chapter 20, you will encounter resources that implement Closeable, rather than AutoCloseable. Since Closeable extends AutoCloseable, they are both supported in try-with-resources statements. The only difference between the two is that Closeable's close() method declares IOException, while AutoCloseable's close() method declares Exception.

Let's define our own custom resource class for use in a try-with-resources statement.

```java
public class MyFileReader implements AutoCloseable {
    private String tag;
    public MyFileReader(String tag) { this.tag = tag;}

    @Override public void close() {
        System.out.println("Closed: "+tag);
    }
}
```

The following code snippet makes use of our custom reader class:

```java
try (var bookReader = new MyFileReader("monkey")) {
    System.out.println("Try Block");
} finally {
    System.out.println("Finally Block");
}
```

The code prints the following at runtime:

```
Try Block
Closed: monkey
Finally Block
```

As you can see, the resources are closed at the end of the try statement, before any catch or finally blocks are executed. Behind the scenes, the JVM calls the close() method inside a hidden finally block, which we can refer to as the *implicit* finally block. The finally block that the programmer declared can be referred to as the *explicit* finally block.

 In a try-with-resources statement, you need to remember that the resource will be closed at the completion of the try block, before any declared catch or finally blocks execute.

The second rule you should be familiar with is: *a try-with-resources statement can include multiple resources, which are closed in the reverse order in which they are declared*. Resources are terminated by a semicolon (;), with the last one being optional.

Consider the following code snippet:

```java
try (var bookReader = new MyFileReader("1");
    var movieReader = new MyFileReader("2");
    var tvReader = new MyFileReader("3");) {
   System.out.println("Try Block");
} finally {
   System.out.println("Finally Block");
}
```

When executed, this code prints the following:

```
Try Block
Closed: 3
Closed: 2
Closed: 1
Finally Block
```

 Real World Scenario

Why You Should Be Using try-with-resources Statements

If you have been working with files and databases and have never used try-with-resources before, you've definitely been missing out. For example, consider this code sample, which does not use automatic resource management:

```java
11: public void copyData(Path path1, Path path2) throws Exception {
12:     BufferedReader in = null;
13:     BufferedWriter out = null;
14:     try {
15:         in = Files.newBufferedReader(path1);
16:         out = Files.newBufferedWriter(path2);
17:         out.write(in.readLine());
18:     } finally {
19:         if (out != null) {
20:             out.close();
21:         }
22:         if (in != null) {
23:             in.close();
```

```
24:         }
25:     }
26: }
```

Switching to the try-with-resources syntax, we can replace it with the following, much shorter implementation:

```
11: public void copyData(Path path1, Path path2) throws Exception {
12:     try (var in = Files.newBufferedReader(path1);
13:          var out = Files.newBufferedWriter(path2)) {
14:         out.write(in.readLine());
15:     }
16: }
```

Excluding the method declaration, that's 14 lines of code to do something that can be done in 4 lines of code. In fact, the first version even contains a bug! If out.close() throws an exception on line 20, the in resource will never be closed. The close() statements would each need to be wrapped in a try/catch block to ensure the resources were properly closed.

The final rule you should know is: *resources declared within a try-with-resources statement are in scope only within the try block.*

This is another way to remember that the resources are closed before any catch or finally blocks are executed, as the resources are no longer available. Do you see why lines 6 and 8 don't compile in this example?

```
3: try (Scanner s = new Scanner(System.in)) {
4:     s.nextLine();
5: } catch(Exception e) {
6:     s.nextInt(); // DOES NOT COMPILE
7: } finally {
8:     s.nextInt(); // DOES NOT COMPILE
9: }
```

The problem is that Scanner has gone out of scope at the end of the try clause. Lines 6 and 8 do not have access to it. This is actually a nice feature. You can't accidentally use an object that has been closed.

Resources do not need to be declared inside a try-with-resources statement, though, as we will see in the next section.

Learning the New Effectively Final Feature

Starting with Java 9, it is possible to use resources declared prior to the try-with-resources statement, provided they are marked final or effectively final. The syntax is just to use the resource name in place of the resource declaration, separated by a semicolon (;).

```
11: public void relax() {
12:    final var bookReader = new MyFileReader("4");
13:    MyFileReader movieReader = new MyFileReader("5");
14:    try (bookReader;
15:        var tvReader = new MyFileReader("6");
16:        movieReader) {
17:      System.out.println("Try Block");
18:    } finally {
19:      System.out.println("Finally Block");
20:    }
21: }
```

Let's take this one line at a time. Line 12 declares a final variable bookReader, while line 13 declares an effectively final variable movieReader. Both of these resources can be used in a try-with-resources statement. We know movieReader is effectively final because it is a local variable that is assigned a value only once. Remember, the test for effectively final is that if we insert the final keyword when the variable is declared, the code still compiles.

Lines 14 and 16 use the new syntax to declare resources in a try-with-resources statement, using just the variable name and separating the resources with a semicolon (;). Line 15 uses the normal syntax for declaring a new resource within the try clause.

On execution, the code prints the following:

```
Try Block
Closed: 5
Closed: 6
Closed: 4
Finally Block
```

If you come across a question on the exam that uses a try-with-resources statement with a variable not declared in the try clause, make sure it is effectively final. For example, the following does not compile:

```
31: var writer = Files.newBufferedWriter(path);
32: try(writer) {  // DOES NOT COMPILE
33:   writer.append("Welcome to the zoo!");
34: }
35: writer = null;
```

The writer variable is reassigned on line 35, resulting in the compiler not considering it effectively final. Since it is not an effectively final variable, it cannot be used in a try-with-resources statement on line 32.

The other place the exam might try to trick you is accessing a resource after it has been closed. Consider the following:

```
41: var writer = Files.newBufferedWriter(path);
42: writer.append("This write is permitted but a really bad idea!");
```

```
43: try(writer) {
44:    writer.append("Welcome to the zoo!");
45: }
46: writer.append("This write will fail!");  // IOException
```

This code compiles but throws an exception on line 46 with the message `Stream closed`. While it was possible to write to the resource before the try-with-resources statement, it is not afterward.

Take Care When Using Resources Declared before try-with-resources Statements

On line 42 of the previous code sample, we used `writer` before the try-with-resources statement. While this is allowed, it's a really bad idea. What happens if line 42 throws an exception? In this case, the resource declared on line 41 will *never* be closed! What about the following code snippet?

```
51: var reader = Files.newBufferedReader(path1);
52: var writer = Files.newBufferedWriter(path2);  // Don't do this!
53: try (reader; writer) {}
```

It has the same problem. If line 52 throws an exception, such as the file cannot be found, then the resource declared on line 51 will never be closed. We recommend you use this new syntax sparingly or with only one resource at a time. For example, if line 52 was removed, then the resource created on line 51 wouldn't have an opportunity to throw an exception before entering the automatic resource management block.

Understanding Suppressed Exceptions

What happens if the `close()` method throws an exception? Let's try an illustrative example:

```
public class TurkeyCage implements AutoCloseable {
    public void close() {
        System.out.println("Close gate");
    }
    public static void main(String[] args) {
        try (var t = new TurkeyCage()) {
            System.out.println("Put turkeys in");
        }
    }
}
```

If the TurkeyCage doesn't close, the turkeys could all escape. Clearly, we need to handle such a condition. We already know that the resources are closed before any programmer-coded catch blocks are run. This means we can catch the exception thrown by close() if we want. Alternatively, we can allow the caller to deal with it.

Let's expand our example with a new JammedTurkeyCage implementation, shown here:

```
1:  public class JammedTurkeyCage implements AutoCloseable {
2:      public void close() throws IllegalStateException {
3:          throw new IllegalStateException("Cage door does not close");
4:      }
5:      public static void main(String[] args) {
6:          try (JammedTurkeyCage t = new JammedTurkeyCage()) {
7:              System.out.println("Put turkeys in");
8:          } catch (IllegalStateException e) {
9:              System.out.println("Caught: " + e.getMessage());
10:         }
11:     }
12: }
```

The close() method is automatically called by try-with-resources. It throws an exception, which is caught by our catch block and prints the following:

```
Caught: Cage door does not close
```

This seems reasonable enough. What happens if the try block also throws an exception? When multiple exceptions are thrown, all but the first are called *suppressed exceptions*. The idea is that Java treats the first exception as the primary one and tacks on any that come up while automatically closing.

What do you think the following implementation of our main() method outputs?

```
5:      public static void main(String[] args) {
6:          try (JammedTurkeyCage t = new JammedTurkeyCage()) {
7:              throw new IllegalStateException("Turkeys ran off");
8:          } catch (IllegalStateException e) {
9:              System.out.println("Caught: " + e.getMessage());
10:             for (Throwable t: e.getSuppressed())
11:                 System.out.println("Suppressed: "+t.getMessage());
12:         }
13:     }
```

Line 7 throws the primary exception. At this point, the try clause ends, and Java automatically calls the close() method. Line 3 of JammedTurkeyCage throws an IllegalStateException, which is added as a suppressed exception. Then line 8 catches the primary exception. Line 9 prints the message for the primary exception. Lines 10–11 iterate through any suppressed exceptions and print them. The program prints the following:

```
Caught: Turkeys ran off
Suppressed: Cage door does not close
```

Keep in mind that the `catch` block looks for matches on the primary exception. What do you think this code prints?

```
5:     public static void main(String[] args) {
6:         try (JammedTurkeyCage t = new JammedTurkeyCage()) {
7:             throw new RuntimeException("Turkeys ran off");
8:         } catch (IllegalStateException e) {
9:             System.out.println("caught: " + e.getMessage());
10:         }
11:     }
```

Line 7 again throws the primary exception. Java calls the `close()` method and adds a suppressed exception. Line 8 would catch the `IllegalStateException`. However, we don't have one of those. The primary exception is a `RuntimeException`. Since this does not match the `catch` clause, the exception is thrown to the caller. Eventually the `main()` method would output something like the following:

```
Exception in thread "main" java.lang.RuntimeException: Turkeys ran off
    at JammedTurkeyCage.main(JammedTurkeyCage.java:7)
    Suppressed: java.lang.IllegalStateException:
        Cage door does not close
    at JammedTurkeyCage.close(JammedTurkeyCage.java:3)
    at JammedTurkeyCage.main(JammedTurkeyCage.java:8)
```

Java remembers the suppressed exceptions that go with a primary exception even if we don't handle them in the code.

If more than two resources throw an exception, the first one to be thrown becomes the primary exception, with the rest being grouped as suppressed exceptions. And since resources are closed in reverse order in which they are declared, the primary exception would be on the last declared resource that throws an exception.

Keep in mind that suppressed exceptions apply only to exceptions thrown in the `try` clause. The following example does not throw a suppressed exception:

```
5:     public static void main(String[] args) {
6:         try (JammedTurkeyCage t = new JammedTurkeyCage()) {
7:             throw new IllegalStateException("Turkeys ran off");
8:         } finally {
9:             throw new RuntimeException("and we couldn't find them");
10:         }
11:     }
```

Line 7 throws an exception. Then Java tries to close the resource and adds a suppressed exception to it. Now we have a problem. The `finally` block runs after all this. Since line 9 also throws an exception, the previous exception from line 7 is lost, with the code printing the following:

```
Exception in thread "main" java.lang.RuntimeException:
    and we couldn't find them
    at JammedTurkeyCage.main(JammedTurkeyCage.java:9)
```

This has always been and continues to be bad programming practice. We don't want to lose exceptions! Although out of scope for the exam, the reason for this has to do with backward compatibility. Automatic resource management was added in Java 7, and this behavior existed before this feature was added.

Declaring Assertions

An *assertion* is a `boolean` expression that you place at a point in your code where you expect something to be `true`. An *assert statement* contains this statement along with an optional message.

An assertion allows for detecting defects in the code. You can turn on assertions for testing and debugging while leaving them off when your program is in production.

Why assert something when you know it is true? It is true only when everything is working properly. If the program has a defect, it might not actually be true. Detecting this earlier in the process lets you know something is wrong.

In the following sections, we cover the syntax for using an assertion, how to turn assertions on/off, and some common uses of assertions.

 Real World Scenario

Assertions vs. Unit Tests

Most developers are more familiar with unit test frameworks, such as JUnit, than with assertions. While there are some similarities, assertions are commonly used to verify the internal state of a program, while unit tests are most frequently used to verify behavior.

Additionally, unit test frameworks tend to be fully featured with lots of options and tools available. While you need to know assertions for the exam, you are far better off writing unit tests when programming professionally.

Validating Data with the *assert* Statement

The syntax for an `assert` statement has two forms, shown in Figure 16.4.

FIGURE 16.4   The syntax of assert statements

When assertions are enabled and the boolean expression evaluates to false, then an AssertionError will be thrown at runtime. Since programs aren't supposed to catch an Error, this means that assertion failures are fatal and end the program!

 Since Java 1.4, assert is a keyword. That means it can't be used as an identifier at compile time, even if assertions will be disabled at runtime. Keep an eye out for questions on the exam that use it as anything other than a statement.

Assertions may include optional parentheses and a message. For example, each of the following is valid:

```
assert 1 == age;
assert(2 == height);
assert 100.0 == length : "Problem with length";
assert ("Cecelia".equals(name)): "Failed to verify user data";
```

When provided, the error message will be sent to the AssertionError constructor. It is commonly a String, although it can be any value.

Recognizing Assertion Syntax Errors

While the preceding examples demonstrate the appropriate syntax, the exam may try to trick you with invalid syntax. See whether you can determine why the following do not compile:

```
assert(1);
assert x -> true;
assert 1==2 ? "Accept" : "Error";
assert.test(5 > age);
```

The first three statements do not compile because they expect a boolean value. The last statement does not compile because the syntax is invalid.

The three possible outcomes of an `assert` statement are as follows:

- If assertions are disabled, Java skips the assertion and goes on in the code.
- If assertions are enabled and the `boolean` expression is `true`, then our assertion has been validated and nothing happens. The program continues to execute in its normal manner.
- If assertions are enabled and the `boolean` expression is `false`, then our assertion is invalid and an `AssertionError` is thrown.

Presuming assertions are enabled, an assertion is a shorter way of writing the following:

```
if (!boolean_expression) throw new AssertionError(error_message);
```

Let's try an example. Consider the following:

```
1: public class Party {
2:     public static void main(String[] args) {
3:         int numGuests = -5;
4:         assert numGuests > 0;
5:         System.out.println(numGuests);
6:     }
7: }
```

We can enable assertions by executing it using the single-file source-code command, as shown here:

```
java -ea Party.java
```

Uh-oh, we made a typo in our `Party` class. We intended for there to be five guests and not negative five guests. The assertion on line 4 detects this problem. Java throws the `AssertionError` at this point. Line 5 never runs since an error was thrown.

The program ends with a stack trace similar to this:

```
Exception in thread "main" java.lang.AssertionError
    at asserts.Assertions.main(Assertions.java:4)
```

If we run the same program using the command line `java Party`, we get a different result. The program prints -5. Now, in this example, it is pretty obvious what the problem is since the program is only seven lines. In a more complicated program, knowing the state of affairs is more useful.

Enabling Assertions

By default, `assert` statements are ignored by the JVM at runtime. To enable assertions, use the -enableassertions flag on the command line.

```
java -enableassertions Rectangle
```

You can also use the shortcut -ea flag.

```
java -ea Rectangle
```

Using the -enableassertions or -ea flag without any arguments enables assertions in all classes (except system classes). You can also enable assertions for a specific class or package. For example, the following command enables assertions only for classes in the com.demos package and any subpackages:

```
java -ea:com.demos... my.programs.Main
```

The ellipsis (...) means any class in the specified package or subpackages. You can also enable assertions for a specific class.

```
java -ea:com.demos.TestColors my.programs.Main
```

Enabling assertions is an important aspect of using them, because if assertions are not enabled, assert statements are ignored at runtime. Keep an eye out for questions that contain an assert statement where assertions are not enabled.

Disabling Assertions

Sometimes you want to enable assertions for the entire application but disable it for select packages or classes. Java offers the -disableassertions or -da flag for just such an occasion. The following command enables assertions for the com.demos package but disables assertions for the TestColors class:

```
java -ea:com.demos... -da:com.demos.TestColors my.programs.Main
```

For the exam, make sure you understand how to use the -ea and -da flags in conjunction with each other.

By default, all assertions are disabled. Then, those items marked with -ea are enabled. Finally, all of the remaining items marked with -da are disabled.

Applying Assertions

Table 16.3 list some of the common uses of assertions. You won't be asked to identify the type of assertion on the exam. This is just to give you some ideas of how they can be used.

TABLE 16.3   Assertion applications

Usage	Description
Internal invariants	Assert that a value is within a certain constraint, such as `assert x < 0`.
Class invariants	Assert the validity of an object's state. Class invariants are typically `private` methods within the class that return a `boolean`.
Control flow invariants	Assert that a line of code you assume is unreachable is never reached.
Pre-conditions	Assert that certain conditions are met before a method is invoked.
Post-conditions	Assert that certain conditions are met after a method executes successfully.

Writing Assertions Correctly

One of the most important rules you should remember from this section is: *assertions should never alter outcomes*. This is especially true because assertions can, should, and probably will be turned off in a production environment.

For example, the following assertion is not a good design because it alters the value of a variable:

```
int x = 10;
assert ++x > 10; // Not a good design!
```

When assertions are turned on, x is incremented to 11; but when assertions are turned off, the value of x is 10. This is not a good use of assertions because the outcome of the code will be different depending on whether assertions are turned on.

Assertions are used for debugging purposes, allowing you to verify that something that you think is true during the coding phase is actually true at runtime.

Working with Dates and Times

The older Java 8 certification exams required you to know a lot about the Date and Time API. This included knowing many of the various date/time classes and their various methods, how to specify amounts of time with the Period and Duration classes, and even how to resolve values across time zones with daylight savings.

For the Java 11 exam, none of those topics is in scope, although strangely enough, you still need to know how to format dates. This just means if you see a date/time on the exam, you aren't being tested about it. Before we learn how to format dates, let's learn what they are and how to create them.

Creating Dates and Times

In the real world, we usually talk about dates and times as relative to our current location. For example, "I'll call you at 11 a.m. on Friday morning." You probably use date and time independently, like this: "The package will arrive by Friday" or "We're going to the movies at 7:15 p.m." Last but not least, you might also use a more absolute time when planning a meeting across a time zone, such as "Everyone in Seattle and Philadelphia will join the call at 10:45 EST."

Understanding Date and Time Types

Java includes numerous classes to model the examples in the previous paragraph. These types are listed in Table 16.4.

TABLE 16.4 Date and time types

Class	Description	Example
java.time.LocalDate	Date with day, month, year	Birth date
java.time.LocalTime	Time of day	Midnight
java.time.LocalDateTime	Day and time with no time zone	10 a.m. next Monday
java.time.ZonedDateTime	Date and time with a specific time zone	9 a.m. EST on 2/20/2021

Each of these types contains a `static` method called now() that allows you to get the current value.

```
System.out.println(LocalDate.now());
System.out.println(LocalTime.now());
System.out.println(LocalDateTime.now());
System.out.println(ZonedDateTime.now());
```

Your output is going to depend on the date/time when you run it and where you live, although it should resemble the following:

```
2020-10-14
12:45:20.854
2020-10-14T12:45:20.854
2020-10-14T12:45:20.854-04:00[America/New_York]
```

The first line contains only a date and no time. The second line contains only a time and no date. The time displays hours, minutes, seconds, and fractional seconds. The third line contains both a date and a time. Java uses T to separate the date and time when converting LocalDateTime to a String. Finally, the fourth line adds the time zone offset and time zone. New York is four time zones away from Greenwich mean time (GMT) for half of the year due to daylight savings time.

Using the *of()* Methods

We can create some date and time values using the of() methods in each class.

```
LocalDate date1 = LocalDate.of(2020, Month.OCTOBER, 20);
LocalDate date2 = LocalDate.of(2020, 10, 20);
```

Both pass in the year, month, and date. Although it is good to use the Month constants (to make the code easier to read), you can pass the int number of the month directly.

While programmers often count from zero, working with dates is one of the few times where it is expected for you to count from 1, just like in the real world.

When creating a time, you can choose how detailed you want to be. You can specify just the hour and minute, or you can include the number of seconds. You can even include nanoseconds if you want to be very precise (a nanosecond is a billionth of a second).

```
LocalTime time1 = LocalTime.of(6, 15);            // hour and minute
LocalTime time2 = LocalTime.of(6, 15, 30);        // + seconds
LocalTime time3 = LocalTime.of(6, 15, 30, 200);   // + nanoseconds
```

These three times are all different but within a minute of each other. You can combine dates and times in multiple ways.

```
var dt1 = LocalDateTime.of(2020, Month.OCTOBER, 20, 6, 15, 30);
```

```
LocalDate date = LocalDate.of(2020, Month.OCTOBER, 20);
LocalTime time = LocalTime.of(6, 15);
var dt2 = LocalDateTime.of(date, time);
```

The dt1 example shows how you can specify all of the information about the LocalDateTime right in the same line. The dt2 example shows how you can create LocalDate and LocalTime objects separately and then combine them to create a LocalDateTime object.

Real World Scenario

The Factory Pattern

Did you notice that we did not use a constructor in any of these examples? Rather than use a constructor, creation of these objects is delegated to a `static` factory method. The *factory pattern*, or factory method pattern, is a creational design pattern in which a factory class is used to provide instances of an object, rather than instantiating them directly. Oftentimes, factory methods return instances that are subtypes of the interface or class you are expecting.

We will be using the factory pattern throughout this book (and even later in this chapter!). In some cases, using a constructor may even be prohibited. For example, you cannot call new `LocalDate()` since all of the constructors in this class are `private`.

Formatting Dates and Times

The date and time classes support many methods to get data out of them.

```
LocalDate date = LocalDate.of(2020, Month.OCTOBER, 20);
System.out.println(date.getDayOfWeek());  // TUESDAY
System.out.println(date.getMonth());      // OCTOBER
System.out.println(date.getYear());       // 2020
System.out.println(date.getDayOfYear());  // 294
```

Java provides a class called DateTimeFormatter to display standard formats.

```
LocalDate date = LocalDate.of(2020, Month.OCTOBER, 20);
LocalTime time = LocalTime.of(11, 12, 34);
LocalDateTime dt = LocalDateTime.of(date, time);

System.out.println(date.format(DateTimeFormatter.ISO_LOCAL_DATE));
System.out.println(time.format(DateTimeFormatter.ISO_LOCAL_TIME));
System.out.println(dt.format(DateTimeFormatter.ISO_LOCAL_DATE_TIME));
```

The code snippet prints the following:

```
2020-10-20
11:12:34
2020-10-20T11:12:34
```

The DateTimeFormatter will throw an exception if it encounters an incompatible type. For example, each of the following will produce an exception at runtime since it attempts to format a date with a time value, and vice versa:

```
System.out.println(date.format(DateTimeFormatter.ISO_LOCAL_TIME));
System.out.println(time.format(DateTimeFormatter.ISO_LOCAL_DATE));
```

If you don't want to use one of the predefined formats, DateTimeFormatter supports a custom format using a date format String.

```
var f = DateTimeFormatter.ofPattern("MMMM dd, yyyy 'at' hh:mm");
System.out.println(dt.format(f));  // October 20, 2020 at 11:12
```

Let's break this down a bit. Java assigns each letter or symbol a specific date/time part. For example, M is used for month, while y is used for year. And case matters! Using m instead of M means it will return the minute of the hour, not the month of the year.

What about the number of symbols? The number often dictates the format of the date/time part. Using M by itself outputs the minimum number of characters for a month, such as 1 for January, while using MM always outputs two digits, such as 01. Furthermore, using MMM prints the three-letter abbreviation, such as Jul for July, while MMMM prints the full month name.

The *Date* and *SimpleDateFormat* Classes

When Java introduced the Date and Time API in Java 8, many developers switched to the new classes, such as DateTimeFormatter. The exam may include questions with the older date/time classes. For example, the previous code snippet could be written using the java.util.Date and java.text.SimpleDateFormat classes.

```
DateFormat s = new SimpleDateFormat("MMMM dd, yyyy 'at' hh:mm");
System.out.println(s.format(new Date()));  // October 20, 2020 at 06:15
```

As we said earlier, if you see dates or times on the exam, regardless of whether they are using the old or new APIs, you are not being tested on them. You only need to know how to format them. For the exam, the rules for defining a custom DateTimeFormatter and SimpleDateFormat symbols are the same.

Learning the Standard Date/Time Symbols

For the exam, you should be familiar enough with the various symbols that you can look at a date/time String and have a good idea of what the output will be. Table 16.5 includes the symbols you should be familiar with for the exam.

TABLE 16.5   Common date/time symbols

Symbol	Meaning	Examples
y	Year	`20, 2020`
M	Month	`1, 01, Jan, January`
d	Day	`5, 05`
h	Hour	`9, 09`
m	Minute	`45`
s	Second	`52`
a	a.m./p.m.	`AM, PM`
z	Time Zone Name	`Eastern Standard Time, EST`
Z	Time Zone Offset	`-0400`

Let's try some examples. What do you think the following prints?

```
var dt = LocalDateTime.of(2020, Month.OCTOBER, 20, 6, 15, 30);

var formatter1 = DateTimeFormatter.ofPattern("MM/dd/yyyy hh:mm:ss");
System.out.println(dt.format(formatter1));

var formatter2 = DateTimeFormatter.ofPattern("MM_yyyy_-_dd");
System.out.println(dt.format(formatter2));

var formatter3 = DateTimeFormatter.ofPattern("h:mm z");
System.out.println(dt.format(formatter3));
```

The output is as follows:

```
10/20/2020 06:15:30
10_2020_-_20
Exception in thread "main" java.time.DateTimeException:
   Unable to extract ZoneId from temporal 2020-10-20T06:15:30
```

The first example prints the date, with the month before the day, followed by the time. The second example prints the date in a weird format with extra characters that are just displayed as part of the output.

The third example throws an exception at runtime because the underlying LocalDateTime does not have a time zone specified. If ZonedDateTime was used instead, then the code would have completed successfully and printed something like 06:15 EDT, depending on the time zone.

As you saw in the previous example, you need to make sure the format String is compatible with the underlying date/time type. Table 16.6 shows which symbols you can use with each of the date/time objects.

TABLE 16.6   Supported date/time symbols

Symbol	LocalDate	LocalTime	LocalDateTime	ZonedDateTime
y	√		√	√
M	√		√	√
d	√		√	√
h		√	√	√
m		√	√	√
s		√	√	√
a		√	√	√
z				√
Z				√

Make sure you know which symbols are compatible with which date/time types. For example, trying to format a month for a LocalTime or an hour for a LocalDate will result in a runtime exception.

Selecting a *format()* Method

The date/time classes contain a format() method that will take a formatter, while the formatter classes contain a format() method that will take a date/time value. The result is that either of the following is acceptable:

```
var dateTime = LocalDateTime.of(2020, Month.OCTOBER, 20, 6, 15, 30);
var formatter = DateTimeFormatter.ofPattern("MM/dd/yyyy hh:mm:ss");
```

```
System.out.println(dateTime.format(formatter)); // 10/20/2020 06:15:30
System.out.println(formatter.format(dateTime)); // 10/20/2020 06:15:30
```

These statements print the same value at runtime. Which syntax you use is up to you.

Adding Custom Text Values

What if you want your format to include some custom text values? If you just type it as part of the format String, the formatter will interpret each character as a date/time symbol. In the best case, it will display weird data based on extra symbols you enter. In the worst case, it will throw an exception because the characters contain invalid symbols. Neither is desirable!

One way to address this would be to break the formatter up into multiple smaller formatters and then concatenate the results.

```
var dt = LocalDateTime.of(2020, Month.OCTOBER, 20, 6, 15, 30);


var f1 = DateTimeFormatter.ofPattern("MMMM dd, yyyy ");
var f2 = DateTimeFormatter.ofPattern(" hh:mm");
System.out.println(dt.format(f1) + "at" + dt.format(f2));
```

This prints October 20, 2020 at 06:15 at runtime.

While this works, it could become difficult if there are a lot of text values and date symbols intermixed. Luckily, Java includes a much simpler solution. You can *escape* the text by surrounding it with a pair of single quotes ('). Escaping text instructs the formatter to ignore the values inside the single quotes and just insert them as part of the final value. We saw this earlier with the 'at' inserted into the formatter.

```
var f = DateTimeFormatter.ofPattern("MMMM dd, yyyy 'at' hh:mm");
System.out.println(dt.format(f));  // October 20, 2020 at 06:15
```

But what if you need to display a single quote in the output too? Welcome to the fun of escaping characters! Java supports this by putting two single quotes next to each other.

We conclude our discussion of date formatting with some various examples of formats and their output that rely on text values, shown here:

```
var g1 = DateTimeFormatter.ofPattern("MMMM dd', Party''s at' hh:mm");
System.out.println(dt.format(g1)); // October 20, Party's at 06:15


var g2 = DateTimeFormatter.ofPattern("'System format, hh:mm: 'hh:mm");
System.out.println(dt.format(g2)); // System format, hh:mm: 06:15


var g3 = DateTimeFormatter.ofPattern("'NEW! 'yyyy', yay!'");
System.out.println(dt.format(g3)); // NEW! 2020, yay!
```

Without escaping the text values with single quotes, an exception will be thrown at runtime if the text cannot be interpreted as a date/time symbol.

```
DateTimeFormatter.ofPattern("The time is hh:mm");  // Exception thrown
```

This line throws an exception since T is an unknown symbol. The exam might also present you with an incomplete escape sequence.

```
DateTimeFormatter.ofPattern("'Time is: hh:mm: ");  // Exception thrown
```

Failure to terminate an escape sequence will trigger an exception at runtime.

Supporting Internationalization and Localization

Many applications need to work in different countries and with different languages. For example, consider the sentence "The zoo is holding a special event on 4/1/15 to look at animal behaviors." When is the event? In the United States, it is on April 1. However, a British reader would interpret this as January 4. A British reader might also wonder why we didn't write "behaviours." If we are making a website or program that will be used in multiple countries, we want to use the correct language and formatting.

Internationalization is the process of designing your program so it can be adapted. This involves placing strings in a properties file and ensuring the proper data formatters are used. *Localization* means actually supporting multiple locales or geographic regions. You can think of a locale as being like a language and country pairing. Localization includes translating strings to different languages. It also includes outputting dates and numbers in the correct format for that locale.

 Initially, your program does not need to support multiple locales. The key is to future-proof your application by using these techniques. This way, when your product becomes successful, you can add support for new languages or regions without rewriting everything.

In this section, we will look at how to define a locale and use it to format dates, numbers, and strings.

Picking a Locale

While Oracle defines a locale as "a specific geographical, political, or cultural region," you'll only see languages and countries on the exam. Oracle certainly isn't going to delve into political regions that are not countries. That's too controversial for an exam!

The Locale class is in the java.util package. The first useful Locale to find is the user's current locale. Try running the following code on your computer:

```
Locale locale = Locale.getDefault();
System.out.println(locale);
```

When we run it, it prints en_US. It might be different for you. This default output tells us that our computers are using English and are sitting in the United States.

Notice the format. First comes the lowercase language code. The language is always required. Then comes an underscore followed by the uppercase country code. The country is optional. Figure 16.5 shows the two formats for Locale objects that you are expected to remember.

FIGURE 16.5   Locale formats

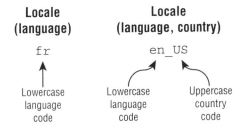

As practice, make sure that you understand why each of these Locale identifiers is invalid:

```
US    // Cannot have country without language
enUS  // Missing underscore
US_en // The country and language are reversed
EN    // Language must be lowercase
```

The corrected versions are en and en_US.

> You do not need to memorize language or country codes. The exam will let you know about any that are being used. You do need to recognize valid and invalid formats. Pay attention to uppercase/lowercase and the underscore. For example, if you see a locale expressed as es_CO, then you should know that the language is es and the country is CO, even if you didn't know they represent Spanish and Colombia, respectively.

As a developer, you often need to write code that selects a locale other than the default one. There are three common ways of doing this. The first is to use the built-in constants in the Locale class, available for some common locales.

```
System.out.println(Locale.GERMAN);  // de
System.out.println(Locale.GERMANY); // de_DE
```

The first example selects the German language, which is spoken in many countries, including Austria (de_AT) and Liechtenstein (de_LI). The second example selects both German the language and Germany the country. While these examples may look similar, they are not the same. Only one includes a country code.

The second way of selecting a Locale is to use the constructors to create a new object. You can pass just a language, or both a language and country:

```
System.out.println(new Locale("fr"));      // fr
System.out.println(new Locale("hi", "IN")); // hi_IN
```

The first is the language French, and the second is Hindi in India. Again, you don't need to memorize the codes. There is another constructor that lets you be even more specific about the locale. Luckily, providing a variant value is not on the exam.

Java will let you create a Locale with an invalid language or country, such as xx_XX. However, it will not match the Locale that you want to use, and your program will not behave as expected.

There's a third way to create a Locale that is more flexible. The builder design pattern lets you set all of the properties that you care about and then build it at the end. This means that you can specify the properties in any order. The following two Locale values both represent en_US:

```
Locale l1 = new Locale.Builder()
    .setLanguage("en")
    .setRegion("US")
    .build();

Locale l2 = new Locale.Builder()
    .setRegion("US")
    .setLanguage("en")
    .build();
```

 Real World Scenario

The Builder Pattern

Another design pattern commonly used in Java APIs is the builder pattern. The *builder pattern* is a creational pattern in which the task of setting the properties to create an object and the actual creation of the object are distinct steps.

In Java, it is often implemented with an instance of a static nested class. Since the builder and the target class tend to be tightly coupled, it makes sense for them to be defined within the same class.

Once all of the properties to create the object are specified, a `build()` method is then called that returns an instance of the desired object. It is commonly used to construct immutable objects with a lot of parameters since an immutable object is created only at the end of a method chain.

When testing a program, you might need to use a `Locale` other than the default of your computer.

```
System.out.println(Locale.getDefault()); // en_US
Locale locale = new Locale("fr");
Locale.setDefault(locale);               // change the default
System.out.println(Locale.getDefault()); // fr
```

Try it, and don't worry—the `Locale` changes for only that one Java program. It does not change any settings on your computer. It does not even change future executions of the same program.

The exam may use `setDefault()` because it can't make assumptions about where you are located. In practice, we rarely write code to change a user's default locale.

Localizing Numbers

It might surprise you that formatting or parsing currency and number values can change depending on your locale. For example, in the United States, the dollar sign is prepended before the value along with a decimal point for values less than one dollar, such as $2.15. In Germany, though, the euro symbol is appended to the value along with a comma for values less than one euro, such as 2,15 €.

Luckily, the `java.text` package includes classes to save the day. The following sections cover how to format numbers, currency, and dates based on the locale.

The first step to formatting or parsing data is the same: obtain an instance of a `NumberFormat`. Table 16.7 shows the available factory methods.

TABLE 16.7 Factory methods to get a `NumberFormat`

Description	Using default `Locale` and a specified `Locale`
A general-purpose formatter	`NumberFormat.getInstance()` `NumberFormat.getInstance(locale)`
Same as getInstance	`NumberFormat.getNumberInstance()` `NumberFormat.getNumberInstance(locale)`
For formatting monetary amounts	`NumberFormat.getCurrencyInstance()` `NumberFormat.getCurrencyInstance(locale)`

TABLE 16.7   Factory methods to get a NumberFormat *(continued)*

Description	Using default Locale **and a specified** Locale
For formatting percentages	NumberFormat.getPercentInstance() NumberFormat.getPercentInstance(locale)
Rounds decimal values before displaying	NumberFormat.getIntegerInstance() NumberFormat.getIntegerInstance(locale)

Once you have the NumberFormat instance, you can call format() to turn a number into a String, or you can use parse() to turn a String into a number.

> The format classes are not thread-safe. Do not store them in instance variables or static variables. You'll learn more about thread safety in Chapter 18, "Concurrency."

Formatting Numbers

When we format data, we convert it from a structured object or primitive value into a String. The NumberFormat.format() method formats the given number based on the locale associated with the NumberFormat object.

Let's go back to our zoo for a minute. For marketing literature, we want to share the average monthly number of visitors to the San Diego Zoo. The following shows printing out the same number in three different locales:

```
int attendeesPerYear = 3_200_000;
int attendeesPerMonth = attendeesPerYear / 12;

var us = NumberFormat.getInstance(Locale.US);
System.out.println(us.format(attendeesPerMonth));

var gr = NumberFormat.getInstance(Locale.GERMANY);
System.out.println(gr.format(attendeesPerMonth));

var ca = NumberFormat.getInstance(Locale.CANADA_FRENCH);
System.out.println(ca.format(attendeesPerMonth));
```

The output looks like this:

```
266,666
266.666
266 666
```

This shows how our U.S., German, and French Canadian guests can all see the same information in the number format they are accustomed to using. In practice, we would just call `NumberFormat.getInstance()` and rely on the user's default locale to format the output.

Formatting currency works the same way.

```
double price = 48;
var myLocale = NumberFormat.getCurrencyInstance();
System.out.println(myLocale.format(price));
```

When run with the default locale of en_US for the United States, it outputs $48.00. On the other hand, when run with the default locale of en_GB for Great Britain, it outputs £48.00.

In the real world, use `int` or `BigDecimal` for money and not `double`. Doing math on amounts with `double` is dangerous because the values are stored as floating-point numbers. Your boss won't appreciate it if you lose pennies or fractions of pennies during transactions!

Parsing Numbers

When we parse data, we convert it from a `String` to a structured object or primitive value. The `NumberFormat.parse()` method accomplishes this and takes the locale into consideration.

For example, if the locale is the English/United States (en_US) and the number contains commas, the commas are treated as formatting symbols. If the locale relates to a country or language that uses commas as a decimal separator, the comma is treated as a decimal point.

The `parse()` method, found in various types, declares a checked exception `ParseException` that must be handled or declared in the method in which they are called.

Let's look at an example. The following code parses a discounted ticket price with different locales. The `parse()` method actually throws a checked `ParseException`, so make sure to handle or declare it in your own code.

```
String s = "40.45";

var en = NumberFormat.getInstance(Locale.US);
System.out.println(en.parse(s));  // 40.45

var fr = NumberFormat.getInstance(Locale.FRANCE);
System.out.println(fr.parse(s));  // 40
```

In the United States, a dot (.) is part of a number, and the number is parsed how you might expect. France does not use a decimal point to separate numbers. Java parses it as a formatting character, and it stops looking at the rest of the number. The lesson is to make sure that you parse using the right locale!

The parse() method is also used for parsing currency. For example, we can read in the zoo's monthly income from ticket sales.

```
String income = "$92,807.99";
var cf = NumberFormat.getCurrencyInstance();
double value = (Double) cf.parse(income);
System.out.println(value); // 92807.99
```

The currency string "$92,807.99" contains a dollar sign and a comma. The parse method strips out the characters and converts the value to a number. The return value of parse is a Number object. Number is the parent class of all the java.lang wrapper classes, so the return value can be cast to its appropriate data type. The Number is cast to a Double and then automatically unboxed into a double.

Writing a Custom Number Formatter

Like you saw earlier when working with dates, you can also create your own number format strings using the DecimalFormat class, which extends NumberFormat. When creating a DecimalFormat object, you use a constructor rather than a factory method. You pass the pattern that you would like to use. The patterns can get complex, but you need to know only about two formatting characters, shown in Table 16.8.

TABLE 16.8   DecimalFormat symbols

Symbol	Meaning	Examples
#	Omit the position if no digit exists for it.	$2.2
0	Put a 0 in the position if no digit exists for it.	$002.20

These examples should help illuminate how these symbols work:

```
12: double d = 1234567.467;
13: NumberFormat f1 = new DecimalFormat("###,###,###.0");
14: System.out.println(f1.format(d));  // 1,234,567.5
15:
```

```
16: NumberFormat f2 = new DecimalFormat("000,000,000.00000");
17: System.out.println(f2.format(d));  // 001,234,567.46700
18:
19: NumberFormat f3 = new DecimalFormat("$#,###,###.##");
20: System.out.println(f3.format(d));  // $1,234,567.47
```

Line 14 displays the digits in the number, rounding to the nearest 10th after the decimal. The extra positions to the left are left off because we used #. Line 17 adds leading and trailing zeros to make the output the desired length. Line 20 shows prefixing a nonformatting character ($ sign) along with rounding because fewer digits are printed than available.

Localizing Dates

Like numbers, date formats can vary by locale. Table 16.9 shows methods used to retrieve an instance of a DateTimeFormatter using the default locale.

TABLE 16.9 Factory methods to get a DateTimeFormatter

Description	Using default Locale
For formatting dates	DateTimeFormatter.ofLocalizedDate(dateStyle)
For formatting times	DateTimeFormatter.ofLocalizedTime(timeStyle)
For formatting dates and times	DateTimeFormatter.ofLocalizedDateTime(dateStyle, timeStyle) DateTimeFormatter.ofLocalizedDateTime(dateTimeStyle)

Each method in the table takes a FormatStyle parameter, with possible values SHORT, MEDIUM, LONG, and FULL. For the exam, you are not required to know the format of each of these styles.

What if you need a formatter for a specific locale? Easy enough—just append withLocale(locale) to the method call.

Let's put it all together. Take a look at the following code snippet, which relies on a static import for the java.time.format.FormatStyle.SHORT value:

```
public static void print(DateTimeFormatter dtf,
    LocalDateTime dateTime, Locale locale) {
  System.out.println(dtf.format(dateTime) + ", "
    + dtf.withLocale(locale).format(dateTime));
}
```

```
public static void main(String[] args) {
   Locale.setDefault(new Locale("en", "US"));
   var italy = new Locale("it", "IT");
   var dt = LocalDateTime.of(2020, Month.OCTOBER, 20, 15, 12, 34);

   // 10/20/20, 20/10/20
   print(DateTimeFormatter.ofLocalizedDate(SHORT),dt,italy);

   // 3:12 PM, 15:12
   print(DateTimeFormatter.ofLocalizedTime(SHORT),dt,italy);

   // 10/20/20, 3:12 PM, 20/10/20, 15:12
   print(DateTimeFormatter.ofLocalizedDateTime(SHORT,SHORT),dt,italy);
}
```

First, we establish en_US as the default locale, with it_IT as the requested locale. We then output each value using the two locales. As you can see, applying a locale has a big impact on the built-in date and time formatters.

Specifying a Locale Category

When you call Locale.setDefault() with a locale, several display and formatting options are internally selected. If you require finer-grained control of the default locale, Java actually subdivides the underlying formatting options into distinct categories, with the Locale.Category enum.

The Locale.Category enum is a nested element in Locale, which supports distinct locales for displaying and formatting data. For the exam, you should be familiar with the two enum values in Table 16.10.

TABLE 16.10 Locale.Category values

Value	Description
DISPLAY	Category used for displaying data about the locale
FORMAT	Category used for formatting dates, numbers, or currencies

When you call Locale.setDefault() with a locale, both the DISPLAY and FORMAT are set together. Let's take a look at an example:

```
10: public static void printCurrency(Locale locale, double money) {
11:     System.out.println(
12:         NumberFormat.getCurrencyInstance().format(money)
13:         + ", " + locale.getDisplayLanguage());
14: }
15: public static void main(String[] args) {
16:     var spain = new Locale("es", "ES");
17:     var money = 1.23;
18:
19:     // Print with default locale
20:     Locale.setDefault(new Locale("en", "US"));
21:     printCurrency(spain, money);  // $1.23, Spanish
22:
23:     // Print with default locale and selected locale display
24:     Locale.setDefault(Category.DISPLAY, spain);
25:     printCurrency(spain, money);  // $1.23, español
26:
27:     // Print with default locale and selected locale format
28:     Locale.setDefault(Category.FORMAT, spain);
29:     printCurrency(spain, money);  // 1,23 €, español
30: }
```

The code prints the same data three times. First, it prints the language of the spain and money variables using the locale en_US. Then, it prints it using the DISPLAY category of es_ES, while the FORMAT category remains en_US. Finally, it prints the data using both categories set to es_ES.

For the exam, you do not need to memorize the various display and formatting options for each category. You just need to know that you can set parts of the locale independently. You should also know that calling Locale.setDefault(us) after the previous code snippet will change both locale categories to en_US.

Loading Properties with Resource Bundles

Up until now, we've kept all of the text strings displayed to our users as part of the program inside the classes that use them. Localization requires externalizing them to elsewhere.

A *resource bundle* contains the locale-specific objects to be used by a program. It is like a map with keys and values. The resource bundle is commonly stored in a properties file. A *properties file* is a text file in a specific format with key/value pairs.

> For the exam, you only need to know about resource bundles that are created from properties files. That said, you can also create a resource bundle from a class by extending ResourceBundle. One advantage of this approach is that it allows you to specify values using a method or in formats other than String, such as other numeric primitives, objects, or lists.

Our zoo program has been successful. We are now getting requests to use it at three more zoos! We already have support for U.S.-based zoos. We now need to add Zoo de La Palmyre in France, the Greater Vancouver Zoo in English-speaking Canada, and Zoo de Granby in French-speaking Canada.

We immediately realize that we are going to need to internationalize our program. Resource bundles will be quite helpful. They will let us easily translate our application to multiple locales or even support multiple locales at once. It will also be easy to add more locales later if we get zoos in even more countries interested. We thought about which locales we need to support, and we came up with four.

```
Locale us            = new Locale("en", "US");
Locale france        = new Locale("fr", "FR");
Locale englishCanada = new Locale("en", "CA");
Locale frenchCanada  = new Locale("fr", "CA");
```

In the next sections, we will create a resource bundle using properties files. A *properties file* is a text file that contains a list of key/value pairs. It is conceptually similar to a Map<String,String>, with each line representing a different key/value. The key and value are separated by an equal sign (=) or colon (:). To keep things simple, we use an equal sign throughout this chapter. We will also look at how Java determines which resource bundle to use.

Creating a Resource Bundle

We're going to update our application to support the four locales listed previously. Luckily, Java doesn't require us to create four different resource bundles. If we don't have a country-specific resource bundle, Java will use a language-specific one. It's a bit more involved than this, but let's start with a simple example.

For now, we need English and French properties files for our Zoo resource bundle. First, create two properties files.

Zoo_en.properties
```
hello=Hello
open=The zoo is open
```

Zoo_fr.properties
```
hello=Bonjour
open=Le zoo est ouvert
```

The filenames match the name of our resource bundle, Zoo. They are then followed by an underscore (_), target locale, and .properties file extension. We can write our very first program that uses a resource bundle to print this information.

```
10: public static void printWelcomeMessage(Locale locale) {
11:     var rb = ResourceBundle.getBundle("Zoo", locale);
12:     System.out.println(rb.getString("hello")
13:         + ", " + rb.getString("open"));
14: }
15: public static void main(String[] args) {
16:     var us = new Locale("en", "US");
17:     var france = new Locale("fr", "FR");
18:     printWelcomeMessage(us);      // Hello, The zoo is open
19:     printWelcomeMessage(france); // Bonjour, Le zoo est ouvert
20: }
```

Lines 16–17 create the two locales that we want to test, but the method on lines 10–14 does the actual work. Line 11 calls a factory method on ResourceBundle to get the right resource bundle. Lines 12 and 13 retrieve the right string from the resource bundle and print the results.

Remember we said you'd see the factory pattern again in this chapter? It will be used a lot in this book, so it helps to be familiar with it.

Since a resource bundle contains key/value pairs, you can even loop through them to list all of the pairs. The ResourceBundle class provides a keySet() method to get a set of all keys.

```
var us = new Locale("en", "US");
ResourceBundle rb = ResourceBundle.getBundle("Zoo", us);
rb.keySet().stream()
   .map(k -> k + ": " + rb.getString(k))
   .forEach(System.out::println);
```

This example goes through all of the keys. It maps each key to a String with both the key and the value before printing everything.

```
hello: Hello
open: The zoo is open
```

Real World Scenario

Loading Resource Bundle Files at Runtime

For the exam, you don't need to know where the properties files for the resource bundles are stored. If the exam provides a properties file, it is safe to assume it exists and is loaded at runtime.

In your own applications, though, the resource bundles can be stored in a variety of places. While they can be stored inside the JAR that uses them, it not recommended. This approach forces you to rebuild the application JAR any time some text changes. One of the benefits of using resource bundles is to decouple the application code from the locale-specific text data.

Another approach is to have all of the properties files in a separate properties JAR or folder and load them in the classpath at runtime. In this manner, a new language can be added without changing the application JAR.

Picking a Resource Bundle

There are two methods for obtaining a resource bundle that you should be familiar with for the exam.

```
ResourceBundle.getBundle("name");
ResourceBundle.getBundle("name", locale);
```

The first one uses the default locale. You are likely to use this one in programs that you write. Either the exam tells you what to assume as the default locale or it uses the second approach.

Java handles the logic of picking the best available resource bundle for a given key. It tries to find the most specific value. Table 16.11 shows what Java goes through when asked for resource bundle Zoo with the locale new Locale("fr", "FR") when the default locale is U.S. English.

TABLE 16.11   Picking a resource bundle for French/France with default locale English/US

Step	Looks for file	Reason
1	Zoo_fr_FR.properties	The requested locale
2	Zoo_fr.properties	The language we requested with no country
3	Zoo_en_US.properties	The default locale
4	Zoo_en.properties	The default locale's language with no country

Step	Looks for file	Reason
5	`Zoo.properties`	No locale at all—the default bundle
6	If still not found, throw `MissingResourceException`.	No locale or default bundle available

As another way of remembering the order of Table 16.11, learn these steps:

1. Look for the resource bundle for the requested locale, followed by the one for the default locale.
2. For each locale, check language/country, followed by just the language.
3. Use the default resource bundle if no matching locale can be found.

As we mentioned earlier, Java supports resource bundles from Java classes and properties alike. When Java is searching for a matching resource bundle, it will first check for a resource bundle file with the matching class name. For the exam, you just need to know how to work with properties files.

Let's see if you understand Table 16.11. What is the maximum number of files that Java would need to consider to find the appropriate resource bundle with the following code?

```
Locale.setDefault(new Locale("hi"));
ResourceBundle rb = ResourceBundle.getBundle("Zoo", new Locale("en"));
```

The answer is three. They are listed here:

1. `Zoo_en.properties`
2. `Zoo_hi.properties`
3. `Zoo.properties`

The requested locale is en, so we start with that. Since the en locale does not contain a country, we move on to the default locale, hi. Again, there's no country, so we end with the default bundle.

Selecting Resource Bundle Values

Got all that? Good—because there is a twist. The steps that we've discussed so far are for finding the matching resource bundle to use as a base. Java isn't required to get all of the keys from the same resource bundle. It can get them from any parent of the matching resource bundle. A parent resource bundle in the hierarchy just removes components of the name until it gets to the top. Table 16.12 shows how to do this.

TABLE 16.12   Selecting resource bundle properties

Matching resource bundle	Properties files keys can come from
Zoo_fr_FR	Zoo_fr_FR.properties Zoo_fr.properties Zoo.properties

Once a resource bundle has been selected, only properties along a single hierarchy will be used. Contrast this behavior with Table 16.11, in which the default en_US resource bundle is used if no other resource bundles are available.

What does this mean exactly? Assume the requested locale is fr_FR and the default is en_US. The JVM will provide data from an en_US *only if there is no matching fr_FR or fr resource bundles.* If it finds a fr_FR or fr resource bundle, then only those bundles, along with the default bundle, will be used.

Let's put all of this together and print some information about our zoos. We have a number of properties files this time.

Zoo.properties
name=Vancouver Zoo

Zoo_en.properties
hello=Hello
open=is open

Zoo_en_US.properties
name=The Zoo

Zoo_en_CA.properties
visitors=Canada visitors

Suppose that we have a visitor from Quebec (which has a default locale of French Canada) who has asked the program to provide information in English. What do you think this outputs?

```
11: Locale.setDefault(new Locale("en", "US"));
12: Locale locale = new Locale("en", "CA");
13: ResourceBundle rb = ResourceBundle.getBundle("Zoo", locale);
14: System.out.print(rb.getString("hello"));
15: System.out.print(". ");
```

```
16: System.out.print(rb.getString("name"));
17: System.out.print(" ");
18: System.out.print(rb.getString("open"));
19: System.out.print(" ");
20: System.out.print(rb.getString("visitors"));
```

The program prints the following:

```
Hello. Vancouver Zoo is open Canada visitors
```

The default locale is en_US, and the requested locale is en_CA. First, Java goes through the available resource bundles to find a match. It finds one right away with Zoo_en_CA.properties. This means the default locale of en_US is irrelevant.

Line 14 doesn't find a match for the key hello in Zoo_en_CA.properties, so it goes up the hierarchy to Zoo_en.properties. Line 16 doesn't find a match for name in either of the first two properties files, so it has to go all the way to the top of the hierarchy to Zoo.properties. Line 18 has the same experience as line 14, using Zoo_en.properties. Finally, line 20 has an easier job of it and finds a matching key in Zoo_en_CA.properties.

In this example, only three properties files were used: Zoo_en_CA.properties, Zoo_en.properties, and Zoo.properties. Even when the property wasn't found in en_CA or en resource bundles, the program preferred using Zoo.properties (the default resource bundle) rather than Zoo_en_US.properties (the default locale).

What if a property is not found in any resource bundle? Then, an exception is thrown. For example, attempting to call rb.getString("close") in the previous program results in a MissingResourceException at runtime.

Formatting Messages

Often, we just want to output the text data from a resource bundle, but sometimes you want to format that data with parameters. In real programs, it is common to substitute variables in the middle of a resource bundle String. The convention is to use a number inside braces such as {0}, {1}, etc. The number indicates the order in which the parameters will be passed. Although resource bundles don't support this directly, the MessageFormat class does.

For example, suppose that we had this property defined:

```
helloByName=Hello, {0} and {1}
```

In Java, we can read in the value normally. After that, we can run it through the MessageFormat class to substitute the parameters. The second parameter to format() is a vararg, allowing you to specify any number of input values.

Given a resource bundle rb:

```
String format = rb.getString("helloByName");
System.out.print(MessageFormat.format(format, "Tammy", "Henry"));
```

that would then print the following:

```
Hello, Tammy and Henry
```

Using the *Properties* Class

When working with the ResourceBundle class, you may also come across the Properties class. It functions like the HashMap class that you learned about in Chapter 14, "Generics and Collections," except that it uses String values for the keys and values. Let's create one and set some values.

```
import java.util.Properties;
public class ZooOptions {
   public static void main(String[] args) {
      var props = new Properties();
      props.setProperty("name", "Our zoo");
      props.setProperty("open", "10am");
   }
}
```

The Properties class is commonly used in handling values that may not exist.

```
System.out.println(props.getProperty("camel"));          // null
System.out.println(props.getProperty("camel", "Bob"));   // Bob
```

If a key were passed that actually existed, both statements would have printed it. This is commonly referred to as providing a default, or backup value, for a missing key.

The Properties class also includes a get() method, but only getProperty() allows for a default value. For example, the following call is invalid since get() takes only a single parameter:

```
props.get("open");                                       // 10am

props.get("open", "The zoo will be open soon");  // DOES NOT COMPILE
```

Using the Property Methods

A Properties object isn't just similar to a Map; it actually inherits Map<Object,Object>. Despite this, you should use the getProperty() and setProperty() methods when working with a Properties object, rather than the get()/put() methods. Besides supporting default values, it also ensures you don't add data to the Properties object that cannot be read.

```
   var props = new Properties();
   props.put("tigerAge", "4");
```

```
props.put("lionAge", 5);
System.out.println(props.getProperty("tigerAge"));  // 4
System.out.println(props.getProperty("lionAge"));   // null
```

Since a `Properties` object works only with `String` values, trying to read a numeric value returns null. Don't worry, you don't have to know this behavior for the exam. The point is to avoid using the get/put() methods when working with `Properties` objects.

Summary

This chapter covered a wide variety of topics centered around building applications that respond well to change. We started our discussion with exception handling. Exceptions can be divided into two categories: checked and unchecked. In Java, checked exceptions inherit `Exception` but not `RuntimeException` and must be handled or declared. Unchecked exceptions inherit `RuntimeException` or `Error` and do not need to be handled or declared. It is considered a poor practice to catch an `Error`.

You can create your own checked or unchecked exceptions by extending `Exception` or `RuntimeException`, respectively. You can also define custom constructors and messages for your exceptions, which will show up in stack traces.

Automatic resource management can be enabled by using a try-with-resources statement to ensure the resources are properly closed. Resources are closed at the conclusion of the `try` block, in the reverse order in which they are declared. A suppressed exception occurs when more than one exception is thrown, often as part of a `finally` block or try-with-resources `close()` operation. The first exception to be encountered will be the primary exception, with the additional exceptions being suppressed. New in Java 9 is the ability to use existing resources in a try-with-resources statement.

An assertion is a `boolean` expression placed at a particular point in your code where you think something should always be true. A failed assertion throws an `AssertionError`. Assertions should not change the state of any variables. You saw how to use the -ea and -enableassertions flags to turn on assertions and how the -disableassertions and -da flags can selectively disable assertions for particular classes or packages.

You can create a `Locale` class with a required lowercase language code and optional uppercase country code. For example, en and en_US are locales for English and U.S. English, respectively. For the exam, you do not need to know how to create dates, but you do need to know how to format them, along with numbers, using a locale. You also need to know how to create custom date and number formatters.

A `ResourceBundle` allows specifying key/value pairs in a properties file. Java goes through candidate resource bundles from the most specific to the most general to find a match. If no matches are found for the requested locale, Java switches to the default locale and then finally the default resource bundle. Once a matching resource bundle is found, Java looks only in the hierarchy of that resource bundle to select values.

By applying the principles you learned about in this chapter to your own projects, you can build applications that last longer, with built-in support for whatever unexpected events may arise.

Exam Essentials

Be able to create custom exception classes.   A new checked exception class can be created by extending Exception, while an unchecked exception class can be created by extending RuntimeException. You can create numerous constructors that call matching parent constructors, with similar arguments. This provides greater control over the exception handling and messages reported in stack traces.

Perform automatic resource management with try-with-resources statements.   A try-with-resources statement supports classes that inherit the AutoCloseable interface. It automatically closes resources in the reverse order in which they are declared. A try-with-resources statement, as well as a try statement with a finally block, may generate multiple exceptions. The first becomes the primary exception, and the rest are suppressed exceptions.

Apply try-with-resources to existing resources.   A try-with-resources statement can use resources declared before the start of the statement, provided they are final or effectively final. They are closed following the execution of the try-with-resources body.

Know how to write assert statements and enable assertions.   Assertions are implemented with the assert keyword, a boolean condition, and an optional message. Assertions are disabled by default. Watch for a question that uses assertions but does not enable them, or a question that tests your knowledge of how assertions are enabled or selectively disabled from the command line.

Identify valid locale strings.   Know that the language code is lowercase and mandatory, while the country code is uppercase and optional. Be able to select a locale using a built-in constant, constructor, or builder class.

Format dates, numbers, and messages.   Be able to format dates, numbers, and messages into various String formats. Also, know how to define a custom date or number formatter using symbols, including how to escape literal values. For messages, you should also be familiar with using the MessageFormat and Properties classes.

Determine which resource bundle Java will use to look up a key.   Be able to create resource bundles for a set of locales using properties files. Know the search order that Java uses to select a resource bundle and how the default locale and default resource bundle are considered. Once a resource bundle is found, recognize the hierarchy used to select values.

Review Questions

The answers to the chapter review questions can be found in the Appendix.

1. Which of the following classes contain at least one compiler error? (Choose all that apply.)

```
class Danger extends RuntimeException {
    public Danger(String message) {
        super();
    }
    public Danger(int value) {
        super((String) null);
    }
}
class Catastrophe extends Exception {
    public Catastrophe(Throwable c) throws RuntimeException {
        super(new Exception());
        c.printStackTrace();
    }
}
class Emergency extends Danger {
    public Emergency() {}
    public Emergency(String message) {
        super(message);
    }
}
```

   A. Danger

   B. Catastrophe

   C. Emergency

   D. All of these classes compile correctly.

   E. The answer cannot be determined from the information given.

2. Which of the following are common types to localize? (Choose all that apply.)

   A. Dates

   B. Lambda expressions

   C. Class names

   D. Currency

   E. Numbers

   F. Variable names

3. What is the output of the following code?

```java
import java.io.*;
public class EntertainmentCenter {
   static class TV implements AutoCloseable {
     public void close() {
        System.out.print("D");
   } }
   static class MediaStreamer implements Closeable {
     public void close() {
        System.out.print("W");
   } }
   public static void main(String[] args) {
     var w = new MediaStreamer();
     try {
        TV d = new TV(); w;
        }
     {
        System.out.print("T");
     } catch (Exception e) {
        System.out.print("E");
     } finally {
        System.out.print("F");
     }
   }
}
```

A. TWF

B. TWDF

C. TWDEF

D. TWF followed by an exception.

E. TWDF followed by an exception.

F. TWEF followed by an exception.

G. The code does not compile.

4. Which statement about the following class is correct?

```java
1:  class Problem extends Exception {
2:      public Problem() {}
3:  }
4:  class YesProblem extends Problem {}
5:  public class MyDatabase {
```

```
6:      public static void connectToDatabase() throw Problem {
7:          throws new YesProblem();
8:      }
9:      public static void main(String[] c) throw Exception {
10:         connectToDatabase();
11:     }
12: }
```

A. The code compiles and prints a stack trace for YesProblem at runtime.

B. The code compiles and prints a stack trace for Problem at runtime.

C. The code does not compile because Problem defines a constructor.

D. The code does not compile because YesProblem does not define a constructor.

E. The code does not compile but would if Problem and YesProblem were switched on lines 6 and 7.

F. None of the above

5. What is the output of the following code?

```
LocalDate date = LocalDate.parse("2020-04-30",
    DateTimeFormatter.ISO_LOCAL_DATE_TIME);
System.out.println(date.getYear() + " "
    + date.getMonth() + " "+ date.getDayOfMonth());
```

A. 2020 APRIL 2

B. 2020 APRIL 30

C. 2020 MAY 2

D. The code does not compile.

E. A runtime exception is thrown.

6. Assume that all of the files mentioned in the answer choices exist and define the same keys. Which one will be used to find the key in line 8?

```
6: Locale.setDefault(new Locale("en", "US"));
7: var b = ResourceBundle.getBundle("Dolphins");
8: System.out.println(b.getString("name"));
```

A. Dolphins.properties

B. Dolphins_US.properties

C. Dolphins_en.properties

D. Whales.properties

E. Whales_en_US.properties

F. The code does not compile.

7. For what value of `pattern` will the following print `<005.21>  <008.49>  <1,234.0>`?

```
String pattern = "_____";
var message = DoubleStream.of(5.21, 8.49, 1234)
    .mapToObj(v -> new DecimalFormat(pattern).format(v))
    .collect(Collectors.joining("> <"));
System.out.println("<"+message+">");
```

A. `##.#`

B. `0,000.0#`

C. `#,###.0`

D. `#,###,000.0#`

E. The code does not compile regardless of what is placed in the blank.

F. None of the above

8. Which of the following prints OhNo with the assertion failure when the number `magic` is positive? (Choose all that apply.)

A. `assert magic < 0: "OhNo";`

B. `assert magic < 0, "OhNo";`

C. `assert magic < 0 ("OhNo");`

D. `assert(magic < 0): "OhNo";`

E. `assert(magic < 0, "OhNo");`

9. Which of the following exceptions must be handled or declared in the method in which they are thrown? (Choose all that apply.)

```
class Apple extends RuntimeException{}
class Orange extends Exception{}
class Banana extends Error{}
class Pear extends Apple{}
class Tomato extends Orange{}
class Peach extends Banana{}
```

A. Apple

B. Orange

C. Banana

D. Pear

E. Tomato

F. Peach

10. Which of the following changes when made independently would make this code compile? (Choose all that apply.)

```
1:  import java.io.*;
2:  public class StuckTurkeyCage implements AutoCloseable {
3:      public void close() throws IOException {
4:          throw new FileNotFoundException("Cage not closed");
5:      }
6:      public static void main(String[] args) {
7:          try (StuckTurkeyCage t = new StuckTurkeyCage()) {
8:              System.out.println("put turkeys in");
9:          }
10:     } }
```

A. Remove throws IOException from the declaration on line 3.

B. Add throws Exception to the declaration on line 6.

C. Change line 9 to } catch (Exception e) {}.

D. Change line 9 to } finally {}.

E. The code compiles as is.

F. None of the above

11. What is the result of running java EnterPark bird.java sing with the following code?

```
public class EnterPark extends Exception {
    public EnterPark(String message) {
        super();
    }
    private static void checkInput(String[] v) {
        if (v.length <= 3)
            assert(false) : "Invalid input";
    }
    public static void main(String... args) {
        checkInput(args);
        System.out.println(args[0] + args[1] + args[2]);
    }
}
```

A. birdsing

B. The assert statement throws an AssertionError.

C. The code throws an ArrayIndexOutOfBoundsException.

D. The code compiles and runs successfully, but there is no output.

E. The code does not compile.

12. Which of the following are true statements about exception handling in Java? (Choose all that apply.)

A. A traditional `try` statement without a `catch` block requires a `finally` block.

B. A traditional `try` statement without a `finally` block requires a `catch` block.

C. A traditional `try` statement with only one statement can omit the `{}`.

D. A try-with-resources statement without a `catch` block requires a `finally` block.

E. A try-with-resources statement without a `finally` block requires a `catch` block.

F. A try-with-resources statement with only one statement can omit the `{}`.

13. Which of the following, when inserted independently in the blank, use locale parameters that are properly formatted? (Choose all that apply.)

```
import java.util.Locale;
public class ReadMap implements AutoCloseable {
    private Locale locale;
    private boolean closed = false;
    void check() {
        assert !closed;
    }
    @Override public void close() {
        check();
        System.out.println("Folding map");
        locale = null;
        closed = true;
    }
    public void open() {
        check();
        this.locale = _____;
    }
    public void use() {
        // Implementation omitted
    }
}
```

A. `new Locale("xM");`

B. `new Locale("MQ", "ks");`

C. `new Locale("qw");`

   D. `new Locale("wp", "VW");`

   E. `Locale.create("zp");`

   F. `Locale.create("FF");`

   G. The code does not compile regardless of what is placed in the blank.

14. Which of the following is true when creating your own exception class?

   A. One or more constructors must be coded.

   B. Only custom checked exception classes may be created.

   C. Only custom unchecked exception classes may be created.

   D. Custom `Error` classes may be created.

   E. The `toString()` method must be coded.

   F. None of the above

15. Which of the following can be inserted into the blank to allow the code to compile and run without throwing an exception? (Choose all that apply.)

```
var f = DateTimeFormatter.ofPattern("hh o'clock");
System.out.println(f.format(_____.now())));
```

   A. `ZonedDateTime`

   B. `LocalDate`

   C. `LocalDateTime`

   D. `LocalTime`

   E. The code does not compile regardless of what is placed in the blank.

   F. None of the above

16. Which of the following command lines cause this program to produce an error when executed? (Choose all that apply.)

```
public class On {
    public static void main(String[] args) {
        String s = null;
        int check = 10;
        assert s != null : check++;
    }
}
```

   A. `java -da On`

   B. `java -ea On`

   C. `java -da -ea:On On`

   D. `java -ea -da:On On`

   E. The code does not compile.

17. Which of the following statements about resource bundles are correct? (Choose all that apply.)

A. All keys must be in the same resource bundle to be used.

B. A resource bundle is loaded by calling the new `ResourceBundle()` constructor.

C. Resource bundle values are always read using the `Properties` class.

D. Changing the default locale lasts for only a single run of the program.

E. If a resource bundle for a specific locale is requested, then the resource bundle for the default locale will not be used.

F. It is possible to use a resource bundle for a locale without specifying a default locale.

18. What is the output of the following code?

```java
import java.io.*;
public class FamilyCar {
    static class Door implements AutoCloseable {
        public void close() {
            System.out.print("D");
    } }
    static class Window implements Closeable {
        public void close() {
            System.out.print("W");
            throw new RuntimeException();
    } }
    public static void main(String[] args) {
        var d = new Door();
        try (d; var w = new Window()) {
            System.out.print("T");
        } catch (Exception e) {
            System.out.print("E");
        } finally {
            System.out.print("F");
} } }
```

A. TWF

B. TWDF

C. TWDEF

D. TWF followed by an exception.

E. TWDF followed by an exception.

F. TWEF followed by an exception.

G. The code does not compile.

19. Suppose that we have the following three properties files and code. Which bundles are used on lines 8 and 9, respectively?

Dolphins.properties
```
name=The Dolphin
age=0
```

Dolphins_en.properties
```
name=Dolly
age=4
```

Dolphins_fr.properties
```
name=Dolly
```

```
5: var fr = new Locale("fr");
6: Locale.setDefault(new Locale("en", "US"));
7: var b = ResourceBundle.getBundle("Dolphins", fr);
8: b.getString("name");
9: b.getString("age");
```

- **A.** `Dolphins.properties` and `Dolphins.properties`
- **B.** `Dolphins.properties` and `Dolphins_en.properties`
- **C.** `Dolphins_en.properties` and `Dolphins_en.properties`
- **D.** `Dolphins_fr.properties` and `Dolphins.properties`
- **E.** `Dolphins_fr.properties` and `Dolphins_en.properties`
- **F.** The code does not compile.
- **G.** None of the above

20. Fill in the blanks: When formatting text data, the _____ class supports parametrized `String` values, while the _____ class has built-in support for missing values.

- **A.** `TextFormat`, `Properties`
- **B.** `MessageFormat`, `Properties`
- **C.** `Properties`, `Formatter`
- **D.** `StringFormat`, `Properties`
- **E.** `Properties`, `TextFormat`
- **F.** `Properties`, `TextHandler`
- **G.** None of the above

21. Which changes, when made independently, allow the following program to compile? (Choose all that apply.)

```
1: public class AhChoo {
2:    static class SneezeException extends Exception {}
3:    static class SniffleException extends SneezeException {}
4:    public static void main(String[] args) {
5:       try {
6:          throw new SneezeException();
7:       } catch (SneezeException | SniffleException e) {
8:       } finally {}
9:    } }
```

A. Add throws SneezeException to the declaration on line 4.

B. Add throws Throwable to the declaration on line 4.

C. Change line 7 to } catch (SneezeException e) {.

D. Change line 7 to } catch (SniffleException e) {.

E. Remove line 7.

F. The code compiles correctly as is.

G. None of the above

22. What is the output of the following code?

```
LocalDateTime ldt = LocalDateTime.of(2020, 5, 10, 11, 22, 33);
var f = DateTimeFormatter.ofLocalizedTime(FormatStyle.SHORT);
System.out.println(ldt.format(f));
```

A. 3/7/19 11:22 AM

B. 5/10/20 11:22 AM

C. 3/7/19

D. 5/10/20

E. 11:22 AM

F. The code does not compile.

G. A runtime exception is thrown.

23. Fill in the blank: A class that implements _____ may be in a try-with-resources statement. (Choose all that apply.)

A. AutoCloseable

B. Resource

C. Exception

D. AutomaticResource

E. Closeable

F. RuntimeException

G. Serializable

24. What is the output of the following method if props contains
`{veggies=brontosaurus, meat=velociraptor}`?

```
private static void print(Properties props) {
    System.out.println(props.get("veggies", "none")
        + " " + props.get("omni", "none"));
}
```

A. brontosaurus none

B. brontosaurus null

C. none none

D. none null

E. The code does not compile.

F. A runtime exception is thrown.

25. What is the output of the following program?

```
public class SnowStorm {
    static class WalkToSchool implements AutoCloseable {
        public void close() {
            throw new RuntimeException("flurry");
        }
    }
    public static void main(String[] args) {
        WalkToSchool walk1 = new WalkToSchool();
        try (walk1; WalkToSchool walk2 = new WalkToSchool()) {
            throw new RuntimeException("blizzard");
        } catch(Exception e) {
            System.out.println(e.getMessage()
                + " " + e.getSuppressed().length);
        }
        walk1 = null;
    }
}
```

A. blizzard 0

B. blizzard 1

C. blizzard 2

D. flurry 0

E. flurry 1

F. flurry 2

G. None of the above

26. Which of the following are true of the code? (Choose all that apply.)

```
4: private int addPlusOne(int a, int b) {
5:     boolean assert = false;
6:     assert a++ > 0;
7:     assert b > 0;
8:     return a + b;
9: }
```

A. Line 5 does not compile.

B. Lines 6 and 7 do not compile because they are missing the `String` message.

C. Lines 6 and 7 do not compile because they are missing parentheses.

D. Line 6 is an appropriate use of an assertion.

E. Line 7 is an appropriate use of an assertion.

27. What is the output of the following program?

```
import java.text.NumberFormat;
import java.util.Locale;
import java.util.Locale.Category;
public class Wallet {
    private double money;
    // Assume getters/setters/constructors provided

    private String openWallet() {
        Locale.setDefault(Category.DISPLAY,
            new Locale.Builder().setRegion("us"));
        Locale.setDefault(Category.FORMAT,
            new Locale.Builder().setLanguage("en"));
        return NumberFormat.getCurrencyInstance(Locale.GERMANY)
            .format(money);
    }
    public void printBalance() {
        System.out.println(openWallet());
    }
    public static void main(String... unused) {
        new Wallet(2.4).printBalance();
    }
}
```

A. 2,40 €

B. $2.40

C. 2.4

D. The output cannot be determined without knowing the locale of the system where it will be run.

E. The code does not compile.

F. None of the above

Chapter

17

Modular Applications

OCP EXAM OBJECTIVES COVERED IN THIS CHAPTER:

✓ **Migration to a Modular Application**

- Migrate the application developed using a Java version prior to SE 9 to SE 11 including top-down and bottom-up migration, splitting a Java SE 8 application into modules for migration

- Use jdeps to determine dependencies and identify ways to address the cyclic dependencies

✓ **Services in a Modular Application**

- Describe the components of Services including directives

- Design a service type, load services using ServiceLoader, check for dependencies of the services including consumer and provider modules

If you took the 1Z0-815 exam, you learned the basics of modules. If not, read Chapter 11, "Modules," before reading this chapter. That will bring you up to speed. Luckily, you don't have to memorize as many command-line options for the 1Z0-816 exam.

This chapter covers strategies for migrating an application to use modules, running a partially modularized application, and dealing with dependencies. We then move on to discuss services and service locators.

You aren't required to create modules by hand or memorize as many commands to compile and run modules on the 1Z0-816 exam. We still include them in the chapter so you can study and follow along. Feel free to use the files we've already set up in the GitHub repo linked to from www.selikoff.net/ocp11-2.

Reviewing Module Directives

Since you are expected to know highlights of the module-info.java file for the 1Z0-816, we have included the relevant parts here as a reference. If anything in Table 17.1 is unclear or unfamiliar, please stop and read Chapter 11 before continuing in this chapter.

TABLE 17.1   Common module directives

Derivative	Description
exports *<package>*	Allows all modules to access the package
exports *<package>* to *<module>*	Allows a specific module to access the package
requires *<module>*	Indicates module is dependent on another module
requires transitive *<module>*	Indicates the module and that all modules that use this module are dependent on another module
uses *<interface>*	Indicates that a module uses a service
provides *<interface>* with *<class>*	Indicates that a module provides an implementation of a service

If you don't have any experience with uses or provides, don't worry—they will be covered in this chapter.

Comparing Types of Modules

The modules you learned about in Chapter 11 are called *named modules*. There are two other types of modules: automatic modules and unnamed modules. In this section, we describe these three types of modules. On the exam, you will need to be able to compare them.

Classpath vs. Module Path

Before we get started, a brief reminder that the Java runtime is capable of using class and interface types from both the classpath and the module path, although the rules for each are a bit different. An application can access any type in the classpath that is exposed via standard Java access modifiers, such as a public class.

On the other hand, public types in the module path are not automatically available. While Java access modifiers must still be used, the type must also be in a package that is exported by the module in which it is defined. In addition, the module making use of the type must contain a dependency on the module.

Named Modules

A *named module* is one containing a module-info file. To review, this file appears in the root of the JAR alongside one or more packages. Unless otherwise specified, a module is a named module. Named modules appear on the module path rather than the classpath. You'll learn what happens if a JAR containing a module-info file is on the classpath. For now, just know it is not considered a named module because it is not on the module path.

As a way of remembering this, a named module has the name inside the module-info file and is on the module path. Figure 17.1 shows the contents of a JAR file for a named module. It contains two packages in addition to the module-info.class.

FIGURE 17.1 A named module

Automatic Modules

An *automatic module* appears on the module path but does not contain a module-info file. It is simply a regular JAR file that is placed on the module path and gets treated as a module.

As a way of remembering this, Java automatically determines the module name. Figure 17.2 shows an automatic module with two packages.

FIGURE 17.2 An automatic module

 Real World Scenario

About the Manifest

A JAR file is a zip file with a special directory named META-INF. This directory contains one or more files. The MANIFEST.MF file is always present. The figure shows how the manifest fits into the directory structure of a JAR file.

The manifest contains extra information about the JAR file. For example, it often contains the version of Java used to build the JAR file. For command-line programs, the class with the `main()` method is commonly specified.

Each line in the manifest is a key/value pair separated by a colon. You can think of the manifest as a map of property names and values. The default manifest in Java 11 looks like this:

```
Manifest-Version: 1.0
Created-By: 11.0.2 (Oracle Corporation)
```

The code referencing an automatic module treats it as if there is a `module-info` file present. It automatically exports all packages. It also determines the module name. How does it determine the module name? you ask. Excellent question.

When Java 9 was released, authors of Java libraries were encouraged to declare the name they intended to use for the module in the future. All they had to do was set a property called `Automatic-Module-Name` in the `MANIFEST.MF` file.

Specifying a single property in the manifest allowed library providers to make things easier for applications that wanted to use their library in a modular application. You can think of it as a promise that when the library becomes a named module, it will use the specified module name.

If the JAR file does not specify an automatic module name, Java will still allow you to use it in the module path. In this case, Java will determine the module name for you. We'd say that this happens automatically, but the joke is probably wearing thin by now.

Java determines the automatic module name by basing it off the filename of the JAR file. Let's go over the rules by starting with an example. Suppose we have a JAR file named `holiday-calendar-1.0.0.jar`.

First, Java will remove the extension `.jar` from the name. Then, Java will remove the version from the end of the JAR filename. This is important because we want module names to be consistent. Having a different automatic module name every time you upgraded to a new version would not be good! After all, this would force you to change the module-info file of your nice, clean, modularized application every time you pulled in a later version of the holiday calendar JAR.

Removing the version and extension gives us holiday-calendar. This leaves us with a problem. Dashes (-) are not allowed in module names. Java solves this problem by converting any special characters in the name to dots (.). As a result, the module name is holiday.calendar. Any characters other than letters and numbers are considered special characters in this replacement. Finally, any adjacent dots or leading/trailing dots are removed.

Since that's a number of rules, let's review the algorithm in a list for determining the name of an automatic module.

- If the MANIFEST.MF specifies an Automatic-Module-Name, use that. Otherwise, proceed with the remaining rules.

- Remove the file extension from the JAR name.

- Remove any version information from the end of the name. A version is digits and dots with possible extra information at the end, for example, -1.0.0 or -1.0-RC.

- Replace any remaining characters other than letters and numbers with dots.

- Replace any sequences of dots with a single dot.

- Remove the dot if it is the first or last character of the result.

Table 17.2 shows how to apply these rules to two examples where there is no automatic module name specified in the manifest.

TABLE 17.2 Practicing with automatic module names

#	Description	Example 1	Example 2
1	Beginning JAR name	commons2-x-1.0.0-SNAPSHOT.jar	mod_$-1.0.jar
2	Remove file extension	commons2-x-1.0.0-SNAPSHOT	mod_$-1.0
3	Remove version information	commons2-x	mod_$
4	Replace special characters	commons2.x	mod..
5	Replace sequence of dots	commons2.x	mod.
6	Remove leading/trailing dots (results in the automatic module name)	commons2.x	mod

While the algorithm for creating automatic module names does its best, it can't always come up with a good name. For example, `1.2.0-calendar-1.2.2-good-1.jar` isn't conducive. Luckily such names are rare and out of scope for the exam.

Unnamed Modules

An *unnamed module* appears on the classpath. Like an automatic module, it is a regular JAR. Unlike an automatic module, it is on the classpath rather than the module path. This means an unnamed module is treated like old code and a second-class citizen to modules. Figure 17.3 shows an unnamed module with one package.

FIGURE 17.3   An unnamed module

Classpath

zoo.legacy.jar

zoo.legacy.util

An unnamed module does not usually contain a `module-info` file. If it happens to contain one, that file will be ignored since it is on the classpath.

Unnamed modules do not export any packages to named or automatic modules. The unnamed module can read from any JARs on the classpath or module path. You can think of an unnamed module as code that works the way Java worked before modules. Yes, we know it is confusing to have something that isn't really a module having the word *module* in its name.

Comparing Module Types

You can expect to get questions on the exam comparing the three types of modules. Please study Table 17.3 thoroughly and be prepared to answer questions about these items in any combination. A key point to remember is that code on the classpath can access the module path. By contrast, code on the module path is unable to read from the classpath.

TABLE 17.3 Properties of modules types

Property	Named	Automatic	Unnamed
A _____ module contains a module-info file?	Yes	No	Ignored if present
A _____ module exports which packages to other modules?	Those in the module-info file	All packages	No packages
A _____ module is readable by other modules on the module path?	Yes	Yes	No
A _____ module is readable by other JARs on the classpath?	Yes	Yes	Yes

Analyzing JDK Dependencies

In this part of the chapter, we look at modules that are supplied by the JDK. We also look at the jdeps command for identifying such module dependencies.

Identifying Built-in Modules

Prior to Java 9, developers could use any package in the JDK by merely importing it into the application. This meant the whole JDK had to be available at runtime because a program could potentially need anything. With modules, your application specifies which parts of the JDK it uses. This allows the application to run on a full JDK or a subset.

You might be wondering what happens if you try to run an application that references a package that isn't available in the subset. No worries! The requires directive in the module-info file specifies which modules need to be present at both compile time and runtime. This means they are guaranteed to be available for the application to run.

The most important module to know is java.base. It contains most of the packages you have been learning about for the exam. In fact, it is so important that you don't even have to use the requires directive; it is available to all modular applications. Your module-info.java file will still compile if you explicitly require java.base. However, it is redundant, so it's better to omit it. Table 17.4 lists some common modules and what they contain.

TABLE 17.4   Common modules

Module name	What it contains	Coverage in book
java.base	Collections, Math, IO, NIO.2, Concurrency, etc.	Most of this book
java.desktop	Abstract Windows Toolkit (AWT) and Swing	Not on the exam beyond the module name
java.logging	Logging	Not on the exam beyond the module name
java.sql	JDBC	Chapter 21, "JDBC"
java.xml	Extensible Markup Language (XML)	Not on the exam beyond the module name

The exam creators feel it is important to recognize the names of modules supplied by the JDK. While you don't need to know the names by heart, you do need to be able to pick them out of a lineup.

For the exam, you need to know that module names begin with java for APIs you are likely to use and with jdk for APIs that are specific to the JDK. Table 17.5 lists all the modules that begin with java.

TABLE 17.5   Java modules prefixed with java

java.base	java.naming	java.smartcardio
java.compiler	java.net.http	java.sql
java.datatransfer	java.prefs	java.sql.rowset
java.desktop	java.rmi	java.transaction.xa
java.instrument	java.scripting	java.xml
java.logging	java.se	java.xml.crypto
java.management	java.security.jgss	
java.management.rmi	java.security.sasl	

Table 17.6 lists all the modules that begin with jdk. We recommend reviewing this right before the exam to increase the chances of them sounding familiar. You don't have to memorize them, but you should be able to pick them out of a lineup.

TABLE 17.6 Java modules prefixed with jdk

jdk.accessiblity	jdk.jconsole	jdk.naming.dns
jdk.attach	jdk.jdeps	jdk.naming.rmi
jdk.charsets	jdk.jdi	jdk.net
jdk.compiler	jdk.jdwp.agent	jdk.pack
jdk.crypto.cryptoki	jdk.jfr	jdk.rmic
jdk.crypto.ec	jdk.jlink	jdk.scripting.nashorn
jdk.dynalink	jdk.jshell	jdk.sctp
jdk.editpad	jdk.jsobject	jdk.security.auth
jdk.hotspot.agent	jdk.jstatd	jdk.security.jgss
jdk.httpserver	jdk.localdata	jdk.xml.dom
jdk.jartool	jdk.management	jdk.zipfs
jdk.javadoc	jdk.management.agent	
jdk.jcmd	jdk.management.jfr	

Using *jdeps*

The jdeps command gives you information about dependencies. Luckily, you are not expected to memorize all the options for the 1Z0-816 exam.

You are expected to understand how to use jdeps with projects that have not yet been modularized to assist in identifying dependencies and problems. First, we will create a JAR file from this class. If you are following along, feel free to copy the class from the online examples referenced at the beginning of the chapter rather than typing it in.

```
// Animatronic.java
package zoo.dinos;

import java.time.*;
import java.util.*;
import sun.misc.Unsafe;
```

```
public class Animatronic {
   private List<String> names;
   private LocalDate visitDate;

   public Animatronic(List<String> names, LocalDate visitDate) {
      this.names = names;
      this.visitDate = visitDate;
   }
   public void unsafeMethod() {
      Unsafe unsafe = Unsafe.getUnsafe();
   }
}
```

This example is silly. It uses a number of unrelated classes. The Bronx Zoo really did have electronic moving dinosaurs for a while, so at least the idea of having dinosaurs in a zoo isn't beyond the realm of possibility.

Now we can compile this file. You might have noticed there is no `module-info.java` file. That is because we aren't creating a module. We are looking into what dependencies we will need when we do modularize this JAR.

```
javac zoo/dinos/*.java
```

Compiling works, but it gives you some warnings about `Unsafe` being an internal API. Don't worry about those for now—we'll discuss that shortly. (Maybe the dinosaurs went extinct because they did something unsafe.)

Next, we create a JAR file.

```
jar -cvf zoo.dino.jar .
```

We can run the `jdeps` command against this JAR to learn about its dependencies. First, let's run the command without any options. On the first two lines, the command prints the modules that we would need to add with a `requires` directive to migrate to the module system. It also prints a table showing what packages are used and what modules they correspond to.

```
jdeps zoo.dino.jar
```

```
zoo.dino.jar -> java.base
zoo.dino.jar -> jdk.unsupported
   zoo.dinos    -> java.lang        java.base
   zoo.dinos    -> java.time        java.base
   zoo.dinos    -> java.util        java.base
   zoo.dinos    -> sun.misc         JDK internal API (jdk.unsupported)
```

If we run in summary mode, we only see just the first part where `jdeps` lists the modules.

```
jdeps -s zoo.dino.jar

zoo.dino.jar -> java.base
zoo.dino.jar -> jdk.unsupported
```

For a real project, the dependency list could include dozens or even hundreds of packages. It's useful to see the summary of just the modules. This approach also makes it easier to see whether jdk.unsupported is in the list.

 You might have noticed that jdk.unsupported is not in the list of modules you saw in Table 17.6. It's special because it contains internal libraries
that developers in previous versions of Java were discouraged from using,
although many people ignored this warning. You should not reference it as it
may disappear in future versions of Java.

The jdeps command has an option to provide details about these unsupported APIs. The output looks something like this:

```
jdeps --jdk-internals zoo.dino.jar

zoo.dino.jar -> jdk.unsupported
   zoo.dinos.Animatronic  -> sun.misc.Unsafe
      JDK internal API (jdk.unsupported)

Warning: <omitted warning>

JDK Internal API      Suggested Replacement
--------------------  --------------------------
sun.misc.Unsafe       See http://openjdk.java.net/jeps/260
```

The --jdk-internals option lists any classes you are using that call an internal API along with which API. At the end, it provides a table suggesting what you should do about it. If you wrote the code calling the internal API, this message is useful. If not, the message would be useful to the team who did write the code. You, on the other hand, might need to update or replace that JAR file entirely with one that fixes the issue. Note that -jdkinternals is equivalent to --jdk-internals.

 Real World Scenario

About *sun.misc.Unsafe*

Prior to the Java Platform Module System, classes had to be public if you wanted them to be used outside the package. It was reasonable to use the class in JDK code since that is low-level code that is already tightly coupled to the JDK. Since it was needed in multiple packages, the class was made `public`. Sun even named it `Unsafe`, figuring that would prevent anyone from using it outside the JDK.

However, developers are clever and used the class since it was available. A number of widely used open source libraries started using `Unsafe`. While it is quite unlikely that you are using this class in your project directly, it is likely you use an open source library that is using it.

The `jdeps` command allows you to look at these JARs to see whether you will have any problems when Oracle finally prevents the usage of this class. If you find any uses, you can look at whether there is a later version of the JAR that you can upgrade to.

Migrating an Application

All applications developed for Java 8 and earlier were not designed to use the Java Platform Module System because it did not exist yet. Ideally, they were at least designed with projects instead of as a big ball of mud. This section will give you an overview of strategies for migrating an existing application to use modules. We will cover ordering modules, bottom-up migration, top-down migration, and how to split up an existing project.

 Real World Scenario

Migrating Your Applications at Work

The exam exists in a pretend universe where there are no open-source dependencies and applications are very small. These scenarios make learning and discussing migration far easier. In the real world, applications have libraries that haven't been updated in 10 or more years, complex dependency graphs, and all sorts of surprises.

Note that you can use all the features of Java 11 without converting your application to modules (except the features in this module chapter, of course!). Please make sure you have a reason for migration and don't think it is required.

This chapter does a great job teaching you what you need to know for the exam. However, it does not adequately prepare you for actually converting real applications to use modules. If you find yourself in that situation, consider reading *The Java Module System* by Nicolai Parlog (Manning Publications, 2019).

Determining the Order

Before we can migrate our application to use modules, we need to know how the packages and libraries in the existing application are structured. Suppose we have a simple application with three JAR files, as shown in Figure 17.4. The dependencies between projects form a graph. Both of the representations in Figure 17.4 are equivalent. The arrows show the dependencies by pointing from the project that will require the dependency to the one that makes it available. In the language of modules, the arrow will go from `requires` to the `exports`.

FIGURE 17.4   Determining the order

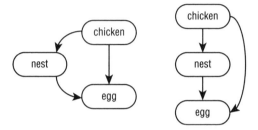

The right side of the diagram makes it easier to identify the top and bottom that top-down and bottom-up migration refer to. Projects that do not have any dependencies are at the bottom. Projects that do have dependencies are at the top.

In this example, there is only one order from top to bottom that honors all the dependencies. Figure 17.5 shows that the order is not always unique. Since two of the projects do not have an arrow between them, either order is allowed when deciding migration order.

FIGURE 17.5   Determining the order when not unique

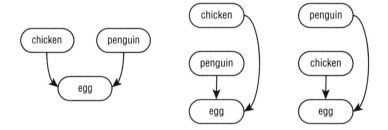

Exploring a Bottom-Up Migration Strategy

The easiest approach to migration is a bottom-up migration. This approach works best when you have the power to convert any JAR files that aren't already modules. For a bottom-up migration, you follow these steps:

1. Pick the lowest-level project that has not yet been migrated. (Remember the way we ordered them by dependencies in the previous section?)

2. Add a `module-info.java` file to that project. Be sure to add any `exports` to expose any package used by higher-level JAR files. Also, add a `requires` directive for any modules it depends on.

3. Move this newly migrated named module from the classpath to the module path.

4. Ensure any projects that have not yet been migrated stay as unnamed modules on the classpath.

5. Repeat with the next-lowest-level project until you are done.

You can see this procedure applied to migrate three projects in Figure 17.6. Notice that each project is converted to a module in turn.

FIGURE 17.6 Bottom-up migration

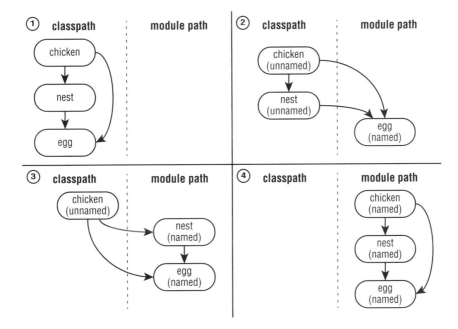

With a bottom-up migration, you are getting the lower-level projects in good shape. This makes it easier to migrate the top-level projects at the end. It also encourages care in what is exposed.

During migration, you have a mix of named modules and unnamed modules. The named modules are the lower-level ones that have been migrated. They are on the module path and not allowed to access any unnamed modules.

The unnamed modules are on the classpath. They can access JAR files on both the classpath and the module path.

Exploring a Top-Down Migration Strategy

A top-down migration strategy is most useful when you don't have control of every JAR file used by your application. For example, suppose another team owns one project. They are just too busy to migrate. You wouldn't want this situation to hold up your entire migration.

For a top-down migration, you follow these steps:

1. Place all projects on the module path.

2. Pick the highest-level project that has not yet been migrated.

3. Add a `module-info` file to that project to convert the automatic module into a named module. Again, remember to add any `exports` or `requires` directives. You can use the automatic module name of other modules when writing the `requires` directive since most of the projects on the module path do not have names yet.

4. Repeat with the next-lowest-level project until you are done.

You can see this procedure applied in order to migrate three projects in Figure 17.7. Notice that each project is converted to a module in turn.

FIGURE 17.7   Top-down migration

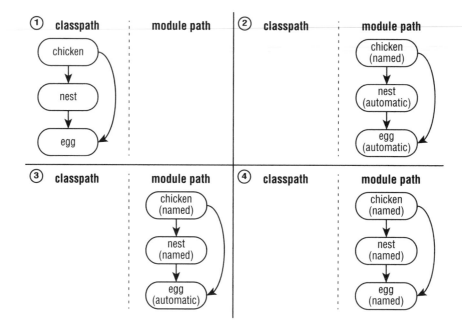

With a top-down migration, you are conceding that all of the lower-level dependencies are not ready but want to make the application itself a module.

During migration, you have a mix of named modules and automatic modules. The named modules are the higher-level ones that have been migrated. They are on the module path and have access to the automatic modules. The automatic modules are also on the module path.

Table 17.7 reviews what you need to know about the two main migration strategies. Make sure you know it well.

TABLE 17.7   Comparing migration strategies

Category	Bottom-Up	Top-Down
A project that depends on all others	Unnamed module on the classpath	Named module on the module path
A project that has no dependencies	Named module on the module path	Automatic module on the module path

Splitting a Big Project into Modules

For the exam, you need to understand the basic process of splitting up a big project into modules. You won't be given a big project, of course. After all, there is only so much space to ask a question. Luckily, the process is the same for a small project.

Suppose you start with an application that has a number of packages. The first step is to break them up into logical groupings and draw the dependencies between them. Figure 17.8 shows an imaginary system's decomposition. Notice that there are seven packages on both the left and right sides. There are fewer modules because some packages share a module.

FIGURE 17.8   First attempt at decomposition

There's a problem with this decomposition. Do you see it? The Java Platform Module System does not allow for *cyclic dependencies*. A cyclic dependency, or *circular dependency*, is when two things directly or indirectly depend on each other. If the zoo.tickets.delivery module requires the zoo.tickets.discount module, the zoo.tickets.discount is not allowed to require the zoo.tickets.delivery module.

Now that we all know that the decomposition in Figure 17.8 won't work, what can we do about it? A common technique is to introduce another module. That module contains the code that the other two modules share. Figure 17.9 shows the new modules without any cyclic dependencies. Notice the new module zoo.tickets.discount. We created a new package to put in that module. This allows the developers to put the common code in there and break the dependency. No more cyclic dependencies!

FIGURE 17.9   Removing the cyclic dependencies

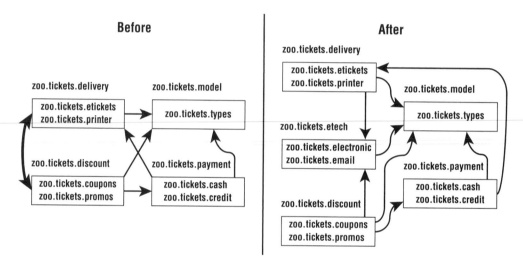

Failing to Compile with a Cyclic Dependency

It is extremely important to understand that Java will not allow you to compile modules that have circular dependencies between each other. In this section, we will look at an example leading to that compiler error.

First, let's create a module named zoo.butterfly that has a single class in addition to the module-info.java file. If you need a reminder where the files go in the directory structure, see Chapter 11 or the online code example.

```
// Butterfly.java
package zoo.butterfly;
public class Butterfly {
}
```

```
// module-info.java
module zoo.butterfly {
   exports zoo.butterfly;
}
```

We can compile the butterfly module and create a JAR file in the mods directory named zoo.butterfly.jar. Remember to create a mods directory if one doesn't exist in your folder structure.

```
javac -d butterflyModule
   butterflyModule/zoo/butterfly/Butterfly.java
   butterflyModule/module-info.java

jar -cvf mods/zoo.butterfly.jar -C butterflyModule/ .
```

Now we create a new module, zoo.caterpillar, that depends on the existing zoo.butterfly module. This time, we will create a module with two classes in addition to the module-info.java file.

```
// Caterpillar.java
package zoo.caterpillar;
public class Caterpillar {
}
```

```
// CaterpillarLifecycle.java
package zoo.caterpillar;
import zoo.butterfly.Butterfly;
public interface CaterpillarLifecycle {
   Butterfly emergeCocoon();
}
```

```
// module-info.java
module zoo.caterpillar {
   requires zoo.butterfly;
}
```

Again, we will compile and create a JAR file. This time it is named zoo.caterpillar.jar.

```
javac -p mods -d caterpillarModule
   caterpillarModule/zoo/caterpillar/*.java
   caterpillarModule/module-info.java
jar -cvf mods/zoo.caterpillar.jar -C caterpillarModule/ .
```

At this point, we want to add a method for a butterfly to make caterpillar eggs. We decide to put it in the Butterfly module instead of the CaterpillarLifecycle class to demonstrate a cyclic dependency.

We know this requires adding a dependency, so we do that first. Updating the module-info.java file in the zoo.butterfly module looks like this:

```
module zoo.butterfly {
    exports zoo.butterfly;
    requires zoo.caterpillar;
}
```

We then compile it with the module path mods so zoo.caterpillar is visible:

```
javac -p mods -d butterflyModule
    butterflyModule/zoo/butterfly/Butterfly.java
    butterflyModule/module-info.java
```

The compiler complains about our cyclic dependency.

```
butterflyModule/module-info.java:3: error:
    cyclic dependence involving zoo.caterpillar
        requires zoo.caterpillar;
```

This is one of the advantages of the module system. It prevents you from writing code that has cyclic dependency. Such code won't even compile!

You might be wondering what happens if three modules are involved. Suppose module ballA requires module ballB and ballB requires module ballC. Can module ballC require module ballA? No. This would create a cyclic dependency. Don't believe us? Try drawing it. You can follow your pencil around the circle from ballA to ballB to ballC to ballA to . . . well, you get the idea. There are just too many balls in the air here!

> Java will still allow you to have a cyclic dependency between packages within a module. It enforces that you do not have a cyclic dependency between modules.

Creating a Service

In this section, you'll learn how to create a service. A *service* is composed of an interface, any classes the interface references, and a way of looking up implementations of the interface. The implementations are not part of the service.

Services are not new to Java. In fact, the ServiceLoader class was introduced in Java 6. It was used to make applications *extensible*, so you could add functionality without recompiling the whole application. What is new is the integration with modules.

We will be using a tour application in the services section. It has four modules shown in Figure 17.10. In this example, the zoo.tours.api and zoo.tours.reservations models make up the service since they consist of the interface and lookup functionality.

FIGURE 17.10   Modules in the tour application

 You aren't required to have four separate modules. We do so to illustrate the concepts. For example, the service provider interface and service locator could be in the same module.

Declaring the Service Provider Interface

First, the zoo.tours.api module defines a Java object called Souvenir. It is considered part of the service because it will be referenced by the interface.

```
// Souvenir.java
package zoo.tours.api;

public class Souvenir {
   private String description;

   public String getDescription() {
      return description;
   }
   public void setDescription(String description) {
      this.description = description;
   }
}
```

Next, the module contains a Java interface type. This interface is called the *service provider interface* because it specifies what behavior our service will have. In this case, it is a simple API with three methods.

```
// Tour.java
package zoo.tours.api;

public interface Tour {
   String name();
   int length();
   Souvenir getSouvenir();
}
```

All three methods use the implicit public modifier, as shown in Chapter 12, "Java Fundamentals." Since we are working with modules, we also need to create a module-info .java file so our module definition exports the package containing the interface.

```
// module-info.java
module zoo.tours.api {
   exports zoo.tours.api;
}
```

Now that we have both files, we can compile and package this module.

```
javac -d serviceProviderInterfaceModule
   serviceProviderInterfaceModule/zoo/tours/api/*.java
   serviceProviderInterfaceModule/module-info.java

jar -cvf mods/zoo.tours.api.jar -C serviceProviderInterfaceModule/ .
```

 A service provider "interface" can be an abstract class rather than an actual interface. Since you will only see it as an interface on the exam, we use that term in the book.

To review, the service includes the service provider interface and supporting classes it references. The service also includes the lookup functionality, which we will define next.

Creating a Service Locator

To complete our service, we need a service locator. A *service locator* is able to find any classes that implement a service provider interface.

Luckily, Java provides a ServiceLocator class to help with this task. You pass the service provider interface type to its load() method, and Java will return any implementation services it can find. The following class shows it in action:

```
// TourFinder.java
package zoo.tours.reservations;

import java.util.*;
import zoo.tours.api.*;

public class TourFinder {
```

```
    public static Tour findSingleTour() {
        ServiceLoader<Tour> loader = ServiceLoader.load(Tour.class);
        for (Tour tour : loader)
            return tour;
        return null;
    }
    public static List<Tour> findAllTours() {
        List<Tour> tours = new ArrayList<>();
        ServiceLoader<Tour> loader = ServiceLoader.load(Tour.class);
        for (Tour tour : loader)
            tours.add(tour);
        return tours;
    }
}
```

As you can see, we provided two lookup methods. The first is a convenience method if you are expecting exactly one Tour to be returned. The other returns a List, which accommodates any number of service providers. At runtime, there may be many service providers (or none) that are found by the service locator.

 The ServiceLoader call is relatively expensive. If you are writing a real application, it is best to cache the result.

Our module definition exports the package with the lookup class TourFinder. It requires the service provider interface package. It also has the uses directive since it will be looking up a service.

```
// module-info.java
module zoo.tours.reservations {
    exports zoo.tours.reservations;
    requires zoo.tours.api;
    uses zoo.tours.api.Tour;
}
```

Remember that both requires and uses are needed, one for compilation and one for lookup. Finally, we compile and package the module.

```
javac -p mods -d serviceLocatorModule
    serviceLocatorModule/zoo/tours/reservations/*.java
    serviceLocatorModule/module-info.java

jar -cvf mods/zoo.tours.reservations.jar -C serviceLocatorModule/ .
```

Now that we have the interface and lookup logic, we have completed our service.

Invoking from a Consumer

Next up is to call the service locator by a consumer. A *consumer* (or *client*) refers to a module that obtains and uses a service. Once the consumer has acquired a service via the service locator, it is able to invoke the methods provided by the service provider interface.

```java
// Tourist.java
package zoo.visitor;

import java.util.*;
import zoo.tours.api.*;
import zoo.tours.reservations.*;

public class Tourist {
   public static void main(String[] args) {
      Tour tour = TourFinder.findSingleTour();
      System.out.println("Single tour: " + tour);

      List<Tour> tours = TourFinder.findAllTours();
      System.out.println("# tours: " + tours.size());
   }
}
```

Our module definition doesn't need to know anything about the implementations since the zoo.tours.reservations module is handling the lookup.

```java
// module-info.java
module zoo.visitor {
   requires zoo.tours.api;
   requires zoo.tours.reservations;
}
```

This time, we get to run a program after compiling and packaging.

```
javac -p mods -d consumerModule
   consumerModule/zoo/visitor/*.java
   consumerModule/module-info.java

jar -cvf mods/zoo.visitor.jar -C consumerModule/ .

java -p mods -m zoo.visitor/zoo.visitor.Tourist
```

The program outputs the following:

```
Single tour: null
# tours: 0
```

Well, that makes sense. We haven't written a class that implements the interface yet.

Adding a Service Provider

A *service provider* is the implementation of a service provider interface. As we said earlier, at runtime it is possible to have multiple implementation classes or modules. We will stick to one here for simplicity.

Our service provider is the zoo.tours.agency package because we've outsourced the running of tours to a third party.

```java
// TourImpl.java
package zoo.tours.agency;

import zoo.tours.api.*;

public class TourImpl implements Tour {
   public String name() {
      return "Behind the Scenes";
   }
   public int length() {
      return 120;
   }
   public Souvenir getSouvenir() {
      Souvenir gift = new Souvenir();
      gift.setDescription("stuffed animal");
      return gift;
   }
}
```

Again, we need a module-info.java file to create a module.

```java
// module-info.java
module zoo.tours.agency {
   requires zoo.tours.api;
   provides zoo.tours.api.Tour with zoo.tours.agency.TourImpl;
}
```

The module declaration requires the module containing the interface as a dependency. We don't export the package that implements the interface since we don't want callers referring to it directly. Instead, we use the provides directive. This allows us to specify that we provide an implementation of the interface with a specific implementation class. The syntax looks like this:

```java
provides interfaceName with className;
```

We have not exported the package containing the implementation. Instead, we have made the implementation available to a service provider using the interface.

Finally, we compile and package it up.

```
javac -p mods -d serviceProviderModule
    serviceProviderModule/zoo/tours/agency/*.java
    serviceProviderModule/module-info.java
jar -cvf mods/zoo.tours.agency.jar -C serviceProviderModule/ .
```

Now comes the cool part. We can run the Java program again.

```
java -p mods -m zoo.visitor/zoo.visitor.Tourist
```

This time we see the following output:

```
Single tour: zoo.tours.agency.TourImpl@1936f0f5
# tours: 1
```

Notice how we didn't recompile the zoo.tours.reservations or zoo.visitor package. The service locator was able to observe that there was now a service provider implementation available and find it for us.

This is useful when you have functionality that changes independently of the rest of the code base. For example, you might have custom reports or logging.

> In software development, the concept of separating out different components into stand-alone pieces is referred to as *loose coupling*. One advantage of loosely coupled code is that it can be easily swapped out or replaced with minimal (or zero) changes to code that uses it. Relying on a loosely coupled structure allows service modules to be easily extensible at runtime.

Java allows only one service provider for a service provider interface in a module. If you wanted to offer another tour, you would need to create a separate module.

Merging Service Locator and Consumer

Now that you understand what all four pieces do, let's see if you understand how to merge pieces. We can even use streams from Chapter 15, "Functional Programming," to implement a method that gets all implementation and the length of the shortest and longest tours.

First, let's create a second service provider. Remember the service provider TourImpl is the implementation of the service interface Tour.

```
package zoo.tours.hybrid;

import zoo.tours.api.*;

public class QuickTourImpl implements Tour {
```

```
   public String name() {
      return "Short Tour";
   }
   public int length() {
      return 30;
   }
   public Souvenir getSouvenir() {
      Souvenir gift = new Souvenir();
      gift.setDescription("keychain");
      return gift;
   }
}
```

Before we introduce the lookup code, it is important to be aware of a piece of trickery. There are two methods in `ServiceLoader` that you need to know for the exam. The declaration is as follows, sans the full implementation:

```
public final class ServiceLoader<S> implements Iterable<S> {

   public static <S> ServiceLoader<S> load(Class<S> service) { ... }

   public Stream<Provider<S>> stream() { ... }

   // Additional methods
}
```

Conveniently, if you call `ServiceLoader.load()`, it returns an object that you can loop through normally. However, requesting a `Stream` gives you a different type. The reason for this is that a `Stream` controls when elements are evaluated. Therefore, a `ServiceLoader` returns a `Stream` of `Provider` objects. You have to call `get()` to retrieve the value you wanted out of each `Provider`.

Now we can create the class that merges the service locator and consumer.

```
package zoo.tours.hybrid;

import java.util.*;
import java.util.ServiceLoader.Provider;
import zoo.tours.api.*;

public class TourLengthCheck {

   public static void main(String[] args) {
      OptionalInt max = ServiceLoader.load(Tour.class)
```

```
      .stream()
      .map(Provider::get)
      .mapToInt(Tour::length)
      .max();
   max.ifPresent(System.out::println);

   OptionalInt min = ServiceLoader.load(Tour.class)
      .stream()
      .map(Provider::get)
      .mapToInt(Tour::length)
      .min();
   min.ifPresent(System.out::println);
   }
}
```

As we mentioned, there is an extra method call to use get() to retrieve the value out of the Provider since we are using a Stream.

Now comes the fun part. What directives do you think we need in module-info.java? It turns out we need three.

```
module zoo.tours.hybrid {
   requires zoo.tours.api;
   provides zoo.tours.api.Tour with zoo.tours.hybrid.QuickTourImpl;
   uses zoo.tours.api.Tour;
}
```

We need requires because we depend on the service provider interface. We still need provides so the ServiceLocator can look up the service. Additionally, we still need uses since we are looking up the service interface from another module.

For the last time, let's compile, package, and run.

```
javac -p mods -d multiPurposeModule
   multiPurposeModule/zoo/tours/hybrid/*.java
   multiPurposeModule/module-info.java

jar -cvf mods/zoo.tours.hybrid.jar -C multiPurposeModule/ .

java -p mods -m zoo.tours.hybrid/zoo.tours.hybrid.TourLengthCheck
```

And it works. The output sees both service providers and prints different values for the maximum and minimum tour lengths:

```
120
30
```

Reviewing Services

Table 17.8 summarizes what we've covered in the section about services. We recommend learning what is needed when each artifact is in a separate module really well. That is most likely what you will see on the exam and will ensure you understand the concepts.

TABLE 17.8 Reviewing services

Artifact	Part of the service	Directives required in `module-info.java`
Service provider interface	Yes	`exports`
Service provider	No	`requires` `provides`

Service locator	Yes	`exports`
		`requires`
		`uses`

Consumer	No	`requires`

Summary

There are three types of modules. Named modules contain a `module-info.java` file and are on the module path. They can read only from the module path. Automatic modules are also on the module path but have not yet been modularized. They might have an automatic module name set in the manifest. Unnamed modules are on the classpath.

The `java.base` module is most common and is automatically supplied to all modules as a dependency. You do have to be familiar with the full list of modules provided in the JDK. The `jdeps` command provides a list of dependencies that a JAR needs. It can do so on a summary level or detailed level. Additionally, it can specify information about JDK internal modules and suggest replacements.

The two most common migration strategies are top-down and bottom-up migration. Top-down migration starts migrating the module with the most dependencies and places all other modules on the module path. Bottom-up migration starts migrating a module with no dependencies and moves one module to the module path at a time. Both of these strategies require ensuring you do not have any cyclic dependencies since the Java Platform Module System will not allow cyclic dependencies to compile.

A service consists of the service provider interface and service locator. The service provider interface is the API for the service. One or more modules contain the service provider. These modules contain the implementing classes of the service provider interface. The service locator calls `ServiceLoader` to dynamically get any service providers. It can return the results so you can loop through them or get a stream. Finally, the consumer calls the service provider interface.

Exam Essentials

Identify the three types of modules.   Named modules are JARs that have been modularized. Unnamed modules have not been modularized. Automatic modules are in between. They are on the module path but do not have a `module-info.java` file.

List built-in JDK modules.   The `java.base` module is available to all modules. There are about 20 other modules provided by the JDK that begin with `java.*` and about 30 that begin with `jdk.*`.

Use *jdeps* to list required packages and internal packages.   The `-s` flag gives a summary by only including module names. The `--jdk-internals` (`-jdkinternals`) flag provides additional information about unsupported APIs and suggests replacements.

Explain top-down and bottom-up migration.   A top-down migration places all JARs on the module path, making them automatic modules while migrating from top to bottom. A bottom-up migration leaves all JARs on the classpath, making them unnamed modules while migrating from bottom to top.

Differentiate the four main parts of a service.   A service provider interface declares the interface that a service must implement. The service locator looks up the service, and a consumer calls the service. Finally, a service provider implements the service.

Code directives for use with services.   A service provider implementation must have the `provides` directive to specify what service provider interface it supplies and what class it implements it `with`. The module containing the service locator must have the `uses` directive to specify which service provider implementation it will be looking up.

Review Questions

The answers to the chapter review questions can be found in the Appendix.

1. Which of the following pairs make up a service?

   A. Consumer and service locator

   B. Consumer and service provider interface

   C. Service locator and service provider

   D. Service locator and service provider interface

   E. Service provider and service provider interface

2. A(n) _____ module is on the classpath while a(n) _____ module is on the module path. (Choose all that apply.)

   A. automatic, named

   B. automatic, unnamed

   C. named, automatic

   D. named, unnamed

   E. unnamed, automatic

   F. unnamed, named

   G. None of the above

3. An automatic module name is generated if one is not supplied. Which of the following JAR filename and generated automatic module name pairs are correct? (Choose all that apply.)

   A. `emily-1.0.0.jar` and `emily`

   B. `emily-1.0.0-SNAPSHOT.jar` and `emily`

   C. `emily_the_cat-1.0.0.jar` and `emily_the_cat`

   D. `emily_the_cat-1.0.0.jar` and `emily-the-cat`

   E. `emily.$.jar` and `emily`

   F. `emily.$.jar` and `emily.`

   G. `emily.$.jar` and `emily..`

4. Which of the following statements are true? (Choose all that apply.)

   A. Modules with cyclic dependencies will not compile.

   B. Packages with a cyclic dependency will not compile.

   C. A cyclic dependency always involves exactly two modules.

   D. A cyclic dependency always involves three or more modules.

   E. A cyclic dependency always involves at least two `requires` statements.

   F. An unnamed module can be involved in a cyclic dependency with an automatic module

5. Which module is available to your named module without needing a `requires` directive?

A. `java.all`

B. `java.base`

C. `java.default`

D. `java.lang`

E. None of the above

6. Suppose you are creating a service provider that contains the following class. Which line of code needs to be in your `module-info.java`?

```
package dragon;
import magic.*;
public class Dragon implements Magic {
    public String getPower() {
        return "breathe fire";
    }
}
```

A. `provides dragon.Dragon by magic.Magic;`

B. `provides dragon.Dragon using magic.Magic;`

C. `provides dragon.Dragon with magic.Magic;`

D. `provides magic.Magic by dragon.Dragon;`

E. `provides magic.Magic using dragon.Dragon;`

F. `provides magic.Magic with dragon.Dragon;`

7. Which of the following modules is provided by the JDK? (Choose all that apply.)

A. `java.base;`

B. `java.desktop;`

C. `java.logging;`

D. `java.util;`

E. `jdk.base;`

F. `jdk.compiler;`

G. `jdk.xerces;`

8. Which of the following compiles and is equivalent to this loop?

```
List<Unicorn> all  = new ArrayList<>();
for (Unicorn current : ServiceLoader.load(Unicorn.class))
   all.add(current);
```

A.

```
List<Unicorn> all = ServiceLoader.load(Unicorn.class)
    .getStream()
    .collect(Collectors.toList());
```

B.

```
List<Unicorn> all = ServiceLoader.load(Unicorn.class)
    .stream()
    .collect(Collectors.toList());
```

C.

```
List<Unicorn> all = ServiceLoader.load(Unicorn.class)
    .getStream()
    .map(Provider::get)
    .collect(Collectors.toList());
```

D.

```
List<Unicorn> all = ServiceLoader.load(Unicorn.class)
    .stream()
    .map(Provider::get)
    .collect(Collectors.toList());
```

E.   None of the above

9. Which command can you run to determine whether you have any code in your JAR file that depends on unsupported internal APIs and suggests an alternative?

   A. `jdeps -internal-jdk`
   B. `jdeps --internaljdk`
   C. `jdeps --internal-jdk`
   D. `jdeps -s`
   E. `jdeps -unsupported`
   F. `jdeps -unsupportedapi`
   G. `jdeps -unsupported-api`
   H. None of the above

10. For a top-down migration, all modules other than named modules are _____ modules and on the _____ .

    A. automatic, classpath
    B. automatic, module path
    C. unnamed, classpath
    D. unnamed, module path
    E. None of the above

11. Suppose you have separate modules for a service provider interface, service provider, service locator, and consumer. If you add a second service provider module, how many of these modules do you need to recompile?

   A. Zero

   B. One

   C. Two

   D. Three

   E. Four

12. Which of the following modules contains the `java.util` package? (Choose all that apply.)

   A. `java.all;`

   B. `java.base;`

   C. `java.main;`

   D. `java.util;`

   E. None of the above

13. Suppose you have separate modules for a service provider interface, service provider, service locator, and consumer. Which are true about the directives you need to specify? (Choose all that apply.)

   A. The service provider interface must use the `exports` directive.

   B. The service provider interface must use the `provides` directive.

   C. The service provider interface must use the `requires` directive.

   D. The service provider must use the `exports` directive.

   E. The service provider must use the `provides` directive.

   F. The service provider must use the `requires` directive.

14. Suppose you have a project with one package named `magic.wand` and another project with one package named `magic.potion`. These projects have a circular dependency, so you decide to create a third project named `magic.helper`. The `magic.helper` module has the common code containing a package named `magic.util`. For simplicity, let's give each module the same name as the package. Which of the following need to appear in your `module-info` files? (Choose all that apply.)

   A. `exports magic.potion;` in the potion project

   B. `exports magic.util;` in the magic helper project

   C. `exports magic.wand;` in the wand project

   D. `requires magic.util;` in the magic helper project

   E. `requires magic.util;` in the potion project

   F. `requires magic.util;` in the wand project

15. Suppose you have separate modules for a service provider interface, service provider, service locator, and consumer. Which module(s) need to specify a `requires` directive on the service provider?

   A. Service locator

   B. Service provider interface

   C. Consumer

   D. Consumer and service locator

   E. Consumer and service provider

   F. Service locator and service provider interface

   G. Consumer, service locator, and service provider interface

   H. None of the above

16. Which are true statements about a package in a JAR on the classpath containing a `module-info` file? (Choose all that apply.)

   A. It is possible to make it available to all other modules on the classpath.

   B. It is possible to make it available to all other modules on the module path.

   C. It is possible to make it available to exactly one other specific module on the classpath.

   D. It is possible to make it available to exactly one other specific module on the module path.

   E. It is possible to make sure it is not available to any other modules on the classpath.

17. Which are true statements? (Choose all that apply.)

   A. An automatic module exports all packages to named modules.

   B. An automatic module exports only the specified packages to named modules.

   C. An automatic module exports no packages to named modules.

   D. An unnamed module exports only the named packages to named modules.

   E. An unnamed module exports all packages to named modules.

   F. An unnamed module exports no packages to named modules.

18. Suppose you have separate modules for a service provider interface, service provider, service locator, and consumer. Which statements are true about the directives you need to specify? (Choose all that apply.)

   A. The consumer must use the `requires` directive.

   B. The consumer must use the `uses` directive.

   C. The service locator must use the `requires` directive.

   D. The service locator must use the `uses` directive.

19. Which statement is true about the `jdeps` command? (Choose all that apply.)

A. It can provide information about dependencies on the class level only.

B. It can provide information about dependencies on the package level only.

C. It can provide information about dependencies on the class or package level.

D. It can run only against a named module.

E. It can run against a regular JAR.

20. Suppose we have a JAR file named `cat-1.2.3-RC1.jar` and `Automatic-Module-Name` in the `MANIFEST.MF` is set to dog. What should an unnamed module referencing this automatic module include in the `module-info.java`?

A. `requires cat;`

B. `requires cat.RC;`

C. `requires cat-RC;`

D. `requires dog;`

E. None of the above

Chapter 18

Concurrency

OCP EXAM OBJECTIVES COVERED IN THIS CHAPTER:

✓ **Concurrency**

- Create worker threads using Runnable, Callable and use an ExecutorService to concurrently execute tasks

- Use java.util.concurrent collections and classes including CyclicBarrier and CopyOnWriteArrayList

- Write thread-safe code

- Identify threading problems such as deadlocks and livelocks

✓ **Parallel Streams**

- Develop code that uses parallel streams

- Implement decomposition and reduction with streams

As you will learn in Chapter 19, "I/O," Chapter 20 "NIO.2," and Chapter 21, "JDBC," computers are capable of reading and writing data to external resources. Unfortunately, as compared to CPU operations, these disk/network operations tend to be extremely slow—so slow, in fact, that if your computer's operating system were to stop and wait for every disk or network operation to finish, your computer would appear to freeze or lock up constantly.

Luckily, all modern operating systems support what is known as *multithreaded processing*. The idea behind multithreaded processing is to allow an application or group of applications to execute multiple tasks at the same time. This allows tasks waiting for other resources to give way to other processing requests.

Since its early days, Java has supported multithreaded programming using the Thread class. More recently, the Concurrency API was introduced. It included numerous classes for performing complex thread-based tasks. The idea was simple: managing complex thread interactions is quite difficult for even the most skilled developers; therefore, a set of reusable features was created. The Concurrency API has grown over the years to include numerous classes and frameworks to assist you in developing complex, multithreaded applications. In this chapter, we will introduce you to the concept of threads and provide numerous ways to manage threads using the Concurrency API.

Threads and concurrency tend to be one of the more challenging topics for many programmers to grasp, as problems with threads can be frustrating even for veteran developers to understand. In practice, concurrency issues are among the most difficult problems to diagnose and resolve.

Previous Java certification exams expected you to know details about threads, such as thread life cycles. The 1Z0-816 exam instead covers the basics of threads but focuses more on your knowledge of the Concurrency API. Since we believe that you need to walk before you can run, we provide a basic overview of threads in the first part of this chapter. Be sure you understand the basics of threads both for exam questions and so you better understand the Concurrency API used throughout the rest of the chapter.

Introducing Threads

We begin this chapter by reviewing common terminology associated with threads. A *thread* is the smallest unit of execution that can be scheduled by the operating system. A *process* is a group of associated threads that execute in the same, shared environment. It follows, then, that a *single-threaded process* is one that contains exactly one thread, whereas a *multithreaded process* is one that contains one or more threads.

By *shared environment*, we mean that the threads in the same process share the same memory space and can communicate directly with one another. Refer to Figure 18.1 for an overview of threads and their shared environment within a process.

FIGURE 18.1   Process model

Figure 18.1 shows a single process with three threads. It also shows how they are mapped to an arbitrary number of *n* CPUs available within the system. Keep this diagram in mind when we discuss task schedulers later in this section.

In this chapter, we will talk a lot about tasks and their relationships to threads. A *task* is a single unit of work performed by a thread. Throughout this chapter, a task will commonly be implemented as a lambda expression. A thread can complete multiple independent tasks but only one task at a time.

By shared memory in Figure 18.1, we are generally referring to `static` variables, as well as instance and local variables passed to a thread. Yes, you will finally see how `static` variables can be useful for performing complex, multithreaded tasks! Remember from Chapter 7, "Methods and Encapsulation" that `static` methods and variables are defined on a single class object that all instances share. For example, if one thread updates the value of a `static` object, then this information is immediately available for other threads within the process to read.

Distinguishing Thread Types

It might surprise you that all Java applications, including all of the ones that we have presented in this book, are all multithreaded. Even a simple Java application that prints Hello World to the screen is multithreaded. To help you understand this, we introduce the concepts of system threads and user-defined threads.

A *system thread* is created by the JVM and runs in the background of the application. For example, the garbage collection is managed by a system thread that is created by the JVM and runs in the background, helping to free memory that is no longer in use. For the most part, the execution of system-defined threads is invisible to the application developer. When a system-defined thread encounters a problem and cannot recover, such as running out of memory, it generates a Java Error, as opposed to an Exception.

> As discussed in Chapter 16, "Exceptions, Assertions, and Localization," even though it is possible to catch an Error, it is considered a poor practice to do so, since it is rare that an application can recover from a system-level failure.

Alternatively, a *user-defined thread* is one created by the application developer to accomplish a specific task. With the exception of parallel streams presented briefly in Chapter 15, "Functional Programming," all of the applications that we have created up to this point have been multithreaded, but they contained only one user-defined thread, which calls the main() method. For simplicity, we commonly refer to threads that contain only a single user-defined thread as a single-threaded application, since we are often uninterested in the system threads.

> Although not required knowledge for the exam, a *daemon thread* is one that will not prevent the JVM from exiting when the program finishes. A Java application terminates when the only threads that are running are daemon threads. For example, if garbage collection is the only thread left running, the JVM will automatically shut down. Both system and user-defined threads can be marked as daemon threads.

Understanding Thread Concurrency

At the start of the chapter, we mentioned that multithreaded processing allows operating systems to execute threads at the same time. The property of executing multiple threads and processes at the same time is referred to as *concurrency*. Of course, with a single-core CPU system, only one task is actually executing at a given time. Even in multicore or multi-CPU systems, there are often far more threads than CPU processors available. How does the system decide what to execute when there are multiple threads available?

Operating systems use a *thread scheduler* to determine which threads should be currently executing, as shown in Figure 18.1. For example, a thread scheduler may employ a *round-robin schedule* in which each available thread receives an equal number of CPU cycles with which to execute, with threads visited in a circular order. If there are 10 available threads, they might each get 100 milliseconds in which to execute, with the process returning to the first thread after the last thread has executed.

When a thread's allotted time is complete but the thread has not finished processing, a context switch occurs. A *context switch* is the process of storing a thread's current state and later restoring the state of the thread to continue execution. Be aware that there is often a cost associated with a context switch by way of lost time saving and reloading a thread's state. Intelligent thread schedules do their best to minimize the number of context switches, while keeping an application running smoothly.

Finally, a thread can interrupt or supersede another thread if it has a higher thread priority than the other thread. A *thread priority* is a numeric value associated with a thread that is taken into consideration by the thread scheduler when determining which threads should currently be executing. In Java, thread priorities are specified as integer values.

 Real World Scenario

The Importance of Thread Scheduling

Even though multicore CPUs are quite common these days, single-core CPUs were the standard in personal computing for many decades. During this time, operating systems developed complex thread-scheduling and context-switching algorithms that allowed users to execute dozens or even hundreds of threads on a single-core CPU system. These scheduling algorithms allowed users to experience the illusion that multiple tasks were being performed at the same time within a single-CPU system. For example, a user could listen to music while writing a paper and receive notifications for new messages.

Since the number of threads requested often far outweighs the number of processors available even in multicore systems, these thread-scheduling algorithms are still employed in operating systems today.

Defining a Task with *Runnable*

As we mentioned in Chapter 15, java.lang.Runnable is a functional interface that takes no arguments and returns no data. The following is the definition of the Runnable interface:

```
@FunctionalInterface public interface Runnable {
    void run();
}
```

The Runnable interface is commonly used to define the task or work a thread will execute, separate from the main application thread. We will be relying on the Runnable interface throughout this chapter, especially when we discuss applying parallel operations to streams.

The following lambda expressions each implement the Runnable interface:

```
Runnable sloth = () -> System.out.println("Hello World");
Runnable snake = () -> {int i=10; i++;};
Runnable beaver = () -> {return;};
Runnable coyote = () -> {};
```

Notice that all of these lambda expressions start with a set of empty parentheses, (). Also, none of the lambda expressions returns a value. The following lambdas, while valid for other functional interfaces, are not compatible with Runnable because they return a value.

```
Runnable capybara = () -> "";              // DOES NOT COMPILE
Runnable Hippopotamus = () -> 5;           // DOES NOT COMPILE
Runnable emu = () -> {return new Object();}; // DOES NOT COMPILE
```

Creating *Runnable* Classes

Even though Runnable is a functional interface, many classes implement it directly, as shown in the following code:

```
public class CalculateAverage implements Runnable {
   public void run() {
      // Define work here
   }
}
```

It is also useful if you need to pass information to your Runnable object to be used by the run() method, such as in the following constructor:

```
public class CalculateAverages implements Runnable {
   private double[] scores;
   public CalculateAverages(double[] scores) {
      this.scores = scores;
   }
   public void run() {
      // Define work here that uses the scores object
   }
}
```

In this chapter, we focus on creating lambda expressions that implicitly implement the Runnable interface. Just be aware that it is commonly used in class definitions.

Creating a Thread

The simplest way to execute a thread is by using the `java.lang.Thread` class. Executing a task with `Thread` is a two-step process. First, you define the `Thread` with the corresponding task to be done. Then, you start the task by using the `Thread.start()` method.

As we will discuss later in the chapter, Java does not provide any guarantees about the order in which a thread will be processed once it is started. It may be executed immediately or delayed for a significant amount of time.

 Remember that order of thread execution is not often guaranteed. The exam commonly presents questions in which multiple tasks are started at the same time, and you must determine the result.

Defining the task that a `Thread` instance will execute can be done two ways in Java:

- Provide a `Runnable` object or lambda expression to the `Thread` constructor.
- Create a class that extends `Thread` and overrides the `run()` method.

The following are examples of these techniques:

```java
public class PrintData implements Runnable {
   @Override public void run() { // Overrides method in Runnable
      for(int i = 0; i < 3; i++)
         System.out.println("Printing record: "+i);
   }
   public static void main(String[] args) {
      (new Thread(new PrintData())).start();
   }
}

public class ReadInventoryThread extends Thread {
   @Override public void run() { // Overrides method in Thread
      System.out.println("Printing zoo inventory");
   }
   public static void main(String[] args) {
      (new ReadInventoryThread()).start();
   }
}
```

The first example creates a `Thread` using a `Runnable` instance, while the second example uses the less common practice of extending the `Thread` class and overriding the `run()` method. Anytime you create a `Thread` instance, make sure that you remember to start the task with the `Thread.start()` method. This starts the task in a separate operating system thread.

Let's try this. What is the output of the following code snippet using these two classes?

```
2: public static void main(String[] args) {
3:     System.out.println("begin");
4:     (new ReadInventoryThread()).start();
5:     (new Thread(new PrintData())).start();
6:     (new ReadInventoryThread()).start();
7:     System.out.println("end");
8: }
```

The answer is that it is unknown until runtime. The following is just one possible output:

```
begin
Printing zoo inventory
Printing record: 0
end
Printing zoo inventory
Printing record: 1
Printing record: 2
```

This sample uses a total of four threads—the main() user thread and three additional threads created on lines 4–6. Each thread created on these lines is executed as an asynchronous task. By *asynchronous*, we mean that the thread executing the main() method does not wait for the results of each newly created thread before continuing. For example, lines 5 and 6 may be executed before the thread created on line 4 finishes. The opposite of this behavior is a *synchronous* task in which the program waits (or blocks) on line 4 for the thread to finish executing before moving on to the next line. The vast majority of method calls used in this book have been synchronous up until now.

While the order of thread execution once the threads have been started is indeterminate, the order within a single thread is still linear. In particular, the for() loop in PrintData is still ordered. Also, begin appears before end in the main() method.

Calling *run()* Instead of *start()*

Be careful with code that attempts to start a thread by calling run() instead of start(). Calling run() on a Thread or a Runnable does not actually start a new thread. While the following code snippets will compile, none will actually execute a task on a separate thread:

```
System.out.println("begin");
(new ReadInventoryThread()).run();
(new Thread(new PrintData())).run();
(new ReadInventoryThread()).run();
System.out.println("end");
```

Unlike the previous example, each line of this code will wait until the run() method is complete before moving on to the next line. Also unlike the previous program, the output for this code sample will be the same each time it is executed.

In general, you should extend the Thread class only under specific circumstances, such as when you are creating your own priority-based thread. In most situations, you should implement the Runnable interface rather than extend the Thread class.

We conclude our discussion of the Thread class here. While previous versions of the exam were quite focused on understanding the difference between extending Thread and implementing Runnable, the exam now strongly encourages developers to use the Concurrency API.

For the exam, you also do not need to know about other thread-related methods, such as Object.wait(), Object.notify(), Thread.join(), etc. In fact, you should avoid them in general and use the Concurrency API as much as possible. It takes a large amount of skill (and some luck!) to use these methods correctly.

 Real World Scenario

For Interviews, Be Familiar with Thread-Creation Options

Despite that the exam no longer focuses on creating threads by extending the Thread class and implementing the Runnable interface, it is extremely common when interviewing for a Java development position to be asked to explain the difference between extending the Thread class and implementing Runnable.

If asked this question, you should answer it accurately. You should also mention that you can now create and manage threads indirectly using an ExecutorService, which we will discuss in the next section.

Polling with Sleep

Even though multithreaded programming allows you to execute multiple tasks at the same time, one thread often needs to wait for the results of another thread to proceed. One solution is to use polling. *Polling* is the process of intermittently checking data at some fixed interval. For example, let's say you have a thread that modifies a shared static counter value and your main() thread is waiting for the thread to increase the value to greater than 100, as shown in the following class:

```
public class CheckResults {
    private static int counter = 0;
    public static void main(String[] args) {
        new Thread(() -> {
            for(int i = 0; i < 500; i++) CheckResults.counter++;
        }).start();
```

```
        while(CheckResults.counter < 100) {
            System.out.println("Not reached yet");
        }
        System.out.println("Reached!");
    }
}
```

How many times does this program print Not reached yet? The answer is, we don't know! It could output zero, ten, or a million times. If our thread scheduler is particularly poor, it could operate infinitely! Using a while() loop to check for data without some kind of delay is considered a bad coding practice as it ties up CPU resources for no reason.

We can improve this result by using the Thread.sleep() method to implement polling. The Thread.sleep() method requests the current thread of execution rest for a specified number of milliseconds. When used inside the body of the main() method, the thread associated with the main() method will pause, while the separate thread will continue to run. Compare the previous implementation with the following one that uses Thread.sleep():

```
public class CheckResults {
    private static int counter = 0;
    public static void main(String[] a) throws InterruptedException {
        new Thread(() -> {
            for(int i = 0; i < 500; i++) CheckResults.counter++;
        }).start();
        while(CheckResults.counter < 100) {
            System.out.println("Not reached yet");
            Thread.sleep(1000); // 1 SECOND
        }
        System.out.println("Reached!");
    }
}
```

In this example, we delay 1,000 milliseconds at the end of the loop, or 1 second. While this may seem like a small amount, we have now prevented a possibly infinite loop from executing and locking up our program. Notice that we also changed the signature of the main() method, since Thread.sleep() throws the checked InterruptedException. Alternatively, we could have wrapped each call to the Thread.sleep() method in a try/catch block.

How many times does the while() loop execute in this revised class? Still unknown! While polling does prevent the CPU from being overwhelmed with a potentially infinite loop, it does not guarantee when the loop will terminate. For example, the separate thread could be losing CPU time to a higher-priority process, resulting in multiple executions of the while() loop before it finishes.

Another issue to be concerned about is the shared counter variable. What if one thread is reading the counter variable while another thread is writing it? The thread reading the shared variable may end up with an invalid or incorrect value. We will discuss these issues in detail in the upcoming section on writing thread-safe code.

Creating Threads with the Concurrency API

Java includes the Concurrency API to handle the complicated work of managing threads for you. The Concurrency API includes the ExecutorService interface, which defines services that create and manage threads for you.

You first obtain an instance of an ExecutorService interface, and then you send the service tasks to be processed. The framework includes numerous useful features, such as thread pooling and scheduling. It is recommended that you use this framework anytime you need to create and execute a separate task, even if you need only a single thread.

Introducing the Single-Thread Executor

Since ExecutorService is an interface, how do you obtain an instance of it? The Concurrency API includes the Executors factory class that can be used to create instances of the ExecutorService object. As you may remember from Chapter 16, the factory pattern is a creational pattern in which the underlying implementation details of the object creation are hidden from us. You will see the factory pattern used again throughout Chapter 20.

Let's start with a simple example using the newSingleThreadExecutor() method to obtain an ExecutorService instance and the execute() method to perform asynchronous tasks.

```java
import java.util.concurrent.*;
public class ZooInfo {
   public static void main(String[] args) {
      ExecutorService service = null;
      Runnable task1 = () ->
         System.out.println("Printing zoo inventory");
      Runnable task2 = () -> {for(int i = 0; i < 3; i++)
            System.out.println("Printing record: "+i);};
      try {
         service = Executors.newSingleThreadExecutor();
         System.out.println("begin");
         service.execute(task1);
         service.execute(task2);
         service.execute(task1);
         System.out.println("end");
      } finally {
         if(service != null) service.shutdown();
      }
   }
}
```

As you may notice, this is just a rewrite of our earlier `PrintData` and `ReadInventoryThread` classes to use lambda expressions and an `ExecutorService` instance.

In this example, we use the `Executors.newSingleThreadExecutor()` method to create the service. Unlike our earlier example, in which we had three extra threads for newly created tasks, this example uses only one, which means that the threads will order their results. For example, the following is a possible output for this code snippet:

```
begin
Printing zoo inventory
Printing record: 0
Printing record: 1
end
Printing record: 2
Printing zoo inventory
```

With a single-thread executor, results are guaranteed to be executed sequentially. Notice that the end text is output while our thread executor tasks are still running. This is because the `main()` method is still an independent thread from the `ExecutorService`.

Shutting Down a Thread Executor

Once you have finished using a thread executor, it is important that you call the `shutdown()` method. A thread executor creates a non-daemon thread on the first task that is executed, so failing to call `shutdown()` will result in your application never terminating.

The shutdown process for a thread executor involves first rejecting any new tasks submitted to the thread executor while continuing to execute any previously submitted tasks. During this time, calling `isShutdown()` will return `true`, while `isTerminated()` will return `false`. If a new task is submitted to the thread executor while it is shutting down, a `RejectedExecutionException` will be thrown. Once all active tasks have been completed, `isShutdown()` and `isTerminated()` will both return `true`. Figure 18.2 shows the life cycle of an `ExecutorService` object.

FIGURE 18.2   ExecutorService life cycle

For the exam, you should be aware that shutdown() does not actually stop any tasks that have already been submitted to the thread executor.

What if you want to cancel all running and upcoming tasks? The ExecutorService provides a method called shutdownNow(), which *attempts to stop* all running tasks and discards any that have not been started yet. It is possible to create a thread that will never terminate, so any attempt to interrupt it may be ignored. Lastly, shutdownNow() returns a List<Runnable> of tasks that were submitted to the thread executor but that were never started.

As you learned in Chapter 16, resources such as thread executors should be properly closed to prevent memory leaks. Unfortunately, the ExecutorService interface does not extend the AutoCloseable interface, so you cannot use a try-with-resources statement. You can still use a finally block, as we do throughout this chapter. While not required, it is considered a good practice to do so.

Submitting Tasks

You can submit tasks to an ExecutorService instance multiple ways. The first method we presented, execute(), is inherited from the Executor interface, which the ExecutorService interface extends. The execute() method takes a Runnable lambda expression or instance and completes the task asynchronously. Because the return type of the method is void, it does not tell us anything about the result of the task. It is considered a "fire-and-forget" method, as once it is submitted, the results are not directly available to the calling thread.

Fortunately, the writers of Java added submit() methods to the ExecutorService interface, which, like execute(), can be used to complete tasks asynchronously. Unlike execute(), though, submit() returns a Future instance that can be used to determine whether the task is complete. It can also be used to return a generic result object after the task has been completed.

Table 18.1 shows the five methods, including execute() and two submit() methods, which you should know for the exam. Don't worry if you haven't seen Future or Callable before; we will discuss them in detail shortly.

In practice, using the submit() method is quite similar to using the execute() method, except that the submit() method returns a Future instance that can be used to determine whether the task has completed execution.

TABLE 18.1 ExecutorService methods

Method name	Description
`void execute(Runnable command)`	Executes a Runnable task at some point in the future
`Future<?> submit(Runnable task)`	Executes a Runnable task at some point in the future and returns a Future representing the task
`<T> Future<T> submit(Callable<T> task)`	Executes a Callable task at some point in the future and returns a Future representing the pending results of the task
`<T> List<Future<T>> invokeAll(Collection<? extends Callable<T>> tasks) throws InterruptedException`	Executes the given tasks and waits for all tasks to complete. Returns a List of Future instances, in the same order they were in the original collection
`<T> T invokeAny(Collection<? extends Callable<T>> tasks) throws InterruptedException, ExecutionException`	Executes the given tasks and waits for at least one to complete. Returns a Future instance for a complete task and cancels any unfinished tasks

---

Submitting Tasks: *execute()* vs. *submit()*

As you might have noticed, the execute() and submit() methods are nearly identical when applied to Runnable expressions. The submit() method has the obvious advantage of doing the same thing execute() does, but with a return object that can be used to track the result. Because of this advantage and the fact that execute() does not support Callable expressions, we tend to prefer submit() over execute(), even if you don't store the Future reference. Therefore, we use submit() in the majority of the examples in this chapter.

For the exam, you need to be familiar with both execute() and submit(), but in your own code we recommend submit() over execute() whenever possible.

Waiting for Results

How do we know when a task submitted to an ExecutorService is complete? As mentioned in the previous section, the submit() method returns a java.util.concurrent.Future<V> instance that can be used to determine this result.

```
Future<?> future = service.submit(() -> System.out.println("Hello"));
```

The Future type is actually an interface. For the exam, you don't need to know any of the classes that implement Future, just that a Future instance is returned by various API methods. Table 18.2 includes useful methods for determining the state of a task.

TABLE 18.2   Future methods

Method name	Description
boolean isDone()	Returns true if the task was completed, threw an exception, or was cancelled
boolean isCancelled()	Returns true if the task was cancelled before it completed normally
boolean cancel(boolean mayInterruptIfRunning)	Attempts to cancel execution of the task and returns true if it was successfully cancelled or false if it could not be cancelled or is complete
V get()	Retrieves the result of a task, waiting endlessly if it is not yet available
V get(long timeout, TimeUnit unit)	Retrieves the result of a task, waiting the specified amount of time. If the result is not ready by the time the timeout is reached, a checked TimeoutException will be thrown.

The following is an updated version of our earlier polling example CheckResults class, which uses a Future instance to wait for the results:

```
import java.util.concurrent.*;
public class CheckResults {
   private static int counter = 0;
   public static void main(String[] unused) throws Exception {
      ExecutorService service = null;
      try {
         service = Executors.newSingleThreadExecutor();
         Future<?> result = service.submit(() -> {
            for(int i = 0; i < 500; i++) CheckResults.counter++;
         });
         result.get(10, TimeUnit.SECONDS);
         System.out.println("Reached!");
      } catch (TimeoutException e) {
         System.out.println("Not reached in time");
      } finally {
         if(service != null) service.shutdown();
      } } }
```

This example is similar to our earlier polling implementation, but it does not use the Thread class directly. In part, this is the essence of the Concurrency API: to do complex things with threads without having to manage threads directly. It also waits at most 10 seconds, throwing a TimeoutException on the call to result.get() if the task is not done.

What is the return value of this task? As Future<V> is a generic interface, the type V is determined by the return type of the Runnable method. Since the return type of Runnable.run() is void, the get() method always returns null when working with Runnable expressions.

The Future.get() method can take an optional value and enum type java.util.concurrent.TimeUnit. We present the full list of TimeUnit values in Table 18.3 in increasing order of duration. Numerous methods in the Concurrency API use the TimeUnit enum.

TABLE 18.3   TimeUnit values

Enum name	Description
TimeUnit.NANOSECONDS	Time in one-billionth of a second (1/1,000,000,000)
TimeUnit.MICROSECONDS	Time in one-millionth of a second (1/1,000,000)
TimeUnit.MILLISECONDS	Time in one-thousandth of a second (1/1,000)
TimeUnit.SECONDS	Time in seconds
TimeUnit.MINUTES	Time in minutes
TimeUnit.HOURS	Time in hours
TimeUnit.DAYS	Time in days

Introducing *Callable*

The java.util.concurrent.Callable functional interface is similar to Runnable except that its call() method returns a value and can throw a checked exception. The following is the definition of the Callable interface:

```
@FunctionalInterface public interface Callable<V> {
   V call() throws Exception;
}
```

The Callable interface is often preferable over Runnable, since it allows more details to be retrieved easily from the task after it is completed. That said, we use both interfaces throughout this chapter, as they are interchangeable in situations where the lambda does not throw an exception and there is no return type. Luckily, the ExecutorService includes an overloaded version of the submit() method that takes a Callable object and returns a generic Future<T> instance.

Unlike Runnable, in which the get() methods always return null, the get() methods on a Future instance return the matching generic type (which could also be a null value).

Let's take a look at an example using Callable.

```java
import java.util.concurrent.*;
public class AddData {
    public static void main(String[] args) throws Exception {
        ExecutorService service = null;
        try {
            service = Executors.newSingleThreadExecutor();
            Future<Integer> result = service.submit(() -> 30 + 11);
            System.out.println(result.get());    // 41
        } finally {
            if(service != null) service.shutdown();
        }
    }
}
```

The results could have also been obtained using Runnable and some shared, possibly static, object, although this solution that relies on Callable is a lot simpler and easier to follow.

Waiting for All Tasks to Finish

After submitting a set of tasks to a thread executor, it is common to wait for the results. As you saw in the previous sections, one solution is to call get() on each Future object returned by the submit() method. If we don't need the results of the tasks and are finished using our thread executor, there is a simpler approach.

First, we shut down the thread executor using the shutdown() method. Next, we use the awaitTermination() method available for all thread executors. The method waits the specified time to complete all tasks, returning sooner if all tasks finish or an InterruptedException is detected. You can see an example of this in the following code snippet:

```java
ExecutorService service = null;
try {
    service = Executors.newSingleThreadExecutor();
    // Add tasks to the thread executor
    ...
```

```
} finally {
   if(service != null) service.shutdown();
}
if(service != null) {
   service.awaitTermination(1, TimeUnit.MINUTES);

   // Check whether all tasks are finished
   if(service.isTerminated()) System.out.println("Finished!");
   else System.out.println("At least one task is still running");
}
```

In this example, we submit a number of tasks to the thread executor and then shut down the thread executor and wait up to one minute for the results. Notice that we can call isTerminated() after the awaitTermination() method finishes to confirm that all tasks are actually finished.

If awaitTermination() is called before shutdown() within the same thread, then that thread will wait the full timeout value sent with awaitTermination().

Submitting Task Collections

The last two methods listed in Table 18.2 that you should know for the exam are invokeAll() and invokeAny(). Both of these methods execute synchronously and take a Collection of tasks. Remember that by synchronous, we mean that unlike the other methods used to submit tasks to a thread executor, these methods will wait until the results are available before returning control to the enclosing program.

The invokeAll() method executes all tasks in a provided collection and returns a List of ordered Future instances, with one Future instance corresponding to each submitted task, in the order they were in the original collection.

```
20: ExecutorService service = ...
21: System.out.println("begin");
22: Callable<String> task = () -> "result";
23: List<Future<String>>  list = service.invokeAll(
24:    List.of(task, task, task));
25: for (Future<String> future : list) {
26:    System.out.println(future.get());
27: }
28: System.out.println("end");
```

In this example, the JVM waits on line 23 for all tasks to finish before moving on to line 25. Unlike our earlier examples, this means that end will always be printed last. Also, even though future.isDone() returns true for each element in the returned List, a task could have completed normally or thrown an exception.

On the other hand, the invokeAny() method executes a collection of tasks and returns the result of one of the tasks that successfully completes execution, cancelling all unfinished tasks. While the first task to finish is often returned, this behavior is not guaranteed, as any completed task can be returned by this method.

```
20: ExecutorService service = ...
21: System.out.println("begin");
22: Callable<String> task = () -> "result";
23: String data = service.invokeAny(List.of(task, task, task));
24: System.out.println(data);
25: System.out.println("end");
```

As before, the JVM waits on line 23 for a completed task before moving on to the next line. The other tasks that did not complete are cancelled.

For the exam, remember that the invokeAll() method will wait indefinitely until all tasks are complete, while the invokeAny() method will wait indefinitely until at least one task completes. The ExecutorService interface also includes overloaded versions of invokeAll() and invokeAny() that take a timeout value and TimeUnit parameter.

Scheduling Tasks

Oftentimes in Java, we need to schedule a task to happen at some future time. We might even need to schedule the task to happen repeatedly, at some set interval. For example, imagine that we want to check the supply of food for zoo animals once an hour and fill it as needed. The ScheduledExecutorService, which is a subinterface of ExecutorService, can be used for just such a task.

Like ExecutorService, we obtain an instance of ScheduledExecutorService using a factory method in the Executors class, as shown in the following snippet:

```
ScheduledExecutorService service
    = Executors.newSingleThreadScheduledExecutor();
```

We could store an instance of ScheduledExecutorService in an ExecutorService variable, although doing so would mean we'd have to cast the object to call any scheduled methods.

Refer to Table 18.4 for our summary of ScheduledExecutorService methods.

TABLE 18.4 ScheduledExecutorService methods

Method Name	Description
schedule(Callable<V> callable, long delay, TimeUnit unit)	Creates and executes a Callable task after the given delay
schedule(Runnable command, long delay, TimeUnit unit)	Creates and executes a Runnable task after the given delay
scheduleAtFixedRate(Runnable command, long initialDelay, long period, TimeUnit unit)	Creates and executes a Runnable task after the given initial delay, creating a new task every period value that passes
scheduleWithFixedDelay(Runnable command, long initialDelay, long delay, TimeUnit unit)	Creates and executes a Runnable task after the given initial delay and subsequently with the given delay between the termination of one execution and the commencement of the next

In practice, these methods are among the most convenient in the Concurrency API, as they perform relatively complex tasks with a single line of code. The delay and period parameters rely on the TimeUnit argument to determine the format of the value, such as seconds or milliseconds.

The first two schedule() methods in Table 18.4 take a Callable or Runnable, respectively; perform the task after some delay; and return a ScheduledFuture instance. The ScheduledFuture interface is identical to the Future interface, except that it includes a getDelay() method that returns the remaining delay. The following uses the schedule() method with Callable and Runnable tasks:

```
ScheduledExecutorService service
    = Executors.newSingleThreadScheduledExecutor();
Runnable task1 = () -> System.out.println("Hello Zoo");
Callable<String> task2 = () -> "Monkey";
ScheduledFuture<?> r1 = service.schedule(task1, 10, TimeUnit.SECONDS);
ScheduledFuture<?> r2 = service.schedule(task2, 8,  TimeUnit.MINUTES);
```

The first task is scheduled 10 seconds in the future, whereas the second task is scheduled 8 minutes in the future.

While these tasks are scheduled in the future, the actual execution may be delayed. For example, there may be no threads available to perform the task, at which point they will just wait in the queue. Also, if the ScheduledExecutorService is shut down by the time the scheduled task execution time is reached, then these tasks will be discarded.

Each of the `ScheduledExecutorService` methods is important and has real-world applications. For example, you can use the `schedule()` command to check on the state of processing a task and send out notifications if it is not finished or even call `schedule()` again to delay processing.

The last two methods in Table 18.4 might be a little confusing if you have not seen them before. Conceptually, they are similar as they both perform the same task repeatedly, after completing some initial delay. The difference is related to the timing of the process and when the next task starts.

The `scheduleAtFixedRate()` method creates a new task and submits it to the executor every period, regardless of whether the previous task finished. The following example executes a `Runnable` task every minute, following an initial five-minute delay:

```
service.scheduleAtFixedRate(command, 5, 1, TimeUnit.MINUTES);
```

The `scheduleAtFixedRate()` method is useful for tasks that need to be run at specific intervals, such as checking the health of the animals once a day. Even if it takes two hours to examine an animal on Monday, this doesn't mean that Tuesday's exam should start any later in the day.

Bad things can happen with `scheduleAtFixedRate()` if each task consistently takes longer to run than the execution interval. Imagine your boss came by your desk every minute and dropped off a piece of paper. Now imagine it took you five minutes to read each piece of paper. Before long, you would be drowning in piles of paper. This is how an executor feels. Given enough time, the program would submit more tasks to the executor service than could fit in memory, causing the program to crash.

On the other hand, the `scheduleWithFixedDelay()` method creates a new task only after the previous task has finished. For example, if a task runs at 12:00 and takes five minutes to finish, with a period between executions of two minutes, then the next task will start at 12:07.

```
service.scheduleWithFixedDelay(command, 0, 2, TimeUnit.MINUTES);
```

The `scheduleWithFixedDelay()` is useful for processes that you want to happen repeatedly but whose specific time is unimportant. For example, imagine that we have a zoo cafeteria worker who periodically restocks the salad bar throughout the day. The process can take 20 minutes or more, since it requires the worker to haul a large number of items from the back room. Once the worker has filled the salad bar with fresh food, he doesn't need to check at some specific time, just after enough time has passed for it to become low on stock again.

If you are familiar with creating Cron jobs in Linux to schedule tasks, then you should know that `scheduleAtFixedRate()` is the closest built-in Java equivalent.

Increasing Concurrency with Pools

All of our examples up until now have been with single-thread executors, which, while interesting, weren't particularly useful. After all, the name of this chapter is "Concurrency," and you can't do a lot of that with a single-thread executor!

We now present three additional factory methods in the Executors class that act on a pool of threads, rather than on a single thread. A *thread pool* is a group of pre-instantiated reusable threads that are available to perform a set of arbitrary tasks. Table 18.5 includes our two previous single-thread executor methods, along with the new ones that you should know for the exam.

TABLE 18.5   Executors factory methods

Method	Description
ExecutorService newSingleThreadExecutor()	Creates a single-threaded executor that uses a single worker thread operating off an unbounded queue. Results are processed sequentially in the order in which they are submitted.
ScheduledExecutorService newSingleThreadScheduledExecutor()	Creates a single-threaded executor that can schedule commands to run after a given delay or to execute periodically
ExecutorService newCachedThreadPool()	Creates a thread pool that creates new threads as needed but will reuse previously constructed threads when they are available
ExecutorService newFixedThreadPool(int)	Creates a thread pool that reuses a fixed number of threads operating off a shared unbounded queue
ScheduledExecutorService newScheduledThreadPool(int)	Creates a thread pool that can schedule commands to run after a given delay or to execute periodically

As shown in Table 18.5, these methods return the same instance types, ExecutorService and ScheduledExecutorService, that we used earlier in this chapter. In other words, all of our previous examples are compatible with these new pooled-thread executors!

The difference between a single-thread and a pooled-thread executor is what happens when a task is already running. While a single-thread executor will wait for a thread to become available before running the next task, a pooled-thread executor can execute the next task concurrently. If the pool runs out of available threads, the task will be queued by the thread executor and wait to be completed.

The newFixedThreadPool() takes a number of threads and allocates them all upon creation. As long as our number of tasks is less than our number of threads, all tasks will be executed concurrently. If at any point the number of tasks exceeds the number of threads in the pool, they will wait in a similar manner as you saw with a single-thread executor. In fact, calling newFixedThreadPool() with a value of 1 is equivalent to calling newSingleThreadExecutor().

The newCachedThreadPool() method will create a thread pool of unbounded size, allocating a new thread anytime one is required or all existing threads are busy. This is commonly used for pools that require executing many short-lived asynchronous tasks. For long-lived processes, usage of this executor is strongly discouraged, as it could grow to encompass a large number of threads over the application life cycle.

The newScheduledThreadPool() is identical to the newFixedThreadPool() method, except that it returns an instance of ScheduledExecutorService and is therefore compatible with scheduling tasks.

 Real World Scenario

Choosing a Pool Size

In practice, choosing an appropriate pool size requires some thought. In general, you want at least a handful more threads than you think you will ever possibly need. On the other hand, you don't want to choose so many threads that your application uses up too many resources or too much CPU processing power. Oftentimes, the number of CPUs available is used to determine the thread pool size using this command:

```
Runtime.getRuntime().availableProcessors()
```

It is a common practice to allocate threads based on the number of CPUs.

Writing Thread-Safe Code

Thread-safety is the property of an object that guarantees safe execution by multiple threads at the same time. Since threads run in a shared environment and memory space, how do we prevent two threads from interfering with each other? We must organize access to data so that we don't end up with invalid or unexpected results.

In this part of the chapter, we show how to use a variety of techniques to protect data including: atomic classes, synchronized blocks, the Lock framework, and cyclic barriers.

Understanding Thread-Safety

Imagine that our zoo has a program to count sheep, preferably one that won't put the zoo workers to sleep! Each zoo worker runs out to a field, adds a new sheep to the flock, counts the total number of sheep, and runs back to us to report the results. We present the following code to represent this conceptually, choosing a thread pool size so that all tasks can be run concurrently:

```java
import java.util.concurrent.*;
public class SheepManager {
   private int sheepCount = 0;
   private void incrementAndReport() {
      System.out.print((++sheepCount)+" ");
   }
   public static void main(String[] args) {
      ExecutorService service = null;
      try {
         service = Executors.newFixedThreadPool(20);
         SheepManager manager = new SheepManager();
         for(int i = 0; i < 10; i++)
            service.submit(() -> manager.incrementAndReport());
      } finally {
         if(service != null) service.shutdown();
      }
   }
}
```

What does this program output? You might think it will output numbers from 1 to 10, in order, but that is far from guaranteed. It may output in a different order. Worse yet, it may print some numbers twice and not print some numbers at all! The following are all possible outputs of this program:

```
1 2 3 4 5 6 7 8 9 10
1 9 8 7 3 6 6 2 4 5
1 8 7 3 2 6 5 4 2 9
```

So, what went wrong? In this example, we use the pre-increment (++) operator to update the sheepCount variable. A problem occurs when two threads both execute the right side of the expression, reading the "old" value before either thread writes the "new" value of the variable. The two assignments become redundant; they both assign the same new value, with one thread overwriting the results of the other. Figure 18.3 demonstrates this problem with two threads, assuming that sheepCount has a starting value of 1.

You can see in Figure 18.3 that both threads read and write the same values, causing one of the two ++sheepCount operations to be lost. Therefore, the increment operator ++ is not thread-safe. As you will see later in this chapter, the unexpected result of two tasks executing at the same time is referred to as a *race condition*.

Conceptually, the idea here is that some zoo workers may run faster on their way to the field but more slowly on their way back and report late. Other workers may get to the field last but somehow be the first ones back to report the results.

FIGURE 18.3   Lack of thread synchronization

Protecting Data with Atomic Classes

One way to improve our sheep counting example is to use the java.util.concurrent.atomic package. As with many of the classes in the Concurrency API, these classes exist to make your life easier.

In our first SheepManager sample output, the same values were printed twice, with the highest counter being 9 instead of 10. As we demonstrated in the previous section, the increment operator ++ is not thread-safe. Furthermore, the reason that it is not thread-safe is that the operation is not atomic, carrying out two tasks, read and write, that can be interrupted by other threads.

Atomic is the property of an operation to be carried out as a single unit of execution without any interference by another thread. A thread-safe atomic version of the increment operator would be one that performed the read and write of the variable as a single operation, not allowing any other threads to access the variable during the operation. Figure 18.4 shows the result of making the sheepCount variable atomic.

Figure 18.4 resembles our earlier Figure 18.3, except that reading and writing the data is atomic with regard to the sheepCount variable. Any thread trying to access the sheepCount variable while an atomic operation is in process will have to wait until the atomic operation on the variable is complete. Conceptually, this is like setting a rule for our zoo workers that there can be only one employee in the field at a time, although they may not each report their result in order.

Since accessing primitives and references in Java is common in shared environments, the Concurrency API includes numerous useful classes that are conceptually the same as our primitive classes but that support atomic operations. Table 18.6 lists the atomic classes with which you should be familiar for the exam.

FIGURE 18.4   Thread synchronization using atomic operations

TABLE 18.6   Atomic classes

Class Name	Description
AtomicBoolean	A boolean value that may be updated atomically
AtomicInteger	An int value that may be updated atomically
AtomicLong	A long value that may be updated atomically

How do we use an atomic class? Each class includes numerous methods that are equivalent to many of the primitive built-in operators that we use on primitives, such as the assignment operator (=) and the increment operators (++). We describe the common atomic methods that you should know for the exam in Table 18.7.

In the following example, we update our `SheepManager` class with an `AtomicInteger`:

```
private AtomicInteger sheepCount = new AtomicInteger(0);
private void incrementAndReport() {
   System.out.print(sheepCount.incrementAndGet()+" ");
}
```

How does this implementation differ from our previous examples? When we run this modification, we get varying output, such as the following:

```
2 3 1 4 5 6 7 8 9 10
1 4 3 2 5 6 7 8 9 10
1 4 3 5 6 2 7 8 10 9
```

Unlike our previous sample output, the numbers 1 through 10 will always be printed, although the order is still not guaranteed. Don't worry, we'll address that issue shortly. The key in this section is that using the atomic classes ensures that the data is consistent between workers and that no values are lost due to concurrent modifications.

TABLE 18.7   Common atomic methods

Method name	Description
get()	Retrieves the current value
set()	Sets the given value, equivalent to the assignment = operator
getAndSet()	Atomically sets the new value and returns the old value
incrementAndGet()	For numeric classes, atomic pre-increment operation equivalent to ++value
getAndIncrement()	For numeric classes, atomic post-increment operation equivalent to value++
decrementAndGet()	For numeric classes, atomic pre-decrement operation equivalent to --value
getAndDecrement()	For numeric classes, atomic post-decrement operation equivalent to value--

Improving Access with Synchronized Blocks

While atomic classes are great at protecting single variables, they aren't particularly useful if you need to execute a series of commands or call a method. How do we improve the results so that each worker is able to increment and report the results in order? The most common technique is to use a monitor, also called a *lock*, to synchronize access. A *monitor* is a structure that supports *mutual exclusion*, which is the property that at most one thread is executing a particular segment of code at a given time.

In Java, any Object can be used as a monitor, along with the synchronized keyword, as shown in the following example:

```
SheepManager manager = new SheepManager();
synchronized(manager) {
    // Work to be completed by one thread at a time
}
```

This example is referred to as a *synchronized block*. Each thread that arrives will first check if any threads are in the block. In this manner, a thread "acquires the lock" for the monitor. If the lock is available, a single thread will enter the block, acquiring the lock and preventing all other threads from entering. While the first thread is executing the block, all threads that arrive will attempt to acquire the same lock and wait for the first thread to finish. Once a thread finishes executing the block, it will release the lock, allowing one of the waiting threads to proceed.

To synchronize access across multiple threads, each thread must have access to the same `Object`. For example, synchronizing on different objects would not actually order the results.

Let's revisit our `SheepManager` example and see whether we can improve the results so that each worker increments and outputs the counter in order. Let's say that we replaced our `for()` loop with the following implementation:

```
for(int i = 0; i < 10; i++) {
   synchronized(manager) {
      service.submit(() -> manager.incrementAndReport());
   }
}
```

Does this solution fix the problem? No, it does not! Can you spot the problem? We've synchronized the *creation* of the threads but not the *execution* of the threads. In this example, each thread would be created one at a time, but they may all still execute and perform their work at the same time, resulting in the same type of output that you saw earlier. Diagnosing and resolving threading problems is often one of the most difficult tasks in any programming language.

We now present a corrected version of the `SheepManager` class, which does order the workers.

```
import java.util.concurrent.*;
public class SheepManager {
   private int sheepCount = 0;
   private void incrementAndReport() {
      synchronized(this) {
         System.out.print((++sheepCount)+" ");
      }
   }
   public static void main(String[] args) {
      ExecutorService service = null;
      try {
         service = Executors.newFixedThreadPool(20);
         var manager = new SheepManager();
         for(int i = 0; i < 10; i++)
```

```
            service.submit(() -> manager.incrementAndReport());
    } finally {
        if(service != null) service.shutdown();
    }
  }
}
```

When this code executes, it will consistently output the following:

1 2 3 4 5 6 7 8 9 10

Although all threads are still created and executed at the same time, they each wait at the synchronized block for the worker to increment and report the result before entering. In this manner, each zoo worker waits for the previous zoo worker to come back before running out on the field. While it's random which zoo worker will run out next, it is guaranteed that there will be at most one on the field and that the results will be reported in order.

We could have synchronized on any object, so long as it was the same object. For example, the following code snippet would have also worked:

```
private final Object herd = new Object();
private void incrementAndReport() {
    synchronized(herd) {
        System.out.print((++sheepCount)+" ");
    }
}
```

Although we didn't need to make the herd variable final, doing so ensures that it is not reassigned after threads start using it.

We could have used an atomic variable along with the synchronized block in this example, although it is unnecessary. Since synchronized blocks allow only one thread to enter, we're not gaining any improvement by using an atomic variable if the only time that we access the variable is within a synchronized block.

Synchronizing on Methods

In the previous example, we established our monitor using synchronized(this) around the body of the method. Java actually provides a more convenient compiler enhancement for doing so. We can add the synchronized modifier to any instance method to synchronize automatically on the object itself. For example, the following two method definitions are equivalent:

```
private void incrementAndReport() {
    synchronized(this) {
        System.out.print((++sheepCount)+" ");
    }
}
```

```java
private synchronized void incrementAndReport() {
    System.out.print((++sheepCount)+" ");
}
```

The first uses a synchronized block, whereas the second uses the synchronized method modifier. Which you use is completely up to you.

We can also apply the synchronized modifier to static methods. What object is used as the monitor when we synchronize on a static method? The class object, of course! For example, the following two methods are equivalent for static synchronization inside our SheepManager class:

```java
public static void printDaysWork() {
    synchronized(SheepManager.class) {
        System.out.print("Finished work");
    }
}
public static synchronized void printDaysWork() {
    System.out.print("Finished work");
}
```

As before, the first uses a synchronized block, with the second example using the synchronized modifier. You can use static synchronization if you need to order thread access across all instances, rather than a single instance.

Avoid Synchronization Whenever Possible

Correctly using the synchronized keyword can be quite challenging, especially if the data you are trying to protect is available to dozens of methods. Even when the data is protected, though, the performance cost for using it can be high.

In this chapter, we present many classes within the Concurrency API that are a lot easier to use and more performant than synchronization. Some you have seen already, like the atomic classes, and others we'll be covering shortly, including the Lock framework, concurrent collections, and cyclic barriers.

While you may not be familiar with all of the classes in the Concurrency API, you should study them carefully if you are writing a lot of multithreaded applications. They contain a wealth of methods that manage complex processes for you in a thread-safe and performant manner.

Understanding the *Lock* Framework

A synchronized block supports only a limited set of functionality. For example, what if we want to check whether a lock is available and, if it is not, perform some other task? Furthermore, if the lock is never available and we synchronize on it, we might hang forever.

The Concurrency API includes the Lock interface that is conceptually similar to using the synchronized keyword, but with a lot more bells and whistles. Instead of synchronizing on any Object, though, we can "lock" only on an object that implements the Lock interface.

Applying a *ReentrantLock* Interface

Using the Lock interface is pretty easy. When you need to protect a piece of code from multithreaded processing, create an instance of Lock that all threads have access to. Each thread then calls lock() before it enters the protected code and calls unlock() before it exits the protected code.

For contrast, the following shows two implementations, one with a synchronized block and one with a Lock instance. As we'll see in the next section, the Lock solution has a number of features not available to the synchronized block.

```
// Implementation #1 with a synchronized block
Object object = new Object();
synchronized(object) {
   // Protected code
}


// Implementation #2 with a Lock
Lock lock = new ReentrantLock();
try {
   lock.lock();
   // Protected code
} finally {
   lock.unlock();
}
```

 While certainly not required, it is a good practice to use a try/finally block with Lock instances. This ensures any acquired locks are properly released.

These two implementations are conceptually equivalent. The ReentrantLock class is a simple monitor that implements the Lock interface and supports mutual exclusion. In other words, at most one thread is allowed to hold a lock at any given time.

The ReentrantLock class ensures that once a thread has called lock() and obtained the lock, all other threads that call lock() will wait until the first thread calls unlock(). As far as which thread gets the lock next, that depends on the parameters used to create the Lock object.

The ReentrantLock class contains a constructor that can be used to send a boolean "fairness" parameter. If set to true, then the lock will usually be granted to each thread in the order it was requested. It is false by default when using the no-argument constructor. In practice, you should enable fairness only when ordering is absolutely required, as it could lead to a significant slowdown.

Besides always making sure to release a lock, you also need to make sure that you only release a lock that you actually have. If you attempt to release a lock that you do not have, you will get an exception at runtime.

```
Lock lock = new ReentrantLock();
lock.unlock();  // IllegalMonitorStateException
```

The Lock interface includes four methods that you should know for the exam, as listed in Table 18.8.

TABLE 18.8 Lock methods

Method	Description
void lock()	Requests a lock and blocks until lock is acquired
void unlock()	Releases a lock
boolean tryLock()	Requests a lock and returns immediately. Returns a boolean indicating whether the lock was successfully acquired
boolean tryLock(long,TimeUnit)	Requests a lock and blocks up to the specified time until lock is required. Returns a boolean indicating whether the lock was successfully acquired

Attempting to Acquire a Lock

While the ReentrantLock class allows you to wait for a lock, it so far suffers from the same problem as a synchronized block. A thread could end up waiting forever to obtain a lock. Luckily, Table 18.8 includes two additional methods that make the Lock interface a lot safer to use than a synchronized block.

For convenience, we'll be using the following printMessage() method for the code in this section:

```
public static void printMessage(Lock lock) {
  try {
    lock.lock();
  } finally {
```

```
      lock.unlock();
   }
}
```

tryLock()

The tryLock() method will attempt to acquire a lock and immediately return a boolean result indicating whether the lock was obtained. Unlike the lock() method, it does not wait if another thread already holds the lock. It returns immediately, regardless of whether or not a lock is available.

The following is a sample implementation using the tryLock() method:

```
Lock lock = new ReentrantLock();
new Thread(() -> printMessage(lock)).start();
if(lock.tryLock()) {
   try {
      System.out.println("Lock obtained, entering protected code");
   } finally {
      lock.unlock();
   }
} else {
   System.out.println("Unable to acquire lock, doing something else");
}
```

When you run this code, it could produce either message, depending on the order of execution. A fun exercise is to insert some Thread.sleep() delays into this snippet to encourage a particular message to be displayed.

Like lock(), the tryLock() method should be used with a try/finally block. Fortunately, you need to release the lock only if it was successfully acquired.

It is imperative that your program always checks the return value of the tryLock() method. It tells your program whether the lock needs to be released later.

tryLock(long,TimeUnit)

The Lock interface includes an overloaded version of tryLock(long,TimeUnit) that acts like a hybrid of lock() and tryLock(). Like the other two methods, if a lock is available, then it will immediately return with it. If a lock is unavailable, though, it will wait up to the specified time limit for the lock.

The following code snippet uses the overloaded version of tryLock(long,TimeUnit):

```
Lock lock = new ReentrantLock();
new Thread(() -> printMessage(lock)).start();
```

```
if(lock.tryLock(10,TimeUnit.SECONDS)) {
   try {
      System.out.println("Lock obtained, entering protected code");
   } finally {
      lock.unlock();
   }
} else {
   System.out.println("Unable to acquire lock, doing something else");
}
```

The code is the same as before, except this time one of the threads waits up to 10 seconds to acquire the lock.

Duplicate Lock Requests

The ReentrantLock class maintains a counter of the number of times a lock has been given to a thread. To release the lock for other threads to use, unlock() must be called the same number of times the lock was granted. The following code snippet contains an error. Can you spot it?

```
Lock lock = new ReentrantLock();
if(lock.tryLock()) {
   try {
      lock.lock();
      System.out.println("Lock obtained, entering protected code");
   } finally {
      lock.unlock();
   }
}
```

The thread obtains the lock twice but releases it only once. You can verify this by spawning a new thread after this code runs that attempts to obtain a lock. The following prints false:

```
new Thread(() -> System.out.print(lock.tryLock())).start();
```

It is critical that you release a lock the same number of times it is acquired. For calls with tryLock(), you need to call unlock() only if the method returned true.

Reviewing the *Lock* Framework

To review, the ReentrantLock class supports the same features as a synchronized block, while adding a number of improvements.

- Ability to request a lock without blocking
- Ability to request a lock while blocking for a specified amount of time
- A lock can be created with a fairness property, in which the lock is granted to threads in the order it was requested.

The Concurrency API includes other lock-based classes, although ReentrantLock is the only one you need to know for the exam.

> While not on the exam, ReentrantReadWriteLock is a really useful class. It includes separate locks for reading and writing data and is useful on data structures where reads are far more common than writes. For example, if you have a thousand threads reading data but only one thread writing data, this class can help you maximize concurrent access.

Orchestrating Tasks with a *CyclicBarrier*

We started thread-safety discussing protecting individual variables and then moved on to blocks of code and locks. We complete our discussion of thread-safety by discussing how to orchestrate complex tasks across many things.

Our zoo workers are back, and this time they are cleaning pens. Imagine that there is a lion pen that needs to be emptied, cleaned, and then filled back up with the lions. To complete the task, we have assigned four zoo workers. Obviously, we don't want to start cleaning the cage while a lion is roaming in it, lest we end up losing a zoo worker! Furthermore, we don't want to let the lions back into the pen while it is still being cleaned.

We could have all of the work completed by a single worker, but this would be slow and ignore the fact that we have three zoo workers standing by to help. A better solution would be to have all four zoo employees work concurrently, pausing between the end of one set of tasks and the start of the next.

To coordinate these tasks, we can use the CyclicBarrier class. For now, let's start with a code sample without a CyclicBarrier.

```
import java.util.concurrent.*;
public class LionPenManager {
    private void removeLions() {System.out.println("Removing lions");}
    private void cleanPen() {System.out.println("Cleaning the pen");}
    private void addLions() {System.out.println("Adding lions");}
    public void performTask() {
        removeLions();
        cleanPen();
        addLions();
    }
    public static void main(String[] args) {
        ExecutorService service = null;
        try {
            service = Executors.newFixedThreadPool(4);
            var manager = new LionPenManager();
```

```
        for (int i = 0; i < 4; i++)
            service.submit(() -> manager.performTask());
    } finally {
        if (service != null) service.shutdown();
    }
  }
}
```

The following is sample output based on this implementation:

```
Removing lions
Removing lions
Cleaning the pen
Adding lions
Removing lions
Cleaning the pen
Adding lions
Removing lions
Cleaning the pen
Adding lions
Cleaning the pen
Adding lions
```

Although within a single thread the results are ordered, among multiple workers the output is entirely random. We see that some lions are still being removed while the cage is being cleaned, and other lions are added before the cleaning process is finished. In our conceptual example, this would be quite chaotic and would not lead to a very clean cage.

We can improve these results by using the CyclicBarrier class. The CyclicBarrier takes in its constructors a limit value, indicating the number of threads to wait for. As each thread finishes, it calls the await() method on the cyclic barrier. Once the specified number of threads have each called await(), the barrier is released, and all threads can continue.

The following is a reimplementation of our LionPenManager class that uses CyclicBarrier objects to coordinate access:

```
import java.util.concurrent.*;
public class LionPenManager {
    private void removeLions() {System.out.println("Removing lions");}
    private void cleanPen() {System.out.println("Cleaning the pen");}
    private void addLions() {System.out.println("Adding lions");}
    public void performTask(CyclicBarrier c1, CyclicBarrier c2) {
        try {
            removeLions();
            c1.await();
            cleanPen();
```

```
            c2.await();
            addLions();
        } catch (InterruptedException | BrokenBarrierException e) {
            // Handle checked exceptions here
        }
    }
    public static void main(String[] args) {
        ExecutorService service = null;
        try {
            service = Executors.newFixedThreadPool(4);
            var manager = new LionPenManager();
            var c1 = new CyclicBarrier(4);
            var c2 = new CyclicBarrier(4,
                () -> System.out.println("*** Pen Cleaned!"));
            for (int i = 0; i < 4; i++)
                service.submit(() -> manager.performTask(c1, c2));
        } finally {
            if (service != null) service.shutdown();
        }
    }
}
```

In this example, we have updated performTask() to use CyclicBarrier objects. Like synchronizing on the same object, coordinating a task with a CyclicBarrier requires the object to be static or passed to the thread performing the task. We also add a try/catch block in the performTask() method, as the await() method throws multiple checked exceptions.

The following is sample output based on this revised implementation of our LionPenManager class:

```
Removing lions
Removing lions
Removing lions
Removing lions
Cleaning the pen
Cleaning the pen
Cleaning the pen
Cleaning the pen
*** Pen Cleaned!
Adding lions
Adding lions
Adding lions
Adding lions
```

As you can see, all of the results are now organized. Removing the lions all happens in one step, as does cleaning the pen and adding the lions back in. In this example, we used two different constructors for our CyclicBarrier objects, the latter of which called a Runnable method upon completion.

Thread Pool Size and Cyclic Barrier Limit

If you are using a thread pool, make sure that you set the number of available threads to be at least as large as your CyclicBarrier limit value. For example, what if we changed the code in the previous example to allocate only two threads, such as in the following snippet?

```
ExecutorService service = Executors.newFixedThreadPool(2);
```

In this case, the code will hang indefinitely. The barrier would never be reached as the only threads available in the pool are stuck waiting for the barrier to be complete. This would result in a deadlock, which will be discussed shortly.

The CyclicBarrier class allows us to perform complex, multithreaded tasks, while all threads stop and wait at logical barriers. This solution is superior to a single-threaded solution, as the individual tasks, such as removing the lions, can be completed in parallel by all four zoo workers.

There is a slight loss in performance to be expected from using a CyclicBarrier. For example, one worker may be incredibly slow at removing lions, resulting in the other three workers waiting for him to finish. Since we can't start cleaning the pen while it is full of lions, though, this solution is about as concurrent as we can make it.

Reusing *CyclicBarrier*

After a CyclicBarrier is broken, all threads are released, and the number of threads waiting on the CyclicBarrier goes back to zero. At this point, the CyclicBarrier may be used again for a new set of waiting threads. For example, if our CyclicBarrier limit is 5 and we have 15 threads that call await(), then the CyclicBarrier will be activated a total of three times.

Using Concurrent Collections

Besides managing threads, the Concurrency API includes interfaces and classes that help you coordinate access to collections shared by multiple tasks. By collections, we are of course referring to the Java Collections Framework that we introduced in Chapter 14,

"Generics and Collections." In this section, we will demonstrate many of the concurrent classes available to you when using the Concurrency API.

Understanding Memory Consistency Errors

The purpose of the concurrent collection classes is to solve common memory consistency errors. A *memory consistency error* occurs when two threads have inconsistent views of what should be the same data. Conceptually, we want writes on one thread to be available to another thread if it accesses the concurrent collection after the write has occurred.

When two threads try to modify the same nonconcurrent collection, the JVM may throw a ConcurrentModificationException at runtime. In fact, it can happen with a single thread. Take a look at the following code snippet:

```
var foodData = new HashMap<String, Integer>();
foodData.put("penguin", 1);
foodData.put("flamingo", 2);
for(String key: foodData.keySet())
    foodData.remove(key);
```

This snippet will throw a ConcurrentModificationException during the second iteration of the loop, since the iterator on keySet() is not properly updated after the first element is removed. Changing the first line to use a ConcurrentHashMap will prevent the code from throwing an exception at runtime.

```
var foodData = new ConcurrentHashMap<String, Integer>();
foodData.put("penguin", 1);
foodData.put("flamingo", 2);
for(String key: foodData.keySet())
    foodData.remove(key);
```

Although we don't usually modify a loop variable, this example highlights the fact that the ConcurrentHashMap is ordering read/write access such that all access to the class is consistent. In this code snippet, the iterator created by keySet() is updated as soon as an object is removed from the Map.

The concurrent classes were created to help avoid common issues in which multiple threads are adding and removing objects from the same collections. At any given instance, all threads should have the same consistent view of the structure of the collection.

Working with Concurrent Classes

You should use a concurrent collection class anytime that you are going to have multiple threads modify a collections object outside a synchronized block or method, even if you don't expect a concurrency problem. On the other hand, immutable or read-only objects can be accessed by any number of threads without a concurrent collection.

Immutable objects can be accessed by any number of threads and do not require synchronization. By definition, they do not change, so there is no chance of a memory consistency error.

In the same way that we instantiate an ArrayList object but pass around a List reference, it is considered a good practice to instantiate a concurrent collection but pass it around using a nonconcurrent interface whenever possible. In some cases, the callers may need to know that it is a concurrent collection so that a concurrent interface or class is appropriate, but for the majority of circumstances, that distinction is not necessary.

Table 18.9 lists the common concurrent classes with which you should be familiar for the exam.

TABLE 18.9 Concurrent collection classes

Class name	Java Collections Framework interfaces	Elements ordered?	Sorted?	Blocking?
ConcurrentHashMap	ConcurrentMap	No	No	No
ConcurrentLinkedQueue	Queue	Yes	No	No
ConcurrentSkipListMap	ConcurrentMap SortedMap NavigableMap	Yes	Yes	No
ConcurrentSkipListSet	SortedSet NavigableSet	Yes	Yes	No
CopyOnWriteArrayList	List	Yes	No	No
CopyOnWriteArraySet	Set	No	No	No
LinkedBlockingQueue	BlockingQueue	Yes	No	Yes

Based on your knowledge of collections from Chapter 14, classes like ConcurrentHashMap and ConcurrentLinkedQueue should be quite easy for you to learn. Take a look at the following code samples:

```
Map<String,Integer> map = new ConcurrentHashMap<>();
map.put("zebra", 52);
map.put("elephant", 10);
System.out.println(map.get("elephant"));  // 10
```

```
Queue<Integer> queue = new ConcurrentLinkedQueue<>();
queue.offer(31);
System.out.println(queue.peek());  // 31
System.out.println(queue.poll());  // 31
```

Like we often did in Chapter 14, we use an interface reference for the variable type of the newly created object and use it the same way as we would a nonconcurrent object. The difference is that these objects are safe to pass to multiple threads.

All of these classes implement multiple interfaces. For example, ConcurrentHashMap implements Map and ConcurrentMap. When declaring methods that take a concurrent collection, it is up to you to determine the appropriate method parameter type. For example, a method signature may require a ConcurrentMap reference to ensure that an object passed to it is properly supported in a multithreaded environment.

Understanding *SkipList* Collections

The SkipList classes, ConcurrentSkipListSet and ConcurrentSkipListMap, are concurrent versions of their sorted counterparts, TreeSet and TreeMap, respectively. They maintain their elements or keys in the natural ordering of their elements. In this manner, using them is the same as the code that you worked with in Chapter 14.

```
Set<String> gardenAnimals = new ConcurrentSkipListSet<>();
gardenAnimals.add("rabbit");
gardenAnimals.add("gopher");
System.out.println(gardenAnimals.stream()
   .collect(Collectors.joining(",")));  // gopher,rabbit

Map<String, String> rainForestAnimalDiet
   = new ConcurrentSkipListMap<>();
rainForestAnimalDiet.put("koala", "bamboo");
rainForestAnimalDiet.entrySet()
   .stream()
   .forEach((e) -> System.out.println(
     e.getKey() + "-" + e.getValue())); // koala-bamboo
```

When you see SkipList or SkipSet on the exam, just think "sorted" concurrent collections, and the rest should follow naturally.

Understanding *CopyOnWrite* Collections

Table 18.9 included two classes, CopyOnWriteArrayList and CopyOnWriteArraySet, that behave a little differently than the other concurrent examples that you have seen. These classes copy all of their elements to a new underlying structure anytime an element is added, modified, or removed from the collection. By a *modified* element, we mean that the reference in the collection is changed. Modifying the actual contents of objects within the collection will not cause a new structure to be allocated.

Although the data is copied to a new underlying structure, our reference to the `Collection` object does not change. This is particularly useful in multithreaded environments that need to iterate the collection. Any iterator established prior to a modification will not see the changes, but instead it will iterate over the original elements prior to the modification.

Let's take a look at how this works with an example. Does the following program terminate? If so, how many times does the loop execute?

```java
List<Integer> favNumbers =
   new CopyOnWriteArrayList<>(List.of(4,3,42));
for(var n: favNumbers) {
   System.out.print(n + " ");
   favNumbers.add(9);
}
System.out.println();
System.out.println("Size: " + favNumbers.size());
```

When executed as part of a program, this code snippet outputs the following:

```
4 3 42
Size: 6
```

Despite adding elements to the array while iterating over it, the `for` loop only iterated on the ones created when the loop started. Alternatively, if we had used a regular `ArrayList` object, a `ConcurrentModificationException` would have been thrown at runtime. With either class, though, we avoid entering an infinite loop in which elements are constantly added to the array as we iterate over them.

The `CopyOnWrite` classes are similar to the immutable object pattern that you saw in Chapter 12, "Java Fundamentals," as a new underlying structure is created every time the collection is modified. Unlike a true immutable object, though, the reference to the object stays the same even while the underlying data is changed.

The `CopyOnWriteArraySet` is used just like a `HashSet` and has similar properties as the `CopyOnWriteArrayList` class.

```java
Set<Character> favLetters =
   new CopyOnWriteArraySet<>(List.of('a','t'));
for(char c: favLetters) {
   System.out.print(c+" ");
   favLetters.add('s');
}
System.out.println();
System.out.println("Size: "+ favLetters.size());
```

This code snippet prints:

```
a t
Size: 3
```

The CopyOnWrite classes can use a lot of memory, since a new collection structure needs be allocated anytime the collection is modified. They are commonly used in multi-threaded environment situations where reads are far more common than writes.

Revisiting Deleting While Looping

In Chapter 14, we showed an example where deleting from an ArrayList while iterating over it triggered a ConcurrentModificationException. Here we present a version that does work using CopyOnWriteArrayList:

```java
List<String> birds = new CopyOnWriteArrayList<>();
birds.add("hawk");
birds.add("hawk");
birds.add("hawk");

for (String bird : birds)
    birds.remove(bird);
System.out.print(birds.size()); // 0
```

As mentioned, though, CopyOnWrite classes can use a lot of memory. Another approach is to use the ArrayList class with an iterator, as shown here:

```java
var iterator = birds.iterator();
while(iterator.hasNext()) {
    iterator.next();
    iterator.remove();
}
System.out.print(birds.size());  // 0
```

Understanding Blocking Queues

The final collection class in Table 18.9 that you should know for the exam is the LinkedBlockingQueue, which implements the BlockingQueue interface. The BlockingQueue is just like a regular Queue, except that it includes methods that will wait a specific amount of time to complete an operation.

Since BlockingQueue inherits all of the methods from Queue, we skip the inherited methods you learned in Chapter 14 and present the new methods in Table 18.10.

TABLE 18.10 BlockingQueue waiting methods

Method name	Description
offer(E e, long timeout, TimeUnit unit)	Adds an item to the queue, waiting the specified time and returning false if the time elapses before space is available
poll(long timeout, TimeUnit unit)	Retrieves and removes an item from the queue, waiting the specified time and returning null if the time elapses before the item is available

The implementation class LinkedBlockingQueue, as the name implies, maintains a linked list between elements. The following sample is using a LinkedBlockingQueue to wait for the results of some of the operations. The methods in Table 18.10 can each throw a checked InterruptedException, as they can be interrupted before they finish waiting for a result; therefore, they must be properly caught.

```
try {
   var blockingQueue = new LinkedBlockingQueue<Integer>();
   blockingQueue.offer(39);
   blockingQueue.offer(3, 4, TimeUnit.SECONDS);
   System.out.println(blockingQueue.poll());
   System.out.println(blockingQueue.poll(10, TimeUnit.MILLISECONDS));
} catch (InterruptedException e) {
   // Handle interruption
}
```

This code snippet prints the following:

```
39
3
```

As shown in this example, since LinkedBlockingQueue implements both Queue and BlockingQueue, we can use methods available to both, such as those that don't take any wait arguments.

Obtaining Synchronized Collections

Besides the concurrent collection classes that we have covered, the Concurrency API also includes methods for obtaining synchronized versions of existing nonconcurrent collection objects. These synchronized methods are defined in the Collections class. They operate on the inputted collection and return a reference that is the same type as the underlying collection. We list these methods in Table 18.11.

TABLE 18.11 Synchronized collections methods

synchronizedCollection(Collection<T> c)
synchronizedList(List<T> list)
synchronizedMap(Map<K,V> m)
synchronizedNavigableMap(NavigableMap<K,V> m)
synchronizedNavigableSet(NavigableSet<T> s)
synchronizedSet(Set<T> s)
synchronizedSortedMap(SortedMap<K,V> m)
synchronizedSortedSet(SortedSet<T> s)

When should you use these methods? If you know at the time of creation that your object requires synchronization, then you should use one of the concurrent collection classes listed in Table 18.9. On the other hand, if you are given an existing collection that is not a concurrent class and need to access it among multiple threads, you can wrap it using the methods in Table 18.11.

Unlike the concurrent collections, the synchronized collections also throw an exception if they are modified within an iterator by a single thread. For example, take a look at the following modification of our earlier example:

```
var foodData = new HashMap<String, Object>();
foodData.put("penguin", 1);
foodData.put("flamingo", 2);
var synFoodData = Collections.synchronizedMap(foodData);
for(String key: synFoodData.keySet())
    synFoodData.remove(key);
```

This loop throws a ConcurrentModificationException, whereas our example that used ConcurrentHashMap did not. Other than iterating over the collection, the objects returned by the methods in Table 18.11 are safe from memory consistency errors and can be used among multiple threads.

Identifying Threading Problems

A threading problem can occur in multithreaded applications when two or more threads interact in an unexpected and undesirable way. For example, two threads may block each other from accessing a particular segment of code.

The Concurrency API was created to help eliminate potential threading issues common to all developers. As you have seen, the Concurrency API creates threads and manages complex thread interactions for you, often in just a few lines of code.

Although the Concurrency API reduces the potential for threading issues, it does not eliminate it. In practice, finding and identifying threading issues within an application is often one of the most difficult tasks a developer can undertake.

Understanding Liveness

As you have seen in this chapter, many thread operations can be performed independently, but some require coordination. For example, synchronizing on a method requires all threads that call the method to wait for other threads to finish before continuing. You also saw earlier in the chapter that threads in a CyclicBarrier will each wait for the barrier limit to be reached before continuing.

What happens to the application while all of these threads are waiting? In many cases, the waiting is ephemeral, and the user has very little idea that any delay has occurred. In other cases, though, the waiting may be extremely long, perhaps infinite.

Liveness is the ability of an application to be able to execute in a timely manner. Liveness problems, then, are those in which the application becomes unresponsive or in some kind of "stuck" state. For the exam, there are three types of liveness issues with which you should be familiar: deadlock, starvation, and livelock.

Deadlock

Deadlock occurs when two or more threads are blocked forever, each waiting on the other. We can illustrate this principle with the following example. Imagine that our zoo has two foxes: Foxy and Tails. Foxy likes to eat first and then drink water, while Tails likes to drink water first and then eat. Furthermore, neither animal likes to share, and they will finish their meal only if they have exclusive access to both food and water.

The zookeeper places the food on one side of the environment and the water on the other side. Although our foxes are fast, it still takes them 100 milliseconds to run from one side of the environment to the other.

What happens if Foxy gets the food first and Tails gets the water first? The following application models this behavior:

```
import java.util.concurrent.*;
class Food {}
class Water {}
public class Fox {
    public void eatAndDrink(Food food, Water water) {
        synchronized(food) {
            System.out.println("Got Food!");
            move();
            synchronized(water) {
```

```
                System.out.println("Got Water!");
            }
        }
    }
    public void drinkAndEat(Food food, Water water) {
        synchronized(water) {
            System.out.println("Got Water!");
            move();
            synchronized(food) {
                System.out.println("Got Food!");
            }
        }
    }
    public void move() {
        try {
            Thread.sleep(100);
        } catch (InterruptedException e) {
            // Handle exception
        }
    }
    public static void main(String[] args) {
        // Create participants and resources
        Fox foxy = new Fox();
        Fox tails = new Fox();
        Food food = new Food();
        Water water = new Water();
        // Process data
        ExecutorService service = null;
        try {
            service = Executors.newScheduledThreadPool(10);
            service.submit(() -> foxy.eatAndDrink(food,water));
            service.submit(() -> tails.drinkAndEat(food,water));
        } finally {
            if(service != null) service.shutdown();
        }
    }
}
```

In this example, Foxy obtains the food and then moves to the other side of the environment to obtain the water. Unfortunately, Tails already drank the water and is waiting for the food to become available. The result is that our program outputs the following, and it hangs indefinitely:

```
Got Food!
Got Water!
```

This example is considered a deadlock because both participants are permanently blocked, waiting on resources that will never become available.

Preventing Deadlocks

How do you fix a deadlock once it has occurred? The answer is that you can't in most situations. On the other hand, there are numerous strategies to help prevent deadlocks from ever happening in the first place. One common strategy to avoid deadlocks is for all threads to order their resource requests. For example, if both foxes have a rule that they need to obtain food before water, then the previous deadlock scenario will not happen again. Once one of the foxes obtained food, the second fox would wait, leaving the water resource available.

There are some advanced techniques that try to detect and resolve a deadlock in real time, but they are often quite difficult to implement and have limited success in practice. In fact, many operating systems ignore the problem altogether and pretend that deadlocks never happen.

Starvation

Starvation occurs when a single thread is perpetually denied access to a shared resource or lock. The thread is still active, but it is unable to complete its work as a result of other threads constantly taking the resource that they are trying to access.

In our fox example, imagine that we have a pack of very hungry, very competitive foxes in our environment. Every time Foxy stands up to go get food, one of the other foxes sees her and rushes to eat before her. Foxy is free to roam around the enclosure, take a nap, and howl for a zookeeper but is never able to obtain access to the food. In this example, Foxy literally and figuratively experiences starvation. It's a good thing that this is just a theoretical example!

Livelock

Livelock occurs when two or more threads are conceptually blocked forever, although they are each still active and trying to complete their task. Livelock is a special case of resource starvation in which two or more threads actively try to acquire a set of locks, are unable to do so, and restart part of the process.

Livelock is often a result of two threads trying to resolve a deadlock. Returning to our fox example, imagine that Foxy and Tails are both holding their food and water resources, respectively. They each realize that they cannot finish their meal in this state, so they both let go of their food and water, run to opposite side of the environment, and pick up the other resource. Now Foxy has the water, Tails has the food, and neither is able to finish their meal!

If Foxy and Tails continue this process forever, it is referred to as livelock. Both Foxy and Tails are active, running back and forth across their area, but neither is able to finish their meal. Foxy and Tails are executing a form of failed deadlock recovery. Each fox notices that they are potentially entering a deadlock state and responds by releasing all of its locked resources. Unfortunately, the lock and unlock process is cyclical, and the two foxes are conceptually deadlocked.

In practice, livelock is often a difficult issue to detect. Threads in a livelock state appear active and able to respond to requests, even when they are in fact stuck in an endless cycle.

Managing Race Conditions

A *race condition* is an undesirable result that occurs when two tasks, which should be completed sequentially, are completed at the same time. We encountered examples of race conditions earlier in the chapter when we introduced synchronization.

While Figure 18.3 shows a classical thread-based example of a race condition, we now provide a more illustrative example. Imagine two zoo patrons, Olivia and Sophia, are signing up for an account on the zoo's new visitor website. Both of them want to use the same username, ZooFan, and they each send requests to create the account at the same time, as shown in Figure 18.5.

What result does the web server return when both users attempt to create an account with the same username in Figure 18.5?

FIGURE 18.5 Race condition on user creation

Possible Outcomes for This Race Condition

- Both users are able to create accounts with username ZooFan.

- Both users are unable to create an account with username ZooFan, returning an error message to both users.

- One user is able to create the account with the username ZooFan, while the other user receives an error message.

Which of these results is most desirable when designing our web server? The first possibility, in which both users are able to create an account with the same username, could cause serious problems and break numerous invariants in the system. Assuming that the username is required to log into the website, how do they both log in with the same username and different passwords? In this case, the website cannot tell them apart. This is the worst possible outcome to this race condition, as it causes significant and potentially unrecoverable data problems.

What about the second scenario? If both users are unable to create the account, both will receive error messages and be told to try again. In this scenario, the data is protected since no two accounts with the same username exist in the system. The users are free to try again with the same username, ZooFan, since no one has been granted access to it. Although this might seem like a form of livelock, there is a subtle difference. When the users try to create their account again, the chances of them hitting a race condition tend to diminish. For example, if one user submits their request a few seconds before the other, they might avoid another race condition entirely by the system informing the second user that the account name is already in use.

The third scenario, in which one user obtains the account while the other does not, is often considered the best solution to this type of race condition. Like the second situation, we preserve data integrity, but unlike the second situation, at least one user is able to move forward on the first request, avoiding additional race condition scenarios. Also unlike the previous scenario, we can provide the user who didn't win the race with a clearer error message because we are now sure that the account username is no longer available in the system.

For the third scenario, which of the two users should gain access to the account? For race conditions, it often doesn't matter as long as only one player "wins" the race. A common practice is to choose whichever thread made the request first, whenever possible.

For the exam, you should understand that race conditions lead to invalid data if they are not properly handled. Even the solution where both participants fail to proceed is preferable to one in which invalid data is permitted to enter the system.

Race conditions tend to appear in highly concurrent applications. As a software system grows and more users are added, they tend to appear more frequently. One solution is to use a monitor to synchronize on the relevant overlapping task. In the previous example, the relevant task is the method that determines whether an account username is in use and reserves it in the system if it is available.

Working with Parallel Streams

One of the most powerful features of the Stream API is built-in concurrency support. Up until now, all of the streams with which you have worked have been serial streams. A *serial stream* is a stream in which the results are ordered, with only one entry being processed at a time.

A *parallel stream* is a stream that is capable of processing results concurrently, using multiple threads. For example, you can use a parallel stream and the map() operation to operate concurrently on the elements in the stream, vastly improving performance over processing a single element at a time.

Using a parallel stream can change not only the performance of your application but also the expected results. As you shall see, some operations also require special handling to be able to be processed in a parallel manner.

The number of threads available in a parallel stream is proportional to the number of available CPUs in your environment.

Creating Parallel Streams

The Stream API was designed to make creating parallel streams quite easy. For the exam, you should be familiar with the two ways of creating a parallel stream.

Calling *parallel()* on an Existing Stream

The first way to create a parallel stream is from an existing stream. You just call parallel() on an existing stream to convert it to one that supports multithreaded processing, as shown in the following code:

```
Stream<Integer> s1 = List.of(1,2).stream();
Stream<Integer> s2 = s1.parallel();
```

Be aware that parallel() is an intermediate operation that operates on the original stream. For example, applying a terminal operation to s2 also makes s1 unavailable for further use.

Calling *parallelStream()* on a *Collection* Object

The second way to create a parallel stream is from a Java Collection class. The Collection interface includes a method parallelStream() that can be called on any collection and returns a parallel stream. The following creates the parallel stream directly from the List object:

```
Stream<Integer> s3 = List.of(1,2).parallelStream();
```

We will use both parallel() and parallelStream() throughout this section.

The Stream interface includes a method isParallel() that can be used to test if the instance of a stream supports parallel processing. Some operations on streams preserve the parallel attribute, while others do not. For example, the Stream.concat(Stream s1, Stream s2) is parallel if either s1 or s2 is parallel. On the other hand, flatMap() creates a new stream that is not parallel by default, regardless of whether the underlying elements were parallel.

Performing a Parallel Decomposition

As you may have noticed, creating the parallel stream is the easy part. The interesting part comes in performing a parallel decomposition. A *parallel decomposition* is the process of taking a task, breaking it up into smaller pieces that can be performed concurrently, and then reassembling the results. The more concurrent a decomposition, the greater the performance improvement of using parallel streams.

Let's try it. For starters, let's define a reusable function that "does work" just by waiting for five seconds.

```
private static int doWork(int input) {
   try {
      Thread.sleep(5000);
   } catch (InterruptedException e) {}
   return input;
}
```

We can pretend that in a real application this might be calling a database or reading a file. Now let's use this method with a serial stream.

```
long start = System.currentTimeMillis();
List.of(1,2,3,4,5)
   .stream()
   .map(w -> doWork(w))
   .forEach(s -> System.out.print(s + " "));

System.out.println();
var timeTaken = (System.currentTimeMillis()-start)/1000;
System.out.println("Time: "+timeTaken+" seconds");
```

What do you think this code will output when executed as part of a main() method? Let's take a look.

```
1 2 3 4 5
Time: 25 seconds
```

As you might expect, the results are ordered and predictable because we are using a serial stream. It also took around 25 seconds to process all five results, one at a time. What happens if we use a parallel stream, though?

```
long start = System.currentTimeMillis();
List.of(1,2,3,4,5)
   .parallelStream()
   .map(w -> doWork(w))
   .forEach(s -> System.out.print(s + " "));
```

```
System.out.println();
var timeTaken = (System.currentTimeMillis()-start)/1000;
System.out.println("Time: "+timeTaken+" seconds");
```

With a parallel stream, the map() and forEach() operations are applied concurrently. The following is sample output:

```
3 2 1 5 4
Time: 5 seconds
```

As you can see, the results are no longer ordered or predictable. The map() and forEach() operations on a parallel stream are equivalent to submitting multiple Runnable lambda expressions to a pooled thread executor and then waiting for the results.

What about the time required? In this case, our system had enough CPUs for all of the tasks to be run concurrently. If you ran this same code on a computer with fewer processors, it might output 10 seconds, 15 seconds, or some other value. The key is that we've written our code to take advantage of parallel processing when available, so our job is done.

Ordering *forEach* Results

The Stream API includes an alternate version of the forEach() operation called forEachOrdered(), which forces a parallel stream to process the results in order at the cost of performance. For example, take a look at the following code snippet:

```
List.of(5,2,1,4,3)
    .parallelStream()
    .map(w -> doWork(w))
    .forEachOrdered(s -> System.out.print(s + " "));
```

Like our starting example, this outputs the results in the order that they are defined in the stream:

```
5 2 1 4 3
Time: 5 seconds
```

With this change, the forEachOrdered() operation forces our stream into a single-threaded process. While we've lost some of the performance gains of using a parallel stream, our map() operation is still able to take advantage of the parallel stream and perform a parallel decomposition in 5 seconds instead of 25 seconds.

Processing Parallel Reductions

Besides possibly improving performance and modifying the order of operations, using parallel streams can impact how you write your application. Reduction operations on parallel streams are referred to as *parallel reductions*. The results for parallel reductions can be different from what you expect when working with serial streams.

Performing Order-Based Tasks

Since order is not guaranteed with parallel streams, methods such as findAny() on parallel streams may result in unexpected behavior. Let's take a look at the results of findAny() applied to a serial stream.

```
System.out.print(List.of(1,2,3,4,5,6)
    .stream()
    .findAny().get());
```

This code frequently outputs the first value in the serial stream, 1, although this is not guaranteed. The findAny() method is free to select any element on either serial or parallel streams.

With a parallel stream, the JVM can create any number of threads to process the stream. When you call findAny() on a parallel stream, the JVM selects the first thread to finish the task and retrieves its data.

```
System.out.print(List.of(1,2,3,4,5,6)
    .parallelStream()
    .findAny().get());
```

The result is that the output could be 4, 1, or really any value in the stream. You can see that with parallel streams, the results of findAny() are not as predictable.

Any stream operation that is based on order, including findFirst(), limit(), or skip(), may actually perform more slowly in a parallel environment. This is a result of a parallel processing task being forced to coordinate all of its threads in a synchronized-like fashion.

On the plus side, the results of ordered operations on a parallel stream will be consistent with a serial stream. For example, calling skip(5).limit(2).findFirst() will return the same result on ordered serial and parallel streams.

 Real World Scenario

Creating Unordered Streams

All of the streams with which you have been working are considered ordered by default. It is possible to create an unordered stream from an ordered stream, similar to how you create a parallel stream from a serial stream:

```
List.of(1,2,3,4,5,6).stream().unordered();
```

This method does not actually reorder the elements; it just tells the JVM that if an order-based stream operation is applied, the order can be ignored. For example, calling skip(5) on an unordered stream will skip any 5 elements, not the first 5 required on an ordered stream.

For serial streams, using an unordered version has no effect, but on parallel streams, the results can greatly improve performance.

```
List.of(1,2,3,4,5,6).stream().unordered().parallel();
```

Even though unordered streams will not be on the exam, if you are developing applications with parallel streams, you should know when to apply an unordered stream to improve performance.

Combining Results with *reduce()*

As you learned in Chapter 15, the stream operation reduce() combines a stream into a single object. Recall that the first parameter to the reduce() method is called the *identity*, the second parameter is called the *accumulator*, and the third parameter is called the *combiner*. The following is the signature for the method:

```
<U> U reduce(U identity,
    BiFunction<U,? super T,U> accumulator,
    BinaryOperator<U> combiner)
```

We can concatenate a list of char values, using the reduce() method, as shown in the following example:

```
System.out.println(List.of('w', 'o', 'l', 'f')
    .parallelStream()
    .reduce("",
        (s1,c) -> s1 + c,
        (s2,s3) -> s2 + s3));   // wolf
```

 The naming of the variables in this stream example is not accidental. We used c for char, whereas s1, s2, and s3 are String values.

On parallel streams, the reduce() method works by applying the reduction to pairs of elements within the stream to create intermediate values and then combining those intermediate values to produce a final result. Put another way, in a serial stream, wolf is built one character at a time. In a parallel stream, the intermediate values wo and lf are created and then combined.

With parallel streams, we now have to be concerned about order. What if the elements of a string are combined in the wrong order to produce wlfo or flwo? The Stream

API prevents this problem, while still allowing streams to be processed in parallel, as long as you follow one simple rule: make sure that the accumulator and combiner work regardless of the order they are called in. For example, if we add numbers, we can do so in any order.

 NOTE While the requirements for the input arguments to the reduce() method hold true for both serial and parallel streams, you may not have noticed any problems in serial streams because the result was always ordered. With parallel streams, though, order is no longer guaranteed, and any argument that violates these rules is much more likely to produce side effects or unpredictable results.

Let's take a look at an example using a problematic accumulator. In particular, order matters when subtracting numbers; therefore, the following code can output different values depending on whether you use a serial or parallel stream. We can omit a combiner parameter in these examples, as the accumulator can be used when the intermediate data types are the same.

```
System.out.println(List.of(1,2,3,4,5,6)
    .parallelStream()
    .reduce(0, (a,b) -> (a - b)));  // PROBLEMATIC ACCUMULATOR
```

It may output −21, 3, or some other value.

You can see other problems if we use an identity parameter that is not truly an identity value. For example, what do you expect the following code to output?

```
System.out.println(List.of("w","o","l","f")
    .parallelStream()
    .reduce("X", String::concat));  // XwXoXlXf
```

On a serial stream, it prints Xwolf, but on a parallel stream the result is XwXoXlXf. As part of the parallel process, the identity is applied to multiple elements in the stream, resulting in very unexpected data.

Selecting a *reduce()* Method

Although the one- and two-argument versions of reduce() do support parallel processing, it is recommended that you use the three-argument version of reduce() when working with parallel streams. Providing an explicit combiner method allows the JVM to partition the operations in the stream more efficiently.

Combining Results with *collect()*

Like reduce(), the Stream API includes a three-argument version of collect() that takes *accumulator* and *combiner* operators, along with a *supplier* operator instead of an identity.

```
<R> R collect(Supplier<R> supplier,
   BiConsumer<R, ? super T> accumulator,
   BiConsumer<R, R> combiner)
```

Also, like reduce(), the accumulator and combiner operations must be able to process results in any order. In this manner, the three-argument version of collect() can be performed as a parallel reduction, as shown in the following example:

```
Stream<String> stream = Stream.of("w", "o", "l", "f").parallel();
SortedSet<String> set = stream.collect(ConcurrentSkipListSet::new,
   Set::add,
   Set::addAll);
System.out.println(set);  // [f, l, o, w]
```

Recall that elements in a ConcurrentSkipListSet are sorted according to their natural ordering. You should use a concurrent collection to combine the results, ensuring that the results of concurrent threads do not cause a ConcurrentModificationException.

Performing parallel reductions with a collector requires additional considerations. For example, if the collection into which you are inserting is an ordered data set, such as a List, then the elements in the resulting collection must be in the same order, regardless of whether you use a serial or parallel stream. This may reduce performance, though, as some operations are unable to be completed in parallel.

Performing a Parallel Reduction on a *Collector*

While we covered the Collector interface in Chapter 15, we didn't go into detail about its properties. Every Collector instance defines a characteristics() method that returns a set of Collector.Characteristics attributes. When using a Collector to perform a parallel reduction, a number of properties must hold true. Otherwise, the collect() operation will execute in a single-threaded fashion.

Requirements for Parallel Reduction with *collect()*

- The stream is parallel.
- The parameter of the collect() operation has the Characteristics.CONCURRENT characteristic.
- Either the stream is unordered or the collector has the characteristic Characteristics.UNORDERED.

For example, while Collectors.toSet() does have the UNORDERED characteristic, it does not have the CONCURRENT characteristic. Therefore, the following is not a parallel reduction even with a parallel stream:

```
stream.collect(Collectors.toSet());  // Not a parallel reduction
```

The Collectors class includes two sets of static methods for retrieving collectors, toConcurrentMap() and groupingByConcurrent(), that are both UNORDERED and CONCURRENT. These methods produce Collector instances capable of performing parallel reductions efficiently. Like their nonconcurrent counterparts, there are overloaded versions that take additional arguments.

Here is a rewrite of an example from Chapter 15 to use a parallel stream and parallel reduction:

```
Stream<String> ohMy = Stream.of("lions","tigers","bears").parallel();
ConcurrentMap<Integer, String> map = ohMy
    .collect(Collectors.toConcurrentMap(String::length,
        k -> k,
        (s1, s2) -> s1 + "," + s2));
System.out.println(map); // {5=lions,bears, 6=tigers}
System.out.println(map.getClass());  // java.util.concurrent.ConcurrentHashMap
```

We use a ConcurrentMap reference, although the actual class returned is likely ConcurrentHashMap. The particular class is not guaranteed; it will just be a class that implements the interface ConcurrentMap.

Finally, we can rewrite our groupingBy() example from Chapter 15 to use a parallel stream and parallel reduction.

```
var ohMy = Stream.of("lions","tigers","bears").parallel();
ConcurrentMap<Integer, List<String>> map = ohMy.collect(
    Collectors.groupingByConcurrent(String::length));
System.out.println(map); // {5=[lions, bears], 6=[tigers]}
```

As before, the returned object can be assigned a ConcurrentMap reference.

Encouraging Parallel Processing

Guaranteeing that a particular stream will perform reductions in parallel, as opposed to single-threaded, is often difficult in practice. For example, the one-argument reduce() operation on a parallel stream may perform concurrently even when there is no explicit combiner argument. Alternatively, you may expect some collectors to perform well on a parallel stream, resorting to single-threaded processing at runtime.

The key to applying parallel reductions is to encourage the JVM to take advantage of the parallel structures, such as using a groupingByConcurrent() collector on a parallel stream rather than a groupingBy() collector. By encouraging the JVM to take advantage of the parallel processing, we get the best possible performance at runtime.

Avoiding Stateful Operations

Side effects can appear in parallel streams if your lambda expressions are stateful. A *stateful lambda expression* is one whose result depends on any state that might change during the execution of a pipeline. On the other hand, a *stateless lambda expression* is one whose result does not depend on any state that might change during the execution of a pipeline.

Let's try an example. Imagine we require a method that keeps only even numbers in a stream and adds them to a list. Also, we want ordering of the numbers in the stream and list to be consistent. The following addValues() method accomplishes this:

```
public List<Integer> addValues(IntStream source) {
   var data = Collections.synchronizedList(new ArrayList<Integer>());
   source.filter(s -> s % 2 == 0)
      .forEach(i -> { data.add(i); });   // STATEFUL: DON'T DO THIS!
   return data;
}
```

Let's say this method is executed with the following stream:

```
var list = addValues(IntStream.range(1, 11));
System.out.println(list);
```

Then, the output would be as follows:

```
[2, 4, 6, 8, 10]
```

But what if someone else wrote an implementation that passed our method a parallel stream?

```
var list = addValues(IntStream.range(1, 11).parallel());
System.out.println(list);
```

With a parallel stream, the order of the output becomes random.

```
[6, 8, 10, 2, 4]
```

The problem is that our lambda expression is stateful and modifies a list that is outside our stream. We could use forEachOrdered() to add elements to the list, but that forces the parallel stream to be serial, potentially losing concurrency enhancements. While these stream operations in our example are quite simple, imagine using them alongside numerous intermediate operations.

We can fix this solution by rewriting our stream operation to no longer have a stateful lambda expression.

```
public static List<Integer> addValues(IntStream source) {
   return source.filter(s -> s % 2 == 0)
      .boxed()
      .collect(Collectors.toList());
}
```

This method processes the stream and then collects all the results into a new list. It produces the same result on both serial and parallel streams.

```
[2, 4, 6, 8, 10]
```

This implementation removes the stateful operation and relies on the collector to assemble the elements. We could also use a concurrent collector to parallelize the building of the list. The goal is to write our code to allow for parallel processing and let the JVM handle the rest.

It is strongly recommended that you avoid stateful operations when using parallel streams, so as to remove any potential data side effects. In fact, they should be avoided in serial streams since doing so limits the code's ability to someday take advantage of parallelization.

Summary

This chapter introduced you to threads and showed you how to process tasks in parallel using the Concurrency API. The work that a thread performs can be expressed as lambda expressions or instances of Runnable or Callable.

For the exam, you should know how to concurrently execute tasks using ExecutorService. You should also know which ExecutorService instances are available, including scheduled and pooled services.

Thread-safety is about protecting data from being corrupted by multiple threads modifying it at the same time. Java offers many tools to keep data safe including atomic classes, synchronized methods/blocks, the Lock framework, and CyclicBarrier. The Concurrency API also includes numerous collections classes that handle multithreaded access for you. For the exam, you should also be familiar with the concurrent collections including the CopyOnWriteArrayList class, which creates a new underlying structure anytime the list is modified.

When processing tasks concurrently, a variety of potential threading issues can arise. Deadlock, starvation, and livelock can result in programs that appear stuck, while race conditions can result in unpredictable data. For the exam, you need to know only the basic theory behind these concepts. In professional software development, however, finding and resolving such problems is often quite challenging.

Finally, we discussed parallel streams and showed you how to use them to perform parallel decompositions and reductions. Parallel streams can greatly improve the performance of your application. They can also cause unexpected results since the results are no longer ordered. Remember to avoid stateful lambda expressions, especially when working with parallel streams.

Exam Essentials

Create concurrent tasks with a thread executor service using *Runnable* and *Callable*.
An ExecutorService creates and manages a single thread or a pool of threads. Instances
of Runnable and Callable can both be submitted to a thread executor and will be
completed using the available threads in the service. Callable differs from Runnable
in that Callable returns a generic data type and can throw a checked exception.
A ScheduledExecutorService can be used to schedule tasks at a fixed rate or a fixed
interval between executions.

Be able to apply the atomic classes. An atomic operation is one that occurs without interference by another thread. The Concurrency API includes a set of atomic classes that are
similar to the primitive classes, except that they ensure that operations on them are performed atomically.

Be able to write thread-safe code. Thread-safety is about protecting shared data
from concurrent access. A monitor can be used to ensure that only one thread processes
a particular section of code at a time. In Java, monitors can be implemented with a
synchronized block or method or using an instance of Lock. ReentrantLock has a
number of advantages over using a synchronized block including the ability to check
whether a lock is available without blocking on it, as well as supporting fair acquisi-
tion of locks. To achieve synchronization, two threads must synchronize on the same
shared object.

Manage a process with a *CyclicBarrier*. The CyclicBarrier class can be used to force a
set of threads to wait until they are at a certain stage of execution before continuing.

Be able to use the concurrent collection classes. The Concurrency API includes numerous
collection classes that include built-in support for multithreaded processing, such as
ConcurrentHashMap. It also includes a class CopyOnWriteArrayList that creates a copy
of its underlying list structure every time it is modified and is useful in highly concurrent
environments.

Identify potential threading problems. Deadlock, starvation, and livelock are three
threading problems that can occur and result in threads never completing their task.
Deadlock occurs when two or more threads are blocked forever. Starvation occurs when
a single thread is perpetually denied access to a shared resource. Livelock is a form of
starvation where two or more threads are active but conceptually blocked forever. Finally,
race conditions occur when two threads execute at the same time, resulting in an unexpected outcome.

Understand the impact of using parallel streams. The Stream API allows for easy
creation of parallel streams. Using a parallel stream can cause unexpected results, since the
order of operations may no longer be predictable. Some operations, such as reduce() and
collect(), require special consideration to achieve optimal performance when applied to a
parallel stream.

Review Questions

The answers to the chapter review questions can be found in the Appendix.

1. Given an instance of a `Stream` s and a `Collection` c, which are valid ways of creating a parallel stream? (Choose all that apply.)

   A. `new ParallelStream(s)`

   B. `c.parallel()`

   C. `s.parallelStream()`

   D. `c.parallelStream()`

   E. `new ParallelStream(c)`

   F. `s.parallel()`

2. Given that the sum of the numbers from 1 (inclusive) to 10 (exclusive) is 45, what are the possible results of executing the following program? (Choose all that apply.)

   ```java
   import java.util.concurrent.locks.*;
   import java.util.stream.*;
   public class Bank {
      private Lock vault = new ReentrantLock();
      private int total = 0;
      public void deposit(int value) {
         try {
            vault.tryLock();
            total += value;
         } finally {
            vault.unlock();
         }
      }
      public static void main(String[] unused) {
         var bank = new Bank();
         IntStream.range(1, 10).parallel()
            .forEach(s -> bank.deposit(s));
         System.out.println(bank.total);
      } }
   ```

   A. 45 is printed.

   B. A number less than 45 is printed.

   C. A number greater than 45 is printed.

   D. An exception is thrown.

   E. None of the above, as the code does not compile

3. Which of the following statements about the `Callable call()` and `Runnable run()` methods are correct? (Choose all that apply.)

    A. Both can throw unchecked exceptions.

    B. `Callable` takes a generic method argument.

    C. `Callable` can throw a checked exception.

    D. Both can be implemented with lambda expressions.

    E. `Runnable` returns a generic type.

    F. `Callable` returns a generic type.

    G. Both methods return `void`.

4. Which lines need to be changed to make the code compile? (Choose all that apply.)

    ```
    ExecutorService service =   // w1
       Executors.newSingleThreadScheduledExecutor();
    service.scheduleWithFixedDelay(() -> {
       System.out.println("Open Zoo");
       return null;   // w2
    }, 0, 1, TimeUnit.MINUTES);
    var result = service.submit(() ->   // w3
       System.out.println("Wake Staff"));
    System.out.println(result.get());   // w4
    ```

    A. It compiles and runs without issue.

    B. Line w1

    C. Line w2

    D. Line w3

    E. Line w4

    F. It compiles but throws an exception at runtime.

    G. None of the above

5. What statement about the following code is true?

    ```
    var value1 = new AtomicLong(0);
    final long[] value2 = {0};
    IntStream.iterate(1, i -> 1).limit(100).parallel()
       .forEach(i -> value1.incrementAndGet());
    IntStream.iterate(1, i -> 1).limit(100).parallel()
       .forEach(i -> ++value2[0]);
    System.out.println(value1+" "+value2[0]);
    ```

    A. It outputs 100 100.

    B. It outputs 100 99.

C. The output cannot be determined ahead of time.

D. The code does not compile.

E. It compiles but throws an exception at runtime.

F. It compiles but enters an infinite loop at runtime.

G. None of the above

6. Which statements about the following code are correct? (Choose all that apply.)

```java
public static void main(String[] args) throws Exception {
    var data = List.of(2,5,1,9,8);
    data.stream().parallel()
        .mapToInt(s -> s)
        .peek(System.out::println)
        .forEachOrdered(System.out::println);
}
```

A. The peek() method will print the entries in the order: 1 2 5 8 9.

B. The peek() method will print the entries in the order: 2 5 1 9 8.

C. The peek() method will print the entries in an order that cannot be determined ahead of time.

D. The forEachOrdered() method will print the entries in the order: 1 2 5 8 9.

E. The forEachOrdered() method will print the entries in the order: 2 5 1 9 8.

F. The forEachOrdered() method will print the entries in an order that cannot be determined ahead of time.

G. The code does not compile.

7. Fill in the blanks: _____ occur(s) when two or more threads are blocked forever but both appear active. _____ occur(s) when two or more threads try to complete a related task at the same time, resulting in invalid or unexpected data.

A. Livelock, Deadlock

B. Deadlock, Starvation

C. Race conditions, Deadlock

D. Livelock, Race conditions

E. Starvation, Race conditions

F. Deadlock, Livelock

8. Assuming this class is accessed by only a single thread at a time, what is the result of calling the countIceCreamFlavors() method?

```java
import java.util.stream.LongStream;
public class Flavors {
    private static int counter;
    public static void countIceCreamFlavors()  {
```

```
            counter = 0;
            Runnable task = () -> counter++;
            LongStream.range(1, 500)
                .forEach(m -> new Thread(task).run());
            System.out.println(counter);
        }
    }
```

A. The method consistently prints 499.

B. The method consistently prints 500.

C. The method compiles and prints a value, but that value cannot be determined ahead of time.

D. The method does not compile.

E. The method compiles but throws an exception at runtime.

F. None of the above

9. Which happens when a new task is submitted to an `ExecutorService`, in which there are no threads available?

A. The executor throws an exception when the task is submitted.

B. The executor discards the task without completing it.

C. The executor adds the task to an internal queue and completes when there is an available thread.

D. The thread submitting the task waits on the submit call until a thread is available before continuing.

E. The executor creates a new temporary thread to complete the task.

10. What is the result of executing the following code snippet?

```
List<Integer> lions = new ArrayList<>(List.of(1,2,3));
List<Integer> tigers = new CopyOnWriteArrayList<>(lions);
Set<Integer> bears = new ConcurrentSkipListSet<>();
bears.addAll(lions);
for(Integer item: tigers) tigers.add(4); // x1
for(Integer item: bears) bears.add(5); // x2
System.out.println(lions.size() + " " + tigers.size()
    + " " + bears.size());
```

A. It outputs 3 6 4.

B. It outputs 6 6 6.

C. It outputs 6 3 4.

D. The code does not compile.

E. It compiles but throws an exception at runtime on line `x1`.

F.   It compiles but throws an exception at runtime on line x2.

G.   It compiles but enters an infinite loop at runtime.

11. What statements about the following code are true? (Choose all that apply.)

```
Integer i1 = List.of(1, 2, 3, 4, 5).stream().findAny().get();
synchronized(i1) { // y1
    Integer i2 = List.of(6, 7, 8, 9, 10)
        .parallelStream()
        .sorted()
        .findAny().get(); // y2
    System.out.println(i1 + " " + i2);
}
```

A.   The first value printed is always 1.

B.   The second value printed is always 6.

C.   The code will not compile because of line y1.

D.   The code will not compile because of line y2.

E.   The code compiles but throws an exception at runtime.

F.   The output cannot be determined ahead of time.

G.   It compiles but waits forever at runtime.

12. Assuming takeNap() is a method that takes five seconds to execute without throwing an exception, what is the expected result of executing the following code snippet?

```
ExecutorService service = null;
try {
    service = Executors.newFixedThreadPool(4);
    service.execute(() -> takeNap());
    service.execute(() -> takeNap());
    service.execute(() -> takeNap());
} finally {
    if (service != null) service.shutdown();
}
service.awaitTermination(2, TimeUnit.SECONDS);
System.out.println("DONE!");
```

A.   It will immediately print DONE!.

B.   It will pause for 2 seconds and then print DONE!.

C.   It will pause for 5 seconds and then print DONE!.

D.   It will pause for 15 seconds and then print DONE!.

E.   It will throw an exception at runtime.

F.   None of the above, as the code does not compile

13. What statements about the following code are true? (Choose all that apply.)

```
System.out.print(List.of("duck","flamingo","pelican")
   .parallelStream().parallel()   // q1
   .reduce(0,
      (c1, c2) -> c1.length() + c2.length(),   // q2
      (s1, s2) -> s1 + s2));   // q3
```

   A. It compiles and runs without issue, outputting the total length of all strings in the stream.

   B. The code will not compile because of line q1.

   C. The code will not compile because of line q2.

   D. The code will not compile because of line q3.

   E. It compiles but throws an exception at runtime.

   F. None of the above

14. What statements about the following code snippet are true? (Choose all that apply.)

```
Object o1 = new Object();
Object o2 = new Object();
var service = Executors.newFixedThreadPool(2);
var f1 = service.submit(() -> {
   synchronized (o1) {
      synchronized (o2) { System.out.print("Tortoise"); }
   }
});
var f2 = service.submit(() -> {
   synchronized (o2) {
      synchronized (o1) { System.out.print("Hare"); }
   }
});
f1.get();
f2.get();
```

   A. The code will always output `Tortoise` followed by `Hare`.

   B. The code will always output `Hare` followed by `Tortoise`.

   C. If the code does output anything, the order cannot be determined.

   D. The code does not compile.

   E. The code compiles but may produce a deadlock at runtime.

   F. The code compiles but may produce a livelock at runtime.

   G. It compiles but throws an exception at runtime.

15. Which statement about the following code snippet is correct?

```
2: var cats = Stream.of("leopard", "lynx", "ocelot", "puma")
3:    .parallel();
4: var bears = Stream.of("panda","grizzly","polar").parallel();
5: var data = Stream.of(cats,bears).flatMap(s -> s)
6:    .collect(Collectors.groupingByConcurrent(
7:       s -> !s.startsWith("p")));
8: System.out.println(data.get(false).size()
9:    + " " + data.get(true).size());
```

A. It outputs 3 4.

B. It outputs 4 3.

C. The code will not compile because of line 6.

D. The code will not compile because of line 7.

E. The code will not compile because of line 8.

F. It compiles but throws an exception at runtime.

16. Which statements about methods in `ReentrantLock` are correct? (Choose all that apply.)

A. The `lock()` method will attempt to acquire a lock without waiting indefinitely for it.

B. The `testLock()` method will attempt to acquire a lock without waiting indefinitely for it.

C. The `attemptLock()` method will attempt to acquire a lock without waiting indefinitely for it.

D. By default, a `ReentrantLock` fairly releases to each thread, in the order that it was requested.

E. Calling the `unlock()` method once will release a resource so that other threads can obtain the lock.

F. None of the above

17. What is the result of calling the following method?

```
3: public void addAndPrintItems(BlockingQueue<Integer> queue) {
4:    queue.offer(103);
5:    queue.offer(20, 1, TimeUnit.SECONDS);
6:    queue.offer(85, 7, TimeUnit.HOURS);
7:    System.out.print(queue.poll(200, TimeUnit.NANOSECONDS));
8:    System.out.print(" " + queue.poll(1, TimeUnit.MINUTES));
9: }
```

A. It outputs 20 85.

B. It outputs 103 20.

C. It outputs 20 103.

D. The code will not compile.

E. It compiles but throws an exception at runtime.

F. The output cannot be determined ahead of time.

G. None of the above

18. Which of the following are valid `Callable` expressions? (Choose all that apply.)

    A. `a -> {return 10;}`

    B. `() -> {String s = "";}`

    C. `() -> 5`

    D. `() -> {return null}`

    E. `() -> "The" + "Zoo"`

    F. `(int count) -> count+1`

    G. `() -> {System.out.println("Giraffe"); return 10;}`

19. What is the result of executing the following application? (Choose all that apply.)

    ```
    import java.util.concurrent.*;
    import java.util.stream.*;
    public class PrintConstants {
        public static void main(String[] args) {
            var s = Executors.newScheduledThreadPool(10);
            DoubleStream.of(3.14159,2.71828)    // b1
                .forEach(c -> s.submit(   // b2
                    () -> System.out.println(10*c)));    // b3
            s.execute(() -> System.out.println("Printed"));    // b4
        }
    }
    ```

    A. It compiles and outputs the two numbers, followed by `Printed`.

    B. The code will not compile because of line b1.

    C. The code will not compile because of line b2.

    D. The code will not compile because of line b3.

    E. The code will not compile because of line b4.

    F. It compiles, but the output cannot be determined ahead of time.

    G. It compiles but throws an exception at runtime.

    H. It compiles but waits forever at runtime.

20. What is the result of executing the following program? (Choose all that apply.)

    ```
    import java.util.*;
    import java.util.concurrent.*;
    import java.util.stream.*;
    ```

```
public class PrintCounter {
   static int count = 0;
   public static void main(String[] args) throws
                     InterruptedException, ExecutionException {
      ExecutorService service = null;
      try {
         service = Executors.newSingleThreadExecutor();
         var r = new ArrayList<Future<?>>();
         IntStream.iterate(0,i -> i+1).limit(5).forEach(
            i -> r.add(service.execute(() -> {count++;})) // n1
         );
         for(Future<?> result : r) {
            System.out.print(result.get()+" "); // n2
         }
      } finally {
         if(service != null) service.shutdown();
      } } }
```

A. It prints 0 1 2 3 4.
B. It prints 1 2 3 4 5.
C. It prints null null null null null.
D. It hangs indefinitely at runtime.
E. The output cannot be determined.
F. The code will not compile because of line n1.
G. The code will not compile because of line n2.

21. Given the following code snippet and blank lines on p1 and p2, which values guarantee 1 is printed at runtime? (Choose all that apply.)

```
var data = List.of(List.of(1,2),
   List.of(3,4),
   List.of(5,6));
data. _____  // p1
   .flatMap(s -> s.stream())
   . _____  // p2
   .ifPresent(System.out::print);
```

A. stream() on line p1, findFirst() on line p2.
B. stream() on line p1, findAny() on line p2.
C. parallelStream() in line p1, findAny() on line p2.
D. parallelStream() in line p1, findFirst() on line p2.

E. The code does not compile regardless of what is inserted into the blank.

F. None of the above

22. Assuming 100 milliseconds is enough time for the tasks submitted to the service executor to complete, what is the result of executing the following method? (Choose all that apply.)

```
private AtomicInteger s1 = new AtomicInteger(0); // w1
private int s2 = 0;

private void countSheep() throws InterruptedException {
   ExecutorService service = null;
   try {
      service = Executors.newSingleThreadExecutor(); // w2
      for (int i = 0; i < 100; i++)
         service.execute(() -> {
            s1.getAndIncrement(); s2++; }); // w3
      Thread.sleep(100);
      System.out.println(s1 + " " + s2);
   } finally {
      if(service != null) service.shutdown();
   }
}
```

A. The method consistently prints 100 99.

B. The method consistently prints 100 100.

C. The output cannot be determined ahead of time.

D. The code will not compile because of line w1.

E. The code will not compile because of line w2.

F. The code will not compile because of line w3.

G. It compiles but throws an exception at runtime.

23. What is the result of executing the following application? (Choose all that apply.)

```
import java.util.concurrent.*;
import java.util.stream.*;
public class StockRoomTracker {
   public static void await(CyclicBarrier cb) { // j1
      try { cb.await(); } catch (Exception e) {}
   }
   public static void main(String[] args) {
      var cb = new CyclicBarrier(10,
         () -> System.out.println("Stock Room Full!")); // j2
```

```
        IntStream.iterate(1, i -> 1).limit(9).parallel()
            .forEach(i -> await(cb)); // j3
    }
}
```

A. It outputs `Stock Room Full!`

B. The code will not compile because of line j1.

C. The code will not compile because of line j2.

D. The code will not compile because of line j3.

E. It compiles but throws an exception at runtime.

F. It compiles but waits forever at runtime.

24. What statements about the following class definition are true? (Choose all that apply.)

```
public class TicketManager {
    private int tickets;
    private static TicketManager instance;
    private TicketManager() {}
    static synchronized TicketManager getInstance() {      // k1
        if (instance==null) instance = new TicketManager(); // k2
        return instance;
    }

    public int getTicketCount() { return tickets; }
    public void addTickets(int value) {tickets += value;}  // k3
    public void sellTickets(int value) {
        synchronized (this) { // k4
            tickets -= value;
        }
    }
}
```

A. It compiles without issue.

B. The code will not compile because of line k2.

C. The code will not compile because of line k3.

D. The locks acquired on k1 and k4 are on the same object.

E. The class correctly protects the tickets data from race conditions.

F. At most one instance of TicketManager will be created in an application that uses this class.

25. Which of the following properties of concurrency are true? (Choose all that apply.)

    A. By itself, concurrency does not guarantee which task will be completed first.

    B. Concurrency always improves the performance of an application.

    C. A computer with a single-processor CPU does not benefit from concurrency.

    D. Applications with many resource-heavy tasks tend to benefit more from concurrency than ones with CPU-intensive tasks.

    E. Concurrent tasks do not share the same memory.

26. Assuming an implementation of the `performCount()` method is provided prior to runtime, which of the following are possible results of executing the following application? (Choose all that apply.)

```
import java.util.*;
import java.util.concurrent.*;
public class CountZooAnimals {
   public static void performCount(int animal) {
      // IMPLEMENTATION OMITTED
   }
   public static void printResults(Future<?> f) {
      try {
         System.out.println(f.get(1, TimeUnit.DAYS)); // o1
      } catch (Exception e) {
         System.out.println("Exception!");
      }
   }
   public static void main(String[] args) throws Exception {
      ExecutorService s = null;
      final var r = new ArrayList<Future<?>>();
      try {
         s = Executors.newSingleThreadExecutor();
         for(int i = 0; i < 10; i++) {
            final int animal = i;
            r.add(s.submit(() -> performCount(animal))); // o2
         }
         r.forEach(f -> printResults(f));
      } finally {
         if(s != null) s.shutdown();
      } } }
```

A. It outputs a number 10 times.

B. It outputs a `Boolean` value 10 times.

C. It outputs a `null` value 10 times.

D. It outputs `Exception!` 10 times.

E. It hangs indefinitely at runtime.

F. The code will not compile because of line o1.

G. The code will not compile because of line o2.

Chapter

19

I/O

OCP EXAM OBJECTIVES COVERED IN THIS CHAPTER:

✓ **I/O (Fundamentals and NIO2)**

- Read data from and write console and file data using I/O Streams

- Use I/O Streams to read and write files

- Read and write objects by using serialization

What can Java applications do outside the scope of managing objects and attributes in memory? How can they save data so that information is not lost every time the program is terminated? They use files, of course! You can design code that writes the current state of an application to a file every time the application is closed and then reloads the data when the application is executed the next time. In this manner, information is preserved between program executions.

This chapter focuses on using the java.io API to interact with files and streams. We start by describing how files and directories are organized within a file system and show how to access them with the java.io.File class. We then show how to read and write file data with the stream classes. We conclude this chapter by discussing ways of reading user input at runtime using the Console class.

In Chapter 20, "NIO.2," we will revisit the discussion of files and directories and show how Java provides more powerful techniques for managing files.

When we refer to streams in this chapter, we are referring to the I/O streams found in the java.io API (unless otherwise specified). I/O streams are completely unrelated to the streams you saw in Chapter 15, "Functional Programming." We agree that the naming can be a bit confusing!

Understanding Files and Directories

We begin this chapter by reviewing what a file and directory are within a file system. We also present the java.io.File class and demonstrate how to use it to read and write file information.

Conceptualizing the File System

We start with the basics. Data is stored on persistent storage devices, such as hard disk drives and memory cards. A *file* is a record within the storage device that holds data. Files are organized into hierarchies using directories. A *directory* is a location that can contain files as well as other directories. When working with directories in Java, we often treat them like files. In fact, we use many of the same classes to operate on files and directories. For example, a file and directory both can be renamed with the same Java method.

To interact with files, we need to connect to the file system. The *file system* is in charge of reading and writing data within a computer. Different operating systems use different file systems to manage their data. For example, Windows-based systems use a different file system than Unix-based ones. For the exam, you just need to know how to issue commands using the Java APIs. The JVM will automatically connect to the local file system, allowing you to perform the same operations across multiple platforms.

Next, the *root directory* is the topmost directory in the file system, from which all files and directories inherit. In Windows, it is denoted with a drive name such as c:\, while on Linux it is denoted with a single forward slash, /.

Finally, a *path* is a String representation of a file or directory within a file system. Each file system defines its own path separator character that is used between directory entries. The value to the left of a separator is the parent of the value to the right of the separator. For example, the path value /user/home/zoo.txt means that the file zoo.txt is inside the home directory, with the home directory inside the user directory. You will see that paths can be absolute or relative later in this chapter.

We show how a directory and file system is organized in a hierarchical manner in Figure 19.1.

FIGURE 19.1   Directory and file hierarchy

This diagram shows the root directory, c:, as containing two directories, app and zoo, along with the file info.txt. Within the app directory, there are two more folders, animals and employees, along with the file java.exe. Finally, the animals directory contains two files, Bear.java and Bear.class.

Storing Data as Bytes

Data is stored in a file system (and memory) as a 0 or 1, called a *bit*. Since it's really hard for humans to read/write data that is just 0s and 1s, they are grouped into a set of 8 bits, called a *byte*.

What about the Java byte primitive type? As you'll see later when we get to I/O streams, values are often read or written streams using byte values and arrays.

Real World Scenario

The ASCII Characters

Using a little arithmetic (2^8), we see a byte can be set in one of 256 possible permutations. These 256 values form the alphabet for our computer system to be able to type characters like a, #, and 7.

Historically, the 256 characters are referred to as ASCII characters, based on the encoding standard that defined them. Given all of the languages and emojis available today, 256 characters is actually pretty limiting. Many newer standards have been developed that rely on additional bytes to display characters.

Introducing the *File* Class

The first class that we will discuss is one of the most commonly used in the java.io API: the java.io.File class. The File class is used to read information about existing files and directories, list the contents of a directory, and create/delete files and directories.

An instance of a File class represents the path to a particular file or directory on the file system. The File class cannot read or write data within a file, although it can be passed as a reference to many stream classes to read or write data, as you will see in the next section.

Remember, a File instance can represent a file or a directory.

Creating a File Object

A File object often is initialized with a String containing either an absolute or relative path to the file or directory within the file system. The *absolute path* of a file or directory is the full path from the root directory to the file or directory, including all subdirectories that contain the file or directory. Alternatively, the *relative path* of a file or directory is the path from the current working directory to the file or directory. For example, the following is an absolute path to the `stripes.txt` file:

```
/home/tiger/data/stripes.txt
```

The following is a relative path to the same file, assuming the user's current directory is set to `/home/tiger`:

```
data/stripes.txt
```

Different operating systems vary in their format of pathnames. For example, Unix-based systems use the forward slash, /, for paths, whereas Windows-based systems use the backslash, \, character. That said, many programming languages and file systems support both types of slashes when writing path statements. For convenience, Java offers two options to retrieve the local separator character: a system property and a `static` variable defined in the `File` class. Both of the following examples will output the separator character for the current environment:

```
System.out.println(System.getProperty("file.separator"));
System.out.println(java.io.File.separator);
```

The following code creates a `File` object and determines whether the path it references exists within the file system:

```
var zooFile1 = new File("/home/tiger/data/stripes.txt");
System.out.println(zooFile1.exists());  // true if the file exists
```

This example provides the absolute path to a file and outputs `true` or `false`, depending on whether the file exists. There are three `File` constructors you should know for the exam.

```
public File(String pathname)
```

```
public File(File parent, String child)
```

```
public File(String parent, String child)
```

The first one creates a `File` from a `String` path. The other two constructors are used to create a `File` from a parent and child path, such as the following:

```
File zooFile2 = new File("/home/tiger", "data/stripes.txt");
```

```
File parent = new File("/home/tiger");
File zooFile3 = new File(parent, "data/stripes.txt");
```

In this example, we create two new `File` instances that are equivalent to our earlier `zooFile1` instance. If the `parent` instance is `null`, then it would be skipped, and the method would revert to the single `String` constructor.

The *File* Object vs. the Actual File

When working with an instance of the `File` class, keep in mind that it only represents a path to a file. Unless operated upon, it is not connected to an actual file within the file system.

For example, you can create a new `File` object to test whether a file exists within the system. You can then call various methods to read file properties within the file system. There are also methods to modify the name or location of a file, as well as delete it.

The JVM and underlying file system will read or modify the file using the methods you call on the `File` class. If you try to operate on a file that does not exist or you do not have access to, some `File` methods will throw an exception. Other methods will return `false` if the file does not exist or the operation cannot be performed.

Working with a *File* Object

The `File` class contains numerous useful methods for interacting with files and directories within the file system. We present the most commonly used ones in Table 19.1. Although this table may seem like a lot of methods to learn, many of them are self-explanatory.

TABLE 19.1 Commonly used java.io.File methods

Method Name	Description
boolean delete()	Deletes the file or directory and returns true only if successful. If this instance denotes a directory, then the directory must be empty in order to be deleted.
boolean exists()	Checks if a file exists
String getAbsolutePath()	Retrieves the absolute name of the file or directory within the file system
String getName()	Retrieves the name of the file or directory.
String getParent()	Retrieves the parent directory that the path is contained in or null if there is none
boolean isDirectory()	Checks if a File reference is a directory within the file system
boolean isFile()	Checks if a File reference is a file within the file system
long lastModified()	Returns the number of milliseconds since the epoch (number of milliseconds since 12 a.m. UTC on January 1, 1970) when the file was last modified
long length()	Retrieves the number of bytes in the file
File[] listFiles()	Retrieves a list of files within a directory
boolean mkdir()	Creates the directory named by this path

Method Name	Description
`boolean mkdirs()`	Creates the directory named by this path including any nonexistent parent directories
`boolean renameTo(File dest)`	Renames the file or directory denoted by this path to `dest` and returns true only if successful

The following is a sample program that given a file path outputs information about the file or directory, such as whether it exists, what files are contained within it, and so forth:

```java
var file = new File("c:\\data\\zoo.txt");
System.out.println("File Exists: " + file.exists());
if (file.exists()) {
   System.out.println("Absolute Path: " + file.getAbsolutePath());
   System.out.println("Is Directory: " + file.isDirectory());
   System.out.println("Parent Path: " + file.getParent());
   if (file.isFile()) {
      System.out.println("Size: " + file.length());
      System.out.println("Last Modified: " + file.lastModified());
   } else {
      for (File subfile : file.listFiles()) {
         System.out.println("   " + subfile.getName());
      }
   }
}
```

If the path provided did not point to a file, it would output the following:

```
File Exists: false
```

If the path provided pointed to a valid file, it would output something similar to the following:

```
File Exists: true
Absolute Path: c:\data\zoo.txt
Is Directory: false
Parent Path: c:\data
Size: 12382
Last Modified: 1606860000000
```

Finally, if the path provided pointed to a valid directory, such as c:\data, it would output something similar to the following:

```
File Exists: true
Absolute Path: c:\data
Is Directory: true
Parent Path: c:\
   employees.txt
   zoo.txt
   zoo-backup.txt
```

In these examples, you see that the output of an I/O-based program is completely dependent on the directories and files available at runtime in the underlying file system.

On the exam, you might get paths that look like files but are directories, or vice versa. For example, /data/zoo.txt could be a file or a directory, even though it has a file extension. Don't assume it is either unless the question tells you it is!

In the previous example, we used two backslashes (\\) in the path String, such as c:\\data\\zoo.txt. When the compiler sees a \\ inside a String expression, it interprets it as a single \ value.

Introducing I/O Streams

Now that we have the basics out of the way, let's move on to I/O streams, which are far more interesting. In this section, we will show you how to use I/O streams to read and write data. The "I/O" refers to the nature of how data is accessed, either by reading the data from a resource (input) or by writing the data to a resource (output).

Understanding I/O Stream Fundamentals

The contents of a file may be accessed or written via a *stream*, which is a list of data elements presented sequentially. Streams should be conceptually thought of as a long, nearly never-ending "stream of water" with data presented one "wave" at a time.

We demonstrate this principle in Figure 19.2. The stream is so large that once we start reading it, we have no idea where the beginning or the end is. We just have a pointer to our current position in the stream and read data one block at a time.

Each type of stream segments data into a "wave" or "block" in a particular way. For example, some stream classes read or write data as individual bytes. Other stream classes read or write individual characters or strings of characters. On top of that, some stream classes read or write larger groups of bytes or characters at a time, specifically those with the word Buffered in their name.

FIGURE 19.2   Visual representation of a stream

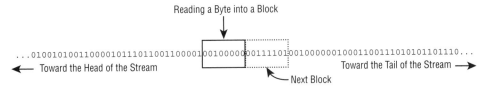

Reading a Byte into a Block

...0100101001100001011101100110000100100000 00111101 00100000010001100111010101101110...

← Toward the Head of the Stream   Toward the Tail of the Stream →

└─ Next Block

 Real World Scenario

All Java I/O Streams Use Bytes

Although the java.io API is full of streams that handle characters, strings, groups of bytes, and so on, nearly all are built on top of reading or writing an individual byte or an array of bytes at a time. The reason higher-level streams exist is for convenience, as well as performance.

For example, writing a file one byte at a time is time-consuming and slow in practice because the round-trip between the Java application and the file system is relatively expensive. By utilizing a BufferedOutputStream, the Java application can write a large chunk of bytes at a time, reducing the round-trips and drastically improving performance.

Although streams are commonly used with file I/O, they are more generally used to handle the reading/writing of any sequential data source. For example, you might construct a Java application that submits data to a website using an output stream and reads the result via an input stream.

I/O Streams Can Be Big

When writing code where you don't know what the stream size will be at runtime, it may be helpful to visualize a stream as being so large that all of the data contained in it could not possibly fit into memory. For example, a 1 terabyte file could not be stored entirely in memory by most computer systems (at the time this book is being written). The file can still be read and written by a program with very little memory, since the stream allows the application to focus on only a small portion of the overall stream at any given time.

Learning I/O Stream Nomenclature

The java.io API provides numerous classes for creating, accessing, and manipulating streams—so many that it tends to overwhelm many new Java developers. Stay calm!

We will review the major differences between each stream class and show you how to distinguish between them.

Even if you come across a particular stream on the exam that you do not recognize, often the name of the stream gives you enough information to understand exactly what it does.

The goal of this section is to familiarize you with common terminology and naming conventions used with streams. Don't worry if you don't recognize the particular stream class names used in this section or their function; we'll be covering each in detail in the next part of the chapter.

Byte Streams vs. Character Streams

The java.io API defines two sets of stream classes for reading and writing streams: byte streams and character streams. We will use both types of streams throughout this chapter.

Differences between Byte and Character Streams

- Byte streams read/write binary data (0s and 1s) and have class names that end in InputStream or OutputStream.

- Character streams read/write text data and have class names that end in Reader or Writer.

The API frequently includes similar classes for both byte and character streams, such as FileInputStream and FileReader. The difference between the two classes is based on how the bytes of the stream are read or written.

It is important to remember that even though character streams do not contain the word Stream in their class name, they are still I/O streams. The use of Reader/Writer in the name is just to distinguish them from byte streams.

Throughout the chapter, we will refer to both InputStream and Reader as *input streams*, and we will refer to both OutputStream and Writer as *output streams*.

The byte streams are primarily used to work with binary data, such as an image or executable file, while character streams are used to work with text files. Since the byte stream classes can write all types of binary data, including strings, it follows that the character stream classes aren't strictly necessary. There are advantages, though, to using the character stream classes, as they are specifically focused on managing character and string data. For example, you can use a Writer class to output a String value to a file without necessarily having to worry about the underlying character encoding of the file.

The *character encoding* determines how characters are encoded and stored in bytes in a stream and later read back or decoded as characters. Although this may sound simple, Java supports a wide variety of character encodings, ranging from ones that may use one byte for Latin characters, UTF-8 and ASCII for example, to using two or more bytes per character, such as UTF-16. For the exam, you don't need to memorize the character encodings, but you should be familiar with the names if you come across them on the exam.

Character Encoding in Java

In Java, the character encoding can be specified using the `Charset` class by passing a name value to the static `Charset.forName()` method, such as in the following examples:

```
Charset usAsciiCharset = Charset.forName("US-ASCII");
Charset utf8Charset = Charset.forName("UTF-8");
Charset utf16Charset = Charset.forName("UTF-16");
```

Java supports numerous character encodings, each specified by a different standard name value.

For character encoding, just remember that using a character stream is better for working with text data than a byte stream. The character stream classes were created for convenience, and you should certainly take advantage of them when possible.

Input vs. Output Streams

Most `InputStream` stream classes have a corresponding `OutputStream` class, and vice versa. For example, the `FileOutputStream` class writes data that can be read by a `FileInputStream`. If you understand the features of a particular `Input` or `Output` stream class, you should naturally know what its complementary class does.

It follows, then, that most `Reader` classes have a corresponding `Writer` class. For example, the `FileWriter` class writes data that can be read by a `FileReader`.

There are exceptions to this rule. For the exam, you should know that `PrintWriter` has no accompanying `PrintReader` class. Likewise, the `PrintStream` is an `OutputStream` that has no corresponding `InputStream` class. It also does not have `Output` in its name. We will discuss these classes later this chapter.

Low-Level vs. High-Level Streams

Another way that you can familiarize yourself with the `java.io` API is by segmenting streams into low-level and high-level streams.

A *low-level stream* connects directly with the source of the data, such as a file, an array, or a `String`. Low-level streams process the raw data or resource and are accessed in a direct and unfiltered manner. For example, a `FileInputStream` is a class that reads file data one byte at a time.

Alternatively, a *high-level stream* is built on top of another stream using wrapping. *Wrapping* is the process by which an instance is passed to the constructor of another class, and operations on the resulting instance are filtered and applied to the original instance. For example, take a look at the `FileReader` and `BufferedReader` objects in the following sample code:

```
try (var br = new BufferedReader(new FileReader("zoo-data.txt"))) {
    System.out.println(br.readLine());
}
```

In this example, FileReader is the low-level stream reader, whereas BufferedReader is the high-level stream that takes a FileReader as input. Many operations on the high-level stream pass through as operations to the underlying low-level stream, such as read() or close(). Other operations override or add new functionality to the low-level stream methods. The high-level stream may add new methods, such as readLine(), as well as performance enhancements for reading and filtering the low-level data.

High-level streams can take other high-level streams as input. For example, although the following code might seem a little odd at first, the style of wrapping a stream is quite common in practice:

```
try (var ois = new ObjectInputStream(
    new BufferedInputStream(
        new FileInputStream("zoo-data.txt")))) {
  System.out.print(ois.readObject());
}
```

In this example, FileInputStream is the low-level stream that interacts directly with the file, which is wrapped by a high-level BufferedInputStream to improve performance. Finally, the entire object is wrapped by a high-level ObjectInputStream, which allows us to interpret the data as a Java object.

For the exam, the only low-level stream classes you need to be familiar with are the ones that operate on files. The rest of the nonabstract stream classes are all high-level streams.

 Real World Scenario

Use Buffered Streams When Working with Files

As briefly mentioned, Buffered classes read or write data in groups, rather than a single byte or character at a time. The performance gain from using a Buffered class to access a low-level file stream cannot be overstated. Unless you are doing something very specialized in your application, you should always wrap a file stream with a Buffered class in practice.

One of the reasons that Buffered streams tend to perform so well in practice is that many file systems are optimized for sequential disk access. The more sequential bytes you read at a time, the fewer round-trips between the Java process and the file system, improving the access of your application. For example, accessing 1,600 sequential bytes is a lot faster than accessing 1,600 bytes spread across the hard drive.

Stream Base Classes

The java.io library defines four abstract classes that are the parents of all stream classes defined within the API: InputStream, OutputStream, Reader, and Writer.

The constructors of high-level streams often take a reference to the abstract class. For example, BufferedWriter takes a Writer object as input, which allows it to take any subclass of Writer.

One common area where the exam likes to play tricks on you is mixing and matching stream classes that are not compatible with each other. For example, take a look at each of the following examples and see whether you can determine why they do not compile:

```
new BufferedInputStream(new FileReader("z.txt"));  // DOES NOT COMPILE
new BufferedWriter(new FileOutputStream("z.txt")); // DOES NOT COMPILE
new ObjectInputStream(
    new FileOutputStream("z.txt"));                 // DOES NOT COMPILE
new BufferedInputStream(new InputStream());        // DOES NOT COMPILE
```

The first two examples do not compile because they mix Reader/Writer classes with InputStream/OutputStream classes, respectively. The third example does not compile because we are mixing an OutputStream with an InputStream. Although it is possible to read data from an InputStream and write it to an OutputStream, wrapping the stream is not the way to do so. As you will see later in this chapter, the data must be copied over, often iteratively. Finally, the last example does not compile because InputStream is an abstract class, and therefore you cannot create an instance of it.

Decoding I/O Class Names

Pay close attention to the name of the I/O class on the exam, as decoding it often gives you context clues as to what the class does. For example, without needing to look it up, it should be clear that FileReader is a class that reads data from a file as characters or strings. Furthermore, ObjectOutputStream sounds like a class that writes object data to a byte stream.

Review of **java.io** Class Name Properties

- A class with the word InputStream or OutputStream in its name is used for reading or writing binary or byte data, respectively.

- A class with the word Reader or Writer in its name is used for reading or writing character or string data, respectively.

- Most, but not all, input classes have a corresponding output class.

- A low-level stream connects directly with the source of the data.

- A high-level stream is built on top of another stream using wrapping.
- A class with `Buffered` in its name reads or writes data in groups of bytes or characters and often improves performance in sequential file systems.
- With a few exceptions, you only wrap a stream with another stream if they share the same abstract parent.

For the last rule, we'll cover some of those exceptions (like wrapping an `OutputStream` with a `PrintWriter`) later in the chapter.

Table 19.2 lists the abstract base classes that all I/O streams inherited from.

TABLE 19.2 The java.io abstract stream base classes

Class Name	Description
InputStream	Abstract class for all input byte streams
OutputStream	Abstract class for all output byte streams
Reader	Abstract class for all input character streams
Writer	Abstract class for all output character streams

Table 19.3 lists the concrete I/O streams that you should be familiar with for the exam. Note that most of the information about each stream, such as whether it is an input or output stream or whether it accesses data using bytes or characters, can be decoded by the name alone.

TABLE 19.3 The java.io concrete stream classes

Class Name	Low/High Level	Description
FileInputStream	Low	Reads file data as bytes
FileOutputStream	Low	Writes file data as bytes
FileReader	Low	Reads file data as characters
FileWriter	Low	Writes file data as characters
BufferedInputStream	High	Reads byte data from an existing InputStream in a buffered manner, which improves efficiency and performance
BufferedOutputStream	High	Writes byte data to an existing OutputStream in a buffered manner, which improves efficiency and performance

Class Name	Low/High Level	Description
BufferedReader	High	Reads character data from an existing Reader in a buffered manner, which improves efficiency and performance
BufferedWriter	High	Writes character data to an existing Writer in a buffered manner, which improves efficiency and performance
ObjectInputStream	High	Deserializes primitive Java data types and graphs of Java objects from an existing InputStream
ObjectOutputStream	High	Serializes primitive Java data types and graphs of Java objects to an existing OutputStream
PrintStream	High	Writes formatted representations of Java objects to a binary stream
PrintWriter	High	Writes formatted representations of Java objects to a character stream

Keep Table 19.2 and Table 19.3 handy throughout this chapter. We will discuss these in more detail including examples of each.

Common I/O Stream Operations

While there are a lot of stream classes, many share a lot of the same operations. In this section, we'll review the common methods among various stream classes. In the next section, we'll cover specific stream classes.

Reading and Writing Data

I/O streams are all about reading/writing data, so it shouldn't be a surprise that the most important methods are read() and write(). Both InputStream and Reader declare the following method to read byte data from a stream:

```
// InputStream and Reader
public int read() throws IOException
```

Likewise, OutputStream and Writer both define the following method to write a byte to the stream:

```
// OutputStream and Writer
public void write(int b) throws IOException
```

Hold on. We said we are reading and writing bytes, so why do the methods use int instead of byte? Remember, the byte data type has a range of 256 characters. They needed an extra value to indicate the end of a stream. The authors of Java decided to use a larger data type, int, so that special values like –1 would indicate the end of a stream. The output stream classes use int as well, to be consistent with the input stream classes.

 Other stream classes you will learn about in this chapter throw exceptions to denote the end of the stream rather than a special value like –1.

The following copyStream() methods show an example of reading all of the values of an InputStream and Reader and writing them to an OutputStream and Writer, respectively. In both examples, –1 is used to indicate the end of the stream.

```
void copyStream(InputStream in, OutputStream out) throws IOException {
    int b;
    while ((b = in.read()) != -1) {
        out.write(b);
    }
}

void copyStream(Reader in, Writer out) throws IOException {
    int b;
    while ((b = in.read()) != -1) {
        out.write(b);
    }
}
```

 Most I/O stream methods declare a checked IOException. File or network resources that a stream relies on can disappear at any time, and our programs need be able to readily adapt to these outages.

The byte stream classes also include overloaded methods for reading and writing multiple bytes at a time.

```
// InputStream
public int read(byte[] b) throws IOException
public int read(byte[] b, int offset, int length) throws IOException
```

```
// OutputStream
public void write(byte[] b) throws IOException
public void write(byte[] b, int offset, int length) throws IOException
```

The offset and length are applied to the array itself. For example, an offset of 5 and length of 3 indicates that the stream should read up to 3 bytes of data and put them into the array starting with position 5.

There are equivalent methods for the character stream classes that use char instead of byte.

```
// Reader
public int read(char[] c) throws IOException
public int read(char[] c, int offset, int length) throws IOException


// Writer
public void write(char[] c) throws IOException
public void write(char[] c, int offset, int length) throws IOException
```

We'll see examples of these methods later in the chapter.

Closing the Stream

All I/O streams include a method to release any resources within the stream when it is no longer needed.

```
// All I/O stream classes
public void close() throws IOException
```

Since streams are considered resources, it is imperative that all I/O streams be closed after they are used lest they lead to resource leaks. Since all I/O streams implement Closeable, the best way to do this is with a try-with-resources statement, which you saw in Chapter 16, "Exceptions, Assertions, and Localization."

```
try (var fis = new FileInputStream("zoo-data.txt")) {
    System.out.print(fis.read());
}
```

In many file systems, failing to close a file properly could leave it locked by the operating system such that no other processes could read/write to it until the program is terminated. Throughout this chapter, we will close stream resources using the try-with-resources syntax since this is the preferred way of closing resources in Java. We will also use var to shorten the declarations, since these statements can get quite long!

What about if you need to pass a stream to a method? That's fine, but the stream should be closed in the method that created it.

```
public void printData(InputStream is) throws IOException {
    int b;
```

```
    while ((b = is.read()) != -1) {
        System.out.print(b);
    }
}

public void readFile(String fileName) throws IOException {
    try (var fis = new FileInputStream(fileName)) {
        printData(fis);
    }
}
```

In this example, the stream is created and closed in the readFile() method, with the printData() processing the contents.

Closing Wrapped Streams

When working with a wrapped stream, you only need to use close() on the topmost object. Doing so will close the underlying streams. The following example is valid and will result in three separate close() method calls but is unnecessary:

```
    try (var fis = new FileOutputStream("zoo-banner.txt"); // Unnecessary
        var bis = new BufferedOutputStream(fis);
        var ois = new ObjectOutputStream(bis)) {
      ois.writeObject("Hello");
    }
```

Instead, we can rely on the ObjectOutputStream to close the BufferedOutputStream and FileOutputStream. The following will call only one close() method instead of three:

```
    try (var ois = new ObjectOutputStream(
        new BufferedOutputStream(
          new FileOutputStream("zoo-banner.txt")))) {
      ois.writeObject("Hello");
    }
```

Manipulating Input Streams

All input stream classes include the following methods to manipulate the order in which data is read from a stream:

```
// InputStream and Reader
public boolean markSupported()
```

```
public void void mark(int readLimit)

public void reset() throws IOException

public long skip(long n) throws IOException
```

The mark() and reset() methods return a stream to an earlier position. Before calling either of these methods, you should call the markSupported() method, which returns true only if mark() is supported. The skip() method is pretty simple; it basically reads data from the stream and discards the contents.

Not all input stream classes support mark() and reset(). Make sure to call markSupported() on the stream before calling these methods or an exception will be thrown at runtime.

mark() and *reset()*

Assume that we have an InputStream instance whose next values are LION. Consider the following code snippet:

```
public void readData(InputStream is) throws IOException {
    System.out.print((char) is.read());      // L
    if (is.markSupported()) {
        is.mark(100);  // Marks up to 100 bytes
        System.out.print((char) is.read());  // I
        System.out.print((char) is.read());  // O
        is.reset();     // Resets stream to position before I
    }
    System.out.print((char) is.read());      // I
    System.out.print((char) is.read());      // O
    System.out.print((char) is.read());      // N
}
```

The code snippet will output LIOION if mark() is supported, and LION otherwise. It's a good practice to organize your read() operations so that the stream ends up at the same position regardless of whether mark() is supported.

What about the value of 100 we passed to the mark() method? This value is called the readLimit. It instructs the stream that we expect to call reset() after at most 100 bytes. If our program calls reset() after reading more than 100 bytes from calling mark(100), then it may throw an exception, depending on the stream class.

In actuality, mark() and reset() are not really putting the data back into the stream but storing the data in a temporary buffer in memory to be read again. Therefore, you should not call the mark() operation with too large a value, as this could take up a lot of memory.

skip()

Assume that we have an `InputStream` instance whose next values are TIGERS. Consider the following code snippet:

```
System.out.print ((char)is.read()); // T
is.skip(2);  // Skips I and G
is.read();   // Reads E but doesn't output it
System.out.print((char)is.read());  // R
System.out.print((char)is.read());  // S
```

This code prints TRS at runtime. We skipped two characters, I and G. We also read E but didn't store it anywhere, so it behaved like calling `skip(1)`.

The return parameter of `skip()` tells us how many values were actually skipped. For example, if we are near the end of the stream and call `skip(1000)`, the return value might be 20, indicating the end of the stream was reached after 20 values were skipped. Using the return value of `skip()` is important if you need to keep track of where you are in a stream and how many bytes have been processed.

Flushing Output Streams

When data is written to an output stream, the underlying operating system does not guarantee that the data will make it to the file system immediately. In many operating systems, the data may be cached in memory, with a write occurring only after a temporary cache is filled or after some amount of time has passed.

If the data is cached in memory and the application terminates unexpectedly, the data would be lost, because it was never written to the file system. To address this, all output stream classes provide a `flush()` method, which requests that all accumulated data be written immediately to disk.

```
// OutputStream and Writer
public void flush() throws IOException
```

In the following sample, 1,000 characters are written to a file stream. The calls to `flush()` ensure that data is sent to the hard drive at least once every 100 characters. The JVM or operating system is free to send the data more frequently.

```
try (var fos = new FileOutputStream(fileName)) {
   for(int i=0; i<1000; i++) {
      fos.write('a');
      if(i % 100 == 0) {
         fos.flush();
      }
   }
}
```

The flush() method helps reduce the amount of data lost if the application terminates unexpectedly. It is not without cost, though. Each time it is used, it may cause a noticeable delay in the application, especially for large files. Unless the data that you are writing is extremely critical, the flush() method should be used only intermittently. For example, it should not necessarily be called after every write.

You also do not need to call the flush() method when you have finished writing data, since the close() method will automatically do this.

Reviewing Common I/O Stream Methods

Table 19.4 reviews the common stream methods you should know for this chapter. For the read() and write() methods that take primitive arrays, the method parameter type depends on the stream type. Byte streams ending in InputStream/OutputStream use byte[], while character streams ending in Reader/Writer use char[].

TABLE 19.4   Common I/O stream methods

Stream Class	Method Name	Description
All streams	void close()	Closes stream and releases resources
All input streams	int read()	Reads a single byte or returns −1 if no bytes were available
InputStream Reader	int read(byte[] b) int read(char[] c)	Reads values into a buffer. Returns number of bytes read
InputStream Reader	int read(byte[] b, int offset, int length) int read(char[] c, int offset, int length)	Reads up to length values into a buffer starting from position offset. Returns number of bytes read
All output streams	void write(int)	Writes a single byte
OutputStream Writer	void write(byte[] b) void write(char[] c)	Writes an array of values into the stream
OutputStream Writer	void write(byte[] b, int offset, int length) void write(char[] c, int offset, int length)	Writes length values from an array into the stream, starting with an offset index

TABLE 19.4   Common I/O stream methods *(continued)*

Stream Class	Method Name	Description
All input streams	boolean markSupported()	Returns true if the stream class supports mark()
All input streams	mark(int readLimit)	Marks the current position in the stream
All input streams	void reset()	Attempts to reset the stream to the mark() position
All input streams	long skip(long n)	Reads and discards a specified number of characters
All output streams	void flush()	Flushes buffered data through the stream

Remember that input and output streams can refer to both byte and character streams throughout this chapter.

Working with I/O Stream Classes

Now that we've reviewed the types of streams and their properties, it's time to jump in and work with concrete I/O stream classes. Some of the techniques for accessing streams may seem a bit new to you, but as you will see, they are similar among different stream classes.

The I/O stream classes include numerous overloaded constructors and methods. Hundreds in fact. Don't panic! In this section, we present the most common constructors and methods that you should be familiar with for the exam.

Reading and Writing Binary Data

The first stream classes that we are going to discuss in detail are the most basic file stream classes, FileInputStream and FileOutputStream. They are used to read bytes from a file or write bytes to a file, respectively. These classes connect to a file using the following constructors:

```
public FileInputStream(File file) throws FileNotFoundException
public FileInputStream(String name) throws FileNotFoundException
```

```
public FileOutputStream(File file) throws FileNotFoundException
public FileOutputStream(String name) throws FileNotFoundException
```

> If you need to append to an existing file, there's a constructor for that. The FileOutputStream class includes overloaded constructors that take a boolean append flag. When set to true, the output stream will append to the end of a file if it already exists. This is useful for writing to the end of log files, for example.

The following code uses FileInputStream and FileOutputStream to copy a file. It's nearly the same as our previous copyStream() method, except that it operates specifically on files.

```
void copyFile(File src, File dest) throws IOException {
    try (var in = new FileInputStream(src);
        var out = new FileOutputStream(dest)) {
        int b;
        while ((b = in.read()) != -1) {
            out.write(b);
        }
    }
}
```

If the source file does not exist, a FileNotFoundException, which inherits IOException, will be thrown. If the destination file already exists, this implementation will overwrite it, since the append flag was not sent. The copy() method copies one byte at a time until it reads a value of −1.

Buffering Binary Data

While our copyFile() method is valid, it tends to perform poorly on large files. As discussed earlier, that's because there is a cost associated with each round-trip to the file system. We can easily enhance our implementation using BufferedInputStream and BufferedOutputStream. As high-level streams, these classes include constructors that take other streams as input.

```
public BufferedInputStream(InputStream in)
public BufferedOutputStream(OutputStream out)
```

Why Use the *Buffered* Classes?

Since the read/write methods that use byte[] exist in InputStream/OutputStream, why use the Buffered classes at all? In particular, we could have rewritten our earlier copyFile() method to use byte[] without introducing the Buffered classes. Put simply, the Buffered classes contain a number of performance improvements for managing data in memory.

For example, the BufferedInputStream class is capable of retrieving and storing in memory more data than you might request with a single read(byte[]) call. For successive calls to the read(byte[]) method with a small byte array, using the Buffered classes would be faster in a wide variety of situations, since the data can be returned directly from memory without going to the file system.

The following shows how to apply these streams:

```
void copyFileWithBuffer(File src, File dest) throws IOException {
    try (var in = new BufferedInputStream(
            new FileInputStream(src));
        var out = new BufferedOutputStream(
            new FileOutputStream(dest))) {
        var buffer = new byte[1024];
        int lengthRead;
        while ((lengthRead = in.read(buffer)) > 0) {
            out.write(buffer, 0, lengthRead);
            out.flush();
        }
    }
}
```

Instead of reading the data one byte at a time, we read and write up to 1024 bytes at a time. The return value lengthRead is critical for determining whether we are at the end of the stream and knowing how many bytes we should write into our output stream. We also added a flush() command at the end of the loop to ensure data is written to disk between each iteration.

Unless our file happens to be a multiple of 1024 bytes, the last iteration of the while loop will write some value less than 1024 bytes. For example, if the buffer size is 1,024 bytes and the file size is 1,054 bytes, then the last read will be only 30 bytes. If we had ignored this return value and instead wrote 1,024 bytes, then 994 bytes from the previous loop would be written to the end of the file.

Real World Scenario

Choosing a Buffer Size

Given the way computers organize data, it is often appropriate to choose a buffer size that is a power of 2, such as 1,024. Performance tuning often involves determining what buffer size is most appropriate for your application.

What buffer size should you use? Any buffer size that is a power of 2 from 1,024 to 65,536 is a good choice in practice. Keep in mind, the biggest performance gain you'll see is from moving from nonbuffered access to buffered access. Once you are using a buffered stream, you're less likely to see a huge performance difference between a buffer size of 1,024 and 2,048, for example.

Reading and Writing Character Data

The FileReader and FileWriter classes, along with their associated buffer classes, are among the most convenient I/O classes because of their built-in support for text data. They include constructors that take the same input as the binary file classes.

```
public FileReader(File file) throws FileNotFoundException
public FileReader(String name) throws FileNotFoundException

public FileWriter(File file) throws FileNotFoundException
public FileWriter(String name) throws FileNotFoundException
```

The following is an example of using these classes to copy a text file:

```
void copyTextFile(File src, File dest) throws IOException {
   try (var reader = new FileReader(src);
        var writer = new FileWriter(dest)) {
      int b;
      while ((b = reader.read()) != -1) {
         writer.write(b);
      }
   }
}
```

Wait a second, this looks identical to our copyFile() method with byte stream! Since we're copying one character at a time, rather than one byte, it is.

The FileReader class doesn't contain any new methods you haven't seen before. The FileWriter inherits a method from the Writer class that allows it to write String values.

```
// Writer
public void write(String str) throws IOException
```

For example, the following is supported in FileWriter but not FileOutputStream:

```
writer.write("Hello World");
```

We'll see even more enhancements for character streams next.

Buffering Character Data

Like we saw with byte streams, Java includes high-level buffered character streams that improve performance. The constructors take existing Reader and Writer instances as input.

```
public BufferedReader(Reader in)
```

```
public BufferedWriter(Writer out)
```

They add two new methods, readLine() and newLine(), that are particularly useful when working with String values.

```
// BufferedReader
public String readLine() throws IOException
```

```
// BufferedWriter
public void newLine() throws IOException
```

Putting it all together, the following shows how to copy a file, one line at a time:

```
void copyTextFileWithBuffer(File src, File dest) throws IOException {
    try (var reader = new BufferedReader(new FileReader(src));
         var writer = new BufferedWriter(new FileWriter(dest))) {
        String s;
        while ((s = reader.readLine()) != null) {
            writer.write(s);
            writer.newLine();
        }
    }
}
```

In this example, each loop iteration corresponds to reading and writing a line of a file. Assuming the length of the lines in the file are reasonably sized, this implementation will perform well.

There are some important distinctions between this method and our earlier copyFileWithBuffer() method that worked with byte streams. First, instead of a buffer array, we are using a String to store the data read during each loop iteration. By storing the data temporarily as a String, we can manipulate it as we would any String value. For example, we can call replaceAll() or toUpperCase() to create new values.

Next, we are checking for the end of the stream with a null value instead of –1. Finally, we are inserting a newLine() on every iteration of the loop. This is because readLine() strips out the line break character. Without the call to newLine(), the copied file would have all of its line breaks removed.

> In the next chapter, we'll show you how to use NIO.2 to read the lines of a file in a single command. We'll even show you how to process the lines of a file using the functional programming streams that you worked with in Chapter 15.

Serializing Data

Throughout this book, we have been managing our data model using classes, so it makes sense that we would want to save these objects between program executions. Data about our zoo animal's health wouldn't be particularly useful if it had to be entered every time the program runs!

You can certainly use the I/O stream classes you've learned about so far to store text and binary data, but you still have to figure out how to put the data in the stream and then decode it later. There are various file formats like XML and CSV you can standardize to, but oftentimes you have to build the translation yourself.

Luckily, we can use serialization to solve the problem of how to convert objects to/from a stream. *Serialization* is the process of converting an in-memory object to a byte stream. Likewise, *deserialization* is the process of converting from a byte stream into an object. Serialization often involves writing an object to a stored or transmittable format, while deserialization is the reciprocal process.

Figure 19.3 shows a visual representation of serializing and deserializing a Giraffe object to and from a giraffe.txt file.

FIGURE 19.3   Serialization process

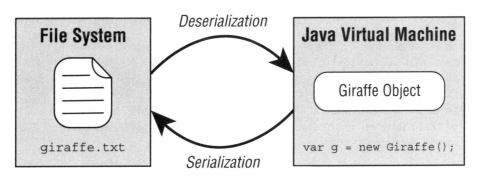

In this section, we will show you how Java provides built-in mechanisms for serializing and deserializing streams of objects directly to and from disk, respectively.

Applying the *Serializable* Interface

To serialize an object using the I/O API, the object must implement the java.io.Serializable interface. The Serializable interface is a marker interface, similar to the marker annotations you learned about in Chapter 13, "Annotations." By marker interface, it means the interface does not have any methods. Any class can implement the Serializable interface since there are no required methods to implement.

 Since Serializable is a marker interface with no abstract members, why not just apply it to every class? Generally speaking, you should only mark data-oriented classes serializable. Process-oriented classes, such as the I/O streams discussed in this chapter, or the Thread instances you learned about in Chapter 18, "Concurrency," are often poor candidates for serialization, as the internal state of those classes tends to be ephemeral or short-lived.

The purpose of using the Serializable interface is to inform any process attempting to serialize the object that you have taken the proper steps to make the object serializable. All Java primitives and many of the built-in Java classes that you have worked with throughout this book are Serializable. For example, this class can be serialized:

```java
import java.io.Serializable;
public class Gorilla implements Serializable {
    private static final long serialVersionUID = 1L;
    private String name;
    private int age;
    private Boolean friendly;
    private transient String favoriteFood;

    // Constructors/Getters/Setters/toString() omitted
}
```

In this example, the Gorilla class contains three instance members (name, age, friendly) that will be saved to a stream if the class is serialized. Note that since Serializable is not part of the java.lang package, it must be imported or referenced with the package name.

What about the favoriteFood field that is marked transient? Any field that is marked transient will not be saved to a stream when the class is serialized. We'll discuss that in more detail next.

Real World Scenario

Maintaining a *serialVersionUID*

It's a good practice to declare a `static serialVersionUID` variable in every class that implements `Serializable`. The version is stored with each object as part of serialization. Then, every time the class structure changes, this value is updated or incremented.

Perhaps our `Gorilla` class receives a new instance member `Double banana`, or maybe the age field is renamed. The idea is a class could have been serialized with an older version of the class and deserialized with a newer version of the class.

The `serialVersionUID` helps inform the JVM that the stored data may not match the new class definition. If an older version of the class is encountered during deserialization, a `java.io.InvalidClassException` may be thrown. Alternatively, some APIs support converting data between versions.

Marking Data *transient*

Oftentimes, the `transient` modifier is used for sensitive data of the class, like a `password`. You'll learn more about this topic in Chapter 22, "Security." There are other objects it does not make sense to serialize, like the state of an in-memory `Thread`. If the object is part of a serializable object, we just mark it `transient` to ignore these select instance members.

What happens to data marked `transient` on deserialization? It reverts to its default Java values, such as `0.0` for `double`, or `null` for an object. We'll see examples of this shortly when we present the object stream classes.

 Marking `static` fields `transient` has little effect on serialization. Other than the `serialVersionUID`, only the instance members of a class are serialized.

Ensuring a Class Is *Serializable*

Since `Serializable` is a marker interface, you might think there are no rules to using it. Not quite! Any process attempting to serialize an object will throw a `NotSerializableException` if the class does not implement the `Serializable` interface properly.

How to Make a Class Serializable

- The class must be marked `Serializable`.
- Every instance member of the class is serializable, marked `transient`, or has a null value at the time of serialization.

Be careful with the second rule. For a class to be serializable, we must apply the second rule recursively. Do you see why the following `Cat` class is not serializable?

```
public class Cat implements Serializable {
    private Tail tail = new Tail();
}

public class Tail implements Serializable {
    private Fur fur = new Fur();
}

public class Fur {}
```

Cat contains an instance of `Tail`, and both of those classes are marked `Serializable`, so no problems there. Unfortunately, `Tail` contains an instance of `Fur` that is not marked `Serializable`.

Either of the following changes fixes the problem and allows `Cat` to be serialized:

```
public class Tail implements Serializable {
    private transient Fur fur = new Fur();
}

public class Fur implements Serializable {}
```

We could also make our `tail` or `fur` instance members `null`, although this would make `Cat` serializable only for particular instances, rather than all instances.

Storing Data with *ObjectOutputStream* and *ObjectInputStream*

The `ObjectInputStream` class is used to deserialize an object from a stream, while the `ObjectOutputStream` is used to serialize an object to a stream. They are high-level streams that operate on existing streams.

```
public ObjectInputStream(InputStream in) throws IOException

public ObjectOutputStream(OutputStream out) throws IOException
```

While both of these classes contain a number of methods for built-in data types like primitives, the two methods you need to know for the exam are the ones related to working with objects.

```
// ObjectInputStream
public Object readObject() throws IOException, ClassNotFoundException

// ObjectOutputStream
public void writeObject(Object obj) throws IOException
```

We now provide a sample method that serializes a List of Gorilla objects to a file.

```
void saveToFile(List<Gorilla> gorillas, File dataFile)
      throws IOException {
   try (var out = new ObjectOutputStream(
         new BufferedOutputStream(
            new FileOutputStream(dataFile)))) {
      for (Gorilla gorilla : gorillas)
         out.writeObject(gorilla);
   }
}
```

Pretty easy, right? Notice we start with a file stream, wrap it in a buffered stream to improve performance, and then wrap that with an object stream. Serializing the data is as simple as passing it to writeObject().

Once the data is stored in a file, we can deserialize it using the following method:

```
List<Gorilla> readFromFile(File dataFile) throws IOException,
      ClassNotFoundException {
   var gorillas = new ArrayList<Gorilla>();
   try (var in = new ObjectInputStream(
         new BufferedInputStream(
            new FileInputStream(dataFile)))) {
      while (true) {
         var object = in.readObject();
         if (object instanceof Gorilla)
            gorillas.add((Gorilla) object);
      }
   } catch (EOFException e) {
      // File end reached
   }
   return gorillas;
}
```

Ah, not as simple as our save method, was it? When calling readObject(), null and −1 do not have any special meaning, as someone might have serialized objects with those values. Unlike our earlier techniques for reading methods from an input stream, we need to use an infinite loop to process the data, which throws an EOFException when the end of the stream is reached.

> If your program happens to know the number of objects in the stream, then you can call readObject() a fixed number of times, rather than using an infinite loop.

Since the return type of readObject() is Object, we need an explicit cast to obtain access to our Gorilla properties. Notice that readObject() declares a checked ClassNotFoundException since the class might not be available on deserialization.

The following code snippet shows how to call the serialization methods:

```
var gorillas = new ArrayList<Gorilla>();
gorillas.add(new Gorilla("Grodd", 5, false));
gorillas.add(new Gorilla("Ishmael", 8, true));
File dataFile = new File("gorilla.data");

saveToFile(gorillas, dataFile);
var gorillasFromDisk = readFromFile(dataFile);
System.out.print(gorillasFromDisk);
```

Assuming the toString() method was properly overridden in the Gorilla class, this prints the following at runtime:

```
[[name=Grodd, age=5, friendly=false],
 [name=Ishmael, age=8, friendly=true]]
```

ObjectInputStream inherits an available() method from InputStream that you might think can be used to check for the end of the stream rather than throwing an EOFException. Unfortunately, this only tells you the number of blocks that can be read without blocking another thread. In other words, it can return 0 even if there are more bytes to be read.

Understanding the Deserialization Creation Process

For the exam, you need to understand how a deserialized object is created. When you deserialize an object, *the constructor of the serialized class, along with any instance initializers, is not called when the object is created.* Java will call the no-arg constructor of the first nonserializable parent class it can find in the class hierarchy. In our Gorilla example, this would just be the no-arg constructor of Object.

As we stated earlier, any static or transient fields are ignored. Values that are not provided will be given their default Java value, such as null for String, or 0 for int values.

Let's take a look at a new Chimpanzee class. This time we do list the constructors to illustrate that none of them is used on deserialization.

```
import java.io.Serializable;
public class Chimpanzee implements Serializable {
    private static final long serialVersionUID = 2L;
    private transient String name;
    private transient int age = 10;
```

```
   private static char type = 'C';
   { this.age = 14; }

   public Chimpanzee() {
      this.name = "Unknown";
      this.age = 12;
      this.type = 'Q';
   }

   public Chimpanzee(String name, int age, char type) {
      this.name = name;
      this.age = age;
      this.type = type;
   }

   // Getters/Setters/toString() omitted
}
```

Assuming we rewrite our previous serialization and deserialization methods to process a Chimpanzee object instead of a Gorilla object, what do you think the following prints?

```
var chimpanzees = new ArrayList<Chimpanzee>();
chimpanzees.add(new Chimpanzee("Ham", 2, 'A'));
chimpanzees.add(new Chimpanzee("Enos", 4, 'B'));
File dataFile = new File("chimpanzee.data");

saveToFile(chimpanzees, dataFile);
var chimpanzeesFromDisk = readFromFile(dataFile);
System.out.println(chimpanzeesFromDisk);
```

Think about it. Go on, we'll wait.

Ready for the answer? Well, for starters, none of the instance members would be serialized to a file. The name and age variables are both marked transient, while the type variable is static. We purposely accessed the type variable using this to see whether you were paying attention.

Upon deserialization, none of the constructors in Chimpanzee is called. Even the no-arg constructor that sets the values [name=Unknown,age=12,type=Q] is ignored. The instance initializer that sets age to 14 is also not executed.

In this case, the name variable is initialized to null since that's the default value for String in Java. Likewise, the age variable is initialized to 0. The program prints the following, assuming the toString() method is implemented:

```
[[name=null,age=0,type=B],
 [name=null,age=0,type=B]]
```

What about the `type` variable? Since it's `static`, it will actually display whatever value was set last. If the data is serialized and deserialized within the same execution, then it will display B, since that was the last `Chimpanzee` we created. On the other hand, if the program performs the deserialization and print on startup, then it will print C, since that is the value the class is initialized with.

For the exam, make sure you understand that the constructor and any instance initializations defined in the serialized class are ignored during the deserialization process. Java only calls the constructor of the first non-serializable parent class in the class hierarchy. In Chapter 22, we will go even deeper into serialization and show you how to write methods to customize the serialization process.

 Real World Scenario

Other Serialization APIs

In this chapter, we focus on serialization using the I/O streams, such as `ObjectInputStream` and `ObjectOutputStream`. While not part of the exam, you should be aware there are many other (often more popular) APIs for serializing Java objects. For example, there are APIs to serialize data to JSON or encrypted data files.

While these APIs might not use I/O stream classes, many make use of the built-in `Serializable` interface and `transient` modifier. Some of these APIs also include annotations to customize the serialization and deserialization of objects, such as what to do when values are missing or need to be translated.

Printing Data

`PrintStream` and `PrintWriter` are high-level output print streams classes that are useful for writing text data to a stream. We cover these classes together, because they include many of the same methods. Just remember that one operates on an `OutputStream` and the other a `Writer`.

The print stream classes have the distinction of being the only I/O stream classes we cover that do not have corresponding input stream classes. And unlike other `OutputStream` classes, `PrintStream` does not have `Output` in its name.

The print stream classes include the following constructors:

```
public PrintStream(OutputStream out)
```

```
public PrintWriter(Writer out)
```

For convenience, these classes also include constructors that automatically wrap the print stream around a low-level file stream class, such as FileOutputStream and FileWriter.

```
public PrintStream(File file) throws FileNotFoundException
public PrintStream(String fileName) throws FileNotFoundException

public PrintWriter(File file) throws FileNotFoundException
public PrintWriter(String fileName) throws FileNotFoundException
```

Furthermore, the PrintWriter class even has a constructor that takes an OutputStream as input. This is one of the few exceptions in which we can mix a byte and character stream.

```
public PrintWriter(OutputStream out)
```

 It may surprise you that you've been regularly using a PrintStream throughout this book. Both System.out and System.err are PrintStream objects. Likewise, System.in, often useful for reading user input, is an InputStream. We'll be covering all three of these objects in the next part of this chapter on user interactions.

Besides the inherited write() methods, the print stream classes include numerous methods for writing data including print(), println(), and format(). Unlike the majority of the other streams we've covered, the methods in the print stream classes do not throw any checked exceptions. If they did, you would have been required to catch a checked exception anytime you called System.out.print()! The stream classes do provide a method, checkError(), that can be used to check for an error after a write.

When working with String data, you should use a Writer, so our examples in this part of the chapter use PrintWriter. Just be aware that many of these examples can be easily rewritten to use a PrintStream.

print()

The most basic of the print-based methods is print(). The print stream classes include numerous overloaded versions of print(), which take everything from primitives and String values, to objects. Under the covers, these methods often just perform String.valueOf() on the argument and call the underlying stream's write() method to add it to the stream. For example, the following sets of print/write code are equivalent:

```
try (PrintWriter out = new PrintWriter("zoo.log")) {
   out.write(String.valueOf(5));   // Writer method
   out.print(5);                   // PrintWriter method
```

```
    var a = new Chimpanzee();
    out.write(a==null ? "null": a.toString()); // Writer method
    out.print(a);                              // PrintWriter method
}
```

println()

The next methods available in the PrintStream and PrintWriter classes are the println() methods, which are virtually identical to the print() methods, except that they also print a line break after the String value is written. These print stream classes also include a no-argument version of println(), which just prints a single line break.

The println() methods are especially helpful, as the line break character is dependent on the operating system. For example, in some systems a line feed symbol, \n, signifies a line break, whereas other systems use a carriage return symbol followed by a line feed symbol, \r\n, to signify a line break. Like the file.separator property, the line.separator value is available from two places, as a Java system property and via a static method.

```
System.getProperty("line.separator");
System.lineSeparator();
```

format()

In Chapter 16, you learned a lot about formatting messages, dates, and numbers to various locales. Each print stream class includes a format() method, which includes an overloaded version that takes a Locale.

```
// PrintStream
public PrintStream format(String format, Object args...)
public PrintStream format(Locale loc, String format, Object args...)

// PrintWriter
public PrintWriter format(String format, Object args...)
public PrintWriter format(Locale loc, String format, Object args...)
```

NOTE   For convenience (as well as to make C developers feel more at home), Java includes printf() methods, which function identically to the format() methods. The only thing you need to know about these methods is that they are interchangeable with format().

The method parameters are used to construct a formatted String in a single method call, rather than via a lot of format and concatenation operations. They return a reference to the instance they are called on so that operations can be chained together.

As an example, the following two `format()` calls print the same text:

```
String name = "Lindsey";
int orderId = 5;

// Both print: Hello Lindsey, order 5 is ready
System.out.format("Hello "+name+", order "+orderId+" is ready");
System.out.format("Hello %s, order %d is ready", name, orderId);
```

In the second `format()` operation, the parameters are inserted and formatted via symbols in the order that they are provided in the vararg. Table 19.5 lists the ones you should know for the exam.

TABLE 19.5 Common print stream `format()` symbols

Symbol	Description
%s	Applies to any type, commonly `String` values
%d	Applies to integer values like `int` and `long`
%f	Applies to floating-point values like `float` and `double`
%n	Inserts a line break using the system-dependent line separator

The following example uses all four symbols from Table 19.5:

```
String name = "James";
double score = 90.25;
int total = 100;
System.out.format("%s:%n   Score: %f out of %d", name, score, total);
```

This prints the following:

```
James:
   Score: 90.250000 out of 100
```

Mixing data types may cause exceptions at runtime. For example, the following throws an exception because a floating-point number is used when an integer value is expected:

```
System.out.format("Food: %d tons", 2.0); // IllegalFormatConversionException
```

Using *format()* with *Flags*

Besides supporting symbols, Java also supports optional flags between the % and the symbol character. In the previous example, the floating-point number was printed as 90.250000. By default, %f displays exactly six digits past the decimal. If you want to display only one digit after the decimal, you could use %.1f instead of %f. The format() method relies on rounding, rather than truncating when shortening numbers. For example, 90.250000 will be displayed as 90.3 (not 90.2) when passed to format() with %.1f.

The format() method also supports two additional features. You can specify the total length of output by using a number before the decimal symbol. By default, the method will fill the empty space with blank spaces. You can also fill the empty space with zeros, by placing a single zero before the decimal symbol. The following examples use brackets, [], to show the start/end of the formatted value:

```
var pi = 3.14159265359;
System.out.format("[%f]",pi);      // [3.141593]
System.out.format("[%12.8f]",pi);  // [  3.14159265]
System.out.format("[%012f]",pi);   // [00003.141593]
System.out.format("[%12.2f]",pi);  // [        3.14]
System.out.format("[%.3f]",pi);    // [3.142]
```

The format() method supports a lot of other symbols and flags. You don't need to know any of them for the exam beyond what we've discussed already.

Sample *PrintWriter* Program

Let's put it altogether. The following sample code shows the PrintWriter class in action:

```
File source = new File("zoo.log");
try (var out = new PrintWriter(
   new BufferedWriter(new FileWriter(source)))) {
   out.print("Today's weather is: ");
   out.println("Sunny");
   out.print("Today's temperature at the zoo is: ");
   out.print(1 / 3.0);
   out.println('C');
```

```
    out.format("It has rained %5.2f inches this year %d", 10.2, 2021);
    out.println();
    out.printf("It may rain %s more inches this year", 1.2);
}
```

After the program runs, zoo.log contains the following:

```
Today's weather is: Sunny
Today's temperature at the zoo is: 0.3333333333333333C
It has rained 10.20 inches this year 2021
It may rain 1.2 more inches this year
```

You should pay close attention to the line breaks in the sample. For example, we called println() after our format(), since format() does not automatically insert a line break after the text. One of the most common bugs with printing data in practice is failing to account for line breaks properly.

Review of Stream Classes

We conclude our discussion of stream classes with Figure 19.4. This diagram shows all of the I/O stream classes that you should be familiar with for the exam, with the exception of the filter streams. FilterInputStream and FilterOutputStream are high-level super-classes that filter or transform data. They are rarely used directly.

InputStreamReader and *OutputStreamWriter*

Most of the time, you can't wrap byte and character streams with each other, although as we mentioned, there are exceptions. The InputStreamReader class wraps an InputStream with a Reader, while the OutputStreamWriter class wraps an OutputStream with a Writer.

```
try (Reader r = new InputStreamReader(System.in);
    Writer w = new OutputStreamWriter(System.out)) {

}
```

These classes are incredibly convenient and are also unique in that they are the only I/O stream classes to have both InputStream/OutputStream and Reader/Writer in their name.

FIGURE 19.4   Diagram of I/O stream classes

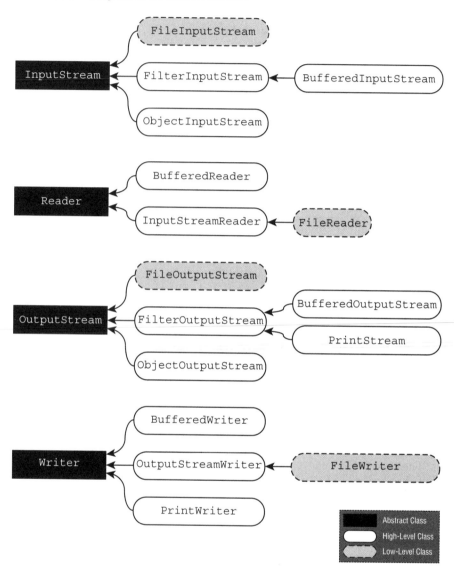

Interacting with Users

The java.io API includes numerous classes for interacting with the user. For example, you might want to write an application that asks a user to log in and prints a success message. This section contains numerous techniques for handling and responding to user input.

Printing Data to the User

Java includes two PrintStream instances for providing information to the user: System.out and System.err. While System.out should be old hat to you, System.err might be new to you. The syntax for calling and using System.err is the same as System.out but is used to report errors to the user in a separate stream from the regular output information.

```
try (var in = new FileInputStream("zoo.txt")) {
    System.out.println("Found file!");
} catch (FileNotFoundException e) {
    System.err.println("File not found!");
}
```

How do they differ in practice? In part, that depends on what is executing the program. For example, if you are running from a command prompt, they will likely print text in the same format. On the other hand, if you are working in an integrated development environment (IDE), they might print the System.err text in a different color. Finally, if the code is being run on a server, the System.err stream might write to a different log file.

 Real World Scenario

Using Logging APIs

While System.out and System.err are incredibly useful for debugging stand-alone or simple applications, they are rarely used in professional software development. Most applications rely on a logging service or API.

While there are many logging APIs available, they tend to share a number of similar attributes. First, you create a static logging object in each class. Then, you log a message with an appropriate logging level: debug(), info(), warn(), or error(). The debug() and info() methods are useful as they allow developers to log things that aren't errors but may be useful.

The log levels can be enabled as needed at runtime. For example, a server might only output warn() and error() to keep the logs clean and easy to read. If an administrator notices a lot of errors, then they might enable debug() or info() logging to help isolate the problem.

Finally, loggers can be enabled for specific classes or packages. While you may be interested in a debug() message for a class you write, you are probably not interested in seeing debug() messages for every third-party library you are using.

Reading Input as a Stream

The System.in returns an InputStream and is used to retrieve text input from the user. It is commonly wrapped with a BufferedReader via an InputStreamReader to use the readLine() method.

```
var reader = new BufferedReader(new InputStreamReader(System.in));
String userInput = reader.readLine();
System.out.println("You entered: " + userInput);
```

When executed, this application first fetches text from the user until the user presses the Enter key. It then outputs the text the user entered to the screen.

Closing *System* Streams

You might have noticed that we never created or closed System.out, System.err, and System.in when we used them. In fact, these are the only I/O streams in the entire chapter that we did not use a try-with-resources block on!

Because these are static objects, the System streams are shared by the entire application. The JVM creates and opens them for us. They can be used in a try-with-resources statement or by calling close(), although *closing them is not recommended*. Closing the System streams makes them permanently unavailable for all threads in the remainder of the program.

What do you think the following code snippet prints?

```
try (var out = System.out) {}
System.out.println("Hello");
```

Nothing. It prints nothing. Remember, the methods of PrintStream do not throw any checked exceptions and rely on the checkError() to report errors, so they fail silently.

What about this example?

```
try (var err = System.err) {}
System.err.println("Hello");
```

This one also prints nothing. Like System.out, System.err is a PrintStream. Even if it did throw an exception, though, we'd have a hard time seeing it since our stream for reporting errors is closed! Closing System.err is a particularly bad idea, since the stack traces from all exceptions will be hidden.

Finally, what do you think this code snippet does?

```
var reader = new BufferedReader(new InputStreamReader(System.in));
try (reader) {}
String data = reader.readLine();  // IOException
```

It prints an exception at runtime. Unlike the PrintStream class, most InputStream implementations will throw an exception if you try to operate on a closed stream.

Acquiring Input with *Console*

The java.io.Console class is specifically designed to handle user interactions. After all, System.in and System.out are just raw streams, whereas Console is a class with numerous methods centered around user input.

The Console class is a singleton because it is accessible only from a factory method and only one instance of it is created by the JVM. For example, if you come across code on the exam such as the following, it does not compile, since the constructors are all private:

```
Console c = new Console();   // DOES NOT COMPILE
```

The following snippet shows how to obtain a Console and use it to retrieve user input:

```
Console console = System.console();
if (console != null) {
   String userInput = console.readLine();
   console.writer().println("You entered: " + userInput);
} else {
   System.err.println("Console not available");
}
```

> The Console object may not be available, depending on where the code is being called. If it is not available, then System.console() returns null. It is imperative that you check for a null value before attempting to use a Console object!

This program first retrieves an instance of the Console and verifies that it is available, outputting a message to System.err if it is not. If it is available, then it retrieves a line of input from the user and prints the result. As you might have noticed, this example is equivalent to our earlier example of reading user input with System.in and System.out.

reader() and *writer()*

The Console class includes access to two streams for reading and writing data.

```
public Reader reader()
```

```
public PrintWriter writer()
```

Accessing these classes is analogous to calling System.in and System.out directly, although they use character streams rather than byte streams. In this manner, they are more appropriate for handling text data.

format()

For printing data with a Console, you can skip calling the writer().format() and output the data directly to the stream in a single call.

```
public Console format(String format, Object... args)
```

The format() method behaves the same as the format() method on the stream classes, formatting and printing a String while applying various arguments. They are so alike, in fact, that there's even an equivalent Console printf() method that does the same thing as format(). We don't want our former C developers to have to learn a new method name!

The following sample code prints information to the user:

```
Console console = System.console();
if (console == null) {
    throw new RuntimeException("Console not available");
} else {
    console.writer().println("Welcome to Our Zoo!");
    console.format("It has %d animals and employs %d people", 391, 25);
    console.writer().println();
    console.printf("The zoo spans %5.1f acres", 128.91);
}
```

Assuming the Console is available at runtime, it prints the following:

```
Welcome to Our Zoo!
It has 391 animals and employs 25 people
The zoo spans 128.9 acres.
```

Using *Console* with a *Locale*

Unlike the print stream classes, Console does not include an overloaded format() method that takes a Locale instance. Instead, Console relies on the system locale. Of course, you could always use a specific Locale by retrieving the Writer object and passing your own Locale instance, such as in the following example:

```
Console console = System.console();
console.writer().format(new Locale("fr", "CA"), "Hello World");
```

readLine() and *readPassword()*

The Console class includes four methods for retrieving regular text data from the user.

```
public String readLine()
public String readLine(String fmt, Object... args)

public char[] readPassword()
public char[] readPassword(String fmt, Object... args)
```

Like using `System.in` with a `BufferedReader`, the `Console` `readLine()` method reads input until the user presses the Enter key. The overloaded version of `readLine()` displays a formatted message prompt prior to requesting input.

The `readPassword()` methods are similar to the `readLine()` method with two important differences.

- The text the user types is not echoed back and displayed on the screen as they are typing.
- The data is returned as a `char[]` instead of a `String`.

The first feature improves security by not showing the password on the screen if someone happens to be sitting next to you. The second feature involves preventing passwords from entering the `String` pool and will be discussed in Chapter 22.

Reviewing *Console* Methods

The last code sample we present asks the user a series of questions and prints results based on this information using many of various methods we learned in this section:

```
Console console = System.console();
if (console == null) {
    throw new RuntimeException("Console not available");
} else {
    String name = console.readLine("Please enter your name: ");
    console.writer().format("Hi %s", name);
    console.writer().println();

    console.format("What is your address? ");
    String address = console.readLine();

    char[] password = console.readPassword("Enter a password "
        + "between %d and %d characters: ", 5, 10);
    char[] verify = console.readPassword("Enter the password again: ");
    console.printf("Passwords "
        + (Arrays.equals(password, verify) ? "match" : "do not match"));
}
```

Assuming a `Console` is available, the output should resemble the following:

```
Please enter your name: Max
Hi Max
What is your address? Spoonerville
Enter a password between 5 and 10 digits:
Enter the password again:
Passwords match
```

Summary

This chapter is all about using classes in the java.io package. We started off showing you how to operate on files and directories using the java.io.File class.

We then introduced I/O streams and explained how they are used to read or write large quantities of data. While there are a lot of I/O streams, they differ on some key points.

- Byte vs. character streams
- Input vs. output streams
- Low-level vs. high-level streams

Oftentimes, the name of the I/O stream can tell you a lot about what it does.

We visited many of the I/O stream classes that you will need to know for the exam in increasing order of complexity. A common practice is to start with a low-level resource or file stream and wrap it in a buffered stream to improve performance. You can also apply a high-level stream to manipulate the data, such as an object or print stream. We described what it means to be serializable in Java, and we showed you how to use the object stream classes to persist objects directly to and from disk.

We concluded the chapter by showing you how to read input data from the user, using both the system stream objects and the Console class. The Console class has many useful features, such as built-in support for passwords and formatting.

Exam Essentials

Understand files, directories, and streams.   Files are records that store data within a persistent storage device, such as a hard disk drive, that is available after the application has finished executing. Files are organized within a file system in directories, which in turn may contain other directories. The root directory is the topmost directory in a file system.

Be able to use the *java.io.File* class.   A java.io.File instance can be created by passing a path String to the File constructor. The File class includes a number of instance methods for retrieving information about both files and directories. It also includes methods to create/delete files and directories, as well as retrieve a list of files within the directory.

Distinguish between byte and character streams.   Streams are either byte streams or character streams. Byte streams operate on binary data and have names that end with Stream, while character streams operate on text data and have names that end in Reader or Writer.

Distinguish between input and output streams.   Operating on a stream involves either receiving or sending data. The InputStream and Reader classes are the topmost abstract classes that receive data, while the OutputStream and Writer classes are the topmost abstract classes that send data. All I/O output streams covered in this chapter have corresponding input streams, with the exception of `PrintStream` and `PrintWriter`. `PrintStream` is also unique in that it is the only `OutputStream` without the word `Output` in its name.

Distinguish between low-level and high-level streams. A low-level stream is one that operates directly on the underlying resource, such as a file or network connection. A high-level stream is one that operates on a low-level or other high-level stream to filter data, convert data, or improve performance.

Be able to perform common stream operations. All streams include a `close()` method, which can be invoked automatically with a try-with-resources statement. Input streams include methods to manipulate the stream including `mark()`, `reset()`, and `skip()`. Remember to call `markSupported()` before using `mark()` and `reset()`, as some streams do not support this operation. Output streams include a `flush()` method to force any buffered data to the underlying resource.

Be able to recognize and know how to use various stream classes. Besides the four top-level abstract classes, you should be familiar with the file, buffered, print, and object stream classes. You should also know how to wrap a stream with another stream appropriately.

Understand how to use Java serialization. A class is considered serializable if it implements the `java.io.Serializable` interface and contains instance members that are either serializable or marked `transient`. All Java primitives and the `String` class are serializable. The `ObjectInputStream` and `ObjectOutputStream` classes can be used to read and write a `Serializable` object from and to a stream, respectively.

Be able to interact with the user. Be able to interact with the user using the system streams (`System.out`, `System.err`, and `System.in`) as well as the `Console` class. The `Console` class includes special methods for formatting data and retrieving complex input such as passwords.

Review Questions

The answers to the chapter review questions can be found in the Appendix.

1. Which class would be best to use to read a binary file into a Java object?

   A. `ObjectWriter`

   B. `ObjectOutputStream`

   C. `BufferedStream`

   D. `ObjectReader`

   E. `FileReader`

   F. `ObjectInputStream`

   G. None of the above

2. Which of the following are methods available on instances of the `java.io.File` class? (Choose all that apply.)

   A. `mv()`

   B. `createDirectory()`

   C. `mkdirs()`

   D. `move()`

   E. `renameTo()`

   F. `copy()`

   G. `mkdir()`

3. What is the value of `name` after the instance of `Eagle` created in the `main()` method is serialized and then deserialized?

   ```
   import java.io.Serializable;
   class Bird {
       protected transient String name;
       public void setName(String name) { this.name = name; }
       public String getName() { return name; }
       public Bird() {
           this.name = "Matt";
       }
   }
   public class Eagle extends Bird implements Serializable {
       { this.name = "Olivia"; }
       public Eagle() {
           this.name = "Bridget";
   ```

```
        }
        public static void main(String[] args) {
            var e = new Eagle();
            e.name = "Adeline";
        }
    }
```

A. Adeline

B. Matt

C. Olivia

D. Bridget

E. null

F. The code does not compile.

G. The code compiles but throws an exception at runtime.

4. Which classes will allow the following to compile? (Choose all that apply.)

```
    var is = new BufferedInputStream(new FileInputStream("z.txt"));
    InputStream wrapper = new _____(is);
    try (wrapper) {}
```

A. BufferedInputStream

B. FileInputStream

C. BufferedWriter

D. ObjectInputStream

E. ObjectOutputStream

F. BufferedReader

G. None of the above, as the first line does not compile.

5. Which of the following are true? (Choose all that apply.)

A. System.console() will throw an IOException if a Console is not available.

B. System.console() will return null if a Console is not available.

C. A new Console object is created every time System.console() is called.

D. Console can be used only for writing output, not reading input.

E. Console includes a format() method to write data to the console's output stream.

F. Console includes a println() method to write data to the console's output stream.

6. Which statements about closing I/O streams are correct? (Choose all that apply.)

A. InputStream and Reader instances are the only I/O streams that should be closed after use.

B. OutputStream and Writer instances are the only I/O streams that should be closed after use.

C. InputStream/OutputStream and Reader/Writer all should be closed after use.

D. A traditional `try` statement can be used to close an I/O stream.

E. A try-with-resources can be used to close an I/O stream.

F. None of the above.

7. Assume that `in` is a valid stream whose next bytes are XYZABC. What is the result of calling the following method on the stream, using a count value of 3?

```java
public static String pullBytes(InputStream in, int count)
        throws IOException {
   in.mark(count);
   var sb = new StringBuilder();
   for(int i=0; i<count; i++)
      sb.append((char)in.read());
   in.reset();
   in.skip(1);
   sb.append((char)in.read());
   return sb.toString();
}
```

A. It will return a `String` value of XYZ.

B. It will return a `String` value of XYZA.

C. It will return a `String` value of XYZX.

D. It will return a `String` value of XYZY.

E. The code does not compile.

F. The code compiles but throws an exception at runtime.

G. The result cannot be determined with the information given.

8. Which of the following are true statements about serialization in Java? (Choose all that apply.)

A. Deserialization involves converting data into Java objects.

B. Serialization involves converting data into Java objects.

C. All nonthread classes should be marked `Serializable`.

D. The `Serializable` interface requires implementing `serialize()` and `deserialize()` methods.

E. `Serializable` is a functional interface.

F. The `readObject()` method of `ObjectInputStream` may throw a `ClassNotFoundException` even if the return object is not cast to a specific type.

9. Assuming / is the root directory within the file system, which of the following are true statements? (Choose all that apply.)

A. /home/parrot is an absolute path.

B. /home/parrot is a directory.

    C. /home/parrot is a relative path.

    D. new File("/home") will throw an exception if /home does not exist.

    E. new File("/home").delete() throws an exception if /home does not exist.

10. What are the requirements for a class that you want to serialize to a stream? (Choose all that apply.)

    A. The class must be marked final.

    B. The class must extend the Serializable class.

    C. The class must declare a static serialVersionUID variable.

    D. All static members of the class must be marked transient.

    E. The class must implement the Serializable interface.

    F. All instance members of the class must be serializable or marked transient.

11. Given a directory /storage full of multiple files and directories, what is the result of executing the deleteTree("/storage") method on it?

```
public static void deleteTree(File file) {
    if(!file.isFile())                      // f1
        for(File entry: file.listFiles())   // f2
            deleteTree(entry);
    else file.delete();
}
```

    A. It will delete only the empty directories.

    B. It will delete the entire directory tree including the /storage directory itself.

    C. It will delete all files within the directory tree.

    D. The code will not compile because of line f1.

    E. The code will not compile because of line f2.

    F. None of the above

12. What are possible results of executing the following code? (Choose all that apply.)

```
public static void main(String[] args) {
    String line;
    var c = System.console();
    Writer w = c.writer();
    try (w) {
        if ((line = c.readLine("Enter your name: ")) != null)
            w.append(line);
        w.flush();
    }
}
```

    A. The code runs but nothing is printed.

    B. The code prints what was entered by the user.

    C. An `ArrayIndexOutOfBoundsException` is thrown.

    D. A `NullPointerException` is thrown.

    E. None of the above, as the code does not compile

13. Suppose that the absolute path /weather/winter/snow.dat represents a file that exists within the file system. Which of the following lines of code creates an object that represents the file? (Choose all that apply.)

    A.   `new File("/weather", "winter", "snow.dat")`

    B.   `new File("/weather/winter/snow.dat")`

    C.   `new File("/weather/winter", new File("snow.dat"))`

    D.   `new File("weather", "/winter/snow.dat")`

    E.   `new File(new File("/weather/winter"), "snow.dat")`

    F. None of the above

14. Which of the following are built-in streams in Java? (Choose all that apply.)

    A. `System.err`

    B. `System.error`

    C. `System.in`

    D. `System.input`

    E. `System.out`

    F. `System.output`

15. Which of the following are not `java.io` classes? (Choose all that apply.)

    A. `BufferedReader`

    B. `BufferedWriter`

    C. `FileReader`

    D. `FileWriter`

    E. `PrintReader`

    F. `PrintWriter`

16. Assuming zoo-data.txt exists and is not empty, what statements about the following method are correct? (Choose all that apply.)

```java
private void echo() throws IOException {
    var o = new FileWriter("new-zoo.txt");
    try (var f = new FileReader("zoo-data.txt");
        var b = new BufferedReader(f); o) {
      o.write(b.readLine());
    }
    o.write("");
}
```

A. When run, the method creates a new file with one line of text in it.

B. When run, the method creates a new file with two lines of text in it.

C. When run, the method creates a new file with the same number of lines as the original file.

D. The method compiles but will produce an exception at runtime.

E. The method does not compile.

F. The method uses byte stream classes.

17. Assume `reader` is a valid stream that supports `mark()` and whose next characters are PEACOCKS. What is the expected output of the following code snippet?

```
var sb = new StringBuilder();
sb.append((char)reader.read());
reader.mark(10);
for(int i=0; i<2; i++) {
    sb.append((char)reader.read());
    reader.skip(2);
}
reader.reset();
reader.skip(0);
sb.append((char)reader.read());
System.out.println(sb.toString());
```

A. PEAE

B. PEOA

C. PEOE

D. PEOS

E. The code does not compile.

F. The code compiles but throws an exception at runtime.

G. The result cannot be determined with the information given.

18. Suppose that you need to write data that consists of `int`, `double`, `boolean`, and `String` values to a file that maintains the data types of the original data. You also want the data to be performant on large files. Which three `java.io` stream classes can be chained together to best achieve this result? (Choose three.)

A. `FileWriter`

B. `FileOutputStream`

C. `BufferedOutputStream`

D. `ObjectOutputStream`

E. `DirectoryOutputStream`

F. `PrintWriter`

G. `PrintStream`

19. Given the following method, which statements are correct? (Choose all that apply.)

```
public void copyFile(File file1, File file2) throws Exception {
    var reader = new InputStreamReader(
        new FileInputStream(file1));
    try (var writer = new FileWriter(file2)) {
        char[] buffer = new char[10];
        while(reader.read(buffer) != -1) {
            writer.write(buffer);
            // n1
        }
    }
}
```

A. The code does not compile because `reader` is not a `Buffered` stream.

B. The code does not compile because `writer` is not a `Buffered` stream.

C. The code compiles and correctly copies the data between some files.

D. The code compiles and correctly copies the data between all files.

E. If we check `file2` on line n1 within the file system after five iterations of the `while` loop, it may be empty.

F. If we check `file2` on line n1 within the file system after five iterations, it will contain exactly 50 characters.

G. This method contains a resource leak.

20. Which values when inserted into the blank independently would allow the code to compile? (Choose all that apply.)

```
Console console = System.console();
String color = console.readLine("Favorite color? ");
console._____("Your favorite color is %s", color);
```

A. `reader().print`

B. `reader().println`

C. `format`

D. `writer().print`

E. `writer().println`

F. None of the above

21. What are some reasons to use a character stream, such as `Reader/Writer`, over a byte stream, such as `InputStream/OutputStream`? (Choose all that apply.)

A. More convenient code syntax when working with `String` data

B. Improved performance

C. Automatic character encoding

  D. Built-in serialization and deserialization

  E. Character streams are high-level streams.

  F. Multithreading support

22. Which of the following fields will be null after an instance of the class created on line 15 is serialized and then deserialized using ObjectOutputStream and ObjectInputStream? (Choose all that apply.)

```
1:  import java.io.Serializable;
2:  import java.util.List;
3:  public class Zebra implements Serializable {
4:      private transient String name = "George";
5:      private static String birthPlace = "Africa";
6:      private transient Integer age;
7:      List<Zebra> friends = new java.util.ArrayList<>();
8:      private Object stripes = new Object();
9:      { age = 10;}
10:     public Zebra() {
11:         this.name = "Sophia";
12:     }
13:     static Zebra writeAndRead(Zebra z) {
14:         // Implementation omitted
15:     }
16:     public static void main(String[] args) {
17:         var zebra = new Zebra();
18:         zebra = writeAndRead(zebra);
19:     } }
```

  A. name

  B. stripes

  C. age

  D. friends

  E. birthPlace

  F. The code does not compile.

  G. The code compiles but throws an exception at runtime.

Chapter

20

NIO.2

OCP EXAM OBJECTIVES COVERED IN THIS CHAPTER:

✓ **I/O (Fundamentals and NIO2)**

- Use the Path interface to operate on file and directory paths

- Use the Files class to check, delete, copy or move a file or directory

- Use the Stream API with Files

In Chapter 19, "I/O," we presented the java.io API and discussed how to use it to interact with files and streams. In this chapter, we focus on the java.nio version 2 API, or NIO.2 for short, to interact with files. NIO.2 is an acronym that stands for the second version of the Non-blocking Input/Output API, and it is sometimes referred to as the "New I/O."

In this chapter, we will show how NIO.2 allows us to do a lot more with files and directories than the original java.io API. We'll also show you how to apply the Streams API to perform complex file and directory operations. We'll conclude this chapter by showing the various ways file attributes can be read and written using NIO.2.

> While Chapter 19 focused on I/O streams, we're back to using streams to refer to the Streams API that you learned about in Chapter 15, "Functional Programming." For clarity, we'll use the phrase *I/O streams* to discuss the ones found in java.io from this point on.

Introducing NIO.2

At its core, NIO.2 is a replacement for the legacy java.io.File class you learned about in Chapter 19. The goal of the API is to provide a more intuitive, more feature-rich API for working with files and directories.

By *legacy*, we mean that the preferred approach for working with files and directories with newer software applications is to use NIO.2, rather than java.io.File. As you'll soon see, the NIO.2 provides many features and performance improvements than the legacy class supported.

What About NIO?

This chapter focuses on NIO.2, not NIO. Java includes an NIO library that uses buffers and channels, in place of I/O streams. The NIO API was never popular, so much so that nothing from the original version of NIO will be on the OCP exam. Many Java developers continue to use I/O streams to manipulate byte streams, rather than NIO.

People sometimes refer to NIO.2 as just NIO, although for clarity and to distinguish it
from the first version of NIO, we will refer to it as NIO.2 throughout the chapter.

Introducing *Path*

The cornerstone of NIO.2 is the `java.nio.file.Path` interface. A `Path` instance represents a hierarchical path on the storage system to a file or directory. You can think of a
`Path` as the NIO.2 replacement for the `java.io.File` class, although how you use it is a bit
different.

Before we get into that, let's talk about what's similar between these two implementations. Both `java.io.File` and `Path` objects may refer to an absolute path or relative
path within the file system. In addition, both may refer to a file or a directory. As we did
in Chapter 19 and continue to do in this chapter, we treat an instance that points to a
directory as a file since it is stored in the file system with similar properties. For example,
we can rename a file or directory with the same commands in both APIs.

Now for something completely different. Unlike the `java.io.File` class, the `Path`
interface contains support for symbolic links. A *symbolic link* is a special file within a file
system that serves as a reference or pointer to another file or directory. Figure 20.1 shows a
symbolic link from `/zoo/favorite` to `/zoo/cats/lion`.

FIGURE 20.1   File system with a symbolic link

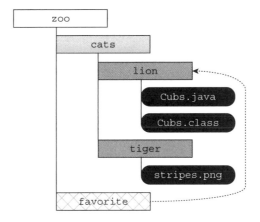

In Figure 20.1, the `lion` folder and its elements can be accessed directly or via the
symbolic link. For example, the following paths reference the same file:

/zoo/cats/lion/Cubs.java
/zoo/favorite/Cubs.java

In general, symbolic links are transparent to the user, as the operating system takes care of resolving the reference to the actual file. NIO.2 includes full support for creating, detecting, and navigating symbolic links within the file system.

Creating Paths

Since Path is an interface, we can't create an instance directly. After all, interfaces don't have constructors! Java provides a number of classes and methods that you can use to obtain Path objects, which we will review in this section.

 You might wonder, why is Path an interface? When a Path is created, the JVM returns a file system–specific implementation, such as a Windows or Unix Path class. In the vast majority of circumstances, we want to perform the same operations on the Path, regardless of the file system. By providing Path as an interface using the factory pattern, we avoid having to write complex or custom code for each type of file system.

Obtaining a *Path* with the *Path* Interface

The simplest and most straightforward way to obtain a Path object is to use the static factory method defined within the Path interface.

```
// Path factory method
public static Path of(String first, String... more)
```

It's easy to create Path instances from String values, as shown here:

```
Path path1 = Path.of("pandas/cuddly.png");
Path path2 = Path.of("c:\\zooinfo\\November\\employees.txt");
Path path3 = Path.of("/home/zoodirectory");
```

The first example creates a reference to a relative path in the current working directory. The second example creates a reference to an absolute file path in a Windows-based system. The third example creates a reference to an absolute directory path in a Linux or Mac-based system.

Absolute vs. Relative Paths

Determining whether a path is relative or absolute is actually file-system dependent. To match the exam, we adopt the following conventions:

- If a path starts with a forward slash (/), it is absolute, with / as the root directory. Examples: /bird/parrot.png and /bird/../data/./info

- If a path starts with a drive letter (c:), it is absolute, with the drive letter as the root directory. Examples: c:/bird/parrot.png and d:/bird/../data/./info

- Otherwise, it is a relative path. Examples: bird/parrot.png and bird/../data/./info

If you're not familiar with path symbols like . and .., don't worry! We'll be covering them in this chapter.

The Path.of() method also includes a varargs to pass additional path elements. The values will be combined and automatically separated by the operating system–dependent file separator you learned about in Chapter 19.

```
Path path1 = Path.of("pandas", "cuddly.png");
Path path2 = Path.of("c:", "zooinfo", "November", "employees.txt");
Path path3 = Path.of("/", "home", "zoodirectory");
```

These examples are just rewrites of our previous set of Path examples, using the parameter list of String values instead of a single String value. The advantage of the varargs is that it is more robust, as it inserts the proper operating system path separator for you.

Obtaining a *Path* with the *Paths* Class

The Path.of() method is actually new to Java 11. Another way to obtain a Path instance is from the java.nio.file.Paths factory class. Note the s at the end of the Paths class to distinguish it from the Path interface.

```
// Paths factory method
public static Path get(String first, String... more)
```

Rewriting our previous examples is easy.

```
Path path1 = Paths.get("pandas/cuddly.png");
Path path2 = Paths.get("c:\\zooinfo\\November\\employees.txt");
Path path3 = Paths.get("/", "home", "zoodirectory");
```

Since Paths.get() is older, the exam is likely to have both. We'll use both Path.of() and Paths.get() interchangeably in this chapter.

Obtaining a *Path* with a *URI* Class

Another way to construct a Path using the Paths class is with a URI value. A *uniform resource identifier* (URI) is a string of characters that identify a resource. It begins with a schema that indicates the resource type, followed by a path value. Examples of schema values include file:// for local file systems, and http://, https://, and ftp:// for remote file systems.

The java.net.URI class is used to create URI values.

```
// URI Constructor
public URI(String str) throws URISyntaxException
```

Java includes multiple methods to convert between Path and URI objects.

```
// URI to Path, using Path factory method
public static Path of(URI uri)
```

```
// URI to Path, using Paths factory method
public static Path get(URI uri)
```

```
// Path to URI, using Path instance method
public URI toURI()
```

The following examples all reference the same file:

```
URI a = new URI("file://icecream.txt");
Path b = Path.of(a);
Path c = Paths.get(a);
URI d = b.toUri();
```

Some of these examples may actually throw an IllegalArgumentException at runtime, as some systems require URIs to be absolute. The URI class does have an isAbsolute() method, although this refers to whether the URI has a schema, not the file location.

Other URI Connection Types

A URI can be used for a web page or FTP connection.

```
    Path path5 = Paths.get(new URI("http://www.wiley.com"));
    Path path6 = Paths.get(new URI("ftp://username:secret@ftp.example.com"));
```

For the exam, you do not need to know the syntax of these types of URIs, but you should be aware they exist.

Obtaining a *Path* from the *FileSystem* Class

NIO.2 makes extensive use of creating objects with factory classes. As you saw already, the Paths class creates instances of the Path interface. Likewise, the FileSystems class creates instances of the abstract FileSystem class.

```
// FileSystems factory method
public static FileSystem getDefault()
```

The FileSystem class includes methods for working with the file system directly. In fact, both Paths.get() and Path.of() are actually shortcuts for this FileSystem method:

```
// FileSystem instance method
public Path getPath(String first, String... more)
```

Let's rewrite our three earlier examples one more time to show you how to obtain a Path instance "the long way."

```
Path path1 = FileSystems.getDefault().getPath("pandas/cuddly.png");
Path path2 = FileSystems.getDefault()
   .getPath("c:\\zooinfo\\November\\employees.txt");
Path path3 = FileSystems.getDefault().getPath("/home/zoodirectory");
```

 Real World Scenario

Connecting to Remote File Systems

While most of the time we want access to a Path object that is within the local file system, the FileSystems class does give us the freedom to connect to a remote file system, as follows:

```
// FileSystems factory method
public static FileSystem getFileSystem(URI uri)
```

The following shows how such a method can be used:

```
FileSystem fileSystem = FileSystems.getFileSystem(
   new URI("http://www.selikoff.net"));
Path path = fileSystem.getPath("duck.txt");
```

This code is useful when we need to construct Path objects frequently for a remote file system. NIO.2 gives us the power to connect to both local and remote file systems, which is a major improvement over the legacy java.io.File class.

Obtaining a *Path* from the *java.io.File* Class

Last but not least, we can obtain Path instances using the legacy java.io.File class. In fact, we can also obtain a java.io.File object from a Path instance.

```
// Path to File, using Path instance method
public default File toFile()
```

```
// File to Path, using java.io.File instance method
public Path toPath()
```

These methods are available for convenience and also to help facilitate integration between older and newer APIs. The following shows examples of each:

```
File file = new File("husky.png");
Path path = file.toPath();
File backToFile = path.toFile();
```

When working with newer applications, though, you should rely on NIO.2's Path interface as it contains a lot more features.

Reviewing NIO.2 Relationships

By now, you should realize that NIO.2 makes extensive use of the factory pattern. You should become comfortable with this paradigm. Many of your interactions with NIO.2 will require two types: an abstract class or interface and a factory or helper class. Figure 20.2 shows the relationships among NIO.2 classes, as well as select java.io and java.net classes.

FIGURE 20.2   NIO.2 class and interface relationships

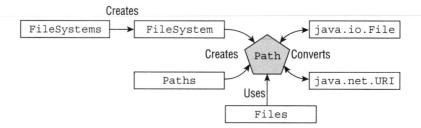

Review Figure 20.2 carefully. When working with NIO.2, keep an eye on whether the class name is singular or plural. The classes with plural names include methods to create or operate on class/interface instances with singular names. Remember, a Path can also be created from the Path interface, using the static factory of() method.

Included in Figure 20.2 is the class java.nio.file.Files, which we'll cover later in the chapter. For now, you just need to know that it is a helper or utility class that operates primarily on Path instances to read or modify actual files and directories.

The java.io.File is the I/O class you worked with in Chapter 19, while Files is an NIO.2 helper class. Files operates on Path instances, not java.io.File instances. We know this is confusing, but they are from completely different APIs! For clarity, we often write out the full name of the java.io.File class in this chapter.

Understanding Common NIO.2 Features

Throughout this chapter, we introduce numerous methods you should know for the exam. Before getting into the specifics of each method, we present many of these common features in this section so you are not surprised when you see them.

Applying Path Symbols

Absolute and relative paths can contain path symbols. A *path symbol* is a reserved series of characters that have special meaning within some file systems. For the exam, there are two path symbols you need to know, as listed in Table 20.1.

TABLE 20.1   File system symbols

Symbol	Description
.	A reference to the current directory
..	A reference to the parent of the current directory

We illuminate using path symbols in Figure 20.3.

FIGURE 20.3   Relative paths using path symbols

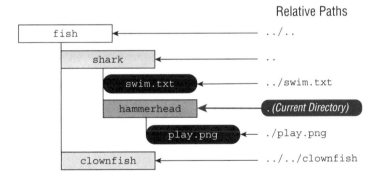

In Figure 20.3, the current directory is /fish/shark/hammerhead. In this case, ../swim.txt refers to the file swim.txt in the parent of the current directory. Likewise, ./play.png refers to play.png in the current directory. These symbols can also be combined for greater effect. For example, ../../clownfish refers to the directory that is two directories up from the current directory.

Sometimes you'll see path symbols that are redundant or unnecessary. For example, the absolute path /fish/shark/hammerhead/../../swim.txt can be simplified to /fish/shark/swim.txt. We'll see how to handle these redundancies later in the chapter when we cover normalize().

Providing Optional Arguments

Many of the methods in this chapter include a varargs that takes an optional list of values. Table 20.2 presents the arguments you should be familiar with for the exam.

TABLE 20.2   Common NIO.2 method arguments

Enum type	Interface inherited	Enum value	Details
LinkOption	CopyOption OpenOption	NOFOLLOW_LINKS	Do not follow symbolic links.
StandardCopyOption	CopyOption	ATOMIC_MOVE	Move file as atomic file system operation.
		COPY_ ATTRIBUTES	Copy existing attributes to new file.
		REPLACE_ EXISTING	Overwrite file if it already exists.
StandardOpenOption	OpenOption	APPEND	If file is already open for write, then append to the end.
		CREATE	Create a new file if it does not exist.
		CREATE_NEW	Create a new file only if it does not exist, fail otherwise.
		READ	Open for read access.
		TRUNCATE_ EXISTING	If file is already open for write, then erase file and append to beginning.
		WRITE	Open for write access.
FileVisitOption	N/A	FOLLOW_LINKS	Follow symbolic links.

With the exceptions of Files.copy() and Files.move() (which we'll cover later), we won't discuss these varargs parameters each time we present a method. The behavior of them should be straightforward, though. For example, can you figure out what the following call to Files.exists() with the LinkOption does in the following code snippet?

```
Path path = Paths.get("schedule.xml");
boolean exists = Files.exists(path, LinkOption.NOFOLLOW_LINKS);
```

The Files.exists() simply checks whether a file exists. If the parameter is a symbolic link, though, then the method checks whether the target of the symbolic link exists instead. Providing LinkOption.NOFOLLOW_LINKS means the default behavior will be overridden, and the method will check whether the symbolic link itself exists.

Note that some of the enums in Table 20.2 inherit an interface. That means some methods accept a variety of enums types. For example, the Files.move() method takes a CopyOption vararg so it can take enums of different types.

```
void copy(Path source, Path target) throws IOException {
    Files.move(source, target,
        LinkOption.NOFOLLOW_LINKS,
        StandardCopyOption.ATOMIC_MOVE);
}
```

 Many of the NIO.2 methods use a varargs for passing options, even when there is only one enum value available. The advantage of this approach, as opposed to say just passing a boolean argument, is future-proofing. These method signatures are insulated from changes in the Java language down the road when future options are available.

Handling Methods That Declare *IOException*

Many of the methods presented in this chapter declare IOException. Common causes of a method throwing this exception include the following:

- Loss of communication to underlying file system.
- File or directory exists but cannot be accessed or modified.
- File exists but cannot be overwritten.
- File or directory is required but does not exist.

In general, methods that operate on abstract Path values, such as those in the Path interface or Paths class, often do not throw any checked exceptions. On the other hand, methods that operate or change files and directories, such as those in the Files class, often declare IOException.

There are exceptions to this rule, as we will see. For example, the method Files.exists() does not declare IOException. If it did throw an exception when the file did not exist, then it would never be able to return false!

Interacting with Paths

Now that we've covered the basics of NIO.2, you might ask, what can we do with it? Short answer: a lot. NIO.2 provides a *rich plethora* of methods and classes that operate on `Path` objects—far more than were available in the `java.io` API. In this section, we present the `Path` methods you should know for the exam, organized by related functionality.

Just like `String` values, `Path` instances are immutable. In the following example, the `Path` operation on the second line is lost since p is immutable:

```
Path p = Path.of("whale");
p.resolve("krill");
System.out.println(p);  // whale
```

Many of the methods available in the `Path` interface transform the path value in some way and return a new `Path` object, allowing the methods to be chained. We demonstrate chaining in the following example, the details of which we'll discuss in this section of the chapter:

```
Path.of("/zoo/../home").getParent().normalize().toAbsolutePath();
```

> If you start to feel overwhelmed by the number of methods available in the `Path` interface, just remember: the function of many of them can be inferred by their method name. For example, what do you think the `Path` method `getParent()` does? It returns the parent directory of a `Path`. Not so difficult, was it?

Many of the code snippets in this part of the chapter can be run without the paths they reference actually existing. The JVM communicates with the file system to determine the path components or the parent directory of a file, without requiring the file to actually exist. As rule of thumb, if the method declares an `IOException`, then it *usually* requires the paths it operates on to exist.

Viewing the Path with *toString()*, *getNameCount()*, and *getName()*

The `Path` interface contains three methods to retrieve basic information about the path representation.

```
public String toString()
```

```
public int getNameCount()
```

```
public Path getName(int index)
```

The first method, toString(), returns a String representation of the entire path. In fact, it is the only method in the Path interface to return a String. Many of the other methods in the Path interface return Path instances.

The getNameCount() and getName() methods are often used in conjunction to retrieve the number of elements in the path and a reference to each element, respectively. These two methods do not include the root directory as part of the path.

```
Path path = Paths.get("/land/hippo/harry.happy");
System.out.println("The Path Name is: " + path);
for(int i=0; i<path.getNameCount(); i++) {
    System.out.println("   Element " + i + " is: " + path.getName(i));
}
```

Notice we didn't call toString() explicitly on the second line. Remember, Java calls toString() on any Object as part of string concatenation. We'll be using this feature throughout the examples in this chapter.

The code prints the following:

```
The Path Name is: /land/hippo/harry.happy
   Element 0 is: land
   Element 1 is: hippo
   Element 2 is: harry.happy
```

Even though this is an absolute path, the root element is not included in the list of names. As we said, these methods do not consider the root as part of the path.

```
var p = Path.of("/");
System.out.print(p.getNameCount()); // 0
System.out.print(p.getName(0));       // IllegalArgumentException
```

Notice that if you try to call getName() with an invalid index, it will throw an exception at runtime.

 Our examples print / as the file separator character because of the system we are using. Your actual output may vary throughout this chapter.

Creating a New Path with *subpath()*

The Path interface includes a method to select portions of a path.

```
public Path subpath(int beginIndex, int endIndex)
```

The references are inclusive of the beginIndex, and exclusive of the endIndex. The subpath() method is similar to the previous getName() method, except that subpath() may return multiple path components, whereas getName() returns only one. Both return Path instances, though.

The following code snippet shows how subpath() works. We also print the elements of the Path using getName() so that you can see how the indices are used.

```
var p = Paths.get("/mammal/omnivore/raccoon.image");
System.out.println("Path is: " + p);
for (int i = 0; i < p.getNameCount(); i++) {
   System.out.println("   Element " + i + " is: " + p.getName(i));
}
System.out.println();
System.out.println("subpath(0,3): " + p.subpath(0, 3));
System.out.println("subpath(1,2): " + p.subpath(1, 2));
System.out.println("subpath(1,3): " + p.subpath(1, 3));
```

The output of this code snippet is the following:

```
Path is: /mammal/omnivore/raccoon.image
   Element 0 is: mammal
   Element 1 is: omnivore
   Element 2 is: raccoon.image

subpath(0,3): mammal/omnivore/raccoon.image
subpath(1,2): omnivore
subpath(1,3): omnivore/raccoon.image
```

Like getNameCount() and getName(), subpath() is 0-indexed and does not include the root. Also like getName(), subpath() throws an exception if invalid indices are provided.

```
var q = p.subpath(0, 4); // IllegalArgumentException
var x = p.subpath(1, 1); // IllegalArgumentException
```

The first example throws an exception at runtime, since the maximum index value allowed is 3. The second example throws an exception since the start and end indexes are the same, leading to an empty path value.

Accessing Path Elements with *getFileName()*, *getParent()*, and *getRoot()*

The Path interface contains numerous methods for retrieving particular elements of a Path, returned as Path objects themselves.

```
public Path getFileName()
```

```
public Path getParent()
```

```
public Path getRoot()
```

The getFileName() returns the Path element of the current file or directory, while getParent() returns the full path of the containing directory. The getParent() returns null if operated on the root path or at the top of a relative path. The getRoot() method returns the root element of the file within the file system, or null if the path is a relative path.

Consider the following method, which prints various Path elements:

```
public void printPathInformation(Path path) {
    System.out.println("Filename is: " + path.getFileName());
    System.out.println("   Root is: " + path.getRoot());
    Path currentParent = path;
    while((currentParent = currentParent.getParent()) != null) {
        System.out.println("   Current parent is: " + currentParent);
    }
}
```

The while loop in the printPathInformation() method continues until getParent() returns null. We apply this method to the following three paths:

```
printPathInformation(Path.of("zoo"));
printPathInformation(Path.of("/zoo/armadillo/shells.txt"));
printPathInformation(Path.of("./armadillo/../shells.txt"));
```

This sample application produces the following output:

```
Filename is: zoo
   Root is: null

Filename is: shells.txt
   Root is: /
   Current parent is: /zoo/armadillo
   Current parent is: /zoo
   Current parent is: /

Filename is: shells.txt
   Root is: null
   Current parent is: ./armadillo/..
   Current parent is: ./armadillo
   Current parent is: .
```

Reviewing the sample output, you can see the difference in the behavior of getRoot() on absolute and relative paths. As you can see in the first and last examples, the getParent() does not traverse relative paths outside the current working directory.

You also see that these methods do not resolve the path symbols and treat them as a distinct part of the path. While most of the methods in this part of the chapter will treat path symbols as part of the path, we will present one shortly that cleans up path symbols.

Checking Path Type with *isAbsolute()* and *toAbsolutePath()*

The Path interface contains two methods for assisting with relative and absolute paths:

```
public boolean isAbsolute()
```

```
public Path toAbsolutePath()
```

The first method, isAbsolute(), returns true if the path the object references is absolute and false if the path the object references is relative. As discussed earlier in this chapter, whether a path is absolute or relative is often file system–dependent, although we, like the exam writers, adopt common conventions for simplicity throughout the book.

The second method, toAbsolutePath(), converts a relative Path object to an absolute Path object by joining it to the current working directory. If the Path object is already absolute, then the method just returns the Path object.

The current working directory can be selected from System.getProperty("user.dir"). This is the value that toAbsolutePath() will use when applied to a relative path.

The following code snippet shows usage of both of these methods when run on a Windows and Linux system, respectively:

```
var path1 = Paths.get("C:\\birds\\egret.txt");
System.out.println("Path1 is Absolute? " + path1.isAbsolute());
System.out.println("Absolute Path1: " + path1.toAbsolutePath());

var path2 = Paths.get("birds/condor.txt");
System.out.println("Path2 is Absolute? " + path2.isAbsolute());
System.out.println("Absolute Path2 " + path2.toAbsolutePath());
```

The output for the code snippet on each respective system is shown in the following sample output. For the second example, assume the current working directory is /home/work.

```
Path1 is Absolute? true
Absolute Path1: C:\birds\egret.txt

Path2 is Absolute? false
Absolute Path2 /home/work/birds/condor.txt
```

Joining Paths with *resolve()*

Suppose you want to concatenate paths in a similar manner as we concatenate strings. The Path interface provides two resolve() methods for doing just that.

```
public Path resolve(Path other)
```

```
public Path resolve(String other)
```

The first method takes a Path parameter, while the overloaded version is a shorthand form of the first that takes a String (and constructs the Path for you). The object on which the resolve() method is invoked becomes the basis of the new Path object, with the input argument being appended onto the Path. Let's see what happens if we apply resolve() to an absolute path and a relative path:

```
Path path1 = Path.of("/cats/../panther");
Path path2 = Path.of("food");
System.out.println(path1.resolve(path2));
```

The code snippet generates the following output:

```
/cats/../panther/food
```

Like the other methods we've seen up to now, resolve() does not clean up path symbols. In this example, the input argument to the resolve() method was a relative path, but what if it had been an absolute path?

```
Path path3 = Path.of("/turkey/food");
System.out.println(path3.resolve("/tiger/cage"));
```

Since the input parameter path3 is an absolute path, the output would be the following:

```
/tiger/cage
```

For the exam, you should be cognizant of mixing absolute and relative paths with the resolve() method. If an absolute path is provided as input to the method, then that is the value that is returned. Simply put, you cannot combine two absolute paths using resolve().

On the exam, when you see Files.resolve(), think concatenation.

Deriving a Path with *relativize()*

The Path interface includes a method for constructing the relative path from one Path to another, often using path symbols.

```
public Path relativize()
```

What do you think the following examples using `relativize()` print?

```
var path1 = Path.of("fish.txt");
var path2 = Path.of("friendly/birds.txt");
System.out.println(path1.relativize(path2));
System.out.println(path2.relativize(path1));
```

The examples print the following:

```
../friendly/birds.txt
../../fish.txt
```

The idea is this: if you are pointed at a path in the file system, what steps would you need to take to reach the other path? For example, to get to `fish.txt` from `friendly/birds.txt`, you need to go up two levels (the file itself counts as one level) and then select `fish.txt`.

If both path values are relative, then the `relativize()` method computes the paths as if they are in the same current working directory. Alternatively, if both path values are absolute, then the method computes the relative path from one absolute location to another, regardless of the current working directory. The following example demonstrates this property when run on a Windows computer:

```
Path path3 = Paths.get("E:\\habitat");
Path path4 = Paths.get("E:\\sanctuary\\raven\\poe.txt");
System.out.println(path3.relativize(path4));
System.out.println(path4.relativize(path3));
```

This code snippet produces the following output:

```
..\sanctuary\raven\poe.txt
..\..\..\habitat
```

The code snippet works even if you do not have an `E:` in your system. Remember, most methods defined in the `Path` interface do not require the path to exist.

The `relativize()` method requires that both paths are absolute or both relative and throws an exception if the types are mixed.

```
Path path1 = Paths.get("/primate/chimpanzee");
Path path2 = Paths.get("bananas.txt");
path1.relativize(path2); // IllegalArgumentException
```

On Windows-based systems, it also requires that if absolute paths are used, then both paths must have the same root directory or drive letter. For example, the following would also throw an `IllegalArgumentException` on a Windows-based system:

```
Path path3 = Paths.get("c:\\primate\\chimpanzee");
Path path4 = Paths.get("d:\\storage\\bananas.txt");
path3.relativize(path4); // IllegalArgumentException
```

Cleaning Up a Path with *normalize()*

So far, we've presented a number of examples that included path symbols that were unnecessary. Luckily, Java provides a method to eliminate unnecessary redundancies in a path.

```
public Path normalize()
```

Remember, the path symbol .. refers to the parent directory, while the path symbol . refers to the current directory. We can apply normalize() to some of our previous paths.

```
var p1 = Path.of("./armadillo/../shells.txt");
System.out.println(p1.normalize()); // shells.txt

var p2 = Path.of("/cats/../panther/food");
System.out.println(p2.normalize()); // /panther/food

var p3 = Path.of("../../fish.txt");
System.out.println(p3.normalize()); // ../../fish.txt
```

The first two examples apply the path symbols to remove the redundancies, but what about the last one? That is as simplified as it can be. The normalize() method does not remove all of the path symbols; only the ones that can be reduced.

The normalize() method also allows us to compare equivalent paths. Consider the following example:

```
var p1 = Paths.get("/pony/../weather.txt");
var p2 = Paths.get("/weather.txt");
System.out.println(p1.equals(p2));                     // false
System.out.println(p1.normalize().equals(p2.normalize())); // true
```

The equals() method returns true if two paths represent the same value. In the first comparison, the path values are different. In the second comparison, the path values have both been reduced to the same normalized value, /weather.txt. This is the primary function of the normalize() method, to allow us to better compare different paths.

Retrieving the File System Path with *toRealPath()*

While working with theoretical paths is useful, sometimes you want to verify the path actually exists within the file system.

```
public Path toRealPath(LinkOption... options) throws IOException
```

This method is similar to normalize(), in that it eliminates any redundant path symbols. It is also similar to toAbsolutePath(), in that it will join the path with the current working directory if the path is relative.

Unlike those two methods, though, toRealPath() will throw an exception if the path does not exist. In addition, it will follow symbolic links, with an optional varargs parameter to ignore them.

Let's say that we have a file system in which we have a symbolic link from /zebra to /horse. What do you think the following will print, given a current working directory of /horse/schedule?

```
System.out.println(Paths.get("/zebra/food.txt").toRealPath());
System.out.println(Paths.get("../../food.txt").toRealPath());
```

The output of both lines is the following:

```
/horse/food.txt
```

In this example, the absolute and relative paths both resolve to the same absolute file, as the symbolic link points to a real file within the file system. We can also use the toRealPath() method to gain access to the current working directory as a Path object.

```
System.out.println(Paths.get(".").toRealPath());
```

Reviewing *Path* Methods

We conclude this section with Table 20.3, which shows the Path methods that you should know for the exam.

TABLE 20.3 *Path* methods

Path of(String, String...)	Path getParent()
URI toURI()	Path getRoot()
File toFile()	boolean isAbsolute()
String toString()	Path toAbsolutePath()
int getNameCount()	Path relativize()
Path getName(int)	Path resolve(Path)
Path subpath(int, int)	Path normalize()
Path getFileName()	Path toRealPath(LinkOption...)

Other than the static method Path.of(), all of the methods in Table 20.3 are instance methods that can be called on any Path instance. In addition, only toRealPath() declares an IOException.

Operating on Files and Directories

Most of the methods we covered in the Path interface operate on theoretical paths, which are not required to exist within the file system. What if you want to rename a directory, copy a file, or read the contents of a file?

Enter the NIO.2 Files class. The Files helper class is capable of interacting with real files and directories within the system. Because of this, most of the methods in this part of the chapter take optional parameters and throw an IOException if the path does not exist. The Files class also replicates numerous methods found in the java.io.File, albeit often with a different name or list of parameters.

Many of the names for the methods in the NIO.2 Files class are a lot more straightforward than what you saw in the java.io.File class. For example, the java.io.File methods renameTo() and mkdir() have been changed to move() and createDirectory(), respectively, in the Files class.

Checking for Existence with *exists()*

The first Files method we present is the simplest. It just checks whether the file exists.

```
public static boolean exists(Path path, LinkOption... options)
```

Let's take a look at some sample code that operates on a features.png file in the /ostrich directory.

```
var b1 = Files.exists(Paths.get("/ostrich/feathers.png"));
System.out.println("Path " + (b1 ? "Exists" : "Missing"));

var b2 = Files.exists(Paths.get("/ostrich"));
System.out.println("Path " + (b2 ? "Exists" : "Missing"));
```

The first example checks whether a file exists, while the second example checks whether a directory exists. This method does not throw an exception if the file does not exist, as doing so would prevent this method from ever returning false at runtime.

Remember, a file and directory may both have extensions. In the last example, the two paths could refer to two files or two directories. Unless the exam tells you whether the path refers to a file or directory, do not assume either.

Testing Uniqueness with *isSameFile()*

Since a path may include path symbols and symbolic links within a file system, it can be difficult to know if two Path instances refer to the same file. Luckily, there's a method for that in the Files class:

```
public static boolean isSameFile(Path path, Path path2)
   throws IOException
```

The method takes two Path objects as input, resolves all path symbols, and follows symbolic links. Despite the name, the method can also be used to determine whether two Path objects refer to the same directory.

While most usages of isSameFile() will trigger an exception if the paths do not exist, there is a special case in which it does not. If the two path objects are equal, in terms of equals(), then the method will just return true without checking whether the file exists.

Assume the file system exists as shown in Figure 20.4 with a symbolic link from /animals/snake to /animals/cobra.

FIGURE 20.4   Comparing file uniqueness

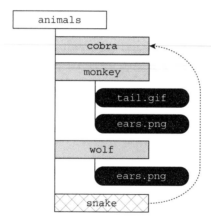

Given the structure defined in Figure 20.4, what does the following output?

```
System.out.println(Files.isSameFile(
   Path.of("/animals/cobra"),
   Path.of("/animals/snake")));
```

```
System.out.println(Files.isSameFile(
    Path.of("/animals/monkey/ears.png"),
    Path.of("/animals/wolf/ears.png")));
```

Since cobra is a symbolic link to snake, the first example outputs true. In the second example, the paths refer to different files, so false is printed.

 This isSameFile() method does not compare the contents of the files. Two files may have identical names, content, and attributes, but if they are in different locations, then this method will return false.

Making Directories with *createDirectory()* and *createDirectories()*

To create a directory, we use these Files methods:

```
public static Path createDirectory(Path dir,
    FileAttribute<?>... attrs) throws IOException
```

```
public static Path createDirectories(Path dir,
    FileAttribute<?>... attrs) throws IOException
```

The createDirectory() will create a directory and throw an exception if it already exists or the paths leading up to the directory do not exist.

The createDirectories() works just like the java.io.File method mkdirs(), in that it creates the target directory along with any nonexistent parent directories leading up to the path. If all of the directories already exist, createDirectories() will simply complete without doing anything. This is useful in situations where you want to ensure a directory exists and create it if it does not.

Both of these methods also accept an optional list of FileAttribute<?> values to apply to the newly created directory or directories. We will discuss file attributes more later in the chapter.

The following shows how to create directories in NIO.2:

```
Files.createDirectory(Path.of("/bison/field"));
Files.createDirectories(Path.of("/bison/field/pasture/green"));
```

The first example creates a new directory, field, in the directory /bison, assuming /bison exists; or else an exception is thrown. Contrast this with the second example, which creates the directory green along with any of the following parent directories if they do not already exist, including bison, field, and pasture.

Copying Files with *copy()*

The NIO.2 Files class provides a method for copying files and directories within the file system.

```
public static Path copy(Path source, Path target,
    CopyOption... options) throws IOException
```

The method copies a file or directory from one location to another using Path objects. The following shows an example of copying a file and a directory:

```
Files.copy(Paths.get("/panda/bamboo.txt"),
    Paths.get("/panda-save/bamboo.txt"));


Files.copy(Paths.get("/turtle"), Paths.get("/turtleCopy"));
```

When directories are copied, the copy is shallow. A *shallow copy* means that the files and subdirectories within the directory are not copied. A *deep copy* means that the entire tree is copied, including all of its content and subdirectories. We'll show how to perform a deep copy of a directory tree using streams later in the chapter.

Copying and Replacing Files

By default, if the target already exists, the copy() method will throw an exception. You can change this behavior by providing the StandardCopyOption enum value REPLACE_EXISTING to the method. The following method call will overwrite the movie.txt file if it already exists:

```
Files.copy(Paths.get("book.txt"), Paths.get("movie.txt"),
    StandardCopyOption.REPLACE_EXISTING);
```

For the exam, you need to know that without the REPLACE_EXISTING option, this method will throw an exception if the file already exists.

Copying Files with I/O Streams

The Files class includes two copy() methods that operate with I/O streams.

```
public static long copy(InputStream in, Path target,
    CopyOption... options) throws IOException
```

```
public static long copy(Path source, OutputStream out)
   throws IOException
```

The first method reads the contents of a stream and writes the output to a file. The second method reads the contents of a file and writes the output to a stream. They are quite convenient if you need to quickly read/write data from/to disk.

The following are examples of each copy() method:

```
try (var is = new FileInputStream("source-data.txt")) {
   // Write stream data to a file
   Files.copy(is, Paths.get("/mammals/wolf.txt"));
}
```

```
Files.copy(Paths.get("/fish/clown.xsl"), System.out);
```

While we used FileInputStream in the first example, the streams could have been any valid I/O stream including website connections, in-memory stream resources, and so forth. The second example prints the contents of a file directly to the System.out stream.

Copying Files into a Directory

For the exam, it is important that you understand how the copy() method operates on both files and directories. For example, let's say we have a file, food.txt, and a directory, /enclosure. Both the file and directory exist. What do you think is the result of executing the following process?

```
var file = Paths.get("food.txt");
var directory = Paths.get("/enclosure");
Files.copy(file, directory);
```

If you said it would create a new file at /enclosure/food.txt, then you're way off. It actually throws an exception. The command tries to create a new file, named /enclosure. Since the path /enclosure already exists, an exception is thrown at runtime.

On the other hand, if the directory did not exist, then it would create a new file with the contents of food.txt, but it would be called /enclosure. Remember, we said files may not need to have extensions, and in this example, it matters.

This behavior applies to both the copy() and the move() methods, the latter of which we will be covering next. In case you're curious, the correct way to copy the file into the directory would be to do the following:

```
var file = Paths.get("food.txt");
var directory = Paths.get("/enclosure/food.txt");
Files.copy(file, directory);
```

You also define directory using the resolve() method we saw earlier, which saves you from having to write the filename twice.

```
var directory = Paths.get("/enclosure").resolve(file.getFileName());
```

Moving or Renaming Paths with *move()*

The Files class provides a useful method for moving or renaming files and directories.

```
public static Path move(Path source, Path target,
    CopyOption... options) throws IOException
```

The following is some sample code that uses the move() method:

```
Files.move(Path.of("c:\\zoo"), Path.of("c:\\zoo-new"));
```

```
Files.move(Path.of("c:\\user\\addresses.txt"),
    Path.of("c:\\zoo-new\\addresses2.txt"));
```

The first example renames the zoo directory to a zoo-new directory, keeping all of the original contents from the source directory. The second example moves the addresses.txt file from the directory user to the directory zoo-new, and it renames it to addresses2.txt.

Similarities between *move()* and *copy()*

Like copy(), move() requires REPLACE_EXISTING to overwrite the target if it exists, else it will throw an exception. Also like copy(), move() will not put a file in a directory if the source is a file and the target is a directory. Instead, it will create a new file with the name of the directory.

Performing an Atomic Move

Another enum value that you need to know for the exam when working with the move() method is the StandardCopyOption value ATOMIC_MOVE.

```
Files.move(Path.of("mouse.txt"), Path.of("gerbil.txt"),
    StandardCopyOption.ATOMIC_MOVE);
```

You may remember the atomic property from Chapter 18, "Concurrency," and the principle of an atomic move is similar. An atomic move is one in which a file is moved within the file system as a single indivisible operation. Put another way, any process monitoring the file system never sees an incomplete or partially written file. If the file system does not support this feature, an AtomicMoveNotSupportedException will be thrown.

Note that while ATOMIC_MOVE is available as a member of the StandardCopyOption type, it will likely throw an exception if passed to a copy() method.

Deleting a File with *delete()* and *deleteIfExists()*

The Files class includes two methods that delete a file or empty directory within the file system.

```
public static void delete(Path path) throws IOException
```

```
public static boolean deleteIfExists(Path path) throws IOException
```

To delete a directory, it must be empty. Both of these methods throw an exception if operated on a nonempty directory. In addition, if the path is a symbolic link, then the symbolic link will be deleted, not the path that the symbolic link points to.

The methods differ on how they handle a path that does not exist. The delete() method throws an exception if the path does not exist, while the deleteIfExists() method returns true if the delete was successful, and false otherwise. Similar to createDirectories(), deleteIfExists() is useful in situations where you want to ensure a path does not exist, and delete it if it does.

Here we provide sample code that performs delete() operations:

```
Files.delete(Paths.get("/vulture/feathers.txt"));
Files.deleteIfExists(Paths.get("/pigeon"));
```

The first example deletes the feathers.txt file in the vulture directory, and it throws a NoSuchFileException if the file or directory does not exist. The second example deletes the pigeon directory, assuming it is empty. If the pigeon directory does not exist, then the second line will not throw an exception.

Reading and Writing Data with *newBufferedReader()* and *newBufferedWriter()*

NIO.2 includes two convenient methods for working with I/O streams.

```
public static BufferedReader newBufferedReader(Path path)
    throws IOException
```

```
public static BufferedWriter newBufferedWriter(Path path,
    OpenOption... options) throws IOException
```

You can wrap I/O stream constructors to produce the same effect, although it's a lot easier to use the factory method.

There are overloaded versions of these methods that take a Charset. You may remember that we briefly discussed character encoding and Charset in Chapter 19. For this chapter, you just need to know that characters can be encoded in bytes in a variety of ways.

The first method, newBufferedReader(), reads the file specified at the Path location using a BufferedReader object.

```
var path = Path.of("/animals/gopher.txt");
try (var reader = Files.newBufferedReader(path)) {
    String currentLine = null;
    while((currentLine = reader.readLine()) != null)
        System.out.println(currentLine);
}
```

This example reads the lines of the files using a BufferedReader and outputs the contents to the screen. As you shall see shortly, there are other methods that do this without having to use an I/O stream.

The second method, newBufferedWriter(), writes to a file specified at the Path location using a BufferedWriter.

```
var list = new ArrayList<String>();
list.add("Smokey");
list.add("Yogi");

var path = Path.of("/animals/bear.txt");
try (var writer = Files.newBufferedWriter(path)) {
   for(var line : list) {
      writer.write(line);
      writer.newLine();
   }
}
```

This code snippet creates a new file with two lines of text in it. Did you notice that both of these methods use buffered streams rather than low-level file streams? As we mentioned in Chapter 19, the buffered stream classes are much more performant, especially when working with files.

Reading a File with *readAllLines()*

The Files class includes a convenient method for turning the lines of a file into a List.

```
public static List<String> readAllLines(Path path) throws IOException
```

The following sample code reads the lines of the file and outputs them to the user:

```
var path = Path.of("/animals/gopher.txt");
final List<String> lines = Files.readAllLines(path);
lines.forEach(System.out::println);
```

Be aware that the entire file is read when readAllLines() is called, with the resulting List<String> storing all of the contents of the file in memory at once. If the file is significantly large, then you may trigger an OutOfMemoryError trying to load all of it into memory. Later in the chapter, we will revisit this method and present a stream-based NIO.2 method that can operate with a much smaller memory footprint.

Reviewing *Files* Methods

Table 20.4 shows the static methods in the Files class that you should be familiar with for the exam.

TABLE 20.4   *Files* methods

boolean exists(Path,
    LinkOption...)
	Path move(Path, Path,
	    CopyOption...)

boolean isSameFile(Path, Path)	void delete(Path)
Path createDirectory(Path, FileAttribute<?>...)	boolean deleteIfExists(Path)

Path createDirectories(Path,
    FileAttribute<?>...)
	BufferedReader
	    newBufferedReader(Path)

Path copy(Path, Path,
    CopyOption...)
	BufferedWriter newBufferedWriter(
	    Path, OpenOption...)

long copy(InputStream, Path, CopyOption...)	List<String> readAllLines(Path)
long copy(Path, OutputStream)	

All of these methods except exists() declare IOException.

Managing File Attributes

The Files class also provides numerous methods for accessing file and directory metadata, referred to as *file attributes*. A file attribute is data about a file within the system, such as its size and visibility, that is not part of the file contents. In this section, we'll show how to read file attributes individually or as a single streamlined call.

Discovering File Attributes

We begin our discussion by presenting the basic methods for reading file attributes. These methods are usable within any file system although they may have limited meaning in some file systems.

Reading Common Attributes with *isDirectory()*, *isSymbolicLink()*, and *isRegularFile()*

The Files class includes three methods for determining type of a Path.

```
public static boolean isDirectory(Path path, LinkOption... options)
```

```
public static boolean isSymbolicLink(Path path)
```

```
public static boolean isRegularFile(Path path, LinkOption... options)
```

The isDirectory() and isSymbolicLink() methods should be self-explanatory, although isRegularFile() warrants some discussion. Java defines a *regular file* as one that can contain content, as opposed to a symbolic link, directory, resource, or other non-regular file that may be present in some operating systems. If the symbolic link points to an actual file, Java will perform the check on the target of the symbolic link. In other words, it is possible for isRegularFile() to return true for a symbolic link, as long as the link resolves to a regular file.

Let's take a look at some sample code.

```
System.out.print(Files.isDirectory(Paths.get("/canine/fur.jpg")));
System.out.print(Files.isSymbolicLink(Paths.get("/canine/coyote")));
System.out.print(Files.isRegularFile(Paths.get("/canine/types.txt")));
```

The first example prints true if fur.jpg is a directory or a symbolic link to a directory and false otherwise. The second example prints true if /canine/coyote is a symbolic link, regardless of whether the file or directory it points to exists. The third example prints true if types.txt points to a regular file or alternatively a symbolic link that points to a regular file.

> While most methods in the Files class declare IOException, these three methods do not. They return false if the path does not exist.

Checking File Accessibility with *isHidden()*, *isReadable()*, *isWritable()*, and *isExecutable()*

In many file systems, it is possible to set a boolean attribute to a file that marks it hidden, readable, or executable. The Files class includes methods that expose this information.

```
public static boolean isHidden(Path path) throws IOException
```

```
public static boolean isReadable(Path path)
```

```
public static boolean isWritable(Path path)
```

```
public static boolean isExecutable(Path path)
```

A hidden file can't normally be viewed when listing the contents of a directory. The readable, writable, and executable flags are important in file systems where the filename can be viewed, but the user may not have permission to open the file's contents, modify the file, or run the file as a program, respectively.

Here we present sample usage of each method:

```
System.out.print(Files.isHidden(Paths.get("/walrus.txt")));
System.out.print(Files.isReadable(Paths.get("/seal/baby.png")));
System.out.print(Files.isWritable(Paths.get("dolphin.txt")));
System.out.print(Files.isExecutable(Paths.get("whale.png")));
```

If the walrus.txt exists and is hidden within the file system, then the first example prints true. The second example prints true if the baby.png file exists and its contents are readable. The third example prints true if the dolphin.txt file is able to be modified. Finally, the last example prints true if the file is able to be executed within the operating system. Note that the file extension does not necessarily determine whether a file is executable. For example, an image file that ends in .png could be marked executable in some file systems.

With the exception of isHidden(), these methods do not declare any checked exceptions and return false if the file does not exist.

Reading File Size with *size()*

The Files class includes a method to determine the size of the file in bytes.

```
public static long size(Path path) throws IOException
```

The size returned by this method represents the conceptual size of the data, and this may differ from the actual size on the persistent storage device. The following is a sample call to the size() method:

```
System.out.print(Files.size(Paths.get("/zoo/animals.txt")));
```

The Files.size() method is defined only on files. Calling Files.size() on a directory is undefined, and the result depends on the file system. If you need to determine the size of a directory and its contents, you'll need to walk the directory tree. We'll show you how to do this later in the chapter.

Checking for File Changes with *getLastModifiedTime()*

Most operating systems support tracking a last-modified date/time value with each file. Some applications use this to determine when the file's contents should be read again. In the majority of circumstances, it is a lot faster to check a single file metadata attribute than to reload the entire contents of the file.

The Files class provides the following method to retrieve the last time a file was modified:

```
public static FileTime getLastModifiedTime(Path path,
    LinkOption... options) throws IOException
```

The method returns a FileTime object, which represents a timestamp. For convenience, it has a toMillis() method that returns the epoch time, which is the number of milliseconds since 12 a.m. UTC on January 1, 1970.

The following shows how to print the last modified value for a file as an epoch value:

```
final Path path = Paths.get("/rabbit/food.jpg");
System.out.println(Files.getLastModifiedTime(path).toMillis());
```

Improving Attribute Access

Up until now, we have been accessing individual file attributes with multiple method calls. While this is functionally correct, there is often a cost each time one of these methods is called. Put simply, it is far more efficient to ask the file system for all of the attributes at once rather than performing multiple round-trips to the file system. Furthermore, some attributes are file system–specific and cannot be easily generalized for all file systems.

NIO.2 addresses both of these concerns by allowing you to construct views for various file systems with a single method call. A *view* is a group of related attributes for a particular file system type. That's not to say that the earlier attribute methods that we just finished discussing do not have their uses. If you need to read only one attribute of a file or directory, then requesting a view is unnecessary.

Understanding Attribute and View Types

NIO.2 includes two methods for working with attributes in a single method call: a read-only attributes method and an updatable view method. For each method, you need to provide a file system type object, which tells the NIO.2 method which type of view you are requesting. By updatable view, we mean that we can both read and write attributes with the same object.

Table 20.5 lists the commonly used attributes and view types. For the exam, you only need to know about the basic file attribute types. The other views are for managing operating system–specific information.

TABLE 20.5   The attributes and view types

Attributes interface	View interface	Description
BasicFileAttributes	BasicFileAttributeView	Basic set of attributes supported by all file systems
DosFileAttributes	DosFileAttributeView	Basic set of attributes along with those supported by DOS/Windows-based systems
PosixFileAttributes	PosixFileAttributeView	Basic set of attributes along with those supported by POSIX systems, such as UNIX, Linux, Mac, etc.

Retrieving Attributes with *readAttributes()*

The Files class includes the following method to read attributes of a class in a read-only capacity:

```
public static <A extends BasicFileAttributes> A readAttributes(
    Path path,
    Class<A> type,
    LinkOption... options) throws IOException
```

Applying it requires specifying the Path and BasicFileAttributes.class parameters.

```
var path = Paths.get("/turtles/sea.txt");
BasicFileAttributes data = Files.readAttributes(path,
    BasicFileAttributes.class);

System.out.println("Is a directory? " + data.isDirectory());
System.out.println("Is a regular file? " + data.isRegularFile());
System.out.println("Is a symbolic link? " + data.isSymbolicLink());
System.out.println("Size (in bytes): " + data.size());
System.out.println("Last modified: " + data.lastModifiedTime());
```

The BasicFileAttributes class includes many values with the same name as the attribute methods in the Files class. The advantage of using this method, though, is that all of the attributes are retrieved at once.

Modifying Attributes with *getFileAttributeView()*

The following Files method returns an updatable view:

```
public static <V extends FileAttributeView> V getFileAttributeView(
    Path path,
    Class<V> type,
    LinkOption... options)
```

We can use the updatable view to increment a file's last modified date/time value by 10,000 milliseconds, or 10 seconds.

```
// Read file attributes
var path = Paths.get("/turtles/sea.txt");
BasicFileAttributeView view = Files.getFileAttributeView(path,
    BasicFileAttributeView.class);
BasicFileAttributes attributes = view.readAttributes();

// Modify file last modified time
FileTime lastModifiedTime = FileTime.fromMillis(
    attributes.lastModifiedTime().toMillis() + 10_000);
view.setTimes(lastModifiedTime, null, null);
```

After the updatable view is retrieved, we need to call readAttributes() on the view to obtain the file metadata. From there, we create a new FileTime value and set it using the setTimes() method.

```
// BasicFileAttributeView instance method
public void setTimes(FileTime lastModifiedTime,
   FileTime lastAccessTime, FileTime createTime)
```

This method allows us to pass null for any date/time value that we do not want to modify. In our sample code, only the last modified date/time is changed.

> Not all file attributes can be modified with a view. For example, you cannot set a property that changes a file into a directory. Likewise, you cannot change the size of the object without modifying its contents.

Applying Functional Programming

We saved the best for last! In this part of the chapter, we'll combine everything we've presented so far with functional programming to perform extremely powerful file operations, often with only a few lines of code. The Files class includes some incredibly useful Stream API methods that operate on files, directories, and directory trees.

Listing Directory Contents

Let's start with a simple Stream API method. The following Files method lists the contents of a directory:

```
public static Stream<Path> list(Path dir) throws IOException
```

The Files.list() is similar to the java.io.File method listFiles(), except that it returns a Stream<Path> rather than a File[]. Since streams use lazy evaluation, this means the method will load each path element as needed, rather than the entire directory at once.

Printing the contents of a directory is easy.

```
try (Stream<Path> s = Files.list(Path.of("/home"))) {
   s.forEach(System.out::println);
}
```

Let's do something more interesting, though. Earlier, we presented the Files.copy() method and showed that it only performed a shallow copy of a directory. We can use the Files.list() to perform a deep copy.

```
public void copyPath(Path source, Path target) {
   try {
      Files.copy(source, target);
      if(Files.isDirectory(source))
         try (Stream<Path> s = Files.list(source)) {
            s.forEach(p -> copyPath(p,
               target.resolve(p.getFileName())));
         }
   } catch(IOException e) {
      // Handle exception
   }
}
```

The method first copies the path, whether it be a file or a directory. If it is a directory, then only a shallow copy is performed. Next, it checks whether the path is a directory and, if it is, performs a recursive copy of each of its elements. What if the method comes across a symbolic link? Don't worry, we'll address that topic in the next section. For now, you just need to know the JVM will not follow symbolic links when using this stream method.

Closing the Stream

Did you notice that in the last two code samples, we put our Stream objects inside a try-with-resources method? The NIO.2 stream-based methods open a connection to the file system *that must be properly closed*, else a resource leak could ensue. A resource leak within the file system means the path may be locked from modification long after the process that used it completed.

If you assumed a stream's terminal operation would automatically close the underlying file resources, you'd be wrong. There was a lot of debate about this behavior when it was first presented, but in short, requiring developers to close the stream won out.

On the plus side, not all streams need to be closed, only those that open resources, like the ones found in NIO.2. For instance, you didn't need to close any of the streams you worked with in Chapter 15.

Finally, the exam doesn't always properly close NIO.2 resources. To match the exam, we will sometimes skip closing NIO.2 resources in review and practice questions. Please, in your own code, always use try-with-resources statements with these NIO.2 methods.

Traversing a Directory Tree

While the Files.list() method is useful, it traverses the contents of only a single directory. What if we want to visit all of the paths within a directory tree? Before we proceed, we need to review some basic concepts about file systems. When we originally described a directory in Chapter 19, we mentioned that it was organized in a hierarchical manner. For example, a directory can contain files and other directories, which can in turn contain other files and directories. Every record in a file system has exactly one parent, with the exception of the root directory, which sits atop everything.

A file system is commonly visualized as a tree with a single root node and many branches and leaves, as shown in Figure 20.5. In this model, a directory is a branch or internal node, and a file is a leaf node.

FIGURE 20.5   File and directory as a tree structure

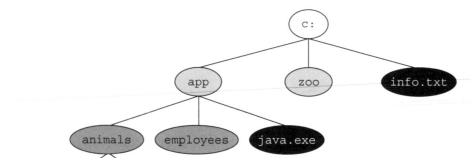

A common task in a file system is to iterate over the descendants of a path, either recording information about them or, more commonly, filtering them for a specific set of files. For example, you may want to search a folder and print a list of all of the .java files. Furthermore, file systems store file records in a hierarchical manner. Generally speaking, if you want to search for a file, you have to start with a parent directory, read its child elements, then read their children, and so on.

Traversing a directory, also referred to as walking a directory tree, is the process by which you start with a parent directory and iterate over all of its descendants until some condition is met or there are no more elements over which to iterate. For example, if we're searching for a single file, we can end the search when the file is found or when we've checked all files and come up empty. The starting path is usually a specific directory; after all, it would be time-consuming to search the entire file system on every request!

Don't Use *DirectoryStream* and *FileVisitor*

While browsing the NIO.2 Javadocs, you may come across methods that use the DirectoryStream and FileVisitor classes to traverse a directory. These methods predate the existence of the Streams API and were even required knowledge for older Java certification exams. Even worse, despite its name, DirectoryStream is not a Stream API class.

The best advice we can give you is to not use them. The newer Stream API–based methods are superior and accomplish the same thing often with much less code.

Selecting a Search Strategy

There are two common strategies associated with walking a directory tree: a depth-first search and a breadth-first search. A *depth-first search* traverses the structure from the root to an arbitrary leaf and then navigates back up toward the root, traversing fully down any paths it skipped along the way. The *search depth* is the distance from the root to current node. To prevent endless searching, Java includes a search depth that is used to limit how many levels (or hops) from the root the search is allowed to go.

Alternatively, a *breadth-first search* starts at the root and processes all elements of each particular depth, before proceeding to the next depth level. The results are ordered by depth, with all nodes at depth 1 read before all nodes at depth 2, and so on. While a breadth-first tends to be balanced and predictable, it also requires more memory since a list of visited nodes must be maintained.

For the exam, you don't have to understand the details of each search strategy that Java employs; you just need to be aware that the NIO.2 Streams API methods use depth-first searching with a depth limit, which can be optionally changed.

Walking a Directory with *walk()*

That's enough background information; let's get to more Steam API methods. The Files class includes two methods for walking the directory tree using a depth-first search.

```
public static Stream<Path> walk(Path start,
    FileVisitOption... options) throws IOException
```

```
public static Stream<Path> walk(Path start, int maxDepth,
    FileVisitOption... options) throws IOException
```

Like our other stream methods, walk() uses lazy evaluation and evaluates a Path only as it gets to it. This means that even if the directory tree includes hundreds or thousands of files, the memory required to process a directory tree is low. The first walk() method relies on a default maximum depth of Integer.MAX_VALUE, while the overloaded version allows the user to set a maximum depth. This is useful in cases where the file system might be large and we know the information we are looking for is near the root.

Java uses an int for its maximum depth rather than a long because most file systems do not support path values deeper than what can be stored in an int. In other words, using Integer.MAX_VALUE is effectively like using an infinite value, since you would be hard-pressed to find a stable file system where this limit is exceeded.

Rather than just printing the contents of a directory tree, we can again do something more interesting. The following getPathSize() method walks a directory tree and returns the total size of all the files in the directory:

```java
private long getSize(Path p) {
   try {
      return  Files.size(p);
   } catch (IOException e) {
      // Handle exception
   }
   return 0L;
}


public long getPathSize(Path source) throws IOException {
   try (var s = Files.walk(source)) {
      return s.parallel()
            .filter(p -> !Files.isDirectory(p))
            .mapToLong(this::getSize)
            .sum();
   }
}
```

The getSize() helper method is needed because Files.size() declares IOException, and we'd rather not put a try/catch block inside a lambda expression. We can print the data using the format() method we saw in the previous chapter:

```java
var size = getPathSize(Path.of("/fox/data"));
System.out.format("Total Size: %.2f megabytes", (size/1000000.0));
```

Depending on the directory you run this on, it will print something like this:

```
Total Directory Tree Size: 15.30 megabytes
```

Applying a Depth Limit

Let's say our directory tree was quite deep, so we apply a depth limit by changing one line of code in our getPathSize() method.

```
try (var s = Files.walk(source, 5)) {
```

This new version checks for files only within 5 steps of the starting node. A depth value of 0 indicates the current path itself. Since the method calculates values only on files, you'd have to set a depth limit of at least 1 to get a nonzero result when this method is applied to a directory tree.

Avoiding Circular Paths

Many of our earlier NIO.2 methods traverse symbolic links by default, with a NOFOLLOW_LINKS used to disable this behavior. The walk() method is different in that it does *not* follow symbolic links by default and requires the FOLLOW_LINKS option to be enabled. We can alter our getPathSize() method to enable following symbolic links by adding the FileVisitOption:

```
try (var s = Files.walk(source,
        FileVisitOption.FOLLOW_LINKS)) {
```

When traversing a directory tree, your program needs to be careful of symbolic links if enabled. For example, if our process comes across a symbolic link that points to the root directory of the file system, then every file in the system would be searched!

Worse yet, a symbolic link could lead to a cycle, in which a path is visited repeatedly. A *cycle* is an infinite circular dependency in which an entry in a directory tree points to one of its ancestor directories. Let's say we had a directory tree as shown in Figure 20.6, with the symbolic link /birds/robin/allBirds that points to /birds.

FIGURE 20.6   File system with cycle

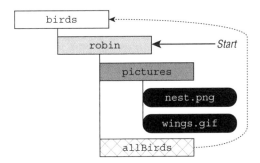

What happens if we try to traverse this tree and follow all symbolic links, starting with /birds/robin? Table 20.6 shows the paths visited after walking a depth of 3. For simplicity, we'll walk the tree in a breadth-first ordering, *although a cycle occurs regardless of the search strategy used.*

TABLE 20.6 Walking a directory with a cycle using breadth-first search

Depth	Path reached
0	/birds/robin
1	/birds/robin/pictures
1	/birds/robin/allBirds ➢ /birds
2	/birds/robin/pictures/nest.png
2	/birds/robin/pictures/nest.gif
2	**/birds/robin/allBirds/robin** ➢ **/birds/robin**
3	/birds/robin/allBirds/robin/pictures ➢ /birds/robin/pictures
3	/birds/robin/allBirds/robin/pictures/allBirds ➢ /birds/robin/allBirds ➢ /birds

After walking a distance of 1 from the start, we hit the symbolic link /birds/robin/allBirds and go back to the top of the directory tree /birds. That's OK because we haven't visited /birds yet, so there's no cycle yet!

Unfortunately, at depth 2, we encounter a cycle. We've already visited the /birds/robin directory on our first step, and now we're encountering it again. If the process continues, we'll be doomed to visit the directory over and over again.

Be aware that when the FOLLOW_LINKS option is used, the walk() method will track all of the paths it has visited, throwing a FileSystemLoopException if a path is visited twice.

Searching a Directory with *find()*

In the previous example, we applied a filter to the Stream<Path> object to filter the results, although NIO.2 provides a more convenient method.

```
public static Stream<Path> find(Path start,
   int maxDepth,
   BiPredicate<Path,BasicFileAttributes> matcher,
   FileVisitOption... options) throws IOException
```

The find() method behaves in a similar manner as the walk() method, except that it takes a BiPredicate to filter the data. It also requires a depth limit be set. Like walk(), find() also supports the FOLLOW_LINK option.

The two parameters of the BiPredicate are a Path object and a BasicFileAttributes object, which you saw earlier in the chapter. In this manner, NIO.2 automatically retrieves the basic file information for you, allowing you to write complex lambda expressions that have direct access to this object. We illustrate this with the following example:

```
Path path = Paths.get("/bigcats");
long minSize = 1_000;
try (var s = Files.find(path, 10,
      (p, a) -> a.isRegularFile()
         && p.toString().endsWith(".java")
         && a.size() > minSize)) {
   s.forEach(System.out::println);
}
```

This example searches a directory tree and prints all .java files with a size of at least 1,000 bytes, using a depth limit of 10. While we could have accomplished this using the walk() method along with a call to readAttributes(), this implementation is a lot shorter and more convenient than those would have been. We also don't have to worry about any methods within the lambda expression declaring a checked exception, as we saw in the getPathSize() example.

Reading a File with *lines()*

Earlier in the chapter, we presented Files.readAllLines() and commented that using it to read a very large file could result in an OutOfMemoryError problem. Luckily, NIO.2 solves this problem with a Stream API method.

```
public static Stream<String> lines(Path path) throws IOException
```

The contents of the file are read and processed lazily, which means that only a small portion of the file is stored in memory at any given time.

```
Path path = Paths.get("/fish/sharks.log");
try (var s = Files.lines(path)) {
   s.forEach(System.out::println);
}
```

Taking things one step further, we can leverage other stream methods for a more powerful example.

```
Path path = Paths.get("/fish/sharks.log");
try (var s = Files.lines(path)) {
   s.filter(f -> f.startsWith("WARN:"))
```

```
    .map(f -> f.substring(5))
    .forEach(System.out::println);
}
```

This sample code searches a log for lines that start with WARN:, outputting the text that follows. Assuming that the input file sharks.log is as follows:

```
INFO:Server starting
DEBUG:Processes available = 10
WARN:No database could be detected
DEBUG:Processes available reset to 0
WARN:Performing manual recovery
INFO:Server successfully started
```

Then, the sample output would be the following:

```
No database could be detected
Performing manual recovery
```

As you can see, functional programming plus NIO.2 gives us the ability to manipulate files in complex ways, often with only a few short expressions.

Files.readAllLines() vs. Files.lines()

For the exam, you need to know the difference between readAllLines() and lines(). Both of these examples compile and run:

```
Files.readAllLines(Paths.get("birds.txt")).forEach(System.out::println);
Files.lines(Paths.get("birds.txt")).forEach(System.out::println);
```

The first line reads the entire file into memory and performs a print operation on the result, while the second line lazily processes each line and prints it as it is read. The advantage of the second code snippet is that it does not require the entire file to be stored in memory at any time.

You should also be aware of when they are mixing incompatible types on the exam. Do you see why the following does not compile?

```
Files.readAllLines(Paths.get("birds.txt"))
    .filter(s -> s.length() > 2)
    .forEach(System.out::println);
```

The readAllLines() method returns a List, not a Stream, so the filter() method is not available.

Comparing Legacy *java.io.File* and NIO.2 Methods

We conclude this chapter with Table 20.7, which shows a comparison between some of the legacy java.io.File methods described in Chapter 19 and the new NIO.2 methods described in this chapter. In this table, file refers to an instance of the java.io.File class, while path and otherPath refer to instances of the NIO.2 Path interface.

TABLE 20.7 Comparison of *java.io.File* and NIO.2 methods

Legacy I/O *File* method	NIO.2 method
file.delete()	Files.delete(path)
file.exists()	Files.exists(path)
file.getAbsolutePath()	path.toAbsolutePath()
file.getName()	path.getFileName()
file.getParent()	path.getParent()
file.isDirectory()	Files.isDirectory(path)
file.isFile()	Files.isRegularFile(path)
file.lastModified()	Files.getLastModifiedTime(path)
file.length()	Files.size(path)
file.listFiles()	Files.list(path)
file.mkdir()	Files.createDirectory(path)
file.mkdirs()	Files.createDirectories(path)
file.renameTo(otherFile)	Files.move(path,otherPath)

Bear in mind that a number of methods and features are available in NIO.2 that are not available in the legacy API, such as support for symbolic links, setting file system–specific attributes, and so on. The NIO.2 is a more developed, much more powerful API than the legacy java.io.File class.

Summary

This chapter introduced NIO.2 for working with files and directories using the Path interface. For the exam, you need to know what the NIO.2 Path interface is and how it differs from the legacy java.io.File class. You should be familiar with how to create and use Path objects, including how to combine or resolve them with other Path objects.

We spent time reviewing various methods available in the Files helper class. As discussed, the name of the function often tells you exactly what it does. We explained that most of these methods are capable of throwing an IOException and many take optional varargs enum values.

We also discussed how NIO.2 provides methods for reading and writing file metadata. NIO.2 includes two methods for retrieving all of the file system attributes for a path in a single call, without numerous round-trips to the operating system. One method requires a read-only attribute type, while the second method requires an updatable view type. It also allows NIO.2 to support operating system–specific file attributes.

Finally, NIO.2 includes Stream API methods that can be used to process files and directories. We discussed methods for listing a directory, walking a directory tree, searching a directory tree, and reading the lines of a file.

Exam Essentials

Understand how to create *Path* objects. An NIO.2 Path instance is an immutable object that is commonly created from the factory method Paths.get() or Path.of(). It can also be created from FileSystem, java.net.URI, or java.io.File instances. The Path interface includes many instance methods for reading and manipulating the abstract path value.

Be able to manipulate *Path* objects. NIO.2 includes numerous methods for viewing, manipulating, and combining Path values. It also includes methods to eliminate redundant or unnecessary path symbols. Most of the methods defined on Path do not declare any checked exceptions and do not require the path to exist within the file system, with the exception of toRealPath().

Be able to operate on files and directories using the *Files* class. The NIO.2 Files helper class includes methods that operate on real files and directories within the file system. For example, it can be used to check whether a file exists, copy/move a file, create a directory, or delete a directory. Most of these methods declare IOException, since the path may not exist, and take a variety of varargs options.

Manage file attributes. The NIO.2 `Files` class includes many methods for reading single file attributes, such as its size or whether it is a directory, a symbolic link, hidden, etc. NIO.2 also supports reading all of the attributes in a single call. An attribute type is used to support operating system–specific views. Finally, NIO.2 supports updatable views for modified select attributes.

Be able to operate on directories using functional programming. NIO.2 includes the Stream API for manipulating directories. The `Files.list()` method iterates over the contents of a single directory, while the `Files.walk()` method lazily traverses a directory tree in a depth-first manner. The `Files.find()` method also traverses a directory but requires a filter to be applied. Both `Files.walk()` and `Files.find()` support a search depth limit. Both methods will also throw an exception if they are directed to follow symbolic links and detect a cycle.

Understand the difference between *readAllLines()* and *lines()*. The `Files.readAllLines()` method reads all the lines of of a file into memory and returns the result as a `List<String>`. The `Files.lines()` method lazily reads the lines of a file, instead returning a functional programming `Stream<Path>` object. While both methods will correctly read the lines of a file, `lines()` is considered safer for larger files since it does not require the entire file to be stored in memory.

Review Questions

The answers to the chapter review questions can be found in the Appendix.

1. What is the output of the following code?

```
4: var path = Path.of("/user/./root","../kodiacbear.txt");
5: path.normalize().relativize("/lion");
6: System.out.println(path);
```

   A. ../../lion
   B. /user/kodiacbear.txt
   C. ../user/kodiacbear.txt
   D. /user/./root/../kodiacbear.txt
   E. The code does not compile.
   F. None of the above

2. For which values of path sent to this method would it be possible for the following code to output Success? (Choose all that apply.)

```
public void removeBadFile(Path path) {
    if(Files.isDirectory(path))
        System.out.println(Files.deleteIfExists(path)
            ? "Success": "Try Again");
}
```

   A. path refers to a regular file in the file system.
   B. path refers to a symbolic link in the file system.
   C. path refers to an empty directory in the file system.
   D. path refers to a directory with content in the file system.
   E. path does not refer to a record that exists within the file system.
   F. The code does not compile.

3. What is the result of executing the following code? (Choose all that apply.)

```
4: var p = Paths.get("sloth.schedule");
5: var a = Files.readAttributes(p, BasicFileAttributes.class);
6: Files.mkdir(p.resolve(".backup"));
7: if(a.size()>0 && a.isDirectory()) {
8:     a.setTimes(null,null,null);
9: }
```

A. It compiles and runs without issue.

B. The code will not compile because of line 5.

C. The code will not compile because of line 6.

D. The code will not compile because of line 7.

E. The code will not compile because of line 8.

F. None of the above

4. If the current working directory is /user/home, then what is the output of the following code?

```
var p = Paths.get("/zoo/animals/bear/koala/food.txt");
System.out.print(p.subpath(1,3).getName(1).toAbsolutePath());
```

A. bear

B. animals

C. /user/home/bear

D. /user/home/animals

E. /user/home/food.txt

F. The code does not compile.

G. The code compiles but throws an exception at runtime.

5. Assume /kang exists as a symbolic link to the directory /mammal/kangaroo within the file system. Which of the following statements are correct about this code snippet? (Choose all that apply.)

```
var path = Paths.get("/kang");
if(Files.isDirectory(path) && Files.isSymbolicLink(path))
    Files.createDirectory(path.resolve("joey"));
```

A. A new directory will always be created.

B. A new directory may be created.

C. If the code creates a directory, it will be reachable at /kang/joey.

D. If the code creates a directory, it will be reachable at /mammal/joey.

E. The code does not compile.

F. The code will compile but always throws an exception at runtime.

6. Assume that the directory /animals exists and is empty. What is the result of executing the following code?

```
Path path = Path.of("/animals");
try (var z = Files.walk(path)) {
    boolean b = z
        .filter((p,a) -> a.isDirectory() && !path.equals(p)) // x
        .findFirst().isPresent();  // y
    System.out.print(b ? "No Sub": "Has Sub");
}
```

A. It prints No Sub.

B. It prints Has Sub.

C. The code will not compile because of line x.

D. The code will not compile because of line y.

E. The output cannot be determined.

F. It produces an infinite loop at runtime.

7. If the current working directory is /zoo and the path /zoo/turkey does not exist, then what is the result of executing the following code? (Choose all that apply.)

```
Path path = Paths.get("turkey");
if(Files.isSameFile(path,Paths.get("/zoo/turkey"))) // z1
    Files.createDirectories(path.resolve("info"));    // z2
```

A. The code compiles and runs without issue, but it does not create any directories.

B. The directory /zoo/turkey is created.

C. The directory /zoo/turkey/info is created.

D. The code will not compile because of line z1.

E. The code will not compile because of line z2.

F. It compiles but throws an exception at runtime.

8. Which of the following correctly create Path instances? (Choose all that apply.)

A. new Path("jaguar.txt")

B. FileSystems.getDefault() .getPath("puma.txt")

C. Path.get("cats","lynx.txt")

D. new java.io.File("tiger.txt").toPath()

E. new FileSystem().getPath("lion")

F. Paths.getPath("ocelot.txt")

G. Path.of(Path.of(".").toUri())

9. What is the output of the following code?

```
var path1 = Path.of("/pets/../cat.txt");
var path2 = Paths.get("./dog.txt");
System.out.println(path1.resolve(path2));
System.out.println(path2.resolve(path1));
```

A. /cats.txt
   /dog.txt

B. /cats.txt/dog.txt
   /cat.txt

C. /pets/../cat.txt/./dog.txt
   /pets/../cat.txt

D. /pets/../cat.txt/./dog.txt
   ./dog.txt/pets/../cat.txt

E. None of the above

10. What are some advantages of using `Files.lines()` over `Files.readAllLines()`? (Choose all that apply.)

    A. It is often faster.

    B. It can be run with little memory available.

    C. It can be chained with functional programming methods like `filter()` and `map()` directly.

    D. It does not modify the contents of the file.

    E. It ensures the file is not read-locked by the file system.

    F. There are no differences, because one method is a pointer to the other.

11. Assume `monkey.txt` is a file that exists in the current working directory. Which statements about the following code snippet are correct? (Choose all that apply.)

    ```
    Files.move(Path.of("monkey.txt"), Paths.get("/animals"),
        StandardCopyOption.ATOMIC_MOVE,
        LinkOption.NOFOLLOW_LINKS);
    ```

    A. If /animals/monkey.txt exists, then it will be overwritten at runtime.

    B. If /animals exists as an empty directory, then /animals/monkey.txt will be the new location of the file.

    C. If monkey.txt is a symbolic link, then the file it points to will be moved at runtime.

    D. If the move is successful and another process is monitoring the file system, then it will not see an incomplete file at runtime.

    E. The code will always throw an exception at runtime.

    F. None of the above

12. What are some advantages of NIO.2 over the legacy `java.io.File` class for working with files? (Choose three.)

    A. NIO.2 supports file system–dependent attributes.

    B. NIO.2 includes a method to list the contents of a directory.

    C. NIO.2 includes a method to traverse a directory tree.

    D. NIO.2 includes a method to delete an entire directory tree.

    E. NIO.2 includes methods that are aware of symbolic links.

    F. NIO.2 supports sending emails.

13. For the `copy()` method shown here, assume that the source exists as a regular file and that the target does not. What is the result of the following code?

    ```
    var p1 = Path.of(".","/","goat.txt").normalize(); // k1
    var p2 = Path.of("mule.png");
    Files.copy(p1, p2, StandardCopyOption.COPY_ATTRIBUTES); //k2
    System.out.println(Files.isSameFile(p1, p2));
    ```

A. It will output `false`.

B. It will output `true`.

C. It does not compile because of line k1.

D. It does not compile because of line k2.

E. None of the above

14. Assume /monkeys exists as a directory containing multiple files, symbolic links, and sub-directories. Which statement about the following code is correct?

```
var f = Path.of("/monkeys");
try (var m =
        Files.find(f, 0, (p,a) -> a.isSymbolicLink())) { // y1
    m.map(s -> s.toString())
        .collect(Collectors.toList())
        .stream()
        .filter(s -> s.toString().endsWith(".txt")) // y2
        .forEach(System.out::println);
}
```

A. It will print all symbolic links in the directory tree ending in `.txt`.

B. It will print the target of all symbolic links in the directory ending in `.txt`.

C. It will print nothing.

D. It does not compile because of line y1.

E. It does not compile because of line y2.

F. It compiles but throws an exception at runtime.

15. Which NIO.2 method is most similar to the legacy `java.io.File` method `listFiles`?

A. `Path.listFiles()`

B. `Files.dir()`

C. `Files.ls()`

D. `Files.files()`

E. `Files.list()`

F. `Files.walk()`

16. What are some advantages of using NIO.2's `Files.readAttributes()` method rather than reading attributes individually from a file? (Choose all that apply.)

A. It can be used on both files and directories.

B. For reading a single attribute, it is often more performant.

C. It allows you to read symbolic links.

D. It makes fewer round-trips to the file system.

E. It can be used to access file system–dependent attributes.

F. For reading multiple attributes, it is often more performant.

17. Assuming the /fox/food-schedule.csv file exists with the specified contents, what is the expected output of calling printData() on it?

/fox/food-schedule.csv

```
6am,Breakfast
9am,SecondBreakfast
12pm,Lunch
6pm,Dinner
```

```
void printData(Path path) throws IOException {
    Files.readAllLines(path) // r1
        .flatMap(p -> Stream.of(p.split(","))) // r2
        .map(q -> q.toUpperCase())  // r3
        .forEach(System.out::println);
}
```

A. The code will not compile because of line r1.

B. The code will not compile because of line r2.

C. The code will not compile because of line r3.

D. It throws an exception at runtime.

E. It does not print anything at runtime.

F. None of the above

18. What are some possible results of executing the following code? (Choose all that apply.)

```
var x = Path.of("/animals/fluffy/..");
Files.walk(x.toRealPath().getParent()) // u1
    .map(p -> p.toAbsolutePath().toString()) // u2
    .filter(s -> s.endsWith(".java")) // u3
    .collect(Collectors.toList())
    .forEach(System.out::println);
```

A. It prints some files in the root directory.

B. It prints all files in the root directory.

C. FileSystemLoopException is thrown at runtime.

D. Another exception is thrown at runtime.

E. The code will not compile because of line u1.

F. The code will not compile because of line u2.

19. Assuming the directories and files referenced exist and are not symbolic links, what is the result of executing the following code?

```
var p1 = Path.of("/lizard",".")
    .resolve(Path.of("walking.txt"));
var p2 = new File("/lizard/./../actions/../walking.txt")
    .toPath();
System.out.print(Files.isSameFile(p1,p2));
System.out.print(" ");
System.out.print(p1.equals(p2));
System.out.print(" ");
System.out.print(p1.normalize().equals(p2.normalize()));
```

A.   true true true

B.   false false false

C.   false true false

D.   true false true

E.   true false false

F.   The code does not compile.

20. Assuming the current directory is /seals/harp/food, what is the result of executing the following code?

```
final Path path = Paths.get(".").normalize();
int count = 0;
for(int i=0; i<path.getNameCount(); ++i) {
    count++;
}
System.out.println(count);
```

A.   0

B.   1

C.   2

D.   3

E.   4

F.   The code compiles but throws an exception at runtime.

21. Assume the `source` instance passed to the following method represents a file that exists. Also, assume /flip/sounds.txt exists as a file prior to executing this method. When this method is executed, which statement correctly copies the file to the path specified by /flip/sounds.txt?

```
void copyIntoFlipDirectory(Path source) throws IOException {
    var dolphinDir = Path.of("/flip");
    dolphinDir = Files.createDirectories(dolphinDir);
    var n = Paths.get("sounds.txt");
    _____;
}
```

A. `Files.copy(source, dolphinDir)`

B. `Files.copy(source, dolphinDir.resolve(n),`
   `StandardCopyOption.REPLACE_EXISTING)`

C. `Files.copy(source, dolphinDir, StandardCopyOption.REPLACE_EXISTING)`

D. `Files.copy(source, dolphinDir.resolve(n))`

E. The method does not compile, regardless of what is placed in the blank.

F. The method compiles but throws an exception at runtime, regardless of what is placed in the blank.

22. Assuming the path referenced by m exists as a file, which statements about the following method are correct? (Choose all that apply.)

```
void duplicateFile(Path m, Path x) throws Exception {
    var r = Files.newBufferedReader(m);
    var w = Files.newBufferedWriter(x,
        StandardOpenOption.APPEND);
    String currentLine = null;
    while ((currentLine = r.readLine()) != null)
        w.write(currentLine);
}
```

A. If the path referenced by x does not exist, then it correctly copies the file.

B. If the path referenced by x does not exist, then a new file will be created.

C. If the path referenced x does not exist, then an exception will be thrown at runtime.

D. If the path referenced x exists, then an exception will be thrown at runtime.

E. The method contains a resource leak.

F. The method does not compile.

Chapter

21

JDBC

THE OCP EXAM TOPICS COVERED IN THIS CHAPTER INCLUDE THE FOLLOWING:

✓ **Database Applications with JDBC**
- Connect to databases using JDBC URLs and DriverManager
- Use PreparedStatement to perform CRUD operations
- Use PreparedStatement and CallableStatement APIs to perform database operations

JDBC stands for Java Database Connectivity. This chapter will introduce you to the basics of accessing databases from Java. We will cover the key interfaces for how to connect, perform queries, and process the results.

If you are new to JDBC, note that this chapter covers only the basics of JDBC and working with databases. What we cover is enough for the exam. To be ready to use JDBC on the job, we recommend that you read books on SQL along with Java and databases. For example, you might try *SQL for Dummies,* 9th edition, Allen G. Taylor (Wiley, 2018) and *Practical Database Programming with Java*, Ying Bai (Wiley-IEEE Press, 2011).

For Experienced Developers

If you are an experienced developer and know JDBC well, you can skip the "Introducing Relational Databases and SQL" section. Read the rest of this chapter carefully, though. We found that the exam covers some topics that developers don't use in practice, in particular these topics:

- You probably set up the URL once for a project for a specific database. Often, developers just copy and paste it from somewhere else. For the exam, you actually have to understand this rather than relying on looking it up.

- You are likely using a DataSource. For the exam, you have to remember or relearn how DriverManager works.

Introducing Relational Databases and SQL

Data is information. A piece of data is one fact, such as your first name. A *database* is an organized collection of data. In the real world, a file cabinet is a type of database. It has file folders, each of which contains pieces of paper. The file folders are organized in some way, often alphabetically. Each piece of paper is like a piece of data. Similarly, the folders on your computer are like a database. The folders provide organization, and each file is a piece of data.

A *relational database* is a database that is organized into *tables*, which consist of rows and columns. You can think of a table as a spreadsheet. There are two main ways to access a relational database from Java.

- *Java Database Connectivity Language (JDBC)*: Accesses data as rows and columns. JDBC is the API covered in this chapter.

- *Java Persistence API (JPA)*: Accesses data through Java objects using a concept called *object-relational mapping* (ORM). The idea is that you don't have to write as much code, and you get your data in Java objects. JPA is not on the exam, and therefore it is not covered in this chapter.

A relational database is accessed through Structured Query Language (*SQL*). SQL is a programming language used to interact with database records. JDBC works by sending a SQL command to the database and then processing the response.

In addition to relational databases, there is another type of database called a *NoSQL database*. This is for databases that store their data in a format other than tables, such as key/value, document stores, and graph-based databases. NoSQL is out of scope for the exam as well.

In the following sections, we introduce a small relational database that we will be using for the examples in this chapter and present the SQL to access it. We will also cover some vocabulary that you need to know.

Picking Database Software

In all of the other chapters of this book, you need to write code and try lots of examples. This chapter is different. It's still nice to try the examples, but you can probably get the JDBC questions correct on the exam from just reading this chapter and mastering the review questions.

In this book we will be using Derby (http://db.apache.org/derby) for most of the examples. It is a small in-memory database. In fact, you need only one JAR file to run it. While the download is really easy, we've still provided instructions on what to do. They are linked from the book page.

www.selikoff.net/ocp11-2

There are also stand-alone databases that you can choose from if you want to install a full-fledged database. We like MySQL (www.mysql.com) or PostgreSQL (www.postgresql.org), both of which are open source and have been around for more than 20 years.

While the major databases all have many similarities, they do have important differences and advanced features. Choosing the correct database for use in your job is an important decision that you need to spend much time researching. For the exam, any database is fine for practice.

There are plenty of tutorials for installing and getting started with any of these. It's beyond the scope of the book and the exam to set up a database, but feel free to ask questions in the database/JDBC section of CodeRanch. You might even get an answer from the authors.

Identifying the Structure of a Relational Database

Our sample database has two tables. One has a row for each species that is in our zoo. The other has a row for each animal. These two relate to each other because an animal belongs to a species. These relationships are why this type of database is called a *relational database*. Figure 21.1 shows the structure of our database.

FIGURE 21.1   Tables in our relational database

As you can see in Figure 21.1, we have two tables. One is named exhibits, and the other is named names. Each table has a *primary key*, which gives us a unique way to reference each row. After all, two animals might have the same name, but they can't have the same ID. You don't need to know about keys for the exam. We mention it to give you a bit of context. In our example, it so happens that the primary key is only one column. In some situations, it is a combination of columns called a *compound key*. For example, a student identifier and year might be a compound key.

There are two rows and three columns in the `exhibits` table and five rows and three columns in the `names` table. You do need to know about rows and columns for the exam.

The Code to Set Up the Database

We provide a program to download, install, and set up Derby to run the examples in this chapter. You don't have to understand it for the exam. Parts of SQL called database definition language (DDL) and database manipulation language (DML) are used to do so. Don't worry—knowing how to read or write SQL is not on the exam!

Before running the following code, you need to add a `.jar` file to your classpath. Add `<PATH TO DERBY>/derby.jar` to your classpath. Just make sure to replace `<PATH TO DERBY>` with the actual path on your file system. You run the program like this:

```
java -cp "<path_to_derby>/derby.jar" SetupDerbyDatabase.java
```

You can also find the code along with more details about setup here:

www.selikoff.net/ocp11-2

For now, you don't need to understand any of the code on the website. It is just to get you set up. In a nutshell, it connects to the database and creates two tables. Then it loads data into those tables. By the end of this chapter, you should understand how to create a `Connection` and `PreparedStatement` in this manner.

Writing Basic SQL Statements

The most important thing that you need to know about SQL for the exam is that there are four types of statements for working with the data in tables. They are referred to as CRUD (Create, Read, Update, Delete). The SQL keywords don't match the acronym, so pay attention to the SQL keyword of each in Table 21.1.

TABLE 21.1   CRUD operations

Operation	SQL Keyword	Description
<u>C</u>reate	INSERT	Adds a new row to the table
<u>R</u>ead	SELECT	Retrieves data from the table
<u>U</u>pdate	UPDATE	Changes zero or more rows in the table
<u>D</u>elete	DELETE	Removes zero or more rows from the table

That's it. You are not expected to determine whether SQL statements are correct. You are not expected to spot syntax errors in SQL statements. You are not expected to write SQL statements. Notice a theme?

If you already know SQL, you can skip to the section on JDBC. We are covering the basics so that newer developers know what is going on, at least at a high level. We promise there is nothing else in this section on SQL that you need to know. In fact, you probably know a lot that isn't covered here. As far as the exam is concerned, joining two tables is a concept that doesn't exist!

Unlike Java, SQL keywords are case insensitive. This means `select`, `SELECT`, and `Select` are all equivalent. Many people use uppercase for the database keywords so that they stand out. It's also common practice to use *snake case* (underscores to separate "words") in column names. We follow these conventions. Note that in some databases, table and column names may be case sensitive.

Like Java primitive types, SQL has a number of data types. Most are self-explanatory, like `INTEGER`. There's also `DECIMAL`, which functions a lot like a `double` in Java. The strangest one is `VARCHAR`, standing for "variable character," which is like a `String` in Java. The *variable* part means that the database should use only as much space as it needs to store the value.

Now it's time to write some code. The `INSERT` statement is usually used to create one new row in a table; here's an example:

```
INSERT INTO exhibits
VALUES (3, 'Asian Elephant', 7.5);
```

If there are two rows in the table before this command is run successfully, then there are three afterward. The `INSERT` statement lists the values that we want to insert. By default, it uses the same order in which the columns were defined. `String` data is enclosed in single quotes.

The `SELECT` statement reads data from the table.

```
SELECT *
FROM exhibits
WHERE ID = 3;
```

The `WHERE` clause is optional. If you omit it, the contents of the entire table are returned. The * indicates to return all of the columns in the order in which they were defined. Alternatively, you can list the columns that you want returned.

```
SELECT name, num_acres
FROM exhibits
WHERE id = 3;
```

It is preferable to list the column names for clarity. It also helps in case the table changes in the database.

You can also get information about the whole result without returning individual rows using special SQL functions.

```
SELECT COUNT(*), SUM(num_acres)
FROM exhibits;
```

This query tells us how many species we have and how much space we need for them. It returns only one row since it is combining information. Even if there are no rows in the table, the query returns one row that contains zero as the answer.

The UPDATE statement changes zero or more rows in the database.

```
UPDATE exhibits
SET num_acres = num_acres + .5
WHERE name = 'Asian Elephant';
```

Again, the WHERE clause is optional. If it is omitted, all rows in the table will be updated. The UPDATE statement always specifies the table to update and the column to update.

The DELETE statement deletes one or more rows in the database.

```
DELETE FROM exhibits
WHERE name = 'Asian Elephant';
```

And yet again, the WHERE clause is optional. If it is omitted, the entire table will be emptied. So be careful!

All of the SQL shown in this section is common across databases. For more advanced SQL, there is variation across databases.

Introducing the Interfaces of JDBC

For the exam you need to know five key interfaces of JDBC. The interfaces are declared in the JDK. This is just like all of the other interfaces and classes that you've seen in this book. For example, in Chapter 14, "Generics and Collections," you worked with the interface List and the concrete class ArrayList.

With JDBC, the concrete classes come from the JDBC driver. Each database has a different JAR file with these classes. For example, PostgreSQL's JAR is called something like postgresql-9.4-1201.jdbc4.jar. MySQL's JAR is called something like mysql-connector-java-5.1.36.jar. The exact name depends on the vendor and version of the driver JAR.

This driver JAR contains an implementation of these key interfaces along with a number of other interfaces. The key is that the provided implementations know how to communicate with a database. There are also different types of drivers; luckily, you don't need to know about this for the exam.

Figure 21.2 shows the five key interfaces that you need to know. It also shows that the implementation is provided by an imaginary Foo driver JAR. They cleverly stick the name Foo in all classes.

FIGURE 21.2   Key JDBC interfaces

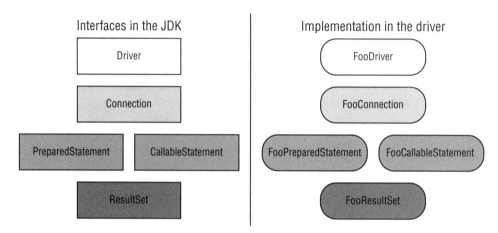

You've probably noticed that we didn't tell you what the implementing classes are called in any real database. The main point is that you shouldn't know. With JDBC, you use only the interfaces in your code and never the implementation classes directly. In fact, they might not even be `public` classes.

What do these five interfaces do? On a very high level, we have the following:

- `Driver`: Establishes a connection to the database
- `Connection`: Sends commands to a database
- `PreparedStatement`: Executes a SQL query
- `CallableStatement`: Executes commands stored in the database
- `ResultSet`: Reads results of a query

All database interfaces are in the package `java.sql`, so we will often omit the imports.

In this next example, we show you what JDBC code looks like end to end. If you are new to JDBC, just notice that three of the five interfaces are in the code. If you are experienced, remember that the exam uses `DriverManager` instead of `DataSource`.

```
public class MyFirstDatabaseConnection {
   public static void main(String[] args) throws SQLException {
      String url = "jdbc:derby:zoo";
      try (Connection conn = DriverManager.getConnection(url);
         PreparedStatement ps = conn.prepareStatement(
           "SELECT name FROM animal");
         ResultSet rs = ps.executeQuery()) {
         while (rs.next())
            System.out.println(rs.getString(1));
      }
   }
}
```

If the URL were using our imaginary Foo driver, DriverManager would return an instance of FooConnection. Calling prepareStatement() would then return an instance of FooPreparedStatement, and calling executeQuery() would return an instance of FooResultSet. Since the URL uses derby instead, it returns the implementations that derby has provided for these interfaces. You don't need to know their names. In the rest of the chapter, we will explain how to use all five of the interfaces and go into more detail about what they do. By the end of the chapter, you'll be writing code like this yourself.

Compiling with Modules

Almost all the packages on the exam are in the java.base module. As you may recall from Chapter 11, "Modules," this module is included automatically when you run your application as a module.

By contrast, the JDBC classes are all in the module java.sql. They are also in the package java.sql. The names are the same, so it should be easy to remember. When working with SQL, you need the java.sql module and import java.sql.*.

We recommend separating your studies for JDBC and modules. You can use the classpath when working with JDBC and reserve your practice with the module path for when you are studying modules.

That said, if you do want to use JDBC code with modules, remember to update your module-info file to include the following:

```
requires java.sql;
```

Connecting to a Database

The first step in doing anything with a database is connecting to it. First, we will show you how to build the JDBC URL. Then, we will show you how to use it to get a Connection to the database.

Building a JDBC URL

To access a website, you need to know the URL of the website. To access your email, you need to know your username and password. JDBC is no different. To access a database, you need to know this information about it.

Unlike web URLs, a JDBC URL has a variety of formats. They have three parts in common, as shown in Figure 21.3. The first piece is always the same. It is the protocol jdbc. The second part is the *subprotocol*, which is the name of the database such as derby, mysql, or postgres. The third part is the *subname*, which is a database-specific format. Colons (:) separate the three parts.

FIGURE 21.3   The JDBC URL format

The subname typically contains information about the database such as the location and/or name of the database. The syntax varies. You need to know about the three main parts. You don't need to memorize the subname formats. Phew! You've already seen one such URL.

```
jdbc:derby:zoo
```

Notice the three parts. It starts with jdbc and then comes the subprotocol derby, and it ends with the subname, which is the database name. The location is not required, because Derby is an in-memory database.

Other examples of subname are shown here:

```
jdbc:postgresql://localhost/zoo
jdbc:oracle:thin:@123.123.123.123:1521:zoo
jdbc:mysql://localhost:3306
jdbc:mysql://localhost:3306/zoo?profileSQL=true
```

You can see that each of these JDBC URLs begins with jdbc, followed by a colon, and then followed by the vendor/product name. After that it varies. Notice how all of them include the location of the database, which are localhost, 123.123.123.123:1521, and localhost:3306. Also, notice that the port is optional when using the default location.

To make sure you get this, do you see what is wrong with each of the following?

```
jdbc:postgresql://local/zoo
jdbc:mysql://123456/zoo
jdbc;oracle;thin;/localhost/zoo
```

The first one uses local instead of localhost. The literal localhost is a specially defined name. You can't just make up a name. Granted, it is possible for our database server to be named *local*, but the exam won't have you assume names. If the database server has a special name, the question will let you know it. The second one says that the location of the database is 123456. This doesn't make sense. A location can be localhost or an IP address or a domain name. It can't be any random number. The third one is no good because it uses semicolons (;) instead of colons (:).

Getting a Database *Connection*

There are two main ways to get a Connection: DriverManager or DataSource. DriverManager is the one covered on the exam. Do not use a DriverManager in code someone is paying you to write. A DataSource has more features than DriverManager. For example, it can pool connections or store the database connection information outside the application.

 Real World Scenario

Using a *DataSource*

In real applications, you should use a DataSource rather than DriverManager to get a Connection. For one thing, there's no reason why you should have to know the database password. It's far better if the database team or another team can set up a data source that you can reference.

Another reason is that a DataSource maintains a connection pool so that you can keep reusing the same connection rather than needing to get a new one each time. Even the Javadoc says DataSource is preferred over DriverManager. But DriverManager is in the exam objectives, so you still have to know it.

The DriverManager class is in the JDK, as it is an API that comes with Java. It uses the factory pattern, which means that you call a static method to get a Connection, rather than calling a constructor. The factory pattern means that you can get any implementation of the interface when calling the method. The good news is that the method has an easy-to-remember name—getConnection().

To get a Connection from the Derby database, you write the following:

```
import java.sql.*;
public class TestConnect {
   public static void main(String[] args) throws SQLException {
      Connection conn =
         DriverManager.getConnection("jdbc:derby:zoo");
      System.out.println(conn);
   }
}
```

Running this example as `java TestConnect.java` will give you an error that looks like this:

```
Exception in thread "main" java.sql.SQLException:
No suitable driver found for jdbc:derby:zoo
    at java.sql/java.sql.DriverManager.getConnection(
        DriverManager.java:702)
    at java.sql/java.sql.DriverManager.getConnection(
        DriverManager.java:251)
    at connection.TestConnect.main(TestConnect.java:9)
```

Seeing `SQLException` means "something went wrong when connecting to or accessing the database." You will need to recognize when a `SQLException` is thrown, but not the exact message. As you learned in Chapter 16, "Exceptions, Assertions, and Localization," `SQLException` is a checked exception.

> If code snippets aren't in a method, you can assume they are in a context where checked exceptions are handled or declared.

In this case, we didn't tell Java where to find the database driver JAR file. Remember that the implementation class for `Connection` is found inside a driver JAR.

We try this again by adding the classpath with the following:

```
java -cp "<path_to_derby>/derby.jar" TestConnect.java
```

Remember to substitute the location of where the Derby JAR is located.

> Notice that we are using single-file source-code execution rather than compiling the code first. This allows us to use a simpler classpath since it has only one element.

This time the program runs successfully and prints something like the following:

```
org.apache.derby.impl.jdbc.EmbedConnection40@1372082959
(XID = 156), (SESSIONID = 1), (DATABASE = zoo), (DRDAID = null)
```

The details of the output aren't important. Just notice that the class is not `Connection`. It is a vendor implementation of `Connection`.

There is also a signature that takes a username and password.

```java
import java.sql.*;
public class TestExternal {
    public static void main(String[] args) throws SQLException {
        Connection conn = DriverManager.getConnection(
            "jdbc:postgresql://localhost:5432/ocp-book",
            "username",
```

```
        "Password20182");
    System.out.println(conn);
  }
}
```

Notice the three parameters that are passed to getConnection(). The first is the JDBC URL that you learned about in the previous section. The second is the username for accessing the database, and the third is the password for accessing the database. It should go without saying that our password is not Password20182. Also, don't put your password in real code. It's a horrible practice. Always load it from some kind of configuration, ideally one that keeps the stored value encrypted.

If you were to run this with the Postgres driver JAR, it would print something like this:

```
org.postgresql.jdbc4.Jdbc4Connection@eed1f14
```

Again, notice that it is a driver-specific implementation class. You can tell from the package name. Since the package is org.postgresql.jdbc4, it is part of the PostgreSQL driver.

Unless the exam specifies a command line, you can assume that the correct JDBC driver JAR is in the classpath. The exam creators explicitly ask about the driver JAR if they want you to think about it.

The nice thing about the factory pattern is that it takes care of the logic of creating a class for you. You don't need to know the name of the class that implements Connection, and you don't need to know how it is created. You are probably a bit curious, though.

DriverManager looks through any drivers it can find to see whether they can handle the JDBC URL. If so, it creates a Connection using that Driver. If not, it gives up and throws a SQLException.

 Real World Scenario

Using *Class.forName()*

You might see Class.forName() in code. It was required with older drivers (that were designed for older versions of JDBC) before getting a Connection. It looks like this:

```
public static void main(String[] args)
    throws SQLException, ClassNotFoundException {

    Class.forName("org.postgresql.Driver");
    Connection conn = DriverManager.getConnection(
        "jdbc:postgresql://localhost:5432/ocp-book",
        "username",
        "password");
}
```

Class.forName() loads a class before it is used. With newer drivers, Class.forName() is no longer required.

Working with a *PreparedStatement*

In Java, you have a choice of working with a Statement, PreparedStatement, or CallableStatement. The latter two are subinterfaces of Statement, as shown in Figure 21.4.

FIGURE 21.4 Types of statements

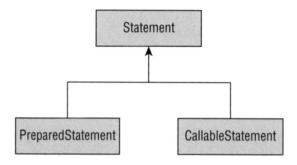

Later in the chapter, you'll learn about using CallableStatement for queries that are inside the database. In this section, we will be looking at PreparedStatement.

What about Statement you ask? It is an interface that both PreparedStatement and CallableStatement extend. A Statement and PreparedStatement are similar to each other, except that a PreparedStatement takes parameters, while a Statement does not. A Statement just executes whatever SQL query you give it.

While it is possible to run SQL directly with Statement, you shouldn't. PreparedStatement is far superior for the following reasons:

- **Performance:** In most programs, you run similar queries multiple times. A PreparedStatement figures out a plan to run the SQL well and remembers it.

- **Security:** As you will see in Chapter 22, "Security," you are protected against an attack called SQL injection when using a PreparedStatement correctly.

- **Readability:** It's nice not to have to deal with string concatenation in building a query string with lots of parameters.

- **Future use:** Even if your query is being run only once or doesn't have any parameters, you should still use a PreparedStatement. That way future editors of the code won't add a variable and have to remember to change to PreparedStatement then.

Using the Statement interface is also no longer in scope for the JDBC exam, so we do not cover it in this book. In the following sections, we will cover obtaining a PreparedStatement, executing one, working with parameters, and running multiple updates.

Obtaining a *PreparedStatement*

To run SQL, you need to tell a PreparedStatement about it. Getting a PreparedStatement from a Connection is easy.

```
try (PreparedStatement ps = conn.prepareStatement(
   "SELECT * FROM exhibits")) {
   // work with ps
}
```

An instance of a PreparedStatement represents a SQL statement that you want to run using the Connection. It does not actually execute the query yet! We'll get to that shortly.

Passing a SQL statement when creating the object is mandatory. You might see a trick on the exam.

```
try (var ps = conn.prepareStatement()) { // DOES NOT COMPILE
}
```

The previous example does not compile, because SQL is not supplied at the time a PreparedStatement is requested. We also used var in this example. We will write JDBC code both using var and the actual class names to get you used to both approaches.

There are overloaded signatures that allow you to specify a ResultSet type and concurrency mode. On the exam, you only need to know how to use the default options, which processes the results in order.

Executing a *PreparedStatement*

Now that we have a PreparedStatement, we can run the SQL statement. The way you run SQL varies depending on what kind of SQL statement it is. Remember that you aren't expected to be able to read SQL, but you do need to know what the first keyword means.

Modifying Data with *executeUpdate()*

Let's start out with statements that change the data in a table. That would be SQL statements that begin with DELETE, INSERT, or UPDATE. They typically use a method called executeUpdate(). The name is a little tricky because the SQL UPDATE statement is not the only statement that uses this method.

The method takes the SQL statement to run as a parameter. It returns the number of rows that were inserted, deleted, or changed. Here's an example of all three update types:

```
10: var insertSql = "INSERT INTO exhibits VALUES(10, 'Deer', 3)";
11: var updateSql = "UPDATE exhibits SET name = '' " +
12:    "WHERE name = 'None'";
13: var deleteSql = "DELETE FROM exhibits WHERE id = 10";
14:
15: try (var ps = conn.prepareStatement(insertSql)) {
16:    int result = ps.executeUpdate();
```

```
17:     System.out.println(result); // 1
18: }
19:
20: try (var ps = conn.prepareStatement(updateSql)) {
21:     int result = ps.executeUpdate();
22:     System.out.println(result); // 0
23: }
24:
25: try (var ps = conn.prepareStatement(deleteSql)) {
26:     int result = ps.executeUpdate();
27:     System.out.println(result); // 1
28: }
```

For the exam, you don't need to read SQL. The question will tell you how many rows are affected if you need to know. Notice how each distinct SQL statement needs its own prepareStatement() call.

Line 15 creates the insert statement, and line 16 runs that statement to insert one row. The result is 1 because one row was affected. Line 20 creates the update statement, and line 21 checks the whole table for matching records to update. Since no records match, the result is 0. Line 25 creates the delete statement, and line 26 deletes the row created on line 16. Again, one row is affected, so the result is 1.

Reading Data with *executeQuery()*

Next, let's look at a SQL statement that begins with SELECT. This time, we use the executeQuery() method.

```
30: var sql = "SELECT * FROM exhibits";
31: try (var ps = conn.prepareStatement(sql);
32:     ResultSet rs = ps.executeQuery() ) {
33:
34:     // work with rs
35: }
```

On line 31, we create a PreparedStatement for our SELECT query. On line 32, we actually run it. Since we are running a query to get a result, the return type is ResultSet. In the next section, we will show you how to process the ResultSet.

Processing Data with *execute()*

There's a third method called execute() that can run either a query or an update. It returns a boolean so that we know whether there is a ResultSet. That way, we can call the proper method to get more detail. The pattern looks like this:

```
boolean isResultSet = ps.execute();
if (isResultSet) {
   try (ResultSet rs = ps.getResultSet()) {
```

```
      System.out.println("ran a query");
   }
} else {
   int result = ps.getUpdateCount();
   System.out.println("ran an update");
}
```

If the PreparedStatement refers to sql that is a SELECT, the boolean is true and we can get the ResultSet. If it is not a SELECT, we can get the number of rows updated.

What do you think happens if we use the wrong method for a SQL statement? Let's take a look.

```
var sql = "SELECT * FROM names";
try (var conn = DriverManager.getConnection("jdbc:derby:zoo");
   var ps = conn.prepareStatement(sql)) {

   var result = ps.executeUpdate();
}
```

This throws a SQLException similar to the following:

```
Statement.executeUpdate() cannot be called with a statement
that returns a ResultSet.
```

We can't get a compiler error since the SQL is a String. We can get an exception, though, and we do. We also get a SQLException when using executeQuery() with SQL that changes the database.

```
Statement.executeQuery() cannot be called with a statement
that returns a row count.
```

Again, we get an exception because the driver can't translate the query into the expected return type.

Reviewing *PreparedStatement* Methods

To review, make sure that you know Table 21.2 and Table 21.3 well. Table 21.2 shows which SQL statements can be run by each of the three key methods on PreparedStatement.

TABLE 21.2　SQL runnable by the execute method

Method	DELETE	INSERT	SELECT	UPDATE
ps.execute()	Yes	Yes	Yes	Yes
ps.executeQuery()	No	No	Yes	No
ps.executeUpdate()	Yes	Yes	No	Yes

Table 21.3 shows what is returned by each method.

TABLE 21.3   Return types of execute methods

Method	Return type	What is returned for SELECT	What is returned for DELETE/INSERT/UPDATE
ps.execute()	boolean	true	false
ps.executeQuery()	ResultSet	The rows and columns returned	n/a
ps.executeUpdate()	int	n/a	Number of rows added/ changed/removed

Working with Parameters

Suppose our zoo acquires a new elephant and we want to register it in our names table. We've already learned enough to do this.

```
public static void register(Connection conn) throws SQLException {
   var sql = "INSERT INTO names VALUES(6, 1, 'Edith')";

   try (var ps = conn.prepareStatement(sql)) {
      ps.executeUpdate();
   }
}
```

However, everything is hard-coded. We want to be able to pass in the values as parameters. However, we don't want the caller of this method to need to write SQL or know the exact details of our database.

Luckily, a PreparedStatement allows us to set parameters. Instead of specifying the three values in the SQL, we can use a question mark (?) instead. A *bind variable* is a placeholder that lets you specify the actual values at runtime. A bind variable is like a parameter, and you will see bind variables referenced as both variables and parameters. We can rewrite our SQL statement using bind variables.

```
String sql = "INSERT INTO names VALUES(?, ?, ?)";
```

Bind variables make the SQL easier to read since you no longer need to use quotes around String values in the SQL. Now we can pass the parameters to the method itself.

```
14: public static void register(Connection conn, int key,
15:    int type, String name) throws SQLException {
16:
```

```
17:     String sql = "INSERT INTO names VALUES(?, ?, ?)";
18:
19:     try (PreparedStatement ps = conn.prepareStatement(sql)) {
20:         ps.setInt(1, key);
21:         ps.setString(3, name);
22:         ps.setInt(2, type);
23:         ps.executeUpdate();
24:     }
25: }
```

Line 19 creates a `PreparedStatement` using our SQL that contains three bind variables. Lines 20, 21, and 22 set those variables. You can think of the bind variables as a list of parameters where each one gets set in turn. Notice how the bind variables can be set in any order. Line 23 actually executes the query and runs the update.

Notice how the bind variables are counted starting with 1 rather than 0. This is really important, so we will repeat it.

 Remember that JDBC starts counting columns with 1 rather than 0. A common exam (and interview) question tests that you know this!

In the previous example, we set the parameters out of order. That's perfectly fine. The rule is only that they are each set before the query is executed. Let's see what happens if you don't set all the bind variables.

```
var sql = "INSERT INTO names VALUES(?, ?, ?)";
try (var ps = conn.prepareStatement(sql)) {
   ps.setInt(1, key);
   ps.setInt(2, type);
   // missing the set for parameter number 3
   ps.executeUpdate();
}
```

The code compiles, and you get a `SQLException`. The message may vary based on your database driver.

```
At least one parameter to the current statement is uninitialized.
```

What about if you try to set more values than you have as bind variables?

```
var sql = "INSERT INTO names VALUES(?, ?)";
try (var ps = conn.prepareStatement(sql)) {
   ps.setInt(1, key);
   ps.setInt(2, type);
   ps.setString(3, name);
   ps.executeUpdate();
}
```

Again, you get a SQLException, this time with a different message. On Derby, that message was as follows:

```
The number of values assigned is not the same as the
number of specified or implied columns.
```

Table 21.4 shows the methods you need to know for the exam to set bind variables. The ones that you need to know for the exam are easy to remember since they are called set, followed by the name of the type you are getting. There are many others, like dates, that are out of scope for the exam.

TABLE 21.4   PreparedStatement methods

Method name	Parameter type	Example database type
setBoolean	Boolean	BOOLEAN
setDouble	Double	DOUBLE
setInt	Int	INTEGER
setLong	Long	BIGINT
setObject	Object	Any type
setString	String	CHAR, VARCHAR

The first column shows the method name, and the second column shows the type that Java uses. The third column shows the type name that could be in the database. There is some variation by databases, so check your specific database documentation. You need to know only the first two columns for the exam.

Notice the setObject() method works with any Java type. If you pass a primitive, it will be autoboxed into a wrapper type. That means we can rewrite our example as follows:

```
String sql = "INSERT INTO names VALUES(?, ?, ?)";
try (PreparedStatement ps = conn.prepareStatement(sql)) {
    ps.setObject(1, key);
    ps.setObject(2, type);
    ps.setObject(3, name);
    ps.executeUpdate();
}
```

Java will handle the type conversion for you. It is still better to call the more specific setter methods since that will give you a compile-time error if you pass the wrong type instead of a runtime error.

Real World Scenario

Compile vs. Runtime Error When Executing

The following code is incorrect. Do you see why?

```
ps.setObject(1, key);
ps.setObject(2, type);
ps.setObject(3, name);
ps.executeUpdate(sql);   // INCORRECT
```

The problem is that the last line passes a SQL statement. With a PreparedStatement, we pass the SQL in when creating the object.

More interesting is that this does not result in a compiler error. Remember that PreparedStatement extends Statement. The Statement interface does accept a SQL statement at the time of execution, so the code compiles. Running this code gives SQLException. The text varies by database.

Updating Multiple Times

Suppose we get two new elephants and want to add both. We can use the same PreparedStatement object.

```
var sql = "INSERT INTO names VALUES(?, ?, ?)";

try (var ps = conn.prepareStatement(sql)) {

    ps.setInt(1, 20);
    ps.setInt(2, 1);
    ps.setString(3, "Ester");
    ps.executeUpdate();

    ps.setInt(1, 21);
    ps.setString(3, "Elias");
    ps.executeUpdate();
}
```

Note that we set all three parameters when adding Ester, but only two for Elias. The PreparedStatement is smart enough to remember the parameters that were already set and retain them. You only have to set the ones that are different.

Real World Scenario

Batching Statements

JDBC supports batching so you can run multiple statements in fewer trips to the database. Often the database is located on a different machine than the Java code runs on. Saving trips to the database saves time because network calls can be expensive. For example, if you need to insert 1,000 records into the database, then inserting them as a single network call (as opposed to 1,000 network calls) is usually *a lot* faster.

You don't need to know the addBatch() and executeBatch() methods for the exam, but they are useful in practice.

```java
public static void register(Connection conn, int firstKey,
    int type, String... names) throws SQLException {

    var sql = "INSERT INTO names VALUES(?, ?, ?)";
    var nextIndex = firstKey;

    try (var ps = conn.prepareStatement(sql)) {
        ps.setInt(2, type);

        for(var name: names) {
            ps.setInt(1, nextIndex);
            ps.setString(3, name);
            ps.addBatch();

            nextIndex++;
        }
        int[] result = ps.executeBatch();
        System.out.println(Arrays.toString(result));
    }
}
```

Now we call this method with two names:

```java
register(conn, 100, 1,  "Elias", "Ester");
```

The output shows the array has two elements since there are two different items in the batch. Each one added one row in the database.

```
[1, 1]
```

When using batching, you should call executeBatch() at a set interval, such as every 10,000 records (rather than after ten million). Waiting too long to send the batch to the database could produce operations that are so large that they freeze the client (or even worse the database!).

Getting Data from a *ResultSet*

A database isn't useful if you can't get your data. We will start by showing you how to go through a ResultSet. Then we will go through the different methods to get columns by type.

Reading a *ResultSet*

When working with a ResultSet, most of the time you will write a loop to look at each row. The code looks like this:

```
20: String sql = "SELECT id, name FROM exhibits";
21: Map<Integer, String> idToNameMap = new HashMap<>();
22:
23: try (var ps = conn.prepareStatement(sql);
24:     ResultSet rs = ps.executeQuery()) {
25:
26:     while (rs.next()) {
27:         int id = rs.getInt("id");
28:         String name = rs.getString("name");
29:         idToNameMap.put(id, name);
30:     }
31:     System.out.println(idToNameMap);
32: }
```

It outputs this:

```
{1=African Elephant, 2=Zebra}
```

There are a few things to notice here. First, we use the executeQuery() method on line 24, since we want to have a ResultSet returned. On line 26, we loop through the results. Each time through the loop represents one row in the ResultSet. Lines 27 and 28 show you the best way to get the columns for a given row.

A ResultSet has a *cursor*, which points to the current location in the data. Figure 21.5 shows the position as we loop through.

FIGURE 21.5   The ResultSet cursor

	Table: exhibits		
Initial position →	id *integer*	name *varchar(255)*	num_acres *numeric*
rs.next() true →	1	African Elephant	7.5
rs.next() true →	2	Zebra	1.2
rs.next() false →			

At line 24, the cursor starts out pointing to the location before the first row in the ResultSet. On the first loop iteration, rs.next() returns true, and the cursor moves to point to the first row of data. On the second loop iteration, rs.next() returns true again, and the cursor moves to point to the second row of data. The next call to rs.next() returns false. The cursor advances past the end of the data. The false signifies that there is no more data available to get.

We did say the "best way." There is another way to access the columns. You can use an index instead of a column name. The column name is better because it is clearer what is going on when reading the code. It also allows you to change the SQL to reorder the columns.

On the exam, either you will be told the names of the columns in a table or you can assume that they are correct. Similarly, you can assume that all SQL is correct.

Rewriting this same example with column numbers looks like the following:

```
20: String sql = "SELECT id, name FROM exhibits";
21: Map<Integer, String> idToNameMap = new HashMap<>();
22:
23: try (var ps = conn.prepareStatement(sql);
24:     ResultSet rs = ps.executeQuery()) {
25:
26:     while (rs.next()) {
27:         int id = rs.getInt(1);
28:         String name = rs.getString(2);
29:         idToNameMap.put(id, name);
30:     }
31:     System.out.println(idToNameMap);
32: }
```

This time, you can see the column positions on lines 27 and 28. Notice how the columns are counted starting with 1 rather than 0. Just like with a PreparedStatement, JDBC starts counting at 1 in a ResultSet.

Sometimes you want to get only one row from the table. Maybe you need only one piece of data. Or maybe the SQL is just returning the number of rows in the table. When you want only one row, you use an `if` statement rather than a `while` loop.

```
var sql = "SELECT count(*) FROM exhibits";

try (var ps = conn.prepareStatement(sql);
   var rs = ps.executeQuery()) {

   if (rs.next()) {
      int count = rs.getInt(1);
      System.out.println(count);
   }
}
```

It is important to check that `rs.next()` returns `true` before trying to call a getter on the `ResultSet`. If a query didn't return any rows, it would throw a `SQLException`, so the `if` statement checks that it is safe to call. Alternatively, you can use the column name.

```
var sql = "SELECT count(*) AS count FROM exhibits";

try (var ps = conn.prepareStatement(sql);
   var rs = ps.executeQuery()) {

   if (rs.next()) {
      var count = rs.getInt("count");
      System.out.println(count);
   }
}
```

Let's try to read a column that does not exist.

```
var sql = "SELECT count(*) AS count FROM exhibits";

try (var ps = conn.prepareStatement(sql);
   var rs = ps.executeQuery()) {

   if (rs.next()) {
      var count = rs.getInt("total");
      System.out.println(count);
   }
}
```

This throws a SQLException with a message like this:

```
Column 'total' not found.
```

Attempting to access a column name or index that does not exist throws a SQLException, as does getting data from a ResultSet when it isn't pointing at a valid row. You need to be able to recognize such code. Here are a few examples to watch out for. Do you see what is wrong here when no rows match?

```
var sql = "SELECT * FROM exhibits where name='Not in table'";

try (var ps = conn.prepareStatement(sql);
    var rs = ps.executeQuery()) {

    rs.next();
    rs.getInt(1); // SQLException
}
```

Calling rs.next() works. It returns false. However, calling a getter afterward does throw a SQLException because the result set cursor does not point to a valid position. If there actually were a match returned, this code would have worked. Do you see what is wrong with the following?

```
var sql = "SELECT count(*) FROM exhibits";

try (var ps = conn.prepareStatement(sql);
    var rs = ps.executeQuery()) {

    rs.getInt(1); // SQLException
}
```

Not calling rs.next() at all is a problem. The result set cursor is still pointing to a location before the first row, so the getter has nothing to point to. How about this one?

```
var sql = "SELECT count(*) FROM exhibits";

try (var ps = conn.prepareStatement(sql);
    var rs = ps.executeQuery()) {

    if (rs.next())
        rs.getInt(0); // SQLException
}
```

Since column indexes begin with 1, there is no column 0 to point to and a SQLException is thrown. Let's try one more example. What is wrong with this one?

```
var sql = "SELECT name FROM exhibits";

try (var ps = conn.prepareStatement(sql);
   var rs = ps.executeQuery()) {

   if (rs.next())
   rs.getInt("badColumn"); // SQLException
}
```

Trying to get a column that isn't in the ResultSet is just as bad as an invalid column index, and it also throws a SQLException.

To sum up this section, it is important to remember the following:

- Always use an if statement or while loop when calling rs.next().

- Column indexes begin with 1.

Getting Data for a Column

There are lots of get methods on the ResultSet interface. Table 21.5 shows the get methods that you need to know. These are the getter equivalents of the setters in Table 21.4.

TABLE 21.5   ResultSet get methods

Method name	Return type
getBoolean	boolean
getDouble	double
getInt	int
getLong	long
getObject	Object
getString	String

You might notice that not all of the primitive types are in Table 21.5. There are getByte() and getFloat() methods, but you don't need to know about them for the exam. There is no getChar() method. Luckily, you don't need to remember this. The exam will not try to trick you by using a get method name that doesn't exist for JDBC. Isn't that nice of the exam creators?

The getObject() method can return any type. For a primitive, it uses the wrapper class. Let's look at the following example:

```
16: var sql = "SELECT id, name FROM exhibits";
17: try (var ps = conn.prepareStatement(sql);
18:    var rs = ps.executeQuery()) {
19:
20:    while (rs.next()) {
21:       Object idField = rs.getObject("id");
22:       Object nameField = rs.getObject("name");
23:       if (idField instanceof Integer) {
24:          int id = (Integer) idField;
25:          System.out.println(id);
26:       }
27:       if (nameField instanceof String) {
28:          String name = (String) nameField;
29:          System.out.println(name);
30:       }
31:    }
32: }
```

Lines 21 and 22 get the column as whatever type of Object is most appropriate. Lines 23–26 show you how to confirm that the type is Integer before casting and unboxing it into an int. Lines 27–30 show you how to confirm that the type is String and cast it as well. You probably won't use getObject() when writing code for a job, but it is good to know about it for the exam.

Using Bind Variables

We've been creating the PreparedStatement and ResultSet in the same try-with-resources statement. This doesn't work if you have bind variables because they need to be set in between. Luckily, we can nest try-with-resources to handle this. This code prints out the ID for any exhibits matching a given name:

```
30: var sql = "SELECT id FROM exhibits WHERE name = ?";
31:
32: try (var ps = conn.prepareStatement(sql)) {
33:    ps.setString(1, "Zebra");
34:
```

```
35:    try (var rs = ps.executeQuery()) {
36:       while (rs.next()) {
37:          int id = rs.getInt("id");
38:          System.out.println(id);
39:       }
40:    }
41: }
```

Pay attention to the flow here. First, we create the `PreparedStatement` on line 32. Then we set the bind variable on line 33. It is only after these are both done that we have a nested try-with-resources on line 35 to create the `ResultSet`.

Calling a *CallableStatement*

Sometimes you want your SQL to be directly in the database instead of packaged with your Java code. This is particularly useful when you have many queries and they are complex. A *stored procedure* is code that is compiled in advance and stored in the database. Stored procedures are commonly written in a database-specific variant of SQL, which varies among database software providers.

Using a stored procedure reduces network round-trips. It also allows database experts to own that part of the code. However, stored procedures are database-specific and introduce complexity of maintaining your application. On the exam, you need to know how to call a stored procedure but not decide when to use one.

You don't need to know how to read or write a stored procedure for the exam. Therefore, we have not included any in the book. If you want to try the examples, the setup procedure and source code is linked from here:

www.selikoff.net/ocp11-2

 You do not need to learn anything database specific for the exam. Since studying stored procedures can be quite complicated, we recommend limiting your studying on `CallableStatement` to what is in this book.

We will be using four stored procedures in this section. Table 21.6 summarizes what you need to know about them. In the real world, none of these would be good implementations since they aren't complex enough to warrant being stored procedures. As you can see in the table, stored procedures allow parameters to be for input only, output only, or both.

In the next four sections, we will look at how to call each of these stored procedures.

TABLE 21.6 Sample stored procedures

Name	Parameter name	Parameter type	Description
read_e_names()	n/a	n/a	Returns all rows in the names table that have a name beginning with an E
read_names_by_ letter()	prefix	IN	Returns all rows in the names table that have a name beginning with the specified parameter
magic_number()	Num	OUT	Returns the number 42
double_number()	Num	INOUT	Multiplies the parameter by two and returns that number

Calling a Procedure without Parameters

Our read_e_names() stored procedure doesn't take any parameters. It does return a ResultSet. Since we worked with a ResultSet in the PreparedStatement section, here we can focus on how the stored procedure is called.

```
12: String sql = "{call read_e_names()}";
13: try (CallableStatement cs = conn.prepareCall(sql);
14:     ResultSet rs = cs.executeQuery()) {
15:
16:     while (rs.next()) {
17:         System.out.println(rs.getString(3));
18:     }
19: }
```

Line 12 introduces a new bit of syntax. A stored procedure is called by putting the word call and the procedure name in braces ({}).

Line 13 creates a CallableStatement object. When we created a PreparedStatement, we used the prepareStatement() method. Here, we use the prepareCall() method instead.

Lines 14–18 should look familiar. They are the standard logic we have been using to get a ResultSet and loop through it. This stored procedure returns the underlying table, so the columns are the same.

Passing an *IN* Parameter

A stored procedure that always returns the same thing is only somewhat useful. We've created a new version of that stored procedure that is more generic. The read_names_ by_letter() stored procedure takes a parameter for the prefix or first letter of the stored procedure. An IN parameter is used for input.

There are two differences in calling it compared to our previous stored procedure.

```
25: var sql = "{call read_names_by_letter(?)}";
26: try (var cs = conn.prepareCall(sql)) {
27:    cs.setString("prefix", "Z");
28:
29:    try (var rs = cs.executeQuery()) {
30:       while (rs.next()) {
31:          System.out.println(rs.getString(3));
32:       }
33:    }
34: }
```

On line 25, we have to pass a ? to show we have a parameter. This should be familiar from bind variables with a PreparedStatement.

On line 27, we set the value of that parameter. Unlike with PreparedStatement, we can use either the parameter number (starting with 1) or the parameter name. That means these two statements are equivalent:

```
cs.setString(1, "Z");
cs.setString("prefix", "Z");
```

Returning an *OUT* Parameter

In our previous examples, we returned a ResultSet. Some stored procedures return other information. Luckily, stored procedures can have OUT parameters for output. The magic_ number() stored procedure sets its OUT parameter to 42. There are a few differences here:

```
40: var sql = "{?= call magic_number(?) }";
41: try (var cs = conn.prepareCall(sql)) {
42:    cs.registerOutParameter(1, Types.INTEGER);
43:    cs.execute();
44:    System.out.println(cs.getInt("num"));
45: }
```

On line 40, we included two special characters (?=) to specify that the stored procedure has an output value. This is optional since we have the OUT parameter, but it does aid in readability.

On line 42, we register the OUT parameter. This is important. It allows JDBC to retrieve the value on line 44. Remember to always call `registerOutParameter()` for each OUT or INOUT parameter (which we will cover next).

On line 43, we call `execute()` instead of `executeQuery()` since we are not returning a ResultSet from our stored procedure.

Database-Specific Behavior

Some databases are lenient about certain things this chapter says are required. For example, some databases allow you to omit the following:

- Braces ({})

- Bind variable (?) if it is an OUT parameter

- Call to `registerOutParameter()`

For the exam, you need to answer according to the full requirements, which are described in this book. For example, you should answer exam questions as if braces are required.

Working with an *INOUT* Parameter

Finally, it is possible to use the same parameter for both input and output. As you read this code, see whether you can spot which lines are required for the IN part and which are required for the OUT part.

```
50: var sql = "{call double_number(?)}";
51: try (var cs = conn.prepareCall(sql)) {
52:     cs.setInt(1, 8);
53:     cs.registerOutParameter(1, Types.INTEGER);
54:     cs.execute();
55:     System.out.println(cs.getInt("num"));
56: }
```

For an IN parameter, line 50 is required since it passes the parameter. Similarly, line 52 is required since it sets the parameter. For an OUT parameter, line 53 is required to register the parameter. Line 54 uses `execute()` again because we are not returning a ResultSet.

Remember that an INOUT parameter acts as both an IN parameter and an OUT parameter, so it has all the requirements of both.

Comparing Callable Statement Parameters

Table 21.7 reviews the different types of parameters. You need to know this well for the exam.

TABLE 21.7   Stored procedure parameter types

	IN	OUT	INOUT
Used for input	Yes	No	Yes
Used for output	No	Yes	Yes
Must set parameter value	Yes	No	Yes
Must call `registerOutParameter()`	No	Yes	Yes
Can include ?=	No	Yes	Yes

Closing Database Resources

As you saw in Chapter 19, "I/O," and Chapter 20, "NIO.2," it is important to close resources when you are finished with them. This is true for JDBC as well. JDBC resources, such as a Connection, are expensive to create. Not closing them creates a *resource leak* that will eventually slow down your program.

Throughout the chapter, we've been using the try-with-resources syntax from Chapter 16. The resources need to be closed in a specific order. The ResultSet is closed first, followed by the PreparedStatement (or CallableStatement) and then the Connection.

While it is a good habit to close all three resources, it isn't strictly necessary. Closing a JDBC resource should close any resources that it created. In particular, the following are true:

- Closing a Connection also closes PreparedStatement (or CallableStatement) and ResultSet.

- Closing a PreparedStatement (or CallableStatement) also closes the ResultSet.

It is important to close resources in the right order. This avoids both resource leaks and exceptions.

Writing a Resource Leak

In Chapter 16, you learned that it is possible to declare a type before a try-with-resources statement. Do you see why this method is bad?

```
40: public void bad() throws SQLException {
41:    var url = "jdbc:derby:zoo";
42:    var sql = "SELECT not_a_column FROM names";
```

```
43:     var conn = DriverManager.getConnection(url);
44:     var ps = conn.prepareStatement(sql);
45:     var rs = ps.executeQuery();
46:
47:     try (conn; ps; rs) {
48:        while (rs.next())
49:           System.out.println(rs.getString(1));
50:     }
51: }
```

Suppose an exception is thrown on line 45. The try-with-resources block is never entered, so we don't benefit from automatic resource closing. That means this code has a resource leak if it fails. Do not write code like this.

There's another way to close a ResultSet. JDBC automatically closes a ResultSet when you run another SQL statement from the same Statement. This could be a PreparedStatement or a CallableStatement. How many resources are closed in this code?

```
14: var url = "jdbc:derby:zoo";
15: var sql = "SELECT count(*) FROM names where id = ?";
16: try (var conn = DriverManager.getConnection(url);
17:     var ps = conn.prepareStatement(sql)) {
18:
19:     ps.setInt(1, 1);
20:
21:     var rs1 = ps.executeQuery();
22:     while (rs1.next()) {
23:        System.out.println("Count: " + rs1.getInt(1));
24:     }
25:
26:     ps.setInt(1, 2);
27:
28:     var rs2 = ps.executeQuery();
29:     while (rs2.next()) {
30:        System.out.println("Count: " + rs2.getInt(1));
31:     }
32:     rs2.close();
33: }
```

The correct answer is four. On line 28, rs1 is closed because the same PreparedStatement runs another query. On line 32, rs2 is closed in the method call. Then the try-with-resources statement runs and closes the PreparedSatement and Connection objects.

 Real World Scenario

Dealing with Exceptions

In most of this chapter, we've lived in a perfect world. Sure, we mentioned that a checked SQLException might be thrown by any JDBC method—but we never actually caught it. We just declared it and let the caller deal with it. Now let's catch the exception.

```
var sql = "SELECT not_a_column FROM names";
var url = "jdbc:derby:zoo";
try (var conn = DriverManager.getConnection(url);
   var ps = conn.prepareStatement(sql);
   var rs = ps.executeQuery()) {

   while (rs.next())
      System.out.println(rs.getString(1));
} catch (SQLException e) {
   System.out.println(e.getMessage());
   System.out.println(e.getSQLState());
   System.out.println(e.getErrorCode());
}
```

The output looks like this:

```
Column 'NOT_A_COLUMN' is either not in any table ...
42X04
30000
```

Each of these methods gives you a different piece of information. The getMessage() method returns a human-readable message as to what went wrong. We've only included the beginning of it here. The getSQLState() method returns a code as to what went wrong. You can Google the name of your database and the SQL state to get more information about the error. By comparison, getErrorCode() is a database-specific code. On this database, it doesn't do anything.

Summary

There are four key SQL statements you should know for the exam, one for each of the CRUD operations: create (INSERT) a new row, read (SELECT) data, update (UPDATE) one or more rows, and delete (DELETE) one or more rows.

For the exam, you should be familiar with five JDBC interfaces: Driver, Connection, PreparedStatement, CallableStatement, and ResultSet. The interfaces are part of the Java API. A database-specific JAR file provides the implementations.

To connect to a database, you need the JDBC URL. A JDBC URL has three parts separated by colons. The first part is jdbc. The second part is the name of the vendor/product. The third part varies by database, but it includes the location and/or name of the database. The location is either localhost or an IP address followed by an optional port.

The DriverManager class provides a factory method called getConnection() to get a Connection implementation. You create a PreparedStatement or CallableStatement using prepareStatement() and prepareCall(), respectively. A PreparedStatement is used when the SQL is specified in your application, and a CallableStatement is used when the SQL is in the database. A PreparedStatement allows you to set the values of bind variables. A CallableStatement also allows you to set IN, OUT, and INOUT parameters.

When running a SELECT SQL statement, the executeQuery() method returns a ResultSet. When running a DELETE, INSERT, or UPDATE SQL statement, the executeUpdate() method returns the number of rows that were affected. There is also an execute() method that returns a boolean to indicate whether the statement was a query.

You call rs.next() from an if statement or while loop to advance the cursor position. To get data from a column, call a method like getString(1) or getString("a"). Column indexes begin with 1, not 0. In addition to getting a String or primitive, you can call getObject() to get any type.

It is important to close JDBC resources when finished with them to avoid leaking resources. Closing a Connection automatically closes the Statement and ResultSet objects. Closing a Statement automatically closes the ResultSet object. Also, running another SQL statement closes the previous ResultSet object from that Statement.

Exam Essentials

Name the core five JDBC interfaces that you need to know for the exam and where they are defined.   The five key interfaces are Driver, Connection, PreparedStatement, CallableStatement, and ResultSet. The interfaces are part of the core Java APIs. The implementations are part of a database driver JAR file.

Identify correct and incorrect JDBC URLs. A JDBC URL starts with `jdbc:`, and it is followed by the vendor/product name. Next comes another colon and then a database-specific connection string. This database-specific string includes the location, such as `localhost` or an IP address with an optional port. It may also contain the name of the database.

Describe how to get a *Connection* using *DriverManager*. After including the driver JAR in the classpath, call `DriverManager.getConnection(url)` or `DriverManager.getConnection(url, username, password)` to get a driver-specific `Connection` implementation class.

Run queries using a *PreparedStatement*. When using a `PreparedStatement`, the SQL contains question marks (`?`) for the parameters or bind variables. This SQL is passed at the time the `PreparedStatement` is created, not when it is run. You must call a setter for each of these with the proper value before executing the query.

Run queries using a *CallableStatement*. When using a `CallableStatement`, the SQL looks like `{ call my_proc(?)}`. If you are returning a value, `{?= call my_proc(?)}` is also permitted. You must set any parameter values before executing the query. Additionally, you must call `registerOutParameter()` for any `OUT` or `INOUT` parameters.

Choose which method to run given a SQL statement. For a `SELECT` SQL statement, use `executeQuery()` or `execute()`. For other SQL statements, use `executeUpdate()` or `execute()`.

Loop through a *ResultSet*. Before trying to get data from a `ResultSet`, you call `rs.next()` inside an `if` statement or `while` loop. This ensures that the cursor is in a valid position. To get data from a column, call a method like `getString(1)` or `getString("a")`. Remember that column indexes begin with 1.

Identify when a resource should be closed. If you're closing all three resources, the `ResultSet` must be closed first, followed by the `PreparedStatement`, `CallableStatement`, and then followed by the `Connection`.

Review Questions

The answers to the chapter review questions can be found in the Appendix.

1. Which interfaces or classes are in a database-specific JAR file? (Choose all that apply.)

   A. Driver

   B. Driver's implementation

   C. DriverManager

   D. DriverManager's implementation

   E. PreparedStatement

   F. PreparedStatement's implementation

2. Which are required parts of a JDBC URL? (Choose all that apply.)

   A. Connection parameters

   B. IP address of database

   C. jdbc

   D. Password

   E. Port

   F. Vendor-specific string

3. Which of the following is a valid JDBC URL?

   A. jdbc:sybase:localhost:1234/db

   B. jdbc::sybase::localhost::/db

   C. jdbc::sybase:localhost::1234/db

   D. sybase:localhost:1234/db

   E. sybase::localhost::/db

   F. sybase::localhost::1234/db

4. Which of the options can fill in the blank to make the code compile and run without error? (Choose all that apply.)

   ```
   var sql = "UPDATE habitat WHERE environment = ?";
   try (var ps = conn.prepareStatement(sql)) {


       _____


       ps.executeUpdate();
   }
   ```

A. `ps.setString(0, "snow");`

B. `ps.setString(1, "snow");`

C. `ps.setString("environment", "snow");`

D. `ps.setString(1, "snow"); ps.setString(1, "snow");`

E. `ps.setString(1, "snow"); ps.setString(2, "snow");`

F. `ps.setString("environment", "snow");`
    `ps.setString("environment", "snow");`

5. Suppose that you have a table named `animal` with two rows. What is the result of the following code?

```
 6:  var conn = new Connection(url, userName, password);
 7:  var ps = conn.prepareStatement(
 8:     "SELECT  count(*) FROM animal");
 9:  var rs = ps.executeQuery();
10: if (rs.next()) System.out.println(rs.getInt(1));
```

A. 0

B. 2

C. There is a compiler error on line 6.

D. There is a compiler error on line 10.

E. There is a compiler error on another line.

F. A runtime exception is thrown.

6. Which of the options can fill in the blanks in order to make the code compile?

```
boolean bool = ps._____();
int num = ps._____();
ResultSet rs = ps._____();
```

A. execute, executeQuery, executeUpdate

B. execute, executeUpdate, executeQuery

C. executeQuery, execute, executeUpdate

D. executeQuery, executeUpdate, execute

E. executeUpdate, execute, executeQuery

F. executeUpdate, executeQuery, execute

7. Which of the following are words in the CRUD acronym? (Choose all that apply.)

   A. Create

   B. Delete

   C. Disable

   D. Relate

   E. Read

   F. Upgrade

8. Suppose that the table `animal` has five rows and the following SQL statement updates all of them. What is the result of this code?

```java
public static void main(String[] args) throws SQLException {
    var sql = "UPDATE names SET name = 'Animal'";
    try (var conn = DriverManager.getConnection("jdbc:derby:zoo");
        var ps = conn.prepareStatement(sql)) {

        var result = ps.executeUpdate();
        System.out.println(result);
    }
}
```

   A. 0

   B. 1

   C. 5

   D. The code does not compile.

   E. A `SQLException` is thrown.

   F. A different exception is thrown.

9. Suppose `learn()` is a stored procedure that takes one `IN` parameter. What is wrong with the following code? (Choose all that apply.)

```java
18: var sql = "call learn()";
19: try (var cs = conn.prepareCall(sql)) {
20:    cs.setString(1, "java");
21:    try (var rs = cs.executeQuery()) {
22:       while (rs.next()) {
23:          System.out.println(rs.getString(3));
24:       }
25:    }
26: }
```

A. Line 18 is missing braces.

B. Line 18 is missing a ?.

C. Line 19 is not allowed to use var.

D. Line 20 does not compile.

E. Line 22 does not compile.

F. Something else is wrong with the code.

G. None of the above. This code is correct.

10. Suppose that the table enrichment has three rows with the animals bat, rat, and snake. How many lines does this code print?

```
var sql = "SELECT toy FROM enrichment WHERE animal = ?";
try (var ps = conn.prepareStatement(sql)) {
   ps.setString(1, "bat");

   try (var rs = ps.executeQuery(sql)) {
      while (rs.next())
         System.out.println(rs.getString(1));
   }
}
```

A. 0

B. 1

C. 3

D. The code does not compile.

E. A SQLException is thrown.

F. A different exception is thrown.

11. Suppose that the table food has five rows and this SQL statement updates all of them. What is the result of this code?

```
public static void main(String[] args) {
   var sql = "UPDATE food SET amount = amount + 1";
   try (var conn = DriverManager.getConnection("jdbc:derby:zoo");
      var ps = conn.prepareStatement(sql)) {

      var result = ps.executeUpdate();
      System.out.println(result);
   }
}
```

A. 0

B. 1

C. 5

D. The code does not compile.

E. A SQLException is thrown.

F. A different exception is thrown.

12. Suppose we have a JDBC program that calls a stored procedure, which returns a set of results. Which is the correct order in which to close database resources for this call?

    A. Connection, ResultSet, CallableStatement

    B. Connection, CallableStatement, ResultSet

    C. ResultSet, Connection, CallableStatement

    D. ResultSet, CallableStatement, Connection

    E. CallableStatement, Connection, ResultSet

    F. CallableStatement, ResultSet, Connection

13. Suppose that the table counts has five rows with the numbers 1 to 5. How many lines does this code print?

    ```
    var sql = "SELECT num FROM counts WHERE num > ?";
    try (var ps = conn.prepareStatement(sql)) {
       ps.setInt(1, 3);

       try (var rs = ps.executeQuery()) {
          while (rs.next())
             System.out.println(rs.getObject(1));
       }

       ps.setInt(1, 100);

       try (var rs = ps.executeQuery()) {
          while (rs.next())
             System.out.println(rs.getObject(1));
       }
    }
    ```

    A. 0

    B. 1

    C. 2

    D. 4

    E. The code does not compile.

    F. The code throws an exception.

14. Which of the following can fill in the blank correctly? (Choose all that apply.)

```
var rs = ps.executeQuery();
if (rs.next()) {

    _____;

}
```

A. `String s = rs.getString(0)`

B. `String s = rs.getString(1)`

C. `String s = rs.getObject(0)`

D. `String s = rs.getObject(1)`

E. `Object s = rs.getObject(0)`

F. `Object s = rs.getObject(1)`

15. Suppose `learn()` is a stored procedure that takes one `IN` parameter and one `OUT` parameter. What is wrong with the following code? (Choose all that apply.)

```
18: var sql = "{?= call learn(?)}";
19: try (var cs = conn.prepareCall(sql)) {
20:    cs.setInt(1, 8);
21:    cs.execute();
22:    System.out.println(cs.getInt(1));
23: }
```

A. Line 18 does not call the stored procedure properly.

B. The parameter value is not set for input.

C. The parameter is not registered for output.

D. The code does not compile.

E. Something else is wrong with the code.

F. None of the above. This code is correct.

16. Which of the following can fill in the blank? (Choose all that apply.)

```
var sql = "_____";
try (var ps = conn.prepareStatement(sql)) {
   ps.setObject(3, "red");
   ps.setInt(2, 8);
   ps.setString(1, "ball");
   ps.executeUpdate();
}
```

A. `{ call insert_toys(?, ?) }`

B. `{ call insert_toys(?, ?, ?) }`

C. `{ call insert_toys(?, ?, ?, ?) }`

D. `INSERT INTO toys VALUES (?, ?)`

E. `INSERT INTO toys VALUES (?, ?, ?)`

F. `INSERT INTO toys VALUES (?, ?, ?, ?)`

17. Suppose that the table `counts` has five rows with the numbers 1 to 5. How many lines does this code print?

```
var sql = "SELECT num FROM counts WHERE num > ?";
try (var ps = conn.prepareStatement(sql)) {
   ps.setInt(1, 3);

   try (var rs = ps.executeQuery()) {
      while (rs.next())
         System.out.println(rs.getObject(1));
   }

   try (var rs = ps.executeQuery()) {
      while (rs.next())
         System.out.println(rs.getObject(1));
   }
}
```

A. 0

B. 1

C. 2

D. 4

E. The code does not compile.

F. The code throws an exception.

18. There are currently 100 rows in the table `species` before inserting a new row. What is the output of the following code?

```
String insert = "INSERT INTO species VALUES (3, 'Ant', .05)";
String select = "SELECT count(*) FROM species";
try (var ps = conn.prepareStatement(insert)) {
   ps.executeUpdate();
}
try (var ps = conn.prepareStatement(select)) {
   var rs = ps.executeQuery();
   System.out.println(rs.getInt(1));
}
```

A. 100

B. 101

C. The code does not compile.

D. A SQLException is thrown.

E. A different exception is thrown.

19. Which of the options can fill in the blank to make the code compile and run without error? (Choose all that apply.)

```
var sql = "UPDATE habitat WHERE environment = ?";
try (var ps = conn.prepareCall(sql)) {


   _____


   ps.executeUpdate();
}
```

A. `ps.setString(0, "snow");`

B. `ps.setString(1, "snow");`

C. `ps.setString("environment", "snow");`

D. The code does not compile.

E. The code throws an exception at runtime.

20. Which of the following could be true of the following code? (Choose all that apply.)

```
var sql = "{call transform(?)}";
try (var cs = conn.prepareCall(sql)) {
   cs.registerOutParameter(1, Types.INTEGER);
   cs.execute();
   System.out.println(cs.getInt(1));
}
```

A. The stored procedure can declare an IN or INOUT parameter.

B. The stored procedure can declare an INOUT or OUT parameter.

C. The stored procedure must declare an IN parameter.

D. The stored procedure must declare an INOUT parameter.

E. The stored procedure must declare an OUT parameter.

21. Which is the first line containing a compiler error?

```
25: String url = "jdbc:derby:zoo";
26: try (var conn = DriverManager.getConnection(url);
27:    var ps = conn.prepareStatement();
28:    var rs = ps.executeQuery("SELECT * FROM swings")) {
29:    while (rs.next()) {
30:       System.out.println(rs.getInteger(1));
31:    }
32: }
```

A. Line 26
B. Line 27
C. Line 28
D. Line 29
E. Line 30
F. None of the above

Chapter

22

Security

OCP EXAM OBJECTIVES COVERED IN THIS CHAPTER:

✓ **Secure Coding in Java SE Application**

- Prevent Denial of Service in Java applications

- Secure confidential information in Java application

- Implement Data integrity guidelines- injections and inclusion and input validation

- Prevent external attack of the code by limiting Accessibility and Extensibility, properly handling input validation, and mutability

- Securely constructing sensitive objects

- Secure Serialization and Deserialization

It's hard to read the news without hearing about a data breach. As developers, it is our job to write secure code that can stand up to attack. In this chapter, you will learn the basics of writing secure code in stand-alone Java applications.

We will learn how Hacker Harry tries to do bad things and Security Sienna protects her application. By the end of the chapter, you should be able to protect an application from Harry just as well as Sienna.

The exam only covers Java SE (Standard Edition) applications. It does not cover web applications or any other advanced Java.

Designing a Secure Object

Java provides us with many tools to protect the objects that we create. In this section, we will look at access control, extensibility, validation, and creating immutable objects. All of these techniques can protect your objects from Hacker Harry.

Limiting Accessibility

Hacker Harry heard that the zoo uses combination locks for the animals' enclosures. He would very much like to get all the combinations.

Let's start with a terrible implementation.

```
package animals.security;
public class ComboLocks {
    public Map<String, String> combos;
}
```

This is terrible because the combos object has public access. This is also poor encapsulation. A key security principle is to limit access as much as possible. Think of it as "need to know" for objects. This is called the *principle of least privilege*.

In Chapter 7, "Methods and Encapsulation," you learned about the four levels of access control. It would be better to make the combos object private and write a method to provide the necessary functionality.

```
package animals.security;
public class ComboLocks {
```

```
    private Map<String, String> combos;

    public boolean isComboValid(String animal, String combo) {
        var correctCombo = combos.get(animal);
        return combo.equals(correctCombo);
    }
}
```

This is far better; we don't expose the combinations map to any classes outside the ComboLocks class. For example, package-private is better than public, and private is better than package-private.

Remember, one good practice to thwart Hacker Harry and his cronies is to limit accessibility by making instance variables private or package-private, whenever possible. If your application is using modules, you can do even better by only exporting the security packages to the specific modules that should have access. Here's an example:

```
exports animals.security to zoo.staff;
```

In this example, only the zoo.staff module can access the public classes in the animals.security package.

Restricting Extensibility

Suppose you are working on a class that uses ComboLocks.

```
public class GrasshopperCage {
    public static void openLock(ComboLocks comboLocks, String combo) {
        if (comboLocks.isComboValid("grasshopper", combo))
            System.out.println("Open!");
    }
}
```

Ideally, the first variable passed to this method is an instance of the ComboLocks class. However, Hacker Harry is hard at work and has created this subclass of ComboLocks.

```
public class EvilComboLocks extends ComboLocks {
    public boolean isComboValid(String animal, String combo) {
        var valid = super.isComboValid(animal, combo);
        if (valid) {
            // email the password to Hacker Harry
        }
        return valid;
    }
}
```

This is great. Hacker Harry can check whether the password is valid and email himself all the valid passwords. Mayhem ensues! Luckily, there is an easy way to prevent this problem. Marking a sensitive class as `final` prevents any subclasses.

```
public final class ComboLocks {
   private Map<String, String> combos;

   // instantiate combos object

   public boolean isComboValid(String animal, String combo) {
      var correctCombo = combos.get(animal);
      return combo.equals(correctCombo);
   }
}
```

Hacker Harry can't create his evil class, and users of the `GrasshopperCage` have the assurance that only the expected `ComboLocks` class can make an appearance.

Creating Immutable Objects

As you might remember from Chapter 12, "Java Fundamentals," an immutable object is one that cannot change state after it is created. Immutable objects are helpful when writing secure code because you don't have to worry about the values changing. They also simplify code when dealing with concurrency.

We worked with some immutable objects in the book. The `String` class used throughout the book is immutable. In Chapter 14, "Generics and Collections," you used `List.of()`, `Set.of()`, and `Map.of()`. All three of these methods return immutable types.

Although there are a variety of techniques for writing an immutable class, you should be familiar with a common strategy for making a class immutable.

1. Mark the class as `final`.
2. Mark all the instance variables `private`.
3. Don't define any setter methods and make fields `final`.
4. Don't allow referenced mutable objects to be modified.
5. Use a constructor to set all properties of the object, making a copy if needed.

The first rule prevents anyone from creating a mutable subclass. You might notice this is the same technique we used to restrict extensibility. The second rule provides good encapsulation. The third rule ensures that callers and the class itself don't make changes to the instance variables.

The fourth rule is subtler. Basically, it means you shouldn't expose a getter method for a mutable object. For example, can you see why the following is not an immutable object?

```
1:  import java.util.*;
2:
3:  public final class Animal {
```

```
4:      private final ArrayList<String> favoriteFoods;
5:
6:      public Animal() {
7:          this.favoriteFoods = new ArrayList<String>();
8:          this.favoriteFoods.add("Apples");
9:      }
10:     public List<String> getFavoriteFoods() {
11:         return favoriteFoods;
12:     }
13: }
```

We carefully followed the first three rules, but unfortunately, Hacker Harry can modify our data by calling getFavoriteFoods().clear() or add a food to the list that our animal doesn't like. It's not an immutable object if we can change it contents! If we don't have a getter for the favoriteFoods object, how do callers access it? Simple, by using delegate methods to read the data, as shown in the following:

```
1:   import java.util.*;
2:
3:   public final class Animal {
4:      private final ArrayList<String> favoriteFoods;
5:
6:      public Animal() {
7:          this.favoriteFoods = new ArrayList<String>();
8:          this.favoriteFoods.add("Apples");
9:      }
10:     public int getFavoriteFoodsCount() {
11:         return favoriteFoods.size();
12:     }
13:     public String getFavoriteFoodsElement(int index) {
14:         return favoriteFoods.get(index);
15:     }
16: }
```

In this improved version, the data is still available. However, it is a true immutable object because the mutable variable cannot be modified by the caller. Another option is to create a copy of the favoriteFoods object and return the copy anytime it is requested, so the original remains safe.

```
10:     public ArrayList<String> getFavoriteFoods() {
11:         return new ArrayList<String>(this.favoriteFoods);
12:     }
```

Of course, changes in the copy won't be reflected in the original, but at least the original is protected from external changes. In the next section, we'll see there is another way to copy an object if the class implements a certain interface.

So, what's this about the last rule for creating immutable objects? Let's say we want to allow the user to provide the favoriteFoods data, so we implement the following:

```
1:  import java.util.*;
2:
3:  public final class Animal {
4:      private final ArrayList<String> favoriteFoods;
5:
6:      public Animal(ArrayList<String> favoriteFoods) {
7:          if(favoriteFoods == null)
8:              throw new RuntimeException("favoriteFoods is required");
9:          this.favoriteFoods = favoriteFoods;
10:     }
11:     public int getFavoriteFoodsCount() {
12:         return favoriteFoods.size();
13:     }
14:     public String getFavoriteFoodsElement(int index) {
15:         return favoriteFoods.get(index);
16:     }
17: }
```

To ensure that favoriteFoods is not null, we validate it in the constructor and throw an exception if it is not provided. Hacker Harry is tricky, though. He decides to send us a favoriteFood object but keep his own secret reference to it, which he can modify directly.

```
void modifyNotSoImmutableObject() {
    var favorites = new ArrayList<String>();
    favorites.add("Apples");
    var animal = new Animal(favorites);
    System.out.print(animal.getFavoriteFoodsCount());
    favorites.clear();
    System.out.print(animal.getFavoriteFoodsCount());
}
```

This method prints 1, followed by 0. Whoops! It seems like Animal is not immutable anymore, since its contents can change after it is created. The solution is to use a *copy constructor* to make a copy of the list object containing the same elements.

```
6:      public Animal(List<String> favoriteFoods) {
7:          if(favoriteFoods == null)
8:              throw new RuntimeException("favoriteFoods is required");
9:          this.favoriteFoods = new ArrayList<String>(favoriteFoods);
10:     }
```

The copy operation is called a *defensive copy* because the copy is being made in case other code does something unexpected. It's the same idea as defensive driving. Security Sienna has to be safe because she can't control what others do. With this approach, Hacker Harry is defeated. He can modify the original favoriteFoods all he wants, but it doesn't change the Animal object's contents.

Cloning Objects

Java has a Cloneable interface that you can implement if you want classes to be able to call the clone() method on your object. This helps with making defensive copies.

The ArrayList class does just that, which means there's another way to write the statement on line 9.

```
9: this.favoriteFoods = (ArrayList) favoriteFoods.clone();
```

The clone() method makes a copy of an object. Let's give it a try by changing line 3 of the previous example to the following:

```
public final class Animal implements Cloneable {
```

Now we can write a method within the Animal class:"

```
public static void main(String... args) throws Exception {
    ArrayList<String> food = new ArrayList<>();
    food.add("grass");
    Animal sheep = new Animal(food);
    Animal clone = (Animal) sheep.clone();
    System.out.println(sheep == clone);
    System.out.println(sheep.favoriteFoods == clone.favoriteFoods);
}
```

This code outputs the following:

```
false
true
```

By default, the clone() method makes a *shallow copy* of the data, which means only the top-level object references and primitives are copied. No new objects from within the cloned object are created. For example, if the object contains a reference to an ArrayList, a shallow copy contains a reference to that same ArrayList. Changes to the ArrayList in one object will be visible in the other since it is the same object.

By contrast, you can write an implementation that does a *deep copy* and clones the objects inside. A deep copy does make a new ArrayList object. Changes to the cloned object do not affect the original.

```
public Animal clone() {
    ArrayList<String> listClone = (ArrayList) favoriteFoods.clone();
    return new Animal(listClone);
}
```

Now the main() method prints false twice because the ArrayList is also cloned.

You might have noticed that the clone() method is declared in the Object class. The default implementation throws an exception that tells you the Object didn't implement Cloneable. If the class implements Cloneable, you can call clone(). Classes that implement Cloneable can also provide a custom implementation of clone(), which is useful when the class wants to make a deep copy. Figure 22.1 reviews how Java decides what to do when clone() is called.

FIGURE 22.1 Cloneable logic

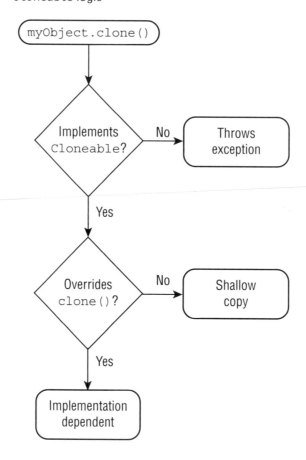

In the last block, implementation-dependent means you should probably check the Javadoc of the overridden clone() method before using it. It may provide a shallow copy, a deep copy, or something else entirely. For example, it may be a shallow copy limited to three levels.

Introducing Injection and Input Validation

Injection is an attack where dangerous input runs in a program as part of a command. For example, user input is often used in database queries or I/O. In this section, we will look at how to protect your code against injection using a PreparedStatement and input validation.

An *exploit* is an attack that takes advantage of weak security. Hacker Harry is ready to try to exploit any code he can find. He especially likes untrusted data.

There are many sources of untrusted data. For the exam, you need to be aware of user input, reading from files, and retrieving data from a database. In the real world, any data that did not originate from your program should be considered suspect.

Preventing Injection with a *PreparedStatement*

Our zoo application has a table named hours that keeps track of when the zoo is open to the public. Figure 22.2 shows the columns in this table.

FIGURE 22.2 Hours table

hours

day varchar(20)	opens integer	closes integer
sunday	9	6
monday	10	4
tuesday	10	4
wednesday	10	5
thursday	10	4
friday	10	6
saturday	9	6

In the following sections, we will look at two examples that are insecure followed by the proper fix.

Using *Statement*

We wrote a method that uses a Statement. In Chapter 21, "JDBC," we didn't use Statement because it is often unsafe.

```
public int getOpening(Connection conn, String day)
      throws SQLException {
```

```
   String sql = "SELECT opens FROM hours WHERE day = '" + day +"'";

   try (var stmt = conn.createStatement();
      var rs = stmt.executeQuery(sql)) {
      if (rs.next())
         return rs.getInt("opens");
   }
   return -1;
}
```

Then, we call the code with one of the days in the table.

```
int opening = attack.getOpening(conn, "monday");  // 10
```

This code does what we want. It queries the database and returns the opening time on the requested day. So far, so good. Then Hacker Harry comes along to call the method. He writes this:

```
int evil = attack.getOpening(conn,
   "monday' OR day IS NOT NULL OR day = 'sunday");  // 9
```

This does not return the expected value. It returned 9 when we ran it. Let's take a look at what Hacker Harry tricked our database into doing.

Hacker Harry's parameter results in the following SQL, which we've formatted for readability:

```
SELECT opens FROM hours
   WHERE day = 'monday'
      OR day IS NOT NULL
      OR day = 'sunday'
```

It says to return any rows where day is sunday, monday, or any value that isn't null. Since none of the values in Figure 22.2 is null, this means all the rows are returned. Luckily, the database is kind enough to return the rows in the order they were inserted; our code reads the first row.

Using *PreparedStatement*

Obviously, we have a problem with using Statement, and we call Security Sienna. She reminds us that Statement is insecure because it is vulnerable to SQL injection. As Hacker Harry just showed us an attack, we have to agree.

We switch our code to use PreparedStatement.

```
public int getOpening(Connection conn, String day)
      throws SQLException {
   String sql = "SELECT opens FROM hours WHERE day = '" + day +"'";
   try (var ps = conn.prepareStatement(sql);
```

```
    var rs = ps.executeQuery()) {
    if (rs.next())
        return rs.getInt("opens");
  }
  return -1;
}
```

Hacker Harry runs his code, and the behavior hasn't changed. We haven't fixed the problem! A PreparedStatement isn't magic. It gives you the capability to be safe, but only if you use it properly.

Security Sienna shows us that we need to rewrite the SQL statement using bind variables like we did in Chapter 21.

```
public int getOpening(Connection conn, String day)
      throws SQLException {
  String sql = "SELECT opens FROM hours WHERE day = ?";
  try (var ps = conn.prepareStatement(sql)) {
      ps.setString(1, day);
      try (var rs = ps.executeQuery()) {
          if (rs.next())
              return rs.getInt("opens");
      }
  }
  return -1;
}
```

This time, Hacker Harry's code does behave differently.

```
int evil = attack.getOpening(conn,
    "monday' or day is not null or day = 'sunday");   // -1
```

The entire string is matched against the day column. Since there is no match, no rows are returned. This is far better!

If you remember only two things about SQL and security, remember to use a PreparedStatement and bind variables.

Little Bobby Tables

SQL injection is often caused by a lack of properly sanitized user input. The author of the popular xkcd.com web comic once asked the question, what would happen if someone's name contained a SQL statement?

"Exploits of a Mom" reproduced with permission from xkcd.com/327/

Oops! Guess the school should have used a PreparedStatement and bound each student's name to a variable. If they had, the entire String would have been properly escaped and stored in the database.

Some databases, like Derby, prevent such an attack. However, it is important to use a PreparedStatement properly to avoid even the possibility of such an attack.

Invalidating Invalid Input with Validation

SQL injection isn't the only type of injection. *Command injection* is another type that uses operating system commands to do something unexpected.

In our example, we will use the Console class from Chapter 19, "I/O," and the Files class from Chapter 20, "NIO.2." Figure 22.3 shows the directory structure we will be using in the example.

The following code attempts to read the name of a subdirectory of diets and print out the names of all the .txt files in that directory:

```
Console console = System.console();
String dirName = console.readLine();
Path path = Paths.get("c:/data/diets/" + dirName);
try (Stream<Path> stream = Files.walk(path)) {
    stream.filter(p -> p.toString().endsWith(".txt"))
        .forEach(System.out::println);
}
```

We tested it by typing in mammals and got the expected output.

```
c:/data/diets/mammals/Platypus.txt
```

FIGURE 22.3 Directory structure

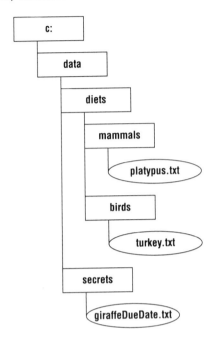

Then Hacker Harry came along and typed `..` as the directory name.

```
c:/data/diets/../secrets/giraffeDueDate.txt
c:/data/diets/../diets/mammals/Platypus.txt
c:/data/diets/../diets/birds/turkey.txt
```

Oh, no! Hacker Harry knows we are expecting a baby giraffe just from the filenames. We were not intending for him to see the `secrets` directory.

We decide to chat with Security Sienna about this problem. She suggests we validate the input. We will use a *whitelist* that allows us to specify which values are allowed.

```
Console console = System.console();
String dirName = console.readLine();
if (dirName.equals("mammal") || dirName.equals("birds")) {
   Path path = Paths.get("c:/data/diets/" + dirName);
   try (Stream<Path> stream = Files.walk(path)) {
      stream.filter(p -> p.toString().endsWith(".txt"))
         .forEach(System.out::println);
   }
}
```

This time when Hacker Harry strikes, he doesn't see any output at all. His input did not match the whitelist. When validation fails, you can throw an exception, log a message, or take any other action of your choosing.

Whitelist vs. Blacklist

A *blacklist* is a list of things that aren't allowed. In the previous example, we could have put the dot (.) character on a blacklist. The problem with a blacklist is that you have to be cleverer than the bad guys. There are a lot of ways to cause harm. For example, you can encode characters.

By contrast, the whitelist is specifying what is allowed. You can supply a list of valid characters. Whitelisting is preferable to blacklisting for security because a whitelist doesn't need to foresee every possible problem.

That said, the whitelist solution could require more frequent updates. In the previous example, we would have to update the code any time we added a new animal type. Security decisions are often about trading convenience for lower risk.

Working with Confidential Information

When working on a project, you will often encounter confidential or sensitive data. Sometimes there are even laws that mandate proper handling of data like the Health Insurance Portability and Accountability Act (HIPAA) in the United States. Table 22.1 lists some examples of confidential information.

TABLE 22.1   Types of confidential data

Category	Examples
Login information	<ul><li>Usernames</li><li>Passwords</li><li>Hashes of passwords</li></ul>
Banking	<ul><li>Credit card numbers</li><li>Account balances</li><li>Credit score</li></ul>
PII (Personal identifiable information)	<ul><li>Social Security number (or other government ID)</li><li>Mother's maiden name</li><li>Security questions/answers</li></ul>

In the following sections, we will look at how to secure confidential data in written form and in log files. We will also show you how to limit access.

Guarding Sensitive Data from Output

Security Sienna makes sure confidential information doesn't leak. The first step she takes is to avoid putting confidential information in a toString() method. That's just inviting the information to wind up logged somewhere you didn't intend.

She is careful what methods she calls in these sensitive contexts to ensure confidential information doesn't escape. Such sensitive contexts include the following:

- Writing to a log file

- Printing an exception or stack trace

- System.out and System.err messages

- Writing to data files

Hacker Harry is on the lookout for confidential information in all of these places. Sometimes you have to process sensitive information. It is important to make sure it is being shared only per the requirements.

Protecting Data in Memory

Security Sienna needs to be careful about what is in memory. If her application crashes, it may generate a dump file. That contains values of everything in memory.

When calling the readPassword() on Console, it returns a char[] instead of a String. This is safer for two reasons.

- It is not stored as a String, so Java won't place it in the String pool, where it could exist in memory long after the code that used it is run.

- You can null out the value of the array element rather than waiting for the garbage collector to do it.

For example, this code overlays the password characters with the letter x:

```
Console console = System.console();
char[] password = console.readPassword();
Arrays.fill(password, 'x');
```

When the sensitive data cannot be overwritten, it is good practice to set confidential data to null when you're done using it. If the data can be garbage collected, you don't have to worry about it being exposed later. Here's an example:

```
LocalDate dateOfBirth = getDateOfBirth();
// use date of birth
dateOfBirth = null;
```

The idea is to have confidential data in memory for as short a time as possible. This gives Hacker Harry less time to make his move.

Limiting File Access

We saw earlier how to prevent command injection by validating requests. Another way is to use a security policy to control what the program can access.

Defense in Depth

It is good to apply multiple techniques to protect your application. This approach is called *defense in depth*. If Hacker Harry gets through one of your defenses, he still doesn't get the valuable information inside. Instead, he is met with another defense.

Validation and using a security policy are good techniques to use together to apply defense in depth.

For the exam, you don't need to know how to write or run a policy. You do need to be able to read one to understand security implications. Luckily, they are fairly self-explanatory. Here's an example of a policy:

```
grant {
    permission java.io.FilePermission
        "C:\\water\\fish.txt",
        "read";
};
```

This policy gives the programmer permission to read, but not update, the fish.txt file. If the program is allowed to read and write the file, we specify the following:

```
grant {
    permission java.io.FilePermission
        "C:\\water\\fish.txt",
        "read, write";
};
```

When looking at a policy, pay attention to whether the policy grants access to more than is needed to run the program. If our application needs to read a file, it should only have read permissions. This is the principle of least privilege we showed you earlier.

Serializing and Deserializing Objects

Imagine we are storing data in an `Employee` record. We want to write this data to a file and read this data back into memory, but we want to do so without writing any potentially sensitive data to disk. From Chapter 19, you should already know how to do this with serialization.

Recall from Chapter 19 that Java skips calling the constructor when deserializing an object. This means it is important not to rely on the constructor for custom validation logic.

Let's define our `Employee` class used throughout this section. Remember, it's important to mark it `Serializable`.

```
import java.io.*;

public class Employee implements Serializable {
    private String name;
    private int age;

    // Constructors/getters/setters
}
```

In the following sections, we will look at how to make serialization safer by specifying which fields get serialized and the process for controlling serialization itself.

Specifying Which Fields to Serialize

Our zoo has decided that employee age information is sensitive and shouldn't be written to disk. From Chapter 19, you should already know how to do this. Security Sienna reminds us that marking a field as `transient` prevents it from being serialized.

```
    private transient int age;
```

Alternatively, you can specify fields to be serialized in an array.

```
private static final ObjectStreamField[] serialPersistentFields =
    { new ObjectStreamField("name", String.class) };
```

You can think of `serialPersistentFields` as the opposite of `transient`. The former is a whitelist of fields that should be serialized, while the latter is a blacklist of fields that should not.

 If you go with the array approach, make sure you remember to use the `private`, `static`, and `final` modifiers. Otherwise, the field will be ignored.

Customizing the Serialization Process

Security may demand custom serialization. In our case, we got a new requirement to add the Social Security number to our object. (For our readers outside the United States, a Social Security number is used for reporting your earnings to the government, among other things.) Unlike age, we do need to serialize this information. However, we don't want to store the Social Security number in plain text, so we need to write some custom code.

Take a look at the following implementation that uses writeObject() and readObject() for serialization, which you learned about in Chapter 19. For brevity, we'll use ssn to stand for Social Security number.

```java
import java.io.*;

public class Employee implements Serializable {
   private String name;
   private String ssn;
   private int age;

   // Constructors/getters/setters

   private static final ObjectStreamField[] serialPersistentFields =
      { new ObjectStreamField("name", String.class),
      new ObjectStreamField("ssn", String.class) };

   private static String encrypt(String input) {
      // Implementation omitted
   }
   private static String decrypt(String input) {
      // Implementation omitted
   }

   private void writeObject(ObjectOutputStream s) throws Exception {
      ObjectOutputStream.PutField fields = s.putFields();
      fields.put("name", name);
      fields.put("ssn", encrypt(ssn));
      s.writeFields();
   }
   private void readObject(ObjectInputStream s) throws Exception {
      ObjectInputStream.GetField fields = s.readFields();
      this.name = (String)fields.get("name", null);
      this.ssn = decrypt((String)fields.get("ssn", null));
   }
}
```

This version skips the age variable as before, although this time without using the `transient` modifier. It also uses custom read and write methods to securely encrypt/decrypt the Social Security number. Notice the `PutField` and `GetField` classes are used in order to write and read the fields easily.

Suppose we were to update our `writeObject()` method with the age variable.

```
fields.put("age", age);
```

When using serialization, the code would result in an exception.

`java.lang.IllegalArgumentException: no such field age with type int`

This shows the `serialPersistentFields` variable is really being used. Java is preventing us from referencing fields that were not declared to be serializable.

 Real World Scenario

Working with Passwords

In this example, we encrypted and then decrypted the Social Security number to show how to perform custom serialization for security reasons. Some fields are too sensitive even for that. In particular, you should never be able to decrypt a password.

When a password is set for a user, it should be converted to a `String` value using a salt (initial random value) and one-way hashing algorithm. Then, when a user logs in, convert the value they type in using the same algorithm and compare it with the stored value. This allows you to authenticate a user without having to expose their password.

Databases of stored passwords can (and very often do) get stolen. Having them properly encrypted means the attacker can't do much with them, like decrypt them and use them to log in to the system. They also can't use them to log in to other systems in which the user used the same password more than once.

Pre/Post-Serialization Processing

Suppose our zoo employee application is having a problem with duplicate records being created for each employee. They decide that they want to maintain a list of all employees in memory and only create users as needed. Furthermore, each employee's name is guaranteed to be unique. Unlikely in practice we know, but this is a special zoo!

From what you learned about concurrent collections in Chapter 18, "Concurrency," and factory methods, we can accomplish this with a `private` constructor and factory method.

```
import java.io.*;
import java.util.Map;
```

```
import java.util.concurrent.ConcurrentHashMap;

public class Employee implements Serializable {
   ...
   private Employee() {}
   private static Map<String,Employee> pool =
      new ConcurrentHashMap<>();

   public synchronized static Employee getEmployee(String name) {
      if(pool.get(name)==null) {
         var e = new Employee();
         e.name = name;
         pool.put(name, e);
      }
      return pool.get(name);
   }
}
```

This method creates a new Employee if one does not exist. Otherwise, it returns the one stored in the memory pool.

Applying *readResolve()*

Now we want to start reading/writing the employee data to disk, but we have a problem. When someone reads the data from the disk, it deserializes it into a new object, not the one in memory pool. This could result in two users holding different versions of the Employee in memory!

Enter the readResolve() method. When this method is present, it is run *after* the readObject() method and is capable of replacing the reference of the object returned by deserialization.

```
import java.io.*;
import java.util.Map;
import java.util.concurrent.ConcurrentHashMap;

public class Employee implements Serializable {
   ...
   public synchronized Object readResolve()
         throws ObjectStreamException {
      var existingEmployee = pool.get(name);
      if(pool.get(name) == null) {
         // New employee not in memory
         pool.put(name, this);
         return this;
```

```
    } else {
      // Existing user already in memory
      existingEmployee.name = this.name;
      existingEmployee.ssn = this.ssn;
      return existingEmployee;
    }
  }
}
```

If the object is not in memory, it is added to the pool and returned. Otherwise, the version in memory is updated, and its reference is returned.

Notice that we added the synchronized modifier to this method. Java allows any method modifiers (except static) for the readResolve() method including any access modifier. This rule applies to writeReplace(), which is up next.

Applying *writeReplace()*

Now, what if we want to write an Employee record to disk but we don't completely trust the instance we are holding? For example, we want to always write the version of the object in the pool rather than the this instance. By construction, there should be only one version of this object in memory, but for this example let's pretend we're not 100 percent confident of that.

The writeReplace() method is run *before* writeObject() and allows us to replace the object that gets serialized.

```
import java.io.*;
import java.util.Map;
import java.util.concurrent.ConcurrentHashMap;

public class Employee implements Serializable {
  ...
  public Object writeReplace() throws ObjectStreamException {
    var e = pool.get(name);
    return e != null ? e : this;
  }
}
```

This implementation checks whether the object is found in the pool. If it is found in the pool, that version is sent for serialization; otherwise, the current instance is used. We could also update this example to add it to the pool if it is somehow missing.

If these last few examples seemed a bit contrived, it's because they are. While the exam is likely to test you on these methods, implementing these advanced serialization methods in detail is way beyond the scope of the exam. Besides, transient will probably meet your needs for customizing what gets serialized.

Reviewing Serialization Methods

You've encountered a lot of methods in this chapter. Table 22.2 summarizes the important features of each that you should know for the exam.

TABLE 22.2   Methods for serialization and deserialization

Return type	Method	Parameters	Description
Object	writeReplace()	None	Allows replacement of object *before* serialization
void	writeObject()	ObjectInputStream	Serializes optionally using PutField
void	readObject()	ObjectOutputStream	Deserializes optionally using GetField
Object	readResolve()	None	Allows replacement of object *after* deserialization

We also provide a visualization of the process of writing and reading a record in Figure 22.4.

FIGURE 22.4   Writing and reading an employee

In Figure 22.4, we show how an employee record for Jane is serialized, written to disk, then read from disk, and returned to the caller. We also show that writeReplace() happens before writeObject(), while readResolve() happens after readObject().

Remember that all four of these methods are optional and must be declared in the `Serializable` object to be used.

Constructing Sensitive Objects

When constructing sensitive objects, you need to ensure that subclasses can't change the behavior. Suppose we have a `FoodOrder` class.

```
public class FoodOrder {
   private String item;
   private int count;

   public FoodOrder(String item, int count) {
      setItem(item);
      setCount(count);
   }
   public String getItem() { return item; }
   public void setItem(String item) { this.item = item; }
   public int getCount() { return count; }
   public void setCount(int count) { this.count = count; }
}
```

This seems simple enough. It is a Java object with two instance variables and corresponding getters/setters. We can even write a method that counts how many items are in our order.

```
public static int total(List<FoodOrder> orders) {
   return orders.stream()
      .mapToInt(FoodOrder::getCount)
      .sum();
}
```

This method signature pleases Hacker Harry because he can pass in his malicious subclass of `FoodOrder`. He overrides the `getCount()` and `setCount()` methods so that `count` is always zero.

```
public class HarryFoodOrder extends FoodOrder {
   public HarryFoodOrder(String item, int count) {
      super(item, count);
   }
   public int getCount() { return 0; }
   public void setCount(int count) { super.setCount(0); }
}
```

Well, that's not good. Now we can't order any food. Luckily, Security Sienna has three techniques to foil Hacker Harry. Let's take a look at each one. If you need to review the `final` modifier, we covered this in detail in Chapter 12.

Making Methods *final*

Security Sienna points out that we are letting Hacker Harry override sensitive methods. If we make the methods `final`, the subclass can't change the behavior on us.

```
public class FoodOrder {
   private String item;
   private int count;

   public FoodOrder(String item, int count) {
      setItem(item);
      setCount(count);
   }
   public final String getItem() { return item; }
   public final void setItem(String item) { this.item = item; }
   public final int getCount() { return count; }
   public final void setCount(int count) { this.count = count; }
}
```

Now the subclass can't provide different behavior for the get and set methods. In general, you should avoid allowing your constructors to call any methods that a subclass can provide its own implementation for.

Making Classes *final*

Remembering to make methods `final` is extra work. Security Sienna points out that we don't need to allow subclasses at all since everything we need is in `FoodOrder`.

```
public final class FoodOrder {
   private String item;
   private int count;

   public FoodOrder(String item, int count) {
      setItem(item);
      setCount(count);
   }
   public String getItem() { return item; }
   public void setItem(String item) { this.item = item; }
   public int getCount() { return count; }
   public void setCount(int count) { this.count = count; }
}
```

Now Hacker Harry can't create his malicious subclass to begin with!

Making the Constructor *private*

Security Sienna notes that another way of preventing or controlling subclasses is to make the constructor private. This technique requires static factory methods to obtain the object.

```java
public class FoodOrder {
    private String item;
    private int count;

    private FoodOrder(String item, int count) {
        setItem(item);
        setCount(count);
    }
    public FoodOrder getOrder(String item, int count) {
        return new FoodOrder(item, count);
    }
    public String getItem() { return item; }
    public void setItem(String item) { this.item = item; }
    public int getCount() { return count; }
    public void setCount(int count) { this.count = count; }
}
```

The factory method technique gives you more control over the process of object creation.

Real World Scenario

How to Protect the Source Code

Since this chapter is about Java SE applications, the person running your program will have access to the code. More specifically, they will have the bytecode (.class) files, typically bundled in a JAR file. With the bytecode, Hacker Harry can decompile your code and get source code. It's not as well written as the code you wrote, but it has equivalent information.

Some people compile their projects with obfuscation tools to try to hide implementation details. *Obfuscation* is the automated process of rewriting source code that purposely makes it more difficult to read. For example, if you try to view JavaScript on a website, entire methods or classes may be on a single line with variable names like aaa, bbb, ccc, and so on. It's harder to know what a method does if it's named gpiomjrqw().

While using an obfuscator makes the decompiled bytecode harder to read and therefore harder to reverse engineer, it doesn't actually provide any security. Remember that security by obscurity will slow down Hacker Harry, but it won't stop him!

Preventing Denial of Service Attacks

A *denial of service* (DoS) attack is when a hacker makes one or more requests with the intent of disrupting legitimate requests. Most denial of service attacks require multiple requests to bring down their targets. Some attacks send a very large request that can even bring down the application in one shot. In this book, we will focus on denial of service attacks.

Unless otherwise specified, a denial of service attack comes from one machine. It may make many requests, but they have the same origin. By contrast, a *distributed denial of service* (DDoS) attack is a denial of service attack that comes from many sources at once. For example, many machines may attack the target. In this section, we will look at some common sources of denial of service issues.

Leaking Resources

One way that Hacker Harry can mount a denial of service attack is to take advantage of poorly written code. This simple method counts the number of lines in a file using NIO.2 methods we saw in Chapter 20:

```
public long countLines(Path path) throws IOException  {
   return Files.lines(path).count();
}
```

Hacker Harry likes this method. He can call it in a loop. Since the method opens a file system resource and never closes it, there is a *resource leak*. After Hacker Harry calls the method enough times, the program crashes because there are no more file handles available.

Luckily, the fix for a resource leak is simple, and it's one you've already seen in Chapter 20. Security Sienna fixes the code by using the try-with-resources statement we saw in Chapter 16, "Exceptions, Assertions, and Localization." Here's an example:

```
public long countLines(Path path) throws IOException  {
   try (var stream = Files.lines(path)) {
      return stream.count();
   }
}
```

Reading Very Large Resources

Another source of a denial of service attacks is very large resources. Suppose we have a simple method that reads a file into memory, does some transformations on it, and writes it to a new file.

```
public void transform(Path in, Path out) throws IOException  {
   var list = Files.readAllLines(in);
```

```
    list.removeIf(s -> s.trim().isBlank());
    Files.write(out, list);
}
```

On a small file, this works just fine. However, on an extremely large file, your program could run out of memory and crash. Hacker Harry strikes again! To prevent this problem, you can check the size of the file before reading it.

Including Potentially Large Resources

An *inclusion* attack is when multiple files or components are embedded within a single file. Any file that you didn't create is suspect. Some types can appear smaller than they really are. For example, some types of images can have a "zip bomb" where the file is heavily compressed on disk. When you try to read it in, the file uses much more space than you thought.

Extensible Markup Language (XML) files can have the same problem. One attack is called the "billion laughs attack" where the file gets expanded exponentially.

The reason these files can become unexpectedly large is that they can include other entities. This means something that is 1 KB can become exponentially larger if it is included enough times.

While handling large files is beyond the scope of the exam, you should understand how and when these issues can come up.

 Inclusion attacks are often known for when they include potentially hosted content. For example, imagine you have a web page that includes a script on another website. You don't control the script, but Hacker Harry does. Including scripts from other websites is dangerous regardless of how big they are.

Overflowing Numbers

When checking file size, be careful with an int type and loops. Since an int has a maximum size, exceeding that size results in integer overflow. Incrementing an int at the maximum value results in a negative number, so validation might not work as expected. In this example, we have a requirement to make sure that we can add a line to a file and have the size stay under a million.

```
public static void main(String[] args) {
    System.out.println(enoughRoomToAddLine(100));
    System.out.println(enoughRoomToAddLine(2_000_000));
    System.out.println(enoughRoomToAddLine(Integer.MAX_VALUE));
}
```

```
public static boolean enoughRoomToAddLine(int requestedSize) {
    int maxLength = 1_000_000;
    String newLine = "END OF FILE";

    int newLineSize = newLine.length();
    return requestedSize + newLineSize < maxLength;
}
```

The output of this program is as follows:

```
true
false
true
```

The first true should make sense. We start with a small file and add a short line to it. This is definitely under a million. The second value is false because two million is already over a million even after adding our short line.

Then we get to the final output of true. We start with a giant number that is over a million. Adding a small number to it exceeds the capacity of an int. Java overflows the number into a very negative number. Since all negative numbers are under a million, the validation doesn't do what we want it to.

When accepting numeric input, you need to verify it isn't too large or too small. In this example, the input value requestedSize should have been checked before adding it to newLineSize.

Wasting Data Structures

One advantage of using a HashMap is that you can look up an element quickly by key. Even if the map is extremely large, a lookup is fast as long as there is a good distribution of hashed keys.

Hacker Harry likes assumptions. He creates a class where hashCode() always returns 42 and puts a million of them in your map. Not so fast anymore.

This one is harder to prevent. However, beware of untrusted classes. Code review can help detect the Hacker Harry in your office.

Similarly, beware of code that attempts to create a very large array or other data structure. For example, if you write a method that lets you set the size of an array, Hacker Harry can repeatedly pick a really large array size and quickly exhaust the program's memory. Input validation is your friend. You could limit the size of an array parameter or, better yet, don't allow the size to be set at all.

Real World Scenario

Learning More

This exam covers security as it applies to stand-alone applications. On a real project, you are likely to be using other technologies. Luckily, there are lists of things to watch out for.

Open Web Application Security Project (OWASP) publishes a top 10 list of security issues. Some will sound familiar from this chapter, like injection. Others, like cross-site scripting (XSS), are specific to web applications. XSS involves malicious JavaScript.

If you are deploying to a cloud provider, like Oracle Cloud or AWS, there is even more to be aware of. The Cloud Security Alliance (CSA) also publishes a security list. Theirs is called the Egregious Eleven. This list covers additional worries such as account hijacking.

We've included links to the OWASP Top 10 and Egregious Eleven on our book page.

`http://www.selikoff.net/ocp11-2`

This chapter is just a taste of security. To learn more about security beyond the scope of the exam, please read *Iron-Clad Java,* Jim Manico and August Detlefsen (Oracle Press, 2014).

Summary

When designing a class, think about what it will be used for. This will allow you to choose the most restrictive access modifiers that meet your requirements. It will also help you determine whether subclasses are needed or whether the class should be `final`. If instances of the class are going to be passed around, it may make sense to make the class immutable so the state is guaranteed not to change.

Injection is an attack where dangerous input can run. SQL injection is prevented using a `PreparedStatement` with bind variables. Command injection is prevented with input validation and security policies. Whitelisting and the principle of least privilege provide the safest combination.

Confidential information must be handled carefully. It should be carefully dealt with in log files, output, and exception stack traces. Confidential information must also be protected in memory through the proper data structures and object lifecycle.

Object serialization and deserialization needs to be designed with security in mind as well. The `transient` modifier flags an instance variable as not being eligible for serialization. More granular control can be provided with the `serialPersistentFields` constant.

It is used to constrain the writeObject() method with PutField and the readObject() method with GetField. Finally, the readResolve() and writeReplace() methods allow you to return a different object or class.

Regardless of whether you are using serialization, objects must take care that the constructor cannot call methods that subclasses can override. Methods that are called from the constructor should be final. Making the constructor private or the class final also meets this requirement.

Finally, applications must protect against denial of service attacks. The most fundamental technique is always using try-with-resources to close resources. Applications should also validate file sizes and input data to ensure data structures are used properly.

Exam Essentials

Identify ways of preventing a denial of service attack.   Using a try-with-resources statement for all I/O and JDBC operations prevents resource leaks. Checking the file size when reading a file prevents it from using an unexpected amount of memory. Confirming large data structures are being used effectively can prevent a performance problem.

Protect confidential information in memory.   Picking a data structure that minimizes exposure is important. The most common one is using char[] for passwords. Additionally, allowing confidential information to be garbage collected as soon as possible reduces the window of exposure.

Compare injection, inclusion, and input validation.   SQL injection and command injection allow an attacker to run expected commands. Inclusion is when one file includes another. Input validation checks for valid or invalid characters from users.

Design secure objects.   Secure objects limit the accessibility of instance variables and methods. They are deliberate about when subclasses are allowed. Often secure objects are immutable and validate any input parameters.

Write serialization and deserializaton code securely.   The transient modifier signifies that an instance variable should not be serialized. Alternatively, serialPersistenceFields specifies what should be. The readObject(), writeObject(), readResolve(), and writeReplace() methods are optional methods that provide further control of the process.

Review Questions

The answers to the chapter review questions can be found in the Appendix.

1. How many requests does it take to have a DDoS attack?

    A. None

    B. One

    C. Two

    D. Many

2. Which of the following is the code an example of? (Choose all that apply.)

    ```java
    public final class Worm {
        private int length;

        public Worm(int length) {
            this.length = length;
        }
        public int getLength() {
            return length;
        }
    }
    ```

    A. Immutability

    B. Input validation

    C. Limiting accessibility

    D. Restricting extensibility

    E. None of the above

3. Which can fill in the blank to make this code compile?

    ```java
    import java.io.*;

    public class AnimalCheckup {
        private String name;
        private int age;

        private static final ObjectStreamField[]
            serialPersistentFields =
            { new ObjectStreamField("name", String.class)};

        private void writeObject(ObjectOutputStream stream)
    ```

```
            throws Exception {

                ObjectOutputStream._____ fields = stream.putFields();
                fields.put("name", name);
                stream.writeFields();
            }
            // readObject method omitted
        }
```

A. PutField

B. PutItem

C. PutObject

D. UpdateField

E. UpdateItem

F. UpdateObject

4. Which of the following can fill in the blank to make a defensive copy of `weights`? (Choose all that apply.)

```
        public class Turkey {
            private ArrayList<Double> weights;
            public Turkey(ArrayList<Double> weights) {
                this.weights = _____;
            }
        }
```

A. weights

B. new ArrayList<>(weights)

C. weights.clone()

D. (ArrayList) weights.clone()

E. weights.copy()

F. (ArrayList) weights.copy()

5. An object has validation code in the constructor. When deserializing an object, the constructor is called with which of the following?

A. readObject()

B. readResolve()

C. Both

D. Neither

6. Which statements are true about the `clone()` method? (Choose all that apply.)

 A. Calling `clone()` on any object will compile.

 B. Calling `clone()` will compile only if the class implements `Cloneable`.

 C. If `clone()` runs without exception, it will always create a deep copy.

 D. If `clone()` runs without exception, it will always create a shallow copy.

 E. If `clone()` is not overridden and runs without exception, it will create a deep copy.

 F. If `clone()` is not overridden and runs without exception, it will create a shallow copy.

7. Which attack could exploit this code?

```
public boolean isValid(String hashedPassword)
    throws SQLException {
    var sql = "SELECT * FROM users WHERE password = ?";
    try (var stmt = conn.prepareStatement(sql)) {
       stmt.setString(1, hashedPassword);
       try (var rs = stmt.executeQuery(sql)) {
          return rs.next();
       }
    }
}
```

 A. Command injection

 B. Confidential data exposure

 C. Denial of service

 D. SQL injection

 E. SQL leak

 F. None of the above

8. You go to the library and want to read a book. Which is true?

```
grant {
    permission java.io.FilePermission
       "/usr/local/library/book.txt",
       "read,write";
};
```

 A. The policy is correct.

 B. The policy is incorrect because file permissions cannot be granted this way.

 C. The policy is incorrect because `read` should not be included.

 D. The policy is incorrect because the permissions should be separated with semicolons.

 E. The policy is incorrect because `write` should not be included.

9. Which are true about securing confidential information? (Choose all that apply.)

   A. It is OK to access it in your program.

   B. It is OK to have it in an exception message.

   C. It is OK to put it in a `char[]`.

   D. It is OK to share it with other users.

   E. None of the above

10. Which types of resources do you need to close to help avoid a denial of service? (Choose all that apply.)

    A. Annotations

    B. Exceptions

    C. I/O

    D. JDBC

    E. String

11. Which of the following are considered inclusion attacks? (Choose all that apply.)

    A. Billion laughs attack

    B. Command injection

    C. CSRF

    D. SQL injection

    E. XSS

    F. Zip bomb

12. What is this code an example of?

    ```
    public void validate(String amount) {
        for (var ch : amount.toCharArray())
            if (ch < '0' || ch > '9')
                throw new IllegalArgumentException("invalid");
    }
    ```

    A. Blacklist

    B. Graylist

    C. Orangelist

    D. Whitelist

    E. None of the above

13. Which of the following are true statements about a class `Camel` with a single instance variable `List<String> species`? (Choose all that apply.)

    A. If `Camel` is well encapsulated, then it must have restricted extensibility.

    B. If `Camel` is well encapsulated, then it must be immutable.

C. If `Camel` has restricted extensibility, then it must have good encapsulation.

D. If `Camel` has restricted extensibility, then it must be immutable.

E. If `Camel` is immutable, then it must have good encapsulation.

F. If `Camel` is immutable, then it must restrict extensibility.

14. Which locations require you to be careful when working with sensitive data to ensure it doesn't leak? (Choose all that apply.)

A. Comments

B. Exception stack traces

C. Log files

D. `System.out`

E. Variable names

F. None of the above

15. What modifiers must be used with the `serialPersistentFields` field in a class? (Choose all that apply.)

A. `final`

B. `private`

C. `protected`

D. `public`

E. `transient`

F. `static`

16. What should your code do when input validation fails? (Choose all that apply.)

A. Call `System.exit()` immediately.

B. Continue execution.

C. Log a message.

D. Throw an exception.

E. None of the above

17. Which techniques can prevent an attacker from creating a top-level subclass that overrides a method called from the constructor? (Choose all that apply.)

A. Adding `final` to the class

B. Adding `final` to the method

C. Adding `transient` to the class

D. Adding `transient` to the method

E. Making the constructor `private`

F. None of the above

18. Which of these attacks is a program trying to prevent when it checks the size of a file?

   A. Denial of service

   B. Inclusion

   C. Injection

   D. None of the above

19. Fill in the blank with the proper method to deserialize an object.

```
public Object _____ throws ObjectStreamException {
    // return an object
}
```

   A. readObject()

   B. readReplace()

   C. readResolve()

   D. writeObject()

   E. writeReplace()

   F. writeResolve()

20. The following code prints true. What is true about the Wombats class implementation of the clone() method?

```
Wombats original = new Wombats();
original.names = new ArrayList<>();
Wombats cloned = (Wombats) original.clone();
System.out.println(original.getNames() == cloned.getNames());
```

   A. It creates a deep copy.

   B. It creates a narrow copy.

   C. It creates a shallow copy.

   D. It creates a wide copy.

Appendix

Answers to Review Questions

Chapter 1: Welcome to Java

1. B, E. C++ has operator overloading and pointers. Java made a point of not having either. Java does have references to objects, but these are pointing to an object that can move around in memory. Option B is correct because Java is platform independent. Option E is correct because Java is object-oriented. While it does support some parts of functional programming, these occur within a class.

2. C, D. Java puts source code in .java files and bytecode in .class files. It does not use a .bytecode file. When running a Java program, you pass just the name of the class without the .class extension.

3. C, D. This example is using the single-file source-code launcher. It compiles in memory rather than creating a .class file, making option A incorrect. To use this launcher, programs can only reference classes built into the JDK or on the classpath. Therefore, option B is incorrect, and options C and D are correct.

4. C, D. The Tank class is there to throw you off since it isn't used by AquariumVisitor. Option C is correct because it imports Jelly by class name. Option D is correct because it imports all the classes in the jellies package, which includes Jelly. Option A is incorrect because it only imports classes in the aquarium package—Tank in this case—and not those in lower-level packages. Option B is incorrect because you cannot use wildcards anywhere other than the end of an import statement. Option E is incorrect because you cannot import parts of a class with a regular import statement. Option F is incorrect because options C and D do make the code compile.

5. A, C, D, E. Eclipse is an integrated development environment (IDE). It is not included in the Java Development Kit (JDK), making option B incorrect. The JDK comes with a number of command-line tools including a compiler, packager, and documentation, making options A, D, and E correct. The JDK also includes the Java Virtual Machine (JVM), making option C correct.

6. E. The first two imports can be removed because java.lang is automatically imported. The following two imports can be removed because Tank and Water are in the same package, making the correct option E. If Tank and Water were in different packages, exactly one of these two imports could be removed. In that case, the answer would be option D.

7. A, B, C. Option A is correct because it imports all the classes in the aquarium package including aquarium.Water. Options B and C are correct because they import Water by class name. Since importing by class name takes precedence over wildcards, these compile. Option D is incorrect because Java doesn't know which of the two wildcard Water classes to use. Option E is incorrect because you cannot specify the same class name in two imports.

8. A, B. The wildcard is configured for files ending in .java, making options E and F incorrect. Additionally, wildcards aren't recursive, making options C and D incorrect. Therefore, options A and B are correct.

9. B. Option B is correct because arrays start counting from zero and strings with spaces must be in quotes. Option A is incorrect because it outputs `Blue`. C is incorrect because it outputs `Jay`. Option D is incorrect because it outputs `Sparrow`. Options E and F are incorrect because they output `java.lang.ClassNotFoundException: BirdDisplay .class`.

10. E. Option E is the canonical `main()` method signature. You need to memorize it. Option A is incorrect because the `main()` method must be public. Options B and F are incorrect because the `main()` method must have a `void` return type. Option C is incorrect because the `main()` method must be static. Option D is incorrect because the `main()` method must be named `main`.

11. C, D. While we wish it were possible to guarantee bug-free code, this is not something a language can ensure, making option A incorrect. Deprecation is an indication that other code should be preferred. It doesn't preclude or require eventual removal, making option B incorrect. Option E is incorrect because backward compatibility is a design goal, not sideways compatibility. Options C and D are correct.

12. C, E. When compiling with `javac`, you can specify a classpath with `-cp` or a directory with `-d`, making options C and E correct. Since the options are case sensitive, option D is incorrect. The other options are not valid on the `javac` command.

13. C. When running a program using `java`, you specify the classpath with `-cp`, making option C correct. Options D and F are incorrect because `-d` and `-p` are used for modules. Options A and B are not valid options on the `java` command.

14. A, B, E. When creating a `jar` file, you use the options `-cf` or `-cvf`, making options A and E correct. It also allows the specification of a directory using `-C`, making option B correct. Options D and F are incorrect because `-d` and `-p` are used for modules.

15. E. The `main()` method isn't `static`. It is a method that happens to be named `main()`, but it's not an application entry point. When the program is run, it gives the error. If the method were `static`, the answer would be option D. Arrays are zero-based, so the loop ignores the first element and throws an exception when accessing the element after the last one.

16. D. The package name represents any folders underneath the current path, which is `named.A` in this case. Option C is incorrect because package names are case sensitive, just like variable names and other identifiers.

17. A, E. Bunny is a class, which can be seen from the declaration: `public class Bunny`. The variable bun is a reference to an object. The method `main()` is the standard entry point to a program. Option G is incorrect because the parameter type matters, not the parameter name.

18. C, D, E. The `package` and `import` statements are both optional. If both are present, the order must be `package`, then `import`, and then `class`. Option A is incorrect because `class` is before `package` and `import`. Option B is incorrect because `import` is before `package`. Option F is incorrect because `class` is before `package`.

19. B, C. Eclipse is an integrated development environment (IDE). It is available from the Eclipse Foundation, not from Oracle, making option C one of the answers. The other answer is option B because the Java Development Kit (JDK) is what you download to get started. The Java Runtime Environment (JRE) was an option for older versions of Java, but it's no longer a download option for Java 11.

20. A, B, E. Unfortunately, this is something you have to memorize. The code with the hyphenated word class-path uses two dashes in front, making option E correct and option D incorrect. The reverse is true for the unhyphenated classpath, making option B correct and option C incorrect. Finally, the short form is option A.

Chapter 2: Java Building Blocks

1. B, E, G. Option A is invalid because a single underscore is no longer allowed as an identifier as of Java 9. Option B is valid because you can use an underscore within identifiers, and a dollar sign ($) is also a valid character. Option C is not a valid identifier because true is a Java reserved word. Option D is not valid because a period (.) is not allowed in identifiers. Option E is valid because Java is case sensitive. Since Public is not a reserved word, it is allowed as an identifier, whereas public would not be allowed. Option F is not valid because the first character is not a letter, dollar sign ($), or underscore (_). Finally, option G is valid as identifiers can contain underscores (_) and numbers, provided the number does not start the identifier.

2. D, F, G. The code compiles and runs without issue, so options A and B are incorrect. A boolean field initializes to false, making option D correct with Empty = false being printed. Object references initialize to null, not the empty String, so option F is correct with Brand = null being printed. Finally, the default value of floating-point numbers is 0.0. Although float values can be declared with an f suffix, they are not printed with an f suffix. For these reasons, option G is correct and Code = 0.0 is printed.

3. B, D, E, H. A var cannot be initialized with a null value without a type, but it can be assigned a null value if the underlying type is not a primitive. For these reasons, option H is correct, but options A and C are incorrect. Options B and D are correct as the underlying types are String and Object, respectively. Option E is correct, as this is a valid numeric expression. You might know that dividing by zero produces a runtime exception, but the question was only about whether the code compiled. Finally, options F and G are incorrect as var cannot be used in a multiple-variable assignment.

4. A, B, D, E. Line 4 does not compile because the L suffix makes the literal value a long, which cannot be stored inside a short directly, making option A correct. Line 5 does not compile because int is an integral type, but 2.0 is a double literal value, making option B correct. Line 6 compiles without issue. Lines 7 and 8 do not compile because numPets and numGrains are both primitives, and you can call methods only on reference types, not primitive values, making options D and E correct, respectively. Finally, line 9 compiles because there is a length() method defined on String.

5. A, D. The class does not compile, so options E, F, G, and H are incorrect. You might notice things like loops and increment/decrement operators in this problem, which we will cover in the next two chapters, but understanding them is not required to answer this question. The first compiler error is on line 3. The variable temp is declared as a float, but the assigned value is 50.0, which is a double without the F/f postfix. Since a double doesn't fit inside a float, line 3 does not compile. Next, depth is declared inside the for loop and only has scope inside this loop. Therefore, reading the value on line 10 triggers a compiler error. Note that the variable Depth on line 2 is never used. Java is case sensitive, so Depth and depth are distinct variables. For these reasons, options A and D are the correct answers.

6. C, E. Option C is correct because float and double primitives default to 0.0, which also makes option A incorrect. Option E is correct because all nonprimitive values default to null, which makes option F incorrect. Option D is incorrect because int primitives default to 0. Option B is incorrect because char defaults to the NUL character, '\u0000'. You don't need to know this value for the exam, but you should know the default value is not null since it is a primitive.

7. G. Option G is correct because local variables do not get assigned default values. The code fails to compile if a local variable is used when not being explicitly initialized. If this question were about instance variables, options B, D, and E would be correct. A boolean primitive defaults to false, and a float primitive defaults to 0.0f.

8. B, E. Option B is correct because boolean primitives default to false. Option E is correct because long values default to 0L.

9. C, E, F. In Java, there are no guarantees when garbage collection will run. The JVM is free to ignore calls to System.gc(). For this reason, options A, B, and D are incorrect. Option C is correct, as the purpose of garbage collection is to reclaim used memory. Option E is also correct that an object may never be garbage collected, such as if the program ends before garbage collection runs. Option F is correct and is the primary means by which garbage collection algorithms determine whether an object is eligible for garbage collection. Finally, option G is incorrect as marking a variable final means it is constant within its own scope. For example, a local variable marked final will be eligible for garbage collection after the method ends, assuming there are no other references to the object that exist outside the method.

10. C. The class does compiles without issue, so options E, F, and G are incorrect. The key thing to notice is line 4 does not define a constructor, but instead a method named PoliceBox(), since it has a return type of void. This method is never executed during the program run, and color and age get assigned the default values null and 0L, respectively. Lines 11 and 12 change the values for an object associated with p, but then on line 13 the p variable is changed to point to the object associated with q, which still has the default values. For this reason, the program prints Q1=null, Q2=0, P1=null, and P2=0, making option C the only correct answer.

11. A, D, E. From Chapter 1, a main() method must have a valid identifier of type String... or String[]. For this reason, option G can be eliminated immediately. Option A is correct because var is not a reserved word in Java and may be used as an identifier. Option B is incorrect as a period (.) may not be used in an identifier. Option C is also incorrect as an identifier may include digits but not start with one. Options D and E are correct as an underscore (_) and dollar sign ($) may appear anywhere in an identifier. Finally, option F is incorrect, as a var may not be used as a method argument.

12. A, E, F. An underscore (_) can be placed in any numeric literal, so long as it is not at the beginning, the end, or next to a decimal point (.). Underscores can even be placed next to each other. For these reasons, options A, E, and F are correct. Options B and D are incorrect, as the underscore (_) is next to a decimal point (.). Options C and G are incorrect, because an underscore (_) cannot be placed at the beginning or end of the literal.

13. B, D, H. The Rabbit object from line 3 has two references to it: one and three. The references are set to null on lines 6 and 8, respectively. Option B is correct because this makes the object eligible for garbage collection after line 8. Line 7 sets the reference four to null, since that is the value of one, which means it has no effect on garbage collection. The Rabbit object from line 4 has only a single reference to it: two. Option D is correct because this single reference becomes null on line 9. The Rabbit object declared on line 10 becomes eligible for garbage collection at the end of the method on line 12, making option H correct. Calling System.gc() has no effect on eligibility for garbage collection.

14. B, C, F. A var cannot be used for a constructor or method parameter or for an instance or class variable, making option A incorrect and option C correct. The type of var is known at compile-time and the type cannot be changed at runtime, although its value can change at runtime. For these reasons, options B and F are correct, and option E is incorrect. Option D is incorrect, as var is not permitted in multiple-variable declarations. Finally, option G is incorrect, as var is not a reserved word in Java.

15. C, F, G. First off, 0b is the prefix for a binary value, and 0x is the prefix for a hexadecimal value. These values can be assigned to many primitive types, including int and double, making options C and F correct. Option A is incorrect because naming the variable Amount will cause the System.out.print(amount) call on the next line to not compile. Option B is incorrect because 9L is a long value. If the type was changed to long amount = 9L, then it would compile. Option D is incorrect because 1_2.0 is a double value. If the type was changed to double amount = 1_2.0, then it would compile. Options E and H are incorrect because the underscore (_) appears next to the decimal point (.), which is not allowed. Finally, option G is correct and the underscore and assignment usage is valid.

16. A, C, D. The code contains three compilation errors, so options E, F, G, and H are incorrect. Line 2 does not compile, as this is incorrect syntax for declaring multiple variables, making option A correct. The data type is declared only once and shared among all variables in a multiple variable declaration. Line 3 compiles without issue, as it declares a local variable inside an instance initializer that is never used. Line 4 does not compile because Java, unlike some other programming languages, does not support setting default method parameter values, making option C correct. Finally, line 7 does not compile because fins is in scope and accessible only inside the instance initializer on line 3, making option D correct.

17. A, E, F, G. The question is primarily about variable scope. A variable defined in a statement such as a loop or initializer block is accessible only inside that statement. For this reason, options A and E are correct. Option B is incorrect because variables can be defined inside initializer blocks. Option C is incorrect, as a constructor argument is accessible only in the constructor itself, not for the life of the instance of the class. Constructors and instance methods can access any instance variable, even ones defined after their declaration, making option D incorrect and options F and G correct.

18. F, G. The code does not compile, so options A, B, C, and D are all incorrect. The first compilation error occurs on line 5. Since char is an unsigned data type, it cannot be assigned a negative value, making option F correct. The second compilation error is on line 9, since mouse is used without being initialized, making option G correct. You could fix this by initializing a value on line 4, but the compiler reports the error where the variable is used, not where it is declared.

19. F. To solve this problem, you need to trace the braces {} and see when variables go in and out of scope. You are not required to understand the various data structures in the question, as this will be covered in the next few chapters. We start with hairs, which goes in and out of scope on line 2, as it is declared in an instance initializer, so it is not in scope on line 14. The three variables—water, air, twoHumps, declared on lines 3 and 4—are instance variables, so all three are in scope in all instance methods of the class, including spit() and on line 14. The distance method parameter is in scope for the life of the spit() method, making it the fourth value in scope on line 14. The path variable is in scope on line 6 and stays in scope until the end of the method on line 16, making it the fifth variable in scope on line 14. The teeth variable is in scope on line 7 and immediately goes out of scope on line 7 since the statement ends. The two variables age and i defined on lines 9 and 10, respectively, both stay in scope until the end of the while loop on line 15, bringing the total variables in scope to seven on line 14. Finally, Private is in scope on 12 but out of scope after the for loop ends on line 13. Since the total in-scope variables is seven, option F is the correct answer.

20. D. The class compiles and runs without issue, so options F and G are incorrect. We start with the main() method, which prints 7- on line 11. Next, a new Salmon instance is created on line 11. This calls the two instance initializers on lines 3 and 4 to be executed in order. The default value of an instance variable of type int is 0, so 0- is printed next and count is assigned a value of 1. Next, the constructor is called. This assigns a value of 4 to count and prints 2-. Finally, line 12 prints 4-, since that is the value of count. Putting it altogether, we have 7-0-2-4-, making option D the correct answer.

21. A, D, F. The class compiles and runs without issue, so option H is incorrect. The program creates two Bear objects, one on line 9 and one on line 10. The first Bear object is accessible until line 13 via the brownBear reference variable. The second Bear object is passed to the first object's roar() method on line 11, meaning it is accessible via both the polarBear reference and the brownBear.pandaBear reference. After line 12, the object is still accessible via brownBear.pandaBear. After line 13, though, it is no longer accessible since brownBear is no longer accessible. In other words, both objects become eligible for garbage collection after line 13, making options A and D correct. Finally, garbage collection is never guaranteed to run or not run, since the JVM decides this for you. For this reason, option F is correct, and options E and G are incorrect. The class contains a finalize() method, although this does not contribute to the answer. For the exam, you may see finalize() in a question, but since it's deprecated as of Java 9, you will not be tested on it.

22. H. None of these declarations is a valid instance variable declaration, as var cannot be used with instance variables, only local variables. For this reason, option H is the only correct answer. If the question were changed to be about local variable declarations, though, then the correct answers would be options C, D, and E. An identifier must start with a letter, $, or _, so options F and G would be incorrect. As of Java 9, a single underscore is not allowed as an identifier, so option A would be incorrect. Options A and G would also be incorrect because their numeric expressions use underscores incorrectly. An underscore cannot appear at the end of literal value, nor next to a decimal point (.). Finally, null is a reserved word, but var is not, so option B would be incorrect, and option E would be correct.

Chapter 3: Operators

1. A, D, G. Option A is the equality operator and can be used on primitives and object references. Options B and C are both arithmetic operators and cannot be applied to a boolean value. Option D is the logical complement operator and is used exclusively with boolean values. Option E is the modulus operator, which can be used only with numeric primitives. Option F is a relational operator that compares the values of two numbers. Finally, option G is correct, as you can cast a boolean variable since boolean is a type.

2. A, B, D. The expression apples + oranges is automatically promoted to int, so int and data types that can be promoted automatically from int will work. Options A, B, and D are such data types. Option C will not work because boolean is not a numeric data type. Options E and F will not work without an explicit cast to a smaller data type.

3. B, C, D, F. The code will not compile as is, so option A is not correct. The value 2 * ear is automatically promoted to long and cannot be automatically stored in hearing, which is in an int value. Options B, C, and D solve this problem by reducing the long value to int. Option E does not solve the problem and actually makes it worse by attempting to place the value in a smaller data type. Option F solves the problem by increasing the data type of the assignment so that long is allowed.

4. B. The code compiles and runs without issue, so option E is not correct. This example is tricky because of the second assignment operator embedded in line 5. The expression (wolf=false) assigns the value false to wolf and returns false for the entire expression. Since teeth does not equal 10, the left side returns true; therefore, the exclusive or (^) of the entire expression assigned to canine is true. The output reflects these assignments, with no change to teeth, so option B is the only correct answer.

5. A, C. Options A and C show operators in increasing or the same order of precedence. Options B and E are in decreasing or the same order of precedence. Options D, F, and G are in neither increasing or decreasing order of precedence. In option D, the assignment operator (=) is between two unary operators, with the multiplication operator (*) incorrectly having the highest order or precedence. In option F, the logical complement operator (!) has the highest order of precedence, so it should be last. In option G, the assignment operators have the lowest order of precedence, not the highest, so the last two operators should be first.

6. F. The code does not compile because line 3 contains a compilation error. The cast (int) is applied to fruit, not the expression fruit+vegetables. Since the cast operator has a higher operator precedence than the addition operator, it is applied to fruit, but the expression is promoted to a float, due to vegetables being float. The result cannot be returned as long in the addCandy() method without a cast. For this reason, option F is correct. If parentheses were added around fruit+vegetables, then the output would be 3-5-6, and option B would be correct. Remember that casting floating point numbers to integral values results in truncation, not rounding.

7. D. In the first boolean expression, vis is 2 and ph is 7, so this expression evaluates to true & (true || false), which reduces to true. The second boolean expression uses the short-circuit operator, and since (vis > 2) is false, the right side is not evaluated, leaving ph at 7. In the last assignment, ph is 7, and the pre-decrement operator is applied first, reducing the expression to 7 <= 6 and resulting in an assignment of false. For these reasons, option D is the correct answer.

8. A. The code compiles and runs without issue, so option E is incorrect. Line 7 does not produce a compilation error since the compound operator applies casting automatically. Line 5 increments pig by 1, but it returns the original value of 4 since it is using the post-increment operator. The pig variable is then assigned this value, and the increment operation is discarded. Line 7 just reduces the value of goat by 1, resulting in an output of 4 - 1 and making option A the correct answer.

9. A, D, E. The code compiles without issue, so option G is incorrect. In the first expression, a > 2 is false, so b is incremented to 5 but since the post-increment operator is used, 4 is printed, making option D correct. The --c was not applied, because only one right side of the ternary expression was evaluated. In the second expression, a!=c is false since c was never modified. Since b is 5 due to the previous line and the post-increment operator is used, b++ returns 5. The result is then assigned to b using the assignment operator, overriding the incremented value for b and printing 5, making option E correct. In the last expression, parentheses are not required but lack of parentheses can make ternary expressions difficult to read. From the previous lines, a is 2, b is 5, and c is 2. We can rewrite this expression with parentheses as (2 > 5 ? (5 < 2 ? 5 : 2) : 1). The second ternary expression is never evaluated since 2 > 5 is false, and the expression returns 1, making option A correct.

10. G. The code does not compile due to an error on the second line. Even though both height and weight are cast to byte, the multiplication operator automatically promotes them to int, resulting in an attempt to store an int in a short variable. For this reason, the code does not compile, and option G is the only correct answer. This line contains the only compilation error. If the code were corrected to add parentheses around the entire expression and cast it to a byte or short, then the program would print 3, 6, and 2 in that order.

11. D. First off, the * and % have the same operator precedence, so the expression is evaluated from left to right unless parentheses are present. The first expression evaluates to 8 % 3, which leaves a remainder of 2. The second expression is just evaluated left to right since * and % have the same operator precedence, and it reduces to 6 % 3, which is 0. The last expression reduces to 5 * 1, which is 5. Therefore, the output on line 6 is 2-0-5, making option D the correct answer.

12. D. The *pre-* prefix indicates the operation is applied first, and the new value is returned, while the *post-* prefix indicates the original value is returned prior to the operation. Next, increment increases the value, while decrement decreases the value. For these reasons, option D is the correct answer.

13. F. The first expression is evaluated from left to right since the operator precedence of & and ^ is the same, letting us reduce it to false ^ sunday, which is true, because sunday is true. In the second expression, we apply the negation operator, (!), first, reducing the expression to sunday && true, which evaluates to true. In the last expression, both variables are true so they reduce to !(true && true), which further reduces to !true, aka false. For these reasons, option F is the correct answer.

14. B, E, G. The return value of an assignment operation in the expression is the same as the value of the newly assigned variable. For this reason, option A is incorrect, and option E is correct. Option B is correct, and the equality (==) and inequality (!=) operators can both be used with objects. Option C is incorrect, as boolean and numeric types are not comparable with each other. For example, you can't say true == 3 without a compilation error. Option D is incorrect, as only the short-circuit operator (&&) may cause only the left side of the expression to be evaluated. The (|) operator will cause both sides to be evaluated. Option F is incorrect, as Java does not accept numbers for boolean values. Finally, option G is correct, as you need to use the negation operator (-) to flip or negate numeric values, not the logical complement operator (!).

15. D. The ternary operator is the only operator that takes three values, making option D the only correct choice. Options A, B, C, E, and G are all binary operators. While they can be strung together in longer expressions, each operation uses only two values at a time. Option F is a unary operator and takes only one value.

16. B. The first line contains a compilation error. The value 3 is cast to long. The 1 * 2 value is evaluated as int but promoted to long when added to the 3. Trying to store a long value in an int variable triggers a compiler error. The other lines do not contain any compilation errors, as they store smaller values in larger or same-size data types, with the third and fourth lines using casting to do so.

17. C, F. The starting values of ticketsTaken and ticketsSold are 1 and 3, respectively. After the first compound assignment, ticketsTaken is incremented to 2. The ticketsSold value is increased from 3 to 5; since the post-increment operator was used the value of ticketsTaken++ returns 1. On the next line, ticketsTaken is doubled to 4. On the final line, ticketsSold is increased by 1 to 6. The final values of the variables are 4 and 6, for ticketsTaken and ticketsSold, respectively, making options C and F the correct answers. Note the last line does not trigger a compilation error as the compound operator automatically casts the right-hand operand.

18. C. Only parentheses, ( ), can be used to change the order of operation in an expression. The other operators, such as [ ], < >, and { }, cannot be used as parentheses in Java.

19. B, F. The code compiles and runs successfully, so options G and H are incorrect. On line 5, the pre-increment operator is executed first, so `start` is incremented to 8, and the new value is returned as the right side of the expression. The value of `end` is computed by adding 8 to the original value of 4, leaving a new value of 12 for `end`, and making option F a correct answer. On line 6, we are incrementing one past the maximum `byte` value. Due to overflow, this will result in a negative number, making option B the correct answer. Even if you didn't know the maximum value of `byte`, you should have known the code compiles and runs and looked for the answer for `start` with a negative number.

20. A, D, E. Unary operators have the highest order of precedence, making option A correct. The negation operator (`-`) is used only for numeric values, while the logical complement operator (`!`) is used exclusively for `boolean` values. For these reasons, option B is incorrect, and option E is correct. Finally, the pre-increment/pre-decrement operators return the new value of the variable, while the post-increment/post-decrement operators return the original variable. For these reasons, option C is incorrect, and option D is correct.

Chapter 4: Making Decisions

1. A, B, C, E, F, G. A `switch` statement supports the primitives `int`, `byte`, `short`, and `char`, along with their associated wrapper classes `Integer`, `Byte`, `Short`, and `Character`, respectively, making options B, C, and F correct. It also supports enum and `String`, making options A and E correct. Finally, `switch` supports `var` if the type can be resolved to a supported `switch` data type, making option G correct. Options D and H are incorrect as `long`, `float`, `double`, and their associated wrapped classes `Long`, `Float`, and `Double`, respectively, are not supported in `switch` statements.

2. B. The code compiles and runs without issue, so options D, E, and F are incorrect. Even though the two consecutive `else` statements on lines 7 and 8 look a little odd, they are associated with separate `if` statements on lines 5 and 6, respectively. The value of `humidity` on line 4 is equal to `-4 + 12`, which is 8. The first `if` statement evaluates to `true` on line 5, so line 6 is executed and its associated `else` statement on line 8 is not. The `if` statement on line 6 evaluates to `false`, causing the `else` statement on line 7 to activate. The result is the code prints `Just Right`, making option B the correct answer.

3. E. The second for-each loop contains a `continue` followed by a `print()` statement. Because the `continue` is not conditional and always included as part of the body of the for-each loop, the `print()` statement is not reachable. For this reason, the `print()` statement does not compile. As this is the only compilation error, option E is correct. The other lines of code compile without issue. In particular, because the data type for the elements of `myFavoriteNumbers` is `Integer`, they can be easily unboxed to `int` or referenced as `Object`. For this reason, the lines containing the for-each expressions each compile.

4. C, E. A for-each loop can be executed on any Collections object that implements `java.lang.Iterable`, such as List or Set, but not all Collections classes, such as Map, so option A is incorrect. The body of a do/while loop is executed one or more times, while the body of a while loop is executed zero or more times, making option E correct and option B incorrect. The conditional expression of for loops is evaluated at the start of the loop execution, meaning the for loop may execute zero or more times, making option C correct. Option D is incorrect, as a default statement is not required in a switch statement. If no case statements match and there is no default statement, then the application will exit the switch statement without executing any branches. Finally, each if statement has at most one matching else statement, making option F incorrect. You can chain multiple if and else statements together, but each else statement requires a new if statement.

5. B, D. Option A is incorrect because on the first iteration it attempts to access weather[weather.length] of the nonempty array, which causes an ArrayIndexOutOfBoundsException to be thrown. Option B is correct and will print the elements in order. It is only a slight modification of a common for loop, with i<weather.length replaced with an equivalent i<=weather.length-1. Option C is incorrect because the snippet creates a compilation problem in the body of the for loop, as i is undefined in weather[i]. For this to work, the body of the for-each loop would have to be updated as well. Option D is also correct and is a common way to print the elements of an array in reverse order. Option E does not compile and is therefore incorrect. You can declare multiple elements in a for loop, but the data type must be listed only once, such as in for(int i=0, j=3; ...). Finally, option F is incorrect because the first element of the array is skipped. The loop update operation is optional, so that part compiles, but the increment is applied as part of the conditional check for the loop. Since the conditional expression is checked before the loop is executed the first time, the first value of i used inside the body of the loop will be 1.

6. B, C, E. The code contains a nested loop and a conditional expression that is executed if the sum of col + row is an even number, else count is incremented. Note that options E and F are equivalent to options B and D, respectively, since unlabeled statements apply to the most inner loop. Studying the loops, the first time the condition is true is in the second iteration of the inner loop, when row is 1 and col is 1. Option A is incorrect, because this causes the loop to exit immediately with count only being set to 1. Options B, C, and E follow the same pathway. First, count is incremented to 1 on the first inner loop, and then the inner loop is exited. On the next iteration of the outer loop, row is 2 and col is 0, so execution exits the inner loop immediately. On the third iteration of the outer loop, row is 3 and col is 0, so count is incremented to 2. In the next iteration of the inner loop, the sum is even, so we exit, and our program is complete, making options B, C, and E each correct. Options D and F are both incorrect, as they cause the outer loops to execute multiple times, with count having a value of 5 when done. You don't need to trace through all the iterations; just stop when the value of count exceeds 2.

7. E. This code contains numerous compilation errors, making options A and H incorrect. All of the compilation errors are contained within the switch statement. The default statement is fine and does not cause any issues. The first case statement does not compile, as continue cannot be used inside a switch statement. The second case statement also does not compile. While the thursday variable is marked final, it is not a compile-time constant required for a switch statement, as any int value can be passed in at runtime. The third case statement is valid and does compile, as break is compatible with switch statements. The fourth case statement does not compile. Even though Sunday is effectively final, it is not a compile-time constant. If it were explicitly marked final, then this case statement would compile. Finally, the last case statement does not compile because DayOfWeek.MONDAY is not an int value. While switch statements do support enum values, each case statement must have the same data type as the switch variable otherDay, which is int. Since exactly four lines do not compile, option E is the correct answer.

8. C. Prior to the first iteration, sing = 8, squawk = 2, and notes = 0. After the iteration of the first loop, sing is updated to 7, squawk to 4, and notes to the sum of the new values for sing + squawk, 7 + 4 = 11. After the iteration of the second loop, sing is updated to 6, squawk to 6, and notes to the sum of itself, plus the new values for sing + squawk, 11 + 6 + 6 = 23. On the third iteration of the loop, sing > squawk evaluates to false, as 6 > 6 is false. The loop ends and the most recent value of sing, 23, is output, so the correct answer is option C.

9. G. This example may look complicated, but the code does not compile. Line 8 is missing the required parentheses around the boolean conditional expression. Since the code does not compile and it is not because of line 6, option G is the correct answer. If line 8 was corrected with parentheses, then the loop would be executed twice, and the output would be 11.

10. B, D, F. The code does compile, making option G incorrect. In the first for-each loop, the right side of the for-each loop has a type of int[], so each element penguin has a type of int, making option B correct. In the second for-each loop, ostrich has a type of Character[], so emu has a data type of Character, making option D correct. In the last for-each loop, parrots has a data type of List. Since no generic type is used, the default type is a List of Object values, and macaw will have a data type of Object, making option F correct.

11. F. The code does not compile, although not for the reason specified in option E. The second case statement contains invalid syntax. Each case statement must have the keyword case—in other words, you cannot chain them with a colon (:) as shown in case 'B' : 'C' :. For this reason, option F is the correct answer. If this line were fixed to add the keyword case before 'C', then the rest of the code would have compiled and printed great good at runtime.

12. A, B, D. To print items in the wolf array in reverse order, the code needs to start with wolf[wolf.length-1] and end with wolf[0]. Option A accomplishes this and is the first correct answer, albeit not using any of for loop structures, and ends when the index is 0. Option B is also correct and is one of the most common ways a reverse loop is written. The termination condition is often m>=0 or m>-1, and both are correct. Options C and F each cause an ArrayIndexOutOfBoundsException at runtime since both read from wolf[wolf.length] first, with an index that is passed the length of the 0-based array wolf. The form of option C would be successful if the value was changed to wolf[wolf.length-z-1]. Option D is also correct, as the j is extraneous and can be ignored in this example. Finally, option E is incorrect and produces an infinite loop at runtime, as w is repeatedly set to r-1, in this case 4, on every loop iteration. Since the update statement has no effect after the first iteration, the condition is never met, and the loop never terminates.

13. B, E. The code compiles without issue and prints three distinct numbers at runtime, so options G and H are incorrect. The first loop executes a total of five times, with the loop ending when participants has a value of 10. For this reason, option E is correct. In the second loop, animals already starts out not less than or equal to 1, but since it is a do/while loop, it executes at least once. In this manner, animals takes on a value of 3 and the loop terminates, making option B correct. Finally, the last loop executes a total of two times, with performers starting with -1, going to 1 at the end of the first loop, and then ending with a value of 3 after the second loop, which breaks the loop. This makes option B a correct answer twice over.

14. E. The variable snake is declared within the body of the do/while statement, so it is out of scope on line 7. For this reason, option E is the correct answer. If snake were declared before line 3 with a value of 1, then the output would have been 1 2 3 4 5 -5.0, and option G would have been the correct answer choice.

15. A, E. The most important thing to notice when reading this code is that the innermost loop is an infinite loop without a statement to branch out of it, since there is no loop termination condition. Therefore, you are looking for solutions that skip the innermost loop entirely or ones that exit that loop. Option A is correct, as break L2 on line 8 causes the second inner loop to exit every time it is entered, skipping the innermost loop entirely. For option B, the first continue on line 8 causes the execution to skip the innermost loop on the first iteration of the second loop, but not the second iteration of the second loop. The innermost loop is executed, and with continue on line 12, it produces an infinite loop at runtime, making option B incorrect. Option C is incorrect because it contains a compiler error. The label L3 is not visible outside its loop. Option D is incorrect, as it is equivalent to option B since unlabeled break and continue apply to the nearest loop and therefore produce an infinite loop at runtime. Like option A, the continue L2 on line 8 allows the innermost loop to be executed the second time the second loop is called. The continue L2 on line 12 exits the infinite loop, though, causing control to return to the second loop. Since the first and second loops terminate, the code terminates, and option E is a correct answer.

16. E. The code compiles without issue, making options F and G incorrect. Since Java 10, var is supported in both switch and while loops, provided the type can be determined by the compiler. In addition, the variable one is allowed in a case statement because it is a final local variable, making it a compile-time constant. The value of tailFeathers is 3, which matches the second case statement, making 5 the first output. The while loop is executed twice, with the pre-increment operator (--) modifying the value of tailFeathers from 3 to 2, and then to 1 on the second loop. For this reason, the final output is 5 2 1, making option E the correct answer.

17. F. Line 19 starts with an else statement, but there is no preceding if statement that it matches. For this reason, line 19 does not compile, making option F the correct answer. If the else keyword was removed from line 19, then the code snippet would print Success.

18. A, D, E. The right side of a for-each statement must be a primitive array or any class that implements java.lang.Iterable, which includes the Collection interface, although not all Collections Framework classes. For these reasons, options A, D, and E are correct. Option B is incorrect as Map does not implement Collection nor Iterable, since it is not a list of items, but a mapping of items to other items. Option C and F are incorrect as well. While you may consider them to be a list of characters, strictly speaking they are not considered Iterable in Java, since they do not implement Iterable. That said, you can iterate over them using a traditional `for` loop and member methods, such as `charAt()` and `length()`.

19. D. The code does compile without issue, so option F is incorrect. The `viola` variable created on line 8 is never used and can be ignored. If it had been used as the `case` value on line 15, it would have caused a compilation error since it is not marked `final`. Since `"violin"` and `"VIOLIN"` are not an exact match, the `default` branch of the `switch` statement is executed at runtime. This execution path increments p a total of three times, bringing the final value of p to 2 and making option D the correct answer.

20. F. The code snippet does not contain any compilation errors, so options D and E are incorrect. There is a problem with this code snippet, though. While it may seem complicated, the key is to notice that the variable r is updated outside of the do/while loop. This is allowed from a compilation standpoint, since it is defined before the loop, but it means the innermost loop never breaks the termination condition `r <= 1`. At runtime, this will produce an infinite loop the first time the innermost loop is entered, making option F the correct answer.

Chapter 5: Core Java APIs

1. F. Line 5 does not compile. This question is checking to see whether you are paying attention to the types. `numFish` is an `int`, and 1 is an `int`. Therefore, we use numeric addition and get 5. The problem is that we can't store an `int` in a `String` variable. Supposing line 5 said `String anotherFish = numFish + 1 + "";`. In that case, the answer would be option A and option C. The variable defined on line 5 would be the string `"5"`, and both output statements would use concatenation.

2. A, C, D. The code compiles fine. Line 3 points to the `String` in the string pool. Line 4 calls the `String` constructor explicitly and is therefore a different object than s. Lines 5 checks for object equality, which is true, and so prints one. Line 6 uses object reference equality, which is not true since we have different objects.

Line 7 calls `intern()`, which returns the value from the string pool and is therefore the same reference as s. Line 8 also compares references but is true since both references point to the object from the string pool. Finally, line 9 is a trick. The string `Hello` is already in the string pool, so calling `intern()` does not change anything. The reference t is a different object, so the result is still `false`.

3. A, C, F. The code does compile, making option G incorrect. In the first for-each loop, `gorillas` has a type of `List<String>`, so each element koko has a type of `String`, making option A correct. In the second for-each loop, you might think that the diamond operator `<>` cannot be used with `var` without a compilation error, but it absolutely can. This result is monkeys having a type of `ArrayList<Object>` with `albert` having a data type of `Object`, making option C correct. While `var` might indicate an ambiguous data type, there is no such thing as an undefined data type in Java, so option D is incorrect.

In the last for-each loop, `chimpanzee` has a data type of `List`. Since the left side does not define a generic type, the compiler will treat this as `List<Object>`, and ham will have a data type of Object, making option F correct. Even though the elements of chimpanzees might be Integer as defined, ham would require an explicit cast to call an Integer method, such as ham.intValue().

4. B. This example uses method chaining. After the call to append(), sb contains "aaa". That result is passed to the first insert() call, which inserts at index 1. At this point sb contains abbaa. That result is passed to the final insert(), which inserts at index 4, resulting in abbaccca.

5. G. The question is trying to distract you into paying attention to logical equality versus object reference equality. The exam creators are hoping you will miss the fact that line 18 does not compile. Java does not allow you to compare String and StringBuilder using ==.

6. B. A String is immutable. Calling concat() returns a new String but does not change the original. A StringBuilder is mutable. Calling append() adds characters to the existing character sequence along with returning a reference to the same object.

7. A, B, F. Remember that indexes are zero-based, which means that index 4 corresponds to 5 and option A is correct. For option B, the replace() method starts the replacement at index 2 and ends before index 4. This means two characters are replaced, and charAt(3) is called on the intermediate value of 1265. The character at index 3 is 5, making option B correct. Option C is similar, making the intermediate value 126 and returning 6.

Option D results in an exception since there is no character at index 5. Option E is incorrect. It does not compile because the parentheses for the length() method are missing. Finally, option F's replace results in the intermediate value 145. The character at index 2 is 5, so option F is correct.

8. A, D, E. substring() has two forms. The first takes the index to start with and the index to stop immediately before. The second takes just the index to start with and goes to the end of the String. Remember that indexes are zero-based. The first call starts at index 1 and ends with index 2 since it needs to stop before index 3. The second call starts at index 7 and ends in the same place, resulting in an empty String. This prints out a blank line. The final call starts at index 7 and goes to the end of the String.

9. C, F. This question is tricky because it has two parts. The first is trying to see if you know that String objects are immutable. Line 17 returns "PURR", but the result is ignored and not stored in s1. Line 18 returns "purr" since there is no whitespace present, but the result is again ignored. Line 19 returns "ur" because it starts with index 1 and ends before index 3 using zero-based indexes. The result is ignored again. Finally, on line 20 something happens. We concatenate three new characters to s1 and now have a String of length 7, making option C correct.

For the second part, a += 2 expands to a = a + 2. A String concatenated with any other type gives a String. Lines 22, 23, and 24 all append to a, giving a result of "2cfalse". The if statement on line 27 returns true because the values of the two String objects are the same using object equality. The if statement on line 26 returns false because the two String objects are not the same in memory. One comes directly from the string pool, and the other comes from building using String operations.

10. A, G. The substring() method includes the starting index but not the ending index. When called with 1 and 2, it returns a single character String, making option A correct and option E incorrect. Calling substring() with 2 as both parameters is legal. It returns an empty String, making options B and F incorrect. Java does not allow the indexes to be specified in reverse order. Option G is correct because it throws a StringIndexOutOfBoundsException. Finally, option H is incorrect because it returns an empty String.

11. A. First, we delete the characters at index 2 until the character one before index 8. At this point, 0189 is in numbers. The following line uses method chaining. It appends a dash to the end of the characters sequence, resulting in 0189-, and then inserts a plus sign at index 2, resulting in 01+89-.

12. F. This is a trick question. The first line does not compile because you cannot assign a String to a StringBuilder. If that line were StringBuilder b = new StringBuilder("rumble"), the code would compile and print rum4. Watch out for this sort of trick on the exam. You could easily spend a minute working out the character positions for no reason at all.

13. A, C. The reverse() method is the easiest way of reversing the characters in a StringBuilder; therefore, option A is correct. In option B, substring() returns a String, which is not stored anywhere. Option C uses method chaining. First, it creates the value "JavavaJ$". Then, it removes the first three characters, resulting in "avaJ$". Finally, it removes the last character, resulting in "avaJ". Option D throws an exception because you cannot delete the character after the last index. Remember that deleteCharAt() uses indexes that are zero-based, and length() counts starting with 1.

14. C, E, F. Option C uses the variable name as if it were a type, which is clearly illegal. Options E and F don't specify any size. Although it is legal to leave out the size for later dimensions of a multidimensional array, the first one is required. Option A declares a legal 2D array. Option B declares a legal 3D array. Option D declares a legal 2D array. Remember that it is normal to see on the exam types you might not have learned. You aren't expected to know anything about them.

15. A, H. Arrays define a property called length. It is not a method, so parentheses are not allowed, making option A correct. The ArrayList class defines a method called size(), making option H the other correct answer.

16. A, F, G. An array is not able to change size, making option A correct and option B incorrect. Neither is immutable, making options C and D incorrect. The elements can change in value. An array does not override equals(), so it uses object equality, making option E incorrect. ArrayList does override equals() and defines it as the same elements in the same order, making option F correct.

    The compiler does not know when an index is out of bounds and thus can't give you a compiler error, making option G correct. The code will throw an exception at runtime, though, making option H the final incorrect answer.

17. F. The code does not compile because list is instantiated using generics. Only String objects can be added to list, and 7 is an int.

18. C. The put() method is used on a Map rather than a List or Set, making options A and D incorrect. The replace() method does not exist on either of these interfaces. Finally, the set method is valid on a List rather than a Set because a List has an index. Therefore, option C is correct.

19. A, F. The code compiles and runs fine. However, an array must be sorted for binarySearch() to return a meaningful result. Option F is correct because line 14 prints a number, but the behavior is undefined. Line 8 creates a list backed by a fixed-size array of 4. Line 10 sorts it. Line 12 converts it back to an array. The brackets aren't in the traditional place, but they are still legal. Line 13 prints the first element, which is now −1, making option A the other correct answer.

20. B, C, E. Remember to watch return types on math operations. One of the tricks is option B on line 24. The round() method returns an int when called with a float. However, we are calling it with a double so it returns a long. The other trick is option C on line 25. The random() method returns a double. Converting from an array to an ArrayList uses Arrays.asList(names). There is no asList() method on an array instance, and option E is correct.

21. D. After sorting, hex contains [30, 3A, 8, FF]. Remember that numbers sort before letters, and strings sort alphabetically. This makes 30 come before 8. A binary search correctly finds 8 at index 2 and 3A at index 1. It cannot find 4F but notices it should be at index 2. The rule when an item isn't found is to negate that index and subtract 1. Therefore, we get −2−1, which is −3.

22. A, B, D. Lines 5 and 7 use autoboxing to convert an int to an Integer. Line 6 does not because valueOf() returns an Integer. Line 8 does not because null is not an int. The code does compile. However, when the for loop tries to unbox null into an int, it fails and throws a NullPointerException.

23. B. The first if statement is false because the variables do not point to the same object. The second if statement is true because ArrayList implements equality to mean the same elements in the same order.

24. D, E. The first line of code in the method creates a fixed size List backed by an array. This means option D is correct, making options B and F incorrect. The second line of code in the method creates an immutable list, which means no changes are allowed. Therefore, option E is correct, making options A and C incorrect.

25. A, B, D. The compare() method returns a positive integer when the arrays are different and s1 is larger. This is the case for option A since the element at index 1 comes first alphabetically. It is not the case for option C because the s4 is longer or option E because the arrays are the same.

    The mismatch() method returns a positive integer when the arrays are different in a position index 1 or greater. This is the case for option B since the difference is at index 1. It is not the case for option D because the s3 is shorter than the s4 or option F because there is no difference.

Chapter 6: Lambdas and Functional Interfaces

1. A. This code is correct. Line 8 creates a lambda expression that checks whether the age is less than 5. Since there is only one parameter and it does not specify a type, the parentheses around the type parameter are optional. Lines 11 and 13 use the `Predicate` interface, which declares a `test()` method.

2. C. The interface takes two `int` parameters. The code on line 7 attempts to use them as if one is a `String`. It is tricky to use types in a lambda when they are implicitly specified. Remember to check the interface for the real type.

3. A, D, F. The `removeIf()` method expects a `Predicate`, which takes a parameter list of one parameter using the specified type. Options B and C are incorrect because they do not use the `return` keyword. This keyword is required to be inside the braces of a lambda body. Option E is incorrect because it is missing the parentheses around the parameter list. This is only optional for a single parameter with an inferred type.

4. A, F. Option B is incorrect because it does not use the `return` keyword. Options C, D, and E are incorrect because the variable e is already in use from the lambda and cannot be redefined. Additionally, option C is missing the `return` keyword, and option E is missing the semicolon.

5. B, D. `Predicate<String>` takes a parameter list of one parameter using the specified type. Options A and F are incorrect because they specify the wrong number of parameters. Option C is incorrect because parentheses are required around the parameter list when the type is specified. Option E is incorrect because the name used in the parameter list does not match the name used in the body.

6. E. While there appears to have been a variable name shortage when this code was written, it does compile. Lambda variables and method names are allowed to be the same. The x lambda parameter is scoped to within each lambda, so it is allowed to be reused. The type is inferred by the method it calls. The first lambda maps x to a `String` and the second to a `Boolean`. Therefore, option E is correct.

7. A, B, E, F. The `forEach()` method with one lambda parameter works with a `List` or a `Set`. Therefore, options A and B are correct. Additionally, options E and F return a `Set` and can be used as well. Options D and G refer to methods that do not exist. Option C is tricky because a `Map` does have a `forEach()` method. However, it uses two lambda parameters rather than one.

8. A, C, F. Option A is correct because a `Supplier` returns a value while a `Consumer` takes one and acts on it. Option C is correct because a `Comparator` returns a negative number, zero, or a positive number depending on the values passed. A `Predicate` always returns a `boolean`. It does have a method named `test()`, making option F correct.

9. A, B, C. Since the scope of start and c is within the lambda, the variables can be declared after it without issue, making options A, B, and C correct. Option D is incorrect because

setting end prevents it from being effectively final. Lambdas are only allowed to reference effectively final variables.

10. C. Since the new `ArrayList<>(set)` constructor makes a copy of set, there are two elements in each of set and list. The `forEach()` methods print each element on a separate line. Therefore, four lines are printed, and option C is the answer.

11. A. The code correctly sorts in descending order. Since uppercase normally sorts before lowercase, the order is reversed here, and option A is correct.

12. C, D, E. The first line takes no parameters, making it a `Supplier`. Option E is correct because Java can autobox from a primitive double to a Double object. Option F is incorrect because it is a `float` rather than a `double`.

    The second line takes one parameter and returns a boolean, making it a `Predicate`. Since the lambda parameter is unused, any generic type is acceptable, and options C and D are both correct.

13. E. Lambdas are only allowed to reference effectively final variables. You can tell the variable j is effectively final because adding a `final` keyword before it wouldn't introduce a compile error. Each time the `else` statement is executed, the variable is redeclared and goes out of scope. Therefore, it is not re-assigned. Similarly, length is effectively final. There are no compile errors, and option E is correct.

14. C. Lambdas are not allowed to redeclare local variables, making options A and B incorrect. Option D is incorrect because setting end prevents it from being effectively final. Lambdas are only allowed to reference effectively final variables. Option C is tricky because it does compile but throws an exception at runtime. Since the question only asks about compilation, option C is correct.

15. C. Set is not an ordered `Collection`. Since it does not have a `sort()` method, the code does not compile, making option C correct.

16. A, D. Method parameters and local variables are effectively final if they aren't changed after initialization. Options A and D meet this criterion.

17. C. Line 8 uses braces around the body. This means the `return` keyword and semicolon are required.

18. D. Lambda parameters are not allowed to use the same name as another variable in the same scope. The variable names s and x are taken from the object declarations and therefore not available to be used inside the lambda.

19. A, C. This interface specifies two `String` parameters. We can provide the parameter list with or without parameter types. However, it needs to be consistent, making option B incorrect. Options D, E, and F are incorrect because they do not use the arrow operator.

20. A, C. `Predicate<String>` takes a parameter list of one parameter using the specified type. Options E and F are incorrect because it specifies the wrong type. Options B and D are incorrect because they use the wrong syntax for the arrow operator.

Chapter 7: Methods and Encapsulation

1. **B, C.** The keyword void is a return type. Only the access modifier or optional specifiers are allowed before the return type. Option C is correct, creating a method with private access. Option B is also correct, creating a method with default access and the optional specifier final. Since default access does not require a modifier, we get to jump right to final. Option A is incorrect because default access omits the access modifier rather than specifying default. Option D is incorrect because Java is case sensitive. It would have been correct if public were the choice. Option E is incorrect because the method already has a void return type. Option F is incorrect because labels are not allowed for methods.

2. **A, D.** Options A and D are correct because the optional specifiers are allowed in any order. Options B and C are incorrect because they each have two return types. Options E and F are incorrect because the return type is before the optional specifier and access modifier, respectively.

3. **A, C, D.** Options A and C are correct because a void method is optionally allowed to have a return statement as long as it doesn't try to return a value. Option B does not compile because null requires a reference object as the return type. Since int is primitive, it is not a reference object. Option D is correct because it returns an int value. Option E does not compile because it tries to return a double when the return type is int. Since a double cannot be assigned to an int, it cannot be returned as one either. Option F does not compile because no value is actually returned.

4. **A, B, F.** Options A and B are correct because the single varargs parameter is the last parameter declared. Option F is correct because it doesn't use any varargs parameters. Option C is incorrect because the varargs parameter is not last. Option D is incorrect because two varargs parameters are not allowed in the same method. Option E is incorrect because the ... for a varargs must be after the type, not before it.

5. **D, F.** Option D passes the initial parameter plus two more to turn into a varargs array of size 2. Option F passes the initial parameter plus an array of size 2. Option A does not compile because it does not pass the initial parameter. Option E does not compile because it does not declare an array properly. It should be new boolean[] {true, true}. Option B creates a varargs array of size 0, and option C creates a varargs array of size 1.

6. **D.** Option D is correct. This is the common implementation for encapsulation by setting all fields to be private and all methods to be public. Option A is incorrect because protected access allows everything that package-private access allows and additionally allows subclasses access. Option B is incorrect because the class is public. This means that other classes can see the class. However, they cannot call any of the methods or read any of the fields. It is essentially a useless class. Option C is incorrect because package-private access applies to the whole package. Option E is incorrect because Java has no such wildcard access capability.

7. **B, C, D, F.** The two classes are in different packages, which means private access and default (package-private) access will not compile. This causes compile errors in lines 5, 6, and 7, making options B, C, and D correct answers. Additionally, protected access will not compile since School does not inherit from Classroom. This causes the compiler error on line 9, making option F a correct answer as well.

8. A, B, E. Encapsulation allows using methods to get and set instance variables so other classes are not directly using them, making options A and B correct. Instance variables must be private for this to work, making option E correct and option D incorrect. While there are common naming conventions, they are not required, making option C incorrect.

9. B, D, F. Option A is incorrect because the methods differ only in return type. Option C is tricky. It is incorrect because var is not a valid return type. Remember that var can be used only for local variables. Option E is incorrect because the method signature is identical once the generic types are erased. Options B and D are correct because they represent interface and superclass relationships. Option F is correct because the arrays are of different types.

10. B. Rope runs line 3, setting LENGTH to 5, and then immediately after runs the static initializer, which sets it to 10. Line 5 in the Chimp class calls the static method normally and prints swing and a space. Line 6 also calls the static method. Java allows calling a static method through an instance variable although it is not recommended. Line 7 uses the static import on line 2 to reference LENGTH.

11. B, E. Line 10 does not compile because static methods are not allowed to call instance methods. Even though we are calling play() as if it were an instance method and an instance exists, Java knows play() is really a static method and treats it as such. If line 10 is removed, the code works. It does not throw a NullPointerException on line 17 because play() is a static method. Java looks at the type of the reference for rope2 and translates the call to Rope.play().

12. D. There are two details to notice in this code. First, note that RopeSwing has an instance initializer and not a static initializer. Since RopeSwing is never constructed, the instance initializer does not run. The other detail is that length is static. Changes from one object update this common static variable.

13. E. If a variable is static final, it must be set exactly once, and it must be in the declaration line or in a static initialization block. Line 4 doesn't compile because bench is not set in either of these locations. Line 15 doesn't compile because final variables are not allowed to be set after that point. Line 11 doesn't compile because name is set twice: once in the declaration and again in the static block. Line 12 doesn't compile because rightRope is set twice as well. Both are in static initialization blocks.

14. B. The two valid ways to do this are import static java.util.Collections.*; and import static java.util.Collections.sort;. Option A is incorrect because you can do a static import only on static members. Classes such as Collections require a regular import. Option C is nonsense as method parameters have no business in an import. Options D, E, and F try to trick you into reversing the syntax of import static.

15. E. The argument on line 17 is a short. It can be promoted to an int, so print() on line 5 is invoked. The argument on line 18 is a boolean. It can be autoboxed to a Boolean, so print() on line 11 is invoked. The argument on line 19 is a double. It can be autoboxed to a Double, so print() on line 11 is invoked. Therefore, the output is int-Object-Object-, and the correct answer is option E.

16. B. Since Java is pass-by-value and the variable on line 8 never gets reassigned, it stays as 9. In the method square, x starts as 9. The y value becomes 81, and then x gets set to −1. Line 9 does set result to 81. However, we are printing out value and that is still 9.

17. B, D, E. Since Java is pass-by-value, assigning a new object to a does not change the caller. Calling append() does affect the caller because both the method parameter and the caller have a reference to the same object. Finally, returning a value does pass the reference to the caller for assignment to s3.

18. B, C, E. The variable value1 is a final instance variable. It can be set only once: in the variable declaration, an instance initializer, or a constructor. Option A does not compile because the final variable was already set in the declaration. The variable value2 is a static variable. Both instance and static initializers are able to access static variables, making options B and E correct. The variable value3 is an instance variable. Options D and F do not compile because a static initializer does not have access to instance variables.

19. A, E. The 100 parameter is an int and so calls the matching int method. When this method is removed, Java looks for the next most specific constructor. Java prefers autoboxing to varargs, so it chooses the Integer constructor. The 100L parameter is a long. Since it can't be converted into a smaller type, it is autoboxed into a Long, and then the method for Object is called.

20. A, C, F. Option B is incorrect because var cannot be a method parameter. It must be a local variable or lambda parameter. Option D is incorrect because the method declarations are identical. Option E is tricky. The variable long is illegal because *long* is a reserved word. Options A, C, and F are correct because they represent different types.

21. A, B, C. Instance variables must include the private access modifier, making option D incorrect. While it is common for methods to be public, this is not required. Options A, B, and C are all correct, although some are more useful than others. Since the class can be written to be encapsulated, options E and F are incorrect.

Chapter 8: Class Design

1. E. Options A and B will not compile because constructors cannot be called without new. Options C and D will compile but will create a new object rather than setting the fields in this one. The result is the program will print 0, not 2, at runtime. Calling an overloaded constructor, using this(), or a parent constructor, using super(), is only allowed on the first line of the constructor, making option E correct and option F incorrect. Finally, option G is incorrect because the program prints 0 without any changes, not 2.

2. B, C. Overloaded methods have the method name but a different signature (the method parameters differ), making option A incorrect. Overridden instance methods and hidden static methods must have the same signature (the name and method parameters must match), making options B and C correct. Overloaded methods can have different return types, while overridden and hidden methods can have covariant return types. None of these methods are required to use the same return type, making options D, E, and F incorrect.

3. F. The code will not compile as is, because the parent class Mammal does not define a no-argument constructor. For this reason, the first line of a Platypus constructor should be an explicit call to super(int), making option F the correct answer. Option E is incorrect, as line 7 compiles without issue. The sneeze() method in the Mammal class is marked private, meaning it is not inherited and therefore is not overridden in the Platypus class. For this reason, the sneeze() method in the Platypus class is free to define the same method with any return type.

4. E. The code compiles, making option F incorrect. An instance variable with the same name as an inherited instance variable is hidden, not overridden. This means that both variables exist, and the one that is used depends on the location and reference type. Because the main() method uses a reference type of Speedster to access the numSpots variable, the variable in the Speedster class, not the Cheetah class, must be set to 50. Option A is incorrect, as it reassigns the method parameter to itself. Option B is incorrect, as it assigns the method parameter the value of the instance variable in Cheetah, which is 0. Option C is incorrect, as it assigns the value to the instance variable in Cheetah, not Speedster. Option D is incorrect, as it assigns the method parameter the value of the instance variable in Speedster, which is 0. Options A, B, C, and D all print 0 at runtime. Option E is the only correct answer, as it assigns the instance variable numSpots in the Speedster class a value of 50. The numSpots variable in the Speedster class is then correctly referenced in the main() method, printing 50 at runtime.

5. A. The code compiles and runs without issue, so options E and F are incorrect. The Arthropod class defines two overloaded versions of the printName() method. The printName() method that takes an int value on line 5 is correctly overridden in the Spider class on line 9. Remember, an overridden method can have a broader access modifier, and protected access is broader than package-private access. Because of polymorphism, the overridden method replaces the method on all calls, even if an Arthropod reference variable is used, as is done in the main() method. For these reasons, the overridden method is called on lines 14 and 15, printing Spider twice. Note that the short value is automatically cast to the larger type of int, which then uses the overridden method. Line 16 calls the overloaded method in the Arthropod class, as the long value 5L does not match the overridden method, resulting in Arthropod being printed. Therefore, option A is the correct answer.

6. B, E. The signature must match exactly, making option A incorrect. There is no such thing as a covariant signature. An overridden method must not declare any new checked exceptions or a checked exception that is broader than the inherited method. For this reason, option B is correct, and option D is incorrect. Option C is incorrect because an overridden method may have the same access modifier as the version in the parent class. Finally, overridden methods must have covariant return types, and only void is covariant with void, making option E correct.

7. A, C. Option A is correct, as this(3) calls the constructor declared on line 5, while this("") calls the constructor declared on line 10. Option B does not compile, as inserting this() at line 3 results in a compiler error, since there is no matching constructor. Option C is correct, as short can be implicitly cast to int, resulting in this((short)1) calling the constructor declared on line 5. In addition, this(null) calls the String constructor declared on line 10. Option D does not compile because inserting super() on line 14 results in an invalid constructor call. The Howler class does not contain a no-argument constructor. Option E is also incorrect. Inserting this(2L) at line 3 results in a recursive constructor definition. The compiler detects this and reports an error. Option F is incorrect, as using super(null) on line 14 does not match any parent constructors. If an explicit cast

was used, such as super((Integer)null), then the code would have compiled but would throw an exception at runtime during unboxing. Finally, option G is incorrect because the superclass Howler does not contain a no-argument constructor. Therefore, the constructor declared on line 13 will not compile without an explicit call to an overloaded or parent constructor.

8. C. The code compiles and runs without issue, making options F and G incorrect. Line 16 initializes a PolarBear instance and assigns it to the bear reference. The variable declaration and instance initializers are run first, setting value to tac. The constructor declared on line 5 is called, resulting in value being set to tacb. Remember, a static main() method can access private constructors declared in the same class. Line 17 creates another PolarBear instance, replacing the bear reference declared on line 16. First, value is initialized to tac as before. Line 17 calls the constructor declared on line 8, since String is the narrowest match of a String literal. This constructor then calls the overloaded constructor declared on line 5, resulting in value being updated to tacb. Control returns to the previous constructor, with line 10 updating value to tacbf, and making option C the correct answer. Note that if the constructor declared on line 8 did not exist, then the constructor on line 12 would match. Finally, the bear reference is properly cast to PolarBear on line 18, making the value parameter accessible.

9. B, F. A valid override of a method with generic arguments must have a return type that is covariant, with matching generic type parameters. Option B is correct, as it is just restating the original return type. Option F is also correct, as ArrayList is a subtype of List. The rest of the method declarations do not compile. Options A and D are invalid because the access levels, package-private and private, are more restrictive than the inherited access modifier, protected. Option C is incorrect because while String is a subtype of CharSequence, the generic type parameters must match exactly. Finally, option E is incorrect as Object is a supertype of List and therefore not covariant.

10. D. The code doesn't compile, so option A is incorrect. The first compilation error is on line 2, as var cannot be used as a constructor argument type. The second compilation error is on line 8. Since Rodent declares at least one constructor and it is not a no-argument constructor, Beaver must declare a constructor with an explicit call to a super() constructor. Line 9 contains two compilation errors. First, the return types are not covariant since Number is a supertype, not a subtype, of Integer. Second, the inherited method is static, but the overridden method is not, making this an invalid override. The code contains four compilation errors, although they are limited to three lines, making option D the correct answer.

11. B, C, E. An object may be cast to a supertype without an explicit cast but requires an explicit cast to be cast to a subtype, making option A incorrect. Option B is correct, as an interface method argument may take any reference type that implements the interface. Option C is also correct, as a method that accepts java.lang.Object can accept any variable since all objects inherit java.lang.Object. This also includes primitives, which can be autoboxed to their wrapper classes. Some cast exceptions can be detected as errors at compile-time, but others can only be detected at runtime, so option D is incorrect. Due to the nature of polymorphism, a final instance method cannot be overridden in a subclass, so calls in the parent class will not be replaced, making option E correct. Finally, polymorphism applies to classes and interfaces alike, making option F incorrect.

12. A, B, E, F. The code compiles if the correct type is inserted in the blank, so option G is incorrect. The setSnake() method requires an instance of Snake or any subtype of Snake. The Cobra class is a subclass of Snake, so it is a subtype. The GardenSnake class is a subclass of Cobra, which, in turn, is a subclass of Snake, also making GardenSnake a subtype of Snake. For these reasons, options A, B, and E are correct. Option C is incorrect because Object is a supertype of Snake, not a subtype, as all instances inherit Object. Option D is incorrect as String is an unrelated class and does not inherit Snake. Finally, a null value can always be passed as an object value, regardless of type, so option F is correct.

13. A, G. The compiler will insert a default no-argument constructor if the class compiles and does not define any constructors. Options A and G fulfill this requirement, making them the correct answers. The bird() declaration in option G is a method declaration, not a constructor. Options B and C do not compile. Since the constructor name does not match the class name, the compiler treats these as methods with missing return types. Options D, E, and F all compile, but since they declare at least one constructor, the compiler does not supply one.

14. B, E, F. A class can only directly extend a single class, making option A incorrect. A class can implement any number of interfaces, though, making option B correct. Option C is incorrect because primitive types do not inherit java.lang.Object. If a class extends another class, then it is a subclass, not a superclass, making option D incorrect. A class that implements an interface is a subtype of that interface, making option E correct. Finally, option F is correct as it is an accurate description of multiple inheritance, which is not permitted in Java.

15. D. The code compiles, so option G is incorrect. Based on order of initialization, the static components are initialized first, starting with the Arachnid class, since it is the parent of the Scorpion class, which initializes the StringBuilder to u. The static initializer in Scorpion then updates sb to contain uq, which is printed twice by lines 13 and 14 along with spaces separating the values. Next, an instance of Arachnid is initialized on line 15. There are two instance initializers in Arachnid, and they run in order, appending cr to the StringBuilder, resulting in a value of uqcr. An instance of Scorpion is then initialized on line 16. The instance initializers in the superclass Arachnid run first, appending cr again and updating the value of sb to uqcrcr. Finally, the instance initializer in Scorpion runs and appends m. The program completes with the final value printed being uq uq uqcrcrm, making option D the correct answer.

16. B. A valid override of a method with generic arguments must have the same signature with the same generic types. For this reason, only option B is correct. Because of type erasure, the generic type parameter will be removed when the code is compiled. Therefore, the compiler requires that the types match. Options A and D do not compile for this reason. Options C, E, and F do compile, but since the generic class changed, they are overloads, not overrides. Remember, covariant types only apply to return values of overridden methods, not method parameters.

17. F. Options A–E are incorrect statements about inheritance and variables, making option F the correct answer. Option A is incorrect because variables can only be hidden, not overridden via inheritance. This means that they are still accessible in the parent class and do not replace the variable everywhere, as overriding does. Options B, C, and E are also incorrect as they more closely match rules for overriding methods. Also, option E is invalid as variables do not throw exceptions. Finally, option D is incorrect as this is a rule for hiding `static` methods.

18. C, F. Calling an overloaded constructor with `this()` may be used only as the first line of a constructor, making options A and B incorrect. Accessing `this.variableName` can be performed from any instance method, constructor, or instance initializer, but not from a `static` method or `static` initializer. For this reason, option C is correct, and option D is incorrect. Option E is tricky. The default constructor is written by the compiler only if no user-defined constructors were provided. And `this()` can only be called from a constructor in the same class. Since there can be no user-defined constructors in the class if a default constructor was created, it is impossible for option E to be true. Since the `main()` method is in the same class, it can call `private` methods in the class, making option F correct.

19. C, F. The `eat()` method is `private` in the `Mammal` class. Since it is not inherited in the `Primate` class, it is neither overridden nor overloaded, making options A and B incorrect. The `drink()` method in `Mammal` is correctly hidden in the `Monkey` class, as the signature is the same, making option C correct and option D incorrect. The version in the `Monkey` class throws a new exception, but it is unchecked; therefore, it is allowed. The `dance()` method in `Mammal` is correctly overloaded in the `Monkey` class because the signatures are not the same, making option E incorrect and option F correct. For methods to be overridden, the signatures must match exactly. Finally, line 12 is an invalid override and does not compile, as `int` is not covariant with `void`, making options G and H both incorrect.

20. F. The `Reptile` class defines a constructor, but it is not a no-argument constructor. Therefore, the `Lizard` constructor must explicitly call `super()`, passing in an `int` value. For this reason, line 9 does not compile, and option F is the correct answer. If the `Lizard` class were corrected to call the appropriate `super()` constructor, then the program would print `BALizard` at runtime, with the `static` initializer running first, followed by the instance initializer, and finally the method call using the overridden method.

21. E. The program compiles and runs without issue, making options A through D incorrect. The `fly()` method is correctly overridden in each subclass since the signature is the same, the access modifier is less restrictive, and the return types are covariant. For covariance, `Macaw` is a subtype of `Parrot`, which is a subtype of `Bird`, so overridden return types are valid. Likewise, the constructors are all implemented properly, with explicit calls to the parent constructors as needed. Line 19 calls the overridden version of `fly()` defined in the `Macaw` class, as overriding replaces the method regardless of the reference type. This results in `feathers` being assigned a value of 3. The `Macaw` object is then cast to `Parrot`, which is allowed because `Macaw` inherits `Parrot`. The `feathers` variable is visible since it is defined in the `Bird` class, and line 19 prints 3, making option E the correct answer.

22. D. The code compiles and runs without issue, making option E incorrect. The `Child` class overrides the `setName()` method and hides the `static` name variable defined in the inherited `Person` class. Since variables are only hidden, not overridden, there are two distinct name variables accessible, depending on the location and reference type. Line 8 creates a `Child` instance, which is implicitly cast to a `Person` reference type on line 9. Line 10 uses the `Child` reference type, updating `Child.name` to `Elysia`. Line 11 uses the `Person` reference type, updating `Person.name` to `Sophia`. Lines 12 and 13 both call the overridden `setName()` instance method declared on line 6. This sets `Child.name` to `Webby` on line 12 and then to `Olivia` on line 13. The final values of `Child.name` and `Person.name` are `Olivia` and `Sophia`, respectively, making option D the correct answer.

23. B. The program compiles, making option F incorrect. The constructors are called from the child class upward, but since each line of a constructor is a call to another constructor, via this() or super(), they are ultimately executed in top-down manner. On line 29, the main() method calls the Fennec() constructor declared on line 19. Remember, integer literals in Java are considered int by default. This constructor calls the Fox() constructor defined on line 12, which in turn calls the overloaded Fox() constructor declared on line 11. Since the constructor on line 11 does not explicitly call a parent constructor, the compiler inserts a call to the no-argument super() constructor, which exists on line 3 of the Canine class. Since Canine does not extend any classes, the compiler will also insert a call to the no-argument super() constructor defined in java.lang.Object, although this has little impact on the output. Line 3 is then executed, adding q to the output, and the compiler chain is unwound. Line 11 then executes, adding p, followed by line 14, adding z. Finally, line 21 is executed, and j is added, resulting in a final value for logger of qpzj, and making option B correct. For the exam, remember to follow constructors from the lowest level upward to determine the correct pathway, but then execute them from the top down using the established order.

24. A, D, F. Polymorphism is the property of an object to take on many forms. Part of polymorphism is that methods are replaced through overriding wherever they are called, regardless of whether they're in a parent or child class. For this reason, option A is correct, and option E incorrect. With hidden static methods, Java relies on the location and reference type to determine which method is called, making option B incorrect and F correct. Finally, making a method final, not static, prevents it from being overridden, making option D correct and option C incorrect.

25. C. The code compiles and runs without issue, making options E and F incorrect. First, the class is initialized, starting with the superclass Antelope and then the subclass Gazelle. This involves invoking the static variable declarations and static initializers. The program first prints 1, followed by 8. Then, we follow the constructor pathway from the object created on line 14 upward, initializing each class instance using a top-down approach. Within each class, the instance initializers are run, followed by the referenced constructors. The Antelope instance is initialized, printing 24, followed by the Gazelle instance, printing 93. The final output is 182493, making option C the correct answer.

26. F. The code does not compile, so options A through C are incorrect. Both lines 5 and 12 do not compile, as this() is used instead of this. Remember, this() refers to calling a constructor, whereas this is a reference to the current instance. Next, the compiler does not allow casting to an unrelated class type. Since Orangutan is not a subclass of Primate, the cast on line 15 is invalid, and the code does not compile. Due to these three lines containing compilation errors, option F is the correct answer. Note that if Orangutan was made a subclass of Primate and the this() references were changed to this, then the code would compile and print 3 at runtime.

Chapter 9: Advanced Class Design

1. B, E. A method that does not declare a body is by definition abstract, making option E correct. All abstract interface methods are assumed to be public, making option B correct. Interface methods cannot be marked protected, so option A is incorrect. Interface methods can be marked static or default, although if they are, they must provide a body, making options C and F incorrect. Finally, void is a return type, not a modifier, so option D is incorrect.

2. A, B, D, E. The code compiles without issue, so option G is incorrect. The blank can be filled with any class or interface that is a supertype of TurtleFrog. Option A is the direct superclass of TurtleFrog, and option B is the same class, so both are correct. BrazilianHornedFrog is not a superclass of TurtleFrog, so option C is incorrect. TurtleFrog inherits the CanHop interface, so option D is correct. All classes inherit Object, so option E is also correct. Finally, Long is an unrelated class that is not a superclass of TurtleFrog and is therefore incorrect.

3. B, C. Concrete classes are, by definition, not abstract, so option A is incorrect. A concrete class must implement all inherited abstract methods, so option B is correct. Concrete classes can be optionally marked final, so option C is correct. Option D is incorrect; a superclass may have already implemented an inherited interface method. The concrete class only needs to implement the inherited abstract methods. Finally, a method in a concrete class that implements an inherited abstract method overrides the method. While the method signature must match, the method declaration does not need to match, such as using a covariant return type or changing the throws declaration. For these reasons, option E is incorrect.

4. E. First, the declarations of HasExoskeleton and Insect are correct and do not contain any errors, making options C and D incorrect. The concrete class Beetle extends Insect and inherits two abstract methods, getNumberOfSections() and getNumberOfLegs(). The Beetle class includes an overloaded version of getNumberOfSections() that takes an int value. The method declaration is valid, making option F incorrect, although it does not satisfy the abstract method requirement. For this reason, only one of the two abstract methods is properly overridden. The Beetle class therefore does not compile, and option E is correct. Since the code fails to compile, options A and B are incorrect.

5. C, F. All interface variables are implicitly assumed to be public, static, and final, making options C and F correct. Option A and G, private and default (package-private), are incorrect since they conflict with the implicit public access modifier. Options B and D are incorrect, as nonstatic and const are not modifiers. Finally, option E is incorrect because a variable cannot be marked abstract.

6. D, E. Lines 1 and 2 are declared correctly, with the implicit modifier abstract being applied to the interface and the implicit modifiers public, static, and final being applied to the interface variable, making options B and C incorrect. Option D is correct, as an abstract method cannot include a body. Option E is also correct because the wrong keyword is used. A class implements an interface; it does not extend it. Option F is incorrect as the implementation of eatGrass() in IsAPlant does not have the same signature; therefore, it is an overload, not an override.

7. C. The code does not compile because the isBlind() method in Nocturnal is not marked abstract and does not contain a method body. The rest of the lines compile without issue, making option C the only correct answer. If the abstract modifier was added to line 2, then the code would compile and print false at runtime, making option B the correct answer.

8. C. The code compiles without issue, so option A is incorrect. Option B is incorrect, as an abstract class could implement HasVocalCords without the need to override the makeSound() method. Option C is correct; a class that implements CanBark automatically inherits its abstract methods, in this case makeSound() and bark(). Option D is incorrect, as a concrete class that implements Dog may be optionally marked final. Finally, an interface can extend multiple interfaces, so option E is incorrect.

9. B, C, E, F. Member inner classes, including both classes and interfaces, can be marked with any of the four access modifiers: public, protected, default (package-private), or private. For this reason, options B, C, E, and F are correct. Options A and D are incorrect as static and final are not access modifiers.

10. C, G. The implicitly abstract interface method on line 6 does not compile because it is missing a semicolon (;), making option C correct. Line 7 compiles, as it provides an overloaded version of the fly() method. Lines 5, 9, and 10 do not contain any compilation errors, making options A, E, and F incorrect. Line 13 does not compile because the two inherited fly() methods, declared on line 6 and 10, conflict with each other. The compiler recognizes that it is impossible to create a class that overrides fly() to return both String and int, since they are not covariant return types, and therefore blocks the Falcon class from compiling. For this reason, option G is correct.

11. A, B, F. The final modifier can be used with private and static, making options A and F correct. Marking a private method final is redundant but allowed. A private method may also be marked static, making option B correct. Options C, D, and E are incorrect because methods marked static, private, or final cannot be overridden; therefore, they cannot be marked abstract.

12. A, E. Line 11 does not compile because a Tangerine and Gala are unrelated types, which the compiler can enforce for classes, making option A correct. Line 12 is valid since Citrus extends Tangerine and would print true at runtime if the rest of the class compiled. Likewise, Gala implements Apple, so line 13 would also print true at runtime if the rest of the code compiled.

Line 14 does compile, even though Apple and Tangerine are unrelated types. While the compiler can enforce unrelated type rules for classes, it has limited ability to do so for interfaces, since there may be a subclass of Tangerine that implements the Apple interface. Therefore, this line would print false if the rest of the code compiled.

Line 15 does not compile. Since Citrus is marked final, the compiler knows that there cannot be a subclass of Citrus that implements Apple, so it can enforce the unrelated type rule. For this reason, option E is correct.

13. G. The interface and classes are structured correctly, but the body of the main() method contains a compiler error. The Orca object is implicitly cast to a Whale reference on line 7. This is permitted because Orca is a subclass of Whale. By performing the cast, the whale reference on line 8 does not have access to the dive(int... depth) method. For this reason, line 8 does not compile. Since this is the only compilation error, option G is the correct answer. If the reference type of whale was changed to Orca, then the main() would compile and print Orca diving deeper 3 at runtime, making option B the correct answer. Note that line 16 compiles because the interface variable MAX is inherited as part of the class structure.

14. A, C, E. A class may extend another class, and an interface may extend another interface, making option A correct. Option B is incorrect. An abstract class can contain concrete instance and `static` methods. Interfaces can also contain nonabstract methods, although knowing this is not required for the 1Z0-815 exam. Option C is correct, as both can contain `static` constants. Option D is incorrect. The compiler only inserts implicit modifiers for interfaces. For abstract classes, the `abstract` keyword must be used on any method that does not define a body. An abstract class must be declared with the `abstract` keyword, while the `abstract` keyword is optional for interfaces. Since both can be declared with the `abstract` keyword, option E is correct. Finally, interfaces do not extend `java.lang.Object`. If they did, then Java would support true multiple inheritance, with multiple possible parent constructors being called as part of initialization. Therefore, option F is incorrect.

15. D. The code compiles without issue. The question is making sure you know that superclass constructors are called in the same manner in abstract classes as they are in nonabstract classes. Line 9 calls the constructor on line 6. The compiler automatically inserts `super()` as the first line of the constructor defined on line 6. The program then calls the constructor on line 3 and prints `Wow-`. Control then returns to line 6, and `Oh-` is printed. Finally, the method call on line 10 uses the version of `fly()` in the `Pelican` class, since it is marked `private` and the reference type of var is resolved as `Pelican`. The final output is `Wow-Oh-Pelican`, making option D the correct answer. Remember that `private` methods cannot be overridden. If the reference type of `chirp` was `Bird`, then the code would not compile as it would not be accessible outside the class.

16. E. The inherited interface method `getNumOfGills(int)` is implicitly `public`; therefore, it must be declared `public` in any concrete class that implements the interface. Since the method uses the default (package-private) modifier in the `ClownFish` class, line 6 does not compile, making option E the correct answer. If the method declaration was corrected to include `public` on line 6, then the program would compile and print 15 at runtime, and option B would be the correct answer.

17. A, E. An inner class can be marked `abstract` or `final`, just like a regular class, making option A correct. A top-level type, such as a class, interface, or enum, can only be marked `public` or default (package-private), making option B incorrect. Option C is incorrect, as a member inner class can be marked `public`, and this would not make it a top-level class. A `.java` file may contain multiple top-level classes, making option D incorrect. The precise rule is that there is at most one `public` top-level type, and that type is used in the filename. Finally, option E is correct. When a member inner class is marked `private`, it behaves like any other `private` members and can be referenced only in the class in which it is defined.

18. A, B, D. The Run interface correctly overrides the inherited method `move()` from the `Walk` interface using a covariant return type. Options A and B are both correct. Notice that the `Leopard` class does not implement or inherit either interface, so the return type of `move()` can be any valid reference type that is compatible with the body returning `null`. Because the `Panther` class inherits both interfaces, it must override a version of `move()` that is covariant with both interfaces. Option C is incorrect, as `List` is not a subtype of `ArrayList`, and using it here conflicts with the Run interface declaration. Option D is correct, as `ArrayList` is compatible with both `List` and `ArrayList` return types. Since the code is capable of compiling, options E and F are incorrect.

19. A, E, F. A class cannot extend any interface, as a class can only extend other classes and interfaces can only extend other interfaces, making option A correct. Java enables only limited multiple inheritance with interfaces, making option B incorrect. True multiple inheritance would be if a class could extend multiple classes directly. Option C is incorrect, as interfaces are implicitly marked abstract. Option D is also incorrect, as interfaces do not contain constructors and do not participate in object initialization. Option E is correct, an interface can extend multiple interfaces. Option F is also correct, as abstract types cannot be instantiated.

20. A, D. The implementation of Elephant and its member inner class SleepsAlot are valid, making options A and D correct. Option B is incorrect, as Eagle must be marked abstract to contain an abstract method. Option C is also incorrect. Since the travel() method does not declare a body, it must be marked abstract in an abstract class. Finally, option E is incorrect, as interface methods are implicitly public. Marking them protected results in a compiler error.

Chapter 10: Exceptions

1. A, C, D, F. Runtime exceptions are unchecked, making option A correct and option B incorrect. Both runtime and checked exceptions can be declared, although only checked exceptions must be handled or declared, making options C and D correct. Legally, you can handle java.lang.Error subclasses, which are not subclasses of Exception, but it's not a good idea, so option E is incorrect. Finally, it is true that all exceptions are subclasses of Throwable, making option F correct.

2. B, D, E. In a method declaration, the keyword throws is used, making option B correct and option A incorrect. To actually throw an exception, the keyword throw is used. The new keyword must be used if the exception is being created. The new keyword is not used when throwing an existing exception. For these reasons, options D and E are correct, while options C and F are incorrect. Since the code compiles with options B, D, and E, option G is incorrect.

3. G. When using a multi-catch block, only one variable can be declared. For this reason, line 9 does not compile and option G correct.

4. B, D. A regular try statement is required to have a catch clause and/or finally clause. If a regular try statement does not have any catch clauses, then it must have a finally block, making option B correct and option A incorrect. Alternatively, a try-with-resources block is not required to have a catch or finally block, making option D correct and option E incorrect. Option C is incorrect, as there is no requirement a program must terminate. Option F is also incorrect. A try-with-resources statement automatically closes all declared resources. While additional resources can be created or declared in a try-with-resources statement, none are required to be closed by a finally block. Option G is also incorrect. The implicit or hidden finally block created by the JVM when a try-with-resources statement is declared is executed first, followed by any programmer-defined finally block.

5. C. Line 5 tries to cast an Integer to a String. Since String does not extend Integer, this is not allowed, and a ClassCastException is thrown, making option C correct. If line 5 were removed, then the code would instead produce a NullPointerException on line 7. Since the program stops after line 5, though, line 7 is never reached.

6. E. The code does not compile, so options A, B, and F are incorrect. The first compiler error is on line 12. Each resource in a try-with-resources statement must have its own data type and be separated by a semicolon (;). The fact that one of the references is declared null does not prevent compilation. Line 15 does not compile because the variable s is already declared in the method. Line 17 also does not compile. The FileNotFoundException, which inherits from IOException and Exception, is a checked exception, so it must be handled in a try/catch block or declared by the method. Because these three lines of code do not compile, option E is the correct answer. Line 14 does compile; since it is an unchecked exception, it does not need to be caught, although in this case it is caught by the catch block on line 15.

7. C. The compiler tests the operation for a valid type but not a valid result, so the code will still compile and run. At runtime, evaluation of the parameter takes place before passing it to the print() method, so an ArithmeticException object is raised, and option C is correct.

8. G. The main() method invokes go(), and A is printed on line 3. The stop() method is invoked, and E is printed on line 14. Line 16 throws a NullPointerException, so stop() immediately ends, and line 17 doesn't execute. The exception isn't caught in go(), so the go() method ends as well, but not before its finally block executes and C is printed on line 9. Because main() doesn't catch the exception, the stack trace displays, and no further output occurs. For these reasons, AEC is printed followed by a stack trace for a NullPointerException, making option G correct.

9. E. The order of catch blocks is important because they're checked in the order they appear after the try block. Because ArithmeticException is a child class of RuntimeException, the catch block on line 7 is unreachable (if an ArithmeticException is thrown in the try block, it will be caught on line 5). Line 7 generates a compiler error because it is unreachable code, making option E correct.

10. B. The main() method invokes start on a new Laptop object. Line 4 prints Starting up_, and then line 5 throws an Exception. Line 6 catches the exception. Line 7 then prints Problem_, and line 8 calls System.exit(0), which terminates the JVM. The finally block does not execute because the JVM is no longer running. For these reasons, option B is correct.

11. D. The runAway() method is invoked within main() on a new Dog object. Line 4 prints 1. The try block executes, and 2 is printed. Line 7 throws a NumberFormatException, so line 8 doesn't execute. The exception is caught on line 9, and line 10 prints 4. Because the exception is handled, execution resumes normally. The runAway() method runs to completion, and line 17 executes, printing 5. That's the end of the program, so the output is 1245, and option D is correct.

12. A. The knockStuffOver() method is invoked on a new Cat object. Line 4 prints 1. The try block is entered, and line 6 prints 2. Line 7 throws a NumberFormatException. It isn't caught, so knockStuffOver() ends. The main() method doesn't catch the exception either, so the program terminates, and the stack trace for the NumberFormatException is printed. For these reasons, option A is correct.

13. A, B, C, D, F. Any Java type, including `Exception` and `RuntimeException`, can be declared as the return type. However, this will simply return the object rather than throw an exception. For this reason, options A and B are correct. Classes listed in the `throws` part of a method declaration must extend `java.lang.Throwable`. This includes `Error`, `Exception`, and `RuntimeException`, making options C, D, and F correct. Arbitrary classes such as `String` can't be declared in a `throws` clause, making option E incorrect.

14. A, C, D, E. A method that declares an exception isn't required to throw one, making option A correct. Unchecked exceptions can be thrown in any method, making options C and E correct. Option D matches the exception type declared, so it's also correct. Option B is incorrect because a broader exception is not allowed.

15. G. The class does not compile because `String` does not implement `AutoCloseable`, making option G the only correct answer.

16. A, B, D, E, F. Any class that extends `RuntimeException` or `Error`, including the classes themselves, is an unchecked exception, making options D and F correct. The classes `ArrayIndexOutOfBoundsException`, `IllegalArgumentException`, and `NumberFormatException` all extend `RuntimeException`, making them unchecked exceptions and options A, B, and E correct. (Sorry, you have to memorize them.) Classes that extend `Exception` but not `RuntimeException` are checked exceptions, making options C and G incorrect.

17. B, F. The `try` block is not capable of throwing an `IOException`. For this reason, declaring it in the `catch` block is considered unreachable code, making option A incorrect. Options B and F are correct, as both are unchecked exceptions that do not extend or inherit from `IllegalArgumentException`. Remember, it is not a good idea to catch `Error` in practice, although because it is possible, it may come up on the exam. Option C is incorrect, but not because of the data type. The variable c is declared already in the method declaration, so it cannot be used again as a local variable in the `catch` block. If the variable name was changed, option C would be correct. Option D is incorrect because the `IllegalArgumentException` inherits from `RuntimeException`, making the first declaration unnecessary. Similarly, option E is incorrect because `NumberFormatException` inherits from `IllegalArgumentException`, making the second declaration unnecessary. Since options B and F are correct, option G is incorrect.

18. B. An `IllegalArgumentException` is used when an unexpected parameter is passed into a method. Option A is incorrect because returning `null` or `-1` is a common return value for searching for data. Option D is incorrect because a `for` loop is typically used for this scenario. Option E is incorrect because you should find out how to code the method and not leave it for the unsuspecting programmer who calls your method. Option C is incorrect because you should run!

19. A, D, E, F. An overridden method is allowed to throw no exceptions at all, making option A correct. It is also allowed to throw new unchecked exceptions, making options E and F correct. Option D is also correct since it matches the signature in the interface. Option B is incorrect because it has the wrong return type for the method signature. Option C is incorrect because an overridden method cannot throw new or broader checked exceptions.

20. B, C, E. Checked exceptions are required to be handled or declared, making option B correct. Unchecked exceptions include both runtime exceptions and errors, both of which may be handled or declared but are not required to be making options C and E correct. Note that handling or declaring `Error` is a bad practice.

21. G. The code does not compile, regardless of what is inserted into the blanks. You cannot add a statement after a line that throws an exception. For this reason, line 8 is unreachable after the exception is thrown on line 7, making option G correct.

22. D, F. A var is not allowed in a `catch` block since it doesn't indicate the exception being caught, making option A incorrect. With multiple `catch` blocks, the exceptions must be ordered from more specific to broader, or be in an unrelated inheritance tree. For these reasons, options D and F are correct, respectively. Alternatively, if a broad exception is listed before a specific exception or the same exception is listed twice, it becomes unreachable. For these reasons, options B and E are incorrect, respectively. Finally, option C is incorrect because the method called inside the `try` block doesn't declare an `IOException` to be thrown. The compiler realizes that `IOException` would be an unreachable `catch` block.

23. A, E. The code begins normally and prints a on line 13, followed by b on line 15. On line 16, it throws an exception that's caught on line 17. Remember, only the most specific matching `catch` is run. Line 18 prints c, and then line 19 throws another exception. Regardless, the `finally` block runs, printing e. Since the `finally` block also throws an exception, that's the one printed.

24. C. The code compiles and runs without issue, so options E and F are incorrect. Since `Sidekick` correctly implements `AutoCloseable`, it can be used in a try-with-resources statement. The first value printed is O on line 9. For this question, you need to remember that a try-with-resources statement executes the resource's `close()` method before a programmer-defined `finally` block. For this reason, L is printed on line 5. Next, the `finally` block is expected, and K is printed. The `requiresAssistance()` method ends, and the `main()` method prints I on line 16. The combined output is `OLKI`, making option C the correct answer.

25. D. The code compiles without issue since `ClassCastException` is a subclass of `RuntimeException` and it is properly listed first, so option E is incorrect. Line 14 executes dividing 1 by itself, resulting in a value of 1. Since no exception is thrown, options B and C are incorrect. The value returned is on track to be 1, but the `finally` block interrupts the flow, causing the method to return 30 instead and making option D correct. Remember, barring use of `System.exit()`, a `finally` block is always executed if the `try` statement is entered, even if no exception is thrown or a `return` statement is used.

Chapter 11: Modules

1. B. Option B is correct since modules allow you to specify which packages can be called by external code. Options C and E are incorrect because they are provided by Java without the module system. Option A is incorrect because there is not a central repository of modules. Option D is incorrect because Java defines types.

2. D. Modules are required to have a module-info.java file at the root directory of the module. Option D matches this requirement.

3. B. Options A, C, and E are incorrect because they refer to keywords that don't exist. The exports keyword is used when allowing a package to be called by code outside of the module, making option B the correct answer. Notice that options D and F are incorrect because requires uses module names and not package names.

4. G. The -m or --module option is used to specify the module and class name. The -p or -module-path option is used to specify the location of the modules. Option D would be correct if the rest of the command were correct. However, running a program requires specifying the package name with periods (.) instead of slashes. Since the command is incorrect, option G is correct.

5. A, F, G. Options C and D are incorrect because there is no use keyword. Options A and F are correct because opens is for reflection and uses declares an API that consumes a service. Option G is also correct as the file can be completely empty. This is just something you have to memorize.

6. B, C. Packages inside a module are not exported by default, making option B correct and option A incorrect. Exporting is necessary for other code to use the packages; it is not necessary to call the main() method at the command line, making option C correct and option D incorrect. The module-info.java file has the correct name and compiles, making options E and F incorrect.

7. D, G. Options A, B, E, and F are incorrect because they refer to keywords that don't exist. The requires transitive keyword is used when specifying a module to be used by the requesting module and any other modules that use the requesting module. Therefore, dog needs to specify the transitive relationship, and option G is correct. The module puppy just needs to require dog, and it gets the transitive dependencies, making option D correct.

8. A, B, D. Options A and B are correct because the -p (--module-path) option can be passed when compiling or running a program. Option D is also correct because jdeps can use the --module-path option when listing dependency information.

9. A, B. The -p specifies the module path. This is just a directory, so all of the options have a legal module path. The -m specifies the module, which has two parts separated by a slash. Options E and F are incorrect since there is no slash. The first part is the module name. It is separated by periods (.) rather than dashes (-), making option C incorrect. The second part is the package and class name, again separated by periods. The package and class names must be legal Java identifiers. Dashes (-) are not allowed, ruling out option D. This leaves options A and B as the correct answers.

10. B. A module claims the packages underneath it. Therefore, options C and D are not good module names. Either would exclude the other package name. Options A and B both meet the criteria of being a higher-level package. However, option A would claim many other packages including `com.sybex`. This is not a good choice, making option B the correct answer.

11. B, D, E, F. This is another question you just have to memorize. The `jmod` command has five modes you need to be able to list: `create`, `extract`, `describe`, `list`, and `hash`. The hash operation is not an answer choice. The other four are making options B, D, E, and F correct.

12. B. The `java` command uses this option to print information when the program loads. You might think `jar` does the same thing since it runs a program too. Alas, this parameter does not exist on `jar`.

13. E. There is a trick here. A module definition uses the keyword `module` rather than `class`. Since the code does not compile, option E is correct. If the code did compile, options A and D would be correct.

14. A. When running `java` with the `-d` option, all the required modules are listed. Additionally, the `java.base` module is listed since it is included automatically. The line ends with `mandated`, making option A correct. The `java.lang` is a trick since that is a package that is imported by default in a class rather than a module.

15. B, D. The `java` command has an `--add-exports` option that allows exporting a package at runtime. However, it is not encouraged to use it, making options B and D the answer.

16. B, C. Option A will run, but it will print details rather than a summary. Options B and C are both valid options for the `jdeps` command. Remember that `-summary` uses a single dash (-).

17. E. The module name is valid as are the `exports` statements. Lines 4 and 5 are tricky because each is valid independently. However, the same module name is not allowed to be used in two `requires` statements. The second one fails to compile on line 5, making option E the answer.

18. A, C. Module names look a lot like package names. Each segment is separated by a period (.) and uses characters valid in Java identifiers. Since identifiers are not allowed to begin with numbers, options E and F are incorrect. Dashes (-) are not allowed either, ruling out options B and D. That leaves options A and C as the correct answers.

19. B, C. Option A is incorrect because JAR files have always been available regardless of the JPMS. Option D is incorrect because bytecode runs on the JVM and is not operating system specific by definition. While it is possible to run the `tar` command, this has nothing to do with Java, making option E incorrect. Option B is one of the correct answers as the `jmod` command creates a JMOD file. Option C is the other correct answer because specifying dependencies is one of the benefits of the JPMS.

20. B, E. Option A is incorrect because describe-module has the d equivalent. Option C is incorrect because module has the m equivalent. Option D is incorrect because module-path has the p equivalent. Option F is incorrect because summary has the s equivalent. Options B and E are the correct answers because they do not have equivalents.

21. G. The -p option is a shorter form of --module-path. Since the same option cannot be specified twice, options B, D, and F are incorrect. The module name and class name are separated with a slash (/). However, the question supplies a package name, not a module name, making option G the answer.

Chapter 12: Java Fundamentals

1. A, D. Instance and static variables can be marked final, making option A correct. Effectively final means a local variable is not marked final but whose value does not change after it is set, making option B incorrect. The final modifier can be applied to classes, but not interfaces, making option C incorrect. Remember, interfaces are implicitly abstract, which is incompatible with final. Option D is correct, as the definition of a final class is that it cannot be extended. Option E is incorrect, as final refers only to the reference to an object, not its contents. Finally, option F is incorrect, as var and final can be used together.

2. C. When an enum contains only a list of values, the semicolon (;) after the list is optional. When an enum contains any other members, such as a constructor or variable, then it is required. Since the code is missing the semicolon, it does not compile, making option C the correct answer. There are no other compilation errors in this code. If the missing semicolon was added, then the program would print 0 1 2 at runtime.

3. C. Popcorn is an inner class. Inner classes are only allowed to contain static variables that are marked final. Since there are no other compilation errors, option C is the only correct answer. If the final modifier was added on line 6, then the code would print 10 at runtime. Note that private constructors can be used by any methods within the same class.

4. B, F. A default interface method is always public, whether you include the identifier or not, making option B correct and option A incorrect. Interfaces cannot contain default static methods, making option C incorrect. Option D is incorrect, as private interface methods are not inherited and cannot be marked abstract. Option E is incorrect, as a method can't be marked both protected and private. Finally, interfaces can include both private and private static methods, making option F correct.

5. B, D. Option B is a valid functional interface, one that could be assigned to a Consumer<Camel> reference. Notice that the final modifier is permitted on variables in the parameter list. Option D is correct, as the exception is being returned as an object and not thrown. This would be compatible with a BiFunction that included RuntimeException as its return type.

Option A is incorrect because it mixes var and non-var parameters. If one argument uses var, then they all must use var. Option C is invalid because the variable b is used twice. Option E is incorrect, as a return statement is permitted only inside braces ({}). Option F is incorrect because the variable declaration requires a semicolon (;) after it. Finally, option G is incorrect. If the type is specified for one argument, then it must be specified for each and every argument.

6. C, E. You can reduce code duplication by moving shared code from `default` or `static` methods into a `private` or `private static` method. For this reason, option C is correct. Option E is also correct, as making interface methods `private` means users of the interface do not have access to them. The rest of the options are not related to `private` methods, although backward compatibility does apply to `default` methods.

7. F. When using an enum in a `switch` statement, the `case` statement must be made up of the enum values only. If the enum name is used in the `case` statement value, then the code does not compile. For example, `VANILLA` is acceptable but `Flavors.VANILLA` is not. For this reason, the three `case` statements do not compile, making option F the correct answer. If these three lines were corrected, then the code would compile and produce a `NullPointerException` at runtime.

8. A, C. A functional interface can contain any number of nonabstract methods including `default`, `private`, `static`, and `private static`. For this reason, option A is correct, and option D is incorrect. Option B is incorrect, as classes are never considered functional interfaces. A functional interface contains exactly one abstract method, although methods that have matching signatures as `public` methods in `java.lang.Object` do not count toward the single method test. For these reasons, option C is correct, and option E is incorrect. Finally, option F is incorrect. While a functional interface can be marked with the `@FunctionalInterface` annotation, it is not required.

9. G. Trick question—the code does not compile! The `Spirit` class is marked `final`, so it cannot be extended. The `main()` method uses an anonymous inner class that inherits from `Spirit`, which is not allowed. If `Spirit` was not marked `final`, then options C and F would be correct. Option A would print `Booo!!!`, while options B, D, and E would not compile for various reasons.

10. E. The code `OstrichWrangler` class is a `static` nested class; therefore, it cannot access the instance member `count`. For this reason, line 6 does not compile, and option E is correct. If the `static` modifier on line 4 was removed, then the class would compile and produce two files: `Ostrich.class` and `Ostrich$OstrichWrangler.class`. You don't need to know that `$` is the syntax, but you do need to know the number of classes and that `OstrichWrangler` is not a top-level class.

11. D. In this example, `CanWalk` and `CanRun` both implement a `default walk()` method. The definition of `CanSprint` extends these two interfaces and therefore won't compile unless the interface overrides both inherited methods. The version of `walk()` on line 12 is an overload, not an override, since it takes an `int` value. Since the interface doesn't override the methods, the compiler can't decide which `default` method to use, leading to a compiler error and making option D the correct answer.

12. C. The functional interface takes two `int` parameters. The code on line m1 attempts to use them as if one is an `Object`, resulting in a compiler error and making option C the correct answer. It also tries to return `String` even though the return data type for the functional interface method is `boolean`. It is tricky to use types in a lambda when they are implicitly specified. Remember to check the interface for the real type.

13. E, G. For this question, it helps to remember which implicit modifiers the compiler will insert and which it will not. Lines 2 and 3 compile with interface variables assumed to be public, static, and final. Line 4 also compiles, as static methods are assumed to be public if not otherwise marked. Line 5 does not compile. Non-static methods within an interface must be explicitly marked private or default. Line 6 compiles, with the public modifier being added by the compiler. Line 7 does not compile, as interfaces do not have protected members. Finally, line 8 compiles, with no modifiers being added by the compiler.

14. E. Diet is an inner class, which requires an instance of Deer to instantiate. Since the main() method is static, there is no such instance. Therefore, the main() method does not compile, and option E is correct. If a reference to Deer were used, such as calling new Deer().new Diet(), then the code would compile and print bc at runtime.

15. G. The isHealthy() method is marked abstract in the enum; therefore, it must be implemented in each enum value declaration. Since only INSECTS implements it, the code does not compile, making option G correct. If the code were fixed to implement the isHealthy() method in each enum value, then the first three values printed would be INSECTS, 1, and true, with the fourth being determined by the implementation of COOK-IES.isHealthy().

16. A, D, E. A valid functional interface is one that contains a single abstract method, excluding any public methods that are already defined in the java.lang.Object class. Transport and Boat are valid functional interfaces, as they each contain a single abstract method: go() and hashCode(String), respectively. Since the other methods are part of Object, they do not count as abstract methods. Train is also a functional interface since it extends Transport and does not define any additional abstract methods.

    Car is not a functional interface because it is an abstract class. Locomotive is not a functional interface because it includes two abstract methods, one of which is inherited. Finally, Spaceship is not a valid interface, let alone a functional interface, because a default method must provide a body. A quick way to test whether an interface is a functional interface is to apply the @FunctionalInterface annotation and check if the code still compiles.

17. A, F. Option A is a valid lambda expression. While main() is a static method, it can access age since it is using a reference to an instance of Hyena, which is effectively final in this method. Remember from your 1Z0-815 studies that var is a reserved type, not a reserved word, and may be used for variable names. Option F is also correct, with the lambda variable being a reference to a Hyena object. The variable is processed using deferred execution in the testLaugh() method.

    Options B and E are incorrect; since the local variable age is not effectively final, this would lead to a compilation error. Option C would also cause a compilation error, since the expression uses the variable name p, which is already declared within the method. Finally, option D is incorrect, as this is not even a lambda expression.

18. C, D, G. Option C is the correct way to create an instance of an inner class Cub using an instance of the outer class Lion. The syntax looks weird, but it creates an object of the outer class and then an object of the inner class from it. Options A, B, and E use incorrect

syntax for creating an instance of the Cub class. Options D and G are the correct way to create an instance of the static nested Den class, as it does not require an instance of Lion, while option F uses invalid syntax. Finally, option H is incorrect since it lacks an instance of Lion. If rest() were an instance method instead of a `static` method, then option H would be correct.

19. D. First off, if a class or interface inherits two interfaces containing `default` methods with the same signature, then it must override the method with its own implementation. The Penguin class does this correctly, so option E is incorrect. The way to access an inherited `default` method is by using the syntax Swim.super.perform(), making option D correct. We agree the syntax is bizarre, but you need to learn it. Options A, B, and C are incorrect and result in compiler errors.

20. A, B, C, D. Effectively final refers to local variables whose value is not changed after it is set. For this reason, option A is correct, and options E and F are incorrect. Options B and C are correct, as lambda expressions can access `final` and effectively final variables. Option D is also correct and is a common test for effectively final variables.

21. B, E. Like classes, interfaces allow instance methods to access `static` members, but not vice versa. Non-`static` `private`, `abstract`, and `default` methods are considered instance methods in interfaces. Line 3 does not compile because the `static` method hunt() cannot access an `abstract` instance method getName(). Line 6 does not compile because the `private static` method sneak() cannot access the `private` instance method roar(). The rest of the lines compile without issue.

22. D, F. Java added `default` methods primarily for backward compatibility. Using a `default` method allows you to add a new method to an interface without having to recompile a class that used an older version of the interface. For this reason, option D is correct. Option F is also correct, as `default` methods in some APIs offer a number of convenient methods to classes that implement the interface. The rest of the options are not related to `default` methods.

23. C, F. Enums are required to have a semicolon (;) after the list of values if there is anything else in the enum. Don't worry, you won't be expected to track down missing semicolons on the whole exam—only on enum questions. For this reason, line 5 should have a semicolon after it since it is the end of the list of enums, making option F correct. Enum constructors are implicitly `private`, making option C correct as well. The rest of the enum compiles without issue.

24. E. Option A does not compile because the second statement within the block is missing a semicolon (;) at the end. Option B is an invalid lambda expression because t is defined twice: in the parameter list and within the lambda expression. Options C and D are both missing a `return` statement and semicolon. Options E and F are both valid lambda expressions, although only option E matches the behavior of the Sloth class. In particular, option F only prints Sleep:, not Sleep: 10.0.

25. B. Zebra.this.x is the correct way to refer to x in the Zebra class. Line 5 defines an abstract local class within a method, while line 11 defines a concrete anonymous class that extends the Stripes class. The code compiles without issue and prints x is 24 at runtime, making option B the correct answer.

Chapter 13: Annotations

1. E. In an annotation, an optional element is specified with the `default` modifier, followed by a constant value. Required elements are specified by not providing a `default` value. Therefore, the lack of the default term indicates the element is required. For this reason, option E is correct.

2. D, F. Line 5 does not compile because = is used to assign a default value, rather than the `default` modifier. Line 7 does not compile because annotation and interface constants are implicitly `public` and cannot be marked `private`. The rest of the lines do not contain any compilation errors.

3. B, D, E. The annotations `@Target` and `@Repeatable` are specifically designed to be applied to annotations, making options D and E correct. Option B is also correct, as `@Deprecated` can be applied to almost any declaration. Option A is incorrect because `@Override` can be applied only to methods. Options C and F are incorrect because they are not the names of built-in annotations.

4. D. Annotations should include metadata (data about data) that is relatively constant, as opposed to attribute data, which is part of the object and can change frequently. The price, sales, inventory, and people who purchased a vehicle could fluctuate often, so using an annotation would be a poor choice. On the other hand, the number of passengers a vehicle is rated for is extra information about the vehicle and unlikely to change once established. Therefore, it is appropriate metadata and best served using an annotation.

5. B, C. Line 4 does not compile because the default value of an element must be a non-`null` constant expression. Line 5 also does not compile because an element type must be one of the predefined immutable types: a primitive, `String`, `Class`, enum, another annotation, or an array of these types. The rest of the lines do not contain any compilation errors.

6. E, G. The annotation declaration includes one required element, making option A incorrect. Options B, C, and D are incorrect because the `Driver` declaration does not contain an element named `value()`. If `directions()` were renamed in `Driver` to `value()`, then options B and D would be correct. The correct answers are options E and G. Option E uses the shorthand form in which the array braces (`{}`) can be dropped if there is only one element. Options C and F are not valid annotation uses, regardless of the annotation declaration. In this question, the `@Documented` and `@Deprecated` annotations have no impact on the solution.

7. A, B, C, D, E, F. Annotations can be applied to all of the declarations listed. If there is a type name used, an annotation can be applied.

8. B, F. In this question, `Ferocious` is the repeatable annotation, while `FerociousPack` is the containing type annotation. The containing type annotation should contain a single `value()` element that is an array of the repeatable annotation type. For this reason, option B is correct. Option A would allow `FerociousPack` to compile, but not `Ferocious`. Option C is an invalid annotation element type.

The repeatable annotation needs to specify the class name of its containing type annotation, making option F correct. While it is expected for repeatable annotations to contain elements to differentiate its usage, it is not required. For this reason, the usage of @Ferocious is a valid marker annotation on the Lion class, making option G incorrect.

9. D. To use an annotation with a value but not element name, the element must be declared with the name value(), not values(), making option A incorrect. The value() annotation may be required or optional, making option B incorrect. The annotation declaration may contain other elements, provided none is required, making option C incorrect. Option D is correct, as the annotation must not include any other values. Finally, option E is incorrect, as this is not a property of using a value() shorthand.

10. G. Furry is an annotation that can be applied only to types. In Bunny, it is applied to a method; therefore, it does not compile. If the @Target value was changed to ElementType.METHOD (or @Target removed entirely), then the rest of the code would compile without issue. The use of the shorthand notation for specifying a value() of an array is correct.

11. C, D, F. The @SafeVarargs annotation can be applied to a constructor or private, static, or final method that includes a varargs parameter. For these reasons, options C, D, and F are correct. Option A is incorrect, as the compiler cannot actually enforce that the operations are safe. It is up to the developer writing the method to verify that. Option B is incorrect as the annotation can be applied only to methods that cannot be overridden and abstract methods can always be overridden. Finally, option E is incorrect, as it is applied to the declaration, not the parameters.

12. B, C, D. Annotations cannot have constructors, so line 5 does not compile. Annotations can have variables, but they must be declared with a constant value. For this reason, line 6 does not compile. Line 7 does not compile as the element unit is missing parentheses after the element name. Lines 8 compiles and shows how to use annotation type with a default value.

13. A, D. An optional annotation element is one that is declared with a default value that may be optionally replaced when used in an annotation. For these reasons, options A and D are correct.

14. D. The @Retention annotation determines whether annotations are discarded when the code is compiled, at runtime, or not at all. The presence, or absence, of the @Documented annotation determines whether annotations are discarded within generated Javadoc. For these reasons, option D is correct.

15. B. A marker annotation is an annotation with no elements. It may or may not have constant variables, making option B correct. Option E is incorrect as no annotation can be extended.

16. F. The @SafeVarargs annotation does not take a value and can be applied only to methods that cannot be overridden (marked private, static, or final). For these reasons, options A and B produce compilation errors. Option C also does not compile, as this annotation can be applied only to other annotations. Even if you didn't remember that, it's clear it has nothing to do with hiding a compiler warning. Option D does not compile

as @SuppressWarnings requires a value. Both options E and F allow the code to compile without error, although only option F will cause a compile without warnings. The unchecked value is required when performing unchecked generic operations.

17. B, E. The @FunctionalInterface marker annotation is used to document that an interface is a valid functional interface that contains exactly one abstract method, making option B correct. It is also useful in determining whether an interface is a valid functional interface, as the compiler will report an error if used incorrectly, making option E correct. The compiler can detect whether an interface is a functional interface even without the annotation, making options A and C incorrect.

18. C, D, E, F. Line 5 and 6 do not compile because Boolean and void are not supported annotation element types. It must be a primitive, String, Class, enum, another annotation, or an array of these types. Line 7 does not compile because annotation elements are implicitly public. Finally, line 8 does not compile because the Strong annotation does not contain a value() element, so the shorthand notation cannot be used. If line 2 were changed from force() to value(), then line 8 would compile. Without the change, though, the compiler error is on line 8. The rest of the lines do not contain any compilation errors, making options C, D, E, and F correct.

19. A, F. The @Override annotation can be applied to a method but will trigger a compiler error if the method signature does not match an inherited method, making option A correct. The annotation @Deprecated can be applied to a method but will not trigger any compiler errors based on the method signature. The annotations @FunctionalInterface, @Repeatable, and @Retention cannot be applied to methods, making these options incorrect. Finally, @SafeVarargs can be applied to a method but will trigger a compiler error if the method does not contain a varargs parameter or is able to be overridden (not marked private, static, or final).

20. D, F. Line 6 contains a compiler error since the element name buoyancy is required in the annotation. If the element were renamed to value() in the annotation declaration, then the element name would be optional. Line 8 also contains a compiler error. While an annotation can be used in a cast operation, it requires a type. If the cast expression was changed to (@Floats boolean), then it would compile. The rest of the code compiles without issue.

21. G. The @Inherited annotation determines whether or not annotations defined in a super type are automatically inherited in a child type. The @Target annotation determines the location or locations an annotation can be applied to. Since this was not an answer choice, option G is correct. Note that ElementType is an enum used by @Target, but it is not an annotation.

22. F. If @SuppressWarnings("deprecation") is applied to a method that is using a deprecated API, then warnings related to the usage will not be shown at compile time, making option F correct. Note that there are no built-in annotations called @Ignore or @IgnoreDeprecated.

23. A. This question, like some questions on the exam, includes extraneous information that you do not need to know to solve it. Therefore, you can assume the reflection code is valid.

That said, this code is not without problems. The default retention policy for all annotations is RetentionPolicy.CLASS if not explicitly stated otherwise. This means the annotation information is discarded at compile time and not available at runtime. For this reason, none of the members will print anything, making option A correct.

If @Retention(RetentionPolicy.RUNTIME) were added to the declaration of Plumber, then the worker member would cause the default annotation value(), Mario, to be printed at runtime, and option B would be the correct answer. Note that foreman would not cause Mario to be printed even with the corrected retention annotation. Setting the value of the annotation is not the same as setting the value of the variable foreman.

24. A, E. The annotation includes only one required element, and it is named value(), so it can be used without an element name provided it is the only value in the annotation. For this reason, option A is correct, and options B and D are incorrect. Since the type of the value() is an array, option B would work if it was changed to @Dance({33, 10}). Option C is incorrect because it attempts to assign a value to fast, which is a constant variable not an element. Option E is correct and is an example of an annotation replacing all of the optional values. Option F is incorrect, as value() is a required element.

25. C. The Javadoc @deprecated annotation should be used, which provides a reason for the deprecation and suggests an alternative. All of the other answers are incorrect, with options A and B having the wrong case too. Those annotations should be written @Repeatable and @Retention since they are Java annotations.

Chapter 14: Generics and Collections

1. B. The answer needs to implement List because the scenario allows duplicates. Since you need a List, you can eliminate options C and D immediately because HashMap is a Map and HashSet is a Set. Option A, Arrays, is trying to distract you. It is a utility class rather than a Collection. An array is not a collection. This leaves you with options B and E. Option B is a better answer than option E because LinkedList is both a List and a Queue, and you just need a regular List.

2. D. The answer needs to implement Map because you are dealing with key/value pairs per the unique id field. You can eliminate options A, C, and E immediately since they are not a Map. ArrayList is a List. HashSet and TreeSet are Sets. Now it is between HashMap and TreeMap. Since the question talks about ordering, you need the TreeMap. Therefore, the answer is option D.

3. C, G. Line 12 creates a List<?>, which means it is treated as if all the elements are of type Object rather than String. Lines 15 and 16 do not compile since they call the String methods isEmpty() and length(), which are not defined on Object. Line 13 creates a List<String> because var uses the type that it deduces from the context. Lines 17 and 18 do compile. However, List.of() creates an immutable list, so both of those lines would throw an UnsupportedOperationException if run. Therefore, options C and G are correct.

4. D. This is a FIFO (first-in, first-out) queue. On line 7, we remove the first element added, which is "hello". On line 8, we look at the new first element ("hi") but don't remove it. On lines 9 and 10, we remove each element in turn until no elements are left, printing hi and ola together. Note that we don't use an Iterator to loop through the LinkedList to avoid concurrent modification issues. The order in which the elements are stored internally is not part of the API contract.

5. B, F. Option A does not compile because the generic types are not compatible. We could say HashSet<? extends Number> hs2 = new HashSet<Integer>();. Option B uses a lower bound, so it allows superclass generic types. Option C does not compile because the diamond operator is allowed only on the right side. Option D does not compile because a Set is not a List. Option E does not compile because upper bounds are not allowed when instantiating the type. Finally, option F does compile because the upper bound is on the correct side of the =.

6. B. The class compiles and runs without issue. Line 10 gives a compiler warning for not using generics but not a compiler error. Line 4 compiles fine because toString() is defined on the Object class and is therefore always available to call.

Line 9 creates the Hello class with the generic type String. It also passes an int to the println() method, which gets autoboxed into an Integer. While the println() method takes a generic parameter of type T, it is not the same <T> defined for the class on line 1. Instead, it is a different T defined as part of the method declaration on line 5. Therefore, the String argument on line 9 applies only to the class. The method can actually take any object as a parameter including autoboxed primitives. Line 10 creates the Hello class with the generic type Object since no type is specified for that instance. It passes a boolean to println(), which gets autoboxed into a Boolean. The result is that hi-1hola-true is printed, making option B correct.

7. A, D. The code compiles fine. It allows any implementation of Number to be added. Lines 5 and 8 succesfully autobox the primitives into an Integer and Long, respectively. HashSet does not guarantee any iteration order, making options A and D correct.

8. B, F. We're looking for a Comparator definition that sorts in descending order by beakLength. Option A is incorrect because it sorts in ascending order by beakLength. Similarly, option C is incorrect because it sorts the beakLength in ascending order within those matches that have the same name. Option E is incorrect because there is no thenComparingNumber() method.

Option B is a correct answer, as it sorts by beakLength in descending order. Options D and F are trickier. First notice that we can call either thenComparing() or thenComparingInt() because the former will simply autobox the int into an Integer. Then observe what reversed() applies to. Option D is incorrect because it sorts by name in ascending order and only reverses the beak length of those with the same name. Option F creates a comparator that sorts by name in ascending order and then by beak size in ascending order. Finally, it reverses the result. This is just what we want, so option F is correct.

9. E. Trick question! The `Map` interface uses `put()` rather than `add()` to add elements to the map. If these examples used `put()`, the answer would be options A and C. Option B is no good because a `long` cannot be placed inside a `Double` without an explicit cast. Option D is no good because a `char` is not the same thing as a `String`.

10. A. The array is sorted using `MyComparator`, which sorts the elements in reverse alphabetical order in a case-insensitive fashion. Normally, numbers sort before letters. This code reverses that by calling the `compareTo()` method on `b` instead of `a`.

11. A. Line 3 uses local variable type inference to create the map. Lines 5 and 7 use autoboxing to convert between the `int` primitive and the `Integer` wrapper class. The keys map to their squared value. 1 maps to 1, 2 maps to 4, 3 maps to 9, 4 maps to 16, and so on.

12. A, B, D. The generic type must be `Exception` or a subclass of `Exception` since this is an upper bound. Options C and E are wrong because `Throwable` is a superclass of `Exception`. Option D uses an odd syntax by explicitly listing the type, but you should be able to recognize it as acceptable.

13. B, E. The `showSize()` method can take any type of `List` since it uses an unbounded wildcard. Option A is incorrect because it is a `Set` and not a `List`. Option C is incorrect because the wildcard is not allowed to be on the right side of an assignment. Option D is incorrect because the generic types are not compatible.

    Option B is correct because a lower-bounded wildcard allows that same type to be the generic. Option E is correct because `Integer` is a subclass of `Number`.

14. C. This question is difficult because it defines both `Comparable` and `Comparator` on the same object. The `t1` object doesn't specify a `Comparator`, so it uses the `Comparable` object's `compareTo()` method. This sorts by the `text` instance variable. The `t2` object did specify a `Comparator` when calling the constructor, so it uses the `compare()` method, which sorts by the `int`.

15. A. When using `binarySearch()`, the `List` must be sorted in the same order that the `Comparator` uses. Since the `binarySearch()` method does not specify a `Comparator` explicitly, the default sort order is used. Only `c2` uses that sort order and correctly identifies that the value 2 is at index 0. Therefore, option A is correct. The other two comparators sort in descending order. Therefore, the precondition for `binarySearch()` is not met, and the result is undefined for those two.

16. B, D, F. The `java.lang.Comparable` interface is implemented on the object to compare. It specifies the `compareTo()` method, which takes one parameter. The `java.util.Comparator` interface specifies the `compare()` method, which takes two parameters.

17. B, D. Line 1 is a generic class that requires specifying a name for the type. Options A and C are incorrect because no type is specified. While you can use the diamond operator `<>` and the wildcard `?` on variables and parameters, you cannot use them in a class declaration. This means option B is the only correct answer for line 1. Knowing this allows you to fill in line 3. Option E is incorrect because `T` is not a class and certainly not one compatible with `String`. Option F is incorrect because a wildcard cannot be specified on the right side when instantiating an object. We're left with the diamond operator, making option D correct.

18. A, B. Y is both a class and a type parameter. This means that within the class Z, when we refer to Y, it uses the type parameter. All of the choices that mention class Y are incorrect because it no longer means the class Y.

19. A, D. A LinkedList implements both List and Queue. The List interface has a method to remove by index. Since this method exists, Java does not autobox to call the other method. Queue has only the remove by object method, so Java does autobox there. Since the number 1 is not in the list, Java does not remove anything for the Queue.

20. E. This question looks like it is about generics, but it's not. It is trying to see whether you noticed that Map does not have a contains() method. It has containsKey() and containsValue() instead. If containsKey() was called, the answer would be false because 123 is an Integer key in the Map, rather than a String.

21. A, E. The key to this question is keeping track of the types. Line 48 is a Map<Integer, Integer>. Line 49 builds a List out of a Set of Entry objects, giving us List<Entry<Integer, Integer>>. This causes a compile error on line 56 since we can't multiply an Entry object by two.

Lines 51 through 54 are all of type List<Integer>. The first three are immutable, and the one on line 54 is mutable. This means line 57 throws an UnsupportedOperationException since we attempt to modify the list. Line 58 would work if we could get to it. Since there is one compiler error and one runtime error, options A and E are correct.

22. B. When using generic types in a method, the generic specification goes before the return type.

23. B, E. Both Comparator and Comparable are functional interfaces. However, Comparable is intended to be used on the object being compared, making option B correct. The removeIf() method allows specifying the lambda to check when removing elements, making option E correct. Option C is incorrect because the remove() method takes an instance of an object to look for in the Collection to remove. Option D is incorrect because removeAll() takes a Collection of objects to look for in the Collection to remove.

24. F. The first two lines correctly create a Set and make a copy of it. Option A is incorrect because forEach takes a Consumer parameter, which requires one parameter. Options B and C are close. The syntax for a lambda is correct. However, s is already defined as a local variable, and therefore the lambda can't redefine it. Options D and E use incorrect syntax for a method reference. Option F is correct.

25. F. The first call to merge() calls the mapping function and adds the two numbers to get 13. It then updates the map. The second call to merge() sees that the map currently has a null value for that key. It does not call the mapping function but instead replaces it with the new value of 3. Therefore, option F is correct.

Chapter 15: Functional Programming

1. D. No terminal operation is called, so the stream never executes. The first line creates an infinite stream reference. If the stream were executed on the second line, it would get the first two elements from that infinite stream, "" and "1", and add an extra character, resulting in "2" and "12", respectively. Since the stream is not executed, the reference is printed instead.

2. F. Both streams created in this code snippet are infinite streams. The variable b1 is set to `true` since `anyMatch()` terminates. Even though the stream is infinite, Java finds a match on the first element and stops looking. However, when `allMatch()` runs, it needs to keep going until the end of the stream since it keeps finding matches. Since all elements continue to match, the program hangs.

3. E. An infinite stream is generated where each element is twice as long as the previous one. While this code uses the three-parameter `iterate()` method, the condition is never `false`. The variable b1 is set to `false` because Java finds an element that matches when it gets to the element of length 4. However, the next line tries to operate on the same stream. Since streams can be used only once, this throws an exception that the "stream has already been operated upon or closed." If two different streams were used, the result would be option B.

4. A, B. Terminal operations are the final step in a stream pipeline. Exactly one is required, because it triggers the execution of the entire stream pipeline. Therefore, options A and B are correct. Option C is true of intermediate operations, rather than terminal operations. Option D is incorrect because `peek()` is an intermediate operation. Finally, option E is incorrect because once a stream pipeline is run, the `Stream` is marked invalid.

5. C, F. Yes, we know this question is a lot of reading. Remember to look for the differences between options rather than studying each line. These options all have much in common. All of them start out with a `LongStream` and attempt to convert it to an `IntStream`. However, options B and E are incorrect because they do not cast the `long` to an `int`, resulting in a compiler error on the `mapToInt()` calls.

    Next, we hit the second difference. Options A and D are incorrect because they are missing `boxed()` before the `collect()` call. Since `groupingBy()` is creating a `Collection`, we need a nonprimitive `Stream`. The final difference is that option F specifies the type of `Collection`. This is allowed, though, meaning both options C and F are correct.

6. A. Options C and D do not compile because these methods do not take a `Predicate` parameter and do not return a `boolean`. When working with streams, it is important to remember the behavior of the underlying functional interfaces. Options B and E are incorrect. While the code compiles, it runs infinitely. The stream has no way to know that a match won't show up later. Option A is correct because it is safe to return `false` as soon as one element passes through the stream that doesn't match.

7.   F. There is no `Stream<T>` method called `compare()` or `compareTo()`, so options A through D can be eliminated. The `sorted()` method is correct to use in a stream pipeline to return a sorted `Stream`. The `collect()` method can be used to turn the stream into a `List`. The `collect()` method requires a collector be selected, making option E incorrect and option F correct.

8.   D, E. The `average()` method returns an `OptionalDouble` since averages of any type can result in a fraction. Therefore, options A and B are both incorrect. The `findAny()` method returns an `OptionalInt` because there might not be any elements to find. Therefore, option D is correct. The `sum()` method returns an `int` rather than an `OptionalInt` because the sum of an empty list is zero. Therefore, option E is correct.

9.   B, D. Lines 4–6 compile and run without issue, making option F incorrect. Line 4 creates a stream of elements [1, 2, 3]. Line 5 maps the stream to a new stream with values [10, 20, 30]. Line 6 filters out all items not less than 5, which in this case results in an empty stream. For this reason, `findFirst()` returns an empty `Optional`.

Option A does not compile. It would work for a `Stream<T>` object, but we have a `LongStream` and therefore need to call `getAsLong()`. Option C also does not compile, as it is missing the `::` that would make it a method reference. Options B and D both compile and run without error, although neither produces any output at runtime since the stream is empty.

10.   F. Only one of the method calls, `forEach()`, is a terminal operation, so any answer in which M is not the last line will not execute the pipeline. This eliminates all but options C, E, and F. Option C is incorrect because `filter()` is called before `limit()`. Since none of the elements of the stream meets the requirement for the `Predicate<String>`, the `filter()` operation will run infinitely, never passing any elements to `limit()`. Option E is incorrect because there is no `limit()` operation, which means that the code would run infinitely. Only option F is correct. It first limits the infinite stream to a finite stream of 10 elements and then prints the result.

11.   B, C, E. As written, the code doesn't compile because the `Collectors.joining()` expects to get a `Stream<String>`. Option B fixes this, at which point nothing is output because the collector creates a `String` without outputting the result. Option E fixes this and causes the output to be `11111`. Since the post-increment operator is used, the stream contains an infinite number of the character `1`. Option C fixes this and causes the stream to contain increasing numbers.

12.   B, F, G. We can eliminate four choices right away. Options A and C are there to mislead you; these interfaces don't actually exist. Option D is incorrect because a `BiFunction<T,U,R>` takes three generic arguments, not two. Option E is incorrect because none of the examples returns a `boolean`.

Moving on to the remaining choices, the declaration on line 6 doesn't take any parameters, and it returns a `String`, so a `Supplier<String>` can fill in the blank, making option F correct. Another clue is that it uses a constructor reference, which should scream `Supplier`! This makes option F correct.

The declaration on line 7 requires you to recognize that `Consumer` and `Function`, along with their binary equivalents, have an `andThen()` method. This makes option B correct.

Finally, line 8 takes a single parameter, and it returns the same type, which is a `UnaryOperator`. Since the types are the same, only one generic parameter is needed, making option G correct.

13. F. If the `map()` and `flatMap()` calls were reversed, option B would be correct. In this case, the `Stream` created from the source is of type `Stream<List>`. Trying to use the addition operator (`+`) on a `List` is not supported in Java. Therefore, the code does not compile, and option F is correct.

14. B, D. Line 4 creates a `Stream` and uses autoboxing to put the `Integer` wrapper of 1 inside. Line 5 does not compile because `boxed()` is available only on primitive streams like `IntStream`, not `Stream<Integer>`. Line 6 converts to a `double` primitive, which works since `Integer` can be unboxed to a value that can be implicitly cast to a `double`. Line 7 does not compile for two reasons. First, converting from a `double` to an `int` would require an explicit cast. Also, `mapToInt()` returns an `IntStream` so the data type of `s3` is incorrect. The rest of the lines compile without issue.

15. B, D. Options A and C do not compile, because they are invalid generic declarations. Primitives are not allowed as generics, and `Map` must have two generic type parameters. Option E is incorrect because partitioning only gives a `Boolean` key. Options B and D are correct because they return a `Map` with a `Boolean` key and a value type that can be customized to any `Collection`.

16. B, C. First, this mess of code does compile. While this code starts out with an infinite stream on line 23, it does become finite on line 24 thanks to `limit()`, making option F incorrect. The pipeline preserves only nonempty elements on line 25. Since there aren't any of those, the pipeline is empty. Line 26 converts this to an empty map.

    Lines 27 and 28 create a `Set` with no elements and then another empty stream. Lines 29 and 30 convert the generic type of the `Stream` to `List<String>` and then `String`. Finally, line 31 gives us another `Map<Boolean, List<String>>`.

    The `partitioningBy()` operation always returns a map with two `Boolean` keys, even if there are no corresponding values. Therefore, option B is correct if the code is kept as is. By contrast, `groupingBy()` returns only keys that are actually needed, making option C correct if the code is modified on line 31.

17. E. The question starts with a `UnaryOperator<Integer>`, which takes one parameter and returns a value of the same type. Therefore, option E is correct, as `UnaryOperator` actually extends `Function`. Notice that other options don't even compile because they have the wrong number of generic types for the functional interface provided. You should know that a `BiFunction<T,U,R>` takes three generic arguments, a `BinaryOperator<T>` takes one generic argument, and a `Function<T,R>` takes two generic arguments.

18. D. The terminal operation is `count()`. Since there is a terminal operation, the intermediate operations run. The `peek()` operation comes before the `filter()`, so both numbers are printed. After the `filter()`, the `count()` happens to be 1 since one of the numbers is filtered out. However, the result of the stream pipeline isn't stored in a variable or printed, and it is ignored.

19. A. The a.compose(b) method calls the Function parameter b before the reference Function variable a. In this case, that means that we multiply by 3 before adding 4. This gives a result of 7, making option A correct.

20. A, C, E. Java includes support for three primitive streams, along with numerous functional interfaces to go with them: int, double, and long. For this reason, options C and E are correct. There is one exception to this rule. While there is no BooleanStream class, there is a BooleanSupplier functional interface, making option A correct. Java does not include primitive streams or related functional interfaces for other numeric data types, making options B and D incorrect. Option F is incorrect because String is not a primitive, but an object. Only primitives have custom suppliers.

21. B. Both lists and streams have forEach() methods. There is no reason to collect into a list just to loop through it. Option A is incorrect because it does not contain a terminal operation or print anything. Options B and C both work. However, the question asks about the simplest way, which is option B.

22. C, E, F. Options A and B compile and return an empty string without throwing an exception, using a String and Supplier parameter, respectively. Option G does not compile as the get() method does not take a parameter. Options C and F throw a NoSuchElementException. Option E throws a RuntimeException. Option D looks correct but will compile only if the throw is removed. Remember, the orElseThrow() should get a lambda expression or method reference that returns an exception, not one that throws an exception.

Chapter 16: Exceptions, Assertions, and Localization

1. C. Exception and RuntimeException, along with many other exceptions in the Java API, define a no-argument constructor, a constructor that takes a String, and a constructor that takes a Throwable. For this reason, Danger compiles without issue. Catastrophe also compiles without issue. Just creating a new checked exception, without throwing it, does not require it to be handled or declared. Finally, Emergency does not compile. The no-argument constructor in Emergency must explicitly call a parent constructor, since Danger does not define a no-argument constructor.

2. A, D, E. Localization refers to user-facing elements. Dates, currency, and numbers are commonly used in different formats for different countries. Class and variable names, along with lambda expressions, are internal to the application, so there is no need to translate them for users.

3. G.A try-with-resources statement uses parentheses, (), rather than braces, {}, for the try section. This is likely subtler than a question that you'll get on the exam, but it is still important to be on alert for details. If parentheses were used instead of braces, then the code would compile and print TWDF at runtime.

4. F. The code does not compile because the `throw` and `throws` keywords are incorrectly used on lines 6, 7, and 9. If the keywords were fixed, then the rest of the code would compile and print a stack track with `YesProblem` at runtime.

5. E. A `LocalDate` does not have a time element. Therefore, a Date/Time formatter is not appropriate. The code compiles but throws an exception at runtime. If `ISO_LOCAL_DATE` was used, then the code would compile and option B would be the correct answer.

6. C. Java will first look for the most specific matches it can find, starting with `Dolphins_en_US.properties`. Since that is not an answer choice, it drops the country and looks for `Dolphins_en.properties`, making option C correct. Option B is incorrect because a country without a language is not a valid locale.

7. D. When working with a custom number formatter, the 0 symbol displays the digit as 0, even if it's not present, while the # symbol omits the digit from the start or end of the `String` if it is not present. Based on the requested output, a `String` that displays at least three digits before the decimal (including a comma) and at least one after the decimal is required. It should display a second digit after the decimal if one is available. For this reason, option D is the correct answer. In case you are curious, option A displays at most only one value to the right of the decimal, printing <5.2> <8.5> <1234>. Option B is close to the correct answer but always displays four digits to the left of the decimal, printing <0,005.21> <0,008.49> <1,234.0>. Finally, option C is missing the zeros padded to the left of the decimal and optional two values to the right of the decimal, printing <5.2> <8.5> <1,234.0>.

8. A, D. An assertion consists of a `boolean` expression followed by an optional colon (:) and message. The `boolean` expression is allowed to be in parentheses, but this is not required. Therefore, options A and D are correct.

9. B, E. An exception that must be handled or declared is a checked exception. A checked exception inherits `Exception` but not `RuntimeException`. The entire hierarchy counts, so options B and E are both correct.

10. B, C. The code does not compile, so option E is incorrect. Option A is incorrect because removing the exception from the declaration causes a compilation error on line 4, as `FileNotFoundException` is a checked exception that must be handled or declared. Option B is correct because the unhandled exception within the `main()` method becomes declared. Option C is also correct because the exception becomes handled. Option D is incorrect because the exception remains unhandled. Finally, option F is incorrect because the changes for option B or C will allow the code to compile.

11. C. The code compiles fine, so option E is incorrect. The command line has only two arguments, so `args.length` is 2 and the `if` statement is `true`. However, because assertions are not enabled, it does not throw an `AssertionError`, so option B is incorrect. The `println()` method attempts to print `args[2]`, which generates an `ArrayIndexOutOfBoundsException`, so the answer is option C.

12. A, B. A try-with-resources statement does not require a `catch` or `finally` block. A traditional `try` statement requires at least one of the two. Neither statement can be written without a body encased in braces, {}.

13. C, D. The code compiles with the appropriate input, so option G is incorrect. A locale consists of a required lowercase language code and optional uppercase country code. In the `Locale()` constructor, the language code is provided first. For these reasons, options C and D are correct. Options E and F are incorrect because a `Locale` is created using a constructor or `Locale.Builder` class.

14. D. You can create custom checked, unchecked exceptions, and even errors. The default constructor is used if one is not supplied. There is no requirement to implement any specific methods.

15. F. The code compiles, but the first line produces a runtime exception regardless of what is inserted into the blank. When creating a custom formatter, any nonsymbol code must be properly escaped using pairs of single quotes (`'`). In this case, it fails because o is not a symbol. Even if you didn't know o wasn't a symbol, the code contains an unmatched single quote. If the properly escaped value of `"hh' o''clock'"` was used, then the correct answers would be `ZonedDateTime`, `LocalDateTime`, and `LocalTime`. Option B would not be correct because `LocalDate` values do not have an hour part.

16. B, C. The code compiles, so option E is incorrect. While it is a poor practice to modify variables in an assertion statement, it is allowed. To enable assertions, use the flag `-ea` or `-enableassertions`. To disable assertions, use the flag `-da` or `-disableassertions`. The colon indicates a specific class. Option A is incorrect, as assertions are already disabled by default. Option B is correct because it turns on assertions for all classes (except system classes). Option C is correct because it disables assertions for all classes but then turns them back on for this class. Finally, option D is incorrect as it enables assertions everywhere except the `On` class.

17. D, F. Option A is incorrect because Java will look at parent bundles if a key is not found in a specified resource bundle. Option B is incorrect because resource bundles are loaded from `static` factory methods. In fact, `ResourceBundle` is an `abstract` class, so calling that constructor is not even possible. Option C is incorrect, as resource bundle values are read from the `ResourceBundle` object directly. Option D is correct because the locale is changed only in memory. Option E is incorrect, as the resource bundle for the default locale may be used if there is no resource bundle for the specified locale (or its locale without a country code). Finally, option F is correct. The JVM will set a default locale automatically, making it possible to use a resource bundle for a locale, even if a locale was not explicitly set.

18. C. After both resources are declared and created in the try-with-resources statement, T is printed as part of the body. Then the try-with-resources completes and closes the resources in reverse order from which they were declared. After W is printed, an exception is thrown. However, the remaining resource still needs to be closed, so D is printed. Once all the resources are closed, the exception is thrown and swallowed in the `catch` block, causing E to be printed. Last, the `finally` block is run, printing F. Therefore, the answer is `TWDEF`.

19. D. Java will use `Dolphins_fr.properties` as the matching resource bundle on line 7 because it is an exact match on the language of the requested locale. Line 8 finds a matching key in this file. Line 9 does not find a match in that file; therefore, it has to look higher up in the hierarchy. Once a bundle is chosen, only resources in that hierarchy are allowed. It cannot use the default locale anymore, but it can use the default resource bundle specified by `Dolphins.properties`.

20. B. The `MessageFormat` class supports parametrized `String` values that take input values, while the `Properties` class supports providing a default value if the property is not set. For this reason, option B is correct.

21. C. The code does not compile because the multi-`catch` on line 7 cannot catch both a superclass and a related subclass. Options A and B do not address this problem, so they are incorrect. Since the `try` body throws `SneezeException`, it can be caught in a `catch` block, making option C correct. Option D allows the `catch` block to compile but causes a compiler error on line 6. Both of the custom exceptions are checked and must be handled or declared in the `main()` method. A `SneezeException` is not a `SniffleException`, so the exception is not handled. Likewise, option E leads to an unhandled exception compiler error on line 6.

22. E. Even though `ldt` has both a date and time, the formatter outputs only time.

23. A, E. Resources must inherit `AutoCloseable` to be used in a try-with-resources block. Since `Closeable`, which is used for I/O classes, extends `AutoCloseable`, both may be used.

24. E. The `Properties` class defines a `get()` method that does not allow for a default value. It also has a `getProperty()` method, which returns the default value if the key is not provided.

25. G. The code does compile because the resource `walk1` is not `final` or effectively final and cannot be used in the declaration of a try-with-resources statement. If the line that set `walk1` to `null` was removed, then the code would compile and print `blizzard 2` at runtime, with the exception inside the `try` block being the primary exception since it is thrown first. Then two suppressed exceptions would be added to it when trying to close the `AutoCloseable` resources.

26. A, E. Line 5 does not compile because `assert` is a keyword, making option A correct. Options B and C are both incorrect because the parentheses and message are both optional. Option D is incorrect because assertions should never alter outcomes, as they may be disabled at runtime. Option E is correct because checking an argument passed from elsewhere in the program is an appropriate use of an assertion.

27. E. The `Locale.Builder` class requires that the `build()` method be called to actually create the `Locale` object. For this reason, the two `Locale.setDefault()` statements do not compile because the input is not a `Locale`, making option E the correct answer. If the proper `build()` calls were added, then the code would compile and print the value for Germany, 2,40 €. As in the exam, though, you did not have to know the format of currency values in a particular locale to answer the question. Note that the default locale category is ignored since an explicit currency locale is selected.

Chapter 17: Modular Applications

1. D. A service consists of the service provider interface and logic to look up implementations using a service locator. This makes option D correct. Make sure you know that the service provider itself is the implementation, which is not considered part of the service.

2. E, F. Automatic modules are on the module path but do not have a module-info file. Named modules are on the module path and do have a module-info. Unnamed modules are on the classpath. Therefore, options E and F are correct.

3. A, B, E. Any version information at the end of the JAR filename is removed, making options A and B correct. Underscores (_) are turned into dots (.), making options C and D incorrect. Other special characters like a dollar sign ($) are also turned into dots. However, adjacent dots are merged, and leading/trailing dots are removed. Therefore, option E is correct.

4. A, E. A cyclic dependency is when a module graph forms a circle. Option A is correct because the Java Platform Module System does not allow cyclic dependencies between modules. No such restriction exists for packages, making option B incorrect. A cyclic dependency can involve two or more modules that require each other, making option E correct, while options C and D are incorrect. Finally. Option F is incorrect because unnamed modules cannot be referenced from an automatic module.

5. B. Option B is correct because java.base is provided by default. It contains the java.lang package among others.

6. F. The provides directive takes the interface name first and the implementing class name second. The with keyword is used. Only option F meets these two criteria, making it the correct answer.

7. A, B, C, F. Option D is incorrect because it is a package name rather than a module name. Option E is incorrect because java.base is the module name, not jdk.base. Option G is wrong because we made it up. Options A, B, C, and F are correct.

8. D. There is no getStream() method on a ServiceLoader, making options A and C incorrect. Option B does not compile because the stream() method returns a list of Provider interfaces and needs to be converted to the Unicorn interface we are interested in. Therefore, option D is correct.

9. C. The jdeps command has an option --internal-jdk that lists any code using unsupported/internal APIs and prints a table with suggested alternatives. This makes option C correct. Option D is incorrect because it does not print out the table with a suggested alternative. Options A, B, E, F, and G are incorrect because those options do not exist.

10. B. A top-down migration strategy first places all JARs on the module path. Then it migrates the top-level module to be a named module, leaving the other modules as automatic modules. Option B is correct as it matches both of those characteristics.

11. A. Since this is a new module, you need to compile the new module. However, none of the existing modules needs to be recompiled, making option A correct. The service locator will see the new service provider simply by having the new service provider on the module path.

12. B. The most commonly used packages are in the `java.base` module, making option B correct.

13. A, E, F. Option A is correct because the service provider interface must specify `exports` for any other modules to reference it. Option F is correct because the service provider needs access to the service provider interface. Option E is also correct because the service provider needs to declare that it provides the service.

14. B, E, F. Since the new project extracts the common code, it must have an `exports` directive for that code, making option B correct. The other two modules do not have to expose anything. They must have a `requires` directive to be able to use the exported code, making options E and F correct.

15. H. This question is tricky. The service provider must have a `uses` directive, but that is on the service provider interface. No modules need to specify `requires` on the service provider since that is the implementation.

16. A. Since the JAR is on the classpath, it is treated as a regular unnamed module even though it has a `module-info` file inside. Remember from learning about top-down migration that modules on the module path are not allowed to refer to the classpath, making options B, and D incorrect. The classpath does not have a facility to restrict packages, making option A correct and options C and E incorrect.

17. A, F. An automatic module exports all packages, making option A correct. An unnamed module is not available to any modules on the module path. Therefore, it doesn't export any packages, and option F is correct.

18. A, C, D. Option A and C are correct because both the consumer and the service locator depend on the service provider interface. Additionally, option D is correct because the service locator must specify that it `uses` the service provider interface to look it up.

19. C, E. The `jdeps` command provides information about the class or package level depending on the options passed, making option C correct. It is frequently used to determine what dependencies you will need when converting to modules. This makes it useful to run against a regular JAR, making option E correct.

20. E. Trick question! An unnamed module doesn't use a `module-info` file. Therefore, option E is correct. An unnamed module can access an automatic module. The unnamed module would simply treat the automatic module as a regular JAR without involving the `module.info` file.

Chapter 18: Concurrency

1. D, F. There is no such class within the Java API called `ParallelStream`, so options A and E are incorrect. The method defined in the `Stream` class to create a parallel stream from an existing stream is `parallel()`; therefore, option F is correct, and option C is incorrect. The method defined in the `Collection` class to create a parallel stream from a collection is `parallelStream()`; therefore, option D is correct, and option B is incorrect.

2. A, D. The `tryLock()` method returns immediately with a value of `false` if the lock cannot be acquired. Unlike `lock()`, it does not wait for a lock to become available. This code fails to check the return value, resulting in the protected code being entered regardless of whether the lock is obtained. In some executions (when `tryLock()` returns `true` on every call), the code will complete successfully and print 45 at runtime, making option A correct. On other executions (when `tryLock()` returns `false` at least once), the `unlock()` method will throw an `IllegalMonitorStateException` at runtime, making option D correct. Option B would be possible if there was no lock at all, although in this case, failure to acquire a lock results in an exception at runtime.

3. A, C, D, F. All methods are capable of throwing unchecked exceptions, so option A is correct. Runnable and Callable statements both do not take any arguments, so option B is incorrect. Only `Callable` is capable of throwing checked exceptions, so option C is also correct. Both Runnable and Callable are functional interfaces that can be implemented with a lambda expression, so option D is also correct. Finally, Runnable returns `void` and Callable returns a generic type, making option F correct and making options E and G incorrect.

4. B, C. The code does not compile, so options A and F are incorrect. The first problem is that although a `ScheduledExecutorService` is created, it is assigned to an `ExecutorService`. The type of the variable on line w1 would have to be updated to `ScheduledExecutorService` for the code to compile, making option B correct. The second problem is that `scheduleWithFixedDelay()` supports only Runnable, not Callable, and any attempt to return a value is invalid in a Runnable lambda expression; therefore, line w2 will also not compile, and option C is correct. The rest of the lines compile without issue, so options D and E are incorrect.

5. C. The code compiles and runs without throwing an exception or entering an infinite loop, so options D, E, and F are incorrect. The key here is that the increment operator ++ is not atomic. While the first part of the output will always be 100, the second part is nondeterministic. It could output any value from 1 to 100, because the threads can overwrite each other's work. Therefore, option C is the correct answer, and options A and B are incorrect.

6. C, E. The code compiles, so option G is incorrect. The `peek()` method on a parallel stream will process the elements concurrently, so the order cannot be determined ahead of time, and option C is correct. The `forEachOrdered()` method will process the elements in the order they are stored in the stream, making option E correct. It does not sort the elements, so option D is incorrect.

7. D. Livelock occurs when two or more threads are conceptually blocked forever, although they are each still active and trying to complete their task. A race condition is an undesirable result that occurs when two tasks are completed at the same time, which should have been completed sequentially.

8. A. The method looks like it executes a task concurrently, but it actually runs synchronously. In each iteration of the forEach() loop, the process waits for the run() method to complete before moving on. For this reason, the code is actually thread-safe. It executes a total of 499 times, since the second value of range() excludes the 500. Since the program consistently prints 499 at runtime, option A is correct. Note that if start() had been used instead of run() (or the stream was parallel), then the output would be indeterminate, and option C would have been correct.

9. C. If a task is submitted to a thread executor, and the thread executor does not have any available threads, the call to the task will return immediately with the task being queued internally by the thread executor. For this reason, option C is the correct answer.

10. A. The code compiles without issue, so option D is incorrect. The CopyOnWriteArrrayList class is designed to preserve the original list on iteration, so the first loop will be executed exactly three times and, in the process, will increase the size of tigers to six elements. The ConcurrentSkipListSet class allows modifications, and since it enforces uniqueness of its elements, the value 5 is added only once leading to a total of four elements in bears. Finally, despite using the elements of lions to populate the collections, tigers and bears are not backed by the original list, so the size of lions is 3 throughout this program. For these reasons, the program prints 3 6 4, and option A is correct.

11. F. The code compiles and runs without issue, so options C, D, E, and G are incorrect. There are two important things to notice. First, synchronizing on the first variable doesn't actually impact the results of the code. Second, sorting on a parallel stream does not mean that findAny() will return the first record. The findAny() method will return the value from the first thread that retrieves a record. Therefore, the output is not guaranteed, and option F is correct. Option A looks correct, but even on serial streams, findAny() is free to select any element.

12. B. The code snippet submits three tasks to an ExecutorService, shuts it down, and then waits for the results. The awaitTermination() method waits a specified amount of time for all tasks to complete, and the service to finish shutting down. Since each five-second task is still executing, the awaitTermination() method will return with a value of false after two seconds but not throw an exception. For these reasons, option B is correct.

13. C. The code does not compile, so options A and E are incorrect. The problem here is that c1 is an int and c2 is a String, so the code fails to combine on line q2, since calling length() on an int is not allowed, and option C is correct. The rest of the lines compile without issue. Note that calling parallel() on an already parallel stream is allowed, and it may in fact return the same object.

14. C, E. The code compiles without issue, so option D is incorrect. Since both tasks are submitted to the same thread executor pool, the order cannot be determined, so options A and B are incorrect, and option C is correct. The key here is that the order in which the resources o1 and o2 are synchronized could result in a deadlock. For example, if the first thread gets a lock on o1 and the second thread gets a lock on o2 before either thread can get their second lock, then the code will hang at runtime, making option E correct. The code cannot produce a livelock, since both threads are waiting, so option F is incorrect. Finally, if a deadlock does occur, an exception will not be thrown, so option G is incorrect.

15. A. The code compiles and runs without issue, so options C, D, E, and F are incorrect. The collect() operation groups the animals into those that do and do not start with the letter p. Note that there are four animals that do not start with the letter p and three animals that do. The logical complement operator (!) before the startsWith() method means that results are reversed, so the output is 3 4 and option A is correct, making option B incorrect.

16. F. The lock() method will wait indefinitely for a lock, so option A is incorrect. Options B and C are also incorrect, as the correct method name to attempt to acquire a lock is tryLock(). Option D is incorrect, as fairness is set to false by default and must be enabled by using an overloaded constructor. Finally, option E is incorrect because a thread that holds the lock may have called lock() or tryLock() multiple times. A thread needs to call unlock() once for each call to lock() and tryLock().

17. D. The methods on line 5, 6, 7, and 8 each throw InterruptedException, which is a checked exception; therefore, the method does not compile, and option D is the only correct answer. If InterruptedException was declared in the method signature on line 3, then the answer would be option F, because adding items to the queue may be blocked at runtime. In this case, the queue is passed into the method, so there could be other threads operating on it. Finally, if the operations were not blocked and there were no other operations on the queue, then the output would be 103 20, and the answer would be option B.

18. C, E, G. A Callable lambda expression takes no values and returns a generic type; therefore, options C, E, and G are correct. Options A and F are incorrect because they both take an input parameter. Option B is incorrect because it does not return a value. Option D is not a valid lambda expression, because it is missing a semicolon at the end of the return statement, which is required when inside braces {}.

19. F, H. The application compiles and does not throw an exception, so options B, C, D, E, and G are incorrect. Even though the stream is processed in sequential order, the tasks are submitted to a thread executor, which may complete the tasks in any order. Therefore, the output cannot be determined ahead of time, and option F is correct. Finally, the thread executor is never shut down; therefore, the code will run but it will never terminate, making option H also correct.

20. F. The key to solving this question is to remember that the execute() method returns void, not a Future object. Therefore, line n1 does not compile, and option F is the correct answer. If the submit() method had been used instead of execute(), then option C would have been the correct answer, as the output of the submit(Runnable) task is a Future<?> object that can only return null on its get() method.

21. A, D. The `findFirst()` method guarantees the first element in the stream will be returned, whether it is serial or parallel, making options A and D correct. While option B may consistently print 1 at runtime, the behavior of `findAny()` on a serial stream is not guaranteed, so option B is incorrect. Option C is likewise incorrect, with the output being random at runtime. Option E is incorrect because any of the previous options will allow the code to compile.

22. B. The code compiles and runs without issue, so options D, E, F, and G are incorrect. The key aspect to notice in the code is that a single-thread executor is used, meaning that no task will be executed concurrently. Therefore, the results are valid and predictable with 100 100 being the output, and option B is the correct answer. If a pooled thread executor was used with at least two threads, then the `sheepCount2++` operations could overwrite each other, making the second value indeterminate at the end of the program. In this case, option C would be the correct answer.

23. F. The code compiles without issue, so options B, C, and D are incorrect. The limit on the cyclic barrier is 10, but the stream can generate only up to 9 threads that reach the barrier; therefore, the limit can never be reached, and option F is the correct answer, making options A and E incorrect. Even if the `limit(9)` statement was changed to `limit(10)`, the program could still hang since the JVM might not allocate 10 threads to the parallel stream.

24. A, F. The class compiles without issue, so option A is correct, and options B and C are incorrect. Since `getInstance()` is a `static` method and `sellTickets()` is an instance method, lines k1 and k4 synchronize on different objects, making option D incorrect. The class is not thread-safe because the `addTickets()` method is not synchronized, and option E is incorrect. For example, one thread could call `sellTickets()` while another thread calls `addTickets()`. These methods are not synchronized with each other and could cause an invalid number of tickets due to a race condition.

Finally, option F is correct because the `getInstance()` method is `synchronized`. Since the constructor is `private`, this method is the only way to create an instance of `TicketManager` outside the class. The first thread to enter the method will set the `instance` variable, and all other threads will use the existing value. This is actually a singleton pattern.

25. A, D. By itself, concurrency does not guarantee which task will be completed first, so option A is correct. Furthermore, applications with numerous resource requests will often be stuck waiting for a resource, which allows other tasks to run. Therefore, they tend to benefit more from concurrency than CPU-intensive tasks, so option D is also correct. Option B is incorrect because concurrency may in fact make an application slower if it is truly single-threaded in nature. Keep in mind that there is a cost associated with allocating additional memory and CPU time to manage the concurrent process. Option C is incorrect because single-processor CPUs have been benefiting from concurrency for decades. Finally, option E is incorrect; there are numerous examples in this chapter of concurrent tasks sharing memory.

26. C, D. The code compiles and runs without issue, so options F and G are incorrect. The return type of performCount() is void, so submit() is interpreted as being applied to a Runnable expression. While submit(Runnable) does return a Future<?>, calling get() on it always returns null. For this reason, options A and B are incorrect, and option C is correct. The performCount() method can also throw a runtime exception, which will then be thrown by the get() call as an ExecutionException; therefore, option D is also a correct answer. Finally, it is also possible for our performCount() to hang indefinitely, such as with a deadlock or infinite loop. Luckily, the call to get() includes a timeout value. While each call to Future.get() can wait up to a day for a result, it will eventually finish, so option E is incorrect.

Chapter 19: I/O

1. F. Since the question asks about putting data into a structured object, the best class would be one that deserializes the data. Therefore, ObjectInputStream is the best choice. ObjectWriter, BufferedStream, and ObjectReader are not I/O stream classes. ObjectOutputStream is an I/O class but is used to serialize data, not deserialize it. FileReader can be used to read text file data and construct an object, but the question asks what would be the best class to use for binary data.

2. C, E, G. The command to move a file or directory using a File is renameTo(), not mv() or move(), making options A and D incorrect, and option E correct. The commands to create a directory using a File are mkdir() and mkdirs(), not createDirectory(), making option B incorrect, and options C and G correct. The mkdirs() differs from mkdir() by creating any missing directories along the path. Finally, option F is incorrect as there is no command to copy a file in the File class. You would need to use an I/O stream to copy the file along with its contents.

3. B. The code compiles and runs without issue, so options F and G are incorrect. The key here is that while Eagle is serializable, its parent class, Bird, is not. Therefore, none of the members of Bird will be serialized. Even if you didn't know that, you should know what happens on deserialization. During deserialization, Java calls the constructor of the first nonserializable parent. In this case, the Bird constructor is called, with name being set to Matt, making option B correct. Note that none of the constructors or instance initializers in Eagle is executed as part of deserialization.

4. A, D. The code will compile if the correct classes are used, so option G is incorrect. Remember, a try-with-resources statement can use resources declared before the start of the statement. The reference type of wrapper is InputStream, so we need a class that inherits InputStream. We can eliminate BufferedWriter, ObjectOutputStream, and BufferedReader since their names do not end in InputStream. Next, we see the class must take another stream as input, so we need to choose the remaining streams that are high-level streams. BufferedInputStream is a high-level stream, so option A is correct. Even though the instance is already a BufferedInputStream, there's no rule that it can't be wrapped multiple times by a high-level stream. Option B is incorrect, as FileInputStream operates on a file, not another stream. Finally, option D is correct—an ObjectInputStream is a high-level stream that operates on other streams.

5. B, E. The JVM creates one instance of the `Console` object as a singleton, making option C incorrect. If the console is unavailable, `System.console()` will return `null`, making option B correct. The method cannot throw an `IOException` because it is not declared as a checked exception. Therefore, option A is incorrect. Option D is incorrect, as a `Console` can be used for both reading and writing data. The `Console` class includes a `format()` method to write data to the output stream, making option E correct. Since there is no `println()` method, as `writer()` must be called first, option F is incorrect.

6. C, D, E. All I/O streams should be closed after use or a resource leak might ensue, making option C correct. While a try-with-resources statement is the preferred way to close an I/O stream, it can be closed with a traditional `try` statement that uses a `finally` block. For this reason, both options D and E are correct.

7. G. Not all I/O streams support the `mark()` operation; therefore, without calling `markSupported()` on the stream, the result is unknown until runtime. If the stream does support the `mark()` operation, then the result would be XYZY, and option D would be correct. The `reset()` operation puts the stream back in the position before the `mark()` was called, and `skip(1)` will skip X. If the stream does not support the `mark()` operation, a runtime exception would likely be thrown, and option F would be correct. Since you don't know if the input stream supports the `mark()` operation, option G is the only correct choice.

8. A, F. In Java, serialization is the process of turning an object to a stream, while deserialization is the process of turning that stream back into an object. For this reason, option A is correct, and option B is incorrect. Option C is incorrect, because many nonthread classes are not marked `Serializable` for various reasons. The `Serializable` interface is a marker interface that does not contain any abstract methods, making options D and E incorrect. Finally, option F is correct, because `readObject()` declares the `ClassNotFoundException` even if the class is not cast to a specific type.

9. A. Paths that begin with the root directory are absolute paths, so option A is correct, and option C is incorrect. Option B is incorrect because the path could be a file or directory within the file system. There is no rule that files have to end with a file extension. Option D is incorrect, as it is possible to create a `File` reference to files and directories that do not exist. Option E is also incorrect. The `delete()` method returns `false` if the file or directory cannot be deleted.

10. E, F. For a class to be serialized, it must implement the `Serializable` interface and contain instance members that are serializable or marked `transient`. For these reasons, options E and F are correct. Marking a class `final` does not impact its ability to be serialized, so option A is incorrect. Option B is incorrect, as `Serializable` is an interface, not a class. Option C is incorrect. While it is a good practice for a serializable class to include a `static serialVersionUID` variable, it is not required. Finally, option D is incorrect as `static` members of the class are ignored on serialization already.

11. C. The code compiles, so options D and E are incorrect. The method looks like it will delete a directory tree but contains a bug. It never deletes any directories, only files. The result of executing this program is that it will delete all files within a directory tree, but none of the directories. For this reason, option C is correct.

12. E. The code does not compile, as the `Writer` methods `append()` and `flush()` both throw an `IOException` that must be handled or declared. Even without those lines of code, the try-with-resources statement itself must be handled or declared, since the `close()` method throws a checked `IOException` exception. For this reason, option E is correct. If the `main()` method was corrected to declare `IOException`, then the code would compile. If the `Console` was not available, it would throw a `NullPointerException` on the call to `c.writer()`; otherwise, it would print whatever the user typed in. For these reasons, options B and D would be correct.

13. B, E. Option A does not compile, as there is no `File` constructor that takes three parameters. Option B is correct and is the proper way to create a `File` instance with a single `String` parameter. Option C is incorrect, as there is no constructor that takes a `String` followed by a `File`. There is a constructor that takes a `File` followed by a `String`, making option E correct. Option D is incorrect because the first parameter is missing a slash (`/`) to indicate it is an absolute path. Since it's a relative path, it is correct only when the user's current directory is the root directory.

14. A, C, E. The `System` class has three streams: `in` is for input, `err` is for error, and `out` is for output. Therefore, options A, C, and E are correct. The others do not exist.

15. E. `PrintStream` and `PrintWriter` are the only I/O classes that you need to know that don't have a complementary `InputStream` or `Reader` class, so option E is correct.

16. A, D. The method compiles, so option E is incorrect. The method creates a `new-zoo.txt` file and copies the first line from `zoo-data.txt` into it, making option A correct. The try-with-resources statement closes all of declared resources including the `FileWriter` `o`. For this reason, the `Writer` is closed when the last `o.write()` is called, resulting in an `IOException` at runtime and making option D correct. Option F is incorrect because this implementation uses the character stream classes, which inherit from `Reader` or `Writer`.

17. C. The code compiles without issue. Since we're told the `Reader` supports `mark()`, the code also runs without throwing an exception. P is added to the `StringBuilder` first. Next, the position in the stream is marked before E. The E is added to the `StringBuilder`, with AC being skipped, then the O is added to the `StringBuilder`, with CK being skipped. The stream is then `reset()` to the position before the E. The call to `skip(0)` doesn't do anything since there are no characters to skip, so E is added onto the `StringBuilder` in the next `read()` call. The value PEOE is printed, and option C is correct.

18. B, C, D. Since you need to write primitives and `String` values, the `OutputStream` classes are appropriate. Therefore, you can eliminate options A and F since they use `Writer` classes. Next, `DirectoryOutputStream` is not a `java.io` class, so option E is incorrect. The data should be written to the file directly using the `FileOutputStream` class, buffered with the `BufferedOutputStream` class, and automatically serialized with the `ObjectOutputStream` class, so options B, C, and D are correct. `PrintStream` is an `OutputStream`, so it could be used to format the data. Unfortunately, since everything is converted to a `String`, the underlying data type information would be lost. For this reason, option G is incorrect.

19. C, E, G. First, the method does compile, so options A and B are incorrect. Methods to read/write `byte[]` values exist in the abstract parent of all I/O stream classes. This implementation is not correct, though, as the return value of `read(buffer)` is not used properly. It will only correctly copy files whose character count is a multiple of 10, making option C correct and option D incorrect. Option E is also correct as the data may not have made it to disk yet. Option F would be correct if the `flush()` method was called after every write. Finally, option G is correct as the `reader` stream is never closed.

20. C. `Console` includes a `format()` method that takes a `String` along with a list of arguments and writes it directly to the output stream, making option C correct. Options A and B are incorrect, as `reader()` returns a `Reader`, which does not define any print methods. Options D and E would be correct if the line was just a `String`. Since neither of those methods take additional arguments, they are incorrect.

21. A, C. Character stream classes often include built-in convenience methods for working with `String` data, so option A is correct. They also handle character encoding automatically, so option C is also correct. The rest of the statements are irrelevant or incorrect and are not properties of all character streams.

22. G. The code compiles, so option F is incorrect. To be serializable, a class must implement the `Serializable` interface, which `Zebra` does. It must also contain instance members that either are marked `transient` or are serializable. The instance member `stripes` is of type `Object`, which is not serializable. If `Object` implemented `Serializable`, then all objects would be serializable by default, defeating the purpose of having the `Serializable` interface. Therefore, the `Zebra` class is not serializable, with the program throwing an exception at runtime if serialized and making option G correct. If `stripes` were removed from the class, then options A and C would be the correct answers, as `name` and `age` are both marked `transient`.

Chapter 20: NIO.2

1. E. The `relativize()` method takes a `Path` value, not a `String`. For this reason, line 5 does not compile, and option E is correct. If line 5 was corrected to use a `Path` value, then the code would compile, but it would print the value of the `Path` created on line 4. Since `Path` is immutable, the operations on line 5 are not saved anywhere. For this reason, option D would be correct. Finally, if the value on line 5 was assigned to `path` and printed on line 6, then option A would be correct.

2. F. The code does not compile, as `Files.deleteIfExists()` declares the checked `IOException` that must be handled or declared. Remember, most `Files` methods declare `IOException`, especially the ones that modify a file or directory. For this reason, option F is correct. If the method was corrected to declare the appropriate exceptions, then option C would be correct. Option B would also be correct, if the method were provided a symbolic link that pointed to an empty directory. Options A and E would not print anything, as `Files.isDirectory()` returns `false` for both. Finally, option D would throw a `DirectoryNotEmptyException` at runtime.

3. C, E. The method to create a directory in the Files class is createDirectory(), not mkdir(). For this reason, line 6 does not compile, and option C is correct. In addition, the setTimes() method is available only on BasicFileAttributeView, not the read-only BasicFileAttributes, so line 8 will also not compile, making option E correct.

4. C. First, the code compiles and runs without issue, so options F and G are incorrect. Let's take this one step at a time. First, the subpath() method is applied to the absolute path, which returns the relative path animals/bear. Next, the getName() method is applied to the relative path, and since this is indexed from zero, it returns the relative path bear. Finally, the toAbsolutePath() method is applied to the relative path bear, resulting in the current directory /user/home being incorporated into the path. The final output is the absolute path /user/home/bear, making option C correct.

5. B, C. The code snippet will attempt to create a directory if the target of the symbolic link exists and is a directory. If the directory already exists, though, it will throw an exception. For this reason, option A is incorrect, and option B is correct. It will be created in /mammal/kangaroo/joey, and also reachable at /kang/joey because of the symbolic link, making option C correct.

6. C. The filter() operation applied to a Stream<Path> takes only one parameter, not two, so the code does not compile, and option C is correct. If the code was rewritten to use the Files.find() method with the BiPredicate as input (along with a maxDepth value), then the output would be option B, Has Sub, since the directory is given to be empty. For fun, we reversed the expected output of the ternary operation.

7. F. The code compiles without issue, so options D and E are incorrect. The method Files.isSameFile() first checks to see whether the Path values are the same in terms of equals(). Since the first path is relative and the second path is absolute, this comparison will return false, forcing isSameFile() to check for the existence of both paths in the file system. Since we know /zoo/turkey does not exist, a NoSuchFileException is thrown, and option F is the correct answer. Options A, B, and C are incorrect since an exception is thrown at runtime.

8. B, D, G. Options A and E are incorrect because Path and FileSystem, respectively, are abstract types that should be instantiated using a factory method. Option C is incorrect because the static method in the Path interface is of(), not get(). Option F is incorrect because the static method in the Paths class is get(), not getPath(). Options B and D are correct ways to obtain a Path instance. Option G is also correct, as there is an overloaded static method in Path that takes a URI instead of a String.

9. C. The code compiles and runs without issue, so option E is incorrect. For this question, you have to remember two things. First, the resolve() method does not normalize any path symbols, so options A and B are not correct. Second, calling resolve() with an absolute path as a parameter returns the absolute path, so option C is correct, and option D is incorrect.

10. B, C. The methods are not the same, because `Files.lines()` returns a `Stream<String>` and `Files.readAllLines()` returns a `List<String>`, so option F is incorrect. Option A is incorrect, because performance is not often the reason to prefer one to the other. `Files.lines()` processes each line via lazy evaluation, while `Files.readAllLines()` reads the entire file into memory all at once. For this reason, `Files.lines()` works better on large files with limited memory available, and option B is correct. Although a `List` can be converted to a stream, this requires an extra step; therefore, option C is correct since the resulting object can be chained directly to a stream. Finally, options D and E are incorrect because they are true for both methods.

11. D. The target path of the file after the `move()` operation is /animals, not /animals/monkey.txt, so options A and B are both incorrect. Option B will actually throw an exception at runtime since /animals already exists and is a directory. Next, the `NOFOLLOW_LINKS` option means that if the source is a symbolic link, the link itself and not the target will be copied at runtime, so option C is also incorrect. The option `ATOMIC_MOVE` means that any process monitoring the file system will not see an incomplete file during the move, so option D is correct. Option E is incorrect, since there are circumstances in which the operation would be allowed. In particular, if /animals did not exist then the operation would complete successfully.

12. A, C, E. Options A, C, and E are all properties of NIO.2 and are good reasons to use it over the `java.io.File` class. Option B is incorrect, as both `java.io.File` and NIO.2 include a method to list the contents of a directory. Option D is also incorrect as both APIs can delete only empty directories, not a directory tree. Finally, option F is incorrect, as sending email messages is not a feature of either API.

13. A. The code compiles and runs without issue, so options C, D, and E are incorrect. Even though the file is copied with attributes preserved, the file is considered a separate file, so the output is `false`, making option A correct and option B incorrect. Remember, `isSameFile()` returns `true` only if the files pointed to in the file system are the same, without regard to the file contents.

14. C. The code compiles and runs without issue, so options D, E, and F are incorrect. The most important thing to notice is that the depth parameter specified as the second argument to `find()` is 0, meaning the only record that will be searched is the top-level directory. Since we know that the top directory is a directory and not a symbolic link, no other paths will be visited, and nothing will be printed. For these reasons, option C is the correct answer.

15. E. The `java.io.File` method `listFiles()` retrieves the members of the current directory without traversing any subdirectories. Option E is correct, as `Files.list()` returns a `Stream<Path>` of a single directory. `Files.walk()` is close, but it iterates over the entire directory tree, not just a single directory. The rest of the methods do not exist.

16. D, E, F. Whether a path is a symbolic link, file, or directory is not relevant, so options A and C are incorrect. Using a view to read multiple attributes leads to fewer round-trips between the process and the file system and better performance, so options D and F are correct. For reading single attributes, there is little or no expected gain, so option B is incorrect. Finally, views can be used to access file system–specific attributes that are not available in `Files` methods; therefore, option E is correct.

17. B. The `readAllLines()` method returns a `List`, not a `Stream`. Therefore, the call to `flatMap()` is invalid, and option B is correct. If the `Files.lines()` method were instead used, it would print the contents of the file one capitalized word at a time, with commas removed.

18. A, D. The code compiles without issue, so options E and F are incorrect. The `toRealPath()` method will simplify the path to `/animals` and throw an exception if it does not exist, making option D correct. If the path does exist, calling `getParent()` on it returns the root directory. Walking the root directory with the filter expression will print all `.java` files in the root directory (along with all `.java` files in the directory tree), making option A correct. Option B is incorrect because it will skip files and directories that do not end in the `.java` extension. Option C is also incorrect as `Files.walk()` does not follow symbolic links by default. Only if the `FOLLOW_LINKS` option is provided and a cycle is encountered will the exception be thrown.

19. D. The code compiles and runs without issue, so option F is incorrect. If you simplify the redundant path symbols, then `p1` and `p2` represent the same path, `/lizard/walking.txt`. Therefore, `isSameFile()` returns `true`. The second output is `false`, because `equals()` checks only if the path values are the same, without reducing the path symbols. Finally, the normalized paths are the same, since all extra symbols have been removed, so the last line outputs `true`. For these reasons, option D is correct.

20. B. The `normalize()` method does not convert a relative path into an absolute path; therefore, the path value after the first line is just the current directory symbol. The `for()` loop iterates the name values, but since there is only one entry, the loop terminates after a single iteration. Therefore, option B is correct.

21. B. The method compiles without issue, so option E is incorrect. Option F is also incorrect. Even though `/flip` exists, `createDirectories()` does not throw an exception if the path already exists. If `createDirectory()` were used instead, then option F would be correct. Next, the `copy()` command takes a target that is the path to the new file location, not the directory to be copied into. Therefore, the target path should be `/flip/sounds.txt`, not `/flip`. For this reason, options A and C are incorrect. Since the question says the file already exists, the `REPLACE_EXISTING` option must be specified or an exception will be thrown at runtime, making option B the correct answer.

22. B, E. Option F is incorrect, as the code does compile. The method copies the contents of a file, but it removes all the line breaks. The `while()` loop would need to include a call to `w.newLine()` to correctly copy the file. For this reason, option A is incorrect. Option B is correct, and options C and D are incorrect. The APPEND option creates the file if it does not exist; otherwise, it starts writing from the end of the file. Option E is correct because the resources created in the method are not closed or declared inside a try-with-resources statement.

Chapter 21: JDBC

1. B, F. The `Driver` and `PreparedStatement` interfaces are part of the JDK, making options A and E incorrect. The concrete `DriverManager` class is also part of the JDK, making options C and D incorrect. Options B and F are correct since the implementation of these interfaces is part of the database-specific driver JAR file.

2. C, F. A JDBC URL has three parts. The first part is the string `jdbc`, making option C correct. The second part is the subprotocol. This is the vendor/product name, which isn't an answer choice. The subname is vendor-specific, making option F correct as well.

3. A. A JDBC URL has three main parts separated by single colons, making options B, C, E, and F incorrect. The first part is always `jdbc`, making option D incorrect. Therefore, the correct answer is option A. Notice that you can get this right even if you've never heard of the Sybase database before.

4. B, D. When setting parameters on a `PreparedStatement`, there are only options that take an index, making options C and F incorrect. The indexing starts with 1, making option A incorrect. This query has only one parameter, so option E is also incorrect. Option B is correct because it simply sets the parameter. Option D is also correct because it sets the parameter and then immediately overwrites it with the same value.

5. C. A `Connection` is created using a `static` method on `DriverManager`. It does not use a constructor. Therefore, option C is correct. If the `Connection` was created properly, the answer would be option B.

6. B. The first line has a return type of `boolean`, making it an `execute()` call. The second line returns the number of modified rows, making it an `executeUpdate()` call. The third line returns the results of a query, making it an `executeQuery()` call.

7. A, B, E. CRUD stands for Create, Read, Update, Delete, making options A, B, and E correct.

8. C. This code works as expected. It updates each of the five rows in the table and returns the number of rows updated. Therefore, option C is correct.

9. A, B. Option A is one of the answers because you are supposed to use braces ({}) for all SQL in a `CallableStatement`. Option B is the other answer because each parameter should be passed with a question mark (?). The rest of the code is correct. Note that your database might not behave the way that's described here, but you still need to know this syntax for the exam.

10. E. The code compiles because `PreparedStatement` extends `Statement` and `Statement` allows passing a `String` in the `executeQuery()` call. While `PreparedStatement` can have bind variables, `Statement` cannot. Since this code uses `executeQuery(sql)` in `Statement`, it fails at runtime. A `SQLException` is thrown, making option E correct.

11. D. JDBC code throws a `SQLException`, which is a checked exception. The code does not handle or declare this exception, and therefore it doesn't compile. Since the code doesn't compile, option D is correct. If the exception were handled or declared, the answer would be option C.

12. D. JDBC resources should be closed in the reverse order from that in which they were opened. The order for opening is `Connection`, `CallableStatement`, and `ResultSet`. The order for closing is `ResultSet`, `CallableStatement`, and `Connection`.

13. C. This code calls the `PreparedStatement` twice. The first time, it gets the numbers greater than 3. Since there are two such numbers, it prints two lines. The second time, it gets the numbers greater than 100. There are no such numbers, so the `ResultSet` is empty. A total of two lines is printed, making option C correct.

14. B, F. In a `ResultSet`, columns are indexed starting with 1, not 0. Therefore, options A, C, and E are incorrect. There are methods to get the column as a `String` or `Object`. However, option D is incorrect because an `Object` cannot be assigned to a `String` without a cast.

15. C. Since an `OUT` parameter is used, the code should call `registerOutParameter()`. Since this is missing, option C is correct.

16. E. First, notice that this code uses a `PreparedStatement`. Options A, B, and C are incorrect because they are for a `CallableStatement`. Next, remember that the number of parameters must be an exact match, making option E correct. Remember that you will not be tested on SQL syntax. When you see a question that appears to be about SQL, think about what it might be trying to test you on.

17. D. This code calls the `PreparedStatement` twice. The first time, it gets the numbers greater than 3. Since there are two such numbers, it prints two lines. Since the parameter is not set between the first and second calls, the second attempt also prints two rows. A total of four lines are printed, making option D correct.

18. D. Before accessing data from a `ResultSet`, the cursor needs to be positioned. The call to `rs.next()` is missing from this code.

19. E. This code should call `prepareStatement()` instead of `prepareCall()` since it not executing a stored procedure. Since we are using `var`, it does compile. Java will happily create a `CallableStatement` for you. Since this compile safety is lost, the code will not cause issues until runtime. At that point, Java will complain that you are trying to execute SQL as if it were a stored procedure, making option E correct.

20. E. Since the code calls `registerOutParameter()`, we know the stored procedure cannot use an `IN` parameter. Further, there is no `setInt()`, so it cannot be an `INOUT` parameter either. Therefore, the stored procedure must use an `OUT` parameter, making option E the answer.

21. B. The `prepareStatement()` method requires SQL be passed in. Since this parameter is omitted, line 27 does not compile, and option B is correct. Line 30 also does not compile as the method should be `getInt()`. However, the question asked about the first compiler error.

Chapter 22: Security

1. D. A distributed denial of service (DDoS) attack requires multiple requests by definition. Even a regular denial of service attack often requires multiple requests. For example, if you forget to close resources, it will take a number of tries for your application to run out resources. Therefore, option D is correct.

2. A, C, D. Since the class is `final`, it restricts extensibility, making option D correct. The `private` variable limits accessibility, making option C correct. Finally, option A is correct. This is an immutable class since it's not possible to change the state after construction. This class does not do any validation, making option B incorrect.

3. A. The `PutField` class is used with the `writeObject()` method, making option A correct. There is also a `GetField` class used with the `readObject()` method.

4. B, D. Option A is incorrect because it does not make a copy. Options E and F are incorrect because `ArrayList` does not have a `copy()` method. Option C is incorrect because the `clone()` method returns an `Object` and needs to be cast, so that option does not compile. Options B and D are correct because they copy the `ArrayList` using the copy constructor and `clone()` method, respectively.

5. D. When deserializing an object, Java does not call the constructor. Therefore, option D is correct.

6. A, F. The `clone()` method is declared on the `Object` class. Option A is correct because it will always compile. However, the call will throw an exception if the class that is being cloned does not implement `Cloneable`. Assuming this interface is implemented, the default implementation creates a shallow copy, making option F correct. If the class wants to implement a deep copy, it must override the `clone()` method with a custom implementation.

7. F. This is a trick question—there is no attack. Option E is incorrect because SQL leak is not the name of an attack. Option C is incorrect because the `PreparedStatement` and `ResultSet` are closed in a try-with-resources block. While we do not see the `Connection` closed, we also don't see it opened. The exam allows us to assume code that we can't see is correct. Option D is an incorrect answer because bind variables are being used properly with a `PreparedStatement`. Options A and B are incorrect because they are not related to the example. Since none of these attacks applies here, option F is correct.

8. E. The policy compiles and uses correct syntax. However, it gives permissions that are too broad. The user needs to be able to read a book, so `write` permissions should not be granted.

9. A, C. Many programs use confidential information securely, making option A correct. After all, you wouldn't be able to bank online if programs couldn't work with confidential information. It is also OK to put it in certain data structures. A built-in Java API puts a password in a `char[]`, making option C correct. Exposing the information unintentionally is not OK, making option B incorrect. Sharing confidential information with others is definitely not OK, making option D incorrect.

10. **C, D.** Any resource accessing things outside your program should be closed. Options C and D are correct because I/O and JDBC meet this criteria.

11. **A, F.** An inclusion attack needs to include something. Options A and F are correct because they are used with XML and ZIP file respectively. Options B and D are incorrect because injection is not an inclusion attack. Options C and E are not inclusion attacks either. In fact, you might not have heard of them. Both are attacks used against web applications. Don't worry if you see something on the exam that you haven't heard of; it isn't a correct answer.

12. **D.** The validation code checks that each character is between 0 and 9. Since it is comparing to allowed values, this is an example of a whitelist, and option D is correct. If it were the opposite, it would be a blacklist. There is no such thing as a gray or orange list.

13. **E, F.** Option A is incorrect because good encapsulation requires `private` state rather than declaring the class `final`. Option B is incorrect because the well-encapsulated `Camel` class can have a getter that exposes the `species` variable to be modified. Options C and D are incorrect because a class can be `final` while having `public` variables and be mutable. Option E is correct because methods that expose `species` could change it, which would prevent immutability. Option F is correct because you cannot enforce immutability in a subclass.

14. **B, C, D.** Any information the user can see requires care. Options B, C, and D are correct for this reason. Comments and variable names are part of the program, not the data it handles, making options A and E incorrect.

15. **A, B, F.** The `serialPersistentFields` field is used to specify which fields should be used in serialization. It must be declared `private static final`, or it will be ignored. Therefore, options A, B, and F are correct.

16. **C, D.** The application should log a message or throw an exception, making options C and D correct. It should not immediately terminate the program with `System.exit()` as that does not execute gracefully, making option A incorrect. It also should not ignore the issue, making option B incorrect.

17. **A, B, E.** Options A and E are correct because they prevent subclasses from being created outside the class definition. Option B is also correct because it prevents overriding the method. Options C and D are incorrect because `transient` is a modifier for variables, not classes or methods.

18. **A.** Reading an extremely large file is a form of a denial of service attack, making option A correct.

19. **C.** Options B and F are incorrect because these method names are not used by any serialization or deserialization process. Options A and D are incorrect because the return type for these methods is `void`, not `Object`. Option E is almost correct, as that is a valid method signature, but our question asks for the method used in deserialization, not serialization. Option C is the correct answer.

20. **C.** A shallow copy does not create copies of the nested objects, making option C correct. Options B and D are incorrect because narrow and wide copies are not terms. Option A is incorrect because a deep copy does copy the nested objects.

Index

Online Test Bank

Register to gain one year of FREE access after activation to the online interactive test bank to help you study for your OCP Java SE 11 Programmer I and Programmer II certification exams—included with your purchase of this book! All of the chapter review questions and the practice tests in this book are included in the online test bank so you can practice in a timed and graded setting.

Register and Access the Online Test Bank

To register your book and get access to the online test bank, follow these steps:

1. Go to bit.ly/SybexTest (this address is case sensitive)!
2. Select your book from the list.
3. Complete the required registration information, including answering the security verification to prove book ownership. You will be emailed a pin code.
4. Follow the directions in the email or go to www.wiley.com/go/sybextestprep.
5. Find your book on that page and click the "Register or Login" link with it. Then enter the pin code you received and click the "Activate PIN" button.
6. On the Create an Account or Login page, enter your username and password, and click Login or, if you don't have an account already, create a new account.
7. At this point, you should be in the test bank site with your new test bank listed at the top of the page. If you do not see it there, please refresh the page or log out and log back in.